THE COMPLETE APOCRYPHA

2018 EDITION

With Enoch, Jasher, & Jubilees

Published by Covenant Press (2018)

of the Covenant Christian Coalition

www.ccc.one

INTRODUCTION

The Deuterocanon, more commonly known as *Apocrypha*, is the collection of writings often sandwiched between the Old and New Testaments. These books are considered by some Christian denominations to be canonical or semi-canonical. While Protestants largely reject the books as spurious or even heretical, and the Roman and Orthodox churches accept them as canonical, it may be wise to recognize that historic Christianity has held to more of a middle ground, including by Reformers such as Martin Luther and early Catholic writers like Jerome. There has always been a distinction between protocanonical books of the Bible and the deuterocanonical books—the former being near-universally attested to as God-breathed by the Church and the latter often questioned for their canonicity. At the same time, the deuterocanonical books are held in higher regard than the truly heretical gnostic works that were written after the advent of Christianity.

While it is unwise to hold the apocryphal Deuterocanon to the same God-breathed standard as the standard 66 books of the Bible, we hold, as Martin Luther did, to their value as possibly true and good to read, but unverified:

> "Apocrypha, that are books which are not considered equal to the
> Holy Scriptures, but are useful and good to read."

Because certain books of the Roman Catholic Deuterocanon do not rise to the level of Holy Scripture, we must reject their canonicity, but that rejection does not exclude their profitability for reading as enlightening works that closely mirror Scripture and inform us about ancient, biblical history. They are lower than Scripture, but not spurious or inherently heretical. The Constitution of the CCC states:

> "The Bible is the final authority for all matters of life, faith, and doctrine and in its original Hebrew, Greek, and Aramaic form is completely infallible. The Bible says that the heart is deceitful above all else (Jer. 17:9) and the understanding of mankind corrupted (1 Cor. 1:20; 3:19), so God's word must inform and ultimately decide all questions of truth and doctrine. The CCC rejects the deuterocanonical books, otherwise known as Apocrypha, because the ancient Jewish canons excluded them, Jesus excludes the time period in which they were written in Luke 11:50–51, no references can be found to them in the New Testament, and early Christians like Jerome fought against their inclusion. However, the Bible mentions and makes allusion to several books that are not in the current Protestant canon such as Jasher, Enoch, and the Wars of the Lord. The true canon begins with Genesis, ends with Revelation, excludes the Apocrypha, and likely includes several of these other referenced books, although it is not clear that the current translations of Jasher, Enoch, and others are accurate translations of the original writings and therefore their authority is in dispute. For this reason only the sixty-six books of the Protestant canon are considered authoritative and divinely inspired, although the study of Jasher, Enoch, and other books that are explicitly mentioned or referenced in Scripture is not precluded, so long as the studier recognizes their current unverifiable state."

With this basic foundation laid, we can now appreciate the deuterocanonical books for what they are: valuable historical and biblical commentaries with perhaps bits of real Scripture intertwined, but not works on which to formulate doctrine. Lastly, it should be noted that the book transliterated "Jasher" is the one most in question in this collection. It was written no later than the mid-16th century AD, but there is debate regarding whether this is in fact the original *Jasher* referenced in the Bible, or, if it is a later, spurious work.

THE GOOD NEWS OF SALVATION

In accordance with the Scriptures, Christ the Messiah, the Son of the living God, became human, incarnate in the person of Jesus of Nazareth, lived a morally perfect and sinless life, died for our sins on the Cross as a substitutionary sacrifice, was buried in a tomb, and was raised bodily from the dead on the third day. Everyone who hears and accepts this message of salvation, believing in their heart that God raised the Christ from the dead, will be pardoned of all their sins, given the gift of the Holy Spirit, and granted everlasting life in perpetual union with God. Salvation is found in Christ alone by grace alone through faith alone and not by works.

BOOKS OF THE APOCRYPHA

UNIVERSAL DEUTEROCANON

EASTERN ORTHODOX DEUTEROCANON

ETHIOPIAN ORTHODOX DEUTEROCANON

JEWISH LEGEND

ADDITIONS TO THE BIBLE

UNIVERSAL DEUTEROCANON

TOBIT

The Book of Tobit, named after its principal character, combines Jewish piety and morality with folklore in a fascinating story that has enjoyed wide popularity in both Jewish and Christian circles. Prayers, psalms, and words of wisdom, as well as the skillfully constructed story itself, provide valuable insights into the faith and the religious milieu of its unknown author. The book was probably written early in the second century BC; it is not known where.

CHAPTER 1

1 The book of the words of Tobit, the son of Tobiel, the son of Ananiel, the son of Aduel, the son of Gabael, of the seed of Asiel, of the tribe of Naphtali; **2** who in the days of Enemessar king of the Assyrians was carried away captive out of Thisbe, which is on the right hand of Kedesh Naphtali in Galilee above Asher. **3** I, Tobit, walked in the ways of truth and righteousness all the days of my life, and I did many alms deeds to my kindred and my nation, who went with me into the land of the Assyrians, to Nineveh. **4** When I was in my own country, in the land of Israel, while I was yet young, all the tribe of Naphtali my father fell away from the house of Jerusalem, which was chosen out of all the tribes of Israel, that all the tribes should sacrifice there, and the temple of the habitation of the Most High was hallowed and built therein for all ages. **5** All the tribes which fell away together sacrificed to the heifer Baal, and so did the house of Naphtali my father. **6** I alone went often to Jerusalem at the feasts, as it has been ordained to all Israel by an everlasting decree, having the first fruits and the tenths of my increase, and that which was first shorn; and I gave them at the altar to the priests the sons of Aaron. **7** I gave a tenth part of all my increase to the sons of Levi, who ministered at Jerusalem. A second tenth part I sold away, and went, and spent it each year at Jerusalem. **8** A third tenth I gave to them to whom it was appropriate, as Deborah my father's mother had commanded me, because I was left an orphan by my father. **9** When I became a man, I took as wife Anna of the seed of our own family. With her, I became the father of Tobias. **10** When I was carried away captive to Nineveh, all my kindred and my relatives ate of the bread of the Gentiles; **11** but I kept myself from eating, **12** because I remembered God with all my soul. **13** So the Most High gave me grace and favor in the sight of Enemessar, and I was his purchasing agent. **14** And I went into Media and left ten talents of silver in trust with Gabael, the brother of Gabrias, at Rages of Media. **15** And when Enemessar was dead, Sennacherib his son reigned in his place. In his time, the highways were troubled, and I could no longer go into Media. **16** In the days of Enemessar, I did many alms deeds to my kindred: I gave my bread to the hungry, **17** and my garments to the naked. If I saw any of my race dead, and thrown out on the wall of Nineveh, I buried him. **18** If Sennacherib the king killed any, when he came fleeing from Judea, I buried them privately; for in his wrath he killed many; and the bodies were sought for by the king and were not found. **19** But one of the Ninevites went and showed to the king concerning me, how I buried them, and hid myself; and when I knew that I was sought for to be put to death, I withdrew myself for fear. **20** And all my goods were forcibly taken away, and there was nothing left to me, save my wife Anna and my son Tobias. **21** No more than fifty-five days passed before two of his sons killed him, and they fled into the mountains of Ararat. And Sarchedonus his son reigned in his place; and he appointed Achiacharus my brother Anael's son over all the accounts of his kingdom, and over all his affairs. **22** Achiacharus requested me, and I came to Nineveh. Now Achiacharus was cupbearer, keeper of the signet, steward, and overseer of the accounts. Sarchedonus appointed him next to himself, but he was my brother's son.

CHAPTER 2

1 Now when I had come home again, and my wife Anna was restored to me, and my son Tobias, in the feast of Pentecost, which is the holy feast of the seven weeks, there was a good dinner prepared me, and I sat down to eat. **2** I saw abundance of meat, and I said to my son, "Go and bring whatever poor man you find of our kindred, who is mindful of the Lord. Behold, I wait for you." **3** Then he came, and said, "Father, one of our race is strangled, and has been cast out in the marketplace." **4** Before I had tasted anything, I sprang up, and took him up into a chamber until the sun had set. **5** Then I returned, washed myself, ate my bread in heaviness, **6** and remembered the prophecy of Amos, as he said, "Your feasts will be turned into mourning, and all your mirth into lamentation." **7** So I wept: and when the sun had set, I went and dug a grave, and buried him. **8** My neighbors mocked me, and said, "He is no longer afraid to be put to death for this matter; and yet he fled away. Behold, he buries the dead again." **9** The same night I returned from burying him, and slept by the wall of my courtyard, being polluted; and my face was uncovered. **10** I didn't know that there were sparrows in the wall. My eyes were open, and the sparrows dropped warm dung into my eyes, and white films came over my eyes. I went to the physicians, and they didn't help me; but Achiacharus nourished me, until I went into Elymais. **11** My wife Anna wove cloth in the women's chambers, **12** and sent the work back to the owners. They on their part paid her wages, and also gave her a kid. **13** But when it came to my house, it began to cry, and I said to her, "Where did this kid come from? Is it stolen? Give it back to the owners; for it is not lawful to eat anything that is stolen." **14** But she said, "It has been given to me for a gift more than the wages." I didn't believe her, and I asked her to return it to the owners; and I was ashamed of her. But she answered and said to me, "Where are your alms and your righteous deeds? Behold, you and all your works are known."

CHAPTER 3

1 I was grieved and wept, and prayed in sorrow, saying, **2** "O Lord, you are righteous, and all your works and all your ways are mercy and truth, and you judge true and righteous judgement forever. **3** Remember me and look at me. Don't take vengeance on me for my sins and my ignorance, and the sins of my fathers who sinned before you. **4** For they disobeyed your commandments. You gave us as plunder, for captivity, for death, and for a proverb of reproach to all the nations among whom we are dispersed. **5** Now your judgments are many and true; that you should deal with me according to my sins and the sins of my fathers; because we didn't keep your commandments, for we didn't walk in truth before you. **6** Now deal with me according to

that which is pleasing in your sight. Command my spirit to be taken from me, that I may be released, and become earth. For it is more profitable for me to die rather than to live, because I have heard false reproaches, and there is much sorrow in me. Command that I be released from my distress, now, and go to the everlasting place. Don't turn your face away from me." **7** The same day it happened to Sarah the daughter of Raguel in Ecbatana of Media, that she also was reproached by her father's maidservants; **8** because that she had been given to seven husbands, and Asmodaeus the evil spirit killed them, before they had lain with her. And they said to her, "Do you not know that you strangle your husbands? You have had already seven husbands, and you haven't borne the name of anyone of them. **9** Why do you scourge us? If they are dead, go your ways with them. Let us never see either son or daughter from you." **10** When she heard these things, she was grieved exceedingly, so that she thought about hanging herself. Then she said, "I am the only daughter of my father. If I do this, it will be a reproach to him, and I will bring down his old age with sorrow to the grave." **11** Then she prayed by the window, and said, "Blessed are you, O Lord my God, and blessed is your holy and honorable name forever! Let all your works praise you forever! **12** And now, Lord, I have set my eyes and my face toward you. **13** Command that I be released from the earth, and that I no longer hear reproach. **14** You know, Lord, that I am pure from all sin with man, **15** and that I never polluted my name or the name of my father, in the land of my captivity. I am the only daughter of my father, and he has no child that will be his heir, nor brother near him, nor son belonging to him, that I should keep myself for a wife to him. Seven husbands of mine are dead already. Why should I live? If it doesn't please you to kill me, command some regard to be had of me, and pity taken of me, and that I hear no more reproach." **16** The prayer of both was heard before the glory of the great God. **17** Raphael also was sent to heal them both, to scale away the white films from Tobit's eyes, and to give Sarah the daughter of Raguel for a wife to Tobias the son of Tobit; and to bind Asmodaeus the evil spirit; because it belonged to Tobias that he should inherit her. At that very time, Tobit returned and entered into his house, and Sarah the daughter of Raguel came down from her upper chamber.

TOBIT

CHAPTER 4

1 In that day Tobit remembered the money which he had left in trust with Gabael in Rages of Media, **2** and he said to himself, I have asked for death; why do I not call my son Tobias, that I may explain to him about the money before I die? **3** And he called him, and said, "My child, if I die, bury me. Don't despise your mother. Honor her all the days of your life, and do that which is pleasing to her, and don't grieve her. **4** Remember, my child, that she has seen many dangers for you, when you were in her womb. When she is dead, bury her by me in one grave. **5** My child, be mindful of the Lord our God all your days, and don't let your will be set to sin and to transgress his commandments: do righteousness all the days of your life, and don't follow the ways of unrighteousness. **6** For if you do what is true, your deeds will prosperously succeed for you, and for all those who do righteousness. **7** Give alms from your possessions. When you give alms, don't let your eye be envious. Don't turn away your face from any poor man, and the face of God won't be turned away from you. **8** As your possessions are, give alms of it according to your abundance. If you have little, don't be afraid to give alms according to that little; **9** for you lay up a good treasure for yourself against the day of necessity; **10** because alms-giving delivers from death, and doesn't allow you to come into darkness. **11** Alms is a good gift in the sight of the Most High for all that give it. **12** Beware, my child, of all whoredom, and take first a wife of the seed of your fathers. Don't take a strange wife, who is not of your father's tribe; for we are the descendants of the prophets. Remember, my child, that Noah, Abraham, Isaac, and Jacob, our fathers of old time, all took wives of their kindred, and were blessed in their children, and their seed will inherit the land. **13** And now, my child, love your kindred, and don't scorn your kindred and the sons and the daughters of your people in your heart, to take a wife of them; for in scornfulness is destruction and much trouble, and in naughtiness is decay and great lack; for naughtiness is the mother of famine. **14** Don't let the wages of any man who works for you wait with you but give it to him out of hand. If you serve God, you will be rewarded. Take heed to yourself, my child, in all your works, and be discreet in all your behavior. **15** And what you yourself hate, do to no man. Don't drink wine to drunkenness, and don't let

drunkenness go with you on your way. **16** Give of your bread to the hungry, and of your garments to those who are naked. Give alms from all your abundance. Don't let your eye be envious when you give alms. **17** Pour out your bread on the burial of the just and give nothing to sinners. **18** Ask counsel of every man who is wise, and don't despise any counsel that is profitable. **19** Bless the Lord your God at all times and ask of him that your ways may be made straight, and that all your paths and counsels may prosper; for every nation has no counsel; but the Lord himself gives all good things, and he humbles whom he will, as he will. And now, my child, remember my commandments, and let them not be blotted out of your mind. **20** And now I explain to you about the ten talents of silver, which I left in trust with Gabael the son of Gabrias at Rages of Media. **21** And fear not, my child, because we are made poor. You have much wealth, if you fear God, and depart from all sin, and do that which is pleasing in his sight."

CHAPTER 5

1 Then Tobias answered and said to him, "Father, I will do all things, whatever you have commanded me. **2** But how could I receive the money, since I don't know him?" **3** He gave him the handwriting, and said to him, "Seek a man who will go with you, and I will give him wages, whiles I yet live; and go and receive the money." **4** He went to seek a man and found Raphael who was an angel; **5** and he didn't know it. He said to him, "Can I go with you to Rages of Media? Do you know those places well?" **6** The angel said to him, "I will go with you. I know the way well. I have lodged with our brother Gabael." **7** Tobias said to him, "Wait for me, and I will tell my father." **8** He said to him, "Go, and don't wait. And he went in and said to his father, "Behold, I have found someone who will go with me." But he said, "Call him to me, that I may know of what tribe he is, and whether he be a trustworthy man to go with you." **9** So he called him, and he came in, and they saluted one another. **10** And Tobit said to him, "Brother, of what tribe and of what family are you? Tell me." **11** He said to him, "Do you seek a tribe and a family, or a hired man which will go with your son?" And Tobit said to him, "I want to know, brother, your kindred and your name." **12** And he said, "I am Azarias, the son of Ananias the great, of your kindred." **13** And he said to him,

11

"Welcome, brother. Don't be angry with me, because I sought to know your tribe and family. You are my brother, of an honest and good lineage; for I knew Ananias and Jathan, the sons of Shemaiah the great, when we went together to Jerusalem to worship, and offered the firstborn, and the tenths of our increase; and they didn't go astray in the error of our kindred. My brother, you are of a great stock. **14** But tell me, what wages will I give you? A drachma a day, and those things that be necessary for you, as to my son? **15** And moreover, if you both return safe and sound, I will add something to your wages." **16** And so they agreed. And he said to Tobias, "Prepare yourself for the journey. May God prosper you." So, his son prepared what was needful for the journey, and his father said to him, "Go with this man; but God, who dwells in heaven, will prosper your journey. May his angel go with you." Then they both departed, and the young man's dog went with them. **17** But Anna his mother wept, and said to Tobit, "Why have you sent away our child? Isn't he the staff of our hand, in going in and out before us? **18** Don't be greedy to add money to money; but let it be as refuse compared to our child. **19** For what the Lord has given us to live is enough for us." **20** Tobit said to her, "Don't worry, my sister. He will return safe and sound, and your eyes will see him. **21** For a good angel will go with him. His journey will be prospered, and he will return safe and sound." **22** So she stopped weeping.

CHAPTER 6

1 Now as they went on their journey, they came at evening to the river Tigris, and they lodged there. **2** But the young man went down to wash himself, and a fish leaped out of the river, and would have swallowed the young man. **3** But the angel said to him, "Grab the fish!" So the young man grabbed the fish, and hauled it up onto the land. **4** And the angel said to him, "Cut the fish open, and take the heart, the liver, and the bile, and keep them with you." **5** And the young man did as the angel commanded him; but they roasted the fish and ate it. And they both went on their way, until they drew near to Ecbatana. **6** The young man said to the angel, "Brother Azarias, of what use is the heart, the liver, and the bile of the fish?" **7** He said to him, "About the heart and the liver: If a demon or an evil spirit troubles anyone, we must burn those and make smoke of them before the man or the woman, and the

affliction will flee. **8** But as for the bile, it is good to anoint a man that has white films in his eyes, and he will be healed." **9** But when they drew near to Rages, **10** the angel said to the young man, "Brother, today we will lodge with Raguel. He is your kinsman. He has an only daughter named Sarah. I will speak about her, that she should be given to you for a wife. **11** For her inheritance belongs to you, and you only are of her kindred. **12** The maid is fair and wise. And now hear me, and I will speak to her father. When we return from Rages we will celebrate the marriage; for I know that Raguel may in no way marry her to another according to the law of Moses, or else he would be liable to death, because it belongs to you to take the inheritance, rather than any other." **13** Then the young man said to the angel, "Brother Azarias, I have heard that this maid has been given to seven men, and that they all perished in the bride-chamber. **14** Now I am the only son of my father, and I am afraid, lest I go in and die, even as those before me. For a demon loves her, which harms no man, but those which come to her. Now I fear lest I die and bring my father's and my mother's life to the grave with sorrow because of me. They have no other son to bury them." **15** But the angel said to him, "Don't you remember the words which your father commanded you, that you should take a wife of your own kindred? Now hear me, brother; for she will be your wife. Don't worry about the demon; for this night she will be given you as wife. **16** And when you come into the bride-chamber, you will take the ashes of incense, and will lay upon them some of the heart and liver of the fish and will make smoke with them. **17** The demon will smell it, and flee away, and never come again any more. But when you go near to her, both of you rise up, and cry to God who is merciful. He will save you and have mercy on you. Don't be afraid, for she was prepared for you from the beginning; and you will save her, and she will go with you. And I suppose that you will have children with her." When Tobias heard these things, he loved her, and his soul was strongly joined to her.

CHAPTER 7

1 They came to Ecbatana and arrived at the house of Raguel. But Sarah met them; and she greeted them, and they her. Then she brought them into the house. **2** Raguel said to Edna his wife, "This young man really resembles Tobit my cousin!" **3** And Raguel asked them,

"Where are you two from, kindred?" They said to him, "We are of the sons of Naphtali, who are captives in Nineveh." **4** He said to them, "Do you know Tobit our brother?" They said, "We know him." Then he said to them, "Is he in good health?" **5** They said, "He is both alive, and in good health." Tobias said, "He is my father." **6** And Raguel sprang up, and kissed him, wept, **7** blessed him, and said to him, "You are the son of an honest and good man." When he had heard that Tobit had lost his sight, he was grieved, and wept; **8** and Edna his wife and Sarah his daughter wept. They received them gladly; and they killed a ram of the flock and served them meat. But Tobias said to Raphael, "Brother Azarias, speak of those things of which you talked about in the way, and let the matter be finished." **9** So he communicated the thing to Raguel. Raguel said to Tobias, "Eat, drink, and make merry: **10** for it belongs to you to take my child. However, I will tell you the truth. **11** I have given my child to seven men of our relatives, and whenever they came in to her, they died in the night. But for the present be merry." And Tobias said, "I will taste nothing here, until you all make a covenant and enter into that covenant with me." **12** Raguel said, "Take her to yourself from now on according to custom. You are her relative, and she is yours. The merciful God will give all good success to you." **13** And he called his daughter Sarah, and took her by the hand, and gave her to be wife of Tobias, and said, "Behold, take her to yourself after the law of Moses, and lead her away to your father." And he blessed them. **14** He called Edna his wife, then took a book, wrote a contract, and sealed it. **15** Then they began to eat. **16** And Raguel called his wife Edna, and said to her, "Sister, prepare the other chamber, and bring her in there." **17** She did as he asked her, and brought her in there. She wept, and she received the tears of her daughter, and said to her, **18** "Be comforted, my child. May the Lord of heaven and earth give you favor for this your sorrow. Be comforted, my daughter."

CHAPTER 8

1 When they had finished their supper, they brought Tobias in to her. **2** But as he went, he remembered the words of Raphael, and took the ashes of the incense, and put the heart and the liver of the fish on them and made smoke with them. **3** When the demon smelled that smell, it fled into the uppermost parts of Egypt, and the angel bound him. **4** But after they were both shut in together, Tobias rose up from the bed, and said, "Sister, arise, and let's pray that the Lord may have mercy on us." **5** And Tobias began to say, "Blessed are you, O God of our fathers, and blessed is your holy and glorious name forever. Let the heavens bless you, and all your creatures. **6** You made Adam and gave him Eve his wife for a helper and support. From them came the seed of men. You said, it is not good that the man should be alone. Let's make him a helper like him. **7** And now, O Lord, I take not this my sister for lust, but in truth. Command that I may find mercy and grow old with her." **8** She said with him, "Amen." And they both slept that night. **9** Raguel arose, and went and dug a grave, **10** saying, "Lest he also should die." **11** And Raguel came into his house, **12** and said to Edna his wife, "Send one of the maidservants, and let them see if he is alive. If not, we will bury him, and no man will know it." **13** So the maidservant opened the door, and went in, and found them both sleeping, **14** and came out, and told them that he was alive. **15** Then Raguel blessed God, saying, "Blessed are you, O God, with all pure and holy blessing! Let your saints bless you, and all your creatures! Let all your angels and your elect bless you forever! **16** Blessed are you, because you have made me glad; and it has not happened to me as I suspected; but you have dealt with us according to your great mercy. **17** Blessed are you, because you have had mercy on two that were the only begotten children of their parents. Show them mercy, O Lord. Fulfill their life in health with gladness and mercy. **18** He commanded his servants to fill the grave. **19** He kept the wedding feast for them fourteen days. **20** Before the days of the wedding feast were finished, Raguel swore to him, that he should not depart until the fourteen days of the wedding feast were fulfilled; **21** and that then he should take half of his goods and go in safety to his father; and the rest, said he, when my wife and I die.

CHAPTER 9

1 And Tobias called Raphael, and said to him, **2** "Brother Azarias, take with you a servant and two camels, and go to Rages of Media to Gabael, and receive the money for me, and bring him to the wedding feast, **3** because Raguel has sworn that I must not depart. **4** My father counts the days; and if I wait long, he will be very grieved. **5** So Raphael went on his way, and lodged with Gabael, and gave him the handwriting; so he brought out the bags with their seals, and gave them to him. **6** Then they rose up early in the morning together and came to the wedding feast. Tobias blessed his wife.

CHAPTER 10

1 Tobit his father counted every day. When the days of the journey were expired, and they didn't come, **2** he said, "Is he perchance detained? Or is Gabael perchance dead, and there is no one to give him the money?" **3** He was very grieved. **4** But his wife said to him, "The child has perished, seeing he waits long." She began to mourn him, and said, **5** "I care about nothing, my child, since I have let you go, the light of my eyes." **6** Tobit said to her, "Hold your peace. Don't worry. He is in good health." **7** And she said to him, "Hold your peace. Don't deceive me. My child has perished." And she went out every day into the way by which they went, and ate no bread in the day-time, and didn't stop mourning her son Tobias for whole nights, until the fourteen days of the wedding feast were expired, which Raguel had sworn that he should spend there. Then Tobias said to Raguel, "Send me away, for my father and my mother look no more to see me." **8** But his father-in-law said to him, "Stay with me, and I will send to your father, and they will declare to him how things go with you." **9** Tobias said, "No. Send me away to my father." **10** Raguel arose, and gave him Sarah his wife, and half his goods, servants and cattle and money; **11** and he blessed them, and sent them away, saying, "The God of heaven will prosper you, my children, before I die." **12** And he said to his daughter, "Honor your father-in-law and your mother-in-law. They are now your parents. Let me hear a good report of you." Then he kissed her. Edna said to Tobias, "May the Lord of heaven restore you, dear brother, and grant to me that I may see your children of my daughter Sarah, that I may rejoice before the Lord. Behold, I commit my daughter to you in special trust. Don't cause her grief.

CHAPTER 11

1 After these things Tobias also went his way, blessing God because he had prospered his journey; and he blessed Raguel and Edna his wife. Then he went on his way until they drew near to Nineveh. **2** Raphael said to Tobias, "Don't you know, brother, how you left your father? **3** Let's run forward before your wife and prepare the house. **4** But take in your hand the bile of the fish." So they went their way, and the dog went after them. **5** Anna sat looking around toward the path for her son. **6** She saw him coming, and said to his father, "Behold, your son is coming with the man that went with him!" **7** Raphael said, "I know, Tobias, that your father will open his eyes. **8** Therefore anoint his eyes with the bile, and being pricked with it, he will rub, and will make the white films fall away. Then he will see you." **9** Anna ran to him, and fell upon the neck of her son, and said to him, "I have seen you, my child! I am ready to die." They wept both. **10** Tobit went toward the door and stumbled; but his son ran to him, **11** and took hold of his father. He rubbed the bile on his father's eyes, saying, "Cheer up, my father." **12** When his eyes began to hurt, he rubbed them. **13** Then the white films peeled away from the corners of his eyes; and he saw his son and fell upon his neck. **14** He wept, and said, "Blessed are you, O God, and blessed is your name forever! Blessed are all your holy angels! **15** For you scourged and had mercy on me. Behold, I see my son Tobias." And his son went in rejoicing and told his father the great things that had happened to him in Media. **16** Tobit went out to meet his daughter-in-law at the gate of Nineveh, rejoicing, and blessing God. Those who saw him go marveled, because he had received his sight. **17** Tobit gave thanks before them, because God had shown mercy on him. When Tobit came near to Sarah his daughter-in-law, he blessed her, saying, "Welcome, daughter! Blessed is God who has brought you to us and blessed are your father and your mother." And there was joy among all his kindred who were at Nineveh. **18** Achiacharus and Nasbas his brother's son came. **19** Tobias' wedding feast was kept seven days with great gladness.

CHAPTER 12

1 And Tobit called his son Tobias, and said to him, "See, my child, that the man which went with you have his wages, and you must give him more." **2** And he said to him, "Father, it is no harm to me to give him the half of those things which I have brought; **3** for he has led me for you in safety, and he cured my wife, and brought my money, and likewise cured you." **4** The old man said, "It is due to him." **5** And he called the angel, and said to him, "Take half of all that you all have brought."

6 Then he called them both privately, and said to them, "Bless God, and give him thanks, and magnify him, and give him thanks in the sight of all that live, for the things which he has done with you. It is good to bless God and exalt his name, showing out with honor the works of God. Don't be slack to give him thanks. **7** It is good to keep close the secret of a king, but to reveal gloriously the works of God. Do good, and evil won't find you. **8** Good is prayer with fasting, alms, and righteousness. A little with righteousness is better than much with unrighteousness. It is better to give alms than to lay up gold. **9** Alms delivers from death, and it purges away all sin. Those who give alms and do righteousness will be filled with life; **10** but those who sin are enemies to their own life. **11** Surely I will keep nothing closed from you. I have said, 'It is good to keep close the secret of a king, but to reveal gloriously the works of God.' **12** And now, when you prayed, and Sarah your daughter-in-law, I brought the memorial of your prayer before the Holy One. When you buried the dead, I was with you likewise. **13** And when you didn't delay to rise up, and leave your dinner, that you might go and cover the dead, your good deed was not hidden from me. I was with you. **14** And now God sent me to heal you and Sarah your daughter-in-law. **15** I am Raphael, one of the seven holy angels, which present the prayers of the saints, and go in before the glory of the Holy One." **16** And they were both troubled and fell upon their faces; for they were afraid. **17** And he said to them, "Don't be afraid. You will all have peace; but bless God forever. **18** For I came not of any favor of my own, but by the will of your God. Therefore bless him forever. **19** All these days I appeared to you. I didn't eat or drink, but you all saw a vision. **20** Now give God thanks, because I ascend to him that sent me. Write in a book all the things which have been done." **21** Then they rose up and saw him no more. **22** They confessed the great and wonderful works of God, and how the angel of the Lord had appeared to them.

CHAPTER 13

1 And Tobit wrote a prayer for rejoicing, and said, "Blessed is God who lives forever! Blessed is his kingdom! **2** For he scourges and shows mercy. He leads down to the grave and brings up again. There is no one that will escape his hand. **3** Give thanks to him before the Gentiles, all you children of Israel! For he has scattered us among them. **4** Declare his greatness, there. Extol him before all the living; because he is our Lord, and God is our Father forever. **5** He will scourge us for our iniquities, and will again show mercy, and will gather us out of all the nations among whom you are all scattered. **6** If you turn to him with your whole heart and with your whole soul, to do truth before him, then he will turn to you, and won't hide his face from you. See what he will do with you. Give him thanks with your whole mouth. Bless the Lord of righteousness. Exalt the everlasting King. I give him thanks in the land of my captivity and show his strength and majesty to a nation of sinners. Turn, you sinners, and do righteousness before him. Who can tell if he will accept you and have mercy on you? **7** I exalt my God. My soul exalts the King of heaven and rejoices in his greatness. **8** Let all men speak and let them give him thanks in Jerusalem. **9** O Jerusalem, the holy city, he will scourge you for the works of your sons and will again have mercy on the sons of the righteous. **10** Give thanks to the Lord with goodness, and bless the everlasting King, that his tabernacle may be built in you again with joy, and that he may make glad in you those who are captives, and love in you forever those who are miserable. **11** Many nations will come from afar to the name of the Lord God with gifts in their hands, even gifts to the King of heaven. Generations of generations will praise you and sing songs of rejoicing. **12** All those who hate you are cursed. All those who love you forever will be blessed. **13** Rejoice and be exceedingly glad for the sons of the righteous; for they will be gathered together and will bless the Lord of the righteous. **14** Oh blessed are those who love you. They will rejoice for your peace. Blessed are all those who sorrowed for all your scourges; because they will rejoice for you when they have seen all your glory. They will be made glad forever. **15** Let my soul bless God the great King. **16** For Jerusalem will be built with sapphires, emeralds, and precious stones; your walls and towers and battlements with pure gold. **17** The streets of Jerusalem will be paved with beryl, carbuncle, and stones of Ophir. **18** All her streets will say, "Hallelujah!" and give praise, saying, "Blessed be God, who has exalted you forever!"

CHAPTER 14

1 Then Tobit finished giving thanks. **2** He was fifty-eight years old when he lost his sight.

After eight years, he received it again. He gave alms and he feared the Lord God more and more and gave thanks to him. **3** Now he grew very old; and he called his son with the six sons of his son, and said to him, "My child, take your sons. Behold, I have grown old, and am ready to depart out of this life. **4** Go into Media, my child, for I surely believe all the things which Jonah the prophet spoke of Nineveh, that it will be overthrown, but in Media there will rather be peace for a season. Our kindred will be scattered in the earth from the good land. Jerusalem will be desolate, and the house of God in it will be burned up and will be desolate for a time. **5** God will again have mercy on them, and bring them back into the land, and they will build the house, but not like to the former house, until the times of that age are fulfilled. Afterward they will return from the places of their captivity and build up Jerusalem with honor. The house of God will be built in it forever with a glorious building, even as the prophets spoke concerning it. **6** And all the nations will turn to fear the Lord God truly and will bury their idols. **7** All the nations will bless the Lord, and his people will give thanks to God, and the Lord will exalt his people; and all those who love the Lord God in truth and righteousness will rejoice, showing mercy to our kindred. **8** And now, my child, depart from Nineveh, because those things which the prophet Jonah spoke will surely come to pass. **9** But you must keep the law and the ordinances, and show yourself merciful and righteous, that it may be well with you. **10** Bury me decently, and your mother with me. Don't stay at Nineveh. See, my child, what Aman did to Achiacharus that nourished him, how out of light he brought him into darkness, and all the recompense that he made him. Achiacharus was saved, but the other had his recompense, and he went down into darkness. Manasses gave alms and escaped the snare of death which he set for him; but Aman fell into the snare and perished. **11** And now, my children, consider what alms does, and how righteousness delivers." While he was saying these things, he gave up the ghost in the bed; but he was one hundred fifty-eight years old. Tobias buried him magnificently. **12** When Anna died, he buried her with his father. But Tobias departed with his wife and his sons to Ecbatana to Raguel his father-in-law, **13** and he grew old in honor, and he buried his father-in-law and mother-in-law magnificently, and he inherited their possessions, and his father Tobit's. **14** He died at Ecbatana of Media, being one hundred twenty-seven years old. **15** Before he died, he heard of the destruction of Nineveh, which Nebuchadnezzar and Ahasuerus took captive. Before his death, he rejoiced over Nineveh.

JUDITH

The Book of Judith relates the story of God's deliverance of the Jewish people. This was accomplished "by the hand of a female"—a constant motif (cf. 8:33; 9:9, 10; 12:4; 13:4, 14, 15; 15:10; 16:5) meant to recall the "hand" of God in the Exodus narrative (cf. Ex. 15:6). The work may have been written around 100 BC. There are four Greek recensions of Judith (Septuagint codices Vaticanus, Sinaiticus, Alexandrinus, and Basiliano-Vaticanus), four ancient translations (Old Latin, Syriac, Sahidic, and Ethiopic), and some late Hebrew versions, apparently translated from the Vulgate. Despite Jerome's claim to have translated an Aramaic text, no ancient Aramaic or Hebrew manuscripts have been found. The oldest extant text of Judith is the preservation of 15:1–7 inscribed on a third-century AD potsherd. Whatever the reasons, the rabbis did not count Judith among their scriptures, and the Reformation adopted that position.

CHAPTER 1

1 In the twelfth year of the reign of Nebuchadnezzar, who reigned over the Assyrians in Nineveh, the great city, in the days of Arphaxad, who reigned over the Medes in Ecbatana, 2 and built around Ecbatana walls of hewn stones three cubits broad and six cubits long, and made the height of the wall seventy cubits, and its breadth fifty cubits; 3 and set its towers at its gates, one hundred cubits high, and its breadth in the foundation was sixty cubits; 4 and made its gates, even gates that were raised to the height of seventy cubits, and their breadth forty cubits, for his mighty army to go out of, and the setting in array of his footmen—5 even in those days king Nebuchadnezzar made war with king Arphaxad in the great plain. This plain is on the borders of Ragau. 6 There came to meet him all that lived in the hill country, and all that lived by Euphrates, Tigris, and Hydaspes, and in the plain of Arioch the king of the Elymaeans. Many nations of the sons of Chelod assembled themselves to the battle. 7 And Nebuchadnezzar king of the Assyrians sent to all who lived in Persia, and to all who lived westward, to those who lived in Cilicia, Damascus, Libanus, and Antilibanus, and to all who lived along the sea coast, 8 and to those among the nations that were of Carmel and Gilead, and to the higher Galilee and the great plain of Esdraelon, 9 and to all who were in Samaria and its cities, and beyond Jordan to Jerusalem, Betane, Chellus, Kadesh, the river of Egypt, Tahpanhes, Rameses, and all the land of Goshen, 10 until you come above Tanis and Memphis, and to all that lived in Egypt, until you come to the borders of Ethiopia. 11 All those who lived in all the land made light of the commandment of Nebuchadnezzar king of the Assyrians and didn't go with him to the war; for they were not afraid of him, but he was before them as one man. They turned away his messengers from their presence without effect, and with disgrace. 12 And Nebuchadnezzar was exceedingly angry with all this land, and he swore by his throne and kingdom, that he would surely be avenged upon all the coasts of Cilicia, Damascus, and Syria, that he would kill with his sword all the inhabitants of the land of Moab, and the children of Ammon, all Judea, and all that were in Egypt, until you come to the borders of the two seas. 13 And he set the battle in array with his army against king Arphaxad in the seventeenth year; and he prevailed in his battle, and turned to flight all the army of Arphaxad, with all his horses and all his chariots. 14 He became master of his cities, and he came even to Ecbatana, and took the towers, plundered its streets, and turned its beauty into shame. 15 He took Arphaxad in the mountains of Ragau, struck him through with his darts, and utterly destroyed him, to this day. 16 He returned with them to Nineveh, he and all his company of sundry nations, an exceedingly great multitude of men of war, and there he took his ease and banqueted, he and his army, for one hundred twenty days.

CHAPTER 2

1 In the eighteenth year, the twenty-second day of the first month, there was talk in the house of Nebuchadnezzar king of the Assyrians, that he should be avenged on all the land, even as he spoke. 2 He called together all his servants and all his great men, and communicated with them his secret counsel,

and concluded the afflicting of all the land out of his own mouth. **3** They decreed to destroy all flesh which didn't follow the word of his mouth. **4** It came to pass, when he had ended his counsel, Nebuchadnezzar king of the Assyrians called Holofernes the chief captain of his army, which was next after himself, and said to him, **5** "The great king, the lord of all the earth, says: Behold, you will go out from my presence, and take with you men who trust in their strength, to one hundred twenty thousand footmen and twelve thousand horses with their riders. **6** And you will go out against all the west country, because they disobeyed the commandment of my mouth. **7** You will declare to them that they should prepare earth and water, because I will go out in my wrath against them and will cover the whole face of the earth with the feet of my army, and I will give them as plunder to them. **8** Their slain will fill their valleys and brooks, and the river will be filled with their dead until it overflows. **9** I will lead them captives to the utmost parts of all the earth. **10** But you will go out and take all their coasts for me first. If they will yield themselves to you, then you must reserve them for me until the day of their reproof. **11** As for those who are disobedient, your eye will not spare; but you will give them up to be slain and to be plundered in all your land. **12** For as I live, and by the power of my kingdom, I have spoken, and I will do this with my hand. **13** Moreover, you will not transgress anything of the commandments of your lord, but you will surely accomplish them, as I have commanded you. You will not defer to do them." **14** So Holofernes went out from the presence of his lord, and called all the governors, the captains, and officers of the army of Asshur. **15** He counted chosen men for the battle, as his lord had commanded him, to one hundred twenty thousand, with twelve thousand archers on horseback. **16** He arranged them as a great multitude is ordered for the war. **17** He took camels and asses and mules for their baggage, an exceedingly great multitude, and sheep and oxen and goats without number for their provision, **18** and great store of rations for every man, and exceedingly much gold and silver out of the king's house. **19** He went out, he and all his army, on their journey, to go before king Nebuchadnezzar, and to cover all the face of the earth westward with their chariots, horsemen, and chosen footmen. **20** A great company of various nations went out with them like locusts, and like the sand of the earth. For they could not be counted by reason of their multitude. **21** And they departed out of Nineveh three days' journey toward the plain of Bectileth and encamped from Bectileth near the mountain which is at the left hand of the upper Cilicia. **22** And he took all his army, his footmen, horsemen, and chariots, and went away from there into the hill country, **23** and destroyed Put and Lud, and plundered all the children of Rasses and the children of Ishmael, which were along the wilderness to the south of the land of the Chellians. **24** And he went over Euphrates, and went through Mesopotamia, and broke down all the high cities that were upon the river Arbonai, until you come to the sea. **25** And he took possession of the borders of Cilicia, and killed all that resisted him, and came to the borders of Japheth, which were toward the south, opposite Arabia. **26** He surrounded all the children of Midian, and set their tents on fire, and plundered their sheepfolds. **27** He went down into the plain of Damascus in the days of wheat harvest, and set all their fields on fire, and utterly destroyed their flocks and herds, and plundered their cities, laid their plains waste, and struck all their young men with the edge of the sword. **28** And the fear and the dread of him fell upon those who lived on the sea coast, upon those who were in Sidon and Tyre, those who lived in Sur and Ocina, and all who lived in Jemnaan. Those who lived in Azotus and Ascalon feared him exceedingly.

CHAPTER 3

1 And they sent to him messengers with words of peace, saying, **2** "Behold, we the servants of Nebuchadnezzar the great king lie before you. Use us as it is pleasing in your sight. **3** Behold, our dwellings, and all our country, and all our fields of wheat, and our flocks and herds, and all the sheepfolds of our tents, lie before your face. Use them as it may please you. **4** Behold, even our cities and those who dwell in them are your servants. Come and deal with them as it is good in your eyes." **5** So the men came to Holofernes and declared to him according to these words. **6** He came down toward the sea coast, he and his army, and set garrisons in the high cities, and took out of them chosen men for allies. **7** They received him, they and all the country around them, with garlands and dances and timbrels. **8** He cast down all their borders and cut down their sacred groves. It had been given to him to destroy all the gods of the land, that all the nations would worship Nebuchadnezzar only, and that all their tongues and their tribes would call upon him as god. **9** Then he came toward Esdraelon near to Dotaea, which is opposite the great ridge of Judea. **10** He encamped between Geba and Scythopolis. He was there a whole month, that he might gather together all the baggage of his army.

CHAPTER 4

1 The children of Israel that lived in Judea heard all that Holofernes the chief captain of Nebuchadnezzar king of the Assyrians had done to the nations, and how he had plundered all their temples and destroyed them utterly. **2** They were exceedingly afraid before him, and were troubled for Jerusalem, and for the temple of the Lord their God; **3** because they had newly come up from the captivity, and all the people of Judea were recently gathered together; and the vessels, the altar, and the house were sanctified after being profaned. **4** And they sent into every coast of Samaria, to Konae, to Beth-horon, Belmaim, Jericho, to Choba, Aesora, and to the valley of Salem; **5** and they occupied beforehand all the tops of the high mountains, fortified the villages that were in them, stored supplies for the provision of war; for their fields were newly reaped. **6** Joakim the high priest, who was in those days at Jerusalem, wrote to those who lived in Bethulia, and Betomesthaim, which is opposite Esdraelon toward the plain that is near to Doesaim, **7** charging them to seize upon the ascents of the hill country; because by them was the entrance into Judea, and it was easy to stop them from approaching, since the approach was narrow, with space for two men at the most. **8** And the children of Israel did as Joakim the high priest had commanded them, as did the senate of all the people of Israel, which lived at Jerusalem. **9** And every man of Israel cried to God with great earnestness, and with great earnestness they humbled their souls. **10** They, their wives, their children, their cattle, and every sojourner, hireling, and servant bought with their money put sackcloth on their loins. **11** Every man and woman of Israel, and the little children, and the inhabitants of Jerusalem, fell before the temple, and cast ashes upon their heads, and spread out their sackcloth before the Lord. They put sackcloth around the altar. **12** They cried to the God of Israel earnestly with one consent, that he would not give their children

as prey, their wives as plunder, the cities of their inheritance to destruction, and the sanctuary to being profaned and being made a reproach, for the nations to rejoice at. **13** The Lord heard their voice and looked at their affliction. The people continued fasting many days in all Judea and Jerusalem before the sanctuary of the Lord Almighty. **14** And Joakim the high priest, and all the priests that stood before the Lord, and those who ministered to the Lord, had their loins dressed in sackcloth, and offered the continual burnt offering, the vows, and the free gifts of the people. **15** They had ashes on their hats. They cried to the Lord with all their power, that he would look upon all the house of Israel for good.

CHAPTER 5

1 Holofernes, the chief captain of the army of Asshur, was told that the children of Israel had prepared for war, had shut up the passages of the hill country, had fortified all the tops of the high hills, and had laid impediments in the plains. **2** Then he was exceedingly angry, and he called all the princes of Moab, and the captains of Ammon, and all the governors of the sea coast, **3** and he said to them, "Tell me now, you sons of Canaan, who are these people who dwell in the hill country? What are the cities that they inhabit? How large is their army? Where is their power and their strength? What king is set over them, to be the leader of their army? **4** Why have they turned their backs, that they should not come and meet me, more than all that dwell in the west?" **5** Then Achior, the leader of all the children of Ammon, said to him, "Let my lord now hear a word from the mouth of your servant, and I will tell you the truth concerning these people who dwell in this hill country, near to the place where you dwell. No lie will come out of the mouth of your servant. **6** These people are descended from the Chaldeans. **7** They sojourned before this in Mesopotamia, because they didn't want to follow the gods of their fathers, which were in the land of the Chaldeans. **8** They departed from the way of their parents, and worshiped the God of heaven, the God whom they knew. Their parents cast them out from the face of their gods, and they fled into Mesopotamia, and sojourned there many days. **9** Then their God commanded them to depart from the place where they sojourned, and to go into the land of Canaan. They lived there, and prospered with gold and silver, and with exceedingly much cattle. **10** Then they went down into Egypt, for a famine covered all the land of Canaan. They sojourned there until they had grown up. They became a great multitude there, so that one could not count the population of their nation. **11** Then the king of Egypt rose up against them, and dealt subtly with them, and brought them low, making them labor in brick, and made them slaves. **12** They cried to their God, and he struck all the land of Egypt with incurable plagues; so the Egyptians cast them out of their sight. **13** God dried up the Red sea before them, **14** and brought them into the way of Sinai Kadesh-Barnea, and they cast out all that lived in the wilderness. **15** They lived in the land of the Amorites, and they destroyed by their strength everyone in Heshbon. Passing over Jordan, they possessed all the hill country. **16** They cast out before them the Canaanite, the Perizzite, the Jebusite, the Shechemite, and all the Girgashites, and they lived in that country many days. **17** And while they didn't sin before their God, they prospered, because God who hates iniquity was with them. **18** But when they departed from the way which he appointed them, they were destroyed in many severe battles, and were led captives into a land that was not theirs. The temple of their God was cast to the ground, and their cities were taken by their adversaries. **19** And now they have returned to their God and have come up from the dispersion where they were dispersed, and have possessed Jerusalem, where their sanctuary is, and are seated in the hill country; for it was desolate. **20** And now, my lord and master, if there is any error in this people, and they sin against their God, we will consider what this thing is in which they stumble, and we will go up and overcome them. **21** But if there is no lawlessness in their nation, let my lord now pass by, lest their Lord defend them, and their God be for them, and we will be a reproach before all the earth." **22** It came to pass, when Achior had finished speaking these words, all the people standing around the tent murmured. The great men of Holofernes, and all that lived by the sea side and in Moab, said that he should kill him. **23** For, they said, "We will not be afraid of the children of Israel, because, behold, they are a people that has no power nor might to make the battle strong. **24** Therefore now we will go up, and they will be a prey to be devoured by all your army, Lord Holofernes."

CHAPTER 6

1 And when the disturbance of the men that were around the council had ceased, Holofernes the chief captain of the army of Asshur said to Achior and to all the children of Moab before all the people of the foreigners, **2** "And who are you, Achior, and the hirelings of Ephraim, that you have prophesied among us as today, and have said that we should not make war with the race of Israel, because their God will defend them? And who is God but Nebuchadnezzar? **3** He will send out his might and will destroy them from the face of the earth, and their God will not deliver them; but we his servants will strike them as one man. They will not sustain the might of our horses. **4** For with them we will burn them up. Their mountains will be drunken with their blood. Their plains will be filled with their dead bodies. Their footsteps will not stand before us, but they will surely perish, says king Nebuchadnezzar, lord of all the earth; for he said, 'The words that I have spoken will not be in vain.' **5** But you, Achior, hireling of Ammon, who have spoken these words in the day of your iniquity, will see my face no more from this day, until I am avenged of the race of those that came out of Egypt. **6** And then the sword of my army, and the multitude of those who serve me, will pass through your sides, and you will fall among their slain when I return. **7** Then my servants will bring you back into the hill country and will set you in one of the cities of the ascents. **8** You will not perish until you are destroyed with them. **9** And if you hope in your heart that they will not be taken, don't let your countenance fall. I have spoken it, and none of my words will fall to the ground." **10** Then Holofernes commanded his servants who waited in his tent to take Achior, and bring him back to Bethulia, and deliver him into the hands of the children of Israel. **11** So his servants took him and brought him out of the camp into the plain, and they moved from the midst of the plains into the hill country and came to the springs that were under Bethulia. **12** When the men of the city saw them on the top of the hill, they took up their weapons, and went out of the city against them to the top of the hill. Every man that used a sling kept them from coming up and cast stones against them. **13** They took cover under the hill, bound Achior, cast him down, left him at the foot of the hill, and went away to their lord. **14** But the children of Israel descended from their city, and came to him, untied him, led him away into Bethulia, and presented him to the rulers of their city; **15** which were in those days Ozias the son of Micah, of the tribe of Simeon, and Chabris the son of Gothoniel, and Charmis the son of Melchiel. **16** Then they called together all the elders of the city; and all their young men ran together, with their women, to the assembly. They set Achior in the midst of all their people. Then Ozias asked him what had happened. **17** He answered and declared to them the words of the council of Holofernes, and all the words that he had spoken in the midst of the princes of the children of Asshur, and all the great words that Holofernes had spoken against the house of Israel. **18** Then the people fell down and worshiped God, and cried, saying, **19** "O Lord God of heaven, behold their arrogance, and pity the low estate of our race. Look upon the face of those who are sanctified to you this day." **20** They comforted Achior and praised him exceedingly. **21** Then Ozias took him out of the assembly into his house and made a feast for the elders. They called on the God of Israel for help all that night.

CHAPTER 7

1 The next day Holofernes commanded all his army and all the people who had come to be his allies, that they should move their camp toward Bethulia, take beforehand the ascents of the hill country, and make war against the children of Israel. **2** Every mighty man of them moved that day. The army of their men of war was one hundred seventy thousand footmen, plus twelve thousand horsemen, besides the baggage, and the men that were on foot among them: an exceedingly great multitude. **3** They encamped in the valley near Bethulia, by the fountain. They spread themselves in breadth over Doesaim even to Belmaim, and in length from Bethulia to Cyamon, which is near Esdraelon. **4** But the children of Israel, when they saw the multitude of them, were troubled exceedingly, and everyone said to his neighbor, "Now these men will lick up the face of all the earth. Neither the high mountains, nor the valleys, nor the hills will be able to bear their weight. **5** Every man took up his weapons of war, and when they had kindled fires upon their towers, they remained and watched all that night. **6** But on the second day Holofernes led out all his cavalry in the sight of the children of Israel which were in Bethulia, **7** viewed the ascents to their city, and searched out the springs of the waters, seized upon them, and set garrisons of men of war over them. Then he departed back to his people. **8** All the rulers of the children of Esau, all the leaders of the people of Moab, and the captains of the sea coast came to him and said, **9** "Let our lord now hear a word, that there be not losses in your army. **10** For this people of the children of Israel do not trust in their spears, but in the height of the mountains wherein they dwell, for it is not easy to come up to the tops of their mountains. **11** And now, my lord, don't fight against them as men fight who join battle, and there will not so much as one man of your people perish. **12** Remain in your camp and keep every man of your army safe. Let your servants get possession of the water spring, which flows from the foot of the mountain, **13** because all the inhabitants of Bethulia get their water from there. Then thirst will kill them, and they will give up their city. Then we and our people will go up to the tops of the mountains that are near, and will encamp upon them, to watch that not one man gets out of the city. **14** They will be consumed with famine, they and their wives and their children. Before the sword comes against them they will be laid low in the streets where they dwell. **15** And you will pay them back with evil, because they rebelled, and didn't meet your face in peace." **16** Their words were pleasing in the sight of Holofernes and in the sight of all his servants; and he ordered them to do as they had spoken. **17** And the army of the children of Ammon moved, and with them five thousand of the children of Asshur, and they encamped in the valley. They seized the waters and the springs of the waters of the children of Israel. **18** The children of Esau went up with the children of Ammon and encamped in the hill country near Doesaim. They sent some of them toward the south, and toward the east, near Ekrebel, which is near Chusi, that is upon the brook Mochmur. The rest of the army of the Assyrians encamped in the plain and covered all the face of the land. Their tents and baggage were pitched upon it in a great crowd. They were an exceedingly great multitude. **19** The children of Israel cried to the Lord their God, for their spirit fainted; for all their enemies had surrounded them. There was no way to escape out from among them. **20** All the army of Asshur remained around them, their footmen and their chariots and their horsemen, thirty-four days. All their vessels of water ran dry for all the inhabitants of Bethulia. **21** The cisterns were emptied, and they had no water to drink their fill for one day; for they rationed drink by measure. **22** Their young children were discouraged. The women and the young men fainted for thirst. They fell down in the streets of the city, and in the passages of the gates. There was no longer any strength in them. **23** All the people, including the young men, the women, and the children, were gathered together against Ozias, and against the rulers of the city. They cried with a loud voice, and said before all the elders, **24** "God be judge between all of you and us, because you have done us great wrong, in that you have not spoken words of peace with the children of Asshur. **25** Now we have no helper; but God has sold us into their hands, that we should be laid low before them with thirst and great destruction. **26** And now summon them and deliver up the whole city as prey to the people of Holofernes, and to all his army. **27** For it is better for us to be made a plunder to them. For we will be servants, and our souls will live, and we will not see the death of our babies before our eyes, and our wives and our children fainting in death. **28** We take to witness against you the heaven and the earth, and our God and the Lord of our fathers, who punishes us according to our sins and the sins of our fathers. Do what we have said today!" **29** And there was great weeping of all with one consent in the midst of the assembly; and they cried to the Lord God with a loud voice. **30** And Ozias said to them, "Brethren, be of good courage! Let us endure five more days, during which the Lord our God will turn his mercy toward us; for he will not forsake us utterly. **31** But if these days pass, and no help comes to us, I will do what you say." **32** Then he dispersed the people, every man to his own camp; and they went away to the walls and towers of their city. He sent the women and children into their houses. They were brought very low in the city.

CHAPTER 8

1 In those days Judith heard about this. She was the daughter of Merari, the son of Ox, the son of Joseph, the son of Oziel, the son of Elkiah, the son of Ananias, the son of Gideon, the son of Raphaim, the son of Ahitub, the son of Elihu, the son of Eliab, the son of Nathanael, the son of Salamiel, the son of Salasadai, the son of Israel. **2** Her husband was Manasses, of her tribe and of her family. He died in the days of barley harvest. **3** For he stood over those who bound sheaves in the field, and the heat came upon his head, and he fell on his bed, and died in his city Bethulia. So they buried him with his fathers in the field which is between Doesaim and Balamon. **4** Judith was a widow in her house three years and four months. **5** She made herself a tent upon the roof of her house and put on sackcloth upon her loins. The garments of her widowhood were upon her. **6** And she fasted all the days of her widowhood, except the eves of the Sabbaths, the Sabbaths, the eves of the new moons, the new moons, and the feasts and joyful days of the house of Israel. **7** She was of a goodly countenance, and exceedingly beautiful to behold. Her husband Manasses had left her gold, silver, menservants, maidservants, cattle, and lands. She remained on those lands. **8** No one said anything evil about her; for she feared God exceedingly. **9** She heard the evil words of the people against the governor, because they fainted for lack of water; and Judith heard all the words that Ozias spoke to them, how he swore to them that he would deliver the city to the Assyrians after five days. **10** So she sent her maid, who was over all things that she had, to summon Ozias, Chabris, and Charmis, the elders of her city. **11** They came to her, and she said to them, "Hear me now, O you rulers of the inhabitants of Bethulia: for your word that you have spoken before the people this day is not right. You have set the oath which you have pronounced between God and you and have promised to deliver the city to our enemies, unless within these days the Lord turns to help you. **12** Now who are you that you have tempted God this day, and stand in the place of God among the children of men? **13** Now try the Lord Almighty, and you will never know anything. **14** For you will not find the depth of the heart of man, and you will not perceive the things that he thinks. How will you search out God, who has made all these things, and know his mind, and comprehend his purpose? No, my kindred, don't provoke the Lord our God to anger! **15** For if he has not decided to help us within these five days, he has power to defend us in such time as he will, or to destroy us before the face of our enemies. **16** But don't you pledge the counsels of the Lord our God! For God is not as man, that he should be threatened; neither as the son of man, that he should be turned by entreaty. **17** Therefore let's wait for the salvation that comes from him and call upon him to help us. He will hear our voice, if it pleases him. **18** For there arose none in our age, neither is there any of us today, tribe, or kindred, or family, or city, which worship gods made with hands, as it was in the former days; 19 for which cause our fathers were given to the sword, and for plunder, and fell with a great fall before our enemies. 20 But we know no other god beside him. Therefore, we hope that he will not despise us, nor any of our race. 21 For if we are taken so, all Judea will sit upon the ground, and our sanctuary will be plundered; and he will require our blood for profaning it. 22 And the slaughter of our kindred, and the captivity of the land, and the desolation of our inheritance, he will turn upon our heads among the Gentiles, wherever we will be in bondage. We will be an offense and a reproach before those who take us for a possession. 23 For our bondage will not be ordered to favor; but the Lord our God will turn it to dishonor. 24 And now, kindred, let's show an example to our kindred, because their soul hangs upon us, and the sanctuary, the house, and the altar rest upon us. 25 Besides all this let's give thanks to the Lord our God, who tries us, even as he did our fathers also. 26 Remember all the things which he did to Abraham, and all the things in which he tried Isaac, and all the things which happened to Jacob in Mesopotamia of Syria, when he kept the sheep of Laban his mother's brother. 27 For he has not tried us in the fire, as he did them, to search out their hearts, neither has he taken vengeance on us; but the Lord does scourge them that come near to him, to admonish them." 28 And Ozias said to her, "All that you have spoken, you have spoken with a good heart. There is no one who will deny your words. 29 For this is not the first day wherein your wisdom is manifested; but from the beginning of your days all the people have known your understanding, because the disposition of your heart is good. 30 But the people were exceedingly thirsty and compelled us to do as we spoke to them, and to bring an oath upon ourselves, which we will not break. 31 And now pray for us, because you are a godly woman, and the Lord will send us rain to fill our cisterns, and we will faint no more." 32 Then Judith said to them, "Hear me, and I will do a thing, which will go down to all generations among the children of our race. 33 You will all stand at the gate tonight. I will go out with my maid. Within the days after which you said that you would deliver the city to our enemies, the Lord will visit Israel by my hand. 34 But you will not inquire of my act;

for I will not declare it to you, until the things are finished that I will do." 35 Then Ozias and the rulers said to her, "Go in peace. May the Lord God be before you, to take vengeance on our enemies." 36 So they returned from the tent and went to their stations.

CHAPTER 9

1 But Judith fell upon her face, and put ashes upon her head, and uncovered the sackcloth with which she was clothed. The incense of that evening was now being offered at Jerusalem in the house of God, and Judith cried to the Lord with a loud voice, and said, 2 "O Lord God of my father Simeon, into whose hand you gave a sword to take vengeance on the strangers who loosened the belt of a virgin to defile her, uncovered the thigh to her shame, and profaned the womb to her reproach; for you said, 'It will not be so;' and they did so. 3 Therefore you gave their rulers to be slain, and their bed, which was ashamed for her who was deceived, to be dyed in blood, and struck the servants with their masters, and the masters upon their thrones; 4 and gave their wives for a prey, and their daughters to be captives, and all their spoils to be divided among your dear children; which were moved with zeal for you, and abhorred the pollution of their blood, and called upon you for aid. O God, O my God, hear me also who am a widow. 5 For you did the things that were before those things, and those things, and such as come after; and you planned the things which are now, and the things which are to come. The things which you planned came to pass. 6 Yes, the things which you determined stood before you, and said, 'Behold, we are here; for all your ways are prepared, and your judgement is with foreknowledge.' 7 For, behold, the Assyrians are multiplied in their power. They are exalted with horse and rider. They were proud of the strength of their footmen. They have trusted in shield, spear, bow, and sling. They don't know that you are the Lord who breaks the battles. 'The Lord' is your name. 8 Break their strength in your power and bring down their force in your wrath; for they intend to profane your sanctuary, and to defile the tabernacle where your glorious name rests, and to destroy the horn of your altar with the sword. 9 Look at their pride and send your wrath upon their heads. Give into my hand, which am a widow, the might that I have conceived. 10 Strike by the deceit of my lips the servant with the

prince, and the prince with his servant. Break down their arrogance by the hand of a woman. 11 For your power stands not in multitude, nor your might in strong men: but you are a God of the afflicted. You are a helper of the minorities, a helper of the weak, a protector of the forsaken, a savior of those who are without hope. 12 Yes, yes, God of my father, and God of the inheritance of Israel, Lord of the heavens and of the earth. Creator of the waters, King of every creature, hear my prayer. 13 Make my speech and deceit to be their wound and stripe, who intend hard things against your covenant, your holy house, the top of Zion, and the house of the possession of your children. 14 Make every nation and tribe of yours to know that you are God, the God of all power and might, and that there is none other that protects the race of Israel but you."

CHAPTER 10

1 It came to pass, when she had ceased to cry to the God of Israel, and had finished saying all these words, 2 that she rose up where she had fallen down, called her maid, and went down into the house that she used to live in on the Sabbath days and on her feast days. 3 She pulled off the sackcloth which she had put on, took off the garments of her widowhood, washed her body all over with water, anointed herself with rich ointment, braided the hair of her head, and put a tiara upon it. She put on her garments of gladness, which she used to wear in the days of the life of Manasses her husband. 4 She took sandals for her feet, and put her chains around her, and her bracelets, her rings, her earrings, and all her jewelry, and decked herself bravely, to deceive the eyes of all men who would see her. 5 She gave her maid a leather container of wine and a flask of oil, and filled a bag with parched corn, lumps of figs, and finebread. She packed all her vessels together and laid them upon her. 6 They went out to the gate of the city of Bethulia, and found Ozias and the elders of the city, Chabris and Charmis standing by it. 7 But when they saw her, that her countenance was altered, and her apparel was changed, they wondered at her beauty very exceedingly, and said to her, 8 "May the God of our fathers give you favor and accomplish your purposes to the glory of the children of Israel, and to the exaltation of Jerusalem." Then she worshiped God, 9 and said to them, "Command that they open the gate of the city for me, and I will go out to accomplish the things you spoke with me about." And they commanded the young men to open to her, as she had spoken; 10 and they did so. Then Judith went out, she, and her handmaid with her. The men of the city watched her until she had gone down the mountain, until she had passed the valley, and they could see her no more. 11 They went straight onward in the valley. The watch of the Assyrians met her; 12 and they took her, and asked her, "Of what people are you? Where are you coming from? Where are you going?" She said, "I am a daughter of the Hebrews. I am fleeing away from their presence, because they are about to be given you to be consumed. 13 I am coming into the presence of Holofernes the chief captain of your army, to declare words of truth. I will show him a way that he can go and win all the hill country, and there will not be lacking his men one person, nor one life." 14 Now when the men heard her words, and considered her countenance, the beauty thereof was exceedingly marvelous in their eyes. They said to her, 15 "You have saved your life, in that you have hurried to come down to the presence of our master. Now come to his tent. Some of us will guide you until they deliver you into his hands. 16 But when you stand before him, don't be afraid in your heart, but declare to him according to your words; and he will treat you well." 17 They chose out of them a hundred men, and appointed them to accompany her and her maid; and they brought them to the tent of Holofernes. 18 And there was great excitement throughout all the camp, for her coming was reported among the tents. They came and surrounded her as she stood outside Holofernes' tent, until they told him about her. 19 They marveled at her beauty and marveled at the children of Israel because of her. Each one said to his neighbor, "Who would despise this people, that have among them such women? For it is not good that one man of them be left, seeing that, if they are let go, they will be able to deceive the whole earth. 20 Those who lay near Holofernes, and all his servants, went out and brought her into the tent. 21 And Holofernes was resting upon his bed under the canopy, which was woven with purple, gold, emeralds, and precious stones. 22 And they told him about her; and he came out into the space before his tent, with silver lamps going before him. 23 But when Judith had come before him and his servants, they all marveled at the beauty of her countenance. She fell down upon her face, and

bowed down to him, but his servants raised her up.

CHAPTER 11

1 Holofernes said to her, "Woman, take courage. Don't be afraid in your heart; for I never hurt anyone who has chosen to serve Nebuchadnezzar, the king of all the earth. **2** And now, if your people who dwell in the hill country had not slighted me, I would not have lifted up my spear against them; but they have done these things to themselves. **3** And now tell me why you fled from them and came to us; for you have come to save yourself. Take courage! You will live tonight, and hereafter; **4** for there is no one that will wrong you, but all will treat you well, as is done to the servants of king Nebuchadnezzar my lord." **5** And Judith said to him, "Receive the words of your servant, and let your handmaid speak in your presence, and I will declare no lie to my lord this night. **6** If you will follow the words of your handmaid, God will bring the thing to pass perfectly with you; and my lord will not fail to accomplish his purposes. **7** As Nebuchadnezzar king of all the earth lives, and as his power lives, who has sent you for the preservation of every living thing, not only do men serve him by you, but also the beasts of the field, the cattle, and the birds of the sky will live through your strength, in the time of Nebuchadnezzar and of all his house. **8** For we have heard of your wisdom and the subtle plans of your soul. It has been reported in all the earth that you only are brave in all the kingdom, mighty in knowledge, and wonderful in feats of war. **9** And now as concerning the matter which Achior spoke in your council, we have heard his words; for the men of Bethulia saved him, and he declared to them all that he had spoken before you. **10** Therefore, O lord and master, don't neglect his word; but lay it up in your heart, for it is true; for our race will not be punished, neither will the sword prevail against them, unless they sin against their God. **11** And now, that my lord be not defeated and frustrate of his purpose, and that death may fall upon them, their sin has overtaken them, with which they will provoke their God to anger, whenever they do wickedness. **12** Since their food failed them, and all their water was scant, they took counsel to lay hands upon their cattle, and determined to consume all those things which God charged them by his laws that they should not eat. **13** They are resolved to spend the first fruits of the corn, and the tenths of the wine and the oil, which they had sanctified and reserved for the priests who stand before the face of our God in Jerusalem; which things it is not fitting for any of the people so much as to touch with their hands. **14** They have sent some to Jerusalem, because they also that dwell there have done this thing, to bring them permission from the council of elders. **15** It will be, when word comes to them and they do it, they will be given to you to be destroyed the same day. **16** Therefore I your servant, knowing all this, fled away from their presence. God sent me to work things with you, at which all the earth will be astonished, even as many as hear it. **17** For your servant is religious and serves the God of heaven day and night. Now, my lord, I will stay with you, and your servant will go out by night into the valley. I will pray to God, and he will tell me when they have committed their sins. **18** Then I will come and show it also to you. Then you will go out with all your army, and there will be none of them that will resist you. **19** And I will lead you through the midst of Judea, until you come to Jerusalem. I will set your seat in the midst of it. You will drive them as sheep that have no shepherd, and a dog will not so much as open his mouth before you; for these things were told me according to my foreknowledge, and were declared to me, and I was sent to tell you." **20** Her words were pleasing in the sight of Holofernes and of all his servants. They marveled at her wisdom, and said, **21** "There is not such a woman from one end of the earth to the other, for beauty of face and wisdom of words." **22** Holofernes said to her, "God did well to send you before the people, that might would be in our hands, and destruction among those who slighted my lord. **23** And now you are beautiful in your countenance, and wise in your words. If you will do as you have spoken, your God will be my God, and you will dwell in the house of king Nebuchadnezzar and will be renowned through the whole earth."

CHAPTER 12

1 He commanded that she should be brought in where his silver vessels were set and asked that his servants should prepare some of his own meats for her, and that she should drink from his own wine. **2** And Judith said, "I will not eat of it, lest there be an occasion of stumbling: but provision will be made for me of the things that have come with me." **3** And

Holofernes said to her, "But if the things that are with you should fail, from where will we be able to give you more like it? For there is none of your race with us." **4** And Judith said to him, "As your soul lives, my lord, your servant will not spend those things that are with me, until the Lord works by my hand the things that he has determined." **5** Then Holofernes' servants brought her into the tent, and she slept until midnight. Then she rose up toward the morning watch, **6** and sent to Holofernes, saying, "Let my lord now command that they allow your servant to go out to pray." **7** Holofernes commanded his guards that they should not stop her. She stayed in the camp three days and went out every night into the valley of Bethulia and washed herself at the fountain of water in the camp. **8** And when she came up, she implored the Lord God of Israel to direct her way to the raising up of the children of his people. **9** She came in clean, and remained in the tent, until she ate her food toward evening. **10** It came to pass on the fourth day, that Holofernes made a feast for his own servants only and called none of the officers to the banquet. **11** And he said to Bagoas the eunuch, who had charge over all that he had, "Go now, and persuade this Hebrew woman who is with you that she come to us and eat and drink with us. **12** For, behold, it is a shame for our person, if we will let such a woman go, not having had her company; for if we don't draw her to ourselves, she will laugh us to scorn." **13** Bagoas went from the presence of Holofernes, and came in to her, and said, "Let this fair lady not fear to come to my lord, and to be honored in his presence, and to drink wine and be merry with us, and to be made this day as one of the daughters of the children of Asshur, which wait in the house of Nebuchadnezzar." **14** Judith said to him, "Who am I, that I should contradict my lord? For whatever would be pleasing in his eyes, I will do speedily, and this will be my joy to the day of my death." **15** She arose and decked herself with her apparel and all her woman's attire; and her servant went and laid fleeces on the ground for her next to Holofernes, which she had received from Bagoas for her daily use, that she might sit and eat upon them. **16** Judith came in and sat down, and Holofernes' heart was ravished with her. His soul was moved, and he exceedingly desired her company. He was watching for a time to deceive her, from the day that he had seen her. **17** Holofernes said to her, "Drink now, and be

merry with us." **18** Judith said, "I will drink now, my lord, because my life is magnified in me this day more than all the days since I was born." **19** Then she took and ate and drank before him what her servant had prepared. **20** Holofernes took great delight in her, and drank exceedingly much wine, more than he had drunk at any time in one day since he was born.

CHAPTER 13

1 But when the evening had come, his servants hurried to depart. Bagoas shut the tent outside and dismissed those who waited from the presence of his lord. They went away to their beds; for they were all weary, because the feast had been long. **2** But Judith was left alone in the tent, with Holofernes lying along upon his bed; for he was drunk with wine. **3** Judith had said to her servant that she should stand outside her bedchamber, and wait for her to come out, as she did daily; for she said she would go out to her prayer. She spoke to Bagoas according to the same words. **4** All went away from her presence, and none was left in the bedchamber, small or great. Judith, standing by his bed, said in her heart, O Lord God of all power, look in this hour upon the works of my hands for the exaltation of Jerusalem. **5** For now is the time to help your inheritance, and to do the thing that I have purposed to the destruction of the enemies which have risen up against us. **6** She came to the rail of the bed, which was at Holofernes' head, and took down his scimitar from there. **7** She drew near to the bed, took hold of the hair of his head, and said, "Strengthen me, O Lord God of Israel, this day." **8** She struck twice upon his neck with all her might, and took away his head from him, **9** tumbled his body down from the bed, and took down the canopy from the pillars. After a little while she went out and gave Holofernes' head to her maid; **10** and she put it in her bag of food. They both went out together to prayer, according to their custom. They passed through the camp, circled around that valley, and went up to the mountain of Bethulia, and came to its gates. **11** Judith said afar off to the watchmen at the gates, "Open, open the gate, now. God is with us, even our God, to show his power yet in Israel, and his might against the enemy, as he has done even this day." **12** It came to pass, when the men of her city heard her voice, they made haste to go down to the gate of their city, and they called together the elders of the city. **13** They all ran together, both small and great, for it was strange to them that she had come. They opened the gate and received them, making a fire to give light, and surrounded them. **14** She said to them with a loud voice, "Praise God! Praise him! Praise God, who has not taken away his mercy from the house of Israel but has destroyed our enemies by my hand tonight!" **15** Then she took the head out of the bag and showed it, and said to them, "Behold, the head of Holofernes, the chief captain of the army of Asshur, and behold, the canopy, in which he laid in his drunkenness. The Lord struck him by the hand of a woman. **16** And as the Lord lives, who preserved me in my way that I went, my countenance deceived him to his destruction, and he didn't commit sin with me, to defile and shame me." **17** All the people were exceedingly amazed, and bowed themselves, and worshiped God, and said with one accord, "Blessed are you, O our God, which have this day brought to nothing the enemies of your people." **18** Ozias said to her, "Blessed are you, daughter, in the sight of the Most High God, above all the women upon the earth; and blessed is the Lord God, who created the heavens and the earth, who directed you to cut off the head of the prince of our enemies. **19** For your hope will not depart from the heart of men that remember the strength of God forever. **20** May God turn these things to you for a perpetual praise, to visit you with good things, because you didn't spare your life by reason of the affliction of our race, but avenged our fall, walking a straight way before our God." And all the people said, "Amen! Amen!"

CHAPTER 14

1 Judith said to them, "Hear me now, my kindred, and take this head, and hang it upon the battlement of your wall. **2** It will be, so soon as the morning appears, and the sun comes up on the earth, you will each take up his weapons of war, and every valiant man of you go out of the city. You will set a captain over them, as though you would go down to the plain toward the watch of the children of Asshur; but you men will not go down. **3** These will take up their full armor and will go into their camp and rouse up the captains of the army of Asshur. They will run together to Holofernes' tent. They won't find him. Fear will fall upon them, and they will flee before your face. **4** You men, and all that inhabit every coast of Israel, will pursue them and overthrow them as they go. **5** But before you do these things, summon Achior the Ammonite to me, that he may see and know him that despised the house of Israel, and that sent him to us, as it were to death. **6** And they called Achior out of the house of Ozias; but when he came and saw the head of Holofernes in a man's hand in the assembly of the people, he fell upon his face, and his spirit failed. **7** But when they had recovered him, he fell at Judith's feet, and bowed down to her, and said, "Blessed are you in every tent of Judah, and in every nation, which hearing your name will be troubled. **8** Now tell me all the things that you have done in these days." And Judith declared to him in the midst of the people all the things that she had done, from the day that she went out until the time that she spoke to them. **9** But when she finished speaking, the people shouted with a loud voice, and made a joyful noise in their city. **10** But when Achior saw all the things that the God of Israel had done, he believed in God exceedingly, and circumcised the flesh of his foreskin, and was joined to the house of Israel, to this day. **11** But as soon as the morning arose, they hanged the head of Holofernes upon the wall, and every man took up his weapons, and they went out by bands to the ascents of the mountain. **12** But when the children of Asshur saw them, they sent word to their leaders; but they went to their captains and tribunes, and to every one of their rulers. **13** They came to Holofernes' tent, and said to him that was over all that he had, "Wake our lord up, now; for the slaves have been bold to come down against us to battle, that they may be utterly destroyed." **14** Bagoas went in and knocked at the outer door of the tent; for he supposed that he was sleeping with Judith. **15** But when no one listened to him, he opened it, and went into the bedchamber, and found him cast upon the threshold dead, and his head had been taken from him. **16** He cried with a loud voice, with weeping and groaning and a mighty cry, and tore his garments. **17** He entered into the tent where Judith lodged, and he didn't find her. He leaped out to the people, and cried aloud, **18** "The slaves have dealt treacherously! One woman of the Hebrews has brought shame upon the house of king Nebuchadnezzar; for, behold, Holofernes lies upon the ground, and his head is not on him!" **19** But when the rulers of the army of Asshur heard the words, they tore their coats, and their soul was troubled exceedingly. There was a cry and an exceedingly great noise in the midst of the camp.

CHAPTER 15

1 When those who were in the tents heard, they were amazed at what happened. 2 Trembling and fear fell upon them, and no man dared stay any more in the sight of his neighbor, but rushing out with one accord, they fled into every way of the plain and of the hill country. 3 Those who had encamped in the hill country around Bethulia fled away. And then the children of Israel, everyone who was a warrior among them, rushed out upon them. 4 Ozias sent to Betomasthaim, Bebai, Chobai, and Chola, and to every coast of Israel, to tell about the things that had been accomplished, and that all should rush upon their enemies to destroy them. 5 But when the children of Israel heard, they all fell upon them with one accord, and struck them to Chobai. Yes, and in like manner also they of Jerusalem and of all the hill country came (for men had told them about what happened in their enemies' camp), and those who were in Gilead and in Galilee fell upon their flank with a great slaughter, until they were past Damascus and its borders. 6 The rest of the people who lived at Bethulia fell upon the camp of Asshur, and plundered them, and were enriched exceedingly. 7 The children of Israel returned from the slaughter and got possession of that which remained. The villages and the cities that were in the hill country and in the plain country, took many spoils; for there was an exceedingly great supply. 8 Joakim the high priest, and the elders of the children of Israel who lived in Jerusalem, came to see the good things which the Lord had showed to Israel, and to see Judith, and to salute her. 9 When they came to her, they all blessed her with one accord, and said to her, "You are the exaltation of Jerusalem! You are the great glory of Israel! You are the great rejoicing of our race! 10 You have done all these things by your hand. You have done with Israel the things that are good, and God is pleased with it. Blessed be you with the Almighty Lord forever. "And all the people said, "Amen!" 11 And the people plundered the camp for the space of thirty days: and they gave Holofernes' tent to Judith, along with all his silver cups, his beds, his bowls, and all his furniture. She took them, and placed them on her mule, and prepared her wagons, and heaped them on it. 12 And all the women of Israel ran together to see her; and

they blessed her and made a dance among them for her. She took branches in her hand and distributed them to the women who were with her. 13 Then they made themselves garlands of olive, she and those who were with her, and she went before all the people in the dance, leading all the women. All the men of Israel followed in their armor with garlands, and with songs in their mouths.

CHAPTER 16

1 And Judith began to sing this song of thanksgiving in all Israel, and all the people sang with loud voices this song of praise. 2 Judith said, "Begin a song to my God with timbrels. Sing to my Lord with cymbals. Make melody to him with psalm and praise. Exalt him and call upon his name. 3 For the Lord is the God that crushes battles. For in his armies in the midst of the people, he delivered me out of the hand of those who persecuted me. 4 Asshur came out of the mountains from the north. He came with tens of thousands of his army. Its multitude stopped the torrents. Their horsemen covered the hills. 5 He said that he would burn up my borders, kill my young men with the sword, throw my nursing children to the ground, give my infants up as prey, and make my virgins a plunder. 6 "The Almighty Lord brought them to nothing by the hand of a woman. 7 For their mighty one didn't fall by young men, neither did sons of the Titans strike him. Tall giants didn't attack him, but Judith the daughter of Merari made him weak with the beauty of her countenance. 8 "For she put off the apparel of her widowhood for the exaltation of those who were distressed in Israel. She anointed her face with ointment, bound her hair in a tiara, and took a linen garment to deceive him. 9 Her sandal ravished his eye. Her beauty took his soul prisoner. The scimitar passed through his neck. 10 "The Persians quaked at her daring. The Medes were daunted at her boldness. 11 "Then my lowly ones shouted aloud. My weak ones were terrified and trembled for fear. They lifted up their voice, and they fled. 12 The sons of ladies pierced them through and wounded them as fugitives' children. They perished by the battle of my Lord. 13 "I will sing to my God a new song: O Lord, you are great and glorious, marvelous in strength, invincible. 14 Let all your creation serve you; for you spoke, and they were made. You sent out your spirit, and it built them. There is no one who can resist your voice. 15 For the mountains

will be moved from their foundations with the waters, and the rocks will melt as wax at your presence: But you are yet merciful to those who fear you. **16** For all sacrifice is little for a sweet savor, and all the fat is very little for a whole burnt offering to you; But he who fears the Lord is great continually. **17** "Woe to the nations who rise up against my race! The Lord Almighty will take vengeance on them in the day of judgement, to put fire and worms in their flesh; and they will weep and feel their pain forever." **18** Now when they came to Jerusalem, they worshiped God. When the people were purified, they offered their whole burnt offerings, their free will offerings, and their gifts. **19** Judith dedicated all Holofernes' stuff, which the people had given her, and gave the canopy, which she had taken for herself out of his bedchamber, for a gift to the Lord. **20** And the people continued feasting in Jerusalem before the sanctuary for three months, and Judith remained with them. **21** But after these days, everyone departed to his own inheritance. Judith went away to Bethulia, and remained in her own possession, and was honorable in her time in all the land. **22** Many desired her, and no man knew her all the days of her life, from the day that Manasses her husband died and was gathered to his people. **23** She increased in greatness exceedingly; and she grew old in her husband's house, to one hundred five years, and let her maid go free. Then she died in Bethulia. They buried her in the cave of her husband Manasses. **24** The house of Israel mourned for her seven days. She distributed her goods before she died to all those who were nearest of kin to Manasses her husband, and to those who were nearest of her own kindred. **25** There was no one that made the children of Israel afraid any more in the days of Judith, nor a long time after her death.

WISDOM

Otherwise known as Wisdom of Solomon

The Book of Wisdom was written as late as fifty years before the coming of Christ. Its author, whose name is not known to us, was probably a member of the Jewish community at Alexandria, in Egypt. He wrote in Greek, in a style patterned on that of Hebrew verse. At times he speaks in the person of Solomon, placing his teachings on the lips of the wise king of Hebrew tradition in order to emphasize their value.

CHAPTER 1

1 Love righteousness, all you who are judges of the earth. Think of the Lord with a good mind. Seek him in singleness of heart, 2 because he is found by those who don't tempt him and is manifested to those who trust him. 3 For crooked thoughts separate from God. His Power convicts when it is tested and exposes the foolish. 4 Because wisdom will not enter into a soul that devises evil, nor dwell in a body that is enslaved by sin. 5 For a holy spirit of discipline will flee deceit, and will depart from thoughts that are without understanding, and will be ashamed when unrighteousness has come in. 6 For wisdom is a spirit who loves man, and she will not hold a blasphemer guiltless for his lips; because God is witness of his inmost self, and is a true overseer of his heart, and a hearer of his tongue: 7 Because the spirit of the Lord has filled the world, and that which holds all things together knows what is said. 8 Therefore no one who utters unrighteous things will be unseen; neither will Justice, when it convicts, pass him by. 9 For in his counsels the ungodly will be searched out, and the sound of his words will come to the Lord to bring his lawless deeds to conviction; 10 because a jealous ear listens to all things, and the noise of murmurings is not hidden. 11 Beware then of unprofitable murmuring and keep your tongue from slander; because no secret utterance will go on its way void, and a lying mouth destroys a soul. 12 Don't court death in the error of your life; and don't draw destruction upon yourselves by the works of your hands, 13 because God didn't make death; neither does he delight when the living

perish. 14 For he created all things that they might have being. The generative powers of the world are wholesome, and there is no poison of destruction in them, nor has Hades royal dominion upon earth; 15 For righteousness is immortal, 16 but ungodly men by their hands and their words summon death; deeming him a friend they pined away. They made a covenant with him, because they are worthy to belong with him.

CHAPTER 2

1 For they said within themselves, with unsound reasoning, "Our life is short and sorrowful. There is no healing when a man comes to his end, and no one was ever known who was released from Hades. 2 Because we were born by mere chance, and hereafter we will be as though we had never been; because the breath in our nostrils is smoke, and reason is a spark kindled by the beating of our heart; 3 which being extinguished, the body will be turned into ashes, and the spirit will be dispersed as thin air. 4 Our name will be forgotten in time. No one will remember our works. Our life will pass away as the traces of a cloud, and will be scattered as is a mist, when it is chased by the rays of the sun and overcome by its heat. 5 For our allotted time is the passing of a shadow, and our end doesn't retreat; because it is securely sealed, and no one turns it back. 6 Come therefore and let's enjoy the good things that exist. Let's use the creation earnestly as in our youth. 7 Let's fill ourselves with costly wine and perfumes and let no Spring flower pass us by. 8 Let's crown ourselves with rosebuds before they wither. 9 Let none of us go without his share in our proud revelry. Let's leave signs of mirth everywhere, because this is our portion, and this is our lot. 10 Let's oppress the righteous poor. Let's not spare the widow, nor reverence the gray hair of the old man. 11 But let our strength be a law of righteousness; for that which is weak is proven useless. 12 But let's lie in wait for the righteous man, because he annoys us, is contrary to our works, reproaches us with sins against the law, and charges us with sins against our training. 13 He professes to have knowledge of God and calls himself a

child of the Lord. **14** He became to us a reproof of our thoughts. **15** He is grievous to us even to look at, because his life is unlike other men's, and his paths are strange. **16** We were regarded by him as worthless metal, and he abstains from our ways as from uncleanness. He calls the latter end of the righteous happy. He boasts that God is his father. **17** Let's see if his words are true. Let's test what will happen at the end of his life. **18** For if the righteous man is God's son, he will uphold him, and he will deliver him out of the hand of his adversaries. **19** Let's test him with outrage and torture, that we may find out how gentle he is, and test his patience. **20** Let's condemn him to a shameful death, for he will be overseen according to his words." **21** So they reasoned, and they were led astray; for their wickedness blinded them, **22** and they didn't know the mysteries of God, neither did they hope for wages of holiness, nor did they discern that there is a prize for blameless souls. **23** Because God created man for incorruption and made him an image of his own everlastingness; **24** but death entered into the world by the envy of the devil, and those who belong to him experience it.

CHAPTER 3

1 But the souls of the righteous are in the hand of God, and no torment will touch them. **2** In the eyes of the foolish they seemed to have died. Their departure was considered affliction, **3** and their travel away from us ruin; But they are in peace. **4** For even if in the sight of men they are punished, their hope is full of immortality. **5** Having borne a little chastening, they will receive great good; because God tested them and found them worthy of himself. **6** He tested them like gold in the furnace, and he accepted them as a whole burnt offering. **7** In the time of their visitation they will shine. They will run back and out like sparks among stubble. **8** They will judge nations and have dominion over peoples. The Lord will reign over them forever. **9** Those who trust him will understand truth. The faithful will live with him in love, because grace and mercy are with his chosen ones. **10** But the ungodly will be punished even as they reasoned, those who neglected righteousness and revolted from the Lord; **11** for he who despises wisdom and discipline is miserable. Their hope is void and their toils unprofitable. Their works are useless. **12** Their wives are foolish and their children are wicked. **13** Their descendants are cursed, because the barren woman who is undefiled is happy, she who has not conceived in transgression. She will have fruit in the visitation of souls. **14** So is the eunuch which has done no lawless deed with his hands, nor imagined wicked things against the Lord; for a precious gift will be given to him for his faithfulness, a special favor, and a delightful inheritance in the Lord's sanctuary. **15** For good labors have fruit of great renown. The root of understanding can't fail. **16** But children of adulterers will not come to maturity. The seed of an unlawful bed will vanish away. **17** For if they live long, they will not be esteemed, and in the end, their old age will be without honor. **18** If they die quickly, they will have no hope, nor consolation in the day of decision. **19** For the end of an unrighteous generation is always grievous.

CHAPTER 4

1 It is better to be childless with virtue, for immortality is in the memory of virtue, because it is recognized both before God and before men. **2** When it is present, people imitate it. They long after it when it has departed. Throughout all time it marches crowned in triumph, victorious in the competition for the prizes that are undefiled. **3** But the multiplying brood of the ungodly will be of no profit, and their illegitimate offshoots won't take deep root, nor will they establish a sure hold. **4** For even if they grow branches and flourish for a season, standing unsure, they will be shaken by the wind. They will be uprooted by the violence of winds. **5** Their branches will be broken off before they come to maturity. Their fruit will be useless, never ripe to eat, and fit for nothing. **6** For unlawfully conceived children are witnesses of wickedness against parents when they are investigated. **7** But a righteous man, even if he dies before his time, will be at rest. **8** For honorable old age is not that which stands in length of time, nor is its measure given by number of years: **9** But understanding is gray hair to men, and an unspotted life is ripe old age. **10** Being found well-pleasing to God, he was loved. While living among sinners he was transported. **11** He was caught away, lest evil should change his understanding, or guile deceive his soul. **12** For the witchcraft of worthlessness obscures the things which are good, and the whirl of desire perverts an innocent mind.

13 Being made perfect quickly, he filled a long time; 14 for his soul was pleasing to the Lord. Therefore he hurried out of the midst of wickedness. 15 But as for the peoples seeing and not understanding, not considering this, that grace and mercy are with his chosen, and that he visits his holy ones— 16 but a righteous man who is dead will condemn the ungodly who are living, and youth that is quickly perfected will condemn the many years of an unrighteous man's old age. 17 For the ungodly will see a wise man's end, and won't understand what the Lord planned for him, and why he safely kept him. 18 They will see, and they will despise; but the Lord will laugh them to scorn. After this, they will become a dishonored carcass and a reproach among the dead forever; 19 because he will dash them speechless to the ground and will shake them from the foundations. They will lie utterly waste. They will be in anguish and their memory will perish. 20 They will come with coward fear when their sins are counted. Their lawless deeds will convict them to their face.

CHAPTER 5

1 Then the righteous man will stand in great boldness before the face of those who afflicted him, and those who make his labors of no account. 2 When they see him, they will be troubled with terrible fear, and will be amazed at the marvel of salvation. 3 They will speak among themselves repenting, and for distress of spirit they will groan, "This was he whom we used to hold in derision, as a parable of reproach. 4 We fools considered his life madness, and his end without honor. 5 How was he counted among sons of God? How is his lot among saints? 6 Truly we went astray from the way of truth. The light of righteousness didn't shine for us. The sun didn't rise for us. 7 We took our fill of the paths of lawlessness and destruction. We traveled through trackless deserts, but we didn't know the Lord's way. 8 What did our arrogance profit us? What good have riches and boasting brought us? 9 Those things all passed away as a shadow, like a message that runs by, 10 like a ship passing through the billowy water, which, when it has gone by, there is no trace to be found, no pathway of its keel in the billows. 11 Or it is like when a bird flies through the air, no evidence of its passage is found, but the light wind, lashed with the stroke of its pinions, and torn apart with the violent rush of the moving wings, is passed

through. Afterwards no sign of its coming remains. 12 Or it is like when an arrow is shot at a mark, the parted air closes up again immediately, so that men don't know where it passed through. 13 So we also, as soon as we were born, ceased to be; and we had no sign of virtue to show, but we were utterly consumed in our wickedness." 14 Because the hope of the ungodly man is like chaff carried by the wind, and as foam vanishing before a tempest; and is scattered like smoke by the wind, and passes by as the remembrance of a guest that waits but a day. 15 But the righteous live forever. Their reward is in the Lord, and the care for them with the Most High. 16 Therefore they will receive the crown of royal dignity and the diadem of beauty from the Lord's hand; because he will cover them with his right hand, and he will shield them with his arm. 17 He will take his jealousy as complete armor and will make the whole creation his weapons to punish his enemies: 18 He will put on righteousness as a breastplate and will wear impartial judgement as a helmet. 19 He will take holiness as an invincible shield. 20 He will sharpen stern wrath for a sword. The world will go with him to fight against his frenzied foes. 21 Shafts of lightning will fly with true aim. They will leap to the mark from the clouds, as from a well-drawn bow. 22 Hailstones full of wrath will be hurled from an engine of war. The water of the sea will be angered against them. Rivers will sternly overwhelm them. 23 A mighty blast will encounter them. It will winnow them away like a tempest. So lawlessness will make all the land desolate. Their evil-doing will overturn the thrones of princes.

CHAPTER 6

1 Hear therefore, you kings, and understand. Learn, you judges of the ends of the earth. 2 Give ear, you rulers who have dominion over many people, and make your boast in multitudes of nations, 3 because your dominion was given to you from the Lord, and your sovereignty from the Most High. He will search out your works and will inquire about your plans; 4 because being officers of his kingdom, you didn't judge rightly, nor did you keep law, nor did you walk according to God's counsel. 5 He will come upon you awfully and swiftly, because a stern judgment comes on those who are in high places. 6 For the man of low estate may be pardoned in mercy, but mighty men will be mightily tested. 7 For the

Sovereign Lord of all will not be impressed with anyone, neither will he show deference to greatness; because it is he who made both small and great, and cares about them all; **8** but the scrutiny that comes upon the powerful is strict. **9** Therefore, my words are to you, O princes, that you may learn wisdom and not fall away. **10** For those who have kept the things that are holy in holiness will be made holy. Those who have been taught them will find what to say in defense. **11** Therefore set your desire on my words. Long for them, and you princes will be instructed. **12** Wisdom is radiant and doesn't fade away; and is easily seen by those who love her and found by those who seek her. **13** She anticipates those who desire her, making herself known. **14** He who rises up early to seek her won't have difficulty, for he will find her sitting at his gates. **15** For to think upon her is perfection of understanding, and he who watches for her will quickly be free from care; **16** because she herself goes around, seeking those who are worthy of her, and in their paths she appears to them graciously, and in every purpose she meets them. **17** For her true beginning is desire for instruction; and desire for instruction is love. **18** And love is observance of her laws. To give heed to her laws confirms immortality. **19** Immortality brings closeness to God. **20** So then desire for wisdom promotes to a kingdom. **21** If therefore you delight in thrones and scepters, you princes of peoples, honor wisdom, that you may reign forever. **22** But what wisdom is, and how she came into being, I will declare. I won't hide mysteries from you; but I will explore from her first beginning, bring the knowledge of her into clear light, and I will not pass by the truth. **23** Indeed, I won't go with consuming envy, because envy will have no fellowship with wisdom. **24** But a multitude of wise men is salvation to the world, and an understanding king is stability for his people. **25** Therefore be instructed by my words, and you will profit.

CHAPTER 7

1 I myself am also mortal, like everyone else, and am a descendant of one formed first and born of the earth. **2** I molded into flesh in the time of ten months in my mother's womb, being compacted in blood from the seed of man and pleasure that came with sleep. **3** I also, when I was born, drew in the common air, and fell upon the kindred earth, uttering, like all, for my first voice, the same cry. **4** I was nursed with care in swaddling clothes. **5** For no king had any other first beginning; **6** but all men have one entrance into life, and a common departure. **7** For this cause I prayed, and understanding was given to me. I asked, and a spirit of wisdom came to me. **8** I preferred her before scepters and thrones. I considered riches nothing in comparison to her. **9** Neither did I liken to her any priceless gem, because all gold in her presence is a little sand, and silver will be considered as clay before her. **10** I loved her more than health and beauty, and I chose to have her rather than light, because her bright shining is never laid to sleep. **11** All good things came to me with her, and innumerable riches are in her hands. **12** And I rejoiced over them all because wisdom leads them; although I didn't know that she was their mother. **13** As I learned without guile, I impart without grudging. I don't hide her riches. **14** For she is a treasure for men that doesn't fail, and those who use it obtain friendship with God, commended by the gifts which they present through discipline. **15** But may God grant that I may speak his judgement, and to conceive thoughts worthy of what has been given me; because he is one who guides even wisdom and who corrects the wise. **16** For both we and our words are in his hand, with all understanding and skill in various crafts. **17** For he himself gave me an unerring knowledge of the things that are, to know the structure of the universe and the operation of the elements; **18** the beginning, end, and middle of times; the alternations of the solstices and the changes of seasons; **19** the circuits of years and the positions of stars; **20** the natures of living creatures and the raging of wild beasts; The violence of winds and the thoughts of men; the diversities of plants and the virtues of roots. **21** All things that are either secret or manifest I learned, **22** for wisdom, that is the architect of all things, taught me. For there is in her a spirit that is quick to understand, holy, unique, manifold, subtle, freely moving, clear in utterance, unpolluted, distinct, unharmed, loving what is good, keen, unhindered, **23** beneficent, loving toward man, steadfast, sure, free from care, all-powerful, all-surveying, and penetrating through all spirits that are quick to understand, pure, most subtle: **24** For wisdom is more mobile than any motion. Yes, she pervades and penetrates all things by reason of her purity. **25** For she is a breath of the power of God, and a clear effluence of the glory of the Almighty. Therefore nothing defiled can find entrance into her. **26** For she is a reflection of everlasting light, an unspotted mirror of the working of God, and an image of his goodness. **27** She, being one, has power to do all things. Remaining in herself, she renews all things. From generation to generation passing into holy souls, she makes friends of God and prophets. **28** For God loves nothing as much as one who dwells with wisdom. **29** For she is fairer than the sun, and above all the constellations of the stars. She is better than light. **30** For daylight yields to night, but evil does not prevail against wisdom.

CHAPTER 8

1 But she reaches from one end to the other with full strength and orders all things well. **2** I loved her and sought her from my youth. I sought to take her for my bride. I became enamored by her beauty. **3** She glorifies her noble birth by living with God. The Sovereign Lord of all loves her. **4** For she is initiated into the knowledge of God, and she chooses his works. **5** But if riches are a desired possession in life, what is richer than wisdom, which makes all things? **6** And if understanding works, who more than wisdom is an architect of the things that exist? **7** If a man loves righteousness, the fruits of wisdom's labor are virtues, for she teaches soberness, understanding, righteousness, and courage. There is nothing in life more profitable for people than these. **8** And if anyone longs for wide experience, she knows the things of old, and infers the things to come. She understands subtleties of speeches and interpretations of dark sayings. She foresees signs and wonders, and the issues of seasons and times. **9** Therefore I determined to take her to live with me, knowing that she is one who would give me good counsel, and encourage me in cares and grief. **10** Because of her, I will have glory among multitudes, and honor in the sight of elders, though I am young. **11** I will be found keen when I give judgement. I will be admired in the presence of rulers. **12** When I am silent, they will wait for me. When I open my lips, they will heed what I say. If I continue speaking, they will put their hands on their mouths. **13** Because of her, I will have immortality, and leave behind an eternal memory to those who come after me. **14** I will govern peoples. Nations will be subjected to me. **15** Dreaded monarchs will fear me when

they hear of me. Among the people, I will show myself to be good, and courageous in war. **16** When I come into my house, I will find rest with her. For conversation with her has no bitterness, and living with her has no pain, but gladness and joy. **17** When I considered these things in myself and thought in my heart how immortality is in kinship to wisdom, **18** and in her friendship is good delight, and in the labors of her hands is wealth that doesn't fail, and understanding is in her companionship, and great renown in having fellowship with her words, I went about seeking how to take her to myself. **19** Now I was a clever child and received a good soul. **20** Or rather, being good, I came into an undefiled body. **21** But perceiving that I could not otherwise possess wisdom unless God gave her to me— yes, and to know and understand by whom the grace is given— I pleaded with the Lord and implored him, and with my whole heart I said,

CHAPTER 9

1 "O God of the fathers, and Lord of mercy, who made all things by your word; **2** and by your wisdom you formed man, that he should have dominion over the creatures that were made by you, **3** and rule the world in holiness and righteousness, and execute judgement in uprightness of soul; **4** give me wisdom, her who sits by you on your thrones. Don't reject me from among your servants, **5** because I am your servant and the son of your handmaid, a weak and short-lived man, with little power to understand judgement and laws. **6** For even if a man is perfect among the sons of men, if the wisdom that comes from you is not with him, he will count for nothing. **7** You chose me to be king of your people, and a judge for your sons and daughters. **8** You gave a command to build a sanctuary on your holy mountain, and an altar in the city where you pitch your tent, a copy of the holy tent which you prepared from the beginning. **9** Wisdom is with you and knows your works, and was present when you were making the world, and understands what is pleasing in your eyes, and what is right according to your commandments. **10** Send her from the holy heavens and ask her to come from the throne of your glory, that being present with me she may work, and I may learn what pleases you well. **11** For she knows all things and understands, and she will guide me soberly in my actions. She will guard me in her glory. **12** So my works will be acceptable. I will judge your people righteously, and I will be worthy of my father's throne. **13** For what man will know the counsel of God? Or who will conceive what the Lord wills? **14** For the thoughts of mortals are unstable, and our plans are prone to fail. **15** For a corruptible body weighs down the soul. The earthy frame lies heavy on a mind that is full of cares. **16** We can hardly guess the things that are on earth, and we find the things that are close at hand with labor; but who has traced out the things that are in the heavens? **17** Who gained knowledge of your counsel, unless you gave wisdom, and sent your holy spirit from the highest? **18** It was so that the ways of those who are on earth were corrected, and men were taught the things that are pleasing to you. They were saved through wisdom."

CHAPTER 10

1 Wisdom guarded to the end the first formed father of the world, who was created alone, and delivered him out of his own transgression, **2** and gave him strength to get dominion over all things. **3** But when an unrighteous man fell away from her in his anger, he perished himself in the rage with which he killed his brother. **4** When for his cause the earth was drowning with a flood, Wisdom again saved it, guiding the righteous man's course by a poor piece of wood. **5** Moreover, when nations consenting together in wickedness had been confounded, Wisdom knew the righteous man, and preserved him blameless to God, and kept him strong when his heart yearned toward his child. **6** While the ungodly were perishing, wisdom delivered a righteous man, when he fled from the fire that descended out of heaven on Pentapolis. **7** To whose wickedness a smoking waste still witnesses, and plants bearing fair fruit that doesn't ripen, a disbelieving soul has a memorial: a standing pillar of salt. **8** For having passed wisdom by, not only were they disabled from recognizing the things which are good, but they also left behind them for their life a monument of their folly, to the end that where they stumbled, they might fail even to be unseen; **9** but wisdom delivered those who waited on her out of troubles. **10** When a righteous man was a fugitive from a brother's wrath, wisdom guided him in straight paths. She showed him God's kingdom and gave him knowledge of holy things. She prospered him in his toils and multiplied the fruits of his labor. **11** When in their covetousness men

dealt harshly with him, she stood by him and made him rich. **12** She guarded him from enemies, and she kept him safe from those who lay in wait. Over his severe conflict, she watched as judge, that he might know that godliness is more powerful than everyone. **13** When a righteous man was sold, Wisdom didn't forsake him, but she delivered him from sin. She went down with him into a dungeon, **14** and in bonds she didn't depart from him, until she brought him the scepter of a kingdom, and authority over those that dealt tyrannously with him. She also showed those who had mockingly accused him to be false and gave him eternal glory. **15** Wisdom delivered a holy people and a blameless seed from a nation of oppressors. **16** She entered into the soul of a servant of the Lord and withstood terrible kings in wonders and signs. **17** She rendered to holy men a reward of their toils. She guided them along a marvelous way and became to them a covering in the daytime, and a flame of stars through the night. **18** She brought them over the Red Sea and led them through much water; **19** but she drowned their enemies, and she cast them up from the bottom of the deep. **20** Therefore the righteous plundered the ungodly, and they sang praise to your holy name, O Lord, and extolled with one accord your hand that fought for them, **21** because wisdom opened the mouth of the mute, and made the tongues of babes to speak clearly.

CHAPTER 11

1 She prospered their works in the hand of a holy prophet. **2** They traveled through a desert without inhabitant, and they pitched their tents in trackless regions. **3** They withstood enemies and repelled foes. **4** They thirsted, and they called upon you, and water was given to them out of the flinty rock, and healing of their thirst out of the hard stone. **5** For by what things their foes were punished, by these they in their need were benefited. **6** When enemies were troubled with clotted blood instead of a river's ever-flowing fountain, **7** to rebuke the decree for the slaying of babies, you gave them abundant water beyond all hope, **8** having shown by the thirst which they had suffered how you punished the adversaries. **9** For when they were tried, although chastened in mercy, they learned how the ungodly were tormented, being judged with wrath. **10** For you tested these as a father admonishing them; but you searched out those as a stern king condemning them. **11** Yes and whether they were far off or near, they were equally distressed; **12** for a double grief seized them, and a groaning at the memory of things past. **13** For when they heard that through their own punishments the others benefited, they recognized the Lord. **14** For him who long before was thrown out and exposed they stopped mocking. In the end of what happened, they marveled, having thirsted in another manner than the righteous. **15** But in return for the senseless imaginings of their unrighteousness, wherein they were led astray to worship irrational reptiles and wretched vermin, you sent upon them a multitude of irrational creatures for vengeance; **16** that they might learn that by what things a man sins, by these he is punished. **17** For your all-powerful hand that created the world out of formless matter didn't lack means to send upon them a multitude of bears, fierce lions, **18** or newly-created and unknown wild beasts, full of rage, either breathing out a blast of fiery breath, or belching out smoke, or flashing dreadful sparks from their eyes; **19** which had power not only to consume them by their violence, but to destroy them even by the terror of their sight. **20** Yes and without these they might have fallen by a single breath, being pursued by Justice, and scattered abroad by the breath of your power; but you arranged all things by measure, number, and weight. **21** For to be greatly strong is yours at all times. Who could withstand the might of your arm? **22** Because the whole world before you is as a grain in a balance, and as a drop of dew that comes down upon the earth in the morning. **23** But you have mercy on all men, because you have power to do all things, and you overlook the sins of men to the end that they may repent. **24** For you love all things that are and abhor none of the things which you made; For you never would have formed anything if you hated it. **25** How would anything have endured unless you had willed it? Or that which was not called by you, how would it have been preserved? **26** But you spare all things, because they are yours, O Sovereign Lord, you lover of lives.

CHAPTER 12

1 For your incorruptible spirit is in all things. **2** Why you convict little by little those who fall from the right way, and, putting them in remembrance by the things wherein they sin, you admonish them, that escaping from their wickedness they may believe in you, O Lord.

3 For truly the old inhabitants of your holy land, **4** hating them because they practiced detestable works of enchantments and unholy rites— **5** merciless slaughters of children and sacrificial banquets of men's flesh and of blood— **6** allies in an impious fellowship, and murderers of their own helpless babes, it was your counsel to destroy by the hands of our fathers; **7** that the land which in your sight is most precious of all might receive a worthy colony of God's servants. **8** Nevertheless you even spared these as men, and you sent hornets as forerunners of your army, to cause them to perish little by little; **9** Not that you were unable to subdue the ungodly under the hand of the righteous in battle, or by terrible beasts or by a stern word to make away with them at once; **10** but judging them little by little you gave them a chance to repent, not being ignorant that their nature by birth was evil, their wickedness inborn, and that their manner of thought would never be changed. **11** For they were a cursed seed from the beginning. It wasn't through fear of any that you left them unpunished for their sins. **12** For who will say, "What have you done?" Or "Who will withstand your judgement?" Who will accuse you for the perishing of nations which you caused? Or who will come and stand before you as an avenger for unrighteous men? **13** For there isn't any God beside you that cares for all, that you might show that you didn't judge unrighteously. **14** No king or prince will be able to look you in the face for those whom you have punished. **15** But being righteous, you rule all things righteously, deeming it a thing alien from your power to condemn one that does not deserve to be punished. **16** For your strength is the beginning of righteousness, and your sovereignty over all makes you to forbear all. **17** For when men don't believe that you are perfect in power, you show your strength, and in dealing with those who think this, you confuse their boldness. **18** But you, being sovereign over strength, judge in gentleness, and with great forbearance do you govern us; for the power is yours whenever you desire it. **19** But you taught your people by such works as these, how the righteous must be a lover of men. You made your sons to have good hope, because you give repentance when men have sinned. **20** For if on those who were enemies of your servants and due to death you took vengeance with so great deliberation and indulgence, giving them times and opportunities when they might escape from their wickedness; **21** with how great carefulness you judged your sons, to whose fathers you gave oaths and covenants of good promises! **22** Therefore while you chasten us, you scourge our enemies ten thousand times more, to the intent that we may ponder your goodness when we judge, and when we are judged may look for mercy. **23** Why also the unrighteous that lived in folly of life, you tormented through their own abominations. **24** For truly they went astray very far in the ways of error, taking as gods those animals which even among their enemies were held in dishonor, deceived like foolish babes. **25** Therefore, as to unreasoning children, you sent your judgement to mock them. **26** But those who would not be admonished by a mocking correction as of children will experience a judgement worthy of God. **27** For through the sufferings they were indignant of, being punished in these creatures which they supposed to be gods, they saw and recognized as the true God him whom they refused to know. Therefore also the result of condemnation came upon them.

CHAPTER 13

1 For truly all men who had no perception of God were vain by nature and didn't gain power to know him who exists from the good things that are seen. They didn't recognize the architect from his works. **2** But they thought that either fire, or wind, or swift air, or circling stars, or raging water, or luminaries of heaven were gods that rule the world. **3** If it was through delight in their beauty that they took them to be gods, let them know how much better their Sovereign Lord is than these, for the first author of beauty created them. **4** But if it was through astonishment at their power and influence, then let them understand from them how much more powerful he who formed them is. **5** For from the greatness of the beauty of created things, mankind forms the corresponding image of their Maker. **6** But yet for these men there is but small blame, for they too perhaps go astray while they are seeking God and desiring to find him. **7** For they diligently search while living among his works, and they trust their sight that the things that they look at are beautiful. **8** But again even they are not to be excused. **9** For if they had power to know so much, that they should be able to explore the world, how is it that they didn't find the Sovereign Lord sooner? **10** But miserable *were* they, and in dead things *were*

their hopes, who called them gods which are works of men's hands, gold and silver, skillfully made, and likenesses of animals, or a useless stone, the work of an ancient hand. **11** Yes and if some woodcutter, having sawn down a tree that is easily moved, skillfully strips away all its bark, and fashioning it in attractive form, makes a useful vessel to serve his life's needs. **12** Burning the scraps from his handiwork to cook his food, he eats his fill. **13** Taking a discarded scrap which served no purpose, a crooked piece of wood and full of knots, carves it with the diligence of his idleness, and shapes it by the skill of his idleness. He shapes it in the image of a man, **14** or makes it like some paltry animal, smearing it with something red, painting it red, and smearing over every stain in it. **15** Having made a worthy chamber for it, he sets it in a wall, securing it with iron. **16** He plans for it that it may not fall down, knowing that it is unable to help itself (for truly it is an image, and needs help). **17** When he makes his prayer concerning goods and his marriage and children, he is not ashamed to speak to that which has no life. **18** Yes, for health, he calls upon that which is weak. For life, he implores that which is dead. For aid, he supplicates that which has no experience. For a good journey, he asks that which can't so much as move a step. **19** And for profit in business and good success of his hands, he asks ability from that which has hands with no ability.

CHAPTER 14

1 Again, one preparing to sail, and about to journey over raging waves, calls upon a piece of wood more rotten than the vessel that carries him. **2** For the hunger for profit planned it, and wisdom was the craftsman who built it. **3** Your providence, O Father, guides it along, because even in the sea you gave a way, and in the waves a sure path, **4** showing that you can save out of every danger, that even a man without skill may put to sea. **5** It is your will that the works of your wisdom should be not idle. Therefore men also entrust their lives to a little piece of wood, and passing through the surge on a raft come safely to land. **6** For in the old time also, when proud giants were perishing, the hope of the world, taking refuge on a raft, your hand guided the seed of generations of the race of men. **7** For blessed is wood through which comes righteousness; **8** but the idol made with hands is accursed, itself and he that made it; because his was the working, and the corruptible thing was called a god: **9** For both the ungodly and his ungodliness are alike hateful to God; **10** for truly the deed will be punished together with him who committed it. **11** Therefore also there will be a visitation among the idols of the nation, because, though formed of things which God created, they were made an abomination, stumbling blocks to the souls of men, and a snare to the feet of the foolish. **12** For the devising of idols was the beginning of fornication, and the invention of them the corruption of life. **13** For they didn't exist from the beginning, and they won't exist forever. **14** For by the vain pride of men they entered into the world, and therefore a speedy end was planned for them. **15** For a father worn with untimely grief, making an image of the child quickly taken away, now honored him as a god which was then a dead man, and delivered to those that were under him mysteries and solemn rites. **16** Afterward the ungodly custom, in process of time grown strong, was kept as a law, and the engraved images received worship by the commandments of princes. **17** And when men could not honor them in presence because they lived far off, imagining the likeness from afar, they made a visible image of the king whom they honored, that by their zeal they might flatter the absent as if present. **18** But worship was raised to a yet higher pitch, even by those who didn't know him, urged forward by the ambition of the architect; **19** for he, wishing perhaps to please one in authority, used his art to force the likeness toward a greater beauty. **20** So the multitude, allured by reason of the grace of his handiwork, now consider an object of devotion him that a little before was honored as a man. **21** And this became an ambush, because men, in bondage either to calamity or to tyranny, invested stones and stocks with the incommunicable Name. **22** Afterward it was not enough for them to go astray concerning the knowledge of God, but also, while they live in a great war of ignorance, they call a multitude of evils peace. **23** For either slaughtering children in solemn rites, or celebrating secret mysteries, or holding frantic revels of strange ordinances, **24** no longer do they guard either life or purity of marriage, but one brings upon another either death by treachery, or anguish by adultery. **25** And all things confusedly are filled with blood and murder, theft and deceit, corruption, faithlessness, tumult, perjury, **26** confusion about what is good, forgetfulness of favors, ingratitude for benefits, defiling of souls, confusion of sex, disorder in marriage, adultery and wantonness. **27** For the worship of idols that may not be named is a beginning and cause and end of every evil. **28** For their worshipers either make merry to madness, or prophesy lies, or live unrighteously, or lightly commit perjury. **29** For putting their trust in lifeless idols, when they have sworn a wicked oath, they expect not to suffer harm. **30** But for both, the just doom will pursue them, because they had evil thoughts of God by giving heed to idols and swore unrighteously in deceit through contempt for holiness. **31** For it is not the power of them by whom men swear, but it is the just penalty for those who sin that always visits the transgression of the unrighteous.

CHAPTER 15

1 But you, our God, are gracious and true, patient, and in mercy ordering all things. **2** For even if we sin, we are yours, knowing your dominion; but we will not sin, knowing that we have been accounted yours. **3** For to be acquainted with you is perfect righteousness, and to know your dominion is the root of immortality. **4** For we weren't led astray by any evil plan of men's, nor yet by painters' fruitless labor, a form stained with varied colors, **5** the sight of which leads fools into lust. Their desire is for the breathless form of a dead image. **6** Lovers of evil things, and worthy of such hopes, are those who make, desire, and worship them. **7** For a potter, kneading soft earth, laboriously molds each article for our service. He fashions out of the same clay both the vessels that minister to clean uses, and those of a contrary sort, all in like manner. What will be the use of each article of either sort, the potter is the judge. **8** Also, laboring to an evil end, he molds a vain god out of the same clay, he who, having but a little before been made of earth, after a short space goes his way to the earth out of which he was taken, when he is required to render back the soul which was lent him. **9** However he has anxious care, not because his powers must fail, nor because his span of life is short; But he compares himself with goldsmiths and silversmiths, and he imitates molders in brass, and esteems it glory that he molds counterfeits. **10** His heart is ashes. His hope is of less value than earth. His life is of less honor than clay; **11** because he was ignorant of him who molded him, and of him that inspired into him an active soul and breathed into him a vital spirit. **12** But he accounted our life to be a game, and our lifetime a festival for profit; for, he says, one must get gain however one can, even if it is by evil. **13** For this man beyond all others knows that he sins, out of earthy matter making brittle vessels and graven images. **14** But most foolish and more miserable than a baby, are the enemies of your people, who oppressed them; **15** because they even considered all the idols of the nations to be gods, which have neither the use of eyes for seeing, nor nostrils for drawing breath, nor ears to hear, nor fingers for handling, and their feet are helpless for walking. **16** For a man made them, and one whose own spirit is borrowed molded them; for no one has power as a man to mold a god like to himself. **17** But, being mortal, he makes a dead thing by the work of lawless hands; for he is better than the objects of his worship, since he indeed had life, but they never did. **18** Yes, and they worship the creatures that are most hateful, for, being compared as to lack of sense, these are worse than all others; **19** Neither, as seen beside other creatures, are they beautiful, so that one should desire them, but they have escaped both the praise of God and his blessing.

CHAPTER 16

1 For this cause, they were deservedly punished through creatures like those which they worship and tormented through a multitude of vermin. **2** Instead of this punishment, you, giving benefits to your people, prepared quails for food, a delicacy to satisfy the desire of their appetite, **3** to the end that your enemies, desiring food, might for the hideousness of the creatures sent among them, loathe even the necessary appetite; but these, your people, having for a short time suffered lack, might even partake of delicacies. **4** For it was necessary that inescapable lack should come upon those oppressors, but that to these it should only be showed how their enemies were tormented. **5** For even when terrible raging of wild beasts came upon your people, and they were perishing by the bites of crooked serpents, your wrath didn't continue to the uttermost; **6** but for admonition were they troubled for a short time, having a token of salvation to put them in remembrance of the commandment of your law; **7** for he who turned toward it was not saved because of that which was seen, but because of you, the Savior

of all. **8** Yes, and in this you persuaded our enemies that you are he who delivers out of every evil. **9** For the bites of locusts and flies truly killed them. No healing for their life was found, because they were worthy to be punished by such things. **10** But your children weren't overcome by the very teeth of venomous dragons, for your mercy passed by where they were and healed them. **11** For they were bitten to put them in remembrance of your oracles, and were quickly saved, lest, falling into deep forgetfulness, they should become unable to respond to your kindness. **12** For truly it was neither herb nor mollifying plaster that cured them, but your word, O Lord, which heals all things. **13** For you have authority over life and death, and you lead down to the gates of Hades, and lead up again. **14** But though a man kills by his wickedness, he can't retrieve the spirit that has departed or release the imprisoned soul. **15** But it is not possible to escape your hand; **16** for ungodly men, refusing to know you, were scourged in the strength of your arm, pursued with strange rains and hails and relentless storms, and utterly consumed with fire. **17** For, what was most marvelous, in the water which quenches all things, the fire burned hotter; for the world fights for the righteous. **18** For at one time the flame lost its fierceness, that it might not burn up the creatures sent against the ungodly, but that these themselves as they looked might see that they were chased through the judgement of God. **19** At another time even in the midst of water it burns above the power of fire, that it may destroy the produce of an unrighteous land. **20** Instead of these things, you gave your people angels' food to eat, and you provided ready-to-eat bread for them from heaven without toil, having the virtue of every pleasant flavor, and agreeable to every taste. **21** For your nature showed your sweetness toward your children, while that bread, serving the desire of the eater, changed itself according to every man's choice. **22** But snow and ice endured fire, and didn't melt, that people might know that fire was destroying the fruits of the enemies, burning in the hail and flashing in the rains; **23** and that this fire again, in order that righteous people may be nourished, has even forgotten its own power. **24** For the creation, ministering to you its maker, strains its force against the unrighteous for punishment and slackens it on behalf of those who trust in you, for kindness. **25** Therefore at that time also, converting itself into all forms, it ministered to your all-nourishing bounty, according to the desire of those who had need, **26** that your sons, whom you loved, O Lord, might learn that it is not the growth of crops that nourishes a man, but that your word preserves those who trust you. **27** For that which was not marred by fire, when it was simply warmed by a faint sunbeam melted away, **28** that it might be known that we must rise before the sun to give you thanks and must plead with you at the dawning of the light; **29** for the hope of the unthankful will melt as the winter's hoar frost and will flow away as water that has no use.

CHAPTER 17

1 For your judgments are great, and hard to interpret; therefore undisciplined souls went astray. **2** For when lawless men had supposed that they held a holy nation in their power, they, prisoners of darkness, and bound in the fetters of a long night, kept close beneath their roofs, lay exiled from the eternal providence. **3** For while they thought that they were unseen in *their* secret sins, they were divided from one another by a dark curtain of forgetfulness, stricken with terrible awe, and very troubled by apparitions. **4** For neither did the dark recesses that held them guard them from fears, but terrifying sounds rang around them, and dismal phantoms appeared with unsmiling faces. **5** And no force of fire prevailed to give light, neither were the brightest flames of the stars strong enough to illuminate that gloomy night; **6** but only the glimmering of a self-kindled fire appeared to them, full of fear. In terror, they considered the things which they saw to be worse than that sight, on which they could not gaze. **7** The mockeries of their magic arts were powerless, now, and a shameful rebuke of their boasted understanding: **8** For those who promised to drive away terrors and disorders from a sick soul, these were sick with a ludicrous fearfulness. **9** For even if no troubling thing frightened them, yet, scared with the creeping of vermin and hissing of serpents, **10** they perished trembling in fear, refusing even to look at the air, which could not be escaped on any side. **11** For wickedness, condemned by a witness within, is a coward thing, and, being pressed hard by conscience, always has added forecasts of the worst. **12** For fear is nothing else but a surrender of the help which reason offers; **13** and from within, the expectation of being less makes of greater account the ignorance of the cause that brings the torment. **14** But they, all through the night which was powerless indeed, and which came upon them out of the recesses of powerless Hades, sleeping the same sleep, **15** now were haunted by monstrous apparitions, and now were paralyzed by their soul's surrendering; for sudden and unexpected fear came upon them. **16** So then whoever it might be, sinking down in his place, was kept captive, shut up in that prison which was not barred with iron; **17** for whether he was a farmer, or a shepherd, or a laborer whose toils were in the wilderness, he was overtaken, and endured that inevitable necessity; for they were all bound with one chain of darkness. **18** Whether there was a whistling wind, or a melodious sound of birds among the spreading branches, or a measured fall of water running violently, **19** or a harsh crashing of rocks hurled down, or the swift course of animals bounding along unseen, or the voice of wild beasts harshly roaring, or an echo rebounding from the hollows of the mountains, all these things paralyzed them with terror. **20** For the whole world was illuminated with clear light, and was occupied with unhindered works, **21** while over them alone was spread a heavy night, an image of the darkness that should afterward receive them; but to themselves, they were heavier than darkness.

CHAPTER 18

1 But for your holy ones there was great light. Their enemies, hearing their voice but seeing not their form, counted it a happy thing that they too had suffered, **2** yet for that they do not hurt them, though wronged by them before, they are thankful; and because they had been at variance with them, they begged for pardon. **3** Whereas you provided a burning pillar of fire, to be a guide for your people's unknown journey, and a harmless sun for their glorious exile. **4** For the Egyptians well deserved to be deprived of light and imprisoned by darkness, they who had imprisoned your children, through whom the incorruptible light of the law was to be given to the race of men. **5** After they had taken counsel to kill the babes of the holy ones, and when a single child had been abandoned and saved to convict them of their sin, you took away from them their multitude of children, and destroyed all their army together in a mighty flood. **6** Our fathers were made aware of that night beforehand, that, having sure knowledge, they might be cheered

by the oaths which they had trusted.
7 Salvation of the righteous and destruction of
the enemies was expected by your people.
8 For as you took vengeance on the
adversaries, by the same means, calling us to
yourself, you glorified us. 9 For holy children
of good men offered sacrifice in secret, and
with one consent they took upon themselves
the covenant of the divine law, that they would
partake alike in the same good things and the
same perils, the fathers already leading the
sacred songs of praise. 10 But the discordant
cry of the enemies echoed back, and a pitiful
voice of lamentation for children was spread
abroad. 11 Both servant and master were
punished with the same just doom, and the
commoner suffering the same as king; 12 Yes,
they all together, under one form of death, had
corpses without number. For the living were
not sufficient even to bury them, since at a
single stroke, their most cherished offspring
was consumed. 13 For while they were
disbelieving all things by reason of the
enchantments, upon the destruction of the
firstborn they confessed the people to be
God's son. 14 For while peaceful silence
wrapped all things, and night in her own
swiftness was in mid-course, 15 your all-
powerful word leaped from heaven out of the
royal thrones, a stern warrior, into the midst of
the doomed land, 16 bearing as a sharp sword
your authentic commandment, and standing, it
filled all things with death, and while it
touched the heaven it stood upon the earth.
17 Then immediately apparitions in dreams
terribly troubled them, and unexpected fears
came upon them. 18 And each, one thrown
here half dead, another there, made known
why he was dying; 19 for the dreams,
disturbing them, forewarned them of this, that
they might not perish without knowing why
they were afflicted. 20 But experience of death
also touched the righteous, and a multitude
were destroyed in the wilderness, however the
wrath didn't last long. 21 For a blameless man
hurried to be their champion, bringing the
weapon of his own ministry, prayer and the
atoning sacrifice of incense, he withstood the
indignation, and set an end to the calamity,
showing that he was your servant. 22 And he
overcame the anger, not by strength of body,
not by force of weapons, but he subdued him
who was punishing by word, by bringing to
remembrance oaths and covenants made with
the fathers. 23 For when the dead had already
fallen in heaps one upon another, standing

between he stopped the wrath, and cut off the
way to the living. 24 For the whole world was
upon his long robe, and the glories of the
fathers were upon the engraving of the four
rows of precious stones, and your majesty was
upon the diadem of his head. 25 The destroyer
yielded to these, and they feared; for it was
enough only to test the wrath.

CHAPTER 19

1 But indignation without mercy came upon
the ungodly to the end; For God also foreknew
their future, 2 how, having changed their
minds to let your people go, and having sped
them eagerly on their way, they would change
their minds and pursue them. 3 For while they
were yet in the midst of their mourning, and
lamenting at the graves of the dead, they drew
upon themselves another counsel of folly, and
pursued as fugitives those whom they had
begged to leave and driven out. 4 For the doom
which they deserved was drawing them to this
end, and it made them forget the things that
had happened to them, that they might fill up
the punishment which was yet lacking to their
torments, 5 and that your people might journey
on by a marvelous road, but they themselves
might find a strange death. 6 For the whole
creation, each part in its diverse kind, was
made new again, complying with your
commandments, that your servants might be
kept unharmed. 7 Then the cloud that
overshadowed the camp was seen, and dry
land rising up out of what had been water, out
of the Red sea an unhindered highway, and a
grassy plain out of the violent surge, 8 by
which they passed over with all their army,
these who were covered with your hand,
having seen strange marvels. 9 For like horses
they roamed at large, and they skipped about
like lambs, praising you, O Lord, who was
their deliverer. 10 For they still remembered
the things that happened in the time of their
sojourning, how instead of bearing cattle, the
land brought out lice, and instead of fish, the
river spewed out a multitude of frogs. 11 But
afterwards, they also saw a new kind of birds,
when, led on by desire, they asked for
luxurious dainties; 12 For, to comfort them,
quails came up for them from the sea.
13 Punishments came upon the sinners, not
without the signs that were given beforehand
by the force of the thunders; for they justly
suffered through their own wickedness, for the
hatred which they practiced toward guests was
grievous indeed. 14 For whereas the others

41

didn't receive the strangers when they came to them, the Egyptians made slaves of guests who were their benefactors. **15** And not only so, but God will visit the men of Sodom another way, since they received as enemies those who were aliens; **16** whereas these first welcomed with feastings, and then afflicted with dreadful toils, those who had already shared with them in the same rights. **17** And moreover they were stricken with loss of sight (even as were those others at the righteous man's doors), when, being surrounded with yawning darkness, they each looked for the passage through his own door. **18** For as the notes of a lute vary the character of the rhythm, even so the elements, changing their order one with another, continuing always in its sound, as may clearly be conjectured from the sight of the things that have happened. **19** For creatures of the dry land were turned into creatures of the waters, and creatures that swim moved upon the land. **20** Fire kept the mastery of its own power in water, and water forgot its quenching nature. **21** On the contrary, flames didn't consume flesh of perishable creatures that walked among them, neither did they melt the ice-like grains of ambrosial food that were apt to melt. **22** For in all things, O Lord, you magnified your people, and you glorified them and didn't lightly regard them, standing by their side in every time and place.

SIRACH

Otherwise known as Ecclesiasticus

The Wisdom of Ben Sira derives its title from the author, "Yeshua [Jesus], son of Eleazar, son of Sira" (50:27). This seems to be the earliest title of the book. The designation "Liber Ecclesiasticus," meaning "Church Book," appended to some Greek and Latin manuscripts, is perhaps due to the extensive use the church made of this book in presenting moral teaching to catechumens and to the faithful. The author, a sage who lived in Jerusalem, was thoroughly imbued with love for the wisdom tradition, and also for the law, priesthood, Temple, and divine worship. Written in Hebrew in the early years of the second century BC, the book was finished by ca. 175.

CHAPTER 1

1 All wisdom comes from the Lord and is with him forever. **2** Who can count the sand of the seas, the drops of rain, and the days of eternity? **3** Who will search out the height of the sky, the breadth of the earth, the deep, and wisdom? **4** Wisdom has been created before all things, and the understanding of prudence from everlasting. **5 6** To whom has the root of wisdom been revealed? Who has known her shrewd counsels? **7 8** There is one wise, greatly to be feared, sitting upon his throne: The Lord. **9** He created her. He saw and measured her. He poured her out upon all his works. **10** She is with all flesh according to his gift. He gave her freely to those who love him. **11** The fear of the Lord is glory, exultation, and gladness, and a crown of rejoicing. **12** The fear of the Lord will delight the heart, and will give gladness, joy, and length of days. **13** Whoever fears the Lord, it will go well with him at the last. He will be blessed in the day of his death. **14** To fear the Lord is the beginning of wisdom. It was created together with the faithful in the womb. **15** She laid an eternal foundation with men. She will be trusted among their offspring. **16** To fear the Lord is the fullness of wisdom. She inebriates men with her fruits. **17** She will fill all her house with desirable things, and her storehouses with her produce. **18** The fear of the Lord is the crown of wisdom, making peace and perfect health to flourish. **19** He both saw and measured her. He rained down skill and knowledge of understanding and exalted the honor of those who hold her fast. **20** To fear the Lord is the root of wisdom. Her branches are length of days. **21 — 22** Unjust wrath can never be justified, for the sway of his wrath is his downfall. **23** A man that is patient will resist for a season, and afterward gladness will spring up to him. **24** He will hide his words for a season, and the lips of many will tell of his understanding. **25** A parable of knowledge is in the treasures of wisdom; but godliness is an abomination to a sinner. **26** If you desire wisdom, keep the commandments and the Lord will give her to you freely; **27** for the fear of the Lord is wisdom and instruction. Faith and humility are his good pleasure. **28** Don't disobey the fear of the Lord. Don't come to him with a double heart. **29** Don't be a hypocrite in the mouths of men. Keep watch over your lips. **30** Don't exalt yourself, lest you fall and bring dishonor upon your soul. The Lord will reveal your secrets and will cast you down in the midst of the congregation, because you didn't come to the fear of the Lord and your heart was full of deceit.

CHAPTER 2

1 My son, if you come to serve the Lord, prepare your soul for temptation. **2** Set your heart aright, constantly endure, and don't make haste in time of calamity. **3** Cling to him, and don't depart, that you may be increased at your latter end. **4** Accept whatever is brought upon you and be patient when you suffer humiliation. **5** For gold is tried in the fire, and acceptable men in the furnace of humiliation. **6** Put your trust in him, and he will help you. Make your ways straight and set your hope on him. **7** All you who fear the Lord, wait for his mercy. Don't turn aside, lest you fall. **8** All you who fear the Lord, put your trust in him, and your reward will not fail. **9** All you who fear the Lord, hope for good things, and for eternal gladness and mercy. **10** Look at the generations of old, and see: Who ever put his trust in the Lord, and was ashamed? Or who remained in his fear, and was forsaken? Or who called upon him, and he despised him?

11 For the Lord is full of compassion and mercy. He forgives sins and saves in time of affliction. 12 Woe to fearful hearts, to faint hands, and to the sinner that goes two ways! 13 Woe to the faint heart! For it doesn't believe. Therefore it won't be defended. 14 Woe to you who have lost your patience! And what will you all do when the Lord visits you? 15 Those who fear the Lord will not disobey his words. Those who love him will keep his ways. 16 Those who fear the Lord will seek his good pleasure. Those who love him will be filled with the law. 17 Those who fear the Lord will prepare their hearts and will humble their souls in his sight. 18 We will fall into the hands of the Lord, and not into the hands of men; for as his majesty is, so also is his mercy.

CHAPTER 3

1 Hear me, your father, O my children, and do what you hear, that you all may be saved. 2 For the Lord has given the father glory concerning the children and has confirmed the judgement of the mother concerning the sons. 3 He who honors his father will make atonement for sins. 4 He that gives glory to his mother is as one who lays up treasure. 5 Whoever honors his father will have joy in his own children. He will be heard in the day of his prayer. 6 He who gives glory to his father will have length of days. He who listens to the Lord will bring rest to his mother, 7 and will serve under his parents, as to masters. 8 Honor your father in deed and word, that a blessing may come upon you from him. 9 For the blessing of the father establishes the houses of children, but the curse of the mother roots out the foundations. 10 Don't glorify yourself in the dishonor of your father, for your father's dishonor is no glory to you. 11 For the glory of a man is from the honor of his father, and a mother in dishonor is a reproach to her children. 12 My son, help your father in his old age, and don't grieve him as long as he lives. 13 If he fails in understanding, have patience with him. Don't dishonor him in your full strength. 14 For the relieving of your father will not be forgotten. Instead of sins it will be added to build you up. 15 In the day of your affliction it will remember you, as fair weather upon ice, so will your sins also melt away. 16 He who forsakes his father is as a blasphemer. He who provokes his mother is cursed by the Lord. 17 My son, go on with your business in humility; so you will be loved by an acceptable

man. 18 The greater you are, humble yourself the more, and you will find favor before the Lord. 19 20 For the power of the Lord is great, and he is glorified by those who are lowly. 21 Don't seek things that are too hard for you, and don't search out things that are above your strength. 22 Think about the things that have been commanded you, for you have no need of the things that are secret. 23 Don't be overly busy in your superfluous works, for more things are showed to you than men can understand. 24 For the conceit of many has led them astray. Evil opinion has caused their judgement to slip. 25 There is no light without eyes. There is no wisdom without knowledge. 26 A stubborn heart will do badly at the end. He who loves danger will perish in it. 27 A stubborn heart will be burdened with troubles. The sinner will heap sin upon sins. 28 The calamity of the proud is no healing, for a weed of wickedness has taken root in him. 29 The heart of the prudent will understand a parable. A wise man desires the ear of a listener. 30 Water will quench a flaming fire; almsgiving will make atonement for sins. 31 He who repays good turns is mindful of that which comes afterward. In the time of his falling he will find a support.

CHAPTER 4

1 My son, don't deprive the poor of his living. Don't make the needy eyes wait long. 2 Don't make a hungry soul sorrowful or provoke a man in his distress. 3 Don't add more trouble to a heart that is provoked. Don't put off giving to him who is in need. 4 Don't reject a suppliant in his affliction. Don't turn your face away from a poor man. 5 Don't turn your eye away from one who asks. Give no occasion to a man to curse you. 6 For if he curses you in the bitterness of his soul, he who made him will hear his supplication. 7 Endear yourself to the assembly. Bow your head to a great man. 8 Incline your ear to a poor man. Answer him with peaceful words in humility. 9 Deliver him who is wronged from the hand of him that wrongs him; Don't be faint-hearted in giving judgement. 10 Be as a father to the fatherless, and like a husband to their mother. So you will be as a son of the Most High, and he will love you more than your mother does. 11 Wisdom exalts her sons and takes hold of those who seek her. 12 He who loves her loves life. Those who seek her early will be filled with gladness. 13 He who holds her fast will inherit glory. Where he enters, the Lord will bless.

14 Those who serve her minister to the Holy One. The Lord loves those who love her. **15** He who gives ear to her will judge the nations. He who heeds her will dwell securely. **16** If he trusts her, he will inherit her, and his generations will possess her. **17** For at the first she will walk with him in crooked ways, and will bring fear and dread upon him, and torment him with her discipline, until she may trust his soul, and try him by her judgments. **18** Then she will return him again to the straight way, and will gladden him, and reveal to him her secrets. **19** If he goes astray, she will forsake him, and hand him over to his fall. **20** Observe the opportunity and beware of evil. Don't be ashamed of your soul. **21** For there is a shame that brings sin, and there is a shame that is glory and grace. **22** Don't show partiality against your soul. Don't revere any man to your falling. **23** Don't refrain from speaking when it is for safety. Don't hide your wisdom for the sake of seeming fair. **24** For wisdom will be known by speech, and instruction by the word of the tongue. **25** Don't speak against the truth and be shamed for your ignorance. **26** Don't be ashamed to confess your sins. Don't fight the river's current. **27** Don't lay yourself down for a fool to tread upon. Don't be partial to one that is mighty. **28** Strive for the truth to death, and the Lord God will fight for you. **29** Don't be hasty with your tongue, or slack and negligent in your deeds. **30** Don't be like a lion in your house, or suspicious of your servants. **31** Don't let your hand be stretched out to receive and closed when you should repay.

CHAPTER 5

1 Don't set your heart upon your goods. Don't say, "They are sufficient for me." **2** Don't follow your own mind and your strength to walk in the desires of your heart. **3** Don't say, "Who will have dominion over me?" for the Lord will surely take vengeance on you. **4** Don't say, "I sinned, and what happened to me?" for the Lord is patient. **5** Don't be so confident of atonement that you add sin upon sins. **6** Don't say, "His compassion is great. He will be pacified for the multitude of my sins," for mercy and wrath are with him, and his indignation will rest on sinners. **7** Don't wait to turn to the Lord. Don't put off from day to day; for suddenly the wrath of the Lord will come on you, and you will perish in the time of vengeance. **8** Don't set your heart upon unrighteous gains, for you will profit nothing in the day of calamity. **9** Don't winnow with every wind. Don't walk in every path. This is what the sinner who has a double tongue does. **10** Be steadfast in your understanding. Let your speech be consistent. **11** Be swift to hear and answer with patience. **12** If you have understanding, answer your neighbor; but if not, put your hand over your mouth. **13** Glory and dishonor is in talk. A man's tongue may be his downfall. **14** Don't be called a whisperer. Don't lie in wait with your tongue; for shame is on the thief, and an evil condemnation is on him who has a double tongue. **15** Don't be ignorant in a great or small matter.

CHAPTER 6

1 Don't become an enemy instead of a friend; for an evil name will inherit shame and reproach. So it is with the sinner who has a double tongue. **2** Don't exalt yourself in the counsel of your soul, that your soul be not torn in pieces as a bull. **3** You will eat up your leaves, destroy your fruit, and leave yourself as a dry tree. **4** A wicked soul will destroy him who has it and will make him a laughing stock to his enemies. **5** Sweet words will multiply a man's friends. A gracious tongue will multiply courtesies. **6** Let those that are at peace with you be many, but your advisers one of a thousand. **7** If you want to gain a friend, get him in a time of testing, and don't be in a hurry to trust him. **8** For there is a friend just for an occasion. He won't continue in the day of your affliction. **9** And there is a friend who turns into an enemy. He will discover strife to your reproach. **10** And there is a friend who is a companion at the table, but he won't continue in the day of your affliction. **11** In your prosperity he will be as yourself and will be bold over your servants. **12** If you are brought low, he will be against you, and will hide himself from your face. **13** Separate yourself from your enemies and beware of your friends. **14** A faithful friend is a strong defense. He who has found him has found a treasure. **15** There is nothing that can be taken in exchange for a faithful friend. His excellency is beyond price. **16** A faithful friend is a life-saving medicine. Those who fear the Lord will find him. **17** He who fears the Lord directs his friendship properly; for as he is, so is his neighbor also. **18** My son, gather instruction from your youth up. Even when you have gray hair you will find wisdom. **19** Come to her as one who plows and sows and wait for her good fruit; for your toil will be little in her tillage, and you will soon eat of her fruit. **20** How exceedingly harsh she is to the unlearned! He who is without understanding will not remain in her. **21** She will rest upon him as a mighty stone of trial. He won't hesitate to cast her from him. **22** For wisdom is according to her name. She isn't manifest to many. **23** Give ear, my son, and accept my judgement. Don't refuse my counsel. **24** Bring your feet into her fetters, and your neck into her chain. **25** Put your shoulder under her and bear her. Don't be grieved with her bonds. **26** Come to her with all your soul. Keep her ways with your whole power. **27** Search and seek, and she will be made known to you. When you get hold of her, don't let her go. **28** For at the last you will find her rest; and she will be turned for you into gladness. **29** Her fetters will be to you for a covering of strength, and her chains for a robe of glory. **30** For there is a golden ornament upon her, and her bands area blue ribbon. **31** You will put her on as a robe of glory and will put her on as a crown of rejoicing. **32** My son, if you are willing, you will be instructed. If you will yield your soul, you will be prudent. **33** If you love to hear, you will receive. If you incline your ear, you will be wise. **34** Stand in the multitude of the elders. Attach yourself to whoever is wise. **35** Be willing to listen to every godly discourse. Don't let the proverbs of understanding escape you. **36** If you see a man of understanding, get to him early. Let your foot wear out the steps of his doors. **37** Let your mind dwell on the ordinances of the Lord and meditate continually on his commandments. He will establish your heart and your desire for wisdom will be given to you.

CHAPTER 7

1 Do no evil, so no evil will overtake you. **2** Depart from wrong, and it will turn away from you. **3** My son, don't sow upon the furrows of unrighteousness, and you won't reap them sevenfold. **4** Don't seek preeminence from the Lord, nor the seat of honor from the king. **5** Don't justify yourself in the presence of the Lord, and don't display your wisdom before the king. **6** Don't seek to be a judge, lest you not be able to take away iniquities, lest perhaps you fear the person of a mighty man and lay a stumbling block in the way of your uprightness. **7** Don't sin against the multitude of the city. Don't cast yourself down in the crowd. **8** Don't commit a sin twice, for even in one you will not be unpunished. **9** Don't say, "He will look upon the multitude of my gifts. When I make an offering to the Most High God, he will accept it." **10** Don't be faint-hearted in your prayer. Don't neglect to give alms. **11** Don't laugh a man to scorn when he is in the bitterness of his soul, for there is one who humbles and exalts. **12** Don't devise a lie against your brother or do the same to a friend. **13** Don't love to make any manner of lie, for that is not a good habit. **14** Don't babble in the multitude of elders. Don't repeat your words in your prayer. **15** Don't hate hard labor or farm work, which the Most High has created. **16** Don't number yourself among the multitude of sinners. Remember that wrath will not wait. **17** Humble your soul greatly, for the punishment of the ungodly man is fire and the worm. **18** Don't exchange a friend for something, neither a true brother for the gold of Ophir. **19** Don't deprive yourself of a wise and good wife, for her grace is worth more than gold. **20** Don't abuse a servant who works faithfully, or a hireling who gives you his life. **21** Let your soul love a wise servant. Don't defraud him of liberty. **22** Do you have cattle? Look after them. If they are profitable to you, let them stay by you. **23** Do you have children? Correct them and bow down their necks from their youth. **24** Do you have daughters? Take care of their bodies, and don't be overly indulgent toward them. **25** Give your daughter in marriage, and you will have accomplished a great matter. Give her to a man of understanding. **26** Do you have a wife after your mind? Don't cast her out. But don't trust yourself to one who is hateful. **27** Give glory to your father with your whole heart, and don't forget the birth pangs of your mother. **28** Remember that you were born of them. What will you repay them for the things that they have done for you? **29** Fear the Lord with all your soul; and revere his priests. **30** With all your strength love him who made you. Don't forsake his ministers. **31** Fear the Lord and honor the priest. Give him his portion, even as it is commanded you: the first fruits, the trespass offering, the gift of the shoulders, the sacrifice of sanctification, and the first fruits of holy things. **32** Also stretch out your hand to the poor man, that your blessing may be perfected. **33** A gift has grace in the sight of every living man. Don't withhold grace for a dead man. **34** Don't be lacking to those who weep and mourn with those who mourn.

46

35 Don't be slow to visit a sick man, for by such things you will gain love. 36 In all your words, remember eternity, and you will never sin.

CHAPTER 8

1 Don't contend with a mighty man, lest perhaps you fall into his hands. 2 Don't strive with a rich man, lest perhaps he overpowers you; for gold has destroyed many and turned away the hearts of kings. 3 Don't contend with a talkative man. Don't heap wood upon his fire. 4 Don't jest with a rude man, lest your ancestors be dishonored. 5 Don't reproach a man when he turns from sin. Remember that we are all worthy of punishment. 6 Don't dishonor a man in his old age; for some of us are also growing old. 7 Don't rejoice over one who is dead. Remember that we all die. 8 Don't neglect the discourse of the wise. Be conversant with their proverbs; for from them you will learn instruction and how to minister to great men. 9 Don't miss the discourse of the aged, for they also learned from their fathers, because from them you will learn understanding, and to give an answer in time of need. 10 Don't kindle the coals of a sinner, lest you be burned with the flame of his fire. 11 Don't rise up from the presence of an insolent man, lest he lie in wait as an ambush for your mouth. 12 Don't lend to a man who is mightier than yourself; and if you lend, be as one who has lost. 13 Don't be a guarantee above your power. If you are a guarantee, think as one who will have to pay. 14 Don't go to law with a judge; for according to his honor they will give judgement for him. 15 Don't go in the way with a rash man, lest he be burdensome to you; for he will do according to his own will, and you will perish with his folly. 16 Don't fight with a wrathful man. Don't travel with him through the desert, for blood is as nothing in his sight. Where there is no help, he will overthrow you. 17 Don't take counsel with a fool, for he will not be able to conceal the matter. 18 Do no secret thing before a stranger, for you don't know what it will cause. 19 Don't open your heart to every man. Don't let him return you a favor.

CHAPTER 9

1 Don't be jealous over the wife of your bosom, and don't teach her an evil lesson against yourself. 2 Don't give your soul to a woman, that she should set her foot upon your strength. 3 Don't go to meet a woman who plays the prostitute, lest perhaps you fall into her snares. 4 Don't use the company of a woman who is a singer, lest perhaps you be caught by her attempts. 5 Don't gaze at a maid, lest perhaps you be trapped in her penalties. 6 Don't give your soul to prostitutes, that you not lose your inheritance. 7 Don't look around you in the streets of the city, neither wander in its solitary places. 8 Turn your eye away from a beautiful woman, and don't gaze at another's beauty. Many have been led astray by the beauty of a woman; and with this, affection is kindled as a fire. 9 Don't sit at all with a woman who has a husband, or revel with her at the wine, lest perhaps your soul turn away to her, and with your spirit you slide into destruction. 10 Don't forsake an old friend; for the new is not comparable to him. A new friend is like new wine: if it becomes old, you will drink it with gladness. 11 Don't envy the glory of a sinner; for you don't know what his overthrow will be. 12 Don't delight in the delights of the ungodly. Remember they will not go unpunished to the grave. 13 Keep yourself far from the man who has power to kill, and you will have no suspicion of the fear of death. If you come to him, commit no fault, lest he take away your life. Know surely that you go about in the midst of snares and walk upon the battlements of a city. 14 As well as you can, aim to know your neighbors, and take counsel with the wise. 15 Let your conversation be with men of understanding. Let all your discourse be in the law of the Most High. 16 Let just men be companions at your table. Let your glorying be in the fear of the Lord. 17 A work is commended because of the hand of the artisan; so he who rules the people will be considered wise for his speech. 18 A talkative man is dangerous in his city. He who is headlong in his speech will be hated.

CHAPTER 10

1 A wise judge will instruct his people. The government of a man of understanding will be well ordered. 2 As is the judge of his people, so are his ministers. As the city's ruler is, so are all those who dwell in it. 3 An uninstructed king will destroy his people. A city will be established through the understanding of the powerful. 4 The authority of the earth is in the Lord's hand. In due time, he will raise up over it one who is profitable. 5 A man's prosperity is in the Lord's hand. He will lay his honor upon the person of the scribe. 6 Don't be angry with your neighbor for every wrong. Do

nothing by works of violence. **7** Pride is hateful before the Lord and men. Unrighteousness is abhorrent in the judgement of both. **8** Sovereignty is transferred from nation to nation because of iniquities, deeds of violence, and greed for money. **9** Why are dirt and ashes proud? Because in life, my body decays. **10** A long disease mocks the physician. He is a king today, and tomorrow he will die. **11** For when a man is dead, he will inherit creeping things, and beasts, and worms. **12** It is the beginning of pride when a man departs from the Lord. His heart has departed from him who made him. **13** For the beginning of pride is sin. He who keeps it will pour out abomination. For this cause the Lord brought upon them strange calamities and utterly overthrew them. **14** The Lord cast down the thrones of rulers and set the meek in their place. **15** The Lord plucked up the roots of nations and planted the lowly in their place. **16** The Lord overthrew the lands of nations and destroyed them to the foundations of the earth. **17** He took some of them away and destroyed them and made their memorial to cease from the earth. **18** Pride has not been created for men, nor wrathful anger for the offspring of women. **19** What manner of seed has honor? The seed of man, those who fear the Lord. What manner of seed has no honor? The seed of man, those who transgress the commandments. **20** In the midst of kindred he who rules them has honor. Those who fear the Lord have honor in his eyes. **21 22** The rich man, the honorable, and the poor all glory in the fear of the Lord. **23** It is not right to dishonor a poor man who has understanding. It is not fitting to glorify a man who is a sinner. **24** The great man, the judge, and the mighty man will be glorified. There is not one of them greater than he who fears the Lord. **25** Free men will minister to a wise servant. A man who has knowledge will not complain. **26** Don't flaunt your wisdom in doing your work. Don't glorify yourself in the time of your distress. **27** Better is he who labors and abounds in all things, than he who glorifies himself and lacks bread. **28** My son, glorify your soul in humility, and esteem yourself honor according to your true worth. **29** Who will justify him who sins against his own soul? Who will glorify him who dishonors his own life? **30** A poor man is glorified for his knowledge. A rich man is glorified for his riches. **31** But he who is glorified in poverty, how much more in riches? He who is

dishonored in riches, how much more in poverty?

CHAPTER 11

1 The wisdom of the lowly will lift up his head and make him sit in the midst of great men. **2** Don't commend a man for his beauty. Don't abhor a man for his outward appearance. **3** The bee is little among flying creatures, but what it produces is the best of confections. **4** Don't boast about the clothes you wear, and don't exalt yourself in the day of honor; for the Lord's works are wonderful, and his works are hidden among men. **5** Many kings have sat down upon the ground, but one who was never thought of has worn a crown. **6** Many mighty men have been greatly disgraced. Men of renown have been delivered into other men's hands. **7** Don't blame before you investigate. Understand first, and then rebuke. **8** Don't answer before you have heard. Don't interrupt while someone else is speaking. **9** Don't argue about a matter that doesn't concern you. Don't sit with sinners when they judge. **10** My son, don't be busy about many matters; for if you meddle much, you will not be unpunished. If you pursue, you will not overtake, and you will not escape by fleeing. **11** There is one who toils, labors, and makes haste, and is even more behind. **12** There is one who is sluggish, and needs help, lacking in strength, and who abounds in poverty, but the Lord's eyes looked upon him for good, and he raised him up from his low condition, **13** and lifted up his head so that many marveled at him. **14** Good things and evil, life and death, poverty and riches, are from the Lord. **15** — **16** — **17** The Lord's gift remains with the godly. His good pleasure will prosper forever. **18** One grows rich by his diligence and self-denial, and this is the portion of his reward: **19** when he says, "I have found rest, and now I will eat of my goods!" he doesn't know how much time will pass until he leaves them to others and dies. **20** Be steadfast in your covenant and be doing it and grow old in your work. **21** Don't marvel at the works of a sinner but trust the Lord and stay in your labor; for it is an easy thing in the sight of the Lord to swiftly and suddenly make a poor man rich. **22** The Lord's blessing is in the reward of the godly. He makes his blessing flourish in an hour that comes swiftly. **23** Don't say, "What use is there of me? What further good things can be mine?" **24** Don't say, "I have enough. What harm could happen to me now?" **25** In the day of good things, evil things are forgotten. In the day of evil things, a man will not remember things that are good. **26** For it is an easy thing in the sight of the Lord to reward a man in the day of death according to his ways. **27** The affliction of an hour causes delights to be forgotten. In the end, a man's deeds are revealed. **28** Call no man happy before his death. A man will be known in his children. **29** Don't bring every man into your house, for many are the plots of a deceitful man. **30** Like a decoy partridge in a cage, so is the heart of a proud man. Like a spy, he looks for your weakness. **31** For he lies in wait to turn things that are good into evil and assigns blame in things that are praiseworthy. **32** From a spark of fire, a heap of many coals is kindled, and a sinful man lies in wait for blood. **33** Take heed of an evil-doer, for he plans wicked things, lest perhaps he ruins your reputation forever. **34** Receive a stranger into your house, and he will distract you with arguments and estrange you from your own.

CHAPTER 12

1 If you do good, know to whom you do it, and your good deeds will have thanks. **2** Do good to a godly man, and you will find a reward— if not from him, then from the Most High. **3** No good will come to him who continues to do evil, nor to him who gives no alms. **4** Give to the godly man, and don't help the sinner. **5** Do good to one who is lowly. Don't give to an ungodly man. Keep back his bread, and don't give it to him, lest he subdue you with it; for you would receive twice as much evil for all the good you would have done to him. **6** For the Most High also hates sinners and will repay vengeance to the ungodly. **7** Give to the good man, and don't help the sinner. **8** A man's friend won't be fully tried in prosperity. His enemy won't be hidden in adversity. **9** In a man's prosperity, his enemies are grieved. In his adversity, even his friend leaves. **10** Never trust your enemy, for his wickedness is like corrosion in copper. **11** Though he humbles himself and walks bowed down, still be careful and beware of him. You will be to him as one who has wiped a mirror, to be sure it doesn't completely tarnish. **12** Don't set him next to you, lest he overthrow you and stand in your place. Don't let him sit on your right hand, lest he seek to take your seat, and at the last you acknowledge my words, and be pricked with my sayings. **13** Who will pity a charmer that is bitten by a snake, or any who come near wild beasts? **14** Even so, who will pity him who

goes to a sinner, and is associated with him in his sins? **15** For a while he will stay with you, and if you falter, he will not stay. **16** The enemy will speak sweetly with his lips, and in his heart plan to throw you into a pit. The enemy may weep with his eyes, but if he finds opportunity, he will want more blood. **17** If adversity meets you, you will find him there before you. Pretending to help you, he will trip you. **18** He will shake his head, clap his hands, whisper much, and change his countenance.

CHAPTER 13

1 He who touches pitch will be defiled. He who has fellowship with a proud man will become like him. **2** Don't take up a burden above your strength. Have no fellowship with one who is mightier and richer than yourself. What fellowship would the earthen pot have with the kettle? The kettle will strike, and the pot will be dashed in pieces. **3** The rich man does a wrong and threatens. The poor is wronged and apologizes. **4** If you are profitable, he will make merchandise of you. If you are in lack, he will forsake you. **5** If you own something, he will live with you. He will drain you bare and will not be sorry. **6** Does he need you? Then he will deceive you, smile at you, and give you hope. He will speak kindly to you and say, "What do you need?" **7** He will shame you by his meats until he has made you bare twice or thrice, and in the end he will laugh you to scorn. Afterward he will see you, will forsake you, and shake his head at you. **8** Beware that you are not deceived and brought low in your mirth. **9** If a mighty man invites you, be reserved, and he will invite you more. **10** Don't press him, lest you be thrust back. Don't stand far off, lest you be forgotten. **11** Don't try to speak with him as an equal, and don't believe his many words; For he will test you with much talk and will examine you in a smiling manner. **12** He who doesn't keep secrets to himself is unmerciful. He won't hesitate to harm and to bind. **13** Keep them to yourself and be careful, for you walk in danger of falling. **14** — **15** Every living creature loves its own kind, and every man loves his neighbor. **16** All flesh associates with their own kind. A man will stick to people like himself. **17** What fellowship would the wolf have with the lamb? So is the sinner to the godly. **18** What peace is there between a hyena and a dog? What peace is there between a rich man and the poor? **19** Wild donkeys are the prey of lions in the wilderness; likewise, poor men are feeding grounds for the rich. 20 Lowliness is an abomination to a proud man; likewise, a poor man is an abomination to the rich. 21 When a rich man is shaken, he is supported by his friends, but when one of low degree is down, he is pushed away even by his friends. 22 When a rich man falls, there are many helpers. He speaks things not to be spoken, and men justify him. A man of low degree falls, and men rebuke him. He utters wisdom and is not listened to. 23 A rich man speaks, and all keep silence. They extol what he says to the clouds. A poor man speaks, and they say, "Who is this?" If he stumbles, they will help to overthrow him. 24 Riches are good if they have no sin. Poverty is evil in the mouth of the ungodly. 25 The heart of a man changes his countenance, whether it is for good or for evil. 26 A cheerful countenance is a sign of a prosperous heart. Devising proverbs takes strenuous thinking.

CHAPTER 14

1 Blessed is the man who has not slipped with his mouth and doesn't suffer from sorrow for sins. 2 Blessed is he whose soul does not condemn him, and who has not given up hope. 3 Riches are not appropriate for a stingy person. What would an envious man do with money? 4 He who gathers by denying himself gathers for others. Others will revel in his goods. 5 If one is mean to himself, to whom will he be good? He won't enjoy his possessions. 6 There is none more evil than he who is stingy with himself. This is a punishment for his wickedness. 7 Even if he does good, he does it in forgetfulness. In the end, he reveals his wickedness. 8 A miser is evil. He turns away and disregards souls. 9 A covetous man's eye is not satisfied with his portion. Wicked injustice dries up his soul. 10 A miser begrudges bread, and it is lacking at his table. 11 My son, according to what you have, treat yourself well, and bring worthy offerings to the Lord. 12 Remember that death will not wait, and that the covenant of Hades hasn't been shown to you. 13 Do good to your friend before you die. According to your ability, reach out and give to him. 14 Don't defraud yourself of a good day. Don't let the portion of a good desire pass you by. 15 Won't you leave your labors to another, and your toils be divided by lot? 16 Give, take, and treat yourself well, because there is no seeking of luxury in Hades. 17 All flesh grows old like a garment, for the covenant from the beginning

is, "You must die." 18 Like the leaves flourishing on a thick tree, some it sheds, and some grow, so also are the generations of flesh and blood: one comes to an end and another is born. 19 Every work rots and falls away, and its builder will depart with it. 20 Blessed is the man who meditates on wisdom, and who reasons by his understanding. 21 He who considers her ways in his heart will also have knowledge of her secrets. 22 Go after her like one who tracks and lie in wait in her ways. 23 He who pries in at her windows will also listen at her doors. 24 He who lodges close to her house will also fasten a nail in her walls. 25 He will pitch his tent near at hand to her and will lodge in a lodging where good things are. 26 He will set his children under her shelter and will rest under her branches. 27 By her he will be covered from heat and will lodge in her glory.

CHAPTER 15

1 He who fears the Lord will do this. He who has possession of the law will obtain her. 2 As a mother will she meet him and receive him as a wife married in her virginity. 3 She will feed him with bread of understanding and give him water of wisdom to drink. 4 He will be stayed upon her and will not be moved. He will rely upon her and will not be confounded. 5 She will exalt him above his neighbors. She will open his mouth in the midst of the congregation. 6 He will inherit joy, a crown of gladness, and an everlasting name. 7 Foolish men will not obtain her. Sinners will not see her. 8 She is far from pride. Liars will not remember her. 9 Praise is not attractive in the mouth of a sinner; for it was not sent to him from the Lord. 10 For praise will be spoken in wisdom; The Lord will prosper it. 11 Don't say, "It is through the Lord that I fell away;" for you will not do the things that he hates. 12 Don't say, "It is he that caused me to err;" for he has no need of a sinful man. 13 The Lord hates every abomination; and those who fear him don't love them. 14 He himself made man from the beginning and left him in the hand of his own counsel. 15 If you will, you will keep the commandments. To be faithful is good pleasure. 16 He has set fire and water before you. You will stretch out your hand to whichever you desire. 17 Before man is life and death. Whichever he likes, it will be given to him. 18 For great is the wisdom of the Lord. He is mighty in power and sees all things. 19 His eyes are upon those who fear him. He

knows every work of man. **20** He has not commanded any man to be ungodly. He has not given any man license to sin.

CHAPTER 16

1 Don't desire a multitude of unprofitable children, neither delight in ungodly sons. **2** If they multiply, don't delight in them unless the fear of the Lord is in them. **3** Don't trust in their life. Don't rely on their condition: for one is better than a thousand, and to die childless than to have ungodly children. **4** For from one who has understanding, a city will be populated, but a race of wicked men will be made desolate. **5** I have seen many such things with my eyes. My ear has heard mightier things than these. **6** In the congregation of sinners, a fire will be kindled. In a disobedient nation, wrath is kindled. **7** He was not pacified toward the giants of old time, who revolted in their strength. **8** He didn't spare Lot's neighbors, whom he abhorred for their pride. **9** He didn't pity the people of perdition who were taken away in their sins, **10** or in like manner, the six hundred thousand footmen who were gathered together in the hardness of their hearts. **11** Even if there is one stiff-necked person, it is a marvel if he will be unpunished, for mercy and wrath are both with him who is mighty to forgive, and he pours out wrath. **12** As his mercy is great, so is his correction also. He judges a man according to his works. **13** The sinner will not escape with plunder. The perseverance of the godly will not be frustrated. **14** He will make room for every work of mercy. Each man will receive according to his works. **15** The Lord made the king of Egypt so stubborn that he would not acknowledge the Lord, in order that the world might know the Lord's works. **16** He shows his mercy to all creation; he has divided his light from darkness with a plumb line. **17** Don't say, "I will be hidden from the Lord," and "Who will remember me from on high?" I will not be known among so many people, for what is my soul in a boundless creation? **18** Behold, the heaven, the heaven of heavens, the deep, and the earth, will be moved when he visits. **19** The mountains and the foundations of the earth together are shaken with trembling when he looks at them. **20** No heart will think about these things. Who could comprehend his ways? **21** Like a tempest which no man can see, Yes, the majority of his works are hidden. **22** Who will declare his works of righteousness? Who will endure them? For his

covenant is far off. **23** He who is lacking in understanding thinks about these things. An unwise and erring man thinks follies. **24** My son, listen to me, learn knowledge, and heed my words with your heart. **25** I will impart instruction with precision and declare knowledge exactly. **26** In the judgement of the Lord are his works from the beginning. From the making of them he determined their parts. **27** He arranged his works for all time, and their beginnings to their generations. They aren't hungry or weary, and they don't cease from their works. **28** No one thrusts aside his neighbor. They will never disobey his word. **29** After this also the Lord looked at the earth and filled it with his blessings. **30** All manner of living things covered its face, and into it is their return.

CHAPTER 17

1 The Lord created mankind out of the earth and turned them back to it again. **2** He gave them days by number, and a set time, and gave them authority over the things that are on it. **3** He endowed them with strength proper to them and made them according to his own image. **4** He put the fear of man upon all flesh and gave him dominion over beasts and birds. **5** The Lord gave them the five senses, but he also gave them a sixth—intelligence, and a seventh—reason, which enables them to interpret what comes to them through the senses. **6** He gave them counsel, tongue, eyes, ears, and heart to have understanding. **7** He filled them with the knowledge of wisdom and showed them good and evil. **8** He set his eye upon their hearts, to show them the majesty of his works. **9** And he allowed them to take pride forever in his marvelous deeds. **10** And they will praise the name of his holiness, that they may declare the majesty of his works. **11** He added to them knowledge and gave them a law of life for a heritage. **12** He made an everlasting covenant with them and showed them his judgments. **13** Their eyes saw the majesty of his glory. Their ears heard the glory of his voice. **14** He said to them, "Beware of all unrighteousness." So he gave them commandment, each man concerning his neighbor. **15** Their ways are ever before him. They will not be hidden from his eyes. **16** From childhood on they tend to be evil; their heart is like stone, and they don't seem to be able to make it more human. **17** He divided the nations of the whole earth. For every nation he appointed a ruler, but Israel is the

Lord's portion. **18** Israel is his first-born, whom he disciplines as he brings him up. He gives him the light of his love and never neglects him. **19** All their works are as clear as the sun before him. His eyes are continually upon their ways. **20** Their iniquities are not hidden from him. All their sins are before the Lord. **21** But the Lord is gracious and knows his creatures; so he has spared them rather than abandon them. **22** With him the alms of a man is as a signet. He will keep the bounty of a man as the apple of the eye. **23** Afterwards he will rise up and recompense them and render their recompense upon their head. **24** However to those who repent he grants a return. He comforts those who are losing patience. **25** Return to the Lord and forsake sins. Make your prayer before his face offend less. **26** Turn again to the Most High and turn away from iniquity. Greatly hate the abominable thing. **27** Who will give praise to the Most High in Hades, in place of those who live and return thanks? **28** Thanksgiving perishes from the dead, as from one who doesn't exist. He who is in life and health will praise the Lord. **29** How great is the mercy of the Lord, and his forgiveness to those who turn to him! **30** For all things can't be in men, because the son of man is not immortal. **31** What is brighter than the sun? Yet even this fails. An evil man thinks about flesh and blood. **32** He looks upon the power of the height of heaven, while all men are earth and ashes.

CHAPTER 18

1 He who lives forever created all things in common. **2** The Lord alone will be justified and there is no other besides him. **3** He guides the world with his hand, and everything obeys him. He is the king of all things, and his power separates what is holy from what is not. **4** He has given power to declare his works to no one. Who could trace out his mighty deeds? **5** Who could measure the strength of his majesty? Who could also proclaim his mercies? **6** As for the wondrous works of the Lord, it is not possible to take from them nor add to them, neither is it possible to explore them. **7** When a man has finished, then he is just at the beginning. When he ceases, then he will be in perplexity. **8** What is mankind, and what purpose do they serve? What is their good, and what is their evil? **9** The number of man's days at the most are a hundred years. **10** As a drop of water from the sea, and a pebble from the sand, so are a few years in the day of eternity. **11** For this cause the Lord was patient over them and poured out his mercy upon them. **12** He saw and perceived their end, that it is evil. Therefore he multiplied his forgiveness. **13** The mercy of a man is upon his neighbor; but the mercy of the Lord is upon all flesh: reproving, chastening, teaching, and bringing back, as a shepherd does his flock. **14** He has mercy on those who accept chastening, and that diligently seek after his judgments. **15** My son, to your good deeds add no blemish, and no grief of words in any of your giving. **16** Doesn't the dew relieve the scorching heat? So a word is better than a gift. **17** Behold, isn't a word better than a gift? Both are with a gracious man. **18** A fool is ungracious and abusive. The gift of an envious man consumes the eyes. **19** Learn before you speak. Take care of your health before you are sick. **20** Before judgement examine yourself, and in the hour of visitation you will find forgiveness. **21** Humble yourself before you become sick. In the time of sins, show repentance. **22** Let nothing hinder you to pay your vow in due time. Don't wait until death to be justified. **23** Before you make a vow, prepare yourself. Don't be like a man who tempts the Lord. **24** Think about the wrath coming in the days of the end, and the time of vengeance, when he turns away his face. **25** In the days of fullness remember the time of hunger. Remember poverty and lack in the days of wealth. **26** From morning until evening, the time changes. All things are speedy before the Lord. **27** A wise man is cautious in everything. In days of sinning, he will beware of offence. **28** Every man of understanding knows wisdom. He will give thanks to him who found her. **29** They who were of understanding in sayings also became wise themselves and poured out apt proverbs. **30** Don't go after your lusts. Refrain yourself from your appetites. **31** If you give fully to your soul the delight of her desire, she will make you the laughing stock of your enemies. **32** Don't make merry in much luxury, neither be tied to the expense thereof. **33** Don't be made a beggar by banqueting upon borrowing when you have nothing in your purse.

CHAPTER 19

1 A workman who is a drunkard will not become rich. He who despises small things will fall little by little. **2** Wine and women will make men of understanding fall away. And he who joins with prostitutes will be more reckless. **3** Moths and worms will have him as their heritage. A reckless soul will be taken away. **4** He who is hasty to trust is willow-hearted. He who sins will offend against his own soul. **5** He who makes merry in his heart will be condemned: **6** He who hates talk has less wickedness. **7** Never repeat what is told you, and you won't be lacking. **8** Whether it is of friend or foe, don't tell it. Unless it is a sin to you, don't reveal it. **9** For he has heard you and observed you, and when the time comes, he will hate you. **10** Have you heard a word? Let it die with you. Be of good courage: it will not burst you. **11** A fool will travail in pain with a word, as a woman in labor with a child. **12** As an arrow that sticks in the flesh of the thigh, so is a word in a fool's belly. **13** Reprove a friend; it may be he didn't do it. If he did something, it may be that he may do it no more. **14** Reprove your neighbor; it may be he didn't say it. If he has said it, it may be that he may not say it again. **15** Reprove a friend; for many times there is slander. Don't trust every word. **16** There is one who slips, and not from the heart. Who is he who hasn't sinned with his tongue? **17** Reprove your neighbor before you threaten him; and give place to the law of the Most High; and don't be angry. **18** Fearing the Lord is the first step toward his accepting you; he will love you if you are wise. **19** Learn the Lord's commands. It is a discipline that gives life. Those who do what pleases him enjoy the fruit of the tree of immortality. **20** All wisdom is the fear of the Lord. In all wisdom is the doing of the law and what the knowledge of his omnipotence means. **21** If a servant refuses to obey his master, but later does obey, the master is still angry. **22** The knowledge of wickedness is not wisdom. The prudence of sinners is not counsel. **23** There is a wickedness, and it is abomination. There is a fool lacking in wisdom. **24** Better is one who has small understanding, and fears, than one who has much prudence, and transgresses the law. **25** There is an exquisite subtlety, and it is unjust. And there is one who perverts favor to gain a judgement. **26** There is one who does wickedly, who hangs down his head with mourning; but inwardly he is full of deceit, **27** bowing down his face, and making as if he were deaf of one ear. Where he isn't known, he will be beforehand with you. **28** And if for lack of power he is hindered from sinning, if he find opportunity, he will do mischief. **29** A man will be known by his look, One who has understanding will be known by his face, when you meet him. **30** A man's attire, grinning laughter, and gait show what he is.

CHAPTER 20

1 There is a reproof that is not timely; and there is a man who keeps silent and is wise. **2** How good is it to reprove, rather than to be angry. He who confesses will be kept back from hurt. **3** Admit when you are wrong, and you will avoid embarrassment. **4** As is the lust of a eunuch to deflower a virgin, so is he who executes judgments with violence. **5** There is one who keeps silent and is found wise; and there is one who is hated for his much talk. **6** There is one who keeps silent, for he has no answer to make; And there is one who keeps silent, as knowing his time. **7** A wise man will be silent until his time has come, but the braggart and fool will miss his time. **8** He who uses many words will be abhorred. He who takes authority for himself will be hated in it. **9** There is a prosperity that a man finds in misfortunes; And there is a gain that turns to loss. **10** There is a gift that will not profit you; and there is a gift pays back double. **11** There is an abasement because of glory; and there is one who has lifted up his head from a low estate. **12** There is one who buys much for a little and pays for it again sevenfold. **13** He who is wise in words will make himself beloved; but the pleasantries of fools will be wasted. **14** The gift of a fool will not profit you; for his eyes are many instead of one. **15** He will give little and insult much. He will open his mouth like a crier. Today he will lend, and tomorrow he will ask for it back. Such a one is a hateful man. **16** The fool will say, "I have no friend, and I have no thanks for my good deeds. They who eat my bread are of evil tongue." **17** How often, and of how many, will he be laughed to scorn! **18** A slip on a pavement is better than a slip with the tongue. So the fall of the wicked will come speedily. **19** A man without grace is a tale out of season. It will be continually in the mouth of the ignorant. **20** A parable from a fool's mouth will be rejected; for he will not speak it in its season. **21** There is one who is hindered from sinning through lack. When he rests, he will not be troubled. **22** There is one who destroys his soul through bashfulness. By a foolish countenance, he will destroy it. **23** There is one who for bashfulness makes promises to his friend; and he makes him his enemy for nothing. **24** A lie is a foul blot in a man. It will be continually in the mouth of the ignorant. 25 A thief is better than a man who is continually lying, but they both will inherit destruction. 26 The disposition of a liar is dishonor. His shame is with him continually. 27 He who is wise in words will advance himself. And one who is prudent will please great men. 28 He who tills his land will raise his heap high. He who pleases great men will get pardon for iniquity. 29 Presents and gifts blind the eyes of the wise, and as a muzzle on the mouth, turn away reproofs. 30 Wisdom that is hidden, and treasure that is out of sight, what profit is in them both? 31 Better is a man who hides his folly than a man who hides his wisdom.

CHAPTER 21

1 My son, have you sinned? Add no more to it; and ask forgiveness for your past sins. 2 Flee from sin as from the face of a serpent; for if you draw near, it will bite you. Its teeth are lion's teeth, slaying men's souls. 3 All iniquity is as a two-edged sword. Its stroke has no healing. 4 Terror and violence will lay waste riches. So the house of an arrogant man will be laid waste. 5 Supplication from a poor man's mouth reaches to the ears of God, and his judgement comes speedily. 6 One who hates reproof is in the path of the sinner. He who fears the Lord will turn again in his heart. 7 He who is mighty in tongue is known far away; but the man of understanding knows when he slips. 8 He who builds his house with other men's money is like one who gathers stones for his own tomb. 9 The congregation of wicked men is as a bundle of tow with a flame of fire at the end of them. 10 The way of sinners is paved with stones; and at the end of it is the pit of Hades. 11 He who keeps the law becomes master of its intent. The end of the fear of the Lord is wisdom. 12 He who is not clever will not be instructed. There is a cleverness which makes bitterness abound. 13 The knowledge of a wise man will be made to abound as a flood, and his counsel as a fountain of life. 14 The inward parts of a fool are like a broken vessel. He will hold no knowledge. 15 If a man of knowledge hears a wise word, he will commend it and add to it. The wanton man hears it, and it displeases him, so he puts it away behind his back. 16 The discourse of a fool is like a burden in the way, but grace will be found on the lips of the wise. 17 The mouth of the prudent man will be sought for in the congregation. They will ponder his words in their heart. 18 As a house that is destroyed, so is wisdom to a fool. The knowledge of an unwise man is talk without sense. 19 Instruction is as fetters on the feet of an unwise man, and as manacles on the right hand. 20 A fool lifts up his voice with laughter, but a clever man smiles quietly. 21 Instruction is to a prudent man as an ornament of gold, and as a bracelet upon his right arm. 22 The foot of a fool rushes into a house, but a man of experience will be ashamed of entering. 23 A foolish man peers into the door of a house, but a man who is instructed will stand outside. 24 It is a lack of instruction in a man to listen at a door, but a prudent man will be grieved with the disgrace. 25 The lips of strangers will be grieved at these things, but the words of prudent men will be weighed in the balance. 26 The heart of fools is in their mouth, but the mouth of wise men is their heart. 27 When the ungodly curses Satan, he curses his own soul. 28 A whisperer defiles his own soul and will be hated wherever he travels.

CHAPTER 22

1 A slothful man is compared to a stone that is defiled. Everyone will at hiss him in his disgrace. 2 A slothful man is compared to the filth of a dunghill. Every man who takes it up will shake out his hand. 3 An uninstructed child is a disgrace to his father, and a foolish daughter is born to his loss. 4 A prudent daughter will inherit a husband of her own. She who brings shame is the grief of her father. 5 She who is bold brings shame upon father and husband. She will be despised by both of them. 6 Unseasonable discourse is as music in mourning, but stripes and correction are wisdom in every season. 7 He who teaches a fool is as one who glues a potsherd together, even as one who wakes a sleeper out of a deep sleep. 8 He who teaches a fool is as one who teaches a man who slumbers. In the end he will say, "What is it?" 9 Children who are brought up well do not show the humble origin of their parents. 10 Children who are not brought up well, who are arrogant and conceited, are a stain on the noblest family. 11 Weep for the dead, for he lacks light. Weep for a fool, for he lacks understanding. Weep more sweetly for the dead, because he has found rest, but the life of the fool is worse than death. 12 Mourning for the dead lasts seven days, but for a fool and an ungodly man, all the days of his life. 13 Don't talk much with a foolish man, and

don't go to one that has no understanding: Beware of him, lest you have trouble and be defiled in his onslaught. Turn away from him, and you will find rest, and you won't be wearied in his madness. **14** What would be heavier than lead? What is its name, but a fool? **15** Sand, salt, and a mass of iron is easier to bear than a man without understanding. **16** Timber girded and bound into a building will not be released with shaking. So a heart established in due season on well advised counsel will not be afraid. **17** A heart settled upon a thoughtful understanding is as an ornament of plaster on a polished wall. **18** Fences set on a high place will not stand against the wind; so a fearful heart in the imagination of a fool will not stand against any fear. **19** He who pricks the eye will make tears fall. He who pricks the heart makes it show feeling. **20** Whoever casts a stone at birds scares them away. He who insults a friend will dissolve friendship. **21** If you have drawn a sword against a friend, don't despair, for there may be a way back. **22** If you have opened your mouth against a friend, don't be afraid, for there may be reconciliation, unless it is for insulting, arrogance, disclosing of a secret, or a treacherous blow— for these things any friend will flee. **23** Gain trust with your neighbor in his poverty, that in his prosperity you may have gladness. Stay steadfast to him in the time of his affliction, that you may be heir with him in his inheritance. **24** Before fire is the vapor and smoke of a furnace, so insults precede bloodshed. **25** I won't be ashamed to shelter a friend. I won't hide myself from his face: **26** If any evil happens to me because of him, everyone that hears it will beware of him. **27** Who will set a watch over my mouth, and a seal of shrewdness upon my lips, that I don't fall from it, and that my tongue not destroy me?

CHAPTER 23

1 O Lord, Father and Master of my life, don't abandon me to their counsel. Don't let me fall by them. **2** Who will set scourges over my thought, and a discipline of wisdom over my heart, that they spare me not for my errors, and not overlook their sins? **3** Otherwise my errors might be multiplied, and my sins abound, I fall before my adversaries, and my enemy rejoice over me. **4** O Lord, Father and God of my life, don't give me haughty eyes, **5** and turn away evil desire from me. **6** Let neither gluttony nor lust overtake me. Don't give me over to a shameless mind. **7** Listen, my children, to the discipline of the mouth. He who keeps it will not be taken. **8** The sinner will be overpowered through his lips. By them, the insulter and the arrogant will stumble. **9** Don't accustom your mouth to an oath, and don't be accustomed to naming the Holy One, **10** for as a servant who is continually scourged will not lack a bruise, so he also who swears and continually utters the Name will not be cleansed from sin. **11** A man of many oaths will be filled with iniquity. The scourge will not depart from his house. If he offends, his sin will be upon him. If he disregards it, he has sinned doubly. If he has sworn in vain, he will not be justified, for his house will be filled with calamities. **12** There is a manner of speech that is clothed with death. Let it not be found in the heritage of Jacob, for all these things will be far from the godly, and they will not wallow in sins. **13** Don't accustom your mouth to gross rudeness, for it involves sinful speech. **14** Remember your father and your mother, for you sit in the midst of great men, that you be not forgetful before them, and become a fool by your custom; so you may wish that you had not been born, and curse the day of your nativity. **15** A man who is accustomed to words of reproach won't be corrected all the days of his life. **16** Two sorts of people multiply sins, and the third will bring wrath: a hot mind, as a burning fire, will not be quenched until it is consumed; a fornicator in the body of his flesh will never cease until he has burned out the fire. **17** All bread is sweet to a fornicator. He will not cease until he dies. **18** A man who goes astray from his own bed, says in his heart, "Who sees me? Darkness is around me, and the walls hide me. No one sees me. Of whom am I afraid? The Most High will not remember my sins." **19** The eyes of men are his terror. He doesn't know that the eyes of the Lord are ten thousand times brighter than the sun, seeing all the ways of men, and looking into secret places. **20** All things were known to him before they were created, and in also after they were completed. **21** This man will be punished in the streets of the city. He will be seized where he least expects it. **22** So also is a wife who leaves her husband and brings in an heir by a stranger. **23** For first, she was disobedient in the law of the Most High. Second, she trespassed against her own husband. Third, she played the adulteress in whoredom, and brought in children by a stranger. **24** She will be brought out into the

55

congregation. Her punishment will extend to her children. **25** Her children will not take root. Her branches will bear no fruit. **26** She will leave her memory for a curse. Her reproach won't be blotted out. **27** And those who are left behind will know that there is nothing better than the fear of the Lord, and nothing sweeter than to heed the commandments of the Lord.

CHAPTER 24

1 Wisdom will praise her own soul and will proclaim her glory in the midst of her people. **2** She will open her mouth in the congregation of the Most High and proclaim her glory in the presence of his power. **3** "I came out of the mouth of the Most High and covered the earth as a mist. **4** I lived in high places, and my throne is in the pillar of the cloud. **5** Alone I surrounded the circuit of heaven and walked in the depth of the abyss. **6** In the waves of the sea, and in all the earth, and in every people and nation, I got a possession. **7** With all these I sought rest. In whose inheritance will I lodge? **8** Then the Creator of all things gave me a commandment. He who created me made my tabernacle to rest, and said, 'Let your tabernacle be in Jacob, and your inheritance in Israel.' **9** He created me from the beginning before the world. For all ages, I will not cease to exist. **10** In the holy tabernacle, I ministered before him. So I was established in Zion. **11** In the beloved city, likewise he gave me rest. In Jerusalem was my domain. **12** I took root in a people that was glorified, even in the portion of the Lord's own inheritance. **13** I was exalted like a cedar in Lebanon, and like a cypress tree on the mountains of Hermon. **14** I was exalted like a palm tree on the seashore, and as rose plants in Jericho, and as a fair olive tree in the plain. I was exalted as a plane tree. **15** As cinnamon and as palathus, I have given a scent to perfumes. As choice myrrh, I spread abroad a pleasant fragrance, as galbanum, onyx, stacte, and as the smell of frankincense in the tabernacle. **16** As the terebinth, I stretched out my branches. My branches are branches of glory and grace. **17** As the vine, I put out grace. My flowers are the fruit of glory and riches. **18** I am the mother of beautiful love, of fear, knowledge, and holy hope. Since I am eternal, I am given to all my children, who are named by him. **19** "Come to me, all you who desire me, and be filled with my fruits. **20** For my memorial is sweeter than honey, and my inheritance than the

honeycomb. **21** Those who eat me will be hungry for more. Those who drink me will be thirsty for more. **22** He who obeys me will not be ashamed. Those who work in me will not sin." **23** All these things are the book of the covenant of the Most High God, the law which Moses commanded us for an inheritance for the assemblies of Jacob. **24** Always be strong in the Lord; stay with him, so that he may make you strong. There is no God but the Lord Almighty, and no savior except him. **25** It is he who makes wisdom abundant, as Pishon, and as Tigris in the days of first fruits. **26** He makes understanding full as Euphrates, and as Jordan in the days of harvest, **27** who makes instruction shine out as the light, as Gihon in the days of vintage. **28** The first man didn't know her perfectly. In like manner, the last has not explored her. **29** For her thoughts are filled from the sea, and her counsels from the great deep. **30** I came out as a canal stream from a river, and as an irrigation ditch into a garden. **31** I said, "I will water my garden, and will drench my garden bed." Behold, my stream became a river, and my river became a sea. **32** I will yet bring instruction to light as the morning and will make these things clear from far away. **33** I will continue to pour out doctrine like prophecy and leave it to generations of ages. **34** Behold that I have not labored for myself only, but for all those who diligently seek her.

CHAPTER 25

1 In three things I was beautified and stood up beautiful before the Lord and men: The concord of kindred, and friendship of neighbors, and a woman and her husband that walk together in agreement. **2** But three sorts *of men* my soul hates, and I am greatly offended at their life: A poor man that is arrogant, and a rich man that is a liar, *and* an old man that is an adulterer lacking understanding. **3** In *your* youth you have not gathered, and how should you find in your old age? **4** How beautiful a thing is judgement for gray hairs, and for elders to know counsel! **5** How beautiful is the wisdom of old men and thought and counsel to men that are in honor! **6** Much experience is the crown of old men; And their glorying is the fear of the Lord. **7** There be nine things that I have thought of, and in my heart counted happy; And the tenth I will utter with my tongue: A man that has joy of his children; A man that lives and looks upon the fall of his enemies: **8** Happy is he that dwells with a wife of understanding; And he that has not slipped with his tongue; And he that has not served a man that is unworthy of him: **9** Happy is he that has found prudence; And he that speaks in the ears of those who listen. **10** How great is he that has found wisdom! Yet is there none above him that fears the Lord. **11** The fear of the Lord passes all things: He that holds it, to whom will he be likened? **12** Fearing the Lord is the first step toward loving him, and faith is the first step toward loyalty to him. **13** *Give me* any plague but the plague of the heart; And any wickedness but the wickedness of a woman; **14** Any calamity, but a calamity from those who hate me; And any vengeance, but the vengeance of enemies. **15** There is no head above the head of a serpent; And there is no wrath above the wrath of an enemy. **16** I will rather dwell with a lion and a dragon, than keep house with a wicked woman. **17** The wickedness of a woman changes her look and darkens her countenance as a bear does. **18** Her husband will sit at meat among his neighbors, and when he hears it he sighs bitterly. **19** All malice is but little to the malice of a woman: Let the portion of a sinner fall on her. **20** *As* the going up a sandy way *is* to the feet of the aged, so is a wife full of words to a quiet man. **21** Throw not yourself upon the beauty of a woman; And desire not a woman for her beauty. **22** There is anger, and impudence, and great reproach, if a woman maintains her husband. **23** A wicked woman is a basement of heart, and sadness of countenance, and a wounded heart: A woman that will not make her husband happy is *as* hands that hang down, and palsied knees. **24** From a woman *was* the beginning of sin; And because of her we all die. **25** Give not water an outlet; Neither to a wicked woman freedom of speech. **26** If she goes not as you would have her, Cut her off from your flesh.

CHAPTER 26

1 Happy is the husband of a good wife; And the number of his days will be doubled. **2** A brave woman rejoices her husband; And he will fulfill his years in peace. **3** A good wife is a good portion: She will be given in the portion of such as fear the Lord. **4** Whether a man be rich or poor, A good heart *makes* at all times a cheerful countenance. **5** Of three things my heart was afraid; And concerning the fourth kind I made supplication: The slander of a city, and the assembly of a multitude, and a false accusation: All these are more grievous than death. **6** A grief of heart and sorrow is a woman that is jealous of *another* woman, and the scourge of a tongue communicating to all. **7** A wicked woman is *as* a yoke of oxen shaken to and fro: He that takes hold of her is as one that grasps a scorpion. **8** A drunken woman *causes* great wrath; And she will not cover her own shame. **9** The whoredom of a woman is in the lifting up of her eyes; And it will be known by her eyelids. **10** Keep strict watch on a headstrong daughter, Lest she find liberty for herself, and use it. **11** Look well after an impudent eye; And marvel not if it trespasses against you. **12** She will open her mouth, as a thirsty traveler, and drink of every water that is near: She will sit down at every post and open her quiver against *any* arrow. **13** The grace of a wife will delight her husband; And her knowledge will fatten his bones. **14** A silent woman is a gift of the Lord; And there is nothing worth so much as a well-instructed soul. **15** A shamefast woman is grace upon grace; And there is no price worthy of a continent soul. **16** As the sun when it arises in the highest places of the Lord, so is the beauty of a good wife in the ordering of a man's house. **17** As the lamp that shines upon the holy candlestick, so is the beauty of the face in ripe age. **18** As the golden pillars are upon a base of silver, so are beautiful feet with the breasts of one that is steadfast. **19** My child, stay healthy while you are young, and don't give your strength to strangers. **20** Search the whole land for a fertile field, and plant it with your own seed, trusting your own good stock. **21** Then your children will survive and grow up confident of their good family. **22** A prostitute is like spit; a married woman who has affairs brings death to her lovers. **23** A lawless man will get a godless wife, as he deserves, but a man who honors the Lord will have a devout wife. **24** A shameless wife enjoys making a disgrace of herself, but a modest wife will act modestly even alone with her husband. **25** A self-willed woman is a bitch, but a woman with a sense of decency honors the Lord. **26** A wife who honors her husband will seem wise to everyone; but if she dishonors him by her overbearing attitude, everyone will know that she is ungodly. Fortunate is the husband of a good wife, because he will live twice as long. **27** A loud-mouthed, talkative woman is like a trumpet sounding the signal for attack, and any man who has such a wife will spend his life at war.

28 For two things my heart is grieved; And for the third anger comes upon me: A man of war that suffers for poverty; And men of understanding that are counted as refuse: One that turns back from righteousness to sin; The Lord will prepare him for the sword. **29** A merchant will hardly keep himself from wrong doing; And a huckster will not be acquitted of sin.

CHAPTER 27

1 Many have sinned for a thing indifferent; And he that seeks to multiply *gain* will turn his eye away. **2** A nail will stick fast between the joining of stones; And sin will thrust itself in between buying and selling. **3** Unless *a man* hold on diligently in the fear of the Lord, His house will soon be overthrown. **4** In the shaking of a sieve, the refuse remains; So the filth of man in his reasoning. **5** The furnace will prove the potter's vessels; And the trial of a man is in his reasoning. **6** The fruit of a tree declares the husbandry thereof; So is the utterance of the thought of the heart of a man. **7** Praise no man before *you hear him* reason; For this is the trial of men. **8** If you follow righteousness, you will obtain her, and put her on, as a long robe of glory. **9** Birds will return to their like; And truth will return to those who practice her. **10** The lion lies in wait for prey; So does sin for those who work iniquity. **11** The discourse of a godly man is always wisdom: But the foolish man changes as the moon. **12** Among men void of understanding observe the opportunity; But stay continually among the thoughtful. **13** The discourse of fools is an offence; And their laughter is in the wantonness of sin. **14** The talk of a man of many oaths will make the hair stand upright; And their strife makes one stop his ears. **15** The strife of the proud is a shedding of blood; And their reviling of each other is a grievous thing to hear. **16** He that reveals secrets destroys credit and will not find a friend to his mind. **17** Love a friend and keep faith with him: But if you reveal his secrets, You will not pursue after him; **18** For as a man has destroyed his enemy, so have you destroyed the friendship of your neighbor. **19** And as a bird which you have released out of your hand, so have you let your neighbor go, and you will not catch him again: **20** Pursue him not, for he is gone far away, and has escaped as a gazelle out of the snare. **21** For a wound may be bound up, and after reviling there may be a reconcilement; But he that reveals secrets has lost hope. **22** One that winks with the eye contrives evil things; And no man will remove him from it. **23** When you are present, he will speak sweetly, and will admire your words; But afterward he will writhe his mouth and set a trap *for you* in your words. **24** I have hated many things, but nothing like him; And the Lord will hate him. **25** One that casts a stone on high casts it on his own head; And a deceitful stroke will open wounds. **26** He that digs a pit will fall into it; And he that sets a snare will be taken therein. **27** He that does evil things, they will roll upon him, and he will not know from where they have come to him. **28** Mockery and reproach are from the arrogant; And vengeance, as a lion, will lie in wait for him. **29** They that rejoice at the fall of the godly will be taken in a snare; And anguish will consume them before they die. **30** Wrath and anger, these also are abominations; And a sinful man will possess them.

CHAPTER 28

1 He that takes vengeance will find vengeance from the Lord; And he will surely make firm his sins. **2** Forgive your neighbor the hurt that he has done *you;* And then your sins will be pardoned when you pray. **3** Man cherishes anger against man; And does he seek healing from the Lord? **4** Upon a man like himself he has no mercy; And does he make supplication for his own sins? **5** He being himself flesh nourishes wrath: Who will make atonement for his sins? **6** Remember your last end, and cease from enmity: *Remember* corruption and death, and remain in the commandments. **7** Remember the commandments and be not angry with your neighbor; And *remember* the covenant of the Highest, and wink at ignorance. **8** Abstain from strife, and you will diminish your sins: For a passionate man will kindle strife; **9** And a man that is a sinner will trouble friends and will make debate among those who are at peace. **10** As is the fuel of the fire, so will it burn; And as the stoutness of the strife is, *so* will it burn: As is the strength of the man, *so* will be his wrath; And as is his wealth, *so* he will exalt his anger. **11** A contention begun in haste kindles a fire; And a hasty fighting sheds blood. **12** If you blow a spark, it will burn; And if you spit upon it, it will be quenched: And both these will come out of your mouth. **13** Curse the whisperer and double-tongued: For he has destroyed many that were at peace. **14** A third person's tongue has shaken many and dispersed them from nation to nation; And it has pulled down strong cities and overthrown the houses of great men. **15** A third person's tongue has cast out brave women and deprived them of their labors. **16** He that listens to it will not find rest, nor will he dwell quietly. **17** The stroke of a whip makes a mark in the flesh; But the stroke of a tongue will break bones. **18** Many have fallen by the edge of the sword: Yet not so many as those who have fallen because of the tongue. **19** Happy is he that is sheltered from it, that has not passed through the wrath thereof; That has not drawn its yoke, and has not been bound with its bands. **20** For the yoke thereof is a yoke of iron, and the bands thereof are bands of brass. **21** The death thereof is an evil death; And Hades were better than it. **22** It will not have rule over godly men; And they will not be burned in its flame. **23** They that forsake the Lord will fall into it; And it will burn among them and will not be quenched: It will be sent out upon them as a lion; And as a leopard it will destroy them. **24** Look that you hedge your possession about with thorns; Bind up your silver and your gold; **25** And make a balance and a weight for your words; And make a door and a bar for your mouth. **26** Take heed lest you slip therein; Lest you fall before one that lies in wait.

CHAPTER 29

1 He that shows mercy will lend to his neighbor; And he that strengthens him with his hand keeps the commandments. **2** Lend to your neighbor in time of his need; And pay you your neighbor again in due season. **3** Confirm your word and keep faith with him; And at all seasons you will find what you need. **4** Many have reckoned a loan as a windfall and have given trouble to those that helped them. **5** until he has received, he will kiss a man's hands; And for his neighbor's money he will speak submissively: And when payment is due, he will prolong the time, and return words of heaviness, and complain of the times. **6** If he prevails, he will hardly receive the half; And he will count it as a windfall: If not, he has deprived him of his money, and he has gotten him for an enemy without cause: He will pay him with cursing and railing; And for honor he will pay him disgrace. **7** Many on account of *men's* ill-dealing have turned away; They have feared to be defrauded for nothing. **8** However with a man in poor estate be patient; And let him not wait for *your* alms. **9** Help a poor man

for the commandment's sake; And according to his need send him not empty away. **10** Lose *your* money for a brother and a friend; And let it not rust under the stone to be lost. **11** Bestow your treasure according to the commandments of the Most High; And it will profit you more than gold. **12** Shut up alms in your store-chambers; And it will deliver you out of all affliction: **13** It will fight for you against your enemy Better than a mighty shield and a ponderous spear. **14** A good man will be a guarantee for his neighbor; And he that has lost shame will fail him. **15** Forget not the good offices of your guarantor; for he has given his life for you. **16** A sinner will overthrow the good estate of his guarantor; **17** And he that is of an unthankful mind will fail him that delivered him. **18** Suretyship has undone many that were prospering and shaken them as a wave of the sea: Mighty men has it driven from their homes; And they wandered among strange nations. **19** A sinner that falls into suretyship, and undertakes contracts for work, will fall into lawsuits. **20** Help your neighbor according to your power and take heed to yourself that you fall not *the same way*. **21** The chief thing for life is water, and bread, and a garment, and a house to cover shame. **22** Better is the life of a poor man under a shelter of logs, than sumptuous fare in another man's house. **23** With little or with much, be well satisfied. **24** It is a miserable life to go from house to house: And where you are a sojourner, you will not *dare to* open your mouth. **25** You will entertain, and give to drink, and have no thanks: And in addition to this you will hear bitter words. **26** Come here, you sojourner, furnish a table, and if you have anything in your hand, feed me with it. **27** Go out, you sojourner, from the face of honor; My brother is come to be my guest; I have need of my house. **28** These things are grievous to a man of understanding; The upbraiding of house-room, and the reproaching of the money-lender.

CHAPTER 30

1 He that loves his son will continue to lay stripes upon him, that he may have joy of him in the end. **2** He that chastises his son will have profit of him and will glory of him among his acquaintance. **3** He that teaches his son will provoke his enemy to jealousy; And before friends he will rejoice of him. **4** His father dies and is as though he had not died; For he has left one behind him like himself. **5** In his life, he saw and rejoiced *in him;* And when he died, he sorrowed not: **6** He left behind him an avenger against his enemies, and one to requite kindness to his friends. **7** He that makes too much of his son will bind up his wounds; And his heart will be troubled at every cry. **8** An unbroken horse becomes stubborn; And a son left at large becomes headstrong. **9** Cocker your child, and he will make you afraid: Play with him, and he will grieve you. **10** Laugh not with him, lest you have sorrow with him; And you will gnash your teeth in the end. **11** Give him no liberty in his youth, and wink not at his follies. **12** Bow down his neck in his youth and beat him on the sides while he is a child, lest he wax stubborn, and be disobedient to you; And there will be sorrow to your soul. **13** Chastise your son, and take pains with him, lest his shameless behavior be an offence to you. **14** Better is a poor man, being sound and strong of constitution, than a rich man that is plagued in his body. **15** Health and a good constitution are better than all gold; And a strong body than wealth without measure. **16** There is no riches better than health of body; And there is no gladness above the joy of the heart. **17** Death is better than a bitter life, and eternal rest than a continual sickness. **18** Good things poured out upon a mouth that is closed are *as* messes of meat laid upon a grave. **19** What does an offering profit an idol? For neither will it eat nor smell: So is he that is afflicted of the Lord, **20** Seeing with his eyes and groaning, as a eunuch embracing a virgin and groaning. **21** Give not over your soul to sorrow; And afflict not yourself in your own counsel. **22** Gladness of heart is the life of a man; And the joyfulness of a man is length of days. **23** Love your own soul and comfort your heart: And remove sorrow far from you; For sorrow has destroyed many, and there is no profit therein. **24** Envy and wrath shorten *a man's* days; And care brings old age before the time. **25** A cheerful and good heart Will have a care of his meat and diet.

CHAPTER 31

1 Wakefulness that comes of riches consumes the flesh, and the anxiety thereof puts away sleep. **2** Wakeful anxiety will crave slumber; Andin a sore disease sleep will be broken. **3** A rich man toils in gathering money together; And when he rests, he is filled with his good things. **4** A poor man toils in lack of substance; And when he rests, he becomes needy. **5** He that loves gold will not be justified; And he

that follows destruction will himself have his fill *of it.* **6** Many have been given over to ruin for the sake of gold; And their perdition meets them face to face. **7** It is a stumbling block to those who sacrifice to it; And every fool will be taken therewith. **8** Blessed is the rich that is found without blemish, and that goes not after gold. **9** Who is he? And we will call him blessed: For wonderful things has he done among his people. **10** Who has been tried by it, and found perfect? Then let him glory. Who has had the power to transgress, and has not transgressed? And to do evil, and has not done it? **11** His goods will be made sure, and the congregation will declare his alms. **12** Do you sit at a great table? Be not greedy upon it, and say not, many are the things upon it. **13** Remember that an evil eye is a wicked thing: What has been created more evil than an eye? Therefore it sheds tears from every face. **14** Stretch not your hand wherever it looks and thrust not yourself with it into the dish. **15** Consider your neighbor's *liking* by your own; And be discreet in every point. **16** Eat, as *becomes* a man, those things which are set before you; And eat not greedily, lest you be hated. **17** Be first to leave off for manners' sake; And be not insatiable, lest you offend. **18** And if you sit among many, Reach not out your hand before them. **19** How sufficient to a well-mannered man is a very little, and he does not breathe hard upon his bed. **20** Heal your sleep comes of moderate eating; He rises early, and his wits are with him: The pain of wakefulness, and colic, and griping, are with an insatiable man. **21** And if you have been forced to eat, Rise up in the midst thereof, and you will have rest. **22** Hear me, my son, and despise me not, and at the last you will find my words *true:* In all your works be quick, and no disease will come to you. **23** Him that is liberal of his meat the lips will bless; And the testimony of his excellence will be believed. **24** The city will murmur at he who is a stingy with his meat; And the testimony of his stinginess will be sure. **25** Show not yourself valiant in wine; For wine has destroyed many. **26** The furnace proves the temper *of steel* by dipping; So does wine *prove* hearts in the quarreling of the proud. **27** Wine is as good as life to men, If you drink it in its measure: What life is there to a man that is without wine? And it has been created to make men glad. **28** Wine drunk in season *and* to satisfy is joy of heart, and gladness of soul: **29** Wine drunk largely is bitterness of soul, With provocation and conflict. **30** Drunkenness increases the rage of a fool to his hurt; It diminishes strength and adds wounds. **31** Rebuke not your neighbor at a banquet of wine, neither set him at nothing in his mirth: Speak not to him a word of reproach and press not upon him by asking back *a debt.*

CHAPTER 32

1 Have they made you ruler *of a feast?* Be not lifted up, be you among them as one of them; Take thought for them, and so sit down. **2** And when you have done all your office, take your place, that you may be gladdened on their account, and receive a crown for your well ordering. **3** Speak, you that are the elder, for it becomes you, *but* with sound knowledge; And hinder not music. **4** Pour not out talk where there is a performance of music and display not your wisdom out of season. **5** *As* a signet of carbuncle in a setting of gold, *so* is a concert of music in a banquet of wine. **6** *As* a signet of emerald in a work of gold, *so* is a strain of music with pleasant wine. **7** Speak, young man, if there be need of you; *Yet* scarcely if you be twice asked. **8** Sum up your speech, many things in few words; Be as one that knows and yet holds his tongue. **9** *If you be* among great men, behave not as their equal; And when another is speaking, make not much babbling. **10** Lightning speeds before thunder; And before a shamefast man favor will go out. **11** Rise up on time and be not the last; Get home quickly and do not loiter: **12** There take your pastime and do what is in your heart; And sin not by proud speech: **13** And for these things bless him that made you and gives you to drink freely of his good things. **14** He that fears the Lord will receive *his* discipline; And those who seek *him* early will find favor. **15** He that seeks the law will be filled therewith: But the hypocrite will stumble thereat. **16** They that fear the Lord will find judgement and will kindle righteous acts as a light. **17** A sinful man shuns reproof and will find a judgement according to his will. **18** A man of counsel will not neglect a thought; A strange and proud man will not crouch in fear, even after he has done a thing by himself without counsel. **19** Do nothing without counsel; And when you have once done, repent not. **20** Go not in a way of conflict; And stumble not in stony places. **21** Be not confident in a smooth way. **22** And beware of your own children. **23** In every work trust your own soul; For this is the keeping of the commandments. **24** He that believes the law gives heed to the commandment; And he that trusts in the Lord will suffer no loss.

CHAPTER 33

1 There will no evil happen to him that fears the Lord; But in temptation once and again he will deliver him. **2** A wise man will not hate the law; But he that is a hypocrite therein is as a ship in a storm. **3** A man of understanding will put his trust in the law; And the law is faithful to him, as when one asks at the oracle. **4** Prepare *your* speech, and so will you be heard; Bind up instruction and make your answer. **5** The heart of a fool is *as* a cartwheel; And his thoughts like a rolling axle tree. **6** A stallion horse is as a mocking friend; He neighs under every one that sits upon him. **7** Why does one day excel another, when all the light of every day in the year is of the sun? **8** By the knowledge of the Lord they were distinguished; And he varied seasons and feasts: **9** Some of them he exalted and hallowed, and some of them has he made ordinary days. **10** And all men are from the ground, and Adam was created of earth. **11** In the abundance of his knowledge the Lord distinguished them and made their ways various: **12** Some of them he blessed and exalted, and some of them he hallowed and brought near to himself: Some of them he cursed and brought low, and overthrew them from their place. **13** As the clay of the potter in his hand, All his ways are according to his good pleasure; So men are in the hand of him that made them, To render to them according to his judgement. **14** Good is the opposite of evil, and life is the opposite of death: So the sinner is the opposite of the godly. **15** And so look upon all the works of the Most High; Two and two, one against another. **16** And I waked up last, as one that gleans after the grape gatherers: By the blessing of the Lord I got before them, and filled my winepress as one that gathers grapes. **17** Consider that I labored not for myself alone, but for all those who seek instruction. **18** Hear me, you great men of the people, and listen with your ears, you rulers of the congregation. **19** To son and wife, to brother and friend, give not power over you while you live; And give not your goods to another, lest you repent and make supplication for them *again.* **20** While you yet live, and breath is in you, Give not yourself over to anybody. **21** For better it is that your children should supplicate you, than that you should look to the hand of your sons. **22** In all your works keep the upper hand; Bring not a stain on your honor. **23** In the day that you end the days of your life, and in the time of death, distribute your inheritance. **24** Fodder, a stick, and burdens, for an ass; Bread, and discipline, and work, for a servant. **25** Set your servant to work, and you will find rest: Leave his hands idle, and he will seek liberty. **26** Yoke and thong will bow the neck: And for an evil servant there are racks and tortures. **27** Send him to labor, that he be not idle; For idleness teaches much mischief. **28** Set him to work, as is fit for him; And if he obeys not, make his fetters heavy. **29** And be not excessive toward any; And without judgement do nothing. **30** If you have a servant, let him be as yourself, because you have bought him with blood. **31** If you have a servant, treat him as yourself; For as your own soul will you have need of him: If you treat him ill, and he depart and run away, which way will you go to seek him?

CHAPTER 34

1 Vain and false hopes are for a man void of understanding; And dreams give wings to fools. **2** As one that catches at a shadow, and follows after the wind, so is he that sets his mind on dreams. **3** The vision of dreams is *as* this thing against that, The likeness of a face near a face. **4** Of an unclean thing what will be cleansed? And of that which is false what will be true? **5** Divinations, and sooth-sayings, and dreams, are vain: And the heart fancies, as a woman's in travail. **6** If they be not sent from the Most High in *your* visitation, Give not your heart to them. **7** For dreams have led many astray: And they have failed by putting their hope in them. **8** Without lying will the law be accomplished; And wisdom is perfection to a faithful mouth. **9** A well-instructed man knows many things; And he that has much experience will declare understanding. **10** He that has no experience knows few things: But he that has wandered will increase *his* skill. **11** In my wandering I have seen many things; And more than my words is my understanding. **12** Often was I in danger even to death; And I was preserved because of these things. **13** The spirit of those that fear the Lord will live; For their hope is upon him that saves them. **14** Whoso fears the Lord will not be afraid and will not play the coward; For he is his hope. **15** Blessed is the soul of him that fears the Lord: To whom does he give heed? And who is his stay? **16** The eyes of the Lord are upon

those who love him, A mighty protection and strong stay, A cover from the hot blast, and a cover from the noonday, A guard from stumbling, and a help from falling. **17** He raises up the soul, and enlightens the eyes: He gives healing, life, and blessing. **18** He that sacrifices of a thing wrongfully gotten, his offering is made in mockery; And the mockeries of wicked men are not well-pleasing. **19** The Most High has no pleasure in the offerings of the ungodly; Neither is he pacified for sins by the multitude of sacrifices. **20** *As* one that kills the son before his father's eyes Is he that brings a sacrifice from the goods of the poor. **21** The bread of the needy is the life of the poor: He that deprives him thereof is a man of blood. **22** *As* one that slays his neighbor is he that takes away his living; And *as* a shedder of blood is he that deprives a hireling of his hire. **23** One building, and another pulling down, what profit have they had but toil? **24** One praying, and another cursing, whose voice will the Lord listen to? **25** He that washes himself after *touching* a dead body, and touches it again, what profit has he in his washing? **26** Even so a man fasting for his sins, and going again, and doing the same; Who will listen to his prayer? And what profit has he in his humiliation?

CHAPTER 35

1 He that keeps the law multiplies offerings; He that takes heed to the commandments sacrifices a peace offering. **2** He that returns a favor offers fine flour; And he that gives alms sacrifices a thank offering. **3** To depart from wickedness is a thing pleasing to the Lord; And to depart from unrighteousness is an atoning sacrifice. **4** See that you appear not in the presence of the Lord empty. **5** For all these things *are to be done* because of the commandment. **6** The offering of the righteous makes the altar fat; And the sweet savor thereof *is* before the Most High. **7** The sacrifice of a righteous man is acceptable; And the memorial thereof will not be forgotten. **8** Glorify the Lord with a good eye, and stint not the first fruits of your hands. **9** In every gift show a cheerful countenance and dedicate your tithe with gladness. **10** Give to the Most High according as he has given; And as your hand has found, *give* with a good eye. **11** For the Lord recompenses, and he will recompense you sevenfold. **12** Think not to corrupt with gifts; for he will not receive them: And set not your mind on an unrighteous sacrifice; For the

Lord is judge, and with him is no respect of persons. **13** He will not accept any person against a poor man; And he will listen to the prayer of him that is wronged. **14** He will in no wise despise the supplication of the fatherless; Nor the widow, when she pours out her tale. **15** Do not the tears of the widow run down her cheek? And is not her cry against him that has caused them to fall? **16** He that serves *God* according to his good pleasure will be accepted, and his supplication will reach to the clouds. **17** The prayer of the humble pierces the clouds; And until it come near, he will not be comforted; And he will not depart, until the Most High will visit; And he will judge righteously and execute judgement. **18** And the Lord will not be slack, neither will he be patient toward them, until he have crushed the loins of the unmerciful; And he will repay vengeance to the heathen; until he have taken away the multitude of the arrogant, and broken in pieces the scepters of the unrighteous; **19** until he have rendered to *every* man according to his doings, and *tot* he works of men according to their plans; until he have judged the cause of his people; And he will make them to rejoice in his mercy. **20** Mercy is seasonable in the time of his afflicting *them,* As clouds of rain in the time of drought.

CHAPTER 36

1 Have mercy upon us, O Lord the God of all, and behold; **2** And send your fear upon all the nations: **3** Lift up your hand against the strange nations; And let them see your mighty power. **4** As you were sanctified in us before them, so be you magnified in them before us. **5** And let them know you, as we also have known you, that there is no God but only you, O God. **6** Show new signs and work various wonders; Glorify your hand and your right arm. **7** Raise up indignation, and pour out wrath; Take away the adversary, and destroy the enemy. **8** hasten the time and remember the oath; And let them declare your mighty works. **9** Let him that escapes be devoured by the rage of fire; And may those who harm your people find destruction. **10** Crush the heads of the rulers of the enemies, that say, there is none but we. **11** Gather all the tribes of Jacob together, and take them for your inheritance, as from the beginning. **12** O Lord, have mercy upon the people that is called by your name, and upon Israel, whom you did liken to a firstborn. **13** Have compassion upon the city of your sanctuary, Jerusalem, the place of your rest.

14 Fill Zion; exalt your oracles and *fill* your people with your glory. **15** Give testimony to those that were your creatures in the beginning and raise up the prophecies that have been in your name. **16** Give reward to those who wait for you: And men will put their trust in your prophets. **17** Listen, O Lord, to the prayer of your suppliants, according to the blessing of Aaron concerning your people; And all those who are on the earth will know That you are the Lord, the eternal God. **18** The belly will eat any meat; Yet is one meat better than another. **19** The mouth tastes meats taken in hunting: So does an understanding heart false speeches. **20** A contrary heart will cause heaviness: And a man of experience will recompense him. **21** A woman will receive any man; But one daughter is better than another. **22** The beauty of a woman cheers the countenance; And a man desires nothing so much. **23** If there is on her tongue mercy and meekness, her husband is not like the sons of men. **24** He that gets a wife enters upon a possession: A help meet for him, and a pillar of rest. **25** Where no hedge is, the possession will be laid waste: And he that has no wife will mourn as he wanders up and down. **26** For who will trust a nimble robber, that skips from city to city? Even so *who will trust* a man that has no nest, and lodges wherever he finds himself at nightfall?

CHAPTER 37

1 Every friend will say, I also am his friend: But there is a friend, which is only a friend in name. **2** Is there not a grief in it even to death, when a companion and friend is turned to enmity? **3** O wicked imagination, from where came you rolling in to cover the dry land with deceitfulness? **4** There is a companion, which rejoices in the gladness of a friend, but in time of affliction will be against him. **5** There is a companion, which for the belly's sake labors with his friend, In the face of battle will take up the buckler. **6** Forget not a friend in your soul; And be not unmindful of him in your riches. **7** Every counselor extols counsel; But there is that counsels for himself. **8** Let your soul beware of a counselor and know beforehand what his interest is (For he will take counsel for himself); Lest he cast the lot upon you, **9** And say to you, your way is good: And he will stand near you, to see what will happen to you. **10** Take not counsel with one that looks askance at you; And hide your counsel from such as are jealous of you. **11** *Take not counsel* with a woman about her rival; Neither with a coward about war; Nor with a merchant about exchange; Nor with a buyer about selling; Nor with an envious man about thankfulness; Nor with an unmerciful man about kindliness; Nor with a sluggard about any kind of work; Nor with a hireling in your house about finishing *his work;* Nor with an idle servant about much business: Give not heed to these in any matter of counsel. **12** But rather be continually with a godly man, whom you will have known to be a keeper of the commandments, who in his soul is as your own soul, and who will grieve with you, if you will miscarry. **13** And make the counsel of your heart to stand; For there is none more faithful to you than it. **14** For a man's soul is sometimes wont to bring him tidings, more than seven watchmen that sit on high on a watch-tower. **15** And above all this entreat the Most High, that he may direct your way in truth. **16** Let reason be the beginning of every work, and let counsel go before every action. **17** As a token of the changing of the heart, **18** four manner of things do rise up, Good and evil, life and death; And that which rules over them continually is the tongue. **19** There is one that is shrewd *and* the instructor of many, and yet is unprofitable to his own soul. **20** There is *one* that is subtle in words and is hated; He will be destitute of all food: **21** For grace was not given him from the Lord; Because he is deprived of all wisdom. **22** There is one that is wise to his own soul; And the fruits of his understanding are trustworthy in the mouth. **23** A wise man will instruct his own people; And the fruits of his understanding are trustworthy. **24** A wise man will be filled with blessing; And all those who see him will call him happy. **25** The life of man is counted by days; And the days of Israel are innumerable. **26** The wise man will inherit confidence among his people, and his name will live forever. **27** My son, prove your soul in your life, and see what is evil for it, and give not that to it. **28** For all things are not profitable for all men, neither has every soul pleasure in everything. **29** Don't be insatiable in any luxury, and don't be greedy in the things that you eat. **30** For in multitude of meats there will be disease, and surfeiting will come near to colic. **31** Because of surfeiting have many perished; But he that takes heed will prolong his life.

CHAPTER 38

1 Honor a physician according to your need *of him* with the honors due to him: For truly the Lord has created him. **2** For from the Most High comes healing; And from the king he will receive a gift. **3** The skill of the physician will lift up his head; And in the sight of great men he will be admired. **4** The Lord created medicines out of the earth; And a prudent man will have no disgust at them. **5** Was not water made sweet with wood, That the virtue thereof might be known? **6** And he gave men skill, that they might be glorified in his marvelous works. **7** With them does he heal *a man and* takes away his pain. **8** With these will the apothecary make a confection; And his works will not be brought to an end; And from him is peace upon the face of the earth. **9** My son, in your sickness be not negligent; But pray to the Lord, and he will heal you. **10** Put away wrong doing, and order your hands aright, and cleanse your heart from all manner of sin. **11** Give a sweet savor, and a memorial of fine flour; And make fat your offering, as one that is not. **12** Then give place to the physician, for truly the Lord has created him; And let him not go from you, for you have need of him. **13** There is a time when in their very hands is the issue for good. **14** For they also will implore the Lord, that he may prosper them in *giving* relief and in healing for the maintenance of life. **15** He that sins before his Maker, let him fall into the hands of the physician. **16** My son, let your tears fall over the dead, and as one that suffers grievously begin lamentation; And wind up his body according to his due, and neglect not his burial. **17** Make bitter weeping, and make passionate wailing, and let your mourning be according to his merit, for one day or two, lest you be spoken evil of: And so be comforted for your sorrow. **18** For of sorrow comes death, and sorrow of heart will bow down the strength. **19** In calamity sorrow also remains: And the poor man's life is grievous to the heart. **20** Don't give your heart to sorrow. Put it away, remembering the last end. **21** Don't forget it, for there is no returning again: Him you will not profit, and you will hurt yourself. **22** Remember the sentence upon him; for so also will yours be; Yesterday for me, and today for you. **23** When the dead is at rest, let his remembrance rest; And be comforted for him, when his spirit departs from him. **24** The wisdom of the scribe comes by opportunity of leisure; And he that has little business will become wise. **25** How will he become wise that holds the plow, that glories in the shaft of the goad, that drives oxen, and is occupied in their labors, and whose discourse is of the stock of bulls? **26** He will set his heart upon turning his furrows; And his wakefulness is to give his heifers their fodder. **27** So is every craftsman and master workman, that passes his time by night as by day; They that cut gravings of signets, and his diligence is to make great variety; He will set his heart to preserve likeness in his portraiture and will be wakeful to finish his work. **28** So is the smith sitting by the anvil and considering the unwrought iron: The vapor of the fire will waste his flesh; And in the heat of the furnace he will wrestle *with his work:* The noise of the hammer will be ever in his ear, and his eyes are upon the pattern of the vessel; He will set his heart upon perfecting his works, and he will be wakeful to adorn them perfectly. **29** So is the potter sitting at his work, and turning the wheel about with his feet, who is always anxiously set at his work, and all his handiwork is by number; **30** He will fashion the clay with his arm and will bend its strength in front of his feet; He will apply his heart to finish the glazing; And he will be wakeful to make clean the furnace. **31** All these put their trust in their hands; And each becomes wise in his own work. **32** Without these will not a city be inhabited, and men will not sojourn nor walk up and down *therein.* **33** They will not be sought for in the council of the people, and in the assembly, they will not mount on high; They will not sit on the seat of the judge, and they will not understand the covenant of judgement: Neither will they declare instruction and judgement; And where parables are they will not be found. **34** But they will maintain the fabric of the world; And in the handiwork of their craft is their prayer.

CHAPTER 39

1 Not so he that has applied his soul and meditates in the law of the Most High; He will seek out the wisdom of all the ancients and will be occupied in prophecies. **2** He will keep the discourse of the men of renown and will enter in amidst the subtleties of parables. **3** He will seek out the hidden meaning of proverbs and be conversant in the dark sayings of parables. **4** He will serve among great men and appear before him that rules: He will travel through the land of strange nations; For he has tried good things and evil among men. **5** He will

apply his heart to return early to the Lord that made him, and will make supplication before the Most High, and will open his mouth in prayer, and will make supplication for his sins. **6** If the great Lord will, He will be filled with the spirit of understanding: He will pour out the words of his wisdom, and in prayer give thanks to the Lord. **7** He will direct his counsel and knowledge, and in his secrets will he meditate. **8** He will show out the instruction which he has been taught and will glory in the law of the covenant of the Lord. **9** Many will commend his understanding; And so long as the world endures, it will not be blotted out: His memorial will not depart, and his name will live from generation to generation. **10** Nations will declare his wisdom, and the congregation will tell out his praise. **11** If he continues, he will leave a greater name than a thousand: And if he dies, he adds thereto. **12** Yet more I will utter, which I have thought upon; And I am filled as the moon at the full. **13** Listen to me, you holy children, and bud out as a rose growing by a brook of water: **14** And give you a sweet savor as frankincense, and put out flowers as a lily, spread abroad a sweet smell, and sing a song of praise; Bless you the Lord for all his works. **15** Magnify his name, and give utterance to his praise with the songs of your lips, and with harps; And so will you say when you utter *his praise:* **16** All the works of the Lord are exceedingly good, and every command will be *accomplished* in his season. **17** None can say, "What is this? What is that?" For in his season they will all be sought out. At his word the waters stood as a heap, and the receptacles of waters at the word of his mouth. **18** At his command is all his good pleasure *done;* And there is none that will hinder his salvation. **19** The works of all flesh are before him; And it is not possible to be hid from his eyes. **20** He sees from everlasting to everlasting; And there is nothing wonderful before him. **21** None can say, "What is this? What is that?" For all things are created for their uses. **22** His blessing covered the dry land as a river and saturated it as a flood. **23** As he has made the waters salty; So will the heathen inherit his wrath. **24** His ways are plain to the holy; So are they stumbling blocks to the wicked. **25** Good things are created from the beginning for the good; So are evil things for sinners. **26** The chief of all things necessary for the life of man Are water, and fire, and iron, and salt, and flour of wheat, and honey, and milk, The blood of the grape, and oil, and clothing. 27 All these things are for good to the godly; So to the sinners they will be turned into evil. 28 There be winds that are created for vengeance, and in their fury lay on their scourges heavily; In the time of consummation they pour out their strength and will appease the wrath of him that made them. 29 Fire, and hail, and famine, and death, all these are created for vengeance; 30 Teeth of wild beasts, and scorpions and adders, and a sword punishing the ungodly to destruction. 31 They will rejoice in his commandment, and will be made ready upon earth, when need is; And in their seasons they will not transgress *his* word. 32 Therefore from the beginning I was resolved, and I thought *this, and* left it in writing; 33 All the works of the Lord are good: And he will supply every need in its season. 34 And none can say, "This is worse than that": For they will all be well approved in their season. 35 And now with all your heart and mouth sing you praises and bless the name of the Lord.

CHAPTER 40

1 Great travail is created for every man, and a heavy yoke is upon the sons of Adam, From the day of their coming out from their mother's womb, Until the day for their burial in the mother of all things. 2 The expectation of things to come, and the day of death, *trouble* their thoughts, and *cause* fear of heart; 3 From him that sits on a throne of glory, even to him that is humbled in earth and ashes; 4 From him that wears purple and a crown, Even to him that is clothed with a hempen frock. 5 *There is* wrath, and jealousy, and trouble, and disquiet, and fear of death, and anger, and strife; And in the time of rest upon his bed His night sleep does change his knowledge. 6 A little or nothing is his resting, and afterward in his sleep, as in a day of keeping watch, He is troubled in the vision of his heart, as one that has escaped from the front of battle. 7 In the very time of his deliverance he awakens, and marvels that the fear is nothing. 8 *It is so* with all flesh, from man to beast, and upon sinners sevenfold more. 9 Death, and bloodshed, and strife, and sword, Calamities, famine, suffering, and the scourge; 10 All these things were created for the wicked, and because of them came the flood. 11 All things that are of the earth turn to the earth again: And *all things that are* of the waters return into the sea. 12 All bribery and injustice will be blotted out; And

good faith will stand forever. 13 The goods of the unjust will be dried up like a river, and like a great thunder in rain will go off in noise. 14 In opening his hands *a man* will be made glad: So will transgressors utterly fail. 15 The children of the ungodly will not put out many branches; And *are as* unclean roots upon a sheer rock. 16 The sedge *that grows* upon every water and bank of a river Will be plucked up before all grass. 17 Bounty is as a garden of blessings, and almsgiving endures forever. 18 The life of one that labors, and is content, will be made sweet; And he that finds a treasure is above both. 19 Children and the building of a city establish a *man's* name; And a blameless wife is counted above both. 20 Wine and music rejoice the heart; And the love of wisdom is above both. 21 The pipe and the lute make pleasant melody; And a pleasant tongue is above both. 22 Your eye will desire grace and beauty; And above both the green blade of corn. 23 A friend and a companion never meet amiss; And a wife with her husband is above both. 24 Brethren and help are for a time of affliction; And almsgiving is a deliverer above both. 25 Gold and silver will make the foot stand sure; And counsel is esteemed above them both. 26 Riches and strength will lift up the heart; And the fear of the Lord is above both: There is nothing lacking in the fear of the Lord, and there is no need to seek help therein. 27 The fear of the Lord is as a garden of blessing and covers a man above all glory. 28 My son, lead not a beggar's life; Better it is to die than to beg. 29 A man that looks to the table of another, His life is not to be counted for a life; He will pollute his soul with another man's meats: But a man wise and well-instructed will beware thereof. 30 In the mouth of the shameless begging will be sweet; And in his belly a fire will be kindled.

CHAPTER 41

1 O death, how bitter is the remembrance of you to a man that is at peace in his possessions, To the man that has nothing to distract him, and has prosperity in all things, and that still has strength to receive meat! 2 O death, acceptable is your sentence to a man that is needy, and that fails in strength, that is in extreme old age, and is distracted about all things, and is perverse, and has lost patience! 3 Don't be afraid of the sentence of death; Remember those who have been before you, and that come after: This is the sentence from

the Lord over all flesh. **4** And why do you refuse, when it is the good pleasure of the Most High? Whether it be ten, or a hundred, or a thousand years, there is no inquisition of life in the grave. **5** The children of sinners are abominable children, and they frequent the dwellings of the ungodly. **6** The inheritance of sinners' children will perish, and with their posterity will be a perpetual reproach. **7** Children will complain of an ungodly father, because they will be reproached for his sake. **8** Woe to you, ungodly men, which have forsaken the law of the Most High God! **9** If you be born, you will be born to a curse; If you die, a curse will be your portion. **10** All things that are of the earth will go back to the earth: So the ungodly will go from a curse to perdition. **11** The mourning of men is about their bodies: But the name of sinners being evil will be blotted out. **12** Have regard to your name; For it continues with you longer than a thousand great treasures of gold. **13** A good life has its number of days; And a good name continues forever. **14** My children, keep instruction in peace: But wisdom that is hid, and a treasure that is not seen, what profit is in them both? **15** Better is a man that hides his foolishness Than a man that hides his wisdom. **16** Why show reverence to my word: For it is not good to retain every kind of shame; And not all things are approved by all in good faith. **17** Be ashamed of whoredom before father and mother: And of a lie before a prince and a mighty man; **18** Of an offence before a judge and ruler; Of iniquity before the congregation and the people; Of unjust dealing before a partner and friend; **19** And of theft in regard of the place where you sojourn, and in regard of the truth of God and his covenant; And of leaning with your elbow at meat; And of scurrility in the matter of giving and taking; **20** And of silence before those who salute you; And of looking upon a woman that is a prostitute; **21** And of turning away your face from a kinsman; Of taking away a portion or a gift; And of gazing upon a woman that has a husband; **22** Of being over busy with his maid; and come not near her bed; Of upbraiding speeches before friends; And after you have given, upbraid not; **23** Of repeating and speaking what you have heard; And of revealing of secrets. **24** So will you be truly shamefast and find favor in the sight of every man.

CHAPTER 42

1 Of these things be not ashamed, and accept no man's person to sin *by it:* **2** Of the law of the Most High, and his covenant; And of judgement to do justice to the ungodly; **3** Of reckoning with a partner and with travelers; And of a gift from the heritage of friends; **4** Of exactness of balance and weights; And of getting much or little; **5** Of indifferent selling of merchants; And of much correction of children; And of making the side of an evil servant to bleed. **6** Sure keeping is good, where an evil wife is; And where many hands are, shut you close. **7** Whatsoever you hand over, let it be by number and weight; And in giving and receiving let all be in writing. **8** *Be not ashamed* to instruct the unwise and foolish, and one of extreme old age that contends with those that are young; And so, will you be well instructed indeed, and approved in the sight of every man living. **9** A daughter is a secret cause of wakefulness to a father; And the care for her puts away sleep; In her youth, lest she pass the flower of her age; And when she is married, lest she should be hated: **10** In her virginity, lest she should be defiled And be with child in her father's house; And when she has a husband, lest she should transgress; And when she is married, lest she should be barren. **11** Keep a strict watch over a headstrong daughter, lest she make you a laughing stock to your enemies, A byword in the city and notorious among the people, and shame you before the multitude. **12** Look not upon everybody in regard of beauty and sit not in the midst of women; **13** For from garments comes a moth, and from a woman a woman's wickedness. **14** Better is the wickedness of a man than a pleasant-dealing woman, and a woman which puts you to shameful reproach. **15** I will make mention now of the works of the Lord and will declare the things that I have seen: In the words of the Lord are his works. **16** The sun that gives light looks upon all things; And the work of the Lord is full of his glory. **17** The Lord has not given power to the saints to declare all his marvelous works; Which the Almighty Lord firmly settled, that whatever is might be established in his glory. **18** He searches out the deep, and the heart, and he has understanding of their cunning plans: For the Most High knows all knowledge, and he looks into the signs of the world, **19** Declaring the things that are past, and the things that will be, and revealing the traces of hidden things. **20** No thought escapes him;

There is not a word hid from him. **21** The mighty works of his wisdom he has ordered, who is from everlasting to everlasting: Nothing has been added to them, nor diminished from them; And he had no need of any counselor. **22** How desirable are all his works! One may behold *this* even to a spark. **23** All these things live and remain forever in all manner of uses, and they are all obedient. **24** All things are double one against another: And he has made nothing imperfect. **25** One thing establishes the good things of another: And who will be filled with beholding his glory?

CHAPTER 43

1 The pride of the height is the firmament in its clearness, The appearance of heaven, in the spectacle of its glory. **2** The sun when he appears, bringing tidings as he goes out, is a marvelous instrument, the work of the Most High: **3** At his noon he dries up the country, and who will stand against his burning heat? **4** A man blowing a furnace is in works of heat, *but* the sun three times more, burning up the mountains: Breathing out fiery vapors, and sending out bright beams, he dims the eyes. **5** Great is the Lord that made him; And at his word he hastens his course. **6** The moon also is in all things for her season, For a declaration of times, and a sign of the world. **7** From the moon is the sign of the feast day; A light that wanes when she is come to the full. **8** The month is called after her name, increasing wonderfully in her changing; An instrument of the army on high, shining out in the firmament of heaven; **9** The beauty of heaven, the glory of the stars, an ornament giving light in the highest places of the Lord. **10** At the word of the Holy One they will stand in due order, and they will not faint in their watches. **11** Look upon the rainbow and praise him that made it; Exceeding beautiful in the brightness thereof. **12** It encircles the heaven around with a circle of glory; The hands of the Most High have stretched it. **13** By his commandment he makes the snow to fall apace and sends swiftly the lightnings of his judgement. **14** By reason thereof the treasure-houses are opened; And clouds fly out as fowls. **15** By his mighty power he makes strong the clouds, and the hailstones are broken small: **16** And at his appearing the mountains will be shaken, and at his will the south wind will blow. **17** The voice of his thunder makes the earth to travail; So does the northern storm and the whirlwind: As

birds flying down he sprinkles the snow; And as the lighting of the locust is the falling down thereof: **18** The eye will marvel at the beauty of its whiteness, and the heart will be astonished at the raining of it. **19** The hoar frost also he pours on the earth as salt; And when it is congealed, it is *as* points of thorns. **20** The cold north wind will blow, and the ice will be congealed on the water: It will lodge upon every gathering together of water, and the water will put on as it were a breastplate. **21** It will devour the mountains, and burn up the wilderness, and consume the green herb as fire. **22** A mist coming speedily is the healing of all things; A dew coming after heat will bring cheerfulness. **23** By his counsel he has stilled the deep, and planted islands therein. **24** They that sail on the sea tell of the danger thereof; And when we hear it with our ears, we marvel. **25** Therein be also those strange and wondrous works, variety of all that has life, the race of sea-monsters. **26** By reason of him his end has success, and by his word all things consist. **27** We may say many things, yet will we not attain; And the sum of our words is, He is all. **28** How will we have strength to glorify him? For he is himself the great one above all his works. **29** The Lord is terrible and exceedingly great; And marvelous is his power. **30** When you glorify the Lord, exalt him as much as you can; For even yet he will exceed: And when you exalt him, put out your full strength: Be not weary; for you will never attain. **31** Who has seen him, that he may declare him? And who will magnify him as he is? **32** Many things are hidden greater than these; For we have seen but a few of his works. **33** For the Lord made all things; And to the godly he gave wisdom.

CHAPTER 44

1 Let us now praise famous men, and our fathers that became the father of us. **2** The Lord manifested *in them* great glory, *even* his mighty power from the beginning. **3** Such as did bear rule in their kingdoms, and were men renowned for their power, Giving counsel by their understanding, Such as have brought tidings in prophecies: **4** Leaders of the people by their counsels, and by their understanding *men of* learning for the people; Wise *were* their words in their instruction: **5** Such as sought out musical tunes, and set out verses in writing: **6** Rich men furnished with ability, Living peaceably in their habitations: **7** All these were honored in their generations, and were a glory in their days. **8** There be of them, that have left a name behind them, To declare their praises. **9** And some there be, which have no memorial; Who are perished as though they had not been and are become as though they had not been born; And their children after them. **10** But these were men of mercy, whose righteous deeds have not been forgotten. **11** With their seed will remain continually a good inheritance; Their children *are* within the covenants. **12** Their seed stands fast, and their children for their sakes. **13** Their seed will remain forever, and their glory will not be blotted out. **14** Their bodies were buried in peace, and their name lives to all generations. **15** Peoples will declare their wisdom, and the congregation tells out their praise. **16** Enoch pleased the Lord, and was translated, *being* an example of repentance to all generations. **17** Noah was found perfect *and* righteous; In the season of wrath he was taken in exchange *for the world;* Therefore was there left a remnant to the earth, when the flood came. **18** Everlasting covenants were made with him, that all flesh should no more be blotted out by a flood. **19** Abraham was a great father of a multitude of nations; And there was none found like him in glory; **20** Who kept the law of the Most High and was taken into covenant with him: In his flesh he established the covenant; And when he was proved, he was found faithful. **21** Therefore he assured him by an oath, That the nations should be blessed in his seed; That he would multiply him as the dust of the earth, and exalt his seed as the stars, and cause them to inherit from sea to sea, and from the River to the utmost part of the earth. **22** In Isaac also did he establish likewise, for Abraham his father's sake, the blessing of all men, and the covenant: **23** And he made it rest upon the head of Jacob; He acknowledged him in his blessings, and gave to him by inheritance, and divided his portions; Among twelve tribes did he part them.

CHAPTER 45

1 And he brought out of him a man of mercy, which found favor in the sight of all flesh; A man beloved of God and men, even Moses, whose memorial is blessed. **2** He made him like to the glory of the saints and magnified him in the fears of his enemies. **3** By his words he caused the wonders to cease; He glorified him in the sight of kings; He gave him commandment for his people and showed him part of his glory. **4** He sanctified him in his

faithfulness and meekness; He chose him out of all flesh. **5** He made him to hear his voice, and led him into the thick darkness, and gave him commandments face to face, Even the law of life and knowledge, that he might teach Jacob the covenant, and Israel his judgments. **6** He exalted Aaron, a holy man like to him, Even his brother, of the tribe of Levi. **7** He established for him an everlasting covenant and gave him the priesthood of the people; He beautified him with comely ornaments and girded him about with a robe of glory. **8** He clothed him with the perfection of exultation; And strengthened him with apparel of honor, The linen trousers, the long robe, and the ephod. **9** And he compassed him with pomegranates of gold, and with many bells round about, to send out a sound as he went, To make a sound that might be heard in the temple, For a memorial to the children of his people; **10** With a holy garment, with gold and blue and purple, the work of the embroiderer, With an oracle of judgement, *even* with the Urim and Thummim; **11** With twisted scarlet, the work of the craftsman; With precious stones graven like a signet, in a setting of gold, the work of the jeweler, For a memorial engraved in writing, after the number of the tribes of Israel; **12** With a crown of gold upon the miter, having graven on it, as on a signet, HOLINESS, An ornament of honor, a work of might, The desires of the eyes, goodly and beautiful. **13** Before him there never have been any such; No stranger put them on, but his sons only, and his offspring perpetually. **14** His sacrifices will be wholly consumed Every day twice continually. **15** Moses consecrated him and anointed him with holy oil: It was to him for an everlasting covenant, and to his seed, all the days of heaven, To minister to him, and to execute also the priest's office, and bless his people in his name. **16** He chose him out of all living to offer sacrifice to the Lord, Incense, and a sweet savor, for a memorial, To make reconciliation for your people. **17** He gave to him in his commandments, *Yes,* authority in the covenants of judgments, to teach Jacob the testimonies, and to enlighten Israel in his law. **18** Strangers gathered themselves together against him, and envied him in the wilderness, *Even* Dathan and Abiram with their company, and the congregation of Korah, with wrath and anger. **19** The Lord saw it, and it displeased him; And in the wrath of his anger they were destroyed: He did wonders upon them, to consume them with flaming fire. **20** And he added glory to Aaron and gave him a heritage: He divided to him the first fruits of the increase; *And* first did he prepare bread in abundance: 21 For they will eat the sacrifices of the Lord, which he gave to him and to his seed. 22 However in the land of the people he will have no inheritance, and he has no portion among the people: For he himself is your portion *and* inheritance. 23 And Phinehas the son of Eleazar is the third in glory, In that he was zealous in the fear of the Lord, and stood fast in the good forwardness of his soul when the people turned away, and he made reconciliation for Israel. 24 Therefore was there a covenant of peace established for him, *that he should be* leader of the saints and of his people; That he and his seed Should have the dignity of the priesthood forever. 25 Also *he made* a covenant with David the son of Jesse, of the tribe of Judah; The inheritance of the king is his alone from son to son; So the inheritance of Aaron is also to his seed. 26 *God* give you wisdom in your heart to judge his people in righteousness, that their good things be not abolished, and *that* their glory *endure* for all their generations.

CHAPTER 46

1 Joshua the son of Nun was valiant in war and was the successor of Moses in prophecies: Who according to his name was made great for the saving of God's elect, to take vengeance of the enemies that rose up against them, That he might give Israel their inheritance. 2 How was he glorified in the lifting up his hands, and in stretching out his sword against the cities! 3 Who before him so stood fast? For the Lord himself brought his enemies to him. 4 Did not the sun go back by his hand? And didn't one day become as two? 5 He called upon the Most High *and* Mighty One, when his foes pressed him round about; And the great Lord heard him. 6 With hailstones of mighty power He caused war to break violently upon the nation, and in the going down he destroyed those who resisted; That the nations might know his armor, how that he fought in the sight of the Lord; For he followed after the Mighty One. 7 Also in the time of Moses he did a work of mercy, He and Caleb the son of Jephunneh, in that they withstood the adversary, Hindered the people from sin, and stilled the murmuring of wickedness. 8 And of six hundred thousand people on foot, they two alone were preserved to bring them into the heritage, Even into a land flowing with milk and honey. 9 Also the Lord gave strength to Caleb, and it remained with him to his old age; So that he entered upon the height of the land, and his seed obtained it for a heritage: 10 That all the children of Israel might see That it is good to walk after the Lord. 11 Also the judges, everyone by his name, all whose hearts went not a whoring, and who turned not away from the Lord, may their memorial be blessed. 12 May their bones flourish again out of their place and may the name of those who have been honored be renewed upon their children. 13 Samuel, the prophet of the Lord, beloved of his Lord, Established a kingdom, and anointed princes over his people. 14 By the law of the Lord he judged the congregation, and the Lord visited Jacob. 15 By his faithfulness he was proved to be a prophet, and by his words he was known to be faithful in vision. 16 Also when his enemies pressed around him he called upon the Lord, the Mighty One, with the offering of the sucking lamb. 17 And the Lord thundered from heaven, and with a mighty sound made his voice to be heard. 18 And he utterly destroyed the rulers of the Tyrians, and all the princes of the Philistines. 19 Also before the time of his long sleep He made protestations in the sight of the lord and *his* anointed, I have not taken any man's goods, so much as a sandal: And no man did accuse him. 20 And after he fell asleep he prophesied, and showed the king his end, and lifted up his voice from the earth in prophecy, to blot out the wickedness of the people.

CHAPTER 47

1 And after him rose up Nathan to prophesy in the days of David. 2 As is the fat when it is separated from the peace offering, so was David *separated* from the children of Israel. 3 He played with lions as with kids, and with bears as with lambs of the flock. 4 In his youth did he not kill a giant, and take away reproach from the people, when he lifted up his hand with a sling stone, and beat down the boasting of Goliath? 5 For he called upon the Most High Lord; And he gave him strength in his right hand, to kill a man mighty in war, to exalt the horn of his people. 6 So they glorified him for *his* tens of thousands, and praised him for the blessings of the Lord, In that there was given him a diadem of glory. 7 For he destroyed the enemies on every side, and brought to nothing the Philistines his adversaries, Brake their horn in pieces to this day. 8 In every work of his he gave thanks to

the Holy One Most High with words of glory; With his whole heart he sang praise and loved him that made him. **9** Also he set singers before the altar, and to make sweet melody by their music. **10** He gave beauty to the feasts, and set in order the seasons to perfection, while they praised his holy name, and the sanctuary sounded from early morning. **11** The Lord took away his sins and exalted his horn forever; And gave him a covenant of kings, and a throne of glory in Israel. **12** After him rose up a son, a man of understanding; And for his sake he lived at large. **13** Solomon reigned in days of peace; And to him God gave rest round about, that he might set up a house for his name and prepare a sanctuary forever. **14** How wise you were made in your youth and filled as a river with understanding! **15** Your soul covered the earth, and you filled it with dark parables. **16** Your name reached to the isles afar off; And for your peace you were beloved. **17** For your songs and proverbs and parables, and for your interpretations, the countries marveled at you. **18** By the name of the Lord God, which is called the God of Israel, you did gather gold as tin, and did multiply silver as lead. **19** You did bow your loins to women, and in your body you were brought into subjection. **20** You did blemish your honor, and profane your seed, to bring wrath upon your children; And I was grieved for your folly: **21** So that the sovereignty was divided, and out of Ephraim ruled a disobedient kingdom. **22** But the Lord will never forsake his mercy; And he will not destroy any of his works, nor blot out the posterity of his elect; And the seed of him that loved him he will not take away; And he gave a remnant to Jacob, and to David a root out of him. **23** And *so* rested Solomon with his fathers; And of his seed he left behind him Rehoboam, *Even* the foolishness of the people, and one that lacked understanding, who made the people to revolt by his counsel. Also, Jeroboam the son of Nebat, who made Israel to sin, and gave to Ephraim a way of sin. **24** And their sins were multiplied exceedingly, to remove them from their land. **25** For they sought out all manner of wickedness, until vengeance should come upon them.

CHAPTER 48

1 Also there arose Elijah the prophet as fire, and his word burned like a torch: **2** Who brought a famine upon them, and by his zeal made them few in number. **3** By the word of the Lord he shut up the heaven: Thrice did he so bring down fire. **4** How you were glorified, O Elijah, in your wondrous deeds! And who will glory like to you? **5** Who did raise up a dead man from death, and from the place of the dead, by the word of the Most High: **6** Who brought down kings to destruction, and honorable men from their bed: **7** Who heard rebuke in Sinai, and judgments of vengeance in Horeb: **8** Who anointed kings for retribution, and prophets to succeed after him: **9** Who was taken up in a tempest of fire, In a chariot of fiery horses: **10** Who was recorded for reproofs in their seasons, To pacify anger, before it brake out into wrath; To turn the heart of the father to the son, and to restore the tribes of Jacob. **11** Blessed are those who saw you, and those who have been beautified with love; For we also will surely live. **12** Elijah *it was,* who was wrapped in a tempest: And Elisha was filled with his spirit; And in *all* his days he was not moved by *the fear of* any ruler, and no one brought him into subjection. **13** Nothing was too high for him; And when he was laid on sleep his body prophesied. **14** As in his life he did wonders, so in death were his works marvelous. **15** For all this the people repented not, and they departed not from their sins, until they were carried away as a plunder from their land and were scattered through all the earth; And the people were left very few in number, and a ruler *was left* in the house of David. **16** Some of them did that which was pleasing *to God, and* some multiplied sins. **17** Hezekiah fortified his city and brought in water into the midst of them: He dug the sheer rock with iron and built up wells for waters. **18** In his days Sennacherib came up, and sent Rabshakeh, and departed; And he lifted up his hand against Zion and boasted great things in his arrogance. **19** Then were their hearts and their hands shaken, and they were in pain, as women in travail; **20** And they called upon the Lord which is merciful, spreading out their hands to him: And the Holy One heard them speedily out of Heaven, and delivered them by the hand of Isaiah. **21** He struck the camp of the Assyrians, and his angel utterly destroyed them. **22** For Hezekiah did that which was pleasing to the Lord and was strong in the ways of David his father, Which Isaiah the prophet commanded, who was great and faithful in his vision. **23** In his days the sun went backward; And he added life to the king. **24** He saw by an excellent spirit what should come to pass at the last; And he comforted those who mourned in Zion. **25** He showed the things that should be to the end of time, and the hidden things or ever they came.

CHAPTER 49

1 The memorial of Josiah is like the composition of incense Prepared by the work of the apothecary: It will be sweet as honey in every mouth, and as music at a banquet of wine. **2** He behaved himself uprightly in the conversion of the people and took away the abominations of iniquity. **3** He set his heart right toward the Lord; In the days of wicked men he made godliness to prevail. **4** Except David and Hezekiah and Josiah, all committed trespass: For they forsook the law of the Most High; The kings of Judah failed. **5** For they gave their power to others, and their glory to a strange nation. **6** They set on fire the chosen city of the sanctuary, and made her streets desolate, *as it was written* by the hand of Jeremiah. **7** For they mistreated him; And yet he was sanctified in the womb to be a prophet, to root out, and to afflict, and to destroy; *And* in like manner to build and to plant. **8** *It was* Ezekiel who saw the vision of glory, Which *God* showed him upon the chariot of the cherubim. **9** For truly he remembered the enemies in storm, and to do good to those who directed their ways aright. **10** Also of the twelve prophets May the bones flourish again out of their place. And he comforted Jacob and delivered them by confidence of hope. **11** How will we magnify Zerubbabel? And he was as a signet on the right hand: **12** So was Jesus the son of Josedek: Who in their days built the house, and exalted a people holy to the Lord, prepared for everlasting glory. **13** Also of Nehemiah the memorial is great; Who raised up for us the walls that were fallen, and set up the gates and bars, and raised up our homes again. **14** No man was created upon the earth such as was Enoch; For he was taken up from the earth. **15** Neither was there a man born like to Joseph, A governor of his kindred, a stay of the people: Yes, his bones were visited. **16** Shem and Seth were glorified among men; And above every living thing in the creation is Adam.

CHAPTER 50

1 *It was* Simon, the son of Onias, the great priest, who in his life repaired the house, and in his days strengthened the temple: **2** And by him was built from the foundation the height of the double *wall,* the lofty underworks of the enclosure of the temple: **3** In his days the cistern of waters was diminished, The brazen vessel in compass as the sea. **4** *It was* he that took thought for his people that they should not fall and fortified the city against besieging: **5** How glorious was he when the people gathered round him at his coming out of the sanctuary! **6** As the morning star in the midst of a cloud, As the moon at the full: **7** As the sun shining out upon the temple of the Most High, and as the rainbow giving light in clouds of glory: **8** As the flower of roses in the days of new *fruits,* As lilies at the water spring, As the shoot of the frankincense tree in the time of summer: **9** As fire and incense in the censer, As a vessel all of beaten gold Adorned with all manner of precious stones: **10** As an olive tree budding out fruits, and as a cypress growing high among the clouds. **11** When he took up the robe of glory, and put on the perfection of exultation, In the ascent of the holy altar, He made glorious the precinct of the sanctuary. **12** And when he received the portions out of the priests' hands, Himself also standing by the hearth of the altar, his kindred as a garland around him, he was as a young cedar in Libanus; And as stems of palm trees compassed around him, **13** And all the sons of Aaron in their glory, and the Lord's offering in their hands, before all the congregation of Israel. **14** And finishing the service at the altars, that he might adorn the offering of the Most High, the Almighty, **15** He stretched out his hand to the cup, and poured out the cup of the grape; He poured out at the foot of the altar A sweet smelling savor to the Most High, the King of all. **16** Then shouted the sons of Aaron, they sounded the trumpets of beaten work, they made a great noise to be heard, For a remembrance before the Most High. **17** Then all the people together hurried and fell down upon the earth on their faces to worship their Lord, the Almighty, God Most High. **18** The singers also praised him with their voices; In the whole house was there made sweet melody. **19** And the people implored the Lord Most High, in prayer before him that is merciful. until the worship of the Lord should be ended; And so, they accomplished his service. **20** Then he went down and lifted up his hands Over the whole congregation of the children of Israel, to give blessing to the Lord with his lips, and to glory in his name. **21** And he bowed himself down in worship the second time, to declare the blessing from the Most High. **22** And now bless the God of all, who everywhere does great things, who exalts our days from the womb, and deals with us according to his mercy. **23** May he grant us joyfulness of heart, and that peace may be in our days in Israel for the days of eternity: **24** To entrust his mercy with us; And let him deliver us in his time! **25** With two nations is my soul vexed, and the third is no nation: **26** They that sit upon the mountain of Samaria, and the Philistines, and that foolish people that dwells in Sichem. **27** I have written in this book the instruction of understanding and knowledge, I Jesus, the son of Sirach Eleazar, of Jerusalem, who out of his heart poured out wisdom. **28** Blessed is he that will be exercised in these things; And he that lays them up in his heart will become wise. **29** For if he do them, he will be strong to all things: For the light of the Lord is his guide.

CHAPTER 51

A Prayer of Jesus the son of Sirach. **1** I will give thanks to you, O Lord, O King, and will praise you, O God my Savior: I do give thanks to your name: **2** For you were my protector and helper, and did deliver my body out of destruction, and out of the snare of a slanderous tongue, From lips that forge lies, and was my helper before those who stood by; **3** And did deliver me, according to the abundance of your mercy, and *greatness* of your name, From the gnashing *of teeth* ready to devour, Out of the hand of such as sought my life, Out of the manifold afflictions which I had; **4** From the choking of a fire on every side, and out of the midst of fire which I kindled not; **5** Out of the depth of the belly of the grave, and from an unclean tongue, and from lying words, **6** The slander of an unrighteous tongue to the king. My soul drew near even to death, and my life was near to the grave beneath. **7** They compassed me on every side, and there was none to help *me. I was* looking for the help of men, and it was not. **8** And I remembered your mercy, O Lord, and your working which has been from everlasting, how you deliver those who wait for you, and save them out of the hand of the enemies. **9** And I lifted up my supplication from the earth and prayed for deliverance from death. **10** I called upon the Lord, the Father of my Lord, that he would not forsake me in the days of affliction, In the time when there was no help against the proud. **11** I will praise your name continually, and will sing praise with thanksgiving; And my supplication was heard: **12** For you saved me from destruction, and delivered me from the evil time: Therefore I will give thanks and praise to you, and bless the name of the Lord. **13** When I was yet young, or ever I went abroad, I sought wisdom openly in my prayer. **14** Before the temple I asked for her, and I will seek her out even to the end. **15** From *her* flower as from the ripening grape my heart delighted in her: My foot trod in uprightness, from my youth I tracked her out. **16** I bowed down my ear a little, and received her, and found for myself much instruction. **17** I profited in her: To him that gives me wisdom I will give glory. **18** For I purposed to practice her, and I was zealous for that which is good; And I will never be put to shame. **19** My soul has wrestled in her, and in my doing I was exact: I spread out my hands to the heaven above and mourned my ignorance of her. **20** I set my soul properly to her, and in pureness I found her. I got me a heart *joined* with her from the beginning: Therefore will I not be forsaken. **21** My inward part also was troubled to seek her: Therefore I have gotten a good possession. **22** The Lord gave me a tongue for my reward; And I will praise him therewith. **23** Draw near to me, you unlearned, and lodge in the house of instruction. **24** Say, why are you lacking in these things, and your souls are very thirsty? **25** I opened my mouth, and spoke, Get her for yourselves without money. **26** Put your neck under the yoke, and let your soul receive instruction: She is hard at hand to find. **27** Behold with your eyes, how that I labored but a little, and found for myself much rest. **28** Get you instruction with a great sum of silver and gain much gold by her. **29** May your soul rejoice in his mercy, and may you not be put to shame in praising him. **30** Work your work before the time comes, and in his time he will give you your reward.

BARUCH

The opening verses ascribe the book to the well-known assistant to Jeremiah (Jer. 32:12; 36:4, 32; 45:1). It is a collection of four very different compositions, ending with a work entitled "The Letter of Jeremiah," which circulated separately in major manuscripts of the Greek tradition. The original language may have been Hebrew, but only the Greek and other versions have been preserved. The setting is Babylon, where Baruch reads his scroll to King Jechoniah (Jehoiachin) and the exiles; they react by sending gifts and the scroll to Jerusalem (1:1–14), presumably by the hand of Baruch (1:7). No certain date can be given for the book, but it may have been edited in final form during the last two centuries BC.

CHAPTER 1

1 These are the words of the book, which Baruch the son of Nerias, the son of Maaseas, the son of Sedekias, the son of Asadias, the son of Helkias, wrote in Babylon, 2 in the fifth year, *and* in the seventh day of the month, what time as the Chaldeans took Jerusalem, and burned it with fire. 3 And Baruch did read the words of this book in the hearing of Jechonias the son of Joakim king of Judah, and in the hearing of all the people that came to *hear* the book, 4 and in the hearing of the mighty men, and of the kings' sons, and in the hearing of the elders, and in the hearing of all the people, from the least to the greatest, even of all those who lived at Babylon by the river Sud. 5 And they wept, and fasted, and prayed before the Lord; 6 they made also a collection of money according to every man's power: 7 and they sent *it* to Jerusalem to Joakim the *high* priest, the son of Helkias, the son of Salom, and to the priests, and to all the people which were found with him at Jerusalem, 8 at the same time when he took the vessels of the house of the Lord, that had been carried out of the temple, to return *them* into the land of Judah, the tenth day of the *month* Sivan, *namely,* silver vessels, which Sedekias the son of Josias king of Judah had made, 9 after Nabuchodonosor king of Babylon had carried away Jechonias, and the princes, and the captives, and the mighty men, and the people of the land, from Jerusalem, and brought them to Babylon. 10 And they said, Behold, we have sent you money; buy you therefore with the money burnt offerings, and sin offerings, and incense, and prepare an oblation, and offer upon the altar of the Lord our God; 11 and pray for the life of Nabuchodonosor king of Babylon, and for the life of Baltasar his son, that their days may be as the days of heaven above the earth: 12 and the Lord will give us strength, and lighten our eyes, and we will live under the shadow of Nabuchodonosor king of Babylon, and under the shadow of Baltasar his son, and we will serve them many days, and find favor in their sight. 13 Pray for us also to the Lord our God, for we have sinned against the Lord our God; and to this day the wrath of the Lord and his indignation is not turned from us. 14 And you will read this book which we have sent to you, to make confession in the house of the Lord, upon the day of the feast and on the days of the solemn assembly. 15 And you will say, To the Lord our God *belongs* righteousness, but to us confusion of face, as at this day, to the men of Judah, and to the inhabitants of Jerusalem, 16 and to our kings, and to our princes, and to our priests, and to our prophets, and to our fathers: 17 for that we have sinned before the Lord, 18 and disobeyed him, and have not listened to the voice of the Lord our God, to walk in the commandments of the Lord that he has set before us: 19 since the day that the Lord brought our fathers out of the land of Egypt, to this present day, we have been disobedient to the Lord our God, and we have dealt unadvisedly in not listening to his voice. 20 Why the plagues clave to us, and the curse, which the Lord commanded Moses his servant *to pronounce* in the day that he brought our fathers out of the land of Egypt, to give us a land that flows with milk and honey, as at this day. 21 Nevertheless we didn't listen to the voice of the Lord our God, according to all the words of the prophets, whom he sent to us: 22 but we walked every man in the imagination of his own wicked heart, to serve strange gods, and to do that which is evil in the sight of the Lord our God.

CHAPTER 2

1 Therefore the Lord has made good his word, which he pronounced against us, and against our judges that judged Israel, and against our kings, and against our princes, and against the men of Israel and Judah, 2 to bring upon us great plagues, such as never happened under the whole heaven, as it came to pass in Jerusalem, according to the things that are written in the law of Moses; 3 That we should eat every man the flesh of his own son, and every man the flesh of his own daughter. 4 Moreover he has given them to be in subjection to all the kingdoms that are around us, to be a reproach and a desolation among all the surrounding people, where the Lord has scattered them. 5 So were they cast down, and not exalted, because we sinned against the Lord our God, in not listening to his voice. 6 To the Lord our God *belongs* righteousness: but to us and to our fathers confusion of face, as at this day. 7 *For* all these plagues are come upon us, which the Lord has pronounced against us. 8 Yet have we not entreated the favor of the Lord, in turning everyone from the thoughts of his wicked heart. 9 Therefore has the Lord kept watch over the plagues, and the Lord has brought *them* upon us; for the Lord is righteous in all his works which he has commanded us. 10 Yet we have not listened to his voice, to walk in the commandments of the Lord that he has set before us. 11 And now, O Lord, you God of Israel, that have brought your people out of the land of Egypt with a mighty hand, and with signs, and with wonders, and with great power, and with a high arm, and have gotten yourself a name, as at this day: 12 O Lord our God, we have sinned, we have been ungodly, we have dealt unrighteously in all your ordinances. 13 Let your wrath turn from us: for we are but a few left among the heathen, where you have scattered us. 14 Hear our prayer, O Lord, and our petition, and deliver us for your own sake, and give us favor in the sight of them which have led us away captive: 15 that all the earth may know that you are the Lord our God, because Israel and his posterity is called by your name. 16 O Lord, look down from your holy house, and consider us: incline your ear, O Lord, and hear: 17 open your eyes, and behold: for the dead that are in the grave, whose breath is taken from their bodies, will give to the Lord neither glory nor righteousness: 18 but the soul that is greatly vexed, which goes stooping and feeble, and the eyes that fail, and the hungry soul, will give you glory and righteousness, O Lord. 19 For we do not present our supplication before you, O Lord our God, for the righteousness of our fathers, and of our kings. 20 For you have sent your wrath and your indignation upon us, as you have spoken by your servants the prophets, *saying,* 21 "The Lord says, bow your shoulders to serve the king of Babylon, and remain in the land that I gave to your fathers. 22 But if you will not hear the voice of the Lord, to serve the king of Babylon, 23 I will cause to cease out of the cities of Judah, and from the region near Jerusalem, the voice of mirth, and the voice of gladness, the voice of the bridegroom, and the voice of the bride: and the whole land will be desolate without inhabitant." 24 But we would not listen to your voice, to serve the king of Babylon: therefore have you made good your words that you spoke by your servants the prophets, *namely,* that the bones of our kings, and the bones of our fathers, should be taken out of their places. 25 And, behold, they are cast out to the heat by day, and to the frost by night, and they died in great miseries by famine, by sword, and by pestilence. 26 And the house which is called by your name have you laid *waste,* as at this day, for the wickedness of the house of Israel and the house of Judah. 27 Yet, O Lord our God, you have dealt with us after all your kindness, and according to all your great mercy, 28 as you spoke by your servant Moses in the day when you did command him to write your law before the children of Israel, saying, 29 If you will not hear my voice, surely this very great multitude will be turned into a small *number* among the nations, where I will scatter them. 30 For I know that they will not hear me, because it is a stiff-necked people: but in the land of their captivity they will take it to heart, 31 and will know that I am the Lord their God: and I will give them a heart, and ears to hear: 32 and they will praise me in the land of their captivity, and think upon my name, 33 and will return from their stiff neck, and from their wicked deeds: for they will remember the way of their fathers, which sinned before the Lord. 34 And I will bring them again into the land which I swore to their fathers, to Abraham, to Isaac, and to Jacob, and they will be lords of it: and I will increase them, and they will not be diminished. 35 And I will make an everlasting covenant with them to be their God, and they will be my people: and I will no

more remove my people Israel out of the land that I have given them.

CHAPTER 3

1 O Lord Almighty, you God of Israel, the soul in anguish, the troubled spirit, cries to you. **2** Hear, O Lord, and have mercy; for you are a merciful God: yes, have mercy upon us, because we have sinned before you. **3** For you sit *as king* forever, and we perish evermore. **4** O Lord Almighty, you God of Israel, hear now the prayer of the dead Israelites, and of the children of them which were sinners before you, that didn't listen to the voice of you their God: for the which cause these plagues clave to us. **5** Remember not the iniquities of our fathers: but remember your power and your name *now* at this time. **6** For you are the Lord our God, and you, O Lord, will we praise. **7** For this cause you have put your fear in our hearts, to the intent that we should call upon your name: and we will praise you in our captivity, for we have called to mind all the iniquity of our fathers, that sinned before you. **8** Behold, we are yet this day in our captivity, where you have scattered us, for a reproach and a curse, and to be subject to penalty, according to all the iniquities of our fathers, which departed from the Lord our God. **9** Hear, O Israel, the commandments of life: give ear to understand wisdom. **10** How is it, O Israel, that you are in your enemies' land, that you have become old in a strange country, that you are defiled with the dead, **11** that you are counted with those who *go down* in to the grave? **12** You have forsaken the fountain of wisdom. **13** *For* if you had walked in the way of God, you should have dwelled in peace forever. **14** Learn where is wisdom, where is strength, where is understanding; that you may know also where is length of days, and life, where is the light of the eyes, and peace. **15** Who has found out her place? And who has come into her treasures? **16** Where are the princes of the heathen, and such as ruled the beasts that are upon the earth; **17** those who had their pastime with the fowls of the air, and those who hoarded up silver and gold, wherein men trust; and of whose getting there is no end? **18** For those who made in silver, and were so careful, and whose works are past finding out, **19** they are vanished and gone down to the grave, and others are come up in their steads. **20** Younger men have seen the light and lived upon the earth: but the way of knowledge have they not known, **21** neither understood they the paths thereof: neither have their children embraced it: they are far off from their way. **22** It has not been heard of in Canaan, neither has it been seen in Teman. **23** The sons also of Agar that seek understanding, which are in the land, the merchants of Merran and Teman, and the authors of fables, and the searchers out of understanding; none of these have known the way of wisdom or remembered her paths. **24** O Israel, how great is the house of God! and how large is the place of his possession! **25** great, and has none end; high, and unmeasurable. **26** There were the giants born that were famous of old, great of stature, *and* expert in war. **27** God didn't choose these, nor did he give the way of knowledge to them; **28** so they perished, because they had no wisdom, they perished through their own foolishness. **29** Who has gone up into heaven, and taken her, and brought her down from the clouds? **30** Who has gone over the sea, and found her, and will bring her for choice gold? **31** There is none that knows her way, nor any that comprehends her path. **32** But he that knows all things knows her, he found her out with his understanding: he that prepared the earth forevermore has filled it with four-footed beasts: **33** he that sends out the light, and it goes; he called it, and it obeyed him with fear: **34** and the stars shone in their watches, and were glad: when he called them, they said, "Here we are." They shone with gladness to him that made them. **35** This is our God, *and* there will none other be accounted of in comparison of him. **36** He has found out all the way of knowledge, and has given it to Jacob his servant, and to Israel that is beloved of him. **37** Afterward did she appear upon earth and was conversant with men.

CHAPTER 4

1 This is the book of the commandments of God, and the law that endures forever: all those who hold it fast *are appointed* to life; but such as leave it will die. **2** Turn you, O Jacob, and take hold of it: walk toward her shining in the presence of the light thereof. **3** Give not your glory to another, nor the things that are profitable to you to a strange nation. **4** O Israel, happy are we: for the things that are pleasing to God are made known to us. **5** Be of good cheer, my people, the memorial of Israel. **6** You were sold to the nations, *but* not for destruction: because you moved God to wrath, you were delivered to your adversaries. **7** For you provoked him that made you by sacrificing to demons, and not to God. **8** You forgot the everlasting God, that brought you up; you grieved also Jerusalem, that nursed you. **9** For she saw the wrath that is come upon you from God, and said, Listen, you *women* that dwell about Zion: for God has brought upon me great mourning; **10** for I have seen the captivity of my sons and daughters, which the Everlasting has brought upon them. **11** For with joy did I nourish them; but sent them away with weeping and mourning. **12** Let no man rejoice over me, a widow, and forsaken of many: for the sins of my children am I left desolate; because they turned away from the law of God, **13** and had no regard to his statutes, neither walked they in the ways of God's commandments, nor trod in the paths of discipline in his righteousness. **14** Let those who dwell about Zion come, and remember you the captivity of my sons and daughters, which the Everlasting has brought upon them. **15** For he has brought a nation upon them from far, a shameless nation, and of a strange language, who neither reverenced old man, nor pitied child. **16** And they have carried away the dear beloved sons of the widow and left her that was alone desolate of her daughters. **17** But I, what can I help you? **18** For he that brought these plagues upon you will deliver you from the hand of your enemies. **19** Go your way, O my children, go your way: for I am left desolate. **20** I have put off the garment of peace and put upon me the sackcloth of my petition: I will cry to the Everlasting as long as I live. **21** Be of good cheer, O my children, cry to God, and he will deliver you from the power and hand of the enemies. **22** For I have trusted in the Everlasting, that he will save you; and joy is come to me from the Holy One, because of the mercy which will soon come to you from your Everlasting Savior. **23** For I sent you out with mourning and weeping: but God will give you to me again with joy and gladness forever. **24** For like as now those who dwell about Zion have seen your captivity: so will they see shortly your salvation from our God, which will come upon you with great glory, and brightness of the Everlasting. **25** My children, suffer patiently the wrath that is come upon you from God: for your enemy has persecuted you; but shortly you will see his destruction, and will tread upon their necks. **26** My delicate ones have gone rough ways; they were taken away as a flock carried off by the enemies. **27** Be of good cheer, O my

children, and cry to God: for you will be remembered of him that has brought *these things* upon you. **28** For as it was your mind to go astray from God: *so,* return and seek him ten times more. **29** For he that brought these plagues upon you will bring you everlasting joy again with your salvation. **30** Be of good cheer, O Jerusalem: for he that called you by name will comfort you. **31** Miserable are those who afflicted you and rejoiced at your fall. **32** Miserable are the cities which your children served: miserable is she that received your sons. **33** For as she rejoiced at your fall, and was glad of your ruin: so will she be grieved for her own desolation. **34** And I will take away her exultation in her great multitude, and her boasting will be turned into mourning. **35** For fire will come upon her from the Everlasting, long to endure; and she will be inhabited of devils for a great time. **36** O Jerusalem look about you toward the east and behold the joy that comes to you from God. **37** Behold, your sons come, whom you sent away, they come gathered together from the east to the west at the word of the Holy One, rejoicing in the glory of God.

CHAPTER 5

1 Put off, O Jerusalem, the garment of your mourning and affliction, and put on the beauty of the glory that *comes* from God forever. **2** Cast about you the robe of the righteousness which *comes* from God; set a diadem on your head of the glory of the Everlasting. **3** For God will show your brightness to every *region* under heaven. **4** For your name will be called of God forever the peace of righteousness, and The glory of godliness. **5** Arise, O Jerusalem, and stand upon the height, and look about you toward the east, and behold your children gathered from the going down of the sun to the rising thereof at the word of the Holy One, rejoicing that God has remembered them. **6** For they went from you on foot, being led away of their enemies: but God brings them in to you borne on high with glory, as *on* a royal throne. **7** For God has appointed that every high mountain, and the everlasting hills, should be made low, and the valleys filled up, to make plain the ground, that Israel may go safely in the glory of God. **8** Moreover the woods and every sweet-smelling tree have overshadowed Israel by the commandment of God. **9** For God will lead Israel with joy in the light of his glory with the mercy and righteousness that comes from him.

CHAPTER 6

1 A copy of a letter, which Jeremy sent to them which were to be led captives into Babylon by the king of the Babylonians, to certify them, as it was commanded him of God. 2 Because of the sins which you have committed before God, you will be led away captives to Babylon by Nabuchodonosor king of the Babylonians. 3 So when you come to Babylon, you will remain there many years, and for a long season, even for seven generations: and after that I will bring you out peaceably from there. 4 But now will you see in Babylon gods of silver, and of gold, and of wood, borne upon shoulders, which cause the nations to fear. 5 Beware therefore that you in no wise become like to the strangers, neither let fear take hold upon you because of them, when you see the multitude before them and behind them, worshiping them. 6 But say you in your hearts, O Lord, we must worship you. 7 For my angel is with you, and I myself do care for your souls. 8 For their tongue is polished by the workman, and they themselves are overlaid with gold and with silver; yet are they but false and can't speak. 9 And taking gold, as it were for a virgin that loves to be happy, they make crowns for the heads of their gods: 10 and sometimes also the priests convey from their gods gold and silver and bestow it upon themselves; 11 and will even give thereof to the common prostitutes: and they deck them as men with garments, *even* the gods of silver, and gods of gold, and of wood. 12 Yet can't these gods save themselves from rust and moths, though they be covered with purple raiment. 13 They wipe their faces because of the dust of the temple, which is thick upon them. 14 And he that can't put to death one that offends against him holds a scepter, as though he were judge of a country. 15 He has also a dagger in his right hand, and an axe: but can't deliver himself from war and robbers. 16 Whereby they are known not to be gods: therefore fear them not. 17 For like as a vessel that a man uses is nothing worth when it is broken; even so it is with their gods: when they be set up in the temples their eyes be full of dust through the feet of those who come in. 18 And as the courts are made sure on every side upon him that offends the king, as being committed to suffer death; *even so* the priests make fast their temples with doors, with locks, and bars, lest they be carried off by robbers. 19 They light the candles, yes, more than for themselves, whereof they can't see one.

20 They are as one of the beams of the temple; and men say their hearts are eaten out, when things creeping out of the earth devour both them and their raiment: 21 they feel it not when their faces are blackened through the smoke that comes out of the temple: 22 bats, swallows, and birds land on their bodies and heads; and in like manner the cats also. 23 Whereby you may know that they are no gods: therefore fear them not. 24 Notwithstanding the gold with which they are beset to make them beautiful, except one wipe off the rust, they will not shine: for not even when they were molten did they feel it. 25 Things wherein there is no breath are bought at any cost. 26 Having no feet, they are borne upon shoulders, whereby they declare to men that they be nothing worth. 27 They also that serve them are ashamed: for if they fall to the ground at any time, they can't rise up again of themselves: neither, if they are bowed down, can they make themselves straight: but the offerings are set before them, as if they were dead men. 28 And the things that are sacrificed to them, their priests sell and spend; and in like manner their wives also lay up part thereof in salt; but to the poor and to the impotent they will give nothing thereof. 29 The menstruous woman and the woman in childbed touch their sacrifices: knowing therefore by these things that they are no gods, fear them not. 30 For how can they be called gods? Because women set meat before the gods of silver, gold, and wood. 31 And in their temples the priests sit on seats, having their clothes tore, and their heads and beards shaven, and nothing upon their heads. 32 They roar and cry before their gods, as men do at the feast when one is dead. 33 The priests also take off garments from them and clothe their wives and children withal. 34 Whether it be evil that one does to them, or good, they are not able to recompense it: they can neither set up a king, nor put him down. 35 In like manner, they can neither give riches nor money: though a man makes a vow to them, and keep it not, they will never exact it. 36 They can save no man from death, neither deliver the weak from the mighty. 37 They can't restore a blind man to his sight, nor deliver any that is in distress. 38 They can show no mercy to the widow, nor do good to the fatherless. 39 They are like the stones that be *hewn* out of the mountain, *these gods* of wood, and that are overlaid with gold and with silver: those who minister to them will be

confounded. **40** How should a man then think or say that they are gods, when even the Chaldeans themselves dishonor them? **41** Who if they will see one mute that can't speak, they bring him, and entreat him to call upon Bel, as though he were able to understand. **42** Yet they can't perceive this themselves and forsake them: for they have no understanding. **43** The women also with cords about them sit in the ways, burning bran for incense: but if any of them, drawn by some that passes by, lie with him, she reproaches her fellow, that she was not thought as worthy as herself, nor her cord broken. **44** Whatsoever is done among them is false: how should a man then think or say that they are gods? **45** They are fashioned by carpenters and goldsmiths: they can be nothing else than the workmen will have them to be. **46** And they themselves that fashioned them can never continue long; how then should the things that are fashioned by them? **47** For they have left lies and reproaches to those who come after. **48** For when there comes any war or plague upon them, the priests consult with themselves, where they may be hidden with them. **49** How then can't men understand that they be no gods, which can neither save themselves from war, nor from plague? **50** For seeing they be but of wood, and overlaid with gold and with silver, it will be known hereafter that they are false: **51** and it will be manifest to all nations and kings that they are no gods, but the works of men's hands, and that there is no work of God in them. **52** Who then may not know that they are no gods? **53** For neither can they set up a king in a land, nor give rain to men. **54** Neither can they judge their own cause, nor redress a wrong, being unable: for they are as crows between heaven and earth. **55** For even when fire falls upon the house of gods of wood, or overlaid with gold or with silver, their priests will flee away, and escape, but they themselves will be burned apart like beams. **56** Moreover they can't withstand any king or enemies: how should a man then allow or think that they be gods? **57** Neither are those gods of wood, and overlaid with silver or with gold, able to escape either from thieves or robbers. **58** Whose gold, and silver, and garments with which they are clothed, they that are strong will take from them, and go away withal: neither will they be able to help themselves. **59** Therefore it is better to be a king that shows his manhood, or else a vessel in a house profitable for that whereof the owner will have need, than such false gods; or even a door in a house, to keep the things safe that be therein, than such false gods; or a pillar of wood in a palace, than such false gods. **60** For sun, and moon, and stars, being bright and sent to do their offices, are obedient. **61** Likewise also the lightning when it glitters is fair to see; and after the same manner the wind also blows in every country. **62** And when God commands the clouds to go over the whole world, they do as they are told. **63** And the fire sent from above to consume mountains and woods does as it is commanded: but these are to be likened to them neither in show nor power. **64** Why a man should neither think nor say that they are gods, seeing they are able neither to judge causes, nor to do good to men. **65** Knowing therefore that they are no gods, fear them not. **66** For they can neither curse nor bless kings: **67** neither can they show signs in the heavens among the nations, nor shine as the sun, nor give light as the moon. **68** The beasts are better than they: for they can get under a covert and help themselves. **69** In no wise then is it manifest to us that they are gods: therefore, fear them not. **70** For as a scarecrow in a garden of cucumbers that keeps nothing, so are their gods of wood, and overlaid with gold and with silver. **71** Likewise also their gods of wood, and overlaid with gold and with silver, are like to a white thorn in an orchard, that every bird sits upon; as also to a dead body, that is cast out into the dark. **72** And you will know them to be no gods by the bright purple that rots upon them: And they themselves afterward will be consumed and will be a reproach in the country. **73** Better therefore is the just man that has none idols: for he will be far from reproach.

1 MACCABEES

The name Maccabee, probably meaning "hammer," is actually applied in the Books of Maccabees to only one man, Judas, third son of the priest Mattathias and first leader of the revolt against the Seleucid kings who persecuted the Jews (1 Mc. 2:4, 66; 2 Mc. 8:5, 16; 10:1, 16). Traditionally the name has come to be extended to the brothers of Judas, his supporters, and even to other Jewish heroes of the period, such as the seven brothers (2 Mc. 7). First Maccabees was written about 100 B.C., in Hebrew, but the original has not come down to us. Instead, we have an early, pre-Christian, Greek translation full of Hebrew idioms. The author, probably a Jew, is unknown. He was familiar with the traditions and sacred books of his people and had access to much reliable information on their recent history (from 175 to 134 B.C.). He may well have played some part in it himself in his youth. His purpose in writing is to record the deliverance of Israel that God worked through the family of Mattathias (5:62)—especially through his three sons, Judas, Jonathan, and Simon, and his grandson, John Hyrcanus.

CHAPTER 1

1 It came to pass, after that Alexander the Macedonian, the son of Philip, who came out of the land of Chittim, and struck Darius king of the Persians and Medes, *it came to pass,* after he had struck him, that he reigned in his stead, in former time, over Greece. 2 And he fought many battles, and won many strongholds, and killed the kings of the earth, 3 and went through to the ends of the earth and took spoils of a multitude of nations. And the earth was quiet before him, and he was exalted, and his heart was lifted up, 4 and he gathered together an exceedingly strong army, and ruled over countries and nations and principalities, and they became tributary to him. 5 And after these things he fell sick, and perceived that he should die. 6 And he called his servants, which were honorable, which had been brought up with him from his youth, and he divided to them his kingdom, while he was yet alive. 7 And Alexander reigned twelve years, and he died. 8 And his servants bare rule, each one in his place. 9 And they did all put diadems upon themselves after that he was dead, and so did their sons after them many years: and they multiplied evils in the earth. 10 And there came out of them a sinful root, Antiochus Epiphanes, son of Antiochus the king, who had been a hostage at Rome, and he reigned in the hundred and thirty and seventh year of the kingdom of the Greeks. 11 In those days came there out of Israel transgressors of the law, and persuaded many, saying, let's go and make a covenant with the Gentiles that are around us; for since we were parted from them many evils have befallen us. 12 And the saying was good in their eyes. 13 And certain of the people were forward *here in* land went to the king, and he gave them license to do after the ordinances of the Gentiles. 14 And they built a place of exercise in Jerusalem according to the laws of the Gentiles; 15 and they made themselves uncircumcised, and forsook the holy covenant, and joined themselves to the Gentiles, and sold themselves to do evil. 16 And the kingdom was well ordered in the sight of Antiochus, and he thought to reign over Egypt, that he might reign over the two kingdoms. 17 And he entered into Egypt with a great multitude, with chariots, and with elephants, and with horsemen, and with a great navy; 18 and he made war against Ptolemy king of Egypt; and Ptolemy was put to shame before him and fled; and many fell wounded to death. 19 And they got possession of the strong cities in the land of Egypt; and he took the spoils of Egypt. 20 And Antiochus, after he had struck Egypt, returned in the hundred and forty and third year, and went up against Israel and Jerusalem with a great multitude, 21 and entered presumptuously into the sanctuary, and took the golden altar, and the candlestick of the light, and all that pertained thereto, 22 and the table of the show bread, and the cups to pour withal, and the bowls, and the golden censers, and the veil, and the crowns, and the adorning of gold which was on the face of the temple, and he peeled it all off. 23 And he took the silver and the gold and the precious vessels; and he took the hidden treasures which he found. 24 And when he had taken all, he went away into his own land, and he made a great slaughter, and spoke very presumptuously.

25 And there came great mourning upon Israel, in every place where they were; 26 and the rulers and elders groaned, the virgins and young men were made feeble, and the beauty of the women was changed. 27 Every bridegroom took up lamentation, she that sat in the marriage chamber was in heaviness. 28 And the land was moved for the inhabitants thereof, and all the house of Jacob was clothed with shame. 29 And after two full years the king sent a chief collector of tribute to the cities of Judah, and he came to Jerusalem with a great multitude. 30 And he spoke words of peace to them in subtlety, and they gave him credence: and he fell upon the city suddenly, and struck it very sore, and destroyed much people out of Israel. 31 And he took the spoils of the city, and set it on fire, and pulled down the houses thereof and the walls thereof on every side. 32 And they led captive the women and the children, and the cattle they took in possession. 33 And they built the city of David with a great and strong wall, with strong towers, and it became to them a citadel. 34 And they put there a sinful nation, transgressors of the law, and they strengthened themselves therein. 35 And they stored up arms and food, and gathering together the spoils of Jerusalem, they laid them up there, and they became a sore snare: 36 and it became a place to lie in wait in against the sanctuary, and an evil adversary to Israel continually. 37 And they shed innocent blood on every side of the sanctuary and defiled the sanctuary. 38 And the inhabitants of Jerusalem fled because of them; and she became a habitation of strangers, and she became strange to those who were born in her, and her children forsook her. 39 Her sanctuary was laid waste like a wilderness, her feasts were turned into mourning, her Sabbaths into reproach, her honor into contempt. 40 According to her glory, so was her dishonor multiplied, and her high estate was turned into mourning. 41 And king Antiochus wrote to his whole kingdom, that all should be one people, 42 and that each should forsake his own laws. And all the nations agreed according to the word of the king; 43 and many of Israel consented to his worship, and sacrificed to the idols, and profaned the Sabbath. 44 And the king sent letters by the hand of messengers to Jerusalem and the cities of Judah, that they should follow laws strange to the land, 45 and should forbid whole burnt offerings and sacrifice and drink offerings in the sanctuary;

and should profane the Sabbaths and feasts, 46 and pollute the sanctuary and those who were holy; 47 that they should build altars, and temples, and shrines for idols, and should sacrifice swine's flesh and unclean beasts: 48 and that they should leave their sons uncircumcised, that they should make their souls abominable with all manner of uncleanness and profanation; 49 so that they might forget the law, and change all the ordinances. 50 And whoever will not do according to the word of the king, he will die. 51 According to all these words wrote he to his whole kingdom; and he appointed overseers over all the people, and he commanded the cities of Judah to sacrifice, city by city. 52 And from the people were gathered together to them many, every one that had forsaken the law; and they did evil things in the land; 53 and they made Israel to hide themselves in every place of refuge which they had. 54 And on the fifteenth day of Chislev, in the hundred and forty and fifth year, they built an abomination of desolation upon the altar, and in the cities of Judah on every side they built *idol* altars. 55 And at the doors of the houses and in the streets they burned incense. 56 And they tore in pieces the books of the law which they found and set them on fire. 57 And wherever was found with any a book of the covenant, and if any consented to the law, the king's sentence delivered him to death. 58 So did they in their might to Israel, to those that were found month by month in the cities. 59 And on the five and twentieth day of the month they sacrificed upon the *idol* altar *of God*. 60 And the women that had circumcised their children they put to death according to the commandment. 61 And they hanged their babes about their necks, and *destroyed* their houses, and those who had circumcised them. 62 And many in Israel were fully resolved and confirmed in themselves not to eat unclean things. 63 And they chose to die, that they might not be defiled with the meats, and that they might not profane the holy covenant: and they died. 64 And there came exceedingly great wrath upon Israel.

CHAPTER 2

1 In those days rose up Mattathias the son of John, the son of Simeon, a priest of the sons of Joarib, from Jerusalem; and he lived at Modin. 2 And he had five sons, John, who was surnamed Gaddis; 3 Simon, who was called Thassi; 4 Judas, who was called Maccabaeus;

5 Eleazar, who was called Avaran; Jonathan, who was called Apphus. 6 And he saw the blasphemies that were committed in Judah and in Jerusalem, 7 and he said, Woe is me! why was I born to see the destruction of my people, and the destruction of the holy city, and to dwell there, when it was given into the hand of the enemy, the sanctuary into the hand of aliens? 8 Her temple is become as a man that was glorious: 9 her vessels of glory are carried away into captivity, her infants are slain in her streets, her young men with the sword of the enemy. 10 What nation has not inherited her palaces, and gotten possession of her spoils? 11 her adorning is all taken away; instead of a free woman she is become a bond woman: 12 and, behold, our holy things and our beauty and our glory are laid waste, and the Gentiles have profaned them. 13 Why should we live any longer? 14 And Mattathias and his sons tore their clothes, and put on sackcloth, and mourned exceedingly. 15 And the king's officers, that were enforcing the apostasy, came into the city Modin to sacrifice. 16 And many of Israel came to them, and Mattathias and his sons were gathered together. 17 And the king's officers answered and spoke to Mattathias, saying, You are a ruler and an honorable and great man in this city, and strengthened with sons and kindred: 18 now therefore come you first and do the commandment of the king, as all the nations have done, and the men of Judah, and those who remain in Jerusalem: and you and your house will be in the number of the king's friends, and you and your sons will be honored with silver and gold and many gifts. 19 And Mattathias answered and said with a loud voice, If all the nations that are in the house of the king's dominion listen to him, to fall away each one from the worship of his fathers, and have made choice to follow his commandments, 20 yet I and my sons and my kindred will walk in the covenant of our fathers. 21 Heaven forbid that we should forsake the law and the ordinances. 22 We will not listen to the king's words, to go aside from our worship, on the right hand, or on the left. 23 And when he had left speaking these words, there came a Jew in the sight of all to sacrifice on the altar which was at Modin, according to the king's commandment. 24 And Mattathias saw it, and his zeal was kindled, and his reins trembled, and he showed out his wrath according to judgement, and ran, and killed him upon the altar. 25 And the king's officer, who compelled men to sacrifice, he killed at that time, and pulled down the altar. 26 And he was zealous for the law, even as Phinehas did to Zimri the son of Salu. 27 And Mattathias cried out in the city with a loud voice, saying, "Whosoever is zealous for the law, and maintains the covenant, let him come out after me." 28 And he and his sons fled into the mountains and forsook all that they had in the city. 29 Then many that sought after justice and judgement went down into the wilderness, to dwell there, 30 they, and their sons, and their wives, and their cattle; because evils were multiplied upon them. 31 And it was told the king's officers, and the forces that were in Jerusalem, the city of David, that certain men, who had broken the king's commandment, were gone down into the secret places in the wilderness; 32 and many pursued after them, and having overtaken them, they encamped against them, and set the battle in array against them on the Sabbath day. 33 And they said to them, so far. Come out, and do according to the word of the king, and you will live. 34 And they said, "We will not come out, neither will we do the word of the king, to profane the Sabbath day." 35 And they hurried to give them battle. 36 And they answered them not, neither cast they a stone at them, nor stopped up the secret places, 37 saying, "Let us die all in our innocence: heaven and earth witness over us, that you put us to death without trial." 38 And they rose up against them in battle on the Sabbath, and they died, they and their wives and their children, and their cattle, to the number of a thousand souls. 39 And Mattathias and his friends knew it, and they mourned over them exceedingly. 40 And one said to another, If we all do as our kindred have done, and fight not against the Gentiles for our lives and our ordinances, they will now quickly destroy us from off the earth. 41 And they took counsel on that day, saying, whoever will come against us to battle on the Sabbath day, let's fight against him, and we will in no wise all die, as our kindred died in the secret places. 42 Then were gathered together to them a company of Hasidaeans, mighty men of Israel, every one that offered himself willingly for the law. 43 And all those who fled from the evils were added to them and became a stay to them. 44 And they mustered an army, and struck sinners in their anger, and lawless men in their wrath: and the rest fled to the Gentiles for safety. 45 And Mattathias and

his friends went around and pulled down the altars; **46** and they circumcised by force the children that were uncircumcised, as many as they found in the coasts of Israel. **47** And they pursued after the sons of pride, and the work prospered in their hand. **48** And they rescued the law out of the hand of the Gentiles, and out of the hand of the kings, neither suffered they the sinner to triumph. **49** And the days of Mattathias drew near that he should die, and he said to his sons, now have pride and rebuke gotten strength, and a season of overthrow, and wrath of indignation. **50** And now, my children, be you zealous for the law, and give your lives for the covenant of your fathers. **51** And call to remembrance the deeds of our fathers which they did in their generations; and receive great glory and an everlasting name. **52** Was not Abraham found faithful in temptation, and it was reckoned to him for righteousness? **53** Joseph in the time of his distress kept the commandment and became lord of Egypt. **54** Phinehas our father, for that he was zealous exceedingly, obtained the covenant of an everlasting priesthood. **55** Joshua for fulfilling the word became a judge in Israel. **56** Caleb for bearing witness in the congregation obtained a heritage in the land. **57** David for being merciful inherited the throne of a kingdom forever and ever. **58** Elijah, for that he was exceedingly zealous for the law, was taken up into heaven. **59** Hananiah, Azariah, Mishael, believed, and were saved out of the flame. **60** Daniel for his innocence was delivered from the mouth of lions. **61** And so consider you from generation to generation, that none that put their trust in him will lack for strength. **62** And be not afraid of the words of a sinful man; for his glory will be dung and worms. **63** To-day he will be lifted up, and tomorrow he will in no wise be found, because he is returned to his dust, and his thought is perished. **64** And you, my children, be strong, and show yourselves men in behalf of the law; for therein will you obtain glory. **65** And, behold, Simon your brother, I know that he is a man of counsel; give ear to him always: he will be a father to you. **66** And Judas Maccabeus, he has been strong and mighty from his youth: he will be your captain and will fight the battle of the people. **67** And take you to you all the doers of the law and avenge the wrong of your people. **68** Render a recompense to the Gentiles and take heed to the commandments of the law. **69** And he blessed them and was gathered to his fathers.

70 And he died in the hundred and forty and sixth year, and his sons buried him in the sepulchers of his fathers at Modin, and all Israel made great lamentation for him.

CHAPTER 3

1 And his son Judas, who was called Maccabaeus, rose up in his stead. **2** And all his kindred helped him, and so did all those who clave to his father, and they fought with gladness the battle of Israel. **3** And he got his people great glory, and put on a breastplate as a giant, and girded his warlike harness about him, and set battles in array, protecting the army with his sword. **4** And he was like a lion in his deeds, and as a lion's whelp roaring for prey. **5** And he pursued the lawless, seeking them out, and he burned up those that troubled his people. **6** And the lawless shrunk for fear of him, and all the workers of lawlessness were sore troubled, and salvation prospered in his hand. **7** And he angered many kings, and made Jacob glad with his acts, and his memorial is blessed forever. **8** And he went about among the cities of Judah, and destroyed the ungodly out of the land, and turned away wrath from Israel: **9** and he was renowned to the utmost part of the earth, and he gathered together such as were ready to perish. **10** And Apollonius gathered the Gentiles together, and a great army from Samaria, to fight against Israel. **11** And Judas perceived it, and he went out to meet him, and struck him, and killed him: and many fell wounded to death, and the rest fled. **12** And they took their spoils, and Judas took the sword of Apollonius, and therewith he fought all his days. **13** And Seron, the commander of the army of Syria, heard say that Judas had gathered a gathering and a congregation of faithful men with him, and of such as went out to war; **14** And he said, I will make myself a name and get me glory in the kingdom; and I will fight against Judas and those who are with him, that set at nothing the word of the king. **15** And there went up with him also a mighty army of the ungodly to help him, to take vengeance on the children of Israel. **16** And he came near to the going up of Bethhoron, and Judas went out to meet him with a small company. **17** But when they saw the army coming to meet them, they said to Judas, "What? Will we be able, being a small company, to fight against so great and strong a multitude? And we for our part are faint, having tasted no food this day." **18** And Judas said, "It is an easy thing for many to be shut up in the hands of a few; and with heaven it is all one, to save by many or by few: **19** for victory in battle stands not in the multitude of an army; but strength is from heaven. **20** They come to us in fullness of insolence and lawlessness, to destroy us and our wives and our children, for to plunder us: **21** but we fight for our lives and our laws. **22** And he himself will discomfit them before our face: but as for you, be you not afraid of them." **23** Now when he had left off speaking, he leapt suddenly upon them, and Seron and his army were discomfited before him. **24** And they pursued them in the going down of Bethhoron to the plain, and there fell of them about eight hundred men; but the residue fled into the land of the Philistines. **25** And the fear of Judas and his kindred, and the dread of them, began to fall upon the nations around them: **26** and his name came near even to the king, and every nation told of the battles of Judas. **27** But when king Antiochus heard these words, he was full of indignation: and he sent and gathered together all the forces of his realm, an exceedingly strong army. **28** And he opened his treasury, and gave his forces pay for a year, and commanded them to be ready for every need. **29** And he saw that the money failed from his treasures, and that the tributes of the country were small, because of the dissension and plague which he had brought upon the land, to the end that he might take away the laws which had been from the first days; **30** and he feared that he should not have enough as at other times for the charges and the gifts which he gave previously with a liberal hand, and he abounded above the kings that were before him. **31** And he was exceedingly perplexed in his mind, and he determined to go into Persia, and to take the tributes of the countries, and to gather much money. **32** And he left Lysias, an honorable man, and one of the seed royal, to be over the affairs of the king from the river Euphrates to the borders of Egypt, **33** and to bring up his son Antiochus, until he came again. **34** And he delivered to him the half of his forces, and the elephants, and gave him charge of all the things that he would have done, and concerning those who lived in Judea and in Jerusalem, **35** that he should send an army against them, to root out and destroy the strength of Israel, and the remnant of Jerusalem, and to take away their memorial from the place; **36** And that he should make strangers to dwell on all their coasts, and should divide their land to them by lot. **37** And

the king took the half that remained of the forces, and removed from Antioch, from his royal city, the hundred and forty and seventh year; and he passed over the river Euphrates and went through the upper countries. **38** And Lysias chose Ptolemy the son of Dorymenes, and Nicanor, and Gorgias, mighty men of the king's friends; **39** and with them he sent forty thousand footmen, and seven thousand horse, to go into the land of Judah, and to destroy it, according to the word of the king. **40** And they removed with all their army and came and pitched near to Emmaus in the plain country. **41** And the merchants of the country heard the fame of them, and took silver and gold exceedingly much, with fetters, and came into the camp to take the children of Israel for servants: and there were added to them the forces of Syria and of the land of the Philistines. **42** And Judas and his kindred saw that evils were multiplied, and that the forces were encamping in their borders; and they took knowledge of the king's words which he had commanded, to destroy the people and make an end of them; **43** and they said each man to his neighbor, "Let's raise up the ruin of our people, and let's fight for our people and the holy place." **44** And the congregation was gathered together, that they might be ready for battle, and that they might pray, and ask for mercy and compassion. **45** And Jerusalem was without inhabitant as a wilderness, there was none of her offspring that went in or went out; and the sanctuary was trodden down, and the sons of strangers were in the citadel, the Gentiles lodged therein; and joy was taken away from Jacob, and the pipe and the harp ceased. **46** And they gathered themselves together, and came to Mizpeh, near Jerusalem; for in Mizpeh was there a place of prayer previously for Israel. **47** And they fasted that day, and put on sackcloth, and *put* ashes upon their heads, and tore their clothes, **48** and laid open the book of the law, concerning which the Gentiles were wont to inquire, seeking the likenesses of their idols. **49** And they brought the priests' garments, and the first fruits, and the tithes: and they stirred up the Nazarites, who had accomplished their days. **50** And they cried aloud toward heaven, saying, "What will we do with these men, and where will we carry them away? **51** And your holy place is trodden down and profaned, and your priests are in heaviness and brought low. **52** And, behold, the Gentiles are assembled together against us to destroy us: you know what things they imagine against us. **53** How will we be able to stand before them, except you be our help?" **54** And they sounded with the trumpets and cried with a loud voice. **55** And after this Judas appointed leaders of the people, captains of thousands, and captains of hundreds, and captains of fifties, and captains of tens. **56** And he said to those who were building houses, and were betrothing wives, and were planting vineyards, and were fearful, that they should return, each man to his own house, according to the law. **57** And the army removed and encamped upon the south side of Emmaus. **58** And Judas said, "Gird yourselves, and be valiant men, and be in readiness against the morning, that you may fight with these Gentiles, that are assembled together against us to destroy us, and our holy place: **59** for it is better for us to die in battle, than to look upon the evils of our nation and the holy place. **60** Nevertheless, as may be the will in heaven, so will he do."

CHAPTER 4

1 And Gorgias took five thousand footmen, and a thousand chosen horse, and the army removed by night, **2** that it might fall upon the army of the Jews and strike them suddenly: and the men of the citadel were his guides. **3** And Judas heard thereof, and removed, he and the valiant men, that he might strike the king's army which was at Emmaus, **4** while as yet the forces were dispersed from the camp. **5** And Gorgias came into the camp of Judas by night and found no man; and he sought them in the mountains; for he said, These men flee from us. **6** And as soon as it was day, Judas appeared in the plain with three thousand men: however, they didn't have the armor and swords they desired. **7** And they saw the camp of the Gentiles strong *and* fortified, and horsemen compassing it around; and these were expert in war. **8** And Judas said to the men that were with him, Fear you not their multitude, neither be you afraid of their onset. **9** Remember how our fathers were saved in the Red sea, when Pharaoh pursued them with an army. **10** And now let's cry to heaven, if he will have us, and will remember the covenant of our fathers, and destroy this army before our face today: **11** and all the Gentiles will know that there is one who redeems and saves Israel. **12** And the strangers lifted up their eyes and saw them coming near them: **13** and they went out of the camp to battle. And those who were with Judas sounded their trumpets, **14** and

joined battle, and the Gentiles were discomfited, and fled into the plain. **15** But all the hindmost fell by the sword: and they pursued them to Gazara, and to the plains of Idumaea and Azotus and Jamnia, and there fell of them about three thousand men. **16** And Judas and his army returned from pursuing after them, **17** and he said to the people, "Be not greedy of the spoils, inasmuch as there is a battle before us; **18** and Gorgias and his army are near to us in the mountain. But stand you now against our enemies, and fight against them, and afterwards take the spoils with boldness." **19** While Judas was yet making an end of these words, there appeared a part of them looking out from the mountain: **20** and they saw that their army had been put to flight, and that the Jews were burning the camp; for the smoke that was seen declared what was done. **21** But when they perceived these things, they were sore afraid; and perceiving also the army of Judas in the plain ready for battle, **22** they fled all of them into the land of the Philistines. **23** And Judas returned to plunder the camp, and they got much gold, and silver, and blue, and sea purple, and great riches. **24** And they returned home, and sang a song of thanksgiving, and gave praise to heaven; because *his mercy* is good, because his mercy endures forever. **25** And Israel had a great deliverance that day. **26** But the strangers, as many as had escaped, came and told Lysias all the things that had happened: **27** but when he heard thereof, he was confounded and discouraged, because neither had such things as he desired been done to Israel, nor had such things as the king commanded him come to pass. **28** And in the next year he gathered together threescore thousand chosen footmen, and five thousand horse, that he might subdue them. **29** And they came into Idumaea and encamped at Bethsura; and Judas met them with ten thousand men. **30** And he saw that the army was strong, and he prayed and said, Blessed are you, O Savior of Israel, who did quell the onset of the mighty man by the hand of your servant David, and did deliver the army of the Philistines into the hands of Jonathan the son of Saul, and of his armor bearer: **31** shut up this army in the hand of your people Israel, and let them be ashamed for their army and their horsemen: **32** give them faintness of heart, and cause the boldness of their strength to melt away, and let them quake at their destruction: **33** cast them down with the sword of those who love you, and let all that know your name praise you with thanksgiving. **34** And they joined battle; and there fell of the army of Lysias about five thousand men, and they fell down near them. **35** But when Lysias saw that his array was put to flight, and the boldness that had come upon those who were with Judas, and how they were ready either to live or to die nobly, he removed to Antioch, and gathered together hired soldiers, that he might come again into Judea with even a greater company. **36** But Judas and his kindred said, Behold, our enemies are discomfited: let's go up to cleanse the holy place, and to dedicate it afresh. **37** And all the army was gathered together, and they went up to Mount Zion. **38** And they saw the sanctuary laid desolate, and the altar profaned, and the gates burned up, and shrubs growing in the courts as in a forest or as on one of the mountains, and the priests' chambers pulled down; **39** and they tore their clothes, and made great lamentation, and put ashes upon their heads, **40** and fell on their faces to the ground, and blew with the solemn trumpets, and cried toward heaven. **41** Then Judas appointed certain men to fight against those that were in the citadel, until he should have cleansed the holy place. **42** And he chose blameless priests, such as had pleasure in the law: **43** and they cleansed the holy place and bare out the stones of defilement into an unclean place. **44** And they took counsel concerning the altar of burnt offerings, which had been profaned, what they should do with it: **45** and there came into their mind a good counsel, that they should pull it down, lest it should be a reproach to them, because the Gentiles had defiled it: and they pulled down the altar, **46** and laid up the stones in the mountain of the house in a convenient place, until there should come a prophet to give an answer concerning them. **47** And they took whole stones according to the law and built a new altar after the fashion of the former; **48** and they built the holy place, and the inner parts of the house; and they hallowed the courts. **49** And they made the holy vessels new, and they brought the candlestick, and the altar of burnt offerings and of incense, and the table, into the temple. **50** And they burned incense upon the altar, and they lighted the lamps that were upon the candlestick, and they gave light in the temple. **51** And they set loaves upon the table, and spread out the veils, and finished all the works which they made. **52** And they rose up early in the morning, on the five and twentieth day of the ninth month,

which is the month Chislev, in the hundred and forty and eighth year, **53** and offered sacrifice according to the law upon the new altar of burnt offerings which they had made. **54** At what time and on what day the Gentiles had profaned it, even on that *day* was it dedicated afresh, with songs and harps and lutes, and with cymbals. **55** And all the people fell upon their faces, and worshiped, and gave praise to heaven, which had given them good success. **56** And they kept the dedication of the altar eight days, and offered burnt offerings with gladness, and sacrificed a sacrifice of deliverance and praise. **57** And they decked the forefront of the temple with crowns of gold and small shields, and dedicated afresh the gates and the priests' chambers, and made doors for them. **58** And there was exceedingly great gladness among the people, and the reproach of the Gentiles was turned away. **59** And Judas and his kindred and the whole congregation of Israel ordained, that the days of the dedication of the altar should be kept in their seasons from year to year by the space of eight days, from the five and twentieth day of the month Chislev, with gladness and joy. **60** And at that season they built up Mount Zion with high walls and strong towers around, lest perhaps the Gentiles should come and tread them down, as they had done previously. **61** And he set there a force to keep it, and they fortified Bethsura to keep it; that the people might have a stronghold near Idumaea.

CHAPTER 5

1 And it came to pass, when the surrounding Gentiles heard that the altar was built, and the sanctuary dedicated as previously, they were exceedingly angry. **2** And they took counsel to destroy the race of Jacob that was in the midst of them, and they began to kill and destroy among the people. **3** And Judas fought against the children of Esau in Idumaea at Akrabattine, because they besieged Israel: and he struck them with a great slaughter, and brought down their pride, and took their spoils. **4** And he remembered the wickedness of the children of Baean, who were to the people a snare and a stumbling block, lying in wait for them in the ways. **5** And they were shut up by him in the towers; and he encamped against them, and destroyed them utterly, and burned with fire the towers of the place, with all that were therein. **6** And he passed over to the children of Ammon, and found a mighty band,

and much people, with Timotheus for their leader. **7** And he fought many battles with them, and they were discomfited before his face; and he struck them, **8** and got possession of Jazer, and the villages thereof, and returned again into Judea. **9** And the Gentiles that were in Gilead gathered themselves together against the Israelites that were on their borders, to destroy them. And they fled to the stronghold of Dathema, **10** and sent letters to Judas and his kindred, saying, The Gentiles that are around us are gathered together against us to destroy us: **11** and they are preparing to come and get possession of the stronghold whereunto we are fled for refuge, and Timotheus is the leader of their army. **12** Now therefore come and deliver us from their hand, for many of us are fallen. **13** And all our kindred that were in the land of Tubias have been put to death; and they have carried into captivity their wives and their children and their stuff; and they destroyed there about a thousand men. **14** While the letters were yet reading, behold, there came other messengers from Galilee with their clothes torn, bringing a report after this wise, **15** saying, That there were gathered together against them those of Ptolemais, and of Tyre, and of Sidon, and all Galilee of the Gentiles to consume them. **16** Now when Judas and the people heard these words, there assembled together a great congregation, to consult what they should do for their kindred, that were in suffering, and were assaulted of them. **17** And Judas said to Simon his brother, "Choose you out men, and go and deliver your kindred that are in Galilee, but I and Jonathan my brother will go into the land of Gilead." **18** And he left Joseph the son of Zacharias, and Azarias, as leaders of the people, with the remnant of the army, in Judea, for to keep it. **19** And he gave commandment to them, saying, "Take you the charge of this people, and fight no battle with the Gentiles until that we come again." **20** And to Simon were divided three thousand men to go into Galilee, but to Judas eight thousand men *to go* into the land of Gilead. **21** And Simon went into Galilee, and fought many battles with the Gentiles, and the Gentiles were discomfited before him. **22** And he pursued them to the gate of Ptolemais; and there fell of the Gentiles about three thousand men, and he took their spoils. **23** And they took to them those that were in Galilee, and in Arbatta, with their wives and their children, and all that they had, and brought them into Judea with great

gladness. **24** And Judas Maccabaeus and his brother Jonathan passed over Jordan, and went three days' journey in the wilderness; **25** and they met with the Nabathaeans, and these met them in a peaceful manner, and told them all things that had befallen their kindred in the land of Gilead: **26** and how that many of them were shut up in Bosora, and Bosor, and Alema, Casphor, Maked, and Carnaim; all these cities are strong and great: **27** and how that they were shut up in the rest of the cities of the land of Gilead, and that tomorrow they have appointed to encamp against the strongholds, and to take them, and to destroy all these men in one day. **28** And Judas and his army turned suddenly by the way of the wilderness to Bosora; and he took the city and killed all the males with the edge of the sword, and took all their spoils, and burned the city with fire. **29** And he left from there by night and went until he came to the stronghold. **30** And the morning came, and they lifted up their eyes, and, behold, much people which could not be counted, bearing ladders and engines of war, to take the stronghold; and they were fighting against them. **31** And Judas saw that the battle was begun, and that the cry of the city went up to heaven, with trumpets and a great sound, **32** and he said to the men of his army, Fight this day for your kindred. **33** And he went out behind them in three companies, and they sounded with their trumpets, and cried out in prayer. **34** And the army of Timotheus perceived that it was Maccabaeus, and they fled from before him: and he struck them with a great slaughter; and there fell of them on that day about eight thousand men. **35** And he turned away to Mizpeh and fought against it, and took it, and killed all the males thereof, and took the spoils thereof, and burned it with fire. **36** From there he left, and took Casphor, Maked, Bosor, and the other cities of the land of Gilead. **37** Now after these things Timotheus gathered another army and encamped near Raphon beyond the brook. **38** And Judas sent men to spy on the army; and they brought him word, saying, All the Gentiles that are around us are gathered together to them, an exceedingly great army. **39** And they have hired Arabians to help them, and are encamping beyond the brook, ready to come against you to battle. And Judas went to meet them. **40** And Timotheus said to the captains of his army, when Judas and his army drew near to the brook of water, If he pass over first to us, we will not be able to withstand him; for he will mightily prevail against us: **41** but if he be afraid, and encamp beyond the river, we will cross over to him, and prevail against him. **42** Now when Judas came near to the brook of water, he caused the scribes of the people to remain by the brook, and gave commandment to them, saying, "Suffer no man to encamp, but let all come to the battle." **43** And he crossed over the first against them, and all the people after him: and all the Gentiles were discomfited before his face, and cast away their arms, and fled to the temple at Carnaim. **44** And they took the city, and burned the temple with fire, together with all that were therein. And Carnaim was subdued, neither could they stand any longer before the face of Judas. **45** And Judas gathered together all Israel, those who were in the land of Gilead, from the least to the greatest, and their wives, and their children, and their stuff, an exceedingly great army, that they might come into the land of Judah. **46** And they came as far as Ephron, and this same city was great, *and it was* in the way as they should go, exceedingly strong: they could not turn away from it on the right hand or on the left but must needs pass through the midst of it. **47** And they of the city shut them out and stopped up the gates with stones. **48** And Judas sent to them with words of peace, saying, "We will pass through your land to go into our own land, and none will do you any hurt, we will only pass by on our feet." And they would not open to him. **49** And Judas commanded proclamation to be made in the army, that each man should encamp in the place where he was. **50** And the men of the army encamped and fought against the city all that day and all that night, and the city was delivered into his hands; **51** and he destroyed all the males with the edge of the sword, and razed the city, and took the spoils thereof, and passed through the city over those who were slain. **52** And they went over Jordan into the great plain near Bethshan. **53** And Judas gathered together those that lagged behind, and encouraged the people all the way through, until he came into the land of Judah. **54** And they went up to mount Zion with gladness and joy, and offered whole burnt offerings, because not so much as one of them was slain until they returned in peace. **55** And in the days when Judas and Jonathan were in the land of Gilead, and Simon his brother in Galilee before Ptolemais, **56** Joseph the son of Zacharias, and Azarias, rulers of the army, heard of their exploits and of the war, what

things they had done; **57** and they said, "Let's also get us a name, and let's go fight against the Gentiles that are around us." **58** And they gave charge to the men of the army that was with them and went toward Jamnia. **59** And Gorgias and his men came out of the city to meet them in battle. **60** And Joseph and Azarias were put to flight and were pursued to the borders of Judea; and there fell on that day of the people of Israel about two thousand men. **61** And there was a great overthrow among the people, because they didn't listen to Judas and his kindred, thinking to do some exploit. **62** But they were not of the seed of those men, by whose hand deliverance was given to Israel. **63** And the man Judas and his kindred were glorified exceedingly in the sight of all Israel, and of all the Gentiles, wherever their name was heard of; **64** and men gathered together to them, acclaiming them. **65** And Judas and his kindred went out and fought against the children of Esau in the land toward the south; and he struck Hebron and the villages thereof, and pulled down the strongholds thereof, and burned the towers thereof. **66** And he left to go into the land of the Philistines, and he went through Samaria. **67** In that day certain priests, desiring to do exploits there, were slain in battle, when he went out to battle unadvisedly. **68** And Judas turned toward Azotus, to the land of the Philistines, and pulled down their altars, and burned the carved images of their gods with fire, and took the plunder of their cities, and returned into the land of Judah.

CHAPTER 6

1 And king Antiochus was journeying through the upper countries; and he heard say, that in Elymais in Persia there was a city renowned for riches, for silver and gold; **2** and that the temple which was in it was rich exceedingly, and that therein were golden shields, and breastplates, and arms, which Alexander, son of Philip, the Macedonian king, who reigned first among the Greeks, left behind there. **3** And he came and sought to take the city, and to pillage it; and he was not able, because the thing was known to them of the city, **4** and they rose up against him to battle: and he fled, and left from there with great heaviness, to return to Babylon. **5** And there came one bringing him tidings into Persia, that the armies, which went against the land of Judah, had been put to flight; **6** and that Lysias went first with a strong army, and was put to shame before them; and that they had waxed strong by reason of arms and power, and with store of spoils, which they took from the armies that they had cut off; 7 and that they had pulled down the abomination which he had built upon the altar that was in Jerusalem; and that they had compassed about the sanctuary with high walls, as before, and Bethsura, his city. 8 And it came to pass, when the king heard these words, he was astonished and moved exceedingly: and he laid him down upon his bed, and fell sick for grief, because it had not befallen him as he looked for. 9 And he was there many days, because great grief was renewed upon him, and he made account that he should die. 10 And he called for all his friends, and said to them, Sleep departs from my eyes, and my heart fails for care. 11 And I said in my heart, To what suffering am I come, and how great a flood is it, wherein I now am! for I was gracious and beloved in my power. 12 But now I remember the evils which I did at Jerusalem, and that I took all the vessels of silver and gold that were therein and sent out to destroy the inhabitants of Judah without a cause. 13 I perceive that on this account these evils are come upon me, and, behold, I perish through great grief in a strange land. 14 And he called for Philip, one of his Friends, and set him over all his kingdom, 15 and gave him his diadem, and his robe, and his signet ring, to the end he should bring Antiochus his son, and nourish him up that he might be king. 16 And king Antiochus died there in the hundred and forty and ninth year. 17 And Lysias knew that the king was dead, and he set up Antiochus his son to reign, whom he had nourished up being young, and he called his name Eupator. 18 And those who were in the citadel shut up Israel around the sanctuary, and sought always their hurt, and the strengthening of the Gentiles. 19 And Judas thought to destroy them and called all the people together to besiege them. 20 And they were gathered together, and besieged them in the hundred and fiftieth year, and he made mounds to shoot from, and engines of war. 21 And there came out some of those who were shut up, and there were joined to them certain ungodly men of Israel. 22 And they went to the king, and said, "How long will you not execute judgement, and avenge our kindred? 23 We were willing to serve your father, and to walk after his words, and to follow his commandments; 24 and for this cause the children of our people besieged the citadel and were alienated from us; but as many of us as they could light on they killed and plundered our inheritances. 25 And not against us only did they stretch out their hand, but also against all their borders. 26 And, behold, they are encamped this day against the citadel at Jerusalem, to take it: and the sanctuary and Bethsura have they fortified. 27 And if you are not beforehand with them quickly, they will do greater things than these, and you will not be able to control them." 28 And when the king heard this, he was angry, and gathered together all his friends, *even the* rulers of his army, and those who were over the horse. 29 And there came to him from other kingdoms, and from isles of the sea, bands of hired soldiers. 30 And the number of his forces was a hundred thousand footmen, and twenty thousand horsemen, and two and thirty elephants trained for war. 31 And they went through Idumaea, and encamped against Bethsura, and fought against it many days, and made engines of war; and they *of Bethsura* came out, and burned them with fire, and fought valiantly. 32 And Judas left from the citadel, and encamped at Bethzacharias, near the king's camp. 33 And the king rose early in the morning and sent his army at full speed along the road to Bethzacharias, and his forces made them ready to battle, and sounded with the trumpets. 34 And they showed the elephants the blood of grapes and mulberries, that they might prepare them for the battle. 35 And they divided the beasts among the phalanxes, and they set by each elephant a thousand men armed with coats of mail, and helmets of brass on their heads; and for each beast were appointed five hundred chosen horsemen. 36 These were ready beforehand, wherever the beast was; and wherever the beast went, they went with him; they departed not from him. 37 And towers of wood were upon them, strong *and* covered, one upon each beast, girded fast upon him with cunning contrivances; and upon each *beast* were two and thirty valiant men that fought upon them, beside his Indian 38 (and the residue of the horsemen he set on this side and that side at the two parts of the army), striking terror *into the enemy,* and protected by the phalanxes. 39 Now when the sun shone upon the shields of gold and brass, the mountains shone therewith, and blazed like torches of fire. 40 And a part of the king's army was spread upon the high mountains, and some on the low ground, and they went on firmly and in order. 41 And all that heard the noise of their multitude, and the marching of the multitude, and the rattling of the arms, did quake: for the army was exceedingly great and strong. **42** And Judas and his army drew near for battle, and there fell of the king's army six hundred men. **43** And Eleazar, who was *called* Avaran, saw one of the beasts armed with royal breastplates, and he was higher than all the beasts, and the king seemed to be upon him; **44** and he gave himself to deliver his people, and to get him an everlasting name; **45** and he ran upon him courageously into the midst of the phalanx, and killed on the right hand and on the left, and they parted asunder from him on this side and on that. **46** And he crept under the elephant, and thrust him from beneath, and killed him; and the *elephant*fell to the earth upon him, and he died there. **47** And they saw the strength of the kingdom, and the fierce onset of the army, and turned away from them. **48** But they of the king's army went up to Jerusalem to meet them, and the king encamped toward Judea, and toward Mount Zion. **49** And he made peace with them of Bethsura; and he came out of the city, because they had no food there to endure the siege, because it was a Sabbath to the land. **50** And the king took Bethsura and appointed a garrison there to keep it. **51** And he encamped against the sanctuary many days; and set there mounds to shoot from, and engines of war, and instruments for casting fire and stones, and pieces to cast darts, and slings. **52** And they also made engines against their engines and fought for many days. **53** But there were no food in the sanctuary, because it was the seventh year, and those who fled for safety into Judea from among the Gentiles had eaten up the residue of the store; **54** and there were but a few left in the sanctuary, because the famine prevailed against them, and they were scattered, each man to his own place. **55** And Lysias heard say, that Philip, whom Antiochus the king, whiles he was yet alive, appointed to nourish up his son Antiochus, that he might be king, **56** was returned from Persia and Media, and with him the forces that went with the king, and that he was seeking to take to him the government. **57** And he made haste, and gave consent to depart; and he said to the king and the leaders of the army and to the men, We decay daily, and our food is scant, and the place where we encamp is strong, and the affairs of the kingdom lie upon us: **58** now therefore let's give the right hand to these men, and make peace with them and with all their nation, **59** and covenant with them, that they will walk after their own laws, as previously: for because of their laws which we abolished they were angered, and did all these things. **60** And the saying pleased the king and the princes, and he sent to them to make peace; and they accepted thereof. **61** And the king and the princes swore to them: immediately they came out from the stronghold. **62** And the king entered into Mount Zion; and he saw the strength of the place and set at nothing the oath which he had sworn and gave commandment to pull down the wall round about. **63** And he left in haste, and returned to Antioch, and found Philip master of the city; and he fought against him and took the city by force.

CHAPTER 7

1 In the hundred and one and fiftieth year Demetrius the son of Seleucus came out from Rome and went up with a few men to a city by the sea and reigned there. **2** And it came to pass, when he would go into the house of the kingdom of his fathers, that the army laid hands on Antiochus and Lysias, to bring them to him. **3** And the thing was known to him, and he said, show me not their faces. **4** And the army killed them. And Demetrius sat upon the throne of his kingdom. **5** And there came to him all the lawless and ungodly men of Israel; and Alcimus was their leader, desiring to be high priest; **6** and they accused the people to the king, saying, Judas and his kindred have destroyed all your friends, and have scattered us from our own land. **7** Now therefore send a man whom you trust and let him go and see all the havock which he has made of us, and of the king's country, and *how* he has punished them and all that helped them. **8** And the king chose Bacchides, one of the king's friends, who was ruler in the country beyond the river, and was a great man in the kingdom, and faithful to the king. **9** And he sent him, and that ungodly Alcimus, and made sure to him the high priesthood, and he commanded him to take vengeance upon the children of Israel. **10** And they went and came with a great army into the land of Judah, and he sent messengers to Judas and his kindred with words of peace deceitfully. **11** And they gave no heed to their words; for they saw that they were come with a great army. **12** And there were gathered together to Alcimus and Bacchides a company of scribes, to seek for justice. **13** And the Hasidaeans were the first among the children of Israel that sought peace of them; **14** for they said, "One that is a priest of the seed of Aaron is come with the forces, and he will do us no wrong." **15** And he spoke with them words of peace, and swore to them, saying, "We will seek the hurt neither of you nor your friends." **16** And they gave him credence: and he laid hands on threescore men of them, and killed them in one day, according to the word which *the psalmist* wrote, **17** The flesh of your saints *did they cast out, and* their blood did they shed around Jerusalem; And there was no man to bury them. **18** And the fear and the dread of them fell upon all the people, for they said, "There is neither truth nor judgement in them; for they have broken the covenant and the oath which they swore." **19** And Bacchides left from Jerusalem and encamped in Bezeth; and he sent and took away many of the deserters that were with him, and certain of the people, and he killed them, and *cast them* into the great pit. **20** And he made sure the country to Alcimus and left with him a force to aid him; and Bacchides went away to the king. **21** And Alcimus strove for his high priesthood. **22** And there were gathered to him all those who troubled their people, and they got the mastery of the land of Judah and did great hurt in Israel. **23** And Judas saw all the mischief that Alcimus and his company had done among the children of Israel, *even* above the Gentiles, **24** and he went out into all the surrounding coasts of Judea and took vengeance on the men that had deserted from him, and they were restrained from going out into the country. **25** But when Alcimus saw that Judas and his company waxed strong and knew that he was not able to withstand them, he returned to the king, and brought evil accusations against them. **26** And the king sent Nicanor, one of his honorable princes, a man that hated Israel and was their enemy, and commanded him to destroy the people. **27** And Nicanor came to Jerusalem with a great army; and he sent to Judas and his kindred deceitfully with words of peace, saying, **28** Let there be no battle between me and you; I will come with a few men, that I may see your faces in peace. **29** And he came to Judas, and they saluted one another peaceably. And the enemies were ready to take away Judas by violence. **30** And the thing was known to Judas, *to wit,* that he came to him with deceit, and he was sore afraid of him, and would see his face no more. **31** And Nicanor knew that his counsel was discovered; and he went out to meet Judas in battle beside Capharsalama;

32 and there fell of Nicanor's side about five hundred men, and they fled into the city of David. **33** And after these things Nicanor went up to Mount Zion: and there came some of the priests out of the sanctuary, and some of the elders of the people, to salute him peaceably, and to show him the whole burned sacrifice that was being offered for the king. **34** And he mocked them, and laughed at them, and entreated them shamefully, and spoke haughtily, **35** and swore in a rage, saying, Unless Judas and his army be now delivered into my hands, it will be that, if I come again in peace, I will burn up this house: and he went out in a great rage. **36** And the priests entered in and stood before the altar and the temple; and they wept, and said, **37** You did choose this house to be called by your name, to be a house of prayer and supplication for your people: **38** take vengeance on this man and his army, and let them fall by the sword: remember their blasphemies, and suffer them not to live any longer. **39** And Nicanor went out from Jerusalem, and encamped in Bethhoron, and there met him the army of Syria. **40** And Judas encamped in Adasa with three thousand men: and Judas prayed and said, **41** When those who came from the king blasphemed, your angel went out, and struck among them a hundred and fourscore and five thousand. **42** Even so discomfit you this army before us today and let all the rest know that he has spoken wickedly against your sanctuary and judge you him according to his wickedness. **43** And on the thirteenth day of the month Adar the armies joined battle: and Nicanor's army was discomfited, and he himself was the first to fall in the battle. **44** Now when his army saw that Nicanor was fallen, they cast away their arms, and fled. **45** And they pursued after them a day's journey from Adasa until you come to Gazara, and they sounded an alarm after them with the solemn trumpets. **46** And they came out of all the surrounding villages of Judea and closed them in; and these turned them back on those, and they all fell by the sword, and there was not one of them left. **47** And they took the spoils, and the booty, and they struck off Nicanor's head, and his right hand, which he stretched out so haughtily, and brought them, and hanged them up beside Jerusalem. **48** And the people were exceedingly glad, and they kept that day as a day of great gladness. **49** And they ordained to keep this day year by year, *to wit,* the thirteenth day of Adar. **50** And the land of Judah had rest a little while.

CHAPTER 8

1 And Judas heard of the fame of the Romans, that they are valiant men, and have pleasure in all that join themselves to them and make friends with all such as come to them, **2** and that they are valiant men. And they told him of their wars and exploits which they do among the Gauls, and how that they conquered them, and brought them under tribute; **3** and what things they did in the land of Spain, that they might become masters of the mines of silver and gold which were there; **4** and how that by their policy and persistence they conquered all the place (and the place was exceedingly far from them), and the kings that came against them from the uttermost part of the earth, until they had discomfited them, and struck them very sore; and how the rest give them tribute year by year: **5** and Philip, and Perseus, king of Chittim, and those who lifted up themselves against them, did they discomfit in battle, and conquered them: **6** Antiochus also, the great king of Asia, who came against them to battle, having a hundred and twenty elephants, with horse, and chariots, and an exceedingly great army, and he was discomfited by them, **7** and they took him alive, and appointed that both he and such as reigned after him should give them a great tribute, and should give hostages, and a parcel *of land, to wit,* **8** the country of India, and Media, and Lydia, and of the goodlie of their countries; and they took them from him, and gave them to king Eumenes: **9** and how they of Greece took counsel to come and destroy them; **10** and the thing was known to them, and they sent against them a captain, and fought against them, and many of them fell down wounded to death, and they made captive their wives and their children, and plundered them, and conquered their land, and pulled down their strongholds, and plundered them, and brought them into bondage to this day: **11** and the residue of the kingdoms and of the isles, as many as rose up against them at any time, they destroyed and made them to be their servants; **12** but with their friends and such as relied upon them they stayed friends; and they conquered the kingdoms that were near and those that were far off, and all that heard of their fame were afraid of them: **13** moreover, whoever they will to help and to make kings, these do they make kings; and whoever they will, do they depose; and they

are exalted exceedingly: **14** and for all this none of them did ever put on a diadem, neither did they clothe themselves with purple, to be magnified by it: **15** and how they had made for themselves a senate house, and day by day three hundred and twenty men sat in council, consulting always for the people, to the end they might be well ordered: **16** and how they commit their government to one man by year, that he should rule over them, and be lord over all their country, and all are obedient to that one, and there is neither envy nor emulation among them. **17** And Judas chose Eupolemus the son of John, the son of Accos, and Jason the son of Eleazar, and sent them to Rome, to establish friendship and alliance with them, **18** and that they should take the yoke from them; for they saw that the kingdom of the Greeks did keep Israel in bondage. **19** And they went to Rome (and the way was exceedingly long), and they entered into the senate house, and answered and said, **20** Judas, who is also *called* Maccabaeus, and his kindred, and the people of the Jews, have sent us to you, to make a confederacy and peace with you, and that we might be registered your allies and friends. **21** And the thing was well-pleasing in their sight. **22** And this is the copy of the writing which they wrote back again on tables of brass, and sent to Jerusalem, that it might be with them there for a memorial of peace and confederacy: **23** Good success be to the Romans, and to the nation of the Jews, by sea and by land forever: the sword also and the enemy be far from them. **24** But if war arise for Rome first, or any of their allies in all their dominion, **25** the nation of the Jews will help them as allies, as the occasion will prescribe to them, with all their heart: **26** and to those who make war upon them they will not give, neither supply, food, arms, money, or ships, as it has seemed good to Rome, and they will keep their ordinances without taking anything therefore. **27** In the same manner, moreover, if war come first upon the nation of the Jews, the Romans will help them as allies with all their soul, as the occasion will prescribe to them: **28** and to those who are allies *with their foes* there will not be given food, arms, money, or ships, as it has seemed good to Rome; and they will keep these ordinances, and that without deceit. **29** According to these words have the Romans made a covenant with the people of the Jews. **30** But if hereafter the one party and the other will take counsel to add or diminish anything, they will do it at their pleasure, and whatever they will add or take away will be established. **31** And as touching the evils which king Demetrius does to them, we have written to him, saying, "Why have you made your yoke heavy upon our friends and allies the Jews? **32** If therefore they plead any more against you, we will do them justice, and fight with you by sea and by land."

CHAPTER 9

1 And Demetrius heard that Nicanor was fallen with his forces in battle, and he sent Bacchides and Alcimus again into the land of Judah a second time, and the right wing *of his army* with them: **2** and they went by the way that leads to Gilgal, and encamped against Mesaloth, which is in Arbela, and got possession of it, and destroyed much people. **3** And the first month of the hundred and fifty and second year they encamped against Jerusalem: **4** and they left, and went to Berea, with twenty thousand footmen and two thousand horses. **5** And Judas was encamped at Elasa, and three thousand chosen men with him: **6** and they saw the multitude of the forces, that they were many, and they feared exceedingly: and many slipped away out of the army; there were not left of them more than eight hundred men. **7** And Judas saw that his army slipped away, and that the battle pressed upon him, and he was sore troubled in heart, for that he had no time to gather them together, and he waxed faint. **8** And he said to those who were left, "Let's arise and go up against our adversaries, if perhaps we may be able to fight with them." **9** And they would have dissuaded him, saying, "We will in no wise be able: but let's rather save our lives now: let's return again, *we* and our kindred, and fight against them: but we are few." **10** And Judas said, "Let it not be so that I should do this thing, to flee from them: and if our time is come, let's die in a manly way for our kindred's sake, and not leave a cause of reproach against our glory." **11** And the army went from the camp, and stood to encounter them, and the horse was parted into two companies, and the slingers and the archers went before the army, and all the mighty men that fought in the front of the battle. **12** But Bacchides was in the right wing; and the phalanx drew near on the two parts, and they blew with their trumpets. **13** And the men of Judas' side, even they sounded with their trumpets, and the earth shook with the shout of the armies, and the battle was joined, and continued from morning until evening. **14** And Judas saw that Bacchides and the strength of his army were on the right side, and there went with him all that were brave in heart, **15** and the right wing was discomfited by them, and he pursued after them to the mount Azotus. **16** And those who were on the left wing saw that the right wing was discomfited, and they turned and followed upon the footsteps of Judas and of those that were with him: **17** and the battle waxed sore, and many on both parts fell wounded to death. **18** And Judas fell, and the rest fled. **19** And Jonathan and Simon took Judas their brother and buried him in the sepulcher of his fathers at Modin. **20** And they mourned him, and all Israel made great lamentation for him, and mourned many days, and said, **21** How is the mighty fallen, the savior of Israel! **22** And the rest of the acts of Judas, and his wars, and the valiant deeds which he did, and his greatness, they are not written; for they were exceedingly many. **23** And it came to pass after the death of Judas, that the lawless put out their heads in all the coasts of Israel, and all those who did iniquity rose up **24** (in those days there was an exceedingly great famine), and the country went over with them. **25** And Bacchides chose out the ungodly men and made them lords of the country. **26** And they sought out and searched for the friends of Judas, and brought them to Bacchides, and he took vengeance on them, and used them despitefully. **27** And there was great suffering in Israel, such as was not since the time that no prophet appeared to them. **28** And all the friends of Judas were gathered together, and they said to Jonathan, **29** Since your brother Judas has died, we have no man like him to go out against our enemies and Bacchides, and among them of our nation that hate us. **30** Now therefore we have chosen you this day to be our prince and leader in his stead, that you may fight our battles. **31** And Jonathan took the governance upon him at that time and rose up in the stead of his brother Judas. **32** And Bacchides knew it, and he sought to kill him. **33** And Jonathan, and Simon his brother, and all that were with him, knew it; and they fled into the wilderness of Tekoah, and encamped by the water of the pool Asphar. **34** And Bacchides knew it on the Sabbath day, and came, he and all his army, over Jordan. **35** And *Jonathan* sent his brother, a leader of the multitude, and implored his friends the Nabathaeans, that they might leave with them their baggage, which was much. **36** And the children of Jambri came out of

Medaba, and took John, and all that he had, and went their way with it. **37** But after these things they brought word to Jonathan and Simon his brother, that the children of Jambri were making a great marriage and were bringing the bride from Nadabath with a great train, a daughter of one of the great nobles of Canaan. **38** And they remembered John their brother, and went up, and hid themselves under the covert of the mountain: **39** and they lifted up their eyes, and saw, and, behold, a great ado and much baggage: and the bridegroom came out, and his friends and his kindred, to meet them with timbrels, and minstrels, and many weapons. **40** And they rose up against them from their ambush, and killed them, and many fell wounded to death, and the remnant fled into the mountain, and they took all their spoils. **41** And the marriage was turned into mourning, and the voice of their minstrels into lamentation. **42** And they avenged fully the blood of their brother and turned back to the marsh of Jordan. **43** And Bacchides heard it, and he came on the Sabbath day to the banks of Jordan with a great army. **44** And Jonathan said to his company, "Let's stand up now and fight for our lives, for it is not *with us* today, as yesterday and the day before. **45** For, behold, the battle is before us and behind us; moreover, the water of the Jordan is on this side and on that side, and marsh and wood; and there is no place to escape. **46** Now therefore cry to heaven, that you may be delivered out of the hand of your enemies." **47** And the battle was joined, and Jonathan stretched out his hand to strike Bacchides, and he turned away back from him. **48** And Jonathan and those who were with him leapt into the Jordan and swam over to the other side: and they didn't pass over Jordan against them. **49** And there fell of Bacchides' company that day about a thousand men; **50** and he returned to Jerusalem. And they built strong cities in Judea, the stronghold that was in Jericho, and Emmaus, and Bethhoron, and Bethel, and Timnath, Pharathon, and Tephon, with high walls and gates and bars. **51** And in them he set a garrison, to vex Israel. **52** And he fortified the city Bethsura, and Gazara, and the citadel, and put forces in them, and store of food. **53** And he took the sons of the chief men of the country for hostages and put them in ward in the citadel at Jerusalem. **54** And in the hundred and fifty and third year, in the second month, Alcimus commanded to pull down the wall of the inner court of the

sanctuary; he pulled down also the works of the prophets; **55** and he began to pull down. At that time was Alcimus stricken, and his works were hindered; and his mouth was stopped, and he was taken with a palsy, and he could no more speak anything and give order concerning his house. **56** And Alcimus died at that time with great torment. **57** And Bacchides saw that Alcimus was dead, and he returned to the king: and the land of Judah had rest two years. **58** And all the lawless men took counsel, saying, Behold, Jonathan and they of his part are dwelling at ease, and in security: now therefore we will bring Bacchides, and he will lay hands on them all in one night. **59** And they went and consulted with him. **60** And he went, and came with a great army, and sent letters privily to all his allies that were in Judea, that they should lay hands on Jonathan and those that were with him: and they could not, because their counsel was known to them. **61** And *those who were of Jonathan's part* laid hands on about fifty of the men of the country, that were authors of the wickedness, and he killed them. **62** And Jonathan, and Simon, and those who were with him, got them away to Bethbasi, which is in the wilderness, and he built up that which had been pulled down thereof, and they made it strong. **63** And Bacchides knew it, and he gathered together all his multitude, and sent word to those who were of Judea. **64** And he went and encamped against Bethbasi, and fought against it many days, and made engines of war. **65** And Jonathan left his brother Simon in the city, and went out into the country, and he went with a few men. **66** And he struck Odomera and his kindred, and the children of Phasiron in their tent. **67** And they began to strike them, and to go up with their forces. And Simon and those who were with him went out of the city, and set on fire the engines of war, **68** and fought against Bacchides, and he was discomfited by them, and they afflicted him sore; for his counsel was in vain, and his inroad. **69** And they were very angry with the lawless men that gave him counsel to come into the country, and they killed many of them. And he took counsel to depart into his own land. **70** And Jonathan had knowledge thereof, and sent ambassadors to him, to the end that they should make peace with him, and that he should restore to them the captives. **71** And he accepted the thing, and did according to his words, and swore to him that he would not seek his hurt all the days of his life. **72** And he restored to him the captives which he had taken previously out of the land of Judah, and he returned and departed into his own land, and came not any more into their borders. 73 And the sword ceased from Israel. And Jonathan lived at Michmash; and Jonathan began to judge the people; and he destroyed the ungodly out of Israel.

CHAPTER 10

1 And in the hundred and sixtieth year Alexander Epiphanes, the son of Antiochus, went up and took possession of Ptolemais: and they received him, and he reigned there. 2 And king Demetrius heard thereof, and he gathered together exceedingly great forces, and went out to meet him in battle. 3 And Demetrius sent letters to Jonathan with words of peace, so as to magnify him. 4 For he said, let's go beforehand to make peace with them, before he makes peace with Alexander against us: 5 for he will remember all the evils that we have done against him, and to his kindred and to his nation. 6 And he gave him authority to gather together forces, and to provide arms, and that he should be his ally: and he commanded that they should deliver up to him the hostages that were in the citadel. 7 And Jonathan came to Jerusalem and read the letters in the audience of all the people, and of those who were in the citadel: 8 and they were sore afraid, when they heard that the king had given him authority to gather together an army. 9 And they of the citadel delivered up the hostages to Jonathan, and he restored them to their parents. 10 And Jonathan lived in Jerusalem and began to build and renew the city. 11 And he commanded those who did the work to build the walls and Mount Zion round about with square stones for defense; and they did so. 12 And the strangers, that were in the strongholds which Bacchides had built, fled away; 13 and each man left his place, and departed into his own land. 14 Only at Bethsura were there left certain of those that had forsaken the law and the commandments; for it was a place of refuge to them. 15 And king Alexander heard all the promises which Demetrius had sent to Jonathan: and they told him of the battles and the valiant deeds which he and his kindred had done, and of the toils which they had endured; 16 And he said, "Will we find such another man? And now we will make him our friend and ally." 17 And he wrote letters, and sent them to him, according to these words, saying, 18 King Alexander to his brother Jonathan, greeting: 19 We have heard of you, that you are a mighty man of valor, and meet to be our friend. 20 And now we have appointed you this day to be high priest of your nation, and to be called the king's friend (and he sent to him a purple robe and a crown of gold), and to take our part, and to keep friendship with us. 21 And Jonathan put on the holy garments in the seventh month of the hundred and sixtieth year, at the feast of tabernacles, and he gathered together forces, and provided arms in abundance. 22 And Demetrius heard these things, and he was grieved, and said, 23 What is this that we have done, that Alexander has been beforehand with us in establishing friendship with the Jews, to strengthen himself? 24 I also will write to them words of encouragement and of honor and of gifts, that they may be with me to aid me. 25 And he sent to them according to these words: King Demetrius to the nation of the Jews, greeting: 26 Forasmuch as you have kept your covenants with us, and continued in our friendship, and have not joined yourselves to our enemies, we have heard of this, and are glad. 27 And now continue you still to keep faith with us, and we will recompense to you good things in return for your dealings with us, 28 and will grant you many immunities, and give you gifts. 29 And now do I free you, and release all the Jews, from the tributes, and from the customs of salt, and from the crowns. 30 And instead of the third part of the seed, and instead of the half of the fruit of the trees, which falls to me to receive, I release it from this day and from now on, so that I will not take it from the land of Judah, and from the three governments which are added thereto from the country of Samaria and Galilee, from this day out and for all time. 31 And let Jerusalem be holy and free, and her borders; the tenths and the tolls *also*. 32 I yield up also my authority over the citadel which is at Jerusalem, and give it to the high priest, that he may appoint in it such men as he will choose to keep it. 33 And every soul of the Jews, that has been carried captive from the land of Judah into any part of my kingdom, I set at liberty without price; and let all remit the tributes of their cattle also. 34 And all the feasts, and the Sabbaths, and new moons, and appointed days, and three days before a feast, and three days after a feast, let them all be days of immunity and release for all the Jews that are in my kingdom. 35 And no man will have authority to exact from any of them, or to

trouble them concerning any matter. **36** And let there be enrolled among the king's forces about thirty thousand men of the Jews, and pay will be given to them, as belongs to all the king's forces. **37** And of them some will be placed in the king's great strongholds, and some of them will be placed over the affairs of the kingdom, which are of trust: and let those that are over them, and their rulers, be of themselves, and let them walk after their own laws, even as the king has commanded in the land of Judah. **38** And the three governments that have been added to Judea from the country of Samaria, let them be added to Judea, that they may be reckoned to be under one, that they may not obey other authority than the high priest's. **39** As for Ptolemais, and the land pertaining thereto, I have given it as a gift to the sanctuary that is at Jerusalem, for the expenses that befit the sanctuary. **40** And I give every year fifteen thousand shekels of silver from the king's revenues from the places that are convenient. **41** And all the overplus, which those who manage the king's affairs paid not in as in the first years, they will give from now on toward the works of the house. **42** And beside this, the five thousand shekels of silver, which they received from the uses of the sanctuary from the revenue year by year, this also is released, because it appertains to the priests that minister. **43** And whoever will flee to the temple that is at Jerusalem, and *be found* within all the borders thereof, whether one owe moneys to the king, or any other matter, let them go free, and all that they have in my kingdom. **44** And for the building and renewing of the works of the sanctuary the expense will be given also out of the king's revenue. **45** And for the building of the walls of Jerusalem, and the fortifying thereof round about, will the expense be given also out of the king's revenue, and for the building of the walls in Judea. **46** Now when Jonathan and the people heard these words, they gave no credence to them, nor received them, because they remembered the great evil which he had done in Israel, and that he had afflicted them very sore. **47** And they were well pleased with Alexander, because he was the first that spoke words of peace to them, and they were allies with him always. **48** And king Alexander gathered together great forces and encamped near Demetrius. **49** And the two kings joined battle, and the army of Alexander fled; and Demetrius followed after him and prevailed against them. **50** And he strengthened the battle exceedingly until the sun went down: and Demetrius fell that day. **51** And Alexander sent ambassadors to Ptolemy king of Egypt according to these words, saying, **52** Forasmuch as I am returned to my kingdom, and am set on the throne of my fathers, and have gotten the dominion, and have overthrown Demetrius, and have gotten possession of our country; **53** yes, I joined the battle with him, and he and his army were discomfited by us, and we sat upon the throne of his kingdom: **54** now also let's make friends with one another, and give me now your daughter to wife: and I will be joined with you, and will give both you and her gifts worthy of you. **55** And Ptolemy the king answered, saying, Happy is the day wherein you did return into the land of your fathers, and did sit on the throne of their kingdom. **56** And now I will do to you, as you have written: but meet me at Ptolemais, that we may see one another; and I will join with you, even as you have said. **57** And Ptolemy went out of Egypt, himself and Cleopatra his daughter, and came to Ptolemais in the hundred and threescore and second year: **58** and king Alexander met him, and he bestowed on him his daughter Cleopatra, and celebrated her wedding at Ptolemais with great pomp, as the manner of kings is. **59** And king Alexander wrote to Jonathan, that he should come to meet him. **60** And he went with pomp to Ptolemais, and met the two kings, and gave them and their friends silver and gold, and many gifts, and found favor in their sight. **61** And there were gathered together against him certain pestilent fellows out of Israel, men that were transgressors of the law, to complain against him: and the king gave no heed to them. **62** And the king commanded, and they took off Jonathan's garments, and clothed him in purple: and so they did. **63** And the king made him sit with him, and said to his princes, Go out with him into the midst of the city, and make proclamation, that no man complain against him of any matter, and let no man trouble him for any manner of cause. **64** And it came to pass, when those who complained against him saw his glory according as *the herald* made proclamation, and *saw* him clothed in purple, they all fled away. **65** And the king gave him honor, and wrote him among his chief friends, and made him a captain, and governor of a province. **66** And Jonathan returned to Jerusalem with peace and gladness. **67** And in the hundred and threescore and fifth year came Demetrius, son of Demetrius, out of Crete into the land of his fathers: **68** and king Alexander heard thereof, and he grieved exceedingly, and returned to Antioch. **69** And Demetrius appointed Apollonius, who was over Coelesyria, and he gathered together a great army, and encamped in Jamnia, and sent to Jonathan the high priest, saying, **70** "You alone lift up yourself against us, but I am had in derision and in reproach because of you. And why do you vaunt your power against us in the mountains? **71** Now therefore, if you trust in your forces, come down to us into the plain, and there let's try the matter together; for with me is the power of the cities. **72** Ask and learn who I am, and the rest that help us; and they say your foot can't stand before our face; for your fathers have been twice put to flight in their own land. **73** And now you will not be able to withstand the horse and such an army as this in the plain, where is neither stone nor flint, nor place to flee to." **74** Now when Jonathan heard the words of Apollonius, he was moved in his mind, and he chose out ten thousand men, and went out from Jerusalem, and Simon his brother met him for to help him. **75** And he encamped against Joppa: and they of the city shut him out, because Apollonius had a garrison in Joppa: **76** and they fought against it. And they of the city were afraid and opened to him: and Jonathan became master of Joppa. **77** And Apollonius heard, and he gathered an army of three thousand horse, and a great army, and went to Azotus as though he were on a journey, and therewithal drew onward into the plain, because he had a multitude of horse, and trusted therein. **78** And he pursued after him to Azotus, and the armies joined battle. **79** And Apollonius had left a thousand horse behind them privily. **80** And Jonathan knew that there was an ambush behind him. And they compassed round his army, and cast their darts at the people, from morning until evening: **81** but the people stood still, as Jonathan commanded them: and their horses were wearied. **82** And Simon drew out his army and joined battle with the phalanx (for the horsemen were spent), and they were discomfited by him, and fled. **83** And the horsemen were scattered in the plain, and they fled to Azotus, and entered into Beth-dagon, their idol's temple, to save themselves. **84** And Jonathan burned Azotus, and the surrounding cities, and took their spoils; and the temple of Dagon, and those who fled into it, he burned with fire. **85** And those who had fallen by the sword, with those who were burned, were about eight thousand men. **86** And from there Jonathan left, and encamped against Ascalon, and they of the city came out to meet him with great pomp. **87** And Jonathan, with those who were on his side, returned to Jerusalem, having many spoils. **88** And it came to pass, when king Alexander heard these things, he honored Jonathan yet more; **89** and he sent to him a buckle of gold, as the use is to give to such as are of the kindred of the kings: and he gave him Ekron and all the coasts thereof for a possession.

CHAPTER 11

1 And the king of Egypt gathered together great forces, as the sand which is by the seashore, and many ships, and sought to make himself master of Alexander's kingdom by deceit, and to add it to his own kingdom. **2** And he went out into Syria with words of peace, and they of the cities opened to him, and met him; For king Alexander's commandment was that they should meet him, because he was his father-in-law. **3** Now as he entered into the cities of Ptolemais, he set his forces for a garrison in each city. **4** But when he came near to Azotus, they showed him the temple of Dagon burned with fire, and Azotus and the pasture lands thereof pulled down, and the bodies cast abroad, and those who had been burned, whom he burned in the war, for they had made heaps of them in his way. **5** And they told the king what things Jonathan had done, that they might cast blame on him: and the king held his peace. **6** And Jonathan met the king with pomp at Joppa, and they saluted one another, and they slept there. **7** And Jonathan went with the king as far as the river that is called Eleutherus and returned to Jerusalem. **8** But king Ptolemy became master of the cities upon the sea coast, to Selucia which is by the sea, and he devised evil plans concerning Alexander. **9** And he sent ambassadors to king Demetrius, saying, Come! Let's make a covenant with one another, and I will give you my daughter whom Alexander has, and you will reign over your father's kingdom; **10** for I have repented that I gave my daughter to him, for he sought to kill me. **11** And he cast blame on him, because he coveted his kingdom. **12** And taking his daughter from him, he gave her to Demetrius, and was estranged from Alexander, and their enmity was openly seen.

13 And Ptolemy entered into Antioch and put on himself the diadem of Asia; and he put two diadems upon his head, the diadem of Egypt and that of Asia. **14** But king Alexander was in Cilicia at that season, because they of those parts were in revolt. **15** And Alexander heard of it, and he came against him in war: and Ptolemy led out *his army, and* met him with a strong force, and put him to flight. **16** And Alexander fled into Arabia, that he might be sheltered there; but king Ptolemy was exalted. **17** And Zabdiel the Arabian took off Alexander's head and sent it to Ptolemy. **18** And king Ptolemy died the third day after, and those who were in his strongholds were slain by those who were in the strongholds. **19** And Demetrius reigned in the hundred and threescore and seventh year. **20** In those days Jonathan gathered together them of Judea, to take the citadel that was at Jerusalem: and he made many engines of war against it. **21** And certain that hated their own nation, men that transgressed the law, went to the king, and reported to him that Jonathan was besieging the citadel. **22** And he heard, and was angered; but when he heard it, he set out immediately, and came to Ptolemais, and wrote to Jonathan, that he should not besiege it, and that he should meet him and speak with him at Ptolemais with all speed. **23** But when Jonathan heard this, he commanded to besiege it *still:* and he chose certain of the elders of Israel and of the priests, and put himself in peril, **24** and taking silver and gold and raiment and various presents besides, went to Ptolemais to the king. And he found favor in his sight. **25** And certain lawless men of those who were of the nation made complaints against him, **26** and the king did to him even as his predecessors had done to him and exalted him in the sight of all his friends, **27** and confirmed to him the high priesthood, and all the other honors that he had before, and gave him preeminence among his chief friends. **28** And Jonathan requested of the king, that he would make Judea free from tribute, and the three provinces, and the country of Samaria; and promised him three hundred talents. **29** And the king consented and wrote letters to Jonathan concerning all these things after this manner: **30** King Demetrius to his brother Jonathan, and to the nation of the Jews, greeting: **31** The copy of the letter which we wrote to Lasthenes our kinsman concerning you, we have written also to you, that you may see it. **32** King Demetrius to Lasthenes his father, greeting: **33** We have determined to do good to the nation of the Jews, who are our friends, and observe what is just toward us, because of their good will toward us. **34** We have confirmed therefore to them the borders of Judea, and also the three governments of Aphaerema and Lydda and Ramathaim (*these* were added to Judea from the country of Samaria), and all things appertaining to them, for all such as do sacrifice in Jerusalem, instead of the king's dues which the king received of them yearly previously from the produce of the earth and the fruits of trees. **35** And as for the other things that pertain to us from now on, of the tenths and the tolls that pertain to us, and the salt pits, and the crowns that pertain to us, all these we will bestow upon them. **36** And not one of these things will be annulled from this time out and forever. **37** Now therefore be careful to make a copy of these things, and let it be given to Jonathan, and let it be set up on the holy mount in a meet and conspicuous place. **38** And king Demetrius saw that the land was quiet before him, and that no resistance was made to him, and he sent away all his forces, each man to his own place, except the foreign forces, which he had raised from the isles of the Gentiles: and all the forces of his fathers hated him. **39** Now Tryphon was of those who previously had been of Alexander's part, and he saw that all the forces murmured against Demetrius, and he went to Imalcue the Arabian, who was nourishing up Antiochus the young child of Alexander, **40** and pressed sore upon him that he should deliver him to him, that he might reign in his father's stead: and he told him all that Demetrius had done, and the hatred with which his forces hated him; and he dwelt there many days. **41** And Jonathan sent to king Demetrius, that he should cast out of Jerusalem them of the citadel, and those who were in the strongholds; for they fought against Israel continually. **42** And Demetrius sent to Jonathan, saying, I will not only do this for you and your nation, but I will greatly honor you and your nation, if I find fair occasion. **43** Now therefore you will do well, if you send me men who will fight for me; for all my forces are revolted. **44** And Jonathan sent him three thousand valiant men to Antioch: and they came to the king, and the king was glad at their coming. **45** And they of the city gathered themselves together into the midst of the city, to the number of a hundred and twenty thousand men, and they were inclined to kill the king. **46** And the king fled into the court of the palace, and they of the city seized the passages of the city and began to fight. **47** And the king called the Jews to help him, and they were gathered together to him all at once, and they dispersed themselves in the city, and killed that day to the number of a hundred thousand. **48** And they set the city on fire, and got many spoils that day, and saved the king. **49** And they of the city saw that the Jews had made themselves masters of the city as they would, and they waxed faint in their hearts, and they cried out to the king with supplication, saying, **50** Give us your right hand, and let the Jews cease from fighting against us and the city. **51** And they cast away their arms and made peace; and the Jews were glorified in the sight of the king, and before all that were in his kingdom; and they returned to Jerusalem, having many spoils. **52** And king Demetrius sat on the throne of his kingdom, and the land was quiet before him. **53** And he lied in all that he spoke, and estranged himself from Jonathan, and recompensed him not according to the benefits with which he had recompensed him and afflicted him exceedingly. **54** Now after this Tryphon returned, and with him the young child Antiochus; and he reigned and put on a diadem. **55** And there were gathered to him all the forces which Demetrius had sent away with disgrace, and they fought against him, and he fled and was put to the rout. **56** And Tryphon took the elephants and became master of Antioch. **57** And the young Antiochus wrote to Jonathan, saying, I confirm to you the high priesthood, and appoint you over the four governments, and to be one of the king's friends. **58** And he sent to him golden vessels and furniture for the table, and gave him leave to drink in golden vessels, and to be clothed in purple, and to have a golden buckle. **59** And his brother Simon he made captain from the Ladder of Tyre to the borders of Egypt. **60** And Jonathan went out and took his journey beyond the river and through the cities; and all the forces of Syria gathered themselves to him for to be his allies. And he came to Ascalon, and they of the city met him honorably. **61** And he departed from there to Gaza, and they of Gaza shut him out; and he laid siege to it, and burned the pasture lands thereof with fire, and plundered them. **62** And they of Gaza made request to Jonathan, and he gave them his right hand, and took the sons of their princes for hostages, and sent them away to Jerusalem; and he passed through the country as far as Damascus. **63** And Jonathan heard that Demetrius' princes were come to Kedesh, which is in Galilee, with a great army, purposing to remove him from his office; **64** and he went to meet them, but Simon his brother he left in the country. **65** And Simon encamped against Bethsura, and fought against it many days, and shut it up: **66** and they made request to him that he would give them his right hand, and he gave it to them; and he put them out from there, and took possession of the city, and set a garrison over it. **67** And Jonathan and his army encamped at the water of Gennesareth, and early in the morning they got them to the plain of Hazor. **68** And, behold, an army of strangers met him in the plain, and they laid an ambush for him in the mountains, but themselves met him face to face. **69** But those who lay in ambush rose out of their places and joined battle; and all those who were of Jonathan's side fled: **70** not one of them was left, except Mattathias the son of Absalom, and Judas the son of Chalphi, captains of the forces. **71** And Jonathan tore his clothes, and put earth upon his head, and prayed. **72** And he turned again to them in battle, and put them to the rout, and they fled. **73** And they of his side that fled saw it, and returned to him, and pursued with him to Kedesh to their camp, and they encamped there. **74** And there fell of the strangers on that day about three thousand men: and Jonathan returned to Jerusalem.

CHAPTER 12

1 And Jonathan saw that the time served him, and he chose men, and sent them to Rome, to confirm and renew the friendship that they had with them. **2** And to the Spartans, and to other places, he sent letters after the same manner. **3** And they went to Rome, and entered into the senate house, and said, Jonathan the high priest, and the nation of the Jews, have sent us, to renew for them the friendship and the confederacy, as in former time. **4** And they gave them letters to the men in every place, that they should bring them on their way to the land of Judah in peace. **5** And this is the copy of the letters which Jonathan wrote to the Spartans: **6** Jonathan the high priest, and the senate of the nation, and the priests, and the rest of the people of the Jews, to their kindred the Spartans, greeting: **7** Even before this time were letters sent to Onias the high priest from Arius, who was reigning among you, to signify that you are our kindred, as the copy written below shows. **8** And Onias entreated honorably the man that was sent, and received the letters, wherein declaration was made of confederacy and friendship. **9** Therefore we also, albeit we need none of these things, having for our encouragement the holy books which are in our hands, **10** have assayed to send that we might renew our brotherhood and friendship with you, to the end that we should not become estranged from you altogether: for long time is passed since you sent to us. **11** We therefore at all times without ceasing, both in our feasts, and on the other convenient days, do remember you in the sacrifices which we offer, and in our prayers, as it is right and meet to be mindful of kindred: **12** and moreover are glad for your glory. **13** But as for ourselves, many afflictions and many wars have encompassed us, and the kings that are around us have fought against us. **14** We were not inclined therefore to be troublesome to you, and to the rest of our allies and friends, in these wars; **15** for we have the help which is from heaven to help us, and we have been delivered from our enemies, and our enemies have been brought low. **16** We chose therefore Numenius the son of Antiochus, and Antipater the son of Jason, and have sent them to the Romans, to renew the friendship that we had with them, and the former confederacy. **17** We commanded them therefore to go also to you, and to salute you, and to deliver you our letters concerning the renewing *of friendship* and our brotherhood. **18** And now you will do well if you give us an answer thereto. **19** And this is the copy of the letters which they sent to Onias: **20** Arius king of the Spartans to Onias the chief priest, greeting: **21** It has been found in writing, concerning the Spartans and the Jews, that they are kindred, and that they are of the stock of Abraham: **22** and now, since this is come to our knowledge, you will do well to write to us of your prosperity. **23** And we moreover do write on our part to you, that your cattle and goods are ours, and ours are yours. We do command therefore that they make report to you on this wise. **24** And Jonathan heard that Demetrius' princes were returned to fight against him with a greater army than before, **25** and he went from Jerusalem, and met them in the country of Hamath; for he gave them no respite to set foot in his country. **26** And he sent spies into his camp, and they came again, and reported to him that they were appointed in such and such

a way to fall upon them in the night season. **27** But as soon as the sun was down, Jonathan commanded his men to watch, and to be in arms, that all the night long they might be ready for battle: and he put out sentinels around the camp. **28** And the adversaries heard that Jonathan and his men were ready for battle, and they feared, and trembled in their hearts, and they kindled fires in their camp, **29** but Jonathan and his men knew it not until the morning; for they saw the lights burning. **30** And Jonathan pursued after them and overtook them not; for they were gone over the river Eleutherus. **31** And Jonathan turned toward the Arabians, who are called Zabadaeans, and struck them, and took their spoils. **32** And he came out from there, and came to Damascus, and took his journey through all the country. **33** And Simon went out, and took his journey as far as Ascalon, and the strongholds that were near to it. And he turned toward Joppa and took possession of it; **34** for he had heard that they were determined to deliver the stronghold to the men of Demetrius; and he set a garrison there to keep it. **35** And Jonathan returned, and called the elders of the people together; and he took counsel with them to build strongholds in Judea, **36** and to make the walls of Jerusalem higher, and to raise a great mound between the citadel and the city, for to separate it from the city, that so it might be all alone, that men might neither buy nor sell. **37** And they were gathered together to build the city, and there fell down part of the wall of the brook that is on the east side, and he repaired that which is called Chaphenatha. **38** And Simon also built Adida in the plain country, and made it strong, and set up gates and bars. **39** And Tryphon sought to reign over Asia and to put on himself the diadem, and to stretch out his hand against Antiochus the king. **40** And he was afraid lest perhaps Jonathan should not suffer him, and lest he should fight against him; and he sought a way how to take him, that he might destroy him. And he went and came to Bethshan. **41** And Jonathan came out to meet him with forty thousand men chosen for battle and came to Bethshan. **42** And Tryphon saw that he came with a great army, and he was afraid to stretch out his hand against him: **43** and he received him honorably, and commended him to all his friends, and gave him gifts, and commanded his forces to be obedient to him, as to himself. **44** And he said to Jonathan, "Why have you put all this people to trouble, seeing there is no war between us? **45** And now send them away to their homes but choose for yourself a few men who will be with you, and come you with me to Ptolemais, and I will give it up to you, and the rest of the strongholds and the rest of the forces, and all the king's officers: and I will return and depart; for this is the cause of my coming." **46** And he put his trust in him, and did even as he said, and sent away his forces, and they departed into the land of Judah. **47** But he reserved to himself three thousand men, of whom he left two thousand in Galilee, but one thousand went with him. **48** Now as soon as Jonathan entered into Ptolemais, they of Ptolemais shut the gates, and laid hands on him; and all those who came in with him they killed with the sword. **49** And Tryphon sent forces and horsemen into Galilee, and into the great plain, to destroy all Jonathan's men. **50** And they perceived that he was taken and had perished, and those who were with him; and they encouraged one another, and went on their way close together, prepared to fight. **51** And those who followed upon them saw that they were ready to fight for their lives and turned back again. **52** And they all came in peace into the land of Judah, and they mourned for Jonathan, and those who were with him, and they were sore afraid; and all Israel mourned with a great mourning. **53** And all the Gentiles that were around them sought to destroy them utterly: for they said, "They have no ruler, nor any to help them: now therefore let's fight against them and take away their memorial from among men."

CHAPTER 13

1 And Simon heard that Tryphon had gathered together a mighty army to come into the land of Judah and destroy it utterly. **2** And he saw that the people trembled and was in great fear; and he went up to Jerusalem, and gathered the people together; **3** and he encouraged them, and said to them, You yourselves know all the things that I, and my kindred, and my father's house, have done for the laws and the sanctuary, and the battles and the distresses which we have seen: **4** by reason of this all my kindred have perished for Israel's sake, and I am left alone. **5** And now be it far from me, that I should spare my own life in any time of affliction; for I am not better than my kindred. **6** However I will take vengeance for my nation, and for the sanctuary, and for our wives and children; because all the Gentiles are

gathered to destroy us of very hatred. **7** And the spirit of the people revived, as soon as they heard these words. **8** And they answered with a loud voice, saying, "You are our leader instead of Judas and Jonathan your brother. **9** Fight you our battles, and all that you will say to us, that will we do." **10** And he gathered together all the men of war, and made haste to finish the walls of Jerusalem, and he fortified it round about. **11** And he sent Jonathan the son of Absalom, and with him a great army, to Joppa: and he cast out those who were therein and dwelt there in it. **12** And Tryphon left from Ptolemais with a mighty army to enter into the land of Judah, and Jonathan was with him in ward. **13** But Simon encamped at Adida, near the plain. **14** And Tryphon knew that Simon was risen up instead of his brother Jonathan, and meant to join battle with him, and he sent ambassadors to him, saying, **15** It is for money which Jonathan your brother owed to the king's treasure, by reason of the offices which he had, that we hold him fast. **16** And now send a hundred talents of silver, and two of his sons for hostages, that when he is set at liberty he may not revolt from us, and we will set him at liberty. **17** And Simon knew that they spoke to him deceitfully; and he sent the money and the children, lest perhaps he should procure to himself great hatred of the people, **18** and they should say, Because I sent him not the money and the children, he perished. **19** And he sent the children and the hundred talents. And he dealt falsely and didn't set Jonathan at liberty. **20** And after this Tryphon came to invade the land, and destroy it, and he went around by the way that leads to Adora: and Simon and his army marched near him to every place, wherever he went. **21** Now they of the citadel sent to Tryphon ambassadors, hastening him to come to them through the wilderness, and to send them food. **22** And Tryphon made ready all his horse to come: and on that night there fell a very great snow, and he came not by reason of the snow. And he left and came into the country of Gilead. **23** But when he came near to Bascama, he killed Jonathan, and he was buried there. **24** And Tryphon returned and went away into his own land. **25** And Simon sent, and took the bones of Jonathan his brother, and buried him at Modin, the city of his fathers. **26** And all Israel made great lamentation over him and mourned for him many days. **27** And Simon built *a monument* upon the sepulcher of his father and his kindred, and raised it aloft to the sight, with polished stone behind and before. **28** And he set up seven pyramids, one near another, for his father, and his mother, and his four kindred. **29** And for these he made cunning devices, setting about them great pillars, and upon the pillars he fashioned all manner of arms for a perpetual memory, and beside the arms ships carved, that they should be seen of all that sail on the sea. **30** This is the sepulcher which he made at Modin, and *it is there* to this day. **31** Now Tryphon dealt deceitfully with the young king Antiochus, and killed him, **32** and reigned in his stead, and put on himself the diadem of Asia, and brought a great calamity upon the land. **33** And Simon built the strongholds of Judea, and fenced them about with high towers, and great walls, and gates, and bars; and he laid up food in the strongholds. **34** And Simon chose men, and sent to king Demetrius, to the end he should give the country an immunity, because all that Tryphon did was to plunder. **35** And king Demetrius sent to him according to these words, and answered him, and wrote a letter to him, after this manner: **36** King Demetrius to Simon the high priest and friend of kings, and to the elders and nation of the Jews, greeting: **37** The golden crown, and the palm branch, which you sent, we have received: and we are ready to make a steadfast peace with you, yes, and to write to our officers, to grant immunities to you. **38** And whatever things we confirmed to you, they are confirmed; and the strongholds, which you have built, let them be your own. **39** As for any oversights and faults committed to this day, we forgive them, and the crown which you owed us: and if there were any other toll exacted in Jerusalem, let it be exacted no longer. **40** And if there be any among you meet to be enrolled in our court, let them be enrolled, and let there be peace between us. **41** In the hundred and seventieth year was the yoke of the heathen taken away from Israel. **42** And the people began to write in their instruments and contracts, In the first year of Simon, the great high priest and captain and leader of the Jews. **43** In those days he encamped against Gazara and compassed it around with armies; and he made an engine of siege, and brought it up to the city, and struck a tower, and took it. **44** And those who were in the engine leaped out into the city; and there was a great uproar in the city: **45** and they of the city tore their clothes and went up on the walls with their wives and children, and cried with a loud voice, making

request to Simon to give them his right hand. **46** And they said, "Deal not with us according to our wickedness, but according to your mercy." **47** And Simon was reconciled to them and didn't fight against them: and he put them out of the city, and cleansed the houses wherein the idols were, and so entered into it with singing and giving praise. **48** And he put all uncleanness out of it and placed in it such men as would keep the law, and made it stronger than it was before, and built therein a dwelling place for himself. **49** But they of the citadel in Jerusalem were hindered from going out, and from going into the country, and from buying and selling; and they hungered exceedingly, and a great number of them perished through famine. **50** And they cried out to Simon, that he should give them his right hand; and he gave it to them: and he put them out from there, and he cleansed the citadel from its pollutions. **51** And he entered into it on the three and twentieth day of the second month, in the hundred and seventy and first year, with praise and palm branches, and with harps, and with cymbals, and with viols, and with hymns, and with songs: because a great enemy was destroyed out of Israel. **52** And he ordained that they should keep that day every year with gladness. And the hill of the temple that was by the citadel he made stronger than before, and there he lived, himself and his men. **53** And Simon saw that John his son was a *valiant* man, and he made him leader of all his forces: and he lived in Gazara.

CHAPTER 14

1 And in the hundred and seventy and second year king Demetrius gathered his forces together, and went into Media, to get him help, that he might fight against Tryphon. **2** And Arsaces, the king of Persia and Media, heard that Demetrius was come into his borders, and he sent one of his princes to take him alive: **3** and he went and struck the army of Demetrius, and took him, and brought him to Arsaces; and he put him in ward. **4** And the land had rest all the days of Simon: and he sought the good of his nation; and his authority and his glory was well-pleasing to them all his days. **5** And amid all his glory he took Joppa for a haven and made it an entrance for the isles of the sea; **6** and he enlarged the borders of his nation and got possession of the country; **7** and he gathered together a great number of captives, and got the dominion of Gazara, and

Bethsura, and the citadel, and he took away from it its uncleanness; and there was none that resisted him. **8** And they tilled their land in peace, and the land gave her increase, and the trees of the plains their fruit. **9** The ancient men sat in the streets, they communed all of them together of good things, and the young men put on glorious and warlike apparel. **10** He provided food for the cities, and furnished them with all manner of munition, until the name of his glory was named to the end of the earth. **11** He made peace in the land, and Israel rejoiced with great joy: **12** and they sat each man under his vine and his fig tree, and there was none to make them afraid: **13** and there ceased in the land any that fought against them: and the kings were discomfited in those days. **14** And he strengthened all those of his people that were brought low: the law he searched out, and every lawless and wicked person he took away. **15** He glorified the sanctuary, and the vessels of the temple he multiplied. **16** And it was heard at Rome that Jonathan was dead, and even to Sparta, and they were exceedingly sorry. **17** But as soon as they heard that his brother Simon was made high priest in his stead, and ruled the country, and the cities therein, **18** they wrote to him on tables of brass, to renew with him the friendship and the confederacy which they had confirmed with Judas and Jonathan his kindred; **19** and they were read before the congregation at Jerusalem. **20** And this is the copy of the letters which the Spartans sent: The rulers of the Spartans, and the city, to Simon the high priest, and to the elders, and the priests, and the residue of the people of the Jews, our kindred, greeting: **21** The ambassadors that were sent to our people made report to us of your glory and honor: and we were glad for their coming, **22** and we did register the things that were spoken by them in the public records after this manner: Numenius son of Antiochus, and Antipater son of Jason, the Jews' ambassadors, came to us to renew the friendship they had with us. **23** And it pleased the people to entertain the men honorably, and to put the copy of their words in the public records, to the end that the people of the Spartans might have a memorial thereof: moreover, they wrote a copy of these things to Simon the high priest. **24** After this Simon sent Numenius to Rome with a great shield of gold of a thousand-pound weight, in order to confirm the confederacy with them. **25** But when the people heard these things, they said,

"What thanks will we give to Simon and his sons? **26** For he and his kindred and the house of his father have made themselves strong and have chased away in fight the enemies of Israel from them, and confirmed liberty to Israel." **27** And they wrote on tables of brass, and set them upon pillars in Mount Zion: and this is the copy of the writing: On the eighteenth day of Elul, in the hundred and seventy and second year, and this is the third year of Simon the high priest, **28** in Asaramel, in a great congregation of priests and people and princes of the nation, and of the elders of the country, was it notified to us: **29** Forasmuch as oftentimes there have been wars in the country, but Simon the son of Mattathias, the son of the sons of Joarib, and his kindred, put themselves in jeopardy, and withstood the enemies of their nation, that their sanctuary and the law might be established, and glorified their nation with great glory: **30** and Jonathan assembled their nation together, and became their high priest, and was gathered to his people: **31** and their enemies purposed to invade their country, that they might destroy their country utterly, and stretch out their hands against their sanctuary: **32** then rose up Simon, and fought for his nation, and spent much of his own substance, and armed the valiant men of his nation, and gave them wages: **33** and he fortified the cities of Judea, and Bethsura that lies upon the borders of Judea, where the arms of the enemies were previously, and set there a garrison of Jews: **34** and he fortified Joppa which is upon the sea, and Gazara which is upon the borders of Azotus, wherein the enemies lived previously, and placed Jews there, and set therein all things convenient for their restoration: **35** and the people saw the faith of Simon, and the glory which he thought to bring to his nation, and they made him their leader and high priest, because he had done all these things, and for the justice and the faith which he kept to his nation, and for that he sought by all means to exalt his people: **36** and in his days things prospered in his hands, so that the Gentiles were taken away out of their country, and they also that were in the city of David, those who were in Jerusalem, who had made themselves a citadel, out of which they issued, and polluted all things around the sanctuary, and did great hurt to its purity; **37** and he placed Jews therein, and fortified it for the safety of the country and the city, and made high the walls of Jerusalem: **38** and king Demetrius confirmed to him the high priesthood according to these things, **39** and made him one of his friends, and honored him with great honor; **40** for he had heard say, that the Jews had been called by the Romans friends and allies and kindred, and that they had met the ambassadors of Simon honorably; **41** and that the Jews and the priests were well pleased that Simon should be their leader and high priest forever, until there should arise a faithful prophet; **42** and that he should be captain over them, and should take charge of the sanctuary, to set them over their works, and over the country, and over the arms, and over the strongholds; and that he should take charge of the sanctuary, **43** and that he should be obeyed by all, and that all instruments in the country should be written in his name, and that he should be clothed in purple, and wear gold; **44** and that it should not be lawful for any of the people or of the priests to set at nothing any of these things, or to gainsay the words that he should speak, or to gather an assembly in the country without him, or to be clothed in purple, or wear a buckle of gold; **45** but whoever should do otherwise, or set at nothing any of these things, he should be liable to punishment. **46** All the people consented to ordain for Simon that he should do according to these words; **47** and Simon accepted this, and consented to be high priest, and to be captain and governor of the Jews and of the priests, and to be protector of all. **48** And they commanded to put this writing on tables of brass, and to set them up within the precinct of the sanctuary in a conspicuous place; **49** and moreover to put the copies thereof in the treasury, to the end that Simon and his sons might have them.

CHAPTER 15

1 And Antiochus son of Demetrius the king sent letters from the isles of the sea to Simon the priest and governor of the Jews, and to all the nation; **2** and the contents thereof were after this manner: King Antiochus to Simon the chief priest and governor, and to the nation of the Jews, greeting: **3** Forasmuch as certain pestilent fellows have made themselves masters of the kingdom of our fathers, but my purpose is to claim the kingdom, that I may restore it as it was before; and moreover I have raised a multitude of foreign soldiers, and have prepared ships of war; **4** moreover I am inclined to land in the country, that I may punish those who have destroyed our country,

and those who have made many cities in the kingdom desolate: **5** Now therefore I confirm to you all the exactions which the kings that were before me remitted to you, and whatever gifts besides they remitted to you: **6** and I give you leave to coin money for your country with your own stamp, **7** but that Jerusalem and the sanctuary should be free: and all the arms that you have prepared, and the strongholds that you have built, which you have in your possession, let them remain to you: **8** and everything owing to the king, and the things that will be owing to the king from now on and forevermore, let them be remitted to you: **9** moreover, when we will have established our kingdom, we will glorify you and your nation and the temple with great glory, so that your glory will be made manifest in all the earth. **10** In the hundred and seventy and fourth year went Antiochus out into the land of his fathers; and all the forces came together to him, so that there were few men with Tryphon. **11** And king Antiochus pursued him, and he came, as he fled, to Dor, which is by the sea: **12** for he knew that troubles were come upon him all at once, and that his forces had forsaken him. **13** And Antiochus encamped against Dor, and with him a hundred and twenty thousand men of war, and eight thousand horses. **14** And he compassed the city round about, and the ships joined in the attack from the sea; and he vexed the city by land and sea, and suffered no man to go out or in. **15** And Numenius and his company came from Rome, having letters to the kings and to the countries, wherein were written these things: **16** Lucius, consul of the Romans, to king Ptolemy, greeting: **17** The Jews' ambassadors came to us as our friends and allies, to renew the old friendship and confederacy, being sent from Simon the high priest, and from the people of the Jews: **18** moreover they brought a shield of gold of a thousand pounds. **19** It pleased us therefore to write to the kings and to the countries, that they should not seek their hurt, nor fight against them, and their cities, and their country, nor be allies with such as fight against them. **20** Moreover it seemed good to us to receive the shield of them. **21** If therefore any pestilent fellows have fled from their country to you, deliver them to Simon the high priest, that he may take vengeance on them according to their law. **22** And the same things wrote he to Demetrius the king, and to Attalus, and to Arathes, and to Arsaces, **23** and to all the countries, and to Sampsames, and to the Spartans, and to Delos, and to Myndos, and to Sicyon, and to Caria, and to Samos, and to Pamphylia, and to Lycia, and to Halicarnassus, and to Rhodes, and to Phaselis, and to Cos, and to Side, and to Aradus, and Gortyna, and Cnidus, and Cyprus, and Cyrene. 24 But they wrote this copy to Simon the high priest. 25 But Antiochus the king encamped against Dor the second day, bringing his forces up to it continually, and making engines of war, and he shut up Tryphon from going in or out. 26 And Simon sent him two thousand chosen men to fight on his side; and silver, and gold, and instruments of war in abundance. 27 And he would not receive them but set at nothing all the covenants which he had made with him previously and was estranged from him. 28 And he sent to him Athenobius, one of his friends, to commune with him, saying, "You hold possession of Joppa and Gazara, and the citadel that is in Jerusalem, cities of my kingdom. 29 The borders thereof you have wasted, and done great hurt in the land, and got the dominion of many places in my kingdom. 30 Now therefore deliver up the cities which you have taken, and the tributes of the places whereof you have gotten dominion without the borders of Judea: 31 or else give me for them five hundred talents of silver; and for the harm that you have done, and the tributes of the cities, other five hundred talents: or else we will come and subdue you." 32 And Athenobius the king's friend came to Jerusalem; and he saw the glory of Simon, and the cupboard of gold and silver vessels, and his great attendance, and he was amazed; and he reported to him the king's words. 33 And Simon answered, and said to him, "We have neither taken other men's land, nor have we possession of that which appertains to others, but of the inheritance of our fathers; however, it was had in possession of our enemies wrongfully for a certain time. 34 But we, having opportunity, hold fast the inheritance of our fathers. 35 But as touching Joppa and Gazara, which you demand, they did great harm among the people throughout our country, we will give a hundred talents for them." And he answered him not a word, 36 but returned in a rage to the king, and reported to him these words, and the glory of Simon, and all that he had seen: and the king was exceedingly angry. 37 But Tryphon embarked on board a ship and fled to Orthosia. 38 And the king appointed Cendebaeus chief captain of the sea coast and gave him forces of foot and horse: 39 and he commanded him to encamp before Judea, and he commanded him to build up Kidron, and to fortify the gates, and that he should fight against the people: but the king pursued Tryphon. 40 And Cendebaeus came to Jamnia, and began to provoke the people, and to invade Judea, and to take the people captive, and to kill them. 41 And he built Kidron, and set horsemen there, and forces of foot, to the end that issuing out they might make excursions upon the ways of Judea, according as the king commanded him.

CHAPTER 16

1 And John went up from Gazara and told Simon his father what Cendebaeus was doing. 2 And Simon called his two oldest sons, Judas and John, and said to them, I and my kindred and my father's house have fought the battles of Israel from our youth, even to this day; and things have prospered in our hands, that we should deliver Israel oftentimes. 3 But now I am old, and you moreover, by *his* mercy, are of a sufficient age: be you instead of me and my brother and go out and fight for our nation; but let the help which is from heaven be with you. 4 And he chose out of the country twenty thousand men of war and horsemen, and they went against Cendebaeus, and slept at Modin. 5 And rising up in the morning, they went into the plain, and, behold, a great army came to meet them, of footmen and horsemen: and there was a brook between them. 6 And he encamped near them, he and his people: and he saw that the people were afraid to pass over the brook, and he passed over first, and the men saw him, and passed over after him. 7 And he divided the people and *set* the horsemen in the midst of the footmen: but the enemies' horsemen were exceedingly many. 8 And they sounded with the trumpets; and Cendebaeus and his army were put to the rout, and there fell of them many wounded to death, but those who were left fled to the stronghold: 9 at that time was Judas, John's brother, wounded: but John pursued after them, until he came to Kidron, which *Cendebaeus* had built; 10 and they fled to the towers that are in the fields of Azotus; and he burned it with fire; and there fell of them about two thousand men. And he returned into Judea in peace. 11 And Ptolemy the son of Abubus had been appointed captain for the plain of Jericho, and he had much silver and gold; 12 for he was the high priest's son in law. 13 And his heart was

lifted up, and he was inclined to make himself master of the country, and he took counsel deceitfully against Simon and his sons, to make away with them. **14** Now Simon was visiting the cities that were in the country, and taking care for the good ordering of them; and he went down to Jericho, himself and Mattathias and Judas his sons, in the hundred and seventy and seventh year, in the eleventh month, which is the month Sebat: **15** and the son of Abubus received them deceitfully into the little stronghold that is called Dok, which he had built, and made them a great banquet, and hid men there. **16** And when Simon and his sons had drunk freely, Ptolemy and his men rose up, and took their arms, and came in upon Simon into the banqueting place, and killed him, and his two sons, and certain of his servants. **17** And he committed a great iniquity, and recompensed evil for good. **18** And Ptolemy wrote these things, and sent to the king, that he should send him forces to aid him, and should deliver him their country and the cities. **19** And he sent others to Gazara to make away with John: and to the captains of thousands he sent letters to come to him, that he might give them silver and gold and gifts. **20** And others he sent to take possession of Jerusalem, and the mount of the temple. **21** And one ran before to Gazara and told John that his father and kindred were perished, and he has sent to kill you also. **22** And when he heard, he was sore amazed; and he laid hands on the men that came to destroy him and killed them; for he perceived that they were seeking to destroy him. **23** And the rest of the acts of John, and of his wars, and of his valiant deeds which he did, and of the building of the walls which he built, and of his doings, **24** behold, they are written in the chronicles of his high priesthood, from the time that he was made high priest after his father.

2 MACCABEES

2 Maccabees is a deuterocanonical book which focuses on the Maccabean Revolt against Antiochus IV Epiphanes and concludes with the defeat of the Seleucid empire general Nicanor in 161 BC by Judas Maccabeus, the hero of the hard work. Unlike 1 Maccabees, 2 Maccabees was written in Koine Greek, probably in Alexandria, Egypt, ca. 124 BC. It presents a revised version of the historical events recounted in the first seven chapters of 1 Maccabees, adding material from the Pharisaic tradition, including prayer for the dead and a resurrection on Judgment Day. Jews and Protestants reject most of the doctrinal issues present in the work, while Catholics and Eastern Orthodox consider the work to be deuterocanonical.

CHAPTER 1

1 The kindred, the Jews that are in Jerusalem and those who are in the country of Judea, send greeting to the kindred, the Jews that are throughout Egypt, and *wish them* good peace: **2** and may God do good to you, and remember his covenant with Abraham and Isaac and Jacob, his faithful servants; **3** and give you all a heart to worship him and do his pleasure with a great heart and a willing soul; **4** and open your heart in his law and in his statutes, and make peace, **5** and listen to your requests, and be reconciled with you, and not forsake you in an evil time. **6** And now we here are praying for you. **7** In the reign of Demetrius, in the hundred threescore and ninth year, we the Jews have *already* written to you in the suffering and in the extremity that has come upon us in these years, from the time that Jason and his company revolted from the holy land and the kingdom, **8** and set the gate on fire, and shed innocent blood: and we implored the Lord, and were heard; and we offered sacrifice and meal *offering, and* we lighted the lamps, and we set out the show bread. **9** And now *see* that you keep the days of the feast of tabernacles of the month Chislev. **10** *Written* in the hundred fourscore and eighth year. THEY that are in Jerusalem and those who are in Judea and the senate and Judas, to Aristobulus, king Ptolemy's teacher, who is also of the stock of the anointed priests, and to

the Jews that are in Egypt, send greeting and health. **11** Having been saved by God out of great perils, as men arrayed against a king, we thank him greatly. **12** For he cast out into Persia those who arrayed themselves *against us* in the holy city. **13** For when the prince had come*, and* the army with him that seemed irresistible, they were cut to pieces in the temple of Nanaea by the treachery of Nanaea's priests. **14** For Antiochus, on the pretense that he would marry her, came into the place, he and his friends that were with him, that they might take a great part of the treasures in name of a dowry. **15** And when the priests of Nanaea's temple had set the treasures out, and he was come there with a small company within the wall of the precincts, they shut to the temple when Antiochus was come in: **16** and opening the secret door of the paneled ceiling, they threw stones and struck down the prince, and they hewed *him and his company* in pieces, and struck off their heads, and cast them to those that were without. **17** Blessed *be* our God in all things, who gave *for a prey* those who had committed impiety. **18** Whereas we are now about to keep the purification of the temple in the *month* Chislev, on the five and twentieth day, we thought it necessary to certify you thereof, that you also may keep a feast of tabernacles, and *a memorial* of the fire *which was given* when Nehemiah offered sacrifices, after he had built both the temple and the altar. **19** For indeed when our fathers were about to be led into the land of Persia, the godly priests of that time took of the fire of the altar and hid it privily in the hollow of a well that was without water, wherein they made *it* sure, so that the place was unknown to all men. **20** Now after many years, when it pleased God, Nehemiah, having received a charge from the king of Persia, sent in quest of the fire the descendants of the priests that hid it. When they declared to us that they had found no fire, but thick water, **21** he commanded them to draw out thereof and bring *to him:* and when the sacrifices had been offered *on the altar,* Nehemiah commanded the priests to sprinkle with the water both the wood and the things laid immediately. **22** And when it was done, and some time had passed, and the sun shone out, which before was hid with clouds, there was kindled a great blaze, so that all men marveled. 23 And the priests made a prayer while the sacrifice was consuming, both the priests and all *others,* Jonathan leading and the rest answering, as Nehemiah did. 24 And the prayer was after this manner: O Lord, Lord God, the Creator of all things, who are terrible and strong and righteous and merciful, who alone are King and gracious, 25 who alone supply *every need,* who alone are righteous and almighty and eternal, you that save Israel out of all evil, who made the fathers *your* chosen, and did sanctify them: 26 accept the sacrifice for all your people Israel, and guard your own portion, and consecrate it. 27 Gather together our Dispersion, set at liberty those who are in bondage among the heathen, look upon those who are despised and abhorred, and let the heathen know that you are our God. 28 Torment those who oppress us and in arrogance shamefully entreat us. 29 Plant your people in your holy place, even as Moses said. 30 And immediately the priests sang the hymns. 31 And as soon as the sacrifice was consumed, then Nehemiah commanded to pour *on* great stones the water that was left. 32 And when this was done, a flame was kindled; but when the light from the altar shone near it, *all* was consumed. 33 And when the matter became known, and it was told the king of the Persians, that, in the place where the priests that were led away had hid the fire, there appeared the water, with which also Nehemiah and those who were with him purified the sacrifice, 34 then the king, inclosing *the place,* made it sacred, after he had proved the matter. 35 And when the king would show favor to any, he would take *from them* many presents and give them some of *this water.* 36 And Nehemiah and those who were with him called this thing Nephthar, which is by interpretation, Cleansing; but most men call it Nephthai.

CHAPTER 2

1 It is also found in the records, that Jeremiah the prophet commanded those who were carried away to take of the fire, as has been signified *above:* 2 and how that the prophet charged those who were carried away, having given them the law, that they should not forget the statutes of the Lord, neither be led astray in their minds, when they saw images of gold and silver, and the adornment thereof. 3 And with other such words exhorted he them, that the law should not depart from their heart. 4 And it was *contained* in the writing, that the prophet, being warned of God, commanded that the tabernacle and the ark should follow with him, when he went out into the mountain where Moses went up and saw the heritage of God. 5 And Jeremiah came and found a chamber in the rock, and there he brought in the tabernacle, and the ark, and the altar of incense; and he made fast the door. 6 And some of those that followed with him came there that they might mark the way and could not find it. 7 But when Jeremiah perceived it, he blamed them, saying, Yes and the place will be unknown until God gather the people again together, and mercy come: 8 and then will the Lord disclose these things, and the glory of the Lord will be seen, and the cloud. As also it was showed with Moses; as also Solomon implored that the place might be consecrated greatly, 9 and it was also declared that he, having wisdom, offered a sacrifice of dedication, and of the finishing of the temple; *so we would have it now.* 10 As Moses prayed to the Lord, and fire came down out of heaven and consumed the sacrifice, even so prayed Solomon also, and the fire came down and consumed the burnt offerings; 11 (and Moses said, Because the sin offering had not been eaten, it was consumed in like manner *with the rest;*)12 and Solomon kept the eight days. 13 And the same things were related both in the public archives and in the records that concern Nehemiah; and how he, founding a library, gathered together the books about the kings and prophets, and the *books* of David, and letters of kings about sacred gifts. 14 And in like manner Judas also gathered together for us all those *writings* that had been scattered by reason of the war that befell, and they are *still* with us. 15 If therefore you have need thereof, send some to fetch them to you. 16 Seeing then that we are about to keep the purification, we write to you; you will therefore do well if you keep the days. 17 Now God, who saved all his people, and restored the heritage to all, and the kingdom, and the priesthood, and the hallowing, 18 even as he promised through the law,— in God have we hope, that he will quickly have mercy upon us, and gather *us* together out of all the earth to the holy place: for he delivered us out of great evils, and purified the place. 19 Now the things concerning Judas Maccabaeus and his kindred, and the purification of the great temple, and the dedication of the altar, 20 and further the

wars against Antiochus Epiphanes, and Eupator his son, **21** and the manifestations that came from heaven to those that vied with one another in manful deeds for the religion of the Jews; so that, being but a few, they rescued the whole country, and chased the barbarous multitudes, **22** and recovered again the temple renowned all the world over, and freed the city, and restored the laws which were like to be overthrown, seeing the Lord became gracious to them with all forbearance: **23** *these things, I say,* which have been declared by Jason of Cyrene in five books, we will assay to abridge in one work. **24** For having in view the confused mass of the numbers, and the difficulty which awaits those who would enter into the narratives of the history, by reason of the abundance of the matter, **25** we were careful that they who choose to read may be attracted, and that they who wish well *to our cause* may find it easy to recall *what we have written, and* that all readers may have profit. **26** And although to us, who have taken upon us the painful labor of the abridgement, the task is not easy, but *matter* of sweat and watching **27** (even as it is no light thing to him that prepares a banquet, and seeks the benefit of others); yet for the sake of the gratitude of the many we will gladly endure the painful labor, **28** leaving to the historian the exact handling of every particular, and again having no strength to fill in the outlines of our abridgement. **29** For as the master builder of a new house must care for the whole structure, and again he that undertakes to decorate and paint it must seek out the things fit for the adorning thereof; even so I think it is also with us. **30** To occupy the ground, and to indulge in long discussions, and to be curious in particulars, becomes the first author of the history: **31** but to strive after brevity of expression, and to avoid a labored fullness in the treatment, is to be granted to him that would bring a writing into a new form. **32** Here then let's begin the narration, only adding so much to that which has been already said; for it is a foolish thing to make a long prologue to the history, and to abridge the history *itself.*

CHAPTER 3

1 WHEN the holy city was inhabited with all peace, and the laws were kept very well, because of the godliness of Onias the high priest, and his hatred of wickedness, **2** it came to pass that even the kings themselves did honor the place and glorify the temple with the noblest presents; **3** insomuch that even Seleucus the king of Asia of his own revenues bare all the costs belonging to the services of the sacrifices. **4** But one Simon of the tribe of Benjamin, having been made guardian of the temple, fell out with the high priest about the ruling of the market in the city. **5** And when he could not overcome Onias, he got him to Apollonius *the son* of Thraseus, who at that time was governor of Coelesyria and Phoenicia: **6** and he brought him word how that the treasury in Jerusalem was full of untold sums of money, so that the multitude of the funds was innumerable, and that they didn't pertain to the account of the sacrifices, but that it was possible that these should fall under the king's power. **7** And when Apollonius met the king, he informed him of the money whereof he had been told; and the king appointed Heliodorus, who was his chancellor, and sent him with a commandment to accomplish the removal of the aforesaid money. **8** So out with Heliodorus took his journey, under a color of visiting the cities of Coelesyria and Phoenicia, but in fact to execute the king's purpose. **9** And when he was come to Jerusalem and had been courteously received by the high priest of the city, he laid before *the m*an account of the information which had been given *him and* declared why he was come; and he inquired if in truth these things were so. **10** And the high priest explained to him that there were *in the treasury* deposits of widows and orphans, **11** and moreover some *money* belonging to Hyrcanus the *son* of Tobias, a man in very high place, and *that the case was* not as that impious Simon falsely alleged; and that in all there were four hundred talents of silver and two hundred of gold; **12** and that it was altogether impossible that wrong should be done to them that had put trust in the holiness of the place, and in the majesty and inviolable sanctity of the temple, honored over all the world. **13** But Heliodorus, because of the king's commandments given him, said that in any case this *money* must be confiscated for the king's treasury. **14** So having appointed a day, he entered in to direct the inquiry concerning these matters; and there was no small distress throughout the whole city. **15** And the priests, prostrating themselves before the altar in their priestly garments, and *looking* toward heaven, called upon him that gave the law concerning deposits, that he should preserve these *treasures* safe for those that had deposited them. **16** And whoever saw the mien of the high priest was wounded in mind; for his countenance and the change of his color betrayed the distress of his soul. **17** For a terror and a shuddering of the body had come over the man, whereby the pain that was in his heart was plainly shown to those who looked upon him. **18** And those who were in the houses rushed flocking out to make a universal supplication, because the place was like to come into contempt. **19** And the women, girded with sackcloth under their breasts, thronged the streets, and the virgins that were kept in ward ran together, some to the gates, others to the walls, and some looked out through the windows. **20** And all, stretching out their hands toward heaven, made their solemn supplication. **21** Then it would have pitied a man to see the multitude prostrating themselves all mixed together, and the expectation of the high priest in his sore distress. **22** While therefore they called upon the Almighty Lord to keep the things entrusted *to them* safe and sure for those that had entrusted them, **23** Heliodorus went on to execute that which had been decreed. **24** But when he was already present there with his guards near the treasury, the Sovereign of spirits and of all authority caused a great apparition, so that all that had presumed to come *in* with him, stricken with dismay at the power of God, fainted and were sore afraid. **25** For there was seen by them a horse with a terrible rider upon him, and adorned with beautiful trappings, and he rushed fiercely and struck at Heliodorus with his forefeet, and it seemed that he that sat upon the horse had complete armor of gold. **26** Two others also appeared to him, young men notable in their strength, and beautiful in their glory, and splendid in their apparel, who stood by him on either side, and scourged him unceasingly, inflicting on him many sore stripes. **27** And when he had fallen suddenly to the ground, and great darkness had come over him, *his guards* caught him up and put him into a litter, **28** and carried him, him that had just now entered with a great train and all his guard into the aforesaid treasury, himself now brought to utter helplessness, manifestly made to recognize the sovereignty of God. **29** And so, while he, through the working of God, speechless and bereft of all hope and deliverance, lay prostrate, **30** they blessed the Lord, that made marvelous his own place; and

the temple, which a little before was full of terror and alarm, was filled with joy and gladness after the Almighty Lord appeared. **31** But quickly certain of Heliodorus's familiar friends implored Onias to call upon the Most High, and grant life to him who lay quite at the last gasp. **32** And the high priest, secretly fearing lest the king might come to think that some treachery toward Heliodorus had been perpetrated by the Jews, brought a sacrifice for the deliverance of the man. **33** But as the high priest was making the atoning sacrifice, the same young men appeared again to Heliodorus, arrayed in the same garments; and they stood and said, Give Onias the high priest great thanks, for his sake the Lord has granted you life; **34** and do you, since you have been scourged from heaven, publish to all men the sovereign majesty of God. And when they had spoken these words, they vanished out of sight. **35** So Heliodorus, having offered a sacrifice to the Lord and vowed great vows to him that had saved his life, and having graciously received Onias, returned with his army to the king. **36** And he testified to all men the works of the great God which he had seen with his eyes. **37** And when the king asked Heliodorus, what manner of man was fit to be sent yet once again to Jerusalem, he said, **38** If you have any enemy or conspirator against the state, send him there, and you will receive him back well scourged, if he even escape with his life; because of a truth there is about the place a power of God. **39** For he that has his dwelling in heaven himself has his eyes upon that place and helps it; and those who come to hurt it he strikes and destroys. **40** And such was the history of Heliodorus and the keeping of the treasury.

CHAPTER 4

1 But the aforesaid Simon, he who had given information of the money, and *had betrayed* his country, slandered Onias, *saying* that it was he who had incited Heliodorus, and made himself the author of these evils. **2** And him that was the benefactor of the city, and the guardian of his fellow countrymen, and a zealot for the laws, he dared to call a conspirator against the state. **3** But when the growing enmity *between them* waxed so great, that even murders were perpetrated through one of Simon's trusted followers, **4** Onias, seeing the danger of the contention, and that Apollonius *the son* of Menestheus, the governor of Coelesyria and Phoenicia, was increasing Simon's malice, **5** betook himself to the king, not to be an accuser of his fellow-citizens, but looking to the good of all the people, both public and private; **6** for he saw that without the king's providence it was impossible for the state to obtain peace any more, and that Simon would not cease from his madness. **7** But when Seleucus was deceased, and Antiochus, who was called Epiphanes, succeeded to the kingdom, Jason the brother of Onias supplanted *his brother* in the high priesthood, **8** having promised to the king at an audience three hundred and threescore talents of silver, and *out* of another fund eighty talents; **9** and beside this, he undertook to assign a hundred and fifty more, if it might be allowed him through the king's authority to set him up a *Greek* place of exercise and *form*a body of youths *to be trained therein, and* to register the inhabitants of Jerusalem as *citizens* of Antioch. **10** And when the king had given assent, and he had gotten possession of the office, he out with brought over them of his own race to the Greek fashion. **11** And setting aside the royal ordinances of special favor to the Jews, granted by the means of John the father of Eupolemus, who went on the embassage to the Romans for friendship and alliance, and seeking to overthrow the lawful modes of life, he brought in new customs forbidden by the law: **12** for he eagerly established a *Greek* place of exercise under the citadel itself; and caused the noblest of the young men to wear the *Greek* cap. **13** And so there was an extreme of hellenization, and an advance of an alien religion, by reason of the exceeding profaneness of Jason, that ungodly man and no high priest; **14** so that the priests had no more any zeal for the services of the altar: but despising the sanctuary, and neglecting the sacrifices, they hastened to enjoy that which was unlawfully provided in the palaestra, after the summons of the discus; **15** making of no account the honors of their fathers, and thinking the glories of the Greeks best of all. **16** By reason whereof sore calamity beset them; and the men whose ways of living they earnestly followed, and to whom they desired to be made like in all things, these became their enemies and punished them. **17** For it is not a light thing to do impiously against the laws of God: but these things the time following will declare. **18** Now when certain games that came every fifth year were kept at Tyre, and the king was present, **19** the vile Jason sent sacred envoys, as being Antiochians of Jerusalem, bearing three hundred drachmas of silver to the sacrifice of Hercules, which even the bearers thereof thought not right to use for *any* sacrifice, because it was not fit, but to expend on another charge. **20** And though in the purpose of the sender this *money was for* the sacrifice of Hercules, yet on account of present circumstances it went to the equipment of the galleys. **21** Now when Apollonius the *son* of Menestheus was sent into Egypt for the enthronement of *Ptolemy* Philometor as king, Antiochus, learning that *Ptolemy* had shown himself ill affected toward the state, took thought for the security of his realm; for that reason, going *by sea* to Joppa, he travelled on to Jerusalem. **22** And being magnificently received by Jason and the city, he was brought in with torches and shouting. This done, he afterward led his army down into Phoenicia. **23** Now after a space of three years Jason sent Menelaus, the aforesaid Simon's brother, to bear the money to the king, and to make reports concerning some necessary matters. **24** But he being commended to the king, and having glorified himself by the display of his authority, got the high priesthood for himself, outbidding Jason by three hundred talents of silver. **25** And having received the royal mandates he came *to Jerusalem,* bringing nothing worthy the high priesthood, but having the passion of a cruel tyrant, and the rage of a savage beast. **26** And whereas Jason, who had supplanted his own brother, was supplanted by another and driven as a fugitive into the country of the Ammonites, **27** Menelaus had possession of the office: but of the money that had been promised to the king nothing was duly paid, and that though Sostratus the governor of the citadel demanded it **28** (for to him appertained the gathering of the revenues); for which cause they were both called by the king to his presence. **29** And Menelaus left his own brother Lysimachus for his deputy in the high priesthood; and Sostratus *left* Crates, who was over the Cyprians. **30** Now while such was the state of things, it came to pass that they of Tarsus and Mallus made insurrection, because they were to be given as a present to Antiochis, the king's concubine. **31** The king therefore came *to Cilicia*in all haste to settle matters, leaving for his deputy Andronicus, a man of high rank. **32** And Menelaus, supposing that he had gotten a favorable opportunity, presented to Andronicus certain vessels of gold belonging to the temple, which he had stolen: other *vessels* also he had already sold into Tyre and the surrounding cities. 33 And when Onias had sure knowledge *of this,* he sharply reproved him, having withdrawn himself into a sanctuary at Daphne, that lies by Antioch. 34 For that reason, Menelaus, taking Andronicus apart, prayed him to kill Onias. And coming to Onias, and being persuaded to use treachery, and being received as a friend, Andronicus gave him his right hand with oaths *of fidelity, and*, though he was suspected *by him, so* persuaded him to come out of the sanctuary; and out with he dispatched him without regard of justice. 35 For the which cause not only Jews, but many also of the other nations, had indignation and displeasure at the unjust murder of the man. 36 And when the king was come back again from the places in Cilicia, the Jews that were in the city pleaded before him *against Andronicus* (the Greeks also joining with them in hatred of the wickedness), urging that Onias had been wrongfully slain. 37 Antiochus therefore was heartily sorry, and was moved to pity, and wept, because of the sober and well-ordered life of him that was dead; 38 and being inflamed with passion, out with he stripped off Andronicus's purple robe, and tore off his under garments, and when he had led him round through the whole city to that very place where he had committed impiety against Onias, there he put the murderer out of the way, the Lord rendering to him the punishment he had deserved. 39 Now when many sacrileges had been committed in the city by Lysimachus with the consent of Menelaus, and when the report of them was spread abroad outside, the people gathered themselves together against Lysimachus, after many vessels of gold had been already dispersed. 40 And when the multitudes were rising against *him, and* were filled with anger, Lysimachus armed about three thousand men, and with unrighteous violence began *the conflict,* one Hauran, a man far gone in years and no less also in madness, leading *the attack.* 41 But when they perceived the assault of Lysimachus, some caught up stones, others logs of wood, and some took handfuls of the ashes that lay near, and they flung them all pell-mell upon Lysimachus and those who were with him; 42 by reason of which they wounded many of them, and some they struck to the ground, and all *of them* they forced to flee, but the author of the sacrilege himself they killed beside the treasury. 43 But touching these matters there was an accusation laid against Menelaus. 44 And when the king was come to Tyre, the three men that were sent by the senate pleaded the cause before him. 45 But Menelaus, seeing himself now defeated, promised much money to Ptolemy the *son* of Dorymenes, that he might win over the king. 46 Whereupon Ptolemy taking the king aside into a cloister, as it were to take the air, brought him to be of another mind: 47 and him that was the cause of all the evil, Menelaus, he discharged from the accusations; but these hapless men, who, if they had pleaded even before Scythians, would have been discharged uncondemned, them he sentenced to death. 48 Soon then did those who were spokesmen for the city and the families *of Israel* and the holy vessels suffer that unrighteous penalty. 49 For which cause even certain Tyrians, moved with hatred of the wickedness, provided magnificently for their burial. 50 But Menelaus through the covetous dealings of those who were in power remained still in his office, growing in wickedness, as a great conspirator against his fellow-citizens.

CHAPTER 5

1 Now about this time Antiochus made his second inroad into Egypt. 2 And it *so* befell that throughout all the city, for the space of almost forty days, there appeared in the midst of the sky horsemen in swift motion, wearing robes inwrought with gold and *carrying* spears, equipped in troops for battle; 3 and drawing of swords; and *on the other side* squadrons of horse in array; and encounters and pursuits of both *armies;* and shaking of shields, and multitudes of lances, and casting of darts, and flashing of golden trappings, and girding on of all sorts of armor. 4 For that reason, all men implored that the vision might have been given for good. 5 But when a false rumor had arisen that Antiochus was deceased, Jason took not less than a thousand men, and suddenly made an assault upon the city; and those who were upon the wall being routed, and the city being now at length well near taken, Menelaus took refuge in the citadel. 6 But Jason slaughtered his own citizens without mercy, not considering that good success against kinsmen is the greatest ill success, but supposing himself to be setting up trophies over enemies, and not over fellow-countrymen. 7 The office *however* he didn't get, but, receiving shame as the end of his

conspiracy, he passed again a fugitive into the country of the Ammonites. **8** At the last therefore he met with a miserable end: having been shut up at the court of Aretas the prince of the Arabians, fleeing from city to city, pursued of all men, hated as an apostate from the laws, and held in abomination as the butcher of his country and his fellow-citizens, he was cast out into Egypt; **9** and he that had driven many from their own country into strange lands perished *himself* in a strange land, having crossed the sea to the Lacedaemonians, as thinking to find shelter *there* because they were near of kin; **10** and he that had cast out a multitude unburied had none to mourn for him, nor had he any funeral at all, or place in the sepulcher of his fathers. **11** Now when tidings came to the king concerning that which was done, he thought that Judea was in revolt; whereupon setting out from Egypt in a furious mind, he took the city by force of arms, **12** and commanded his soldiers to cut down without mercy such as came in their way, and to kill such as went up upon the houses; **13** and there was killing of young and old, making away of boys, women, and children, slaying of virgins and infants. **14** And in all the three days *of the slaughter* there were destroyed fourscore thousand, *where of* forty thousand *were slain* in close combat, and no fewer were sold than slain. **15** But not content with this he presumed to enter into the most holy temple of all the earth, having Menelaus for his guide (him that had proved himself a traitor both to the laws and to his country), **16** even taking the sacred vessels with his polluted hands, and dragging down with his profane hands the offerings that had been dedicated by other kings to the augmentation and glory and honor of the place. **17** And Antiochus was lifted up in mind, not seeing that because of the sins of those who lived in the city the Sovereign Lord had been provoked to anger a little while, and therefore his eye was *then* turned away from the place. **18** But had it not so been that they were already bound by many sins, this man, even as Heliodorus who was sent by Seleucus the king to view the treasury, would, so soon as he pressed forward, have been scourged and turned back from his daring deed. **19** However the Lord didn't choose the nation for the place's sake, but the place for the nation's sake. **20** For that reason, also the place itself, having shared in the calamities that befell the nation, did afterward share in *its* benefits; and

the *place* which was forsaken in the wrath of the Almighty was, at the reconciliation of the great Sovereign, restored again with all glory. **21** As for Antiochus, when he had carried away out of the temple a thousand and eight hundred talents, he departed in all haste to Antioch, thinking in his arrogance to make the land navigable and the sea passable by foot, because his heart was lifted up. **22** And moreover he left governors to afflict the race: at Jerusalem, Philip, by race a Phrygian, and in character more barbarous than him that set him there; **23** and at Gerizim, Andronicus; and besides these, Menelaus, who worse than all the rest exalted himself against his fellow-citizens. And having a malicious mind toward the Jews *whom he had made* his citizens, **24** he sent that lord of pollutions Apollonius with an army of two and twenty thousand, commanding him to kill all those that were of full age, and to sell the women and the younger men. **25** And he coming to Jerusalem, and playing the man of peace, waited until the holy day of the Sabbath, and finding the Jews at rest from work, he commanded his men to parade in arms. **26** And he put to the sword all those who came out to the spectacle; and running into the city with the armed men he killed great multitudes. **27** But Judas, who is also *called* Maccabaeus, with nine others or thereabout, withdrew himself, and with his company kept himself alive in the mountains after the manner of wild beasts; and they continued feeding on such poor herbs as grew there, that they might not be partakers of the *threatened* pollution.

CHAPTER 6

1 And not long after this the king sent out an old man of Athens to compel the Jews to depart from the laws of their fathers, and not to live after the laws of God; **2** and also to pollute the sanctuary in Jerusalem, and to call it by the name of Jupiter Olympius, and *to call* the *sanctuary* in Gerizim by the name of Jupiter the Protector of strangers, even as they were that lived in the place. **3** But sore and utterly grievous was the visitation of this evil. **4** For the temple was filled with riot and reveling by the heathen, who dallied with prostitutes, and had to do with women within the sacred precincts, and moreover brought inside things that were not befitting; **5** and the place of sacrifice was filled with those abominable things which had been prohibited by the laws. **6** And a man could neither keep the Sabbath, nor observe the feasts of the fathers, nor so much as confess himself to be a Jew. **7** And on the day of the king's birth every month they were led along with bitter constraint to eat of the sacrifices; and when the feast of Bacchus came, they were compelled to go in procession in honor of Bacchus, wearing wreaths of ivy. **8** A decree went out to the neighboring Greek cities, by the suggestion of Ptolemy, that they should observe the same conduct against the Jews and should make them eat of the sacrifices; **9** and that they should kill such as didn't choose to go over to the Greek rites. So the present misery was for all to see: **10** for two women were brought up for having circumcised their children; and these, when they had led them publicly around the city, with the babes hung from their breasts, they cast down headlong from the wall. **11** And others, that had run together into the caves nearby to keep the seventh day secretly, being betrayed to Philip were all burned together, because they scrupled to defend themselves, from regard to the honor of that most solemn day. **12** I implore therefore those that read this book, that they be not discouraged because of the calamities, but account that these punishments were not for the destruction, but for the chastening of our race. **13** For indeed that those who act impiously be not let alone any long time, but immediately meet with retribution, is a sign of great beneficence. **14** For in the case of the other nations the Sovereign Lord does with patience forbear, until that he punishes them when they have attained to the full measure of *their* sins; but not so judged he as touching us, **15** that he may not take vengeance on us afterward, when we come to the height of our sins. **16** For that reason, he never withdraws his mercy from us; but though he chastens with calamity, yet does he not forsake his own people. **17** However let this that we have spoken suffice to put *you* in remembrance; but after *these* few words we must come to the narrative. **18** Eleazar, one of the principal scribes, a man already well stricken in years, and of a noble countenance, was compelled to open his mouth to eat swine's flesh. **19** But he, welcoming death with renown rather than life with pollution, advanced of his own accord to the instrument of torture, but first spat out *the flesh,* **20** *coming forward* as men ought to come that are resolute to repel such things as not *even* for the natural love of life is it lawful to taste. **21** But those who had the charge of

that forbidden sacrificial feast took the man aside, for the acquaintance which of old times they had with him, and privately implored him to bring flesh of his own providing, such as was befitting for him to use, and to make as if he did eat of the flesh from the sacrifice, as had been commanded by the king; **22** that by so doing he might be delivered from death, and for his ancient friendship with them might be treated kindly. **23** But he, having formed a high resolve, and one that became his years, and the dignity of old age, and the gray hairs which he had reached with honor, and his excellent education from a child, or rather *that became* the holy laws of God's ordaining, declared his mind accordingly, bidding them quickly send him to Hades. **24** For it becomes not our years to dissemble, *said he,* that *through this* many of the young should suppose that Eleazar, the man of fourscore years and ten, had gone over to an alien religion; **25** and *so* they, by reason of my dissimulation, and for the sake of this brief and momentary life, should be led astray because of me, and *so* I get to myself a pollution and a stain of my old age. **26** For even if for the present time I will remove from me the punishment of men, yet will I not escape the hands of the Almighty, either living or dead. **27** For that reason, by manfully parting with my life now, I will show myself worthy of my old age, **28** and leave behind a noble example to the young to die willingly and nobly a glorious death for the reverend and holy laws. And when he had said these words, he went immediately to the instrument of torture. **29** And when they changed the good will they bore toward him a little before into ill will, because these words of his were, as they thought, sheer madness, **30** and when he was at the point to die with the stripes, he groaned aloud and said, "To the Lord, who has the holy knowledge, it is manifest that, whereas I might have been delivered from death, I endure sore pains in my body by being scourged; but in soul I gladly suffer these things for my fear of him." **31** So this man also died after this manner, leaving his death for an example of nobleness and a memorial of virtue, not only to the young but also to the great body of his nation.

CHAPTER 7

1 And it came to pass that seven kindred also with their mother were at the king's command taken and shamefully handled with scourges and cords, to compel them to taste of the abominable swine's flesh. **2** But one of them made himself the spokesman and said, "What would you ask and learn of us? For we are ready to die rather than transgress the laws of our fathers." **3** And the king fell into a rage and commanded to heat pans and caldrons: **4** and when these were heated, he commanded to cut out the tongue of him that had been their spokesman, and to scalp him, and to cut off his extremities, the rest of his kindred and his mother looking on. **5** And when he was utterly maimed, *the king* commanded to bring him to the fire, being yet alive, and to fry him in the pan. And as the vapor of the pan spread far, they and their mother also exhorted one another to die nobly, saying: **6** The Lord God sees, and in truth is entreated for us, as Moses declared in his song, which witnesses against *the people* to their faces, saying, and he will be treated for his servants. **7** And when the first had died after this manner, they brought the second to the mocking; and they pulled off the skin of his head with the hair and asked him, "Will you eat, before your body is punished in every limb?" **8** But he answered in the language of his fathers and said to them, "No." Therefore he also underwent the next torture in succession, as the first had done. **9** And when he was at the last gasp, he said, "You, miscreant, release us out of this present life, but the King of the world will raise us up, who have died for his laws, to an eternal renewal of life." **10** And after him was the third made a mocking-stock. And when he was required, he quickly put out his tongue, and stretched out his hands courageously, **11** and nobly said, "From heaven I possess these; and for his laws' sake I treat these with contempt; and from him I hope to receive these back again": **12** insomuch that the king himself and those who were with him were astonished at the young man's soul, for he regarded the pain as nothing. **13** And when he too was dead, they shamefully handled and tortured the fourth in like manner. **14** And being come near to death he said: It is good to die at the hands of men and look for the hopes which are *given* by God, that we will be raised up again by him; for as for you, you will have no resurrection to life. **15** And next after him they brought the fifth, and shamefully handled him. **16** But he looked toward the king and said, "Because you have authority among men, though you are *yourself* corruptible, you do what you will; yet think not that our race has been forsaken of God;

17 but hold you on your way, and behold his sovereign majesty, how it will torture you and your seed." **18** And after him they brought the sixth. And when he was at the point to die he said, "Be not vainly deceived, for we suffer these things for our own doings, as sinning against our own God: marvelous things are come to pass; **19** but do not think that you will be unpunished, having assayed to fight against God." **20** But above all was the mother marvelous and worthy of honorable memory; for when she looked on seven sons perishing within the space of one day, she bare *the sight* with a good courage for the hopes *that she had set* on the Lord. **21** And she exhorted each one of them in the language of their fathers, filled with a noble temper and stirring up her womanish thought with manly passion, saying to them, **22** "I know not how you came into my womb, neither was it I that bestowed on you your spirit and your life, and it was not I that brought into order the first elements of each one of you. **23** Therefore the Creator of the world, who fashioned the generation of man and devised the generation of all things, in mercy gives back to you again both your spirit and your life, as you now treat yourselves with contempt for his laws' sake." **24** But Antiochus, thinking himself to be despised, and suspecting the reproachful voice, while the youngest was yet alive didn't only make his appeal *to him* by words, but also at the same time promised with oaths that he would enrich him and raise him to high estate, if he would turn from the *customs* of his fathers, and that he would take him for his friend and entrust him with affairs. **25** But when the young man would in no wise give heed, the king called to him his mother, and exhorted her that she would counsel the lad to save himself. **26** And when he had exhorted her with many words, she undertook to persuade her son. **27** But bending toward him, laughing the cruel tyrant to scorn, she spoke this in the language of her fathers: "My son, have pity upon me that carried you nine months in my womb, and gave you suck three years, and nourished and brought you up to this age, and sustained you. **28** I implore you, my child, to lift your eyes to the heaven and the earth, and to see all things that are in it, and so to recognize that God made them not of things that were, and *that* the race of men in this way comes into being. **29** Don't be afraid of this butcher, but, proving yourself worthy of your kindred, accept your death, that in the mercy *of God* I may receive you again with your kindred." **30** But before she had yet ended speaking, the young man said, "Whom do you wait for? I obey not the commandment of the king, but I listen to the commandment of the law that was given to our fathers through Moses. **31** But you, that have devised all manner of evil against the Hebrews, will in no wise escape the hands of God. **32** For we are suffering because of our own sins; **33** and if for rebuke and chastening our living Lord has been angered a little while, yet will he again be reconciled with his own servants. **34** But you, O unholy man and of all most vile, be not vainly lifted up in your wild pride with uncertain hopes, raising your hand against the heavenly children; **35** For not yet have you escaped the judgement of the Almighty God that sees *all things.* **36** For these our kindred, having endured a short pain that brings everlasting life, have now died under God's covenant; But you, through the judgement of God, will receive in just measure the penalties of your arrogance. **37** But I, as my kindred, give up both body and soul for the laws of our fathers, calling upon God that he may speedily become gracious to the nation; and that you amidst trials and plagues may confess that he alone is God; **38** and that in me and my kindred you may stay the wrath of the Almighty, which has been justly brought upon our whole race." **39** But the king, falling into a rage, handled him worse than all the rest, being exasperated at his mocking. **40** So he also died pure *from pollution,* putting his whole trust in the Lord. **41** And last of all after her sons the mother died. **42** Let it then suffice to have said so much concerning the *enforcement of* sacrificial feasts and the *king's* exceeding barbarities.

CHAPTER 8

1 But Judas, who is also *called* Maccabaeus, and those who were with him, making their way privily into the villages, called to them their kinsfolk; and taking to them such as had continued in the Jews' religion, gathered together as many as six thousand. **2** And they called upon the Lord, *imploreing him* to look upon the people that was oppressed by all; and to have compassion on the sanctuary also that had been profaned by the ungodly men; **3** and to have pity on the city also that was suffering ruin and ready to be made level with the ground; and to listen to the blood that cried to him; **4** and to remember also the lawless slaughter of the innocent infants, and the blasphemies that had been committed against his name; and to show his hatred of wickedness. **5** And when Maccabaeus had trained his men for service, the heathen at once found him irresistible, for that the wrath of the Lord was turned into pity. **6** And coming unawares he set fire to cities and villages. And in winning back the most important positions, putting to flight no small number of the enemies, **7** he especially took advantage of the nights for such assaults. And his courage was loudly talked of everywhere. **8** But when Philip saw the man gaining ground by little and little, and increasing more and more in his prosperity, he wrote to Ptolemy, the governor of Coelesyria and Phoenicia, that he should support the king's cause. **9** And *Ptolemy* quickly appointed Nicanor the *son* of Patroclus, one of the king's chief friends, and sent him, in command of no fewer than twenty thousand of all nations, to destroy the whole race of Judea; and with him he joined Gorgias also, a captain and one that had experience in matters of war. **10** And Nicanor undertook by *the sale of the* captive Jews to make up for the king the tribute of two thousand talents which he was to pay to the Romans. **11** And immediately he sent to the cities upon the sea coast, inviting them to buy Jewish slaves, promising to allow fourscore and ten slaves for a talent, not expecting the judgement that was to follow upon him from the Almighty. **12** But tidings came to Judas concerning the inroad of Nicanor; and when he communicated to those who were with him the presence of the army, **13** those who were cowardly and distrustful of the judgement of God ran away and left the country. **14** And others sold all that was left over to them, and withal implored the Lord to deliver those who had been sold *as slaves* by the impious Nicanor before he ever met them; **15** and *this,* if not for their own sakes, yet for the covenants made with their fathers, and because he had called them by his reverend and glorious name. **16** And Maccabaeus gathered his men together, six thousand in number, and exhorted them not to be stricken with dismay at the enemy, nor to fear the great multitude of the heathen who came wrongfully against them; but to contend nobly, **17** setting before their eyes the outrage that had been lawlessly perpetrated upon the holy place, and the shameful handling of the city that had been turned to mockery, and further the overthrow of the mode of life received from their ancestors. **18** For they, said he, trust to arms, and withal to deeds of daring; but we trust on the almighty God, since he is able at a beck to cast down those who are coming against us, and even the whole world. **19** And moreover he recounted to them the help given from time to time in the days of their ancestors, both the *help given* in the days of Sennacherib, how that a hundred fourscore and five thousand perished, **20** and the *help given* in the land of Babylon, even the battle that was fought against the Gauls, how that they came to the engagement eight thousand in all, with four thousand Macedonians, and *how that,* the Macedonians being hard pressed, the six thousand destroyed the hundred and twenty thousand, because of the help which they had from heaven, and took great booty. **21** And when he had with these words made them of good courage, and ready to die for the laws and their country, he divided his army into four parts; **22** appointing his kindred to be with himself leaders of the several bands, *to wit,* Simon and Joseph and Jonathan, giving each the command of fifteen hundred men, **23** and moreover Eleazer also: *then,* having read aloud the sacred book, and having given as watchword, THE HELP OF GOD, leading the first band himself, he joined battle with Nicanor. **24** And, since the Almighty fought on their side, they killed of the enemy above nine thousand, and wounded and disabled the more part of Nicanor's army and compelled all to flee: **25** and they took the money of those that had come there to buy them. And after they had pursued them for some distance, they returned, being constrained by the time of the day; **26** for it was the day before the Sabbath, and for this cause they made no effort to chase them far. **27** And when they had gathered the arms of the enemy together, and had stripped off their spoils, they occupied themselves about the Sabbath, blessing and thanking the Lord exceedingly, who had saved them to this day, for that he had caused a beginning of mercy to distil upon them. **28** And after the Sabbath, when they had given of the spoils to the maimed, and to the widows and orphans, the residue they distributed among themselves and their children. **29** And when they had accomplished these things, and had made a common supplication, they implored the merciful Lord to be wholly reconciled with his servants. **30** And having had an encounter with the forces of Timotheus and Bacchides, they killed above twenty thousand of them, and made themselves masters of strongholds exceedingly high, and divided very much plunder, giving the maimed and orphans and widows, and moreover the aged also, an equal share with themselves. **31** And when they had gathered the arms of the enemy together, they stored them all up carefully in the most important positions, and the residue of the spoils they carried to Jerusalem. **32** And they killed the phylarch of Timotheus's forces, a most unholy man, and one who had done the Jews much hurt. **33** And as they kept the feast of victory in the city of their fathers, they burned those that had set the sacred gates on fire, and *among them* Callisthenes, who had fled into an outhouse; and *so* they received the meet reward of their impiety. **34** And the thrice-accursed Nicanor, who had brought the thousand merchants to buy the Jews *for slaves,* **35** being through the help of the Lord humbled by them who in his eyes were held to be of least account, put off his glorious apparel, and *passing* through the midland, shunning all company like a fugitive slave, arrived at Antioch, having, *as he thought,* had the greatest possible good fortune, though his army was destroyed. **36** And he that had taken upon him to make tribute sure for the Romans by the captivity of the men of Jerusalem published abroad that the Jews had One who fought for them, and that because this was so the Jews were invulnerable, because they followed the laws ordained by him.

CHAPTER 9

1 Now about that time it befell that Antiochus had returned in disorder from the region of Persia. **2** For he had entered into the city called Persepolis, and he assayed to rob a temple and to hold down the city. Whereupon there was an onset of the multitudes, and *Antiochus and his men* turned to make defense with arms; and it came to pass that Antiochus was put to flight by the people of the country and broke up his camp with disgrace. **3** And while he was at Ecbatana, news was brought him what had happened to Nicanor and the forces of Timotheus. **4** And being lifted up by his passion he thought to make the Jews suffer even for the evil-doing of those that had put him to rout. For that reason, the judgement from heaven even now accompanying him, he gave order to his charioteer to drive without ceasing and dispatch the journey; for so he arrogantly spoke: I will make Jerusalem a common graveyard of Jews, when I come there. **5** But the All-seeing Lord, the God of Israel, struck him with a fatal and invisible stroke; and as soon as he had ceased speaking this word, an incurable pain of the bowels seized him, and bitter torments of the inner parts; **6** and that most justly, for he had tormented other men's bowels with many and strange sufferings. **7** But he in no wise ceased from his rude insolence; no, still more was he filled with arrogance, breathing fire in his passion against the Jews, and commanding to haste the journey. But it came to pass moreover that he fell from his chariot as it rushed along, and having a grievous fall was racked in all the members of his body. **8** And he that but now supposed himself to have the waves of the sea at his bidding, so vainglorious was he beyond the condition of a man, and that thought to weigh the heights of the mountains in a balance, was now brought to the ground and carried in a litter, showing to all that the power was manifestly God's; **9** so that out of the body of the impious man worms swarmed, and while he was still living in anguish and pains, his flesh fell off, and by reason of the stench all the army turned with loathing from his corruption. **10** And the man that a little before supposed himself to touch the stars of heaven, no one could endure to carry for his intolerable stench. **11** Therefore he began in great part to cease from his arrogance, being broken *in spirit, and* to come to knowledge under the scourge of God, his pains increasing every moment. **12** And when he himself could not stand his own smell, he said these words: It is right to be subject to God, and that one who is mortal should not be inclined arrogantly. **13** And the vile man vowed to the sovereign Lord, who now no more would have pity upon him, saying on this wise: **14** that the holy city, to the which he was going in haste, to lay it even with the ground and to make it a common graveyard, he would declare free; **15** and as touching the Jews, whom he had decided not even to count worthy of burial, but to cast them out to the beasts with their infants, for the birds to devour, he would make them all equal to citizens of Athens; **16** and the holy sanctuary, which before he had plundered, he would adorn with goodlie offerings, and would restore all the sacred vessels many times multiplied, and out of his own revenues would defray the charges that were required for the sacrifices; **17** and, beside all this, that he would become a Jew, and would visit every inhabited place, publishing abroad the might of God. **18** But when his sufferings did in no wise cease, for the judgement of God had come upon him in righteousness, having given up all hope of himself, he wrote to the Jews the letter written below, having the nature of a supplication, to this effect: **19** To the worthy Jews, his fellow-citizens, Antiochus, king and general, wishes much joy and health and prosperity. **20** May you and your children fare well; and your affairs will be to your mind. Having my hope in heaven, **21** I remembered with affection your honor and good will *toward me.* Returning out of the region of Persia, and being taken with a noisome sickness, I deemed it necessary to take thought for the common safety of all, **22** not despairing of myself, but having great hope to escape from the sickness. **23** But considering that my father also, at what time he led an army into the upper country, appointed his successor, **24** to the end that, if anything fell out contrary to expectation, or if any unwelcome tidings were brought, they *that remained* in the country, knowing to whom the state had been left, might not be troubled; **25** and, besides all this, observing how that the princes that are borderers and neighbors to my kingdom watch opportunities, and look for the future event, I have appointed my son Antiochus *to be* king, whom I often committed and commended to most of you, when I was hastening to the upper provinces; and I have written to him what is written below. **26** I exhort you therefore and implore you, having in your remembrance the benefits done to you in common and severally, to preserve each of you your present good will toward me and my son. **27** For I am persuaded that he in gentleness and kindness will follow my purpose and treat you with indulgence. **28** So the murderer and blasphemer, having endured the most intense sufferings, even as he had dealt with other men, ended his life among the mountains by a most piteous fate in a strange land. **29** And Philip his foster brother conveyed the body *home;* and then, fearing the son of Antiochus, he betook himself to Ptolemy Philometor in Egypt.

CHAPTER 10

1 And Maccabaeus and those who were with him, the Lord leading them on, recovered the temple and the city; **2** and they pulled down the altars that had been built in the marketplace by the aliens, and also *the walls of* sacred enclosures. **3** And having cleansed the sanctuary they made another altar of sacrifice;

and striking stones and taking fire out of them, they offered sacrifices, after *they had ceased for* two years, and *burned* incense, and *lighted* lamps, and set out the show bread. 4 And when they had done these things, they fell prostrate and implored the Lord that they might fall no more into such evils; but that, if ever they should sin, they might be chastened by him with forbearance, and not be delivered to blaspheming and barbarous heathen. 5 Now on the same day that the sanctuary was profaned by aliens, upon that very day did it come to pass that the cleansing of the sanctuary was made, even on the five and twentieth day of the same month, which is Chislev. 6 And they kept eight days with gladness in the manner *of the feast* of tabernacles, remembering how that not long before, during the feast of tabernacles, they were wandering in the mountains and in the caves after the manner of wild beasts. 7 For that reason, bearing wands wreathed with leaves, and fair boughs, and palms also, they offered up hymns of thanksgiving to him that had prosperously brought to pass the cleansing of his own place. 8 They ordained also with a common statute and decree, for all the nation of the Jews, that they should keep these days every year. 9 And such was the end of Antiochus, who was called Epiphanes. 10 But now will we declare what came to pass under Antiochus *named* Eupator, who proved himself a *true* son of that ungodly man and will gather up briefly the successive evils of the wars. 11 For this man, when he succeeded to the kingdom, appointed one Lysias *to be* chancellor, and supreme governor of Coelesyria and Phoenicia. 12 For Ptolemy that was called Macron, setting an example of observing justice toward the Jews because of the wrong that had been done to them, endeavored to conduct his dealings with them on peaceful terms. 13 Whereupon being accused by the king*'s friend*s before Eupator, and hearing himself called traitor at every turn, because he had abandoned Cyprus which Philometor had entrusted to him, and had withdrawn himself to Antiochus *called* Epiphanes, and failing to uphold the honor of his office, he took poison and made away with himself. 14 But Gorgias, when he was made governor of the district, maintained a force of mercenaries, and at every turn kept up war with the Jews. 15 And together with him the Idumaeans also, being masters of important strongholds, harassed the Jews; and receiving to them those that had taken refuge *there* from Jerusalem, they assayed to keep up war. 16 But Maccabaeus and his men, having made solemn supplication and having implored God to fight on their side, rushed upon the strongholds of the Idumaeans; 17 and assaulting them vigorously they made themselves masters of the positions, and kept off all that fought upon the wall, and killed those that fell in their way, and killed no fewer than twenty thousand. 18 And because no less than nine thousand were fled into two towers exceedingly strong and having all things *needed* for a siege, 19 Maccabaeus, having left Simon and Joseph, and Zacchaeus besides and those who were with him, a force sufficient to besiege them, departed himself to places where he was most needed. 20 But Simon and those who were with him, yielding to covetousness, were bribed by certain of those that were in the towers, and receiving seventy thousand drachmas let some of them slip away. 21 But when word was brought to Maccabaeus of what was done, he gathered the leaders of the people together, and accused *those men* of having sold their kindred for money, by setting their enemies free *to fight* against them. 22 So he killed these men for having turned traitors, and out with took possession of the two towers. 23 And prospering with his arms in all things he took in hand, he destroyed in the two strongholds more than twenty thousand. 24 Now Timotheus, who had been before defeated by the Jews, having gathered together foreign forces in great multitudes, and having collected the horsemen which belonged to Asia, not a few, came as though he would take Judea by force of arms. 25 But as he drew near, Maccabaeus and his men sprinkled earth upon their heads and girded their loins with sackcloth, in supplication to God, 26 and falling down upon the step in front of the altar, implored him to become gracious to them, and be an enemy to their enemies and an adversary to their adversaries, as the law declares. 27 And rising from their prayer they took up their arms and advanced some distance from the city; and when they had come near to their enemies they halted. 28 And when the dawn was now spreading, the two *armies* joined battle; the one part having this, beside *their* virtue, for a pledge of success and victory, that they had fled to the Lord for refuge, the others making their passion their leader in the strife. 29 But when the battle waxed strong, there appeared out of heaven to their adversaries five men on horses with bridles of gold, *in splendid array;* and two of them, leading on the Jews, 30 and taking Maccabaeus in the midst of them, and covering him with their own armor, guarded him from wounds, while on the adversaries they shot out arrows and thunderbolts; by reason whereof they were blinded and thrown into confusion, and were cut to pieces, filled with bewilderment. 31 And there were slain twenty thousand and five hundred, beside six hundred horsemen. 32 But Timotheus himself fled into a stronghold called Gazara, a fortress of exceedingly strength, Chaereas being in command there. 33 But Maccabaeus and his men were glad and laid siege to the fortress four and twenty days. 34 And those who were within, trusting to the strength of the place, blasphemed exceedingly, and hurled out impious words. 35 But at dawn of the five and twentieth day certain young men of the company of Maccabaeus, inflamed with passion because of the blasphemies, assaulted the wall with masculine force and with furious passion, and cut down whoever came in their way. 36 And others climbing up in like manner, while *the besieged* were distracted with them *that had made their way* within, set fire to the towers, and kindling fires burned the blasphemers alive; while others broke open the gates, and, having given entrance to the rest of the band, occupied the city. 37 And they killed Timotheus, who was hidden in a cistern, and his brother Chaereas, and Apollophanes. 38 And when they had accomplished these things, they blessed the Lord with hymns and thanksgiving, him who does great benefits to Israel, and gives them the victory.

CHAPTER 11

1 Now after a very little time Lysias, the king's guardian and kinsman and chancellor, being sore displeased for the things that had come to pass, 2 collected about fourscore thousand *footmen* and all his horsemen and came against the Jews, thinking to make the city a place for Greeks to dwell in, 3 and to levy tribute on the temple, a son the other sacred places of the nations, and to put up the high priesthood to sale every year; 4 holding in no account the might of God, but puffed up with his tens of thousands of footmen, and his thousands of horsemen, and his fourscore elephants. 5 And coming into Judea and drawing near to Bethsuron, which was a strong place and distant from Jerusalem about five leagues, he pressed it hard. 6 But when Maccabaeus and his men learned that he was besieging the strongholds, they and all the people with lamentations and tears made supplication to the Lord to send a good angel to save Israel. 7 And Maccabaeus himself took up arms first and exhorted the others to put themselves in jeopardy together with him and help their kindred; and they went out with him very willingly. 8 And as they were there, close to Jerusalem, there appeared at their head one on horseback in white apparel, brandishing weapons of gold. 9 And they all together praised the merciful God and were yet more strengthened in heart: being ready to assail not men only but the wildest beasts, and walls of iron, 10 they advanced in array, having him that is in heaven to fight on their side, for the Lord had mercy on them. 11 And hurling *themselves* like lions upon the enemy, they killed of them eleven thousand *footmen* and sixteen hundred horsemen and forced all *the rest* to flee. 12 But the more part of them escaped wounded *and* naked; and Lysias also himself escaped by shameful flight. 13 But as he was a man not void of understanding, weighing with himself the defeat which had befallen him, and considering that the Hebrews could not be overcome, because the Almighty God fought on their side, he sent again *to them,* 14 and persuaded them to come to terms on condition that all their rights were acknowledged, and *promised* that he would also persuade the king to become their friend. 15 And Maccabaeus gave consent upon all the conditions which Lysias proposed to him, being careful of the *common* good; for whatever *requests* Maccabaeus delivered in writing to Lysias concerning the Jews the king allowed. 16 For the letters written to the Jews from Lysias were to this effect: Lysias to the people of the Jews, greeting. 17 John and Absalom, who were sent from you, having delivered the petition written below, made request concerning the things signified therein. 18 Whatever things therefore had need to be brought before the king I declared *to him, and* what things were possible he allowed. 19 If then you will preserve your good will toward the state, henceforward I will also endeavor to contribute to *your* good. 20 And on this behalf I have given order in detail, both to these men and to those *that are sent* from me, to confer with you. 21 Fare you well. *Written* in the hundred forty and eighth year, on the four and

twentieth day of the *month* Dioscorinthius. **22** And the king's letter was in these words: King Antiochus to his brother Lysias, greeting. **23** Seeing that our father passed to the gods having the wish that the subjects of his kingdom should be undisturbed and give themselves to the care of their own affairs, **24** we, having heard that the Jews do not consent to our father's purpose to turn them to the *customs* of the Greeks, but choose rather their own manner of living, and make request that the *customs* of their law be allowed to them,—**25** choosing therefore that this nation also should be free from disturbance, we determine that their temple be restored to them, and that they live according to the customs that were in the days of their ancestors. **26** You will therefore do well to send *messengers* to them and give them the right hand *of friendship,* that they, knowing our mind, may be of good heart, and gladly occupy themselves with the conduct of their own affairs. **27** And to the nation the king's letter was after this manner: King Antiochus to the senate of the Jews and to the other Jews, greeting. **28** If you fare well, we have our desire: we ourselves also are in good health. **29** Menelaus informed us that your desire was to return home and follow your own business. **30** They therefore that depart home up to the thirtieth day of Xanthicus will have *our* friendship, with full permission **31** that the Jews use their own *proper* meats and *observe their own* laws, even as formerly; and none of them will be in any way molested for the things that have been ignorantly done. **32** Moreover I have sent Menelaus also, that he may encourage you. **33** Fare you well. *Written* in the hundred forty and eighth year, on the fifteenth day of Xanthicus. **34** And the Romans also sent to them a letter in these words: Quintus Memmius *and* Titus Manius, ambassadors of the Romans, to the people of the Jews, greeting. **35** In regard to the things which Lysias the king's kinsman granted you, we also give consent. **36** But as for the things which he judged should be referred to the king, send one out with, after you have advised thereof, that we may publish such *decrees* as befit your case; for we are on our way to Antioch. **37** For that reason, send some with speed, that we also may learn what is your mind. **38** Farewell. *Written* in the hundred forty and eighth year, on the fifteenth day of Xanthicus.

CHAPTER 12

1 So when these covenants had been made, Lysias departed to the king, and the Jews went about their husbandry. **2** But *certain* of the governors of districts, Timotheus and Apollonius the *son* of Gennaeus, and Hieronymus also and Demophon, and beside them Nicanor the governor of Cyprus, would not suffer them to enjoy tranquility and live in peace. **3** And men of Joppa perpetrated this great impiety: they invited the Jews that lived among them to go with their wives and children into the boats which they had provided, as though they had no ill will toward them; **4** and when the Jews, relying on the common decree of the city, accepted *the invitation,* as men desiring to live in peace and suspecting nothing, they took them out to sea and drowned them, *in number* not less than two hundred. **5** But when Judas heard of the cruelty done to his fellow-countrymen, giving command to the men that were with him **6** and calling upon God the righteous Judge, he came against the murderers of his kindred, and set the haven on fire by night, and burned the boats, and put to the sword those that had fled there. **7** But when the town was closed *against him,* he withdrew, intending to come again to root out the whole community of the men of Joppa. **8** But learning that the men of Jamnia were inclined to do in like manner to the Jews that sojourned among them, **9** he fell upon the Jamnites also by night, and set fire to the haven together with the fleet, so that the glare of the light was seen at Jerusalem, two hundred and forty furlongs distant. **10** Now when they had drawn off nine furlongs from there, as they marched against Timotheus, *an army of* Arabians attacked him, no fewer than five thousand *footmen* and five hundred horsemen. **11** And when a sore battle had been fought, and Judas and his company by the help of God had good success, the nomads being overcome implored Judas to grant them friendship, promising to give *him* cattle, and to help his people in all other ways. **12** So Judas, thinking that they would indeed be profitable in many things, agreed to live in peace with them; and receiving pledges of friendship they departed to their tents. **13** And he also fell upon a certain city Gephyrun, strong and fenced about with walls, and inhabited by a mixed multitude of various nations; and it was named Caspin. **14** But those who were within, trusting to the strength of the walls and to their store of provisions, behaved themselves rudely toward

Judas and those who were with him, railing, and furthermore blaspheming and speaking impious words. **15** But Judas and his company, calling upon the great sovereign of the world, who without rams and cunning engines of war hurled down Jericho in the times of Joshua, rushed wildly against the wall; **16** and having taken the city by the will of God, they made unspeakable slaughter, insomuch that the adjoining lake, which was two furlongs broad, appeared to be filled with the deluge of blood. **17** And when they had drawn off seven hundred and fifty furlongs from there, they made their way to Charax, to the Jews that are called Tubieni. **18** And Timotheus they found not in occupation of that district, for he had then departed from the district without accomplishing anything, but had left behind a garrison, and that a very strong one, in a certain post. **19** But Dositheus and Sosipater, who were of Maccabaeus's captains, went out and destroyed those that had been left by Timotheus in the stronghold, above ten thousand men. **20** And Maccabaeus, ranging his own army by bands, set these two over the bands, and marched in haste against Timotheus, who had with him a hundred and twenty thousand footmen and two thousand and five hundred horsemen. **21** But when Timotheus heard of the inroad of Judas, he at once sent away the women and the children and also the baggage into the *fortress* called Carnion; for the place was hard to besiege and difficult of access by reason of the narrowness of the approaches on all sides. **22** But when the band of Judas, who led the van, appeared in sight, and when terror came upon the enemy and fear, because the manifestation of him who sees all things came upon them, they fled a main, carried this way and that, so that they were often hurt of their own men, and pierced with the points of their swords. **23** And Judas continued the pursuit the more hotly, putting the wicked wretches to the sword, and he destroyed as many as thirty thousand men. **24** But Timotheus himself, falling in with the company of Dositheus and Sosipater, implored them with much crafty guile to let him go with his life, because he had in *his power* the parents of many *of them* and the kindred of some: otherwise, *said he,* little regard will be shown to these. **25** So when he had with many words confirmed the agreement to restore them without hurt, they let him go that they might save their kindred. **26** And *Judas,* marching against Carnion and the temple of Atergatis, killed five and twenty thousand persons. **27** And after he had put these to flight and destroyed them, he marched against Ephron also, a strong city, wherein were multitudes of people of all nations; and stalwart young men placed on the walls made a vigorous defense; and there were great stores of engines and darts there. **28** But calling upon the Sovereign who with might breaks in pieces the strength of the enemy, they got the city into their hands, and killed as many as twenty and five thousand of those who were within. **29** And setting out from there they marched in haste against Scythopolis, which is distant from Jerusalem six hundred furlongs. **30** But when the Jews that were settled there testified of the good will that the Scythopolitans had shown toward them, and of their kindly bearing *toward them* in the times of their misfortune, **31** they gave thanks, and further exhorted them to remain well affected toward the race for the future; and they went up to Jerusalem, the feast of weeks being close to hand. **32** But after the *feast* called Pentecost they marched in haste against Gorgias the governor of Idumaea: **33** and he came out with three thousand footmen and four hundred horsemen. **34** And when they had set themselves in array, it came to pass that a few of the Jews fell. **35** And a certain Dositheus, one of Bacenor's company, who was on horseback and a strong man, pressed hard on Gorgias, and taking hold of his cloak drew him along by main force; and while he was inclined to take the accursed man alive, one of the Thracian horsemen bore down upon him and disabled his shoulder, and so Gorgias escaped to Marisa. **36** And when those who were with Esdris had been fighting long and were wearied out, Judas called upon the Lord to show himself, fighting on their side and leading the van of the battle; **37** and *then* in the language of his fathers he raised the battle-cry joined with hymns, and rushing unawares upon the troops of Gorgias put them to flight. **38** And Judas gathering his army came to the city of Adullam; and as the seventh day was coming on, they purified themselves according to the custom, and kept the Sabbath there. **39** And on the day following, at which time it had become necessary, Judas and his company came to take up the bodies of those who had fallen, and in company with their kinsmen to bring them back to the sepulchers of their fathers. **40** But under the garments of each one of the dead they found consecrated signs of the idols of Jamnia, which the law forbids the Jews to have anything to do with; and it became clear to all that it was for this cause that they had fallen. **41** All therefore, blessing the *works* of the Lord, the righteous Judge, who makes manifest the things that are hid, **42** betook themselves to supplication, imploreing that the sin committed might be wholly blotted out. And the noble Judas exhorted the multitude to keep themselves from sin, for so much as they had seen before their eyes what things had come to pass because of the sin of those who had fallen. **43** And when he had made a collection man by man to the sum of two thousand drachmas of silver, he sent to Jerusalem to offer a sacrifice for sin, doing therein right well and honorably, in that he took thought for a resurrection. **44** For if he were not expecting that those who had fallen would rise again, it was superfluous and idle to pray for the dead. **45** (And if *he did it* looking to an honorable memorial of gratitude laid up for those who die in godliness, holy and godly was the thought.) For that reason, he made the atoning sacrifice for those who had died, that they might be released from their sin.

CHAPTER 13

1 In the hundred forty and ninth year tidings were brought to Judas and his company that Antiochus Eupator was coming with *great* multitudes against Judea, **2** and with him Lysias his guardian and chancellor, each having a Greek force, a hundred and ten thousand footmen, and five thousand and three hundred horsemen, and two and twenty elephants, and three hundred chariots armed with scythes. **3** And Menelaus also joined himself with them, and with great dissimulation encouraged Antiochus, not for the saving of his country, but because he thought that he would be set over the government. **4** But the King of kings stirred up the passion of Antiochus against the wicked wretch; and when Lysias informed him that this man was the cause of all the evils, *the king* commanded to bring him to Beroea, and to put him to death after the manner of that place. **5** Now there is in that place a tower of fifty cubits high, full of ashes, and it had all round it a gallery descending sheer on every side into the ashes. **6** Here him that is guilty of sacrilege or has attained a preeminence in any other evil deeds, they all push forward into destruction. **7** By such a fate it befell the breaker of the law,

Menelaus, to die, without obtaining so much as *a grave in* the earth, and that right justly; **8** for since he had perpetrated many sins against the altar, whose fire and whose ashes were holy, in ashes did he receive his death. **9** Now the king, infuriated in spirit, was coming with intent to inflict on the Jews the very worst of the sufferings that had befallen *them* in his father's time. **10** But when Judas heard of these things, he gave charge to the multitude to call upon the Lord day and night, *imploreing him,* if ever at any other time, so now to help those who were at the point to be deprived of the law and their country and the holy temple, **11** and not to suffer the people that had been but now a little while revived to fall into the hands of those profane heathen. **12** So when they had all done the same thing together, imploreing the merciful Lord with weeping and fasting and prostration for three days without ceasing, Judas exhorted them and commanded they should join him *for service.* **13** And having gone apart with the elders he resolved that, before the king's army should enter into Judea and make themselves masters of the city, they should go out and try the matter *in fight* by the help of God. **14** And committing the decision to the Lord of the world and exhorting those who were with him to contend nobly even to death for laws, temple, city, country, commonwealth, he pitched his camp by Modin. **15** And given out to his men the watchword, VICTORY IS GOD's, with a chosen body of the bravest young men he fell upon *the camp* by night *and penetrated* to the king's tent and killed *of* the army as many as two thousand men and brought down the mightiest elephant with him that was in the tower upon him. **16** And at last they filled the army with terror and alarm and departed with good success. **17** And this had been accomplished when the day was but now dawning, because of the Lord's protection that gave Judas help. **18** But the king, having had a taste of the exceeding boldness of the Jews, made attempts by stratagem upon their positions, **19** and *upon* a strong fortress of the Jews at Bethsura; he advanced, was turned back, failed, was defeated, **20** And Judas conveyed such things as were necessary to those who were within. **21** But Rhodocus, from the Jewish ranks, made known to the enemy the secrets *of his countrymen.* He was sought out, and taken, and shut up in prison. **22** The king treated with them in Bethsura the second time, gave his hand, took theirs, departed, attacked the forces of Judas, was put to the worse, **23** heard that Philip who had been left as chancellor in Antioch had become reckless, was confounded, made to the Jews an overture *of peace,* submitted himself and swore to acknowledge all their rights, came to terms with them and offered sacrifice, honored the sanctuary and the place, **24** showed kindness and graciously received Maccabaeus, left Hegemonides governor from Ptolemais even to the Gerrenians, **25** came to Ptolemais. The men of Ptolemais were displeased at the treaty, for they had exceedingly great indignation *against the Jews:* they desired to annul the articles of the agreement. **26** Lysias came forward to speak, made the best defense that was possible, persuaded, pacified, made them well affected, departed to Antioch. This was the issue of the inroad and departure of the king.

CHAPTER 14

1 Now after a space of three years tidings were brought to Judas and his company that Demetrius the *son* of Seleucus, having sailed into the haven of Tripolis with a mighty army and a fleet, **2** had gotten possession of the country, having made away with Antiochus and Lysias his guardian. **3** But one Alcimus, who had formerly been high priest, and had willfully polluted himself in the times when there was no mingling *with the Gentiles,* considering that there was no deliverance for him in any way, nor any more access to the holy altar, **4** came to king Demetrius in about the hundred fifty first year, presenting to him a crown of gold and a palm, and beside these some of the festal olive boughs of the temple. And for that day he held his peace; **5** but having gotten opportunity to further his own madness, being called by Demetrius into a meeting of his council and asked how the Jews stood affected and what they purposed, he answered thereto. **6** Those of the Jews that he called Hasidaeans, whose leader is Judas Maccabaeus, keep up war, and are seditious, not suffering the kingdom to find tranquility. **7** For that reason, having laid aside my ancestral glory, I mean the high priesthood, I am now come here; **8** first for the unfeigned care I have for the things that concern the king, and secondly because I have regard also to my own fellow-citizens: for, through the unadvised dealing of those of whom I spoke before, our whole race is in no small misfortune. **9** But do you, O king, having

informed yourself of these things severally, take thought both for our country and for our race, which is surrounded *by foes,* according to the gracious kindness with which you receive all. **10** For as long as Judas remains alive, it is impossible that the state should find peace. **11** And when he had spoken such words as these, at once the rest of the *king's* friends, having ill will against Demetrius, inflamed Demetrius yet more. **12** And out with appointing Nicanor, who had been master of the elephants, and making him governor of Judea, he sent him out, **13** giving him written instructions to make away with Judas himself and to scatter those who were with him, and to set up Alcimus as high priest of the great temple. **14** And those in Judea that had *before* driven Judas into exile thronged to Nicanor in flocks, supposing that the misfortunes and calamities of the Jews would be successes to themselves. **15** But when *the Jews* heard of Nicanor's inroad and the assault of the heathen, they sprinkled earth *upon their heads* and made solemn supplication to him who had established his own people forevermore, and who always, making manifest his presence, upholds *those who are* his own portion. **16** And when the leader had given *his* commands, he immediately set out from there, and joined battle with them at a village *called* Lessau. **17** But Simon, the brother of Judas, had encountered Nicanor, yet not until late, having received a check by reason of the sudden consternation caused by his adversaries. **18** Nevertheless Nicanor, hearing of the manliness of those who were with Judas, and their courage in fighting for their country, shrank from bringing the matter to the decision of the sword. **19** For that reason, he sent Posidonius and Theodotus and Mattathias to give and receive pledges of friendship. **20** So when these proposals had been long considered, and the leader had made the troops acquainted therewith, and it appeared that they were all of like mind, they consented to the covenants. **21** And they appointed a day on which to meet together by themselves. And a litter was borne forward from each *army;* they set chairs of state; **22** Judas stationed armed men ready in convenient places, lest perhaps there should suddenly be treachery on the part of the enemy; they held such conference as was meet. **23** Nicanor waited in Jerusalem, and did nothing to cause disturbance, but dismissed the flocks of people that had gathered together. **24** And he kept Judas always in his presence; he had gained a hearty affection for the man; **25** he urged him to marry and beget children; he married, settled quietly, took part in common life. **26** But Alcimus, perceiving the good will that was between them, and having got possession of the covenants that had been made, came to Demetrius and told him that Nicanor was ill affected toward the state, for he had appointed that conspirator against his kingdom, Judas, to be his successor. **27** And the king, falling into a rage, and being exasperated by the false accusations of that most wicked man, wrote to Nicanor, signifying that he was displeased at the covenants, and commanding him to send Maccabaeus prisoner to Antioch in all haste. **28** And when this message came to Nicanor, he was confounded, and was sore troubled at the thought of annulling the articles that had been agreed upon, the man having done no wrong; **29** but because there was no dealing against the king, he watched his time to execute this purpose by stratagem. **30** But Maccabaeus, when he perceived that Nicanor was behaving more harshly in his dealings with him, and that he had become ruler in his customary bearing, understanding that this harshness came not of good, gathered together not a few of his men, and concealed himself from Nicanor. **31** But the other, when he became aware that he had been bravely defeated by the stratagem of Judas, came to the great and holy temple, while the priests were offering the usual sacrifices, and commanded them to deliver up the man. **32** And when they declared with oaths that they had no knowledge where the man was whom he sought, **33** he stretched out his right hand toward the sanctuary and swore this oath: If you will not deliver up to me Judas as a prisoner, I will lay this temple of God even with the ground, and will break down the altar, and I will erect here a temple to Bacchus for all to see. **34** And having said this, he departed. But the priests, stretching out their hands toward heaven, called upon him that ever fights for our nation, in these words: **35** You, O Lord of the universe, who in yourself have need of nothing, was well pleased that a sanctuary of your habitation should be set among us; **36** so now, O holy Lord of all hallowing, keep undefiled forever this house that has been lately cleansed. **37** Now information was given to Nicanor against one Razis, an elder of Jerusalem, as being a lover of his countrymen and a man of very good

report, and one called Father of the Jews for his good will *toward them.* **38** For in the former times when there was no mingling *with the Gentiles* he had been accused of *cleaving to the* Jews' religion, and had jeoparded body and life with all earnestness for the religion of the Jews. **39** And Nicanor, wishing to make evident the ill will that he bore to the Jews, sent above five hundred soldiers to take him; **40** for he thought by taking him to inflict a calamity upon them. **41** But when the troops were on the point of taking the tower, and were forcing the door of the court, and bade bring fire and burn the doors, he being surrounded on every side fell upon his sword, **42** choosing rather to die nobly than to fall into the hands of the wicked wretches, and suffer outrage unworthy of his own nobleness: **43** but since he missed his stroke through the excitement of the struggle, and the crowds were now rushing within the door, he ran bravely up to the wall and cast himself down manfully among the crowds. **44** But as they quickly gave back, a space was made, and he fell on the middle of his side. **45** And having yet breath within him, and being inflamed with passion, he rose up, and though his blood gushed out in streams and his wounds were grievous, he ran through the crowds, and standing upon a steep rock, **46** when as his blood was now well near spent, he drew out his bowels *through the wound, and* taking them in both his hands he shook them at the crowds; and calling upon him who is Lord of the life and the spirit to restore these again, he thus died.

CHAPTER 15

1 But Nicanor, hearing that Judas and his company were in the region of Samaria, resolved to set upon them with all security on the day of rest. **2** And when the Jews that were compelled to follow him said, O destroy not so savagely and barbarously, but give due glory to the day which he that sees all things has honored and hallowed above *other days;* **3** then the thrice-accursed wretch asked if there were a Sovereign in heaven that had commanded to keep the Sabbath day. **4** And when they declared, there is the Lord, living himself a Sovereign in heaven, who commanded *us* to observe the seventh day; **5** then says the other, I also am a sovereign upon the earth, who *now* command to take up arms and execute the king's business. Nevertheless, he prevailed not to execute his cruel purpose. **6** And Nicanor, bearing himself haughtily in all vain pride, had determined to set up a monument of complete victory over Judas and all those who were with him: **7** but Maccabaeus still trusted unceasingly, with all hope that he should obtain help from the Lord. **8** And he exhorted his company not to be fearful at the inroad of the heathen, but, keeping in mind the help which of old they had oftentimes received from heaven, so now also to look for the victory which would come to them from the Almighty; **9** and comforting them out of the law and the prophets, and withal putting them in mind of the conflicts that they had maintained, he made them more eager *for the battle.* **10** And when he had roused their spirit, he gave them *his* commands, at the same time pointing out the perfidiousness of the heathen and their breach of their oaths. **11** And arming each one of them, not so much with the sure defense of shields and spears as with the encouragement *that lies* in good words, and moreover relating to them a dream worthy to be believed, he made them all exceedingly glad. **12** And the vision of that *dream* was this: *He saw* Onias, him that was high priest, a noble and good man, reverend in bearing, yet gentle in manner and well-spoken, and exercised from a child in all points of virtue, with outstretched hands invoking *blessings* on the whole body of the Jews: **13** there upon *he saw* a man appear, of venerable age and exceeding glory, and wonderful and most majestic was the dignity around him: **14** and Onias answered and said, This is the lover of the kindred, he who prays much for the people and the holy city, Jeremiah the prophet of God: **15** and Jeremiah stretching out his right hand delivered to Judas a sword of gold, and in giving it addressed *him* saying, **16** Take the holy sword, a gift from God, with which you will strike down the adversaries. **17** And being encouraged by the words of Judas, which were of a lofty strain, and able to incite to virtue and to stir the souls of the young to manly courage, they determined not to carry on a campaign, but nobly to bear down upon *the enemy, and* fighting hand to hand with all courage bring the matter to an issue, because the city and the sanctuary and the temple were in danger. **18** For their fear for wives and children, and furthermore for kindred and kinsfolk, was in less account with them; but greatest and first was their fear for the consecrated sanctuary. **19** And they also that were shut up in the city were in no light distress, being troubled because of the encounter in the open ground. **20** And when all were now waiting for the decision of the issue, and the enemy had already joined battle, and the army had been set in array, and the elephants brought back to a convenient post, and the horsemen drawn upon the flank, **21** Maccabaeus, perceiving the presence of the troops, and the various arms with which they were equipped, and the savageness of the elephants, holding up his hands to heaven called upon the Lord that works wonders, recognizing that *success* comes not by arms, but that, according as *the Lord* will judge, he gains the victory for those who are worthy. **22** And calling upon *God* he said after this manner: You, O Sovereign Lord, did send your angel in the time of Hezekiah king of Judea, and he killed of the army of Sennacherib as many as a hundred fourscore and five thousand; **23** so now also, O Sovereign of the heavens, send a good angel before us to bring terror and trembling: **24** through the greatness of your arm let them be stricken with dismay that with blasphemy are come here against your holy people. And as he ended with these words, **25** Nicanor and his company advanced with trumpets and victory songs; **26** but Judas and his company joined battle with the enemy with invocation and prayers. **27** And contending with their hands, and praying to God with their hearts, they killed no less than thirty-five thousand men, being made exceedingly glad by the manifestation of God. **28** And when the engagement was over, and they were returning again with joy, they recognized Nicanor lying dead in full armor; **29** and there arose a shout and tumult, and then they blessed the Sovereign *Lord* in the language of their fathers. **30** And he that in all things was in body and soul the foremost champion of his fellow-citizens, he that kept through life the good will of his youth toward his countrymen, commanded to cut off Nicanor's head, and his hand with the shoulder, and bring them to Jerusalem. **31** And when he had arrived there, and had called his countrymen together and set the priests before the altar, he sent for those who were in the citadel; **32** and showing the head of the vile Nicanor, and the hand of that profane man, which with proud brags he had stretched out against the holy house of the Almighty, **33** and cutting out the tongue of the impious Nicanor, he said that he would give it by pieces to the birds, and hang up the rewards of his madness near the sanctuary. **34** And they all *looking up* to heaven blessed the Lord who had manifested himself, saying, "Blessed be he that has preserved his own place undefiled." **35** And he hanged Nicanor's head and shoulder from the citadel, a sign, evident to all and manifest, of the help of the Lord. **36** And they all ordained with a common decree in no wise to let this day pass undistinguished, but to mark with honor the thirteenth day of the twelfth month (it is called Adar in the Syrian tongue), the day before the day of Mordecai. **37** THIS then having been the issue of the attempt of Nicanor, and the city having from those times been held by the Hebrews, I also will here make an end of my book. **38** And if *I have written* well and to the point in my story, this is what I myself desired; but if meanly and indifferently, this is all I could attain to. **39** For as it is distasteful to drink wine alone and in like manner again *to drink* water *alone,* while the mingling of wine with water at once gives full pleasantness to the flavor; so also the fashioning of the language delights the ears of those who read the story. And here will be the end.

EASTERN ORTHODOX DEUTEROCANON

1 ESDRAS

Otherwise known as 3 Esdras

1 Esdras, also called Greek Esdras, Greek Ezra, or 3 Esdras, is an ancient Greek version of the biblical Book of Ezra in use among the early church, and many modern Christians with varying degrees of canonicity. First Esdras is substantially the same as Masoretic Ezra. As part of the Septuagint translation of the Old Testament, it is regarded as deuterocanonical in the churches of the East, but apocryphal in the West. First Esdras is found in Origen's Hexapla. Greek and related versions of the Bible include both Esdras A (English title: 1 Esdras) and Esdras B (Ezra–Nehemiah) in parallel.

CHAPTER 1

1 Josias held the Passover in Jerusalem to his Lord and offered the Passover the fourteenth day of the first month; 2 having set the priests according to their daily courses, being arrayed in their vestments, in the temple of the Lord. 3 And he spoke to the Levites, the temple-servants of Israel, that they should make themselves holy to the Lord, to set the holy ark of the Lord in the house that King Solomon the son of David had built: 4 *and said,* "You will no more have need to bear it upon your shoulders: now therefore serve the Lord your God, and minister to his people Israel, and prepare you after your fathers' houses and kindred, 5 according to the writing of David king of Israel, and according to the magnificence of Solomon his son: and standing in the holy place according to the several divisions of the families of you the Levites, who *minister* in the presence of your kindred the children of Israel, 6 offer the Passover in order, and make ready the sacrifices for your kindred, and keep the Passover according to the commandment of the Lord, which was given to Moses." 7 And to the people which were present Josias gave thirty thousand lambs and kids, and three thousand calves: these things were given of the king's substance, according as he promised, to the people, and to the priests and Levites. 8 And Helkias, and Zacharias, and Esyelus, the rulers of the temple, gave to the priests for the Passover two thousand *and* six hundred sheep, and three hundred calves. 9 And Jeconias, and Samaias and Nathanael his brother, and Sabias, and Ochielus, and Joram, captains over thousands, gave to the Levites for the Passover five thousand sheep, and seven hundred calves. 10 And when these things were done, the priests and Levites, having the unleavened bread, stood in comely order according to the kindred, 11 and according to the several divisions by fathers' houses, before the people, to offer to the Lord, as it is written in the book of Moses: and so did *they in* the morning. 12 And they roasted the Passover with fire, as appertains: and the sacrifices they sod in the brazen vessels and caldrons with a good savor, 13 and set them before all the people: and afterward they prepared for themselves, and for the priests their kindred, the sons of Aaron. 14 For the priests offered the fat until night: and the Levites prepared for themselves, and for the priests their kindred, the sons of Aaron. 15 The holy singers also, the sons of Asaph, were in their order, according to the appointment of David, *to wit,* Asaph, Zacharias, and Eddinus, who was of the king's retinue. 16 Moreover the gatekeepers were at every gate; none had need to depart from his daily course: for their kindred the Levites prepared for them. 17 So were the things that belonged to the sacrifices of the Lord accomplished in that day, in holding the Passover, 18 and offering sacrifices upon the altar of the Lord, according to the commandment of King Josias. 19 So the children of Israel which were present at that time held the Passover, and the feast of unleavened bread seven days. 20 And such a Passover was not held in Israel since the time of the prophet Samuel. 21 Yes, all the kings of Israel held not such a Passover as Josias, and the priests, and the Levites, and the Jews, held with all Israel that were present in their dwelling place at Jerusalem. 22 In the eighteenth year of the reign of Josias was this Passover held. 23 And the works of Josias were upright before his Lord with a heart full of godliness. 24 Moreover the things that came to pass in his days have been written in times past, concerning those that sinned, and did wickedly against the Lord above every people

and kingdom, and how they grieved him exceedingly, so that the words of the Lord were confirmed against Israel. **25** Now after all these acts of Josias it came to pass, that Pharaoh the king of Egypt came to raise war at Carchemish upon Euphrates: and Josias went out against him. **26** But the king of Egypt sent to him, saying, "What have I to do with you, O king of Judea? **27** I am not sent out from the Lord God against you; for my war is upon Euphrates: and now the Lord is with me, yes, the Lord is with me hastening me forward: depart from me and be not against the Lord." **28** However Josias didn't turn back to his chariot, but undertook to fight with him, not regarding the words of the prophet Jeremy *spoken* by the mouth of the Lord: **29** but joined battle with him in the plain of Megiddo, and the princes came down against King Josias. **30** Then said the king to his servants, "Carry me away out of the battle; for I am very weak. And immediately his servants carried him away out of the army." **31** Then he got up upon his second chariot; and being brought back to Jerusalem he died and was buried in the sepulcher of his fathers. **32** And in all Jewry they mourned for Josias; and Jeremy the prophet lamented for Josias, and the chief men with the women made lamentation for him, to this day: and this was given out for an ordinance to be done continually in all the nation of Israel. **33** These things are written in the book of the histories of the kings of Judea, and every one of the acts that Josias did, and his glory, and his understanding in the law of the Lord, and the things that he had done before, and the things now *recited*, are reported in the book of the kings of Israel and Judah. **34** And the people took Joachaz the son of Josias, and made him king instead of Josias his father, when he was twenty and three years old. **35** And he reigned in Judah and in Jerusalem three months: and then the king of Egypt deposed him from reigning in Jerusalem. **36** And he set a tax upon the people of a hundred talents of silver and one talent of gold. **37** The king of Egypt also made King Joakim his brother king of Judea and Jerusalem. **38** And Joakim bound the nobles: but Zarakes his brother he apprehended and brought him up out of Egypt. **39** Five and twenty years old was Joakim when he began to reign in Judea and Jerusalem; and he did that which was evil in the sight of the Lord. **40** And against him Nabuchodonosor the king of Babylon came up, and bound him with a chain

of brass, and carried him to Babylon. **41** Nabuchodonosor also took of the holy vessels of the Lord, and carried them away, and set them up in his own temple at Babylon. **42** But those things that are reported of him, and of his uncleanness and impiety, are written in the chronicles of the kings. **43** And Joakim his son reigned in his stead: for when he was made king he was eighteen years old; **44** and he reigned three months and ten days in Jerusalem; and did that which was evil before the Lord. **45** So after a year Nabuchodonosor sent and caused him to be brought to Babylon with the holy vessels of the Lord; **46** and made Sedekias king of Judea and Jerusalem, when he was one and twenty years old; and he reigned eleven years: **47** and he also did that which was evil in the sight of the Lord and cared not for the words that were spoken by Jeremy the prophet from the mouth of the Lord. **48** And after king Nabuchodonosor had made him to swear by the name of the Lord, he forswore himself, and rebelled; and hardening his neck, and his heart, he transgressed the laws of the Lord, the God of Israel. **49** Moreover the governors of the people and of the priests did many things wickedly, and passed all the pollutions of all nations, and defiled the temple of the Lord, which was sanctified in Jerusalem. **50** And the God of their fathers sent by his messenger to call them back, because he had compassion on them and on his dwelling place. **51** But they mocked his messengers; and in the day when the Lord spoke *to them,* they scoffed at his prophets: **52** so far out, that he, being angry with his people for their great ungodliness, commanded to bring up the kings of the Chaldeans against them; **53** who killed their young men with the sword, around their holy temple, and spared neither young man nor maid, old man nor child; but he delivered all into their hands. **54** And they took all the holy vessels of the Lord, both great and small, with the vessels of the ark of the Lord, and the king's treasures, and carried them away to Babylon. **55** And they burned the house of the Lord, and brake down the walls of Jerusalem, and burned the towers thereof with fire: **56** and as for her glorious things, they never ceased until they had brought them all to nothing: and the people that were not slain with the sword he carried to Babylon: **57** and they were servants to him and to his children, until the Persians reigned, to fulfill the word of the Lord by the mouth of Jeremy: **58** Until the land has enjoyed her Sabbaths, the whole time of her desolation will she keep Sabbath, to fulfill threescore and ten years.

CHAPTER 2

1 In the first year of Cyrus king of the Persians, that the word of the Lord by the mouth of Jeremy might be accomplished, 2 the Lord stirred up the spirit of Cyrus king of the Persians, and he made proclamation through all his kingdom, and also by writing, 3 saying, "Cyrus king of the Persians says: The Lord of Israel, the Most High Lord, has made me king of the whole world, 4 and commanded me to build him a house at Jerusalem that is in Judea. 5 If therefore there be any of you that are of his people, let the Lord, even his Lord, be with him, and let him go up to Jerusalem that is in Judea, and build the house of the Lord of Israel: he is the Lord that dwells in Jerusalem. 6 Of such therefore as dwell in various places, let those who are in his own place help each one with gold, and with silver, 7 with gifts, with horses also and cattle, beside the other things which have been added by vow for the temple of the Lord which is in Jerusalem." 8 Then the chief of the families of Judah and of the tribe of Benjamin stood up; the priests also, and the Levites, and all they whose spirit the Lord had stirred to go up, to build the house for the Lord which is in Jerusalem. 9 And those who lived around them helped them in all things with silver and gold, with horses and cattle, and with very many gifts that were vowed of a great number whose minds were stirred up *there to.* 10 King Cyrus also brought out the holy vessels of the Lord, which Nabuchodonosor had carried away from Jerusalem, and had set up in his temple of idols. 11 Now when Cyrus king of the Persians had brought them out, he delivered them to Mithradates his treasurer, 12 and by him they were delivered to Sanabassar the governor of Judea. 13 And this was the number of them: A thousand golden cups, a thousand cups of silver, censers of silver twenty-nine, vials of gold thirty, and of silver two thousand four hundred and ten, and other vessels a thousand. 14 So all the vessels of gold and of silver were brought up, even five thousand four hundred threescore and nine, 15 and were carried back by Sanabassar, together with them of the captivity, from Babylon to Jerusalem. 16 But in the time of Artaxerxes king of the Persians Belemus, and Mithradates, and Tabellius, and Rathumus, and Beeltethmus, and Samellius

the scribe, with the others that were in commission with them, dwelling in Samaria and other places, wrote to him against those who lived in Judea and Jerusalem the letter following: 17 To king Artaxerxes our Lord, Your servants, Rathumus the recorder, and Samellius the scribe, and the rest of their council, and the judges that are in Coelesyria and Phoenicia. 18 Be it now known to our lord the king, that the Jews that have come up from you to us, having come to Jerusalem, are building that rebellious and wicked city, and are repairing its marketplaces and walls, and are laying the foundation of a temple. 19 Now if this city is built and the walls *thereof* are finished, they will not only refuse to give tribute, but will even stand up against kings. 20 And forasmuch as the things pertaining to the temple are now in hand, we think it meet not to neglect such a matter, 21 but to speak to our lord the king, to the intent that, if it be your pleasure, search may be made in the books of your fathers: 22 and you will find in the chronicles what is written concerning these things, and will understand that that city was rebellious, troubling both kings and cities: 23 and that the Jews were rebellious, and raised always wars therein of old time; for which cause even this city was laid waste. 24 For that reason, now we do declare to you, O lord the king, that if this city be built again, and the walls thereof set up anew, you will from now on have no passage into Coelesyria and Phoenicia. 25 Then the king wrote back again to Rathumus the recorder, and Beeltethmus, and Samellius the scribe, and to the rest that were in commission, and lived in Samaria and Syria and Phoenicia, after this manner: 26 I have read the letter which you have sent to me: therefore I commanded to make search, and it has been found that that city of old time has made insurrection against kings; 27 and the men were given to rebellion and war therein: and that mighty kings and fierce were in Jerusalem, who reigned and exacted tribute in Coelesyria and Phoenicia. 28 Now therefore I have commanded to hinder those men from building the city, and heed to be taken that there be nothing done contrary to this *order;* 29 and that those wicked doings proceed no further to the annoyance of kings. 30 Then king Artaxerxes, his letters being read, Rathumus, and Samellius the scribe, and the rest that were in commission with them, removing in haste to Jerusalem with horsemen and a multitude of people in battle array, began to hinder the builders; and the building of the temple in Jerusalem ceased until the second year of the reign of Darius king of the Persians.

CHAPTER 3

1 Now king Darius made a great feast to all his subjects, and to all that were born in his house, and to all the princes of Media and of Persia, 2 and to all the local governors and captains and governors that were under him, from India to Ethiopia, in the hundred twenty and seven provinces. 3 And when they had eaten and drunken, and being satisfied were gone home, then Darius the king went into his bedchamber, and slept, and awaked out of his sleep. 4 Then the three young men of the body-guard, that kept the king's person, spoke one to another: 5 Let every one of us say one thing which will be strongest: and he whose sentence will seem wiser than the others, to him will Darius the king give great gifts, and great honors in token of victory: 6 as, to be clothed in purple, to drink in gold, and to sleep upon gold, and a chariot with bridles of gold, and a turban of fine linen, and a chain about his neck: 7 and he will sit next to Darius because of his wisdom, and will be called Darius his cousin. 8 And then they wrote everyone his sentence, and set to their seals, and laid *the writing* under king Darius his pillow, 9 and said, When the king is risen, some will give him the writing; and of whose side the king and the three princes of Persia will judge that his sentence is the wisest, to him will the victory be given, as it is written. 10 The first wrote, Wine is the strongest. 11 The second wrote, The king is strongest. 12 The third wrote, Women are strongest: but above all things Truth bears away the victory. 13 Now when the king was risen up, they took the writing, and gave it to him, and so he read it: 14 and sending out he called all the princes of Persia and of Media, and the local governors, and the captains, and the governors, and the chief officers; 15 and sat him down in the royal seat of judgment; and the writing was read before them. 16 And he said, Call the young men, and they will explain their own sentences. So they were called, and came in. 17 And they said to them, Declare to us your mind concerning the things you have written. Then began the first, who had spoken of the strength of wine, 18 and said, O sirs, how exceedingly strong is wine! it causes all men to err that drink it: 19 it makes the mind of the king and of the fatherless child to be all one; of the bondman and of the freeman, of the poor man and of the rich: 20 it turns also every thought into cheer and mirth, so that a man remembers neither sorrow nor debt: 21 and it makes every heart rich, so that a man remembers neither king nor local governor; and it makes to speak all things by talents: 22 and when they are in their cups, they forget their love both to friends and kindred, and a little after draw their swords: 23 but when they awake from their wine, they remember not what they have done. 24 O sirs, is not wine the strongest, seeing that it enforces to do so? And when he had so spoken, he held his peace.

CHAPTER 4

1 Then the second, that had spoken of the strength of the king, began to say, 2 O sirs, do not men excel in strength, that bear rule over the sea and land, and all things in them? 3 But yet is the king stronger: and he is their lord and has dominion over them; and in whatever he commands them they obey him. 4 If he bid them make war the one against the other, they do it: and if he sends them out against the enemies, they go, and overcome mountains, walls, and towers. 5 They kill and are slain and transgress not the king's commandment: if they get the victory, they bring all to the king, as well the plunder, as all things else. 6 Likewise for those that are no soldiers, and have not to do with wars, but use husbandry, when they have reaped again that which they had sown, they bring it to the king, and compel one another to pay tribute to the king. 7 And he is but one man: if he commands to kill, they kill; if he command to spare, they spare; 8 if he command to strike, they strike; if he command to make desolate, they make desolate; if he command to build, they build; 9 if he command to cut down, they cut down; if he command to plant, they plant. 10 So all his people and his armies obey him: furthermore, he lies down, he eats and drinks, and takes his rest: 11 and these keep watch around him, neither may anyone depart, and do his own business, neither disobey they him in *anything*. 12 O sirs, how should not the king be strongest, seeing that in such sort he is obeyed? And he held his peace. 13 Then the third, who had spoken of women, and of truth, (this was Zorobabel) began to speak. 14 O sirs, is not the king great, and men are many, and wine is strong? Who is it then that rules them, or has the lordship over them? Are they not women? 15 Women have borne the king and

all the people that bear rule by sea and land. **16** Even of them came they: and they nourished them up that planted the vineyards, from where the wine comes. **17** These also make garments for men; these bring glory to men; and without women can't men be. **18** Yes, and if men have gathered together gold and silver and any other goodly thing and see a woman which is comely in favor and beauty, **19** they let all those things go, and gape after her, and even with open mouth fix their eyes fast on her; and have all more desire to her than to gold or silver, or any goodly thing whatever. **20** A man leaves his own father that brought him up, and his own country, and joins with his wife. **21** And with his wife he ends his days, and remembers neither father, nor mother, nor country. **22** By this also you must know that women have dominion over you: do you not labor and toil, and give and bring all to women? **23** Yes, a man takes his sword, and goes out to make excursions, and to rob and to steal, and to sail upon the sea and upon rivers; **24** and looks upon a lion and walks in the darkness; and when he has stolen, plundered, and robbed, he brings it to his love. **25** For that reason, a man loves his wife better than father or mother. **26** Yes, many there be that have run out of their wits for women and become bondmen for their sakes. **27** Many also have perished, have stumbled, and sinned, for women. **28** And now do you not believe me? Is not the king great in his power? Do not all regions fear to touch him? **29** Yet did I see him and Apame the king's concubine, the daughter of the illustrious Barticus, sitting at the right hand of the king, **30** and taking the crown from the king's head, and setting it upon her own head; yes, she struck the king with her left hand: **31** and therewithal the king gaped and gazed upon her with open mouth: if she laughed upon him, he laughed also: but if she took any displeasure at him, he was fain to flatter, that she might be reconciled to him again. **32** O sirs, how can it be but women should be strong, seeing they do so? **33** Then the king and the nobles looked one upon another: so he began to speak concerning truth. **34** O sirs, are not women strong? Great is the earth, high is the heaven, swift is the sun in his course, for he encircles the heavens round about, and fetches his course again to his own place in one day. **35** Is he not great that makes these things? Therefore great is truth, and stronger than all things. **36** All the earth calls upon truth, and

the heaven blesses her: all works shake and tremble, but with her is no unrighteous thing. **37** Wine is unrighteous, the king is unrighteous, women are unrighteous, all the children of men are unrighteous, and unrighteous are all such their works; and there is no truth in them; in their unrighteousness also, they will perish. **38** But truth remains and is strong forever; she lives and conquers forevermore. **39** With her there is no accepting of persons or rewards; but she does the things that are just, and *refrains* from all unrighteous and wicked things; and all men do well like of her works. **40** Neither in her judgment is any unrighteousness; and she is the strength, and the kingdom, and the power, and the majesty, of all ages. Blessed be the God of truth. **41** And with that he held his tongue. And all the people then shouted, and said, Great is truth, and strong above all things. **42** Then said the king to him, "Ask what you will more than is appointed in writing, and we will give it you, inasmuch as you are found wisest; and you will sit next me, and will be called my cousin." **43** Then said he to the king, "Remember your vow, which you did vow to build Jerusalem, in the day when you came to your kingdom, **44** and to send away all the vessels that were taken out of Jerusalem, which Cyrus set apart, when he vowed to destroy Babylon, and vowed to send them again there. **45** You did also vow to build up the temple, which the Edomites burned when Judea was made desolate by the Chaldeans. **46** And now, O lord the king, this is that which I require, and which I desire of you, and this is the princely generosity that will proceed from you: I pray therefore that you make good the vow, the performance whereof you have vowed to the King of heaven with your own mouth." **47** Then Darius the king stood up, and kissed him, and wrote letters for him to all the treasurers and governors and captains and local governors, that they should safely bring on their way both him, and all those that should go up with him to build Jerusalem. **48** He wrote letters also to all the governors that were in Coelesyria and Phoenicia, and to them in Libanus, that they should bring cedar wood from Libanus to Jerusalem, and that they should build the city with him. **49** Moreover he wrote for all the Jews that should go out of his realm up into Jewry, concerning their freedom, that no officer, no governor, no local governor, nor treasurer, should forcibly enter into their doors; **50** and that all the country which they occupied should be free to them without tribute; and that the Edomites should give over the villages of the Jews which then they held: **51** and that there should be yearly given twenty talents to the building of the temple, until the time that it were built; **52** and other ten talents yearly, for burnt offerings to be presented upon the altar every day, as they had a commandment to offer seventeen: **53** and that all those who should come from Babylonia to build the city should have their freedom, as well they as their posterity, and all the priests that came. **54** He wrote also *to give them* their charges, and the priests' vestments wherein they minister; **55** and for the Levites he wrote that their charges should be given them until the day that the house were finished, and Jerusalem built up. **56** And he commanded to give to all that kept the city lands and wages. **57** He sent away also all the vessels from Babylon, that Cyrus had set apart; and all that Cyrus had given in commandment, he charged also to be done, and sent to Jerusalem. **58** Now when this young man was gone out, he lifted up his face to heaven toward Jerusalem, and praised the King of heaven, **59** and said, "From you comes victory, from you comes wisdom, and yours is the glory, and I am your servant. **60** Blessed are you, who have given me wisdom: and to you I give thanks, O Lord of our fathers." **61** And so he took the letters, and went out, and came to Babylon, and told it all his kindred. **62** And they praised the God of their fathers, because he had given them freedom and liberty **63** to go up, and to build Jerusalem, and the temple which is called by his name: and they feasted with instruments of music and gladness seven days.

CHAPTER 5

1 After this were the chiefs of fathers' houses chosen to go up according to their tribes, with their wives and sons and daughters, with their menservants and maidservants, and their cattle. **2** And Darius sent with them a thousand horsemen, until they had brought them back to Jerusalem safely, and with musical instruments, tabrets and flutes. **3** And all their kindred played, and he made them go up together with them. **4** And these are the names of the men which went up, according to their families among their tribes, after their several divisions. **5** The priests, the sons of Phinees, the sons of Aaron: Jesus the son of Josedek, the son of Saraias, and Joakim the son of Zorobabel, the son of Salathiel, of the house of David, of the lineage of Phares, of the tribe of Judah; **6** who spoke wise sentences before Darius the king of Persia in the second year of his reign, in the month Nisan, which is the first month. **7** And these are they of Jewry that came up from the captivity, where they lived as strangers, whom Nabuchodonosor the king of Babylon had carried away to Babylon. **8** And they returned to Jerusalem, and to the other parts of Jewry, every man to his own city, who came with Zorobabel, with Jesus, Nehemias, and Zaraias, Resaias, Eneneus, Mardocheus, Beelsarus, Aspharsus, Reelias, Roimus, and Baana, their leaders. **9** The number of them of the nation, and their leaders: the sons of Phoros, two thousand a hundred seventy and two: the sons of Saphat, four hundred seventy and two: **10** the sons of Ares, seven hundred fifty and six: **11** the sons of Phaath Moab, of the sons of Jesus and Joab, two thousand eight hundred and twelve: **12** the sons of Elam, a thousand two hundred fifty and four: the sons of Zathui, nine hundred forty and five: the sons of Chorbe, seven hundred and five: the sons of Bani, six hundred forty and eight: **13** the sons of Bebai, six hundred twenty and three: the sons of Astad, a thousand three hundred twenty and two: **14** the sons of Adonikam, six hundred sixty and seven: the sons of Bagoi, two thousand sixty and six: the sons of Adinu, four hundred fifty and four: **15** the sons of Ater, of Ezekias, ninety and two: the sons of Kilan and Azetas, three score and seven: the sons of Azaru, four hundred thirty and two: **16** the sons of Annis, a hundred and one: the sons of Arom: the sons of Bassai, three hundred twenty and three: the sons of Arsiphurith, a hundred and twelve: **17** the sons of Baiterus, three thousand and five: the sons of Bethlomon, a hundred twenty and three: **18** they of Netophas, fifty and five: they of Anathoth, a hundred fifty and eight: they of Bethasmoth, forty and two: **19** they of Kariathiarius, twenty and five: they of Caphira and Beroth, seven hundred forty and three: **20** the Chadiasai and Ammidioi, four hundred twenty and two: they of Kirama and Gabbe, six hundred twenty and one: **21** they of Macalon, a hundred twenty and two: they of Betolion, fifty and two: the sons of Niphis, a hundred fifty and six: **22** the sons of Calamolalus and Onus, seven hundred twenty and five: the sons of Jerechu, three hundred forty and five: **23** the sons of Sanaas, three thousand three hundred and thirty. **24** The priests: the sons of Jeddu, the son of Jesus, among the sons of Sanasib, nine hundred seventy and two: the sons of Emmeruth, a thousand fifty and two: **25** the sons of Phassurus, a thousand two hundred forty and seven: the sons of Charme, a thousand and seventeen. **26** The Levites: the sons of Jesus, and Kadmiel, and Bannas, and Sudias, seventy and four. **27** The holy singers: the sons of Asaph, a hundred twenty and eight. **28** The gatekeepers: the sons of Salum, the sons of Atar, the sons of Tolman, the sons of Dacubi, the sons of Ateta, the sons of Sabi, in all a hundred thirty and nine. **29** The temple servants: the sons of Esau, the sons of Asipha, the sons of Tabaoth, the sons of Keras, the sons of Sua, the sons of Phaleas, the sons of Labana, the sons of Aggaba. **30** the sons of Acud, the sons of Uta, the sons of Ketab, the sons of Accaba, the sons of Subai, the sons of Anan, the sons of Cathua, the sons of Geddur, **31** the sons of Jairus, the sons of Daisan, the sons of Noeba, the sons of Chaseba, the sons of Gazera, the sons of Ozias, the sons of Phinoe, the sons of Asara, the sons of Basthai, the sons of Asana, the sons of Maani, the sons of Naphisi, the sons of Acub, the sons of Achipha, the sons of Asur, the sons of Pharakim, the sons of Basaloth, **32** the sons of Meedda, the sons of Cutha, the sons of Charea, the sons of Barchus, the sons of Serar, the sons of Thomei, the sons of Nasi, the sons of Atipha. **33** The sons of the servants of Solomon: the sons of Assaphioth, the sons of Pharida, the sons of Jeeli, the sons of Lozon, the sons of Isdael, the sons of Saphuthi, **34** the sons of Agia, the sons of Phacareth, the sons of Sabie, the sons of Sarothie, the sons of Masias, the sons of Gas, the sons of Addus, the sons of Subas, the sons of Apherra, the sons of Barodis, the sons of Saphat, the sons of Allon. **35** All the temple-servants, and the sons of the servants of Solomon, were three hundred seventy and two. **36** These came up from Thermeleth, and Thelersas, Charaathalan leading them, and Allar; **37** and they could not show their families, nor their stock, how they were of Israel: the sons of Dalan the son of Ban, the sons of Nekodan, six hundred fifty and two. **38** And of the priests, those who usurped the office of the priesthood and were not found: the sons of Obdia, the sons of Akkos, the sons of Jaddus, who married Augia one of the daughters of Zorzelleus, and was called after his name. **39** And when the description of the kindred of these men was sought in the register, and was not found, they were removed from executing the office of the priesthood: **40** for to them said Nehemias and Attharias, that they should not be partakers of the holy things, until there arose up a high priest wearing Urim and Thummim. **41** So all they of Israel, from twelve years old *and upward,* beside menservants and womenservants, were in *number forty* and two thousand three hundred and sixty. **42** Their menservants and handmaids were seven thousand three hundred thirty and seven: the minstrels and singers, two hundred forty and five: **43** four hundred thirty and five camels, seven thousand thirty and six horses, two hundred forty and five mules, five thousand five hundred twenty and five beasts of burden. **44** And certain of the chief men of their families, when they came to the temple of God that is in Jerusalem, vowed to set up the house again in its own place according to their ability, **45** and to give into the holy treasury of the works a thousand pounds of gold, five thousand of silver, and a hundred priestly vestments. **46** And the priests and the Levites and those who were of the people lived in Jerusalem and the country; the holy singers also and the gatekeepers and all Israel in their villages. **47** But when the seventh month was at hand, and when the children of Israel were every man in his own place, they came all together with one consent into the broad place before the first porch which is toward the east. **48** Then stood up Jesus the son of Josedek, and his kindred the priests, and Zorobabel the son of Salathiel, and his kindred, and made ready the altar of the God of Israel, **49** to offer burned sacrifices upon it, according as it is expressly commanded in the book of Moses the man of God. **50** And certain were gathered to them out of the other nations of the land, and they erected the altar upon its own place, because all the nations of the land were at enmity with them and oppressed them; and they offered sacrifices according to the time and burnt offerings to the Lord both morning and evening. **51** Also they held the feast of tabernacles, as it is commanded in the law, and *offered* sacrifices daily, as was meet: **52** and after that, the continual oblations, and the sacrifices of the Sabbaths, and of the new moons, and of all the consecrated feasts. **53** And all those who had made any vow to God began to offer sacrifices to God from the new moon of the seventh month, although the temple of God was not yet built. **54** And they gave money to the masons and carpenters; and meat and drink, **55** and cars to them of Sidon and Tyre, that they should bring cedar trees from Libanus, and convey them in floats to the haven of Joppa, according to the commandment which was written for them by Cyrus king of the Persians. **56** And in the second year after his coming to the temple of God at Jerusalem, in the second month, began Zorobabel the son of Salathiel, and Jesus the son of Josedek, and their kindred, and the Levitical priests, and all those who were come to Jerusalem out of the captivity: **57** and they laid the foundation of the temple of God on the new moon of the second month, in the second year after they were come to Jewry and Jerusalem. **58** And they appointed the Levites from twenty years old over the works of the Lord. Then stood up Jesus, and his sons and kindred, and Kadmiel his brother, and the sons of Jesus, Emadabun, and the sons of Joda the son of Iliadun, and their sons and kindred, all the Levites, with one accord started the business, laboring to advance the works in the house of God. So the builders built the temple of the Lord. **59** And the priests stood arrayed in their vestments with musical instruments and trumpets, and the Levites the sons of Asaph with their cymbals, **60** singing songs of thanksgiving, and praising the Lord, after the order of David king of Israel. **61** And they sang aloud, praising the Lord in songs of thanksgiving, because his goodness and his glory are forever in all Israel. **62** And all the people sounded trumpets, and shouted with a loud voice, singing songs of thanksgiving to the Lord for the rearing up of the house of the Lord. **63** Also of the Levitical priests, and of the heads of their families, the ancients who had seen the former house came to the building of this with lamentation and great weeping. **64** But many with trumpets and joy *shouted* with loud voice, **65** insomuch that the people heard not the trumpets for the weeping of the people: for the multitude sounded marvelously, so that it was heard afar off. **66** For that reason, when the enemies of the tribe of Judah and Benjamin heard it, they came to know what that noise of trumpets should mean. **67** And they perceived that those who were of the captivity did build the temple to the Lord, the God of Israel. **68** So they went to Zorobabel and Jesus, and to the chief men of the families, and said to them, we will build together with you. **69** For we likewise, as you,

do obey your Lord, and do sacrifice to him from the days of Asbasareth the king of the Assyrians, who brought us here. **70** Then Zorobabel and Jesus and the chief men of the families of Israel said to them, It is not for you to build the house to the Lord our God. **71** We ourselves alone will build to the Lord of Israel, according as Cyrus the king of the Persians has commanded us. **72** But the heathen of the land lying heavy upon the inhabitants of Judea, and holding them strait, hindered their building; **73** and by their secret plots, and popular persuasions and commotions, they hindered the finishing of the building all the time that King Cyrus lived: so they were hindered from building for the space of two years, until the reign of Darius.

CHAPTER 6

1 Now in the second year of the reign of Darius, Aggaeus and Zacharius the son of Addo, the prophets, prophesied to the Jews in Jewry and Jerusalem; in the name of the Lord, the God of Israel, *prophesied they* to them. **2** Then stood up Zorobabel the son of Salathiel, and Jesus the son of Josedek, and began to build the house of the Lord at Jerusalem, the prophets of the Lord being with them, and helping them. **3** At the same time came to them Sisinnes the governor of Syria and Phoenicia, with Sathrabuzanes and his companions, and said to them, **4** By whose appointment do you build this house and this roof, and perform all the other things? And who are the builders that perform these things? **5** Nevertheless the elders of the Jews obtained favor, because the Lord had visited the captivity; **6** and they were not hindered from building, until such time as communication was made to Darius concerning them, and his answer signified. **7** The copy of the letter which Sisinnes, governor of Syria and Phoenicia, and Sathrabuzanes, with their companions, the rulers in Syria and Phoenicia, wrote and sent to Darius; **8** To king Darius, greeting: Let all things be known to our lord the king, that being come into the country of Judea, and entered into the city of Jerusalem, we found in the city of Jerusalem the elders of the Jews that were of the captivity **9** building a house to the Lord, great *and* new, of hewn and costly stones, with timber laid in the walls. **10** And those works are done with great speed, and the work goes on prosperously in their hands, and with all glory and diligence it is accomplished. **11** Then asked we these elders, saying, By whose commandment build you this house, and lay the foundations of these works? **12** Therefore, to the intent that we might give knowledge to you by writing who were the chief doers, we questioned them, and we required of them the names in writing of their principal men. **13** So they gave us this answer, "We are the servants of the Lord which made heaven and earth. **14** And as for this house, it was built many years ago by a king of Israel great and strong and was finished. **15** But when our fathers sinned against the Lord of Israel which is in heaven, and provoked him to wrath, he gave them over into the hands of Nabuchodonosor king of Babylon, king of the Chaldeans; **16** and they pulled down the house, and burned it, and carried away the people captives to Babylon. **17** But in the first year that Cyrus reigned over the country of Babylon, king Cyrus wrote to build up this house. **18** And the holy vessels of gold and of silver, that Nabuchodonosor had carried away out of the house at Jerusalem, and had set up in his own temple, those Cyrus the king brought out again out of the temple in Babylonia, and they were delivered to Zorobabel and to Sanabassarus the governor, **19** with commandment that he should carry away all these vessels, and put them in the temple at Jerusalem; and that the temple of the Lord should be built in its place. **20** Then Sanabassarus, being come here, laid the foundations of the house of the Lord which is in Jerusalem; and from that time to this being still a building, it is not yet fully ended. **21** Now therefore, if it seem good, O king, let search be made among the royal archives of our lord the king that are in Babylon: **22** and if it be found that the building of the house of the Lord which is in Jerusalem has been done with the consent of king Cyrus, and it seem good to our lord the king, let him signify to us thereof." **23** Then commanded King Darius to seek among the archives that were laid up at Babylon: and so at Ekbatana the palace, which is in the country of Media, there was found a scroll where these things were recorded. **24** In the first year of the reign of Cyrus king Cyrus commanded to build up the house of the Lord which is in Jerusalem, where they do sacrifice with continual fire: **25** whose height will be sixty cubits, and the breadth sixty cubits, with three rows of hewn stones, and one row of new wood of that country; and the expenses thereof to be given out of the house of king Cyrus: **26** and that the holy vessels of the house of the

Lord, both gold and silver, that Nabuchodonosor took out of the house at Jerusalem, and carried away to Babylon, should be restored to the house at Jerusalem, and be set in the place where they were before. **27** And also he commanded that Sisinnes the governor of Syria and Phoenicia, and Sathrabuzanes, and their companions, and those which were appointed rulers in Syria and Phoenicia, should be careful not to meddle with the place, but suffer Zorobabel, the servant of the Lord, and governor of Judea, and the elders of the Jews, to build that house of the Lord in its place. **28** And I also do command to have it built up whole again; and that they look diligently to help those that be of the captivity of Judea, until the house of the Lord be finished: **29** and that out of the tribute of Coelesyria and Phoenicia a portion be carefully given these men for the sacrifices of the Lord, *that is,* to Zorobabel the governor, for bullocks, and rams, and lambs; **30** and also corn, salt, wine and oil, and that continually every year without further question, according as the priests that be in Jerusalem will signify to be daily spent: **31** that drink offerings may be made to the Most High God for the king and for his children, and that they may pray for their lives. **32** And that commandment be given that whoever will transgress, yes, or neglect anything written here, out of his own *house* will a tree be taken, and he be hanged on it, and all his goods seized for the king. **33** The Lord therefore, whose name is there called upon, utterly destroy every king and nation, that will stretch out his hand to hinder or damage that house of the Lord in Jerusalem. **34** I Darius the king have ordained that according to these things it be done with diligence.

CHAPTER 7

1 Then Sisinnes the governor of Coelesyria and Phoenicia, and Sathrabuzanes, with their companions, following the commandments of king Darius, **2** did very carefully oversee the holy works, assisting the elders of the Jews and rulers of the temple. **3** And so the holy works prospered, while Aggaeus and Zacharias the prophets prophesied. **4** And they finished these things by the commandment of the Lord, the God of Israel, and with the consent of Cyrus, Darius, and Artaxerxes, kings of the Persians. **5** *And so* was the house finished by the three and twentieth day of the month Adar, in the sixth year of king Darius.

6 And the children of Israel, the priests, and the Levites, and the other that were of the captivity, that were added *to them,* did according to the things *written* in the book of Moses. 7 And to the dedication of the temple of the Lord they offered a hundred bullocks, two hundred rams, four hundred lambs; 8 *and* twelve he-goats for the sin of all Israel, according to the number of the twelve princes of the tribes of Israel. 9 The priests also and the Levites stood arrayed in their vestments, according to their kindred, for the services of the Lord, the God of Israel, according to the book of Moses: and the gatekeepers at every gate. 10 And the children of Israel that came out of the captivity held the Passover the fourteenth day of the first month, when the priests and the Levites were sanctified together, 11 and all those who were of the captivity; for they were sanctified. For the Levites were all sanctified together, 12 and they offered the Passover for all them of the captivity, and for their kindred the priests, and for themselves. 13 And the children of Israel that came out of the captivity did eat, even all those who had separated themselves from the abominations of the heathen of the land and sought the Lord. 14 And they kept the feast of unleavened bread seven days, making merry before the Lord, 15 for that he had turned the counsel of the king of Assyria toward them, to strengthen their hands in the works of the Lord, the God of Israel.

CHAPTER 8

1 And after these things, when Artaxerxes the king of the Persians reigned, came Esdras the son of Azaraias, the son of Zechrias, the son of Helkias, the son of Salem, 2 the son of Sadduk, the son of Ahitob, the son of Amarias, the son of Ozias,the son of Memeroth, the son of Zaraias, the son of Savias, the son of Boccas, the son of Abisne, the son of Phinees, the son of Eleazar, the son of Aaron, the chief priest. 3 This Esdras went up from Babylon, as being a ready scribe in the law of Moses, that was given by the God of Israel. 4 And the king did him honor: for he found grace in his sight in all his requests. 5 There went up with him also certain of the children of Israel, and of the priests, and Levites, and holy singers, and gatekeepers, and temple servants, to Jerusalem, 6 in the seventh year of the reign of Artaxerxes, in the fifth month, this was the king's seventh year; for they went from Babylon on the new moon of the first month,

and came to Jerusalem, according to the prosperous journey which the Lord gave them for his sake. 7 For Esdras had very great skill, so that he omitted nothing of the law and commandments of the Lord but taught all Israel the ordinances and judgments. 8 Now the commission, which was written from Artaxerxes the king, came to Esdras the priest and reader of the law of the Lord, whereof this that follows is a copy; 9 King Artaxerxes to Esdras the priest and reader of the law of the Lord, greeting: 10 Having determined to deal graciously, I have given order, that such of the nation of the Jews, and of the priests and Levites, and of those within our realm, as are willing and desirous, should go with you to Jerusalem. 11 As many therefore as have a mind *there to,* let them depart with you, as it has seemed good both to me and my seven friends the counselors; 12 that they may look to the affairs of Judea and Jerusalem, agreeably to that which is in the law of the Lord, 13 and carry the gifts to the Lord of Israel to Jerusalem, which I and my friends have vowed; and that all the gold and silver that can be found in the country of Babylonia for the Lord in Jerusalem, 14 with that also which is given of the people for the temple of the Lord their God that is at Jerusalem, be collected: even the gold and silver for bullocks, rams, and lambs, and things thereto appertaining; 15 to the end that they may offer sacrifices to the Lord upon the altar of the Lord their God, which is in Jerusalem. 16 And whatever you and your kindred are inclined to do with gold and silver, that perform, according to the will of your God. 17 And the holy vessels of the Lord, which are given you for the use of the temple of your God, which is in Jerusalem: 18 and whatever thing else you will remember for the use of the temple of your God, you will give it out of the king's treasury. 19 And I king Artaxerxes have also commanded the keepers of the treasures in Syria and Phoenicia, that whatever Esdras the priest and reader of the law of the Most High God will send for, they should give it him with all diligence, 20 to the sum of a hundred talents of silver, likewise also of wheat even to a hundred measures, and a hundred firkins of wine, and salt in abundance. 21 Let all things be performed after the law of God diligently to the most high God, that wrath come not upon the kingdom of the king and his sons. 22 I command you also, that no tax, nor any other imposition, be laid upon any of the priests, or

Levites, or holy singers, or gatekeepers, or temple servants, or any that have employment in this temple, and that no man have authority to impose anything upon them. **23** And you, Esdras, according to the wisdom of God ordain judges and justices, that they may judge in all Syria and Phoenicia all those that know the law of your God; and those that know it not you will teach. **24** And whoever will transgress the law of your God, and of the king, will be punished diligently, whether it be by death, or other punishment, by penalty of money, or by imprisonment. **25** Then said Esdras the scribe, "Blessed be the only Lord, the God of my fathers, who has put these things into the heart of the king, to glorify his house that is in Jerusalem: **26** and has honored me in the sight of the king, and his counselors, and all his friends and nobles. **27** Therefore was I encouraged by the help of the Lord my God and gathered together out of Israel men to go up with me. **28** And these are the chief according to their families and the several divisions thereof, that went up with me from Babylon in the reign of king Artaxerxes: **29** of the sons of Phinees, Gerson: of the sons of Ithamar, Gamael: of the sons of David, Attus the son of Sechenias: **30** of the sons of Phoros, Zacharais; and with him were counted a hundred and fifty men: **31** of the sons of Phaath-moab, Eliaonias the son of Zaraias, and with him two hundred men: **32** of the sons of Zathoes, Sechenias the son of Jezelus, and with him three hundred men: of the sons of Adin, Obeth the son of Jonathan, and with him two hundred and fifty men: **33** of the sons of Elam, Jesias son of *Athaliah,* Gotholia's son, and with him seventy men: **34** of the sons of Saphatias, *Zebadiah,* Zaraias son of Michael, and with him threescore and ten men: **35** of the sons of Joab, *Obadiah,* Abadias son of *Jehiel.* Jezelus, and with him two hundred and twelve men: **36** of the sons of Banias, Salimoth son of Josaphias, and with him a hundred and threescore men: **37** of the sons of Babi, Zacharias son of Bebai, and with him twenty and eight men: **38** of the sons of *Azgad,* Joannes son of *Hakkatan,* and with him a hundred and ten men: **39** of the sons of Adonikam, the last, and these are the names of them, Eliphalat, Jeuel, and *Shemaiah,* and with them seventy men: **40** of the sons of *Bigvai.* Bago, Uthi the son of Istalcurus, and with him seventy men. **41** And I gathered them together to the river called Theras; and there we pitched our tents three days, and I surveyed them.

42 But when I had found there none of the priests and Levites, **43** then sent I to Eleazar and Iduel, and Maasmas, **44** and Elnathan, and Samaias, and *Jarib,* Nathan, Ennatan, Zacharias, and Mosollamus, principal men and men of understanding. **45** And I bade those who they should go to *Iddo,* Loddeus the captain, who was in the place of *Casiphia,* the treasury: **46** and commanded them that they should speak to Loddeus, and to his kindred, and to the treasurers in that place, to send us such men as might execute the priests' office in the house of our Lord. **47** And by the mighty hand of our Lord they brought to us men of understanding of the sons of Mooli the son of Levi, the son of Israel, Asebebias, and his sons, and his kindred, who were eighteen, **48** and Asebias, and Annuus, and Osaias his brother, of the sons of Chanuneus, and their sons were twenty men; **49** and of the temple-servants whom David and the principal men had appointed for the servants of the Levites, two hundred and twenty temple-servants, the catalogue of all their names was showed. **50** And there I vowed a fast for the young men before our Lord, to desire of him a prosperous journey both for us and for our children and cattle that were with us: **51** for I was ashamed to ask of the king footmen, and horsemen, and conduct for protection against our adversaries. **52** For we had said to the king, that the power of our Lord would be with those who seek him, to support them in all ways. **53** And again we implored our lord as touching these things and found him favorable *to us.* **54** Then I separated twelve men of the chiefs of the priests, Eserebias, and Assamias, and ten men of their kindred with them: **55** and I weighed them the silver, and the gold, and the holy vessels of the house of our Lord, which the king, and his counselors, and the nobles, and all Israel, had given. **56** And when I had weighed it, I delivered to them six hundred and fifty talents of silver, and silver vessels of a hundred talents, and a hundred talents of gold, **57** and twenty golden vessels, and twelve vessels of brass, even of fine brass, glittering like gold. **58** And I said to them, Both you are holy to the Lord, and the vessels are holy, and the gold and the silver are a vow to the Lord, the Lord of our fathers. **59** Watch you and keep them until you deliver them to the chiefs of the priests and Levites, and to the principal men of the families of Israel, in Jerusalem, in the chambers of the house of our Lord. **60** So the priests and the Levites, who received the silver and the gold and the vessels which were in Jerusalem, brought them into the temple of the Lord. **61** And from the river Theras we departed the twelfth day of the first month, until we came to Jerusalem, by the mighty hand of our Lord which was upon us: and the Lord delivered us from *assault by* the way, from every enemy, and so we came to Jerusalem. **62** And when we had been there three days, the silver and gold was weighed and delivered in the house of our Lord on the fourth day to Marmoth the priest the son of Urias. **63** And with him was Eleazar the son of Phinees, and with them were Josabdus the son of Jesus and Moeth the son of Sabannus, the Levites: all *was delivered them* by number and weight. **64** And all the weight of them was written up the same hour. **65** Moreover those who were come out of the captivity offered sacrifices to the Lord, the God of Israel, even twelve bullocks for all Israel, fourscore and sixteen rams, **66** threescore and twelve lambs, goats for a peace offering, twelve; all of them a sacrifice to the Lord. **67** And they delivered the king's commandments to the king's stewards, and to the governors of Coelesyria and Phoenicia; and they honored the people and the temple of the Lord. **68** Now when these things were done, the principal men came to me, and said, **69** The nation of Israel, and the princes, and the priests and the Levites, have not put away *from them* the strange people of the land, nor the uncleanness of the Gentiles, *to wit,* of the Canaanites, Hittites, Pherezites, Jebusites, and the Moabites, Egyptians, and Edomites. **70** For both they and their sons have married with their daughters, and the holy seed is mixed with the strange people of the land; and from the beginning of this matter the rulers and the nobles have been partakers of this iniquity. **71** And as soon as I had heard these things, I tore my clothes, and my holy garment, and plucked the hair from off my head and beard and sat me down sad and full of heaviness. **72** So all those who were moved at the word of the Lord, the God of Israel, assembled to me, while I mourned for the iniquity: but I sat still full of heaviness until the evening sacrifice. **73** Then rising up from the fast with my clothes and my holy garment tore, and bowing my knees, and stretching out my hands to the Lord, **74** I said, O Lord, I am ashamed and confounded before your face; **75** for our sins are multiplied above our heads, and our errors have reached up to heaven, **76** ever since the time of our fathers; and we

are in great sin, even to this day. **77** And for our sins and our fathers' we with our kindred and our kings and our priests were given up to the kings of the earth, to the sword, and to captivity, and for a prey with shame, to this day. **78** And now in some measure has mercy been showed to us from you, O Lord, that there should be left us a root and a name in the place of your sanctuary; **79** and to discover to us a light in the house of the Lord our God, and to give us food in the time of our servitude. **80** Yes, when we were in bondage, we were not forsaken of our Lord; but he made us gracious before the kings of Persia, so that they gave us food, **81** and glorified the temple of our Lord, and raised up the desolate Zion, to give us a sure dwelling in Jewry and Jerusalem. **82** And now, O Lord, what will we say, having these things? For we have transgressed your commandments, which you gave by the hand of your servants the prophets, saying, **83** That the land, which you enter into to possess as a heritage, is a land polluted with the pollutions of the strangers of the land, and they have filled it with their uncleanness. **84** Therefore now will you not join your daughters to their sons, neither will you take their daughters to your sons. **85** Neither will you seek to have peace with them forever, that you may be strong, and eat the good things of the land, and that you may leave it for an inheritance to your children forevermore. **86** And all that is befallen is done to us for our wicked works and great sins: for you, O Lord, did make our sins light, **87** and did give to us such a root: *but* we have turned back again to transgress your law, in mingling ourselves with the uncleanness of the heathen of the land. **88** You were not angry with us to destroy us, until you had left us neither root, seed, nor name. **89** O Lord of Israel, you are true: for we are left a root this day. **90** Behold, now are we before you in our iniquities, for we can't stand any longer before you by reason of these things. **91** And as Esdras in his prayer made his confession, weeping, and lying flat upon the ground before the temple, there gathered to him from Jerusalem a very great throng of men and women and children: for there was great weeping among the multitude. **92** Then Jechonias the son of Jeelus, one of the sons of Israel, called out, and said, O Esdras, we have sinned against the Lord God, we have married strange women of the heathen of the land, and now is all Israel aloft. **93** Let's make an oath to the Lord herein, that we will put away all our wives, which *we have taken* of the strangers, with their children, **94** like as seems good to you, and to as many as do obey the Law of the Lord. **95** Arise and put in execution: for to you does this matter appertain, and we will be with you to do valiantly. **96** So Esdras arose, and took an oath of the chief of the priests and Levites of all Israel to do after these things; and *so* they swore.

CHAPTER 9

1 Then Esdras rising from the court of the temple went to the chamber of Jonas the son of Eliasib, **2** and lodged there, and did eat no bread nor drink water, mourning for the great iniquities of the multitude. **3** And there was made proclamation in all Jewry and Jerusalem to all those who were of the captivity, that they should be gathered together at Jerusalem: **4** and that whoever met not there within two or three days, according as the elders that bare rule appointed, their cattle should be seized to the use of the temple, and himself cast out from the multitude of those who were of the captivity. **5** And in three days were all they of the tribe of Judah and Benjamin gathered together at Jerusalem: this was the ninth month, on the twentieth day of the month. **6** And all the multitude sat together trembling in the broad place before the temple because of the present foul weather. **7** So Esdras arose up and said to them, you have transgressed the law and married strange wives to increase the sins of Israel. **8** And now make confession and give glory to the Lord, the God of our fathers, **9** and do his will, and separate yourselves from the heathen of the land, and from the strange women. **10** Then cried the whole multitude, and said with a loud voice, Just as you have spoken, so will we do. **11** But forasmuch as the multitude is great, and it is foul weather, so that we can't stand without, and this is not a work of one day or two, seeing our sin in these things is spread far: **12** therefore let the rulers of the multitude stay, and let all them of our habitations that have strange wives come at the time appointed, **13** and with them the rulers and judges of every place, until we turn away the wrath of the Lord from us for this matter. **14** *Then* Jonathan the son of Azael and Ezekias the son of Thocanus accordingly took the matter upon them: and Mosollamus and Levis and Sabbateus were assessors to them. **15** And those who were of the captivity did according to all these things. **16** And Esdras the priest chose to him principal men of their families, all by name: and on the new moon of the tenth month they were shut in together to examine the matter. **17** So their cause that held strange wives was brought to an end by the new moon of the first month. **18** And of the priests that were come together, and had strange wives, there were found; **19** of the sons of Jesus the son of Josedek, and his kindred; Mathelas, and Eleazar, and Joribus, and Joadanus. **20** And they gave their hands to put away their wives, and to *offer* rams to make reconciliation for their error. **21** And of the sons of Emmer; Ananias, and Zabdeus, and Manes, and Sameus, and Hiereel, and Azarias. **22** And of the sons of Phaisur; Elionas, Massias, Ishmael, and Nathanael, and Ocidelus, and Saloas. **23** And of the Levites; Jozabdus, and Semeis, and Colius, who was called Calitas, and Patheus, and Judas, and Jonas. **24** Of the holy singers; Eliasibus, Bacchurus. **25** Of the gatekeepers: Sallumus, and tolbanes. **26** Of Israel, of the sons of Phoros; Hiermas, and Ieddias, and Melchias, and Maelus, and Eleazar, and Asibas, and Banneas. **27** Of the sons of Ela; Matthanias, Zacharias, and Jezrielus, and Oabdius, and Hieremoth, and Aedias. **28** And of the sons of Zamoth; Eliadas, Eliasimus, Othonias, Jarimoth, and Sabathus, and Zardeus. **29** Of the sons of Bebai; Joannes, and Ananias, and Jozabdus, and Ematheis. **30** Of the sons of Mani; Olamus, Mamuchus, Jedeus, Jasubas, and Jasaelus, and Hieremoth. **31** And of the sons of Addi; Naathus, and Moossias, Laccunus, and Naidus, and Matthanias, and Sesthel, Balnuus, and Manasseas. **32** And of the sons of Annas; Elionas, and Aseas, and Melchias, and Sabbeus, and Simon Chosameus. **33** And of the sons of Asom; Maltanneus, and Mattathias, and Sabanneus, Eliphalat, and Manasses, and Semei. **34** And of the sons of Baani; Jeremias, Momdis, Ismaerus, Juel, Mamdai, and Pedias, and Anos, Carabasion, and Enasibus, and Mamnitamenus, Eliasis, Bannus, Eliali, someis, Selemias, Nathanias: and of the sons of Ezora; Sesis, Ezril, Azaelus, Samatus, Zambri, Josephus. **35** And of the sons of Nooma; Mazitias, Zabadeas, Edos, Juel, Banaias. **36** All these had taken strange wives, and they put them away with their children. **37** And the priests and Levites, and those who were of Israel, lived in Jerusalem, and in the country, on the new moon of the seventh month, and the children of Israel in their habitations. **38** And the whole multitude were gathered together with one accord into the broad place before the porch of the temple toward the east: **39** and they said to Esdras the priest and reader, Bring the law of Moses, that was given of the Lord, the God of Israel. **40** So Esdras the chief priest brought the law to the whole multitude both of men and women, and to all the priests, to hear the law on the new moon of the seventh month. **41** And he read in the broad place before the porch of the temple from morning to mid-day, before both men and women; and all the multitude gave heed to the law. **42** And Esdras the priest and reader of the law stood up upon the pulpit of wood, which was made *for that purpose.* **43** And there stood up by him Mattathias, Sammus, Ananias, Azarias, Urias, Ezekias, Baalsamus, upon the right hand: **44** and upon his left hand, Phaldeus, Misael, Melchias, Lothasubus, Nabarias, Zacharias. **45** Then took Esdras the book of the law before the multitude and sat honorably in the first place before all. **46** And when he opened the law, they stood all straight up. So Esdras blessed the Lord God Most High, the God of armies, Almighty. **47** And all the people answered, Amen; and lifting up their hands they fell to the ground, and worshiped the Lord. **48** Also Jesus, Annus, Sarabias, Iadinus, Jacubus, Sabateus, Auteas, Maiannas, and Calitas, Azarias, and Jozabdus, and Ananias, Phalias, the Levites, taught the law of the Lord, and read to the multitude the law of the Lord, making them withal to understand it. **49** Then said Attharates to Esdras the chief priest and reader, and to the Levites that taught the multitude, even to all, **50** This day is holy to the Lord; (now they all wept when they heard the law:)**51** go then, and eat the fat, and drink the sweet, and send portions to those who have nothing; **52** for the day is holy to the Lord: and be not sorrowful; for the Lord will bring you to honor. **53** So the Levites published all things to the people, saying, "This day is holy; be not sorrowful." **54** Then they went their way, everyone to eat and drink, and make merry, and to give portions to those who had nothing, and to make great cheer; **55** because they understood the words wherein they were instructed, and for the which they had been assembled.

3 MACCABEES

The book of 3 Maccabees is found in most Orthodox Bibles as a part of the deuterocanon. Catholics consider it to be an example of pseudepigrapha and do not regard it as canonical. Protestants, with the exception of the Moravian Brethren who include it in the Apocrypha of the Czech Kralice Bible and Polish Gdańsk Bible, likewise regard it as non-canonical. Despite the title, the book has nothing to do with the Maccabees or their revolt against the Seleucid Empire, as described in 1 Maccabees and 2 Maccabees. Instead it tells the story of persecution of the Jews under Ptolemy IV Philopator (222–205 BC), some decades before the Maccabee uprising. The name of the book apparently comes from the similarities between this book and the stories of the martyrdom of Eleazar and the Maccabeean youths in 2 Maccabees; the High Priest Shimon is also mentioned.

CHAPTER 1

1 Now Philopater, on learning from those who came back that Antiochus had made himself master of the places which belonged to himself, sent orders to all his footmen and horsemen, took with him his sister Arsinoe, and marched out as far as the parts of Raphia, where Antiochus and his forces encamped. **2** And one Theodotus, intending to carry out his design, took with him the bravest of the armed men who had been before committed to his trust by Ptolemy, and got through at night to the tent of Ptolemy, to kill him on his own responsibility, and so to end the war. **3** But Dositheus, called the son of Drimulus, by birth a Jew, afterward a renegade from the laws and observances of his country, conveyed Ptolemy away, and made an obscure person lie down in his stead in the tent. It befell this man to receive the fate which was meant for the other. **4** A fierce battle then took place; and the men of Antiochus prevailing, Arsinoe continually went up and down the ranks, and with disheveled hair, with tears and entreaties, begged the soldiers to fight manfully for themselves, their children, and wives; and promised that if they proved conquerors, she would give them each two minas of gold. **5** It then happened that their enemies were defeated in hand-to-hand encounter, and that many of them were taken prisoners. **6** Having vanquished this attempt, the king then decided to proceed to the neighboring cities and encourage them. **7** By doing this, and by making donations to their temples, he inspired his subjects with confidence. **8** The Jews sent some of their council and of their elders to him. The greetings, guest-gifts, and congratulations of the past, bestowed by them, filled him with the greater eagerness to visit their city. **9** Having arrived at Jerusalem, sacrificed, and offered thank-offerings to the Greatest God, and done whatever else was suitable to the sanctity of the place, and entered the inner court, **10** he was so struck with the magnificence of the place, and so wondered at the orderly arrangements of the temple, that he considered entering the sanctuary itself. **11** And when they told him that this was not permissible, none of the nation, no, nor even the priests in general, but only the supreme high priest of all, and he only once in a year, being allowed to go in, he would by no means give way. **12** Then they read the law to him; but he persisted in obtruding himself, exclaiming, that he ought to be allowed: and saying Be it that they were deprived of this honor, I ought not to be. **13** And he put the question, Why, when he entered all the temples, none of the priests who were present forbade him? **14** He was thoroughly answered by someone, that he did wrong to boast of this. **15** Well; since I have done this, said he, be the cause what it may, will I not enter with or without your consent? **16** And when the priests fell down in their sacred vestments imploring the Greatest God to come and help in time of need, and to avert the violence of the fierce aggressor, and when they filled the temple with lamentations and tears, **17** then those who had been left behind in the city were scared, and rushed out, uncertain of the event. **18** Virgins, who had been shut up within their chambers, came out with their mothers, scattering dust and ashes on their heads, and filling the streets with outcries. **19** Women, but recently separated off, left their bridal chambers, left the reserve that befitted them, and ran about the city in a disorderly manner. **20** New-born babes were deserted by the mothers or nurses who waited upon them; some here, some there, in houses, or in fields; these now, with an ardor which could not be checked, swarmed into the Most High temple. 21 Various were the prayers offered up by those who assembled in this place, on account of the unholy attempt of the king. 22 Along with these there were some of the citizens who took courage, and would not submit to his obstinacy, and his intention of carrying out his purpose. 23 Calling out to arms, and to die bravely in defense of the law of their fathers, they created a great uproar in the place, and were with difficulty brought back by the aged and the elders to the station of prayer which they had occupied before. 24 During this time the multitude kept on praying. 25 The elders who surrounded the king tried in many ways to divert his arrogant mind from the design which he had formed. 26 He, in his hardened mood, insensible to all persuasion, was going onward with the view of carrying out this design. 27 Yet even his own officers, when they saw this, joined the Jews in an appeal to Him who has all power, to aid in the present crisis, and not wink at such overweening lawlessness. 28 Such was the frequency and the vehemence of the cry of the assembled crowd, that an indescribable noise ensued. 29 Not the men only, but the very walls and floor seemed to sound out; all things preferring dissolution rather than to see the place defiled.

CHAPTER 2

1 Now was it that the high priest Simon bowed his knees near the holy place, and spread out his hands in reverent form, and uttered the following supplication: 2 O Lord, Lord, King of the heavens, and Ruler of the whole creation, Holy among the holy, sole Governor, Almighty, give ear to us who are oppressed by a wicked and profane one, who celebrates in his confidence and strength. 3 It is you, the Creator of all, the Lord of the universe, who are a righteous Governor, and judge all who act with pride and insolence. 4 It was you who did destroy the former workers of unrighteousness, among whom were the giants, who trusted in their strength and daring, by covering them with a measureless flood. 5 It was you who did make the Sodomites, those workers of exceedingly iniquity, men notorious for their vices, an example to after generations, when you did cover them with fire and brimstone. 6 You did

make known your power when you caused the bold Pharaoh, the enslaver of your people, to pass through the ordeal of many and diverse inflictions. 7 And you rolled the depths of the sea over him, when he made pursuit with chariots, and with a multitude of followers, and gave a safe passage to those who put their trust in you, the Lord of the whole creation. 8 These saw and felt the works of your hands, and praised you the Almighty. 9 You, O King, when you created the illimitable and measureless earth, did choose out this city: you did make this place sacred to your name, albeit you need nothing: you did glorify it with your illustrious presence, after constructing it to the glory of your great and honorable name. 10 And you did promise, out of love to the people of Israel, that should we fall away from you, and become afflicted, and then come to this house and pray, you would hear our prayer. 11 Truly you are faithful and true. 12 And when you did often aid our fathers when hard pressed, and in low estate, and delivered them out of gret dangers, 13 see now, holy King, how through our many and great sins we are borne down, and made subject to our enemies, and are become weak and powerless. 14 We being in this low condition, this bold and profane man seeks to dishonor this your holy place, consecrated out of the earth to the name of your Majesty. 15 Your dwelling place, the heaven of heavens, is indeed unapproachable to men. 16 But since it seemed good to you to exhibit your glory among your people Israel, you did sanctify this place. 17 Punish us not by means of the uncleanness of their men, nor chastise us by means of their profanity; lest the lawless ones should boast in their rage, and exult in exuberant pride of speech, and say, 18 We have trampled upon the holy house, as idolatrous houses are trampled upon. 19 Blot out our iniquities, and do away with our errors, and show out your compassion in this hour. 20 Let your mercies quickly go before us. Grant us peace, that the cast down and broken hearted may praise you with their mouth. 21 At that time God, who sees all things, who is beyond all Holy among the holy, heard that prayer, so suitable; and scourged the man greatly uplifted with scorn and insolence. 22 Shaking him to and fro as a reed is shaken with the wind, he cast him upon the pavement, powerless, with limbs paralyzed; by a righteous judgment deprived of the faculty of speech. 23 His friends and bodyguards, beholding the swift recompense which had suddenly overtaken him, struck with exceeding terror, and fearing that he would die, speedily removed him. **24** When in course of time he had come to himself, this severe check caused no repentance within him, but he departed with bitter threats. **25** He proceeded to Egypt, grew worse in wickedness through his before mentioned companions in wine, who were lost to all goodness; **26** and not satisfied with countless acts of impiety, his audacity so increased that he raised evil reports there, and many of his friends, watching his purpose attentively, joined in furthering his will. **27** His purpose was to indict a public stigma upon our race; for that reason, he erected a pillar at the tower-porch, and caused the following inscription to be engraved upon it: **28** That entrance to their own temple was to be refused to all those who would not sacrifice; that all the Jews were to be registered among the common people; that those who resisted were to be forcibly seized and put to death; **29** that those who were so registered, were to be marked on their persons by the ivy-leaf symbol of Dionysus, and to be set apart with these limited rights. **30** To do away with the appearance of hating them all, he had it written underneath, that if any of them should elect to enter the community of those initiated in the rites, these should have equal rights with the Alexandrians. **31** Some of those who were over the city, therefore, abhorring any approach to the city of piety, unhesitatingly gave in to the king, and expected to derive some great honor from a future connection with him. **32** A nobler spirit, however, prompted the majority to cling to their religious observances, and by paying money that they might live unmolested, these sought to escape the registration: **33** cheerfully looking forward to future aid, they abhorred their own apostates, considering them to be national foes, and debarring them from the common usages of social intercourse.

CHAPTER 3

1 On discovering this, so incensed was the wicked king, that he no longer confined his rage to the Jews in Alexandria. Laying his hand more heavily upon those who lived in the country, he gave orders that they should be quickly collected into one place, and most cruelly deprived of their lives. **2** While this was going on, an invidious rumor was uttered abroad by men who had banded together to injure the Jewish race. The purport of their charge was, that the Jews kept them away from the ordinances of the law. **3** Now, while the Jews always maintained a feeling of unwavering loyalty toward the kings, **4** yet, as they worshiped God, and observed his law, they made certain distinctions, and avoided certain things. Hence some persons held them in revulsion; **5** although, as they adorned their conversation with works of righteousness, they had established themselves in the good opinion of the world. **6** What all the rest of mankind said, was, however, made of no account by the foreigners; **7** who said much of the exclusiveness of the Jews with regard to their worship and meats; they alleged that they were men unsociable, hostile to the king's interests, refusing to associate with him or his troops. By this way of speaking, they brought much odium upon them. **8** Nor was this unexpected uproar and sudden conflux of people unobserved by the Greeks who lived in the city, concerning men who had never harmed them: yet to aid them was not in their power, since all was oppression around; but they encouraged them in their troubles, and expected a favorable turn of affairs: **9** He who knows all things, will not, *said they,* disregard so great a people. **10** Some of the neighbors, friends, and fellow dealers of the Jews, even called them secretly to an interview, pledged them their assistance, and promised to do their very utmost for them. **11** Now the king, elated with his prosperous fortune, and not regarding the superior power of God, but thinking to persevere in his present purpose, wrote the following letter to the prejudice of the Jews. **12** King Ptolemy Philopater, to the commanders and soldiers in Egypt, and in all places, health and happiness! **13** I am right well; and so, too, are my affairs. **14** Since our Asiatic campaign, the particulars of which you know, and which by the aid of the gods, not lightly given, and by our own vigor, has been brought to a successful issue according to our expectation, **15** we resolved, not with strength of spear, but with gentleness and much humanity, as it were to nurse the inhabitants of Coele-Syria and Phoenicia, and to be their willing benefactors. **16** So, having bestowed considerable sums of money upon the temples of the several cities, we proceeded even as far as Jerusalem; and went up to honor the temple of these wretched beings who never cease from their folly. **17** To outward appearance they received us willingly; but belied that appearance by their deeds. When we were eager to enter their temple, and to honor it with the most beautiful and exquisite gifts, **18** they were so carried away by their old arrogance, as to forbid us the entrance; while we, out of our forbearance toward all men, refrained from exercising our power upon them. **19** And so, exhibiting their enmity against us, they alone among the nations lift up their heads against kings and benefactors, as men unwilling to submit to anything reasonable. **20** We then, having endeavored to make allowance for the madness of these persons, and on our victorious return treating all people in Egypt courteously, acted in a manner which was befitting. **21** Accordingly, bearing no ill-will against their kinsmen *at Jerusalem,* but rather remembering our connection with them, and the numerous matters with sincere heart from a remote period entrusted to them, we wished to venture a total alteration of their state, by giving them the rights of citizens of Alexandria, and to admit them to the everlasting rites of our solemnities. **22** All this, however, they have taken in a very different spirit. With their innate malignity, they have spurned the fair offer; and constantly inclining to evil, **23** have rejected the inestimable rights. Not only so, but by using speech, and by refraining from speech, they abhor the few among them who are heartily disposed toward us; ever deeming that their ignoble course of procedure will force us to do away with our reform. **24** Having then, received certain proofs that these *Jews* bear us every sort of ill-will, we must look forward to the possibility of some sudden tumult among ourselves, when these impious men may turn traitors and barbarous enemies. **25** As soon, therefore, as the contents of this letter become known to you, in that same hour we order those *Jews* who dwell among you, with wives and children, to be sent to us, vilified and abused, in chains of iron, to undergo a death, cruel and ignominious, suitable to men disaffected. **26** For by the punishment of them in one body we perceive that we have found the only means of establishing our affairs for the future on a firm and satisfactory basis. **27** Whosoever will shield a Jew, whether it be old man, child, or nursing baby, will with his whole house be tortured to death. **28** Whoever will inform against the *Jews,* besides receiving the property of the person charged, will be presented with two thousand drachmas from the royal treasury, will be made free, and will

be crowned. **29** Whatever place will shelter a Jew, will, when he is hunted out, be put under the ban of fire, and be forever rendered useless to every living being for all time to come. **30** Such was the purport of the king's letter.

CHAPTER 4

1 Wherever this decree was received, the people kept up a revelry of joy and shouting; as if their long-pent-up, hardened hatred, were now to show itself openly. **2** The Jews suffered great throes of sorrow, and wept much; while their hearts, all things around being lamentable, were set on fire as they mourned the sudden destruction which was decreed against them. **3** What home, or city, or place at all inhabited, or what streets were there, which their condition didn't fill with wailing and lamentation? **4** They were sent out unanimously by the generals in the several cities, with such stern and pitiless feeling, that the exceptional nature of the infliction moved even some of their enemies. These influenced by sentiments of common humanity, and reflecting upon the uncertain issue of life, shed tears at this their miserable expulsion. **5** A multitude of aged hoary-haired old men, were driven along with halting bending feet, urged onward by the impulse of a violent, shameless force to quick speed. **6** Girls who had entered the bridal chamber quite lately, to enjoy the partnership of marriage, exchanged pleasure for misery; and with dust scattered upon their myrrh-anointed heads, were hurried along unveiled; and, in the midst of outlandish insults, set up with one accord a lamentable cry instead of the marriage hymn. **7** Bound, and exposed to public gaze, they were hurried violently on board ship. **8** The husbands of these, in the prime of their youthful vigor, instead of crowns wore halters round their necks; instead of feasting and youthful celebration, spent the rest of their nuptial days in wailing, and saw only the grave at hand. **9** They were dragged along by unyielding chains, like wild beasts: of these, some had their necks thrust into the benches of the rowers; while the feet of others were enclosed in hard fetters. **10** The planks of the deck above them blocked out the light, and shut out the day on every side, so that they might be treated like traitors during the whole voyage. **11** They were conveyed accordingly in this vessel, and at the end of it arrived at Schedia. The king had ordered them to be cast into the vast hippodrome, which was built in front of the city. This place was well adapted by its situation to expose them to the gaze of all comers into the city, and of those who went from the city into the country. So they could hold no communication with his forces; no, were deemed unworthy of any civilized accommodation. **12** When this was done, the king, hearing that their kindred in the city often went out and lamented the melancholy distress of these victims, **13** was full of rage, and commanded that they should be carefully subjected to the same (and not one bit milder) treatment. **14** The whole nation was now to be registered. Every individual was to be specified by name; not for that hard servitude of labor which we have a little before mentioned, but that he might expose them to the before-mentioned tortures; and finally, in the short space of a day, might extirpate them by his cruelties. **15** The registering of these men was carried on cruelly, zealously, assiduously, from the rising of the sun to its going down and was not brought to an end in forty days. **16** The king was filled with great and constant joy, and celebrated banquets before the temple idols. His erring heart, far from the truth, and his profane mouth, gave glory to idols, deaf and incapable of speaking or aiding, and uttered unworthy speech against the Greatest God. **17** At the end of the above-mentioned interval of time, the registrars brought word to the king that the multitude of the Jews was too great for registration, **18** inasmuch as there were many still left in the land, of whom some were in inhabited houses, and others were scattered about in various places; so that all the commanders in Egypt were insufficient for the work. **19** The king threatened them, and charged them with taking bribes, in order to contrive the escape of the Jews: but was clearly convinced of the truth of what had been said. **20** They said, and proved, that paper and pens had failed them for the carrying out of their purpose. **21** Now this was an active interference of the unconquerable Providence which assisted the Jews from heaven.

CHAPTER 5

1 Then he called Hermon, who had charge of the elephants. Full of rage, altogether fixed in his furious design, **2** he commanded him, with a quantity of unmixed wine and handfuls of incense *infused* to drug the elephants early on the following day. These five hundred elephants were, when infuriated by the copious draughts of frankincense, to be led up to the execution of death upon the Jews. **3** The king, after issuing these orders, went to his feasting, and gathered together all those of his friends and of the army who hated the Jews the most. **4** The master of the elephants, Hermon, fulfilled his commission punctually. **5** The underlings appointed for the purpose went out about evening and bound the hands of the miserable victims, and took other precautions for their security at night, thinking that the whole race would perish together. **6** The heathen believed the Jews to be destitute of all protection; for chains fettered them about. **7** they invoked the Almighty Lord, and ceaselessly implored with tears their merciful God and Father, Ruler of all, Lord of every power, **8** to overthrow the evil purpose which was gone out against them, and to deliver them by extraordinary manifestation from that death which was in store for them. **9** Their litany so earnest went up to heaven. **10** Then Hermon, who had filled his merciless elephants with copious draughts of mixed wine and frankincense, came early to the palace to certify the kind thereof. **11** He, however, who has sent his good creature sleep from all time by night or by day so gratifying whom he wills, diffused a portion thereof now upon the king. **12** By this sweet and profound influence of the Lord he was held fast, and so his unjust purpose was quite frustrated, and his unflinching resolve greatly falsified. **13** But the Jews, having escaped the hour which had been fixed, praised their holy God, and again prayed him who is easily reconciled to display the power of his powerful hand to the overweening Gentiles. **14** The middle of the tenth hour had well near arrived, when the person who sent invitations, seeing the guests who were invited present, came and shook the king. **15** He gained his attention with difficulty, and hinting that the mealtime was getting past, talked the matter over with him. **16** The king listened to this, and then turning aside to his potations, commanded the guests to sit down before him. **17** This done, he asked them to enjoy themselves, and to indulge in mirth at this somewhat late hour of the banquet. **18** Conversation grew on, and the king sent for Hermon, and inquired of him, with fierce denunciations, why the Jews had been allowed to outlive that day. **19** Hermon explained that he had done his bidding over night; and in this he was confirmed by his friends. **20** The king, then, with a barbarity exceeding that of Phalaris, said, that they might thank his sleep of that day, "Lose no time, and get ready the elephants against tomorrow, as you did before, for the destruction of these accursed Jews." 21 When the king said this, the company present were glad, and approved; and then each man went to his own home. 22 Nor did they employ the night in sleep, so much as in contriving cruel mockeries for those deemed miserable. 23 The morning cock had just crowed, and Hermon, having harnessed the brutes, was stimulating them in the great colonnade. 24 The city crowds were collected together to see the hideous spectacle and waited impatiently for the dawn. 25 The Jews, breathless with momentary suspense, stretched out their hands, and prayed the Greatest God, in mournful strains, again to help them speedily. 26 The sun's rays were not yet shed abroad, and the king was waiting for his friends, when Hermon came to him, calling him out, and saying, That his desires could now be realized. 27 The king, receiving him, was astonished at his unwonted exit; and, overwhelmed with a spirit of oblivion about everything, inquired the object of this earnest preparation. 28 But this was the working of that Almighty God who had made him forget all his purpose. 29 Hermon, and all his friends, pointed out the preparation of the animals. They are ready, O king, according to your own strict injunction. 30 The king was filled with fierce anger at these words; for, by the Providence of God regarding these things, his mind had become entirely confused. He looked hard at Hermon, and threatened him as follows: 31 Your parents, or your children, were they here, to these wild beasts a large repast they should have furnished; not these innocent Jews, who me and my forefathers loyally have served. 32 Had it not been for familiar friendship, and the claims of your office, your life should have gone for theirs. 33 Hermon, being threatened in this unexpected and alarming manner, was troubled in visage, and depressed in countenance. 34 The friends, too, stole out one by one, and dismissed the assembled multitudes to their respective occupations. 35 The Jews, having heard of these events, praised the glorious God and King of kings, because they had obtained this help, too, from him. 36 Now the king arranged another banquet after the same manner and proclaimed an invitation to mirth. 37 And he summoned Hermon to his presence, and said, with threats,

"How often, O wretch, must I repeat my orders to you about these same persons? 38 Once more, arm the elephants for the extermination of the Jews tomorrow." 39 His kinsmen, who were reclining with him, wondered at his instability, and so expressed themselves: 40 "O king, how long do you make trial of us, as of men bereft of reason? This is the third time that you have ordered their destruction. When the thing is to be done, you change your mind, and recall your instructions. 41 For this cause the feeling of expectation causes tumult in the city: it swarms with factions; and is continually on the point of being plundered." 42 The king, just like another Phalaris, a prey to thoughtlessness, made no account of the changes which his own mind had undergone, issuing in the deliverance of the Jews. He swore a fruitless oath, and determined out with to send them to hades, crushed by the knees and feet of the elephants. 43 He would also invade Judea, and level its towns with fire and the sword; and destroy that temple which the heathen might not enter and prevent sacrifices ever after being offered up there. 44 Joyfully his friends broke up, together with his kinsmen; and, trusting in his determination, arranged their forces in guard at the most convenient places of the city. 45 And the master of the elephants urged the beasts into an almost maniacal state, drenched them with incense and wine, and decked them with frightful instruments. 46 About early morning, when the city was now filled with an immense number of people at the hippodrome, he entered the palace, and called the king to the business in hand. 47 The king's heart teemed with impious rage; and he rushed out with the mass, along with the elephants. With feelings unsoftened, and eyes pitiless, he longed to gaze at the hard and wretched doom of the above-mentioned *Jews*. 48 But the *Jews*, when the elephants went out at the gate, followed by the armed force; and when they saw the dust raised by the throng, and heard the loud cries of the crowd, 49 thought that they had come to the last moment of their lives, to the end of what they had tremblingly expected. They gave way, therefore, to lamentations and moans: they kissed each other: those nearest of kin to each other hung about one another's necks: fathers about their sons, mother their daughters: other women held their infants to their breasts, which drew what seemed their last milk. 50 Nevertheless, when they reflected upon the help previously granted them from heaven, they prostrated themselves with one accord; removed even the sucking children from the breasts, **51** and sent up an exceedingly great cry asking the Lord of all power to reveal himself and have mercy upon those who now lay at the gates of hades.

CHAPTER 6

1 And Eleazar, an illustrious priest of the country, who had attained to length of days, and whose life had been adorned with virtue, caused the elders who were around him to cease to cry out to the holy God, and prayed this: **2** O king, mighty in power, most high, Almighty God, who regulates the whole creation with your tender mercy, **3** look upon the seed of Abraham, upon the children of the sanctified Jacob, your sanctified inheritance, O Father, now being wrongfully destroyed as strangers in a strange land. **4** You destroyed Pharaoh, with his army of chariots, when that lord of this same Egypt was uplifted with lawless daring and loud-sounding tongue. Shedding the beams of your mercy upon the race of Israel, you did overwhelm him with his proud army. **5** When Sennacherim, the grievous king of the Assyrians, exulting in his countless army, had subdued the whole land with his spear, and was lifting himself against your holy city, with boastings grievous to be endured, you, O Lord, did demolish him and did show your might to many nations. **6** When the three friends in the land of Babylon of their own will exposed their lives to the fire rather than serve vain things, you did send a moist coolness through the fiery furnace and bring the fire upon all their adversaries. **7** It was you who, when Daniel was hurled, through slander and envy, as a prey to lions down below, did bring him back against unhurt to light. **8** When Jonah was pining away in the belly of the sea-bred monster, you did look upon him, O Father, and recover him to the sight of his own. **9** And now, you who hate insolence; you who do abound in mercy; you who are the protector of all things; appear quickly to those of the race of Israel, who are insulted by abhorred, lawless gentiles. **10** If our life has during our exile been stained with iniquity, deliver us from the hand of the enemy, and destroy us, O Lord, by the death which you prefer. **11** Let not the vain-minded congratulate vain idols at the destruction of your beloved, saying, neither did their god deliver them. **12** You, who are All-powerful and Almighty, O Eternal One, behold! have mercy upon us who are

being withdrawn from life, like traitors, by the unreasoning insolence of lawless men. **13** Let the heathen cower before your invincible might today, O glorious One, who have all power to save the race of Jacob. **14** The whole band of infants and their parents with tears implore you. **15** Let it be shown to all the nations that you are with us, O Lord, and have not turned your face away from us; but as you said that you would not forget them even in the land of their enemies, so do you fulfill this saying, O Lord. **16** Now, at the time that Eleazar had ended his prayer, the king came along to the hippodrome, with the wild beasts, and with his tumultuous power. **17** When the Jews saw this, they uttered a loud cry to heaven, so that the adjacent valleys resounded, and caused an irrepressible lamentation throughout the army. **18** Then the all-glorious, all-powerful, and true God, displayed his holy countenance, and opened the gates of heaven, from which two angels, dreadful of form, came down and were visible to all but the Jews. **19** And they stood opposite and filled the enemies' army with confusion and cowardice; and bound them with immoveable fetters. **20** And a cold shudder came over the person of the king, and oblivion paralyzed the vehemence of his spirit. **21** They turned back the animals upon the armed forces which followed them; and the animals trod them down and destroyed them. **22** The king's wrath was converted into compassion; and he wept at his own machinations. **23** For when he heard the cry, and saw them all on the verge of destruction, with tears he angrily threatened his friends, saying, **24** You have governed badly; and have exceeded tyrants in cruelty; and me your benefactor you have labored to deprive at once of my dominion and my life, by secretly devising measures injurious to the kingdom. **25** Who has gathered here, unreasonably removing each from his home, those who, in fidelity to us, had held the fortresses of the country? **26** Who has so consigned to unmerited punishments those who in good will toward us from the beginning have in all things surpassed all nations, and who often have engaged in the most dangerous undertakings? **27** Loose, loose the unjust bonds; send them to their homes in peace, and deprecate what has been done. **28** Release the sons of the almighty living God of heaven, who from our ancestors' times until now has granted a glorious and uninterrupted prosperity to our affairs. **29** These things he said; and they, released the same moment, having now escaped death, praised God their holy Savior. **30** The king then departed to the city, and called his financier to him, and asked him provide a seven days' quantity of wine and other materials for feasting for the Jews. He decided that they should keep a gladsome festival of deliverance in the very place in which they expected to meet with their destruction. **31** Then they who were before despised and near to hades, yes, rather advanced into it, partook of the cup of salvation, instead of a grievous and lamentable death. Full of exultation, they parted out the place intended for their fall and burial into banqueting booths. **32** Ceasing their miserable strain of woe, they took up the subject of their fatherland, hymning in praise God their wonder-working Savior. All groans, all wailing, were laid aside: they formed dances in token of serene joy. **33** So, also, the king collected a number of guests for the occasion and returned unceasing thanks with much magnificence for the unexpected deliverance afforded him. **34** Those who had marked them out as for death and for carrion, and had registered them with joy, howled aloud, and were clothed with shame, and had the fire of their rage ingloriously put out. **35** But the Jews, as we just said, instituted a dance, and then gave themselves up to feasting, glad thanksgiving, and psalms. **36** They made a public ordinance to commemorate these things for generations to come, as long as they should be sojourners. They therefore established these days as days of mirth, not for the purpose of drinking or luxury, but because God had saved them. **37** They requested the king to send them back to their homes. **38** They were being enrolled from the twenty-fifth of Pachon to the fourth of Epiphi, a period of forty days: the measures taken for their destruction lasted from the fifth of Epiphi until the seventh, that is, three days. **39** The Ruler over all did during this time manifest out his mercy gloriously and did deliver them all together unharmed. **40** They feasted upon the king's provision up to the fourteenth day, and then asked to be sent away. **41** The king commended them, and wrote the following letter, of magnanimous import for them, to the commanders of every city.

CHAPTER 7

1 King Ptolemy Philopator to the commanders throughout Egypt, and to all who are set over affairs, joy and strength. **2** We, too, and our children are well; and God has directed our affairs as we wish. **3** Certain of our friends did of malice vehemently urge us to punish the Jews of our realm in a body, with the infliction of a monstrous punishment. **4** They pretended that our affairs would never be in a good state until this took place. Such, they said, was the hatred borne by the Jews to all other people. **5** They brought them fettered in grievous chains as slaves, no, as traitors. Without enquiry or examination they endeavored to annihilate them. They buckled themselves with a savage cruelty, worse than Scythian custom. **6** For this cause we severely threatened them; yet, with the clemency which we are wont to extend to all men, we at length permitted them to live. Finding that the God of heaven cast a shield of protection over the Jews so as to preserve them, and that he fought for them as a father always fights for his sons; **7** and taking into consideration their constancy and fidelity toward us and toward our ancestors, we have, as we ought, acquitted them of every sort of charge. **8** And we have dismissed them to their several homes; bidding all men everywhere to do them no wrong, or unrighteously revile them about the past. **9** Know that should we conceive any evil design, or in any way aggrieve them, we will ever have as our opposite, not man, but the highest God, the ruler of all might. From Him there will be no escape, as the avenger of such deeds. Fare you well. **10** When they had received this letter, they were not forward to depart immediately. They petitioned the king to be allowed to inflict fitting punishment upon those of their race who had willingly transgressed the holy god, and the law of God. **11** They alleged that men who had for their bellies' sake transgressed the ordinances of God, would never be faithful to the interests of the king. **12** The king admitted the truth of this reasoning and commended them. Full power was given them, without warrant or special commission, to destroy those who had transgressed the law of God boldly in every part of the king's dominions. **13** Their priests, then, as it was meet, saluted him with good wishes, and all the people echoed with the Hallelujah. They then joyfully departed. **14** Then they punished and destroyed with ignominy every polluted Jew that fell in their way; **15** slaying therefore, in that day, above three hundred men, and esteeming this destruction of the wicked a season of joy.

16 They themselves having held fast their God to death, and having enjoyed a full deliverance, departed from the city garlanded with sweet-flowered wreaths of every kind. Uttering exclamations of joy, with songs of praise, and melodious hymns they thanked the God of their fathers, the eternal Savior of Israel. **17** Having arrived at Ptolemais, called from the specialty of that district Rose-bearing, where the fleet, in accordance with the general wish, waited for them seven days, **18** they partook of a banquet of deliverance, for the king generously granted them severally the means of securing a return home. **19** They were accordingly brought back in peace, while they gave utterance to becoming thanks; and they determined to keep these days during their sojourn as days of joyfulness. **20** These they registered as sacred upon a pillar, when they had dedicated the place of their festivity to be one of prayer. They departed unharmed, free, abundant in joy, preserved by the king's command, by land, by sea, and by river, each to his own home. **21** They had more weight than before among their enemies; and were honored and feared, and no one in any way robbed them of their goods. **22** Every man received back his own, according to inventory; those who had obtained their goods, giving them up with the greatest terror. For the greatest God made perfect wonders for their salvation. **23** Blessed be the Redeemer of Israel to everlasting. Amen.

4 MACCABEES

The book of 4 Maccabees is a homily or philosophic discourse praising the supremacy of pious reason over passion. It is not in the Bible for most churches, but is an appendix to the Greek Bible, and in the canon of the Georgian Orthodox Bible. It was included in the 1688 Romanian Orthodox and the 18th-century Romanian Catholic Bibles where it was called "Iosip" (Joseph). It is no longer printed in Romanian Bibles today. The book was ascribed to Josephus by Eusebius and Jerome, and this opinion was accepted for many years, leading to its inclusion in many editions of Josephus' works. Scholars have however pointed to perceived differences of language and style. The book is generally dated between 20 and 130 AD, likely in the later half of that range.

CHAPTER 1

1 As I am going to demonstrate a most philosophical proposition, namely, that religious reasoning is absolute master of the passions, I would willingly advise you to give the utmost heed to philosophy. 2 For reason is necessary to everyone as a step to science: and more especially does it embrace the praise of prudence, the highest virtue. 3 If, then, reasoning appears to hold the mastery over the passions which stand in the way of temperance, such as gluttony and lust, 4 it surely also and manifestly has the rule over the affections which are contrary to justice, such as malice; and of those which are hindrances to manliness, as wrath, and pain, and fear. 5 How, then, is it, perhaps some may say, that reasoning, if it rules the affections, is not also master of forgetfulness and ignorance? They attempt a ridiculous argument. 6 For reasoning does not rule over its own affections, but over such as are contrary to justice, and manliness and temperance, and prudence; and yet over these, so as to withstand, without destroying them. 7 I might prove to you, from many other considerations, that religious reasoning is sole master of the passions; 8 but I will prove it with the greatest force from the fortitude of Eleazar, and seven kindred, and their mother, who suffered death in defense of virtue. 9 For all these, treating pains with contempt even to death, by this contempt, demonstrated that reasoning has command over the passions. 10 For their virtues, then, it is right that I should commend those men who died with their mother at this time in behalf of rectitude; and for their honors, I may count them happy. 11 For they, winning admiration not only from men in general, but even from the persecutors, for their manliness and endurance, became the means of the destruction of the tyranny against their nation, having conquered the tyrant by their endurance, so that by them their country was purified. 12 But we may now at once enter upon the question, having commenced, as is our wont, with laying down the doctrine, and so proceed to the account of these persons, giving glory to the all wise God. 13 The question, therefore, is, whether reasoning be absolute master of the passions. 14 Let's determine, then, what is reasoning? And what passion? And how many forms of the passions? And whether reasoning bears sway over all of these? 15 Reasoning is, then, intellect accompanied by a life of rectitude, putting foremost the consideration of wisdom. 16 And wisdom is a knowledge of divine and human things, and of their causes. 17 And this is contained in the education of the law; by means of which we learn divine things reverently, and human things profitably. 18 And the forms of wisdom are prudence, and justice, and manliness, and temperance. 19 The leading one of these is prudence; by whose means, indeed, it is that reasoning bears rule over the passions. 20 Of the passions, pleasure and pain are the two most comprehensive; and they also by nature refer to the soul. 21 And there are many attendant affections surrounding pleasure and pain. 22 Before pleasure is lust; and after pleasure, joy. 23 And before pain is fear; and after pain is sorrow. 24 Wrath is an affection, common to pleasure and to pain, if anyone will pay attention when it comes upon him. 25 And there exists in pleasure a malicious disposition, which is the most multiform of all the affections. 26 In the soul it is arrogance, and love of money, and vain pride, and contention, and faithlessness, and the evil eye. 27 In the body it is greediness and gormandizing, and solitary gluttony. 28 As

pleasure and pain are, therefore, two growth of the body and the soul, so there are many offshoots of these passions. **29** And reasoning, the universal husbandman, purging, and pruning these severally, and binding round, and watering, and transplanting, in every way improves the materials of the morals and affections. **30** For reasoning is the leader of the virtues, but it is the sole ruler of the passions. Observe then first, through the very things which stand in the way of temperance, that reasoning is absolute ruler of the passions. **31** Now temperance consists of a command over the lusts. **32** But of the lusts, some belong to the soul, others to the body: and over each of these classes the reasoning appears to bear sway. **33** For where is it, otherwise, that when urged on to forbidden meats, we reject the gratification which would ensue from them? Is it not because reasoning is able to command the appetites? I believe so. **34** Hence it is, then, that when lusting after water-animals and birds, and four-footed beasts, and all kinds of food which are forbidden us by the law, we withhold ourselves through the mastery of reasoning. **35** For the affections of our appetites are resisted by the temperate understanding, and bent back again, and all the impulses of the body are reined in by reasoning.

CHAPTER 2

1 And what wonder? If the lusts of the soul, after participation with what is beautiful, are frustrated, **2** on this ground, therefore, the temperate Joseph is praised in that by reasoning, he subdued, on reflection, the indulgence of sense. **3** For, although young, and ripe for sexual intercourse, he abrogated by reasoning the stimulus of his passions. **4** And it is not merely the stimulus of sensual indulgence, but that of every desire, that reasoning is able to master. **5** For instance, the law says, "You will not covet your neighbor's wife, nor anything that belongs to your neighbor." **6** Now, then, since it is the law which has forbidden us to desire, I will much the more easily persuade you, that reasoning is able to govern our lusts, just as it does the affections which are impediments to justice. **7** Since in what way is a solitary eater, and a glutton, and a drunkard reclaimed, unless it be clear that reasoning is lord of the passions? **8** A man, therefore, who regulates his course by the law, even if he be a lover of money, immediately puts force upon his own disposition; lending to the needy without interest and cancelling the debt of the incoming Sabbath. **9** And should a man be parsimonious, he is ruled by the law acting through reasoning; so that he does not glean his harvest crops, nor vintage: and in reference to other points we may perceive that it is reasoning that conquers his passions. **10** For the law conquers even affection toward parents, not surrendering virtue on their account. **11** And it prevails over marriage love, condemning it when transgressing law. **12** And it lords it over the love of parents toward their children, for they punish them for vice; and it domineers over the intimacy of friends, reproving them when wicked. **13** And think it not a strange assertion that reasoning can in behalf of the law conquer even enmity. **14** It allows not to cut down the cultivated herbage of an enemy, but preserves it from the destroyers, and collects their fallen ruins. **15** And reason appears to be master of the more violent passions, as love of empire and empty boasting, and slander. **16** For the temperate understanding repels all these malignant passions, as it does wrath: for it masters even this. **17** So Moses, when angered against Dathan and Abiram, did nothing to them in wrath, but regulated his anger by reasoning. **18** For the temperate mind is able, as I said, to be superior to the passions, and to transfer some, and destroy others. **19** For why, else, does our most wise father Jacob blame Simeon and Levi for having irrationally slain the whole race of the Shechemites, saying, "Cursed be their anger." **20** For if reasoning didn't possess the power of subduing angry affections, he would not have spoken like this. **21** For at the time when God created man, He implanted within him his passions and moral nature. **22** And at that time He enthroned above all the holy leader mind, through the medium of the senses. **23** And He gave a law to this mind, by living according to which it will maintain a temperate, and just, and good, and manly reign. **24** How, then, a man may say, if reasoning be master of the passions, has it no control over forgetfulness and ignorance?

CHAPTER 3

1 The argument is exceedingly ridiculous: for reasoning does not appear to bear sway over its own affections, but over those of the body, **2** in such a way as that anyone of you may not be able to root out desire, but reasoning will enable you to avoid being enslaved to it. **3** One may not be able to root out anger from the soul, but it is possible to withstand anger. **4** Anyone of you may not be able to eradicate malice, but reasoning has force to work with you to prevent you yielding to malice. **5** For reasoning is not an eradicator, but an antagonist of the passions. **6** And this may be more clearly comprehended from the thirst of king David. **7** For after David had been attacking the Philistines the whole day, he with the soldiers of his nation killed many of them; **8** then when evening came, sweating and very weary, he came to the royal tent, about which the entire army of our ancestors was encamped. **9** Now all the rest of them were at supper; **10** but the king, being very much thirsty, although he had numerous springs, could not by their means quench his thirst; **11** but a certain irrational longing for the water in the enemy's camp grew stronger and fiercer upon him, and consumed him with languish. **12** For that reason, his bodyguards being troubled at this longing of the king, two valiant young soldiers, reverencing the desire of the king, put on their panoplies, and taking a pitcher, got over the ramparts of the enemies: **13** and unperceived by the guardians of the gate, they went throughout the whole camp of the enemy in quest. **14** And having boldly discovered the fountain, they filled out of it the draught for the king. **15** But he, though parched with thirst, reasoned that a draught reputed of equal value to blood, would be terribly dangerous to his soul. **16** For that reason, setting up reasoning in opposition to his desire, he poured out the draught to God. **17** For the temperate mind has power to conquer the pressure of the passions, and to quench the fires of excitement, **18** and to wrestle down the pains of the body, however excessive; and, through the excellency of reasoning, to abominate all the assaults of the passions. **19** But the occasion now invites us to give an illustration of temperate reasoning from history. **20** For at a time when our fathers were in possession of undisturbed peace through obedience to the law, and were prosperous, so that Seleucus Nicanor, the king of Asia, both assigned them money for divine service, and accepted their form of government, **21** then certain persons, bringing in new things contrary to the general unanimity, in various ways fell into calamities.

CHAPTER 4

1 For a certain man named Simon, who was in opposition to Onias, who once held the high priesthood for life, and was an honorable and good man, after slandering him in every way, he could not injure him with the people, went away as an exile, with the intention of betraying his country. **2** When coming to Apollonius, the military governor of Syria, and Phoenicia, and Cilicia, he said, **3** Having good will to the king's affairs, I have come to inform you that infinite private wealth is laid up in the treasuries of Jerusalem which do not belong to the temple but pertain to king Seleucus. **4** Apollonius, acquainting himself with the particulars of this, praised Simon for his care of the king's interests, and going up to Seleucus informed him of the treasure; **5** and getting authority about it, and quickly advancing into our country with the accursed Simon and a very heavy force, **6** he said that he came with the commands of the king that he should take the private money of the treasure. **7** And the nation, indignant at this proclamation, and replying to the effect that it was extremely unfair that those who had committed deposits to the sacred treasury should be deprived of them, resisted as well as they could. **8** But Appolonius went away with threats into the temple. **9** And the priests, with the women and children, having supplicated God to throw his shield over the holy, despised place, **10** and Appolonius going up with his armed force to the seizure of the treasure, — there appeared from heaven angels riding on horseback, all radiant in armor, filling them with much fear and trembling. **11** And Apollonius fell half dead upon the court which is open to all nations, and extended his hands to heaven, and implored the Hebrews, with tears, to pray for him, and propitiate the heavenly army. **12** For he said that he had sinned, so as to be consequently worthy of death; and that if he were saved, he would celebrate to all men the blessedness of the holy place. **13** Onias the high priest, induced by these words, although for other reasons anxious that king Seleucus should not suppose that Apollonius was slain by human device and not by Divine punishment, prayed for him; **14** and he being unexpectedly saved, departed to manifest to the king what had happened to him. **15** But on the death of Seleucus the king, his son Antiochus Epiphanes succeeds to the kingdom: a man of arrogant pride and terrible. **16** Who having deposed Onias from the high priesthood, appointed his brother Jason to be high priest: **17** who had made a covenant, if he would give him this authority, to pay yearly three thousand six hundred and sixty talents. **18** And he committed to him the high priesthood and rulership over the nation. **19** And he both changed the manner of living of the people and perverted their civil customs into all lawlessness. **20** So that he not only erected a gymnasium on the very citadel of our country but *neglected* the guardianship of the temple. **21** At which Divine vengeance being grieved, instigated Antiochus himself against them. **22** For being at war with Ptolemy in Egypt, he heard that on a report of his death being spread abroad, the inhabitants of Jerusalem had exceedingly rejoiced, and he quickly marched against them. **23** And having subdued them, he established a decree that if any of them lived according to the laws of his country he should die. **24** And when he could by no means destroy by his decrees the obedience to the law of the nation, but saw all his threats and punishments without effect, **25** for even women, because they continued to circumcise their children, were flung down a precipice along with them, knowing beforehand of the punishment. **26** When, therefore, his decrees were disregarded by the people, he himself compelled by means of tortures every one of this race, by tasting forbidden meats, to renounce the Jewish religion.

CHAPTER 5

1 The tyrant Antiochus, therefore, sitting in public state with his assessors upon a certain lofty place, with his armed troops standing in a circle around him, **2** commanded his spear-bearers to seize every one of the Hebrews, and to compel them to taste swine's flesh, and things offered to idols. **3** And should any of them be unwilling to eat the accursed food, they were to be tortured on the wheel, and so killed. **4** And when many had been seized, a foremost man of the assembly, a Hebrew, by name Eleazar, a priest by family, by profession a lawyer, and advanced in years, and for this reason known to many of the king's followers, was brought near to him. **5** And Antiochus seeing him, said, **6** I would counsel you, old man, before your tortures begin, to taste the swine's flesh, and save your life; for I feel respect for your age and hoary head, which since you have had so long, you appear to me to be no philosopher in retaining the superstition of the Jews. **7** For that reason, since nature has conferred upon you the most excellent flesh of this animal, do you loathe it? **8** It seems senseless to not enjoy what is pleasant, yet not disgraceful; and from notions of sinfulness, to reject the boons of nature. **9** And you will be acting, I think, still more senselessly, if you follow vain conceits about the truth. **10** And you will, moreover, be despising me to your own punishment. **11** Will you not awake from your trifling philosophy? And give up the folly of your notions; and, regaining understanding worthy of your age, search into the truth of an expedient course? **12** and, reverencing my kindly admonition, have pity upon your own years? **13** For, bear in mind, that if there be any power which watches over this religion of yours, it will pardon you for all transgressions of the law which you commit through compulsion. **14** While the tyrant incited him in this manner to the unlawful eating of flesh, Eleazar begged permission to speak. **15** And having received power to speak, he began deliver himself like this: **16** We, O Antiochus, who are persuaded that we live under a divine law, consider no compulsion to be so forcible as obedience to that law; **17** for this reason we consider that we ought not in any point to transgress the law. **18** And indeed, were our law (as you suppose) not truly divine, and if we wrongly think it divine, we should have no right even in that case to destroy our sense of religion. **19** Think not eating the unclean, then, a trifling offense. **20** For transgression of the law, whether in small or great matters, is of equal moment; **21** for in either case the law is equally slighted. **22** But you deride our philosophy, as though we lived irrationally in it. **23** Yet it instructs us in temperance, so that we are superior to all pleasures and lusts; and it exercises us in manliness, so that we cheerfully undergo every grievance. **24** And it instructs us in justice, so that in all our dealings we render what is due; and it teaches us piety, so that we worship the one only God becomingly. **25** For that reason it is that we eat not the unclean; for believing that the law was established by God, we are convinced that the Creator of the world, in giving his laws, sympathizes with our nature. **26** Those things which are convenient to our souls, he has directed us to eat; but those which are repugnant to them, he has interdicted. **27** But, tyrant-like, you not only force us to break the law, but also to eat, that you may ridicule us as we so profanely eat:

28 but you will not have this cause of laughter against me; 29 nor will I transgress the sacred oaths of my forefathers to keep the law. 30 No, not if you pluck out my eyes, and consume my entrails. 31 I am not so old, and void of manliness, but that my rational powers are youthful in defense of my religion. 32 Now then; prepare your wheels and kindle a fiercer flame. 33 I will not so compassionate my old age, as on my account to break the law of my country. 34 I will not belie you, O law, my instructor! or forsake you, O beloved self-control! 35 I will not put you to shame, O philosopher Reason; or deny you, O honored priesthood, and science of the law. 36 Mouth! you will not pollute my old age, nor the full stature of a perfect life. 37 My fathers will receive me pure, not having quailed before your compulsion, though to death. 38 For over the ungodly you will tyrannize; but you will not lord it over my thoughts about religion, either by your arguments, or through deeds.

CHAPTER 6

1 When Eleazar had in this manner answered the exhortations of the tyrant, the spear-bearers came up, and rudely haled Eleazar to the instruments of torture. 2 And first, they stripped the old man, adorned as he was with the beauty of piety. 3 Then tying back his arms and hands, they disdainfully used him with stripes; 4 a herald opposite crying out, Obey the commands of the king. 5 But Eleazar, the high-minded and truly noble, as one tortured in a dream, regarded it not all. 6 But raising his eyes on high to heaven, the old man's flesh was stripped off by the scourges, and his blood streamed down, and his sides were pierced through. 7 And falling upon the ground, from his body having no power to support the pains, he yet kept his reasoning upright and unbending. 8 then one of the harsh spear-bearers leaped upon his belly as he was falling, to force him upright. 9 But he endured the pains, and despised the cruelty, and persevered through the indignities; 10 and like a noble athlete, the old man, when struck, vanquished his torturers. 11 His countenance sweating, and he panting for breath, he was admired by the very torturers for his courage. 12 For that reason, partly in pity for his old age, 13 partly from the sympathy of acquaintance, and partly in admiration of his endurance, some of the attendants of the king said, 14 "Why do you unreasonably destroy yourself, O Eleazar, with these miseries? 15 We will bring you some meat cooked by yourself, and do you save yourself by pretending that you have eaten swine's flesh." 16 And Eleazar, as though the advice more painfully tortured him, cried out, 17 "Let not us who are children of Abraham be so evil advised as by giving way to make use of an unbecoming pretense; 18 for it were irrational, if having lived up to old age in all truth, and having scrupulously guarded our character for it, we should now turn back, 19 and ourselves should become a pattern of impiety to the young, as being an example of pollution eating. 20 It would be disgraceful if we should live on some short time, and that scorned by all men for cowardice, 21 and be condemned by the tyrant for unmanliness, by not contending to the death for our divine law. 22 For this reason do you, O children of Abraham, die nobly for your religion. 23 You spear-bearers of the tyrant, why do you linger?" 24 Beholding him so high-minded against misery, and not changing at their pity, they led him to the fire: 25 then with their wickedly contrived instruments they burned him on the fire and poured stinking fluids down into his nostrils. 26 And he being at length burned down to the bones, and about to expire, raised his eyes Godward, and said, 27 "You know, O God, that when I might have been saved, I am slain for the sake of the law by tortures of fire. 28 Be merciful to your people and be satisfied with the punishment of me on their account. 29 Let my blood be a purification for them and take my life in recompense for theirs." 30 Therefore speaking, the holy man departed, noble in his torments, and even to the agonies of death resisted in his reasoning for the sake of the law. 31 Confessedly, therefore, religious reasoning is master of the passions. 32 For had the passions been superior to reasoning, I would have given them the witness of this mastery. 33 But now, since reasoning conquered the passions, we befittingly awarded it the authority of first place. 34 And it is but fair that we should allow, that the power belongs to reasoning, since it masters external miseries. 35 Ridiculous would it be were it not so; and I prove that reasoning has not only mastered pains, but that it is also superior to the pleasures, and withstands them.

CHAPTER 7

1 The reasoning of our father Eleazar, like a first-rate pilot, steering the vessel of piety in the sea of passions, 2 and flouted by the threats

of the tyrant, and overwhelmed with the breakers of torture, **3** in no way shifted the rudder of piety until it sailed into the harbor of victory over death. **4** Not so has ever a city, when besieged, held out against many and various machines, as did that holy man, when his pious soul was tried with the fiery trial of tortures and racking, move his besiegers through the religious reasoning that shielded him. **5** For father Eleazar, projecting his disposition, broke the raging waves of the passions as with a jutting promontory. **6** O priest worthy of the priesthood! you didn't pollute your sacred teeth; nor make your appetite, which had always embraced the clean and lawful, a partaker of profanity. **7** O harmonizer with the law, and sage devoted to a divine life! **8** Of such a character ought those to be who perform the duties of the law at the risk of their own blood and defend it with generous sweat by sufferings even to death. **9** You, father, have gloriously established our right government by your endurance; and making of much account our service past, prevented its destruction, and, by your deeds, have made credible the words of philosophy. **10** O aged man of more power than tortures, elder more vigorous than fire, greatest king over the passions, Eleazar! **11** For as father Aaron, armed with a censer, hastening through the consuming fire, vanquished the flame-bearing angel, **12** so, Eleazar, the descendant of Aaron, wasted away by the fire, didn't give up his reasoning. **13** And, what is most wonderful, though an old man, though the labors of his body were now spent, and his muscles were relaxed, and his sinews worn out, he recovered youth. **14** By the spirit of reasoning, and the reasoning of Isaac, he rendered powerless the many-headed instrument. **15** O blessed old age, and reverend hoar head, and life obedient to the law, which the faithful seal of death perfected. **16** If, then, an old man, through religion, despised tortures even to death, confessedly religious reasoning is ruler of the passions. **17** But perhaps some might say, It is not all who conquer passions, as all do not possess wise reasoning. **18** But they who have meditated upon religion with their whole heart, these alone can master the passions of the flesh; **19** they who believe that to God they die not; for, as our forefathers, Abraham, Isaac, Jacob, they live to God. **20** This circumstance, then, is by no means an objection, that some who have weak reasoning, are governed by their passions:

21 since what person, walking religiously by the whole rule of philosophy, and believing in God, **22** and knowing that it is a blessed thing to endure all kinds of hardships for virtue, would not, for the sake of religion, master his passion? **23** For the wise and brave man only is lord over his passions. **24** From where it is, that even boys, trained with the philosophy of religious reasoning, have conquered still more bitter tortures: **25** for when the tyrant was manifestly vanquished in his first attempt, in being unable to force the old man to eat the unclean thing,—

CHAPTER 8

1 Then, indeed, vehemently swayed with passion, he commanded to bring others of the adult Hebrews, and if they would eat of the unclean thing, to let them go when they had eaten; but if they objected, to torment them more grievously. **2** The tyrant having given this charge, seven kindred were brought into his presence, along with their aged mother, handsome, and modest, and well-born, and altogether comely. **3** When the tyrant saw them encircling their mother as in a dance, he was pleased at them; and being struck with their becoming and innocent manner, smiled upon them, and calling them near, said: **4** O youths, with favorable feelings, I admire the beauty of each of you; and greatly honoring so numerous a band of kindred, I not only counsel you not to share the madness of the old man who has been tortured before, **5** but I do beg you to yield, and to enjoy my friendship; for I possess the power, not only of punishing those who disobey my commands, but of doing good to those who obey them. **6** Put confidence in me, then, and you will receive places of authority in my government, if you forsake your national ordinance, **7** and, conforming to the Greek mode of life, alter your rule, and revel in youth's delights. **8** For if you provoke me by your disobedience, you will compel me to destroy you, everyone, with terrible punishments by tortures. **9** Have mercy, then, upon your own selves, whom I, although an enemy, compassionate for your age and attractive appearance. **10** Will you not reason upon this—that if you disobey, there will be nothing left for you but to die in tortures? **11** So speaking, he ordered the instruments of torture to be brought forward, that very fear might prevail upon them to eat unclean meat. **12** And when the spearman brought forward the wheels, and the racks, and the hooks, and catapults, and caldrons, pans, and finger-racks, and iron hands and wedges, and bellows, the tyrant continue: **13** Fear, young men, and the righteousness which you worship will be merciful to you if you err from compulsion. **14** Now they having listened to these words of persuasion, and seeing the fearful instruments, not only were not afraid, but even answered the arguments of the tyrant, and through their good reasoning destroyed his power. **15** Now let's consider the matter: had any of them been weak-spirited and cowardly among them, what reasoning would they have employed but these? **16** O wretched that we are, and exceedingly senseless! when the king exhorts us, and calls us to his bounty, should we not obey him? **17** Why do we cheer ourselves with vain counsels, and venture upon a disobedience bringing death? **18** Will we not fear, O kindred, the instruments of torture and weigh the threats of torment and shun this vain-glory and destructive pride? **19** Let's have compassion upon our age and relent over the years of our mother. **20** And let's bear in mind that we will be dying as rebels. **21** And Divine Justice will pardon us if we fear the king through necessity. **22** Why withdraw ourselves from a most sweet life, and deprive ourselves of this pleasant world? **23** Let's not oppose necessity, nor seek vain-glory by our own excrucition. **24** The law itself is not forward to put us to death, if we dread torture. **25** From where has such angry zeal taken root in us, and such fatal obstinacy approved itself to us, when we might live unmolested by the king? **26** But nothing of this kind did the young men say or think when about to be tortured. **27** For they were well aware of the sufferings, and masters of the pains. **28-29** So that as soon as the tyrant had ceased counselling them to eat the unclean, they altogether with one voice, as from the same heart said:

CHAPTER 9

1 Why delay you, O tyrant? For we are more ready to die than to transgress the injunctions of our fathers. **2** And we should be disgracing our fathers if we didn't obey the law and take knowledge for our guide. **3** O tyrant, counselor of law-breaking, do not, hating us as you do, pity us more than we pity ourselves. **4** For we account escape to be worse than death. **5** And you think to scare us, by threatening us with death by tortures, as though you had learned nothing by the death of Eleazar. **6** But if aged

men of the Hebrews have died in the cause of religion after enduring torture, more rightly should we younger men die, scorning your cruel tortures, which our aged instructor overcame. **7** Make the attempt, then, O tyrant; and if you put us to death for our religion, think not that you harm us by torturing us. **8** For we through this ill-treatment and endurance will bear off the rewards of virtue. **9** But you, for the wicked and despotic slaughter of us, will, from the Divine vengeance, endure eternal torture by fire. **10** When they had so spoken, the tyrant was not only exasperated against them as being refractory but enraged with them as being ungrateful. **11** So that, at his bidding, the torturers brought out the oldest of them, and tearing through his tunic, bound his hands and arms on each side with thongs. **12** And when they had labored hard without effect in scourging him, they hurled him upon the wheel. **13** And the noble youth, extended upon this, became dislocated. **14** And with every member disjointed, he exclaimed in expostulation, **15** O most accursed tyrant, and enemy of heavenly justice, and cruel-hearted, I am no murderer, nor sacrilegious man, whom you so ill-used; but a defender of the Divine law. **16** And when the spearmen said, "Consent to eat, that you may be released from your tortures," **17** he answered, "Not so powerful, O accursed ministers, is your wheel, as to stifle my reasoning; cut my limbs, and burn my flesh, and twist my joints. **18** For through all my torments I will convince you that the children of the Hebrews are alone unconquered in behalf of virtue." **19** While he was saying this, they heaped up fuel, and setting fire to it, strained him upon the wheel still more. **20** And the wheel was defiled all over with blood, and the hot ashes were quenched by the droppings of gore, and pieces of flesh were scattered about the axles of the machine. **21** And although the framework of his bones was now destroyed the high-minded and Abrahamic youth didn't groan. **22** But, as though transformed by fire into immortality, he nobly endured the racking, saying **23** "Imitate me, O kindred, nor ever desert your station, nor renounce my brotherhood in courage: fight the holy and honorable fight of religion; **24** by which means our just and paternal Providence, becoming merciful to the nation, will punish the pestilent tyrant." **25** And saying this, the revered youth abruptly closed his life. **26** And when all admired his courageous soul, the spearmen brought forward him who was second in point of age, and having put on iron hands, bound him with pointed hooks to the torture device. **27** And when, on enquiring whether he would eat before he was tortured, they heard his noble sentiment, **28** after they with the iron hands had violently dragged all the flesh from the neck to the chin, the panther-like beasts tore off the very skin of his head: but he, bearing with firmness this misery, said, **29** "How sweet is every form of death for the religion of our fathers!" And he said to the tyrant, **30** "Do you think, most cruel of all tyrants, that you are now tortured more than I, finding your overweening conception of tyranny conquered by our perseverance in behalf of our religion? **31** For I lighten my suffering by the pleasures which are connected with virtue. **32** But you are tortured with threats for impiety; and you will not escape, most corrupt tyrant, the vengeance of Divine wrath."

CHAPTER 10

1 Now this one, having endured this praiseworthy death, the third was brought along, and exhorted by many to taste and save his life. **2** But he cried out and said, "Do you not know that the father of those who are dead, became the father of me also; and that the same mother bore me; and that I was brought up in the same tenets? **3** I renounce not the noble relationship of my kindred. **4** Now then, whatever instrument of vengeance you have, apply it to my body, for you are not able to touch, even if you wish it, my soul. **5** But they, highly incensed at his boldness of speech, dislocated his hands and feet with racking engines, and wrenching them from their sockets, dismembered him." **6** And they dragged round his fingers, and his arms, and his legs, and his ankles. **7** And not being able by any means to strangle him, they tore off his skin, together with the extreme tips of his fingers and then dragged him to the wheel; **8** around which his vertebral joints were loosened, and he saw his own flesh torn to shreds, and streams of blood flowing from his entrails. **9** And when about to die, he said, **10** "We, O accursed tyrant, suffer this for the sake of Divine education and virtue. **11** But you, for your impiety and blood shedding, will endure indissoluble torments." **12** And having died worthily of his kindred, they dragged forward the fourth, saying, **13** "Do not share the madness of your kindred: but give regard to the king, and save yourself." **14** But he said

to them, "You have not a fire so scorching as to make me play the coward. **15** By the blessed death of my kindred, and the eternal punishment of the tyrant, and the glorious life of the pious, I will not repudiate the noble brotherhood. **16** Invent, O tyrant, tortures; that you may learn, even through them, that I am the brother of those tormented before." **17** When he had said this, the blood-thirsty, and murderous, and unhallowed Antiochus ordered his tongue to be cut out. **18** But he said, "Even if you take away the organ of speech, yet God hears the silent. **19** Behold, my tongue is extended, cut it off; for by that you won't halt my reasoning. **20** Gladly do we lose our limbs in behalf of God. **21** But God will speedily find you, since you cut off the tongue, the instrument of divine melody."

CHAPTER 11

1 And when he had died, disfigured in his torments, the fifth leaped forward, and said, **2** "I intend not, O tyrant, to get excused from the torment which is in behalf of virtue. **3** But I have come of my own accord, that by the death of me, you may owe heavenly vengeance a punishment for more crimes. **4** O you hater of virtue and of men, what have we done that you so revel in our blood? **5** Does it seem evil to you that we worship the Founder of all things, and live according to his surpassing law? **6** But this is worthy of honors, not torments; **7** had you been capable of the higher feelings of men and possessed the hope of salvation from God. **8** Behold now, being alien from God, you make war against those who are religious toward God." **9** As he said this, the spear-bearers bound him, and drew him to the torture device: **10** to which binding him at his knees, and fastening them with iron fetters, they bent down his loins upon the wedge of the wheel; and his body was then dismembered, scorpion-fashion. **11** With his breath so confined, and his body strangled, he said, **12** "A great favor you bestow upon us, O tyrant, by enabling us to manifest our adherence to the law by means of nobler sufferings." **13** He also being dead, the sixth, quite a youth, was brought out; and on the tyrant asking him whether he would eat and be delivered, he said, **14** "I am indeed younger than my brothers, but in understanding I am as old; **15** for having been born and reared to the same end, we are bound to die also in behalf of the same cause. **16** So that if you think proper to torment us for not eating the unclean, then torment!" **17** As he said this, they brought him to the wheel. **18** Extended upon which, with limbs racked and dislocated, he was gradually roasted from beneath. **19** And having heated sharp spits, they approached them to his back; and having transfixed his sides, they burned away his entrails. **20** And he, while tormented, said, "O period good and holy, in which, for the sake of religion, we kindred have been called to the contest of pain, and have not been conquered. **21** For religious understanding, O tyrant, is unconquered. **22** Armed with upright virtue, I also will depart with my kindred. **23** I, too, bearing with me a great avenger, O inventor of tortures, and enemy of the truly pious. **24** We six youths have destroyed your tyranny. **25** For is not your inability to overrule our reasoning, and to compel us to eat the unclean, your destruction? **26** Your fire is cold to us, your devices are painless, and your violence harmless. **27** For the guards not of a tyrant but of a divine law are our defenders: through this we keep our reasoning unconquered."

CHAPTER 12

1 When he, too, had undergone blessed martyrdom, and died in the cauldron into which he had been thrown, the seventh, the youngest of all, came forward: **2** whom the tyrant pitying, though he had been dreadfully reproached by his kindred, **3** seeing him already encompassed with chains, had him brought nearer, and endeavored to counsel him, saying, **4** "You see the end of the madness of your kindred: for they have died in torture through disobedience; and you, if disobedient, having been miserably tormented, will yourself perish prematurely. **5** But if you obey, you will be my friend, and have a charge over the affairs of the kingdom." **6** And having so exhorted him, he sent for the mother of the boy; that, by condoling with her for the loss of so many sons, he might incline her, through the hope of safety, to render the survivor obedient. **7** And he, after his mother had urged him on in the Hebrew tongue, (as we will soon relate) says, **8** "Release me that I may speak to the king and all his friends." **9** And they, rejoicing exceedingly at the promise of the youth, quickly let him go. **10** And he, running up to the pans, said, **11** "Impious tyrant, and most blasphemous man, were you not ashamed, having received prosperity and a kingdom from God, to kill His servants, and to rack the doers of godliness?

12 For this reason the divine vengeance is reserving you for eternal fire and torments, which will cling to you for all time. **13** Were you not ashamed, man as you are, yet most savage, to cut out the tongues of men of like feeling and origin, and having so abused to torture them? **14** But they, bravely dying, fulfilled their religion toward God. **15** But you will groan according to your deserts for having slain without cause the champions of virtue." **16** For this reason, he continued, "I myself, being about to die, **17** will not forsake my kindred. **18** And I call upon the God of my fathers to be merciful to my race. **19** But you, both living and dead, he will punish." **20** So having prayed, he hurled himself into the pans; and so expired.

CHAPTER 13

1 If then, the seven kindred despised troubles even to death, it is confessed on all sides that righteous reasoning is absolute master over the passions. **2** For just as if, had they as slaves to the passions, eaten of the unholy, we should have said that they had been conquered; **3** now it is not so: but by means of the reasoning which is praised by God, they mastered their passions. **4** And it is impossible to overlook the leadership of reflection: for it gained the victory over both passions and troubles. **5** How, then, can we avoid according to these men mastery of passion through right reasoning, since they drew not back from the pains of fire? **6** For just as by means of towers projecting in front of harbors men break the threatening waves, and therefore assure a still course to vessels entering port, **7** so that seven-towered right-reasoning of the young men, securing the harbor of religion, conquered the intemperance of passions. **8** For having arranged a holy choir of piety, they encouraged one another, saying, **9** "Brothers, may we die brotherly for the law. Let us imitate the three young men in Assyria who despised the equally afflicting furnace. **10** Let's not be cowards in the manifestation of piety." **11** And one said, "Courage, brother"; and another, "Nobly endure." **12** And another, "Remember of what stock you are; and by the hand of our father Isaac endured to be slain for the sake of piety." **13** And one and all, looking on each other serene and confident, said, "Let us sacrifice with all our heart our souls to God who gave them, and employ our bodies for the keeping of the law. **14** Let's not fear him who thinks he kills; **15** for great is the trial of soul and danger of eternal torment laid up for those who transgress the commandment of God. **16** Let's arm ourselves, therefore, in the self-control, which is divine reasoning. **17** If we suffer like this, Abraham, and Isaac, and Jacob will receive us, and all the fathers will commend us." **18** And as each one of the kindred was hauled away, the rest exclaimed, "Disgrace us not, O brother, nor falsify those who died before you. **19** Now you are not ignorant of the charm of brotherhood, which the Divine and all wise Providence has imparted through fathers to children and has engendered through the mother's womb." **20** In which these brothers having remained an equal time, and having been formed for the same period, and been increased by the same blood, and having been perfected through the same principle of life, **21** and having been brought out at equal intervals, and having sucked milk from the same springs, hence their brotherly souls are reared up lovingly together; **22** and increase the more powerfully by reason of this simultaneous rearing, and by daily intercourse, and by other education, and exercise in the law of God. **23** Brotherly love being so sympathetically constituted, the seven kindred had a more sympathetic mutual harmony. **24** For being educated in the same law, and practicing the same virtues, and reared up in a just course of life, they increased this harmony with each other. **25** For a like ardor for what is right and honorable increased their fellow-feeling toward each other. **26** For it acting along with religion, made their brotherly feeling more desirable to them. **27** And yet, although nature and intercourse and virtuous morals increased their brotherly love, those who were left endured to behold their kindred, who were ill-used for their religion, tortured even to death.

CHAPTER 14

1 And more than this, they even urged them on to this ill-treatment; so that they not only despised pains themselves, but they even got the better of their affections of brotherly love. **2** O reasoning more royal than a king, and freer than freemen! **3** Sacred and harmonious concert of the seven kindred as concerning piety! **4** None of the seven youths turned cowardly or shrank back from death. **5** But all of them, as though running the road to immortality, hastened on to death through tortures. **6** For just as hands and feet are moved sympathetically with the directions of the soul, so those holy youths agreed to death for religion's sake, as through the immortal soul of religion. **7** O holy seven of harmonious kindred! for as the seven days of creation, about religion, **8** so the youths, circling around the number seven, annulled the fear of torments. **9** We now shudder at the recital of the affliction of those young men; but they not only saw, and not only heard the immediate execution of the threat, but undergoing it, persevered; and that through the pains of fire. **10** And what could be more painful? For the power of fire, being sharp and quick, speedily dissolved their bodies. **11** And think it not wonderful that reasoning bore rule over those men in their torments, when even a woman's mind despised more manifold pains. **12** For the mother of those seven youths endured the rackings of each of her children. **13** And consider how comprehensive is the love of offspring, which draws everyone to sympathy of affection, **14** where irrational animals possess a similar sympathy and love for their offspring with men. **15** The tame birds frequenting the roofs of our houses, defend their fledglings. **16** Others build their nests, and hatch their young, in the tops of mountains and in the precipices of valleys, and the holes and tops of trees, and keep off the intruder. **17** And if not able to do this, they fly circling round them in agony of affection, calling out in their own note, and save their offspring in whatever manner they are able. **18** But why should we point attention to the sympathy toward children shown by irrational animals? **19** The very bees, at the season of honey-making, attack all who approach; and pierce with their sting, as with a sword, those who draw near their hive, and repel them even to death. **20** But sympathy with her children didn't turn away the mother of the young men, who had a spirit kindred with that of Abraham.

CHAPTER 15

1 O reasoning of the sons, lord over the passions, and religion more desirable to a mother than progeny! **2** The mother, when two things were set before here, religion and the safety of her seven sons for a time, on the conditional promise of a tyrant, **3** rather elected the religion which according to God preserves to eternal life. **4** O in what way can I describe ethically the affections of parents toward their children, the resemblance of soul and of form engrafted into the small type of a child in a wonderful manner, especially through the greater sympathy of mothers with the feelings of those born of them! **5** for by how much mothers are by nature weak in disposition and prolific in offspring, by so much the fonder they are of children. **6** And of all mothers the mother of the seven was the fondest of children, who in seven childbirths had deeply engendered love toward them; **7** and through her many pains undergone in connection with each one, was compelled to feel sympathy with them; **8** yet, through fear of God, she neglected the temporary salvation of her children. **9** Not but that, on account of the excellent disposition to the law, her maternal affection toward them was increased. **10** For they were both just and temperate, and manly, and high-minded, and fond of their kindred, and so fond of their mother that even to death they obeyed her by observing the law. **11** And yet, though there were so many circumstances connected with love of children to draw on a mother to sympathy, in the case of none of them were the various tortures able to pervert her principle. **12** But she inclined each one separately and all together to death for religion. **13** O holy nature and parental feeling, and reward of bringing up children, and unconquerable maternal affection! **14** At the racking and roasting of each one of them, the observant mother was prevented by religion from changing. **15** She saw her children's flesh dissolving around the fire; and their extremities quivering on the ground, and the flesh of their heads dropped forward down to their beards, like masks. **16** O you mother, who was tried at this time with bitterer pangs than those of parturition! **17** O you only woman who have brought out perfect holiness! **18** Your firstborn, expiring, turned you not; nor the second, looking miserable in his torments; nor the third, breathing out his soul. **19** Nor when you did behold the eyes of each of them looking sternly upon their tortures, and their nostrils foreboding death, did you weep! **20** When you did see children's flesh heaped upon children's flesh that had been torn off, heads decapitated upon heads, dead falling upon the dead, and a choir of children turned through torture into a burying ground, you lamented not. **21** Not so do siren melodies, or songs of swans, attract the hearers to listening, O voices of children calling upon your mother in the midst of torments! **22** With what and what manner of torments was the mother herself tortured, as her sons were undergoing the wheel and the fires! **23** But religious reasoning, having strengthened her courage in the midst of sufferings, enabled her to forego, for the time, parental love. **24** Although beholding the destruction of seven children, the noble mother, after one embrace, stripped off *her feelings* through faith in God. **25** For just as in a council-room, beholding in her own soul vehement counselors, nature and parentage and love of her children, and the racking of her children, **26** she holding two votes, one for the death, the other for the preservation of her children, **27** didn't lean to that which would have saved her children for the safety of a brief space. **28** But this daughter of Abraham remembered his holy fortitude. **29** O holy mother of a nation avenger of the law, and defender of religion, and prime bearer in the battle of the affections! **30** O you nobler in endurance than males, and more manly than men in perseverance! **31** For as the ark of Noah, bearing the world in the world-filling flood, bore up against the waves, **32** so you, the guardian of the law, when surrounded on every side by the flood of passions, and straitened by violent storms which were the torments of those children, did bear up nobly against the storms against religion.

CHAPTER 16

1 If, then, even a woman, and that an aged one, and the mother of seven children, endured to see her children's torments even to death, confessedly religious reasoning is master even of the passions. **2** I have proved, then, that not only men have obtained the mastery of their passions, but also that a woman despised the greatest torments. **3** And not so fierce were the lions round Daniel, nor the furnace of Misael burning with most vehement fires as that natural love of children burned within her, when she saw her seven sons tortured. **4** But with the reasoning of religion the mother quenched passions so great and powerful. **5** For we must consider also this: that, had the woman been faint hearted, as being their other, she would have lamented over them; and perhaps might have spoken like this: **6** Ah! wretched I, and many times miserable; who having born seven sons, have become the mother of none. **7** O seven useless childbirths, and seven profitless periods of labor, and fruitless giving of suck, and miserable nursing at the breast. **8** Vainly, for your sakes, O sons, have I endured many pangs, and the more difficult anxieties of rearing. **9** Alas, of my children, some of you unmarried, and some who have married to no profit, I will not see your children, nor be felicitated as a grandmother. **10** Ah, that I who had many and fair children, should be a lone widow full of sorrows! **11** Nor, should I die, will I have a son to bury me. But with such a lament as this the holy and God-fearing mother mourned none of them. **12** Nor did she divert any of them from death, nor grieve for them as for the dead. **13** But as one possessed with an adamantine mind, and as one bringing out again her full number of sons to immortality, she rather with supplication exhorted them to death in behalf of religion. **14** O woman, soldier of God for religion, you, aged and a female, have conquered through endurance even a tyrant; and though but weak, have been found more powerful in deeds and words. **15** For when you were seized along with your children, you stood looking upon Eleazar in torments, and said to your sons in the Hebrew tongue, **16** O sons, noble is the contest; to which you being called as a witness for the nation, strive zealously for the laws of your country. **17** For it were disgraceful that this old man should endure pains for the sake of righteousness, and that you who are younger should be afraid of the tortures. **18** Remember that through God you obtained existence and have enjoyed it. **19** And on this second account you ought to bear every affliction because of God. **20** For whom also our father Abraham was forward to sacrifice Isaac our progenitor and shuddered not at the sight of his own paternal hand descending down with the sword upon him. **21** And the righteous Daniel was cast to the lions; and Ananias, and Azarias, and Misael, were slung out into a furnace of fire; yet they endured through God. **22** You, then, having the same faith toward God, be not troubled. **23** For it is unreasonable that they who know religion should not stand up against troubles. **24** With these arguments, the mother of seven, exhorting each of her sons, over-persuaded them from transgressing the commandment of God. **25** And they saw this, too, that they who die for God, live to God; as Abraham, and Isaac, and Jacob, and all the patriarchs.

CHAPTER 17

1 And some of the spear-bearers said, that when she herself was about to be seized for the purpose of being put to death, she threw herself upon the pile, rather than they should touch her person. **2** O you mother, who together with seven children did destroy the violence of the tyrant, and render void his wicked intentions, and exhibit the nobleness of faith! **3** For you, as a house bravely built upon the pillar of your children, did bear without swaying, the shock of tortures. **4** Be of good cheer, therefore, O holy-minded mother! holding the firm *substance of the* hope of your steadfastness with God. **5** Not so gracious does the moon appear with the stars in heaven, as you are established honorable before God, and fixed in the firmament with your sons who you did illuminate with religion to the stars. **6** For your bearing of children was after the fashion of a child of Abraham. **7** And, were it lawful for us to paint as on a tablet the religion of your story, the spectators would not shudder at beholding the mother of seven children enduring for the sake of religion various tortures even to death. **8** And it had been a worth thing to have inscribed upon the tomb itself these words as a memorial to those of the nation, **9** Here an aged priest, and an aged woman, and seven sons, are buried through the violence of a tyrant, who wished to destroy the society of the Hebrews. **10** These also avenged their nation, looking to God, and enduring torments to death. **11** For it was truly a divine contest which was carried through by them. **12** For at that time virtue presided over the contest, approving the victory through endurance, namely, immortality, eternal life. **13** Eleazar was the first to contend: and the mother of the seven children entered the contest; and the kindred contended. **14** The tyrant was the opposite; and the world and living men were the spectators. **15** And reverence for God conquered and crowned her own athletes. **16** Who didn't admire those champions of true legislation? Who were not astonied? **17** The tyrant himself, and all their council, admired their endurance; **18** through which, also, they now stand beside the divine throne, and live a blessed life. **19** For Moses says, and all the saints are under your hands. **20** These, therefore, having been sanctified through God, have been honored not only with this honor, but that also by their means the enemy didn't overcome our nation; **21** and that the tyrant was punished, and their country purified. **22** For they became the ransom to the sin of the nation; and the Divine Providence saved Israel, previously afflicted, by the blood of those pious ones, and the propitiatory death. **23** For the tyrant Antiochus, looking to their manly virtue, and to their endurance in torture, proclaimed that endurance as an example to his soldiers. 24 And they proved to be to him noble and brave for land battles and for sieges; and he conquered and stormed the towns of all his enemies.

CHAPTER 18

1 O Israelitish children, descendants of the seed of Abraham, obey this law, and in every way be religious. 2 Knowing that religious reasoning is lord of the passions, and those not only inward but outward. 3 When those persons giving up their bodies to pains for the sake of religion, were not only admired by men, but were deemed worthy of a divine portion. 4 And the nation through them obtained peace and having renewed the observance of the law in their country, drove the enemy out of the land. 5 And the tyrant Antiochus was both punished upon earth and is punished now he is dead; for when he was quite unable to compel the Israelites to adopt foreign customs, and to desert the manner of life of their fathers, 6 then, departing from Jerusalem, he made war against the Persians. 7 And the righteous mother of the seven children spoke also as follows to her offspring: I was a pure virgin and went not beyond my father's house; but I took care of the built-up rib. 8 No destroyer of the desert, *or* ravisher of the plain, injured me; nor did the destructive, deceitful snake, make plunder of my chaste virginity; and I remained with my husband during the period of my prime. 9 And these my children, having arrived at maturity, their father died: blessed was he! for having sought out a life of fertility in children, he was not grieved with a period of loss of children. 10 And he used to teach you, when yet with you, the law and the prophets. 11 He used to read to you the slaying of Abel by Cain, and the offering up of Isaac, and the imprisonment of Joseph. 12 And he used to tell you of the zealous Phinehas; and informed you of Ananias and Azarias, and Misael in the fire. 13 And he used to glorify Daniel, who was in the den of lions, and pronounce him blessed. 14 And he used to put you in mind of the scripture of Esaias, which says, "Even if you pass through the fire, it will not burn you." 15 He chanted to you David, the hymn-writer, who says, "Many are the afflictions of the just." 16 He declared the proverbs of Solomon, who says, "He is a tree of life to all those who do His will." 17 He used to verify Ezekiel, who said, "Will these dry bones live?" 18 For he didn't forget the song which Moses taught, proclaiming, "I will kill, and I will make to live." 19 This is our life, and the length of our days. 20 O that bitter, and yet not bitter, day when the bitter tyrant of the Greeks, quenching fire with fire in his cruel caldrons, brought with boiling rage the seven sons of the daughter of Abraham to the torture device, and to all his torments! 21 He pierced the balls of their eyes, and cut out their tongues, and put them to death with varied tortures. 22 For this reason divine retribution pursued and will pursue the pestilent wretch. 23 But the children of Abraham, with their victorious mother, are assembled together to the choir of their father; having received pure and immortal souls from God. 24 To whom be glory forever and ever. Amen.

PRAYER OF MANASSES

The Prayer of Manasses (or Manasseh) is a short work of 15 verses recording a penitential prayer attributed to King Manasseh of Judah. Most scholars believe that the Prayer of Manasseh was written, in Greek, in the first or second century BC. Another work by the same title, written in Hebrew and containing distinctly different content, was found among the Dead Sea Scrolls.

CHAPTER 1

1 O LORD Almighty, that are in heaven, you God of our fathers, of Abraham, and Isaac, and Jacob, and of their righteous seed; 2 who have made heaven and earth, with all the ornament thereof; 3 who have bound the sea by the word of your commandment; who have shut up the deep, and sealed it by your terrible and glorious name; 4 whom all things fear, yes, tremble before your power; 5 for the majesty of your glory can't be borne, and the anger of your threatening toward sinners is importable: 6 your merciful promise is unmeasurable and unsearchable; 7 for you are the Lord Most High, of great compassion, patient and abundant in mercy, and repent of bringing evils upon men. 8 You, O Lord, according to your great goodness have promised repentance and forgiveness to those who have sinned against you: and of your infinite mercies have appointed repentance to sinners, that they may be saved. You therefore, O Lord, that are the God of the just, have not appointed repentance to the just, to Abraham, and Isaac, and Jacob, which have not sinned against you; but you have appointed repentance to me that am a sinner: 9 for I have sinned above the number of the sands of the sea. My transgressions are multiplied, O Lord: my transgressions are multiplied, and I am not worthy to behold and see the height of heaven for the multitude of my iniquities. 10 I am bowed down with many iron bands, that I can't lift up my head by reason of my sins, neither have I any respite: for I have provoked your wrath and done that which is evil before you: I didn't do your will, neither did I keep your commandments: I have set up abominations and have multiplied detestable things. 11 Now therefore I bow the knee of my heart, imploreing you of grace. 12 I have sinned, O Lord, I have sinned, and I acknowledge my iniquities: 13 but, I humbly implore you, forgive me, O Lord, forgive me, and destroy me not with my iniquities. Be not angry with me forever, by reserving evil for me; neither condemn me into the lower parts of the earth. For you, O Lord, are the God of those who repent; 14 and in me you will show all your goodness: for you will save me, that am unworthy, according to your great mercy. 15 And I will praise you forever all the days of my life: for all the army of heaven sings your praise, and yours is the glory forever and ever. Amen.

ETHIOPIAN ORTHODOX DEUTEROCANON

2 ESDRAS

Otherwise known as 4 Esdras

2 Esdras (also called 4 Esdras, Latin Esdras, or Latin Ezra) is the name of an apocalyptic book in many English versions of the Bible. Its authorship is ascribed to Ezra, a scribe and priest of the 5th century BC, although modern scholarship places its composition between 70 and 218 AD. It is reckoned among the apocrypha by Roman Catholics, Protestants, and most Eastern Orthodox Christians. Although 2 Esdras was preserved in Latin as an appendix to the Vulgate and passed down as a unified book, it is generally considered to be a tripartite work.

CHAPTER 1

1 The second book of the prophet Esdras, the son of Saraias, the son of Azaraias, the son of Helkias, the son of Salemas, the son of Sadoc, the son of Ahitob, 2 the son of Achias, the son of Phinees, the son of Heli, the son of Amarias, the son of Aziei, the son of Marimoth, the son of Arna, the son of Ozias, the son of Borith, the son of Abissei, the son of Phinees, the son of Eleazar, 3 the son of Aaron, of the tribe of Levi; which was captive in the land of the Medes, in the reign of Artaxerxes king of the Persians. 4 And the word of the Lord came to me, saying, 5 "Go your way, and show my people their sinful deeds, and their children their wickedness which they have done against me; that they may tell their children's children: 6 because the sins of their fathers are increased in them: for they have forgotten me, and have done sacrifice to strange gods. 7 Did I not bring them out of the land of Egypt, out of the house of bondage? But they have provoked me to wrath and have despised my counsels. 8 Shake you then the hair of your head, and cast all evils upon them, for they have not been obedient to my law, but it is a rebellious people. 9 How long will I forbear them, to whom I have done so much good? 10 I have overthrown many kings for their sakes; I have struck down Pharaoh with his servants and all his army. 11 I have destroyed all the nations before them, and in the east, I have scattered the people of two provinces, even of Tyre and Sidon, and have slain all their adversaries. 12 Speak therefore to them, saying, 13 'The

Lord says, of a truth I brought you through the sea, and where there was no path I made for you highways; I gave you Moses for a leader, and Aaron for a priest. 14 I gave you light in a pillar of fire, and great wonders have I done among you; yet have you forgotten me,' says the Lord." 15 The Lord Almighty says, "The quails were for a token to you; I gave you a camp for your protection, nevertheless you murmured there: 16 and you triumphed not in my name for the destruction of your enemies, but ever to this day do you yet murmur. 17 Where are the benefits that I have done for you? When you were hungry and thirsty in the wilderness, did you not cry to me, 18 saying, 'Why have you brought us into this wilderness to kill us? It had been better for us to have served the Egyptians, than to die in this wilderness.' 19 I had pity upon your mourning and gave you manna for food; you did eat angels' bread. 20 When you were thirsty, did I not cleave the rock, and waters flowed out to your fill? For the heat I covered you with the leaves of the trees. 21 I divided among you fruitful lands; I cast out the Canaanites, the Pherezites, and the Philistines, before you: what will I yet do more for you?" says the Lord. 22 The Lord Almighty says, "When you were in the wilderness, at the bitter river, being thirsty, and blaspheming my name, 23 I gave you not fire for your blasphemies, but cast a tree in the water, and made the river sweet. 24 What will I do to you, O Jacob? You, Judah, would not obey me: I will turn me to other nations, and I will give my name to them, that they may keep my statutes. 25 Seeing you have forsaken me, I also will forsake you; when you ask me to be merciful to you, I will have no mercy upon you. 26 Whenever you will call upon me, I will not hear you: for you have defiled your hands with blood, and your feet are swift to commit manslaughter. 27 You have not as it were forsaken me, but your own selves," says the Lord. 28 The Lord Almighty says, "Have I not prayed you as a father his sons, as a mother her daughters, and a nurse her young babes, 29 that you would be my people, and I should be your God; that you would be my children, and I should be your father? 30 I gathered you together, as a hen *gathers* her chickens under her wings: but now, what will I do to you? I will cast you out from my presence. **31** When you offer oblations to me, I will turn my face from you: for your solemn feast days, your new moons, and your circumcisions of the flesh, have I rejected. **32** I sent to you my servants the prophets, whom you have taken and slain, and torn their bodies in pieces, whose blood I will require *of your hands,*" says the Lord. **33** The Lord Almighty says, "Your house is desolate, I will cast you out as the wind does stubble. **34** And your children will not be fruitful; for they have neglected my commandment to you and done that which is evil before me. **35** I will give your houses to a people that will come; which not having heard of me yet believe me; they to whom I have showed no signs will do that which I have commanded. **36** They have seen no prophets, yet they will call their former estate to remembrance. **37** I take to witness the grace of the people that will come, whose little ones rejoice with gladness: and though they see me not with bodily eyes, yet in spirit they will believe the thing that I say. **38** And now, O father, behold with glory; and see the people that come from the east: **39** to whom I will give for leaders, Abraham, Isaac, and Jacob, Oseas, Amos, and Micheas, Joel, Abdias, and Jonas, **40** Nahum, and Abacuc, Sophonias, Aggaeus, Zachary, and Malachy, which is called also the angel of the Lord."

CHAPTER 2

1 The Lord says, "I brought this people out of bondage, and I gave them my commandments by my servants the prophets; whom they would not hear but set my counsels at nothing. **2** The mother that bare them says to them, go your way, O my children; for I am a widow and forsaken. **3** I brought you up with gladness, and with sorrow and heaviness have I lost you: for you have sinned before the Lord God and done that which is evil before me. **4** But what will I now do to you? For I am a widow and forsaken: go your way, O my children, and ask mercy of the Lord. **5** As for me, O father, I call upon you for a witness over the mother of *these* children, because they would not keep my covenant, **6** that you bring them to confusion, and their mother to a plunder, that there may be no offspring of them. **7** Let them be scattered abroad among the heathen, let their names be blotted out of the earth: for they have despised my covenant. **8** Woe to you, Assur, you that hide the unrighteous with you! O you wicked nation, remember what I did to Sodom and Gomorrah; **9** whose land lies in clods of pitch and heaps of ashes: even so I will also do to those who have not listened to me," says the Lord Almighty. **10** The Lord says to Esdras, "Tell my people that I will give them the kingdom of Jerusalem, which I would have given to Israel. **11** I will also take their glory, and give these the everlasting tabernacles, which I had prepared for them. **12** They will have the tree of life for an ointment of sweet savor; they will neither labor, nor be weary. **13** Ask, and you will receive: pray for few days for you, that they may be shortened: the kingdom is already prepared for you: watch. **14** Take heaven and earth to witness, take them to witness; for I have given up the evil, and created the good: for I live," says the Lord. **15** "Mother, embrace your children; I will bring them out with gladness like a dove; establish their feet; for I have chosen you," says the Lord. **16** "And I will raise those who are dead up again from their places, and bring them out from their tombs: for I have known my name in them. **17** Don't be afraid, you mother of the children: for I have chosen you," says the Lord. **18** "For your help I will send my servants Esaias and Jeremy, after whose counsel I have sanctified and prepared for you twelve trees laden with various fruits, **19** and as many springs flowing with milk and honey, and seven mighty mountains, whereupon there grow roses and lilies, whereby I will fill your children with joy. **20** Do right to the widow, judge the fatherless, give to the poor, defend the orphan, clothe the naked, **21** heal the broken and the weak, laugh not a lame man to scorn, defend the maimed, and let the blind man come to the sight of my glory. **22** Keep the old and young within your walls. **23** Wherever you find the dead, set a sign upon them and commit them to the grave, and I will give you the first place in my resurrection. **24** Stay still, O my people, and take your rest, for your quietness will come. **25** Nourish your children, O you good nurse, and establish their feet. **26** As for the servants whom I have given you, there will not one of them perish; for I will require them from among your number. **27** Be not careful overmuch: for when the day of suffering and anguish comes, others will weep and be sorrowful, but you will be merry and have abundance. **28** The nations will envy you, but they will be able to do nothing against you," says the Lord. **29** "My hands will cover you, so that your children see not hell. **30** Be joyful, O you mother, with your children; for I will deliver you," says the Lord. **31** "Remember your children that sleep, for I will bring them out of the secret places of the earth and show mercy to them: for I am merciful," says the Lord Almighty. **32** "Embrace your children until I come and proclaim mercy to them: for my wells run over, and my grace will not fail." **33** I Esdras received a charge from the Lord upon the mount Horeb, that I should go to Israel; but when I came to them, they would have none of me, and rejected the commandment of the Lord. **34** And therefore I say to you, O you nations, that hear and understand, look for your shepherd, he will give you everlasting rest; for he is near at hand, that will come in the end of the world. **35** Be ready to the rewards of the kingdom, for the everlasting light will shine upon you forevermore. **36** Flee the shadow of this world, receive the joyfulness of your glory: I call to witness my savior openly. **37** O receive that which is given you of the Lord, and be joyful, giving thanks to him that has called you to heavenly kingdoms. **38** Arise up and stand and behold the number of those that be sealed in the feast of the Lord; **39** those who withdrew them from the shadow of the world have received glorious garments of the Lord. **40** Look upon your number, O Zion, and make up the reckoning of those of you that are clothed in white, which have fulfilled the law of the Lord. **41** The number of your children, whom you long for, is fulfilled: implore the power of the Lord, that your people, which have been called from the beginning, may be hallowed. **42** I Esdras saw upon Mount Zion a great multitude, whom I could not number, and they all praised the Lord with songs. **43** And in the midst of them there was a young man of a high stature, taller than all the rest, and upon every one of their heads he set crowns and was more exalted. I marveled greatly at this. **44** So I asked the angel, and said, "What are these, my Lord?" **45** He answered and said to me, "These be those who have put off the mortal clothing, and put on the immortal, and have confessed the name of God: now are they crowned, and receive palms." **46** Then said I to the angel, "What young man is he that sets crowns upon them, and gives them palms in their hands?" **47** So he answered and said to me, "It is the Son of God, whom they have confessed in the world." Then began I greatly to commend those who stood so stiffly for the name of the Lord. **48** Then the angel said to me, "Go your way, and tell my people what manner of things, and how great wonders of the Lord God you have seen."

CHAPTER 3

1 In the thirty years after the ruin of the city, I Salathiel (also called Esdras) was in Babylon, and lay troubled upon my bed, and my thoughts came up over my heart: **2** for I saw the desolation of Zion, and the wealth of those who lived at Babylon. **3** And my spirit was sore moved, so that I began to speak words full of fear to the Most High, and said, **4** O Lord that bear rule, did you not speak at the beginning, when you did fashion the earth, and that yourself alone, and command the dust. **5** and it gave you Adam, a body without a soul? Yet it was the workmanship of your hands, and you did breathe into him the breath of life, and he was made living before you. **6** And you led him into paradise, which your right hand did plant, before ever the earth came forward. **7** And to him you gave your one commandment: which he transgressed, and immediately you appointed death for him and in his generations; and there were born of him nations and tribes, peoples and kindred, out of number. **8** And every nation walked after their own will, and did ungodly things before you, and despised *your commandments, and* you didn't forbid them. **9** Nevertheless again in process of time you brought the flood upon those that lived in the world and destroyed them. **10** And it came to pass that the same hap befell them; like as death was to Adam, so was the flood to these. **11** Nevertheless one of them you left, Noah with his household, *even* all the righteous men *that came* of him. **12** And it came to pass, that when those who lived upon the earth began to multiply, they multiplied also children, and peoples, and many nations, and began again to be more ungodly than the first. **13** And it came to pass, when they did wickedly before you, you did choose you one from among them, whose name was Abraham; **14** and him you loved, and to him only you showed the end of the times secretly by night: **15** and made an everlasting covenant with him, promising him that you would never forsake his seed. **16** And to him you gave Isaac, and to Isaac you gave Jacob and Esau. And you did set apart Jacob for yourself but did put by Esau: and Jacob became a great multitude. **17** And it came to pass, that when

173

you led his seed out of Egypt, you brought them up to the mount Sinai. **18** You bowed the heavens also, and did shake the earth, and moved the whole world, and made the depths to tremble, and troubled the *course of that* age. **19** And your glory went through four gates, of fire, and of earthquake, and of wind, and of cold; that you might give the law to the seed of Jacob, and the commandment to the generation of Israel. **20** And yet took you not away from them *their* wicked heart, that your law might bring out fruit in them. **21** For the first Adam bearing a wicked heart transgressed, and was overcome; *and not he only,* but all they also that are born of him. **22** Therefore disease was made permanent; and the law was in the heart of the people along with the wickedness of the root; so the good departed away, and that which was wicked dwelt still. **23** So the times passed away, and the years were brought to an end: then did you raise you up a servant, called David, **24** whom you commanded to build a city to your name, and to offer oblations to you therein of your own. **25** When this was done many years, then those who inhabited the city did evil, **26** in all things doing even as Adam and all his generations had done: for they also bare a wicked heart: **27** and so you gave your city over into the hands of your enemies. **28** And I said then in my heart, are their deeds any better that inhabit Babylon? And has she therefore dominion over Zion? **29** For it came to pass when I came here, that I saw also impieties without number, and my soul saw many evil-doers in this thirties year, so that my heart failed me. **30** For I have seen how you suffer them sinning, and have spared the ungodly doers, and have destroyed your people, and have preserved your enemies; and you have not signified **31** to anyhow your way may be comprehended. Are the deeds of Babylon better than those of Zion? **32** Or is there any other nation that knows you beside Israel? Or what tribes have so believed your covenants as these *tribes of* Jacob? **33** And yet their reward appears not, and their labor has no fruit: for I have gone here and there through the nations, and I see that they abound *in wealth, and* think not upon your commandments. **34** Weigh you therefore our iniquities now in the balance, and theirs also that dwell in the world; and so will it be found which way the scale inclines. **35** Or when was it that they which dwell upon the earth have not sinned in your sight? Or what nation has so

kept your commandments? **36** You will find that men *who may be reckoned* by name have kept your precepts; but nations you will not find.

CHAPTER 4

1 And the angel that was sent to me, whose name was Uriel, gave me an answer, **2** and said to me, "Your heart has utterly failed you in *regarding* this world, and think you to comprehend the way of the Most High?" **3** Then said I, "Yes my Lord." And he answered me, and said, "I am sent to show you three ways, and to set out three similitudes before you: **4** whereof if you can declare me one, I also will show you the way that you desire to see, and I will teach you why the heart is wicked." **5** And I said, "Speak, my Lord." Then he said to me, "Go to, weigh me a weight of fire, or measure me a measure of wind, or call me again the day that is past." **6** Then answered I and said, "Who of the sons *of men* is able to do this, that you should ask me of such things?" **7** And he said to me, "If I had asked you, saying, How many dwellings are there in the heart of the sea? Or how many springs are there at the fountain head of the deep? Or how many ways are above the firmament? Or which are the exits of hell? Or which are the paths of paradise? **8** Perhaps you would say to me, 'I never went down into the deep, nor as yet into hell, neither did I ever climb up into heaven.' **9** Nevertheless now have I asked you but only of the fire and wind, and of the day, things you have experienced, and without which you cannot be, and yet you have given me no answer about them." **10** He said moreover to me, "Your own things, that are grown up with you, can you not know; **11** how then can you comprehend the way of the Most High? And how can he that is already worn out with the corrupted world understand incorruption?" **12** And when I heard these things I fell upon my face, and said to him, "It were better that we were not here at all, than that we should come here and live in the midst of ungodliness, and suffer, and not know why. **13** He answered me, and said, "The woods of the trees of the field went out, and took counsel together, **14** and said, 'Come! Let's go and make war against the sea, that it may depart away before us, and that we may make us more woods.' **15** The waves of the sea also in like manner took counsel together, and said, 'Come! Let's go up and subdue the wood of the plain, that there also we may make us another country.' **16** The counsel of the wood was in vain, for the fire came and consumed it: **17** likewise also the counsel of the waves of the sea, for the sand stood up and stopped them. **18** If you were judge now between these two, whom would you justify, or whom condemn?" **19** I answered and said, "It is a foolish counsel that they both have taken, for the ground is given to the wood, and the place of the sea *is given* to bear his waves." **20** Then he answered me, and said, "You have given a right judgement, and why judge you not in your own case? **21** For like as the ground is given to the wood, and the sea to his waves, even so those who dwell upon the earth may understand nothing but that which is upon the earth: and he *only that dwells* above the heavens *may understand the* things that are above the height of the heavens." **22** Then answered I and said, I implore you, O Lord, why is the power of understanding given to me? **23** For it was not in my mind to be curious of the ways above, but of such things as pass by us daily; because Israel is given up as a reproach to the heathen, and the people whom you have loved is given over to ungodly nations, and the law of our forefathers is made of none effect, and the written covenants are nowhere *regarded,* **24** and we pass away out of the world as grasshoppers, and our life is as a vapor, neither are we worthy to obtain mercy. **25** What will he then do for his name whereby we are called? Of these things have I asked." **26** Then he answered me, and said, "If you be *alive* you will see, and if you live long, you will marvel; for the world hastens fast to pass away. **27** For it is not able to bear the things that are promised to the righteous in the times *to come:* for this world is full of sadness and infirmities. **28** For the evil whereof you asked me is sown, but the gathering thereof is not yet come. **29** If therefore that which is sown be not reaped, and if the place where the evil is sown pass not away, there can't come the field where the good is sown. **30** For a grain of evil seed was sown in the heart of Adam from the beginning, and how much wickedness has it brought out to this time! And how much will it yet bring out until the time of threshing comes! **31** Ponder now by yourself, how great fruit of wickedness a grain of evil seed has brought out. **32** When the ears which are without number will be sown, how great a floor will they fill!" **33** Then I answered and said, "How long? And when will these things come to pass? Why are our years few and

evil?" **34** And he answered me, and said, "You do not hasten more than the Most High: for your haste is for your own self, but he that is above hasten*s* on behalf of many. **35** Did not the souls of the righteous ask questions of these things in their chambers, saying, 'How long are we here? When comes the fruit of the threshing time of our reward?' " **36** And to them Jeremiel the archangel gave answer, and said, "When the number is fulfilled of those who are like to you. For he has weighed the world in the balance; **37** and by measure has he measured the times, and by number has he counted the seasons; and he will not move nor stir them, until the said measure be fulfilled." **38** Then answered I and said, "O Lord that bear rule, yet even we all are full of impiety: **39** and for our sakes perhaps it is that the threshing time of the righteous is kept back, because of the sins of those who dwell upon the earth." **40** So he answered me, and said, "Go your way to a woman with child, and ask of her when she has fulfilled her nine months, if her womb may keep the birth any longer within her." **41** Then said I, "No, Lord, that can it not." And he said to me, "In the grave the chambers of souls are like the womb: **42** for like as a woman that travails makes haste to escape the anguish of the travail: even so do these places hasten to deliver those things that are committed to them from the beginning. **43** Then will it be showed you concerning those things which you desire to see." **44** Then answered I and said, "If I have found favor in your sight, and if it be possible, and if I be meet therefore, **45** show me this also, whether there be more to come than is past, or whether the more part is gone over us. **46** For what is gone I know, but what is for to come I know not." **47** And he said to me, "Stand up upon the right side, and I will expound the similitude to you." **48** So I stood, and saw, and, behold, a hot burning oven passed by before me: and it happened, that when the flame was gone by I looked, and, behold, the smoke remained still. **49** After this there passed by before me a watery cloud and sent down much rain with a storm; and when the stormy rain was past, the drops remained therein still. **50** Then said he to me, "Consider with yourself; as the rain is more than the drops, and the fire is greater than the smoke, so the quantity which is past did more exceed; but the drops and the smoke remained still." **51** Then I prayed, and said, "Will I live until that time? Or who will be alive in those days?"

52 He answered me, and said, "As for the signs whereof you asked me, I may tell you of them in part: but as touching your life, I am not sent to show you; for I do not know it."

CHAPTER 5

1 "Nevertheless as concerning the signs, behold, the days will come, that they which dwell upon earth will be taken with great amazement, and the way of truth will be hidden, and the land will be barren of faith. **2** But iniquity will be increased above that which now you see, or that you have heard long ago. **3** And the land, that you see now to have rule, will be waste and untrodden, and men will see it desolate. **4** But if the Most High grant you to live, you will see that which is after the third *kingdom* to be troubled; and the sun will suddenly shine out in the night, and the moon in the day: **5** and blood will drop out of wood, and the stone will give his voice, and the peoples will be troubled; and their goings will be changed: **6** and he will rule, whom those who dwell upon the earth look not for, and the fowls will take their flight away together: **7** and the Sodomite sea will cast out fish, and make a noise in the night, which many have not known: but all will hear the voice thereof. **8** There will be chaos also in many places, and the fire will be often sent out, and the wild beasts will change their places, and women will bring out monsters: **9** and salt waters will be found in the sweet, and all friends will destroy one another; then will wit hide itself, and understanding withdraw itself into its chamber; **10** and it will be sought of many, and will not be found: and unrighteousness and incontinency will be multiplied upon earth. **11** One land also will ask another, and say, Is righteousness, is a man that does righteousness, gone through you? And it will say, No. **12** And it will come to pass at that time that men will hope, but will not obtain: they will labor, but their ways will not prosper. **13** To show you such signs I have leave; and if you will pray again, and weep as now, and fast seven days, you will hear yet greater things than these." **14** Then I awaked, and an extreme trembling went through my body, and my mind was troubled, so that it fainted. **15** So the angel that was come to talk with me held me, comforted me, and set me up upon my feet. **16** And in the second night it came to pass, that Phaltiel the captain of the people came to me, saying, "Where have you been? And why is your countenance sad?

17 Or do you not know that Israel is committed to you in the land of their captivity? **18** Get up then, and eat some bread, and forsake us not, as the shepherd *that leaves* in the hands of cruel wolves." **19** Then I said to him, "Go your ways from me, and come not near me for seven days, and then will you come to me." And he heard what I said and went from me. **20** And so I fasted seven days, mourning and weeping, like as Uriel the angel commanded me. **21** And after seven days, so it was, that the thoughts of my heart were very grievous to me again, **22** and my soul recovered the spirit of understanding, and I began to speak words before the Most High again, **23** and said, "O Lord that bear rule, of all the woods of the earth, and of all the trees thereof, you have chosen you one vine: **24** and of all the lands of the world you have chosen you one country: and of all the flowers of the world you have chosen you one lily: **25** and of all the depths of the sea you have filled you one river: and of all built cities you have hallowed Zion to yourself: **26** and of all the fowls that are created you have named you one dove: and of all the cattle that are made you have provided you one sheep: **27** and among all the multitudes of peoples you have gotten you one people: and to this people, whom you loved, you gave a law that is approved of all. **28** And now, O Lord, why have you given this one people over to many, and have dishonored the one root above others, and have scattered your only one among many? **29** And they which did gainsay your promises have trodden them down that believed your covenants. **30** If you do so much hate your people, they should be punished with your own hands." **31** Now when I had spoken these words, the angel that came to me the night before was sent to me, **32** and said to me, "Hear me, and I will instruct you; listen to me, and I will tell you more." **33** And I said, "Speak, my Lord." Then he said to me, "You are sore troubled in mind for Israel's sake: do you that people better than he that made them?" **34** And I said, "No, Lord: but in great grief have I spoken: for my reins torment me every hour, while I labor to comprehend the way of the Most High, and to seek out part of his judgement." **35** And he said to me, "You cannot." And I said, "Why, Lord, or for what purpose was I born? Or why was not my mother's womb then my grave, that I might not have seen the travail of Jacob, and the wearisome toil of the stock of Israel?" **36** And he said to me, "Number me those who are not yet come, gather me together the drops that are scattered abroad, make me the flowers green again that are withered, **37** open me the chambers that are closed, and bring me out the winds that in them are shut up, or show me the image of a voice: and then I will declare to you the travail that you asked to see." **38** And I said, "O Lord that bear rule, who may know these things, but he that has not his dwelling with men? **39** As for me, I am unwise: how may I then speak of these things whereof you asked me?" **40** Then said he to me, "Just as you can do none of these things that I have spoken of, even so can you not find out my judgement, or the end of the love that I have promised to my people." **41** And I said, "But, behold, O Lord, you have made the promise to those who be in the end: and what will they do that have been before us, or we *that be now,* or those who will come after us?" **42** And he said to me, "I will liken my judgement to a ring: like as there is no slackness of those who are last, even so there is no swiftness of those who be first." **43** So I answered and said, "Could you not make them *to be* at once that have been made, and that be now, and that are still to come; that you might show your judgment sooner?" **44** Then answered he me, and said, "The creature may not hasten above the Creator; neither may the world hold them at once that will be created therein." **45** And I said, "How have you said to your servant, that you will surely make alive at once the creature that you have created? If therefore they will be alive at once, and the creature will sustain them: even so it might now also support them to be present at once." **46** And he said to me, "Ask the womb of a woman, and say to her, 'If you bring out ten children, why *do you do it* several times?' Pray instead to bring out ten children at once." **47** And I said, "She can't: but must do it by distance of time." **48** Then said he to me, "Even so have I given the womb of the earth to those that be sown therein in their several times. **49** For like as a young child may not bring out, neither she that is grown old *bring out* any more, even so have I disposed the world which I created." **50** And I asked, and said, "Seeing you have now showed me the way, I will speak before you: Is our mother, of whom you have told me, still young? Or does she now draw near to age?" **51** He answered me, and said, "Ask a woman that bears children, and she will tell you. **52** Say to her, why are not they whom you have now brought out like those that were before, but less of stature? **53** And she also will answer you, 'They that be born in the strength of youth are of one fashion, and those who are born in the time of age, when the womb fails, are otherwise.' **54** Consider therefore you also, how that you are less of stature than those that were before you. **55** And so are those who come after you less than you, as *born* of the creature which now begins to be old and is past the strength of youth." **56** Then I said, "Lord, I implore you, if I have found favor in your sight, show your servant by whom you visit your creature."

CHAPTER 6

1 And he said to me, "In the beginning, when the earth was made, before the portals of the world were fixed, or ever the gatherings of the winds blew, **2** before the voices of the thunder sounded and before the flashes of the lightning shone, or ever the foundations of paradise were laid, **3** before the fair flowers were seen, or ever the powers of the earthquake were established, before the innumerable army of angels were gathered together, **4** or ever the heights of the air were lifted up, before the measures of the firmament were named, or ever the footstool of Zion was established, **5** and before the present years were sought out, and or ever the imaginations of those who now sin were estranged, before they were sealed that have gathered faith for a treasure: **6** then did I consider these things, and they all were made through me alone, and through none other: as by me also they will be ended, and by none other." **7** Then I answered and said, "What will be the parting asunder of the times? Or when will be the end of the first, and the beginning of it that follows?" **8** And he said to me, "From Abraham to Abraham, inasmuch as Jacob and Esau were born of him, for Jacob's hand held the heel of Esau from the beginning. **9** For Esau is the end of this world, and Jacob is the beginning of it that follows. **10** The beginning of a man is his hand, and the end of a man is his heel; between the heel and the hand seek you nothing else, Esdras." **11** I answered then and said, "O Lord that bear rule, If I have found favor in your sight, **12** I implore you, show your servant the end of your signs, whereof you showed me part the last night." **13** So he answered and said to me, "Stand up upon your feet, and you will hear a mighty sounding voice; **14** and if the place you stand on is greatly moved, **15** when it speaks be you not afraid: for the word is of the end, and the foundations of the earth will understand, **16** that the speech is of them: they will tremble and be moved: for they know that their end must be changed." **17** And it happened, that when I had heard it I stood up upon my feet, and listened, and, behold, there was a voice that spoke, and the sound of it was like the sound of many waters. **18** And it said, "Behold, the days come, and it will be that when I draw near to visit those who dwell upon the earth, **19** and when I will make inquisition of those who have done hurt unjustly with their unrighteousness, and when the affliction of Zion will be fulfilled, **20** and when the seal will be set upon the world that is to pass away, then I will show these signs: the books will be opened before the firmament, and all will see together: **21** and the children of a year old will speak with their voices, the women with child will bring out untimely children at three or four months, and they will live, and dance. **22** And suddenly will the sown places appear unsown, the full storehouses will suddenly be found empty: **23** and the trumpet will give a sound, which when every man hears, they will be suddenly afraid. **24** At that time will friends make war one against another like enemies, and the earth will stand in fear with those that dwell therein, the springs of the springs will stand still, so that for three hours they will not run. **25** And it will be that whoever remains after all these things that I have told you of, he will be saved, and will see my salvation, and the end of my world. **26** And they will see the men that have been taken up, who have not tasted death from their birth: and the heart of the inhabitants will be changed and turned into another meaning. **27** For evil will be blotted out, and deceit will be quenched; **28** and faith will flourish, and corruption will be overcome, and the truth, which has been so long without fruit, will be declared." **29** And when he talked with me, behold, by little and little the place I stood on rocked to and fro. **30** And he said to me, "These things I came to show you this night. **31** If therefore you will pray yet again, and fast seven days more, I will yet tell you greater things than these. **32** For your voice has surely been heard before the Most High: for the Mighty has seen your righteous dealing, he has seen previously also your chastity, which you have had ever since your youth. **33** And therefore has he sent me to show you all these things, and to say to you, 'Be of good comfort, and fear not.' **34** And be not hasty in *regard of the* former times, to think vain things, that you may not hasten in the latter times." **35** And it came to pass after this, that I wept again, and fasted seven days in like manner, that I might fulfill the three weeks which he told me. **36** And in the eighth night was my heart vexed within me again, and I began to speak before the Most High. **37** For my spirit was greatly set on fire, and my soul was in distress. **38** And I said, "O Lord, of a truth you spoke at the beginning of the creation, upon the first day, and said this; 'Let heaven and earth be made'; and your word perfected the work. **39** And then was the spirit hovering, and darkness and silence were on every side; the sound of man's voice was not yet. **40** Then command you a ray of light to be brought out of your treasures, that then your works might appear. **41** Upon the second day again you made the spirit of the firmament and commanded it to part asunder, and to make a division between the waters, that the one part might go up, and the other remain beneath. **42** Upon the third day you did command that the waters should be gathered together in the seventh part of the earth: six parts did you dry up, and keep them, to the intent that of these some being both planted and tilled might serve before you. **43** For as soon as your word went out the work was done. **44** For immediately there came out great and innumerable fruit, and manifold pleasures for the taste, and flowers of inimitable color, and odors of most exquisite smell: and this was done the third day. **45** Upon the fourth day you commanded that the sun should shine, and the moon give her light, and the stars should be in their order: **46** and gave them a charge to do service to man, that was to be made. **47** Upon the fifth day you said to the seventh part, where the water was gathered together, that it should bring out living creatures, fowls and fishes: and so it came to pass, **48** that the mute water and without life brought out living things as it was told, that the peoples might therefore praise your wondrous works. **49** Then did you preserve two living creatures, the one you called Behemoth, and the other you called Leviathan: **50** and you did separate the one from the other: for the seventh part, namely, where the water was gathered together, might not hold them both. **51** To Behemoth you gave one part, which was dried up on the third day, that he should dwell in it, wherein are a thousand hills: **52** but to Leviathan you gave the seventh part, namely, the moist; and you have kept them to be devoured of whom you will, and when. **53** But upon the sixth day you gave commandment to the earth, that it should bring out before you cattle, beasts, and creeping things: **54** and over these Adam, whom you ordain lord over all the works that you have made: of him come we all, the people whom you have chosen. **55** All this have I spoken before you, O Lord, because you have said that for our sakes you made this world. **56** As for the other nations, which also come of Adam, you have said that they are nothing, and are like to spittle: and you have likened the abundance of them to a drop that falls from a vessel. **57** And now, O Lord, behold these nations, which are reputed as nothing, be lords over us, and devour us. **58** But we your people, whom you have called your firstborn, your only begotten, and your fervent lover, are given into their hands. **59** If the world now be made for our sakes, why do we not possess for an inheritance our world? How long will this endure?"

CHAPTER 7

1 And when I had made an end of speaking these words, there was sent to me the angel which had been sent to me the nights before: **2** and he said to me, "Get up, Esdras, and hear the words that I am come to tell you." **3** And I said, "Speak, my Lord." Then he said to me, "There is a sea set in a wide place, that it might be broad and vast. **4** But the entrance thereof will be set in a narrow place so as to be like a river; **5** whoso then should desire to go into the sea to look upon it, or to rule it, if he went not through the narrow, how could he come into the broad? **6** Another thing also: There is a city built and set in a plain country, and full of all good things; **7** but the entrance thereof is narrow, and is set in a dangerous place to fall, having a fire on the right hand, and on the left a deep water: **8** and there is one only path between them both, even between the fire and the water, *so small* that there could but one man go there at once. **9** If this city now be given to a man for an inheritance, if the heir pass not the danger before him, how will he receive his inheritance?" **10** And I said, "It is so, Lord." Then he said to me, "Even so also is Israel's portion. **11** Because for their sakes I made the world: and when Adam transgressed my statutes, then was decreed that now is done. **12** Then were the entrances of this world made narrow, and sorrowful and toilsome: they are but few and evil, full of perils, and charged with great toils. **13** For the entrances

of the greater world are wide and sure and bring out fruit of immortality. **14** If then those who live enter not these strait and vain things, they can never receive those that are laid up for them. **15** Now therefore why do you disquiet yourself, seeing you are but a corruptible man? And why are you moved, whereas you are but mortal? **16** And why have you not considered in your mind that which is to come, rather than that which is present?" **17** Then I answered and said, "O Lord that bear rule, behold, you have ordained in your law, that the righteous should inherit these things, but that the ungodly should perish. **18** The righteous therefore will suffer strait things, and hope for wide: but those who have done wickedly have suffered the strait things, and yet will not see the wide." **19** And he said to me, "You are not a judge above God, neither have you understanding above the Most High. **20** Yes, rather let many that now be perish, than that the law of God which is set before them be despised. **21** For God strictly commanded such as came, even as they came, what they should do to live, and what they should observe to avoid punishment. **22** Nevertheless they were not obedient to him; but spoke against him and imagined for themselves vain things; **23** and framed cunning plans of wickedness; and said moreover of the Most High, that he is not; and knew not his ways: **24** but they despised his law and denied his covenants; they have not been faithful to his statutes and have not performed his works. **25** Therefore, Esdras, for the empty are empty things, and for the full are the full things. **26** For behold, the time will come, and it will be, when these signs, of which I told you before, will come to pass, that the bride will appear, even the city coming out, and she will be seen, that now is withdrawn from the earth. **27** And whoever is delivered from the previously mentioned evils will see my wonders. **28** For my son the Christ will be revealed with those that be with him and will rejoice with those who remain four hundred years. **29** After these years will my son the Christ die for those who, and all that have the breath of life. **30** And the world will be turned into the old silence seven days, like as in the first beginning: so that no man will remain. **31** And after seven days the world, that yet awakens not, will be raised up, and that will die that is corruptible. **32** And the earth will restore those that are asleep in her, and so will the dust those that dwell therein in silence, and the secret places will deliver those souls that were committed to them. **33** And the Most High will be revealed upon the seat of judgement, and compassion will pass away, and patience will be withdrawn: **34** but judgement only will remain, truth will stand, and faith will wax strong: **35** and the work will follow, and the reward will be showed, and good deeds will awake, and wicked deeds will not sleep. **36** And the pit of torment will appear, and near it will be the place of rest: and the furnace will be showed, and near it the paradise of delight. **37** And then will the Most High say to the nations that are raised from the dead, 'see you and understand whom you have denied, or whom you have not served, or whose commandments you have despised. **38** Look on this side and on that: here is delight and rest, and there fire and torments.' This will he speak to them in the day of judgement: **39** This is a day that has neither sun, nor moon, nor stars, **40** neither cloud, nor thunder, nor lightning, neither wind, nor water, nor air, neither darkness, nor evening, nor morning, **41** neither summer, nor spring, nor heat, nor winter, neither frost, nor cold, nor hail, nor rain, nor dew, **42** neither noon, nor night, nor dawn, neither shining, nor brightness, nor light, save only the splendor of the glory of the Most High, whereby all will see the things that are set before them: **43** for it will endure as it were a week of years. **44** This is my judgement and the ordinance thereof; but to you only have I showed these things." **45** And I answered, I said even then, "O Lord, and I say now: blessed are those who are now alive and keep the *statutes* ordained of you. **46** But as touching them for whom my prayer was made, *what will I say?* For who is there of those who are alive that has not sinned, and who of the sons *of men* that has not transgressed your covenant? **47** And now I see, that the world to come will bring delight to few, but torments to many. **48** For an evil heart has grown up in us, which has led us astray from these *statutes, and* has brought us into corruption and into the ways of death, has showed us the paths of perdition and removed us far from life; and that, not a few only, but well near all that have been created." **49** And he answered me, and said, "Listen to me, and I will instruct you; and I will admonish you yet again: **50** for this cause the Most High has not made one world, but two. **51** For whereas you have said that the just are not many, but few, and the ungodly abound, hear *the answer*

thereto. **52** If you have exceedingly few choice stones, will you set for you near them according to their number *things of* lead and clay?" **53** And I said, "Lord, how will this be?" **54** And he said to me, "Not only this, but ask the earth, and she will tell you; entreat her, and she will declare to you. **55** For you will say to her, 'You bring out gold and silver and brass, and iron also and lead and clay:' **56** but silver is more abundant than gold, and brass than silver, and iron than brass, lead than iron, and clay than lead. **57** Judge you therefore which things are precious and to be desired, what is abundant or what is rare." **58** And I said, "O Lord that bear rule, that which is plentiful is of less worth, for that which is more rare is more precious." **59** And he answered me, and said, "Weigh within yourself the things that you have thought, for he that has what is hard to get rejoices over him that has what is plentiful. **60** So also is the judgement which I have promised: for I will rejoice over the few that will be saved, inasmuch as these are those who have made my glory now to prevail, and of whom my name is now named. **61** And I will not grieve over the multitude of those who perish; for these are those who are now like to vapor and are become as flame and smoke; they are set on fire and burn hotly and are quenched." **62** And I answered and said, "O you earth, why have you brought out, if the mind is made out of dust, like as all other created things? **63** For it were better that the dust itself had been unborn, so that the mind might not have been made from it. **64** But now the mind grows with us, and by reason of this we are tormented, because we perish and know it. **65** Let the race of men lament and the beasts of the field be glad; let all that are born lament but let the four-footed beasts and the cattle rejoice. **66** For it is far better with them than with us; for they look not for judgement, neither do they know of torments or of salvation promised to them after death. **67** For what does it profit us, that we will be preserved alive, but yet be afflicted with torment? **68** For all that are born are defiled with iniquities and are full of sins and laden with offences: **69** and if after death we were not to come into judgement, perhaps it had been better for us." **70** And he answered me, and said, "When the Most High made the world, and Adam and all those who came of him, he first prepared the judgement and the things that pertain to the judgement. **71** And now understand from your own words, for you have said that the mind grows with us. **72** They therefore that dwell upon the earth will be tormented for this reason, that having understanding they have done iniquity, and receiving commandments have not kept them, and having obtained a law they dealt unfaithfully with that which they received. **73** What then will they have to say in the judgement, or how will they answer in the last times? **74** For how great a time has the Most High been patient with those who inhabit the world, and not for their sakes, but because of the times which he has foreordained!" **75** And I answered and said, "If I have found grace in your sight, O Lord, show this also to your servant, whether after death, even now when every one of us gives up his soul, we will be kept in rest until those times come, in which you will renew the creation, or whether we will be tormented immediately." **76** And he answered me, and said, "I will show you this also; but join not yourself with those who are scorners, nor count yourself with those who are tormented. **77** For you have a treasure of *good* works laid up with the Most High, but it will not be showed you until the last times. **78** For concerning death the teaching is: When the determinate sentence has gone out from the Most High that a man should die, as the spirit leaves the body to return again to him who gave it, it adores the glory of the Most High first of all. **79** And if it be one of those that have been scorners and have not kept the way of the Most High, and that have despised his law, and that hate those who fear God, **80** these spirits will not enter into habitations, but will wander and be in torments immediately, ever grieving and sad, in seven ways. **81** The first way, because they have despised the law of the Most High. **82** The second way, because they can't now make a good returning that they may live. **83** The third way, they will see the reward laid up for those who have believed the covenants of the Most High. **84** The fourth way, they will consider the torment laid up for themselves in the last days. **85** The fifth way, they will see the dwelling places of the others guarded by angels, with great quietness. **86** The sixth way, they will see how immediately some of them will pass into torment. **87** The seventh way, which is more grievous than all the aforesaid ways, because they will pine away in confusion and be consumed with shame, and will be withered up by fears, seeing the glory of the Most High before whom they have sinned while living, and before whom they will be judged in the last times. **88** Now this is the order of those who have kept the ways of the Most High, when they will be separated from the corruptible vessel. **89** In the time that they lived therein they painfully served the Most High, and were in jeopardy every hour, that they might keep the law of the lawgiver perfectly. **90** Here then is the teaching concerning them: **91** First of all they will see with great joy the glory of him who takes them up, for they will have rest in seven orders. **92** The first order, because they have labored with great effort to overcome the evil thought which was fashioned together with them, that it might not lead them astray from life into death. **93** The second order, because they see the perplexity in which the souls of the ungodly wander, and the punishment that awaits them. **94** The third order, they see the witness which he that fashioned them bears concerning them, that while they lived they kept the law which was given them in trust. **95** The fourth order, they understand the rest which, being gathered in their chambers, they now enjoy with great quietness, guarded by angels, and the glory that awaits them in the last days. **96** The fifth order, they rejoice, *seeing* how they have now escaped from that which is corruptible, and how they will inherit that which is to come, while they see moreover the narrowness and the painfulness from which they have been delivered, and the large room which they will receive with joy and immortality. **97** The sixth order, when it is showed to them how their face will shine as the sun, and how they will be made like to the light of the stars, being from now on incorruptible. **98** The seventh order, which is greater than all the previous orders, because they will rejoice with confidence, and because they will be bold without confusion, and will be glad without fear, for they hasten to behold the face of him whom in their lifetime they served, and from whom they will receive *their* reward in glory. **99** This is the order of the souls of the just, as from now on is announced to them, and announced are the ways of torture which those who would not give heed will suffer from now on." **100** And I answered and said, "Will time therefore be given to the souls after they are separated from the bodies, that they may see what you have spoken to me?" **101** And he said, "Their freedom will be for seven days, that for seven days they may see the things that you have been told, and afterwards they will be gathered together in their habitations." **102** And I answered and said, "If I have found favor in your sight, show further to me your servant whether in the day of judgment the just will be able to intercede for the ungodly or to entreat the Most High for them, **103** whether fathers for children, or children for parents, or kindred for kindred, or kinsfolk for their next of kin, or friends for those who are most dear." **104** And he answered me, and said, "Since you have found favor in my sight, I will show you this also: The day of judgement is a day of decision, and displays to all the seal of truth; even as now a father sends not his son, or a son his father, or a master his slave, or a friend him that is most dear, that in his stead he may be sick, or sleep, or eat, or be healed: **105** so never will anyone pray for another in that day, neither will one lay a burden on another, for then will everyone bear his own righteousness or unrighteousness." **106** And I answered and said, "How do we now find that first Abraham prayed for the people of Sodom, and Moses for the fathers that sinned in the wilderness: **107** and Joshua after him for Israel in the days of Achar: **108** and Samuel in the days of Saul; and David for the plague: and Solomon for those who *should worship* in the sanctuary: **109** and Elijah for those that received rain; and for the dead, that he might live: **110** and Hezekiah for the people in the days of Sennacherib: and many for many? **111** If therefore now, when corruption is grown up, and unrighteousness increased, the righteous have prayed for the ungodly, why will it not be so then also?" **112** He answered me, and said, "This present world is not the end; the full glory remains not therein: therefore have they who were able prayed for the weak. **113** But the day of judgement will be the end of this time, and the beginning of the immortality for to come, wherein corruption is passed away, **114** intemperance is at an end, infidelity is cut off, but righteousness is grown, and truth is sprung up. **115** Then will no man be able to have mercy on him that is cast in judgement, nor to thrust down him that has gotten the victory." **116** I answered then and said, "This is my first and last saying, that it had been better that the earth had not given *you* Adam: or else, when it had given *him,* to have restrained him from sinning. **117** For what profit is it for all that are in this present time to live in heaviness, and after death to look for punishment? **118** O you Adam, what have you done? For though it was you that sinned, the evil is not fallen on you alone, but upon all of us that come of you. **119** For what profit is it to us, if there be promised us an immortal time, whereas we have done the works that bring death? **120** And that there is promised us an everlasting hope, whereas ourselves most miserably are become vain? **121** And that there are reserved habitations of health and safety, whereas we have lived wickedly? **122** And that the glory of the Most High will defend them which have led a pure life, whereas we have walked in the most wicked ways of all? **123** And that there will be showed a paradise, whose fruit endures without decay, wherein is abundance and healing, but we will not enter into it, **124** for we have walked in unpleasant places? **125** And that the faces of them which have used abstinence will shine above the stars, whereas our faces will be blacker than darkness? **126** For while we lived and committed iniquity, we considered not what we should have to suffer after death." **127** Then he answered and said, "This is the condition of the battle, which man that is born upon the earth will fight; **128** that, if he be overcome, he will suffer as you have said: but if he get the victory, he will receive the thing that I say. **129** For this is the way whereof Moses spoke to the people while he lived, saying, 'Choose you life, that you may live.' **130** Nevertheless they did not believe him, nor yet the prophets after him, no, nor me which have spoken to them; **131** so that there will not be such heaviness in their destruction, as there will be joy over those who are persuaded to salvation." **132** I answered then and said, "I know, Lord, that the Most High is now called merciful, in that he has mercy upon them which are not yet come into the world; **133** and compassionate, in that he has compassion upon those that turn to his law; **134** and patient, for that he long suffers those that have sinned, as his creatures; **135** and bountiful, for that he is ready to give rather than to exact; **136** and of great mercy, for that he multiplies more and more mercies to those who are present, and that are past, and also to them which are to come; **137** (for if he multiplied no *this mercies,* the world would not continue with those who dwell therein;) **138** and one that forgives, for if he didn't forgive of his goodness, that they which have committed iniquities might be eased of them, the ten thousandth part of men would not remain living; **139** and a judge, *for* if he didn't pardon those who were created by his word, and blot out the multitude of offenses, **140** there would perhaps be very few left in an innumerable multitude."

CHAPTER 8

1 And he answered me, and said, "The Most High has made this world for many, but the world to come for few. **2** I will tell you now a similitude, Esdras; As when you ask the earth, it will say to you, that it gives very much mold whereof earthen vessels are made, and little dust that gold comes of: even so is the course of the present world. **3** There are many created, but few will be saved." **4** And I answered and said, "Swallow down understanding then, O my soul, and let *my heart* devour wisdom. **5** For you are come here without your will and depart when you would not: for there is given you no longer space than only to live a short time. **6** O Lord, that are over us, suffer your servant, that we may pray before you, and give us seed to our heart, and culture to our understanding, that there may come fruit of it, whereby everyone will live that is corrupt, who bears the likeness of a man. **7** For you are alone, and we are all one workmanship of your hands, like as you have said. **8** Forasmuch as you quicken the body that is fashioned now in the womb, and give it members, your creature is preserved in fire and water, and nine months does your workmanship endure your creature which is created in her. **9** But that which keeps and that which is kept will both be kept by your keeping: and when the womb gives up again that which has grown in it, **10** you have commanded that out of the parts of the body, that is to say, out of the breasts, be given milk, which is the fruit of the breasts, **11** that the thing which is fashioned may be nourished for a time, and afterwards you will order it in your mercy. **12** Yes, you have brought it up in your righteousness, and nurtured it in your law, and corrected it with your judgement. **13** And you will mortify it as your creature and quicken it as your work. **14** If therefore you will lightly and suddenly destroy him which with so great labor was fashioned by your commandment, to what purpose was he made? **15** Now therefore I will speak; touching man in general, you know best; but touching your people *I will speak,* for whose sake I am sorry; **16** and for your inheritance, for whose cause I mourn; and for Israel, for whom I am heavy; and for the seed of Jacob, for whose sake I am troubled; **17** therefore I will begin to pray before you for

myself and for them: for I see the falls of us that dwell in the land; **18** but I have heard the swiftness of the judgment which is to come. **19** Therefore hear my voice, and understand my saying, and I will speak before you." The beginning of the words of Esdras, before he was taken up. And he said, **20** "O Lord, you who remain forever, whose eyes are exalted, and whose chambers are in the air; **21** whose throne is inestimable; whose glory may not be comprehended; before whom the army of angels stand with trembling, **22** at whose bidding they are changed to wind and fire; whose word is sure, and sayings constant; whose ordinance is strong, and commandment fearful; **23** whose look dries up the depths, and whose indignation makes the mountains to melt away, and whose truth bears witness: **24** hear, O Lord, the prayer of your servant, and give ear to the petition of your handiwork; **25** attend to my words, for so long as I live I will speak, and so long as I have understanding I will answer. **26** O look not upon the sins of your people; but on those who have served you in truth, **27** Regard not the doings of those who deal wickedly, but of those who have kept your covenants in affliction. **28** Think not upon those that have walked feignedly before you; but remember them which have willingly known your fear. **29** Let it not be your will to destroy them which have lived like cattle; but look upon those who have clearly taught your law. **30** Take you no indignation at them which are deemed worse than beasts; but love those who have always put their trust in your glory. **31** For we and our fathers have passed our lives in ways that bring death: but you because of us sinners are called merciful. **32** For if you have a desire to have mercy upon us, then will you be called merciful, to us, namely, that have no works of righteousness. **33** For the just, which have many *good* works laid up with you, will for their own deeds receive reward. **34** For what is man, that you should take displeasure at him? Or what is a corruptible race, that you should be so bitter toward it? **35** For in truth there is no man among those who are born, but he has dealt wickedly; and among them that have lived there is none which have not done amiss. **36** For in this, O Lord, your righteousness and your goodness will be declared, if you be merciful to them which have no store of good works." **37** Then answered he me, and said, "Some things have you spoken correctly, and according to your words so will it come to pass. **38** For indeed I will not think on the fashioning of them which have sinned, or their death, their judgement, or their destruction; **39** but I will rejoice over the framing of the righteous, their pilgrimage also, and the salvation, and the reward, that they will have. **40** Like therefore as I have spoken, so will it be. **41** For as the husbandman sows much seed upon the ground, and plants many trees, and yet not all that is sown will come up in due season, neither will all that is planted take root: even so those who are sown in the world will not all be saved." **42** I answered then and said, "If I have found favor, let me speak before you. **43** Forasmuch as the husbandman's seed, if it come not up, seeing that it has not received your rain in due season, or if it be corrupted through too much rain, so perishes; **44** likewise man, which is formed with your hands, and is called your own image, because he is made like *to you,* for whose sake you have formed all things, even him have you made like to the husbandman's seed. **45** Be not angry with us, but spare your people, and have mercy upon your inheritance; for you have mercy upon your own creation." **46** Then he answered me, and said, "Things present are for those who now be, and things to come for such as will be hereafter. **47** For you come far short that you should be able to love my creature more than I. But you have brought yourself full near to the unrighteous. *Let this* never *be.* **48** Yet in this will you be admirable to the Most High; **49** in that you have humbled yourself, as it becomes you, and have not judged yourself *worthy to be* among the righteous, so as to be much glorified. **50** For many grievous miseries will fall on those who in the last times dwell in the world, because they have walked in great pride. **51** But understand you for yourself, and of such as be like you seek out the glory. **52** For to you is paradise opened, the tree of life planted, the time to come is prepared, bounty is made ready, a city is built, and rest is allowed, goodness is perfected, wisdom being perfect beforehand. **53** The root *of evil* is sealed up from you, weakness is done away from you, and [death] is hidden; hell and corruption are fled into forgetfulness: **54** sorrows are passed away, and in the end is showed the treasure of immortality. **55** Therefore do not ask any more questions concerning the multitude of them that perish. **56** For when they had received liberty, they despised the Most High, thought scorn of his law, and forsook his ways.

57 Moreover they have trodden down his righteous, **58** and said in their heart, that there is no God; yes, and that knowing they must die. **59** For as the things previously said you will receive, so thirst and pain which are prepared *will they receive*: for the Most High willed not that men should come to nothing: **60** but they which be created have themselves defiled the name of him that made them and were unthankful to him which prepared life for them. **61** And therefore is my judgement now at hand, **62** which I have not showed to all men, but to you, and a few like you." Then I answered and said, **63** "Behold, O Lord, now have you showed me the multitude of the wonders, which you will do in the last times: but at what time, you have not showed me."

CHAPTER 9

1 And he answered me, and said, "Measure you diligently within yourself: and when you see that a certain part of the signs are past, which have been told you beforehand, **2** then will you understand, that it is the very time, wherein the Most High will visit the world which was made by him. **3** And when there will be seen in the world earthquakes, disquietude of peoples, plans of nations, wavering of leaders, disquietude of princes, **4** then will you understand, that the Most High spoke of these things from the days that were previously from the beginning. **5** For like as all that is made in the world, the beginning is evident, and the end manifest; **6** so also are the times of the Most High: the beginnings are manifest in wonders and mighty works, and the end in effects and signs. **7** And everyone that will be saved, and will be able to escape by his works, or by faith, whereby he has believed, **8** will be preserved from the said perils, and will see my salvation in my land, and within my borders, which I have sanctified for me from the beginning. **9** Then will they be amazed, which now have abused my ways: and those who have cast them away despitefully will dwell in torments. **10** For as many as in their life have received benefits, and yet have not known me; **11** and as many as have scorned my law, while they still had liberty, and, when repentance was open to them, understood not, but despised *it,* **12** must know *it* after death by torment. **13** And therefore no longer be curious how the ungodly will be punished; but inquire how the righteous will be saved, they whose the world *is, and* for whom the world *was created.*"

14 And I answered and said, **15** "I have said before, and now do speak, and will speak it also hereafter, that there be more of them which perish, than of those which will be saved: **16** like as a wave is greater than a drop." **17** And he answered me, saying, "Just as the field is, so also the seed; and as the flowers be, such are the colors also; and such as the work is, such also is the judgement *on it;* and as is the husbandman, so is his threshing floor also. For there was a time in the world, **18** even then when I was preparing for those who now live, before the world was made for them to dwell in; and then no man spoke against me, **19** there was not any: but now they which are created in this world that is prepared, both with a table that fails not, and a law which is unsearchable, are corrupted in their manners. **20** So I considered my world, and, behold, it was destroyed, and my earth, and, behold, it was in peril, because of the plans that had come into it. **21** And I saw, and spared them, but not greatly, and saved me a grape out of a cluster, and a plant out of a great forest. **22** Let the multitude perish then, which was born in vain; and let my grape be saved, and my plant; for with great labor have I made them perfect. **23** Nevertheless if you will cease yet seven days more, (however you will not fast in them, **24** but will go into a field of flowers, where no house is built, and eat only of the flowers of the field; and you will taste no flesh, and will drink no wine, but *will eat* flowers only;) **25** and pray to the Most High continually, then I will come and talk with you." **26** So I went my way, like as he commanded me, into the field which is called Ardat; and there I sat among the flowers, and did eat of the herbs of the field, and its meat satisfied me. **27** And it came to pass after seven days that I lay upon the grass, and my heart was vexed again, like as before: **28** and my mouth was opened, and I began to speak before the Lord Most High, and said, **29** "O Lord, you did show yourself among us, to our fathers in the wilderness, when they went out of Egypt, and when they came into the wilderness, where no man treads and that bears no fruit; **30** and you did say, 'Hear me, you Israel; and mark my words, O seed of Jacob. **31** For, behold, I sow my law in you, and it will bring out fruit in you, and you will be glorified in it forever.' **32** But our fathers, which received the law, kept it not, and observed not the statutes: and the fruit of the law didn't perish, neither could it, for it was

yours; **33** yet those who received it perished, because they kept not the thing that was sown in them. **34** And, behold, it is a custom, that when the ground has received seed, or the sea a ship, or any vessel meat or drink, and when it comes to pass that that which is sown, or that which is launched, **35** or the things which have been received, should come to an end, these come to an end, but the receptacles remain: yet with us it has not happened so. **36** For we that have received the law will perish by sin, and our heart also which received it. **37** Notwithstanding the law perishes not but remains in its honor." **38** And when I spoke these things in my heart, I looked about me with my eyes, and upon the right side I saw a woman, and, behold, she mourned and wept with a loud voice, and was much grieved in mind, and her clothes were torn, and she had ashes upon her head. **39** Then I let my thoughts go wherein I was occupied, and I turned to her, **40** and said to her, "Why do you weep? And why are you grieved in your mind?" **41** And she said to me, "Leave me alone, my Lord, that I may mourn myself, and add to my sorrow, for I am sore vexed in my mind, and brought very low." **42** And I said to her, "What ails you? Tell me." **43** She said to me, "I your servant was barren, and had no child, though I had a husband thirty years. **44** And every hour and every day these thirty years did I make my prayer to the Most High day and night. **45** And it came to pass after thirty years that God heard me your handmaid, and looked upon my low estate, and considered my trouble, and gave me a son: and I rejoiced in him greatly, I and my husband, and all my neighbors: and we gave great honor to the Mighty. **46** And I nourished him with great travail. **47** So when he grew up, and I came to take him a wife, I made him a feast day."

CHAPTER 10

1 "And it so came to pass, that when my son was entered into his wedding chamber, he fell down, and died. **2** Then we all overthrew the lights, and all my neighbors rose up to comfort me: and I remained quiet to the second day at night. **3** And it came to pass, when they had all left off to comfort me, to the end I might be quiet, then rose I up by night, and fled, and came here into this field, as you see. **4** And I do now purpose not to return into the city, but here to stay, and neither to eat nor drink, but continually to mourn and to fast until I die." **5** Then I left the meditations wherein I was, and answered her in anger, and said, **6** "You foolish woman above all others, do you not see our mourning, and what has happened to us? **7** how Zion the mother of us all is full of sorrow, and much humbled. **8** It is right now to mourn very sore, seeing we all mourn, and to be sorrowful, seeing we are all in sorrow, but you mourn for one son. **9** For ask the earth, and she will tell you, that it is she which ought to mourn for so many that grow upon her. **10** For out of her all had their beginnings, and others will come; and, behold, they walk almost all into destruction, and the multitude of them is utterly rooted out. **11** Who then should make more mourning, she, that has lost so great a multitude, or you, which are grieved but for one? **12** But if you say to me, 'My lamentation is not like the earth's, for I have lost the fruit of my womb, which I brought out with pains, and bore with sorrows': **13** but *it is with the* earth after the manner of the earth; the multitude present in it is gone, as it came: **14** then say I to you, just as you have brought out with sorrow; even so the earth also has given her fruit, namely, man, ever since the beginning to him that made her. **15** Now therefore keep your sorrow to yourself, and bear with a good courage the adversities which have befallen you. **16** For if you will acknowledge the decree of God to be just, you will both receive your son in time, and will be praised among women. **17** Go your way then into the city to your husband." **18** And she said to me, "I won't do that. I will not go into the city, but I will die here." **19** So I proceeded to speak further to her, and said, **20** "Do not do that, but suffer yourself to be prevailed on by reason of the adversities of Zion; and be comforted by reason of the sorrow of Jerusalem. **21** For you see that our sanctuary is laid waste, our altar broken down, our temple destroyed; **22** our lute is brought low, our song is put to silence, our rejoicing is at an end; the light of our candlestick is put out, the ark of our covenant is plundered, our holy things are defiled, and the name that is called upon us is profaned; our freemen are despitefully treated, our priests are burned, our Levites are gone into captivity, our virgins are defiled, and our wives ravished; our righteous men carried away, our little ones betrayed, our young men are brought into bondage, and our strong men have become weak; **23** and, what is more than all, the seal of Zion—for she has now lost the seal of her honor, and is delivered into the hands of those who hate us. **24** You therefore

shake off your great heaviness, and put away from you the multitude of sorrows, that the Mighty may be merciful to you again, and the Most High may give you rest, even ease from your travails." **25** And it came to pass, while I was talking with her, behold, her face suddenly shined exceedingly, and her countenance radiated like lightning, so that I was terrified of her, and wondered what this might be; **26** and, behold, suddenly she made a great cry very fearful; so that the earth shook at the noise. **27** And I looked, and, behold, the woman appeared to me no more, but there was a city built, and a place showed itself from large foundations: then was I afraid, and cried with a loud voice, and said, **28** "Where is Uriel the angel, who came to me at the first? For he has caused me to fall into this great trance, and my end is turned into corruption, and my prayer to rebuke." **29** And as I was speaking these words, behold, the angel who had come to me at the first came to me, and he looked upon me: **30** and, behold, I lay as one that had been dead, and my understanding was taken from me; and he took me by the right hand, and comforted me, and set me upon my feet, and said to me, **31** "What ails you? And why are you so disquieted? And why is your understanding troubled, and the thoughts of your heart?" **32** And I said, "Because you have forsaken me: yet I did according to your words, and went into the field, and, behold, I have seen, and yet see, that which I am not able to express." **33** And he said to me, "Stand up like a man, and I will advise you." **34** Then said I, "Speak, my Lord; only forsake me not, lest I die without hope. **35** For I have seen and heard that I do not understand. **36** Or is my sense deceived, or my soul in a dream? **37** Now therefore I implore you to show your servant concerning this vision." **38** And he answered me, and said, "Hear me, and I will inform you, and tell you concerning the things whereof you are afraid: For the Most High has revealed many secret things to you. **39** He has seen that your way is right: for that you mourn continually for your people and make great lamentation for Zion. **40** This therefore is the meaning of the vision. **41** The woman which appeared to you a little while ago, whom you saw mourning, and began to comfort her: **42** but now you see the likeness of the woman no more, but there appeared to you a city in building: **43** and whereas she told you of the death of her son, this is the solution: **44** This woman, whom you saw, is Zion, whom you now see as a city built; **45** and whereas she said to you, that she has been thirty years barren, *it is,* because there were three thousand years in the world wherein there was no offering as yet offered in her. **46** And it came to pass after three thousand years that Solomon built the city and offered offerings: then it was that the barren bore a son. **47** And whereas she told you that she nourished him with travail: that was the dwelling in Jerusalem. **48** And whereas she said to you, 'My son coming into his marriage chamber died', and that misfortune befell her: this was the destruction that came to Jerusalem. **49** And, behold, you saw her likeness, how she mourned for her son, and you began to comfort her for what has befallen her; these were the things to be opened to you. **50** For now the Most High, seeing that you are grieved, and suffer from your whole heart for her, has showed you the brightness of her glory, and the attractiveness of her beauty: **51** and therefore I bade you remain in the field where no house was built: **52** for I knew that the Most High would show this to you. **53** Therefore I commanded you to come into the field, where no foundation of any building was. **54** For in the place wherein the city of the Most High was to be showed, the work of no man's building could stand. **55** Therefore fear you not, nor let your heart be affrighted, but go your way in, and see the beauty and greatness of the building, as much as your eyes be able to see: **56** and then will you hear as much as your ears may comprehend. **57** For you are blessed above many, and with the Most High are called by name, like as but few. **58** But tomorrow at night you will remain here; **59** and so will the Most High show you those visions in dreams, of what the Most High will do to those who dwell upon the earth in the last days." So I slept that night and another, like as he commanded me.

CHAPTER 11

1 And it came to pass the second night that I saw a dream, and, behold, there came up from the sea an eagle, which had twelve feathered wings, and three heads. **2** And I saw, and, behold, she spread her wings over all the earth, and all the winds of heaven blew on her, and the clouds were gathered together against her. **3** And I saw, and out of her wings there grew *other* wings near them; and they became little wings and small. **4** But her heads were at rest: the head in the midst was greater than the other heads yet rested with them. **5** Moreover I saw, and, behold, the eagle flew with her wings, to reign over the earth, and over those who dwell therein. **6** And I saw how all things under heaven were subject to her, and no man spoke against her, no, not one creature upon earth. **7** And I saw, and, behold, the eagle rose upon her talons, and uttered her voice to her wings, saying, **8** "Watch not all at once: sleep everyone in his own place, and watch by course: **9** but let the heads be preserved for the last." **10** And I saw, and, behold, the voice went not out of her heads, but from the midst of her body. **11** And I counted her wings that were near the other, and, behold, there were eight of them. **12** And I saw, and, behold, on the right side there arose one wing, and reigned over all the earth; **13** and so it was, that when it reigned, the end of it came, and it appeared not, so that the place thereof appeared no more: and the next following rose up, and reigned, and it ruled a great time; **14** and it happened, that when it reigned, the end of it came also, so that it appeared no more, like as the first. **15** And, behold, there came a voice to it, and said, **16** "Hear you that have borne rule over the earth all this time: this I proclaim to you, before you will appear no more, **17** There will none after you attain to your time, neither to the half thereof." **18** Then arose the third, and had the rule as the others before, and it also appeared no more. **19** So it went with all the wings one after another, as that everyone bare rule, and then appeared no more. **20** And I saw, and, behold, in process of time the wings that followed were set up upon the right side, that they might rule also; and some of them ruled, but within a while they appeared no more: **21** some of them were also set up, but ruled not. **22** After this I saw, and, behold, the twelve wings appeared no more, nor two of the little wings: **23** and there was no more left upon the eagle's body, but the three heads that rested, and six little wings. **24** And I saw, and, behold, two little wings divided themselves from the six, and remained under the head that was upon the right side: but four remained in their place. **25** And I saw, and, behold, these under wings thought to set up themselves, and to have the rule. **26** And I saw, and, behold, there was one set up, but within a while it appeared no more. **27** A second also, and it was sooner away than the first. **28** And I saw, and, behold, the two that remained thought also in themselves to reign: **29** and while they so thought, behold, there awakened one of the heads that were at rest, *namely, it* that was in the midst; for that was greater than the two *other* heads. **30** And I saw how it joined the two *other* heads with it. **31** And, behold, the head was turned with those who were with it, and did eat up the two under wings that thought to have reigned. **32** But this head held the whole earth in possession, and bare rule over those that dwell therein with much oppression; and it had the governance of the world more than all the wings that had been. **33** And after this I saw, and, behold, the head also that was in the midst suddenly appeared no more, like as the wings. **34** But there remained the two heads, which also in like sort reigned over the earth, and over those that dwell therein. **35** And I saw, and, behold, the head upon the right side devoured it that was upon the left side. **36** Then I heard a voice, which said to me, "Look before you, and consider the thing that you see." **37** And I saw, and, behold, as it were a lion roused out of the wood roaring: and I heard how that he sent out a man's voice to the eagle, and spoke, saying, **38** "Hear you, I will talk with you, and the Most High will say to you, **39** 'Are you not it that remain of the four beasts, whom I made to reign in my world, that the end of my times might come through them?' " **40** And the fourth came, and overcame all the beasts that were past, and held the world in governance with great trembling, and the whole compass of the earth with grievous oppression; and so long time lived he upon the earth with deceit. **41** And you have judged the earth, but not with truth. **42** For you have afflicted the meek, you have hurt the peaceful, you have hated those who speak truth, you have loved liars, and destroyed the dwellings of those who brought out fruit and cast down the walls of such as did you no harm. **43** Therefore is your insolent dealing come up to the Most High, and your pride to the Mighty. **44** The Most High also has looked upon his times, and, behold, they are ended, and his ages are fulfilled. **45** And therefore appear no more, you eagle, nor your horrible wings, nor your evil little wings, nor your cruel heads, nor your hurtful talons, nor all your vain body: **46** that all the earth may be refreshed, and be eased, being delivered from your violence, and that she may hope for the judgement and mercy of him that made her.

CHAPTER 12

1 And it came to pass, while the lion spoke these words to the eagle, I saw, **2** and, behold, the head that remained appeared no more, and the two wings which went over to it arose and set themselves up to reign, and their kingdom was small, and full of uproar. **3** And I saw, and, behold, they appeared no more, and the whole body of the eagle was burned, so that the earth was in great fear: then awaked I by reason of great ecstasy of mind, and from great fear, and said to my spirit, **4** Behold, this have you done to me, in that you search out the ways of the Most High. **5** Behold, I am yet weary in my mind, and very weak in my spirit; nor is there the least strength in me, for the great fear with which I was affrighted this night. **6** Therefore I will now implore the Most High, that he will strengthen me to the end. **7** And I said, "O Lord that bear rule, if I have found favor in your sight, and if I am justified with you above many others, and if my prayer indeed has come up before your face; **8** strengthen me then and show me your servant the interpretation and plain meaning of this fearful vision, that you may perfectly comfort my soul. **9** For you have judged me worthy to show me the end of time and the last times." **10** And he said to me, "This is the interpretation of this vision which you saw: **11** The eagle, whom you saw come up from the sea, is the fourth kingdom which appeared in vision to your brother Daniel. **12** But it was not expounded to him, as I now expound it to you or have expounded it. **13** Behold, the days come, that there will rise up a kingdom upon earth, and it will be feared above all the kingdoms that were before it. **14** Twelve kings will reign in it, one after another: **15** whereof the second will begin to reign and will have a longer time than *any of the* twelve. **16** This is the interpretation of the twelve wings, which you saw. **17** And whereas you heard a voice which spoke, not going out from the heads, but from the midst of the body thereof, this is the interpretation: **18** That after the time of that kingdom there will arise no small contentions, and it will stand in peril of falling: nevertheless, it will not then fall, but will be restored again to its first estate. **19** And whereas you saw the eight under wings sticking to her wings, this is the interpretation: **20** That in it there will arise eight kings, whose times will be but small, and their years swift. **21** And two of them will perish, when the middle time approaches: four will be kept for a while until the time of the ending thereof will approach: but two will be kept to the end. **22** And whereas you saw three heads resting, this is the interpretation: **23** In the last days thereof will the Most High raise up three kingdoms, and renew many things therein, and they will bear rule over the earth, **24** and over those that dwell therein, with much oppression, above all those that were before them: therefore are they called the heads of the eagle. **25** For these are those who will accomplish her wickedness, and that will finish her last end. **26** And whereas you saw that the great head appeared no more, *it signifies* that one of them will die upon his bed, and yet with pain. **27** But for the two that remained, the sword will devour them. **28** For the sword of the one will devour him that was with him: but he also will fall by the sword in the last days. **29** And whereas you saw two under wings passing over to the head that is on the right side, **30** this is the interpretation: These are they, whom the Most High has kept to his end: this is the small kingdom and full of trouble, as you saw. **31** And the lion, whom you saw rising up out of the wood, and roaring, and speaking to the eagle, and rebuking her for her unrighteousness, and all her words which you have heard; **32** this is the anointed one, whom the Most High has kept to the end of days, who will spring up out of the seed of David, and he will come and speak to them and reprove them for their wickedness and unrighteousness, and will heap up before them their contemptuous dealings. **33** For at the first he will set them alive in his judgement, and when he has reproved them, he will destroy them. **34** For the rest of my people will he deliver with mercy, those that have been preserved throughout my borders, and he will make them joyful until the coming of the end, even the day of judgment, whereof I have spoken to you from the beginning. **35** This is the dream that you saw, and this is the interpretation thereof: **36** and you only have been chosen to know the secret of the Most High. **37** Therefore write all these things that you have seen in a book and put them in a secret place: **38** and you will teach them to the wise of your people, whose hearts you know are able to comprehend and keep these secrets. **39** But wait here yourself yet seven days more, that there may be showed to you whatever it pleases the Most High to show you." And he departed from me. **40** And it came to pass, when all the people saw that the seven days were past, and I had not come again into the city, they gathered them all together, from the least to the greatest, and came to me, and spoke to me, saying, **41** "How have we offended you? And what evil have we done against you, that you have utterly forsaken us, and sit in this place? **42** For of all the prophets you alone are left to us, as a cluster of the vintage, and as a lamp in a dark place, and as a haven for a ship saved from the tempest. **43** Are not the evils which are come to us sufficient? **44** If you will forsake us, how much better had it been for us, if we also had been consumed in the burning of Zion! **45** For we are not better than those who died there." And they wept with a loud voice. And I answered them, and said, **46** "Be of good comfort, O Israel; and be not sorrowful, you house of Jacob: **47** for the Most High has you in remembrance, and the Mighty has not forgotten you forever. **48** As for me, I have not forsaken you, neither am I departed from you: but am come into this place, to pray for the desolation of Zion, and that I might seek mercy for the low estate of your sanctuary. **49** And now go your way every man to his own house, and after these days I will come to you." **50** So the people went their way into the city, like as I said to them: **51** but I sat in the field seven days, as *the angel* commanded me; and in those days I did eat only of the flowers of the field and had my meat of the herbs.

CHAPTER 13

1 And it came to pass after seven days, I dreamed a dream by night: **2** and, behold, there arose a wind from the sea, that it moved all the waves thereof. **3** And I saw, and, behold, this wind caused to come up from the midst of the sea as it were the likeness of a man, and I saw, and, behold, that man flew with the clouds of heaven: and when he turned his countenance to look, all things trembled that were seen under him. **4** And whenever the voice went out of his mouth, all they burned that heard his voice, like as the wax melts when it feels the fire. **5** And after this I saw, and, behold, there was gathered together a multitude of men, out of number, from the four winds of heaven, to make war against the man that came out of the sea. **6** And I saw, and, behold, he carved himself a great mountain, and flew upon it. **7** But I sought to see the region or place where the mountain was graven, and I could not. **8** And after this I saw, and, behold, all they which were gathered together to fight against him were sore afraid, and yet dared fight. **9** And, behold, as he saw the assault of the multitude that came, he neither lifted up his hand, nor held spear, nor any instrument of war: **10** but only I saw how that he sent out of his mouth as it had been a flood of fire, and out of his lips a flaming breath, and out of his tongue he cast out sparks of the storm. **11** And these were all mixed together; the flood of fire, the flaming breath, and the great storm; and fell upon the assault of the multitude which was prepared to fight, and burned all of them up, so that upon a sudden of an innumerable multitude nothing was to be perceived, but only dust of ashes and smell of smoke: when I saw this I was amazed. **12** Afterward I saw the same man come down from the mountain, and call to him another multitude which was peaceful. **13** And many people came to him, whereof some were glad, some were sorry, some of them were bound, and some brought of those who were offered: then through great fear I awakened, and prayed to the Most High, and said, **14** "You have showed your servant these wonders from the beginning, and have counted me worthy that you should receive my prayer: **15** and now show me moreover the interpretation of this dream. **16** For as I conceive in my understanding, woe to those who will be left in those days! and much more woe to those who are not left! **17** for those who were not left will be in heaviness, **18** understanding the things that are laid up in the latter days, but not attaining to them. **19** But woe to them also that are left, for this cause; for they will see great perils and many necessities, like as these dreams declare. **20** Yet it is better for one to be in peril and to come into these things, than to pass away as a cloud out of the world, and not to see the things that will happen in the last days." And he answered to me, and said, **21** "The interpretation of the vision will I tell you, and I will also open to you the things whereof you have made mention. **22** Whereas you have spoken of those who are left behind, this is the interpretation: **23** He that will endure the peril in that time will keep those who are fallen into danger, even such as have works, and faith toward the Almighty. **24** Know therefore, that they which are left behind are more blessed than those who are dead. **25** These are the interpretations of the vision: Whereas you saw a man coming up from the midst of the sea, **26** this is he whom the Most High has kept a great season, which by his own self will deliver his creature: and he will order those who are left behind. **27** And whereas you saw, that out of his mouth there came wind, and fire,

and storm; **28** and whereas he held neither spear, nor any instrument of war, but destroyed the assault of that multitude which came to fight against him; this is the interpretation: **29** Behold, the days come, when the Most High will begin to deliver those who are upon the earth. **30** And there will come astonishment of mind upon those who dwell on the earth. **31** And one will think to war against another, city against city, place against place, people against people, and kingdom against kingdom. **32** And it will be, when these things will come to pass, and the signs will happen which I showed you before, then will my Son be revealed, whom you saw *as* a man ascending. **33** And it will be, when all the nations hear his voice, every man will leave his own land and the battle they have against one another. **34** And an innumerable multitude will be gathered together, as you saw, desiring to come, and to fight against him. **35** But he will stand upon the top of Mount Zion. **36** And Zion will come, and will be showed to all men, being prepared and built, like as you saw the mountain graven without hands. **37** And this my Son will rebuke the nations which are come for their wickedness, *with plagues* that are like to a tempest; **38** and will taunt them to their face with their evil thoughts, and the torments with which they will be tormented, which are likened to a flame: and he will destroy them without labor by the law, which is likened to fire. **39** And whereas you saw that he gathered to him another multitude that was peaceful; **40** these are the ten tribes, which were led away out of their own land in the time of Osea the king, whom Salmananser the king of the Assyrians led away captive, and he carried them beyond the River, and they were carried into another land. **41** But they took this counsel among themselves, that they would leave the multitude of the heathen, and go out into a further country, where never mankind lived, **42** that they might there keep their statutes, which they had not kept in their own land. **43** And they entered by the narrow passages of the river Euphrates. **44** For the Most High then performed signs for them, and held back the springs of the River, until they had passed over. **45** For through that country there was a great way to go, namely, of a year and a half: and the same region is called Arzareth. **46** Then they lived there until the latter time; and now when they begin to come again, **47** the Most High holds back the springs of the River again, that they may go through: therefore you saw the multitude gathered together with peace. **48** But those that are left behind of your people are those who are found within my holy border. **49** It will be therefore when he will destroy the multitude of the nations that are gathered together, he will defend the people that remain. **50** And then will he show them very many wonders." **51** Then said I, "O Lord that bear rule, show me this: why I have seen the man coming up from the midst of the sea." **52** And he said to me, "Like as one can neither seek out nor know what is in the deep of the sea, even so can no man upon earth see my Son, or those that be with him, but in the time of his day. **53** This is the interpretation of the dream which you saw, and for this you only are enlightened herein. **54** For you have forsaken your own *ways, and* applied your diligence to mine, and have sought out my law. **55** Your life have you ordered in wisdom, and have called understanding your mother. **56** And therefore have I showed you this; for there is a reward laid up with the Most High: and it will be, after another three days I will speak other things to you and declare to you mighty and wondrous things." **57** Then I went out and passed into the field, giving praise and thanks greatly to the Most High because of his wonders, which he did from time to time; **58** and because he governs the time, and such things as fall in their seasons. And there I sat three days.

CHAPTER 14

1 And it came to pass upon the third day, I sat under an oak, and, behold, there came a voice out of a bush near me, and said, "Esdras, Esdras." **2** And I said, "Here am I, Lord." And I stood up upon my feet. **3** Then he said to me, "In the bush I did manifestly reveal myself, and talked with Moses, when my people were in bondage in Egypt: **4** and I sent him, and he led my people out of Egypt; and I brought him up to the mount of Sinai, where I held him by me for many days; **5** and told him many wondrous things, and showed him the secrets of the times, and the end of the seasons; and commanded him, saying, **6** 'These words will you publish openly, and these will you hide.' **7** And now I say to you, **8** Lay up in your heart the signs that I have showed, and the dreams that you have seen, and the interpretations which you have heard: **9** for you will be taken away from men, and from now on you will

remain with my Son, and with such as be like you, until the times be ended. **10** For the world has lost its youth, and the times begin to wax old. **11** For the world is divided into twelve parts, and ten parts of it are gone already, even the half of the tenth part: **12** and there remain of it two parts after the middle of the tenth part. **13** Now therefore set your house in order, and reprove your people, comfort the lowly among them, and instruct such of them as be wise, and now renounce the life that is corruptible, **14** and let go from the mortal thoughts, cast away from you the burdens of man, put off now your weak nature, **15** and lay aside the thoughts that are most grievous to you, and haste you to remove from these times. **16** For yet worse evils than those which you have seen happen will be done hereafter. **17** For look, how much the world will be weaker through age, so much the more will evils increase upon those who dwell therein. **18** For the truth will withdraw itself further off, and falsehood will be hard at hand: for now hastens the eagle to come, which you saw in vision." **19** Then answered I and said, "I will speak before you, O Lord. **20** Behold, I will go, as you have commanded me, and reprove the people that now be: but those who will be born afterward, who will admonish them? For the world is set in darkness, and those who dwell therein are without light. **21** For your law is burned, therefore no man knows the things that you have done, or the works that will be done. **22** But if I have found favor before you, send the Holy Spirit to me, and I will write all that has been done in the world since the beginning, even the things that were written in your law, that men may be able to find the path, and that they which would live in the latter days may live." **23** And he answered me and said, "Go your way, gather the people together, and say to them, that they seek you not for forty days. **24** But prepare many tablets, and take with you Sarea, Dabria, Selemia, Ethanus, and Asiel, these five, which are ready to write swiftly; **25** and come here, and I will light a lamp of understanding in your heart, which will not be put out, until the things be ended which you will write. **26** And when you have done this, some things will you publish openly, and some things will you deliver in secret to the wise: tomorrow this hour will you begin to write." **27** Then I went out, as he commanded me, and gathered all the people together, and said, **28** "Hear these words, O Israel. **29** Our fathers at the beginning were strangers in Egypt, and they were delivered from there, **30** and received the law of life, which they kept not, which you also have transgressed after them. **31** Then was the land, even the land of Zion, given you for a possession: but you yourselves, and your fathers, have done unrighteousness, and have not kept the ways which the Most High commanded you. **32** And forasmuch as he is a righteous judge, he took from you for a while the thing that he had given you. **33** And now you are here, and your kindred are among you. **34** Therefore if so be that you will rule over your own understanding, and instruct your hearts, you will be kept alive, and after death you will obtain mercy. **35** For after death will the judgement come, when we will live again: and then will the names of the righteous be manifest, and the works of the ungodly will be declared. **36** Let no man therefore come to me now, nor seek after me these forty days." **37** So I took the five men, as he commanded me, and we went out into the field, and remained there. **38** And it came to pass on the next day that, behold, a voice called me, saying, "Esdras, open your mouth, and drink what I give you to drink. **39** Then I opened my mouth, and, behold, there was given to me a full cup, which was full as it were with water, but the color of it was like fire. **40** And I took it and drank: and when I had drunk of it, my heart uttered understanding, and wisdom grew in my breast, for my spirit retained its memory: **41** and my mouth was opened and shut no more. **42** The Most High gave understanding to the five men, and they wrote by course the things that were told them, in characters which they knew not, and they sat forty days: now they wrote in the daytime, and at night they ate bread. **43** As for me, I spoke in the day, and by night I held not my tongue. **44** So in forty days were written fourscore and fourteen books. **45** And it came to pass, when the forty days were fulfilled, that the Most High spoke to me, saying, "The first that you have written publish openly, and let the worthy and unworthy read it: **46** but keep the seventy last, that you may deliver them to such as be wise among your people: **47** for in them is the spring of understanding, the fountain of wisdom, and the stream of knowledge." **48** And I did so.

CHAPTER 15

1 "Behold, speak you in the ears of my people the words of prophecy, which I will put in your mouth, says the Lord: **2** and cause you them to be written in paper: for they are faithful and true. **3** Don't be afraid of their imaginations against you, don't let the unbelief of them that speak against you trouble you. **4** For all the unbelievers will die in their unbelief. **5** Behold, says the Lord, I bring evils upon the whole earth; sword and famine, and death and destruction. **6** For wickedness has prevailed over every land, and their hurtful works are come to the full. **7** Therefore says the Lord, **8** I will hold my peace no more as touching their wickedness, which they profanely commit, neither will I suffer them in these things, which they wickedly practice: behold, the innocent and righteous blood cries to me, and the souls of the righteous cry out continually. **9** I will surely avenge them, says the Lord, and will receive to me all the innocent blood from among them. **10** Behold, my people are led as a flock to the slaughter: I will not suffer them now to dwell in the land of Egypt: **11** but I will bring them out with a mighty hand and with a high arm, and will strike Egypt with plagues, as previously, and will destroy all the land thereof. **12** Let Egypt mourn, and the foundations thereof, for the plague of the chastisement and the punishment that God will bring upon it. **13** Let the farmers that till the ground mourn: for their seeds will fail and their trees will be laid waste through the blasting and hail, and a terrible star. **14** Woe to the world and those who dwell therein! **15** for the sword and their destruction draws near, and nation will rise up against nation to battle with weapons in their hands. **16** For there will be sedition among men; and waxing strong one against another, they will not regard their king nor the chief of their great ones, in their might. **17** For a man will desire to go into a city and will not be able. **18** For because of their pride the cities will be troubled, the houses will be destroyed, and men will be afraid. **19** A man will have no pity upon his neighbor but will make an assault on their houses with the sword, and plunder their goods, because of the lack of bread, and for great suffering. **20** Behold, says God, I call together all the kings of the earth, to stir up those who are from the rising of the sun, from the south, from the east, and Libanus; to turn themselves one against another, and repay the things that they have done to them. **21** Just as they do yet this day to my chosen, so I will do also, and recompense in their bosom." The Lord God says: **22** "My right hand will not spare the sinners, and my sword will not cease over those who shed innocent blood upon the earth. **23** And a fire is gone out from his wrath, and has consumed the foundations of the earth, and the sinners, like the straw that is kindled. **24** Woe to those who sin and keep not my commandments!" says the Lord. **25** "I will not spare them: go your way, you rebellious children, defile not my sanctuary. **26** For the Lord knows all those who trespass against him, therefore has he delivered them to death and destruction. **27** For now are the evils come upon the whole earth, and you will remain in them: for God will not deliver you, because you have sinned against him. **28** Behold, a vision horrible, and the appearance thereof from the east! **29** And the nations of the dragons of Arabia will come out with many chariots, and from the day that they set out the hissing of them is carried over the earth, so that all they which will hear them may fear also and tremble. **30** Also the Carmonians raging in wrath will go out as the wild boars of the wood, and with great power will they come, and join battle with them, and will waste a portion of the land of the Assyrians with their teeth. **31** And then will the dragons have the upper hand, remembering their nature; and if they will turn themselves, conspiring together in great power to persecute them, **32** then these will be troubled, and keep silence through their power, and will turn and flee. **33** And from the land of the Assyrians will the ambusher in wait besiege them, and consume one of them, and upon their army will be fear and trembling, and sedition against their kings. **34** Behold, clouds from the east and from the north to the south, and they are very horrible to look upon, full of wrath and storm. **35** They will dash one against another, and they will pour out a plentiful storm upon the earth, even their own star; and there will be blood from the sword to the horse's belly, **36** and to the thigh of man, and to the camel's hough. **37** And there will be fearfulness and great trembling upon earth: and they that see that wrath will be afraid, and trembling will take hold upon them. **38** And after this will there be stirred up great storms from the south, and from the north, and another part from the west. **39** And strong winds will arise from the east, and will shut it up, even the cloud which he raised up in wrath; and the star that was to cause destruction by the east wind will be violently driven toward the south and west. **40** And great clouds and mighty and full of wrath will be lifted up, and the star, that they may destroy all the earth, and those who dwell therein; and they will pour out over every high and eminent one a terrible star, **41** fire, and hail, and flying swords, and many waters, that all plains may be full, and all rivers, with the abundance of those waters. **42** And they will break down the cities and walls, mountains and hills, trees of the wood, and grass of the meadows, and their corn. **43** And they will go on steadfastly to Babylon and destroy her. **44** They will come to her and compass her about; the star and all wrath will they pour out upon her: then will the dust and smoke go up to the heaven, and all those who are about her will mourn her. **45** And those who remain will do service to those who have put her in fear. **46** And you, Asia, that are partaker in the beauty of Babylon, and in the glory of her person: **47** woe to you, you wretch, because you have made yourself like to her; you have decked your daughters in whoredom, that they might please and glory in your lovers, which have always desired you to commit whoredom with! **48** You have followed her that is hateful in all her works and inventions: therefore says God, **49** I will send evils upon you; widowhood, poverty, famine, sword, and pestilence, to waste your houses to destruction and death. **50** And the glory of your power will be dried up as a flower, when the heat will arise that is sent over you. **51** You will be weakened as a poor woman with stripes, and as one chastened with wounds, so that your mighty ones and *your* lovers you will not be able to receive. **52** Would I with jealousy have so proceeded against you," says the Lord, **53** "if you had not always slain my chosen, exalting the stroke of your hands, and saying over their dead, when you were drunken, **54** 'set out the beauty of your countenance?' **55** The reward of a prostitute will be in your bosom, therefore will you receive recompense. **56** Just as you will do to my chosen," says the Lord, "even so will God do to you, and will deliver you into mischief. **57** And your children will die of hunger, and you will fall by the sword: and your cities will be broken down, and all your will perish by the sword in the field. **58** And those who are in the mountains will die of hunger, and eat their own flesh, and drink *their own* blood, for very hunger of bread, and thirst of water. **59** You unhappy above all will come and will again receive evils. **60** And in the passage, they will rush on the idle city, and will destroy some portion of your land, and mar part of your glory, and will return again to Babylon that was destroyed. **61** And you will be cast down by them as stubble, and they will be to you as fire; **62** and will devour you, and your cities, your land, and your mountains; all your woods and your fruitful trees will they burn up with fire. **63** They will carry your children away captive, and will plunder your wealth, and mar the glory of your face."

CHAPTER 16

1 "Woe to you, Babylon, and Asia! woe to you, Egypt, and Syria! **2** Gird up yourselves with sackcloth and garments of hair, and mourn your children, and lament; for your destruction is at hand. **3** A sword is sent upon you, and who is he that may turn it back? **4** A fire is sent upon you, and who is he that may quench it? **5** Evils are sent upon you, and who is he that may drive them away? **6** May one drive away a hungry lion in the wood? Or may one quench the fire in stubble, when it has once begun to burn? **7** May one turn again the arrow that is shot of a strong archer? **8** The Lord God sends the evils, and who will drive them away? **9** A fire will go out from his wrath, and who is he that may quench it? **10** He will cast lightning, and who will not fear? He will thunder, and who will not tremble? **11** The Lord will threaten, and who will not be utterly broken in pieces at his presence? **12** The earth quakes, and the foundations thereof; the sea arises up with waves from the deep, and the waves of it will be troubled, and the fishes thereof also, at the presence of the Lord, and before the glory of his power: **13** for strong is his right hand that bends the bow, his arrows that he shoots are sharp, and will not miss, when they begin to be shot into the ends of the world. **14** Behold, the evils are sent out, and will not return again, until they come upon the earth. **15** The fire is kindled, and will not be put out, until it consumes the foundations of the earth. **16** Just as an arrow which is shot of a mighty archer returns not backward, even so the evils that are sent out upon earth will not return again. **17** Woe is me! woe is me! who will deliver me in those days? **18** The beginning of sorrows, and the*re will be* great mourning; the beginning of famine, and many will perish; the beginning of wars, and the powers will stand in fear; the beginning of evils, and all will tremble! what will they do in *all* this when the evils will come? **19** Behold, famine and plague, suffering and anguish! they are sent as

scourges for amendment. **20** But for all these things they will not turn them from their wickedness, nor be always mindful of the scourges. **21** Behold, food will be so good cheap upon earth, that they will think themselves to be in good case, and even then, will evils grow upon earth, sword, famine, and great confusion. **22** For many of those who dwell upon earth will perish of famine; and the other, that escape the famine, will the sword destroy. **23** And the dead will be cast out as dung, and there will be no man to comfort them: for the earth will be left desolate, and the cities thereof will be cast down. **24** There will be no husbandman left to until the earth, and to sow it. **25** The trees will give fruit, and who will gather them? **26** The grapes will ripen, and who will tread them? For in *all* places there will be a great forsaking: **27** for one man will desire to see another, or to hear his voice. **28** For of a city there will be ten left, and two of the field, which have hidden themselves in the thick groves, and in the clefts of the rocks. **29** As in an orchard of olives upon every tree there be left three or four olives, **30** or as when a vineyard is gathered there be some clusters left by those who diligently seek through the vineyard; **31** even so in those days there will be three or four left by those who search their houses with the sword. **32** And the earth will be left desolate, and the fields thereof will be for briers, and her ways and all her paths will bring out thorns, because no sheep will pass therethrough. **33** The virgins will mourn, having no bridegrooms; the women will mourn, having no husbands; their daughters will mourn, having no helpers. **34** In the wars will their bridegrooms be destroyed, and their husbands will perish of famine. **35** Hear now these things, and understand them, you servants of the Lord. **36** Behold, the word of the Lord, receive it: disbelieve not the things whereof the Lord speaks. **37** Behold, the evils draw near, and are not slack. **38** Just as a woman with child in the ninth month, when the hour of her delivery draws near, within two or three hours doleful pains surround her womb, and when the child comes out from the womb, there will be no waiting for a moment: **39** even so will not the evils be slack to come upon the earth, and the world will groan, and sorrows will take hold of it on every side. **40** O my people, hear my word: make you ready to the battle, and in those evils be even as pilgrims upon the earth. **41** He that sells, let him be as he that flees away: and he that buys, as one that will lose: **42** he that occupies merchandise, as he that has no profit by it: and he that builds, as he that will not dwell therein: **43** he that sows, as if he should not reap: so also he that prunes *the vines,* as he that will not gather the grapes: **44** those who marry, as those who will get no children; and those who marry not, as the widowed. **45** Inasmuch as those who labor labor in vain; **46** for strangers will reap their fruits, and plunder their goods, overthrow their houses, and take their children captive, for in captivity and famine will they beget their children: **47** and those who traffic traffic to become a plunder: the more they deck their cities, their houses, their possessions, and their own persons, **48** the more I will hate them for their sins," says the Lord. **49** "Just as a right honest and virtuous woman hates a prostitute, **50** so will righteousness hate iniquity, when she decks herself, and will accuse her to her face, when he comes that will defend him that diligently searches out every sin upon earth. **51** Therefore be not like them, nor do the works thereof. **52** For yet a little while, and iniquity will be taken away out of the earth, and righteousness will reign over us. **53** Let not the sinner say that he has not sinned: for he will burn coals of fire upon his head, which says, 'I have not sinned before God and his glory.' **54** Behold, the Lord knows all the works of men, their imaginations, their thoughts, and their hearts. **55** Who said, 'Let the earth be made'; and it was made: 'Let the heaven be made'; and it was made. **56** And at his word were the stars established, and he knows the number of the stars. **57** Who searches the deep, and the treasures thereof; he has measured the sea, and what it contains. **58** Who has shut the sea in the midst of the waters, and with his word has he hanged the earth upon the waters. **59** Who spreads out the heaven like a vault; upon the waters has he founded it. **60** Who has made in the desert springs of water, and pools upon the tops of the mountains, to send out rivers from the height to water the earth. **61** Who framed man and put a heart in the midst of the body, and gave him breath, life, and understanding, **62** yes, the spirit of God Almighty. He who made all things, and searches out hidden things in hidden places, **63** surely he knows your imagination, and what you think in your hearts. Woe to those who sin and would fain hide their sin! **64** Forasmuch as the Lord will exactly search out all your works, and he will put you all to shame. **65** And when your sins are brought out before men, you will be ashamed, and your own iniquities will stand as your accusers in that day. **66** What will you do? Or how will you hide your sins before God and his angels? **67** Behold, God is the judge, fear him: leave off from your sins, and forget your iniquities, to meddle no more with them forever: so will God lead you out, and deliver you from all suffering. **68** For, behold, the burning wrath of a great multitude is kindled over you, and they will take away certain of you, and feed you with that which is slain to idols. **69** And those who consent to them will be had in derision and in reproach and be trodden under foot of them. **70** For there will be in various places, and in the next cities, a great insurrection upon those that fear the Lord. **71** They will be like mad men, sparing none, but spoiling and destroying those who still fear the Lord. **72** For they will waste and take away their goods and cast them out of their houses. **73** Then will be manifest the trial of my elect; even as the gold that is tried in the fire. **74** Hear, O you my elect," says the Lord: "behold, the days of suffering are at hand, and I will deliver you from them. **75** Be you not afraid, neither doubt; for God is your guide: **76** and you who keep my commandments and precepts," says the Lord God, "don't let your sins weigh you down, and don't let your iniquities lift up themselves. **77** Woe to those who are fast bound with their sins, and covered with their iniquities, like as a field is fast bound with bushes, and the path thereof covered with thorns, that no man may travel through! **78** It is even shut off and given up to be consumed of fire.

ENOCH

The Book of Enoch (also called 1 Enoch) is an ancient Jewish religious work, ascribed by tradition to Enoch, the great-grandfather of Noah. Enoch contains unique material on the origins of supernatural demons and giants, why some angels fell from heaven, an explanation of why the Great Flood was morally necessary, and prophetic exposition of the thousand-year reign of the Messiah. It is wholly extant only in the Ge'ez language, with Aramaic fragments from the Dead Sea Scrolls and a few Greek and Latin fragments. Jd. 1:14–15 is a direct quote of Enoch 1:9 (see also Enoch 60:8). Enoch is composed of five sections.

SECTION 1:
THE BOOK OF THE WATCHERS

CHAPTER 1

1 The words of the blessing of Enoch, with which he blessed the elect and righteous, who will be living in the day of tribulation, when all the wicked and godless are to be removed. 2 And he took up his parable and spoke— Enoch a righteous man, whose eyes were opened by God, saw the vision of the Holy One in the heavens, which the angels showed me, and from them I heard everything, and from them I understood as I saw, but not for this generation, but for a remote one which is to come. 3 Concerning the elect I spoke and took up my parable concerning them: The Holy Great One will come out from His dwelling, 4 And the eternal God will tread upon the earth, (even) on Mount Sinai, [And appear from His camp] And appear in the strength of His might from the heaven of heavens. 5 And all will be smitten with fear and the Watchers will quake, and great fear and trembling will seize them unto the ends of the earth. 6 And the high mountains will be shaken, and the high hills will be made low, and will melt like wax before the flame 7 And the earth will be wholly rent in sunder, and all that is upon the earth will perish, and there will be a judgement upon all (men). 8 But with the righteous He will make peace. And will protect the elect, and mercy will be upon them. And they will all belong to God, and they will

be prospered, and they will all be blessed. And He will help them all, and light will appear unto them, and He will make peace with them. 9 And, behold, He comes with tens of thousands of His holy ones to execute judgement upon all, and to destroy all the ungodly: And to convict all flesh of all the works of their ungodliness which they have ungodly committed, and of all the hard things which ungodly sinners have spoken against Him.

CHAPTER 2

1 Observe you everything that takes place in the heaven, how they do not change their orbits, and the luminaries which are in the heaven, how they all rise and set in order each in its season, and transgress not against their appointed order. 2 Behold you the earth and give heed to the things which take place upon it from first to last, how steadfast they are, how none of the things upon earth change, but all the works of God appear to you. 3 Behold the summer and the winter, how the whole earth is filled with water, and clouds and dew and rain lie upon it.

CHAPTER 3

1 Observe and see how (in the winter) all the trees seem as though they had withered and shed all their leaves, 2 except fourteen trees, which do not lose their foliage but retain the old foliage from two to three years until the new comes.

CHAPTER 4

1 And again, observe you the days of summer how the sun is above the earth over against it. 2 And you seek shade and shelter by reason of the heat of the sun, and the earth also burns with growing heat, and so you cannot tread on the earth, or on a rock by reason of its heat.

CHAPTER 5

1 Observe you how the trees cover themselves with green leaves and bear fruit: for what reason give you heed and know with regard to all His works and recognize how He that lives forever has made them so. 2 And all His works go on like this from year to year forever, and all the tasks which they accomplish for Him,

and their tasks change not, but according as God has ordained so is it done. **3** And behold how the sea and the rivers in like manner accomplish and change not their tasks from His commandments. **4** But you have not been steadfast, nor done the commandments of the Lord, but you have turned away and spoken proud and hard words with your impure mouths against His greatness. Oh, you hard-hearted, you will find no peace. **5** Therefore will you execrate your days, and the years of your life will perish, and the years of your destruction will be multiplied in eternal execration, and you will find no mercy. **6** In those days you will make your names an eternal execration unto all the righteous, and by you will all who curse, curse, and all the sinners and godless will imprecate by you, and for you the godless there will be a curse. And all the [righteous] will rejoice, and there will be forgiveness of sins, and every mercy and peace and forbearance: There will be salvation unto them, a goodly light. And for all of you sinners there will be no salvation, but on you all will abide a curse. **7** But for the elect there will be light and joy and peace, and they will inherit the earth. **8** And then there will be bestowed upon the elect wisdom, and they will all live and never again sin, either through ungodliness or through pride: But they who are wise will be humble. **9** And they will not again transgress, nor will they sin all the days of their life, nor will they die of (the divine) anger or wrath, but they will complete the number of the days of their life. And their lives will be increased in peace, and the years of their joy will be multiplied, in eternal gladness and peace, all the days of their life.

CHAPTER 6

1 And it came to pass when the children of men had multiplied that in those days were born unto them beautiful and comely daughters. **2** And the angels, the children of the heaven, saw and lusted after them, and said to one another: "Come, let us choose us wives from among the children of men and beget us children." **3** And Semjaza, who was their leader, said unto them: "I fear you will not indeed agree to do this deed, and I alone will have to pay the penalty of a great sin." **4** And they all answered him and said: "Let us all swear an oath, and all bind ourselves by mutual imprecations not to abandon this plan but to do this thing." **5** Then swore they all together and bound themselves by mutual

imprecations upon it. **6** And they were in all two hundred; who descended in the days of Jared on the summit of Mount Hermon, and they called it Mount Hermon, because they had sworn and bound themselves by mutual imprecations upon it. **7** And these are the names of their leaders: Samlazaz, their leader, Araklba, Rameel, Kokablel, Tamlel, Ramlel, Danel, Ezeqeel, Baraqijal, Asael, Armaros, Batarel, Ananel, Zaqiel, Samsapeel, Satarel, Turel, Jomjael, Sariel. **8** These are their chiefs of tens.

CHAPTER 7

1 And all the others together with them took unto themselves wives, and each chose for himself one, and they began to go in unto them and to defile themselves with them, and they taught them charms and enchantments, and the cutting of roots, and made them acquainted with plants. **2** And they became pregnant, and they bare great giants, whose height was three thousand ells: **3** Who consumed all the acquisitions of men. And when men could no longer sustain them, **4** the giants turned against them and devoured mankind. **5** And they began to sin against birds, and beasts, and reptiles, and fish, and to devour one another's flesh, and drink the blood. **6** Then the earth laid accusation against the lawless ones.

CHAPTER 8

1 And Azazel taught men to make swords, and knives, and shields, and breastplates, and made known to them the metals of the earth and the art of working them, and bracelets, and ornaments, and the use of antimony, and the beautifying of the eyelids, and all kinds of costly stones, and all coloring tinctures. **2** And there arose much godlessness, and they committed fornication, and they were led astray, and became corrupt in all their ways. **3** Semjaza taught enchantments, and root-cuttings, 'Armaros the resolving of enchantments, Baraqijal (taught) astrology, Kokabel the constellations, Ezeqeel the knowledge of the clouds, Araqiel the signs of the earth, Shamsiel the signs of the sun, and Sariel the course of the moon. And as men perished, they cried, and their cry went up to heaven.

CHAPTER 9

1 And then Michael, Uriel, Raphael, and Gabriel looked down from heaven and saw much blood being shed upon the earth, and all lawlessness being wrought upon the earth. 2 And they said one to another: "The earth made without inhabitant cries the voice of their crying up to the gates of heaven." 3 And now to you, the holy ones of heaven, the souls of men make their suit, saying, "Bring our cause before the Most High." 4 And they said to the Lord of the ages: "Lord of lords, God of gods, King of kings, and God of the ages, the throne of Your glory stands unto all the generations of the ages, and Your name holy and glorious and blessed unto all the ages! 5 You have made all things and have power over all things: and all things are naked and open in Your sight, and You see all things, and nothing can hide itself from You. 6 You see what Azazel has done, who has taught all unrighteousness on earth and revealed the eternal secrets which were (preserved) in heaven, which men were striving to learn: 7 And Semjaza, to whom You have given authority to bear rule over his associates. 8 And they have gone to the daughters of men upon the earth, and have slept with the women, and have defiled themselves, and revealed to them all kinds of sins. 9 And the women have borne giants, and the whole earth has thereby been filled with blood and unrighteousness. 10 And now, behold, the souls of those who have died are crying and making their suit to the gates of heaven, and their lamentations have ascended: and cannot cease because of the lawless deeds which are wrought on the earth. 11 And You know all things before they come to pass, and You see these things and You do suffer them, and You do not say to us what we are to do to them in regard to these."

CHAPTER 10

1 Then said the Most High, the Holy and Great One spoke, and sent Uriel to the son of Lamech, and said to him: 2 "Go to Noah and tell him in my name 'Hide yourself!' and reveal to him the end that is approaching: that the whole earth will be destroyed, and a deluge is about to come upon the whole earth and will destroy all that is on it. 3 And now instruct him that he may escape and his seed may be preserved for all the generations of the world." 4 And again, the Lord said to Raphael: "Bind Azazel hand and foot and cast him into the darkness: and make an opening in the desert, which is in Dudael, and cast him therein. 5 And place upon him rough and jagged rocks, and cover him with darkness, and let him abide there forever, and cover his face that he may

not see light. 6 And on the day of the great judgement he will be cast into the fire. 7 And heal the earth which the angels have corrupted, and proclaim the healing of the earth, that they may heal the plague, and that all the children of men may not perish through all the secret things that the Watchers have disclosed and have taught their sons. 8 And the whole earth has been corrupted through the works that were taught by Azazel: to him ascribe all sin." 9 And to Gabriel said the Lord: "Proceed against the bastards and the reprobates, and against the children of fornication: and destroy [the children of fornication and] the children of the Watchers from among men [and cause them to go out]: send them one against the other that they may destroy each other in battle: for length of days will they not have. 10 And no request that they (i.e. their fathers) make of you will be granted unto their fathers on their behalf; for they hope to live an eternal life, and that each one of them will live five hundred years." 11 And the Lord said unto Michael: "Go, bind Semjaza and his associates who have united themselves with women so as to have defiled themselves with them in all their uncleanness. 12 And when their sons have slain one another, and they have seen the destruction of their beloved ones, bind them fast for seventy generations in the valleys of the earth, until the day of their judgement and of their consummation, until the judgement that is for ever and ever is consummated. 13 In those days they will be led off to the abyss of fire: and to the torment and the prison in which they will be confined forever. 14 And whosoever will be condemned and destroyed will from then on be bound together with them to the end of all generations. 15 And destroy all the spirits of the reprobate and the children of the Watchers, because they have wronged mankind. 16 Destroy all wrong from the face of the earth and let every evil work come to an end: and let the plant of righteousness and truth appear: and it will prove a blessing; the works of righteousness and truth will be planted in truth and joy forevermore. 17 And then will all the righteous escape and will live until they beget thousands of children and all the days of their youth and their old age will they complete in peace. 18 And then will the whole earth be tilled in righteousness and will all be planted with trees and be full of blessing. 19 And all desirable trees will be planted on it, and they will plant vines on it: and the vine which they plant thereon will yield wine in abundance, and as for all the seed which is sown thereon each measure (of it) will bear a thousand, and each measure of olives will yield ten presses of oil. **20** And You will cleanse the earth from all oppression, and from all unrighteousness, and from all sin, and from all godlessness: and all the uncleanness that is wrought upon the earth destroy from off the earth. **21** And all the children of men will become righteous, and all nations will offer adoration and will praise Me, and all will worship Me. **22** And the earth will be cleansed from all defilement, and from all sin, and from all punishment, and from all torment, and I will never again send (them) upon it from generation to generation and forever."

CHAPTER 11

1 "And in those days I will open the store chambers of blessing which are in the heaven, so as to send them down upon the earth over the work and labor of the children of men. **2** And truth and peace will be associated together throughout all the days of the world and throughout all the generations of men."

CHAPTER 12

1 Before these things Enoch was hidden, and no one of the children of men knew where he was hidden, and where he dwelt, and what had become of him. **2** And his activities had to do with the Watchers, and his days were with the holy ones. **3** And I Enoch was blessing the Lord of majesty and the King of the ages, and the Watchers called me—Enoch the scribe— and said to me: **4** "Enoch, you scribe of righteousness, go, declare to the Watchers of the heaven who have left the high heaven, the holy eternal place, and have defiled themselves with women, and have done as the children of earth do, and have taken unto themselves wives: **5** 'You have wrought great destruction on the earth: And you will have no peace nor forgiveness of sin: **6** and inasmuch as they delight themselves in their children, the murder of their beloved ones will they see, and over the destruction of their children will they lament, and will make supplication unto eternity, but mercy and peace will you not attain.' "

CHAPTER 13

1 And Enoch went and said: "Azazel, you will have no peace: a severe sentence has gone out against you to put you in bonds: **2** And you will not have toleration nor request granted to you, because of the unrighteousness which you have taught, and because of all the works of godlessness and unrighteousness and sin which you have shown to men." **3** Then I went and spoke to them all together, and they were all afraid, and fear and trembling seized them. **4** And they besought me to draw up a petition for them that they might find forgiveness, and to read their petition in the presence of the Lord of heaven. **5** For from that point forward they could not speak (with Him) nor lift up their eyes to heaven for shame of their sins for which they had been condemned. **6** Then I wrote out their petition, and the prayer in regard to their spirits and their deeds individually and in regard to their requests that they should have forgiveness and length. **7** And I went off and sat down at the waters of Dan, in the land of Dan, to the south of the west of Hermon: I read their petition until I fell asleep. **8** And behold a dream came to me, and visions fell down upon me, and I saw visions of chastisement, and a voice came bidding me to tell it to the sons of heaven and reprimand them. **9** And when I awaked, I came unto them, and they were all sitting gathered together, weeping in 'Abelsjail, which is between Lebanon and Seneser, with their faces covered. **10** And I recounted before them all the visions which I had seen in sleep, and I began to speak the words of righteousness, and to reprimand the heavenly Watchers.

CHAPTER 14

1 The book of the words of righteousness, and of the reprimand of the eternal Watchers in accordance with the command of the Holy Great One in that vision. **2** I saw in my sleep what I will now say with a tongue of flesh and with the breath of my mouth: which the Great One has given to men to converse therewith and understand with the heart. **3** As He has created and given to man the power of understanding the word of wisdom, so has He created me also and given me the power of reprimanding the Watchers, the children of heaven. **4** I wrote out your petition, and in my vision it appeared like this, that your petition will not be granted unto you throughout all the days of eternity, and that judgement has been finally passed upon you: yea (your petition) will not be granted unto you. **5** And from now on you will not ascend into heaven unto all eternity, and in bonds of the earth the decree has gone out to bind you for all the days of the world. **6** And (that) previously you will have seen the destruction of your beloved sons and you will have no pleasure in them, but they will fall before you by the sword. **7** And your petition on their behalf will not be granted, nor yet on your own: even though you weep and pray and speak all the words contained in the writing which I have written. **8** And the vision was shown to me like this: Behold, in the vision clouds invited me and a mist summoned me, and the course of the stars and the lightnings sped towards me, and the winds in the vision caused me to fly and lifted me upward and bore me into heaven. **9** And I went in until I drew nigh to a wall which is built of crystals and surrounded by tongues of fire: and it began to affright me. **10** And I went into the tongues of fire and drew nigh to a large house which was built of crystals: and the walls of the house were like a tessellated floor (made) of crystals, and its groundwork was of crystal. **11** Its ceiling was like the path of the stars and the lightnings, and between them were fiery cherubim, and their heaven was (clear as) water. **12** A flaming fire surrounded the walls, and its portals blazed with fire. **13** And I entered into that house, and it was hot as fire and cold as ice: there **14** were no delights of life therein: fear covered me, and trembling got hold upon me. **15** And as I quaked and trembled, I fell upon my face. And I beheld a vision, and, behold, there was a second house, greater than the former, and the entire portal stood open before me, and it was built of flames of fire. **16** And in every respect it so excelled in splendor and magnificence and extent that I cannot describe to you its splendor and its extent. **17** And its floor was of fire, and above it were lightnings and the path of the stars, and its ceiling also was flaming fire. **18** And I looked and saw therein a lofty throne: its appearance was as crystal, and the wheels thereof as the shining sun, and there was the vision of cherubim. **19** And from underneath the throne came streams of flaming fire so that I could not look thereon. **20** And the Great Glory sat thereon, and His raiment shone more brightly than the sun and was whiter than any snow. **21** None of the angels could enter and could behold His face by reason of the magnificence and glory and no flesh could behold Him. **22** The flaming fire was around Him, and a great fire stood before Him, and none around could draw nigh Him: ten thousand times ten thousand (stood) before Him, yet He needed no counselor. **23** And the most holy ones who were nigh to Him did not leave by night nor depart from Him. **24** And until then I had been prostrate on my face, trembling: and the Lord called me with His own mouth, and said to me: "Come here, Enoch, and hear my word." **25** And one of the holy ones came to me and waked me, and He made me rise up and approach the door: and I bowed my face downwards.

CHAPTER 15

1 And He answered and said to me, and I heard His voice: "Fear not, Enoch, you righteous man and scribe of righteousness: approach here and hear my voice. **2** And go, say to the Watchers of heaven, who have sent you to intercede for them: 'You should intercede for men, and not men for you': **3** Why have you left the high, holy, and eternal heaven, and lain with women, and defiled yourselves with the daughters of men and taken to yourselves wives, and done like the children of earth, and begotten giants (as your) sons? **4** And though you were holy, spiritual, living the eternal life, you have defiled yourselves with the blood of women, and have begotten (children) with the blood of flesh, and, as the children of men, have lusted after flesh and blood as those also do who die and perish. **5** Therefore have I given them wives also that they might impregnate them, and beget children by them, that nothing might be wanting to them on earth. **6** But you were formerly spiritual, living the eternal life, and immortal for all generations of the world. **7** And therefore I have not appointed wives for you; for as for the spiritual ones of the heaven, in heaven is their dwelling. **8** And now, the giants, who are produced from the spirits and flesh, will be called evil spirits upon the earth, and on the earth will be their dwelling. **9** Evil spirits have proceeded from their bodies; because they are born from men and from the holy Watchers is their beginning and primal origin; they will be evil spirits on earth, and evil spirits will they be called. **10** [As for the spirits of heaven, in heaven will be their dwelling, but as for the spirits of the earth which were born upon the earth, on the earth will be their dwelling.] **11** And the spirits of the giants afflict, oppress, destroy, attack, do battle, and work destruction on the earth, and cause trouble: they take no food, but nevertheless hunger and thirst, and cause offences. **12** And these spirits will rise up against the children of men and against the women, because they have proceeded from them."

CHAPTER 16

1 From the days of the slaughter and destruction and death of the giants, from the souls of whose flesh the spirits, having gone out, will destroy without incurring judgement -therefore will they destroy until the day of the consummation, the great judgement in which the age will be consummated, over the Watchers and the godless, yea, will be wholly consummated. **2** And now as to the watchers who have sent you to intercede for them, who had been previously in heaven, (say to them): **3** "You have been in heaven, but all the mysteries had not yet been revealed to you, and you knew worthless ones, and these in the hardness of your hearts you have made known to the women, and through these mysteries women and men work much evil on earth." **4** Say to them therefore: "You have no peace."

CHAPTER 17

1 And they took and brought me to a place in which those who were there were like flaming fire, and, when they wished, they appeared as men. **2** And they brought me to the place of darkness, and to a mountain the point of whose summit reached to heaven. **3** And I saw the places of the luminaries and the treasuries of the stars and of the thunder and in the uttermost depths, where were a fiery bow and arrows and their quiver, and a fiery sword and all the lightnings. **4** And they took me to the living waters, and to the fire of the west, which receives every setting of the sun. **5** And I came to a river of fire in which the fire flows like water and discharges itself into the great sea towards the west. **6** I saw the great rivers and came to the great river and to the great darkness and went to the place where no flesh walks. **7** I saw the mountains of the darkness of winter and the place from where all the waters of the deep flow. **8** I saw the mouths of all the rivers of the earth and the mouth of the deep.

CHAPTER 18

1 I saw the treasuries of all the winds: I saw how He had furnished with them the whole creation and the firm foundations of the earth. **2** And I saw the corner-stone of the earth: I saw the four winds which bear [the earth and] the firmament of the heaven. **3** And I saw how the winds stretch out the vaults of heaven and

have their station between heaven and earth: these are the pillars of the heaven. **4** I saw the winds of heaven which turn and bring the circumference of the sun and all the stars to their setting. **5** I saw the winds on the earth carrying the clouds: I saw the paths of the angels. **6** I saw at the end of the earth the firmament of the heaven above. And I proceeded and saw a place which burns day and night, where there are seven mountains of magnificent stones, three towards the east, and three towards the south. **7** And as for those towards the east, was of colored stone, and one of pearl, and one of jacinth, and those towards the south of red stone. **8** But the middle one reached to heaven like the throne of God, of alabaster, and the summit of the throne was of sapphire. **9** And I saw a flaming fire. **10** And beyond these mountains is a region at the end of the great earth: there the heavens were completed. **11** And I saw a deep abyss, with columns of heavenly fire, and among them I saw columns of fire fall, which were beyond measure alike towards the height and towards the depth. **12** And beyond that abyss I saw a place which had no firmament of the heaven above, and no firmly founded earth beneath it: there was no water upon it, and no birds, but it was a waste and horrible place. **13** I saw there seven stars like great burning mountains, and to me, when I inquired regarding them, **14** the angel said: "This place is the end of heaven and earth: this has become a prison for the stars and the host of heaven. **15** And the stars which roll over the fire are they which have transgressed the commandment of the Lord in the beginning of their rising, because they did not come out at their appointed times. **16** And He was angry with them and bound them until the time when their guilt should be consummated (even) for ten thousand years."

CHAPTER 19

1 And Uriel said to me: 'Here will stand the angels who have connected themselves with women, and their spirits assuming many different forms are defiling mankind and will lead them astray into sacrificing to demons as gods, (here will they stand,) until the day of the great judgement in which they will be judged until they are made an end of. **2** And the women also of the angels who went astray will become sirens.' **3** And I, Enoch, alone saw the vision, the ends of all things: and no man will see as I have seen.

CHAPTER 20

1 And these are the names of the holy angels who watch. 2 Uriel, one of the holy angels, who is over the world and over Tartarus. 3 Raphael, one of the holy angels, who is over the spirits of men. 4 Raguel, one of the holy angels who takes vengeance on the world of the luminaries. 5 Michael, one of the holy angels, to wit, he that is set over the best part of mankind and over chaos. 6 Saraqael, one of the holy angels, who is set over the spirits, who sin in the spirit. 7 Gabriel, one of the holy angels, who is over Paradise and the serpents and the Cherubim. 8 Remiel, one of the holy angels, whom God set over those who rise.

CHAPTER 21

1 And I proceeded to where things were chaotic. 2 And I saw there something horrible: I saw neither a heaven above nor a firmly founded earth, but a place chaotic and horrible. 3 And there I saw seven stars of the heaven bound together in it, like great mountains and burning with fire. 4 Then I said: "For what sin are they bound, and on what account have they been cast in here?" 5 Then said Uriel, one of the holy angels, who was with me, and was chief over them, and said: "Enoch, why do you ask, and why are you eager for the truth? 6 These are of the number of the stars of heaven, which have transgressed the commandment of the Lord, and are bound here until ten thousand years, the time entailed by their sins, are consummated." 7 And from there I went to another place, which was still more horrible than the former, and I saw a horrible thing: a great fire there which burnt and blazed, and the place was cleft as far as the abyss, being full of great descending columns of fire: neither its extent or magnitude could I see, nor could I conjecture. 8 Then I said: "How fearful is the place and how terrible to look upon!" 9 Then Uriel answered me, one of the holy angels who was with me, and said unto me: "Enoch, why have you such fear and affright?" And I answered: "Because of this fearful place, and because of the spectacle of the pain." 10 And he said unto me: "This place is the prison of the angels, and here they will be imprisoned forever."

CHAPTER 22

1 And then I went to another place—the mountain of hard rock. 2 And there was in it four hollow places, deep and wide and very smooth. How smooth are the hollow places and deep and dark to look at. 3 Then Raphael answered, one of the holy angels who was with me, and said unto me: "These hollow places have been created for this very purpose, that the spirits of the souls of the dead should assemble therein, yea that all the souls of the children of men should assemble here. 4 And these places have been made to receive them until the day of their judgement and until their appointed period [till the period appointed], until the great judgement (comes) upon them." 5 I saw (the spirit of) a dead man making suit, and his voice went out to heaven and made suit. 6 And I asked Raphael the angel who was with me, and I said unto him: "This spirit which makes suit, whose is it, whose voice goes out and makes suit to heaven?" 7 And he answered me saying: "This is the spirit which went out from Abel, whom his brother Cain slew, and he makes his suit against him until his seed is destroyed from the face of the earth, and his seed is annihilated from among the seed of men." 8 Then I asked regarding it, and regarding all the hollow places: "Why is one separated from the other?" 9 And he answered me and said unto me: "These three have been made that the spirits of the dead might be separated. And such a division has been made (for) the spirits of the righteous, in which there is the bright spring of water. 10 And such has been made for sinners when they die and are buried in the earth and judgement has not been executed on them in their lifetime. 11 Here their spirits will be set apart in this great pain until the great day of judgement and punishment and torment of those who curse forever and retribution for their spirits. 12 There He will bind them forever. And such a division has been made for the spirits of those who make their suit, who make disclosures concerning their destruction, when they were slain in the days of the sinners. 13 Such has been made for the spirits of men who were not righteous but sinners, who were complete in transgression, and of the transgressors they will be companions: but their spirits will not be slain in the day of judgement nor will they be raised from there." 14 Then I blessed the Lord of glory and said: "Blessed be my Lord, the Lord of righteousness, who rules forever."

CHAPTER 23

1 From there I went to another place to the west of the ends of the earth. 2 And I saw a burning fire which ran without resting and

paused not from its course day or night but (ran) regularly. **3** And I asked saying: "What is this which rests not?" **4** Then Raguel, one of the holy angels who was with me, answered me and said unto me: "This course of fire which you have seen is the fire in the west which persecutes all the luminaries of heaven."

CHAPTER 24

1 And from there I went to another place of the earth, and he showed me a mountain range of fire which burnt day and night. **2** And I went beyond it and saw seven magnificent mountains all differing each from the other, and the stones (thereof) were magnificent and beautiful, magnificent as a whole, of glorious appearance and fair exterior: three towards the east, one founded on the other, and three towards the south, one upon the other, and deep rough ravines, no one of which joined with any other. **3** And the seventh mountain was in the midst of these, and it excelled them in height, resembling the seat of a throne: and fragrant trees encircled the throne. **4** And among them was a tree such as I had never yet smelt, neither was any among them nor were others like it: it had a fragrance beyond all fragrance, and its leaves and blooms and wood wither not forever: and its fruit is beautiful, and its fruit n resembles the dates of a palm. **5** Then I said: "How beautiful is this tree, and fragrant, and its leaves are fair, and its blooms very delightful in appearance." **6** Then answered Michael, one of the holy and honored angels who was with me and was their leader.

CHAPTER 25

1 And he said unto me: "Enoch, why do you ask me regarding the fragrance of the tree, and why do you wish to learn the truth?" **2** Then I answered him saying: "I wish to know about everything, but especially about this tree." **3** And he answered saying: "This high mountain which you have seen, whose summit is like the throne of God, is His throne, where the Holy Great One, the Lord of Glory, the Eternal King, will sit, when He will come down to visit the earth with goodness. **4** And as for this fragrant tree no mortal is permitted to touch it until the great judgement, when He will take vengeance on all and bring (everything) to its consummation forever. **5** It will then be given to the righteous and holy. Its fruit will be for food to the elect: it will be

transplanted to the holy place, to the temple of the Lord, the Eternal King. **6** Then will they rejoice with joy and be glad, and into the holy place will they enter; And its fragrance will be in their bones, and they will live a long life on earth, such as your fathers lived: And in their days will no sorrow or plague Or torment or calamity touch them." **7** Then I blessed the God of Glory, the Eternal King, who has prepared such things for the righteous, and has created them and promised to give to them.

CHAPTER 26

1 And I went from there to the middle of the earth, and I saw a blessed place in which there were trees with branches abiding and blooming [of a dismembered tree]. **2** And there I saw a holy mountain, and underneath the mountain to the east there was a stream and it flowed towards the south. **3** And I saw towards the east another mountain higher than this, and between them a deep and narrow ravine: in it also ran a stream underneath the mountain. **4** And to the west thereof there was another mountain, lower than the former and of small elevation, and a ravine deep and dry between them: and another deep and dry ravine was at the extremities of the three mountains. **5** And all the ravines were deep and narrow, (being formed) of hard rock, and trees were not planted upon them. **6** And I marveled at the rocks, and I marveled at the ravine, yea, I marveled very much.

CHAPTER 27

1 Then I said: "For what object is this blessed land, which is entirely filled with trees, and this accursed valley between?" **2** Then Uriel, one of the holy angels who was with me, answered and said: "This accursed valley is for those who are accursed forever: Here will all the accursed be gathered together who utter with their lips against the Lord unseemly words and of His glory speak hard things. Here will they be gathered together, and here will be their place of judgement. **3** In the last days there will be upon them the spectacle of righteous judgement in the presence of the righteous forever: here will the merciful bless the Lord of glory, the Eternal King. **4** In the days of judgement over the former, they will bless Him for the mercy in accordance with which He has assigned them (their lot)." **5** Then I blessed the Lord of Glory and set out His glory and lauded Him gloriously.

CHAPTER 28

1 And then I went towards the east, into the midst of the mountain range of the desert, and I saw a wilderness and it was solitary, full of trees and plants. 2 And water gushed out from above. 3 Rushing like a copious watercourse [which flowed] towards the north-west it caused clouds and dew to ascend on every side.

CHAPTER 29

1 And then I went to another place in the desert and approached to the east of this mountain range. 2 And there I saw aromatic trees exhaling the fragrance of frankincense and myrrh, and the trees also were similar to the almond tree.

CHAPTER 30

1 And beyond these, I went afar to the east, and I saw another place, a valley (full) of water. 2 And therein there was a tree, the color of fragrant trees such as the mastic. 3 And on the sides of those valleys I saw fragrant cinnamon. And beyond these I proceeded to the east.

CHAPTER 31

1 And I saw other mountains, and among them were groves of trees, and there flowed out from them nectar, which is called sarara and galbanum. 2 And beyond these mountains I saw another mountain to the east of the ends of the earth, on which were aloe-trees, and all the trees were full of stacte, being like almond-trees. 3 And when one burnt it, it smelt sweeter than any fragrant odor.

CHAPTER 32

1 And after these fragrant odors, as I looked towards the north over the mountains I saw seven mountains full of choice nard and fragrant trees and cinnamon and pepper. 2 And then I went over the summits of all these mountains, far towards the east of the earth, and passed above the Erythraean sea and went far from it and passed over the angel Zotiel. 3 And I came to the Garden of Righteousness and saw beyond those trees many large trees growing there and of goodly fragrance, large, very beautiful and glorious, and the tree of wisdom whereof they eat and know great wisdom. 4 That tree is in height like the fir, and its leaves are like (those of) the Carob tree: and its fruit is like the clusters of the vine, very beautiful: and the fragrance of the tree penetrates afar. 5 Then I said: "How beautiful

is the tree, and how attractive is its look!" 6 Then Raphael the holy angel, who was with me, answered me and said: "This is the tree of wisdom, of which your father old (in years) and your aged mother, who were before you, have eaten, and they learnt wisdom and their eyes were opened, and they knew that they were naked, and they were driven out of the garden."

CHAPTER 33

1 And from there I went to the ends of the earth and saw there great beasts, and each differed from the other; and (I saw) birds also differing in appearance and beauty and voice, the one differing from the other. 2 And to the east of those beasts I saw the ends of the earth on which the heaven rests, and the portals of the heaven open. 3 And I saw how the stars of heaven come out, and I counted the portals out of which they proceed, and wrote down all their outlets, of each individual star by itself, according to their number and their names, their courses and their positions, and their times and their months, as Uriel the holy angel who was with me showed me. 4 He showed all things to me and wrote them down for me: also their names he wrote for me, and their laws and their companies.

CHAPTER 34

1 And from there I went towards the north to the ends of the earth, and there I saw a great and glorious device at the ends of the whole earth. 2 And here I saw three portals of heaven open in the heaven: through each of them proceed north winds: when they blow there is cold, hail, frost, snow, dew, and rain. 3 And out of one portal they blow for good: but when they blow through the other two portals, it is with violence and affliction on the earth, and they blow with violence.

CHAPTER 35

1 And from there I went towards the west to the ends of the earth and saw there three portals of the heaven open such as I had seen in the east, the same number of portals, and the same number of outlets.

CHAPTER 36

1 And from there I went to the south to the ends of the earth and saw there three open portals of the heaven: and then there came dew, rain, and wind. 2 And from there I went to the east to the ends of the heaven and saw

here the three eastern portals of heaven open and small portals above them. **3** Through each of these small portals pass the stars of heaven and run their course to the west on the path which is shown to them. **4** And as often as I saw I blessed always the Lord of Glory, and I continued to bless the Lord of Glory who has wrought great and glorious wonders, to show the greatness of His work to the angels and to spirits and to men, that they might praise His work and all His creation: that they might see the work of His might and praise the great work of His hands and bless Him forever.

SECTION 2:
THE BOOK OF PARABLES OF ENOCH

CHAPTER 37

1 The second vision which he saw, the vision of wisdom, which Enoch the son of Jared, the son of Mahalalel, the son of Cainan, the son of Enos, the son of Seth, the son of Adam, saw. **2** And this is the beginning of the words of wisdom which I lifted up my voice to speak and say to those which dwell on earth: Hear, you men of old time, and see, you that come after, the words of the Holy One which I will speak before the Lord of Spirits. **3** It were better to declare (them only) to the men of old time, but even from those that come after we will not withhold the beginning of wisdom. **4** Until the present day such wisdom has never been given by the Lord of Spirits as I have received according to my insight, according to the good pleasure of the Lord of Spirits by whom the lot of eternal life has been given to me. **5** Now three parables were imparted to me, and I lifted up my voice and recounted them to those that dwell on the earth.

CHAPTER 38

1 The first Parable. When the congregation of the righteous will appear, and sinners will be judged for their sins, and will be driven from the face of the earth: **2** And when the Righteous One will appear before the eyes of the righteous, whose elect works hang upon the Lord of Spirits, and light will appear to the righteous and the elect who dwell on the earth, where then will be the dwelling of the sinners, and where the resting-place of those who have denied the Lord of Spirits? It had been good for them if they had not been born. **3** When the secrets of the righteous will be revealed and the sinners judged, and the godless driven from the presence of the righteous and elect,

4 from that time those that possess the earth will no longer be powerful and exalted: And they will not be able to behold the face of the holy, for the Lord of Spirits has caused His light to appear on the face of the holy, righteous, and elect. **5** Then will the kings and the mighty perish and be given into the hands of the righteous and holy. **6** And from then on none will seek for themselves mercy from the Lord of Spirits For their life is at an end.

CHAPTER 39

1 [And it will come to pass in those days that elect and holy children will descend from the high heaven, and their seed will become one with the children of men. **2** And in those days Enoch received books of zeal and wrath, and books of disquiet and expulsion.] And mercy will not be accorded to them, says the Lord of Spirits. **3** And in those days a whirlwind carried me off from the earth and set me down at the end of the heavens. **4** And there I saw another vision, the dwelling-places of the holy, and the resting-places of the righteous. **5** Here mine eyes saw their dwellings with His righteous angels, and their resting-places with the holy. And they petitioned and interceded and prayed for the children of men, and righteousness flowed before them as water, and mercy like dew upon the earth: So it is among them forever and ever. **6** And in that place mine eyes saw the Elect One of righteousness and of faith, and I saw his dwelling-place under the wings of the Lord of Spirits. And righteousness will prevail in his days, and the righteous and elect will be without number before Him forever and ever. **7** And all the righteous and elect before Him will be strong as fiery lights, and their mouth will be full of blessing, and their lips extol the name of the Lord of Spirits, and righteousness before Him will never fail, [And uprightness will never fail before Him.] **8** There I wished to dwell, and my spirit longed for that dwelling-place: And there heretofore has been my portion, for so has it been established concerning me before the Lord of Spirits. **9** In those days I praised and extolled the name of the Lord of Spirits with blessings and praises, because He has destined me for blessing and glory according to the good pleasure of the Lord of Spirits. **10** For a long time my eyes regarded that place, and I blessed Him and praised Him, saying: "Blessed is He, and may He be blessed from the beginning and forevermore. And before Him there is no ceasing. He knows before the world was created what is forever and what will be from generation unto generation. **12** Those who sleep not bless You: they stand before Your glory and bless, praise, and extol, saying: 'Holy, holy, holy, is the Lord of Spirits: He fills the earth with spirits.' " And here my eyes saw all those who sleep not: they stand before Him and bless and say: "Blessed be You and blessed be the name of the Lord forever and ever." And my face was changed; for I could no longer behold.

CHAPTER 40

1 And after that I saw thousands of thousands and ten thousand times ten thousand, I saw a multitude beyond number and reckoning, who stood before the Lord of Spirits. **2** And on the four sides of the Lord of Spirits I saw four presences, different from those that sleep not, and I learnt their names: for the angel that went with me made known to me their names and showed me all the hidden things. **3** And I heard the voices of those four presences as they uttered praises before the Lord of glory. **4** The first voice blesses the Lord of Spirits forever and ever. **5** And the second voice I heard blessing the Elect One and the elect ones who hang upon the Lord of Spirits. **6** And the third voice I heard pray and intercede for those who dwell on the earth and supplicate in the name of the Lord of Spirits. **7** And I heard the fourth voice fending off the devils and forbidding them to come before the Lord of Spirits to accuse them who dwell on the earth. **8** After that I asked the angel of peace who went with me, who showed me everything that is hidden: "Who are these four presences which I have seen and whose words I have heard and written down?" **9** And he said to me: "This first is Michael, the merciful and long-suffering: and the second, who is set over all the diseases and all the wounds of the children of men, is Raphael: and the third, who is set over all the powers, is Gabriel: and the fourth, who is set over the repentance unto hope of those who inherit eternal life, is named Phanuel." **10** And these are the four angels of the Lord of Spirits and the four voices I heard in those days.

CHAPTER 41

1 And after that I saw all the secrets of the heavens, and how the kingdom is divided, and how the actions of men are weighed in the balance. **2** And there I saw the mansions of the elect and the mansions of the holy, and mine eyes saw there all the sinners being driven from there which deny the name of the Lord of Spirits and being dragged off: and they could not abide because of the punishment which proceeds from the Lord of Spirits. **3** And there mine eyes saw the secrets of the lightning and of the thunder, and the secrets of the winds, how they are divided to blow over the earth, and the secrets of the clouds and dew, and there I saw from where they proceed in that place and from where they saturate the dusty earth. **4** And there I saw closed chambers out of which the winds are divided, the chamber of the hail and winds, the chamber of the mist, and of the clouds, and the cloud thereof hovers over the earth from the beginning of the world. **5** And I saw the chambers of the sun and moon, from where they proceed and where they come again, and their glorious return, and how one is superior to the other, and their stately orbit, and how they do not leave their orbit, and they add nothing to their orbit and they take nothing from it, and they keep faith with each other, in accordance with the oath by which they are bound together. **6** And first the sun goes out and traverses his path according to the commandment of the Lord of Spirits, and mighty is His name forever and ever. **7** And after that I saw the hidden and the visible path of the moon, and she accomplishes the course of her path in that place by day and by night-the one holding a position opposite to the other before the Lord of Spirits. And they give thanks and praise and rest not; For unto them is their thanksgiving rest. **8** For the sun changes oft for a blessing or a curse, and the course of the path of the moon is light to the righteous and darkness to the sinners in the name of the Lord, who made a separation between the light and the darkness, and divided the spirits of men, and strengthened the spirits of the righteous, In the name of His righteousness. **9** For no angel hinders and no power is able to hinder; for He appoints a judge for them all and He judges them all before Him.

CHAPTER 42

1 Wisdom found no place where she might dwell; Then a dwelling-place was assigned her in the heavens. **2** Wisdom went out to make her dwelling among the children of men and found no dwelling-place: Wisdom returned to her place and took her seat among the angels. **3** And unrighteousness went out from her chambers: Whom she sought not she found, and dwelt with them, as rain in a desert and dew on a thirsty land.

CHAPTER 43

1 And I saw other lightnings and the stars of heaven, and I saw how He called them all by their names and they hearkened unto Him. 2 And I saw how they are weighed in a righteous balance according to their proportions of light: (I saw) the width of their spaces and the day of their appearing, and how their revolution produces lightning: and (I saw) their revolution according to the number of the angels, and (how) they keep faith with each other. 3 And I asked the angel who went with me who showed me what was hidden: "What are these?" 4 And he said to me: "The Lord of Spirits has showed you their parabolic meaning: these are the names of the holy who dwell on the earth and believe in the name of the Lord of Spirits forever and ever."

CHAPTER 44

1 Also another phenomenon I saw in regard to the lightnings: how some of the stars arise and become lightnings and cannot part with their new form.

CHAPTER 45

1 And this is the second parable concerning those who deny the name of the dwelling of the holy ones and the Lord of Spirits. 2 And into the heaven they will not ascend, and on the earth they will not come: Such will be the lot of the sinners who have denied the name of the Lord of Spirits, who are therefore preserved for the day of suffering and tribulation. 3 On that day Mine Elect One will sit on the throne of glory and will try their works, and their places of rest will be innumerable. And their souls will grow strong within them when they see Mine Elect Ones, and those who have called upon My glorious name: 4 Then will I cause Mine Elect One to dwell among them. And I will transform the heaven and make it an eternal blessing and light and I will transform the earth and make it a blessing: 5 And I will cause Mine elect ones to dwell upon it: But the sinners and evil-doers will not set foot thereon. 6 For I have provided and satisfied with peace My righteous ones and have caused them to dwell before Me: But for the sinners there is judgement impending with Me, so that I will destroy them from the face of the earth.

CHAPTER 46

1 And there I saw One who had a head of days, and His head was white like wool, and with Him was another being whose countenance had the appearance of a man, and his face was full of graciousness, like one of the holy angels. 2 And I asked the angel who went with me and showed me all the hidden things, concerning that Son of Man, who he was, and from where he was, (and) why he went with the Head of Days? 3 And he answered and said unto me: "This is the Son of Man who has righteousness, with whom dwells righteousness, and who reveals all the treasures of that which is hidden, because the Lord of Spirits has chosen him, and whose lot has the pre-eminence before the Lord of Spirits in uprightness forever. 4 And this Son of Man whom you have seen will raise up the kings and the mighty from their seats, [And the strong from their thrones] and will loosen the reins of the strong and break the teeth of the sinners. 5 [And he will put down the kings from their thrones and kingdoms] Because they do not extol and praise Him, nor humbly acknowledge from where the kingdom was bestowed upon them. 6 And he will put down the countenance of the strong and will fill them with shame. And darkness will be their dwelling, and worms will be their bed, and they will have no hope of rising from their beds, because they do not extol the name of the Lord of Spirits. 7 [And raise their hands against the Most High], and tread upon the earth and dwell upon it. And all their deeds manifest unrighteousness, and their power rests upon their riches, and their faith is in the gods which they have made with their hands, and they deny the name of the Lord of Spirits, 8 And they persecute the houses of His congregations, and the faithful who hang upon the name of the Lord of Spirits.

CHAPTER 47

1 And in those days will have ascended the prayer of the righteous, and the blood of the righteous from the earth before the Lord of Spirits. 2 In those days the holy ones who dwell above in the heavens Will unite with one voice and supplicate and pray [and praise and give thanks and bless the name of the Lord of Spirits On behalf of the blood of the righteous which has been shed, and that the prayer of the righteous may not be in vain before the Lord of Spirits, that judgement may be done unto them, and that they may not have to suffer

forever. **3** In those days I saw the Head of Days when He seated himself upon the throne of His glory, and the books of the living were opened before Him: And all His host which is in heaven above and His counselors stood before Him, **4** And the hearts of the holy were filled with joy; Because the number of the righteous had been offered, and the prayer of the righteous had been heard, and the blood of the righteous been required before the Lord of Spirits.

CHAPTER 48

1 And in that place I saw the fountain of righteousness which was inexhaustible: And around it were may fountains of wisdom: And all the thirsty drank of them, and were filled with wisdom, and their dwellings were with the righteous and holy and elect. **2** And at that hour that Son of Man was named in the presence of the Lord of Spirits, and his name before the Head of Days. **3** Yea, before the sun and the signs were created, before the stars of the heaven were made, His name was named before the Lord of Spirits. **4** He will be a staff to the righteous on which to stay themselves and not fall, and he will be the light of the Gentiles, and the hope of those who are troubled of heart. **5** All who dwell on earth will fall down and worship before him and will praise and bless and celebrate with song the Lord of Spirits. **6** And for this reason has he been chosen and hidden before Him, before the creation of the world and forevermore. **7** And the wisdom of the Lord of Spirits has revealed him to the holy and righteous; For he has preserved the lot of the righteous, because they have hated and despised this world of unrighteousness and have hated all its works and ways in the name of the Lord of Spirits: For in his name they are saved, and according to his good pleasure has it been in regard to their life. **8** In these days downcast in countenance will the kings of the earth have become, and the strong who possess the land because of the works of their hands, for on the day of their anguish and affliction they will not (be able to) save themselves. And I will give them over into the hands of Mine elect: **9** As straw in the fire so will they burn before the face of the holy: As lead in the water will they sink before the face of the righteous, and no trace of them will any more be found. **10** And on the day of their affliction there will be rest on the earth, and before them they will fall and not rise again: And there will be no one to take

them with his hands and raise them: For they have denied the Lord of Spirits and His Anointed. The name of the Lord of Spirits be blessed.

CHAPTER 49

1 For wisdom is poured out like water, and glory fails not before him forevermore. **2** For he is mighty in all the secrets of righteousness, and unrighteousness will disappear as a shadow, and have no continuance; Because the Elect One stands before the Lord of Spirits, and his glory is forever and ever, and his might unto all generations. **3** And in him dwells the spirit of wisdom, and the spirit which gives insight, and the spirit of understanding and of might, and the spirit of those who have fallen asleep in righteousness. **4** And he will judge the secret things, and none will be able to utter a lying word before him; For he is the Elect One before the Lord of Spirits according to His good pleasure.

CHAPTER 50

1 And in those days a change will take place for the holy and elect, and the light of days will abide upon them, and glory and honor will turn to the holy, on the day of affliction on which evil will have been treasured up against the sinners. **2** And the righteous will be victorious in the name of the Lord of Spirits: And He will cause the others to witness (this) that they may repent and forgo the works of their hands. **3** They will have no honor through the name of the Lord of Spirits, yet through His name will they be saved, and the Lord of Spirits will have compassion on them, for His compassion is great. **4** And He is righteous also in His judgement, and in the presence of His glory unrighteousness also will not maintain itself: At His judgement the unrepentant will perish before Him. **5** And from now on I will have no mercy on them, says the Lord of Spirits.

CHAPTER 51

1 And in those days will the earth also give back that which has been entrusted to it, and Sheol also will give back that which it has received, and hell will give back that which it owes. For in those days the Elect One will arise, **2** and he will choose the righteous and holy from among them: For the day has drawn nigh that they should be saved. **3** And the Elect One will in those days sit on My throne, and his mouth will pour out all the secrets of wisdom and counsel: For the Lord of Spirits

208

has given (them) to him and has glorified him.
4 And in those days will the mountains leap like rams, and the hills also will skip like lambs satisfied with milk, and the faces of [all] the angels in heaven will be lighted up with joy. **5** And the earth will rejoice, and the righteous will dwell upon it, and the elect will walk thereon.

CHAPTER 52

1 And after those days in that place where I had seen all the visions of that which is hidden, I had been carried off in a whirlwind and they had borne me towards the west. **2** There mine eyes saw all the secret things of heaven that will be, a mountain of iron, and a mountain of copper, and a mountain of silver, and a mountain of gold, and a mountain of soft metal, and a mountain of lead. **3** And I asked the angel who went with me, saying, "What things are these which I have seen in secret?" **4** And he said unto me: "All these things which you have seen will serve the dominion of His Anointed that he may be potent and mighty on the earth." **5** And that angel of peace answered, saying unto me: "Wait a little, and there will be revealed unto you all the secret things which surround the Lord of Spirits. **6** And these mountains which your eyes have seen, the mountain of iron, and the mountain of copper, and the mountain of silver, and the mountain of gold, and the mountain of soft metal, and the mountain of lead, all these will be in the presence of the Elect One As wax: before the fire, and like the water which streams down from above [upon those mountains], and they will become powerless before his feet. **7** And it will come to pass in those days that none will be saved, either by gold or by silver, and none be able to escape. **8** And there will be no iron for war, nor will one clothe oneself with a breastplate. Bronze will be of no service, and tin [will be of no service and] will not be esteemed, and lead will not be desired. **9** And all these things will be [denied and] destroyed from the surface of the earth, when the Elect One will appear before the face of the Lord of Spirits."

CHAPTER 53

1 There mine eyes saw a deep valley with open mouths, and all who dwell on the earth and sea and islands will bring to him gifts and presents and signs of homage, but that deep valley will not become full. **2** And their hands commit lawless deeds, and the sinners devour all whom they lawlessly oppress: Yet the sinners will be destroyed before the face of the Lord of Spirits, and they will be banished from off the face of His earth, and they will perish forever and ever. **3** For I saw all the angels of punishment abiding (there) and preparing all the instruments of Satan. **4** And I asked the angel of peace who went with me: "For whom are they preparing these Instruments?" **5** And he said unto me: "They prepare these for the kings and the mighty of this earth, that they may thereby be destroyed. **6** And after this the Righteous and Elect One will cause the house of his congregation to appear: from now on they will be no more hindered in the name of the Lord of Spirits. **7** And these mountains will not stand as the earth before his righteousness, but the hills will be as a fountain of water, and the righteous will have rest from the oppression of sinners."

CHAPTER 54

1 And I looked and turned to another part of the earth and saw there a deep valley with burning fire. **2** And they brought the kings and the mighty and began to cast them into this deep valley. **3** And there mine eyes saw how they made these their instruments, iron chains of immeasurable weight. **4** And I asked the angel of peace who went with me, saying: "For whom are these chains being prepared?" And he said unto me: "These are being prepared for the hosts of Azazel, so that they may take them and cast them into the abyss of complete condemnation, and they will cover their jaws with rough stones as the Lord of Spirits commanded. **6** And Michael, and Gabriel, and Raphael, and Phanuel will take hold of them on that great day, and cast them on that day into the burning furnace, that the Lord of Spirits may take vengeance on them for their unrighteousness in becoming subject to Satan and leading astray those who dwell on the earth." **7** And in those days will punishment come from the Lord of Spirits, and he will open all the chambers of waters which are above the heavens, and of the fountains which are beneath the earth. **8** And all the waters will be joined with the waters: that which is above the heavens is the masculine, and the water which is beneath the earth is the feminine. **9** And they will destroy all who dwell on the earth and those who dwell under the ends of the heaven. **10** And when they have recognized their unrighteousness which they have wrought on the earth, then by these will they perish.

CHAPTER 55

1 And after that the Head of Days repented and said: "In vain have I destroyed all who dwell on the earth." 2 And He swore by His great name: "From now on I will not do so to all who dwell on the earth, and I will set a sign in the heaven: and this will be a pledge of good faith between Me and them forever, so long as heaven is above the earth. And this is in accordance with My command. 3 When I have desired to take hold of them by the hand of the angels on the day of tribulation and pain because of this, I will cause My chastisement and My wrath to abide upon them," says God, the Lord of Spirits. 4 "You mighty kings who dwell on the earth, you will have to behold Mine Elect One, how he sits on the throne of glory and judges Azazel, and all his associates, and all his hosts in the name of the Lord of Spirits."

CHAPTER 56

1 And I saw there the hosts of the angels of punishment going, and they held scourges and chains of iron and bronze. 2 And I asked the angel of peace who went with me, saying: "To whom are these who hold the scourges going?" 3 And he said unto me: "To their elect and beloved ones, that they may be cast into the chasm of the abyss of the valley. 4 And then that valley will be filled with their elect and beloved, and the days of their lives will be at an end, and the days of their leading astray will no longer be reckoned. 5 And in those days the angels will return and hurl themselves to the east upon the Parthians and Medes: They will stir up the kings, so that a spirit of unrest will come upon them, and they will rouse them from their thrones, that they may break out as lions from their lairs, and as hungry wolves among their flocks. 6 And they will go up and tread underfoot the land of His elect ones [And the land of His elect ones will be before them a threshing-floor and a highway:] 7 But the city of my righteous will be a hindrance to their horses. And they will begin to fight among themselves, and their right hand will be strong against themselves, and a man will not know his brother, nor a son his father or his mother, until there be no number of the corpses through their slaughter, and their punishment be not in vain. 8 In those days Sheol will open its jaws, and they will be

swallowed up therein and their destruction will be at an end; Sheol will devour the sinners in the presence of the elect."

CHAPTER 57

1 And it came to pass after this that I saw another host of wagons, and men riding thereon, and coming on the winds from the east, and from the west to the south. 2 And the noise of their wagons was heard, and when this turmoil took place the holy ones from heaven remarked it, and the pillars of the earth were moved from their place, and the sound thereof was heard from the one end of heaven to the other, in one day. 3 And they will all fall down and worship the Lord of Spirits. And this is the end of the second Parable.

CHAPTER 58

1 And I began to speak the third Parable concerning the righteous and elect. 2 Blessed are you, you righteous and elect, for glorious will be your lot. 3 And the righteous will be in the light of the sun. And the elect in the light of eternal life: The days of their life will be unending, and the days of the holy without number. 4 And they will seek the light and find righteousness with the Lord of Spirits: There will be peace to the righteous in the name of the Eternal Lord. 5 And after this it will be said to the holy in heaven That they should seek out the secrets of righteousness, the heritage of faith: For it has become bright as the sun upon earth, and the darkness is past. 6 And there will be a light that never ends, and to a limit of days they will not come, for the darkness will first have been destroyed, [And the light established before the Lord of Spirits] and the light of uprightness established forever before the Lord of Spirits.

CHAPTER 59

1 [In those days mine eyes saw the secrets of the lightnings, and of the lights, and the judgements they execute: and they lighten for a blessing or a curse as the Lord of Spirits wills. 2 And there I saw the secrets of the thunder, and how when it resounds above in the heaven, the sound thereof is heard, and he caused me to see the judgements executed on the earth, whether they be for well-being and blessing, or for a curse according to the word of the Lord of Spirits. 3 And after that all the secrets of the lights and lightnings were shown to me, and they lighten for blessing and for satisfying.]

CHAPTER 60

1 In the year 500, in the seventh month, on the fourteenth day of the month in the life of Enoch. In that parable I saw how a mighty quaking made the heaven of heavens to quake, and the host of the Most High, and the angels, a thousand thousands and ten thousand times ten thousand, were disquieted with a great disquiet. 2 And the Head of Days sat on the throne of His glory, and the angels and the righteous stood around Him. 3 And a great trembling seized me, and fear took hold of me, and my loins gave way, and dissolved were my reins, and I fell upon my face. 4 And Michael sent another angel from among the holy ones and he raised me up, and when he had raised me up my spirit returned; for I had not been able to endure the look of this host, and the commotion and the quaking of the heaven. 5 And Michael said unto me: "Why are you disquieted with such a vision? Until this day lasted the day of His mercy; and He has been merciful and long-suffering towards those who dwell on the earth. 6 And when the day, and the power, and the punishment, and the judgement come, which the Lord of Spirits has prepared for those who worship not the righteous law, and for those who deny the righteous judgement, and for those who take His name in vain-that day is prepared, for the elect a covenant, but for sinners an inquisition. When the punishment of the Lord of Spirits will rest upon them, it will rest in order that the punishment of the Lord of Spirits may not come, in vain, and it will slay the children with their mothers and the children with their fathers. Afterwards the judgement will take place according to His mercy and His patience." 7 And on that day were two monsters parted, a female monster named Leviathan, to dwell in the abysses of the ocean over the fountains of the waters. 8 But the male is named Behemoth, who occupied with his breast a waste wilderness named Duidain, on the east of the garden where the elect and righteous dwell, where my grandfather was taken up, the seventh from Adam, the first man whom the Lord of Spirits created. 9 And I sought the other angel that he should show me the might of those monsters, how they were parted on one day and cast, the one into the abysses of the sea, and the other unto the dry land of the wilderness. 10 And he said to me: "You son of man, herein you do seek to know what is hidden." 11 And the other angel who went with me and showed me what was hidden told me what is first and last in the heaven in the height, and beneath the earth in the depth, and at the ends of the heaven, and on the foundation of the heaven. 12 And the chambers of the winds, and how the winds are divided, and how they are weighed, and (how) the portals of the winds are reckoned, each according to the power of the wind, and the power of the lights of the moon, and according to the power that is fitting: and the divisions of the stars according to their names, and how all the divisions are divided. 13 And the thunders according to the places where they fall, and all the divisions that are made among the lightnings that it may lighten, and their host that they may at once obey. 14 For the thunder has places of rest (which) are assigned (to it) while it is waiting for its peal; and the thunder and lightning are inseparable, and although not one and undivided, they both go together through the spirit and separate not. 15 For when the lightning lightens, the thunder utters its voice, and the spirit enforces a pause during the peal, and divides equally between them; for the treasury of their peals is like the sand, and each one of them as it peals is held in with a bridle, and turned back by the power of the spirit, and pushed forward according to the many quarters of the earth. 16 And the spirit of the sea is masculine and strong, and according to the might of his strength he draws it back with a rein, and in like manner it is driven forward and disperses amid all the mountains of the earth. 17 And the spirit of the hoar-frost is his own angel, and the spirit of the hail is a good angel. 18 And the spirit of the snow has forsaken his chambers on account of his strength. There is a special spirit therein, and that which ascends from it is like smoke, and its name is frost. 19 And the spirit of the mist is not united with them in their chambers, but it has a special chamber; for its course is glorious both in light and in darkness, and in winter and in summer, and in its chamber is an angel. 20 And the spirit of the dew has its dwelling at the ends of the heaven, and is connected with the chambers of the rain, and its course is in winter and summer: and its clouds and the clouds of the mist are connected, and the one gives to the other. 21 And when the spirit of the rain goes out from its chamber, the angels come and open the chamber and lead it out, and when it is diffused over the whole earth it unites with the water on the earth. 22 For the waters are for those who dwell on the earth; for they are nourishment

for the earth from the Most High who is in heaven: therefore there is a measure for the rain, and the angels take it in charge. **23** And these things I saw towards the Garden of the Righteous. **24** And the angel of peace who was with me said to me: "These two monsters, prepared conformably to the greatness of God, will feed."

CHAPTER 61

1 And I saw in those days how long cords were given to those angels, and they took to themselves wings and flew, and they went towards the north. **2** And I asked the angel, saying unto him: "Why have those (angels) taken these cords and gone off?" And he said unto me: "They have gone to measure." **3** And the angel who went with me said unto me: "These will bring the measures of the righteous, and the ropes of the righteous to the righteous, that they may stay themselves on the name of the Lord of Spirits forever and ever. **4** The elect will begin to dwell with the elect, and those are the measures which will be given to faith and which will strengthen righteousness. **5** And these measures will reveal all the secrets of the depths of the earth, and those who have been destroyed by the desert, and those who have been devoured by the beasts, and those who have been devoured by the fish of the sea, that they may return and stay themselves on the day of the Elect One; for none will be destroyed before the Lord of Spirits, and none can be destroyed. **6** And all who dwell above in the heaven received a command and power and one voice and one light like unto fire. **7** And that One (with) their first words they blessed, and extolled and lauded with wisdom, and they were wise in utterance and in the spirit of life. **8** And the Lord of Spirits placed the Elect one on the throne of glory. And he will judge all the works of the holy above in the heaven, and in the balance will their deeds be weighed **9** and when he will lift up his countenance to judge their secret ways according to the word of the name of the Lord of Spirits, and their path according to the way of the righteous judgement of the Lord of Spirits, then will they all with one voice speak and bless, and glorify and extol and sanctify the name of the Lord of Spirits. **10** And He will summon all the host of the heavens, and all the holy ones above, and the host of God, the Cherubim, Seraphim and Ophanim, and all the angels of power, and all the angels of principalities, and the Elect One,

and the other powers on the earth (and) over the water On that day will raise one voice, and bless and glorify and exalt in the spirit of faith, and in the spirit of wisdom, and in the spirit of patience, and in the spirit of mercy, and in the spirit of judgement and of peace, and in the spirit of goodness, and will all say with one voice: 'Blessed is He, and may the name of the Lord of Spirits be blessed forever and ever.' **12** All who sleep not above in heaven will bless Him: All the holy ones who are in heaven will bless Him, and all the elect who dwell in the garden of life: And every spirit of light who is able to bless, and glorify, and extol, and hallow Your blessed name, and all flesh will beyond measure glorify and bless Your name forever and ever. **13** For great is the mercy of the Lord of Spirits, and He is long-suffering, and all His works and all that He has created He has revealed to the righteous and elect in the name of the Lord of Spirits."

CHAPTER 62

1 And so the Lord commanded the kings and the mighty and the exalted, and those who dwell on the earth, and said: "Open your eyes and lift up your horns if you are able to recognize the Elect One." **2** And the Lord of Spirits seated him on the throne of His glory, and the spirit of righteousness was poured out upon him, and the word of his mouth slays all the sinners, and all the unrighteous are destroyed from before his face. **3** And there will stand up in that day all the kings and the mighty, and the exalted and those who hold the earth, and they will see and recognize How he sits on the throne of his glory, and righteousness is judged before him, and no lying word is spoken before him. **4** Then will pain come upon them as on a woman in travail, [And she has pain in bringing out] When her child enters the mouth of the womb, and she has pain in bringing out. **5** And one portion of them will look on the other, and they will be terrified, and they will be downcast of countenance, and pain will seize them, when they see that Son of Man Sitting on the throne of his glory. **6** And the kings and the mighty and all who possess the earth will bless and glorify and extol him who rules over all, who was hidden. **7** For from the beginning the Son of Man was hidden, and the Most High preserved him in the presence of His might and revealed him to the elect. **8** And the congregation of the elect and holy will be sown, and all the elect will stand before him on that day. **9** And all the kings and the mighty and the exalted and those who rule the earth Will fall down before him on their faces, and worship and set their hope upon that Son of Man and petition him and supplicate for mercy at his hands. **10** Nevertheless that Lord of Spirits will so press them that they will have to go out from His presence, and their faces will be filled with shame, and the darkness grow deeper on their faces. **11** And He will deliver them to the angels for punishment, to execute vengeance on them because they have oppressed His children and His elect **12** and they will be a spectacle for the righteous and for His elect: They will rejoice over them, because the wrath of the Lord of Spirits rests upon them, and His sword is drunk with their blood. **13** And the righteous and elect will be saved on that day, and they will never again see the face of the sinners and unrighteous. **14** And the Lord of Spirits will abide over them, and with that Son of Man will they eat and lie down and rise up forever and ever. **15** And the righteous and elect will have risen from the earth and ceased to be of downcast countenance. And they will have been clothed with garments of glory, **16** and these will be the garments of life from the Lord of Spirits: And your garments will not grow old, nor your glory pass away before the Lord of Spirits.

CHAPTER 63

1 In those days will the mighty and the kings who possess the earth implore (Him) to grant them a little respite from His angels of punishment to whom they were delivered, that they might fall down and worship before the Lord of Spirits and confess their sins before Him. **2** And they will bless and glorify the Lord of Spirits and say: "Blessed is the Lord of Spirits and the Lord of kings, and the Lord of the mighty and the Lord of the rich, and the Lord of glory and the Lord of wisdom, **3** and splendid in every secret thing is Your power from generation to generation, and Your glory forever and ever: Deep are all Your secrets and innumerable, and Your righteousness is beyond reckoning. **4** we have now learnt that we should glorify and bless the Lord of kings and Him who is king over all kings." **5** And they will say: "Would that we had rest to glorify and give thanks and confess our faith before His glory! **6** And now we long for a little rest but find it not: We follow hard upon and obtain (it) not: And light has vanished from before us, and darkness is our dwelling-

place forever and ever: **7** For we have not believed before Him nor glorified the name of the Lord of Spirits, [nor glorified our Lord] but our hope was in the scepter of our kingdom, and in our glory. **8** And in the day of our suffering and tribulation He saves us not, and we find no respite for confession that our Lord is true in all His works, and in His judgements and His justice, and His judgements have no respect of persons. And we pass away from before His face on account of our works, and all our sins are reckoned up in righteousness." **10** Now they will say unto themselves: "Our souls are full of unrighteous gain, but it does not prevent us from descending from the midst thereof into the burden of Sheol." **11** And after that their faces will be filled with darkness and shame before that Son of Man, and they will be driven from his presence, and the sword will abide before his face in their midst. **12** So spoke the Lord of Spirits: "This is the ordinance and judgement with respect to the mighty and the kings and the exalted and those who possess the earth before the Lord of Spirits."

CHAPTER 64

1 And other forms I saw hidden in that place. **2** I heard the voice of the angel saying: "These are the angels who descended to the earth and revealed what was hidden to the children of men and seduced the children of men into committing sin."

CHAPTER 65

1 And in those days, Noah saw the earth that it had sunk down and its destruction was nigh. **2** And he arose from there and went to the ends of the earth and cried aloud to his grandfather Enoch: **3** and Noah said three times with an embittered voice: "Hear me, hear me, hear me." And I said unto him: "Tell me what it is that is falling out on the earth that the earth is in such evil plight and shaken, lest perhaps I will perish with it?" **4** And there was a great commotion, on the earth, and a voice was heard from heaven, and I fell on my face. **5** And Enoch my grandfather came and stood by me, and said unto me: "Why have you cried unto me with a bitter cry and weeping **6** and a command has gone out from the presence of the Lord concerning those who dwell on the earth that their ruin is accomplished because they have learnt all the secrets of the angels, and all the violence of the devils, and all their powers—the most secret ones—and all the power of those who practice sorcery, and the power of witchcraft, and the power of those who make molten images for the whole earth: **7** And how silver is produced from the dust of the earth, and how soft metal originates in the earth. **8** For lead and tin are not produced from the earth like the first: it is a fountain that produces them, and an angel stands therein, and that angel is pre-eminent." **9** And after that my grandfather Enoch took hold of me by my hand and raised me up, and said unto me: "Go, for I have asked the Lord of Spirits as touching this commotion on the earth." **10** And He said unto me: "Because of their unrighteousness their judgement has been determined upon and will not be withheld by Me forever. Because of the sorceries which they have searched out and learnt, the earth and those who dwell upon it will be destroyed. **11** And these-they have no place of repentance forever, because they have shown them what was hidden, and they are the damned: but as for you, my son, the Lord of Spirits knows that you are pure, and guiltless of this reproach concerning the secrets. **12** And He has destined your name to be among the holy and will preserve you among those who dwell on the earth and has destined your righteous seed both for kingship and for great honors, and from your seed will proceed a fountain of the righteous and holy without number forever."

CHAPTER 66

1 And after that he showed me the angels of punishment who are prepared to come and let loose all the powers of the waters which are beneath in the earth in order to bring judgement and destruction on all who [abide and] dwell on the earth. **2** And the Lord of Spirits gave commandment to the angels who were going out, that they should not cause the waters to rise but should hold them in check; for those angels were over the powers of the waters. **3** And I went away from the presence of Enoch.

CHAPTER 67

1 And in those days the word of God came unto me, and He said unto me: "Noah, your lot has come up before Me, a lot without blame, a lot of love and uprightness. **2** And now the angels are making a wooden (building), and when they have completed that task I will place My hand upon it and preserve it, and there will come out from it the seed of life, and a change will set in so that the earth will not

remain without inhabitant. **3** And I will make fast your sed before me forever and ever, and I will spread abroad those who dwell with you: it will not be unfruitful on the face of the earth, but it will be blessed and multiply on the earth in the name of the Lord." **4** And He will imprison those angels, who have shown unrighteousness, in that burning valley which my grandfather Enoch had formerly shown to me in the west among the mountains of gold and silver and iron and soft metal and tin. **5** And I saw that valley in which there was a great convulsion and a convulsion of the waters. **6** And when all this took place, from that fiery molten metal and from the convulsion thereof in that place, there was produced a smell of sulfur, and it was connected with those waters, and that valley of the angels who had led astray (mankind) burned beneath that land. **7** And through its valleys proceed streams of fire, where these angels are punished who had led astray those who dwell upon the earth. **8** But those waters will in those days serve for the kings and the mighty and the exalted, and those who dwell on the earth, for the healing of the body, but for the punishment of the spirit; now their spirit is full of lust, that they may be punished in their body, for they have denied the Lord of Spirits and see their punishment daily, and yet believe not in His name. **9** And in proportion as the burning of their bodies becomes severe, a corresponding change will take place in their spirit forever and ever; for before the Lord of Spirits none will utter an idle word. **10** For the judgement will come upon them, because they believe in the lust of their body and deny the Spirit of the Lord. **11** And those same waters will undergo a change in those days; for when those angels are punished in these waters, these water-springs will change their temperature, and when the angels ascend, this water of the springs will change and become cold. **12** And I heard Michael answering and saying: "This judgement with which the angels are judged is a testimony for the kings and the mighty who possess the earth." **13** Because these waters of judgement minister to the healing of the body of the kings and the lust of their body; therefore they will not see and will not believe that those waters will change and become a fire which burns forever.

CHAPTER 68

1 And after that my grandfather Enoch gave me the teaching of all the secrets in the book in the Parables which had been given to him, and he put them together for me in the words of The Book of the Parables. **2** And on that day Michael answered Raphael and said: "The power of the spirit transports and makes me to tremble because of the severity of the judgement of the secrets, the judgement of the angels: who can endure the severe judgement which has been executed, and before which they melt away?" **3** And Michael answered again, and said to Raphael: "Who is he whose heart is not softened concerning it, and whose reins are not troubled by this word of judgement (that) has gone out upon them because of those who have so led them out?" **4** And it came to pass when he stood before the Lord of Spirits, Michael said this to Raphael: "I will not take their part under the eye of the Lord; for the Lord of Spirits has been angry with them because they do as if they were the Lord. **5** Therefore all that is hidden will come upon them forever and ever; for neither angel nor man will have his portion (in it), but alone they have received their judgement forever and ever."

CHAPTER 69

1 And after this judgement they will terrify and make them to tremble because they have shown this to those who dwell on the earth. **2** And behold the names of those angels [and these are their names: the first of them is Samjaza, the second Artaqifa, and the third Armen, the fourth Kokabel, the fifth Turael, the sixth Rumjal, the seventh Danjal, the eighth Neqael, the ninth Baraqel, the tenth Azazel, the eleventh Armaros, the twelfth Batarjal, the thirteenth Busasejal, the fourteenth Hananel, the fifteenth Turel, and the sixteenth Simapesiel, the seventeenth Jetrel, the eighteenth Tumael, the nineteenth Turel, the twentieth Rumael, the twenty-first Azazel. **3** And these are the chiefs of their angels and their names, and their chief ones over hundreds and over fifties and over tens]. **4** The name of the first Jeqon: that is, the one who led astray [all] the sons of God, and brought them down to the earth, and led them astray through the daughters of men. **5** And the second was named Asbeel: he imparted to the holy sons of God evil counsel and led them astray so that they defiled their bodies with the daughters of men. **6** And the third was named Gadreel: he it is who showed the children of men all the blows of death, and he led astray Eve, and showed [the weapons of death to the

sons of men] the shield and the coat of mail, and the sword for battle, and all the weapons of death to the children of men. **7** And from his hand they have proceeded against those who dwell on the earth from that day and forevermore. **8** And the fourth was named Penemue: he taught the children of men the bitter and the sweet, and he taught them all the secrets of their wisdom. **9** And he instructed mankind in writing with ink and paper, and thereby many sinned from eternity to eternity and until this day. **10** For men were not created for such a purpose, to give confirmation to their good faith with pen and ink. **11** For men were created exactly like the angels, to the intent that they should continue pure and righteous, and death, which destroys everything, could not have taken hold of them, but through this their knowledge they are perishing, and through this power it is consuming me. **12** And the fifth was named Kasdeja: this is he who showed the children of men all the wicked smiting of spirits and demons, and the smiting of the embryo in the womb, that it may pass away, and [the smiting of the soul] the bites of the serpent, and the smiting which befall through the noontide heat, the son of the serpent named Taba'et. **13** And this is the task of Kasbeel, the chief of the oath which he showed to the holy ones when he dwelt high above in glory, and its name is Biqa. **14** This (angel) requested Michael to show him the hidden name, that he might enunciate it in the oath, so that those might quake before that name and oath who revealed all that was in secret to the children of men. **15** And this is the power of this oath, for it is powerful and strong, and he placed this oath Akae in the hand of Michael. **16** And these are the secrets of this oath, and they are strong through his oath: And the heaven was suspended before the world was created, and forever **17** and through it the earth was founded upon the water, and from the secret recesses of the mountains come beautiful waters, from the creation of the world and unto eternity. **18** And through that oath the sea was created, and at its foundation He set for it the sand against the time of (its) anger, and it dare not pass beyond it from the creation of the world unto eternity. **19** And through that oath are the depths made fast and abide and stir not from their place from eternity to eternity. **20** And through that oath the sun and moon complete their course and deviate not from their ordinance from eternity to eternity.

21 And through that oath the stars complete their course, and He calls them by their names, and they answer Him from eternity to eternity. 22 [And in like manner the spirits of the water, and of the winds, and of all zephyrs, and (their) paths from all the quarters of the winds. 23 And there are preserved the voices of the thunder and the light of the lightnings: and there are preserved the chambers of the hail and the chambers of the hoarfrost, and the chambers of the mist, and the chambers of the rain and the dew. 24 And all these believe and give thanks before the Lord of Spirits, and glorify (Him) with all their power, and their food is in every act of thanksgiving: they thank and glorify and extol the name of the Lord of Spirits forever and ever.] 25 And this oath is mighty over them and through it [they are preserved and] their paths are preserved, and their course is not destroyed. 26 And there was great joy among them, and they blessed and glorified and extolled Because the name of that Son of Man had been revealed unto them. 27 And he sat on the throne of his glory, and the sum of judgement was given unto the Son of Man, and he caused the sinners to pass away and be destroyed from off the face of the earth, and those who have led the world astray. 28 With chains will they be bound, and in their assemblage-place of destruction will they be imprisoned, and all their works vanish from the face of the earth. 29 And from now on there will be nothing corruptible; for that Son of Man has appeared and has seated himself on the throne of his glory, and all evil will pass away before his face, and the word of that Son of Man will go out and be strong before the Lord of Spirits.

CHAPTER 70

1 And it came to pass after this that his name during his lifetime was raised aloft to that Son of Man and to the Lord of Spirits from among those who dwell on the earth. 2 And he was raised aloft on the chariots of the spirit and his name vanished among them. 3 And from that day I was no longer numbered among them: and he set me between the two winds, between the North and the West, where the angels took the cords to measure for me the place for the elect and righteous. 4 And there I saw the first fathers and the righteous who from the beginning dwell in that place.

CHAPTER 71

1 And it came to pass after this that my spirit was translated and it ascended into the heavens: And I saw the holy sons of God. They were stepping on flames of fire: Their garments were white [and their raiment], and their faces shone like snow. 2 And I saw two streams of fire, and the light of that fire shone like hyacinth, and I fell on my face before the Lord of Spirits. 3 And the angel Michael [one of the archangels] seized me by my right hand and lifted me up and led me out into all the secrets, and he showed me all the secrets of righteousness. 4 And he showed me all the secrets of the ends of the heaven, and all the chambers of all the stars, and all the luminaries, from where they proceed before the face of the holy ones. 5 And he translated my spirit into the heaven of heavens, and I saw there as it were a structure built of crystals, and between those crystals tongues of living fire. 6 And my spirit saw the girdle which girt that house of fire, and on its four sides were streams full of living fire, and they girt that house. 7 And around were Seraphim, Cherubim, and Ophanim: And these are they who sleep not and guard the throne of His glory. 8 And I saw angels who could not be counted, a thousand thousands, and ten thousand times ten thousand, encircling that house. And Michael, and Raphael, and Gabriel, and Phanuel, and the holy angels who are above the heavens, go in and out of that house. 9 And they came out from that house, and Michael and Gabriel, Raphael and Phanuel, and many holy angels without number. 10 And with them the Head of Days, His head white and pure as wool, and His raiment indescribable. 11 And I fell on my face, and my whole body became relaxed, and my spirit was transfigured; and I cried with a loud voice, with the spirit of power, and blessed and glorified and extolled. 12 And these blessings which went out of my mouth were well pleasing before that Head of Days. 13 And that Head of Days came with Michael and Gabriel, Raphael and Phanuel, thousands and tens of thousands of angels without number. 14 And he came to me and greeted me with His voice, and said unto me "This is the Son of Man who is born unto righteousness, and righteousness abides over him, and the righteousness of the Head of Days forsakes him not." 15 And he said unto me: "He proclaims unto you peace in the name of the world to come; for from hence has proceeded

peace since the creation of the world, and so will it be unto you forever and forever and ever. **16** And all will walk in his ways since righteousness never forsakes him: With him will be their dwelling-places, and with him their heritage, and they will not be separated from him forever and ever and ever. And so there will be length of days with that Son of Man, and the righteous will have peace and an upright way in the name of the Lord of Spirits forever and ever."

SECTION 3:
THE ASTRONOMICAL BOOK

CHAPTER 72

1 The book of the courses of the luminaries of the heaven, the relations of each, according to their classes, their dominion and their seasons, according to their names and places of origin, and according to their months, which Uriel, the holy angel, who was with me, who is their guide, showed me; and he showed me all their laws exactly as they are, and how it is with regard to all the years of the world and unto eternity, until the new creation is accomplished which endures until eternity. **2** And this is the first law of the luminaries: the luminary the Sun has its rising in the eastern portals of the heaven, and its setting in the western portals of the heaven. **3** And I saw six portals in which the sun rises, and six portals in which the sun sets and the moon rises and sets in these portals, and the leaders of the stars and those whom they lead: six in the east and six in the west, and all following each other in accurately corresponding order: also many windows to the right and left of these portals. **4** And first there goes out the great luminary, named the Sun, and his circumference is like the circumference of the heaven, and he is quite filled with illuminating and heating fire. **5** The chariot on which he ascends, the wind drives, and the sun goes down from the heaven and returns through the north in order to reach the east and is so guided that he comes to the appropriate portal and shines in the face of the heaven. **6** In this way he rises in the first month in the great portal, which is the fourth [those six portals in the east]. **7** And in that fourth portal from which the sun rises in the first month are twelve window-openings, from which proceed a flame when they are opened in their season. **8** When the sun rises in the heaven, he comes out through that fourth portal thirty, mornings in succession, and sets accurately in the fourth portal in the west of the heaven. **9** And during this period the day becomes daily longer and the night nightly shorter to the thirtieth morning. **10** On that day the day is longer than the night by a ninth part, and the day amounts exactly to ten parts and the night to eight parts. **11** And the sun rises from that fourth portal and sets in the fourth and returns to the fifth portal of the east thirty mornings and rises from it and sets in the fifth portal. **12** And then the day becomes longer by two parts and amounts to eleven parts, and the night becomes shorter and amounts to seven parts. **13** And it returns to the east and enters into the sixth portal and rises and sets in the sixth portal one-and-thirty mornings on account of its sign. **14** On that day the day becomes longer than the night, and the day becomes double the night, and the day becomes twelve parts, and the night is shortened and becomes six parts. **15** And the sun mounts up to make the day shorter and the night longer, and the sun returns to the east and enters into the sixth portal and rises from it and sets thirty mornings. **16** And when thirty mornings are accomplished, the day decreases by exactly one part, and becomes eleven parts, and the night seven. **17** And the sun goes out from that sixth portal in the west and goes to the east and rises in the fifth portal for thirty mornings and sets in the west again in the fifth western portal. **18** On that day the day decreases by two parts and amounts to ten parts and the night to eight parts. **19** And the sun goes out from that fifth portal and sets in the fifth portal of the west and rises in the fourth portal for thirty-one mornings on account of its sign and sets in the west. **20** On that day the day is equalized with the night, [and becomes of equal length], and the night amounts to nine parts and the day to nine parts. **21** And the sun rises from that portal and sets in the west and returns to the east and rises thirty mornings in the third portal and sets in the west in the third portal. **22** And on that day the night becomes longer than the day, and night becomes longer than night, and day shorter than day until the thirtieth morning, and the night amounts exactly to ten parts and the day to eight parts. **23** And the sun rises from that third portal and sets in the third portal in the west and returns to the east, and for thirty mornings rises in the second portal in the east, and in like manner sets in the second portal in the west of the heaven. **24** And on that day the night amounts to eleven parts and the day to seven parts. **25** And the sun rises on that day from that second portal and sets in the west in the second portal and returns to the east into the first portal for one-and-thirty mornings and sets in the first portal in the west of the heaven. **26** And on that day the night becomes longer and amounts to the double of the day: and the night amounts exactly to twelve parts and the day to six. **27** And the sun has (therewith) traversed the divisions of his orbit and turns again on those divisions of his orbit and enters that portal thirty mornings and sets also in the west opposite to it. **28** And on that night has the night decreased in length by a ninth part, and the night has become eleven parts and the day seven parts. **29** And the sun has returned and entered into the second portal in the east and returns on those his divisions of his orbit for thirty mornings, rising and setting. **30** And on that day the night decreases in length, and the night amounts to ten parts and the day to eight. **31** And on that day the sun rises from that portal, and sets in the west, and returns to the east, and rises in the third portal for one-and-thirty mornings and sets in the west of the heaven. **32** On that day the night decreases and amounts to nine parts, and the day to nine parts, and the night is equal to the day and the year is exactly as to its days three hundred and sixty-four. **33** And the length of the day and of the night, and the shortness of the day and of the night arise-through the course **34** of the sun these distinctions are made. **34** So it comes that its course becomes daily longer, and its course nightly shorter. **35** And this is the law and the course of the sun, and his return as often as he returns sixty times and rises, i.e. the great luminary which is named the sun, forever and ever. **36** And that which rises is the great luminary, and is so named according to its appearance, according as the Lord commanded. **37** As he rises, so he sets and decreases not, and rests not, but runs day and night, and his light is sevenfold brighter than that of the moon; but as regards size they are both equal.

CHAPTER 73

1 And after this law I saw another law dealing with the smaller luminary, which is named the Moon. **2** And her circumference is like the circumference of the heaven, and her chariot in which she rides is driven by the wind, and light is given to her in (definite) measure. **3** And her rising and setting change every month: and her days are like the days of the

sun, and when her light is uniform (i.e. full) it amounts to the seventh part of the light of the sun. **4** And so she rises. And her first phase in the east comes out on the thirtieth morning: and on that day she becomes visible and constitutes for you the first phase of the moon on the thirtieth day together with the sun in the portal where the sun rises. **5** And the one half of her goes out by a seventh part, and her whole circumference is empty, without light, with the exception of one-seventh part of it, (and) the fourteenth part of her light. **6** And when she receives one-seventh part of the half of her light, her light amounts to one-seventh part and the half thereof. **7** And she sets with the sun, and when the sun rises the moon rises with him and receives the half of one part of light, and in that night in the beginning of her morning [in the commencement of the lunar day] the moon sets with the sun and is invisible that night with the fourteen parts and the half of one of them. **8** And she rises on that day with exactly a seventh part and comes out and recedes from the rising of the sun, and in her remaining days she becomes bright in the (remaining) thirteen parts.

CHAPTER 74

1 And I saw another course, a law for her, (and) how according to that law she performs her monthly revolution. **2** And all these Uriel, the holy angel who is the leader of them all, showed to me, and their positions, and I wrote down their positions as he showed them to me, and I wrote down their months as they were, and the appearance of their lights until fifteen days were accomplished. **3** In single seventh parts she accomplishes all her light in the east, and in single seventh parts accomplishes all her darkness in the west. **4** And in certain months she alters her settings, and in certain months she pursues her own peculiar course. **5** In two months the moon sets with the sun: in those two middle portals the third and the fourth. **6** She goes out for seven days and turns about and returns again through the portal where the sun rises and accomplishes all her light: and she recedes from the sun, and in eight days enters the sixth portal from which the sun goes out. **7** And when the sun goes out from the fourth portal she goes out seven days, until she goes out from the fifth and turns back again in seven days into the fourth portal and accomplishes all her light: and she recedes and enters into the first portal in eight days. **8** And she returns again in seven days into the fourth portal from which the sun goes out. **9** So I saw their position—how the moons rose and the sun set in those days. **10** And if five years are added together the sun has an overplus of thirty days, and all the days which accrue to it for one of those five years, when they are full, amount to 364 days. **11** And the overplus of the sun and of the stars amounts to six days: in 5 years 6 days every year come to 30 days: and the moon falls behind the sun and stars to the number of 30 days. **12** And the sun and the stars bring in all the years exactly, so that they do not advance or delay their position by a single day unto eternity; but complete the years with perfect justice in 364 days. **13** In 3 years there are 1,092 days, and in 5 years 1,820 days, so that in 8 years there are 2,912 days. **14** For the moon alone the days amount in 3 years to 1,062 days, and in 5 years she falls 50 days behind: there is 5 to be added (1,000 and) 62 days. **15** And in 5 years there are 1,770 days, so that for the moon the days 6 in 8 years amount to 21,832 days. **16** [For in 8 years she falls behind to the amount of 80 days], all the 17 days she falls behind in 8 years are 80. **17** And the year is accurately completed in conformity with their world-stations and the stations of the sun, which rise from the portals through which it (the sun) rises and sets 30 days.

CHAPTER 75

1 And the leaders of the heads of the thousands, who are placed over the whole creation and over all the stars, have also to do with the four intercalary days, being inseparable from their office, according to the reckoning of the year, and these render service on the four days which are not reckoned in the reckoning of the year. **2** And owing to them men go wrong therein, for those luminaries truly render service on the world-stations, one in the first portal, one in the third portal of the heaven, one in the fourth portal, and one in the sixth portal, and the exactness of the year is **3** accomplished through its separate three hundred and sixty-four stations. **3** For the signs and the times and the years and the days the angel Uriel showed to me, whom the Lord of glory has set forever over all the luminaries of the heaven, in the heaven and in the world, that they should rule on the face of the heaven and be seen on the earth, and be leaders for the day and the night, i.e. the sun, moon, and stars, and all the ministering creatures which make their revolution in all the chariots of the

heaven. **4** In like manner twelve doors Uriel showed me, open in the circumference of the sun's chariot in the heaven, through which the rays of the sun break out: and from them is warmth diffused over the earth, when they are opened at their appointed seasons. **5** [And for the winds and the spirit of the dew when they are opened, standing open in the heavens at the ends.] **6** As for the twelve portals in the heaven, at the ends of the earth, out of which go out the sun, moon, and stars, and all the works of heaven in the east and in the west, **7** there are many windows open to the left and right of them, and one window at its (appointed) season produces warmth, corresponding (as these do) to those doors from which the stars come out according as He has commanded them, and wherein they set corresponding to their number. **8** And I saw chariots in the heaven, running in the world, above those portals in which revolve the stars that never set. **9** And one is larger than all the rest, and it is that that makes its course through the entire world.

CHAPTER 76

1 And at the ends of the earth I saw twelve portals open to all the quarters (of the heaven), from which the winds go out and blow over the earth. **2** Three of them are open on the face (i.e. the east) of the heavens, and three in the west, and three on the right (i.e. the south) of the heaven, and three on the left (i.e. the north). **3** And the three first are those of the east, and three are of the north, and three [after those on the left] of the south, and three of the west. **4** Through four of these come winds of blessing and prosperity, and from those eight come hurtful winds: when they are sent, they bring destruction on all the earth and on the water upon it, and on all who dwell thereon, and on everything which is in the water and on the land. **5** And the first wind from those portals, called the east wind, comes out through the first portal which is in the east, inclining towards the south: from it come out desolation, drought, heat, and destruction. **6** And through the second portal in the middle comes what is fitting, and from it there come rain and fruitfulness and prosperity and dew; and through the third portal which lies toward the north come cold and drought. **7** And after these come the south winds through three portals: through the first portal of them inclining to the east comes out a hot wind. **8** And through the middle portal next to it there come out fragrant smells, and dew and rain, and prosperity and health. **9** And through the third portal lying to the west come out dew and rain, locusts and desolation. **10** And after these the north winds: from the seventh portal in the east come dew and rain, locusts and desolation. **11** And from the middle portal come in a direct direction health and rain and dew and prosperity; and through the third portal in the west come cloud and hoar-frost, and snow and rain, and dew and locusts. **12** And after these [four] are the west winds: through the first portal adjoining the north come out dew and hoar-frost, and cold and snow and frost. **13** And from the middle portal come out dew and rain, and prosperity and blessing; and through the last portal which adjoins the south come out drought and desolation and burning and destruction. **14** And the twelve portals of the four quarters of the heaven are therewith completed, and all their laws and all their plagues and all their benefactions have I shown to you, my son Methuselah.

CHAPTER 77

1 And the first quarter is called the east, because it is the first: and the second, the south, because the Most High will descend there, yea, there in quite a special sense will He who is blessed forever descend. **2** And the west quarter is named the diminished, because there all the luminaries of the heaven wane and go down. **3** And the fourth quarter, named the north, is divided into three parts: the first of them is for the dwelling of men: and the second contains seas of water, and the abysses and forests and rivers, and darkness and clouds; and the third part contains the garden of righteousness. **4** I saw seven high mountains, higher than all the mountains which are on the earth: and there comes out hoar-frost, and days, seasons, and years pass away. **5** I saw seven rivers on the earth larger than all the rivers: one of them coming from the west pours its waters into the Great Sea. **6** And these two come from the north to the sea and pour their waters into the Erythraean Sea in the east. **7** And the remaining, four come out on the side of the north to their own sea, two of them to the Erythraean Sea, and two into the Great Sea and discharge themselves there [and some say: into the desert]. **8** Seven great islands I saw in the sea and in the mainland: two in the mainland and five in the Great Sea.

CHAPTER 78

1 And the names of the sun are the following: the first Orjares, and the second Tomas. **2** And the moon has four names: the first name is Asonja, the second Ebla, the third Benase, and the fourth Erae. **3** These are the two great luminaries: their circumference is like the circumference of the heaven, and the size of the circumference of both is alike. **4** In the circumference of the sun there are seven portions of light which are added to it more than to the moon, and in definite measures it is s transferred until the seventh portion of the sun is exhausted. **5** And they set and enter the portals of the west, and make their revolution by the north, and come out through the eastern portals on the face of the heaven. **6** And when the moon rises one-fourteenth part appears in the heaven: [the light becomes full in her]: on the fourteenth day she accomplishes her light. **7** And fifteen parts of light are transferred to her until the fifteenth day (when) her light is accomplished, according to the sign of the year, and she becomes fifteen parts, and the moon grows by (the addition of) fourteenth parts. **8** And in her waning (the moon) decreases on the first day to fourteen parts of her light, on the second to thirteen parts of light, on the third to twelve, on the fourth to eleven, on the fifth to ten, on the sixth to nine, on the seventh to eight, on the eighth to seven, on the ninth to six, on the tenth to five, on the eleventh to four, on the twelfth to three, on the thirteenth to two, on the fourteenth to the half of a seventh, and all her remaining light disappears wholly on the fifteenth. **9** And in certain months the month has twenty-nine days and once twenty-eight. **10** And Uriel showed me another law: when light is transferred to the moon, and on which side it is transferred to her by the sun. **11** During all the period during which the moon is growing in her light, she is transferring it to herself when opposite to the sun during fourteen days [her light is accomplished in the heaven, and when she is illumined throughout, her light is accomplished full in the heaven. **12** And on the first day she is called the new moon, for on that day the light rises upon her. **13** She becomes full moon exactly on the day when the sun sets in the west, and from the east she rises at night, and the moon shines the whole night through until the sun rises over against her and the moon is seen over against the sun. **14** On the side from where the light of the moon comes out, there again she wanes until all the light vanishes and all the days of the month are at an end, and her circumference is empty, void of light. 15 And three months she makes of thirty days, and at her time she makes three months of twenty- nine days each, in which she accomplishes her waning in the first period of time, and in the first portal for one hundred and seventy-seven days. 16 And in the time of her going out she appears for three months (of) thirty days each, and for three months she appears (of) twenty-nine each. 17 At night she appears like a man for twenty days each time, and by day she appears like the heaven, and there is nothing else in her save her light.

CHAPTER 79

1 And now, my son, I have shown you everything, and the law of all the stars of the heaven is completed. 2 And he showed me all the laws of these for every day, and for every season of bearing rule, and for every year, and for its going out, and for the order prescribed to it every month and every week: 3 And the waning of the moon which takes place in the sixth portal: for in this sixth portal her light is accomplished, and after that there is the beginning of the waning: 4 (And the waning) which takes place in the first portal in its season, until one hundred and seventy-seven days are accomplished: reckoned according to weeks, twenty-five (weeks) and two days. 5 She falls behind the sun and the order of the stars exactly five days in the course of one period, and when this place which you see has been traversed. 6 Such is the picture and sketch of every luminary which Uriel the archangel, who is their leader, showed unto me.

CHAPTER 80

1 And in those days the angel Uriel answered and said to me: "Behold, I have shown you everything, Enoch, and I have revealed everything to you that you should see this sun and this moon, and the leaders of the stars of the heaven and all those who turn them, their tasks and times and departures. 2 And in the days of the sinners the years will be shortened, and their seed will be tardy on their lands and fields, and all things on the earth will alter, and will not appear in their time: And the rain will be kept back, and the heaven will withhold (it). 3 And in those times the fruits of the earth will be backward, and will not grow in their time, and the fruits of the trees will be withheld in

their time. 4 And the moon will alter her order, and not appear at her time. 5 [And in those days the sun will be seen, and he will journey in the evening on the extremity of the great chariot in the west] And will shine more brightly than accords with the order of light. 6 And many chiefs of the stars will transgress the order (prescribed). And these will alter their orbits and tasks, and not appear at the seasons prescribed to them. 7 And the whole order of the stars will be concealed from the sinners, and the thoughts of those on the earth will err concerning them, [And they will be altered from all their ways], yea, they will err and take them to be gods. 8 And evil will be multiplied upon them, and punishment will come upon them so as to destroy all."

CHAPTER 81

1 And he said unto me: "Observe, Enoch, these heavenly tablets, and read what is written thereon, and mark every individual fact." 2 And I observed the heavenly tablets and read everything which was written (thereon) and understood everything and read the book of all the deeds of mankind, and of all the children of flesh that will be upon the earth to the remotest generations. 3 And out with I blessed the great Lord the King of glory forever, in that He has made all the works of the world, and I extolled the Lord because of His patience, and blessed Him because of the children of men. 4 And after that I said: "Blessed is the man who dies in righteousness and goodness, concerning whom there is no book of unrighteousness written, and against whom no day of judgement will be found." 5 And those seven holy ones brought me and placed me on the earth before the door of my house, and said to me: "Declare everything to your son Methuselah, and show to all your children that no flesh is righteous in the sight of the Lord, for He is their Creator. 6 One year we will leave you with your son, until you give your (last) commands, that you may teach your children and record (it) for them and testify to all your children; and in the second year they will take you from their midst. 7 Let your heart be strong, for the good will announce righteousness to the good; The righteous with the righteous will rejoice and will offer congratulation to one another. 8 But the sinners will die with the sinners, and the apostate go down with the apostate. 9 And those who practice righteousness will die on account of the deeds of men and be taken away

on account of the doings of the godless." **10** And in those days they ceased to speak to me, and I came to my people, blessing the Lord of the world.

CHAPTER 82

1 And now, my son Methuselah, all these things I am recounting to you and writing down for you! and I have revealed to you everything, and given you books concerning all these: so preserve, my son Methuselah, the books from your father's hand, and (see) that you deliver them to the generations of the world. **2** I have given Wisdom to you and to your children, [And your children that will be to you], that they may give it to their children for generations, this wisdom (namely) that passes their thought. **3** And those who understand it will not sleep but will listen with the ear that they may learn this wisdom, and it will please those that eat thereof better than good food. **4** Blessed are all the righteous, blessed are all those who walk in the way of righteousness and sin not as the sinners, in the reckoning of all their days in which the sun traverses the heaven, entering into and departing from the portals for thirty days with the heads of thousands of the order of the stars, together with the four which are intercalated which divide the four portions of the year, which lead them and enter with them four days. **5** Owing to them men will be at fault and not reckon them in the whole reckoning of the year: yea, men will be at fault, and not recognize them accurately. **6** For they belong to the reckoning of the year and are truly recorded (thereon) forever, one in the first portal and one in the third, and one in the fourth and one in the sixth, and the year is completed in three hundred and sixty-four days. **7** And the account thereof is accurate and the recorded reckoning thereof exact; for the luminaries, and months and festivals, and years and days, has Uriel shown and revealed to me, to whom the Lord of the whole creation of the world has subjected the host of heaven. **8** And he has power over night and day in the heaven to cause the light to give light to men - sun, moon, and stars, and all the powers of the heaven which revolve in their circular chariots. **9** And these are the orders of the stars, which set in their places, and in their seasons and festivals and months. **10** And these are the names of those who lead them, who watch that they enter at their times, in their orders, in their seasons, in their months, in their periods of dominion, and in their positions. **11** Their four leaders who divide the four parts of the year enter first; and after them the twelve leaders of the orders who divide the months; and for the three hundred and sixty (days) there are heads over thousands who divide the days; and for the four intercalary days there are the leaders which sunder **12** the four parts of the year. **12** And these heads over thousands are intercalated between leader and leader, each behind a station, but their leaders make the division. **13** And these are the names of the leaders who divide the four parts of the year which are ordained: Milki'el, Hel'emmelek, and Mel'ejal, and Narel. **14** And the names of those who lead them: Adnar'el, and Ijasusa'el, and 'Elome'el- these three follow the leaders of the orders, and there is one that follows the three leaders of the orders which follow those leaders of stations that divide the four parts of the year. **15** In the beginning of the year Melkejal rises first and rules, who is named Tam'aini and sun, and all the days of his dominion while he bears rule are ninety-one days. **16** And these are the signs of the days which are to be seen on earth in the days of his dominion: sweat, and heat, and calms; and all the trees bear fruit, and leaves are produced on all the trees, and the harvest of wheat, and the rose-flowers, and all the flowers which come out in the field, but the trees of the winter season become withered. **17** And these are the names of the leaders which are under them: Berka'el, Zelebs'el, and another who is added a head of a thousand, called Hilujaseph: and the days of the dominion of this (leader) are at an end. **18** The next leader after him is Hel'emmelek, whom one names the shining sun, and all the days of his light are ninety-one days. **19** And these are the signs of (his) days on the earth: glowing heat and dryness, and the trees bear their fruits and produce all their fruits ripe and ready, and the sheep pair and become pregnant, and all the fruits of the earth are gathered in, and everything that is in the fields, and the winepress: these things take place in the days of his dominion. **20** These are the names, and the orders, and the leaders of those heads of thousands: Gida'ljal, Ke'el, and He'el, and the name of the head of a thousand which is added to them, Asfa'el: and the days of his dominion are at an end.

SECTION 4:
THE BOOK OF DREAM VISIONS

CHAPTER 83

1 And now, my son Methuselah, I will show you all my visions which I have seen, recounting them before you. 2 Two visions I saw before I took a wife, and the one was quite unlike the other: the first when I was learning to write: the second before I took your mother, (when) I saw a terrible vision. 3 And regarding them I prayed to the Lord. I had laid me down in the house of my grandfather Mahalalel, (when) I saw in a vision how the heaven collapsed and was borne off and fell to the earth. 4 And when it fell to the earth I saw how the earth was swallowed up in a great abyss, and mountains were suspended on mountains, and hills sank down on hills, and high trees were rent from their stems, and hurled down and sunk in the abyss. 5 And immediately a word fell into my mouth, and I lifted up (my voice) to cry aloud and said: "The earth is destroyed." 6 And my grandfather Mahalalel waked me as I lay near him, and said unto me: "Why do you cry so, my son, and why do you make such lamentation?" 7 And I recounted to him the whole vision which I had seen, and he said to me: "A terrible thing have you seen, my son, and of grave moment is your dream-vision as to the secrets of all the sin of the earth: it must sink into the abyss and be destroyed with a great destruction. 8 And now, my son, arise and make petition to the Lord of glory, since you are a believer, that a remnant may remain on the earth, and that He may not destroy the whole earth. 9 My son, from heaven all this will come upon the earth, and upon the earth there will be great destruction. 10 After that I arose and prayed and implored and sought and wrote down my prayer for the generations of the world, and I will show everything to you, my son Methuselah. 11 And when I had gone out below and seen the heaven, and the sun rising in the east, and the moon setting in the west, and a few stars, and the whole earth, and everything as He had known it in the beginning, then I blessed the Lord of judgement and extolled Him because He had made the sun to go out from the windows of the east, and he ascended and rose on the face of the heaven, and set out and kept traversing the path shown unto him.

CHAPTER 84

1 And I lifted up my hands in righteousness and blessed the Holy and Great One, and spoke with the breath of my mouth, and with the tongue of flesh, which God has made for the children of the flesh of men, that they should speak therewith, and He gave them breath and a tongue and a mouth that they should speak therewith: 2 "Blessed be You, O Lord, King, great and mighty in Your greatness, Lord of the whole creation of the heaven, King of kings and God of the whole world. And Your power and kingship and greatness abide forever and ever, and throughout all generations Your dominion; And all the heavens are Your throne forever, and the whole earth Your footstool forever and ever. 3 For You have made and You rule all things, and nothing is too hard for You, wisdom departs not from the place of Your throne, nor turns away from Your presence. And You know and see and hear everything, and there is nothing hidden from You [for You see everything] 4 And now the angels of Your heavens are guilty of trespass, and upon the flesh of men abides Your wrath until the great day of judgement. 5 And now, O God and Lord and Great King, I implore and implore You to fulfil my prayer, to leave me a posterity on earth, and not destroy all the flesh of man, and make the earth without inhabitant, so that there should be an eternal destruction. 6 And now, my Lord, destroy from the earth the flesh which has aroused Your wrath, but the flesh of righteousness and uprightness establish as a plant of the eternal seed, and hide not Your face from the prayer of Your servant, O Lord."

CHAPTER 85

1 And after this I saw another dream, and I will show the whole dream to you, my son. 2 And Enoch lifted up (his voice) and spoke to his son Methuselah: "To you, my son, will I speak: hear my words and incline your ear to the dream-vision of your father. 3 Before I took your mother Edna, I saw in a vision on my bed, and behold a bull came out from the earth, and that bull was white; and after it came out a heifer, and along with this (latter) came out two bulls, one of them black and the other red. 4 And that black bull gored the red one and pursued him over the earth, and immediately I could no longer see that red bull. 5 But that black bull grew and that heifer went with him, and I saw that many oxen proceeded from him which resembled and followed him. 6 And that

223

cow, that first one, went from the presence of that first bull in order to seek that red one, but found him not, and lamented with a great lamentation over him and sought him. **7** And I looked until that first bull came to her and quieted her, and from that time onward she cried no more. **8** And after that she bore another white bull, and after him she bore many bulls and black cows. **9** And I saw in my sleep that white bull likewise grow and become a great white bull, and from Him proceeded many white bulls, and they resembled him. **10** And they began to beget many white bulls, which resembled them, one following the other, (even) many.

CHAPTER 86

1 And again I saw with mine eyes as I slept, and I saw the heaven above, and behold a star fell from heaven, and it arose and eat and pastured among those oxen. **2** And after that I saw the large and the black oxen and behold they all changed their stalls and pastures and their cattle and began to live with each other. **3** And again, I saw in the vision, and looked towards the heaven, and behold I saw many stars descend and cast themselves down from heaven to that first star, and they became bulls among those cattle and pastured with them [among them]. **4** And I looked at them and saw, and behold they all let out their privy members, like horses, and began to cover the cows of the oxen, and they all became pregnant and bare elephants, camels, and asses. **5** And all the oxen feared them and were affrighted at them and began to bite with their teeth and to devour, and to gore with their horns. **6** And they began, moreover, to devour those oxen; and behold all the children of the earth began to tremble and quake before them and to flee from them.

CHAPTER 87

1 And again I saw how they began to gore each other and to devour each other, and the earth began to cry aloud. **2** And I raised mine eyes again to heaven, and I saw in the vision, and behold there came out from heaven beings who were like white men: and four went out from that place and three with them. **3** And those three that had last come out grasped me by my hand and took me up, away from the generations of the earth, and raised me up to a lofty place, and showed me a tower raised high above the earth, and all the hills were lower. **4** And one said unto me: "Remain here until

you see everything that befalls those elephants, camels, and asses, and the stars and the oxen, and all of them."

CHAPTER 88

1 And I saw one of those four who had come out first, and he seized that first star which had fallen from the heaven, and bound it hand and foot and cast it into an abyss: now that abyss was narrow and deep, and horrible and dark. **2** And one of them drew a sword and gave it to those elephants and camels and asses: then they began to smite each other, and the whole earth quaked because of them. **3** And as I was beholding in the vision one of those four who had come out stoned (them) from heaven and gathered and took all the great stars whose privy members were like those of horses, and bound them all hand and foot, and cast them in an abyss of the earth.

CHAPTER 89

1 And one of those four went to that white bull and instructed him in a secret, without his being terrified: he was born a bull and became a man and built for himself a great vessel and dwelt thereon; and three bulls dwelt with him in that vessel and they were covered in. **2** And again, I raised mine eyes towards heaven and saw a lofty roof, with seven water torrents thereon, and those torrents flowed with much water into an enclosure. **3** And I saw again, and behold fountains were opened on the surface of that great enclosure, and that water began to swell and rise upon the surface, and I saw that enclosure until all its surface was covered with water. **4** And the water, the darkness, and mist increased upon it; and as I looked at the height of that water, that water had risen above the height of that enclosure, and was streaming over that enclosure, and it stood upon the earth. **5** And all the cattle of that enclosure were gathered together until I saw how they sank and were swallowed up and perished in that water. **6** But that vessel floated on the water, while all the oxen and elephants and camels and asses sank to the bottom with all the animals, so that I could no longer see them, and they were not able to escape, (but) perished and sank into the depths. **7** And again, I saw in the vision until those water torrents were removed from that high roof, and the chasms of the earth were leveled up and other abysses were opened. **8** Then the water began to run down into these, until the earth became visible; but that vessel settled on the earth, and the darkness retired, and light appeared. **9** But that white bull which had become a man came out of that vessel, and the three bulls with him, and one of those three was white like that bull, and one of them was red as blood, and one black: and that white bull departed from them. **10** And they began to bring out beasts of the field and birds, so that there arose different genera: lions, tigers, wolves, dogs, hyenas, wild boars, foxes, squirrels, swine, falcons, vultures, kites, eagles, and ravens; and among them was born a white bull. **11** And they began to bite one another; but that white bull which was born among them begat a wild ass and a white bull with it, and the wild asses multiplied. **12** But that bull which was born from him begat a black wild boar and a white sheep; and the former begat many boars, but that sheep begat twelve sheep. **13** And when those twelve sheep had grown, they gave up one of them to the asses, and those asses again gave up that sheep to the wolves, and that sheep grew up among the wolves. **14** And the Lord brought the eleven sheep to live with it and to pasture with it among the wolves: and they multiplied and became many flocks of sheep. **15** And the wolves began to fear them, and they oppressed them until they destroyed their little ones, and they cast their young into a river of much water: but those sheep began to cry aloud on account of their little ones, and to complain unto their Lord. **16** And a sheep which had been saved from the wolves fled and escaped to the wild asses; and I saw the sheep how they lamented and cried, and besought their Lord with all their might, until that Lord of the sheep descended at the voice of the sheep from a lofty abode and came to them and pastured them. **17** And He called that sheep which had escaped the wolves and spoke with it concerning the wolves that it should admonish them not to touch the sheep. **18** And the sheep went to the wolves according to the word of the Lord, and another sheep met it and went with it, and the two went and entered together into the assembly of those wolves and spoke with them and admonished them not to touch the sheep from now on. **19** And immediately I saw the wolves, and how they oppressed the sheep exceedingly with all their power; and the sheep cried aloud. **20** And the Lord came to the sheep and they began to smite those wolves: and the wolves began to make lamentation; but the sheep became quiet and out with ceased to cry out. **21** And I saw the sheep until they departed from among the wolves; but the eyes of the wolves were blinded, and those wolves departed in pursuit of the sheep with all their power. **22** And the Lord of the sheep went with them, as their leader, and all His sheep followed Him: and his face was dazzling and glorious and terrible to behold. **23** But the wolves began to pursue those sheep until they reached a sea of water. **24** And that sea was divided, and the water stood on this side and on that before their face, and their Lord led them and placed Himself between them and the wolves. **25** And as those wolves did not yet see the sheep, they proceeded into the midst of that sea, and the wolves followed the sheep, and [those wolves] ran after them into that sea. **26** And when they saw the Lord of the sheep, they turned to flee before His face, but that sea gathered itself together, and became as it had been created, and the water swelled and rose until it covered those wolves. **27** And I saw until all the wolves who pursued those sheep perished and were drowned. **28** But the sheep escaped from that water and went out into a wilderness, where there was no water and no grass; and they began to open their eyes and to see; and I saw the Lord of the sheep pasturing them and giving them water and grass, and that sheep going and leading them. **29** And that sheep ascended to the summit of that lofty rock, and the Lord of the sheep sent it to them. **30** And after that I saw the Lord of the sheep who stood before them, and His appearance was great and terrible and majestic, and all those sheep saw Him and were afraid before His face. **31** And they all feared and trembled because of Him, and they cried to that sheep with them [which was among them]: "We are not able to stand before our Lord or to behold Him." **32** And that sheep which led them again ascended to the summit of that rock, but the sheep began to be blinded and to wander from the way which he had showed them, but that sheep wot not thereof. **33** And the Lord of the sheep was wrathful exceedingly against them, and that sheep discovered it, and went down from the summit of the rock, and came to the sheep, and found the greatest part of them blinded and fallen away. **34** And when they saw it they feared and trembled at its presence and desired to return to their folds. **35** And that sheep took other sheep with it, and came to those sheep which had fallen away, and began to slay them; and the sheep feared its presence, and so that sheep brought back those sheep that had fallen away, and they returned to their folds. **36** And I saw in this vision until that sheep became a man and built a house for the Lord of the sheep and placed all the sheep in that house. **37** And I saw until this sheep which had met that sheep which led them fell asleep: and I saw until all the great sheep perished and little ones arose in their place, and they came to a pasture, and approached a stream of water. **38** Then that sheep, their leader which had become a man, withdrew from them and fell asleep, and all the sheep sought it and cried over it with a great crying. **39** And I saw until they left off crying for that sheep and crossed that stream of water, and there arose the two sheep as leaders in the place of those which had led them and fallen asleep. **40** And I saw until the sheep came to a goodly place, and a pleasant and glorious land, and I saw until those sheep were satisfied; and that house stood among them in the pleasant land. **41** And sometimes their eyes were opened, and sometimes blinded, until another sheep arose and led them and brought them all back, and their eyes were opened. **42** And the dogs and the foxes and the wild boars began to devour those sheep until the Lord of the sheep raised up [another sheep] a ram from their midst, which led them. **43** And that ram began to butt on either side those dogs, foxes, and wild boars until he had destroyed them all. **44** And that sheep whose eyes were opened saw that ram, which was among the sheep, until it forsook its glory and began to butt those sheep, and trampled upon them, and behaved itself unseemly. **45** And the Lord of the sheep sent the lamb to another lamb and raised it to be a ram and leader of the sheep instead of that ram which had forsaken its glory. **46** And it went to it and spoke to it alone, and raised it to be a ram, and made it the prince and leader of the sheep; but during all these things those dogs oppressed the sheep. **47** And the first ram pursued that second ram, and that second ram arose and fled before it; and I saw until those dogs pulled down the first ram. **48** And that second ram arose and led the [little] sheep. And those sheep grew and multiplied; but all the dogs, and foxes, and wild boars feared and fled before it, and that ram butted and killed the wild beasts, and those wild beasts had no longer any power among the sheep and robbed them no more of ought. **49** And that ram begat many sheep and fell asleep; and a little sheep became ram in its stead and became prince and leader of those sheep. **50** And that house became great and broad, and it was built for those sheep: (and) a tower lofty and great was built on the house for the Lord of the sheep, and that house was low, but the tower was elevated and lofty, and the Lord of the sheep stood on that tower and they offered a full table before Him. **51** And again I saw those sheep that they again erred and went many ways, and forsook that their house, and the Lord of the sheep called some from among the sheep and sent them to the sheep, but the sheep began to slay them. **52** And one of them was saved and was not slain, and it sped away and cried aloud over the sheep; and they sought to slay it, but the Lord of the sheep saved it from the sheep, and brought it up to me, and caused it to dwell there. **53** And many other sheep He sent to those sheep to testify unto them and lament over them. **54** And after that I saw that when they forsook the house of the Lord and His tower they fell away entirely, and their eyes were blinded; and I saw the Lord of the sheep how He wrought much slaughter among them in their herds until those sheep invited that slaughter and betrayed His place. **55** And He gave them over into the hands of the lions and tigers, and wolves and hyenas, and into the hand of the foxes, and to all the wild beasts, and those wild beasts began to tear in pieces those sheep. **56** And I saw that He forsook that their house and their tower and gave them all into the hand of the lions, to tear and devour them, into the hand of all the wild beasts. **57** And I began to cry aloud with all my power, and to appeal to the Lord of the sheep, and to represent to Him in regard to the sheep that they were devoured by all the wild beasts. **58** But He remained unmoved, though He saw it, and rejoiced that they were devoured and swallowed and robbed and left them to be devoured in the hand of all the beasts. **59** And He called seventy shepherds and cast those sheep to them that they might pasture them, and He spoke to the shepherds and their companions: "Let each individual of you pasture the sheep from now on and do everything that I will command you to do. And I will deliver them over unto you duly numbered and tell you which of them are to be destroyed-and them destroy you." **60** And He gave over unto them those sheep. **61** And He called another and spoke unto him: "Observe and mark everything that the shepherds will do to those sheep; for they will destroy more of them than I have commanded them. **62** And every excess and the destruction which will be wrought through the shepherds, record (namely) how many they destroy according to my command, and how many according to their own caprice: record against every individual shepherd all the destruction he effects. 63 And read out before me by number how many they destroy, and how many they deliver over for destruction, that I may have this as a testimony against them, and know every deed of the shepherds, that I may comprehend and see what they do, whether or not they abide by my command which I have commanded them. 64 But they will not know it, and you will not declare it to them, nor admonish them, but only record against each individual all the destruction which the shepherds effect each in his time and lay it all before me." 65 And I saw until those shepherds pastured in their season, and they began to slay and to destroy more than they were bidden, and they delivered those sheep into the hand of the lions. 66 And the lions and tigers eat and devoured the greater part of those sheep, and the wild boars eat along with them; and they burnt that tower and demolished that house. 67 And I became exceedingly sorrowful over that tower because that house of the sheep was demolished, and afterwards I was unable to see if those sheep entered that house. 68 And the shepherds and their associates delivered over those sheep to all the wild beasts, to devour them, and each one of them received in his time a definite number: it was written by the other in a book how many each one of them destroyed of them. 69 And each one slew and destroyed many more than was prescribed; and I began to weep and lament on account of those sheep. 70 And so in the vision I saw that one who wrote, how he wrote down every one that was destroyed by those shepherds, day by day, and carried up and laid down and showed actually the whole book to the Lord of the sheep-(even) everything that they had done, and all that each one of them had made away with, and all that they had given over to destruction. 71 And the book was read before the Lord of the sheep, and He took the book from his hand and read it and sealed it and laid it down. 72 And out with I saw how the shepherds pastured for twelve hours and behold three of those sheep turned back and came and entered and began to build up all that had fallen down of that house; but the wild boars tried to hinder them, but they were not able. 73 And they began again to build as before, and they reared up

that tower, and it was named the high tower; and they began again to place a table before the tower, but all the bread on it was polluted and not pure. 74 And as touching all this the eyes of those sheep were blinded so that they saw not, and (the eyes of) their shepherds likewise; and they delivered them in large numbers to their shepherds for destruction, and they trampled the sheep with their feet and devoured them. 75 And the Lord of the sheep remained unmoved until all the sheep were dispersed over the field and mingled with them, and they did not save them out of the hand of the beasts. 76 And this one who wrote the book carried it up and showed it and read it before the Lord of the sheep, and implored Him on their account, and besought Him on their account as he showed Him all the doings of the shepherds and gave testimony before Him against all the shepherds. 77 And he took the actual book and laid it down beside Him and departed.

CHAPTER 90

1 And I saw until that in this manner thirty-five shepherds undertook the pasturing (of the sheep), and they severally completed their periods as did the first; and others received them into their hands, to pasture them for their period, each shepherd in his own period. 2 And after that I saw in my vision all the birds of heaven coming, the eagles, the vultures, the kites, the ravens; but the eagles led all the birds; and they began to devour those sheep, and to pick out their eyes and to devour their flesh. 3 And the sheep cried out because their flesh was being devoured by the birds, and as for me I looked and lamented in my sleep over that shepherd who pastured the sheep. 4 And I saw until those sheep were devoured by the dogs and eagles and kites, and they left neither flesh nor skin nor sinew remaining on them until only their bones stood there: and their bones too fell to the earth and the sheep became few. 5 And I saw until that twenty-three had undertaken the pasturing and completed in their several periods fifty-eight times. 6 But behold lambs were borne by those white sheep, and they began to open their eyes and to see, and to cry to the sheep. 7 Yea, they cried to them, but they did not hearken to what they said to them, but were exceedingly deaf, and their eyes were very exceedingly blinded. 8 And I saw in the vision how the ravens flew upon those lambs and took one of those lambs and dashed the sheep in pieces and devoured

them. **9** And I saw until horns grew upon those lambs, and the ravens cast down their horns; and I saw until there sprouted a great horn of one of those sheep, and their eyes were opened. **10** And it looked at them [and their eyes opened], and it cried to the sheep, and the rams saw it and all ran to it. **11** And notwithstanding all this those eagles and vultures and ravens and kites still kept tearing the sheep and swooping down upon them and devouring them: still the sheep remained silent, but the rams lamented and cried out. **12** And those ravens fought and battled with it and sought to lay low its horn, but they had no power over it. **13** And I saw till the shepherds and eagles and those vultures and kites came, and they cried to the ravens that they should break the horn of that ram, and they battled and fought with it, and it battled with them and cried that its help might come. **14** And I saw till that man, who wrote down the names of the shepherds [and] carried up into the presence of the Lord of the sheep [came and helped it and showed it everything: he had come down for the help of that ram]. **15** And I saw till the Lord of the sheep came unto them in wrath, and all who saw Him fled, and they all fell into His shadow from before His face. **16** All the eagles and vultures and ravens and kites were gathered together, and there came with them all the sheep of the field, yea, they all came together, and helped each other to break that horn of the ram. **17** And I saw that man, who wrote the book according to the command of the Lord, till he opened that book concerning the destruction which those twelve last shepherds had wrought and showed that they had destroyed much more than their predecessors, before the Lord of the sheep. **18** And I saw till the Lord of the sheep came unto them and took in His hand the staff of His wrath, and smote the earth, and the earth clave asunder, and all the beasts and all the birds of the heaven fell from among those sheep and were swallowed up in the earth and it covered them. **19** And I saw until a great sword was given to the sheep, and the sheep proceeded against all the beasts of the field to slay them, and all the beasts and the birds of the heaven fled before their face. **20** And I saw until a throne was erected in the pleasant land, and the Lord of the sheep sat Himself thereon, and the other took the sealed books and opened those books before the Lord of the sheep. **21** And the Lord called those men the seven first white ones, and commanded that they should bring

before Him, beginning with the first star which led the way, all the stars whose privy members were like those of horses, and they brought them all before Him. **22** And He said to that man who wrote before Him, being one of those seven white ones, and said unto him: "Take those seventy shepherds to whom I delivered the sheep, and who taking them on their own authority slew more than I commanded them." **23** And behold they were all bound, I saw, and they all stood before Him. **24** And the judgement was held first over the stars, and they were judged and found guilty, and went to the place of condemnation, and they were cast into an abyss, full of fire and flaming, and full of pillars of fire. **25** And those seventy shepherds were judged and found guilty, and they were cast into that fiery abyss. **26** And I saw at that time how a like abyss was opened in the midst of the earth, full of fire, and they brought those blinded sheep, and they were all judged and found guilty and cast into this fiery abyss, and they burned; now this abyss was to the right of that house. **27** And I saw those sheep burning and their bones burning. **28** And I stood up to see until they folded up that old house; and carried off all the pillars, and all the beams and ornaments of the house were at the same time folded up with it, and they carried it off and laid it in a place in the south of the land. **29** And I saw until the Lord of the sheep brought a new house greater and loftier than that first and set it up in the place of the first which had beer folded up: all its pillars were new, and its ornaments were new and larger than those of the first, the old one which He had taken away, and all the sheep were within it. **30** And I saw all the sheep which had been left, and all the beasts on the earth, and all the birds of the heaven, falling down and doing homage to those sheep and making petition to and obeying them in everything. **31** And thereafter those three who were clothed in white and had seized me by my hand [who had taken me up before], and the hand of that ram also seizing hold of me, they took me up and set me down in the midst of those sheep before the judgement took place. **32** And those sheep were all white, and their wool was abundant and clean. **33** And all that had been destroyed and dispersed, and all the beasts of the field, and all the birds of the heaven, assembled in that house, and the Lord of the sheep rejoiced with great joy because they were all good and had returned to His house. **34** And I saw until they laid down that sword, which had been given to the sheep, and they brought it back into the house, and it was sealed before the presence of the Lord, and all the sheep were invited into that house, but it held them not. **35** And the eyes of them all were opened, and they saw the good, and there was not one among them that did not see. **36** And I saw that that house was large and broad and very full. **37** And I saw that a white bull was born, with large horns and all the beasts of the field and all the birds of the air feared him and made petition to him all the time. **38** And I saw until all their generations were transformed, and they all became white bulls; and the first among them became a lamb, and that lamb became a great animal and had great black horns on its head; and the Lord of the sheep rejoiced over it and over all the oxen. **39** And I slept in their midst: and I awoke and saw everything. **40** This is the vision which I saw while I slept, and I awoke and blessed the Lord of righteousness and gave Him glory. **41** Then I wept with a great weeping and my tears stayed not until I could no longer endure it: when I saw, they flowed on account of what I had seen; for everything will come and be fulfilled, and all the deeds of men in their order were shown to me. **42** On that night I remembered the first dream, and because of it I wept and was troubled-because I had seen that vision.

SECTION 5:
THE EPISTLE OF ENOCH

CHAPTER 91

1 "And now, my son Methuselah, call to me all your brothers and gather together to me all the sons of your mother; for the word calls me, and the Spirit is poured out upon me, that I may show you everything that will befall you forever." **2** And there upon Methuselah went and summoned to him all his brothers and assembled his relatives. **3** And he spoke unto all the children of righteousness and said: "Hear, you sons of Enoch, all the words of your father, and hearken to the voice of my mouth; for I exhort you and say unto you, beloved: **4** Love uprightness and walk therein. And draw not nigh to uprightness with a double heart, and associate not with those of a double heart, but walk in righteousness, my sons. And it will guide you on good paths, and righteousness will be your companion. **5** For I know that violence must increase on the earth, and a great chastisement be executed on the

earth, yea, it will be cut off from its roots, and its whole structure be destroyed. **6** And unrighteousness will again be consummated on the earth, and all the deeds of unrighteousness and of violence and transgression will prevail in a twofold degree. **7** And when sin and unrighteousness and blasphemy and violence in all kinds of deeds increase, and apostasy and transgression and uncleanness increase, a great chastisement will come from heaven upon all these, and the holy Lord will come out with wrath and chastisement to execute judgement on earth. **8** In those days violence will be cut off from its roots, and the roots of unrighteousness together with deceit, and they will be destroyed from under heaven. **9** And all the idols of the heathen will be abandoned, and the temples burned with fire, and they will remove them from the whole earth, and they will be cast into the judgement of fire and will perish in wrath and in grievous judgement forever. **10** And the righteous will arise from their sleep, and wisdom will arise and be given unto them. [And after that the roots of unrighteousness will be cut off, and the sinners will be destroyed by the sword [and] will be cut off from the blasphemers in every place, and those who plan violence and those who commit blasphemy will perish by the sword.] **12** And after that there will be another, the eighth week, that of righteousness, and a sword will be given to it that a righteous judgement may be executed on the oppressors, and sinners will be delivered into the hands of the righteous. **13** And at its close they will acquire houses through their righteousness, and a house will be built for the Great King in glory forevermore, and all mankind will look to the path of uprightness. **14** And after that, in the ninth week, the righteous judgement will be revealed to the whole world, and all the works of the godless will vanish from all the earth, and the world will be written down for destruction. **15** And after this, in the tenth week in the seventh part, there will be the great eternal judgement, in which He will execute vengeance among the angels. **16** And the first heaven will depart and pass away, and a new heaven will appear, and all the powers of the heavens will give sevenfold light. **17** And after that there will be many weeks without number forever, and all will be in goodness and righteousness, and sin will no more be mentioned forever. **18** And now I tell you, my sons, and show you the paths of righteousness and the paths of violence. Yea, I will show them to you again That you may know what will come to pass. **19** And now, hearken unto me, my sons, and walk in the paths of righteousness, and walk not in the paths of violence; for all who walk in the paths of unrighteousness will perish forever."

CHAPTER 92

1 The book written by Enoch—[Enoch indeed wrote this complete doctrine of wisdom, (which is) praised of all men and a judge of all the earth]—for all my children who will dwell on the earth. And for the future generations who will observe uprightness and peace. **2** Let not your spirit be troubled on account of the times; For the Holy and Great One has appointed days for all things. **3** And the righteous one will arise from sleep, [Will arise] and walk in the paths of righteousness, and all his path and conversation will be in eternal goodness and grace. **4** He will be gracious to the righteous and give him eternal uprightness, and He will give him power so that he will be (endowed) with goodness and righteousness. And he will walk in eternal light. **5** And sin will perish in darkness forever and will no more be seen from that day forevermore.

CHAPTER 93

1 And after that Enoch both gave and began to recount from the books. **2** And Enoch said: "Concerning the children of righteousness and concerning the elect of the world, and concerning the plant of uprightness, I will speak these things, yea, I Enoch will declare (them) unto you, my sons: According to that which appeared to me in the heavenly vision, and which I have known through the word of the holy angels, and have learnt from the heavenly tablets." **3** And Enoch began to recount from the books and said: "I was born the seventh in the first week, while judgement and righteousness still endured. **4** And after me there will arise in the second week great wickedness, and deceit will have sprung up; And in it there will be the first end. And in it a man will be saved; and after it is ended unrighteousness will grow up, and a law will be made for the sinners. **5** And after that in the third week at its close a man will be elected as the plant of righteous judgement, and his posterity will become the plant of righteousness forevermore. **6** And after that in the fourth week, at its close, visions of the holy

and righteous will be seen, and a law for all generations and an enclosure will be made for them. **7** And after that in the fifth week, at its close, the house of glory and dominion will be built forever. **8** And after that in the sixth week all who live in it will be blinded, and the hearts of all of them will godlessly forsake wisdom. And in it a man will ascend; And at its close the house of dominion will be burnt with fire, and the whole race of the chosen root will be dispersed. **9** And after that in the seventh week will an apostate generation arise, and many will be its deeds, and all its deeds will be apostate. **10** And at its close will be elected the elect righteous of the eternal plant of righteousness, to receive sevenfold instruction concerning all His creation. **11** [For who is there of all the children of men that is able to hear the voice of the Holy One without being troubled? And who can think His thoughts? And who is there that can behold all the works of heaven? **12** And how should there be one who could behold the heaven, and who is there that could understand the things of heaven and see a soul or a spirit and could tell thereof, or ascend and see all their ends and think them or do like them? **13** And who is there of all men that could know what is the breadth and the length of the earth, and to whom has been shown the measure of all of them? **14** Or is there anyone who could discern the length of the heaven and how great is its height, and upon what it is founded, and how great is the number of the stars, and where all the luminaries rest?]"

CHAPTER 94

1 And now I say unto you, my sons, love righteousness and walk therein; For the paths of righteousness are worthy of acceptation, but the paths of unrighteousness will suddenly be destroyed and vanish. **2** And to certain men of a generation will the paths of violence and of death be revealed, and they will hold themselves afar from them, and will not follow them. **3** And now I say unto you the righteous: Walk not in the paths of wickedness, nor in the paths of death, and draw not nigh to them, lest you be destroyed. **4** But seek and choose for yourselves righteousness and an elect life, and walk in the paths of peace, and you will live and prosper. **5** And hold fast my words in the thoughts of your hearts and suffer them not to be effaced from your hearts; for I know that sinners will tempt men to mistreat wisdom, so that no place may be found for her, and no manner of temptation may diminish. **6** Woe to those who build unrighteousness and oppression and lay deceit as a foundation; for they will be suddenly overthrown, and they will have no peace. **7** Woe to those who build their houses with sin; For from all their foundations will they be overthrown, and by the sword will they fall. [And those who acquire gold and silver in judgement suddenly will perish.] **8** Woe to you, you rich, for you have trusted in your riches, and from your riches will you depart, because you have not remembered the Most High in the days of your riches. **9** You have committed blasphemy and unrighteousness, and have become ready for the day of slaughter, and the day of darkness and the day of the great judgement. **10** So I speak and declare unto you: He who has created you will overthrow you, and for your fall there will be no compassion, and your Creator will rejoice at your destruction. **11** And your righteous ones in those days will be A reproach to the sinners and the godless.

CHAPTER 95

1 Oh that mine eyes were [a cloud of] waters That I might weep over you and pour down my tears as a cloud of waters: That so I might rest from my trouble of heart! **2** Who has permitted you to practice reproaches and wickedness? And so judgement will overtake you, sinners. **3** Fear not the sinners, you righteous; For again will the Lord deliver them into your hands, that you may execute judgement upon them according to your desires. **4** Woe to you who fulminate anathemas which cannot be reversed: Healing will therefore be far from you because of your sins. **5** Woe to you who requite your neighbor with evil; For you will be requited according to your works. **6** Woe to you, lying witnesses, and to those who weigh out injustice, for suddenly will you perish. **7** Woe to you, sinners, for you persecute the righteous; for you will be delivered up and persecuted because of injustice, and heavy will its yoke be upon you.

CHAPTER 96

1 Be hopeful, you righteous; for suddenly will the sinners perish before you, and you will have lordship over them according to your desires. **2** [And in the day of the tribulation of the sinners, Your children will mount and rise as eagles, and higher than the vultures will be your nest, and you will ascend and enter the crevices of the earth, and the clefts of the rock

forever as coneys before the unrighteous, and the sirens will sigh because of you and weep.] **3** So fear not, you that have suffered; For healing will be your portion, and a bright light will enlighten you, and the voice of rest you will hear from heaven. **4** Woe unto you, you sinners, for your riches make you appear like the righteous, but your hearts convict you of being sinners, and this fact will be a testimony against you for a memorial of (your) evil deeds. **5** Woe to you who devour the finest of the wheat, and drink wine in large bowls, and tread underfoot the lowly with your might. **6** Woe to you who drink water from every fountain, for suddenly will you be consumed and wither away, because you have forsaken the fountain of life. **7** Woe to you who work unrighteousness and deceit and blasphemy: It will be a memorial against you for evil. **8** Woe to you, you mighty, who with might oppress the righteous; for the day of your destruction is coming. In those days many and good days will come to the righteous-in the day of your judgement.

CHAPTER 97

1 Believe, you righteous, that the sinners will become a shame and perish in the day of unrighteousness. **2** Be it known unto you (ye sinners) that the Most High is mindful of your destruction, and the angels of heaven rejoice over your destruction. **3** What will you do, you sinners, and where will you flee on that day of judgement, when you hear the voice of the prayer of the righteous? **4** Yea, you will fare like unto them, against whom this word will be a testimony: "You have been companions of sinners." **5** And in those days the prayer of the righteous will reach unto the Lord, and for you the days of your judgement will come. **6** And all the words of your unrighteousness will be read out before the Great Holy One, and your faces will be covered with shame, and He will reject every work which is grounded on unrighteousness. **7** Woe to you, you sinners, who live on the mid ocean and on the dry land, whose remembrance is evil against you. **8** Woe to you who acquire silver and gold in unrighteousness and say: "We have become rich with riches and have possessions; and have acquired everything we have desired. **9** And now let us do what we purposed: For we have gathered silver, and many are the husbandmen in our houses." And our granaries are (brim) full as with water, **10** yea and like water your lies will flow away; for your riches will not abide but speedily ascend from you; for you have acquired it all in unrighteousness, and you will be given over to a great curse.

CHAPTER 98

1 And now I swear unto you, to the wise and to the foolish, for you will have manifold experiences on the earth. 2 For you men will put on more adornments than a woman, and colored garments more than a virgin: In royalty and in grandeur and in power, and in silver and in gold and in purple, and in splendor and in food they will be poured out as water. 3 Therefore they will be wanting in doctrine and wisdom, and they will perish thereby together with their possessions; and with all their glory and their splendor, and in shame and in slaughter and in great destitution, their spirits will be cast into the furnace of fire. 4 I have sworn unto you, you sinners, as a mountain has not become a slave, and a hill does not become the handmaid of a woman, even so sin has not been sent upon the earth, but man of himself has created it, and under a great curse will they fall who commit it. 5 And barrenness has not been given to the woman, but on account of the deeds of her own hands she dies without children. 6 I have sworn unto you, you sinners, by the Holy Great One, that all your evil deeds are revealed in the heavens, and that none of your deeds of oppression are covered and hidden. 7 And do not think in your spirit nor say in your heart that you do not know and that you do not see that every sin is every day recorded in heaven in the presence of the Most High. 8 From now on you know that all your oppression with which you oppress is written down every day until the day of your judgement. 9 Woe to you, you fools, for through your folly will you perish: and you transgress against the wise, and so good hap will not be your portion. 10 And now, know that you are prepared for the day of destruction: for that reason, do not hope to live, you sinners, but you will depart and die; for you know no ransom; for you are prepared for the day of the great judgement, for the day of tribulation and great shame for your spirits. 11 Woe to you, you obstinate of heart, who work wickedness and eat blood: From where have you good things to eat and to drink and to be filled? From all the good things which the Lord the Most High has placed in abundance on the earth; therefore, you will have no peace. 12 Woe to you who love the deeds of unrighteousness: why do you hope for good

for yourselves? Know that you will be delivered into the hands of the righteous, and they will cut off your necks and slay you and have no mercy upon you. 13 Woe to you who rejoice in the tribulation of the righteous; for no grave will be dug for you. 14 Woe to you who set as nothing the words of the righteous; for you will have no hope of life. 15 Woe to you who write down lying and godless words; for they write down their lies that men may hear them and act godlessly towards (their) neighbor. 16 Therefore they will have no peace but die a sudden death.

CHAPTER 99

1 Woe to you who work godlessness, and glory in lying and extol them: you will perish, and no happy life will be yours. 2 Woe to them who pervert the words of uprightness, and transgress the eternal law, and transform themselves into what they were not [into sinners]: They will be trodden under foot upon the earth. 3 In those days make ready, you righteous, to raise your prayers as a memorial, and place them as a testimony before the angels, that they may place the sin of the sinners for a memorial before the Most High. 4 In those days the nations will be stirred up, and the families of the nations will arise on the day of destruction. 5 And in those days the destitute will go out and carry off their children, and they will abandon them, so that their children will perish through them: Yea, they will abandon their children (that are still) sucklings, and not return to them, and will have no pity on their beloved ones. 6 And again I swear to you, you sinners, that sin is prepared for a day of unceasing bloodshed. 7 And they who worship stones, and grave images of gold and silver and wood (and stone) and clay, and those who worship impure spirits and demons, and all kinds of idols not according to knowledge, will get no manner of help from them. 8 And they will become godless by reason of the folly of their hearts, and their eyes will be blinded through the fear of their hearts and through visions in their dreams. 9 Through these they will become godless and fearful; For they will have wrought all their work in a lie, and will have worshiped a stone: Therefore, in an instant will they perish. 10 But in those days blessed are all they who accept the words of wisdom, and understand them, and observe the paths of the Most High, and walk in the path of His righteousness, and become not godless with

the godless; For they will be saved. **11** Woe to you who spread evil to your neighbors; For you will be slain in Sheol. **12** Woe to you who make deceitful and false measures, and (to them) who cause bitterness on the earth; For they will thereby be utterly consumed. **13** Woe to you who build your houses through the grievous toil of others, and all their building materials are the bricks and stones of sin; I tell you that you will have no peace. **14** Woe to them who reject the measure and eternal heritage of their fathers and whose souls follow after idols; For they will have no rest. **15** Woe to them who work unrighteousness and help oppression and slay their neighbors until the day of the great judgement. **16** For He will cast down your glory, and bring affliction on your hearts, and will arouse His fierce indignation and destroy you all with the sword; and all the holy and righteous will remember your sins.

CHAPTER 100

1 And in those days in one place the fathers together with their sons will be smitten and brothers one with another will fall in death until the streams flow with their blood. **2** For a man will not withhold his hand from slaying his sons and his sons' sons, and the sinner will not withhold his hand from his honored brother: From dawn until sunset they will slay one another. **3** And the horse will walk up to the breast in the blood of sinners, and the chariot will be submerged to its height. **4** In those days the angels will descend into the secret places and gather together into one place all those who brought down sin And the Most High will arise on that day of judgement to execute great judgement among sinners. **5** And over all the righteous and holy He will appoint guardians from among the holy angels to guard them as the apple of an eye, until He makes an end of all wickedness and all sin, and though the righteous sleep a long sleep, they have nothing to fear. **6** And (then) the children of the earth will see the wise in security, and will understand all the words of this book, and recognize that their riches will not be able to save them in the overthrow of their sins. **7** Woe to you, sinners, on the day of strong anguish, you who afflict the righteous and burn them with fire: you will be requited according to your works. **8** Woe to you, you obstinate of heart, who watch in order to devise wickedness: Therefore, will fear come upon you and there will be none to help you.

9 Woe to you, you sinners, on account of the words of your mouth, and on account of the deeds of your hands which your godlessness as wrought, in blazing flames burning worse than fire will you burn. **10** And now, know that from the angels He will inquire as to your deeds in heaven, from the sun and from the moon and from the stars in reference to your sins because upon the earth you execute judgement on the righteous. **11** And He will summon to testify against you every cloud and mist and dew and rain; for they will all be withheld because of you from descending upon you, and they will be mindful of your sins. **12** And now give presents to the rain that it be not withheld from descending upon you, nor yet the dew, when it has received gold and silver from you that it may descend. **13** When the hoar-frost and snow with their chilliness, and all the snow-storms with all their plagues fall upon you, in those days you will not be able to stand before them.

CHAPTER 101

1 Observe the heaven, you children of heaven, and every work of the Most High, and fear you Him and work no evil in His presence. **2** If He closes the windows of heaven, and withholds the rain and the dew from descending on the earth on your account, what will you do then? **3** And if He sends His anger upon you because of your deeds, you cannot petition Him; for you spoke proud and insolent words against His righteousness: therefore, you will have no peace. **4** And see you not the sailors of the ships, how their ships are tossed to and fro by the waves, and are shaken by the winds, and are in sore trouble? **5** And therefore, do they fear because all their goodly possessions go upon the sea with them, and they have evil forebodings of heart that the sea will swallow them and they will perish therein. **6** Are not the entire sea and all its waters, and all its movements, the work of the Most High, and has He not set limits to its doings, and confined it throughout by the sand? **7** And at His reproof it is afraid and dries up, and all its fish die and all that is in it; But you sinners that are on the earth fear Him not. **8** Has He not made the heaven and the earth, and all that is therein? Who has given understanding and wisdom to everything that moves on the earth and in the sea. **9** Do not the sailors of the ships fear the sea? Yet sinners fear not the Most High.

CHAPTER 102

1 In those days when He has brought a grievous fire upon you, where will you flee, and where will you find deliverance? And when He launches out His Word against you Will you not be affrighted and fear? 2 And all the luminaries will be frightened with great fear, and all the earth will be frightened and tremble and be alarmed. 3 And all the angels will execute their commands and will seek to hide themselves from the presence of the Great Glory, and the children of earth will tremble and quake; and you sinners will be cursed forever, and you will have no peace. 4 Fear you not, you souls of the righteous, and be hopeful you that have died in righteousness. 5 And grieve not if your soul into Sheol has descended in grief, and that in your life your body fared not according to your goodness but wait for the day of the judgement of sinners and for the day of cursing and chastisement. 6 And yet when you die the sinners speak over you: "As we die, so die the righteous, and what benefit do they reap for their deeds? 7 Behold, even as we, so do they die in grief and darkness, and what have they more than we? From now on we are equal. 8 And what will they receive and what will they see forever? Behold, they too have died, and from now on and forever will they see no light." 9 I tell you, you sinners, you are content to eat and drink, and rob and sin, and strip men naked, and acquire wealth and see good days. 10 Have you seen the righteous how their end falls out, that no manner of violence is found in them until their death? 11 "Nevertheless they perished and became as though they had not been, and their spirits descended into Sheol in tribulation."

CHAPTER 103

1 Now, therefore, I swear to you, the righteous, by the glory of the Great and Honored and Mighty One in dominion, and by His greatness I swear to you. 2 I know a mystery and have read the heavenly tablets, and have seen the holy books, and have found written therein and inscribed regarding them: 3 That all goodness and joy and glory are prepared for them and written down for the spirits of those who have died in righteousness, and that manifold good will be given to you in recompense for your labors, and that your lot is abundantly beyond the lot of the living. 4 And the spirits of you who have died in righteousness will live and rejoice, and their spirits will not perish, nor

their memorial from before the face of the Great One unto all the generations of the world: for that reason, no longer fear their insolence. 5 Woe to you, you sinners, when you have died, if you die in the wealth of your sins, and those who are like you say regarding you: "Blessed are the sinners: they have seen all their days. 6 And how they have died in prosperity and in wealth and have not seen tribulation or murder in their life; And they have died in honor, and judgement has not been executed on them during their life." 7 Know that their souls will be made to descend into Sheol and they will be wretched in their great tribulation. 8 And into darkness and chains and a burning flame where there is grievous judgement will your spirits enter; and the great judgement will be for all the generations of the world. Woe to you, for you will have no peace. 9 Say not in regard to the righteous and good who are in life: "In our troubled days we have toiled laboriously and experienced every trouble, and have met with much evil and been consumed, and have become few and our spirit small. 10 And we have been destroyed and have not found any to help us even with a word: We have been tortured [and destroyed], and not hoped to see life from day to day. 11 We hoped to be the head and have become the tail: We have toiled laboriously and had no satisfaction in our toil; and we have become the food of the sinners and the unrighteous, and they have laid their yoke heavily upon us. 12 They have had dominion over us that hated us and smote us; and to those that hated us we have bowed our necks but they pitied us not. 13 We desired to get away from them that we might escape and be at rest but found no place where we should flee and be safe from them. 14 And are complained to the rulers in our tribulation, and cried out against those who devoured us, but they did not attend to our cries and would not hearken to our voice. 15 And they helped those who robbed us and devoured us and those who made us few; and they concealed their oppression, and they did not remove from us the yoke of those that devoured us and dispersed us and murdered us, and they concealed their murder, and remembered not that they had lifted up their hands against us."

CHAPTER 104

1 I swear unto you, that in heaven the angels remember you for good before the glory of the Great One: and your names are written before

the glory of the Great One. **2** Be hopeful; for previously you were put to shame through ill and affliction; but now you will shine as the lights of heaven, you will shine, and you will be seen, and the portals of heaven will be opened to you. **3** And in your cry, cry for judgement, and it will appear to you; for all your tribulation will be visited on the rulers, and on all who helped those who plundered you. **4** Be hopeful and cast not away your hopes for you will have great joy as the angels of heaven. **5** What will you be obliged to do? You will not have to hide on the day of the great judgement and you will not be found as sinners, and the eternal judgement will be far from you for all the generations of the world. **6** And now fear not, you righteous, when you see the sinners growing strong and prospering in their ways: be not companions with them but keep afar from their violence; for you will become companions of the hosts of heaven. **7** And, although you sinners say: "All our sins will not be searched out and be written down," nevertheless they will write down all your sins every day. **8** And now I show unto you that light and darkness, day and night, see all your sins. **9** Be not godless in your hearts and lie not and alter not the words of uprightness, nor charge with lying the words of the Holy Great One, nor take account of your idols; for all your lying and all your godlessness issue not in righteousness but in great sin. **10** And now I know this mystery, that sinners will alter and pervert the words of righteousness in many ways, and will speak wicked words, and lie, and practice great deceits, and write books concerning their words. **11** But when they write down truthfully all my words in their languages, and do not change or diminish from my words but write them all down truthfully— all that I first testified concerning them. **12** Then, I know another mystery, that books will be given to the righteous and the wise to become a cause of joy and uprightness and much wisdom. **13** And to them will the books be given, and they will believe in them and rejoice over them, and then will all the righteous who have learnt therefrom all the paths of uprightness be recompensed."

CHAPTER 105

1 In those days the Lord bade (them) to summon and testify to the children of earth concerning their wisdom: Show (it) unto them; for you are their guides, and a recompense over the whole earth. **2** For I and My son will be united with them forever in the paths of uprightness in their lives; and you will have peace: rejoice, you children of uprightness. Amen.

CHAPTER 106

1 And after some days my son Methuselah took a wife for his son Lamech, and she became pregnant by him and bore a son. **2** And his body was white as snow and red as the blooming of a rose, and the hair of his head and his long locks were white as wool, and his eyes beautiful. And when he opened his eyes, he lighted up the whole house like the sun, and the whole house was very bright. **3** And immediately he arose in the hands of the midwife, opened his mouth, and conversed with the Lord of righteousness. **4** And his father Lamech was afraid of him and fled and came to his father Methuselah. **5** And he said unto him: "I have begotten a strange son, diverse from and unlike man, and resembling the sons of the God of heaven; and his nature is different, and he is not like us, and his eyes are as the rays of the sun, and his countenance is glorious. **6** And it seems to me that he is not sprung from me but from the angels, and I fear that in his days a wonder may be wrought on the earth. **7** And now, my father, I am here to petition you and implore you that you may go to Enoch, our father, and learn from him the truth, for his dwelling-place is among the angels." **8** And when Methuselah heard the words of his son, he came to me to the ends of the earth; for he had heard that I was there, and he cried aloud, and I heard his voice and I came to him. And I said unto him: "Behold, here am I, my son, why have you come to me?" **9** And he answered and said: "Because of a great cause of anxiety have I come to you, and because of a disturbing vision have I approached. **10** And now, my father, hear me: unto Lamech my son there has been born a son, the like of whom there is none, and his nature is not like man's nature, and the color of his body is whiter than snow and redder than the bloom of a rose, and the hair of his head is whiter than white wool, and his eyes are like the rays of the sun, and he opened his eyes and immediately lighted up the whole house. **11** And he arose in the hands of the midwife and opened his mouth and blessed the Lord of heaven. **12** And his father Lamech became afraid and fled to me and did not believe that he was sprung from him, but that he was in the likeness of the angels of heaven; and behold I have come to you that you may make known to me the truth." **13** And I, Enoch, answered and said unto him: "The Lord will do a new thing on the earth, and this I have already seen in a vision, and make known to you that in the generation of my father Jared some of the angels of heaven transgressed the word of the Lord. **14** And behold they commit sin and transgress the law and have united themselves with women and commit sin with them, and have married some of them, and have begot children by them. And they will produce on the earth giants not according to the spirit, but according to the flesh, and there will be a great punishment on the earth, and the earth will be cleansed from all impurity. **15** Yea, there will come a great destruction over the whole earth, and there will be a deluge and a great destruction for one year. **16** And this son who has been born unto you will be left on the earth, **17** and his three children will be saved with him: when all mankind that are on the earth will die [he and his sons will be saved]. **18** And now make known to your son Lamech that he who has been born is in truth his son and call his name Noah; for he will be left to you, and he and his sons will be saved from the destruction, which will come upon the earth on account of all the sin and all the unrighteousness, which will be consummated on the earth in his days. **19** And after that there will be still more unrighteousness than that which was first consummated on the earth; for I know the mysteries of the holy ones; for He, the Lord, has showed me and informed me, and I have read (them) in the heavenly tablets."

CHAPTER 107

1 "And I saw written on them that generation upon generation will transgress, until a generation of righteousness arises, and transgression is destroyed, and sin passes away from the earth, and all manner of good comes upon it. **2** And now, my son, go and make known to your son Lamech that this son, which has been born, is in truth his son, and that (this) is no lie." **3** And when Methuselah had heard the words of his father Enoch—for he had shown to him everything in secret—he returned and showed (them) to him and called the name of that son Noah; for he will comfort the earth after all the destruction.

CHAPTER 108

1 Another book which Enoch wrote for his son Methuselah and for those who will come after

him and keep the law in the last days. **2** You who have done good will wait for those days until an end is made of those who work evil; and an end of the might of the transgressors. **3** And wait you indeed until sin has passed away, for their names will be blotted out of the book of life and out of the holy books, and their seed will be destroyed forever, and their spirits will be slain, and they will cry and make lamentation in a place that is a chaotic wilderness, and in the fire will they burn; for there is no earth there. **4** And I saw there something like an invisible cloud; for by reason of its depth I could not look over, and I saw a flame of fire blazing brightly, and things like shining mountains circling and sweeping to and fro. **5** And I asked one of the holy angels who was with me and said unto him: "What is this shining thing? For it is not a heaven but only the flame of a blazing fire, and the voice of weeping and crying and lamentation and strong pain." **6** And he said unto me: "This place which you see here are cast the spirits of sinners and blasphemers, and of those who work wickedness, and of those who pervert everything that the Lord has spoken through the mouth of the prophets—(even) the things that will be. **7** For some of them are written and inscribed above in the heaven, in order that the angels may read them and know that which will befall the sinners, and the spirits of the humble, and of those who have afflicted their bodies, and been recompensed by God; and of those who have been put to shame by wicked men: **8** Who love God and loved neither gold nor silver nor any of the good things which are in the world, but gave over their bodies to torture. **9** Who, since they came into being, longed not after earthly food, but regarded everything as a passing breath, and lived accordingly, and the Lord tried them much, and their spirits were found pure so that they should bless His name. **10** And all the blessings destined for them I have recounted in the books. And he has assigned them their recompense, because they have been found to be such as loved heaven more than their life in the world, and though they were trodden under foot of wicked men, and experienced abuse and reviling from them and were put to shame, yet they blessed Me. **11** And now I will summon the spirits of the good who belong to the generation of light, and I will transform those who were born in darkness, who in the flesh were not recompensed with such honor as their faithfulness deserved. **12** And I will bring out in shining light those who have loved My holy name, and I will seat each on the throne of his honor. **13** And they will be resplendent for times without number; for righteousness is the judgement of God; for to the faithful He will give faithfulness in the habitation of upright paths. **14** And they will see those who were, born in darkness led into darkness, while the righteous will be resplendent. **15** And the sinners will cry aloud and see them resplendent, and they indeed will go where days and seasons are prescribed for them."

JUBILEES

The Book of Jubilees, sometimes called Lesser Genesis (Leptogenesis), is an ancient Jewish religious work of 50 chapters, considered canonical by the Ethiopian Orthodox Church as well as Beta Israel (Ethiopian Jews), where it is known as the Book of Division. Jubilees is considered one of the pseudepigrapha by Protestant, Roman Catholic, and Eastern Orthodox Churches. It is also not considered canonical within Judaism outside of Beta Israel.

This is the history of the division of the days of the law and of the testimony, of the events of the years, of their (year) weeks, of their Jubilees throughout all the years of the world, as the Lord spoke to Moses on Mount Sinai when he went up to receive the tables of the law and of the commandment, according to the voice of God as he said unto him, "Go up to the top of the Mount."

CHAPTER 1

1 And it came to pass in the first year of the exodus of the children of Israel out of Egypt, in the third month, on the sixteenth day of the month, that God spoke to Moses, saying: "Come up to Me on the Mount, and I will give you two tables of stone of the law and of the commandment, which I have written, that you may teach them." **2** And Moses went up into the mount of God, and the glory of the Lord abode on Mount Sinai, and a cloud overshadowed it six days. **3** And He called to Moses on the seventh day out of the midst of the cloud, and the appearance of the glory of the Lord was like a flaming fire on the top of the Mount. **4** And Moses was on the Mount forty days and forty nights, and God taught him the earlier and the later history of the division of all the days of the law and of the testimony. **5** And He said: "Incline your heart to every word which I shall speak to you on this Mount and write them in a book in order that their generations may see how I have not forsaken them for all the evil which they have wrought in transgressing the covenant which I establish between Me and you for their generations this day on Mount Sinai. **6** And thus it will come to pass when all these things

come upon them, that they will recognize that I am more righteous than they in all their judgments and in all their actions, and they will recognize that I have been truly with them. **7** And do you write for thyself all these words which I declare unto you this day, for I know their rebellion and their stiff neck, before I bring them into the land of which I swore to their fathers, to Abraham and to Isaac and to Jacob, saying: "Unto your seed will I give a land flowing with milk and honey. **8** And they will eat and be satisfied, and they will turn to strange gods, to (gods) which cannot deliver them from aught of their tribulation: "and this witness shall be heard for a witness against them. **9** For they will forget all My commandments, (even) all that I command them, and they will walk after the Gentiles, and after their uncleanness, and after their shame, and will serve their gods, and these will prove unto them an offence and a tribulation and an affliction and a snare. **10** And many will perish and they will be taken captive, and will fall into the hands of the enemy, because they have forsaken My ordinances and My commandments, and the festivals of My covenant, and My sabbaths, and My holy place which I have hallowed for Myself in their midst, and My tabernacle, and My sanctuary, which I have hallowed for Myself in the midst of the land, that I should set My name upon it, and that it should dwell (there). **11** And they will make to themselves high places and groves and graven images, and they will worship, each his own (graven image), so as to go astray, and they will sacrifice their children to demons, and to all the works of the error of their hearts. **12** And I will send witnesses unto them, that I may witness against them, but they will not hear, and will slay the witnesses also, and they will persecute those who seek the law, and they will abrogate and change everything so as to work evil before My eyes. **13** And I shall hide My face from them, and I shall deliver them into the hand of the Gentiles for captivity, and for a prey, and for devouring, and I shall remove them from the midst of the land, and I shall scatter them among the Gentiles. **14** And they will forget all My law and all My commandments and all My judgments, and will go astray as to new moons, and sabbaths, and festivals, and jubilees, and ordinances. 15 And after this they will turn to Me from among the Gentiles with all their heart and with all their soul and with all their strength, and I shall gather them from among all the Gentiles, and they will seek Me, so that I shall be found of them, when they seek Me with all their heart and with all their soul. 16 And I shall disclose to them abounding peace with righteousness, and I shall remove them the plant of uprightness with all My heart and with all My soul, and they will be for a blessing and not for a curse, and they will be the head and not the tail. 17 And I shall build My sanctuary in their midst, and I shall dwell with them, and I shall be their God and they will be My people in truth and righteousness. 18 And I shall not forsake them nor fail them; for I am the Lord their God." 19 And Moses fell on his face and prayed and said, "O Lord my God, do not forsake your people and your inheritance, so that they should wander in the error of their hearts, and do not deliver them into the hands of their enemies, the Gentiles, lest they should rule over them and cause them to sin against you. 20 Let your mercy, O Lord, be lifted up upon your people, and create in them an upright spirit, and let not the spirit of Belial rule over them to accuse them before you, and to ensnare them from all the paths of righteousness, so that they may perish from before your face. 21 But they are your people and your inheritance, which you have delivered with your great power from the hands of the Egyptians: create in them a clean heart and a holy Spirit, and let them not be ensnared in their sins from now on until eternity." 22 And the Lord said unto Moses: "I know their contrariness and their thoughts and their stubbornness, and they will not be obedient until they confess their own sin and the sin of their fathers. 23 And after this they will turn to Me in all uprightness and with all (their) heart and with all (their) soul, and I shall circumcise the foreskin of their heart and the foreskin of the heart of their seed, and I shall create in them a holy spirit, and I shall cleanse them so that they shall not turn away from Me from that day unto eternity. 24 And their souls will cleave to Me and to all My commandments, and they will fulfil My commandments, and I shall be their Father and they will be My children. 25 And they will all be called children of the living God, and every angel and every spirit will know, yea, they will know that these are My children, and that I am their Father in uprightness and righteousness, and that I love them. 26 And do you write down for thyself all these words which I declare unto you on this mountain, the first and the last, which shall come to pass in all the divisions of the days in the law and in the testimony and in the weeks and the jubilees unto eternity, until I descend and dwell with them throughout eternity." 27 And He said to the angel of the presence: "Write for Moses from the beginning of creation until My sanctuary has been built among them for all eternity. 28 And the Lord will appear to the eyes of all, and all will know that I am the God of Israel and the Father of all the children of Jacob, and King on Mount Zion for all eternity. And Zion and Jerusalem will be holy." 29 And the angel of the presence who went before the camp of Israel took the tables of the divisions of the years—from the time of the creation—of the law and of the testimony of the weeks, of the jubilees, according to the individual years, according to all the number of the jubilees [according to the individual years], from the day of the [new] creation when the heavens and the earth shall be renewed and all their creation according to the powers of the heaven, and according to all the creation of the earth, until the sanctuary of the Lord shall be made in Jerusalem on Mount Zion, and all the luminaries be renewed for healing and for peace and for blessing for all the elect of Israel, and that thus it may be from that day and unto all the days of the earth.

CHAPTER 2

1 And the angel of the presence spoke to Moses according to the word of the Lord, saying: Write the complete history of the creation, how in six days the Lord God finished all His works and all that He created, and kept Sabbath on the seventh day and hallowed it for all ages, and appointed it as a sign for all His works. 2 For on the first day He created the heavens which are above and the earth and the waters and all the spirits which serve before Him—the angels of the presence, and the angels of sanctification, and the angels [of the spirit of fire and the angels] of the spirit of the winds, and the angels of the spirit of the clouds, and of darkness, and of snow and of hail and of hoar frost, and the angels of the voices and of the thunder and of the lightning, and the angels of the spirits of cold and of heat, and of winter and of spring

and of autumn and of summer, and of all the spirits of His creatures which are in the heavens and on the earth, (He created) the abysses and the darkness, eventide (and night), and the light, dawn and day, which He has prepared in the knowledge of His heart. 3 And immediately we saw His works, and praised Him, and lauded before Him on account of all His works; for seven great works did He create on the first day. 4 And on the second day He created the firmament in the midst of the waters, and the waters were divided on that day—half of them went up above and half of them went down below the firmament (that was) in the midst over the face of the whole earth. And this was the only work (God) created on the second day. 5 And on the third day He commanded the waters to pass from off the face of the whole earth into one place, and the dry land to appear. 6 And the waters did so as He commanded them, and they retired from off the face of the earth into one place outside of this firmament, and the dry land appeared. 7 And on that day He created for them all the seas according to their separate gathering-places, and all the rivers, and the gatherings of the waters in the mountains and on all the earth, and all the lakes, and all the dew of the earth, and the seed which is sown, and all sprouting things, and fruit-bearing trees, and trees of the wood, and the garden of Eden, in Eden, and all (plants after their kind). These four great works God created on the third day. 8 And on the fourth day He created the sun and the moon and the stars, and set them in the firmament of the heaven, to give light upon all the earth, and to rule over the day and the night, and divide the light from the darkness. 9 And God appointed the sun to be a great sign on the earth for days and for sabbaths and for months and for feasts and for years and for sabbaths of years and for jubilees and for all seasons of the years. 10 And it divides the light from the darkness [and] for prosperity, that all things may prosper which shoot and grow on the earth. These three kinds He made on the fourth day. 11 And on the fifth day He created great sea monsters in the depths of the waters, for these were the first things of flesh that were created by His hands, the fish and everything that moves in the waters, and everything that flies, the birds and all their kind. 12 And the sun rose above them to prosper (them), and above everything that was on the earth, everything that shoots out of the earth, and all fruit-bearing trees, and all flesh. These three

kinds He created on the fifth day. 13 And on the sixth day He created all the animals of the earth, and all cattle, and everything that moves on the earth. 14 And after all this He created man, a man and a woman created He them, and gave him dominion over all that is upon the earth, and in the seas, and over everything that flies, and over beasts and over cattle, and over everything that moves on the earth, and over the whole earth, and over all this He gave him dominion. And these four kinds He created on the sixth day. 15 And there were altogether two and twenty kinds. 16 And He finished all His work on the sixth day—all that is in the heavens and on the earth, and in the seas and in the abysses, and in the light and in the darkness, and in everything. 17 And He gave us a great sign, the Sabbath day, that we should work six days, but keep Sabbath on the seventh day from all work. 18 And all the angels of the presence, and all the angels of sanctification, these two great classes—He has bidden us to keep the Sabbath with Him in heaven and on earth. 19 And He said unto us: "Behold, I will separate unto Myself a people from among all the peoples, and these will keep the Sabbath day, and I will sanctify them unto Myself as My people and will bless them; as I have sanctified the Sabbath day and do sanctify (it) unto Myself, even so shall I bless them, and they will be My people and I shall be their God. 20 And I have chosen the seed of Jacob from among all that I have seen, and have written him down as My firstborn son, and have sanctified him unto Myself forever and ever; and I will teach them the Sabbath day, that they may keep Sabbath thereon from all work." 21 And thus He created therein a sign in accordance with which they should keep Sabbath with us on the seventh day, to eat and to drink, and to bless Him who has created all things as He has blessed and sanctified unto Himself a peculiar people above all peoples, and that they should keep Sabbath together with us. 22 And He caused His commands to ascend as a sweet savor acceptable before Him all the days. 23 There (were) two and twenty heads of mankind from Adam to Jacob, and two and twenty kinds of work were made until the seventh day; this is blessed and holy; and the former also is blessed and holy; and this one serves with that one for sanctification and blessing. 24 And to this (Jacob and his seed) it was granted that they should always be the blessed and holy ones of the first testimony and law, even as He had sanctified and blessed the Sabbath day on the seventh day. **25** He created heaven and earth and everything that He created in six days, and God made the seventh day holy, for all His works; therefore, He commanded on its behalf that, whoever doth any work thereon shall die, and that he who defiles it shall surely die. **26** For that reason do you command the children of Israel to observe this day that they may keep it holy and not do thereon any work, and not to defile it, as it is holier than all other days. **27** And whoever profanes it shall surely die, and whoever doeth thereon any work shall surely die eternally, that the children of Israel may observe this day throughout their generations, and not be rooted out of the land; for it is a holy day and a blessed day. **28** And everyone who observes it and keeps Sabbath thereon from all his work, will be holy and blessed throughout all days like unto us. **29** Declare and say to the children of Israel the law of this day both that they should keep Sabbath thereon, and that they should not forsake it in the error of their hearts; (and) that it is not lawful to do any work thereon which is unseemly, to do thereon their own pleasure, and that they should not prepare thereon anything to be eaten or drunk. and (that it is not lawful) to draw water or bring in or take out thereon through their gates any burden, which they had not prepared for themselves on the sixth day in their dwellings. **30** And they shall not bring in nor take out from house to house on that day; for that day is more holy and blessed than any jubilee day of the jubilees: on this we kept Sabbath in the heavens before it was made known to any flesh to keep Sabbath thereon on the earth. **31** And the Creator of all things blessed it, but He did not sanctify all peoples and nations to keep Sabbath thereon, but Israel alone: them alone He permitted to eat and drink and to keep Sabbath thereon on the earth. **32** And the Creator of all things blessed this day which He had created for a blessing and a sanctification and a glory above all days. **33** This law and testimony was given to the children of Israel as a law forever unto their generations.

CHAPTER 3

1 And on the six days of the second week we brought, according to the word of God, unto Adam all the beasts, and all the cattle, and all the birds, and everything that moves on the earth, and everything that moves in the water, according to their kinds, and according to their types: the beasts on the first day; the cattle on the second day; the birds on the third day; and all that which moves on the earth on the fourth day; and that which moves in the water on the fifth day. **2** And Adam named them all by their respective names, and as he called them, so was their name. **3** And on these five days Adam saw all these, male and female, according to every kind that was on the earth, but he was alone and found no helpmeet for him. **4** And the Lord said unto us: "It is not good that the man should be alone: let us make a helpmeet for him." **5** And the Lord our God caused a deep sleep to fall upon him, and he slept, and He took for the woman one rib from among his ribs, and this rib was the origin of the woman from among his ribs, and He built up the flesh in its stead, and built the woman. **6** And He awaked Adam out of his sleep and on awaking he rose on the sixth day, and He brought her to him, and he knew her, and said unto her: "This is now bone of my bones and flesh of my flesh; she will be called [my] wife; because she was taken from her husband." **7** Therefore shall man and wife be one, and therefore shall a man leave his father and his mother, and cleave unto his wife, and they shall be one flesh. **8** In the first week was Adam created, and the rib—his wife: in the second week He showed her unto him: and for this reason, the commandment was given to keep in their defilement, for a male seven days, and for a female twice seven days. **9** And after Adam had completed forty days in the land where he had been created, we brought him into the Garden of Eden to until and keep it, but his wife they brought in on the eightieth day, and after this she entered into the Garden of Eden. **10** And for this reason the commandment is written on the heavenly tables in regard to her that giveth birth: "if she bears a male, she shall remain in her uncleanness seven days according to the first week of days, and thirty and three days shall she remain in the blood of her purifying, and she shall not touch any hallowed thing, nor enter into the sanctuary, until she accomplishes these days which (are enjoined) in the case of a male child. **11** But in the case of a female child she shall remain in her uncleanness two weeks of days, according to the first two weeks, and sixty-six days in the blood of her purification, and they will be in all eighty days." **12** And when she had completed these eighty days we brought her into the Garden of Eden, for it is holier than all the earth besides, and every tree that is planted in it is holy. **13** Therefore, there was ordained regarding her who bears a male or a female child the statute of those days that she should touch no hallowed thing, nor enter into the sanctuary until these days for the male or female child are accomplished. **14** This is the law and testimony which was written down for Israel, in order that they should observe (it) all the days. **15** And in the first week of the first jubilee, Adam and his wife were in the Garden of Eden for seven years tilling and keeping it, and we gave him work and we instructed him to do everything that is suitable for tillage. **16** And he tilled (the garden), and was naked and knew it not, and was not ashamed, and he protected the garden from the birds and beasts and cattle, and gathered its fruit, and ate, and put aside the residue for himself and for his wife [and put aside that which was being kept]. **17** And after the completion of the seven years, which he had completed there, seven years exactly, and in the second month, on the seventeenth day (of the month), the serpent came and approached the woman, and the serpent said to the woman, "Hath God commanded you, saying, you shall not eat of every tree of the garden?" **18** And she said to it, "Of all the fruit of the trees of the garden God has said unto us, Eat; but of the fruit of the tree which is in the midst of the garden God has said unto us, you shall not eat thereof, neither shall you touch it, lest you die." **19** And the serpent said unto the woman, "Ye shall not surely die: for God doth know that on the day you shall eat thereof, your eyes will be opened, and you will be as gods, and you will know good and evil." **20** And the woman saw the tree that it was agreeable and pleasant to the eye, and that its fruit was good for food, and she took thereof and ate. **21** And when she had first covered her shame with fig-leaves, she gave thereof to Adam and he ate, and his eyes were opened, and he saw that he was naked. **22** And he took fig-leaves and sewed (them) together, and made an apron for himself, and covered his shame. **32** And God cursed the serpent and was angry with it forever. **24** And He was angry with the woman, because she hearkened to the voice of the serpent, and did eat; and He said unto her: I shall greatly multiply your sorrow and your pains in sorrow you shall bring out children, and your return shall be unto your husband, and he will rule over you." **25** And to Adam also He said, "Because you have hearkened unto the voice of your wife, and have eaten of the tree of which I commanded you that you should not eat thereof, cursed be the ground for your sake: thorns and thistles shall it bring out to you, and you shall eat your bread in the sweat of your face, until you return to the earth from where you were taken; for earth you art, and unto earth shall you return." **26** And He made for them coats of skin, and clothed them, and sent them out from the Garden of Eden. **27** And on that day on which Adam went out from the garden, he offered as a sweet savor an offering, frankincense, galbanum, and stacte, and spices in the morning with the rising of the sun from the day when he covered his shame. **28** And on that day was closed the mouth of all beasts, and of cattle, and of birds, and of whatever walketh, and of whatever moves, so that they could no longer speak: for they had all spoken one with another with one lip and with one tongue. **29** And He sent out of the Garden of Eden all flesh that was in the Garden of Eden, and all flesh was scattered according to its kinds, and according to its types unto the places which had been created for them. **30** And to Adam alone did He give (the wherewithal) to cover his shame, of all the beasts and cattle. **31** On this account, it is prescribed on the heavenly tables as touching all those who know the judgment of the law, that they should cover their shame, and should not uncover themselves as the Gentiles uncover themselves. **32** And on the new moon of the fourth month, Adam and his wife went out from the Garden of Eden, and they dwelt in the land of 'Eldâ, in the land of their creation. **33** And Adam called the name of his wife Eve. **34** And they had no son until the first jubilee, and after this he knew her. **35** Now he tilled the land as he had been instructed in the Garden of Eden.

CHAPTER 4

1 And in the third week in the second jubilees he gave birth to Cain, and in the fourth she gave birth to Abel, and in the fifth she gave birth to her daughter 'Âwân. **2** And in the first (year) of the third jubilee, Cain slew Abel because (God) accepted the sacrifice of Abel and did not accept the offering of Cain. **3** And he slew him in the field: and his blood cried from the ground to heaven, complaining because he had slain him. **4** And the Lord reproved Cain because of Abel, because he had slain him, and he made him a fugitive on the earth because of the blood of his brother, and he cursed him upon the earth. **5** And on this account, it is written on the heavenly tables, "Cursed is he who smites his neighbor treacherously, and let all who have seen and heard say, so be it; and the man who has seen and not declared (it), let him be accursed as the other." And for this reason, we announce when we come before the Lord our God all the sin which is committed in heaven and on earth, and in light and in darkness, and everywhere. 7 And Adam and his wife mourned for Abel four weeks of years, and in the fourth year of the fifth week they became joyful, and Adam knew his wife again, and she bore him a son, and he called his name Seth; for he said "God has raised up a second seed unto us on the earth instead of Abel; for Cain slew him." 8 And in the sixth week he begat his daughter 'Azûrâ. 9 And Cain took 'Âwân his sister to be his wife and she bore him Enoch at the close of the fourth jubilee. And in the first year of the first week of the fifth jubilee, houses were built on the earth, and Cain built a city, and called its name after the name of his son Enoch. 10 And Adam knew Eve his wife and she bare yet nine sons. 11 And in the fifth week of the fifth jubilee Seth took 'Azûrâ his sister to be his wife, and in the fourth (year of the sixth week) she bore him Enos. 12 He began to call on the name of the Lord on the earth. 13 And in the seventh jubilee in the third week Enos took Nôâm his sister to be his wife, and she bore him a son in the third year of the fifth week, and he called his name Kenan. 14 And at the close of the eighth jubilee Kenan took Mûalêlêth his sister to be his wife, and she bore him a son in the ninth jubilee, in the first week in the third year of this week, and he called his name Mahalalel. 15 And in the second week of the tenth jubilee Mahalalel took unto him to wife Dînâh, the daughter of Barâkî'êl the daughter of his father's brother, and she bore him a son in the third week in the sixth year, and he called his name Jared; for in his days the angels of the Lord descended on the earth, those who are named the Watchers, that they should instruct the children of men, and that they should do judgment and uprightness on the earth. 16 And in the eleventh jubilee Jared took to himself a wife, and her name was Bâraka, the daughter of Râsûjâl, a daughter of his father's brother, in the fourth week of this jubilee, and she bore him a son in the fifth week, in the fourth year of the jubilee, and he called his name Enoch. 17 And he was the first among men that are born on earth who learnt writing and

knowledge and wisdom and who wrote down the signs of heaven according to the order of their months in a book, that men might know the seasons of the years according to the order of their separate months. 18 And he was the first to write a testimony, and he testified to the sons of men among the generations of the earth, and recounted the weeks of the jubilees, and made known to them the days of the years and set in order the months and recounted the Sabbaths of the years as we made (them) known to him. 19 And what was and what will be he saw in a vision of his sleep, as it will happen to the children of men throughout their generations until the day of judgment; he saw and understood everything, and wrote his testimony, and placed the testimony on earth for all the children of men and for their generations. 20 And in the twelfth jubilee, in the seventh week thereof, he took to himself a wife, and her name was Ednî, the daughter of Dânêl, the daughter of his father's brother, and in the sixth year in this week she bore him a son and he called his name Methuselah. 21 And he was moreover with the angels of God these six jubilees of years, and they showed him everything which is on earth and in the heavens, the rule of the sun, and he wrote down everything. 22 And he testified to the Watchers, who had sinned with the daughters of men; for these had begun to unite themselves, so as to be defiled, with the daughters of men, and Enoch testified against (them) all. 23 And he was taken from among the children of men, and we conducted him into the Garden of Eden in majesty and honor and behold there he wrote down the condemnation and judgment of the world, and all the wickedness of the children of men. 24 And on account of it (God) brought the waters of the flood upon all the land of Eden; for there he was set as a sign and that he should testify against all the children of men, that he should recount all the deeds of the generations until the day of condemnation. 25 And he burnt the incense of the sanctuary, (even) sweet spices, acceptable before the Lord on the Mount. 26 For the Lord has four places on the earth, the Garden of Eden, and the Mount of the East, and this mountain on which you are this day, Mount Sinai, and Mount Zion (which) will be sanctified in the new creation for a sanctification of the earth; through it will the earth be sanctified from all (its) guilt and its uncleanness throughout the generations of the world. 27 And in the fourteenth jubilee

Methuselah took unto himself a wife, Ednâ the daughter of 'Âzrîâl, the daughter of his father's brother, in the third week, in the first year of this week, and he begat a son and called his name Lamech. **28** And in the fifteenth jubilee in the third week Lamech took to himself a wife, and her name was Bêtênôs the daughter of Bârâkî'îl, the daughter of his father's brother, and in this week she bore him a son and he called his name Noah, saying, "This one will comfort me for my trouble and all my work, and for the ground which the Lord has cursed." **29** And at the close of the nineteenth jubilee, in the seventh week in the sixth year thereof, Adam died, and all his sons buried him in the land of his creation, and he was the first to be buried in the earth. **30** And he lacked seventy years of one thousand years; for one thousand years are as one day in the testimony of the heavens and therefore was it written concerning the tree of knowledge: "On the day that you eat thereof you will die." For this reason he did not complete the years of this day; for he died during it. **31** At the close of this jubilee Cain was killed after him in the same year; for his house fell upon him and he died in the midst of his house, and he was killed by its stones, for with a stone he had killed Abel, and by a stone was he killed in righteous judgment. **32** For this reason it was ordained on the heavenly tables: "With the instrument with which a man kills his neighbor with the same shall he be killed; after the manner that he wounded him, in like manner shall they deal with him." **33** And in the twenty-fifth jubilee Noah took to himself a wife, and her name was 'Ĕmzârâ, the daughter of Râkê'êl, the daughter of his father's brother, in the first year in the fifth week: and in the third year thereof she bore him Shem, in the fifth year thereof she bore him Ham, and in the first year in the sixth week she bore him Japheth

CHAPTER 5

1 And it came to pass when the children of men began to multiply on the face of the earth and daughters were born unto them, that the angels of God saw them on a certain year of this jubilee, that they were beautiful to look upon; and they took themselves wives of all whom they chose, and they bare unto them sons and they were giants. **2** And lawlessness increased on the earth and all flesh corrupted its way, alike men and cattle and beasts and birds and everything that walks on the earth—

all of them corrupted their ways and their orders, and they began to devour each other, and lawlessness increased on the earth and every imagination of the thoughts of all men was evil continually. **3** And God looked upon the earth, and behold it was corrupt, and all flesh had corrupted its orders, and all that were upon the earth had wrought all manner of evil before His eyes. **4** And He said that He would destroy man and all flesh upon the face of the earth which He had created. **5** But Noah found grace before the eyes of the Lord. **6** And against the angels whom He had sent upon the earth, He was exceedingly angry, and He gave commandment to root them out of all their dominion, and He bade us to bind them in the depths of the earth, and behold they are bound in the midst of them and are (kept) separate. **7** And against their sons went out a command from before His face that they should be smitten with the sword and be removed from under heaven. **8** And He said "My spirit will not always abide on man; for they also are flesh and their days will be one hundred and twenty years." **9** And He sent His sword into their midst that each should slay his neighbor, and they began to slay each other until they all fell by the sword and were destroyed from the earth. **10** And their fathers were witnesses (of their destruction), and after this they were bound in the depths of the earth forever, until the day of the great condemnation, when judgment is executed on all those who have corrupted their ways and their works before the Lord. **11** And He destroyed all from their places, and there was not left one of them whom He judged not according to all their wickedness. **12** And he made for all his works a new and righteous nature, so that they should not sin in their whole nature forever but should be all righteous each in his kind always. **13** And the judgment of all is ordained and written on the heavenly tablets in righteousness -even (the judgment of) all who depart from the path which is ordained for them to walk in; and if they walk not therein, judgment is written down for every creature and for every kind. **14** And there is nothing in heaven or on earth, or in light or in darkness, or in Sheol or in the depth, or in the place of darkness (which is not judged); and all their judgments are ordained and written and engraved. **15** In regard to all He will judge, the great according to his greatness, and the small according to his smallness, and each according to his way. **16** And He is not one who will regard the person (of any), nor is He one who will receive gifts, if He says that He will execute judgment on each: if one gave everything that is on the earth, He will not regard the gifts or the person (of any), nor accept anything at his hands, for He is a righteous judge. 17 And of the children of Israel it has been written and ordained: If they turn to him in righteousness He will forgive all their transgressions and pardon all their sins. 18 It is written and ordained that He will show mercy to all who turn from all their guilt once each year. 19 And as for all those who corrupted their ways and their thoughts before the flood, no man's person was accepted save that of Noah alone; for his person was accepted in behalf of his sons, whom (God) saved from the waters of the flood on his account; for his heart was righteous in all his ways, according as it was commanded regarding him, and he had not departed from aught that was ordained for him. 20 And the Lord said that he would destroy everything which was upon the earth, both men and cattle, and beasts, and fowls of the air, and that which moves on the earth. 21 And He commanded Noah to make him an ark, that he might save himself from the waters of the flood. 22 And Noah made the ark in all respects as He commanded him, in the twenty-seventh jubilee of years, in the fifth week in the fifth year (on the new moon of the first month). [1307 A.M.] 23 And he entered in the sixth (year) thereof, [1308 A.M.] in the second month, on the new moon of the second month, until the sixteenth; and he entered, and all that we brought to him, into the ark, and the Lord closed it from without on the seventeenth evening. 24 And the Lord opened seven floodgates of heaven, and the mouths of the fountains of the great deep, seven mouths in number. 25 And the floodgates began to pour down water from the heaven forty days and forty nights, and the fountains of the deep also sent up waters, until the whole world was full of water. 26 And the waters increased upon the earth: Fifteen cubits did the waters rise above all the high mountains, and the ark was lift up above the earth, and it moved upon the face of the waters. 27 And the water prevailed on the face of the earth five months—one hundred and fifty days. 28 And the ark went and rested on the top of Lubar, one of the mountains of Ararat. 29 And (on the new moon) in the fourth month the fountains of the great deep were closed and the flood-gates of heaven were restrained; and

on the new moon of the seventh month all the mouths of the abysses of the earth were opened, and the water began to descend into the deep below. 30 And on the new moon of the tenth month the tops of the mountains were seen, and on the new moon of the first month the earth became visible. 31 And the waters disappeared from above the earth in the fifth week in the seventh year [1309 A.M.] thereof, and on the seventeenth day in the second month the earth was dry. 32 And on the twenty-seventh thereof he opened the ark, and sent out from it beasts, and cattle, and birds, and every moving thing.

CHAPTER 6

1 And on the new moon of the third month he went out from the ark and built an altar on that mountain. 2 And he made atonement for the earth and took a kid and made atonement by its blood for all the guilt of the earth; for everything that had been on it had been destroyed, save those that were in the ark with Noah. 3 And he placed the fat thereof on the altar, and he took an ox, and a goat, and a sheep and kids, and salt, and a turtle-dove, and the young of a dove, and placed a burnt sacrifice on the altar, and poured thereon an offering mingled with oil, and sprinkled wine and strewed frankincense over everything, and caused a goodly savor to arise, acceptable before the Lord. 4 And the Lord smelt the goodly savor and He made a covenant with him that there should not be any more a flood to destroy the earth; that all the days of the earth seed-time and harvest should never cease; cold and heat, and summer and winter, and day and night should not change their order, nor cease forever. 5 "And you, increase you and multiply upon the earth, and become many upon it, and be a blessing upon it. The fear of you and the dread of you I shall inspire in everything that is on earth and in the sea. 6 And behold I have given unto you all beasts, and all winged things, and everything that moves on the earth, and the fish in the waters, and all things for food; as the green herbs, I have given you all things to eat. 7 But flesh, with the life thereof, with the blood, you shall not eat; for the life of all flesh is in the blood, lest your blood of your lives be required. At the hand of every man, at the hand of every (beast), shall I require the blood of man. 8 Whoso sheds man's blood by man shall his blood be shed; for in the image of God made He man. 9 And you, increase ye, and multiply

on the earth." **10** And Noah and his sons swore that they would not eat any blood that was in any flesh, and he made a covenant before the Lord God forever throughout all the generations of the earth in this month. **11** On this account He spoke to you that you should make a covenant with the children of Israel in this month upon the mountain with an oath, and that you should sprinkle blood upon them because of all the words of the covenant, which the Lord made with them forever. **12** And this testimony is written concerning you that you should observe it continually, so that you should not eat on any day any blood of beasts or birds or cattle during all the days of the earth, and the man who eats the blood of beast or of cattle or of birds during all the days of the earth, he and his seed shall be rooted out of the land. **13** And do you command the children of Israel to eat no blood, so that their names and their seed may be before the Lord our God continually. **14** And for this law there is no limit of days, for it is forever. They shall observe it throughout their generations, so that they may continue supplicating on your behalf with blood before the altar; every day and at the time of morning and evening they shall seek forgiveness on your behalf perpetually before the Lord that they may keep it and not be rooted out. **15** And He gave to Noah and his sons a sign that there should not again be a flood on the earth. **16** He set His bow in the cloud for a sign of the eternal covenant that there should not again be a flood on the earth to destroy it all the days of the earth. **17** For this reason it is ordained and written on the heavenly tables, that they should celebrate the feast of weeks in this month once a year, to renew the covenant every year. **18** And this whole festival was celebrated in heaven from the day of creation until the days of Noah-twenty-six jubilees and five weeks of years: and Noah and his sons observed it for seven jubilees and one week of years, until the day of Noah's death, and from the day of Noah's death his sons did away with (it) until the days of Abraham, and they ate blood. **19** But Abraham observed it, and Isaac and Jacob and his children observed it up to your days, and in your days the children of Israel forgot it until you celebrated it anew on this mountain. **20** And do you command the children of Israel to observe this festival in all their generations for a commandment unto them: one day in the year in this month they shall celebrate the festival. **21** For it is the feast of weeks and the feast of first-fruits: this feast is twofold and of a double nature: according to what is written and engraved concerning it celebrate it. **22** For I have written in the book of the first law, in that which I have written for you, that you should celebrate it in its season, one day in the year, and I explained to you its sacrifices that the children of Israel should remember and should celebrate it throughout their generations in this month, one day in every year. **23** And on the new moon of the first month, and on the new moon of the fourth month, and on the new moon of the seventh month, and on the new moon of the tenth month are the days of remembrance, and the days of the seasons in the four divisions of the year. These are written and ordained as a testimony forever. **24** And Noah ordained them for himself as feasts for the generations forever, so that they have become thereby a memorial unto him. **25** And on the new moon of the first month he was bidden to make for himself an ark, and on that (day) the earth became dry and he opened (the ark) and saw the earth. **26** And on the new moon of the fourth month the mouths of the depths of the abysses beneath were closed. And on the new moon of the seventh month all the mouths of the abysses of the earth were opened, and the waters began to descend into them. **27** And on the new moon of the tenth month the tops of the mountains were seen, and Noah was glad. **28** And on this account he ordained them for himself as feasts for a memorial forever, and thus are they ordained. **29** And they placed them on the heavenly tables, each had thirteen weeks; from one to another (passed) their memorial, from the first to the second, and from the second to the third, and from the third to the fourth. **30** And all the days of the commandment will be two and fifty weeks of days, and (these will make) the entire year complete. **31** Thus it is engraved and ordained on the heavenly tables. And there is no neglecting (this commandment) for a single - year or from year to year. **32** And command you the children of Israel that they observe the years according to this reckoning-three hundred and sixty-four days, and (these) will constitute a complete year, and they will not disturb its time from its days and from its feasts; for everything will fall out in them according to their testimony, and they will not leave out any day nor disturb any feasts. **33** But if they do neglect and do not observe them according to His commandment, then they will disturb all their seasons, and the years will be dislodged from this (order), [and they will disturb the seasons and the years will be dislodged] and they will neglect their ordinances. **34** And all the children of Israel will forget, and will not find the path of the years, and will forget the new moons, and seasons, and sabbaths, and they will go wrong as to all the order of the years. **35** For I know and from now on shall I declare it unto you, and it is not of my own devising; for the book (lies) written before me, and on the heavenly tables the division of days is ordained, lest they forget the feasts of the covenant and walk according to the feasts of the Gentiles after their error and after their ignorance. **36** For there will be those who will assuredly make observations of the moon—now (it) disturbs the seasons and comes in from year to year ten days too soon. **37** For this reason the years will come upon them when they will disturb (the order) and make an abominable (day) the day of testimony, and an unclean day a feast day, and they will confound all the days, the holy with the unclean, and the unclean day with the holy; for they will go wrong as to the months and sabbaths and feasts and jubilees. **38** For this reason I command and testify to you that you may testify to them; for after your death your children will disturb (them), so that they will not make the year three hundred and sixty-four days only, and for this reason they will go wrong as to the new moons and seasons and sabbaths and festivals, and they will eat all kinds of blood with all kinds of flesh.

CHAPTER 7

1 And in the seventh week in the first year thereof, in this jubilee, Noah planted vines on the mountain on which the ark had rested, named Lûbâr, one of the Ararat Mountains, and they produced fruit in the fourth year, and he guarded their fruit, and gathered it in this year in the seventh month. **2** And he made wine therefrom and put it into a vessel, and kept it until the fifth year, until the first day, on the new moon of the first month. **3** And he celebrated with joy the day of this feast, and he made a burnt sacrifice unto the Lord, one young ox and one ram, and seven sheep, each a year old, and a kid of the goats, that he might make atonement thereby for himself and his sons. **4** And he prepared the kid first and placed some of its blood on the flesh that was on the altar which he had made, and all the fat he laid on the altar where he made the burnt

sacrifice, and the ox and the ram and the sheep, and he laid all their flesh upon the altar. **5** And he placed all their offerings mingled with oil upon it, and afterwards he sprinkled wine on the fire which he had previously made on the altar, and he placed incense on the altar and caused a sweet savor to ascend acceptable before the Lord his God. **6** And he rejoiced and drank of this wine, he and his children with joy. **7** And it was evening, and he went into his tent, and being drunken he lay down and slept, and was uncovered in his tent as he slept. **8** And Ham saw Noah his father naked and went out and told his two brethren without. **9** And Shem took his garment and arose, he and Japheth, and they placed the garment on their shoulders and went backward and covered the shame of their father, and their faces were backward. **10** And Noah awoke from his sleep and knew all that his younger son had done unto him, and he cursed his son and said: "Cursed be Canaan; an enslaved servant shall he be unto his brethren." **11** And he blessed Shem and said: "Blessed be the Lord God of Shem, and Canaan shall be his servant. **12** God shall enlarge Japheth, and God shall dwell in the dwelling of Shem, and Canaan shall be his servant." **13** And Ham knew that his father had cursed his younger son, and he was displeased that he had cursed his son, and he parted from his father, he and his sons with him, Cush and Mizraim and Put and Canaan. **14** And he built for himself a city and called its name after the name of his wife Nê'êlâtamâ'ûk. **15** And Japheth saw it, and became envious of his brother, and he too built for himself a city, and he called its name after the name of his wife 'Adâtanêsês. **16** And Shem dwelt with his father Noah, and he built a city close to his father on the mountain, and he too called its name after the name of his wife Sêdêqêtêlêbâb. **17** And behold these three cities are near Mount Lûbâr; Sêdêqêtêlêbâb fronting the mountain on its east; and Na'êlâtamâ'ûk on the south; 'Adatanêsês towards the west. **18** And these are the sons of Shem: Elam, and Asshur, and Arpachshad—this (son) was born two years after the flood—and Lud, and Aram. **19** The sons of Japheth: Gomer and Magog and Madai and Javan, Tubal and Meshech and Tiras: these are the sons of Noah. **20** And in the twenty-eighth jubilee Noah began to enjoin upon his sons' sons the ordinances and commandments, and all the judgments that he knew, and he exhorted his sons to observe righteousness, and to cover the shame of their flesh, and to bless their Creator, and honor father and mother, and love their neighbor, and guard their souls from fornication and uncleanness and all iniquity. **21** For owing to these three things came the flood upon the earth, namely, owing to the fornication wherein the Watchers against the law of their ordinances went a whoring after the daughters of men, and took themselves wives of all which they chose: and they made the beginning of uncleanness. **22** And they begat sons the Nâphîdîm, and they were all unlike, and they devoured one another: and the Giants slew the Nâphîl, and the Nâphîl slew the Eljô, and the Eljô mankind, and one man another. **23** And everyone sold himself to work iniquity and to shed much blood, and the earth was filled with iniquity. **24** And after this they sinned against the beasts and birds, and all that moves and walketh on the earth: and much blood was shed on the earth, and every imagination and desire of men imagined vanity and evil continually. **25** And the Lord destroyed everything from off the face of the earth; because of the wickedness of their deeds, and because of the blood which they had shed in the midst of the earth He destroyed everything. **26** "And we were left, I and you, my sons, and everything that entered with us into the ark, and behold I see your works before me that you do not walk in righteousness; for in the path of destruction you have begun to walk, and you are parting one from another, and are envious one of another, and (so it comes) that you are not in harmony, my sons, each with his brother. **27** For I see and behold the demons have begun (their) seductions against you and against your children, and now I fear on your behalf, that after my death you will shed the blood of men upon the earth, and that ye, too, will be destroyed from the face of the earth. **28** For whoso sheds man's blood, and whoso eats the blood of any flesh, will all be destroyed from the earth. **29** And there will not be left any man that eats blood. Or that sheds the blood of man on the earth, nor will there be left to him any seed or descendants living under heaven; For into Sheol will they go, and into the place of condemnation will they descend. And into the darkness of the deep will they all be removed by a violent death. **30** There shall be no blood seen upon you of all the blood there shall be all the days in which you have killed any beasts or cattle or whatever flies upon the earth and work you a good work to your souls by covering that which has been shed on the face of the earth. **31** And you shall not be like him who eats with blood, but guard yourselves that none may eat blood before you: cover the blood, for thus have I been commanded to testify to you and your children, together with all flesh. **32** And suffer not the soul to be eaten with the flesh, that your blood, which is your life, may not be required at the hand of any flesh that sheds (it) on the earth. **33** For the earth will not be clean from the blood which has been shed upon it; for (only) through the blood of him that shed it will the earth be purified throughout all its generations. **34** And now, my children, hearken: work judgment and righteousness that you may be planted in righteousness over the face of the whole earth, and your glory lifted up before my God, who saved me from the waters of the flood. **35** And behold, you will go and build for yourselves cities, and plant in them all the plants that are upon the earth, and moreover all fruit-bearing trees. **36** For three years the fruit of everything that is eaten will not be gathered: and in the fourth year its fruit will be accounted holy [and they will offer the first-fruits], acceptable before the Most High God, who created heaven and earth and all things. Let them offer in abundance the first of the wine and oil (as) first-fruits on the altar of the Lord, who receives it, and what is left let the servants of the house of the Lord eat before the altar which receives (it). **37** And in the fifth year make you the release so that you release it in righteousness and uprightness, and you shall be righteous, and all that you plant will prosper. **38** For thus did Enoch, the father of your father command Methuselah, his son, and Methuselah his son Lamech, and Lamech commanded me all the things which his fathers commanded him. **39** And I also will give you commandment, my sons, as Enoch commanded his son in the first jubilees: while still living, the seventh in his generation, he commanded and testified to his son and to his sons' sons until the day of his death."

CHAPTER 8

1 In the twenty-ninth jubilee, in the first week, in the beginning thereof Arpachshad took to himself a wife and her name was Râsû'ĕjâ, [the daughter of Sûsân,] the daughter of Elam, and she bore him a son in the third year in this week, and he called his name Kâinâm. **2** And the son grew, and his father taught him writing, and he went to seek for himself a place where he might seize for himself a city. 3 And he found a writing which former (generations) had carved on the rock, and he read what was thereon, and he transcribed it and sinned owing to it; for it contained the teaching of the Watchers in accordance with which they used to observe the omens of the sun and moon and stars in all the signs of heaven. 4 And he wrote it down and said nothing regarding it; for he was afraid to speak to Noah about it lest he should be angry with him on account of it. 5 And in the thirtieth jubilee, in the second week, in the first year thereof, he took to himself a wife, and her name was Mêlkâ, the daughter of Madai, the son of Japheth, and in the fourth year he begat a son, and called his name Shelah; for he said: "Truly I have been sent." 6 [And in the fourth year he was born], and Shelah grew up and took to himself a wife, and her name was Mû'ak, the daughter of Kêsêd, his father's brother, in the one and thirtieth jubilee, in the fifth week, in the first year thereof. 7 And she bore him a son in the fifth year thereof, and he called his name Eber: and he took unto himself a wife, and her name was 'Azûrâd the daughter of Nêbrôd, in the thirty-second jubilee, in the seventh week, in the third year thereof. 8 And in the sixth year thereof, she bore him a son, and he called his name Peleg; for in the days when he was born the children of Noah began to divide the earth among themselves: for this reason he called his name Peleg. 9 And they divided (it) secretly among themselves and told it to Noah. 10 And it came to pass in the beginning of the thirty-third jubilee that they divided the earth into three parts, for Shem and Ham and Japheth, according to the inheritance of each, in the first year in the first week, when one of us, who had been sent, was with them. 11 And he called his sons, and they drew nigh to him, they and their children, and he divided the earth into the lots, which his three sons were to take in possession, and they reached out their hands, and took the writing out of the bosom of Noah, their father. 12 And there came out on the writing as Shem's lot the middle of the earth which he should take as an inheritance for himself and for his sons for the generations of eternity, from the middle of the mountain range of Râfâ, from the mouth of the water from the river Tînâ. and his portion goes towards the west through the midst of this river, and it extends until it reaches the water

of the abysses, out of which this river goes out and pours its waters into the sea Mê'at, and this river flows into the great sea. And all that is towards the north is Japheth's, and all that is towards the south belongs to Shem. 13 And it extends until it reaches Kârâsô: this is in the bosom of the tongue which looks towards the south. 14 And his portion extends along the great sea, and it extends in a straight line until it reaches the west of the tongue which looks towards the south; for this sea is named the tongue of the Egyptian Sea. 15 And it turns from here towards the south towards the mouth of the great sea on the shore of (its) waters, and it extends to the west to 'Afrâ and it extends until it reaches the waters of the river Gihon, and to the south of the waters of Gihon, to the banks of this river. 16 And it extends towards the east, until it reaches the Garden of Eden, to the south thereof, [to the south] and from the east of the whole land of Eden and of the whole cast, it turns to the east, and proceeds until it reaches the east of the mountain named Râfâ, and it descends to the bank of the mouth of the river Tînâ. 17 This portion came out by lot for Shem and his sons, that they should possess it forever unto his generations forevermore. 18 And Noah rejoiced that this portion came out for Shem and for his sons, and he remembered all that he had spoken with his mouth in prophecy; for he had said: Blessed be the Lord God of Shem, and may the Lord dwell in the dwelling of Shem." 19 And he knew that the Garden of Eden is the holy of holies, and the dwelling of the Lord, and Mount Sinai the center of the desert, and Mount Zion—the center of the navel of the earth: these three were created as holy places facing each other. 20 And he blessed the God of gods, who had put the word of the Lord into his mouth, and the Lord forevermore. 21 And he knew that a blessed portion and a blessing had come to Shem and his sons unto the generations forever—the whole land of Eden and the whole land of the Red Sea, and the whole land of the east, and India, and on the Red Sea and the mountains thereof, and all the land of Bashan, and all the land of Lebanon and the islands of Kaftûr, and all the mountains of Sanîr and 'Amânâ, and the mountains of Asshur in the north, and all the land of Elam, Asshur, and Bâbêl, and Sûsân and Mâ'ĕdâi and all the mountains of Ararat, and all the region beyond the sea, which is beyond the mountains of Asshur towards the north, a blessed and spacious land, and all that is in it is very good. **22** And for Ham came out the second portion, beyond the Gihon towards the south to the right of the Garden, and it extends towards the south and it extends to all the mountains of fire, and it extends towards the west to the sea of 'Atêl and it extends towards the west until it reaches the sea of Mâ'ûk—that (sea) into which everything which is not destroyed descends. **23** And it goes out towards the north to the limits of Gâdir, and it goes out to the coast of the waters of the sea to the waters of the great sea until it draws near to the river Gihon and goes along the river Gihon until it reaches the right of the Garden of Eden. **24** And this is the land which came out for Ham as the portion which he was to occupy forever for himself and his sons unto their generations forever. **25** And for Japheth came out the third portion beyond the river Tînâ to the north of the outflow of its waters, and it extends north-easterly to the whole region of Gog and to all the country east thereof. **26** And it extends northerly to the north, and it extends to the mountains of Qêlt towards the north, and towards the sea of Mâ'ûk, and it goes out to the east of Gâdir as far as the region of the waters of the sea. **27** And it extends until it approaches the west of Fârâ and it returns towards 'Afêrâg, and it extends easterly to the waters of the sea of Mê'at. **28** And it extends to the region of the river Tînâ in a northeasterly direction until it approaches the boundary of its waters towards the mountain Râfâ, and it turns towards the north. **29** This is the land which came out for Japheth and his sons as the portion of his inheritance which he should possess for himself and his sons, for their generations forever; five great islands, and a great land in the north. **30** But it is cold, and the land of Ham is hot, and the land of Shem is neither hot nor cold, but it is of blended cold and heat.

CHAPTER 9

1 And Ham divided among his sons, and the first portion came out for Cush towards the east, and to the west of him for Mizraim, and to the west of him for Put, and to the west of him [and to the west thereof] on the sea for Canaan. **2** And Sherri also divided among his sons, and the first portion came out for Elam and his sons, to the east of the river Tigris until it approaches the east, the whole land of India, and on the Red Sea on its coast, and the waters of Dêdân, and all the mountains of Mebrî and 'Êlâ, and all the land of Sûsân and all that is on

the side of Pharnâk to the Red Sea and the river Tînâ. **3** And for Asshur came out the second portion, all the land of Asshur and Nineveh and Shinar and to the border of India, and it ascends and skirts the river. **4** And for Arpachshad came out the third portion, all the land of the region of the Chaldees to the east of the Euphrates, bordering on the Red Sea, and all the waters of the desert close to the tongue of the sea which looks towards Egypt, all the land of Lebanon and Sanîr and 'Amânâ to the border of the Euphrates. **5** And for Aram there came out the fourth portion, all the land of Mesopotamia between the Tigris and the Euphrates to the north of the Chaldees to the border of the mountains of Asshur and the land of 'Arârâ. **6** And there came out for Lud the fifth portion, the mountains of Asshur and all appertaining to them until it reaches the Great Sea, and until it reaches the east of Asshur his brother. **7** And Japheth also divided the land of his inheritance among his sons. **8** And the first portion came out for Gomer to the east from the north side to the river Tînâ; and in the north there came out for Magog all the inner portions of the north until it reaches to the sea of Mê'at. **9** And for Madai came out as his portion that he should possess from the west of his two brothers to the islands, and to the coasts of the islands. **10** And for Javan came out the fourth portion every island and the islands which are towards the border of Lud. **11** And for Tubal there came out the fifth portion in the midst of the tongue which approaches towards the border of the portion of Lud to the second tongue, to the region beyond the second tongue unto the third tongue. **12** And for Meshech came out the sixth portion, all the region beyond the third tongue until it approaches the east of Gâdir. **13** And for Tiras there came out the seventh portion, four great islands in the midst of the sea, which reach to the portion of Ham [and the islands of Kamâtûrî came out by lot for the sons of Arpachshad as his inheritance]. **14** And thus the sons of Noah divided unto their sons in the presence of Noah their father, and he bound them all by an oath, imprecating a curse on every one that sought to seize the portion which had not fallen (to him) by his lot. **15** And they all said, "So be it; so be it," for themselves and their sons forever throughout their generations until the day of judgment, on which the Lord God shall judge them with a sword and with fire, for all the unclean wickedness of their errors, with which they have filled the earth with transgression and uncleanness and fornication and sin.

CHAPTER 10

1 And in the third week of this jubilee the unclean demons began to lead astray the children of the sons of Noah; and to make to err and destroy them. **2** And the sons of Noah came to Noah their father, and they told him concerning the demons which were, leading astray and blinding and slaying his sons' sons. **3** And he prayed before the Lord his God, and said: God of the spirits of all flesh, who have shown mercy unto me, and have saved me and my sons from the waters of the flood, and have not caused me to perish as you did the sons of perdition; For your grace has been great towards me, and great has been your mercy to my soul; Let your grace be lift up upon my sons, and let not wicked spirits rule over them Lest they should destroy them from the earth. **4** But do you bless me and my sons, that we may increase and multiply and replenish the earth. **5** And you know how your Watchers, the fathers of these spirits, acted in my day: and as for these spirits which are living, imprison them and hold them fast in the place of condemnation, and let them not bring destruction on the sons of your servant, my God; for these are malignant, and created in order to destroy. **6** And let them not rule over the spirits of the living; for you alone can exercise dominion over them. And let them not have power over the sons of the righteous from now on and forevermore." **7** And the Lord our God bade us to bind all. **8** And the chief of the spirits, Mastêmâ, came and said: "Lord, Creator, let some of them remain before me, and let them hearken to my voice, and do all that I shall say unto them; for if some of them are not left to me, I shall not be able to execute the power of my will on the sons of men; for these are for corruption and leading astray before my judgment, for great is the wickedness of the sons of men." **9** And He said: "Let the tenth part of them remain before him, and let nine parts descend into the place of condemnation." **10** And one of us He commanded that we should teach Noah all their medicines; for He knew that they would not walk in uprightness, nor strive in righteousness. **11** And we did according to all His words: all the malignant evil ones we bound in the place of condemnation, and a tenth part of them we left that they might be subject before Satan on the earth. **12** And we

explained to Noah all the medicines of their diseases, together with their seductions, how he might heal them with herbs of the earth. **13** And Noah wrote down all things in a book as we instructed him concerning every kind of medicine. Thus, the evil spirits were precluded from (hurting) the sons of Noah. **14** And he gave all that he had written to Shem, his eldest son; for he loved him exceedingly above all his sons. **15** And Noah slept with his fathers and was buried on Mount Lûbâr in the land of Ararat. **16** Nine hundred and fifty years he completed in his life, nineteen jubilees and two weeks and five years. **17** And in his life on earth he excelled the children of men save Enoch because of the righteousness, wherein he was perfect. For Enoch's office was ordained for a testimony to the generations of the world, so that he should recount all the deeds of generation unto generation, until the day of judgment. **18** And in the three and thirtieth jubilee, in the first year in the second week, Peleg took to himself a wife, whose name was Lômnâ the daughter of Sînâ'ar, and she bore him a son in the fourth year of this week, and he called his name Reu; for he said: "Behold the children of men have become evil through the wicked purpose of building for themselves a city and a tower in the land of Shinar." **19** For they departed from the land of Ararat eastward to Shinar; for in his days they built the city and the tower, saying, "Go to, let us ascend thereby into heaven." **20** And they began to build, and in the fourth week they made brick with fire, and the bricks served them for stone, and the clay with which they cemented them together was asphalt which comes out of the sea, and out of the fountains of water in the land of Shinar. **21** And they built it: forty and three years were they building it; its breadth was 203 bricks, and the height (of a brick) was the third of one; its height amounted to 5433 cubits and **2** palms, and (the extent of one wall was) thirteen stadia (and of the other thirty stadia). **22** And the Lord our God said unto us: "Behold, they are one people, and (this) they begin to do, and now nothing will be withheld from them. Go to, let us go down and confound their language, that they may not understand one another's speech, and they may be dispersed into cities and nations, and one purpose will no longer abide with them until the day of judgment." **23** And the Lord descended, and we descended with Him to see the city and the tower which the children of men had built.

24 And He confounded their language, and they no longer understood one another's speech, and they ceased then to build the city and the tower. 25 For this reason the whole land of Shinar is called Babel, because the Lord did there confound all the language of the children of men, and from there they were dispersed into their cities, each according to his language and his nation. 26 And the Lord sent a mighty wind against the tower and overthrew it upon the earth, and behold it was between Asshur and Babylon in the land of Shinar, and they called its name "Overthrow." 27 In the fourth week in the first year in the beginning thereof in the four and thirtieth jubilee, were they dispersed from the land of Shinar. 28 And Ham and his sons went into the land which he was to occupy, which he acquired as his portion in the land of the south. 29 And Canaan saw the land of Lebanon to the river of Egypt that it was very good, and he went not into the land of his inheritance to the west (that is to) the sea, and he dwelt in the land of Lebanon, eastward and westward from the border of Jordan and from the border of the sea. 30 And Ham, his father, and Cush and Mizraim, his brothers, said unto him: "You have settled in a land which. is not your, and which did not fall to us by lot: do not do so; for if you do do so, you and your sons will fall in the land and (be) accursed through sedition; for by sedition you have settled, and by sedition will your children fall, and you shall be rooted out forever. 31 Dwell not in the dwelling of Shem; for to Shem and to his sons did it come by their lot. 32 Cursed are you and cursed shall you be beyond all the sons of Noah, by the curse by which we bound ourselves by an oath in the presence of the holy judge, and in the presence of Noah our father." 33 But he did not hearken unto them and dwelt in the land of Lebanon from Hamath to the entering of Egypt, he and his sons until this day. 34 And for this reason that land is named Canaan. 35 And Japheth and his sons went towards the sea and dwelt in the land of their portion, and Madai saw the land of the sea and it did not please him, and he begged a (portion) from Elam and Asshur and Arpachshad, his wife's brother, and he dwelt in the land of Media, near to his wife's brother until this day. 36 And he called his dwelling-place, and the dwelling-place of his sons, Media, after the name of their father Madai.

CHAPTER 11

1 And in the thirty-fifth jubilee, in the third week, in the first year thereof, Reu took to himself a wife, and her name was 'Ôrâ, the daughter of 'Ûr, the son of Kêsêd, and she bore him a son, and he called his name Sêrôḫ, in the seventh year of this week in this jubilee. 2 And the sons of Noah began to war on each other, to take captive and to slay each other, and to shed the blood of men on the earth, and to eat blood, and to build strong cities, and walls, and towers, and individuals (began) to exalt themselves above the nation, and to found the beginnings of kingdoms, and to go to war people against people, and nation against nation, and city against city, and all (began) to do evil, and to acquire arms, and to teach their sons war, and they began to capture cities, and to sell male and female slaves. 3 And 'Ûr, the son of Kêsêd, built the city of 'Arâ of the Chaldees, and called its name after his own name and the name of his father. 4 And they made for themselves molten images, and they worshipped each the idol, the molten image which they had made for themselves, and they began to make graven images and unclean simulacra, and malignant spirits assisted and seduced (them) into committing transgression and uncleanness. 5 And the prince Mastêmâ exerted himself to do all this, and he sent out other spirits, those which were put under his hand, to do all manner of wrong and sin, and all manner of transgression, to corrupt and destroy, and to shed blood upon the earth. 6 For this reason he called the name of Sêrôḫ, Serug, for everyone turned to do all manner of sin and transgression. 7 And he grew up, and dwelt in Ur of the Chaldees, near to the father of his wife's mother, and he worshipped idols, and he took to himself a wife in the thirty-sixth jubilee, in the fifth week, in the first year thereof, and her name was Mêlkâ, the daughter of Kâbêr, the daughter of his father's brother. 8 And she bore him Nahor, in the first year of this week, and he grew and dwelt in Ur of the Chaldees, and his father taught him the researches of the Chaldees to divine and augur, according to the signs of heaven. 9 And in the thirty-seventh jubilee, in the sixth week, in the first year thereof, he took to himself a wife, and her name was 'Îjâskâ, the daughter of Nêstâg of the Chaldees. 10 And she bore him Terah in the seventh year of this week. 11 And the prince Mastêmâ sent ravens and birds to devour the seed which was sown in the land, in order to destroy the land, and rob the

children of men of their labors. Before they could plough in the seed, the ravens picked (it) from the surface of the ground. 12 And for this reason he called his name Terah, because the ravens and the birds reduced them to destitution and devoured their seed. 13 And the years began to be barren, owing to the birds, and they devoured all the fruit of the trees from the trees: it was only with great effort that they could save a little of all the fruit of the earth in their days. 14 And in this thirty-ninth jubilee, in the second week in the first year, Terah took to himself a wife, and her name was 'Êdnâ, the daughter of 'Abrâm the daughter of his father's sister. 15 And in the seventh year of this week she bore him a son, and he called his name Abram, by the name of the father of his mother; for he had died before his daughter had conceived a son. 16 And the child began to understand the errors of the earth that all went astray after graven images and after uncleanness, and his father taught him writing, and he was two weeks of years old, and he separated himself from his father that he might not worship idols with him. 17 And he began to pray to the Creator of all things that He might save him from the errors of the children of men, and that his portion should not fall into error after uncleanness and vileness. 18 And the seed time came for the sowing of seed upon the land, and they all went out together to protect their seed against the ravens, and Abram went out with those that went, and the child was a lad of fourteen years. 19 And a cloud of ravens came to devour the seed, and Abram ran to meet them before they settled on the ground and cried to them before they settled on the ground to devour the seed, and said, "Descend not: return to the place where you came," and they proceeded to turn back. 20 And he caused the clouds of ravens to turn back that day seventy times, and of all the ravens throughout all the land where Abram was there settled there not so much as one. 21 And all who were with him throughout all the land saw him cry out, and all the ravens turn back, and his name became great in all the land of the Chaldees. 22 And there came to him this year all those that wished to sow, and he went with them until the time of sowing ceased: and they sowed their land, and that year they brought enough grain home and ate and were satisfied. 23 And in the first year of the fifth week Abram taught those who made implements for oxen, the artificers in wood, and they made a vessel above the ground,

facing the frame of the plough, in order to put the seed thereon, and the seed fell down therefrom upon the share of the plough, and was hidden in the earth, and they no longer feared the ravens. 24 And after this manner they made (vessels) above the ground on all the frames of the ploughs, and they sowed and tilled all the land, according as Abram commanded them, and they no longer feared the birds.

CHAPTER 12

1 And it came to pass in the sixth week, in the seventh year thereof, that Abram said to Terah his father, saying, "Father!" And he said, "Behold, here am I, my son." 2 And he said, "What help and profit have we from those idols which you do worship, and before which you do bow thyself? 3 For there is no spirit in them, for they are dumb forms, and a misleading of the heart. Worship them not: 4 Worship the God of heaven, who causes the rain and the dew to descend on the earth, and doeth everything upon the earth, and has created everything by His word, and all life is from before His face. 5 Why do you worship things that have no spirit in them? For they are the work of (men's) hands, and on your shoulders do you bear them, and you have no help from them, But they are a great cause of shame to those who make them, and a misleading of the heart to those who worship them: Worship them not." 6 And his father said unto him, "I also know it, my son, but what shall I do with a people who have made me to serve before them? 7 And if I tell them the truth, they will slay me; for their soul cleaved to them to worship them and honor them. Keep silent, my son, lest they slay you." 8 And these words he spoke to his two brothers, and they were angry with him and he kept silent. 9 And in the fortieth jubilee, in the second week, in the seventh year thereof, Abram took to himself a wife, and her name was Sarai, the daughter of his father, and she became his wife. 10 And Haran, his brother, took to himself a wife in the third year of the third week, and she bore him a son in the seventh year of this week and he called his name Lot. 11 And Nahor, his brother, took to himself a wife. 12 And in the sixtieth year of the life of Abram, that is, in the fourth week, in the fourth year thereof, Abram arose by night, and burned the house of the idols, and he burned all that was in the house, and no man knew it. 13 And they arose in the night and

sought to save their gods from the midst of the fire. 14 And Haran tried to save them, but the fire flamed over him, and he was burnt in the fire, and he died in Ur of the Chaldees before Terah his father, and they buried him in Ur of the Chaldees. 15 And Terah went out from Ur of the Chaldees, he and his sons, to go into the land of Lebanon and into the land of Canaan, and he dwelt in the land of Haran, and Abram, dwelt with Terah his father in Haran two weeks of years. 16 And in the sixth week, in the fifth year thereof, Abram sat up throughout the night on the new moon of the seventh month to observe the stars from the evening to the morning, in order to see what would be the character of the year with regard to the rains, and he was alone as he sat and observed. 17 And a word came into his heart and he said: "All the signs of the stars, and the signs of the moon and of the sun are all in the hand of the Lord. Why do I search (them) out? 18 If He desires, He causes it to rain, morning and evening; And if He desires, He withholds it, and all things are in His hand." 19 And he prayed that night and said "My God, God Most High, you alone are my God, and you and your dominion have I chosen. And you have created all things, and all things that are, are the work of your hands. 20 Deliver me from the hands of evil spirits who have sway over the thoughts of men's hearts, and let them not lead me astray from you, my God. And stablish you me and my seed forever That we go not astray from now and forevermore." 21 And he said Shall I return unto Ur of the Chaldees who seek my face that I may return to them, or am I to remain here in this place? The right path before you prosper it in the hands of your servant that he may fulfil (it) and that I may not walk in the deceitfulness of my heart, O my God." 22 And he made an end of speaking and praying, and behold the word of the Lord was sent to him through me, saying: "Get you up from your country, and from your kindred and from the house of your father unto a land which I shall show you, and I shall make you a great and numerous nation. 23 And I shall bless you And I shall make your name great, and you will be blessed in the earth, and in you will all families of the earth be blessed, and I shall bless them that bless you, and curse them that curse you. 24 And I shall be a God to you and your son, and to your son's son, and to all your seed: fear not, from now and unto all generations of the earth I am your God." 25 And the Lord God said: "Open his mouth

and his ears, that he may hear and speak with his mouth, with the language which has been revealed"; for it had ceased from the mouths of all the children of men from the day of the overthrow (of Babel). 26 And I opened his mouth, and his ears and his lips, and I began to speak with him in Hebrew in the tongue of the creation. 27 And he took the books of his fathers, and these were written in Hebrew and he transcribed them, and he began from then to study them, and I made known to him that which he could not (understand), and he studied them during the six rainy months. 28 And it came to pass in the seventh year of the sixth week that he spoke to his father and informed him that he would leave Haran to go into the land of Canaan to see it and return to him. 29 And Terah his father said unto him; "Go in peace: May the eternal God make your path straight, and the Lord [(be) with you, and] protect you from all evil, and grant unto you grace, mercy and favor before those who see you, and may none of the children of men have power over you to harm you; Go in peace. 30 And if you see a land pleasant to your eyes to dwell in, then arise and take me to you and take Lot with you, the son of Haran your brother, as your own son: the Lord be with you. 31 And Nahor your brother leave with me until you return in peace, and we go with you all together."

CHAPTER 13

1 And Abram journeyed from Haran, and he took Sarai, his wife, and Lot his brother Haran's son, to the land of Canaan, and he came into Asshur, and proceeded to Shechem, and dwelt near a lofty oak. 2 And he saw, and, behold, the land was very pleasant from the entering of Hamath to the lofty oak. 3 And the Lord said to him: "To you and to your seed will I give this land." 4 And he built an altar there, and he offered thereon a burnt sacrifice to the Lord, who had appeared to him. 5 And he left from there unto the mountain [with] Bethel on the west and Ai on the east and pitched his tent there. 6 And he saw and behold, the land was very wide and good, and everything grew thereon—vines and figs and pomegranates, oaks and ilexes, and terebinths and oil trees, and cedars and cypresses and date trees, and all trees of the field, and there was water on the mountains. 7 And he blessed the Lord who had led him out of Ur of the Chaldees and had brought him to this land. 8 And it came to pass in the first year, in the

seventh week, on the new moon of the first month, that he built an altar on this mountain, and called on the name of the Lord: "You, the eternal God, are my God." 9 And he offered on the altar a burnt sacrifice unto the Lord that He should be with him and not forsake him all the days of his life. 10 And he left from there and went towards the south, and he came to Hebron, and Hebron was built at, that time, and he dwelt there two years, and he went into the land of the south, to Bealoth and there was a famine in the land. 11 And Abram went into Egypt in the third year of the week, and he dwelt in Egypt five years before his wife was torn away from him. 12 Now Tanais in Egypt was at that time built—seven years after Hebron. 11 And it came to pass when Pharaoh seized Sarai, the wife of Abram, that the Lord plagued Pharaoh and his house with great plagues because of Sarai, Abram's wife. 14 And Abram was very glorious by reason of possessions in sheep, and cattle, and asses, and horses, and camels, and menservants, and maidservants, and in silver and gold exceedingly. And Lot also, his brother's son, was wealthy. 15 And Pharaoh gave back Sarai, the wife of Abram, and he sent him out of the land of Egypt, and he journeyed to the place where he had pitched his tent at the beginning, to the place of the altar, with Ai on the east, and Bethel on the west, and he blessed the Lord his God who had brought him back in peace. 16 And it came to pass in the forty-first jubilee, in the third year of the first week, that he returned to this place and offered thereon a burnt sacrifice, and called on the name of the Lord, and said: "You, the most high God, are my God forever and ever." 17 And in the fourth year of this week Lot parted from him, and Lot dwelt in Sodom, and the men of Sodom were sinners exceedingly. 18 And it grieved him in his heart that his brother's son had parted from him; for he had no children. 19 In that year when Lot was taken captive, the Lord said unto Abram, after that Lot had parted from him, in the fourth year of this week: "Lift up your eyes from the place where you are dwelling, northward and southward, and westward and eastward. 20 For all the land which you see I shall give to you and to your seed forever, and I shall make your seed as the sand of the sea: though a man may number the dust of the earth, yet your seed shall not be numbered. 21 Arise, walk (through the land) in the length of it and the breadth of it, and see it all; for to your seed shall I give it." And

Abram went to Hebron and dwelt there. 22 And in this year came Chedorlaomer, king of Elam, and Amraphel, king of Shinar, and Arioch, king of Sêllâsar and Têrgâl, king of nations, and slew the king of Gomorrah, and the king of Sodom fled, and many fell through wounds in the valley of Siddim, by the Salt Sea. 23 And they took captive Sodom and Adam and Zeboim, and they took captive Lot also, the son of Abram's brother, and all his possessions, and they went to Dan. 24 And one who had escaped came and told Abram that his brother's son had been taken captive and (Abram) armed his household servants. 25 For Abram, and for his seed, a tenth of the first-fruits to the Lord, and the Lord ordained it as an ordinance forever that they should give it to the priests who served before Him, that they should possess it forever. 26 And to this law there is no limit of days; for He has ordained it for the generations forever that they should give to the Lord the tenth of everything, of the seed and of the wine and of the oil and of the cattle and of the sheep. 27 And He gave (it) unto His priests to eat and to drink with joy before Him. 28 And the king of Sodom came to him and bowed himself before him, and said: "Our Lord Abram, give unto us the souls which you have rescued, but let the booty be yours." 29 And Abram said unto him: "I lift up my hands to the Most High God, that from a thread to a shoe-latchet I shall not take aught that is your, lest you should say I have made Abram rich; save only what the young men have eaten, and the portion of the men who went with me—Aner, Eschol, and Mamre. These will take their portion."

CHAPTER 14

1 After these things, in the fourth year of this week, on the new moon of the third month, the word of the Lord came to Abram in a dream, saying: "Fear not, Abram; I am your defender, and your reward will be exceeding great." 2 And he said: "Lord, Lord, what will you give me, seeing I go hence childless, and the son of Mâsêq, the son of my handmaid, is the Dammasek Eliezer: he will be my heir, and to me you have given no seed." 3 And He said unto him: "This (man) will not be your heir, but one that will come out of your own bowels; he will be your heir." 4 And He brought him out abroad, and said unto him: "Look toward heaven and number the stars, if you are able to number them." 5 And he looked toward heaven, and beheld the stars. And He said unto

him: "So shall your seed be." **6** And he believed in the Lord, and it was counted to him for righteousness. **7** And He said unto him: "I am the Lord that brought you out of Ur of the Chaldees, to give you the land of the Canaanites to possess it forever; and I shall be God unto you and to your seed after you." **8** And he said: "Lord, Lord, whereby shall I know that I shall inherit (it)?" **9** And he said unto him: "Take Me an heifer of three years, and a goat of three years, and a sheep of three years, and a turtle-dove, and a pigeon." **10** And he took all these in the middle of the month; and he dwelt at the oak of Mamre, which is near Hebron. **11** And he built there an altar and sacrificed all these; and he poured their blood upon the altar, and divided them in the midst, and laid them over against each other; but the birds divided he not. **12** And birds came down upon the pieces, and Abram drove them away, and did not suffer the birds to touch them. **13** And it came to pass, when the sun had set, that an ecstasy fell upon Abram, and, behold, a horror of great darkness fell upon him, and it was said unto Abram: "Know for sure that your seed shall be a stranger in a land (that is) not theirs, and they will bring them into bondage, and afflict them four hundred years. **14** And the nation also to whom they will be in bondage shall I judge, and after that they will come out from there with much substance. **15** And you will go to your fathers in peace and be buried in a good old age. **16** But in the fourth generation they will return here; for the iniquity of the Amorites is not yet full." **17** And he awoke from his sleep, and he arose, and the sun had set; and there was a flame, and behold! a furnace was smoking, and a flame of fire passed between the pieces. **18** And on that day the Lord made a covenant with Abram, saying: "To your seed will I give this land, from the river of Egypt unto the great river, the river Euphrates, the Kenites, the Kenizzites, the Kadmonites, the Perizzites, and the Rephaim, the Phakorites, and the Hivites, and the Amorites, and the Canaanites, and the Girgashites, and the Jebusites." **19** And the day passed, and Abram offered the pieces, and the birds, and their fruit-offerings, and their drink-offerings, and the fire devoured them. **20** And on that day we made a covenant with Abram, according as we had covenanted with Noah in this month; and Abram renewed the festival and ordinance for himself forever. **21** And Abram rejoiced, and made all these things known to Sarai his wife; and he believed that he would have seed, but she did not bear. **22** And Sarai advised her husband Abram and said unto him: "Go in unto Hagar, my Egyptian maid: it may be that I shall build up seed unto you by her." **23** And Abram hearkened unto the voice of Sarai his wife, and said unto her, "Do (so)." And Sarai took Hagar, her maid, the Egyptian, and gave her to Abram, her husband, to be his wife. **24** And he went in unto her, and she conceived and bore him a son, and he called his name Ishmael, in the fifth year of this week; and this was the eighty-sixth year in the life of Abram.

CHAPTER 15

1 And in the fifth year of the fourth week of this jubilee, in the third month, in the middle of the month, Abram celebrated the feast of the first-fruits of the grain harvest. **2** And he offered new offerings on the altar, the first-fruits of the produce, unto the Lord, a heifer and a goat and a sheep on the altar as a burnt sacrifice unto the Lord; their fruit-offerings and their drink-offerings he offered upon the altar with frankincense. **3** And the Lord appeared to Abram and said unto him: "I am God Almighty; approve thyself before Me and be you perfect. **4** And I will make My covenant between Me and you, and I will multiply you exceedingly." **5** And Abram fell on his face, and God talked with him, and said: **6** "Behold My ordinance is with you, and you will be the father of many nations. **7** Neither will your name any more be called Abram, But your name from now on, even forever, shall be Abraham. For the father of many nations have I made you. **8** And I shall make you very great, and I shall make you into nations, and kings will come out from you. **9** And I shall establish My covenant between Me and you, and your seed after you, throughout their generations, for an eternal covenant, so that I may be a God unto you, and to your seed after you. **10** (And I shall give to you and to your seed after you) the land where you have been a sojourner, the land of Canaan, that you may possess it forever, and I shall be their God." **11** And the Lord said unto Abraham: "And as for you, do you keep My Covenant, you and your seed after you, and circumcise you every male among you, and circumcise your foreskins, and it will be a token of an eternal covenant between Me and you. **12** And the child on the eighth day you will circumcise, every male throughout your generations, him that is born in the house, or whom you have bought with money from any stranger, whom you have acquired who is not of your seed. **13** He that is born in your house will surely be circumcised, and those whom you have bought with money will be circumcised, and My covenant will be in your flesh for an eternal ordinance. **14** And the uncircumcised male who is not circumcised in the flesh of his foreskin on the eighth day, that soul will be cut off from his people, for he has broken My covenant." **15** And God said unto Abraham: "As for Sarai your wife, her name will no more be called Sarai, but Sarah will be her name. **16** And I shall bless her, and give you a son by her, and I shall bless him, and he will become a nation, and kings of nations will proceed from him." **17** And Abraham fell on his face, and rejoiced, and said in his heart: "Shall a son be born to him that is a hundred years old, and shall Sarah, who is ninety years old, bring out?" **18** And Abraham said unto God: "O that Ishmael might live before you!" **19** And God said: "Yea, and Sarah also will bear you a son, and you will call his name Isaac, and I shall establish My covenant with him, an everlasting covenant, and for his seed after him. **20** And as for Ishmael also have I heard you, and behold I shall bless him, and make him great, and multiply him exceedingly, and he will beget twelve princes, and I shall make him a great nation. **21** But My covenant shall I establish with Isaac, whom Sarah will bear to you, in these days, in the next year." **22** And He left off speaking with him, and God went up from Abraham. **23** And Abraham did according as God had said unto him, and he took Ishmael his son, and all that were born in his house, and whom he had bought with his money, every male in his house, and circumcised the flesh of their foreskin. **24** And on the selfsame day was Abraham circumcised, and all the men of his house, (and those born in the house), and all those, whom he had bought with money from the children of the stranger, were circumcised with him. **25** This law is for all the generations forever, and there is no circumcision of the days, and no omission of one day out of the eight days; for it is an eternal ordinance, ordained and written on the heavenly tables. **26** And every one that is born, the flesh of whose foreskin is not circumcised on the eighth day, belongs not to the children of the covenant which the Lord made with Abraham, but to the children of destruction; nor is there, moreover, any sign on him that he is the Lord's, but (he is destined) to be destroyed and slain from the earth, and to be rooted out of the earth, for he has broken the covenant of the Lord our God. **27** For all the angels of the presence and all the angels of sanctification have been so created from the day of their creation, and before the angels of the presence and the angels of sanctification He has sanctified Israel, that they should be with Him and with His holy angels. **28** And do you command the children of Israel and let them observe the sign of this covenant for their generations as an eternal ordinance, and they will not be rooted out of the land. **29** For the command is ordained for a covenant, that they should observe it forever among all the children of Israel. **30** For Ishmael and his sons and his brothers and Esau, the Lord did not cause to approach Him, and he chose them not because they are the children of Abraham, because He knew them, but He chose Israel to be His people. **31** And He sanctified it and gathered it from among all the children of men; for there are many nations and many peoples, and all are His, and over all has He placed spirits in authority to lead them astray from Him. **32** But over Israel He did not appoint any angel or spirit, for He alone is their ruler, and He will preserve them and require them at the hand of His angels and His spirits, and at the hand of all His powers in order that He may preserve them and bless them, and that they may be His and He may be theirs from now on and forever. **33** And now I announce unto you that the children of Israel will not keep true to this ordinance, and they will not circumcise their sons according to all this law; for in the flesh of their circumcision they will omit this circumcision of their sons, and all of them, sons of Belial, will leave their sons uncircumcised as they were born. **34** And there will be great wrath from the Lord against the children of Israel, because they have forsaken His covenant and turned aside from His word, and provoked and blasphemed, inasmuch as they do not observe the ordinance of this law; for they have treated their members like the Gentiles, so that they may be removed and rooted out of the land. And there will no more be pardon or forgiveness unto them [so that there should be forgiveness and pardon] for all the sin of this eternal error.

CHAPTER 16

1 And on the new moon of the fourth month we appeared unto Abraham, at the oak of

Mamre, and we talked with him, and we announced to him that a son would be given to him by Sarah his wife. 2 And Sarah laughed, for she heard that we had spoken these words with Abraham, and we admonished her, and she became afraid, and denied that she had laughed on account of the words. 3 And we told her the name of her son, as his name is ordained and written in the heavenly tables (*i.e.*) Isaac. 4 And (that) when we returned to her at a set time, she would have conceived a son. 5 And in this month the Lord executed his judgments on Sodom, and Gomorrah, and Zeboim, and all the region of the Jordan, and He burned them with fire and brimstone, and destroyed them until this day, even as [lo] I have declared unto you all their works, that they are wicked and sinners exceedingly, and that they defile themselves and commit fornication in their flesh, and work uncleanness on the earth. 6 And, in like manner, God will execute judgment on the places where they have done according to the uncleanness of the Sodomites, like unto the judgment of Sodom. 7 But Lot we saved; for God remembered Abraham and sent him out from the midst of the overthrow. 8 And he and his daughters committed sin upon the earth, such as had not been on the earth since the days of Adam until his time; for the man lay with his daughters. 9 And, behold, it was commanded and engraved concerning all his seed, on the heavenly tables, to remove them and root them out, and to execute judgment upon them like the judgment of Sodom, and to leave no seed of the man on earth on the day of condemnation. 10 And in this month Abraham moved from Hebron, and departed and dwelt between Kadesh and Shur in the mountains of Gerar. 11 And in the middle of the fifth month he moved from there and dwelt at the Well of the Oath. 12 And in the middle of the sixth month the Lord visited Sarah and did unto her as He had spoken, and she conceived. 13 And she bore a son in the third month, and in the middle of the month, at the time of which the Lord had spoken to Abraham, on the festival of the first-fruits of the harvest, Isaac was born. 14 And Abraham circumcised his son on the eighth day: he was the first that was circumcised according to the covenant which is ordained forever. 15 And in the sixth year of the fourth week we came to Abraham, to the Well of the Oath, and we appeared unto him [as we had told Sarah that we should return to her, and she would have conceived a son. 16 And we returned in the seventh month, and found Sarah with child before us] and we blessed him, and we announced to him all the things which had been decreed concerning him, that he should not die until he should beget six sons more, and should see (them) before he died; but (that) in Isaac should his name and seed be called: 17 And (that) all the seed of his sons should be Gentiles, and be reckoned with the Gentiles; but from the sons of Isaac one should become a holy seed, and should not be reckoned among the Gentiles. 18 For he should become the portion of the Most High, and all his seed had fallen into the possession of God, that it should be unto the Lord a people for (His) possession above all nations and that it should become a kingdom and priests and a holy nation. 19 And we went our way, and we announced to Sarah all that we had told him, and they both rejoiced with exceeding great joy. 20 And he built there an altar to the Lord who had delivered him, and who was making him rejoice in the land of his sojourning, and he celebrated a festival of joy in this month seven days, near the altar which he had built at the Well of the Oath. 21 And he built booths for himself and for his servants on this festival, and he was the first to celebrate the feast of tabernacles on the earth. 22 And during these seven days he brought each day to the altar a burnt-offering to the Lord, two oxen, two rams, seven sheep, one he-goat, for a sin-offering, that he might atone thereby for himself and for his seed. 23 And, as a thank-offering, seven rams, seven kids, seven sheep, and seven he-goats, and their fruit-offerings and their drink-offerings; and he burnt all the fat thereof on the altar, a chosen offering unto the Lord for a sweet-smelling savor. 24 And morning and evening he burnt fragrant substances, frankincense and galbanum, and stacte, and nard, and myrrh, and spice, and costum; all these seven he offered, crushed, mixed together in equal parts (and) pure. 25 And he celebrated this feast during seven days, rejoicing with all his heart and with all his soul, he and all those who were in his house; and there was no stranger with him, nor any that was uncircumcised. 26 And he blessed his Creator who had created him in his generation, for He had created him according to His good pleasure; for He knew and perceived that from him would arise the plant of righteousness for the eternal generations, and from him a holy seed, so that it should become like Him who had made all things. 27 And he blessed and rejoiced, and he called the name of this festival the festival of the Lord, a joy acceptable to the Most High God. 28 And we blessed him forever, and all his seed after him throughout all the generations of the earth, because he celebrated this festival in its season, according to the testimony of the heavenly tables. 29 For this reason it is ordained on the heavenly tables concerning Israel, that they shall celebrate the feast of tabernacles seven days with joy, in the seventh month, acceptable before the Lord—a statute forever throughout their generations every year. 30 And to this there is no limit of days; for it is ordained forever regarding Israel that they should celebrate it and dwell in booths, and set wreaths upon their heads, and take leafy boughs, and willows from the brook. 31 And Abraham took branches of palm trees, and the fruit of goodly trees, and every day going around the altar with the branches seven times [a day] in the morning, he praised and gave thanks to his God for all things in joy.

CHAPTER 17

1 And in the first year of the fifth week Isaac was weaned in this jubilee, and Abraham made a great banquet in the third month, on the day his son Isaac was weaned. 2 And Ishmael, the son of Hagar, the Egyptian, was before the face of Abraham, his father, in his place, and Abraham rejoiced and blessed God because he had seen his sons and had not died childless. 3 And he remembered the words which He had spoken to him on the day on which Lot had parted from him, and he rejoiced because the Lord had given him seed upon the earth to inherit the earth, and he blessed with all his mouth the Creator of all things. 4 And Sarah saw Ishmael playing and dancing and Abraham rejoicing with great joy, and she became jealous of Ishmael and said to Abraham, "Cast out this bondwoman and her son; for the son of this bondwoman will not be heir with my son, Isaac." 5 And the thing was grievous in Abraham's sight, because of his maidservant and because of his son, that he should drive them from him. 6 And God said to Abraham "Let it not be grievous in your sight, because of the child and because of the bondwoman; in all that Sarah has said unto you, hearken to her words and do (them); for in Isaac shall your name and seed be called. 7 But as for the son of this bondwoman I will make him a great nation, because he is of your seed." 8 And Abraham rose up early in the morning and took bread and a bottle of water and placed them on the shoulders of Hagar and the child and sent her away. 9 And she departed and wandered in the wilderness of Beersheba, and the water in the bottle was spent, and the child thirsted, and was not able to go on, and fell down. 10 And his mother took him and cast him under an olive tree, and went and sat her down over against him, at the distance of a bow-shot; for she said, "Let me not see the death of my child," and as she sat she wept. 11 And an angel of God, one of the holy ones, said unto her, "Why do you weep, Hagar? Arise, take the child, and hold him in your hand; for God has heard your voice, and has seen the child." 12 And she opened her eyes, and she saw a well of water, and she went and filled her bottle with water, and she gave her child to drink, and she arose and went towards the wilderness of Paran. 13 And the child grew and became an archer, and God was with him; and his mother took him a wife from among the daughters of Egypt. 14 And she bore him a son, and he called his name Nebaioth; for she said, "The Lord was nigh to me when I called upon him." 15 And it came to pass in the seventh week, in the first year thereof, in the first month in this jubilee, on the twelfth of this month, there were voices in heaven regarding Abraham, that he was faithful in all that He told him, and that he loved the Lord, and that in every affliction he was faithful. 16 And the prince Mastêmâ came and said before God, "Behold, Abraham loves Isaac his son, and he delights in him above all things else; bid him offer him as a burnt-offering on the altar, and you will see if he will do this command, and you will know if he is faithful in everything wherein you do try him." 17 And the Lord knew that Abraham was faithful in all his afflictions; for He had tried him through his country and with famine, and had tried him with the wealth of kings, and had tried him again through his wife, when she was torn (from him), and with circumcision, and had tried him through Ishmael and Hagar, his maid-servant, when he sent them away. 18 And in everything wherein He had tried him, he was found faithful, and his soul was not impatient, and he was not slow to act; for he was faithful and a lover of the Lord.

CHAPTER 18

1 And God said to him, "Abraham, Abraham"; and he said, "Behold, (here) am I." 2 And He

said, "Take your beloved son whom you love, (even) Isaac, and go unto the high country, and offer him on one of the mountains which I will point out unto you." 3 And he rose early in the morning and saddled his ass, and took his two young men with him, and Isaac his son, and clave the wood of the burnt-offering, and he went to the place on the third day, and he saw the place afar off. 4 And he came to a well of water, and he said to his young men, "Abide you here with the ass, and I and the lad shall go (yonder), and when we have worshipped we shall come again to you." 5 And he took the wood of the burnt-offering and laid it on Isaac his son, and he took in his hand the fire and the knife, and they went both of them together to that place. 6 And Isaac said to his father, "Father"; and he said, "Here am I, my son." And he said unto him, "Behold the fire, and the knife, and the wood; but where is the sheep for the burnt-offering, father?" 7 And he said, "God will provide for himself a sheep for a burnt-offering, my son." And he drew near to the place of the mount of God. 8 And he built an altar, and he placed the wood on the altar, and bound Isaac his son, and placed him on the wood which was upon the altar and stretched out his hand to take the knife to slay Isaac his son. 9 And I stood before him, and before the prince of the Mastêmâ, and the Lord said, "Bid him not to lay his hand on the lad, nor to do anything to him, for I have shown that he fears the Lord." 10 And I called to him from heaven, and said unto him: "Abraham, Abraham"; and he was terrified and said: "Behold, (here) am I." 11 And I said unto him: "Lay not your hand upon the lad, neither do you anything to him; for now I have shown that you fear the Lord, and have not withheld your son, your first-born son, from me." 12 And the prince of the Mastêmâ was put to shame; and Abraham lifted up his eyes and looked, and, behold, a single ram caught . . . by his horns, and Abraham went and took the ram and offered it for a burnt-offering in the stead of his son. 13 And Abraham called that place "The Lord has seen," so that it is said "(in the mount) the Lord has seen": that is Mount Zion. 14 And the Lord called Abraham by his name a second time from heaven, as he caused us to appear to speak to him in the name of the Lord. 15 And He said: "By Myself have I sworn, saith the Lord, because you have done this thing, and have not withheld your son, your beloved son, from Me, that in blessing I shall bless you and in multiplying I

shall multiply your seed As the stars of heaven, and as the sand which is on the seashore. And your seed will inherit the cities of its enemies, 16 And in your seed will all nations of the earth be blessed; Because you have obeyed My voice, and I have shown to all that you are faithful unto Me in all that I have said unto you: Go in peace." 17 And Abraham went to his young men, and they arose and went together to Beersheba, and Abraham dwelt by the Well of the Oath. 18 And he celebrated this festival every year, seven days with joy, and he called it the festival of the Lord according to the seven days during which he went and returned in peace. 19 And accordingly has it been ordained and written on the heavenly tables regarding Israel and its seed that they should observe this festival seven days with the joy of festival.

CHAPTER 19

1 And in the first year of the first week in the forty-second jubilee, Abraham returned and dwelt opposite Hebron, that is Kirjath Arba, two weeks of years. 2 And in the first year of the third week of this jubilee the days of the life of Sarah were accomplished, and she died in Hebron. 3 And Abraham went to mourn over her and bury her, and we tried him [to see] if his spirit were patient and he were not indignant in the words of his mouth; and he was found patient in this and was not disturbed. 4 For in patience of spirit he conversed with the children of Heth, to the intent that they should give him a place in which to bury his dead. 5 And the Lord gave him grace before all who saw him, and he besought in gentleness the sons of Heth, and they gave him the land of the double cave over against Mamre, that is Hebron, for four hundred pieces of silver. 6 And they besought him, saying, "We shall give it to you for nothing"; but he would not take it from their hands for nothing, for he gave the price of the place, the money in full, and he bowed down before them twice; and after this he buried his dead in the double cave. 7 And all the days of the life of Sarah were one hundred and twenty-seven years, that is, two jubilees and four weeks and one year: these are the days of the years of the life of Sarah. 8 This is the tenth trial with which Abraham was tried, and he was found faithful, patient in spirit. 9 And he said not a single word regarding the rumor in the land how that God had said that He would give it to him and to his seed after him, and he

begged a place there to bury his dead; for he was found faithful and was recorded on the heavenly tables as the friend of God. **10** And in the fourth year thereof he took a wife for his son Isaac and her name was Rebecca [the daughter of Bethuel, the son of Nahor, the brother of Abraham] the sister of Laban and daughter of Bethuel; and Bethuel was the son of Mêlcâ, who was the wife of Nahor, the brother of Abraham. **11** And Abraham took to himself a third wife, and her name was Keturah, from among the daughters of his household servants, for Hagar had died before Sarah. **12** And she bore him six sons, Zimram, and Jokshan, and Medan, and Midian, and Ishbak, and Shuah, in the two weeks of years. **13** And in the sixth week, in the second year thereof, Rebecca bore to Isaac two sons, Jacob and Esau, and Jacob was a smooth and upright man, and Esau was fierce, a man of the field, and hairy, and Jacob dwelt in tents. **14** And the youths grew, and Jacob learned to write; but Esau did not learn, for he was a man of the field and a hunter, and he learnt war, and all his deeds were fierce. **15** And Abraham loved Jacob, but Isaac loved Esau. **16** And Abraham saw the deeds of Esau, and he knew that in Jacob should his name and seed be called; and he called Rebecca and gave commandment regarding Jacob, for he knew that she (too) loved Jacob much more than Esau. **17** And he said unto her: "My daughter, watch over my son Jacob, for he shall be in my stead on the earth, and for a blessing in the midst of the children of men, and for the glory of the whole seed of Shem. **18** For I know that the Lord will choose him to be a people for possession unto Himself, above all peoples that are upon the face of the earth. **19** And behold, Isaac my son loves Esau more than Jacob, but I see that you truly love Jacob. **20** Add still further to your kindness to him, and let your eyes be upon him in love; For he will be a blessing unto us on the earth from now on and unto all generations of the earth. **21** Let your hands be strong and let your heart rejoice in your son Jacob; For I have loved him far beyond all my sons. He will be blessed forever, and his seed will fill the whole earth. **22** If a man can number the sand of the earth, His seed also will be numbered. **23** And all the blessings with which the Lord has blessed me, and my seed shall belong to Jacob and his seed always. **24** And in his seed shall my name be blessed, and the name of my fathers, Shem, and Noah, and Enoch, and Mahalalel, and Enos, and Seth, and Adam.

25 And these shall serve to lay the foundations of the heaven, and to strengthen the earth, and to renew all the luminaries which are in the firmament." **26** And he called Jacob before the eyes of Rebecca his mother, and kissed him, and blessed him, and said: **27** "Jacob, my beloved son, whom my soul loves, may God bless you from above the firmament, and may He give you all the blessings with which He blessed Adam, and Enoch, and Noah, and Shem; and all the things of which He told me, and all the things which He promised to give me, may He cause to cleave to you and to your seed forever, according to the days of heaven above the earth. **28** And the spirits of Mastêmâ shall not rule over you or over your seed to turn you from the Lord, who is your God from now on and forever. **29** And may the Lord God be a father to you and you the first-born son, and to the people always. Go in peace, my son." **30** And they both went out together from Abraham. **31** And Rebecca loved Jacob, with all her heart and with all her soul, very much more than Esau; but Isaac loved Esau much more than Jacob.

CHAPTER 20

1 And in the forty-second jubilee, in the first year of the seventh week, Abraham called Ishmael, and his twelve sons, and Isaac and his two sons, and the six sons of Keturah, and their sons. **2** And he commanded them that they should observe the way of the Lord; that they should work righteousness, and love each his neighbor, and act on this manner among all men; that they should each so walk with regard to them as to do judgment and righteousness on the earth. **3** That they should circumcise their sons, according to the covenant which He had made with them, and not deviate to the right hand or the left of all the paths which the Lord had commanded us; and that we should keep ourselves from all fornication and uncleanness, [and renounce from among us all fornication and uncleanness]. **4** And if any woman or maid commit fornication among you, burn her with fire, and let them not commit fornication with her after their eyes and their heart; and let them not take to themselves wives from the daughters of Canaan; for the seed of Canaan will be rooted out of the land. **5** And he told them of the judgment of the giants, and the judgment of the Sodomites, how they had been judged on account of their wickedness, and had died on account of their fornication, and uncleanness, and mutual corruption through fornication. 6 "And guard yourselves from all fornication and uncleanness, and from all pollution of sin, lest you make our name a curse, and your whole life a hissing, and all your sons be destroyed by the sword, and you become accursed like Sodom, and all your remnant as the sons of Gomorrah. 7 I implore you, my sons, love the God of heaven, and cleave you to all His commandments. And walk not after their idols, and after their uncleanness, 8 and make not for yourselves molten or graven gods; For they are vanity, and there is no spirit in them; For they are work of (men's) hands, and all who trust in them, trust in nothing. Serve them not, nor worship them, 9 but serve you the Most High God, and worship Him continually: And hope for His countenance always, and work uprightness and righteousness before Him, That He may have pleasure in you and grant you His mercy, and send rain upon you morning and evening, and bless all your works which you have wrought upon the earth, and bless your bread and your water, and bless the fruit of your womb and the fruit of your land, and the herds of your cattle, and the flocks of your sheep. 10 And you will be for a blessing on the earth, and all nations of the earth will desire you, and bless your sons in my name, that they may be blessed as I am." 11 And he gave to Ishmael and to his sons, and to the sons of Keturah, gifts, and sent them away from Isaac his son, and he gave everything to Isaac his son. 12 And Ishmael and his sons, and the sons of Keturah and their sons, went together and dwelt from Paran to the entering in of Babylon in all the land which is towards the East facing the desert. 13 And these mingled with each other, and their name was called Arabs, and Ishmaelites.

CHAPTER 21

1 And in the sixth year of the seventh week of this jubilee Abraham called Isaac his son, and commanded him, saying: "I am become old, and. know not the day of my death, and am full of my days. 2 And behold, I am one hundred and seventy-five years old, and throughout all the days of my life I have remembered the Lord and sought with all my heart to do His will, and to walk uprightly in all His ways. 3 My soul has hated idols, (and I have despised those that served them, and I have given my heart and spirit) that I might observe to do the will of Him who created me. 4 For He is the living God, and He is holy and faithful, and He is righteous beyond all, and there is with Him no accepting of (men's) persons and no accepting of gifts; for God is righteous and executes judgment on all those who transgress His commandments and despise His covenant. 5 And do you, my son, observe His commandments and His ordinances and His judgments, and walk not after the abominations and after the graven images and after the molten images. 6 And eat no blood at all of animals or cattle, or of any bird which flies in the heaven. 7 And if you do slay a victim as an acceptable peace-offering, slay you it, and pour out its blood upon the altar, and all the fat of the offering offer on the altar with fine flour (and the meat-offering) mingled with oil, with its drink-offering— offer them all together on the altar of burnt-offering; it is a sweet savor before the Lord. 8 And you will offer the fat of the sacrifice of thank-offerings on the fire which is upon the altar, and the fat which is on the belly, and all the fat on the inwards and the two kidneys, and all the fat that is upon them, and upon the loins and liver you shall remove together with the kidneys. 9 And offer all these for a sweet savor acceptable before the Lord, with its meat-offering and with its drink-offering, for a sweet savor, the bread of the offering unto the Lord, 10 And eat its meat on that day and on the second day, and let not the sun on the second day go down upon it until it is eaten, and let nothing be left over for the third day; for it is not acceptable [for it is not approved] and let it no longer be eaten, and all who eat thereof will bring sin upon themselves; for thus I have found it written in the books of my forefathers, and in the words of Enoch, and in the words of Noah. 11 And on all your oblations you shall strew salt and let not the salt of the covenant be lacking in all your oblations before the Lord. 12 And as regards the wood of the sacrifices, beware lest you bring (other) wood for the altar in addition to these: cypress, dêfrân, sagâd, pine, fir, cedar, savin, palm, olive, myrrh, laurel, and citron, juniper, and balsam. 13 And of these kinds of wood lay upon the altar under the sacrifice, such as have been tested as to their appearance, and do not lay (thereon) any split or dark wood, (but) hard and clean, without fault, a sound and new growth; and do not lay (thereon) old wood, [for its fragrance is gone] for there is no longer fragrance in it as before. 14 Besides these kinds of wood there is none other that you shall place (on the altar), for the

fragrance is dispersed, and the smell of its fragrance goes not up to heaven. **15** Observe this commandment and do it, my son, that you may be upright in all your deeds. **16** And at all times be clean in your body and wash thyself with water before you approach to offer on the altar and wash your hands and your feet before you draws near to the altar; and when you are done sacrificing, wash again your hands and your feet. **17** And let no blood appear upon you nor upon your clothes; be on your guard, my son, against blood, be on your guard exceedingly; cover it with dust. **18** And do not eat any blood, for it is the soul; eat no blood whatever. **19** And take no gifts for the blood of man, lest it be shed with impunity, without judgment; for it is the blood that is shed that causes the earth to sin, and the earth cannot be cleansed from the blood of man save by the blood of him who shed it. **20** And take no present or gift for the blood of man: blood for blood, that you may be accepted before the Lord, the Most High God; for He is the defense of the good: and that you may be preserved from all evil, and that He may save you from every kind of death. **21** I see, my son, that all the works of the children of men are sin and wickedness, and all their deeds are uncleanness and an abomination and a pollution, and there is no righteousness with them. **22** Beware, lest you shouldest walk in their ways and tread in their paths and sin a sin unto death before the Most High God. Else He will [hide His face from you, and] give you back into the hands of your transgression, and root you out of the land, and your seed likewise from under heaven, and your name and your seed will perish from the whole earth. **23** Turn away from all their deeds and all their uncleanness, and observe the ordinance of the Most High God, and do His will and be upright in all things. **24** And He will bless you in all your deeds and will raise up from you the plant of righteousness through all the earth, throughout all generations of the earth, and my name and your name will not be forgotten under heaven forever. **25** Go, my son, in peace. May the Most High God, my God and your God, strengthen you to do His will, and may He bless all your seed and the residue of your seed for the generations forever, with all righteous blessings, that you may be a blessing on all the earth." **26** And he went out from him rejoicing.

CHAPTER 22

1 And it came to pass in the first week in the forty-fourth jubilee, in the second year, that is, the year in which Abraham died, that Isaac and Ishmael came from the Well of the Oath to celebrate the feast of weeks—that is, the feast of the first-fruits of the harvest—to Abraham, their father, and Abraham rejoiced because his two sons had come. **2** For Isaac had many possessions in Beersheba, and Isaac was wont to go and see his possessions and to return to his father. **3** And in those days Ishmael came to see his father, and they both came together, and Isaac offered a sacrifice for a burnt-offering, and presented it on the altar of his father which he had made in Hebron. **4** And he offered a thank-offering and made a feast of joy before Ishmael, his brother: and Rebecca made new cakes from the new grain, and gave them to Jacob, her son, to take them to Abraham, his father, from the first-fruits of the land, that he might eat and bless the Creator of all things before he died. **5** And Isaac, too, sent by the hand of Jacob to Abraham a best thank-offering, that he might eat and drink. **6** And he ate and drank, and blessed the Most High God, who has created heaven and earth, who has made all the fat things of the earth and given them to the children of men That they might eat and drink and bless their Creator. **7** "And now I give thanks unto you, my God, because you have caused me to see this day: behold, I am one hundred three score and fifteen years, an old man and full of days, and all my days have been unto me peace. **8** The sword of the adversary has not overcome me in all that you have given me and my children all the days of my life until this day. **9** My God, may your mercy and your peace be upon your servant, and upon the seed of his sons, that they may be to you a chosen nation and an inheritance from among all the nations of the earth from now on and unto all the days of the generations of the earth, unto all the ages." **10** And he called Jacob and said My son Jacob, may the God of all bless you and strengthen you to do righteousness, and His will before Him, and may He choose you and your seed that you may become a people for His inheritance according to His will always. And do you, my son, Jacob, draw near and kiss me." **11** And he drew near and kissed him, and he said: "Blessed be my son Jacob And all the sons of God Most High, unto all the ages: May God give unto you a seed of righteousness; And some of your sons may He sanctify in the midst of the whole earth; May nations serve you, and all the nations bow themselves before your seed. **12** Be strong in the presence of men, and exercise authority over all the seed of Seth. Then your ways and the ways of your sons will be justified, so that they shall become a holy nation. **13** May the Most High God give you all the blessings with which he has blessed me and with which He blessed Noah and Adam; May they rest on the sacred head of your seed from generation to generation forever. **14** And may He cleanse you from all unrighteousness and impurity, that you may be forgiven all (thy) transgressions; (and) your sins of ignorance. And may He strengthen you and bless you. And may you inherit the whole earth, **15** And may He renew His covenant with you, that you may be to Him a nation for His inheritance for all the ages, and that He may be to you and to your seed a God in truth and righteousness throughout all the days of the earth. **16** And do you, my son Jacob, remember my words, and observe the commandments of Abraham, your father: Separate thyself from the nations, and eat not with them: And do not according to their works, and become not their associate; For their works are unclean, and all their ways are a pollution and an abomination and uncleanness. **17** They offer their sacrifices to the dead and they worship evil spirits, and they eat over the graves, and all their works are vanity and nothingness. **18** They have no heart to understand and their eyes do not see what their works are, and how they err in saying to a piece of wood: 'You are my God,' And to a stone: 'You are my Lord and you are my deliverer.' [And they have no heart.] **19** And as for you, my son Jacob, May the Most High God help you And the God of heaven bless you and remove you from their uncleanness and from all their error. **20** Be you ware, my son Jacob, of taking a wife from any seed of the daughters of Canaan; For all his seed is to be rooted out of the earth. **21** For, owing to the transgression of Ham, Canaan erred, and all his seed will be destroyed from off the earth and all the residue thereof, and none springing from him will be saved on the day of judgment. **22** And as for all the worshippers of idols and the profane: There will be no hope for them in the land of the living; And there will be no remembrance of them on the earth; For they will descend into Sheol, and into the place of condemnation will they go, As the children of Sodom were taken away from the

earth So will all those who worship idols be taken away. **23** Fear not, my son Jacob, and be not dismayed, O son of Abraham: May the Most High God preserve you from destruction, and from all the paths of error may He deliver you. **24** This house have I built for myself that I might put my name upon it in the earth: [it is given to you and to your seed forever], and it will be named the house of Abraham; it is given to you and to your seed forever; for you will build my house and establish my name before God forever: your seed and your name will stand throughout all generations of the earth." **25** And he ceased commanding him and blessing him. **26** And the two lay together on one bed, and Jacob slept in the bosom of Abraham, his father's father and he kissed him seven times, and his affection and his heart rejoiced over him. **27** And he blessed him with all his heart and said: "The Most High God, the God of all, and Creator of all, who brought me out from Ur of the Chaldees, that He might give me this land to inherit it forever, and that I might establish a holy seed—blessed be the Most High forever." **28** And he blessed Jacob and said: "My son, over whom with all my heart and my affection I rejoice, may your grace and your mercy be lift up upon him and upon his seed always. **29** And do not forsake him, nor set him at nothing from now on and unto the days of eternity, and may Your eyes be opened upon him and upon his seed, that you may preserve him, and bless him, and may sanctify him as a nation for Your inheritance; **30** And bless him with all your blessings from now on and unto all the days of eternity, and renew your covenant and your grace with him and with his seed according to all your good pleasure unto all the generations of the earth."

CHAPTER 23

1 And he placed two fingers of Jacob on his eyes, and he blessed the God of gods, and he covered his face and stretched out his feet and slept the sleep of eternity and was gathered to his fathers. **2** And notwithstanding all this Jacob was lying in his bosom, and knew not that Abraham, his father's father, was dead. **3** And Jacob awoke from his sleep, and behold Abraham was cold as ice, and he said: "Father, father!"; but there was none that spoke, and he knew that he was dead. **4** And he arose from his bosom and ran and told Rebecca, his mother; and Rebecca went to Isaac in the night and told him; and they went together, and Jacob with them, and a lamp was in his hand,

and when they had gone in they found Abraham lying dead. **5** And Isaac fell on the face of his father and wept and kissed him. **6** And the voices were heard in the house of Abraham, and Ishmael his son arose, and went to Abraham his father, and wept over Abraham his father, he and all the house of Abraham, and they wept with a great weeping. **7** And his sons Isaac and Ishmael buried him in the double cave, near Sarah his wife, and they wept for him forty days, all the men of his house, and Isaac and Ishmael, and all their sons, and all the sons of Keturah in their places, and the days of weeping for Abraham were ended. **8** And he lived three jubilees and four weeks of years, one hundred and seventy-five years, and completed the days of his life, being old and full of days. **9** For the days of the forefathers, of their life, were nineteen jubilees; and after the Flood they began to grow less than nineteen jubilees, and to decrease in jubilees, and to grow old quickly, and to be full of their days by reason of manifold tribulation and the wickedness of their ways, with the exception of Abraham. **10** For Abraham was perfect in all his deeds with the Lord, and well-pleasing in righteousness all the days of his life; and behold, he did not complete four jubilees in his life, when he had grown old by reason of the wickedness and was full of his days. **11** And all the generations which will arise from this time until the day of the great judgment will grow old quickly, before they complete two jubilees, and their knowledge will forsake them by reason of their old age [and all their knowledge will vanish away]. **12** And in those days, if a man live a jubilee and a half of years, they will say regarding him: "He has lived long, and the greater part of his days are pain and sorrow and tribulation, and there is no peace: **13** For calamity follows on calamity, and wound on wound, and tribulation on tribulation, and evil tidings on evil tidings, and illness on illness, and all evil judgments such as these, one with another, illness and overthrow, and snow and frost and ice, and fever, and chills, and torpor, and famine, and death, and sword, and captivity, and all kinds of calamities and pains." **14** And all these will come on an evil generation, which transgresses on the earth: their works are uncleanness and fornication, and pollution and abominations. **15** Then they will say: "The days of the forefathers were many (even), unto a thousand years, and were good; but, behold, the days of our life, if a man has lived many, are three score years and ten, and, if he is strong, four score years, and those evil and there is no peace in the days of this evil generation." **16** And in that generation the sons will convict their fathers and their elders of sin and unrighteousness, and of the words of their mouth and the great wickedness which they perpetrate, and concerning their forsaking the covenant which the Lord made between them and Him, that they should observe and do all His commandments and His ordinances and all His laws, without departing either to the right hand or to the left. **17** For all have done evil, and every mouth speaks iniquity and all their works are an uncleanness and an abomination, and all their ways are pollution, uncleanness and destruction. **18** Behold the earth will be destroyed on account of all their works, and there will be no seed of the vine, and no oil; for their works are altogether faithless, and they will all perish together, beasts and cattle and birds, and all the fish of the sea, on account of the children of men. **19** And they will strive one with another, the young with the old, and the old with the young, the poor with the rich, and the lowly with the great, and the beggar with the prince, on account of the law and the covenant; for they have forgotten commandment, and covenant, and feasts, and months, and Sabbaths, and jubilees, and all judgments. **20** And they will stand (with bows and) swords and war to turn them back into the way; but they will not return until much blood has been shed on the earth, one by another. **21** And those who have escaped will not return from their wickedness to the way of righteousness, but they will all exalt themselves to deceit and wealth, that they may each take all that is his neighbor's, and they will name the great name, but not in truth and not in righteousness, and they will defile the holy of holies with their uncleanness and the corruption of their pollution. **22** And a great punishment will befall the deeds of this generation from the Lord, and He will give them over to the sword and to judgment and to captivity, and to be plundered and devoured. **23** And He will wake up against them the sinners of the Gentiles, who have neither mercy nor compassion, and who will respect the person of none, neither old nor young, nor anyone, for they are more wicked and strong to do evil than all the children of men. And they will use violence against Israel and transgression against Jacob, and much blood will be shed upon the earth, and there will be none to gather and none to bury. **24** In those days they will cry aloud, and call and pray that they may be saved from the hand of the sinners, the Gentiles; But none will be saved. **25** And the heads of the children will be white with grey hair, and a child of three weeks will appear old like a man of one hundred years, and their stature will be destroyed by tribulation and oppression. **26** And in those days the children will begin to study the laws, and to seek the commandments, and to return to the path of righteousness. **27** And the days will begin to grow many and increase among those children of men [until] their days draw nigh to one thousand years, and to a greater number of years than (before) was the number of the days. **28** And there will be no old man nor one who is not satisfied with his days, for all will be (as) children and youths. **29** And all their days they will complete and live in peace and in joy, and there will be no Satan nor any evil destroyer; For all their days will be days of blessing and healing, **30** and at that time the Lord will heal His servants, and they will rise up and see great peace, and drive out their adversaries. And the righteous will see and be thankful, and rejoice with joy forever and ever, and will see all their judgments and all their curses on their enemies. **31** And their bones will rest in the earth, and their spirits will have much joy, and they will know that it is the Lord who executes judgment and shows mercy to hundreds and thousands and to all that love Him. **32** And do you, Moses, write down these words; for thus are they written, and they record (them) on the heavenly tables for a testimony for the generations forever.

CHAPTER 24

1 And it came to pass after the death of Abraham, that the Lord blessed Isaac his son, and he arose from Hebron and went and dwelt at the Well of the Vision in the first year of the third week of this jubilee, seven years. **2** And in the first year of the fourth week a famine began in the land, besides the first famine, which had been in the days of Abraham. **3** And Jacob sod lentil pottage, and Esau came from the field hungry. And he said to Jacob his brother: "Give me of this red pottage." And Jacob said to him: "Sell to me your [primogeniture, this] birthright and I will give you bread, and also some of this lentil pottage." **4** And Esau said in his heart: "I shall die; of what profit to me is this birthright?"

And he said to Jacob: "I give it to you." **5** And Jacob said, "Swear to me, this day," and he swore unto him. **6** And Jacob gave his brother Esau bread and pottage, and he ate until he was satisfied, and Esau despised his birthright; for this reason was Esau's name called Edom, on account of the red pottage which Jacob gave him for his birthright. **7** And Jacob became the elder, and Esau was brought down from his dignity. **8** And the famine was over the land, and Isaac departed to go down into Egypt in the second year of this week and went to the king of the Philistines to Gerar, unto Abimelech. **9** And the Lord appeared unto him and said unto him: "Go not down into Egypt; dwell in the land that I shall tell you of, and sojourn in this land, and I shall be with you and bless you. **10** For to you and to your seed shall I give all this land, and I shall establish My oath which I swore unto Abraham your father, and I shall multiply your seed as the stars of heaven and shall give unto your seed all this land. **11** And in your seed will all the nations of the earth be blessed, because your father obeyed My voice, and kept My charge and My commandments, and My laws, and My ordinances, and My covenant; and now obey My voice and dwell in this land." **12** And he dwelt in Gerar three weeks of years. **13** And Abimelech charged concerning him, and concerning all that was his, saying: "Any man that shall touch him or aught that is his shall surely die." **14** And Isaac waxed strong among the Philistines, and he got many possessions, oxen and sheep and camels and asses and a great household. **15** And he sowed in the land of the Philistines and brought in a hundred-fold, and Isaac became exceedingly great, and the Philistines envied him. **16** Now all the wells which the servants of Abraham had dug during the life of Abraham, the Philistines had stopped them after the death of Abraham and filled them with earth. **17** And Abimelech said unto Isaac: "Go from us, for you are much mightier than we"; and Isaac departed from there in the first year of the seventh week and sojourned in the valleys of Gerar. **18** And they dug again the wells of water which the servants of Abraham, his father, had dug, and which the Philistines had closed after the death of Abraham his father, and he called their names as Abraham his father had named them. **19** And the servants of Isaac dug a well in the valley, and found living water, and the shepherds of Gerar strove with the shepherds of Isaac, saying: "The water is ours "; and

Isaac called the name of the well "Perversity," because they had been perverse with us. 20 And they dug a second well, and they strove for that also, and he called its name "Enmity." And he arose from there and they dug another well, and for that they strove not, and he called the name of it "Room," and Isaac said: "Now the Lord has made room for us, and we have increased in the land." 21 And he went up from there to the Well of the Oath in the first year of the first week in the forty-fourth jubilee. 22 And the Lord appeared to him that night, on the new moon of the first month, and said unto him: "I am the God of Abraham your father; fear not, for I am with you, and shall bless you and shall surely multiply your seed as the sand of the earth, for the sake of Abraham my servant." 23 And he built an altar there, which Abraham his father had first built, and he called upon the name of the Lord, and he offered sacrifice to the God of Abraham his father. 24 And they dug a well and they found living water. 25 And the servants of Isaac dug another well and did not find water, and they went and told Isaac that they had not found water, and Isaac said: "I have sworn this day to the Philistines and this thing has been announced to us." 26 And he called the name of that place the "Well of the Oath"; for there he had sworn to Abimelech and Ahuzzath his friend and Phicol the prefect of his host. 27 And Isaac knew that day that under constraint he had sworn to them to make peace with them. 28 And Isaac on that day cursed the Philistines and said: "Cursed be the Philistines unto the day of wrath and indignation from the midst of all nations; may God make them a derision and a curse and an object of wrath and indignation in the hands of the sinners the Gentiles and in the hands of the Kittim. 29 And whoever escapes the sword of the enemy and the Kittim, may the righteous nation root out in judgment from under heaven; for they will be the enemies and foes of my children throughout their generations upon the earth. 30 And no remnant will be left to them, nor one that will be saved on the day of the wrath of judgment; for destruction and rooting out and expulsion from the earth is the whole seed of the Philistines (reserved), and there will no longer be left for these Caphtorim a name or a seed on the earth. 31 For though he ascends into heaven, from there will he be brought down, and though he makes himself strong on earth, from there will he be dragged out, and though he hides himself among the nations, even from there will he be rooted out; And though he descends into Sheol, there also will his condemnation be great, and there also he will have no peace. 32 And if he goes into captivity, By the hands of those that seek his life will they slay him on the way, and neither name nor seed will be left to him on all the earth; for into eternal malediction will he depart." 33 And thus is it written and engraved concerning him on the heavenly tables, to do unto him on the day of judgment, so that he may be rooted out of the earth.

CHAPTER 25

1 And in the second year of this week in this jubilee, Rebecca called Jacob her son, and spoke unto him, saying: "My son, do not take you a wife of the daughters of Canaan, as Esau, your brother, who took him two wives of the daughters of Canaan, and they have embittered my soul with all their unclean deeds: for all their deeds are fornication and lust, and there is no righteousness with them, for (their deeds) are evil. 2 And I, my son, love you exceedingly, and my heart and my affection bless you every hour of the day and watch of the night. 3 And now, my son, hearken to my voice, and do the will of your mother, and do not take you a wife of the daughters of this land, but only of the house of my father, and of my father's kindred. you will take you a wife of the house of my father, and the Most High God will bless you, and your children will be a righteous generation and a holy seed." 4 And then spoke Jacob to Rebecca, his mother, and said unto her: "Behold, mother, I am nine weeks of years old, and I neither know nor have I touched any woman, nor have I betrothed myself to any, nor even think of taking me a wife of the daughters of Canaan. 5 For I remember, mother, the words of Abraham, our father, for he commanded me not to take a wife of the daughters of Canaan, but to take me a wife from the seed of my father's house and from my kindred. 6 I have heard before that daughters have been born to Laban, your brother, and I have set my heart on them to take a wife from among them. 7 And for this reason I have guarded myself in my spirit against sinning or being corrupted in all my ways throughout all the days of my life; for with regard to lust and fornication, Abraham, my father, gave me many commands. 8 And, despite all that he has commanded me, these two and twenty years my brother has striven with me and spoken

frequently to me and said: 'My brother, take to wife a sister of my two wives'; but I refuse to do as he has done. **9** I swear before you, mother, that all the days of my life I will not take me a wife from the daughters of the seed of Canaan, and I will not act wickedly as my brother has done. **10** Fear not, mother; be assured that I shall do your will and walk in uprightness, and not corrupt my ways forever." **11** And immediately she lifted up her face to heaven and extended the fingers of her hands and opened her mouth and blessed the Most High God, who had created the heaven and the earth, and she gave Him thanks and praise. **12** And she said: "Blessed be the Lord God, and may His holy name be blessed forever and ever, who has given me Jacob as a pure son and a holy seed; for He is Yours, and Yours shall his seed be continually and throughout all the generations forevermore. **13** Bless him, O Lord, and place in my mouth the blessing of righteousness, that I may bless him." **14** And at that hour, when the spirit of righteousness descended into her mouth, she placed both her hands on the head of Jacob, and said: **15** "Blessed are you, Lord of righteousness and God of the ages; And may He bless you beyond all the generations of men. May He give you, my son, the path of righteousness, and reveal righteousness to your seed. **16** And may He make your sons many during your life, and may they arise according to the number of the months of the year. And may their sons become many and great beyond the stars of heaven, and their numbers be more than the sand of the sea. **17** And may He give them this goodly land—as He said He would give it to Abraham and to his seed after him always— And may they hold it as a possession forever. **18** And may I see (born) unto you, my son, blessed children during my life, and a blessed and holy seed may all your seed be. **19** And as you have refreshed your mother's spirit during my life, the womb of her that bare you blesses you, [My affection] and my breasts bless you, and my mouth and my tongue praise you greatly. **20** Increase and spread over the earth, and may your seed be perfect in the joy of heaven and earth forever; And may your seed rejoice, and on the great day of peace may it have peace. **21** And may your name and your seed endure to all the ages, and may the Most High God be their God, and may the God of righteousness dwell with them, and by them may His sanctuary be built unto all the ages. **22** Blessed be he that blesses you, and all flesh that curses you falsely may it be cursed." **23** And she kissed him and said to him "May the Lord of the world love you as the heart of your mother and her affection rejoice in you and bless you." And she ceased from blessing.

CHAPTER 26

1 And in the seventh year of this week Isaac called Esau, his elder son, and said unto him: "I am old, my son, and behold my eyes are dim in seeing, and I know not the day of my death. **2** And now take your hunting weapons, your quiver and your bow, and go out to the field, and hunt and catch me (venison), my son, and make me savory meat, such as my soul loves, and bring it to me that I may eat, and that my soul may bless you before I die." **3** But Rebecca heard Isaac speaking to Esau. **4** And Esau went out early to the field to hunt and catch and bring home to his father. **5** And Rebecca called Jacob, her son, and said unto him: "Behold, I heard Isaac, your father, speak unto Esau, your brother, saying: 'Hunt for me, and make me savory meat, and bring (it) to me that I may eat and bless you before the Lord before I die.' **6** And now, my son, obey my voice in that which I command you: Go to your flock and fetch me two good kids of the goats, and I will make them savory meat for your father, such as he loves, and you shall bring (it) to your father that he may eat and bless you before the Lord before he die, and that you may be blessed." **7** And Jacob said to Rebecca his mother: "Mother, I shall not withhold anything which my father would eat, and which would please him: only I fear, my mother, that he will recognize my voice and wish to touch me. **8** And you know that I am smooth, and Esau, my brother, is hairy, and I shall appear before his eyes as an evildoer, and shall do a deed which he had not commanded me, and he will be angry with me, and I shall bring upon myself a curse, and not a blessing." **9** And Rebecca, his mother, said unto him: "Upon me be your curse, my son, only obey my voice." **10** And Jacob obeyed the voice of Rebecca, his mother, and went and fetched two good and fat kids of the goats, and brought them to his mother, and his mother made them (savory meat) such as he loved. **11** And Rebecca took the goodly raiment of Esau, her elder son, which was with her in the house, and she clothed Jacob, her younger son, (with them), and she put the skins of the kids upon his hands and on the exposed parts of his neck.

12 And she gave the meat and the bread which she had prepared into the hand of her son Jacob. **13** And Jacob went in to his father and said: "I am your son: I have done according as you commanded me: arise and sit and eat of that which I have caught, father, that your soul may bless me." **14** And Isaac said to his son: "How have you found so quickly, my son?" **15** And Jacob said: "Because (the Lord) your God caused me to find." **16** And Isaac said unto him: "Come near, that I may feel you, my son, if you are my son Esau or not." **17** And Jacob went near to Isaac, his father, and he felt him and said: **18** "The voice is Jacob's voice, but the hands are the hands of Esau," and he discerned him not, because it was a dispensation from heaven to remove his power of perception and Isaac discerned not, for his hands were hairy as (his brother) Esau's, so that he blessed him. **19** And he said: "Art you my son Esau?" and he said: "I am your son and he said, "Bring near to me that I may eat of that which you have caught, my son, that my soul may bless you." **20** And he brought near to him, and he did eat, and he brought him wine and he drank. **21** And Isaac, his father, said unto him: "Come near and kiss me, my son." And he came near and kissed him. **22** And he smelled the smell of his raiment, and he blessed him and said: "Behold, the smell of my son is as the smell of a (full) field which the Lord has blessed. **23** And may the Lord give you of the dew of heaven and of the dew of the earth, and plenty of corn and oil: Let nations serve you, and peoples bow down to you. **24** Be lord over your brethren and let your mother's sons bow down to you; And may all the blessings with which the Lord has blessed me and blessed Abraham, my father, Be imparted to you and to your seed forever Cursed be he that curses you, and blessed be he that blesses you." **25** And it came to pass as soon as Isaac had made an end of blessing his son Jacob, and Jacob had gone out from Isaac his father he hid himself and Esau, his brother, came in from his hunting. **26** And he also made savory meat, and brought (it) to his father, and said unto his father: "Let my father arise and eat of my venison that your soul may bless me." **27** And Isaac, his father, said unto him: "Who are you?" And he said unto him: "I am your firstborn, your son Esau: I have done as you have commanded me." **28** And Isaac was very greatly astonished, and said: "Who is he that has hunted and caught and brought (it) to me, and I have eaten of all before you came, and have blessed him: (and) he shall be blessed, and all his seed forever." **29** And it came to pass when Esau heard the words of his father Isaac that he cried with an exceeding great and bitter cry, and said unto his father: "Bless me, (even) me also, father." **30** And he said unto him: "Your brother came with guile, and has taken away your blessing." And he said: "Now I know why his name is named Jacob: behold, he has supplanted me these two times: he took away my birth-right, and now he has taken away my blessing." **31** And he said: "Hast you not reserved a blessing for me, father?" and Isaac answered and said unto Esau: "Behold, I have made him your lord, and all his brethren have I given to him for servants, and with plenty of corn and wine and oil have I strengthened him: And what now shall I do for you, my son?" **32** And Esau said to Isaac, his father: "Hast you but one blessing, O father? Bless me, (even) me also, father": And Esau lifted up his voice and wept. **33** And Isaac answered and said unto him: "Behold, far from the dew of the earth shall be your dwelling, and far from the dew of heaven from above. **34** And by your sword will you live, and you will serve your brother. And it shall come to pass when you become great, and do shake his yoke from off your neck, you will sin a complete sin unto death, and your seed will be rooted out from under heaven." **35** And Esau kept threatening Jacob because of the blessing with which his father blessed him, and he said in his heart: "May the days of mourning for my father now come, so that I may slay my brother Jacob."

CHAPTER 27

1 And the words of Esau, her elder son, were told to Rebecca in a dream, and Rebecca sent and called Jacob her younger son, and said unto him: **2** "Behold Esau your brother will take vengeance on you so as to kill you. **3** Now, therefore, my son, obey my voice, and arise and flee you to Laban, my brother, to Haran, and tarry with him a few days until your brother's anger turns away, and he remove his anger from you, and forget all that you have done; then I will send and fetch you from there." **4** And Jacob said: "I am not afraid; if he wishes to kill me, I will kill him." **5** But she said unto him: "Let me not be bereft of both my sons on one day." **6** And Jacob said to Rebecca his mother: "Behold, you know that my father has become old, and doth not see because his eyes are dull, and if I leave him it will be evil in his eyes, because I leave him and go away from you, and my father will be angry, and will curse me. I will not go; when he sends me, then only will I go." 7 And Rebecca said to Jacob: "I will go in and speak to him, and he will send you away." 8 And Rebecca went in and said to Isaac: "I loathe my life because of the two daughters of Heth, whom Esau has taken him as wives; and if Jacob take a wife from among the daughters of the land such as these, for what purpose do I further live; for the daughters of Canaan are evil." 9 And Isaac called Jacob and blessed him, and admonished him and said unto him: 10 "Do not take you a wife of any of the daughters of Canaan; arise and go to Mesopotamia, to the house of Bethuel, your mother's father, and take you a wife from there of the daughters of Laban, your mother's brother. 11 And God Almighty bless you and increase and multiply you that you may become a company of nations, and give you the blessings of my father Abraham, to you and to your seed after you, that you may inherit the land of your sojournings and all the land which God gave to Abraham: go, my son, in peace." 12 And Isaac sent Jacob away, and he went to Mesopotamia, to Laban the son of Bethuel the Syrian, the brother of Rebecca, Jacob's mother. 13 And it came to pass after Jacob had arisen to go to Mesopotamia that the spirit of Rebecca was grieved after her son, and she wept. 14 And Isaac said to Rebecca: "My sister, weep not on account of Jacob, my son; for he goes in peace, and in peace will he return. 15 The Most High God will preserve him from all evil and will be with him; for He will not forsake him all his days; 16 For I know that his ways will be prospered in all things wherever he goes, until he returns in peace to us, and we see him in peace. 17 Fear not on his account my sister, for he is on the upright path and he is a perfect man: and he is faithful and will not perish. Weep not." 18 And Isaac comforted Rebecca on account of her son Jacob and blessed him. 19 And Jacob went from the Well of the Oath to go to Haran on the first year of the second week in the forty-fourth Jubilee, and he came to Luz on the mountains, that is, Bethel, on the new moon of the first month of this week, and he came to the place at even and turned from the way to the west of the road that night: and he slept there; for the sun had set. 20 And he took one of the stones of that place and laid it (at his head) under the tree, and he was journeying alone, and he slept. 21 And he dreamt that night, and behold a ladder set up on the earth, and the top of it reached to heaven, and behold, the angels of the Lord ascended and descended on it: and behold, the Lord stood upon it. 22 And He spoke to Jacob and said: "I am the Lord God of Abraham, your father, and the God of Isaac; the land on which you are sleeping, to you shall I give it, and to thy-seed after you. 23 And your seed will be as the dust of the earth, and you will increase to the west and to the east, to the north and the south, and in you and in your seed will all the families of the nations be blessed. 24 And behold, I shall be with you, and shall keep you wheresoever you go, and I shall bring you again into this land in peace; for I shall not leave you until I do everything that I told you of." 25 And Jacob awoke from his sleep, and said, "Truly this place is the house of the Lord, and I knew it not." And he was afraid and said:" Dreadful is this place which is none other than the house of God, and this is the gate of heaven." 26 And Jacob arose early in the morning and took the stone which he had put under his head and set it up as a pillar for a sign, and he poured oil upon the top of it. And he called the name of that place Bethel; but the name of the place was Luz at the first. 27 And Jacob vowed a vow unto the Lord, saying: "If the Lord will be with me, and will keep me in this way that I go, and give me bread to eat and raiment to put on, so that I come again to my father's house in peace, then shall the Lord be my God, and this stone which I have set up as a pillar for a sign in this place, shall be the Lord's house, and of all that you give me, I shall give the tenth to you, my God."

CHAPTER 28

1 And he went on his journey, and came to the land of the east, to Laban, the brother of Rebecca, and he was with him, and served him for Rachel his daughter one week. 2 And in the first year of the third week he said unto him: "Give me my wife, for whom I have served you seven years;" and Laban said unto Jacob. "I will give you your wife." 3 And Laban made a feast, and took Leah his elder daughter, and gave (her) to Jacob as a wife and gave her Zilpah his handmaid for a handmaid; and Jacob did not know, for he thought that she was Rachel. 4 And he went in unto her, and behold, she was Leah; and Jacob was angry with Laban, and said unto him: "Why have you dealt thus with me? Did not I serve you for

Rachel and not for Leah? Why have you wronged me? Take your daughter, and I will go; for you have done evil to me." **5** For Jacob loved Rachel more than Leah; for Leah's eyes were weak, but her form was very handsome; but Rachel had beautiful eyes and a beautiful and very handsome form. **6** And Laban said to Jacob: "It is not so done in our country, to give the younger before the elder." And it is not right to do this; for thus it is ordained and written in the heavenly tables, that no one should give his younger daughter before the elder—but the elder one giveth first and after her the younger—and the man who doeth so, they set down guilt against him in heaven, and none is righteous that doeth this thing, for this deed is evil before the Lord. **7** And command you the children of Israel that they do not this thing; let them neither take nor give the younger before they have given the elder, for it is very wicked. **8** And Laban said to Jacob: "Let the seven days of the feast of this one pass by, and I shall give you Rachel, that you may serve me another seven years, that you may pasture my sheep as you did in the former week." **9** And on the day when the seven days of the feast of Leah had passed, Laban gave Rachel to Jacob, that he might serve him another seven years, and he gave to Rachel Bilhah, the sister of Zilpah as a handmaid. **10** And he served yet other seven years for Rachel, for Leah had been given to him for nothing. **11** And the Lord opened the womb of Leah, and she conceived and bare Jacob a son, and he called his name Reuben, on the fourteenth day of the ninth month, in the first year of the third week. **12** But the womb of Rachel was closed, for the Lord saw that Leah was hated and Rachel loved. **13** And again Jacob went in unto Leah, and she conceived, and bare Jacob a second son, and he called his name Simeon, on the twenty-first of the tenth month, and in the third year of this week. **14** And again Jacob went in unto Leah, and she conceived, and bore him a third son, and he called his name Levi, in the new moon of the first month in the sixth year of this week. **15** And again Jacob went in unto her, and she conceived, and bore him a fourth son, and he called his name Judah, on the fifteenth of the third month, in the first year of the fourth week. **16** And on account of all this Rachel envied Leah, for she did not bear, and she said to Jacob: "Give me children "; and Jacob said: "Have I withheld from you the fruits of your womb? Have I forsaken you?" **17** And when

Rachel saw that Leah had borne four sons to Jacob, Reuben and Simeon and Levi and Judah, she said unto him: "Go in unto Bilhah my handmaid, and she will conceive, and bear a son unto me." **18** (And she gave (him) Bilhah her handmaid to wife.) And he went in unto her, and she conceived, and bore him a son, and he called his name Dan, on the ninth of the sixth month, in the sixth year of the third week. **19** And Jacob went in again unto Bilhah a second time, and she conceived, and bare Jacob another son, and Rachel called his name Naphtali, on the fifth of the seventh month, in the second year of the fourth week. **20** And when Leah saw that she had become sterile and did not bear, she envied (Rachel) and she also gave her handmaid Zilpah to Jacob to wife, and she conceived, and bore a son, and Leah called his name Gad, on the twelfth of the eighth month, in the third year of the fourth week. **21** And he went in again unto her, and she conceived, and bore him a second son, and Leah called his name Asher, on the second of the eleventh month, in the fifth year of the fourth week. **22** And Jacob went in unto Leah, and she conceived, and bore a son, and she called his name Issachar, on the fourth of the fifth month, in the fourth year of the fourth week, and she gave him to a nurse. **23** And Jacob went in again unto her, and she conceived, and bare two (children), a son and a daughter, and she called the name of the son Zebulon, and the name of the daughter Dinah, in the seventh of the seventh month, in the sixth year of the fourth week. **24** And the Lord was gracious to Rachel, and opened her womb, and she conceived, and bore a son, and she called his name Joseph, on the new moon of the fourth month, in the sixth year in this fourth week. **25** And in the days when Joseph was born, Jacob said to Laban: "Give me my wives and sons, and let me go to my father Isaac, and let me make me an house; for I have completed the years in which I have served you for your two daughters, and I will go to the house of my father." **26** And Laban said to Jacob: "Tarry with me for your wages , and pasture my flock for me again, and take your wages." **27** And they agreed with one another that he should give him as his wages those of the lambs and kids which were born black and spotted and white, (these) were to be his wages. **28** And all the sheep brought out spotted and speckled and black, variously marked, and they brought out again lambs like themselves, and all that were spotted were

Jacob's and those which were not were Laban's. **29** And Jacob's possessions multiplied exceedingly, and he possessed oxen and sheep and asses and camels, and menservants and maidservants. **30** And Laban and his sons envied Jacob, and Laban took back his sheep from him, and he observed him with evil intent.

CHAPTER 29

1 And it came to pass when Rachel had borne Joseph, that Laban went to shear his sheep; for they were distant from him a three days' journey. **2** And Jacob saw that Laban was going to shear his sheep, and Jacob called Leah and Rachel, and spoke kindly unto them that they should come with him to the land of Canaan. **3** For he told them how he had seen everything in a dream, even all that He had spoken unto him that he should return to his father's house; and they said: "To every place where you go we will go with you." **4** And Jacob blessed the God of Isaac his father, and the God of Abraham his father's father, and he arose and mounted his wives and his children, and took all his possessions and crossed the river, and came to the land of Gilead, and Jacob hid his intention from Laban and told him not. **5** And in the seventh year of the fourth week Jacob turned (his face) toward Gilead in the first month, on the twenty-first thereof. And Laban pursued after him and overtook Jacob in the mountain of Gilead in the third month, on the thirteenth thereof. **6** And the Lord did not suffer him to injure Jacob; for He appeared to him in a dream by night. And Laban spoke to Jacob, **7** and on the fifteenth of those days Jacob made a feast for Laban, and for all who came with him, and Jacob swore to Laban that day, and Laban also to Jacob, that neither should cross the mountain of Gilead to the other with evil purpose. **8** And he made there a heap for a witness; for that reason the name of that place is called: "The Heap of Witness," after this heap. **9** But before they used to call the land of Gilead the land of the Rephaim; for it was the land of the Rephaim, and the Rephaim were born (there), giants whose height was ten, nine, eight down to seven cubits. **10** And their habitation was from the land of the children of Ammon to Mount Hermon, and the seats of their kingdom were Karnaim and Ashtaroth, and Edrei, and Mîsûr, and Beon. **11** And the Lord destroyed them because of the evil of their deeds; for they were very malignant, and

the Amorites dwelt in their stead, wicked and sinful, and there is no people to-day which has wrought to the full all their sins, and they have no longer length of life on the earth. **12** And Jacob sent away Laban, and he departed into Mesopotamia, the land of the East, and Jacob returned to the land of Gilead. **13** And he passed over the Jabbok in the ninth month, on the eleventh thereof. And on that day Esau, his brother, came to him, and he was reconciled to him, and departed from him unto the land of Seir, but Jacob dwelt in tents. **14** And in the first year of the fifth week in this jubilee he crossed the Jordan, and dwelt beyond the Jordan, and he pastured his sheep from the sea of the heap unto Bethshan, and unto Dothan and unto the forest of Akrabbim. **15** And he sent to his father Isaac of all his substance, clothing, and food, and meat, and drink, and milk, and butter, and cheese, and some dates of the valley, **16** And to his mother Rebecca also four times a year, between the times of the months, between ploughing and reaping, and between autumn and the rain (season) and between winter and spring, to the tower of Abraham. **17** For Isaac had returned from the Well of the Oath and gone up to the tower of his father Abraham, and he dwelt there apart from his son Esau. **18** For in the days when Jacob went to Mesopotamia, Esau took to himself a wife Mahalath, the daughter of Ishmael, and he gathered together all the flocks of his father and his wives, and went up and dwelt on Mount Seir, and left Isaac his father at the Well of the Oath alone. **19** And Isaac went up from the Well of the Oath and dwelt in the tower of Abraham his father on the mountains of Hebron, **20** And there Jacob sent all that he did send to his father and his mother from time to time, all they needed, and they blessed Jacob with all their heart and with all their soul.

CHAPTER 30

1 And in the first year of the sixth week he went up to Salem, to the east of Shechem, in peace, in the fourth month. **2** And there they carried off Dinah, the daughter of Jacob, into the house of Shechem, the son of Hamor, the Hivite, the prince of the land, and he lay with her and defiled her, and she was a little girl, a child of twelve years. **3** And he besought his father and her brothers that she might be given to him to wife. And Jacob and his sons were angry because of the men of Shechem; for they had defiled Dinah, their sister, and they spoke to them with evil intent and dealt deceitfully with them and beguiled them. **4** And Simeon and Levi came unexpectedly to Shechem and executed judgment on all the men of Shechem and slew all the men whom they found in it and left not a single one remaining in it: they slew all in torments because they had dishonored their sister Dinah. **5** And thus let it not again be done from now on that a daughter of Israel be defiled; for judgment is ordained in heaven against them that they should destroy with the sword all the men of the Shechemites because they had wrought shame in Israel. **6** And the Lord delivered them into the hands of the sons of Jacob that they might exterminate them with the sword and execute judgment upon them, and that it might not thus again be done in Israel that a virgin of Israel should be defiled. **7** And if there is any man who wishes in Israel to give his daughter or his sister to any man who is of the seed of the Gentiles he shall surely die, and they shall stone him with stones; for he has wrought shame in Israel; and they shall burn the woman with fire, because she has dishonored the name of the house of her father, and she shall be rooted out of Israel. **8** And let not an adulteress and no uncleanness be found in Israel throughout all the days of the generations of the earth; for Israel is holy unto the Lord, and every man who has defiled (it) shall surely die: they shall stone him with stones. **9** For thus has it been ordained and written in the heavenly tables regarding all the seed of Israel: he who defiles (it) shall surely die, and he shall be stoned with stones. **10** And to this law there is no limit of days, and no remission, nor any atonement: but the man who has defiled his daughter shall be rooted out in the midst of all Israel, because he has given of his seed to Moloch, and wrought impiously so as to defile it. **11** And do you, Moses, command the children of Israel and exhort them not to give their daughters to the Gentiles, and not to take for their sons any of the daughters of the Gentiles, for this is abominable before the Lord. **12** For this reason I have written for you in the words of the Law all the deeds of the Shechemites, which they wrought against Dinah, and how the sons of Jacob spoke, saying: "We shall not give our daughter to a man who is uncircumcised; for that were a reproach unto us." **13** And it is a reproach to Israel, to those who give, and to those who take the daughters of the Gentiles; for this is unclean and abominable to Israel. **14** And Israel will not be free from this uncleanness if it has a wife of the daughters of the Gentiles or has given any of its daughters to a man who is of any of the Gentiles. **15** For there will be plague upon plague, and curse upon curse, and every judgment and plague and curse will come (upon him): if he do this thing, or hide his eyes from those who commit uncleanness, or those who defile the sanctuary of the Lord, or those who profane His holy name, (then) will the whole nation together be judged for all the uncleanness and profanation of this (man). **16** And there will be no respect of persons [and no consideration of persons], and no receiving at his hands of fruits and offerings and burnt-offerings and fat, nor the fragrance of sweet savor, so as to accept it: and so fare every man or woman in Israel who defiles the sanctuary. **17** For this reason I have commanded you, saying: "Testify this testimony to Israel: see how the Shechemites fared and their sons: how they were delivered into the hands of two sons of Jacob, and they slew them under tortures, and it was (reckoned) unto them for righteousness, and it is written down to them for righteousness. **18** And the seed of Levi was chosen for the priesthood, and to be Levites, that they might minister before the Lord, as we, continually, and that Levi and his sons may be blessed forever; for he was zealous to execute righteousness and judgment and vengeance on all those who arose against Israel. **19** And so they inscribe as a testimony in his favor on the heavenly tables blessing and righteousness before the God of all: **20** And we remember the righteousness which the man fulfilled during his life, at all periods of the year; until a thousand generations they will record it, and it will come to him and to his descendants after him, and he has been recorded on the heavenly tables as a friend and a righteous man. **21** All this account I have written for you and have commanded you to say to the children of Israel, that they should not commit sin nor transgress the ordinances nor break the covenant which has been ordained for them, (but) that they should fulfil it and be recorded as friends. **22** But if they transgress and work uncleanness in every way, they will be recorded on the heavenly tables as adversaries, and they will be destroyed out of the book of life, and they will be recorded in the book of those who will be destroyed and with those who will be rooted out of the earth. **23** And on the day when the sons of Jacob slew Shechem a writing was recorded in their favor in heaven that they had executed righteousness and uprightness and vengeance on the sinners, and it was written for a blessing. **24** And they brought Dinah, their sister, out of the house of Shechem, and they took captive everything that was in Shechem, their sheep and their oxen and their asses, and all their wealth, and all their flocks, and brought them all to Jacob their father. **25** And he reproached them because they had put the city to the sword; for he feared those who dwelt in the land, the Canaanites and the Perizzites. **26** And the dread of the Lord was upon all the cities which are around Shechem, and they did not rise to pursue after the sons of Jacob; for terror had fallen upon them.

CHAPTER 31

1 And on the new moon of the month Jacob spoke to all the people of his house, saying: "Purify yourselves and change your garments, and let us arise and go up to Bethel, where I vowed a vow to Him on the day when I fled from the face of Esau my brother, because He has been with me and brought me into this land in peace, and put you away the strange gods that are among you." **2** And they gave up the strange gods and that which was in their ears and which was on their necks, and the idols which Rachel stole from Laban her brother she gave wholly to Jacob. And he burnt and brake them to pieces and destroyed them and hid them under an oak which is in the land of Shechem. **3** And he went up on the new moon of the seventh month to Bethel. And he built an altar at the place where he had slept, and he set up a pillar there, and he sent word to his father Isaac to come to him to his sacrifice, and to his mother Rebecca. **4** And Isaac said: "Let my son Jacob come, and let me see him before I die." **5** And Jacob went to his father Isaac and to his mother Rebecca, to the house of his father Abraham, and he took two of his sons with him, Levi and Judah, and he came to his father Isaac and to his mother Rebecca. **6** And Rebecca came out from the tower to the front of it to kiss Jacob and embrace him; for her spirit had revived when she heard: "Behold Jacob your son has come"; and she kissed him. **7** And she saw his two sons, and she recognized them, and said unto him: "Are these your sons, my son?" and she embraced them and kissed them, and blessed them, saying: "In you shall the seed of Abraham become illustrious, and you will prove a blessing on the earth." **8** And Jacob went in to Isaac his father, to the chamber where he lay, and his two sons were with him, and he took the hand of his father, and stooping down he kissed him, and Isaac clung to the neck of Jacob his son, and wept upon his neck. **9** And the darkness left the eyes of Isaac, and he saw the two sons of Jacob, Levi and Judah, and he said: "Are these your sons, my son? For they are like you." **10** And he said unto him that they were truly his sons: "And you have truly seen that they are truly my sons." **11** And they came near to him, and he turned and kissed them and embraced them both together. **12** And the spirit of prophecy came down into his mouth, and he took Levi by his right hand and Judah by his left. **13** And he turned to Levi first, and began to bless him first, and said unto him: "May the God of all, the very Lord of all the ages, bless you and your children throughout all the ages. **14** And may the Lord give to you and to your seed greatness and great glory, and cause you and your seed, from among all flesh, to approach Him to serve in His sanctuary as the angels of the presence and as the holy ones. (Even) as they, will the seed of your sons be for glory and greatness and holiness, and may He make them great unto all the ages. **15** And they will be princes and judges, and chiefs of all the seed of the sons of Jacob; They will speak the word of the Lord in righteousness, and they will judge all His judgments in righteousness. And they will declare My ways to Jacob And My paths to Israel. The blessing of the Lord will be given in their mouths to bless all the seed of the beloved. **16** your mother has called your name Levi, and justly has she called your name; you will be joined to the Lord And be the companion of all the sons of Jacob; Let His table be yours and do you and your sons eat thereof; And may your table be full unto all generations, and your food fail not unto all the ages. **17** And let all who hate you fall down before you and let all your adversaries be rooted out and perish; And blessed be he that blesses you and cursed be every nation that curses you." **18** And to Judah he said: "May the Lord give you strength and power to tread down all that hate you; A prince shall you be, you and one of your sons, over the sons of Jacob; May your name and the name of your sons go out and traverse every land and region. Then will the Gentiles fear before your face, and all the nations will quake [And all the peoples will quake]. **19** In you shall be the help of Jacob, and in you be found the salvation of

Israel. **20** And when you sit on the throne of the honor of your righteousness, there will be great peace for all the seed of the sons of the beloved, and blessed will he be that blesses you; And all that hate you and afflict you and curse you shall be rooted out and destroyed from the earth and accursed." **21** And turning he kissed him again and embraced him, and rejoiced greatly; for he had seen the sons of Jacob his son in very truth. **22** And he went out from between his feet and fell down and worshipped him. And he blessed them. And (Jacob) rested there with Isaac his father that night, and they ate and drank with joy. **23** And he made the two sons of Jacob sleep, the one on his right hand and the other on his left and it was counted to him for righteousness. **24** And Jacob told his father everything during the night, how the Lord had shown him great mercy, and how He had prospered (him in) all his ways and protected him from all evil. **25** And Isaac blessed the God of his father Abraham, who had not withdrawn His mercy and His righteousness from the sons of His servant Isaac. **26** And in the morning Jacob told his father Isaac the vow which he had vowed to the Lord, and the vision which he had seen, and that he had built an altar, and that everything was ready for the sacrifice to be made before the Lord as he had vowed, and that he had come to set him on an ass. **27** And Isaac said unto Jacob his son: "I am not able to go with you; for I am old, and not able to bear the way: go, my son, in peace; for I am one hundred and sixty-five years this day; I am no longer able to journey, set your mother (on an ass) and let her go with you. **28** And I know, my son, that you have come on my account, and may this day be blessed on which you have seen me alive, and I also have seen you, my son. **29** May you prosper and fulfil the vow which you have vowed, and put not off your vow; for you will be called to account as touching the vow; now therefore make have to perform it, and may He be pleased who has made all things, to whom you have vowed the vow." **30** And he said to Rebecca: "Go with Jacob your son"; and Rebecca went with Jacob her son, and Deborah with her, and they came to Bethel. **31** And Jacob remembered the prayer with which his father had blessed him and his two sons, Levi and Judah, and he rejoiced and blessed the God of his fathers, Abraham and Isaac. **32** And he said: "Now I know that I have an eternal hope, and my sons also, before the God of all;" and thus is it ordained concerning the two; and they record it as an eternal testimony unto them on the heavenly tables how Isaac blessed them.

CHAPTER 32

1 And he stayed that night at Bethel, and Levi dreamed that they had ordained and made him the priest of the Most High God, him and his sons forever; and he awoke from his sleep and blessed the Lord. **2** And Jacob rose early in the morning, on the fourteenth of this month, and he gave a tithe of all that came with him, both of men and cattle, both of gold and every vessel and garment, yea, he gave tithes of all. **3** And in those days Rachel became pregnant with her son Benjamin. And Jacob counted his sons from him upwards and Levi fell to the portion of the Lord, and his father clothed him in the garments of the priesthood and filled his hands. **4** And on the fifteenth of this month, he brought to the altar fourteen oxen from among the cattle, and twenty-eight rams, and forty-nine sheep, and seven lambs, and twenty-one kids of the goats as a burnt-offering on the altar of sacrifice, well pleasing for a sweet savor before God. **5** This was his offering, in consequence of the vow which he had vowed that he would give a tenth, with their fruit-offerings and their drink-offerings. **6** And when the fire had consumed it, he burnt incense on the fire over the fire, and for a thank-offering two oxen and four rams and four sheep, four he-goats, and two sheep of a year old, and two kids of the goats; and thus, he did daily for seven days. **7** And he and all his sons and his men were eating (this) with joy there for seven days and blessing and thanking the Lord, who had delivered him out of all his tribulation and had given him his vow. **8** And he tithed all the clean animals, and made a burnt sacrifice, but the unclean animals he gave (not) to Levi his son, and he gave him all the souls of the men. **9** And Levi discharged the priestly office at Bethel before Jacob his father in preference to his ten brothers, and he was a priest there, and Jacob gave his vow: thus, he tithed again the tithe to the Lord and sanctified it, and it became holy unto Him. **10** And for this reason it is ordained on the heavenly tables as a law for the tithing again the tithe to eat before the Lord from year to year, in the place where it is chosen that His name should dwell, and to this law there is no limit of days forever. **11** This ordinance is written that it may be fulfilled from year to year in eating the second tithe before the Lord in the place where it has been chosen, and nothing shall remain over from it from this year to the year following. 12 For in its year shall the seed be eaten until the days of the gathering of the seed of the year, and the wine until the days of the wine, and the oil until the days of its season. 13 And all that is left thereof and becomes old, let it be regarded as polluted: let it be burnt with fire, for it is unclean. 14 And thus let them eat it together in the sanctuary and let them not suffer it to become old. 15 And all the tithes of the oxen and sheep shall be holy unto the Lord, and shall belong to His priests, which they will eat before Him from year to year; for thus is it ordained and engraved regarding the tithe on the heavenly tables. 16 And on the following night, on the twenty-second day of this month, Jacob resolved to build that place, and to surround the court with a wall, and to sanctify it and make it holy forever, for himself and his children after him. 17 And the Lord appeared to him by night and blessed him and said unto him: "Your name shall not be called Jacob, but Israel shall they name your name." 18 And He said unto him again: "I am the Lord who created the heaven and the earth, and I shall increase you and multiply you exceedingly, and kings will come out from you, and they will judge everywhere wherever the foot of the sons of men has trodden. 19 And I shall give to your seed all the earth which is under heaven, and they will judge all the nations according to their desires, and after that they will get possession of the whole earth and inherit it forever." 20 And He finished speaking with him, and He went up from him, and Jacob looked until He had ascended into heaven. 21 And he saw in a vision of the night, and behold an angel descended from heaven with seven tablets in his hands, and he gave them to Jacob, and he read them and knew all that was written therein which would befall him and his sons throughout all the ages. 22 And he showed him all that was written on the tablets and said unto him: "Do not build this place, and do not make it an eternal sanctuary, and do not dwell here; for this is not the place. Go to the house of Abraham your father and dwell with Isaac your father until the day of the death of your father. 23 For in Egypt you will die in peace, and in this land you will be buried with honor in the sepulcher of your fathers, with Abraham and Isaac. 24 Fear not, for as you have seen and read it, thus will. it all be; and do you write down

everything as you have seen and read." 25 And Jacob said: "Lord, how can I remember all that I have read and seen?" And he said unto him: "I will bring all things to your remembrance." 26 And he went up from him, and he awoke from his sleep, and he remembered everything which he had read and seen, and he wrote down all the words which he had read and seen. 27 And he celebrated there yet another day, and he sacrificed thereon according to all that he sacrificed on the former days, and called its name "Addition," for this day was added, and the former days he called "The Feast." 28 And thus it was manifested that it should be, and it is written on the heavenly tables: for that reason it was revealed to him that he should celebrate it, and add it to the seven days of the feast. 29 And its name was called "Addition," because that it was recorded among the days of the feast days, according to the number of the days of the year. 30 And in the night, on the twenty-third of this month, Deborah Rebecca's nurse died, and they buried her beneath the city under the oak of the river, and he called the name of this place, "The river of Deborah," and the oak, "The oak of the mourning of Deborah." 31 And Rebecca went and returned to her house to her father Isaac, and Jacob sent by her hand rams and sheep and he-goats that she should prepare a meal for his father such as he desired. 32 And he went after his mother until he came to the land of Kabrâtân, and he dwelt there. 33 And Rachel bore a son in the night and called his name "Son of my sorrow"; for she suffered in giving him birth: but his father called his name Benjamin, on the eleventh of the eighth month in the first of the sixth week of this jubilee. 34 And Rachel died there, and she was buried in the land of Ephrath, the same is Bethlehem, and Jacob built a pillar on the grave of Rachel, on the road above her grave.

CHAPTER 33

1 And Jacob went and dwelt to the south of Magdalâdrâ'êf. And he went to his father Isaac, he and Leah his wife, on the new moon of the tenth month. 2 And Reuben saw Bilhah, Rachel's maid, the concubine of his father, bathing in water in a secret place, and he loved her. 3 And he hid himself at night, and he entered the house of Bilhah [at night], and he found her sleeping alone on a bed in her house. 4 And he lay with her, and she awoke and saw, and behold Reuben was lying with her in the bed, and she uncovered the border of her

covering and seized him, and cried out, and discovered that it was Reuben. **5** And she was ashamed because of him, and released her hand from him, and he fled. **6** And she lamented because of this thing exceedingly and did not tell it to anyone. **7** And when Jacob returned and sought her, she said unto him: "I am not clean for you, for I have been defiled as regards you; for Reuben has defiled me, and has lain with me in the night, and I was asleep, and did not discover until he uncovered my skirt and slept with me." **8** And Jacob was exceedingly angry with Reuben because he had lain with Bilhah, because he had uncovered his father's skirt. **9** And Jacob did not approach her again because Reuben had defiled her. And as for any man who uncovers his father's skirt his deed is wicked exceedingly, for he is abominable before the Lord. **10** For this reason it is written and ordained on the heavenly tables that a man should not lie with his father's wife, and should not uncover his father's skirt, for this is unclean: they shall surely die together, the man who lies with his father's wife and the woman also, for they have wrought uncleanness on the earth. **11** And there shall be nothing unclean before our God in the nation which He has chosen for Himself as a possession. **12** And again, it is written a second time: "Cursed he be who lies with the wife of his father, for he has uncovered his father's shame"; and all the holy ones of the Lord said "So be it; so be it." **13** And do you, Moses, command the children of Israel that they observe this word; for it (entails) a punishment of death; and it is unclean, and there is no atonement forever to atone for the man who has committed this, but he is to be put to death and slain, and stoned with stones, and rooted out from the midst of the people of our God. **14** For to no man who doeth so in Israel is it permitted to remain alive a single day on the earth, for he is abominable and unclean. **15** And let them not say: to Reuben was granted life and forgiveness after he had lain with his father's concubine, and to her also though she had a husband, and her husband Jacob, his father, was still alive. **16** For until that time there had not been revealed the ordinance and judgment and law in its completeness for all, but in your days (it has been revealed) as a law of seasons and of days, and an everlasting law for the everlasting generations. **17** And for this law there is no consummation of days, and no atonement for it, but they must both be rooted out in the midst

of the nation: on the day on which they committed it they shall slay them. **18** And do you, Moses, write (it) down for Israel that they may observe it, and do according to these words, and not commit a sin unto death; for the Lord our God is judge, who respects not persons and accepts not gifts. **19** And tell them these words of the covenant, that they may hear and observe, and be on their guard with respect to them, and not be destroyed and rooted out of the land; for an uncleanness, and an abomination, and a contamination, and a pollution are all they who commit it on the earth before our God. **20** And there is no greater sin than the fornication which they commit on earth; for Israel is a holy nation unto the Lord its God, and a nation of inheritance, and a priestly and royal nation and for (His own) possession; and there shall no such uncleanness appear in the midst of the holy nation. **21** And in the third year of this sixth week Jacob and all his sons went and dwelt in the house of Abraham, near Isaac his father and Rebecca his mother. **22** And these were the names of the sons of Jacob: the first-born Reuben, Simeon, Levi, Judah, Issachar, Zebulon, the sons of Leah; and the sons of Rachel, Joseph and Benjamin; and the sons of Bilhah, Dan and Naphtali, and the sons of Zilpah, Gad and Asher; and Dinah, the daughter of Leah, the only daughter of Jacob. **23** And they came and bowed themselves to Isaac and Rebecca, and when they saw them they blessed Jacob and all his sons, and Isaac rejoiced exceedingly, for he saw the sons of Jacob, his younger son, and he blessed them.

CHAPTER 34

1 And in the sixth year of this week of this forty-fourth jubilee Jacob sent his sons to pasture their sheep, and his servants with them, to the pastures of Shechem. **2** And the seven kings of the Amorites assembled themselves together against them, to slay them, hiding themselves under the trees, and to take their cattle as a prey. **3** And Jacob and Levi and Judah and Joseph were in the house with Isaac their father; for his spirit was sorrowful, and they could not leave him: and Benjamin was the youngest, and for this reason remained with his father. **4** And there came the king[s] of Tâphû, and the king[s] of 'Arêsa, and the king[s] of Sêragân, and the king[s] of Sêlô, and the king[s] of Gâ'as, and the king of Bêthôrôn, and the king of Ma'anîsâkîr, and all those who dwell in these mountains (and) who dwell in the woods in the land of Canaan. 5 And they announced this to Jacob saying: "Behold, the kings of the Amorites have surrounded your sons, and plundered their herds." 6 And he arose from his housel he and his three sons and all the servants of his father, and his own servants, and he went against them with six thousand men, who carried swords. 7 And he slew them in the pastures of Shechem, and pursued those who fled, and he slew them with the edge of the sword, and he slew 'Arêsa and Tâphû and Sarêgân and Sêlô and 'Amânîsakîr and Gâ[gâ]'as, and he recovered his herds. 8 And he prevailed over them, and imposed tribute on them that they should pay him tribute, five fruit products of their land, and he built Rôbêl and Tamnâtârês 9 And he returned in peace, and made peace with them, and they became his servants, until the day that he and his sons went down into Egypt. 10 And in the seventh year of this week he sent Joseph to learn about the welfare of his brothers from his house to the land of Shechem, and he found them in the land of Dothan. 11 And they dealt treacherously with him, and formed a plot against him to slay him, but changing their minds, they sold him to Ishmaelite merchants, and they brought him down into Egypt, and they sold him to Potiphar, the eunuch of Pharaoh, the chief of the cooks, priest of the city of 'Êlêw. 12 And the sons of Jacob slaughtered a kid, and dipped the coat of Joseph in the blood, and sent (it) to Jacob their father on the tenth of the seventh month. 13 And he mourned all that night, for they had brought it to him in the evening, and he became feverish with mourning for his death, and he said: "An evil beast has devoured Joseph"; and all the members of his house [mourned with him that day, and they] were grieving and mourning with him all that day. 14 And his sons and his daughter rose up to comfort him, but he refused to be comforted for his son. 15 And on that day Bilhah heard that Joseph had perished, and she died mourning him, and she was living in Qafrâtêf and Dinah also, his daughter, died after Joseph had perished. And there came these three mournings upon Israel in one month. 16 And they buried Bilhah over against the tomb of Rachel, and Dinah also, his daughter, they buried there. 17 And he mourned for Joseph one year, and did not cease, for he said "Let me go down to the grave mourning for my son." 18 For this reason it is ordained for the children of Israel that they should afflict themselves on the tenth of the seventh month—on the day that the news which made him weep for Joseph came to Jacob his father—that they should make atonement for themselves thereon with a young goat on the tenth of the seventh month, once a year, for their sins; for they had grieved the affection of their father regarding Joseph his son. 19 And this day has been ordained that they should grieve thereon for their sins, and for all their transgressions and for all their errors, so that they might cleanse themselves on that day once a year. 20 And after Joseph perished, the sons of Jacob took unto themselves wives. The name of Reuben's wife is 'Adâ and the name of Simeon's wife is 'Adîbâ'a, a Canaanite; and the name of Levi's wife is Mêlkâ, of the daughters of Aram, of the seed of the sons of Terah; and the name of Judah's wife, Bêtasû'êl, a Canaanite; and the name of Issachar's wife, Hêzaqâ; and the name of Zebulon's wife, Nî'îmân; and the name of Dan's wife, 'Êglâ; and the name of Naphtali's wife, Rasû'û, of Mesopotamia; and the name of Gad's wife, Mâka; and the name of Asher's wife, 'Îjônâ; and the name of Joseph's wife, Asenath, the Egyptian; and the name of Benjamin's wife, 'Îjasaka. 21 And Simeon repented, and took a second wife from Mesopotamia as his brothers.

CHAPTER 35

1 And in the first year of the first week of the forty-fifth jubilee Rebecca called Jacob, her son, and commanded him regarding his father and regarding his brother, that he should honor them all the days of his life. 2 And Jacob said: "I will do everything as you have commanded me; for this thing will be honor and greatness to me, and righteousness before the Lord, that I should honor them. 3 And you too, mother, know from the time I was born until this day, all my deeds and all that is in my heart, that I always think good concerning all. 4 And how should I not do this thing which you have commanded me, that I should honor my father and my brother! 5 Tell me, mother, what perversity have you seen in me and I shall turn away from it, and mercy will be upon me." 6 And she said unto him: "My son, I have not seen in you all my days any perverse but (only) upright deeds. And yet I shall tell you the truth, my son: I shall die this, year, and I shall not survive this year in my life; for I have seen in a dream the day of my death, that I should not

live beyond a hundred and fifty-five years: and behold I have completed all the days of my life which I am to live." **7** And Jacob laughed at the words of his mother, because his mother had said unto him that she should die; and she was sitting opposite to him in possession of her strength, and she was not infirm in her strength; for she went in and out and saw, and her teeth were strong, and no ailment had touched her all the days of her life. **8** And Jacob said unto her: "Blessed am I, mother, if my days approach the days of your life, and my strength remain with me thus as your strength: and you will not die, for you are jesting idly with me regarding your death." **9** And she went in to Isaac and said unto him: "One petition I make unto you: make Esau swear that he will not injure Jacob, nor pursue him with enmity; for you know Esau's thoughts that they are perverse from his youth, and there is no goodness in him; for he desires after your death to kill him. **10** And you know all that he has done since the day Jacob his brother went to Haran until this day; how he has forsaken us with his whole heart and has done evil to us; your flocks he has taken to himself, and carried off all your possessions from before your face. **11** And when we implored and besought him for what was our own, he did as a man who was taking pity on us. **12** And he is bitter against you because you did bless Jacob your perfect and upright son; for there is no evil but only goodness in him, and since he came from Haran unto this day he has not robbed us of aught, for he bringeth us everything in its season always, and rejoices with all his heart when we take at his hands, and he blesses us, and has not parted from us since he came from Haran until this day, and he remains with us continually at home honoring us." **13** And Isaac said unto her: "I, too, know and see the deeds of Jacob who is with us, how that with all his heart he honors us; but I loved Esau formerly more than Jacob, because he was the first-born; but now I love Jacob more than Esau, for he has done manifold evil deeds, and there is no righteousness in him, for all his ways are unrighteousness and violence, [and there is no righteousness around him]. **14** And now my heart is troubled because of all his deeds, and neither he nor his seed is to be saved, for they are those who will be destroyed from the earth, and who will be rooted out from under heaven, for he has forsaken the God of Abraham and gone after his wives and after their uncleanness and after their error, he and his children. **15** And you do bid me make him swear that he will not slay Jacob, his brother; even if he swears he will not abide by his oath, and he will not do good but evil only. **16** But if he desires to slay Jacob, his brother, into Jacob's hands will he be given, and he will not escape from his hands, [for he will descend into his hands.] **17** And fear you not on account of Jacob; for the guardian of Jacob is great and powerful and honored, and praised more than the guardian of Esau." **18** And Rebecca sent and called Esau, and he came to her, and she said unto him: "I have a petition, my son, to make unto you, and do you promise to do it, my son." **19** And he said: "I will do everything that you say unto me, and I will not refuse your petition." **20** And she said unto him: "I ask you that the day I die, you will take me in and bury me near Sarah, your father's mother, and that you and Jacob will love each other, and that neither will desire evil against the other, but mutual love only, and (so) you will prosper, my sons, and be honored in the midst of the land, and no enemy will rejoice over you, and you will be a blessing and a mercy in the eyes of all those that love you." **21** And he said: "I will do all that you have told me, and I shall bury you on the day you die near Sarah, my father's mother, as you have desired that her bones may be near your bones. **22** And Jacob, my brother, also, I shall love above all flesh; for I have not a brother in all the earth but him only: and this is no great merit for me if I love him; for he is my brother, and we were sown together in your body, and together came we out from your womb, and if I do not love my brother, whom shall I love? **23** And I, myself, beg you to exhort Jacob concerning me and concerning my sons, for I know that he will assuredly be king over me and my sons, for on the day my father blessed him he made him the higher and me the lower. **24** And I swear unto you that I shall love him, and not desire evil against him all the days of my life but good only." And he swore unto her regarding all this matter. **25** And she called Jacob before the eyes of Esau and gave him commandment according to the words which she had spoken to Esau. **26** And he said: "I shall do your pleasure; believe me that no evil will proceed from me or from my sons against Esau, and I shall be first in naught save in love only." **27** And they ate and drank, she and her sons that night, and she died, three jubilees and one week and one year old, on that night, and her two sons, Esau and Jacob, buried her in the double cave near Sarah, their father's mother.

CHAPTER 36

1 And in the sixth year of this week Isaac called his two sons, Esau and Jacob, and they came to him, and he said unto them: "My sons, I am going the way of my fathers, to the eternal house where my fathers are. **2** For that reason, bury me near Abraham my father, in the double cave in the field of Ephron the Hittite, where Abraham purchased a sepulcher to bury in; in the sepulcher which I dug for myself, there bury me. **3** And this I command you, my sons, that you practice righteousness and uprightness on the earth, so that the Lord may bring upon you all that the Lord said that he would do to Abraham and to his seed. **4** And love one another, my sons, your brothers as a man who loves his own soul and let each seek in what he may benefit his brother, and act together on the earth; and let them love each other as their own souls. **5** And concerning the question of idols, I command and admonish you to reject them and hate them and love them not; for they are full of deception for those that worship them and for those that bow down to them. **6** Remember ye, my sons, the Lord God of Abraham your father, and how I too worshipped Him and served Him in righteousness and in joy, that He might multiply you and increase your seed as the stars of heaven in multitude and establish you on the earth as the plant of righteousness which will not be rooted out unto all the generations forever. **7** And now I shall make you swear a great oath—for there is no oath which is greater than it by the name glorious and honored and great and splendid and wonderful and mighty, which created the heavens and the earth and all things together—that you will fear Him and worship Him. **8** And that each will love his brother with affection and righteousness, and that neither will desire evil against his brother from now on and forever all the days of your life, so that you may prosper in all your deeds and not be destroyed. **9** And if either of you devises evil against his brother, know that from now on everyone that devises evil against his brother will fall into his hand, and will be rooted out of the land of the living, and his seed will be destroyed from under heaven. **10** But on the day of turbulence and execration and indignation and anger, with flaming devouring fire as He burnt Sodom, so likewise will He burn his land and his city and all that is his, and he will be blotted out of the book of the discipline of the children of men, and not be recorded in the book of life, but in that which is appointed to destruction, and he will depart into eternal execration; so that their condemnation may be always renewed in hate and in execration and in wrath and in torment and in indignation and in plagues and in disease forever. **11** I say and testify to you, my sons, according to the judgment which will come upon the man who wishes to injure his brother." **12** And he divided all his possessions between the two on that day, and he gave the larger portion to him that was the first-born, and the tower and all that was about it, and all that Abraham possessed at the Well of the Oath. **13** And he said, "This larger portion I shall give to the first-born." **14** And Esau said, "I have sold to Jacob and given my birthright to Jacob; to him let it be given, and I have not a single word to say regarding it, for it is his." **15** And Isaac said, "May a blessing rest upon you, my sons, and upon your seed this day, for you have given me rest, and my heart is not pained concerning the birthright, lest you shouldest work wickedness on account of it. **16** May the Most High God bless the man that worketh righteousness, him and his seed forever." **17** And he ended commanding them and blessing them, and they ate and drank together before him, and he rejoiced because there was one mind between them, and they went out from him and rested that day and slept. **18** And Isaac slept on his bed that day rejoicing; and he slept the eternal sleep and died one hundred and eighty years old. He completed twenty-five weeks and five years; and his two sons Esau and Jacob buried him. **19** And Esau went to the land of Edom, to the mountains of Seir, and dwelt there. **20** And Jacob dwelt in the mountains of Hebron, in the tower of the land of the sojournings of his father Abraham, and he worshipped the Lord with all his heart and according to the visible commands according as He had divided the days of his generations. **21** And Leah his wife died in the fourth year of the second week of the forty-fifth jubilee, and he buried her in the double cave near Rebecca his mother, to the left of the grave of Sarah, his father's mother. **22** And all her sons and his sons came to mourn over Leah his wife with him, and to comfort him regarding her, for he was lamenting her. **23** For he loved her exceedingly after Rachel her sister died; for she was perfect and upright in all her ways and honored Jacob, and all the days that she lived with him he did not hear from her mouth a harsh word, for she was gentle and peaceable and upright and honorable. 24 And he remembered all her deeds which she had done during her life, and he lamented her exceedingly; for he loved her with all his heart and with all his soul.

CHAPTER 37

1 And on the day that Isaac the father of Jacob and Esau died, the sons of Esau heard that Isaac had given the portion of the elder to his younger son Jacob and they were very angry. 2 And they strove with their father, saying: "Why has your father given Jacob the portion of the elder and passed over you, although you are the elder and Jacob the younger?" 3 And he said unto them "Because I sold my birthright to Jacob for a small mess of lentils; and on the day my father sent me to hunt and catch and bring him something that he should eat and bless me, he came with guile and brought my father food and drink, and my father blessed him and put me under his hand. 4 And now our father has caused us to swear, me and him, that we shall not mutually devise evil, either against his brother, and that we shall continue in love and in peace each with his brother and not make our ways corrupt." 5 And they said unto him, "We shall not hearken unto you to make peace with him; for our strength is greater than his strength, and we are more powerful than he; we shall go against him and slay him, and destroy him and his sons. And if you will not go with us, we shall do hurt to you also. 6 And now hearken unto us: Let us send to Aram and Philistia and Moab and Ammon, and let us choose for ourselves chosen men who are ardent for battle, and let us go against him and do battle with him, and let us exterminate him from the earth before he grows strong." 7 And their father said unto them, "Do not go and do not make war with him lest you fall before him." 8 And they said unto him, "This too, is exactly your mode of action from your youth until this day, and you are putting your neck under his yoke. We shall not hearken to these words." 9 And they sent to Aram, and to 'Adurâm to the friend of their father, and they hired along with them one thousand fighting men, chosen men of war. 10 And there came to them from Moab and from the children of Ammon, those who were hired, one thousand chosen men,

and from Philistia, one thousand chosen men of war, and from Edom and from the Horites one thousand chosen fighting men, and from the Kittim mighty men of war. 11 And they said unto their father: "Go out with them and lead them, else we shall slay you." 12 And he was filled with wrath and indignation on seeing that his sons were forcing him to go before (them) to lead them against Jacob his brother. 13 But afterward he remembered all the evil which lay hidden in his heart against Jacob his brother; and he remembered not the oath which he had sworn to his father and to his mother that he would devise no evil all his days against Jacob his brother. 14 And notwithstanding all this, Jacob knew not that they were coming against him to battle, and he was mourning for Leah, his wife, until they approached very near to the tower with four thousand warriors and chosen men of war. 15 And the men of Hebron sent to him saying, "Behold your brother has come against you, to fight you, with four thousand girt with the sword, and they carry shields and weapons"; for they loved Jacob more than Esau. So they told him; for Jacob was a more liberal and merciful man than Esau. 16 But Jacob would not believe until they came very near to the tower. 17 And he closed the gates of the tower; and he stood on the battlements and spoke to his brother Esau and said, "Noble is the comfort with which you have come to comfort me for my wife who has died. Is this the oath that you did swear to your father and again to your mother before they died? You have broken the oath, and on the moment that you did swear to your father was you condemned." 18 And then Esau answered and said unto him, "Neither the children of men nor the beasts of the earth have any oath of righteousness which in swearing they have sworn (an oath valid) forever; but every day they devise evil one against another, and how each may slay his adversary and foe. 19 And you do hate me and my children forever. And there is no observing the tie of brotherhood with you. 20 Hear these words which I declare unto you, If the boar can change its skin and make its bristles as soft as wool, or if it can cause horns to sprout out on its head like the horns of a stag or of a sheep, then shall I observe the tie of brotherhood with you. [And if the breasts separated themselves from their mother; for you have not been a brother to me.] 21 And if the wolves make peace with the lambs so as not to devour or do them violence, and if their hearts are towards them for good, then there will be peace in my heart towards you. 22 And if the lion becomes the friend of the ox and makes peace with him, and if he is bound under one yoke with him and ploughs with him, then shall I make peace with you. 23 And when the raven becomes white as the râzâ, then know that I have loved you and shall make peace with you. You shall be rooted out, and your sons shall be rooted out, and there shall be no peace for you." 24 And when Jacob saw that he was (so) evilly disposed towards him with his heart, and with all his soul as to slay him, and that he had come springing like the wild boar which comes upon the spear that pierces and kills it, and recoils not from it; 25 Then he spoke to his own and to his servants that they should attack him and all his companions.

CHAPTER 38

1 And after that Judah spoke to Jacob, his father, and said unto him: "Bend your bow, father, and send out your arrows and cast down the adversary and slay the enemy; and may you have the power, for we shall not slay your brother, for he is such as you, and he is like you: let us give him (this) honor." 2 Then Jacob bent his bow and sent out the arrow and struck Esau, his brother, (on his right breast) and slew him. 3 And again he sent out an arrow and struck 'Adôrân the Aramaean, on the left breast, and drove him backward and slew him. 4 And then went out the sons of Jacob, they and their servants, dividing themselves into companies on the four sides of the tower. 5 And Judah went out in front, and Naphtali and Gad with him and fifty servants with him on the south side of the tower, and they slew all they found before them, and not one individual of them escaped. 6 And Levi and Dan and Asher went out on the east side of the tower, and fifty (men) with them, and they slew the fighting men of Moab and Ammon. 7 And Reuben and Issachar and Zebulon went out on the north side of the tower, and fifty men with them, and they slew the fighting men of the Philistines. 8 And Simeon and Benjamin and Enoch, Reuben's son, went out on the west side of the tower, and fifty (men) with them, and they slew of Edom and of the Horites four hundred men, stout warriors; and six hundred fled, and four of the sons of Esau fled with them, and left their father lying slain, as he had fallen on the hill which is in 'Adûrâm. 9 And the sons of Jacob pursued after them to the mountains of Seir.

And Jacob buried his brother on the hill which is in 'Adûrâm, and he returned to his house. 10 And the sons of Jacob pressed hard upon the sons of Esau in the mountains of Seir and bowed their necks so that they became servants of the sons of Jacob. 11 And they sent to their father (to inquire) whether they should make peace with them or slay them. 12 And Jacob sent word to his sons that they should make peace, and they made peace with them, and placed the yoke of servitude upon them, so that they paid tribute to Jacob and to his sons always. 13 And they continued to pay tribute to Jacob until the day that he went down into Egypt. 14 And the sons of Edom have not got quit of the yoke of servitude which the twelve sons of Jacob had imposed on them until this day. 15 And these are the kings that reigned in Edom before there reigned any king over the children of Israel [until this day] in the land of Edom. 16 And Bâlâq, the son of Beor, reigned in Edom, and the name of his city was Danâbâ. 17 And Bâlâq died, and Jobab, the son of Zârâ of Bôsêr, reigned in his stead. 18 And Jobab died, and 'Asâm, of the land of Têmân, reigned in his stead. 19 And 'Asâm died, and 'Adâth, the son of Barad, who slew Midian in the field of Moab, reigned in his stead, and the name of his city was Avith. 20 And 'Adâth died, and Salman, from 'Amâsêqâ, reigned in his stead. 21 And Salman died, and Saul of Râ'abôth (by the) river, reigned in his stead. 22 And Saul died, and Ba'êlûnân, the son of Achbor, reigned in his stead. 23 And Ba'êlûnân, the son of Achbor, died, and 'Adâth reigned in his stead, and the name of his wife was Maiṭabîth, the daughter of Mâṭarat, the daughter of Mêtabêdzâ'ab. 24 These are the kings who reigned in the land of Edom.

CHAPTER 39

1 And Jacob dwelt in the land of his father's sojournings in the land of Canaan. 2 These are the generations of Jacob. And Joseph was seventeen years old when they took him down into the land of Egypt, and Potiphar, an eunuch of Pharaoh, the chief cook bought him. 3 And he set Joseph over all his house, and the blessing of the Lord came upon the house of the Egyptian on account of Joseph, and the Lord prospered him in all that he did. 4 And the Egyptian committed everything into the hands of Joseph; for he saw that the Lord was with him, and that the Lord prospered him in all that he did. 5 And Joseph's appearance was

comely and very beautiful was his appearance, and his master's wife lifted up her eyes and saw Joseph, and she loved him, and besought him to lie with her. 6 But he did not surrender his soul, and he remembered the Lord and the words which Jacob, his father, used to read from among the words of Abraham, that no man should commit fornication with a woman who has a husband; that for him the punishment of death has been ordained in the heavens before the Most High God, and the sin will be recorded against him in the eternal books continually before the Lord. 7 And Joseph remembered these words and refused to lie with her. 8 And she besought him for a year, but he refused and would not listen. 9 But she embraced him and held him fast in the house in order to force him to lie with her and closed the doors of the house and held him fast; but he left his garment in her hands and broke through the door and fled without from her presence. 10 And the woman saw that he would not lie with her, and she calumniated him in the presence of his lord, saying: "Your Hebrew servant, whom you love, sought to force me so that he might lie with me; and it came to pass when I lifted up my voice that he fled and left his garment in my hands when I held him, and he brake through the door." 11 And the Egyptian saw the garment of Joseph and the broken door, and heard the words of his wife, and cast Joseph into prison into the place where the prisoners were kept whom the king imprisoned. 12 And he was there in the prison; and the Lord gave Joseph favor in the sight of the chief of the prison guards and compassion before him, for he saw that the Lord was with him, and that the Lord made all that he did to prosper. 13 And he committed all things into his hands, and the chief of the prison guards knew of nothing that was with him, for Joseph did everything, and the Lord perfected it. 14 And he remained there two years. And in those days Pharaoh, king of Egypt, was angry against his two eunuchs, against the chief butler and against the chief baker, and he put them in ward in the house of the chief cook, in the prison where Joseph was kept. 15 And the chief of the prison guards appointed Joseph to serve them; and he served before them. 16 And they both dreamed a dream, the chief butler and the chief baker, and they told it to Joseph. 17 And as he interpreted to them so it befell them, and Pharaoh restored the chief butler to his office, and the (chief) baker he slew, as Joseph had interpreted to them. 18 But the chief butler forgot Joseph in the prison, although he had informed him what would befall him, and did not remember to inform Pharaoh how Joseph had told him for he forgot.

CHAPTER 40

1 And in those days Pharaoh dreamed two dreams in one night concerning a famine which was to be in all the land, and he awoke from his sleep and called all the interpreters of dreams that were in Egypt, and magicians, and told them his two dreams, and they were not able to declare (them). 2 And then the chief butler remembered Joseph and spoke of him to the king, and he brought him out from the prison, and he told his two dreams before him. 3 And he said before Pharaoh that his two dreams were one, and he said unto him: "Seven years will come (in which there will be) plenty over all the land of Egypt, and after that seven years of famine, such a famine as has not been in all the land. 4 And now let Pharaoh appoint overseers in all the land of Egypt, and let them store up food in every city throughout the days of the years of plenty, and there will be food for the seven years of famine, and the land will not perish through the famine, for it will be very severe." 5 And the Lord gave Joseph favor and mercy in the eyes of Pharaoh, and Pharaoh said unto his servants: "We shall not find such a wise and discreet man as this man, for the spirit of the Lord is with him." 6 And he appointed him the second in all his kingdom and gave him authority over all Egypt, and caused him to ride in the second chariot of Pharaoh. 7 And he clothed him with byssus garments, and he put a gold chain upon his neck, and (a herald) proclaimed before him "'Êl 'Êl wa' Abîrĕr," and he placed a ring on his hand and made him ruler over all his house, and magnified him, and said unto him: "Only on the throne shall I be greater than you." 8 And Joseph ruled over all the land of Egypt, and all the princes of Pharaoh, and all his servants, and all who did the king's business loved him, for he walked in uprightness, for he was without pride and arrogance, and he had no respect of persons, and did not accept gifts, but he judged in uprightness all the people of the land. 9 And the land of Egypt was at peace before Pharaoh because of Joseph, for the Lord was with him, and gave him favor and mercy for all his generations before all those who knew him and those who heard concerning him, and

Pharaoh's kingdom was well ordered, and there was no Satan and no evil person (therein). 10 And the king called Joseph's name Sĕphânṭîphâns, and gave Joseph to wife the daughter of Potiphar, the daughter of the priest of Heliopolis, the chief cook. 11 And on the day that Joseph stood before Pharaoh he was thirty years old [when he stood before Pharaoh]. 12 And in that year Isaac died. And it came to pass as Joseph had said in the interpretation of his two dreams, according as he had said it, there were seven years of plenty over all the land of Egypt, and the land of Egypt produced abundantly, one measure (producing) eighteen hundred measures. 13 And Joseph gathered food into every city until they were full of corn until they could no longer count and measure it for its multitude.

CHAPTER 41

1 And in the forty-fifth jubilee, in the second week, (and) in the second year, Judah took for his first-born Er, a wife from the daughters of Aram, named Tamar. 2 But he hated, and did not lie with her, because his mother was of the daughters of Canaan, and he wished to take him a wife of the kinsfolk of his mother, but Judah, his father, would not permit him. 3 And this Er, the first-born of Judah, was wicked, and the Lord slew him. 4 And Judah said unto Onan, his brother: "Go in unto your brother's wife and perform the duty of a husband's brother unto her, and raise up seed unto your brother." 5 And Onan knew that the seed would not be his, (but) his brother's only, and he went into the house of his brother's wife, and spilt the seed on the ground, and he was wicked in the eyes of the Lord, and He slew him. 6 And Judah said unto Tamar, his daughter-in-law: "Remain in your father's house as a widow until Shelah my son be grown up, and I shall give you to him to wife." 7 And he grew up; but Bêdsû'êl, the wife of Judah, did not permit her son Shelah to marry. And Bêdsû'êl, the wife of Judah, died in the fifth year of this week. 8 And in the sixth year Judah went up to shear his sheep at Timnah. And they told Tamar: "Behold your father-in-law goes up to Timnah to shear his sheep." 9 And she put off her widow's clothes, and put on a veil, and adorned herself, and sat in the gate adjoining the way to Timnah. 10 And as Judah was going along he found her, and thought her to be an harlot, and he said unto her: "Let me come in unto you"; and she said unto him: "Come in," and he went in. 11 And

she said unto him: "Give me my hire"; and he said unto her: "I have nothing in my hand save my ring that is on my finger, and my necklace, and my staff which is in my hand." 12 And she said unto him: "Give them to me until you do send me my hire"; and he said unto her: "I will send unto you a kid of the goats"; and he gave them to her, (and he went in unto her,) and she conceived by him. 13 And Judah went unto his sheep, and she went to her father's house. 14 And Judah sent a kid of the goats by the hand of his shepherd, an Adullamite, and he found her not; and he asked the people of the place, saying: "Where is the harlot who was here?" And they said unto him: "There is no harlot here with us." 15 And he returned and informed him, and said unto him that he had not found her; "I asked the people of the place, and they said unto me: 'There is no harlot here.' " And he said: "Let her keep (them) lest we become a cause of derision." 16 And when she had completed three months, it was manifest that she was with child, and they told Judah, saying: "Behold Tamar, your daughter-in-law, is with child by whoredom." 17 And Judah went to the house of her father, and said unto her father and her brothers: "Bring her out, and let them burn her, for she has wrought uncleanness in Israel." 18 And it came to pass when they brought her out to burn her that she sent to her father-in-law the ring and the necklace, and the staff, saying: "Discern whose are these, for by him am I with child." 19 And Judah acknowledged, and said: "Tamar is more righteous than I am. And therefore, let them burn her not." 20 And for that reason she was not given to Shelah, and he did not again approach her. 21 And after that she bore two sons, Perez and Zerah, in the seventh year of this second week. 22 And immediately the seven years of fruitfulness were accomplished, of which Joseph spoke to Pharaoh. 23 And Judah acknowledged that the deed which he had done was evil, for he had lain with his daughter-in-law, and he esteemed it hateful in his eyes, and he acknowledged that he had transgressed and gone astray; for he had uncovered the skirt of his son, and he began to lament and to supplicate before the Lord because of his transgression. 24 And we told him in a dream that it was forgiven him because he supplicated earnestly, and lamented, and did not again commit it. 25 And he received forgiveness because he turned from his sin and from his ignorance, for he transgressed greatly before our God; and everyone that acts this way, everyone who lies with his mother-in-law, let them burn him with fire that he may burn therein, for there is uncleanness and pollution upon them; with fire let them burn them. 26 And do you command the children of Israel that there be no uncleanness among them, for everyone who lies with his daughter-in-law or with his mother-in-law has wrought uncleanness; with fire let them bum the man who has lain with her, and likewise the woman, and He will turn away wrath and punishment from Israel. 27 And unto Judah we said that his two sons had not lain with her, and for this reason his seed was established for a second generation and would not be rooted out. 28 For in singleness of eye he had gone and sought for punishment, namely, according to the judgment of Abraham, which he had commanded his sons, Judah had sought to burn her with fire.

CHAPTER 42

1 And in the first year of the third week of the forty-fifth jubilee the famine began to come into the land, and the rain refused to be given to the earth, for none whatever fell. 2 And the earth grew barren, but in the land of Egypt there was food, for Joseph had gathered the seed of the land in the seven years of plenty and had preserved it. 3 And the Egyptians came to Joseph that he might give them food, and he opened the storehouses where was the grain of the first year, and he sold it to the people of the land for gold. 4 (Now the famine was very sore in the land of Canaan), and Jacob heard that there was food in Egypt, and he sent his ten sons that they should procure food for him in Egypt; but Benjamin he did not send, and (the ten sons of Jacob) arrived (in Egypt) among those that went (there.) 5 And Joseph recognized them, but they did not recognize him, and he spoke unto them and questioned them, and he said unto them: "Are you not spies, and have you not come to explore the approaches of the land?" And he put them in ward. 6 And after that he set them free again, and detained Simeon alone and sent off his nine brothers. 7 And he filled their sacks with corn, and he put their gold in their sacks, and they did not know. 8 And he commanded them to bring their younger brother, for they had told him their father was living and their younger brother. 9 And they went up from the land of Egypt and they came to the land of Canaan; and they told their father

all that had befallen them, and how the lord of the country had spoken roughly to them and had seized Simeon until they should bring Benjamin. 10 And Jacob said: "Me have you bereaved of my children! Joseph is not, and Simeon also is not, and you will take Benjamin away. On me has your wickedness come." 11 And he said: "My son will not go down with you lest perchance he falls sick; for their mother gave birth to two sons, and one has perished, and this one also you will take from me. If perchance he took a fever on the road, you would bring down my old age with sorrow unto death." 12 For he saw that their money had been returned to every man in his sack, and for this reason he feared to send him. 13 And the famine increased and became sore in the land of Canaan, and in all lands save in the land of Egypt, for many of the children of the Egyptians had stored up their seed for food from the time when they saw Joseph gathering seed together and putting it in storehouses and preserving it for the years of famine. 14 And the people of Egypt fed themselves thereon during the first year of their famine. 15 But when Israel saw that the famine was very sore in the land, and there was no deliverance, he said unto his sons: "Go again, and procure food for us that we die not." 16 And they said: "We shall not go; unless our youngest brother go with us, we shall not go." 17 And Israel saw that if he did not send him with them, they should all perish by reason of the famine. 18 And Reuben said: "Give him into my hand, and if I do not bring him back to you, slay my two sons instead of his soul." And he said unto him He will not go with you." 19 And Judah came near and said: "Send him with me, and if I do not bring him back to you, let me bear the blame before you all the days of my life." 20 And he sent him with them in the second year of this week on the first day of the month, and they came to the land of Egypt with all those who went, and (they had) presents in their hands, stacte and almonds and terebinth nuts and pure honey. 21 And they went and stood before Joseph, and he saw Benjamin his brother, and he knew him, and said unto them: "Is this your youngest brother?" And they said unto him: "It is he." And he said: "The Lord be gracious to you, my son!" 22 And he sent him into his house and he brought out Simeon unto them and he made a feast for them, and they presented to him the gift which they had brought in their hands. 23 And they ate before him and he gave them all a portion, but the portion of Benjamin was seven times larger than that of any of theirs. **24** And they ate and drank and arose and remained with their asses. **25** And Joseph devised a plan whereby he might learn their thoughts as to whether thoughts of peace prevailed among them, and he said to the steward who was over his house: "Fill all their sacks with food, and return their money unto them into their vessels, and my cup, the silver cup out of which I drink, put it in the sack of the youngest, and send them away."

CHAPTER 43

1 And he did as Joseph had told him and filled all their sacks for them with food and put their money in their sacks and put the cup in Benjamin's sack. **2** And early in the morning they departed, and it came to pass that, when they had gone from there, Joseph said unto the steward of his house: "Pursue them, run and seize them, saying, 'For good you have requited me with evil; you have stolen from me the silver cup out of which my lord drinks.' And bring back to me their youngest brother, and fetch (him) quickly before I go out to my seat of judgment." **3** And he ran after them and said unto them according to these words. **4** And they said unto him: "God forbid that your servants should do this thing, and steal from the house of your lord any utensil, and the money also which we found in our sacks the first time, we your servants brought back from the land of Canaan. **5** How then should we steal any utensil? Behold here are we and our sacks; search, and wherever you find the cup in the sack of any man among us, let him be slain, and we and our asses will serve your lord." **6** And he said unto them: "Not so, the man with whom I find, him only shall I take as a servant, and you will return in peace unto your house." **7** And as he was searching in their vessels, beginning with the eldest and ending with the youngest, it was found in Benjamin's sack. **8** And they rent their garments, and laded their asses, and returned to the city and came to the house of Joseph, and they all bowed themselves on their faces to the ground before him. **9** And Joseph said unto them: "Ye have done evil." And they said: "What shall we say and how shall we defend ourselves? Our lord has discovered the transgression of his servants; behold we are the servants of our lord, and our asses also." **10** And Joseph said unto them: "I too fear the Lord; as for you, go you to your homes and let

your brother be my servant, for you have done evil. Do you not know that a man delights in his cup as I with this cup? And yet you have stolen it from me." **11** And Judah said: "O my lord, let your servant, I pray you, speak a word in my lord's ear; two brothers did your servant's mother bear to our father; one went away and was lost, and has not been found, and he alone is left of his mother, and your servant our father loves him, and his life also is bound up with the life of this (lad). **12** And it will come to pass, when we go to your servant our father, and the lad is not with us, that he will die, and we shall bring down our father with sorrow unto death. **13** Now rather let me, your servant, abide instead of the boy as a bondsman unto my lord, and let the lad go with his brethren, for I became a guarantee for him at the hand of your servant our father, and if I do not bring him back, your servant will bear the blame to our father forever." **14** And Joseph saw that they were all accordant in goodness one with another, and he could not refrain himself, and he told them that he was Joseph. **15** And he conversed with them in the Hebrew tongue and fell on their neck and wept. But they knew him not and they began to weep. **16** And he said unto them: "Weep not over me, but hasten and bring my father to me; and you see that it is my mouth that speaks, and the eyes of my brother Benjamin see. **17** For behold this is the second year of the famine, and there are still five years without harvest or fruit of trees or ploughing. **18** Come down quickly you and your households, so that you perish not through the famine, and do not be grieved for your possessions, for the Lord sent me before you to set things in order that many people might live. **19** And tell my father that I am still alive, and ye, behold, you see that the Lord has made me as a father to Pharaoh, and ruler over his house and over all the land of Egypt. **20** And tell my father of all my glory, and all the riches and glory that the Lord has given Me." **21** And by the command of the mouth of Pharaoh he gave them chariots and provisions for the way, and he gave them all many-colored raiment and silver. **22** And to their father he sent raiment and silver and ten asses which carried com, and he sent them away. **23** And they went up and told their father that Joseph was alive and was measuring out corn to all the nations of the earth, and that he was ruler over all the land of Egypt. **24** And their father did not believe it, for he was beside himself in his mind; but when he saw the wagons which Joseph had sent, the life of his spirit revived, and he said: "It is enough for me if Joseph lives; I will go down and see him before I die."

CHAPTER 44

1 And Israel took his journey from Haran from his house on the new moon of the third month, and he went on the way of the Well of the Oath, and he offered a sacrifice to the God of his father Isaac on the seventh of this month. 2 And Jacob remembered the dream that he had seen at Bethel, and he feared to go down into Egypt. 3 And while he was thinking of sending word to Joseph to come to him, and that he would not go down, he remained there seven days, if perchance he should see a vision as to whether he should remain or go down. 4 And he celebrated the harvest festival of the first-fruits with old grain, for in all the land of Canaan there was not a handful of seed (in the land), for the famine was over all the beasts and cattle and birds, and also over man. 5 And on the sixteenth the Lord appeared unto him, and said unto him, "Jacob, Jacob"; and he said, "Here am I." And He said unto him: "I am the God of your fathers, the God of Abraham and Isaac; fear not to go down into Egypt, for I will there make of you a great nation. 6 I shall go down with you, and I shall bring you up (again), and in this land will you be buried, and Joseph will put his hands upon your eyes. Fear not; go down into Egypt." 7 And his sons rose up, and his sons' sons, and they placed their father and their possessions upon wagons. 8 And Israel rose up from the Well of the Oath on the sixteenth of this third month, and he went to the land of Egypt. 9 And Israel sent Judah before him to his son Joseph to examine the Land of Goshen, for Joseph had told his brothers that they should come and dwell there that they might be near him. 10 And this was the goodlie (land) in the land of Egypt, and near to him, for all (of them) and also for the cattle. 11 And these are the names of the sons of Jacob who went into Egypt with Jacob their father. 12 Reuben, the first-born of Israel; and these are the names of his sons: Enoch, and Pallu, and Hezron and Carmi—five. 13 Simeon and his sons; and these are the names of his sons: Jemuel, and Jamin, and Ohad, and Jachin, and Zohar, and Shaul, the son of the Zephathite woman—seven. 14 Levi and his sons; and these are the names of his sons: Gershon, and Kohath, and Merari—four. 15 Judah and his sons; and these are the names

of his sons: Shela, and Perez, and Zerah—four. 16 Issachar and his sons; and these are the names of his sons: Tola, and Phûa, and Jâsûb, and Shimron—five. 17 Zebulon and his sons; and these are the names of his sons: Sered, and Elon, and Jahleel—four. 18 And these are the sons of Jacob, and their sons, whom Leah bore to Jacob in Mesopotamia, six, and their one sister, Dinah: and all the souls of the sons of Leah, and their sons, who went with Jacob their father into Egypt, were twenty-nine, and Jacob their father being with them, they were thirty. 19 And the sons of Zilpah, Leah's handmaid, the wife of Jacob, whom she bore unto Jacob, Gad and Asher. 20 And these are the names of their sons who went with him into Egypt: the sons of Gad: Ziphion, and Haggi, and Shuni, and Ezbon, (and Eri) and Areli, and Arodi—eight. 21 And the sons of Asher: Imnah, and Ishvah, (and Ishvi), and Beriah, and Serah, their one sister—six. 22 All the souls were fourteen, and all those of Leah were forty-four. 23 And the sons of Rachel, the wife of Jacob: Joseph and Benjamin. 24 And there were born to Joseph in Egypt before his father came into Egypt, those whom Asenath, daughter of Potiphar priest of Heliopolis bore unto him, Manasseh, and Ephraim—three. 25 And the sons of Benjamin: Bela and Becher, and Ashbel, Gera, and Naaman, and Ehi, and Rosh, and Muppim, and Huppim, and Ard—eleven. 26 And all the souls of Rachel were fourteen. 27 And the sons of Bilhah, the handmaid of Rachel, the wife of Jacob, whom she bore to Jacob, were Dan and Naphtali. 28 And these are the names of their sons who went with them into Egypt. And the sons of Dan were Hushim, and Sâmon, and Asûdî, and 'Îjâka, and Salômôn—six. 29 And they died the year in which they entered into Egypt, and there was left to Dan Hushim alone. 30 And these are the names of the sons of Naphtali: Jahziel, and Guni, and Jezer, and Shallum, and 'Îv. 31 And 'Îv, who was born after the years of famine, died in Egypt. 32 And all the souls of Rachel were twenty-six. 33 And all the souls of Jacob which went into Egypt were seventy souls. These are his children and his children's children, in all seventy; but five died in Egypt before Joseph and had no children. 34 And in the land of Canaan two sons of Judah died, Er and Onan, and they had no children, and the children of Israel buried those who perished, and they were reckoned among the seventy Gentile nations.

CHAPTER 45

1 And Israel went into the country of Egypt, into the land of Goshen, on the new moon of the fourth month, in the second year of the third week of the forty-fifth jubilee. 2 And Joseph went to meet his father Jacob, to the land of Goshen, and he fell on his father's neck and wept. 3 And Israel said unto Joseph: "Now let me die since I have seen you, and now may the Lord God of Israel be blessed, the God of Abraham and the God of Isaac who has not withheld His mercy and His grace from His servant Jacob. 4 It is enough for me that I have seen your face while I am yet alive; yea, true is the vision which I saw at Bethel. Blessed be the Lord my God forever and ever and blessed be His name." 5 And Joseph and his brothers ate bread before their father and drank wine, and Jacob rejoiced with exceeding great joy because he saw Joseph eating with his brothers and drinking before him, and he blessed the Creator of all things who had preserved him and had preserved for him his twelve sons. 6 And Joseph had given to his father and to his brothers as a gift the right of dwelling in the land of Goshen and in Rameses and all the surrounding region, which he ruled over before Pharaoh. And Israel and his sons dwelt in the land of Goshen, the best part of the land of Egypt; and Israel was one hundred and thirty years old when he came into Egypt, 7 And Joseph nourished his father and his brethren and also their possessions with bread as much as sufficed them for the seven years of the famine. 8 And the land of Egypt suffered by reason of the famine, and Joseph acquired all the land of Egypt for Pharaoh in return for food, and he got possession of the people and their cattle and everything for Pharaoh. 9 And the years of the famine were accomplished, and Joseph gave to the people in the land seed and food that they might sow (the land) in the eighth year, for the river had overflowed all the land of Egypt. 10 For in the seven years of the famine it had not overflowed and had irrigated only a few places on the banks of the river, but now it overflowed, and the Egyptians sowed the land, and it bore much corn that year. 11 And this was the first year of the fourth week of the forty-fifth jubilee. 12 And Joseph took of the corn of the harvest the fifth part for the king and left four parts for them for food and for seed, and Joseph made it an ordinance for the land of Egypt until this day. 13 And Israel lived in the land of Egypt seventeen years, and all the days which he lived were three jubilees, one hundred and forty-seven years, and he died in the fourth year of the fifth week of the forty-fifth jubilee. 14 And Israel blessed his sons before he died and told them everything that would befall them in the land of Egypt; and he made known to them what would come upon them in the last days and blessed them and gave to Joseph two portions in the land. 15 And he slept with his fathers, and he was buried in the double cave in the land of Canaan, near Abraham his father in the grave which he dug for himself in the double cave in the land of Hebron. 16 And he gave all his books and the books of his fathers to Levi his son that he might preserve them and renew them for his children until this day.

CHAPTER 46

1 And it came to pass that after Jacob died the children of Israel multiplied in the land of Egypt, and they became a great nation, and they were of one accord in heart, so that brother loved brother and every man helped his brother, and they increased abundantly and multiplied exceedingly, ten weeks of years, all the days of the life of Joseph. 2 And there was no Satan nor any evil all the days of the life of Joseph which he lived after his father Jacob, for all the Egyptians honored the children of Israel all the days of the life of Joseph. 3 And Joseph died being a hundred and ten years old; seventeen years he lived in the land of Canaan, and ten years he was a servant, and three years in prison, and eighty years he was under the king, ruling all the land of Egypt. 4 And he died and all his brethren and all that generation. 5 And he commanded the children of Israel before he died that they should carry his bones with them when they went out from the land of Egypt. 6 And he made them swear regarding his bones, for he knew that the Egyptians would not again bring out and bury him in the land of Canaan, for Mâkamârôn, king of Canaan, while dwelling in the land of Assyria, fought in the valley with the king of Egypt and slew him there, and pursued after the Egyptians to the gates of 'Êrmôn. 7 But he was not able to enter, for another, a new king, had become king of Egypt, and he was stronger than he, and he returned to the land of Canaan, and the gates of Egypt were closed, and none went out and none came into Egypt. 8 And Joseph died in the forty-sixth jubilee, in the sixth week, in the second year, and they buried him in the land of Egypt, and his

brethren died after him. **9** And the king of Egypt went out to war with the king of Canaan in the forty-seventh jubilee, in the second week in the second year, and the children of Israel brought out all the bones of the children of Jacob save the bones of Joseph, and they buried them in the field in the double cave in the mountain. **10** And the most (of them) returned to Egypt, but a few of them remained in the mountains of Hebron, and Amram your father remained with them. **11** And the king of Canaan was victorious over the king of Egypt, and he closed the gates of Egypt. **12** And he devised an evil device against the children of Israel of afflicting them; and he said unto the people of Egypt: **13** "Behold the people of the children of Israel have increased and multiplied more than we. Come and let us deal wisely with them before they become too many and let us afflict them with slavery before war come upon us and before they too fight against us; else they will join themselves unto our enemies and get them up out of our land, for their hearts and faces are towards the land of Canaan." **14** And he set over them taskmasters to afflict them with slavery; and they built strong cities for Pharaoh, Pithom and Raamses, and they built all the walls and all the fortifications which had fallen in the cities of Egypt. **15** And they made them serve with rigor, and the more they dealt evilly with them, the more they increased and multiplied. **16** And the people of Egypt abominated the children of Israel.

CHAPTER 47

1 And in the seventh week, in the seventh year, in the forty-seventh jubilee, your father went out from the land of Canaan, and you were born in the fourth week, in the sixth year thereof, in the forty-eighth jubilee; this was the time of tribulation on the children of Israel. **2** And Pharaoh, king of Egypt, issued a command regarding them that they should cast all their male children which were born into the river. **3** And they cast them in for seven months until the day that you were born. And your mother hid you for three months, and they told regarding her. **4** And she made an ark for you, and covered it with pitch and asphalt, and placed it in the flags on the bank of the river, and she placed you in it seven days, and your mother came by night and suckled you, and by day Miriam, your sister, guarded you from the birds. **5** And in those days Tharmuth, the daughter of Pharaoh, came to bathe in the river, and she heard your voice crying, and she told her maidens to bring you out, and they brought you unto her. **6** And she took you out of the ark, and she had compassion on you. **7** And your sister said unto her: "Shall I go and call unto you one of the Hebrew women to nurse and suckle this babe for you?" And she said (unto her): "Go." **8** And she went and called your mother Jochebed, and she gave her wages, and she nursed you. **9** And afterwards, when you were grown up, they brought you unto the daughter of Pharaoh, and you did become her son, and Amram your father taught you writing, and after you had completed three weeks they brought you into the royal court. **10** And you were three weeks of years at court until the time when you did go out from the royal court and did see an Egyptian smiting your friend who was of the children of Israel, and you did slay him and hide him in the sand. **11** And on the second day you did find two of the children of Israel striving together, and you did say to him who was doing the wrong: "Why do you smite your brother? **12** And he was angry and indignant, and said "Who made you a prince and a judge over us? Think you to kill me as you killed the Egyptian yesterday?" And you did fear and flee on account of these words.

CHAPTER 48

1 And in the sixth year of the third week of the forty-ninth jubilee you did depart and dwell in the land of Midian five weeks and one year. And you did return into Egypt in the second week in the second year in the fiftieth jubilee. **2** And you yourself know what He spoke unto you on Mount Sinai, and what prince Mastêmâ desired to do with you when you were returning into Egypt on the way when you did meet him at the lodging-place. **3** Did he not with all his power seek to slay you and deliver the Egyptians out of your hand when he saw that you were sent to execute judgment and vengeance on the Egyptians? **4** And I delivered you out of his hand, and you did perform the signs and wonders which you were sent to perform in Egypt against Pharaoh, and against all his house, and against his servants and his people. **5** And the Lord executed a great vengeance on them for Israel's sake, and smote them through (the plagues of) blood and frogs, lice and dog-flies, and malignant boils breaking out in blains; and their cattle by death; and by hail-stones, thereby He destroyed everything that grew for them; and by locusts which devoured the residue which had been left by the hail, and by darkness; and (by the death) of the first-born of men and animals, and on all their idols the Lord took vengeance and burned them with fire. 6 And everything was sent through your hand, that you should declare (these things) before they were done, and you did speak with the king of Egypt before all his servants and before his people. 7 And everything took place according to your words; ten great and terrible judgments came on the land of Egypt that you might execute vengeance on it for Israel. 8 And the Lord did everything for Israel's sake, and according to His covenant, which He had ordained with Abraham that He would take vengeance on them as they had brought them by force into bondage. 9 And the prince of the Mastêmâ stood up against you and sought to cast you into the hands of Pharaoh, and he helped the Egyptian sorcerers, and they stood up and wrought before you. 10 The evils indeed we permitted them to work, but the remedies we did not allow to be wrought by their hands. 11 And the Lord smote them with malignant ulcers, and they were not able to stand for we destroyed them so that they could not perform a single sign. 12 And notwithstanding all (these) signs and wonders the prince of the Mastêmâ was not put to shame because he took courage and cried to the Egyptians to pursue after you with all the powers of the Egyptians, with their chariots, and with their horses, and with all the hosts of the peoples of Egypt. 13 And I stood between the Egyptians and Israel, and we delivered Israel out of his hand, and out of the hand of his people, and the Lord brought them through the midst of the sea as if it were dry land. 14 And all the peoples whom he brought to pursue after Israel, the Lord our God cast them into the midst of the sea, into the depths of the abyss beneath the children of Israel, even as the people of Egypt had cast their children into the river. He took vengeance on 1,000,000 of them, and one thousand strong and energetic men were destroyed on account of one suckling of the children of your people which they had thrown into the river. 15 And on the fourteenth day and on the fifteenth and on the sixteenth and on the seventeenth and on the eighteenth the prince of the Mastêmâ was bound and imprisoned behind the children of Israel that he might not accuse them. 16 And on the nineteenth we let them loose that they might help the Egyptians and pursue the children of Israel. 17 And he hardened their hearts and made them stubborn, and the device was devised by the Lord our God that He might smite the Egyptians and cast them into the sea. 18 And on the fourteenth we bound him that he might not accuse the children of Israel on the day when they asked the Egyptians for vessels and garments, vessels of silver, and vessels of gold, and vessels of bronze, in order to despoil the Egyptians in return for the bondage in which they had forced them to serve. 19 And we did not lead out the children of Israel from Egypt empty handed.

CHAPTER 49

1 Remember the commandment which the Lord commanded you concerning the Passover, that you should celebrate it in its season on the fourteenth of the first month, that you should kill it before it is evening, and that they should eat it by night on the evening of the fifteenth from the time of the setting of the sun. 2 For on this night—the beginning of the festival and the beginning of the joy—you were eating the Passover in Egypt, when all the powers of Mastêmâ had been let loose to slay all the first-born in the land of Egypt, from the firstborn of Pharaoh to the first-born of the captive maidservant in the mill, and to the cattle. 3 And this is the sign which the Lord gave them: Into every house on the lintels of which they saw the blood of a lamb of the first year, into (that) house they should not enter to slay, but should pass by (it), that all those should be saved that were in the house because the sign of the blood was on its lintels. 4 And the powers of the Lord did everything according as the Lord commanded them, and they passed by all the children of Israel, and the plague came not upon them to destroy from among them any soul either of cattle, or man, or dog. 5 And the plague was very grievous in Egypt, and there was no house in Egypt where there was not one dead and weeping and lamentation. 6 And all Israel was eating the flesh of the paschal lamb, and drinking the wine, and was lauding and blessing, and giving thanks to the Lord God of their fathers, and was ready to go out from under the yoke of Egypt; and from the evil bondage. 7 And remember you this day all the days of your life and observe it from year to year all the days of your life, once a year, on its day, according to all the law thereof, and do not adjourn (it) from day to day, or from month to month. 8 For it is

an eternal ordinance and engraved on the heavenly tables regarding all the children of Israel that they should observe it every year on its day once a year, throughout all their generations; and there is no limit of days, for this is ordained forever. **9** And the man who is free from uncleanness, and doth not come to observe it on occasion of its day, so as to bring an acceptable offering before the Lord, and to eat and to drink before the Lord on the day of its festival, that man who is clean and close at hand will be cut off; because he offered not the oblation of the Lord in its appointed season, he will take the guilt upon himself. **10** Let the children of Israel come and observe the Passover on the day of its fixed time, on the fourteenth day of the first month, between the evenings, from the third part of the day to the third part of the night, for two portions of the day are given to the light, and a third part to the evening. **11** That is that which the Lord commanded you that you should observe it between the evenings. **12** And it is not permissible to slay it during any period of the light, but during the period bordering on the evening, and let them eat it at the time of the evening until the third part of the night, and whatever is leftover of all its flesh from the third part of the night and onwards, let them burn it with fire. **13** And they shall not cook it with water, nor shall they eat it raw, but roast on the fire: they shall eat it with diligence, its head with the inwards thereof and its feet they shall roast with fire, and not break any bone thereof; for of the children of Israel no bone shall be crushed. **14** For this reason the Lord commanded the children of Israel to observe the Passover on the day of its fixed time, and they shall not break a bone thereof; for it is a festival day, and a day commanded, and there may be no passing over from day to day, and month to month, but on the day of its festival let it be observed. **15** And do you command the children of Israel to observe the Passover throughout their days, every year, once a year on the day of its fixed time, and it will come for a memorial well pleasing before the Lord, and no plague will come upon them to slay or to smite in that year in which they celebrate the Passover in its season in every respect according to His command. **16** And they shall not eat it outside the sanctuary of the Lord, but before the sanctuary of the Lord, and all the people of the congregation of Israel shall celebrate it in its appointed season. **17** And every man who has come upon its day shall eat it in the sanctuary of your God before the Lord from twenty years old and upward; for thus is it written and ordained that they should eat it in the sanctuary of the Lord. **18** And when the children of Israel come into the land which they are to possess, into the land of Canaan, and set up the tabernacle of the Lord in the midst of the land in one of their tribes until the sanctuary of the Lord has been built in the land, let them come and celebrate the Passover in the midst of the tabernacle of the Lord, and let them slay it before the Lord from year to year. **19** And in the days when the house has been built in the name of the Lord in the land of their inheritance, they shall go there and slay the Passover in the evening, at sunset, at the third part of the day. **20** And they will offer its blood on the threshold of the altar and shall place its fat on the fire which is upon the altar, and they shall eat its flesh roasted with fire in the court of the house which has been sanctified in the name of the Lord. **21** And they may not celebrate the Passover in their cities, nor in any place save before the tabernacle of the Lord, or before His house where His name has dwelt; and they will not go astray from the Lord. **22** And do you, Moses, command the children of Israel to observe the ordinances of the Passover, as it was commanded unto you; declare you unto them every year and the day of its days, and the festival of unleavened bread, that they should eat unleavened bread seven days, (and) that they should observe its festival, and that they bring an oblation every day during those seven days of joy before the Lord on the altar of your God. **23** For you celebrated this festival when you went out from Egypt until you entered into the wilderness of Shur; for on the shore of the sea you completed it.

CHAPTER 50

1 And after this law I made known to you the days of the Sabbaths in the desert of Sin[ai], which is between Elim and Sinai. **2** And I told you of the Sabbaths of the land on Mount Sinai, and I told you of the jubilee years in the sabbaths of years: but the year thereof have I not told you until you enter the land which you are to possess. **3** And the land also will keep its sabbaths while they dwell upon it, and they will know the jubilee year. **4** For that reason I have ordained for you the year-weeks and the years and the jubilees: there are forty-nine jubilees from the days of Adam until this day, and one week and two years and there are yet forty years to come (lit. "distant for learning the commandments of the Lord, until they pass over into the land of Canaan, crossing the Jordan to the west. 5 And the jubilees will pass by, until Israel is cleansed from all guilt of fornication, and uncleanness, and pollution, and sin, and error, and dwells with confidence in all the land, and there will be no more a Satan or any evil one, and the land will be clean from that time forevermore. 6 And behold the commandment regarding the Sabbaths—I have written (them) down for you and all the judgments of its laws. 7 Six days will you labor, but on the seventh day is the Sabbath of the Lord your God. In it you shall do no manner of work, you and your sons, and your men-servants and your maid-servants, and all your cattle and the sojourner also who is with you. 8 And the man that does any work on it shall die: whoever desecrates that day, whoever lies with (his) wife or whoever saith he will do something on it, that he will set out on a journey thereon in regard to any buying or selling: and whoever draws water thereon which he had not prepared for himself on the sixth day, and whoever takes up any burden to carry it out of his tent or out of his house shall die. 9 You shall do no work whatever on the Sabbath day save that you have prepared for yourselves on the sixth day, so as to eat, and drink, and rest, and keep Sabbath from all work on that day, and to bless the Lord your God, who has given you a day of festival, and a holy day: and a day of the holy kingdom for all Israel is this day among their days forever. 10 For great is the honor which the Lord has given to Israel that they should eat and drink and be satisfied on this festival day, and rest thereon from all labor which belongs to the labor of the children of men, save burning frankincense and bringing oblations and sacrifices before the Lord for days and for Sabbaths. 11 This work alone shall be done on the Sabbath-days in the sanctuary of the Lord your God; that they may atone for Israel with sacrifice continually from day to day for a memorial well-pleasing before the Lord, and that He may receive them always from day to day according as you have been commanded. 12 And every man who does any work thereon, or goes a journey, or tills (his) farm, whether in his house or any other place, and whoever lights a fire, or rides on any beast, or travels by ship on the sea, and whoever strikes or kills anything, or slaughters a beast or a bird, or whoever catches an animal or a bird or a fish, or whoever fasts or makes war on the Sabbaths: 13 The man who doeth any of these things on the Sabbath shall die, so that the children of Israel shall observe the Sabbaths according to the commandments regarding the Sabbaths of the land, as it is written in the tables, which He gave into my hands that I should write out for you the laws of the seasons, and the seasons according to the division of their days. Here is completed the account of the division of the days.

JEWISH LEGEND

JASHER

Otherwise known as Sefer haYashar

The Sefer haYashar (first edition 1552) is a Hebrew midrash also known as the Toledot Adam and Dibre ha-Yamim be-'Aruk. The Hebrew title may be translated Sefer haYashar "Book of the Correct Record," but it is known in English translation mostly as the Book of Jasher following English tradition. The book is named after the Book of Jasher mentioned in Joshua and 2 Samuel. Although it is presented as the original "Book of Jasher" in the translations such as that of Moses Samuel (1840), it is not accepted as such in rabbinical Judaism, nor does the original Hebrew text make such a claim.

CHAPTER 1

1 And God said, "Let us make man in our image, after our likeness," and God created man in his own image. 2 And God formed man from the ground, and he blew into his nostrils the breath of life, and man became a living soul endowed with speech. 3 And the Lord said, "It is not good for man to be alone; I will make unto him a helpmate." 4 And the Lord caused a deep sleep to fall upon Adam, and he slept, and he took away one of his ribs, and he built flesh upon it, and formed it and brought it to Adam, and Adam awoke from his sleep, and behold a woman was standing before him. 5 And he said, "This is a bone of my bones and it will be called woman, for this has been taken from man; and Adam called her name Eve, for she was the mother of all living." 6 And God blessed them and called their names Adam and Eve in the day that he created them, and the Lord God said, "Be fruitful and multiply and fill the earth." 7 And the Lord God took Adam and his wife, and he placed them in the garden of Eden to dress it and to keep it; and he commanded them and said unto them, "From every tree of the garden you may eat, but from the tree of the knowledge of good and evil you will not eat, for in the day that you eat thereof you will surely die." 8 And when God had blessed and commanded them, he went from them, and Adam and his wife dwelt in the garden according to the command which the Lord had commanded them. 9 And the serpent, which God had created with them in the earth, came to them to incite them to transgress the command of God which he had commanded them. 10 And the serpent enticed and persuaded the woman to eat from the tree of knowledge, and the woman hearkened to the voice of the serpent, and she transgressed the word of God, and took from the tree of the knowledge of good and evil, and she ate, and she took from it and gave also to her husband and he ate. 11 And Adam and his wife transgressed the command of God which he commanded them, and God knew it, and his anger was kindled against them and he cursed them. 12 And the Lord God drove them that day from the garden of Eden, to until the ground from which they were taken, and they went and dwelt at the east of the garden of Eden; and Adam knew his wife Eve and she bore two sons and three daughters. 13 And she called the name of the first-born Cain, saying, "I have obtained a man from the Lord," and the name of the other she called Abel, for she said, "In vanity we came into the earth, and in vanity we will be taken from it." 14 And the boys grew up and their father gave them a possession in the land; and Cain was a tiller of the ground, and Abel a keeper of sheep. 15 And it was at the expiration of a few years, that they brought an approximating offering to the Lord, and Cain brought from the fruit of the ground, and Abel brought from the firstlings of his flock from the fat thereof, and God turned and inclined to Abel and his offering, and a fire came down from the Lord from heaven and consumed it. 16 And unto Cain and his offering the Lord did not turn, and he did not incline to it, for he had brought from the inferior fruit of the ground before the Lord, and Cain was jealous against his brother Abel on account of this, and he sought a pretext to slay him. 17 And in some time after, Cain and Abel his brother, went one day into the field to do their work; and they were both in the field, Cain tilling and ploughing his ground, and Abel feeding his flock; and the flock passed that part which Cain had ploughed in the ground, and it sorely grieved Cain on this account. 18 And Cain approached his brother Abel in anger, and he said unto him, "What is there between me and you, that you come to

dwell and bring your flock to feed in my land?" **19** And Abel answered his brother Cain and said unto him, "What is there between me and you, that you will eat the flesh of my flock and clothe yourself with their wool? **20** And now therefore, put off the wool of my sheep with which you have clothed yourself, and recompense me for their fruit and flesh which you have eaten, and when you will have done this, I will then go from your land as you have said." **21** And Cain said to his brother Abel, "Surely if I slay you this day, who will require your blood from me?" **22** And Abel answered Cain, saying, "Surely God who has made us in the earth, he will avenge my cause, and he will require my blood from you should you slay me, for the Lord is the judge and arbiter, and it is he who will pay back man according to his evil, and the wicked man according to the wickedness that he may do upon earth. **23** And now, if you should slay me here, surely God knows your secret views, and will judge you for the evil which you did declare to do unto me this day." **24** And when Cain heard the words which Abel his brother had spoken, behold the anger of Cain was kindled against his brother Abel for declaring this thing. **25** And Cain hastened and rose up, and took the iron part of his ploughing instrument, with which he suddenly smote his brother and he slew him, and Cain spilt the blood of his brother Abel upon the earth, and the blood of Abel streamed upon the earth before the flock. **26** And after this Cain repented having slain his brother, and he was sadly grieved, and he wept over him and it vexed him exceedingly. **27** And Cain rose up and dug a hole in the field, wherein he put his brother's body, and he turned the dust over it. **28** And the Lord knew what Cain had done to his brother, and the Lord appeared to Cain and said unto him, "Where is Abel your brother that was with you?" **29** And Cain concealed his true motives, and said, I do not know, am I my brother's keeper? And the Lord said unto him, "What have you done? The voice of your brother's blood cries unto me from the ground where you have slain him. **30** For you have slain your brother and have concealed your intentions before me and did imagine in your heart that I saw you not, nor knew all your actions. **31** But you did this thing and did slay your brother for no reason and because he spoke rightly to you, and now, therefore, cursed be you from the ground which opened its mouth to receive your brother's blood from

your hand, and wherein you did bury him. **32** And it will be when you will till it, it will no more give you its strength as in the beginning, for thorns and thistles will the ground produce, and you will be moving and wandering in the earth until the day of your death." **33** And at that time Cain went out from the presence of the Lord, from the place where he was, and he went moving and wandering in the land toward the east of Eden, he and all belonging to him. **34** And Cain knew his wife in those days, and she conceived and bore a son, and he called his name Enoch, saying, "In that time the Lord began to give him rest and quiet in the earth." **35** And at that time Cain also began to build a city: and he built the city and he called the name of the city Enoch, according to the name of his son; for in those days the Lord had given him rest upon the earth, and he did not move about and wander as in the beginning. **36** And Irad was born to Enoch, and Irad begat Mechuyael and Mechuyael begat Methusael.

CHAPTER 2

1 And it was in the hundred and thirtieth year of the life of Adam upon the earth, that he again knew Eve his wife, and she conceived and bore a son in his likeness and in his image, and she called his name Seth, saying, "Because God has appointed me another seed in the place of Abel, for Cain has slain him." **2** And Seth lived one hundred and five years, and he begat a son; and Seth called the name of his son Enosh, saying, "Because in that time the sons of men began to multiply, and to afflict their souls and hearts by transgressing and rebelling against God." **3** And it was in the days of Enosh that the sons of men continued to rebel and transgress against God, to increase the anger of the Lord against the sons of men. **4** And the sons of men went and they served other gods, and they forgot the Lord who had created them in the earth: and in those days the sons of men made images of brass and iron, wood and stone, and they bowed down and served them. **5** And every man made his god and they bowed down to them, and the sons of men forsook the Lord all the days of Enosh and his children; and the anger of the Lord was kindled on account of their works and abominations which they did in the earth. **6** And the Lord caused the waters of the river Gihon to overwhelm them, and he destroyed and consumed them, and he destroyed the third part of the earth, and notwithstanding this, the sons of men did not turn from their evil ways, and their hands were yet extended to do evil in the sight of the Lord. **7** And in those days there was neither sowing nor reaping in the earth; and there was no food for the sons of men and the famine was very great in those days. **8** And the seed which they sowed in those days in the ground became thorns, thistles and briers; for from the days of Adam was this declaration concerning the earth, of the curse of God, which he cursed the earth, on account of the sin which Adam sinned before the Lord. **9** And it was when men continued to rebel and transgress against God, and to corrupt their ways, that the earth also became corrupt. **10** And Enosh lived ninety years and he begat Cainan; **11** And Cainan grew up and he was forty years old, and he became wise and had knowledge and skill in all wisdom, and he reigned over all the sons of men, and he led the sons of men to wisdom and knowledge; for Cainan was a very wise man and had understanding in all wisdom, and with his wisdom he ruled over spirits and demons; **12** And Cainan knew by his wisdom that God would destroy the sons of men for having sinned upon earth, and that the Lord would in the latter days bring upon them the waters of the flood. **13** And in those days Cainan wrote upon tablets of stone, what was to take place in time to come, and he put them in his treasures. **14** And Cainan reigned over the whole earth, and he turned some of the sons of men to the service of God. **15** And when Cainan was seventy years old, he begat three sons and two daughters. **16** And these are the names of the children of Cainan; the name of the firstborn Mahlallel, the second Enan, and the third Mered, and their sisters were Adah and Zillah; these are the five children of Cainan that were born to him. **17** And Lamech, the son of Methusael, became related to Cainan by marriage, and he took his two daughters for his wives, and Adah conceived and bore a son to Lamech, and she called his name Jabal. **18** And she again conceived and bore a son, and called his name Jubal; and Zillah, her sister, was barren in those days and had no offspring. **19** For in those days the sons of men began to trespass against God, and to transgress the commandments which he had commanded to Adam, to be fruitful and multiply in the earth. **20** And some of the sons of men caused their wives to drink a draught that would render them barren, in order that they might retain their figures and whereby

their beautiful appearance might not fade. **21** And when the sons of men caused some of their wives to drink, Zillah drank with them. **22** And the child-bearing women appeared abominable in the sight of their husbands as widows, while their husbands lived, for to the barren ones only they were attached. **23** And in the end of days and years, when Zillah became old, the Lord opened her womb. **24** And she conceived and bore a son and she called his name Tubal Cain, saying, After I had withered away have I obtained him from the Almighty God. **25** And she conceived again and bare a daughter, and she called her name Naamah, for she said, After I had withered away have I obtained pleasure and delight. **26** And Lamech was old and advanced in years, and his eyes were dim that he could not see, and Tubal Cain, his son, was leading him and it was one day that Lamech went into the field and Tubal Cain his son was with him, and while they were walking in the field, Cain the son of Adam advanced towards them; for Lamech was very old and could not see much, and Tubal Cain his son was very young. **27** And Tubal Cain told his father to draw his bow, and with the arrows he smote Cain, who was yet far off, and he slew him, for he appeared to them to be an animal. **28** And the arrows entered Cain's body although he was distant from them, and he fell to the ground and died. **29** And the Lord pay backd Cain's evil according to his wickedness, which he had done to his brother Abel, according to the word of the Lord which he had spoken. **30** And it came to pass when Cain had died, that Lamech and Tubal went to see the animal which they had slain, and they saw, and behold Cain their grandfather was fallen dead upon the earth. **31** And Lamech was very much grieved at having done this, and in clapping his hands together he struck his son and caused his death. **32** And the wives of Lamech heard what Lamech had done, and they sought to kill him. **33** And the wives of Lamech hated him from that day, because he slew Cain and Tubal Cain, and the wives of Lamech separated from him, and would not hearken to him in those days. **34** And Lamech came to his wives, and he pressed them to listen to him about this matter. **35** And he said to his wives Adah and Zillah, "Hear my voice O wives of Lamech, attend to my words, for now you have imagined and said that I slew a man with my wounds, and a child with my stripes for their having done no violence, but surely know that

I am old and grey-headed, and that my eyes are heavy through age, and I did this thing unknowingly." **36** And the wives of Lamech listened to him in this matter, and they returned to him with the advice of their father Adam, but they bore no children to him from that time, knowing that God's anger was increasing in those days against the sons of men, to destroy them with the waters of the flood for their evil doings. **37** And Mahlallel the son of Cainan lived sixty-five years and he begat Jared; and Jared lived sixty-two years and he begat Enoch.

CHAPTER 3

1 And Enoch lived sixty-five years and he begat Methuselah; and Enoch walked with God after having begot Methuselah, and he served the Lord, and despised the evil ways of men. **2** And the soul of Enoch was wrapped up in the instruction of the Lord, in knowledge and in understanding; and he wisely retired from the sons of men and secreted himself from them for many days. **3** And it was at the expiration of many years, while he was serving the Lord, and praying before him in his house, that an angel of the Lord called to him from Heaven, and he said, "Here am I." **4** And he said, "Rise, go out from your house and from the place where you do hide yourself, and appear to the sons of men, in order that you may teach them the way in which they should go and the work which they must accomplish to enter in the ways of God." **5** And Enoch rose up according to the word of the Lord, and went out from his house, from his place and from the chamber in which he was concealed; and he went to the sons of men and taught them the ways of the Lord, and at that time assembled the sons of men and acquainted them with the instruction of the Lord. **6** And he ordered it to be proclaimed in all places where the sons of men dwelt, saying, "Where is the man who wishes to know the ways of the Lord and good works? Let him come to Enoch." **7** And all the sons of men then assembled to him, for all who desired this thing went to Enoch, and Enoch reigned over the sons of men according to the word of the Lord, and they came and bowed to him and they heard his word. **8** And the spirit of God was upon Enoch, and he taught all his men the wisdom of God and his ways, and the sons of men served the Lord all the days of Enoch, and they came to hear his wisdom. **9** And all the kings of the sons of men, both first and last, together with their princes and

judges, came to Enoch when they heard of his wisdom, and they bowed down to him, and they also required of Enoch to reign over them, to which he consented. **10** And they assembled in all, one hundred and thirty kings and princes, and they made Enoch king over them and they were all under his power and command. **11** And Enoch taught them wisdom, knowledge, and the ways of the Lord; and he made peace among them, and peace was throughout the earth during the life of Enoch. **12** And Enoch reigned over the sons of men two hundred and forty-three years, and he did justice and righteousness with all his people, and he led them in the ways of the Lord. **13** And these are the generations of Enoch, Methuselah, Elisha, and Elimelech, three sons; and their sisters were Melca and Nahmah, and Methuselah lived eighty-seven years and he begat Lamech. **14** And it was in the fifty-sixth year of the life of Lamech when Adam died; nine hundred and thirty years old was he at his death, and his two sons, with Enoch and Methuselah his son, buried him with great pomp, as at the burial of kings, in the cave which God had told him. **15** And in that place all the sons of men made a great mourning and weeping on account of Adam; it has therefore become a custom among the sons of men to this day. **16** And Adam died because he ate of the tree of knowledge; he and his children after him, as the Lord God had spoken. **17** And it was in the year of Adam's death which was the two hundred and forty-third year of the reign of Enoch, in that time Enoch resolved to separate himself from the sons of men and to secret himself as at first in order to serve the Lord. **18** And Enoch did so, but did not entirely secret himself from them, but kept away from the sons of men three days and then went to them for one day. **19** And during the three days that he was in his chamber, he prayed to, and praised the Lord his God, and the day on which he went and appeared to his subjects he taught them the ways of the Lord, and all they asked him about the Lord he told them. **20** And he did in this manner for many years, and he afterward concealed himself for six days, and appeared to his people one day in seven; and after that once in a month, and then once in a year, until all the kings, princes and sons of men sought for him, and desired again to see the face of Enoch, and to hear his word; but they could not, as all the sons of men were greatly afraid of Enoch, and they feared to approach him on account of the Godlike awe that was seated upon his countenance; therefore no man could look at him, fearing he might be punished and die. 21 And all the kings and princes resolved to assemble the sons of men, and to come to Enoch, thinking that they might all speak to him at the time when he should come out among them, and they did so. 22 And the day came when Enoch went out and they all assembled and came to him, and Enoch spoke to them the words of the Lord and he taught them wisdom and knowledge, and they bowed down before him and they said, May the king live! May the king live! 23 And in some time after, when the kings and princes and the sons of men were speaking to Enoch, and Enoch was teaching them the ways of God, behold an angel of the Lord then called unto Enoch from heaven, and wished to bring him up to heaven to make him reign there over the sons of God, as he had reigned over the sons of men upon earth. 24 When at that time Enoch heard this he went and assembled all the inhabitants of the earth and taught them wisdom and knowledge and gave them divine instructions, and he said to them, "I have been required to ascend into heaven, I therefore do not know the day of my going. 25 And now therefore I will teach you wisdom and knowledge and will give you instruction before I leave you, how to act upon earth whereby you may live"; and he did so. 26 And he taught them wisdom and knowledge, and gave them instruction, and he reproved them, and he placed before them statutes and judgments to do upon earth, and he made peace among them, and he taught them everlasting life, and dwelt with them some time teaching them all these things. 27 And at that time the sons of men were with Enoch, and Enoch was speaking to them, and they lifted up their eyes and the likeness of a great horse descended from heaven, and the horse paced in the air; 28 And they told Enoch what they had seen, and Enoch said to them, "On my account does this horse descend upon earth; the time is come when I must go from you and I will no more be seen by you." 29 And the horse descended at that time and stood before Enoch, and all the sons of men that were with Enoch saw him. 30 And Enoch then again ordered a voice to be proclaimed, saying, "Where is the man who delights to know the ways of the Lord his God, let him come this day to Enoch before he is taken from us." 31 And all the sons of men assembled and came to Enoch that day; and all the kings of the earth with their princes and counsellors remained with him that day; and Enoch then taught the sons of men wisdom and knowledge, and gave them divine instruction; and he command them to serve the Lord and walk in his ways all the days of their lives, and he continued to make peace among them. 32 And it was after this that he rose up and rode upon the horse; and he went out and all the sons of men went after him, about eight hundred thousand men; and they went with him one day's journey. 33 And the second day he said to them, "Return home to your tents, why will you go? Perhaps you may die"; and some of them went from him, and those that remained went with him six day's journey; and Enoch said to them every day, Return to your tents, lest you may die; but they were not willing to return, and they went with him. 34 And on the sixth day some of the men remained and clung to him, and they said to him, "We will go with you to the place where you go; as the Lord lives, death only will separate us." 35 And they urged so much to go with him, that he ceased speaking to them; and they went after him and would not return; 36 And when the kings returned they caused a census to be taken, in order to know the number of remaining men that went with Enoch; and it was upon the seventh day that Enoch ascended into heaven in a whirlwind, with horses and chariots of fire. 37 And on the eighth day all the kings that had been with Enoch sent to bring back the number of men that were with Enoch, in that place from which he ascended into heaven. 38 And all those kings went to the place and they found the earth there filled with snow, and upon the snow were large stones of snow, and one said to the other, Come, let us break through the snow and see, perhaps the men that remained with Enoch are dead, and are now under the stones of snow, and they searched but could not find him, for he had ascended into heaven.

CHAPTER 4

1 And all the days that Enoch lived upon earth, were three hundred and sixty-five years. 2 And when Enoch had ascended into heaven, all the kings of the earth rose and took Methuselah his son and anointed him, and they caused him to reign over them in the place of his father. 3 And Methuselah acted uprightly in the sight of God, as his father Enoch had taught him, and he likewise during the whole of his life taught the sons of men wisdom, knowledge

and the fear of God, and he did not turn from the good way either to the right or to the left. **4** But in the latter days of Methuselah, the sons of men turned from the Lord, they corrupted the earth, they robbed and plundered each other, and they rebelled against God and they transgressed, and they corrupted their ways, and would not hearken to the voice of Methuselah, but rebelled against him. **5** And the Lord was exceedingly angry against them, and the Lord continued to destroy the seed in those days, so that there was neither sowing nor reaping in the earth. **6** For when they sowed the ground in order that they might obtain food for their support, behold, thorns and thistles were produced which they did not sow. **7** And still the sons of men did not turn from their evil ways, and their hands were still extended to do evil in the sight of God, and they provoked the Lord with their evil ways, and the Lord was very angry, and repented that he had made man. **8** And he thought to destroy and annihilate them and he did so. **9** In those days when Lamech the son of Methuselah was one hundred and sixty years old, Seth the son of Adam died. **10** And all the days that Seth lived, were nine hundred and twelve years, and he died. **11** And Lamech was one hundred and eighty years old when he took Ashmua, the daughter of Elishaa the son of Enoch his uncle, and she conceived. **12** And at that time the sons of men sowed the ground, and a little food was produced, yet the sons of men did not turn from their evil ways, and they trespassed and rebelled against God. **13** And the wife of Lamech conceived and bore him a son at that time, at the revolution of the year. **14** And Methuselah called his name Noah, saying, "The earth was in his days at rest and free from corruption," and Lamech his father called his name Menachem, saying, "This one will comfort us in our works and miserable toil in the earth," which God had cursed. **15** And the child grew up and was weaned, and he went in the ways of his father Methuselah, perfect and upright with God. **16** And all the sons of men departed from the ways of the Lord in those days as they multiplied upon the face of the earth with sons and daughters, and they taught one another their evil practices and they continued sinning against the Lord. **17** And every man made unto himself a god, and they robbed and plundered every man his neighbor as well as his relative, and they corrupted the earth, and the earth was filled with violence. **18** And their judges and rulers went to the daughters of men and took their wives by force from their husbands according to their choice, and the sons of men in those days took from the cattle of the earth, the beasts of the field and the fowls of the air, and taught the mixture of animals of one species with the other, in order therewith to provoke the Lord; and God saw the whole earth and it was corrupt, for all flesh had corrupted its ways upon earth, all men and all animals. **19** And the Lord said, "I will blot out man that I created from the face of the earth, yea from man to the birds of the air, together with cattle and beasts that are in the field for I repent that I made them." **20** And all men who walked in the ways of the Lord, died in those days, before the Lord brought the evil upon man which he had declared, for this was from the Lord, that they should not see the evil which the Lord spoke of concerning the sons of men. **21** And Noah found grace in the sight of the Lord, and the Lord chose him and his children to raise up seed from them upon the face of the whole earth.

CHAPTER 5

1 And it was in the eighty-fourth year of the life of Noah, that Enoch the son of Seth died, he was nine hundred and five years old at his death. **2** And in the one hundred and seventy ninth year of the life of Noah, Cainan the son of Enosh died, and all the days of Cainan were nine hundred and ten years, and he died. **3** And in the two hundred and thirty fourth year of the life of Noah, Mahlalel the son of Cainan died, and the days of Mahlalel were eight hundred and ninety-five years, and he died. **4** And Jared the son of Mahlalel died in those days, in the three hundred and thirty-sixth year of the life of Noah; and all the days of Jared were nine hundred and sixty-two years, and he died. **5** And all who followed the Lord died in those days, before they saw the evil which God declared to do upon earth. **6** And after the lapse of many years, in the four hundred and eightieth year of the life of Noah, when all those men, who followed the Lord had died away from among the sons of men, and only Methuselah was then left, God said unto Noah and Methuselah, saying, **7** Speak ye, and proclaim to the sons of men, saying, Thus says the Lord, return from your evil ways and forsake your works, and the Lord will repent of the evil that he declared to do to you, so that it will not come to pass. **8** For thus says the Lord, Behold I give you a period of one hundred and twenty years; if you will turn to me and forsake your evil ways, then will I also turn away from the evil which I told you, and it will not exist, says the Lord. **9** And Noah and Methuselah spoke all the words of the Lord to the sons of men, day after day, constantly speaking to them. **10** But the sons of men would not hearken to them, nor incline their ears to their words, and they were stiffnecked. **11** And the Lord granted them a period of one hundred and twenty years, saying, If they will return, then will God repent of the evil, so as not to destroy the earth. **12** Noah the son of Lamech refrained from taking a wife in those days, to beget children, for he said, "Surely now God will destroy the earth, why then will I beget children?" **13** And Noah was a just man, he was perfect in his generation, and the Lord chose him to raise up seed from his seed upon the face of the earth. **14** And the Lord said unto Noah, "Take unto you a wife, and beget children, for I have seen you righteous before me in this generation. **15** And you will raise up seed, and your children with you, in the midst of the earth; and Noah went and took a wife, and he chose Naamah the daughter of Enoch, and she was five hundred and eighty years old. **16** And Noah was four hundred and ninety-eight years old, when he took Naamah for a wife." **17** And Naamah conceived and bore a son, and he called his name Japheth, saying, "God has enlarged me in the earth"; and she conceived again and bore a son, and he called his name Shem, saying, "God has made me a remnant, to raise up seed in the midst of the earth." **18** And Noah was five hundred and two years old when Naamah bare Shem, and the boys grew up and went in the ways of the Lord, in all that Methuselah and Noah their father taught them. **19** And Lamech the father of Noah, died in those days; yet verily he did not go with all his heart in the ways of his father, and he died in the hundred and ninety-fifth year of the life of Noah. **20** And all the days of Lamech were seven hundred and seventy years, and he died. **21** And all the sons of men who knew the Lord, died in that year before the Lord brought evil upon them; for the Lord willed them to die, so as not to behold the evil that God would bring upon their brothers and relatives, as he had so declared to do. **22** In that time, the Lord said to Noah and Methuselah, "Stand out and proclaim to the sons of men all the words that I spoke to you in those days, perhaps they may turn from their evil ways, and I will then repent of the evil and will not bring it." **23** And Noah and Methuselah stood out, and said in the ears of the sons of men, all that God had spoken concerning them. **24** But the sons of men would not hearken, neither would they incline their ears to all their declarations. **25** And it was after this that the Lord said to Noah, "The end of all flesh is come before me, on account of their evil deeds, and behold I will destroy the earth. **26** So take unto you gopher wood and go to a certain place and make a large ark and place it in that spot. **27** And thus will you make it; three hundred cubits its length, fifty cubits broad and thirty cubits high. **28** And you will make unto you a door, open at its side, and to a cubit you will finish above, and cover it within and without with pitch. **29** And behold I will bring the flood of waters upon the earth, and all flesh be destroyed, from under the heavens all that is upon earth will perish. **30** And you and your household will go and gather two couple of all living things, male and female, and will bring them to the ark, to raise up seed from them upon earth. **31** And gather unto you all food that is eaten by all the animals, that there may be food for you and for them. **32** And you will choose for your sons three maidens, from the daughters of men, and they will be wives to your sons." **33** And Noah rose up, and he made the ark, in the place where God had commanded him, and Noah did as God had ordered him. **34** In his five hundred and ninety-fifth year Noah commenced to make the ark, and he made the ark in five years, as the Lord had commanded. **35** Then Noah took the three daughters of Eliakim, son of Methuselah, for wives for his sons, as the Lord had commanded Noah. **36** And it was at that time Methuselah the son of Enoch died, nine hundred and sixty years old was he, at his death.

CHAPTER 6

1 At that time, after the death of Methuselah, the Lord said to Noah, "Go you with your household into the ark; behold I will gather to you all the animals of the earth, the beasts of the field and the fowls of the air, and they will all come and surround the ark. **2** And you will go and seat yourself by the doors of the ark, and all the beasts, the animals, and the fowls, will assemble and place themselves before you, and such of them as will come and crouch before you, will you take and deliver into the hands of your sons, who will bring them to the ark, and all that will stand before you you will leave." **3** And the Lord brought this about on the next day, and animals, beasts and fowls came in great multitudes and surrounded the ark. **4** And Noah went and seated himself by the door of the ark, and of all flesh that crouched before him, he brought into the ark, and all that stood before him he left upon earth. **5** And a lioness came, with her two whelps, male and female, and the three crouched before Noah, and the two whelps rose up against the lioness and smote her, and made her flee from her place, and she went away, and they returned to their places, and crouched upon the earth before Noah. **6** And the lioness ran away and stood in the place of the lions. **7** And Noah saw this, and wondered greatly, and he rose and took the two whelps, and brought them into the ark. **8** And Noah brought into the ark from all living creatures that were upon earth, so that there was none left but which Noah brought into the ark. **9** Two and two came to Noah into the ark, but from the clean animals, and clean fowls, he brought seven couples, as God had commanded him. **10** And all the animals, and beasts, and fowls, were still there, and they surrounded the ark at every place, and the rain had not descended until seven days after. **11** And on that day, the Lord caused the whole earth to shake, and the sun darkened, and the foundations of the world raged, and the whole earth was moved violently, and the lightning flashed, and the thunder roared, and all the fountains in the earth were broken up, such as was not known to the inhabitants before; and God did this mighty act, in order to terrify the sons of men, that there might be no more evil upon earth. **12** And still the sons of men would not return from their evil ways, and they increased the anger of the Lord at that time and did not even direct their hearts to all this. **13** And at the end of seven days, in the six hundredth year of the life of Noah, the waters of the flood were upon the earth. **14** And all the fountains of the deep were broken up, and the windows of heaven were opened, and the rain was upon the earth forty days and forty nights. **15** And Noah and his household, and all the living creatures that were with him, came into the ark on account of the waters of the flood, and the Lord shut him in. **16** And all the sons of men that were left upon the earth, became exhausted through evil on account of the rain, for the waters were coming more violently upon the earth, and the animals and beasts were still surrounding the ark. **17** And the sons of men assembled together, about seven hundred thousand men and women, and they came unto Noah to the ark. **18** And they called to Noah, saying, "Open for us that we may come to you in the ark—and why will we die?" **19** And Noah, with a loud voice, answered them from the ark, saying, "Have you not all rebelled against the Lord, and said that he does not exist? And therefore, the Lord brought upon you this evil, to destroy and cut you off from the face of the earth. **20** Is not this the thing that I spoke to you of one hundred and twenty years back, and you would not hearken to the voice of the Lord, and now do you desire to live upon earth?" **21** And they said to Noah, "We are ready to return to the Lord; only open for us that we may live and not die." **22** And Noah answered them, saying, "Behold now that you see the trouble of your souls, you wish to return to the Lord; why did you not return during these hundred and twenty years, which the Lord granted you as the determined period? **23** But now you come and tell me this on account of the troubles of your souls, now also the Lord will not listen to you, neither will he give ear to you on this day, so that you will not now succeed in your wishes." **24** And the sons of men approached in order to break into the ark, to come in on account of the rain, for they could not bear the rain upon them. **25** And the Lord sent all the beasts and animals that stood round the ark. And the beasts overpowered them and drove them from that place, and every man went his way and they again scattered themselves upon the face of the earth. **26** And the rain was still descending upon the earth, and it descended forty days and forty nights, and the waters prevailed greatly upon the earth; and all flesh that was upon the earth or in the waters died, whether men, animals, beasts, creeping things or birds of the air, and there only remained Noah and those that were with him in the ark. **27** And the waters prevailed and they greatly increased upon the earth, and they lifted up the ark and it was raised from the earth. **28** And the ark floated upon the face of the waters, and it was tossed upon the waters so that all the living creatures within were turned about like pottage in a cauldron. **29** And great anxiety seized all the living creatures that were in the ark, and the ark was like to be broken. **30** And all the living creatures that were in the ark were terrified, and the lions roared, and the oxen lowed, and the wolves howled, and every living creature in the ark spoke and lamented in its own language, so that their voices reached to a great distance, and Noah and his sons cried and wept in their troubles; they were greatly afraid that they had reached the gates of death. **31** And Noah prayed unto the Lord, and cried unto him on account of this, and he said, "O Lord help us, for we have no strength to bear this evil that has encompassed us, for the waves of the waters have surrounded us, mischievous torrents have terrified us, the snares of death have come before us; answer us, O Lord, answer us, light up your countenance toward us and be gracious to us, redeem us and deliver us." **32** And the Lord hearkened to the voice of Noah, and the Lord remembered him. **33** And a wind passed over the earth, and the waters were still and the ark rested. **34** And the fountains of the deep and the windows of heaven were stopped, and the rain from heaven was restrained. **35** And the waters decreased in those days, and the ark rested upon the mountains of Ararat. **36** And Noah then opened the windows of the ark, and Noah still called out to the Lord at that time and he said, "O Lord, who did form the earth and the heavens and all that are therein, bring out our souls from this confinement, and from the prison wherein you have placed us, for I am much wearied with sighing." **37** And the Lord hearkened to the voice of Noah, and said to him, "When you will have completed a full year you will then go out." **38** And at the revolution of the year, when a full year was completed to Noah's dwelling in the ark, the waters were dried from off the earth, and Noah put off the covering of the ark. **39** At that time, on the twenty-seventh day of the second month, the earth was dry, but Noah and his sons, and those that were with him, did not go out from the ark until the Lord told them. **40** And the day came that the Lord told them to go out, and they all went out from the ark. **41** And they went and returned everyone to his way and to his place, and Noah and his sons dwelt in the land that God had told them, and they served the Lord all their days, and the Lord blessed Noah and his sons on their going out from the ark. **42** And he said to them, "Be fruitful and fill all the earth; become strong and increase abundantly in the earth and multiply therein."

CHAPTER 7

1 And these are the names of the sons of Noah: Japheth, Ham and Shem; and children were born to them after the flood, for they had taken wives before the flood. **2** These are the sons of Japheth; Gomer, Magog, Madai, Javan, Tubal, Meshech, and Tiras, seven sons. **3** And the sons of Gomer were Askinaz, Rephas and Tegarmah. **4** And the sons of Magog were Elichanaf and Lubal. **5** And the children of Madai were Achon, Zeelo, Chazoni and Lot. **6** And the sons of Javan were Elisha, Tarshish, Chittim and Dudonim. **7** And the sons of Tubal were Ariphi, Kesed and Taari. **8** And the sons of Meshech were Dedon, Zaron and Shebashni. **9** And the sons of Tiras were Benib, Gera, Lupirion and Gilak; these are the sons of Japheth according to their families, and their numbers in those days were about four hundred and sixty men. **10** And these are the sons of Ham; Cush, Mitzraim, Phut and Canaan, four sons; and the sons of Cush were Seba, Havilah, Sabta, Raama and Satecha, and the sons of Raama were Sheba and Dedan. **11** And the sons of Mitzraim were Lud, Anom and Pathros, Chasloth and Chaphtor. **12** And the sons of Phut were Gebul, Hadan, Benah and Adan. **13** And the sons of Canaan were Zidon, Heth, Amori, Gergashi, Hivi, Arkee, Seni, Arodi, Zimodi and Chamothi. **14** These are the sons of Ham, according to their families, and their numbers in those days were about seven hundred and thirty men. **15** And these are the sons of Shem; Elam, Ashur, Arpachshad, Lud and Aram, five sons; and the sons of Elam were Shushan, Machul and Harmon. **16** And the sons of Ashar were Mirus and Mokil, and the sons of Arpachshad were Shelach, Anar and Ashcol. **17** And the sons of Lud were Pethor and Bizayon, and the sons of Aram were Uz, Chul, Gather and Mash. **18** These are the sons of Shem, according to their families; and their numbers in those days were about three hundred men. **19** These are the generations of Shem; Shem begat Arpachshad and Arpachshad begat Shelach, and Shelach begat Eber and to Eber were born two children, the name of one was Peleg, for in his days the sons of men were divided, and in the latter days, the earth was divided. **20** And the name of the second was Yoktan, meaning that in his day the lives of the sons of men were diminished and lessened. **21** These are the sons of Yoktan; Almodad, Shelaf, Chazarmoves, Yerach, Hadurom, Ozel, Diklah, Obal, Abimael, Sheba, Ophir, Havilah and Jobab; all these are the sons of Yoktan. **22** And Peleg his brother begat Yen, and Yen begat Serug, and Serug begat Nahor and Nahor begat Terah, and Terah was thirty-eight years old, and he begat Haran and Nahor. **23** And

Cush the son of Ham, the son of Noah, took a wife in those days in his old age, and she bore a son, and they called his name Nimrod, saying, "At that time the sons of men again began to rebel and transgress against God," and the child grew up, and his father loved him exceedingly, for he was the son of his old age. 24 And the garments of skin which God made for Adam and his wife, when they went out of the garden, were given to Cush. 25 For after the death of Adam and his wife, the garments were given to Enoch, the son of Jared, and when Enoch was taken up to God, he gave them to Methuselah, his son. 26 And at the death of Methuselah, Noah took them and brought them to the ark, and they were with him until he went out of the ark. 27 And in their going out, Ham stole those garments from Noah his father, and he took them and hid them from his brothers. 28 And when Ham begat his firstborn Cush, he gave him the garments in secret, and they were with Cush many days. 29 And Cush also concealed them from his sons and brothers, and when Cush had begotten Nimrod, he gave him those garments through his love for him, and Nimrod grew up, and when he was twenty years old he put on those garments. 30 And Nimrod became strong when he put on the garments, and God gave him might and strength, and he was a mighty hunter in the earth, yea, he was a mighty hunter in the field, and he hunted the animals and he built altars, and he offered upon them the animals before the Lord. 31 And Nimrod strengthened himself, and he rose up from among his brethren, and he fought the battles of his brethren against all their surrounding enemies. 32 And the Lord delivered all the enemies of his brethren in his hands, and God prospered him from time to time in his battles, and he reigned upon earth. 33 Therefore it became current in those days, when a man ushered out those that he had trained up for battle, he would say to them, "Like God did to Nimrod, who was a mighty hunter in the earth, and who succeeded in the battles that prevailed against his brethren, that he delivered them from the hands of their enemies, so may God strengthen us and deliver us this day." 34 And when Nimrod was forty years old, at that time there was a war between his brethren and the children of Japheth, so that they were in the power of their enemies. 35 And Nimrod went out at that time, and he assembled all the sons of Cush and their families, about four hundred and sixty men, and he hired also from some of his friends and acquaintances about eighty men, and he gave them their hire, and he went with them to battle, and when he was on the road, Nimrod strengthened the hearts of the people that went with him. 36 And he said to them, "Do not fear, neither be alarmed, for all our enemies will be delivered into our hands, and you may do with them as you please." 37 And all the men that went were about five hundred, and they fought against their enemies, and they destroyed them, and subdued them, and Nimrod placed standing officers over them in their respective places. 38 And he took some of their children as security, and they were all servants to Nimrod and to his brethren, and Nimrod and all the people that were with him turned homeward. 39 And when Nimrod had joyfully returned from battle, after having conquered his enemies, all his brethren, together with those who knew him before, assembled to make him king over them, and they placed the regal crown upon his head. 40 And he set over his subjects and people, princes, judges, and rulers, as is the custom among kings. 41 And he placed Terah the son of Nahor the prince of his host, and he dignified him and elevated him above all his princes. 42 And while he was reigning according to his heart's desire, after having conquered all his enemies around, he advised with his counselors to build a city for his palace, and they did so. 43 And they found a large valley opposite to the east, and they built him a large and extensive city, and Nimrod called the name of the city that he built Shinar, for the Lord had vehemently shaken his enemies and destroyed them. 44 And Nimrod dwelt in Shinar, and he reigned securely, and he fought with his enemies and he subdued them, and he prospered in all his battles, and his kingdom became very great. 45 And all nations and tongues heard of his fame, and they gathered themselves to him, and they bowed down to the earth, and they brought him offerings, and he became their lord and king, and they all dwelt with him in the city at Shinar, and Nimrod reigned in the earth over all the sons of Noah, and they were all under his power and counsel. 46 And all the earth was of one tongue and words of union, but Nimrod did not go in the ways of the Lord, and he was more wicked than all the men that were before him, from the days of the flood until those days. 47 And he made gods of wood and stone, and he bowed down to them, and he rebelled against the Lord, and taught all his subjects and the people of the earth his wicked ways; and Mardon his son was more wicked than his father. **48** And every one that heard of the acts of Mardon the son of Nimrod would say, concerning him, "From the wicked goes out wickedness"; therefore, it became a proverb in the whole earth, saying, "From the wicked goes out wickedness," and it was current in the words of men from that time to this. **49** And Terah the son of Nahor, prince of Nimrod's host, was in those days very great in the sight of the king and his subjects, and the king and princes loved him, and they elevated him very high. **50** And Terah took a wife and her name was Amthelo the daughter of Cornebo; and the wife of Terah conceived and bore him a son in those days. **51** Terah was seventy years old when he begat him, and Terah called the name of his son that was born to him Abram, because the king had raised him in those days, and dignified him above all his princes that were with him.

CHAPTER 8

1 And it was in the night that Abram was born, that all the servants of Terah, and all the wise men of Nimrod, and his conjurors came and ate and drank in the house of Terah, and they rejoiced with him on that night. **2** And when all the wise men and conjurors went out from the house of Terah, they lifted up their eyes toward heaven that night to look at the stars, and they saw, and behold one very large star came from the east and ran in the heavens, and he swallowed up the four stars from the four sides of the heavens. **3** And all the wise men of the king and his conjurors were astonished at the sight, and the sages understood this matter, and they knew its import. **4** And they said to each other, "This only signifies the child that has been born to Terah this night, who will grow up and be fruitful, and multiply, and possess all the earth, he and his children forever, and he and his seed will slay great kings, and inherit their lands." **5** And the wise men and conjurors went home that night, and in the morning all these wise men and conjurors rose up early and assembled in an appointed house. **6** And they spoke and said to each other, "Behold the sight that we saw last night is hidden from the king, it has not been made known to him. **7** And should this thing get known to the king in the latter days, he will say to us, 'Why have you concealed this matter from me,' and then we will all suffer death;

therefore, now let us go and tell the king the sight which we saw, and the interpretation thereof, and we will then remain clear." **8** And they did so, and they all went to the king and bowed down to him to the ground, and they said, "May the king live, may the king live. **9** We heard that a son was born to Terah the son of Nahor, the prince of your host, and we last night came to his house, and we ate and drank and rejoiced with him that night. **10** And when your servants went out from the house of Terah, to go to our respective homes to abide there for the night, we lifted up our eyes to heaven, and we saw a great star coming from the east, and the same star ran with great speed, and swallowed up four great stars, from the four sides of the heavens. **11** And your servants were astonished at the sight which we saw, and were greatly terrified, and we made our judgment upon the sight, and knew by our wisdom the proper interpretation thereof, that this thing applies to the child that is born to Terah, who will grow up and multiply greatly, and become powerful, and kill all the kings of the earth, and inherit all their lands, he and his seed forever. **12** And now our lord and king, behold we have truly acquainted you with what we have seen concerning this child. **13** If it seems good to the king to give his father value for this child, we will slay him before he will grow up and increase in the land, and his evil increase against us, that we and our children perish through his evil." **14** And the king heard their words and they seemed good in his sight, and he sent and called for Terah, and Terah came before the king. **15** And the king said to Terah, "I have been told that a son was last night born to you, and after this manner was observed in the heavens at his birth. **16** And now therefore give me the child, that we may slay him before his evil springs up against us, and I will give you for his value, your house full of silver and gold." **17** And Terah answered the king and said to him: "My Lord and king, I have heard your words, and your servant will do all that his king desires. **18** But my lord and king, I will tell you what happened to me last night, that I may see what advice the king will give his servant, and then I will answer the king upon what he has just spoken"; and the king said, "Speak." **19** And Terah said to the king, "Ayon, son of Mored, came to me last night, saying, **20** 'Give unto me the great and beautiful horse that the king gave you, and I will give you silver and gold, and straw and provender for its value'; and I said to him, 'Wait until I see the king concerning your words, and behold whatever the king says, that will I do.' **21** And now my lord and king, behold I have made this thing known to you, and the advice which my king will give unto his servant, that will I follow." **22** And the king heard the words of Terah, and his anger was kindled, and he considered him in the light of a fool. **23** And the king answered Terah, and he said to him, "Are you so silly, ignorant, or deficient in understanding, to do this thing, to give your beautiful horse for silver and gold or even for straw and provender? **24** Are you so short of silver and gold, that you should do this thing, because you cannot obtain straw and provender to feed your horse? And what is silver and gold to you, or straw and provender, that you should give away that fine horse which I gave you, like which there is none to be had on the whole earth?" **25** And the king left off speaking, and Terah answered the king, saying, "Like unto this has the king spoken to his servant; **26** I implore you, my lord and king, what is this which you did say unto me, saying, 'Give your son that we may slay him, and I will give you silver and gold for his value; what will I do with silver and gold after the death of my son? Who will inherit me? Surely then at my death, the silver and gold will return to my king who gave it." **27** And when the king heard the words of Terah, and the parable which he brought concerning the king, it grieved him greatly and he was vexed at this thing, and his anger burned within him. **28** And Terah saw that the anger of the king was kindled against him, and he answered the king, saying, "All that I have is in the king's power; whatever the king desires to do to his servant, that let him do, yea, even my son, he is in the king's power, without value in exchange, he and his two brothers that are older than he." **29** And the king said to Terah, "No, but I will purchase your younger son for a price." **30** And Terah answered the king, saying, "I implore you my lord and king to let your servant speak a word before you, and let the king hear the word of his servant," and Terah said, "Let my king give me three days' time until I consider this matter within myself, and consult with my family concerning the words of my king"; and he pressed the king greatly to agree to this. **31** And the king hearkened to Terah, and he did so and he gave him three days' time, and Terah went out from the king's presence, and he came home to his family and spoke to them

all the words of the king; and the people were greatly afraid. **32** And it was in the third day that the king sent to Terah, saying, "Send me your son for a price as I spoke to you; and should you not do this, I will send and slay all you have in your house, so that you will not even have a dog remaining." **33** And Terah hastened, (as the thing was urgent from the king), and he took a child from one of his servants, which his handmaid had born to him that day, and Terah brought the child to the king and received value for him. **34** And the Lord was with Terah in this matter, that Nimrod might not cause Abram's death, and the king took the child from Terah and with all his might dashed his head to the ground, for he thought it had been Abram; and this was concealed from him from that day, and it was forgotten by the king, as it was the will of Providence not to suffer Abram's death. **35** And Terah took Abram his son secretly, together with his mother and nurse, and he concealed them in a cave, and he brought them their provisions monthly. **36** And the Lord was with Abram in the cave and he grew up, and Abram was in the cave ten years, and the king and his princes, soothsayers and sages, thought that the king had killed Abram.

CHAPTER 9

1 And Haran, the son of Terah, Abram's oldest brother, took a wife in those days. **2** Haran was thirty-nine years old when he took her; and the wife of Haran conceived and bore a son, and he called his name Lot. **3** And she conceived again and bare a daughter, and she called her name Milca; and she again conceived and bare a daughter, and she called her name Sarai. **4** Haran was forty-two years old when he begat Sarai, which was in the tenth year of the life of Abram; and in those days Abram and his mother and nurse went out from the cave, as the king and his subjects had forgotten the affair of Abram. **5** And when Abram came out from the cave, he went to Noah and his son Shem, and he remained with them to learn the instruction of the Lord and his ways, and no man knew where Abram was, and Abram served Noah and Shem his son for a long time. **6** And Abram was in Noah's house thirty-nine years, and Abram knew the Lord from three years old, and he went in the ways of the Lord until the day of his death, as Noah and his son Shem had taught him; and all the sons of the earth in those days greatly transgressed against the Lord, and they rebelled against him and they served other gods, and they forgot the Lord who had created them in the earth; and the inhabitants of the earth made unto themselves, at that time, every man his god; gods of wood and stone which could neither speak, hear, nor deliver, and the sons of men served them and they became their gods. 7 And the king and all his servants, and Terah with all his household were then the first of those that served gods of wood and stone. 8 And Terah had twelve gods of large size, made of wood and stone, after the twelve months of the year, and he served each one monthly, and every month Terah would bring his meat offering and drink offering to his gods; thus did Terah all the days. 9 And all that generation were wicked in the sight of the Lord, and they thus made every man his god, but they forsook the Lord who had created them. 10 And there was not a man found in those days in the whole earth, who knew the Lord (for they served each man his own God) except Noah and his household, and all those who were under his counsel knew the Lord in those days. 11 And Abram the son of Terah was waxing great in those days in the house of Noah, and no man knew it, and the Lord was with him. 12 And the Lord gave Abram an understanding heart, and he knew all the works of that generation were vain, and that all their gods were vain and were of no avail. 13 And Abram saw the sun shining upon the earth, and Abram said unto himself "Surely now this sun that shines upon the earth is God, and him will I serve." 14 And Abram served the sun in that day and he prayed to him, and when evening came the sun set as usual, and Abram said within himself, "Surely this cannot be God?" 15 And Abram still continued to speak within himself, "Who is he who made the heavens and the earth? Who created upon earth? Where is he?" 16 And night darkened over him, and he lifted up his eyes toward the west, north, south, and east, and he saw that the sun had vanished from the earth, and the day became dark. 17 And Abram saw the stars and moon before him, and he said, "Surely this is the God who created the whole earth as well as man and behold these his servants are gods around him": and Abram served the moon and prayed to it all that night. 18 And in the morning when it was light, and the sun shone upon the earth as usual, Abram saw all the things that the Lord God had made upon earth. 19 And Abram said unto himself "Surely these are not gods that made the earth and all mankind, but

these are the servants of God," and Abram remained in the house of Noah and there knew the Lord and his ways, and he served the Lord all the days of his life, and all that generation forgot the Lord, and served other gods of wood and stone, and rebelled all their days. 20 And king Nimrod reigned securely, and all the earth was under his control, and all the earth was of one tongue and words of union. 21 And all the princes of Nimrod and his great men took counsel together; Phut, Mitzraim, Cush and Canaan with their families, and they said to each other, "Come let us build ourselves a city and in it a strong tower, and its top reaching heaven, and we will make ourselves famed, so that we may reign upon the whole world, in order that the evil of our enemies may cease from us, that we may reign mightily over them, and that we may not become scattered over the earth on account of their wars." 22 And they all went before the king, and they told the king these words, and the king agreed with them in this affair, and he did so. 23 And all the families assembled consisting of about six hundred thousand men, and they went to seek an extensive piece of ground to build the city and the tower, and they sought in the whole earth and they found none like one valley at the east of the land of Shinar, about two days' walk, and they journeyed there and they dwelt there. 24 And they began to make bricks and burn fires to build the city and the tower that they had imagined to complete. 25 And the building of the tower was unto them a transgression and a sin, and they began to build it, and while they were building against the Lord God of heaven, they imagined in their hearts to war against him and to ascend into heaven. 26 And all these people and all the families divided themselves in three parts; the first said "We will ascend into heaven and fight against him"; the second said, "We will ascend to heaven and place our own gods there and serve them"; and the third part said, "We will ascend to heaven and smite him with bows and spears"; and God knew all their works and all their evil thoughts, and he saw the city and the tower which they were building. 27 And when they were building they built themselves a great city and a very high and strong tower; and on account of its height the mortar and bricks did not reach the builders in their ascent to it, until those who went up had completed a full year, and after that, they reached to the builders and gave them the mortar and the bricks; thus was it done daily. 28 And behold these ascended and others descended the whole day; and if a brick should fall from their hands and get broken, they would all weep over it, and if a man fell and died, none of them would look at him. **29** And the Lord knew their thoughts, and it came to pass when they were building they cast the arrows toward the heavens, and all the arrows fell upon them filled with blood, and when they saw them they said to each other, "Surely we have slain all those that are in heaven." **30** For this was from the Lord in order to cause them to err, and in order; to destroy them from off the face of the ground. **31** And they built the tower and the city, and they did this thing daily until many days and years were elapsed. **32** And God said to the seventy angels who stood foremost before him, to those who were near to him, saying, "Come let us descend and confuse their tongues, that one man will not understand the language of his neighbor," and they did so unto them. **33** And from that day following, they forgot each man his neighbor's tongue, and they could not understand to speak in one tongue, and when the builder took from the hands of his neighbor lime or stone which he did not order, the builder would cast it away and throw it upon his neighbor, that he would die. **34** And they did so many days, and they killed many of them in this manner. **35** And the Lord smote the three divisions that were there, and he punished them according to their works and designs; those who said, "We will ascend to heaven and serve our gods," became like apes and elephants; and those who said, "We will smite the heaven with arrows," the Lord killed them, one man through the hand of his neighbor; and the third division of those who said, "We will ascend to heaven and fight against him," the Lord scattered them throughout the earth. **36** And those who were left among them, when they knew and understood the evil which was coming upon them, they forsook the building, and they also became scattered upon the face of the whole earth. **37** And they ceased building the city and the tower; therefore, he called that place Babel, for there the Lord confounded the Language of the whole earth; behold it was at the east of the land of Shinar. **38** And as to the tower which the sons of men built, the earth opened its mouth and swallowed up one third part thereof, and a fire also descended from heaven and burned another third, and the other third is left to this day, and it is of that part which was aloft, and its circumference is three days' walk. **39** And many of the sons of men died in that tower, a people without number.

CHAPTER 10

1 And Peleg the son of Eber died in those days, in the forty-eighth year of the life of Abram son of Terah, and all the days of Peleg were two hundred and thirty-nine years. **2** And when the Lord had scattered the sons of men on account of their sin at the tower, behold they spread out into many divisions, and all the sons of men were dispersed into the four corners of the earth. **3** And all the families became each according to its language, its land, or its city. **4** And the sons of men built many cities according to their families, in all the places where they went, and throughout the earth where the Lord had scattered them. **5** And some of them built cities in places from which they were afterward extirpated, and they called these cities after their own names, or the names of their children, or after their particular occurrences. **6** And the sons of Japheth the son of Noah went and built themselves cities in the places where they were scattered, and they called all their cities after their names, and the sons of Japheth were divided upon the face of the earth into many divisions and languages. **7** And these are the sons of Japheth according to their families, Gomer, Magog, Medai, Javan, Tubal, Meshech and Tiras; these are the children of Japheth according to their generations. **8** And the children of Gomer, according to their cities, were the Francum, who dwell in the land of Franza, by the river Franza, by the river Senah. **9** And the children of Rephas are the Bartonim, who dwell in the land of Bartonia by the river Ledah, which empties its waters in the great sea Gihon, that is, oceanus. **10** And the children of Tugarma are ten families, and these are their names: Buzar, Parzunac, Balgar, Elicanum, Ragbib, Tarki, Bid, Zebuc, Ongal and Tilmaz; all these spread and rested in the north and built themselves cities. **11** And they called their cities after their own names, those are they who abide by the rivers Hithlah and Italac unto this day. **12** But the families of Angoli, Balgar and Parzunac, they dwell by the great river Dubnee; and the names of their cities are also according to their own names. **13** And the children of Javan are the Javanim who dwell in the land of Makdonia, and the children of Medaiare are the Orelum that dwell in the land of Curson, and the children of Tubal are those that dwell in the land of Tuskanah by the river Pashiah. **14** And the children of Meshech are the Shibashni and the children of Tiras are Rushash, Cushni, and Ongolis; all these went and built themselves cities; those are the cities that are situate by the sea Jabus by the river Cura, which empties itself in the river Tragan. **15** And the children of Elishah are the Almanim, and they also went and built themselves cities; those are the cities situate between the mountains of Job and Shibathmo; and of them were the people of Lumbardi who dwell opposite the mountains of Job and Shibathmo, and they conquered the land of Italia and remained there unto this day. **16** And the children of Chittim are the Romim who dwell in the valley of Canopia by the river Tibreu. **17** And the children of Dudonim are those who dwell in the cities of the sea Gihon, in the land of Bordna. **18** These are the families of the children of Japheth according to their cities and languages, when they were scattered after the tower, and they called their cities after their names and occurrences; and these are the names of all their cities according to their families, which they built in those days after the tower. **19** And the children of Ham were Cush, Mitzraim, Phut and Canaan according to their generation and cities. **20** All these went and built themselves cities as they found fit places for them, and they called their cities after the names of their fathers Cush, Mitzraim, Phut and Canaan. **21** And the children of Mitzraim are the Ludim, Anamim, Lehabim, Naphtuchim, Pathrusim, Casluchim and Caphturim, seven families. **22** All these dwell by the river Sihor, that is the brook of Egypt, and they built themselves cities and called them after their own names. **23** And the children of Pathros and Casloch intermarried together, and from them went out the Pelishtim, the Azathim, and the Gerarim, the Githim and the Ekronim, in all five families; these also built themselves cities, and they called their cities after the names of their fathers unto this day. **24** And the children of Canaan also built themselves cities, and they called their cities after their names, eleven cities and others without number. **25** And four men from the family of Ham went to the land of the plain; these are the names of the four men, sodom, Gomorrah, Admah and Zeboyim. **26** And these men built themselves four cities in the land of the plain, and they called the names of their cities after their own names. **27** And they and their children and all belonging to them dwelt in those cities, and they were fruitful and multiplied greatly and dwelt peaceably. **28** And Seir the son of Hur, son of Hivi, son of Canaan, went and found a valley opposite to Mount Paran, and he built a city there, and he and his seven sons and his household dwelt there, and he called the city which he built Seir, according to his name; that is the land of Seir unto this day. **29** These are the families of the children of Ham, according to their languages and cities, when they were scattered to their countries after the tower. **30** And some of the children of Shem son of Noah, father of all the children of Eber, also went and built themselves cities in the places wherein they were scattered, and they called their cities after their names. **31** And the sons of Shem were Elam, Ashur, Arpachshad, Lud and Aram, and they built themselves cities and called the names of all their cities after their names. **32** And Ashur son of Shem and his children and household went out at that time, a very large body of them, and they went to a distant land that they found, and they met with a very extensive valley in the land that they went to, and they built themselves four cities, and they called them after their own names and occurrences. **33** And these are the names of the cities which the children of Ashur built, Ninevah, Resen, Calach and Rehobother; and the children of Ashur dwell there unto this day. **34** And the children of Aram also went and built themselves a city, and they called the name of the city Uz after their eldest brother, and they dwell therein; that is the land of Uz to this day. **35** And in the second year after the tower a man from the house of Ashur, whose name was Bela, went from the land of Ninevah to sojourn with his household wherever he could find a place; and they came until opposite the cities of the plain against Sodom, and they dwelt there. **36** And the man rose up and built there a small city, and called its name Bela, after his name; that is the land of Zoar unto this day. **37** And these are the families of the children of Shem according to their language and cities, after they were scattered upon the earth after the tower. **38** And every kingdom, city, and family of the families of the children of Noah built themselves many cities after this. **39** And they established governments in all their cities, in order to be regulated by their orders; so did all the families of the children of Noah forever.

CHAPTER 11

1 And Nimrod son of Cush was still in the land of Shinar, and he reigned over it and dwelt there, and he built cities in the land of Shinar. 2 And these are the names of the four cities which he built, and he called their names after the occurrences that happened to them in the building of the tower. 3 And he called the first Babel, saying, "Because the Lord there confounded the language of the whole earth"; and the name of the second he called Erech, because from there God dispersed them. 4 And the third he called Eched, saying, "There was a great battle at that place"; and the fourth he called Calnah, because his princes and mighty men were consumed there, and they vexed the Lord, they rebelled and transgressed against him. 5 And when Nimrod had built these cities in the land of Shinar, he placed in them the remainder of his people, his princes and his mighty men that were left in his kingdom. 6 And Nimrod dwelt in Babel, and he there renewed his reign over the rest of his subjects, and he reigned securely, and the subjects and princes of Nimrod called his name Amraphel, saying that at the tower his princes and men fell through his means. 7 And notwithstanding this, Nimrod did not return to the Lord, and he continued in wickedness and teaching wickedness to the sons of men; and Mardon, his son, was worse than his father, and continued to add to the abominations of his father. 8 And he caused the sons of men to sin, therefore it is said, "From the wicked goes out wickedness." 9 At that time there was war between the families of the children of Ham, as they were dwelling in the cities which they had built. 10 And Chedorlaomer, king of Elam, went away from the families of the children of Ham, and he fought with them and he subdued them, and he went to the five cities of the plain and he fought against them and he subdued them, and they were under his control. 11 And they served him twelve years, and they gave him a yearly tax. 12 At that time died Nahor, son of Serug, in the forty-ninth year of the life of Abram son of Terah. 13 And in the fiftieth year of the life of Abram son of Terah, Abram came out from the house of Noah, and went to his father's house. 14 And Abram knew the Lord, and he went in his ways and instructions, and the Lord his God was with him. 15 And Terah his father was in those days, still captain of the host of king Nimrod, and he still followed strange gods. 16 And Abram came to his father's house and saw twelve gods standing there in their temples, and the anger of Abram was kindled when he saw these images in his father's house. 17 And Abram said, "As the Lord lives these images will not remain in my father's house; so will the Lord who created me do unto me if in three days' time I do not break them all." 18 And Abram went from them, and his anger burned within him. And Abram hastened and went from the chamber to his father's outer court, and he found his father sitting in the court, and all his servants with him, and Abram came and sat before him. 19 And Abram asked his father, saying, "Father, tell me where is God who created heaven and earth, and all the sons of men upon earth, and who created you and me." And Terah answered his son Abram and said, "Behold those who created us are all with us in the house." 20 And Abram said to his father, "My lord, shew them to me I pray you"; and Terah brought Abram into the chamber of the inner court, and Abram saw, and behold the whole room was full of gods of wood and stone, twelve great images and others less than they without number. 21 And Terah said to his son, "Behold these are they which made all you see upon earth, and which created me and you, and all mankind." 22 And Terah bowed down to his gods, and he then went away from them, and Abram, his son, went away with him. 23 And when Abram had gone from them he went to his mother and sat before her, and he said to his mother, "Behold, my father has shown me those who made heaven and earth, and all the sons of men. 24 Now, therefore, hasten and fetch a kid from the flock, and make of it savory meat, that I may bring it to my father's gods as an offering for them to eat; perhaps I may thereby become acceptable to them." 25 And his mother did so, and she fetched a kid, and made savory meat thereof, and brought it to Abram, and Abram took the savory meat from his mother and brought it before his father's gods, and he drew nigh to them that they might eat; and Terah his father, did not know of it. 26 And Abram saw on the day when he was sitting among them, that they had no voice, no hearing, no motion, and not one of them could stretch out his hand to eat. 27 And Abram mocked them, and said, "Surely the savory meat that I prepared has not pleased them, or perhaps it was too little for them, and for that reason they would not eat; therefore tomorrow I will prepare fresh savory meat, better and more plentiful than this, in order that I may see the result." 28 And it was

JASHER

on the next day that Abram directed his mother concerning the savory meat, and his mother rose and fetched three fine kids from the flock, and she made of them some excellent savory meat, such as her son was fond of, and she gave it to her son Abram; and Terah his father did not know of it. **29** And Abram took the savory meat from his mother and brought it before his father's gods into the chamber; and he came nigh unto them that they might eat, and he placed it before them, and Abram sat before them all day, thinking perhaps they might eat. **30** And Abram viewed them, and behold they had neither voice nor hearing, nor did one of them stretch out his hand to the meat to eat. **31** And in the evening of that day in that house Abram was clothed with the spirit of God. **32** And he called out and said, "Woe unto my father and this wicked generation, whose hearts are all inclined to vanity, who serve these idols of wood and stone which can neither eat, smell, hear nor speak, who have mouths without speech, eyes without sight, ears without hearing, hands without feeling, and legs which cannot move; like them are those that made them and that trust in them." **33** And when Abram saw all these things his anger was kindled against his father, and he hastened and took a hatchet in his hand, and came unto the chamber of the gods, and he broke all his father's gods. **34** And when he had done breaking the images, he placed the hatchet in the hand of the great god which was there before them, and he went out; and Terah his father came home, for he had heard at the door the sound of the striking of the hatchet; so Terah came into the house to know what this was about. **35** And Terah, having heard the noise of the hatchet in the room of images, ran to the room to the images, and he met Abram going out. **36** And Terah entered the room and found all the idols fallen down and broken, and the hatchet in the hand of the largest, which was not broken, and the savory meat which Abram his son had made was still before them. **37** And when Terah saw this his anger was greatly kindled, and he hastened and went from the room to Abram. **38** And he found Abram his son still sitting in the house; and he said to him, "What is this work you have done to my gods?" **39** And Abram answered Terah his father and he said, "Not so my lord, for I brought savory meat before them, and when I came nigh to them with the meat that they might eat, they all at once stretched out their hands to eat before the great

one had put out his hand to eat. **40** And the large one saw their works that they did before him, and his anger was violently kindled against them, and he went and took the hatchet that was in the house and came to them and broke them all, and behold the hatchet is yet in his hand as you see." **41** And Terah's anger was kindled against his son Abram, when he spoke this; and Terah said to Abram his son in his anger, "What is this tale that you have told? You speak lies to me. **42** Is there in these gods spirit, soul or power to do all you have told me? Are they not wood and stone, and have I not myself made them, and can you speak such lies, saying that the large god that was with them smote them? It is you that did place the hatchet in his hands, and then say he smote them all." **43** And Abram answered his father and said to him, "And how can you then serve these idols in whom there is no power to do anything? Can those idols in which you trust deliver you? Can they hear your prayers when you call upon them? Can they deliver you from the hands of your enemies, or will they fight your battles for you against your enemies, that you should serve wood and stone which can neither speak nor hear? **44** And now surely it is not good for you nor for the sons of men that are connected with you, to do these things; are you so silly, so foolish or so short of understanding that you will serve wood and stone, and do after this manner? **45** And forget the Lord God who made heaven and earth, and who created you in the earth, and thereby bring a great evil upon your souls in this matter by serving stone and wood? **46** Did not our fathers in days of old sin in this matter, and the Lord God of the universe brought the waters of the flood upon them and destroyed the whole earth? **47** And how can you continue to do this and serve gods of wood and stone, who cannot hear, or speak, or deliver you from oppression, thereby bringing down the anger of the God of the universe upon you? **48** Now therefore my father refrain from this and bring not evil upon your soul and the souls of your household." **49** And Abram hastened and sprang from before his father, and took the hatchet from his father's largest idol, with which Abram broke it and ran away. **50** And Terah, seeing all that Abram had done, hastened to go from his house, and he went to the king and he came before Nimrod and stood before him, and he bowed down to the king; and the king said, "What do you want?" **51** And he said, I implore you my lord, to hear me—Now fifty years back a child was born to me, and thus has he done to my gods and thus has he spoken; and now therefore, my lord and king, send for him that he may come before you, and judge him according to the law, that we may be delivered from his evil. **52** And the king sent three men of his servants, and they went and brought Abram before the king. And Nimrod and all his princes and servants were that day sitting before him, and Terah sat also before them. **53** And the king said to Abram, "What is this that you have done to your father and to his gods?" And Abram answered the king in the words that he spoke to his father, and he said, "The large god that was with them in the house did to them what you have heard." **54** And the king said to Abram, "Had they power to speak and eat and do as you have said?" And Abram answered the king, saying, "And if there be no power in them why do you serve them and cause the sons of men to err through your follies? **55** Do you imagine that they can deliver you or do anything small or great, that you should serve them? And why will you not sense the God of the whole universe, who created you and in whose power it is to kill and keep alive? **56** O foolish, simple, and ignorant king, woe unto you forever. **57** I thought you would teach your servants the upright way, but you have not done this, but have filled the whole earth with your sins and the sins of your people who have followed your ways. **58** Do you not know, or have you not heard, that this evil which you do, our ancestors sinned therein in days of old, and the eternal God brought the waters of the flood upon them and destroyed them all, and also destroyed the whole earth on their account? And will you and your people rise up now and do like unto this work, in order to bring down the anger of the Lord God of the universe, and to bring evil upon you and the whole earth? **59** Now therefore put away this evil deed which you do, and serve the God of the universe, as your soul is in his hands, and then it will be well with you. **60** And if your wicked heart will not hearken to my words to cause you to forsake your evil ways, and to serve the eternal God, then will you die in shame in the latter days, you, your people and all who are connected with you, hearing your words or walking in your evil ways." **61** And when Abram had ceased speaking before the king and princes, Abram lifted up his eyes to the heavens, and he said, "The Lord sees all the wicked, and he will judge them."

CHAPTER 12

1 And when the king heard the words of Abram he ordered him to be put into prison; and Abram was ten days in prison. **2** And at the end of those days the king ordered that all the kings, princes and governors of different provinces and the sages should come before him, and they sat before him, and Abram was still in the house of confinement. **3** And the king said to the princes and sages, "Have you heard what Abram, the son of Terah, has done to his father? Thus has he done to him, and I ordered him to be brought before me, and thus has he spoken; his heart did not misgive him, neither did he stir in my presence, and behold now he is confined in the prison. **4** And therefore decide what judgment is due to this man who reviled the king; who spoke and did all the things that you heard." **5** And they all answered the king saying, "The man who reviles the king should be hanged upon a tree; but having done all the things that he said, and having despised our gods, he must therefore be burned to death, for this is the law in this matter. **6** If it pleases the king to do this, let him order his servants to kindle a fire both night and day in your brick furnace, and then we will cast this man into it." And the king did so, and he commanded his servants that they should prepare a fire for three days and three nights in the king's furnace, that is in Casdim; and the king ordered them to take Abram from prison and bring him out to be burned. **7** And all the king's servants, princes, lords, governors, and judges, and all the inhabitants of the land, about nine hundred thousand men, stood opposite the furnace to see Abram. **8** And all the women and little ones crowded upon the roofs and towers to see what was happening with Abram, and they all stood together at a distance; and there was not a man left that did not come on that day to behold the scene. **9** And when Abram was come, the conjurors of the king and the sages saw Abram, and they cried out to the king, saying, "Our sovereign lord, surely this is the man whom we know to have been the child at whose birth the great star swallowed the four stars, which we declared to the king now fifty years since. **10** And behold now his father has also transgressed your commands, and mocked you by bringing you another child, which you did kill. **11** And when the king heard their words, he was exceedingly angry, and he ordered Terah to be brought before him. **12** And the king said, "Have you heard what the conjurors have spoken? Now tell me truly, how did you; and if you will speak truth you will be acquitted." 13 And seeing that the king's anger was so much kindled, Terah said to the king, "My lord and king, you have heard the truth, and what the sages have spoken is right." And the king said, "How could you do this thing, to transgress my orders and to give me a child that you did not beget, and to take value for him?" 14 And Terah answered the king, "Because my tender feelings were excited for my son, at that time, and I took a son of my handmaid, and I brought him to the king." 15 And the king said, "Who advised you to this? Tell me, do not hide it from me, and then you will not die." 16 And Terah was greatly terrified in the king's presence, and he said to the king, "It was Haran my eldest son who advised me to this"; and Haran was in those days that Abram was born, two and thirty years old. 17 But Haran did not advise his father to anything, for Terah said this to the king in order to deliver his soul from the king, for he feared greatly; and the king said to Terah, "Haran your son who advised you to this will die through fire with Abram; for the sentence of death is upon him for having rebelled against the king's desire in doing this thing." 18 And Haran at that time felt inclined to follow the ways of Abram, but he kept it within himself. 19 And Haran said in his heart, "Behold now the king has seized Abram on account of these things which Abram did, and it will come to pass, that if Abram prevail over the king I will follow him, but if the king prevail I will go after the king." 20 And when Terah had spoken this to the king concerning Haran his son, the king ordered Haran to be seized with Abram. 21 And they brought them both, Abram and Haran his brother, to cast them into the fire; and all the inhabitants of the land and the king's servants and princes and all the women and little ones were there, standing that day over them. 22 And the king's servants took Abram and his brother, and they stripped them of all their clothes excepting their lower garments which were upon them. 23 And they bound their hands and feet with linen cords, and the servants of the king lifted them up and cast them both into the furnace. 24 And the Lord loved Abram and he had compassion over him, and the Lord came down and delivered Abram from the fire and he was not burned. 25 But all the cords with which they bound him were burned, while Abram remained and walked about in the fire.

26 And Haran died when they had cast him into the fire, and he was burned to ashes, for his heart was not perfect with the Lord; and those men who cast him into the fire, the flame of the fire spread over them, and they were burned, and twelve men of them died. 27 And Abram walked in the midst of the fire three days and three nights, and all the servants of the king saw him walking in the fire, and they came and told the king, saying, "Behold we have seen Abram walking about in the midst of the fire, and even the lower garments which are upon him are not burned, but the cord with which he was bound is burned." 28 And when the king heard their words his heart fainted and he would not believe them; so he sent other faithful princes to see this matter, and they went and saw it and told it to the king; and the king rose to go and see it, and he saw Abram walking to and fro in the midst of the fire, and he saw Haran's body burned, and the king wondered greatly. 29 And the king ordered Abram to be taken out from the fire; and his servants approached to take him out and they could not, for the fire was round about and the flame ascending toward them from the furnace. 30 And the king's servants fled from it, and the king rebuked them, saying, "Make haste and bring Abram out of the fire that you will not die." 31 And the servants of the king again approached to bring Abram out, and the flames came upon them and burned their faces so that eight of them died. 32 And when the king saw that his servants could not approach the fire lest they should be burned, the king called to Abram, "O servant of the God who is in heaven, go out from amidst the fire and come here before me"; and Abram hearkened to the voice of the king, and he went out from the fire and came and stood before the king. 33 And when Abram came out the king and all his servants saw Abram coming before the king, with his lower garments upon him, for they were not burned, but the cord with which he was bound was burned. 34 And the king said to Abram, "How is it that you were not burned in the fire?" 35 And Abram said to the king, "The God of heaven and earth in whom I trust and who has all in his power, he delivered me from the fire into which you did cast me." 36 And Haran the brother of Abram was burned to ashes, and they sought for his body, and they found it consumed. 37 And Haran was eighty-two years old when he died in the fire of Casdim. And the king, princes, and inhabitants of the land, seeing that Abram

was delivered from the fire, they came and bowed down to Abram. **38** And Abram said to them, "Do not bow down to me, but bow down to the God of the world who made you, and serve him, and go in his ways for it is he who delivered me from out of this fire, and it is he who created the souls and spirits of all men, and formed man in his mother's womb, and brought him out into the world, and it is he who will deliver those who trust in him from all pain." **39** And this thing seemed very wonderful in the eyes of the king and princes, that Abram was saved from the fire and that Haran was burned; and the king gave Abram many presents and he gave him his two head servants from the king's house; the name of one was Oni and the name of the other was Eliezer. **40** And all the kings, princes and servants gave Abram many gifts of silver and gold and pearl, and the king and his princes sent him away, and he went in peace. **41** And Abram went out from the king in peace, and many of the king's servants followed him, and about three hundred men joined him. **42** And Abram returned on that day and went to his father's house, he and the men that followed him, and Abram served the Lord his God all the days of his life, and he walked in his ways and followed his law. **43** And from that day forward Abram inclined the hearts of the sons of men to serve the Lord. **44** And at that time Nahor and Abram took unto themselves wives, the daughters of their brother Haran; the wife of Nahor was Milca and the name of Abram's wife was Sarai. And Sarai, wife of Abram, was barren; she had no offspring in those days. **45** And at the expiration of two years from Abram's going out of the fire, that is in the fifty-second year of his life, behold king Nimrod sat in Babel upon the throne, and the king fell asleep and dreamed that he was standing with his troops and hosts in a valley opposite the king's furnace. **46** And he lifted up his eyes and saw a man in the likeness of Abram coming out from the furnace, and that he came and stood before the king with his drawn sword, and then sprang to the king with his sword, when the king fled from the man, for he was afraid; and while he was running, the man threw an egg upon the king's head, and the egg became a great river. **47** And the king dreamed that all his troops sank in that river and died, and the king took flight with three men who were before him and he escaped. **48** And the king looked at these men and they were clothed in princely dresses as the garments of kings and had the appearance and majesty of kings. **49** And while they were running, the river again turned to an egg before the king, and there came out from the egg a young bird which came before the king and flew at his head and plucked out the king's eye. **50** And the king was grieved at the sight, and he awoke out of his sleep and his spirit was agitated; and he felt a great terror. **51** And in the morning the king rose from his couch in fear, and he ordered all the wise men and magicians to come before him, when the king related his dream to them. **52** And a wise servant of the king, whose name was Anuki, answered the king, saying, "This is nothing else but the evil of Abram and his seed which will spring up against my Lord and king in the latter days. **53** And behold the day will come when Abram and his seed and the children of his household will war with my king, and they will smite all the king's hosts and his troops. **54** And as to what you have said concerning three men which you did see like unto yourself, and which did escape, this means that only you will escape with three kings from the kings of the earth who will be with you in battle. **55** And that which you saw of the river which turned to an egg as at first, and the young bird plucking out your eye, this means nothing else but the seed of Abram which will slay the king in latter days. **56** This is my king's dream, and this is its interpretation, and the dream is true, and the interpretation which your servant has given you is right. **57** Now therefore my king, surely you know that it is now fifty-two years since your sages saw this at the birth of Abram, and if my king will suffer Abram to live in the earth it will be to the injury of my lord and king, for all the days that Abram lives neither you nor your kingdom will be established, for this was known formerly at his birth; and why will not my king slay him, that his evil may be kept from you in latter days?" **58** And Nimrod hearkened to the voice of Anuki, and he sent some of his servants in secret to go and seize Abram, and bring him before the king to suffer death. **59** And Eliezer, Abram's servant whom the king had given him, was at that time in the presence of the king, and he heard what Anuki had advised the king, and what the king had said to cause Abram's death. **60** And Eliezer said to Abram, "Hasten, rise up and save your soul, that you may not die through the hands of the king, for thus did he see in a dream concerning you, and thus did Anuki interpret it, and thus also did Anuki advise the king concerning you." **61** And Abram hearkened to the voice of Eliezer, and Abram hastened and ran for safety to the house of Noah and his son Shem, and he concealed himself there and found a place of safety; and the king's servants came to Abram's house to seek him, but they could not find him, and they searched through out the country and he was not to be found, and they went and searched in every direction and he was not to be met with. **62** And when the king's servants could not find Abram they returned to the king, but the king's anger against Abram was stilled, as they did not find him, and the king drove from his mind this matter concerning Abram. **63** And Abram was concealed in Noah's house for one month, until the king had forgotten this matter, but Abram was still afraid of the king; and Terah came to see Abram his son secretly in the house of Noah, and Terah was very great in the eyes of the king. **64** And Abram said to his father, "Do you not know that the king thinks to slay me, and to annihilate my name from the earth by the advice of his wicked counsellors? **65** Now whom have you here and what have you in this land? Arise, let us go together to the land of Canaan, that we may be delivered from his hand, lest you perish also through him in the latter days. **66** Do you not know or have you not heard, that it is not through love that Nimrod gives you all this honor, but it is only for his benefit that he bestows all this good upon you? **67** And if he do unto you greater good than this, surely these are only vanities of the world, for wealth and riches cannot avail in the day of wrath and anger. **68** Now therefore hearken to my voice and let us arise and go to the land of Canaan, out of the reach of injury from Nimrod; and serve you the Lord who created you in the earth and it will be well with you; and cast away all the vain things which you pursue." **69** And Abram ceased to speak, when Noah and his son Shem answered Terah, saying, "True is the word which Abram has said unto you." **70** And Terah hearkened to the voice of his son Abram, and Terah did all that Abram said, for this was from the Lord, that the king should not cause Abram's death.

CHAPTER 13

1 And Terah took his son Abram and his grandson Lot, the son of Haran, and Sarai his daughter-in-law, the wife of his son Abram, and all the souls of his household and went with them from Ur Casdim to go to the land of Canaan. And when they came as far as the land of Haran they remained there, for it was exceedingly good land for pasture, and of sufficient extent for those who accompanied them. **2** And the people of the land of Haran saw that Abram was good and upright with God and men, and that the Lord his God was with him, and some of the people of the land of Haran came and joined Abram, and he taught them the instruction of the Lord and his ways; and these men remained with Abram in his house and they adhered to him. **3** And Abram remained in the land three years, and at the expiration of three years the Lord appeared to Abram and said to him, "I am the Lord who brought you out from Ur Casdim and delivered you from the hands of all your enemies. **4** And now therefore if you will hearken to my voice and keep my commandments, my statutes and my laws, then will I cause your enemies to fall before you, and I will multiply your seed like the stars of heaven, and I will send my blessing upon all the works of your hands, and you will lack nothing. **5** Arise now, take your wife and all belonging to you and go to the land of Canaan and remain there, and I will there be unto you for a God, and I will bless you." And Abram rose and took his wife and all belonging to him, and he went to the land of Canaan as the Lord had told him; and Abram was fifty years old when he went from Haran. **6** And Abram came to the land of Canaan and dwelt in the midst of the city, and he there pitched his tent among the children of Canaan, inhabitants of the land. **7** And the Lord appeared to Abram when he came to the land of Canaan, and said to him, "This is the land which I gave unto you and to your seed after you forever, and I will make your seed like the stars of heaven, and I will give unto your seed for an inheritance all the lands which you see." **8** And Abram built an altar in the place where God had spoken to him, and Abram there called upon the name of the Lord. **9** At that time, at the end of three years of Abram's dwelling in the land of Canaan, in that year Noah died, which was the fifty-eighth year of the life of Abram; and all the days that Noah lived were nine hundred and fifty years and he died. **10** And Abram dwelt in the land of Canaan, he, his wife, and all belonging to him, and all those that accompanied him, together with those that joined him from the people of the land; but Nahor, Abram's brother, and Terah his father, and Lot the son of Haran and all belonging to them dwelt in Haran. **11** In the fifth year of Abram's dwelling in the land of Canaan the people of Sodom and Gomorrah and all the cities of the plain revolted from the power of Chedorlaomer, king of Elam; for all the kings of the cities of the plain had served Chedorlaomer for twelve years, and given him a yearly tax, but in those days in the thirteenth year, they rebelled against him. **12** And in the tenth year of Abram's dwelling in the land of Canaan there was war between Nimrod king of Shinar and Chedorlaomer king of Elam, and Nimrod came to fight with Chedorlaomer and to subdue him. **13** For Chedorlaomer was at that time one of the princes of the hosts of Nimrod, and when all the people at the tower were dispersed and those that remained were also scattered upon the face of the earth, Chedorlaomer went to the land of Elam and reigned over it and rebelled against his lord. **14** And in those days when Nimrod saw that the cities of the plain had rebelled, he came with pride and anger to war with Chedorlaomer, and Nimrod assembled all his princes and subjects, about seven hundred thousand men, and went against Chedorlaomer, and Chedorlaomer went out to meet him with five thousand men, and they prepared for battle in the valley of Babel which is between Elam and Shinar. **15** And all those kings fought there, and Nimrod and his people were smitten before the people of Chedorlaomer, and there fell from Nimrod's men about six hundred thousand, and Mardon the king's son fell among them. **16** And Nimrod fled and returned in shame and disgrace to his land, and he was under subjection to Chedorlaomer for a long time, and Chedorlaomer returned to his land and sent princes of his host to the kings that dwelt around him, to Arioch king of Elasar, and to Tidal king of Goyim, and made a covenant with them, and they were all obedient to his commands. **17** And it was in the fifteenth year of Abram's dwelling in the land of Canaan, which is the seventieth year of the life of Abram, and the Lord appeared to Abram in that year and he said to him, "I am the Lord who brought you out from Ur Casdim to give you this land for an inheritance. **18** Now therefore walk before me and be perfect and keep my commands, for to you and to your seed I will give this land for an inheritance, from the river Mitzraim unto the great river Euphrates. **19** And you will come to your fathers in peace and in good age, and the fourth generation will return here in this land and will

inherit it forever"; and Abram built an altar, and he called upon the name of the Lord who appeared to him, and he brought up sacrifices upon the altar to the Lord. **20** At that time Abram returned and went to Haran to see his father and mother, and his father's household, and Abram and his wife and all belonging to him returned to Haran, and Abram dwelt in Haran five years. **21** And many of the people of Haran, about seventy-two men, followed Abram and Abram taught them the instruction of the Lord and his ways, and he taught them to know the Lord. **22** In those days the Lord appeared to Abram in Haran, and he said to him, "Behold, I spoke unto you these twenty years back saying, **23** Go out from your land, from your birth-place and from your father's house, to the land which I have shown you to give it to you and to your children, for there in that land will I bless you, and make you a great nation, and make your name great, and in you will the families of the earth be blessed. **24** Now therefore arise, go out from this place, you, your wife, and all belonging to you, also everyone born in your house and all the souls you have made in Haran, and bring them out with you from here, and rise to return to the land of Canaan." **25** And Abram arose and took his wife Sarai and all belonging to him and all that were born to him in his house and the souls which they had made in Haran, and they came out to go to the land of Canaan. **26** And Abram went and returned to the land of Canaan, according to the word of the Lord. And Lot the son of his brother Haran went with him, and Abram was seventy-five years old when he went out from Haran to return to the land of Canaan. **27** And he came to the land of Canaan according to the word of the Lord to Abram, and he pitched his tent and he dwelt in the plain of Mamre, and with him was Lot his brother's son, and all belonging to him. **28** And the Lord again appeared to Abram and said, "To your seed will I give this land"; and he there built an altar to the Lord who appeared to him, which is still to this day in the plains of Mamre.

CHAPTER 14

1 In those days there was in the land of Shinar a wise man who had understanding in all wisdom, and of a beautiful appearance, but he was poor and indigent; his name was Rikayon and he was hard set to support himself. **2** And he resolved to go to Egypt, to Oswiris the son of Anom king of Egypt, to show the king his wisdom; for perhaps he might find grace in his sight, to raise him up and give him maintenance; and Rikayon did so. **3** And when Rikayon came to Egypt he asked the inhabitants of Egypt concerning the king, and the inhabitants of Egypt told him the custom of the king of Egypt, for it was then the custom of the king of Egypt that he went from his royal palace and was seen abroad only one day in the year, and after that the king would return to his palace to remain there. **4** And on the day when the king went out he passed judgment in the land, and everyone having a suit came before the king that day to obtain his request. **5** And when Rikayon heard of the custom in Egypt and that he could not come into the presence of the king, he grieved greatly and was very sorrowful. **6** And in the evening Rikayon went out and found a house in ruins, formerly a bake house in Egypt, and he remained there all night in bitterness of soul and pinched with hunger, and sleep was removed from his eyes. **7** And Rikayon considered within himself what he should do in the town until the king made his appearance, and how he might maintain himself there. **8** And he rose in the morning and walked about and met in his way those who sold vegetables and various sorts of seed with which they supplied the inhabitants. **9** And Rikayon wished to do the same in order to get a maintenance in the city, but he was unacquainted with the custom of the people, and he was like a blind man among them. **10** And he went and obtained vegetables to sell them for his support, and the rabble assembled about him and ridiculed him, and took his vegetables from him and left him nothing. **11** And he rose up from there in bitterness of soul and went sighing to the bake house in which he had remained all the night before, and he slept there the second night. **12** And on that night again he reasoned within himself how he could save himself from starvation, and he devised a scheme how to act. **13** And he rose up in the morning and acted ingeniously and went and hired thirty strong men of the rabble, carrying their war instruments in their hands, and he led them to the top of the Egyptian sepulcher, and he placed them there. **14** And he commanded them, saying, "Thus says the king, strengthen yourselves and be valiant men, and let no man be buried here until two hundred pieces of silver be given, and then he may be buried"; and those men did according to the order of Rikayon to the people of Egypt the whole of that year. **15** And in eight months time Rikayon and his men gathered great riches of silver and gold, and Rikayon took a great quantity of horses and other animals, and he hired more men, and he gave them horses and they remained with him. **16** And when the year came round, at the time the king went out into the town, all the inhabitants of Egypt assembled together to speak to him concerning the work of Rikayon and his men. **17** And the king went out on the appointed day, and all the Egyptians came before him and cried unto him, saying, **18** "May the king live forever. What is this thing you do in the town to your servants, not to suffer a dead body to be buried until so much silver and gold be given? Was there ever the like unto this done in the whole earth, from the days of former kings yea even from the days of Adam, unto this day, that the dead should not be buried only for a set price? **19** We know it to be the custom of kings to take a yearly tax from the living, but you do not only do this, but from the dead also you exact a tax day by day. **20** Now, O king, we can no more bear this, for the whole city is ruined on this account, and do you not know it?" **21** And when the king heard all that they had spoken he was very angry, and his anger burned within him at this affair, for he had known nothing of it. **22** And the king said, "Who and where is he that dares to do this wicked thing in my land without my command? Surely you will tell me." **23** And they told him all the works of Rikayon and his men, and the king's anger was aroused, and he ordered Rikayon and his men to be brought before him. **24** And Rikayon took about a thousand children, sons and daughters, and clothed them in silk and embroidery, and he set them upon horses and sent them to the king by means of his men, and he also took a great quantity of silver and gold and precious stones, and a strong and beautiful horse, as a present for the king, with which he came before the king and bowed down to the earth before him; and the king, his servants and all the inhabitants of Egypt wondered at the work of Rikayon, and they saw his riches and the present that he had brought to the king. **25** And it greatly pleased the king and he wondered at it; and when Rikayon sat before him the king asked him concerning all his works, and Rikayon spoke all his words wisely before the king, his servants and all the inhabitants of Egypt. **26** And when the king heard the words of Rikayon and his wisdom, Rikayon found grace in his sight, and he met with grace and kindness from all the servants of the king and from all the inhabitants of Egypt, on account of his wisdom and excellent speeches, and from that time they loved him exceedingly. 27 And the king answered and said to Rikayon, "Your name will no more be called Rikayon but Pharaoh will be your name, since you did exact a tax from the dead"; and he called his name Pharaoh. 28 And the king and his subjects loved Rikayon for his wisdom, and they consulted with all the inhabitants of Egypt to make him prefect under the king. 29 And all the inhabitants of Egypt and its wise men did so, and it was made a law in Egypt. 30 And they made Rikayon Pharaoh prefect under Oswiris king of Egypt, and Rikayon Pharaoh governed over Egypt, daily administering justice to the whole city, but Oswiris the king would judge the people of the land one day in the year, when he went out to make his appearance. 31 And Rikayon Pharaoh cunningly usurped the government of Egypt, and he exacted a tax from all the inhabitants of Egypt. 32 And all the inhabitants of Egypt greatly loved Rikayon Pharaoh, and they made a decree to call every king that should reign over them and their seed in Egypt, Pharaoh. 33 Therefore all the kings that reigned in Egypt from that time forward were called Pharaoh unto this day.

CHAPTER 15

1 And in that year there was a heavy famine throughout the land of Canaan, and the inhabitants of the land could not remain on account of the famine for it was very grievous. 2 And Abram and all belonging to him rose and went down to Egypt on account of the famine, and when they were at the brook Mitzraim they remained there some time to rest from the fatigue of the road. 3 And Abram and Sarai were walking at the border of the brook Mitzraim, and Abram beheld his wife Sarai that she was very beautiful. 4 And Abram said to his wife Sarai, "Since God has created you with such a beautiful countenance, I am afraid of the Egyptians lest they should slay me and take you away, for the fear of God is not in these places. 5 Surely then you will do this, say you are my sister to all that may ask you, in order that it may be well with me, and that we may live and not be put to death." 6 And Abram commanded the same to all those that came with him to Egypt on account

of the famine; also his nephew Lot he commanded, saying, "If the Egyptians asks you concerning Sarai say she is the sister of Abram." 7 And yet with all these orders Abram did not put confidence in them, but he took Sarai and placed her in a chest and concealed it among their vessels, for Abram was greatly concerned about Sarai on account of the wickedness of the Egyptians. 8 And Abram and all belonging to him rose up from the brook Mitzraim and came to Egypt; and they had scarcely entered the gates of the city when the guards stood up to them saying, "Give tithe to the king from what you have, and then you may come into the town"; and Abram and those that were with him did so. 9 And Abram with the people that were with him came to Egypt, and when they came they brought the chest in which Sarai was concealed and the Egyptians saw the chest. 10 And the king's servants approached Abram, saying, "What have you here in this chest which we have not seen? Now open you the chest and give tithe to the king of all that it contains." 11 And Abram said, "This chest I will not open, but all you demand upon it I will give." And Pharaoh's officers answered Abram, saying, "It is a chest of precious stones, give us the tenth thereof." 12 Abram said, "All that you desire I will give, but you must not open the chest." 13 And the king's officers pressed Abram, and they reached the chest and opened it with force, and they saw, and behold a beautiful woman was in the chest. 14 And when the officers of the king beheld Sarai they were struck with admiration at her beauty, and all the princes and servants of Pharaoh assembled to see Sarai, for she was very beautiful. And the king's officers ran and told Pharaoh all that they had seen, and they praised Sarai to the king; and Pharaoh ordered her to be brought, and the woman came before the king. 15 And Pharaoh beheld Sarai and she pleased him exceedingly, and he was struck with her beauty, and the king rejoiced greatly on her account, and made presents to those who brought him the tidings concerning her. 16 And the woman was then brought to Pharaoh's house, and Abram grieved on account of his wife, and he prayed to the Lord to deliver her from the hands of Pharaoh. 17 And Sarai also prayed at that time and said, "O Lord God you did tell my Lord Abram to go from his land and from his father's house to the land of Canaan, and you did promise to do well with him if he would perform your commands; now behold we have done that which you did command us, and we left our land and our families, and we went to a strange land and to a people whom we have not known before. **18** And we came to this land to avoid the famine, and this evil accident has befallen me; now therefore, O Lord God, deliver us and save us from the hand of this oppressor, and do well with me for the sake of your mercy." **19** And the Lord hearkened to the voice of Sarai, and the Lord sent an angel to deliver Sarai from the power of Pharaoh. **20** And the king came and sat before Sarai and behold an angel of the Lord was standing over them, and he appeared to Sarai and said to her, "Do not fear, for the Lord has heard your prayer." **21** And the king approached Sarai and said to her, "What is that man to you who brought you here?" and she said, "He is my brother." **22** And the king said, "It is incumbent upon us to make him great, to elevate him and to do unto him all the good which you will command us"; and at that time the king sent to Abram silver and gold and precious stones in abundance, together with cattle, menservants and maidservants; and the king ordered Abram to be brought, and he sat in the court of the king's house, and the king greatly exalted Abram on that night. **23** And the king approached to speak to Sarai, and he reached out his hand to touch her, when the angel smote him heavily, and he was terrified and he refrained from reaching to her. **24** And when the king came near to Sarai, the angel smote him to the ground, and acted thus to him the whole night, and the king was terrified. **25** And the angel on that night smote heavily all the servants of the king, and his whole household, on account of Sarai, and there was a great lamentation that night among the people of Pharaoh's house. **26** And Pharaoh, seeing the evil that befell him, said, "Surely on account of this woman has this thing happened to me," and he removed himself at some distance from her and spoke pleasing words to her. **27** And the king said to Sarai, "Tell me I pray you concerning the man with whom you came here"; and Sarai said, "This man is my husband, and I said to you that he was my brother for I was afraid, lest you should put him to death through wickedness." **28** And the king kept away from Sarai, and the plagues of the angel of the Lord ceased from him and his household; and Pharaoh knew that he was smitten on account of Sarai, and the king was greatly astonished at this. **29** And in the morning the king called for Abram and said to him, "What is this you have done to me? Why did you say, 'she is my sister,' owing to which I took her unto me for a wife, and this heavy plague has therefore come upon me and my household? **30** Now therefore here is your wife, take her and go from our land lest we all die on her account." And Pharaoh took more cattle, menservants and maidservants, and silver and gold, to give to Abram, and he returned unto him Sarai his wife. **31** And the king took a maiden whom he begat by his concubines, and he gave her to Sarai for a handmaid. **32** And the king said to his daughter, "It is better for you my daughter to be a handmaid in this man's house than to be mistress in my house, after we have beheld the evil that befell us on account of this woman." **33** And Abram arose, and he and all belonging to him went away from Egypt; and Pharaoh ordered some of his men to accompany him and all that went with him. **34** And Abram returned to the land of Canaan, to the place where he had made the altar, where he at first had pitched his tent. **35** And Lot the son of Haran, Abram's brother, had a heavy stock of cattle, flocks and herds and tents, for the Lord was bountiful to them on account of Abram. **36** And when Abram was dwelling in the land the herdsmen of Lot quarrelled with the herdsmen of Abram, for their property was too great for them to remain together in the land, and the land could not bear them on account of their cattle. **37** And when Abram's herdsmen went to feed their flock they would not go into the fields of the people of the land, but the cattle of Lot's herdsmen did otherwise, for they were suffered to feed in the fields of the people of the land. **38** And the people of the land saw this occurrence daily, and they came to Abram and quarrelled with him on account of Lot's herdsmen. **39** And Abram said to Lot, "What is this you are doing to me, to make me despicable to the inhabitants of the land, that you orderest your herdsman to feed your cattle in the fields of other people? Do you not know that I am a stranger in this land among the children of Canaan, and why will you do this unto me?" **40** And Abram quarrelled daily with Lot on account of this, but Lot would not listen to Abram, and he continued to do the same and the inhabitants of the land came and told Abram. **41** And Abram said unto Lot, "How long will you be to me for a stumbling block with the inhabitants of the land? Now I implore you let there be no more quarrelling between us, for we are kinsmen. **42** But I pray you separate from me, go and choose a place where you may dwell with your cattle and all belonging to you, but keep yourself at a distance from me, you and your household. **43** And be not afraid in going from me, for if anyone do an injury to you, let me know and I will avenge your cause from him, only remove from me." **44** And when Abram had spoken all these words to Lot, then Lot arose and lifted up his eyes toward the plain of Jordan. **45** And he saw that the whole of this place was well watered, and good for man as well as affording pasture for the cattle. **46** And Lot went from Abram to that place, and he there pitched his tent and he dwelt in Sodom, and they were separated from each other. **47** And Abram dwelt in the plain of Mamre, which is in Hebron, and he pitched his tent there, and Abram remained in that place many years.

CHAPTER 16

1 At that time Chedorlaomer king of Elam sent to all the neighboring kings, to Nimrod, king of Shinar who was then under his power, and to Tidal, king of Goyim, and to Arioch, king of Elasar, with whom he made a covenant, saying, "Come up to me and assist me, that we may smite all the towns of Sodom and its inhabitants, for they have rebelled against me these thirteen years." **2** And these four kings went up with all their camps, about eight hundred thousand men, and they went as they were, and smote every man they found in their road. **3** And the five kings of Sodom and Gomorrah, Shinab king of Admah, Shemeber king of Zeboyim, Bera king of Sodom, Bersha king of Gomorrah, and Bela king of Zoar, went out to meet them, and they all joined together in the valley of Siddim. **4** And these nine kings made war in the valley of Siddim; and the kings of Sodom and Gomorrah were smitten before the kings of Elam. **5** And the valley of Siddim was full of lime pits and the kings of Elam pursued the kings of Sodom, and the kings of Sodom with their camps fled and fell into the lime pits, and all that remained went to the mountain for safety, and the five kings of Elam came after them and pursued them to the gates of Sodom, and they took all that there was in Sodom. **6** And they plundered all the cities of Sodom and Gomorrah, and they also took Lot, Abram's brother's son, and his property, and they seized all the goods of the cities of Sodom, and they went away; and Unic, Abram's servant, who was in the battle,

saw this, and told Abram all that the kings had done to the cities of Sodom, and that Lot was taken captive by them. **7** And Abram heard this, and he rose up with about three hundred and eighteen men that were with him, and he that night pursued these kings and smote them, and they all fell before Abram and his men, and there was none remaining but the four kings who fled, and they went each his own road. **8** And Abram recovered all the property of Sodom, and he also recovered Lot and his property, his wives and little ones and all belonging to him, so that Lot lacked nothing. **9** And when he returned from smiting these kings, he and his men passed the valley of Siddim where the kings had made war together. **10** And Bera king of Sodom, and the rest of his men that were with him, went out from the lime pits into which they had fallen, to meet Abram and his men. **11** And Adonizedek king of Jerusalem, the same was Shem, went out with his men to meet Abram and his people, with bread and wine, and they remained together in the valley of Melech. **12** And Adonizedek blessed Abram, and Abram gave him a tenth from all that he had brought from the spoil of his enemies, for Adonizedek was a priest before God. **13** And all the kings of Sodom and Gomorrah who were there, with their servants, approached Abram and begged of him to return them their servants whom he had made captive, and to take unto himself all the property. **14** And Abram answered the kings of Sodom, saying, "As the Lord lives who created heaven and earth, and who redeemed my soul from all affliction, and who delivered me this day from my enemies, and gave them into my hand, I will not take anything belonging to you, that you may not boast tomorrow, saying, 'Abram became rich from our property that he saved.' **15** For the Lord my God in whom I trust said unto me, 'You will lack nothing, for I will bless you in all the works of your hands.' **16** And now therefore behold, here is all belonging to you, take it and go; as the Lord lives I will not take from you from a living soul down to a shoetie or thread, excepting the expense of the food of those who went out with me to battle, as also the portions of the men who went with me, Anar, Ashcol, and Mamre, they and their men, as well as those also who had remained to watch the baggage, they will take their portion of the spoil." **17** And the kings of Sodom gave Abram according to all that he had said, and they pressed him to take of whatever he chose, but he would not. 18 And he sent away the kings of Sodom and the remainder of their men, and he gave them orders about Lot, and they went to their respective places. 19 And Lot, his brother's son, he also sent away with his property, and he went with them, and Lot returned to his home, to Sodom, and Abram and his people returned to their home to the plains of Mamre, which is in Hebron. 20 At that time the Lord again appeared to Abram in Hebron, and he said to him, "Do not fear, your reward is very great before me, for I will not leave you, until I will have multiplied you, and blessed you and made your seed like the stars in heaven, which cannot be measured nor numbered. 21 And I will give unto your seed all these lands that you see with your eyes, to them will I give them for an inheritance forever, only be strong and do not fear, walk before me and be perfect." 22 And in the seventy-eighth year of the life of Abram, in that year died Reu, the son of Peleg, and all the days of Reu were two hundred and thirty-nine years, and he died. 23 And Sarai, the daughter of Haran, Abram's wife, was still barren in those days; she did not bear to Abram either son or daughter. 24 And when she saw that she bore no children she took her handmaid Hagar, whom Pharaoh had given her, and she gave her to Abram her husband for a wife. 25 For Hagar learned all the ways of Sarai as Sarai taught her, she was not in any way deficient in following her good ways. 26 And Sarai said to Abram, "Behold here is my handmaid Hagar, go to her that she may bring out upon my knees, that I may also obtain children through her." 27 And at the end of ten years of Abram's dwelling in the land of Canaan, which is the eighty-fifth year of Abram's life, Sarai gave Hagar unto him. 28 And Abram hearkened to the voice of his wife Sarai, and he took his handmaid Hagar and Abram came to her and she conceived. 29 And when Hagar saw that she had conceived she rejoiced greatly, and her mistress was despised in her eyes, and she said within herself, "This can only be that I am better before God than Sarai my mistress, for all the days that my mistress has been with my lord, she did not conceive, but me the Lord has caused in so short a time to conceive by him." 30 And when Sarai saw that Hagar had conceived by Abram, Sarai was jealous of her handmaid, and Sarai said within herself, "This is surely nothing else but that she must be better than I am." 31 And Sarai said unto Abram, "My wrong be upon you, for at the time when you did pray before the Lord for children why did you not pray on my account, that the Lord should give me seed from you? 32 And when I speak to Hagar in your presence, she despises my words, because she has conceived, and you will say nothing to her; may the Lord judge between me and you for what you have done to me." 33 And Abram said to Sarai, "Behold your handmaid is in your hands, do unto her as it may seem good in your eyes"; and Sarai afflicted her, and Hagar fled from her to the wilderness. 34 And an angel of the Lord found her in the place where she had fled, by a well, and he said to her, "Do not fear, for I will multiply your seed, for you will bear a son and you will call his name Ishmael; now then return to Sarai your mistress, and submit yourself under her hands." 35 And Hagar called the place of that well Beer-lahai-roi, it is between Kadesh and the wilderness of Bered. 36 And Hagar at that time returned to her master's house, and at the end of days Hagar bore a son to Abram, and Abram called his name Ishmael; and Abram was eighty-six years old when he begat him.

CHAPTER 17

1 And in those days, in the ninety-first year of the life of Abram, the children of Chittim made war with the children of Tubal, for when the Lord had scattered the sons of men upon the face of the earth, the children of Chittim went and embodied themselves in the plain of Canopia, and they built themselves cities there and dwelt by the river Tibreu. 2 And the children of Tubal dwelt in Tuscanah, and their boundaries reached the river Tibreu, and the children of Tubal built a city in Tuscanan, and they called the name Sabinah, after the name of Sabinah son of Tubal their father, and they dwelt there unto this day. 3 And it was at that time the children of Chittim made war with the children of Tubal, and the children of Tubal were smitten before the children of Chittim, and the children of Chittim caused three hundred and seventy men to fall from the children of Tubal. 4 And at that time the children of Tubal swore to the children of Chittim, saying, "You will not intermarry among us, and no man will give his daughter to any of the sons of Chittim." 5 For all the daughters of Tubal were in those days fair, for no women were then found in the whole earth so fair as the daughters of Tubal. 6 And all who delighted in the beauty of women went to

the daughters of Tubal and took wives from them, and the sons of men, kings and princes, who greatly delighted in the beauty of women, took wives in those days from the daughters of Tubal. 7 And at the end of three years after the children of Tubal had sworn to the children of Chittim not to give them their daughters for wives, about twenty men of the children of Chittim went to take some of the daughters of Tubal, but they found none. 8 For the children of Tubal kept their oaths not to intermarry with them, and they would not break their oaths. 9 And in the days of harvest the children of Tubal went into their fields to get in their harvest, when the young men of Chittim assembled and went to the city of Sabinah, and each man took a young woman from the daughters of Tubal, and they came to their cities. 10 And the children of Tubal heard of it and they went to make war with them, and they could not prevail over them, for the mountain was exceedingly high from them, and when they saw they could not prevail over them they returned to their land. 11 And at the revolution of the year the children of Tubal went and hired about ten thousand men from those cities that were near them, and they went to war with the children of Chittim. 12 And the children of Tubal went to war with the children of Chittim, to destroy their land and to distress them, and in this engagement the children of Tubal prevailed over the children of Chittim, and the children of Chittim, seeing that they were greatly distressed, lifted up the children which they had had by the daughters of Tubal, upon the wall which had been built, to be before the eyes of the children of Tubal. 13 And the children of Chittim said to them, "Have you come to make war with your own sons and daughters, and have we not been considered your flesh and bones from that time until now?" 14 And when the children of Tubal heard this they ceased to make war with the children of Chittim, and they went away. 15 And they returned to their cities, and the children of Chittim at that time assembled and built two cities by the sea, and they called one Purtu and the other Ariza. 16 And Abram the son of Terah was then ninety-nine years old. 17 At that time the Lord appeared to him and he said to him, "I will make my covenant between me and you, and I will greatly multiply your seed, and this is the covenant which I make between me and you, that every male child be circumcised, you and your seed after you. 18 At eight days old will it be circumcised, and this covenant will be in your flesh for an everlasting covenant. 19 And now therefore your name will no more be called Abram but Abraham, and your wife will no more be called Sarai but Sarah. 20 For I will bless you both, and I will multiply your seed after you that you will become a great nation, and kings will come out from you."

CHAPTER 18

1 And Abraham rose and did all that God had ordered him, and he took the men of his household and those bought with his money, and he circumcised them as the Lord had commanded him. 2 And there was not one left whom he did not circumcise, and Abraham and his son Ishmael were circumcised in the flesh of their foreskin; thirteen years old was Ishmael when he was circumcised in the flesh of his foreskin. 3 And in the third day Abraham went out of his tent and sat at the door to enjoy the heat of the sun, during the pain of his flesh. 4 And the Lord appeared to him in the plain of Mamre and sent three of his ministering angels to visit him, and he was sitting at the door of the tent, and he lifted his eyes and saw, and, behold, three men were coming from a distance, and he rose up and ran to meet them, and he bowed down to them and brought them into his house. 5 And he said to them, "If now I have found favor in your sight, turn in and eat a morsel of bread"; and he pressed them, and they turned in and he gave them water and they washed their feet, and he placed them under a tree at the door of the tent. 6 And Abraham ran and took a calf, tender and good, and he hastened to kill it, and gave it to his servant Eliezer to dress. 7 And Abraham came to Sarah into the tent, and he said to her, "Make ready quickly three measures of fine meal, knead it and make cakes to cover the pot containing the meat," and she did so. 8 And Abraham hastened and brought before them butter and milk, beef and mutton, and gave it before them to eat before the flesh of the calf was sufficiently done, and they did eat. 9 And when they had done eating one of them said to him, "I will return to you according to the time of life, and Sarah your wife will have a son." 10 And the men afterward departed and went their ways, to the places to which they were sent. 11 In those days all the people of Sodom and Gomorrah, and of the whole five cities, were exceedingly wicked and sinful against the Lord and they provoked the Lord with their abominations, and they strengthened in aging

abominably and scornfully before the Lord, and their wickedness and crimes were in those days great before the Lord. **12** And they had in their land a very extensive valley, about half a day's walk, and in it there were fountains of water and a great deal of herbage surrounding the water. **13** And all the people of Sodom and Gomorrah went there four times in the year, with their wives and children and all belonging to them, and they rejoiced there with timbrels and dances. **14** And in the time of rejoicing they would all rise and lay hold of their neighbor's wives, and some, the virgin daughters of their neighbors, and they enjoyed them, and each man saw his wife and daughter in the hands of his neighbor and did not say a word. **15** And they did so from morning to night, and they afterward returned home each man to his house and each woman to her tent; so they always did four times in the year. **16** Also when a stranger came into their cities and brought goods which he had purchased with a view to dispose of there, the people of these cities would assemble, men, women and children, young and old, and go to the man and take his goods by force, giving a little to each man until there was an end to all the goods of the owner which he had brought into the land. **17** And if the owner of the goods quarreled with them, saying, "What is this work which you have done to me," then they would approach to him one by one, and each would show him the little which he took and taunt him, saying, "I only took that little which you did give me"; and when he heard this from them all, he would arise and go from them in sorrow and bitterness of soul, when they would all arise and go after him, and drive him out of the city with great noise and tumult. **18** And there was a man from the country of Elam who was leisurely going on the road, seated upon his ass, which carried a fine mantle of varying colors, and the mantle was bound with a cord upon the ass. **19** And the man was on his journey passing through the street of Sodom when the sun set in the evening, and he remained there in order to abide during the night, but no one would let him into his house; and at that time there was in Sodom a wicked and mischievous man, one skillful to do evil, and his name was Hedad. **20** And he lifted up his eyes and saw the traveler in the street of the city, and he came to him and said, "From where do you come and to where do you go?" **21** And the man said to him, "I am traveling from Hebron to Elam

where I belong, and as I passed the sun set and no one would suffer me to enter his house, though I had bread and water and also straw and provender for my ass, and am short of nothing." **22** And Hedad answered and said to him, "All that you will want will be supplied by me, but in the street you will not abide all night." **23** And Hedad brought him to his house, and he took off the mantle from the ass with the cord, and brought them to his house, and he gave the ass straw and provender while the traveler ate and drank in Hedad's house, and he stayed there that night. **24** And in the morning the traveler rose up early to continue his journey, when Hedad said to him, "Wait, comfort your heart with a morsel of bread and then go," and the man did so; and he remained with him, and they both ate and drank together during the day, when the man rose up to go. **25** And Hedad said to him, "Behold now the day is declining, you had better remain all night that your heart may be comforted"; and he pressed him so that he tarried there all night, and on the second day he rose up early to go away, when Hedad pressed him, saying, "Comfort your heart with a morsel of bread and then go," and he remained and ate with him also the second day, and then the man rose up to continue his journey. **26** And Hedad said to him, "Behold now the day is declining, remain with me to comfort your heart and in the morning rise up early and go your way." **27** And the man would not remain, but rose and saddled his ass, and while he was saddling his ass the wife of Hedad said to her husband, "Behold this man has remained with us for two days eating and drinking and he has given us nothing, and now will he go away from us without giving anything?" and Hedad said to her, "Be silent." **28** And the man saddled his ass to go, and he asked Hedad to give him the cord and mantle to tie it upon the ass. **29** And Hedad said to him, "What say you?" And he said to him, "That you my lord will give me the cord and the mantle made with varying colors which you did conceal with you in your house to take care of it." **30** And Hedad answered the man, saying, "This is the interpretation of your dream, the cord which you did see, means that your life will be lengthened out like a cord, and having seen the mantle colored with all sorts of colors, means that you will have a vineyard in which you will plant trees of all fruits." **31** And the traveler answered, saying, "Not so my lord, for I was awake when I gave you the cord and also a mantle woven with different colors, which you did take off the ass to put them by for me"; and Hedad answered and said, "Surely I have told you the interpretation of your dream and it is a good dream, and this is the interpretation thereof. 32 Now the sons of men give me four pieces of silver, which is my charge for interpreting dreams, and of you only I require three pieces of silver." 33 And the man was provoked at the words of Hedad, and he cried bitterly, and he brought Hedad to Serak judge of Sodom. 34 And the man laid his cause before Serak the judge, when Hedad replied, saying, "It is not so, but thus the matter stands"; and the judge said to the traveler, "This man Hedad tells you the truth, for he is famed in the cities for the accurate interpretation of dreams." 35 And the man cried at the word of the judge, and he said, "Not so my Lord, for it was in the day that I gave him the cord and mantle which was upon the ass, in order to put them by in his house"; and they both disputed before the judge, the one saying, "Thus the matter was," and the other declaring otherwise. 36 And Hedad said to the man, "Give me four pieces of silver that I charge for my interpretations of dreams; I will not make any allowance; and give me the expense of the four meals that you did eat in my house." 37 And the man said to Hedad, "Truly I will pay you for what I ate in your house, only give me the cord and mantle which you did conceal in your house." 38 And Hedad replied before the judge and said to the man, "Did I not tell you the interpretation of your dream? The cord means that your days will be prolonged like a cord, and the mantle, that you will have a vineyard in which you will plant all kinds of fruit trees. 39 This is the proper interpretation of your dream, now give me the four pieces of silver that I require as a compensation, for I will make you no allowance." 40 And the man cried at the words of Hedad and they both quarreled before the judge, and the judge gave orders to his servants, who drove them rashly from the house. 41 And they went away quarreling from the judge, when the people of Sodom heard them, and they gathered about them and they exclaimed against the stranger, and they drove him rashly from the city. 42 And the man continued his journey upon his ass with bitterness of soul, lamenting and weeping. 43 And while he was going along he wept at what had happened to him in the corrupt city of Sodom.

CHAPTER 19

1 And the cities of Sodom had four judges to four cities, and these were their names, Serak in the city of Sodom, Sharkad in Gomorrah, Zabnac in Admah, and Menon in Zeboyim. 2 And Eliezer Abraham's servant applied to them different names, and he converted Serak to Shakra, Sharkad to Shakrura, Zebnac to Kezobim, and Menon to Matzlodin. 3 And by desire of their four judges the people of Sodom and Gomorrah had beds erected in the streets of the cities, and if a man came to these places they laid hold of him and brought him to one of their beds, and by force made him to lie in them. 4 And as he lay down, three men would stand at his head and three at his feet, and measure him by the length of the bed, and if the man was less than the bed these six men would stretch him at each end, and when he cried out to them they would not answer him. 5 And if he was longer than the bed they would draw together the two sides of the bed at each end, until the man had reached the gates of death. 6 And if he continued to cry out to them, they would answer him, saying, "Thus will it be done to a man that comes into our land." 7 And when men heard all these things that the people of the cities of Sodom did, they refrained from coming there. 8 And when a poor man came to their land they would give him silver and gold, and cause a proclamation in the whole city not to give him a morsel of bread to eat, and if the stranger should remain there some days, and die from hunger, not having been able to obtain a morsel of bread, then at his death all the people of the city would come and take their silver and gold which they had given to him. 9 And those that could recognize the silver or gold which they had given him took it back, and at his death they also stripped him of his garments, and they would fight about them, and he that prevailed over his neighbor took them. 10 They would after that carry him and bury him under some of the shrubs in the deserts; so they did all the days to anyone that came to them and died in their land. 11 And in the course of time Sarah sent Eliezer to Sodom, to see Lot and inquire after his welfare. 12 And Eliezer went to Sodom, and he met a man of Sodom fighting with a stranger, and the man of Sodom stripped the poor man of all his clothes and went away. 13 And this poor man cried to Eliezer and supplicated his favor on account of what the man of Sodom had done to him. 14 And he said to him, "Why do you

act thus to the poor man who came to your land?" **15** And the man of Sodom answered Eliezer, saying, "Is this man your brother, or have the people of Sodom made you a judge this day, that you speak about this man?" **16** And Eliezer strove with the man of Sodom on account of the poor man, and when Eliezer approached to recover the poor man's clothes from the man of Sodom, he hastened and with a stone smote Eliezer in the forehead. **17** And the blood flowed copiously from Eliezer's forehead, and when the man saw the blood he caught hold of Eliezer, saying, "Give me my hire for having rid you of this bad blood that was in your forehead, for such is the custom and the law in our land." **18** And Eliezer said to him, "You have wounded me and require me to pay you your hire"; and Eliezer would not hearken to the words of the man of Sodom. **19** And the man laid hold of Eliezer and brought him to Shakra the judge of Sodom for judgment. **20** And the man spoke to the judge, saying, "I implore you my lord, thus has this man done, for I smote him with a stone that the blood flowed from his forehead, and he is unwilling to give me my hire." **21** And the judge said to Eliezer, "This man speaks truth to you, give him his hire, for this is the custom in our land"; and Eliezer heard the words of the judge, and he lifted up a stone and smote the judge, and the stone struck on his forehead, and the blood flowed copiously from the forehead of the judge, and Eliezer said, "If this then is the custom in your land give you unto this man what I should have given him, for this has been your decision, you did decree it." **22** And Eliezer left the man of Sodom with the judge, and he went away. **23** And when the kings of Elam had made war with the kings of Sodom, the kings of Elam captured all the property of Sodom, and they took Lot captive, with his property, and when it was told to Abraham he went and made war with the kings of Elam, and he recovered from their hands all the property of Lot as well as the property of Sodom. **24** At that time the wife of Lot bore him a daughter, and he called her name Paltith, saying, Because God had delivered him and his whole household from the kings of Elam; and Paltith daughter of Lot grew up, and one of the men of Sodom took her for a wife. **25** And a poor man came into the city to seek a maintenance, and he remained in the city some days, and all the people of Sodom caused a proclamation of their custom not to give this man a morsel of bread to eat, until he dropped

dead upon the earth, and they did so. **26** And Paltith the daughter of Lot saw this man lying in the streets starved with hunger, and no one would give him anything to keep him alive, and he was just upon the point of death. **27** And her soul was filled with pity on account of the man, and she fed him secretly with bread for many days, and the soul of this man was revived. **28** For when she went out to fetch water she would put the bread in the water pitcher, and when she came to the place where the poor man was, she took the bread from the pitcher and gave it to him to eat; so she did many days. **29** And all the people of Sodom and Gomorrah wondered how this man could bear starvation for so many days. **30** And they said to each other, "This can only be that he eats and drinks, for no man can bear starvation for so many days or live as this man has, without even his countenance changing"; and three men concealed themselves in a place where the poor man was stationed, to know who it was that brought him bread to eat. **31** And Paltith daughter of Lot went out that day to fetch water, and she put bread into her pitcher of water, and she went to draw water by the poor man's place, and she took out the bread from the pitcher and gave it to the poor man and he ate it. **32** And the three men saw what Paltith did to the poor man, and they said to her, "It is you then who have supported him, and therefore has he not starved, nor changed in appearance nor died like the rest." **33** And the three men went out of the place in which they were concealed, and they seized Paltith and the bread which was in the poor man's hand. **34** And they took Paltith and brought her before their judges, and they said to them, "Thus did she do, and it is she who supplied the poor man with bread, therefore did he not die all this time; now therefore declare to us the punishment due to this woman for having transgressed our law." **35** And the people of Sodom and Gomorrah assembled and kindled a fire in the street of the city, and they took the woman and cast her into the fire and she was burned to ashes. **36** And in the city of Admah there was a woman to whom they did the like. **37** For a traveler came into the city of Admah to abide there all night, with the intention of going home in the morning, and he sat opposite the door of the house of the young woman's father, to remain there, as the sun had set when he had reached that place; and the young woman saw him sitting by the door of the house. **38** And he asked her for a drink of water and she said to him, "Who are you?" And he said to her, "I was this day going on the road, and reached here when the sun set, so I will abide here all night, and in the morning I will arise early and continue my journey." 39 And the young woman went into the house and fetched the man bread and water to eat and drink. 40 And this affair became known to the people of Admah, and they assembled and brought the young woman before the judges, that they should judge her for this act. 41 And the judge said, "The judgment of death must pass upon this woman because she transgressed our law, and this therefore is the decision concerning her." 42 And the people of those cities assembled and brought out the young woman, and anointed her with honey from head to foot, as the judge had decreed, and they placed her before a swarm of bees which were then in their hives, and the bees flew upon her and stung her that her whole body was swelled. 43 And the young woman cried out on account of the bees, but no one took notice of her or pitied her, and her cries ascended to heaven. 44 And the Lord was provoked at this and at all the works of the cities of Sodom, for they had abundance of food, and had tranquility among them, and still would not sustain the poor and the needy, and in those days their evil doings and sins became great before the Lord. 45 And the Lord sent for two of the angels that had come to Abraham's house, to destroy Sodom and its cities. 46 And the angels rose up from the door of Abraham's tent, after they had eaten and drunk, and they reached Sodom in the evening, and Lot was then sitting in the gate of Sodom, and when he saw them he rose to meet them, and he bowed down to the ground. 47 And he pressed them greatly and brought them into his house, and he gave them victuals which they ate, and they stayed all night in his house. 48 And the angels said to Lot, "Arise, go out from this place, you and all belonging to you, lest you be consumed in the iniquity of this city, for the Lord will destroy this place." 49 And the angels laid hold upon the hand of Lot and upon the hand of his wife, and upon the hands of his children, and all belonging to him, and they brought him out and set him outside the cities. 50 And they said to Lot, "Escape for your life," and he fled and all belonging to him. 51 Then the Lord rained upon Sodom and upon Gomorrah and upon all these cities brimstone and fire from the Lord out of heaven. 52 And he overthrew these cities, all the plain and all the inhabitants

of the cities, and that which grew upon the ground; and Ado the wife of Lot looked back to see the destruction of the cities, for her compassion was moved on account of her daughters who remained in Sodom, for they did not go with her. 53 And when she looked back she became a pillar of salt, and it is yet in that place unto this day. 54 And the oxen which stood in that place daily licked up the salt to the extremities of their feet, and in the morning it would spring out afresh, and they again licked it up unto this day. 55 And Lot and two of his daughters that remained with him fled and escaped to the cave of Adullam, and they remained there for some time. 56 And Abraham rose up early in the morning to see what had been done to the cities of Sodom; and he looked and beheld the smoke of the cities going up like the smoke of a furnace. 57 And Lot and his two daughters remained in the cave, and they made their father drink wine, and they lay with him, for they said there was no man upon earth that could raise up seed from them, for they thought that the whole earth was destroyed. 58 And they both lay with their father, and they conceived and bore sons, and the firstborn called the name of her son Moab, saying, "From my father did I conceive him"; he is the father of the Moabites unto this day. 59 And the younger also called her son Benami; he is the father of the children of Ammon unto this day. 60 And after this Lot and his two daughters went away from there, and he dwelt on the other side of the Jordan with his two daughters and their sons, and the sons of Lot grew up, and they went and took themselves wives from the land of Canaan, and they begat children and they were fruitful and multiplied.

CHAPTER 20

1 And at that time Abraham journeyed from the plain of Mamre, and he went to the land of the Philistines, and he dwelt in Gerar; it was in the twenty-fifth year of Abraham's being in the land of Canaan, and the hundredth year of the life of Abraham, that he came to Gerar in the land of the Philistines. 2 And when they entered the land he said to Sarah his wife, "Say you are my sister, to anyone that will ask you, in order that we may escape the evil of the inhabitants of the land." 3 And as Abraham was dwelling in the land of the Philistines, the servants of Abimelech, king of the Philistines, saw that Sarah was exceedingly beautiful, and they asked Abraham concerning her, and he

said, "She is my sister." **4** And the servants of Abimelech went to Abimelech, saying, "A man from the land of Canaan is come to dwell in the land, and he has a sister that is exceedingly fair." **5** And Abimelech heard the words of his servants who praised Sarah to him, and Abimelech sent his officers, and they brought Sarah to the king. **6** And Sarah came to the house of Abimelech, and the king saw that Sarah was beautiful, and she pleased him exceedingly. **7** And he approached her and said to her, "What is that man to you with whom you did come to our land? And Sarah answered and said, "He is my brother, and we came from the land of Canaan to dwell wherever we could find a place." **8** And Abimelech said to Sarah, "Behold my land is before you, place your brother in any part of this land that pleases you, and it will be our duty to exalt and elevate him above all the people of the land since he is your brother." **9** And Abimelech sent for Abraham, and Abraham came to Abimelech. **10** And Abimelech said to Abraham, "Behold I have given orders that you will be honored as you desire on account of your sister Sarah." **11** And Abraham went out from the king, and the king's present followed him. **12** As at evening time, before men lie down to rest, the king was sitting upon his throne, and a deep sleep fell upon him, and he lay upon the throne and slept until morning. **13** And he dreamed that an angel of the Lord came to him with a drawn sword in his hand, and the angel stood over Abimelech, and wished to slay him with the sword, and the king was terrified in his dream, and said to the angel, "In what have I sinned against you that you come to slay me with your sword?" **14** And the angel answered and said to Abimelech, "Behold you die on account of the woman which you did last night bring to your house, for she is a married woman, the wife of Abraham who came to your house; now therefore return that man his wife, for she is his wife; and should you not return her, know that you will surely die, you and all belonging to you." **15** And on that night there was a great outcry in the land of the Philistines, and the inhabitants of the land saw the figure of a man standing with a drawn sword in his hand, and he smote the inhabitants of the land with the sword, yea he continued to smite them. **16** And the angel of the Lord smote the whole land of the Philistines on that night, and there was a great confusion on that night and on the following morning. **17** And every womb was closed, and all their issues, and the hand of the Lord was upon them on account of Sarah, wife of Abraham, whom Abimelech had taken. **18** And in the morning Abimelech rose with terror and confusion and with a great dread, and he sent and had his servants called in, and he related his dream to them, and the people were greatly afraid. **19** And one man standing among the servants of the king answered the king, saying, "O sovereign king, restore this woman to her husband, for he is her husband, for the like happened to the king of Egypt when this man came to Egypt." **20** And he said concerning his wife, "She is my sister, for such is his manner of doing when he comes to dwell in the land in which he is a stranger. **21** And Pharaoh sent and took this woman for a wife and the Lord brought upon him grievous plagues until he returned the woman to her husband. **22** Now therefore, O sovereign king, know what happened last night to the whole land, for there was a very great consternation and great pain and lamentation, and we know that it was on account of the woman which you did take. **23** Now, therefore, restore this woman to her husband, lest it should befall us as it did to Pharaoh king of Egypt and his subjects, and that we may not die"; and Abimelech hastened and called and had Sarah called for, and she came before him, and he had Abraham called for, and he came before him. **24** And Abimelech said to them, "What is this work you have been doing in saying you are brother and sister, and I took this woman for a wife?" **25** And Abraham said, "Because I thought I should suffer death on account of my wife"; and Abimelech took flocks and herds, and menservants and maidservants, and a thousand pieces of silver, and he gave them to Abraham, and he returned Sarah to him. **26** And Abimelech said to Abraham, "Behold the whole land is before you, dwell in it wherever you will choose." **27** And Abraham and Sarah, his wife, went out from the king's presence with honor and respect, and they dwelt in the land, even in Gerar. **28** And all the inhabitants of the land of the Philistines and the king's servants were still in pain, through the plague which the angel had inflicted upon them the whole night on account of Sarah. **29** And Abimelech sent for Abraham, saying, "Pray now for your servants to the Lord your God, that he may put away this mortality from among us." **30** And Abraham prayed on account of Abimelech and his subjects, and the

Lord heard the prayer of Abraham, and he healed Abimelech and all his subjects.

CHAPTER 21

1 And it was at that time at the end of a year and four months of Abraham's dwelling in the land of the Philistines in Gerar, that God visited Sarah, and the Lord remembered her, and she conceived and bore a son to Abraham. 2 And Abraham called the name of the son which was born to him, which Sarah bore to him, Isaac. 3 And Abraham circumcised his son Isaac at eight days old, as God had commanded Abraham to do unto his seed after him; and Abraham was one hundred, and Sarah ninety years old, when Isaac was born to them. 4 And the child grew up and he was weaned, and Abraham made a great feast upon the day that Isaac was weaned. 5 And Shem and Eber and all the great people of the land, and Abimelech king of the Philistines, and his servants, and Phicol, the captain of his host, came to eat and drink and rejoice at the feast which Abraham made upon the day of his son Isaac's being weaned. 6 Also Terah, the father of Abraham, and Nahor his brother, came from Haran, they and all belonging to them, for they greatly rejoiced on hearing that a son had been born to Sarah. 7 And they came to Abraham, and they ate and drank at the feast which Abraham made upon the day of Isaac's being weaned. 8 And Terah and Nahor rejoiced with Abraham, and they remained with him many days in the land of the Philistines. 9 At that time Serug the son of Reu died, in the first year of the birth of Isaac son of Abraham. 10 And all the days of Serug were two hundred and thirty-nine years, and he died. 11 And Ishmael the son of Abraham was grown up in those days; he was fourteen years old when Sarah bare Isaac to Abraham. 12 And God was with Ishmael the son of Abraham, and he grew up, and he learned to use the bow and became an archer. 13 And when Isaac was five years old he was sitting with Ishmael at the door of the tent. 14 And Ishmael came to Isaac and seated himself opposite to him, and he took the bow and drew it and put the arrow in it and intended to slay Isaac. 15 And Sarah saw the act which Ishmael desired to do to her son Isaac, and it grieved her exceedingly on account of her son, and she sent for Abraham, and said to him, "Cast out this bondwoman and her son, for her son will not be heir with my son, for thus did he seek to do unto him this day." 16 And Abraham hearkened to the voice of Sarah, and

he rose up early in the morning, and he took twelve loaves and a bottle of water which he gave to Hagar, and sent her away with her son, and Hagar went with her son to the wilderness, and they dwelt in the wilderness of Paran with the inhabitants of the wilderness, and Ishmael was an archer, and he dwelt in the wilderness a long time. 17 And he and his mother afterward went to the land of Egypt, and they dwelt there, and Hagar took a wife for her son from Egypt, and her name was Meribah. 18 And the wife of Ishmael conceived and bare four sons and two daughters, and Ishmael and his mother and his wife and children afterward went and returned to the wilderness. 19 And they made themselves tents in the wilderness, in which they dwelt, and they continued to travel and then to rest monthly and yearly. 20 And God gave Ishmael flocks and herds and tents on account of Abraham his father, and the man increased in cattle. 21 And Ishmael dwelt in deserts and in tents, traveling and resting for a long time, and he did not see the face of his father. 22 And in some time after, Abraham said to Sarah his wife, "I will go and see my son Ishmael, for I have a desire to see him, for I have not seen him for a long time." 23 And Abraham rode upon one of his camels to the wilderness to seek his son Ishmael, for he heard that he was dwelling in a tent in the wilderness with all belonging to him. 24 And Abraham went to the wilderness, and he reached the tent of Ishmael about noon, and he asked after Ishmael, and he found the wife of Ishmael sitting in the tent with her children, and Ishmael her husband and his mother were not with them. 25 And Abraham asked the wife of Ishmael, saying, "Where has Ishmael gone?" And she said, "He has gone to the field to hunt," and Abraham was still mounted upon the camel, for he would not get off to the ground as he had sworn to his wife Sarah that he would not get off from the camel. 26 And Abraham said to Ishmael's wife, "My daughter, give me a little water that I may drink, for I am fatigued from the journey." 27 And Ishmael's wife answered and said to Abraham, "We have neither water nor bread," and she continued sitting in the tent and did not notice Abraham, neither did she ask him who he was. 28 But she was beating her children in the tent, and she was cursing them, and she also cursed her husband Ishmael and reproached him, and Abraham heard the words of Ishmael's wife to her children, and he was very angry and displeased. 29 And Abraham called to the woman to come out to him from the tent, and the woman came and stood opposite to Abraham, for Abraham was still mounted upon the camel. **30** And Abraham said to Ishmael's wife, "When your husband Ishmael returns home say to him that **31** a very old man from the land of the Philistines came here to seek you, and thus was his appearance and figure; I did not ask him who he was, and seeing you were not here he spoke unto me and said, 'When Ishmael your husband returns tell him thus did this man say, *When you come home put away this nail of the tent which you have placed here, and place another nail in its stead.'* " **32** And Abraham finished his instructions to the woman, and he turned and went off on the camel homeward. **33** And after that Ishmael came from the chase he and his mother, and returned to the tent, and his wife spoke these words to him, **34** "A very old man from the land of the Philistines came to seek you, and thus was his appearance and figure; I did not ask him who he was, and seeing you were not at home he said to me, 'When your husband comes home tell him, thus says the old man, *Put away the nail of the tent which you have placed here and place another nail in its stead.'* " **35** And Ishmael heard the words of his wife, and he knew that it was his father, and that his wife did not honor him. **36** And Ishmael understood his father's words that he had spoken to his wife, and Ishmael hearkened to the voice of his father, and Ishmael cast off that woman and she went away. **37** And Ishmael afterward went to the land of Canaan, and he took another wife and he brought her to his tent to the place where he then dwelt. **38** And at the end of three years Abraham said, "I will go again and see Ishmael my son, for I have not seen him for a long time." **39** And he rode upon his camel and went to the wilderness, and he reached the tent of Ishmael about noon. **40** And he asked after Ishmael, and his wife came out of the tent and she said, "He is not here my lord, for he has gone to hunt in the fields, and to feed the camels," and the woman said to Abraham, "Turn in my lord into the tent, and eat a morsel of bread, for your soul must be wearied on account of the journey." **41** And Abraham said to her, "I will not stop for I am in haste to continue my journey, but give me a little water to drink, for I have thirst"; and the woman hastened and ran into the tent and she brought out water and bread to Abraham, which she placed before him and she urged him to eat, and he ate and drank and his heart was comforted and he blessed his son Ishmael. **42** And he finished his meal and he blessed the Lord, and he said to Ishmael's wife, "When Ishmael comes home say these words to him, **43** 'A very old man from the land of the Philistines came here and asked after you, and you were not here; and I brought him out bread and water and he ate and drank and his heart was comforted. **44** And he spoke these words to me: *When Ishmael your husband comes home, say unto him, The nail of the tent which you have is very good, do not put it away from the tent.'* " **45** And Abraham finished commanding the woman, and he rode off to his home to the land of the Philistines; and when Ishmael came to his tent his wife went out to meet him with joy and a cheerful heart. **46** And she said to him, "An old man came here from the land of the Philistines and thus was his appearance, and he asked after you and you were not here, so I brought out bread and water, and he ate and drank and his heart was comforted. **47** And he spoke these words to me, 'When Ishmael your husband comes home say to him, *The nail of the tent which you have is very good, do not put it away from the tent.'* " **48** And Ishmael knew that it was his father, and that his wife had honored him, and the Lord blessed Ishmael.

CHAPTER 22

1 And Ishmael then rose up and took his wife and his children and his cattle and all belonging to him, and he journeyed from there and he went to his father in the land of the Philistines. **2** And Abraham related to Ishmael his son the transaction with the first wife that Ishmael took, according to what she did. **3** And Ishmael and his children dwelt with Abraham many days in that land, and Abraham dwelt in the land of the Philistines a long time. **4** And the days increased and reached twenty six years, and after that Abraham with his servants and all belonging to him went from the land of the Philistines and removed to a great distance, and they came near to Hebron, and they remained there, and the servants of Abraham dug wells of water, and Abraham and all belonging to him dwelt by the water, and the servants of Abimelech king of the Philistines heard the report that Abraham's servants had dug wells of water in the borders of the land. **5** And they came and quarreled with the servants of Abraham, and they robbed them of the great well which they had dug. **6** And Abimelech king of the Philistines heard of this affair, and he with Phicol the captain of his host and twenty of his men came to Abraham, and Abimelech spoke to Abraham concerning his servants, and Abraham rebuked Abimelech concerning the well of which his servants had robbed him. **7** And Abimelech said to Abraham, "As the Lord lives who created the whole earth, I did not hear of the act which my servants did unto your servants until this day." **8** And Abraham took seven ewe lambs and gave them to Abimelech, saying, "Take these, I pray you, from my hands that it may be a testimony for me that I dug this well." **9** And Abimelech took the seven ewe lambs which Abraham had given to him, for he had also given him cattle and herds in abundance, and Abimelech swore to Abraham concerning the well, therefore he called that well Beersheba, for there they both swore concerning it. **10** And they both made a covenant in Beersheba, and Abimelech rose up with Phicol the captain of his host and all his men, and they returned to the land of the Philistines, and Abraham and all belonging to him dwelt in Beersheba and he was in that land a long time. **11** And Abraham planted a large grove in Beersheba, and he made to it four gates facing the four sides of the earth, and he planted a vineyard in it, so that if a traveler came to Abraham he entered any gate which was in his road and remained there and ate and drank and satisfied himself and then departed. **12** For the house of Abraham was always open to the sons of men that passed and repassed, who came daily to eat and drink in the house of Abraham. **13** And any man who had hunger and came to Abraham's house, Abraham would give him bread that he might eat and drink and be satisfied, and anyone that came naked to his house he would clothe with garments as he might choose and give him silver and gold and make known to him the Lord who had created him in the earth; this did Abraham all his life. **14** And Abraham and his children and all belonging to him dwelt in Beersheba, and he pitched his tent as far as Hebron. **15** And Abraham's brother Nahor and his father and all belonging to them dwelt in Haran, for they did not come with Abraham to the land of Canaan. **16** And children were born to Nahor which Milca the daughter of Haran, and sister to Sarah, Abraham's wife, bore to him. **17** And these are the names of those that were born to him, Uz, Buz, Kemuel, Kesed, Chazo, Pildash, Tidlaf, and Bethuel, being eight sons, these are the children of Milca which she bore to Nahor, Abraham's brother. **18** And Nahor had a concubine and her name was Reumah, and she also bore to Nahor, Zebach, Gachash, Tachash and Maacha, being four sons. **19** And the children that were born to Nahor were twelve sons besides his daughters, and they also had children born to them in Haran. **20** And the children of Uz the firstborn of Nahor were Abi, Cheref, Gadin, Melus, and Deborah their sister. **21** And the sons of Buz were Berachel, Naamath, Sheva, and Madonu. **22** And the sons of Kemuel were Aram and Rechob. **23** And the sons of Kesed were Anamlech, Meshai, Benon and Yifi; and the sons of Chazo were Pildash, Mechi and Opher. **24** And the sons of Pildash were Arud, Chamum, Mered and Moloch. **25** And the sons of Tidlaf were Mushan, Cushan and Mutzi. **26** And the children of Bethuel were Sechar, Laban and their sister Rebecca. **27** These are the families of the children of Nahor, that were born to them in Haran; and Aram the son of Kemuel and Rechob his brother went away from Haran, and they found a valley in the land by the river Euphrates. **28** And they built a city there, and they called the name of the city after the name of Pethor the son of Aram, that is Aram Naharayim unto this day. **29** And the children of Kesed also went to dwell where they could find a place, and they went and they found a valley opposite to the land of Shinar, and they dwelt there. **30** And they there built themselves a city, and they called the name at the city Kesed after the name of their father, that is the land Kasdim unto this day, and the Kasdim dwelt in that land and they were fruitful and multiplied exceedingly. **31** And Terah, father of Nahor and Abraham, went and took another wife in his old age, and her name was Pelilah, and she conceived and bore him a son and he called his name Zoba. **32** And Terah lived twenty-five years after he begat Zoba. **33** And Terah died in that year, that is in the thirty-fifth year of the birth of Isaac son of Abraham. **34** And the days of Terah were two hundred and five years, and he was buried in Haran. **35** And Zoba the son of Terah lived thirty years and he begat Aram, Achlis and Merik. **36** And Aram son of Zoba son of Terah, had three wives and he begat twelve sons and three daughters, and the Lord gave to Aram the son of Zoba, riches and possessions, and abundance of cattle, and flocks and herds, and the man increased greatly. **37** And Aram the son of Zoba and his brother and all his household journeyed from Haran, and they went to dwell where they should find a place, for their property was too great to remain in Haran; for they could not stop in Haran together with their brethren the children of Nahor. **38** And Aram the son of Zoba went with his brethren, and they found a valley at a distance toward the eastern country and they dwelt there. **39** And they also built a city there, and they called the name thereof Aram, after the name of their eldest brother; that is Aram Zoba to this day. **40** And Isaac the son of Abraham was growing up in those days, and Abraham his father taught him the way of the Lord to know the Lord, and the Lord was with him. **41** And when Isaac was thirty-seven years old, Ishmael his brother was going about with him in the tent. **42** And Ishmael boasted of himself to Isaac, saying, "I was thirteen years old when the Lord spoke to my father to circumcise us, and I did according to the word of the Lord which he spoke to my father, and I gave my soul unto the Lord, and I did not transgress his word which he commanded my father." **43** And Isaac answered Ishmael, saying, "Why do you boast to me about this, about a little bit of your flesh which you did take from your body, concerning which the Lord commanded you? **44** As the Lord lives, the God of my father Abraham, if the Lord should say unto my father, 'Take now your son Isaac and bring him up an offering before me,' I would not refrain but I would joyfully accede to it." **45** And the Lord heard the word that Isaac spoke to Ishmael, and it seemed good in the sight of the Lord, and he thought to try Abraham in this matter. **46** And the day arrived when the sons of God came and placed themselves before the Lord, and Satan also came with the sons of God before the Lord. **47** And the Lord said unto Satan, "From where do you come?" And Satan answered the Lord and said, "From going to and fro in the earth, and from walking up and down in it." **48** And the Lord said to Satan, "What is your word to me concerning all the children of the earth?" And Satan answered the Lord and said, "I have seen all the children of the earth who serve you and remember you when they require anything from you. **49** And when you give them the thing which they require from you, they sit at their ease, and forsake you and they remember you no more. **50** Have you seen Abraham the son of Terah, who at first had no children, and he served you and erected altars to you wherever he came, and he brought up offerings

upon them, and he proclaimed your name continually to all the children of the earth. **51** And now that his son Isaac is born to him, he has forsaken you, he has made a great feast for all the inhabitants of the land, and the Lord he has forgotten. **52** For amidst all that he has done he brought you no offering; neither burnt offering nor peace offering, neither ox, lamb nor goat of all that he killed on the day that his son was weaned. **53** Even from the time of his son's birth until now, being thirty-seven years, he built no altar before you, nor brought any offering to you, for he saw that you did give what he requested before you, and he therefore forsook you." **54** And the Lord said to Satan, "Have you thus considered my servant Abraham? For there is none like him upon earth, a perfect and an upright man before me, one that fears God and avoids evil; as I live, were I to say unto him, 'Bring up Isaac your son before me,' he would not withhold him from me, much more if I told him to bring up a burnt offering before me from his flock or herds." **55** And Satan answered the Lord and said, "Speak then now unto Abraham as you have said, and you will see whether he will not this day transgress and cast aside your words."

CHAPTER 23

1 At that time the word of the Lord came to Abraham, and he said unto him, "Abraham," and he said, "Here I am." **2** And he said to him, "Take now your son, your only son whom you love, even Isaac, and go to the land of Moriah, and offer him there for a burnt offering upon one of the mountains which will be shown to you, for there will you see a cloud and the glory of the Lord." **3** And Abraham said within himself, "How will I separate my son Isaac from Sarah his mother, in order to bring him up for a burnt offering before the Lord?" **4** And Abraham came into the tent, and he sat before Sarah his wife, and he spoke these words to her, **5** "My son Isaac is grown up and he has not for some time studied the service of his God, now tomorrow I will go and bring him to Shem, and Eber his son, and there he will learn the ways of the Lord, for they will teach him to know the Lord as well as to know that when he prays continually before the Lord, he will answer him, therefore there he will know the way of serving the Lord his God." **6** And Sarah said, "You have spoken well, go my lord and do unto him as you have said, but remove him not at a great distance from me, neither let him remain there too long, for my soul is bound within his soul." **7** And Abraham said unto Sarah, "My daughter, let us pray to the Lord our God that he may do good with us." **8** And Sarah took her son Isaac and he remained all that night with her, and she kissed and embraced him, and gave him instructions until morning. **9** And she said to him, "O my son, how can my soul separate itself from you?" And she still kissed him and embraced him, and she gave Abraham instructions concerning him. **10** And Sarah said to Abraham, "O my lord, I pray you take heed of your son, and place your eyes over him, for I have no other son nor daughter but him. **11** O forsake him not. If he be hungry give him bread, and if he be thirsty give him water to drink; do not let him go on foot, neither let him sit in the sun. **12** Neither let him go by himself in the road, neither force him from whatever he may desire, but do unto him as he may say to you." **13** And Sarah wept bitterly the whole night on account of Isaac, and she gave him instructions until morning. **14** And in the morning Sarah selected a very fine and beautiful garment from those garments which she had in the house, that Abimelech had given to her. **15** And she dressed Isaac her son therewith, and she put a turban upon his head, and she enclosed a precious stone in the top of the turban, and she gave them provision for the road, and they went out, and Isaac went with his father Abraham, and some of their servants accompanied them to see them off the road. **16** And Sarah went out with them, and she accompanied them upon the road to see them off, and they said to her, "Return to the tent." **17** And when Sarah heard the words of her son Isaac she wept bitterly, and Abraham her husband wept with her, and their son wept with them a great weeping; also those who went with them wept greatly. **18** And Sarah caught hold of her son Isaac, and she held him in her arms, and she embraced him and continued to weep with him, and Sarah said, "Who knows if after this day I will ever see you again?" **19** And they still wept together, Abraham, Sarah and Isaac, and all those that accompanied them on the road wept with them, and Sarah afterward turned away from her son, weeping bitterly, and all her menservants and maidservants returned with her to the tent. **20** And Abraham went with Isaac his son to bring him up as an offering before the Lord, as He had commanded him. **21** And Abraham took two of his young men

with him, Ishmael the son of Hagar and Eliezer his servant, and they went together with them, and while they were walking in the road the young men spoke these words to themselves, **22** and Ishmael said to Eliezer, "Now my father Abraham is going with Isaac to bring him up for a burnt offering to the Lord, as He commanded him. **23** Now when he returns he will give unto me all that he possesses, to inherit after him, for I am his firstborn." **24** And Eliezer answered Ishmael and said, "Surely Abraham did cast you away with your mother, and swear that you should not inherit anything of all he possesses, and to whom will he give all that he has, with all his treasures, but unto me his servant, who has been faithful in his house, who has served him night and day, and has done all that he desired me? To me will he bequeath at his death all that he possesses." **25** And while Abraham was proceeding with his son Isaac along the road, Satan came and appeared to Abraham in the figure of a very aged man, humble and of contrite spirit, and he approached Abraham and said to him, "Are you silly or brutish, that you go to do this thing this day to your only son? **26** For God gave you a son in your latter days, in your old age, and will you go and slaughter him this day because he committed no violence, and will you cause the soul of your only son to perish from the earth? **27** Do you not know and understand that this thing cannot be from the Lord? For the Lord cannot do unto man such evil upon earth to say to him, 'Go slaughter your child.' " **28** And Abraham heard this and knew that it was the word of Satan who endeavored to draw him aside from the way of the Lord, but Abraham would not hearken to the voice of Satan, and Abraham rebuked him so that he went away. **29** And Satan returned and came to Isaac; and he appeared unto Isaac in the figure of a young man comely and well favored. **30** And he approached Isaac and said unto him, "Do you not know and understand that your old silly father brings you to the slaughter this day for no reason? **31** Now therefore, my son, do not listen nor attend to him, for he is a silly old man, and let not your precious soul and beautiful figure be lost from the earth." **32** And Isaac heard this, and said unto Abraham, "Have you heard, my father, that which this man has spoken? Even thus has he spoken." **33** And Abraham answered his son Isaac and said to him, "Take heed of him and do not listen to his words, nor attend to him, for he is Satan, endeavoring to draw us aside this day from the commands of God." **34** And Abraham still rebuked Satan, and Satan went from them, and seeing he could not prevail over them he hid himself from them, and he went and passed before them in the road; and he transformed himself to a large brook of water in the road, and Abraham and Isaac and his two young men reached that place, and they saw a brook large and powerful as the mighty waters. **35** And they entered the brook and passed through it, and the waters at first reached their legs. **36** And they went deeper in the brook and the waters reached up to their necks, and they were all terrified on account of the water; and while they were going over the brook Abraham recognized that place, and he knew that there was no water there before. **37** And Abraham said to his son Isaac, "I know this place in which there was no brook nor water, now therefore it is this Satan who does all this to us, to draw us aside this day from the commands of God." **38** And Abraham rebuked him and said unto him, "The Lord rebuke you, O Satan, begone from us for we go by the commands of God." **39** And Satan was terrified at the voice of Abraham, and he went away from them, and the place again became dry land as it was at first. **40** And Abraham went with Isaac toward the place that God had told him. **41** And on the third day Abraham lifted up his eyes and saw the place at a distance which God had told him of. **42** And a pillar of fire appeared to him that reached from the earth to heaven, and a cloud of glory upon the mountain, and the glory of the Lord was seen in the cloud. **43** And Abraham said to Isaac, "My son, do you see in that mountain, which we perceive at a distance, that which I see upon it?" **44** And Isaac answered and said unto his father, "I see and, behold, a pillar of fire and a cloud, and the glory of the Lord is seen upon the cloud." **45** And Abraham knew that his son Isaac was accepted before the Lord for a burnt offering. **46** And Abraham said unto Eliezer and unto Ishmael his son, "Do you also see that which we see upon the mountain which is at a distance? **47** And they answered and said, "We see nothing more than like the other mountains of the earth." And Abraham knew that they were not accepted before the Lord to go with them, and Abraham said to them, "Abide here with the ass while I and Isaac my son will go to yonder mount and worship there before the Lord and then return to you." **48** And Eliezer and Ishmael remained

in that place, as Abraham had commanded. **49** And Abraham took wood for a burnt offering and placed it upon his son Isaac, and he took the fire and the knife, and they both went to that place. **50** And when they were going along Isaac said to his father, "Behold, I see here the fire and wood, and where then is the lamb that is to be the burnt offering before the Lord?" **51** And Abraham answered his son Isaac, saying, "The Lord has made choice of you my son, to be a perfect burnt offering instead of the lamb." **52** And Isaac said unto his father, "I will do all that the Lord spoke to you with joy and cheerfulness of heart." **53** And Abraham again said unto Isaac his son, "Is there in your heart any thought or counsel concerning this, which is not proper? Tell me my son, I pray you, O my son conceal it not from me." **54** And Isaac answered his father Abraham and said unto him, "O my father, as the Lord lives and as your soul lives, there is nothing in my heart to cause me to deviate either to the right or to the left from the word that he has spoken to you. **55** Neither limb nor muscle has moved or stirred at this, nor is there in my heart any thought or evil counsel concerning this. **56** But I am of joyful and cheerful heart in this matter, and I say, 'Blessed is the Lord who has this day chosen me to be a burnt offering before Him.' " **57** And Abraham greatly rejoiced at the words of Isaac, and they went on and came together to that place that the Lord had spoken of. **58** And Abraham approached to build the altar in that place, and Abraham was weeping, and Isaac took stones and mortar until they had finished building the altar. **59** And Abraham took the wood and placed it in order upon the altar which he had built. **60** And he took his son Isaac and bound him in order to place him upon the wood which was upon the altar, to slay him for a burnt offering before the Lord. **61** And Isaac said to his father, "Bind me securely and then place me upon the altar lest I should turn and move and break loose from the force of the knife upon my flesh and thereof profane the burnt offering"; and Abraham did so. **62** And Isaac still said to his father, "O my father, when you will have slain me and burnt me for an offering, take with you that which will remain of my ashes to bring to Sarah my mother, and say to her, 'This is the sweet smelling savor of Isaac; but do not tell her this if she should sit near a well or upon any high place, lest she should cast her soul after me and die.' " **63** And Abraham heard the words of Isaac, and he lifted up his voice and wept when Isaac spoke these words; and Abraham's tears gushed down upon Isaac his son, and Isaac wept bitterly, and he said to his father, "Hasten you, O my father, and do with me the will of the Lord our God as He has commanded you." **64** And the hearts of Abraham and Isaac rejoiced at this thing which the Lord had commanded them; but the eye wept bitterly while the heart rejoiced. **65** And Abraham bound his son Isaac, and placed him on the altar upon the wood, and Isaac stretched out his neck upon the altar before his father, and Abraham stretched out his hand to take the knife to slay his son as a burnt offering before the Lord. **66** At that time the angels of mercy came before the Lord and spoke to him concerning Isaac, saying, **67** "O Lord, you are a merciful and compassionate King over all that you have created in heaven and in earth, and you support them all; give therefore ransom and redemption instead of your servant Isaac, and pity and have compassion upon Abraham and Isaac his son, who are this day performing your commands. **68** Have you seen, O Lord, how Isaac the son of Abraham your servant is bound down to the slaughter like an animal? Now therefore let your pity be roused for them, O Lord." **69** At that time the Lord appeared unto Abraham, and called to him, from heaven, and said unto him, "Lay not your hand upon the lad, neither do you anything unto him, for now I know that you fear God in performing this act, and in not withholding your son, your only son, from me." **70** And Abraham lifted up his eyes and saw, and behold, a ram was caught in a thicket by his horns; that was the ram which the Lord God had created in the earth in the day that he made earth and heaven. **71** For the Lord had prepared this ram from that day, to be a burnt offering instead of Isaac. **72** And this ram was advancing to Abraham when Satan caught hold of him and entangled his horns in the thicket, that he might not advance to Abraham, in order that Abraham might slay his son. **73** And Abraham, seeing the ram advancing to him and Satan withholding him, fetched him and brought him before the altar, and he loosened his son Isaac from his binding, and he put the ram in his stead, and Abraham killed the ram upon the altar, and brought it up as an offering in the place of his son Isaac. **74** And Abraham sprinkled some of the blood of the ram upon the altar, and he exclaimed and said, "This is in the place of my son, and may this

be considered this day as the blood of my son before the Lord." **75** And all that Abraham did on this occasion by the altar, he would exclaim and say, "This is in the room of my son, and may it this day be considered before the Lord in the place of my son"; and Abraham finished the whole of the service by the altar, and the service was accepted before the Lord, and was accounted as if it had been Isaac; and the Lord blessed Abraham and his seed on that day. **76** And Satan went to Sarah, and he appeared to her in the figure of an old man very humble and meek, and Abraham was yet engaged in the burnt offering before the Lord. **77** And he said unto her, "Do you not know all the work that Abraham has made with your only son this day? For he took Isaac and built an altar, and killed him, and brought him up as a sacrifice upon the altar, and Isaac cried and wept before his father, but he looked not at him, neither did he have compassion over him." **78** And Satan repeated these words, and he went away from her, and Sarah heard all the words of Satan, and she imagined him to be an old man from among the sons of men who had been with her son and had come and told her these things. **79** And Sarah lifted up her voice and wept and cried out bitterly on account of her son; and she threw herself upon the ground and she cast dust upon her head, and she said, "O my son, Isaac my son, O that I had this day died instead of you." And she continued to weep and said, "It grieves me for you, O my son, my son Isaac, O that I had died this day in your stead." **80** And she still continued to weep, and said, "It grieves me for you after that I have reared you and have brought you up; now my joy is turned into mourning over you, I that had a longing for you, and cried and prayed to God until I bare you at ninety years old; and now have you served this day for the knife and the fire, to be made an offering. **81** But I console myself with you, my son, in its being the word of the Lord, for you did perform the command of your God; for who can transgress the word of our God, in whose hands is the soul of every living creature? **82** You are just, O Lord our God, for all your works are good and righteous; for I also am rejoiced with your word which you did command, and while mine eye weeps bitterly my heart rejoices." **83** And Sarah laid her head upon the bosom of one of her handmaids, and she became as still as a stone. **84** She afterward rose up and went about making inquiries until she came to Hebron, and she inquired of all those whom she met walking in the road, and no one could tell her what had happened to her son. **85** And she came with her maidservants and menservants to Kireath-arba, which is Hebron, and she asked concerning her Son, and she remained there while she sent some of her servants to seek where Abraham had gone with Isaac; they went to seek him in the house of Shem and Eber, and they could not find him, and they sought throughout the land and he was not there. **86** And behold, Satan came to Sarah in the shape of an old man, and he came and stood before her, and he said unto her, "I spoke falsely unto you, for Abraham did not kill his son and he is not dead"; and when she heard the word her joy was so exceedingly violent on account of her son, that her soul went out through joy; she died and was gathered to her people. **87** And when Abraham had finished his service he returned with his son Isaac to his young men, and they rose up and went together to Beersheba, and they came home. **88** And Abraham sought for Sarah, and could not find her, and he made inquiries concerning her, and they said unto him, "She went as far as Hebron to seek you both where you had gone, for thus was she informed." **89** And Abraham and Isaac went to her to Hebron, and when they found that she was dead they lifted up their voices and wept bitterly over her; and Isaac fell upon his mother's face and wept over her, and he said, "O my mother, my mother, how have you left me, and where have you gone? O how, how have you left me!" **90** And Abraham and Isaac wept greatly and all their servants wept with them on account of Sarah, and they mourned over her a great and heavy mourning.

CHAPTER 24

1 And the life of Sarah was one hundred and twenty-seven years, and Sarah died; and Abraham rose up from before his dead to seek a burial place to bury his wife Sarah; and he went and spoke to the children of Heth, the inhabitants of the land, saying, **2** "I am a stranger and a sojourner with you in your land; give me a possession of a burial place in your land, that I may bury my dead from before me." **3** And the children of Heth said unto Abraham, "Behold the land is before you, in the choice of our sepulchers bury your dead, for no man will withhold you from burying your dead." **4** And Abraham said unto them, "If you are agreeable to this go and entreat for me to Ephron, the son of Zochar, requesting

that he may give me the cave of Machpelah, which is in the end of his field, and I will purchase it of him for whatever he desires for it." **5** And Ephron dwelt among the children of Heth, and they went and called for him, and he came before Abraham, and Ephron said unto Abraham, "Behold all you require your servant will do"; and Abraham said, "No, but I will buy the cave and the field which you have for value, in order that it may be for a possession of a burial place forever." **6** And Ephron answered and said, "Behold the field and the cave are before you, give whatever you desire"; and Abraham said, "Only at full value will I buy it from your hand, and from the hands of those that go in at the gate of your city, and from the hand of your seed forever." **7** And Ephron and all his brethren heard this, and Abraham weighed to Ephron four hundred shekels of silver in the hands of Ephron and in the hands of all his brethren; and Abraham wrote this transaction, and he wrote it and testified to it with four witnesses. **8** And these are the names of the witnesses, Amigal son of Abishna the Hittite, Adichorom son of Ashunach the Hivite, Abdon son of Achiram the Gomerite, Bakdil the son of Abudish the Zidonite. **9** And Abraham took the book of the purchase, and placed it in his treasures, and these are the words that Abraham wrote in the book, namely: **10** That the cave and the field Abraham bought from Ephron the Hittite, and from his seed, and from those that go out of his city, and from their seed forever, are to be a purchase to Abraham and to his seed and to those that go out from his loins, for a possession of a burial place forever; and he put a signet to it and testified to it with witnesses. **11** And the field and the cave that was in it and all that place were made sure unto Abraham and unto his seed after him, from the children of Heth; behold it is before Mamre in Hebron, which is in the land of Canaan. **12** And after this Abraham buried his wife Sarah there, and that place and all its boundary became to Abraham and unto his seed for a possession of a burial place. **13** And Abraham buried Sarah with pomp as observed at the interment of kings, and she was buried in very fine and beautiful garments. **14** And at her bier was Shem, his sons Eber and Abimelech, together with Anar, Ashcol and Mamre, and all the noblemen of the land followed her bier. **15** And the days of Sarah were one hundred and twenty-seven years and she died, and Abraham made a great and heavy mourning, and he performed the rites of mourning for seven days. **16** And all the inhabitants of the land comforted Abraham and Isaac his son on account of Sarah. **17** And when the days of their mourning passed by Abraham sent away his son Isaac, and he went to the house of Shem and Eber, to learn the ways of the Lord and his instructions, and Abraham remained there three years. **18** At that time Abraham rose up with all his servants, and they went and returned homeward to Beersheba, and Abraham and all his servants remained in Beersheba. **19** And at the revolution of the year Abimelech king of the Philistines died in that year; he was one hundred and ninety-three years old at his death; and Abraham went with his people to the land of the Philistines, and they comforted the whole household and all his servants, and he then turned and went home. **20** And it was after the death of Abimelech that the people of Gerar took Benmalich his son, and he was only twelve years old, and they made him lie in the place of his father. **21** And they called his name Abimelech after the name of his father, for thus was it their custom to do in Gerar, and Abimelech reigned instead of Abimelech his father, and he sat upon his throne. **22** And Lot the son of Haran also died in those days, in the thirty-ninth year of the life of Isaac, and all the days that Lot lived were one hundred and forty years and he died. **23** And these are the children of Lot, that were born to him by his daughters, the name of the firstborn was Moab, and the name of the second was Benami. **24** And the two sons of Lot went and took themselves wives from the land of Canaan, and they bore children to them, and the children of Moab were Ed, Mayon, Tarsus, and Kanvil, four sons, these are fathers to the children of Moab unto this day. **25** And all the families of the children of Lot went to dwell wherever they should light upon, for they were fruitful and increased abundantly. **26** And they went and built themselves cities in the land where they dwelt, and they called the names of the cities which they built after their own names. **27** And Nahor the son of Terah, brother to Abraham, died in those days in the fortieth year of the life of Isaac, and all the days of Nahor were one hundred and seventy-two years and he died and was buried in Haran. **28** And when Abraham heard that his brother was dead he grieved sadly, and he mourned over his brother many days. **29** And Abraham called for Eliezer his head servant, to give him orders concerning his house, and he came and stood before him. **30** And Abraham said to him, "Behold I am old, I do not know the day of my death; for I am advanced in days; now therefore rise up, go out and do not take a wife for my son from this place and from this land, from the daughters of the Canaanites among whom we dwell. **31** But go to my land and to my birthplace, and take from there a wife for my son, and the Lord God of Heaven and earth who took me from my father's house and brought me to this place, and said unto me, 'To your seed will I give this land for an inheritance forever,' he will send his angel before you and prosper your way, that you may obtain a wife for my son from my family and from my father's house." **32** And the servant answered his master Abraham and said, "Behold I go to your birthplace and to your father's house, and take a wife for your son from there; but if the woman be not willing to follow me to this land, will I take your son back to the land of your birthplace?" **33** And Abraham said unto him, "Take heed that you bring not my son here again, for the Lord before whom I have walked he will send his angel before you and prosper your way." **34** And Eliezer did as Abraham ordered him, and Eliezer swore unto Abraham his master upon this matter; and Eliezer rose up and took ten camels of the camels of his master, and ten men from his master's servants with him, and they rose up and went to Haran, the city of Abraham and Nahor, in order to fetch a wife for Isaac the son of Abraham; and while they were gone Abraham sent to the house of Shem and Eber, and they brought from there his son Isaac. **35** And Isaac came home to his father's house to Beersheba, while Eliezer and his men came to Haran; and they stopped in the city by the watering place, and he made his camels to kneel down by the water and they remained there. **36** And Eliezer, Abraham's servant, prayed and said, "O God of Abraham my master; send me I pray you good speed this day and show kindness unto my master, that you will appoint this day a wife for my master's son from his family." **37** And the Lord hearkened to the voice of Eliezer, for the sake of his servant Abraham, and he happened to meet with the daughter of Bethuel, the son of Milcah, the wife of Nahor, brother to Abraham, and Eliezer came to her house. **38** And Eliezer related to them all his concerns, and that he was Abraham's servant, and they greatly rejoiced at him. **39** And they all blessed the Lord who brought this thing about, and they gave him Rebecca, the daughter of Bethuel, for a wife for Isaac. **40** And the young woman was of very comely appearance, she was a virgin, and Rebecca was ten years old in those days. **41** And Bethuel and Laban and his children made a feast on that night, and Eliezer and his men came and ate and drank and rejoiced there on that night. **42** And Eliezer rose up in the morning, he and the men that were with him, and he called to the whole household of Bethuel, saying, "Send me away that I may go to my master"; and they rose up and sent away Rebecca and her nurse Deborah, the daughter of Uz, and they gave her silver and gold, menservants and maidservants, and they blessed her. **43** And they sent Eliezer away with his men; and the servants took Rebecca, and he went and returned to his master to the land of Canaan. **44** And Isaac took Rebecca and she became his wife, and he brought her into the tent. **45** And Isaac was forty years old when he took Rebecca, the daughter of his uncle Bethuel, for a wife.

CHAPTER 25

1 And it was at that time that Abraham again took a wife in his old age, and her name was Keturah, from the land of Canaan. **2** And she bore unto him Zimran, Jokshan, Medan, Midian, Ishbak and Shuach, being six sons. And the children of Zimran were Abihen, Molich and Narim. **3** And the sons of Jokshan were Sheba and Dedan, and the sons of Medan were Amida, Joab, Gochi, Elisha and Nothach; and the sons of Midian were Ephah, Epher, Chanoch, Abida and Eldaah. **4** And the sons of Ishbak were Makiro, Beyodua and Tator. **5** And the sons of Shuach were Bildad, Mamdad, Munan and Meban; all these are the families of the children of Keturah the Canaanite woman which she bore unto Abraham the Hebrew. **6** And Abraham sent all these away, and he gave them gifts, and they went away from his son Isaac to dwell wherever they should find a place. **7** And all these went to the mountain at the east, and they built themselves six cities in which they dwelt unto this day. **8** But the children of Sheba and Dedan, children of Jokshan, with their children, did not dwell with their brethren in their cities, and they journeyed and encamped in the countries and wildernesses unto this day. **9** And the children of Midian, son of Abraham, went to the east of the land of Cush, and they

there found a large valley in the eastern country, and they remained there and built a city, and they dwelt therein, that is the land of Midian unto this day. **10** And Midian dwelt in the city which he built, he and his five sons and all belonging to him. **11** And these are the names of the sons of Midian according to their names in their cities, Ephah, Epher, Chanoch, Abida and Eldaah. **12** And the sons of Ephah were Methach, Meshar, Avi and Tzanua, and the sons of Epher were Ephron, Zur, Alirun and Medin, and the sons of Chanoch were Reuel, Rekem, Azi, Alyoshub and Alad. **13** And the sons of Abida were Chur, Melud, Kerury, Molchi; and the sons of Eldaah were Miker, and Reba, and Malchiyah and Gabol; these are the names of the Midianites according to their families; and afterward the families of Midian spread throughout the land of Midian. **14** And these are the generations of Ishmael the son Abraham, whom Hagar, Sarah's handmaid, bare unto Abraham. **15** And Ishmael took a wife from the land of Egypt, and her name was Ribah, the same is Meribah. **16** And Ribah bare unto Ishmael Nebayoth, Kedar, Adbeel, Mibsam and their sister Bosmath. **17** And Ishmael cast away his wife Ribah, and she went from him and returned to Egypt to the house of her father, and she dwelt there, for she had been very bad in the sight of Ishmael, and in the sight of his father Abraham. **18** And Ishmael afterward took a wife from the land of Canaan, and her name was Malchuth, and she bare unto him Nishma, Dumah, Masa, Chadad, Tema, Yetur, Naphish and Kedma. **19** These are the sons of Ishmael, and these are their names, being twelve princes according to their nations; and the families of Ishmael afterward spread out, and Ishmael took his children and all the property that he had gained, together with the souls of his household and all belonging to him, and they went to dwell where they should find a place. **20** And they went and dwelt near the wilderness of Paran, and their dwelling was from Havilah unto Shur, that is before Egypt as you come toward Assyria. **21** And Ishmael and his sons dwelt in the land, and they had children born to them, and they were fruitful and increased abundantly. **22** And these are the names of the sons of Nebayoth the firstborn of Ishmael; Mend, Send, Mayon; and the sons of Kedar were Alyon, Kezem, Chamad and Eli. **23** And the sons of Adbeel were Chamad and Jabin; and the sons of Mibsam were Obadiah, Ebedmelech and

Yeush; these are the families of the children of Ribah the wife of Ishmael. 24 And the sons of Mishma the son of Ishmael were Shamua, Zecaryon and Obed; and the sons of Dumah were Kezed, Eli, Machmad and Amed. 25 And the sons of Masa were Melon, Mula and Ebidadon; and the sons of Chadad were Azur, Minzar and Ebedmelech; and the sons of Tema were Seir, Sadon and Yakol. 26 And the sons of Yetur were Merith, Yaish, Alyo, and Pachoth; and the sons of Naphish were Ebed-Tamed, Abiyasaph and Mir; and the sons of Kedma were Calip, Tachti, and Omir; these were the children of Malchuth the wife of Ishmael according to their families. 27 All these are the families of Ishmael according to their generations, and they dwelt in those lands wherein they had built themselves cities unto this day. 28 And Rebecca the daughter of Bethuel, the wife of Abraham's son Isaac, was barren in those days, she had no offspring; and Isaac dwelt with his father in the land of Canaan; and the Lord was with Isaac; and Arpachshad the son of Shem the son of Noah died in those days, in the forty-eighth year of the life of Isaac, and all the days that Arpachshad lived were four hundred and thirty-eight years, and he died.

CHAPTER 26

1 And in the fifty-ninth year of the life of Isaac the son of Abraham, Rebecca his wife was still barren in those days. 2 And Rebecca said unto Isaac, "Truly I have heard, my lord, that your mother Sarah was barren in her days until my Lord Abraham, your father, prayed for her and she conceived by him. 3 Now therefore stand up, pray you also to God and he will hear your prayer and remember us through his mercies." 4 And Isaac answered his wife Rebecca, saying, "Abraham has already prayed for me to God to multiply his seed, now therefore this barrenness must proceed to us from you." 5 And Rebecca said unto him, "But arise now you also and pray, that the Lord may hear your prayer and grant me children," and Isaac hearkened to the words of his wife, and Isaac and his wife rose up and went to the land of Moriah to pray there and to seek the Lord, and when they had reached that place Isaac stood up and prayed to the Lord on account of his wife because she was barren. 6 And Isaac said, "O Lord God of heaven and earth, whose goodness and mercies fill the earth, you who did take my father from his father's house and from his birthplace, and did bring him unto

this land, and did say unto him, 'To your seed will I give the land, and you did promise him and did declare unto him, I will multiply your seed as the stars of heaven and as the sand of the sea,' now may your words be verified which you did speak unto my father. 7 For you are the Lord our God, our eyes are toward you to give us seed of men, as you did promise us, for you are the Lord our God and our eyes are directed toward you only." 8 And the Lord heard the prayer of Isaac the son of Abraham, and the Lord was entreated of him and Rebecca his wife conceived. 9 And in about seven months after the children struggled together within her, and it pained her greatly that she was wearied on account of them, and she said to all the women who were then in the land, "Did such a thing happen to you as it has to me?" And they said unto her, "No." 10 And she said unto them, "Why am I alone in this among all the women that were upon earth?" And she went to the land of Moriah to seek the Lord on account of this; and she went to Shem and Eber his son to make inquiries of them in this matter, and that they should seek the Lord in this thing respecting her. 11 And she also asked Abraham to seek and inquire of the Lord about all that had befallen her. 12 And they all inquired of the Lord concerning this matter, and they brought her word from the Lord and told her, "Two children are in your womb, and two nations will rise from them; and one nation will be stronger than the other, and the greater will serve the younger." 13 And when her days to be delivered were completed, she knelt down, and behold there were twins in her womb, as the Lord had spoken to her. 14 And the first came out red all over like a hairy garment, and all the people of the land called his name Esau, saying, "That this one was made complete from the womb." 15 And after that came his brother, and his hand took hold of Esau's heel, therefore they called his name Jacob. 16 And Isaac, the son of Abraham, was sixty years old when he begat them. 17 And the boys grew up to their fifteenth year, and they came among the society of men. Esau was a designing and deceitful man, and an expert hunter in the field, and Jacob was a man perfect and wise, dwelling in tents, feeding flocks and learning the instructions of the Lord and the commands of his father and mother. 18 And Isaac and the children of his household dwelt with his father Abraham in the land of Canaan, as God had commanded them. 19 And Ishmael the son of Abraham went with his children and all belonging to them, and they returned there to the land of Havilah, and they dwelt there. **20** And all the children of Abraham's concubines went to dwell in the land of the east, for Abraham had sent them away from his son, and had given them presents, and they went away. **21** And Abraham gave all that he had to his son Isaac, and he also gave him all his treasures. **22** And he commanded him saying, "Do you not know and understand the Lord is God in heaven and in earth, and there is no other beside him? **23** And it was he who took me from my father's house, and from my birth place, and gave me all the delights upon earth; who delivered me from the counsel of the wicked, for in him did I trust. **24** And he brought me to this place, and he delivered me from Ur Casdim; and he said unto me, 'To your seed will I give all these lands, and they will inherit them when they keep my commandments, my statutes and my judgments that I have commanded you, and which I will command them.' **25** Now therefore my son, hearken to my voice, and keep the commandments of the Lord your God, which I commanded you, do not turn from the right way either to the right or to the left, in order that it may be well with you and your children after you forever. **26** And remember the wonderful works of the Lord, and his kindness that he has shown toward us, in having delivered us from the hands of our enemies, and the Lord our God caused them to fall into our hands; and now therefore keep all that I have commanded you, and turn not away from the commandments of your God, and serve none beside him, in order that it may be well with you and your seed after you. **27** And teach your children and your seed the instructions of the Lord and his commandments and teach them the upright way in which they should go, in order that it may be well with them forever." **28** And Isaac answered his father and said unto him, "That which my Lord has commanded that will I do, and I will not depart from the commands of the Lord my God, I will keep all that he commanded me"; and Abraham blessed his son Isaac, and also his children; and Abraham taught Jacob the instruction of the Lord and his ways. **29** And it was at that time that Abraham died, in the fifteenth year of the life of Jacob and Esau, the sons of Isaac, and all the days of Abraham were one hundred and seventy-five years, and he died and was gathered to his people in good old age, old and satisfied with

days, and Isaac and Ishmael his sons buried him. **30** And when the inhabitants of Canaan heard that Abraham was dead, they all came with their kings and princes and all their men to bury Abraham. **31** And all the inhabitants of the land of Haran, and all the families of the house of Abraham, and all the princes and noblemen, and the sons of Abraham by the concubines, all came when they heard of Abraham's death, and they pay backd Abraham's kindness, and comforted Isaac his son, and they buried Abraham in the cave which he bought from Ephron the Hittite and his children, for the possession of a burial place. **32** And all the inhabitants of Canaan, and all those who had known Abraham, wept for Abraham a whole year, and men and women mourned over him. **33** And all the little children, and all the inhabitants of the land wept on account of Abraham, for Abraham had been good to them all, and because he had been upright with God and men. **34** And there arose not a man who feared God like unto Abraham, for he had feared his God from his youth, and had served the Lord, and had gone in all his ways during his life, from his childhood to the day of his death. **35** And the Lord was with him and delivered him from the counsel of Nimrod and his people, and when he made war with the four kings of Elam he conquered them. **36** And he brought all the children of the earth to the service of God, and he taught them the ways of the Lord, and caused them to know the Lord. **37** And he formed a grove and he planted a vineyard therein, and he had always prepared in his tent meat and drink to those that passed through the land, that they might satisfy themselves in his house. **38** And the Lord God delivered the whole earth on account of Abraham. **39** And it was after the death of Abraham that God blessed his son Isaac and his children, and the Lord was with Isaac as he had been with his father Abraham, for Isaac kept all the commandments of the Lord as Abraham his father had commanded him; he did not turn to the right or to the left from the right path which his father had commanded him.

CHAPTER 27

1 And Esau at that time, after the death of Abraham, frequently went in the field to hunt. **2** And Nimrod king of Babel, the same was Amraphel, also frequently went with his mighty men to hunt in the field, and to walk about with his men in the cool of the day.

3 And Nimrod was observing Esau all the days, for a jealousy was formed in the heart of Nimrod against Esau all the days. 4 And on a certain day Esau went in the field to hunt, and he found Nimrod walking in the wilderness with his two men. 5 And all his mighty men and his people were with him in the wilderness, but they removed at a distance from him, and they went from him in different directions to hunt, and Esau concealed himself for Nimrod, and he lurked for him in the wilderness. 6 And Nimrod and his men that were with him did not know him, and Nimrod and his men frequently walked about in the field at the cool of the day, and to know where his men were hunting in the field. 7 And Nimrod and two of his men that were with him came to the place where they were, when Esau started suddenly from his lurking place, and drew his sword, and hastened and ran to Nimrod and cut off his head. 8 And Esau fought a desperate fight with the two men that were with Nimrod, and when they called out to him, Esau turned to them and smote them to death with his sword. 9 And all the mighty men of Nimrod, who had left him to go to the wilderness, heard the cry at a distance, and they knew the voices of those two men, and they ran to know the cause of it, when they found their king and the two men that were with him lying dead in the wilderness. 10 And when Esau saw the mighty men of Nimrod coming at a distance, he fled, and thereby escaped; and Esau took the valuable garments of Nimrod, which Nimrod's father had bequeathed to Nimrod, and with which Nimrod prevailed over the whole land, and he ran and concealed them in his house. 11 And Esau took those garments and ran into the city on account of Nimrod's men, and he came unto his father's house wearied and exhausted from fight, and he was ready to die through grief when he approached his brother Jacob and sat before him. 12 And he said unto his brother Jacob, "Behold I will die this day, and why then do I want the birthright?" And Jacob acted wisely with Esau in this matter, and Esau sold his birthright to Jacob, for it was so brought about by the Lord. 13 And Esau's portion in the cave of the field of Machpelah, which Abraham had bought from the children of Heth for the possession of a burial ground, Esau also sold to Jacob, and Jacob bought all this from his brother Esau for value given. 14 And Jacob wrote the whole of this in a book, and he testified the same with witnesses, and he sealed it, and the book remained in the hands of Jacob. 15 And when Nimrod the son of Cush died, his men lifted him up and brought him in consternation, and buried him in his city, and all the days that Nimrod lived were two hundred and fifteen years and he died. 16 And the days that Nimrod reigned upon the people of the land were one hundred and eighty-five years; and Nimrod died by the sword of Esau in shame and contempt, and the seed of Abraham caused his death as he had seen in his dream. 17 And at the death of Nimrod his kingdom became divided into many divisions, and all those parts that Nimrod reigned over were restored to the respective kings of the land, who recovered them after the death of Nimrod, and all the people of the house of Nimrod were for a long time enslaved to all the other kings of the land.

CHAPTER 28

1 And in those days, after the death of Abraham, in that year the Lord brought a heavy famine in the land, and while the famine was raging in the land of Canaan, Isaac rose up to go down to Egypt on account of the famine, as his father Abraham had done. 2 And the Lord appeared that night to Isaac and he said to him, "Do not go down to Egypt but rise and go to Gerar, to Abimelech king of the Philistines, and remain there until the famine will cease." 3 And Isaac rose up and went to Gerar, as the Lord commanded him, and he remained there a full year. 4 And when Isaac came to Gerar, the people of the land saw that Rebecca his wife was of a beautiful appearance, and the people of Gerar asked Isaac concerning his wife, and he said, "She is my sister," for he was afraid to say she was his wife lest the people of the land should slay him on account of her. 5 And the princes of Abimelech went and praised the woman to the king, but he answered them not, neither did he attend to their words. 6 But he heard them say that Isaac declared her to be his sister, so the king reserved this within himself. 7 And when Isaac had remained three months in the land, Abimelech looked out at the window, and he saw, and behold Isaac was sporting with Rebecca his wife, for Isaac dwelt in the outer house belonging to the king, so that the house of Isaac was opposite the house of the king. 8 And the king said unto Isaac, "What is this you have done to us in saying of your wife, 'she is my sister?' How easily might one of the great men of the people have lain with her, and

you would then have brought guilt upon us." 9 And Isaac said unto Abimelech, "Because I was afraid lest I die on account of my wife, therefore I said, 'she is my sister.' " 10 At that time Abimelech gave orders to all his princes and great men, and they took Isaac and Rebecca his wife and brought them before the king. 11 And the king commanded that they should dress them in princely garments and make them ride through the streets of the city, and proclaim before them throughout the land, saying, "This is the man and this is his wife; whoever touches this man or his wife will surely die." And Isaac returned with his wife to the king's house, and the Lord was with Isaac and he continued to wax great and lacked nothing. 12 And the Lord caused Isaac to find favor in the sight of Abimelech, and in the sight of all his subjects, and Abimelech acted well with Isaac, for Abimelech remembered the oath and the covenant that existed between his father and Abraham. 13 And Abimelech said unto Isaac, "Behold the whole earth is before you; dwell wherever it may seem good in your sight until you will return to your land"; and Abimelech gave Isaac fields and vineyards and the best part of the land of Gerar, to sow and reap and eat the fruits of the ground until the days of the famine should have passed by. 14 And Isaac sowed in that land and received a hundred-fold in the same year, and the Lord blessed him. 15 And the man waxed great, and he had possession of flocks and possession of herds and great store of servants. 16 And when the days of the famine had passed away the Lord appeared to Isaac and said unto him, "Rise up, go out from this place and return to your land, to the land of Canaan"; and Isaac rose up and returned to Hebron which is in the land of Canaan, he and all belonging to him as the Lord commanded him. 17 And after this Shelach the son of Arpachshad died in that year, which is the eighteenth year of the lives of Jacob and Esau; and all the days that Shelach lived were four hundred and thirty-three years and he died. 18 At that time Isaac sent his younger son Jacob to the house of Shem and Eber, and he learned the instructions of the Lord, and Jacob remained in the house of Shem and Eber for thirty-two years, and Esau his brother did not go, for he was not willing to go, and he remained in his father's house in the land of Canaan. 19 And Esau was continually hunting in the fields to bring home what he could get, so did Esau all the days. 20 And Esau was a designing and deceitful man, one who hunted after the hearts of men and persuaded them through deceit, and Esau was a valiant man in the field, and in the course of time went as usual to hunt; and he came as far as the field of Seir, the same is Edom. 21 And he remained in the land of Seir hunting in the field a year and four months. 22 And Esau there saw in the land of Seir the daughter of a man of Canaan, and her name was Jehudith, the daughter of Beeri, son of Epher, from the families of Heth the son of Canaan. 23 And Esau took her for a wife, and he came unto her; forty years old was Esau when he took her, and he brought her to Hebron, the land of his father's dwelling place, and he dwelt there. 24 And it came to pass in those days, in the hundred and tenth year of the life of Isaac, that is in the fiftieth year of the life of Jacob, in that year died Shem the son of Noah; Shem was six hundred years old at his death. 25 And when Shem died Jacob returned to his father to Hebron which is in the land of Canaan. 26 And in the fifty-sixth year of the life of Jacob, people came from Haran, and Rebecca was told concerning her brother Laban the son of Bethuel. 27 For the wife of Laban was barren in those days, and bare no children, and also all his handmaids bore none to him. 28 And the Lord afterward remembered Adinah the wife of Laban, and she conceived and bore twin daughters, and Laban called the names of his daughters, the name of the elder Leah, and the name of the younger Rachel. 29 And those people came and told these things to Rebecca, and Rebecca rejoiced greatly that the Lord had visited her brother and that he was given children.

CHAPTER 29

1 And Isaac the son of Abraham became old and advanced in days, and his eyes became heavy through age; they were dim and could not see. 2 At that time Isaac called unto Esau his son, saying, "Get I pray you your weapons, your quiver and your bow, rise up and go out into the field and get me some venison, and make me savory meat and bring it to me, that I may eat in order that I may bless you before my death, as I have now become old and gray-headed." 3 And Esau did so; and he took his weapon and went out into the field to hunt for venison, as usual, to bring to his father as he had ordered him, so that he might bless him. 4 And Rebecca heard all the words that Isaac had spoken unto Esau, and she hastened and called her son Jacob, saying, "Thus did your

father speak unto your brother Esau, and thus did I hear, now therefore hasten you and make that which I will tell you. **5** Rise up and go, I pray you, to the flock and fetch me two fine kids of the goats, and I will get the savory meat for your father, and you will bring the savory meat that he may eat before your brother will have come from the chase, in order that your father may bless you." **6** And Jacob hastened and did as his mother had commanded him, and he made the savory meat and brought it before his father before Esau had come from his chase. **7** And Isaac said unto Jacob, "Who are you, my son?" And he said, "I am your firstborn Esau, I have done as you did order me, now therefore rise up I pray you, and eat of my hunt, in order that your soul may bless me as you did speak unto me." **8** And Isaac rose up and he ate and he drank, and his heart was comforted, and he blessed Jacob and Jacob went away from his father; and as soon as Isaac had blessed Jacob and he had gone away from him, behold Esau came from his hunt from the field, and he also made savory meat and brought it to his father to eat thereof and to bless him. **9** And Isaac said unto Esau, "And who was he that has taken venison and brought it to me before you came and whom I did bless?" And Esau knew that his brother Jacob had done this, and the anger of Esau was kindled against his brother Jacob that he had acted thus toward him. **10** And Esau said, "Is he not rightly called Jacob? For he has supplanted me twice, he took away my birthright and now he has taken away my blessing"; and Esau wept greatly; and when Isaac heard the voice of his son Esau weeping, Isaac said unto Esau, "What can I do, my son, your brother came with subtlety and took away your blessing"; and Esau hated his brother Jacob on account of the blessing that his father had given him, and his anger was greatly roused against him. **11** And Jacob was very much afraid of his brother Esau, and he rose up and fled to the house of Eber the son of Shem, and he concealed himself there on account of his brother, and Jacob was sixty-three years old when he went out from the land of Canaan from Hebron, and Jacob was concealed in Eber's house fourteen years on account of his brother Esau, and he there continued to learn the ways of the Lord and his commandments. **12** And when Esau saw that Jacob had fled and escaped from him, and that Jacob had cunningly obtained the blessing, then Esau grieved exceedingly, and he was

also vexed at his father and mother; and he also rose up and took his wife and went away from his father and mother to the land of Seir, and he dwelt there; and Esau saw there a woman from among the daughters of Heth whose name was Bosmath, the daughter of Elon the Hittite, and he took her for a wife in addition to his first wife, and Esau called her name Adah, saying the blessing had in that time passed from him. **13** And Esau dwelt in the land of Seir six months without seeing his father and mother, and afterward Esau took his wives and rose up and returned to the land of Canaan, and Esau placed his two wives in his father's house in Hebron. **14** And the wives of Esau vexed and provoked Isaac and Rebecca with their works, for they walked not in the ways of the Lord but served their father's gods of wood and stone as their father had taught them, and they were more wicked than their father. **15** And they went according to the evil desires of their hearts, and they sacrificed and burnt incense to the Baalim, and Isaac and Rebecca became weary of them. **16** And Rebecca said, "I am weary of my life because of the daughters of Heth; if Jacob takes a wife from the daughters of Heth, such as these which are of the daughters of the land, what good then is life unto me?" **17** And in those days Adah the wife of Esau conceived and bore him a son, and Esau called the name of the son that was born unto him Eliphaz, and Esau was sixty-five years old when she bore him. **18** And Ishmael the son of Abraham died in those days, in the sixtieth year of the life of Jacob, and all the days that Ishmael lived were one hundred and thirty-seven years and he died. **19** And when Isaac heard that Ishmael was dead he mourned for him, and Isaac lamented over him many days. **20** And at the end of fourteen years of Jacob's residing in the house of Eber, Jacob desired to see his father and mother, and Jacob came to the house of his father and mother to Hebron, and Esau had in those days forgotten what Jacob had done to him in having taken the blessing from him in those days. **21** And when Esau saw Jacob coming to his father and mother he remembered what Jacob had done to him, and he was greatly incensed against him and he sought to slay him. **22** And Isaac the son of Abraham was old and advanced in days, and Esau said, "Now my father's time is drawing nigh that he must die, and when he will die I will slay my brother Jacob." **23** And this was told to Rebecca, and she hastened and sent and called for Jacob her son, and she said unto him, "Arise, go and flee to Haran to my brother Laban, and remain there for some time, until your brother's anger be turned from you and then will you come back." 24 And Isaac called unto Jacob and said unto him, "Take not a wife from the daughters of Canaan, for thus did our father Abraham command us according to the word of the Lord which he had commanded him, saying, 'Unto your seed will I give this land; if your children keep my covenant that I have made with you, then will I also perform to your children that which I have spoken unto you and I will not forsake them.' 25 Now therefore my son hearken to my voice, to all that I will command you, and refrain from taking a wife from among the daughters of Canaan; arise, go to Haran to the house of Bethuel your mother's father, and take unto you a wife from there from the daughters of Laban your mother's brother. 26 Therefore take heed lest you should forget the Lord your God and all his ways in the land to which you go and should get connected with the people of the land and pursue vanity and forsake the Lord your God. 27 But when you come to the land serve there the Lord, do not turn to the right or to the left from the way which I commanded you and which you did learn. 28 And may the Almighty God grant you favor in the sight of the people of the earth, that you may take there a wife according to your choice; one who is good and upright in the ways of the Lord. 29 And may God give unto you and your seed the blessing of your father Abraham, and make you fruitful and multiply you, and may you become a multitude of people in the land where you go, and may God cause you to return to this land, the land of your father's dwelling, with children and with great riches, with joy and with pleasure." 30 And Isaac finished commanding Jacob and blessing him, and he gave him many gifts, together with silver and gold, and he sent him away; and Jacob hearkened to his father and mother; he kissed them and arose and went to Padan-aram; and Jacob was seventy-seven years old when he went out from the land of Canaan from Beersheba. 31 And when Jacob went away to go to Haran Esau called unto his son Eliphaz, and secretly spoke unto him, saying, "Now hasten, take your sword in your hand and pursue Jacob and pass before him in the road, and lurk for him, and slay him with your sword in one of the mountains, and take all belonging to him and come back." 32 And

Eliphaz the son of Esau was an active man and expert with the bow as his father had taught him, and he was a noted hunter in the field and a valiant man. 33 And Eliphaz did as his father had commanded him, and Eliphaz was at that time thirteen years old, and Eliphaz rose up and went and took ten of his mother's brothers with him and pursued Jacob. 34 And he closely followed Jacob, and he lurked for him in the border of the land of Canaan opposite to the city of Shechem. 35 And Jacob saw Eliphaz and his men pursuing him, and Jacob stood still in the place in which he was going, in order to know what this was, for he did not know the thing; and Eliphaz drew his sword and he went on advancing, he and his men, toward Jacob; and Jacob said unto them, "What are you doing that you have come here, and what do you intend that you pursue with your swords." 36 And Eliphaz came near to Jacob and he answered and said unto him, "Thus did my father command me, and now therefore I will not deviate from the orders which my father gave me"; and when Jacob saw that Esau had spoken to Eliphaz to employ force, Jacob then approached and supplicated Eliphaz and his men, saying to him, 37 "Behold all that I have and which my father and mother gave unto me, that take unto you and go from me, and do not slay me, and may this thing be accounted unto you a righteousness." 38 And the Lord caused Jacob to find favor in the sight of Eliphaz the son of Esau, and his men, and they hearkened to the voice of Jacob, and they did not put him to death, and Eliphaz and his men took all belonging to Jacob together with the silver and gold that he had brought with him from Beersheba; they left him nothing. 39 And Eliphaz and his men went away from him and they returned to Esau to Beersheba, and they told him all that had occurred to them with Jacob, and they gave him all that they had taken from Jacob. 40 And Esau was indignant at Eliphaz his son, and at his men that were with him, because they had not put Jacob to death. 41 And they answered and said unto Esau, "Because Jacob supplicated us in this matter not to slay him, our pity was excited toward him, and we took all belonging to him and brought it unto you; and Esau took all the silver and gold which Eliphaz had taken from Jacob and he put them by in his house." 42 At that time when Esau saw that Isaac had blessed Jacob, and had commanded him, saying, "You will not take a wife from among the daughters of Canaan," and that the daughters of Canaan were bad in the sight of Isaac and Rebecca, **43** Then he went to the house of Ishmael his uncle, and in addition to his older wives he took Machlath the daughter of Ishmael, the sister of Nebayoth, for a wife.

CHAPTER 30

1 And Jacob went out continuing his road to Haran, and he came as far as Mount Moriah, and he tarried there all night near the city of Luz; and the Lord appeared there unto Jacob on that night, and he said unto him, "I am the Lord God of Abraham and the God of Isaac your father; the land upon which you lie I will give unto you and your seed. **2** And behold I am with you and will keep you wherever you go, and I will multiply your seed as the stars of Heaven, and I will cause all your enemies to fall before you; and when they will make war with you they will not prevail over you, and I will bring you again unto this land with joy, with children, and with great riches." **3** And Jacob awoke from his sleep and he rejoiced greatly at the vision which he had seen; and he called the name of that place Bethel. **4** And Jacob rose up from that place quite rejoiced, and when he walked his feet felt light to him for joy, and he went from there to the land of the children of the East, and he returned to Haran and he sat by the shepherd's well. **5** And there he found some men; going from Haran to feed their flocks, and Jacob made inquiries of them, and they said, "We are from Haran." **6** And he said unto them, "Do you know Laban, the son of Nahor?" And they said, "We know him, and behold his daughter Rachel is coming along to feed her father's flock." **7** While he was yet speaking with them, Rachel the daughter of Laban came to feed her father's sheep, for she was a shepherdess. **8** And when Jacob saw Rachel, the daughter of Laban, his mother's brother, he ran and kissed her, and lifted up his voice and wept. **9** And Jacob told Rachel that he was the son of Rebecca, her father's sister, and Rachel ran and told her father, and Jacob continued to cry because he had nothing with him to bring to the house of Laban. **10** And when Laban heard that his sister's son Jacob had come, he ran and kissed him and embraced him and brought him into the house and gave him bread, and he ate. **11** And Jacob related to Laban what his brother Esau had done to him, and what his son Eliphaz had done to him in the road. **12** And Jacob resided in Laban's house for one month,

and Jacob ate and drank in the house of Laban, and afterward Laban said unto Jacob, "Tell me what will be your wages, for how can you serve me for nothing?" **13** And Laban had no sons but only daughters, and his other wives and handmaids were still barren in those days; and these are the names of Laban's daughters which his wife Adinah had bore unto him; the name of the elder was Leah and the name of the younger was Rachel; and Leah was tender-eyed, but Rachel was beautiful and well favored, and Jacob loved her. **14** And Jacob said unto Laban, "I will serve you seven years for Rachel your younger daughter"; and Laban consented to this and Jacob served Laban seven years for his daughter Rachel. **15** And in the second year of Jacob's dwelling in Haran, that is in the seventy ninth year of the life of Jacob, in that year died Eber the son of Shem, he was four hundred and sixty-four years old at his death. **16** And when Jacob heard that Eber was dead he grieved exceedingly, and he lamented and mourned over him many days. **17** And in the third year of Jacob's dwelling in Haran, Bosmath, the daughter of Ishmael, the wife of Esau, bore unto him a son, and Esau called his name Reuel. **18** And in the fourth year of Jacob's residence in the house of Laban, the Lord visited Laban and remembered him on account of Jacob, and sons were born unto him, and his firstborn was Beor, his second was Alib, and the third was Chorash. **19** And the Lord gave Laban riches and honor, sons and daughters, and the man increased greatly on account of Jacob. **20** And Jacob in those days served Laban in all manner of work, in the house and in the field, and the blessing of the Lord was in all that belonged to Laban in the house and in the field. **21** And in the fifth year died Jehudith, the daughter of Beeri, the wife of Esau, in the land of Canaan, and she had no sons but daughters only. **22** And these are the names of her daughters which she bore to Esau, the name of the elder was Marzith, and the name of the younger was Puith. **23** And when Jehudith died, Esau rose up and went to Seir to hunt in the field, as usual, and Esau dwelt in the land of Seir for a long time. **24** And in the sixth year Esau took for a wife, in addition to his other wives, Ahlibamah, the daughter of Zebeon the Hivite, and Esau brought her to the land of Canaan. **25** And Ahlibamah conceived and bore unto Esau three sons, Yeush, Yaalan, and Korah. **26** And in those days, in the land of Canaan, there was a quarrel between the herdsmen of

Esau and the herdsmen of the inhabitants of the land of Canaan, for Esau's cattle and goods were too abundant for him to remain in the land of Canaan, in his father's house, and the land of Canaan could not bear him on account of his cattle. **27** And when Esau saw that his quarreling increased with the inhabitants of the land of Canaan, he rose up and took his wives and his sons and his daughters, and all belonging to him, and the cattle which he possessed, and all his property that he had acquired in the land of Canaan, and he went away from the inhabitants of the land to the land of Seir, and Esau and all belonging to him dwelt in the land of Seir. **28** But from time to time Esau would go and see his father and mother in the land of Canaan, and Esau intermarried with the Horites, and he gave his daughters to the sons of Seir, the Horite. **29** And he gave his elder daughter Marzith to Anah, the son of Zebeon, his wife's brother, and Puith he gave to Azar, the son of Bilhan the Horite; and Esau dwelt in the mountain, he and his children, and they were fruitful and multiplied.

CHAPTER 31

1 And in the seventh year, Jacob's service which he served Laban was completed, and Jacob said unto Laban, "Give me my wife, for the days of my service are fulfilled"; and Laban did so, and Laban and Jacob assembled all the people of that place and they made a feast. **2** And in the evening Laban came to the house, and afterward Jacob came there with the people of the feast, and Laban extinguished all the lights that were there in the house. **3** And Jacob said unto Laban, "Why do you do this thing unto us?" And Laban answered, "Such is our custom to act in this land." **4** And afterward Laban took his daughter Leah, and he brought her to Jacob, and he came to her and Jacob did not know that she was Leah. **5** And Laban gave his daughter Leah his maid Zilpah for a handmaid. **6** And all the people at the feast knew what Laban had done to Jacob, but they did not tell the thing to Jacob. **7** And all the neighbors came that night to Jacob's house, and they ate and drank and rejoiced, and played before Leah upon timbrels, and with dances, and they responded before Jacob, Heleah, Heleah. **8** And Jacob heard their words but did not understand their meaning, but he thought such might be their custom in this land. **9** And the neighbors spoke these words before Jacob during the night, and all the lights that were in the house Laban had that night extinguished. **10** And in the morning, when daylight appeared, Jacob turned to his wife and he saw, and behold it was Leah that had been lying in his bosom, and Jacob said, "Behold now I know what the neighbors said last night, Heleah, they said, and I knew it not." **11** And Jacob called unto Laban, and said unto him, "What is this that you did unto me? Surely I served you for Rachel, and why did you deceive me and did give me Leah?" **12** And Laban answered Jacob, saying, "Not so is it done in our place to give the younger before the elder now therefore if you desire to take her sister likewise, take her unto you for the service which you will serve me for another seven years." **13** And Jacob did so, and he also took Rachel for a wife, and he served Laban seven years more, and Jacob also came to Rachel, and he loved Rachel more than Leah, and Laban gave her his maid Bilhah for a handmaid. **14** And when the Lord saw that Leah was hated, the Lord opened her womb, and she conceived and bore Jacob four sons in those days. **15** And these are their names, Reuben, Simeon, Levi, and Judah, and she afterward left bearing. **16** And at that time Rachel was barren, and she had no offspring, and Rachel envied her sister Leah, and when Rachel saw that she bore no children to Jacob, she took her handmaid Bilhah, and she bore Jacob two sons, Dan and Naphtali. **17** And when Leah saw that she had left bearing, she also took her handmaid Zilpah, and she gave her to Jacob for a wife, and Jacob also came to Zilpah, and she also bore Jacob two sons, Gad and Asher. **18** And Leah again conceived and bore Jacob in those days two sons and one daughter, and these are their names, Issachar, Zebulon, and their sister Dinah. **19** And Rachel was still barren in those days, and Rachel prayed unto the Lord at that time, and she said, "O Lord God remember me and visit me, I implore you, for now my husband will cast me off, for I have borne him no children. **20** Now O Lord God, hear my supplication before you, and see my affliction, and give me children like one of the handmaids, that I may no more bear my reproach." **21** And God heard her and opened her womb, and Rachel conceived and bore a son, and she said, "The Lord has taken away my reproach," and she called his name Joseph, saying, "May the Lord add to me another son"; and Jacob was ninety-one years old when she bore him. **22** At that time Jacob's mother, Rebecca, sent her nurse

Deborah the daughter of Uz, and two of Isaac's servants unto Jacob. **23** And they came to Jacob to Haran and they said unto him, "Rebecca has sent us to you that you will return to your father's house to the land of Canaan"; and Jacob hearkened unto them in this which his mother had spoken. **24** At that time, the other seven years which Jacob served Laban for Rachel were completed, and it was at the end of fourteen years that he had dwelt in Haran that Jacob said unto Laban, "give me my wives and send me away, that I may go to my land, for behold my mother did send unto me from the land at Canaan that I should return to my father's house." **25** And Laban said unto him, "Not so I pray you; if I have found favor in your sight do not leave me; appoint me your wages and I will give them, and remain with me." **26** And Jacob said unto him, "This is what you will give me for wages, that I will this day pass through all your flock and take away from them every lamb that is speckled and spotted and such as are brown among the sheep, and among the goats, and if you will do this thing for me I will return and feed your flock and keep them as at first." **27** And Laban did so, and Laban removed from his flock all that Jacob had said and gave them to him. **28** And Jacob placed all that he had removed from Laban's flock in the hands of his sons, and Jacob was feeding the remainder of Laban's flock. **29** And when the servants of Isaac which he had sent unto Jacob saw that Jacob would not then return with them to the land of Canaan to his father, they then went away from him, and they returned home to the land of Canaan. **30** And Deborah remained with Jacob in Haran, and she did not return with the servants of Isaac to the land of Canaan, and Deborah resided with Jacob's wives and children in Haran. **31** And Jacob served Laban six years longer, and when the sheep brought out, Jacob removed from them such as were speckled and spotted, as he had determined with Laban, and Jacob did so at Laban's for six years, and the man increased abundantly, and he had cattle and maidservants and menservants, camels, and asses. **32** And Jacob had two hundred drove of cattle, and his cattle were of large size and of beautiful appearance and were very productive, and all the families of the sons of men desired to get some of the cattle of Jacob, for they were exceedingly prosperous. **33** And many of the sons of men came to procure some of Jacob's flock, and Jacob gave them a sheep for a manservant or a maidservant or for an ass or a camel, or whatever Jacob desired from them they gave him. **34** And Jacob obtained riches and honor and possessions by means of these transactions with the sons of men, and the children of Laban envied him of this honor. **35** And in the course of time he heard the words of Laban's sons, saying, "Jacob has taken away all that was our father's, and of that which was our father's has he acquired all this glory." **36** And Jacob beheld the countenance of Laban and of his children, and behold it was not toward him in those days as it had been before. **37** And the Lord appeared to Jacob at the expiration of the six years, and said unto him, "Arise, go out out of this land, and return to the land of your birthplace and I will be with you." **38** And Jacob rose up at that time and he mounted his children and wives and all belonging to him upon camels, and he went out to go to the land of Canaan to his father Isaac. **39** And Laban did not know that Jacob had gone from him, for Laban had been that day sheep-shearing. **40** And Rachel stole her father's images, and she took them and she concealed them upon the camel upon which she sat, and she went on. **41** And this is the manner of the images; in taking a man who is the firstborn and slaying him and taking the hair off his head, and taking salt and salting the head and anointing it in oil, then taking a small tablet of copper or a tablet of gold and writing the name upon it, and placing the tablet under his tongue, and taking the head with the tablet under the tongue and putting it in the house, and lighting up lights before it and bowing down to it. **42** And at the time when they bow down to it, it speaks to them in all matters that they ask of it, through the power of the name which is written in it. **43** And some make them in the figures of men, of gold and silver, and go to them in times known to them, and the figures receive the influence of the stars, and tell them future things, and in this manner were the images which Rachel stole from her father. **44** And Rachel stole these images which were her father's, in order that Laban might not know through them where Jacob had gone. **45** And Laban came home and he asked concerning Jacob and his household, and he was not to be found, and Laban sought his images to know where Jacob had gone, and could not find them, and he went to some other images, and he inquired of them and they told him that Jacob had fled from him to his father's, to the land of Canaan. **46** And Laban then rose up and he took his brothers and all his servants, and he went out and pursued Jacob, and he overtook him in Mount Gilead. 47 And Laban said unto Jacob, "What is this you have done to me to flee and deceive me, and lead my daughters and their children as captives taken by the sword? 48 And you did not suffer me to kiss them and send them away with joy, and you did steal my gods and did go away." 49 And Jacob answered Laban, saying, "Because I was afraid lest you would take your daughters by force from me; and now with whomsoever you find your gods he will die. 50 And Laban searched for the images and he examined in all Jacob's tents and furniture but could not find them. 51 And Laban said unto Jacob, "We will make a covenant together and it will be a testimony between me and you; if you will afflict my daughters, or will take other wives besides my daughters, even God will be a witness between me and you in this matter." 52 And they took stones and made a heap, and Laban said, "This heap is a witness between me and you, therefore he called the name thereof Gilead. 53 And Jacob and Laban offered sacrifice upon the mount, and they ate there by the heap, and they tarried in the mount all night, and Laban rose up early in the morning, and he wept with his daughters and he kissed them, and he returned unto his place. 54 And he hastened and sent off his son Beor, who was seventeen years old, with Abichorof the son of Uz, the son of Nahor, and with them were ten men. 55 And they hastened and went and passed on the road before Jacob, and they came by another road to the land of Seir. 56 And they came unto Esau and said unto him, "Thus says your brother and relative, your mother's brother Laban, the son of Bethuel, saying, 57 'Have you heard what Jacob your brother has done unto me, who first came to me naked and bare, and I went to meet him, and brought him to my house with honor, and I made him great, and I gave him my two daughters for wives and also two of my maids. 58 And God blessed him on my account, and he increased abundantly, and had sons, daughters and maidservants. 59 He has also an immense stock of flocks and herds, camels and asses, also silver and gold in abundance; and when he saw that his wealth increased, he left me while I went to shear my sheep, and he rose up and fled in secrecy. 60 And he lifted his wives and children upon camels, and he led away all his cattle and property which he acquired in my land, and he lifted up his

countenance to go to his father Isaac, to the land of Canaan. 61 And he did not suffer me to kiss my daughters and their children, and he led my daughters as captives taken by the sword, and he also stole my gods and he fled. 62 And now I have left him in the mountain of the brook of Jabuk, him and all belonging to him; he lacks nothing. 63 If it be your wish to go to him, go then and there will you find him, and you can do unto him as your soul desires' "; and Laban's messengers came and told Esau all these things. 64 And Esau heard all the words of Laban's messengers, and his anger was greatly kindled against Jacob, and he remembered his hatred, and his anger burned within him. 65 And Esau hastened and took his children and servants and the souls of his household, being sixty men, and he went and assembled all the children of Seir the Horite and their people, being three hundred and forty men, and took all this number of four hundred men with drawn swords, and he went unto Jacob to smite him. 66 And Esau divided this number into several parts, and he took the sixty men of his children and servants and the souls of his household as one head and gave them in care of Eliphaz his eldest son. 67 And the remaining heads he gave to the care of the six sons of Seir the Horite, and he placed every man over his generations and children. 68 And the whole of this camp went as it was, and Esau went among them toward Jacob, and he conducted them with speed. 69 And Laban's messengers departed from Esau and went to the land of Canaan, and they came to the house of Rebecca the mother of Jacob and Esau. 70 And they told her saying, "Behold your son Esau has gone against his brother Jacob with four hundred men, for he heard that he was coming, and he is gone to make war with him, and to smite him and to take all that he has." 71 And Rebecca hastened and sent seventy-two men from the servants of Isaac to meet Jacob on the road; for she said, "Perhaps Esau may make war in the road when he meets him." 72 And these messengers went on the road to meet Jacob, and they met him in the road of the brook on the opposite side of the brook Jabuk, and Jacob said when he saw them, "This camp is destined to me from God," and Jacob called the name of that place Machnayim. 73 And Jacob knew all his father's people, and he kissed them and embraced them and came with them, and Jacob asked them concerning his father and mother, and they said they were well. 74 And these messengers said unto Jacob, "Rebecca your mother has sent us to you, saying, 'I have heard, my son, that your brother Esau has gone out against you on the road with men from the children of Seir the Horite. **75** And therefore, my son, hearken to my voice and see with your counsel what you will do, and when he comes up to you, supplicate him, and do not speak rashly to him, and give him a present from what you possess, and from what God has favored you with. **76** And when he asks you concerning your affairs, conceal nothing from him, perhaps he may turn from his anger against you and you will thereby save your soul, you and all belonging to you, for it is your duty to honor him, for he is your elder brother.' " **77** And when Jacob heard the words of his mother which the messengers had spoken to him, Jacob lifted up his voice and wept bitterly, and did as his mother then commanded him.

CHAPTER 32

1 And at that time Jacob sent messengers to his brother Esau toward the land of Seir, and he spoke to him words of supplication. **2** And he commanded them, saying, "Thus will you say to my lord, to Esau, 'Thus says your servant Jacob, let not my lord imagine that my father's blessing with which he did bless me has proved beneficial to me. **3** For I have been these twenty years with Laban, and he deceived me and changed my wages ten times, as it has all been already told unto my lord. **4** And I served him in his house very laboriously, and God afterward saw my affliction, my labor and the work of my hands, and he caused me to find grace and favor in his sight. **5** And I afterward through God's great mercy and kindness acquired oxen and asses and cattle, and menservants and maidservants. **6** And now I am coming to my land and my home to my father and mother, who are in the land of Canaan; and I have sent to let my lord know all this in order to find favor in the sight of my lord, so that he may not imagine that I have of myself obtained wealth, or that the blessing with which my father blessed me has benefited me.' " **7** And those messengers went to Esau and found him on the borders of the land of Edom going toward Jacob, and four hundred men of the children of Seir the Horite were standing with drawn swords. **8** And the messengers of Jacob told Esau all the words that Jacob had spoken to them concerning Esau. **9** And Esau answered them with pride and contempt, and said unto them, "Surely I have heard and truly it has been told unto me what Jacob has done to Laban, who exalted him in his house and gave him his daughters for wives, and he begat sons and daughters, and abundantly increased in wealth and riches in Laban's house through his means. **10** And when he saw that his wealth was abundant and his riches great he fled with all belonging to him, from Laban's house, and he led Laban's daughters away from the face of their father, as captives taken by the sword without telling him of it. **11** And not only to Laban has Jacob done thus but also unto me has he done so and has twice supplanted me, and will I be silent? **12** Now therefore I have this day come with my camps to meet him, and I will do unto him according to the desire of my heart." **13** And the messengers returned and came to Jacob and said unto him, "We came to your brother, to Esau, and we told him all your words, and thus has he answered us, and behold he comes to meet you with four hundred men. **14** Now then know and see what you will do and pray before God to deliver you from him." **15** And when he heard the words of his brother which he had spoken to the messengers of Jacob, Jacob was greatly afraid, and he was distressed. **16** And Jacob prayed to the Lord his God, and he said, "O Lord God of my fathers, Abraham and Isaac, you did say unto me when I went away from my father's house, saying, **17** 'I am the Lord God of your father Abraham and the God of Isaac, unto you do I give this land and your seed after you, and I will make your seed as the stars of heaven, and you will spread out to the four sides of heaven, and in you and in your seed will all the families of the earth be blessed.' **18** And you did establish your words and did give unto me riches and children and cattle, as the utmost wishes of my heart did you give unto your servant; you did give unto me all that I asked from you, so that I lacked nothing. **19** And you did afterward say unto me, 'Return to your parents and to your birth place and I will still do well with you.' **20** And now that I have come, and you did deliver me from Laban, I will fall in the hands of Esau who will slay me, yea, together with the mothers of my children. **21** Now therefore, O Lord God, deliver me, I pray you, also from the hands of my brother Esau, for I am greatly afraid of him. **22** And if there is no righteousness in me, do it for the sake of Abraham and my father Isaac. **23** For I know that through kindness and mercy have I acquired this wealth; now therefore I implore you to deliver me this day with your kindness and to answer me." **24** And Jacob ceased praying to the Lord, and he divided the people that were with him with the flocks and cattle into two camps, and he gave the half to the care of Damesek, the son of Eliezer, Abraham's servant, for a camp, with his children, and the other half he gave to the care of his brother Elianus the son of Eliezer, to be for a camp with his children. **25** And he commanded them, saying, "Keep yourselves at a distance with your camps, and do not come too near each other, and if Esau come to one camp and slay it, the other camp at a distance from it will escape him." **26** And Jacob tarried there that night, and during the whole night he gave his servants instructions concerning the forces and his children. **27** And the Lord heard the prayer of Jacob on that day, and the Lord then delivered Jacob from the hands of his brother Esau. **28** And the Lord sent three angels of the angels of heaven, and they went before Esau and came to him. **29** And these angels appeared unto Esau and his people as two thousand men, riding upon horses furnished with all sorts of war instruments, and they appeared in the sight of Esau and all his men to be divided into four camps, with four chiefs to them. **30** And one camp went on and they found Esau coming with four hundred men toward his brother Jacob, and this camp ran toward Esau and his people and terrified them, and Esau fell off the horse in alarm, and all his men separated from him in that place, for they were greatly afraid. **31** And the whole of the camp shouted after them when they fled from Esau, and all the warlike men answered, saying, **32** "Surely we are the servants of Jacob, who is the servant of God, and who then can stand against us?" And Esau said unto them, "O then, my lord and brother Jacob is your lord, whom I have not seen for these twenty years, and now that I have this day come to see him, do you treat me in this manner?" **33** And the angels answered him saying, "As the Lord lives, were not Jacob of whom you speak your brother, we had not let one remaining from you and your people, but only on account of Jacob we will do nothing to them." **34** And this camp passed from Esau and his men and it went away, and Esau and his men had gone from them about a league when the second camp came toward him with all sorts of weapons, and they also did unto Esau and his men as the first camp had done to them. **35** And when they had left it to go on, behold the third camp came toward him and they were all terrified, and Esau fell off the horse, and the whole camp cried out, and said, "Surely we are the servants of Jacob, who is the servant of God, and who can stand against us?" **36** And Esau again answered them saying, "O then, Jacob my lord and your lord is my brother, and for twenty years I have not seen his countenance and hearing this day that he was coming, I went this day to meet him, and do you treat me in this manner?" **37** And they answered him, and said unto him, "As the Lord lives, were not Jacob your brother as you did say, we had not left a remnant from you and your men, but on account of Jacob of whom you speak being your brother, we will not meddle with you or your men." **38** And the third camp also passed from them, and he still continued his road with his men toward Jacob, when the fourth camp came toward him, and they also did unto him and his men as the others had done. **39** And when Esau beheld the evil which the four angels had done to him and to his men, he became greatly afraid of his brother Jacob, and he went to meet him in peace. **40** And Esau concealed his hatred against Jacob, because he was afraid of his life on account of his brother Jacob, and because he imagined that the four camps that he had lighted upon were Jacob's servants. **41** And Jacob tarried that night with his servants in their camps, and he resolved with his servants to give unto Esau a present from all that he had with him, and from all his property; and Jacob rose up in the morning, he and his men, and they chose from among the cattle a present for Esau. **42** And this is the amount of the present which Jacob chose from his flock to give unto his brother Esau: and he selected two hundred and forty head from the flocks, and he selected from the camels and asses thirty each, and of the herds he chose fifty kine. **43** And he put them all in ten droves, and he placed each sort by itself, and he delivered them into the hands of ten of his servants, each drove by itself. **44** And he commanded them, and said unto them, "Keep yourselves at a distance from each other, and put a space between the droves, and when Esau and those who are with him will meet you and ask you, saying, 'Whose are you, and where do you go, and to whom belongs all this before you,' you will say unto them, 'We are the servants of Jacob, and we come to meet Esau in peace, and behold Jacob comes behind us. **45** And that which is before us is a present sent from Jacob to his brother Esau.' **46** And if they will say unto you, 'Why does he delay behind you, from coming to meet his brother and to see his face,' then you will say unto them, 'surely he comes joyfully behind us to meet his brother, for he said, I will appease him with the present that goes to him, and after this I will see his face, perhaps he will accept of me.' " **47** So the whole present passed on in the hands of his servants, and went before him on that day, and he lodged that night with his camps by the border of the brook of Jabuk, and he rose up in the midst of the night, and he took his wives and his maidservants, and all belonging to him, and he that night passed them over the ford Jabuk. **48** And when he passed all belonging to him over the brook, Jacob was left by himself, and a man met him, and he wrestled with him that night until the breaking of the day, and the hollow of Jacob's thigh was out of joint through wrestling with him. **49** And at the break of day the man left Jacob there, and he blessed him and went away, and Jacob passed the brook at the break of day, and he halted upon his thigh. **50** And the sun rose upon him when he had passed the brook, and he came up to the place of his cattle and children. **51** And they went on until midday, and while they were going the present was passing on before them. **52** And Jacob lifted up his eyes and looked, and behold Esau was at a distance, coming along with many men, about four hundred, and Jacob was greatly afraid of his brother. **53** And Jacob hastened and divided his children unto his wives and his handmaids, and his daughter Dinah he put in a chest, and delivered her into the hands of his servants. **54** And he passed before his children and wives to meet his brother, and he bowed down to the ground. He bowed down seven times until he approached his brother, and God caused Jacob to find grace and favor in the sight of Esau and his men, for God had heard the prayer of Jacob. **55** And the fear of Jacob and his terror fell upon his brother Esau, for Esau was greatly afraid of Jacob for what the angels of God had done to Esau, and Esau's anger against Jacob was turned into kindness. **56** And when Esau saw Jacob running toward him, he also ran toward him and he embraced him, and he fell upon his neck, and they kissed and they wept. **57** And God put fear and kindness toward Jacob in the hearts of the men that came with Esau, and they also kissed Jacob and embraced him. **58** And also Eliphaz, the son of Esau, with his four brothers, sons of Esau, wept with Jacob, and they kissed him and embraced him, for the fear of Jacob had fallen upon them all. **59** And Esau lifted up his eyes and saw the women with their offspring, the children of Jacob, walking behind Jacob and bowing along the road to Esau. **60** And Esau said unto Jacob, "Who are these with you, my brother? Are they your children or your servants?" And Jacob answered Esau and said, "They are my children which God has graciously given to your servant." **61** And while Jacob was speaking to Esau and his men, Esau beheld the whole camp, and he said unto Jacob, "From where did you get the whole of the camp that I met last night?" And Jacob said, "To find favor in the sight of my lord, it is that which God graciously gave to your servant." **62** And the present came before Esau, and Jacob pressed Esau, saying, "Take I pray you the present that I have brought to my lord," and Esau said, "Why is this my purpose? Keep that which you have unto yourself." **63** And Jacob said, "It is incumbent upon me to give all this, since I have seen your face, that you still live in peace." **64** And Esau refused to take the present, and Jacob said unto him, "I implore you my lord, if now I have found favor in your sight, then receive my present at my hand, for I have therefore seen your face, as though I had seen a god-like face, because you were pleased with me." **65** And Esau took the present, and Jacob also gave unto Esau silver and gold and bdellium, for he pressed him so much that he took them. **66** And Esau divided the cattle that were in the camp, and he gave the half to the men who had come with him, for they had come on hire, and the other half he delivered unto the hands of his children. **67** And the silver and gold and bdellium he gave in the hands of Eliphaz his eldest son, and Esau said unto Jacob, "Let us remain with you, and we will go slowly along with you until you come to my place with me, that we may dwell there together." **68** And Jacob answered his brother and said, "I would do as my lord speaks unto me, but my lord knows that the children are tender, and the flocks and herds with their young who are with me, go but slowly, for if they went swiftly they would all die, for you know their burdens and their fatigue. **69** Therefore let my lord pass on before his servant, and I will go on slowly for the sake of the children and the flock, until I come to my lord's place to Seir." **70** And Esau said unto Jacob, "I will place with you some of the people that are with me to take care of you in the road, and to bear your fatigue and burden," and he said, "What need is there of that my lord, if I may find grace in your sight? **71** Behold I will come unto you to Seir to dwell there together as you have spoken, go you then with your people for I will follow you." **72** And Jacob said this to Esau in order to remove Esau and his men from him, so that Jacob might afterward go to his father's house to the land of Canaan. **73** And Esau hearkened to the voice of Jacob, and Esau returned with the four hundred men that were with him on their road to Seir, and Jacob and all belonging to him went that day as far as the extremity of the land of Canaan in its borders, and he remained there some time.

CHAPTER 33

1 And some time after Jacob went away from the borders of the land, he came to the land of Shalem, that is the city of Shechem, which is in the land of Canaan, and he rested in front of the city. **2** And he bought a parcel of the field which was there, from the children of Hamor the people of the land, for five shekels. **3** And Jacob there built himself a house, and he pitched his tent there, and he made booths for his cattle, therefore he called the name of that place Succoth. **4** And Jacob remained in Succoth a year and six months. **5** At that time some of the women of the inhabitants of the land went to the city of Shechem to dance and rejoice with the daughters of the people of the city, and when they went out then Rachel and Leah the wives of Jacob with their families also went to behold the rejoicing of the daughters of the city. **6** And Dinah the daughter of Jacob also went along with them and saw the daughters of the city, and they remained there before these daughters while all the people of the city were standing by them to behold their rejoicings, and all the great people of the city were there. **7** And Shechem the son of Hamor, the prince of the land was also standing there to see them. **8** And Shechem beheld Dinah the daughter of Jacob sitting with her mother before the daughters of the city, and the damsel pleased him greatly, and he there asked his friends and his people, saying, "Whose daughter is that sitting among the women, whom I do not know in this city?" **9** And they said unto him, "Surely this is the daughter of Jacob the son of Isaac the Hebrew, who has dwelt in this city for some time, and when it was reported that the daughters of the

land were going out to rejoice she went with her mother and maidservants to sit among them as you see." **10** And Shechem beheld Dinah the daughter of Jacob, and when he looked at her his soul became fixed upon Dinah. **11** And he sent and had her taken by force, and Dinah came to the house of Shechem and he seized her forcibly and lay with her and humbled her, and he loved her exceedingly and placed her in his house. **12** And they came and told the thing unto Jacob, and when Jacob heard that Shechem had defiled his daughter Dinah, Jacob sent twelve of his servants to fetch Dinah from the house of Shechem, and they went and came to the house of Shechem to take away Dinah from there. **13** And when they came Shechem went out to them with his men and drove them from his house, and he would not suffer them to come before Dinah, but Shechem was sitting with Dinah kissing and embracing her before their eyes. **14** And the servants of Jacob came back and told him, saying, "When we came, he and his men drove us away, and thus did Shechem do unto Dinah before our eyes." **15** And Jacob knew moreover that Shechem had defiled his daughter, but he said nothing, and his sons were feeding his cattle in the field, and Jacob remained silent until their return. **16** And before his sons came home Jacob sent two maidens from his servants' daughters to take care of Dinah in the house of Shechem, and to remain with her, and Shechem sent three of his friends to his father Hamor the son of Chiddekem, the son of Pered, saying, "Get me this damsel for a wife." **17** And Hamor the son of Chiddekem the Hivite came to the house of Shechem his son, and he sat before him, and Hamor said unto his son, "Shechem, is there then no woman among the daughters of your people that you will take an Hebrew woman who is not of your people?" **18** And Shechem said to him, "Her only must you get for me, for she is delightful in my sight"; and Hamor did according to the word of his son, for he was greatly beloved by him. **19** And Hamor went out to Jacob to commune with him concerning this matter, and when he had gone from the house of his son Shechem, before he came to Jacob to speak unto him, behold the sons of Jacob had come from the field, as soon as they heard the thing that Shechem the son of Hamor had done. **20** And the men were very much grieved concerning their sister, and they all came home fired with anger, before the time of gathering in their cattle. **21** And they came and sat before their father and they spoke unto him kindled with wrath, saying, "Surely death is due to this man and to his household, because the Lord God of the whole earth commanded Noah and his children that man will never rob, nor commit adultery; now behold Shechem has both ravaged and committed fornication with our sister, and not one of all the people of the city spoke a word to him. **22** Surely you know and understandest that the judgment of death is due to Shechem, and to his father, and to the whole city on account of the thing which he has done." **23** And while they were speaking before their father in this matter, behold Hamor the father of Shechem came to speak to Jacob the words of his son concerning Dinah, and he sat before Jacob and before his sons. **24** And Hamor spoke unto them, saying, "The soul of my son Shechem longs for your daughter; I pray you give her unto him for a wife and intermarry with us; give us your daughters and we will give you our daughters, and you will dwell with us in our land and we will be as one people in the land. **25** For our land is very extensive, so dwell you and trade therein and get possessions in it, and do therein as you desire, and no one will prevent you by saying a word to you." **26** And Hamor ceased speaking unto Jacob and his sons, and behold Shechem his son had come after him, and he sat before them. **27** And Shechem spoke before Jacob and his sons, saying, "May I find favor in your sight that you will give me your daughter, and whatever you say unto me that will I do for her. **28** Ask me for abundance of dowry and gift, and I will give it, and whatever you will say unto me that will I do, and whoever he be that will rebel against your orders, he will die; only give me the damsel for a wife." **29** And Simeon and Levi answered Hamor and Shechem his son deceitfully, saying, "All you have spoken unto us we will do for you. **30** And behold our sister is in your house but keep away from her until we send to our father Isaac concerning this matter, for we can do nothing without his consent. **31** For he knows the ways of our father Abraham, and whatever he says unto us we will tell you, we will conceal nothing from you." **32** And Simeon and Levi spoke this unto Shechem and his father in order to find a pretext, and to seek counsel what was to be done to Shechem and to his city in this matter. **33** And when Shechem and his father heard the words of Simeon and Levi, it seemed good in their sight,

and Shechem and his father came out to go home. **34** And when they had gone, the sons of Jacob said unto their father, saying, "Behold, we know that death is due to these wicked ones and to their city, because they transgressed that which God had commanded unto Noah and his children and his seed after them. **35** And also because Shechem did this thing to our sister Dinah in defiling her, for such vileness will never be done among us. **36** Now therefore know and see what you will do and seek counsel and pretext what is to be done to them, in order to kill all the inhabitants of this city." **37** And Simeon said to them, "Here is a proper advice for you: tell them to circumcise every male among them as we are circumcised, and if they do not wish to do this, we will take our daughter from them and go away. **38** And if they consent to do this and will do it, then when they are sunk down with pain, we will attack them with our swords, as upon one who is quiet and peaceable, and we will slay every male person among them." **39** And Simeon's advice pleased them, and Simeon and Levi resolved to do unto them as it was proposed. **40** And on the next morning Shechem and Hamor his father came again unto Jacob and his sons, to speak concerning Dinah, and to hear what answer the sons of Jacob would give to their words. **41** And the sons of Jacob spoke deceitfully to them, saying, "We told our father Isaac all your words, and your words pleased him. **42** But he spoke unto us, saying, 'Thus did Abraham his father command him from God the Lord of the whole earth, that any man who is not of his descendants that should wish to take one of his daughters, will cause every male belonging to him to be circumcised, as we are circumcised, and then we may give him our daughter for a wife.' **43** Now we have made known to you all our ways that our father spoke unto us, for we cannot do this of which you spoke unto us, to give our daughter to an uncircumcised man, for it is a disgrace to us. **44** But herein will we consent to you, to give you our daughter, and we will also take unto ourselves your daughters, and will dwell among you and be one people as you have spoken, if you will hearken to us, and consent to be like us, to circumcise every male belonging to you, as we are circumcised. **45** And if you will not hearken unto us, to have every male circumcised as we are circumcised, as we have commanded, then we will come to you, and take our daughter from you and go away."

46 And Shechem and his father Hamor heard the words of the sons of Jacob, and the thing pleased them exceedingly, and Shechem and his father Hamor hastened to do the wishes of the sons of Jacob, for Shechem was very fond of Dinah, and his soul was riveted to her. **47** And Shechem and his father Hamor hastened to the gate of the city, and they assembled all the men of their city and spoke unto them the words of the sons of Jacob, saying, **48** "We came to these men, the sons of Jacob, and we spoke unto them concerning their daughter, and these men will consent to do according to our wishes, and behold our land is of great extent for them, and they will dwell in it, and trade in it, and we will be one people; we will take their daughters, and our daughters we will give unto them for wives. **49** But only on this condition will these men consent to do this thing, that every male among us be circumcised as they are circumcised, as their God commanded them, and when we will have done according to their instructions to be circumcised, then will they dwell among us, together with their cattle and possessions, and we will be as one people with them." **50** And when all the men of the city heard the words of Shechem and his father Hamor, then all the men of their city were agreeable to this proposal, and they obeyed to be circumcised, for Shechem and his father Hamor were greatly esteemed by them, being the princes of the land. **51** And on the next day, Shechem and Hamor his father rose up early in the morning, and they assembled all the men of their city into the middle of the city, and they called for the sons of Jacob, who circumcised every male belonging to them on that day and the next. **52** And they circumcised Shechem and Hamor his father, and the five brothers of Shechem, and then everyone rose up and went home, for this thing was from the Lord against the city of Shechem, and from the Lord was Simeon's counsel in this matter, in order that the Lord might deliver the city of Shechem into the hands of Jacob's two sons.

CHAPTER 34

1 And the number of all the males that were circumcised, were six hundred and forty-five men, and two hundred and forty-six children. **2** But Chiddekem, son of Pered, the father of Hamor, and his six brothers, would not listen unto Shechem and his father Hamor, and they would not be circumcised, for the proposal of the sons of Jacob was loathsome in their sight, and their anger was greatly roused at this, that the people of the city had not hearkened to them. **3** And in the evening of the second day, they found eight small children who had not been circumcised, for their mothers had concealed them from Shechem and his father Hamor, and from the men of the city. **4** And Shechem and his father Hamor sent to have them brought before them to be circumcised, when Chiddekem and his six brothers sprang at them with their swords and sought to slay them. **5** And they sought to slay also Shechem and his father Hamor and they sought to slay Dinah with them on account of this matter. **6** And they said unto them, "What is this thing that you have done? Are there no women among the daughters of your brethren the Canaanites, that you wish to take unto yourselves daughters of the Hebrews, whom you knew not before, and will do this act which your fathers never commanded you? **7** Do you imagine that you will succeed through this act which you have done? And what will you answer in this affair to your brethren the Canaanites, who will come tomorrow and ask you concerning this thing? **8** And if your act will not appear just and good in their sight, what will you do for your lives, and me for our lives, in your not having hearkened to our voices? **9** And if the inhabitants of the land and all your brethren the children of Ham, will hear of your act, saying, **10** 'On account of a Hebrew woman did Shechem and Hamor his father, and all the inhabitants of their city, do that with which they had been unacquainted and which their ancestors never commanded them,' where then will you fly or where conceal your shame, all your days before your brethren, the inhabitants of the land of Canaan? **11** Now therefore we cannot bear up against this thing which you have done, neither can we be burdened with this yoke upon us, which our ancestors did not command us. **12** Behold tomorrow we will go and assemble all our brethren, the Canaanite brethren who dwell in the land, and we will all come and smite you and all those who trust in you, that there will not be a remnant left from you or them." **13** And when Hamor and his son Shechem and all the people of the city heard the words of Chiddekem and his brothers, they were terribly afraid of their lives at their words, and they repented of what they had done. **14** And Shechem and his father Hamor answered their father Chiddekem and his brethren, and they said unto them, "All the words which you spoke unto us are true. 15 Now do not say, nor imagine in your hearts that on account of the love of the Hebrews we did this thing that our ancestors did not command us. 16 But because we saw that it was not their intention and desire to accede to our wishes concerning their daughter as to our taking her, except on this condition, so we hearkened to their voices and did this act which you saw, in order to obtain our desire from them. 17 And when we will have obtained our request from them, we will then return to them and do unto them that which you say unto us. 18 We implore you then to wait and tarry until our flesh will be healed and we again become strong, and we will then go together against them, and do unto them that which is in your hearts and in ours." 19 And Dinah the daughter of Jacob heard all these words which Chiddekem and his brothers had spoken, and what Hamor and his son Shechem and the people of their city had answered them. 20 And she hastened and sent one of her maidens, that her father had sent to take care of her in the house of Shechem, to Jacob her father and to her brethren, saying: 21 "Thus did Chiddekem and his brothers advise concerning you, and thus did Hamor and Shechem and the people of the city answer them." 22 And when Jacob heard these words he was filled with wrath, and he was indignant at them, and his anger was kindled against them. 23 And Simeon and Levi swore and said, "As the Lord lives, the God of the whole earth, by this time tomorrow, there will not be a remnant left in the whole city." 24 And twenty young men had concealed themselves who were not circumcised, and these young men fought against Simeon and Levi, and Simeon and Levi killed eighteen of them, and two fled from them and escaped to some lime pits that were in the city, and Simeon and Levi sought for them, but could not find them. 25 And Simeon and Levi continued to go about in the city, and they killed all the people of the city at the edge of the sword, and they left none remaining. 26 And there was a great consternation in the midst of the city, and the cry of the people of the city ascended to heaven, and all the women and children cried aloud. 27 And Simeon and Levi slew all the city; they left not a male remaining in the whole city. 28 And they slew Hamor and Shechem his son at the edge of the sword, and they brought away Dinah from the house of Shechem and they went from there. 29 And the sons of Jacob went and returned, and came upon the slain, and spoiled all their property which was in the city and the field. 30 And while they were taking the spoil, three hundred men stood up and threw dust at them and struck them with stones, when Simeon turned to them and he slew them all with the edge of the sword, and Simeon turned before Levi, and came into the city. 31 And they took away their sheep and their oxen and their cattle, and also the remainder of the women and little ones, and they led all these away, and they opened a gate and went out and came unto their father Jacob with vigor. 32 And when Jacob saw all that they had done to the city, and saw the spoil that they took from them, Jacob was very angry at them, and Jacob said unto them, "What is this that you have done to me? Behold I obtained rest among the Canaanite inhabitants of the land, and none of them meddled with me. 33 And now you have done to make me obnoxious to the inhabitants of the land, among the Canaanites and the Perizzites, and I am but of a small number, and they will all assemble against me and slay me when they hear of your work with their brethren, and I and my household will be destroyed." 34 And Simeon and Levi and all their brothers with them answered their father Jacob and said unto him, "Behold we live in the land, and will Shechem do this to our sister? Why are you silent at all that Shechem has done? And will he deal with our sister as with a harlot in the streets?" 35 And the number of women whom Simeon and Levi took captives from the city of Shechem, whom they did not slay, was eighty-five who had not known man. 36 And among them was a young damsel of beautiful appearance and well favored, whose name was Bunah, and Simeon took her for a wife, and the number of the males which they took captives and did not slay, was forty-seven men, and the rest they slew. 37 And all the young men and women that Simeon and Levi had taken captives from the city of Shechem, were servants to the sons of Jacob and to their children after them, until the day of the sons of Jacob going out from the land of Egypt. 38 And when Simeon and Levi had gone out from the city, the two young men that were left, who had concealed themselves in the city, and did not die among the people of the city, rose up, and these young men went into the city and walked about in it, and found the city desolate without man, and only women weeping, and these young men cried out and said, "Behold, this is the evil which the sons of Jacob the Hebrew did to this city in their having this day destroyed one of the Canaanite cities, and were not afraid of their lives of all the land of Canaan." **39** And these men left the city and went to the city of Tapnach, and they came there and told the inhabitants of Tapnach all that had befallen them, and all that the sons of Jacob had done to the city of Shechem. **40** And the information reached Jashub king of Tapnach, and he sent men to the city of Shechem to see those young men, for the king did not believe them in this account, saying, "How could two men lay waste such a large town as Shechem?" **41** And the messengers of Jashub came back and told him, saying, "We came unto the city, and it is destroyed, there is not a man there; only weeping women; neither is any flock or cattle there, for all that was in the city the sons of Jacob took away." **42** And Jashub wondered at this, saying, "How could two men do this thing, to destroy so large a city, and not one man able to stand against them? **43** For the like has not been from the days of Nimrod, and not even from the remotest time, has the like taken place"; and Jashub, king of Tapnach, said to his people, "Be courageous and we will go and fight against these Hebrews, and do unto them as they did unto the city, and we will avenge the cause of the people of the city." **44** And Jashub, king of Tapnach, consulted with his counsellors about this matter, and his advisers said unto him, "Alone you will not prevail over the Hebrews, for they must be powerful to do this work to the whole city. **45** If two of them laid waste the whole city, and no one stood against them, surely if you will go against them, they will all rise against us and destroy us likewise. **46** But if you will send to all the kings that surround us, and let them come together, then we will go with them and fight against the sons of Jacob; then will you prevail against them." **47** And Jashub heard the words of his counsellors, and their words pleased him and his people, and he did so; and Jashub king of Tapnach sent to all the kings of the Amorites that surrounded Shechem and Tapnach, saying, **48** "Go up with me and assist me, and we will smite Jacob the Hebrew and all his sons, and destroy them from the earth, for thus did he do to the city of Shechem, and do you not know of it?" **49** And all the kings of the Amorites heard the evil that the sons of Jacob had done to the city of Shechem, and they were greatly astonished at them. **50** And the seven kings of the Amorites assembled with all their armies, about ten thousand men with drawn swords, and they came to fight against the sons of Jacob; and Jacob heard that the kings of the Amorites had assembled to fight against his sons, and Jacob was greatly afraid, and it distressed him. **51** And Jacob exclaimed against Simeon and Levi, saying, "What is this act that you did? Why have you injured me, to bring against me all the children of Canaan to destroy me and my household? For I was at rest, even I and my household, and you have done this thing to me, and provoked the inhabitants of the land against me by your proceedings." **52** And Judah answered his father, saying, "Was it for naught my brothers Simeon and Levi killed all the inhabitants of Shechem? Surely it was because Shechem had humbled our sister and transgressed the command of our God to Noah and his children, for Shechem took our sister away by force, and committed adultery with her. **53** And Shechem did all this evil and not one of the inhabitants of his city interfered with him, to say, 'Why will you do this?' Surely for this my brothers went and smote the city, and the Lord delivered it into their hands, because its inhabitants had transgressed the commands of our God. Is it then for naught that they have done all this? **54** And now why are you afraid or distressed, and why are you displeased at my brothers, and why is your anger kindled against them? **55** Surely our God who delivered into their hand the city of Shechem and its people, he will also deliver into our hands all the Canaanite kings who are coming against us, and we will do unto them as my brothers did unto Shechem. **56** Now be tranquil about them and cast away your fears, but trust in the Lord our God, and pray unto him to assist us and deliver us and deliver our enemies into our hands." **57** And Judah called to one of his father's servants, "Go now and see where those kings, who are coming against us, are situated with their armies." **58** And the servant went and looked far off, and went up opposite Mount Sihon, and saw all the camps of the kings standing in the fields, and he returned to Judah and said, "Behold the kings are situated in the field with all their camps, a people exceedingly numerous, like unto the sand upon the seashore." **59** And Judah said unto Simeon and Levi, and unto all his brothers, "Strengthen yourselves and be sons of valor, for the Lord our God is with us, do not fear them. **60** Stand out each man, girt with his weapons of war, his bow and his sword, and we will go and fight against these uncircumcised men; the Lord is our God, He will save us." 61 And they rose up, and each girt on his weapons of war, great and small, eleven sons of Jacob, and all the servants of Jacob with them. 62 And all the servants of Isaac who were with Isaac in Hebron, all came to them equipped in all sorts of war instruments, and the sons of Jacob and their servants, being one hundred and twelve men, went towards these kings, and Jacob also went with them. 63 And the sons of Jacob sent unto their father Isaac the son of Abraham to Hebron, the same is Kireath-arba, saying, 64 "Pray we implore you for us unto the Lord our God, to protect us from the hands of the Canaanites who are coming against us, and to deliver them into our hands." 65 And Isaac the son of Abraham prayed unto the Lord for his sons, and he said, "O Lord God, you did promise my father, saying, 'I will multiply your seed as the stars of heaven,' and you did also promise me, and establish you your word, now that the kings of Canaan are coming together, to make war with my children because they committed no violence. 66 Now therefore, O Lord God, God of the whole earth, pervert, I pray you, the counsel of these kings that they may not fight against my sons. 67 And impress the hearts of these kings and their people with the terror of my sons and bring down their pride that they may turn away from my sons. 68 And with your strong hand and outstretched arm deliver my sons and their servants from them, for power and might are in your hands to do all this." 69 And the sons of Jacob and their servants went toward these kings, and they trusted in the Lord their God, and while they were going, Jacob their father also prayed unto the Lord and said, "O Lord God, powerful and exalted God, who has reigned from days of old, from then until now and forever; 70 You are He who stirs up wars and causes them to cease, in your hand are power and might to exalt and to bring down; O may my prayer be acceptable before you that you may turn to me with your mercies, to impress the hearts of these kings and their people with the terror of my sons, and terrify them and their camps, and with your great kindness deliver all those that trust in you, for it is you who can bring people under us and reduce nations under our power."

CHAPTER 35

1 And all the kings of the Amorites came and took their stand in the field to consult with their counsellors what was to be done with the sons of Jacob, for they were still afraid of them, saying, "Behold, two of them slew the whole of the city of Shechem." 2 And the Lord heard the prayers of Isaac and Jacob, and he filled the hearts of all these kings' advisers with great fear and terror that they unanimously exclaimed, 3 "Are you silly this day, or is there no understanding in you, that you will fight with the Hebrews, and why will you take a delight in your own destruction this day? 4 Behold two of them came to the city of Shechem without fear or terror, and they killed all the inhabitants of the city, that no man stood up against them, and how will you be able to fight with them all? 5 Surely you know that their God is exceedingly fond of them, and has done mighty things for them, such as have not been done from days of old, and among all the gods of nations, there is none can do like unto his mighty deeds. 6 Surely he delivered their father Abraham, the Hebrew, from the hand of Nimrod, and from the hand of all his people who had many times sought to slay him. 7 He delivered him also from the fire in which king Nimrod had cast him, and his God delivered him from it. 8 And who else can do the like? Surely it was Abraham who slew the five kings of Elam, when they had touched his brother's son who in those days dwelt in Sodom. 9 And took his servant that was faithful in his house and a few of his men, and they pursued the kings of Elam in one night and killed them and restored to his brother's son all his property which they had taken from him. 10 And surely you know the God of these Hebrews is much delighted with them, and they are also delighted with him, for they know that he delivered them from all their enemies. 11 And behold through his love toward his God, Abraham took his only and precious son and intended to bring him up as a burnt offering to his God, and had it not been for God who prevented him from doing this, he would then have done it through his love to his God. 12 And God saw all his works, and swore unto him, and promised him that he would deliver his sons and all his seed from every trouble that would befall them, because he had done this thing, and through his love to his God stifled his compassion for his child. 13 And have you not heard what their God did to Pharaoh king of Egypt, and to Abimelech

king of Gerar, through taking Abraham's wife, who said of her, 'she is my sister,' lest they might slay him on account of her, and think of taking her for a wife? And God did unto them and their people all that you heard of. **14** And behold, we ourselves saw with our eyes that Esau, the brother of Jacob, came to him with four hundred men, with the intention of slaying him, for he called to mind that he had taken away from him his father's blessing. **15** And he went to meet him when he came from Syria, to smite the mother with the children, and who delivered him from his hands but his God in whom he trusted? He delivered him from the hand of his brother and also from the hands of his enemies, and surely he again will protect them. **16** Who does not know that it was their God who inspired them with strength to do to the town of Shechem the evil which you heard of? **17** Could it then be with their own strength that two men could destroy such a large city as Shechem had it not been for their God in whom they trusted? He said and did unto them all this to slay the inhabitants of the city in their city. **18** And can you then prevail over them who have come out together from your city to fight with the whole of them, even if a thousand times as many more should come to your assistance? **19** Surely you know and understand that you do not come to fight with them, but you come to war with their God who made choice of them, and you have therefore all come this day to be destroyed. **20** Now therefore refrain from this evil which you are endeavoring to bring upon yourselves, and it will be better for you not to go to battle with them, although they are but few in numbers, because their God is with them." **21** And when the kings of the Amorites heard all the words of their advisers, their hearts were filled with terror, and they were afraid of the sons of Jacob and would not fight against them. **22** And they inclined their ears to the words of their advisers, and they listened to all their words, and the words of the counsellors greatly pleased the kings, and they did so. **23** And the kings turned and refrained from the sons of Jacob, for they dared not approach them to make war with them, for they were greatly afraid of them, and their hearts melted within them from their fear of them. **24** For this proceeded from the Lord to them, for he heard the prayers of his servants Isaac and Jacob, for they trusted in him; and all these kings returned with their camps on that day, each to his own city, and they did not

at that time fight with the sons of Jacob. **25** And the sons of Jacob kept their station that day until evening opposite Mount Sihon and seeing that these kings did not come to fight against them, the sons of Jacob returned home.

CHAPTER 36

1 At that time the Lord appeared unto Jacob saying, "Arise, go to Bethel and remain there, and make there an altar to the Lord who appears unto you, who delivered you and your sons from affliction." **2** And Jacob rose up with his sons and all belonging to him, and they went and came to Bethel according to the word of the Lord. **3** And Jacob was ninety-nine years old when he went up to Bethel, and Jacob and his sons and all the people that were with him, remained in Bethel in Luz, and he there built an altar to the Lord who appeared unto him, and Jacob and his sons remained in Bethel six months. **4** At that time died Deborah the daughter of Uz, the nurse of Rebecca, who had been with Jacob; and Jacob buried her beneath Bethel under an oak that was there. **5** And Rebecca the daughter of Bethuel, the mother of Jacob, also died at that time in Hebron, the same is Kireath-arba, and she was buried in the cave of Machpelah which Abraham had bought from the children of Heth. **6** And the life of Rebecca was one hundred and thirty-three years, and she died and when Jacob heard that his mother Rebecca was dead he wept bitterly for his mother, and made a great mourning for her, and for Deborah her nurse beneath the oak, and he called the name of that place Allon-bachuth. **7** And Laban the Syrian died in those days, for God smote him because he transgressed the covenant that existed between him and Jacob. **8** And Jacob was a hundred years old when the Lord appeared unto him, and blessed him and called his name Israel, and Rachel the wife of Jacob conceived in those days. **9** And at that time Jacob and all belonging to him journeyed from Bethel to go to his father's house, to Hebron. **10** And while they were going on the road, and there was yet but a little way to come to Ephrath, Rachel bore a son and she had hard labor and she died. **11** And Jacob buried her in the way to Ephrath, which is Bethlehem, and he set a pillar upon her grave, which is there unto this day; and the days of Rachel were forty-five years and she died. **12** And Jacob called the name of his son that was born to him, which Rachel bare unto him, Benjamin, for he was born to him in the land on the right hand. **13** And it was after the death of Rachel, that Jacob pitched his tent in the tent of her handmaid Bilhah. **14** And Reuben was jealous for his mother Leah on account of this, and he was filled with anger, and he rose up in his anger and went and entered the tent of Bilhah and he there removed his father's bed. **15** At that time the portion of birthright, together with the kingly and priestly offices, was removed from the sons of Reuben, for he had profaned his father's bed, and the birthright was given unto Joseph, the kingly office to Judah, and the priesthood unto Levi, because Reuben had defiled his father's bed. **16** And these are the generations of Jacob who were born to him in Padan-aram, and the sons of Jacob were twelve. **17** The sons of Leah were Reuben the firstborn, and Simeon, Levi, Judah, Issachar, Zebulun, and their sister Dinah; and the sons of Rachel were Joseph and Benjamin. **18** The sons of Zilpah, Leah's handmaid, were Gad and Asher, and the sons of Bilhah, Rachel's handmaid, were Dan and Naphtali; these are the sons of Jacob which were born to him in Padan-aram. **19** And Jacob and his sons and all belonging to him journeyed and came to Mamre, which is Kireath-arba, that is in Hebron, where Abraham and Isaac sojourned, and Jacob with his sons and all belonging to him, dwelt with his father in Hebron. **20** And his brother Esau and his sons, and all belonging to him went to the land of Seir and dwelt there, and had possessions in the land of Seir, and the children of Esau were fruitful and multiplied exceedingly in the land of Seir. **21** And these are the generations of Esau that were born to him in the land of Canaan, and the sons of Esau were five. **22** And Adah bore to Esau his firstborn Eliphaz, and she also bore to him Reuel, and Ahlibamah bore to him Jeush, Yaalam and Korah. **23** These are the children of Esau who were born to him in the land of Canaan; and the sons of Eliphaz the son of Esau were Teman, Omar, Zepho, Gatam, Kenaz and Amalex, and the sons of Reuel were Nachas, Zerach, Shamah and Mizzah. **24** And the sons of Jeush were Timnah, Alvah, Jetheth; and the sons of Yaalam were Alah, Phinor and Kenaz. **25** And the sons of Korah were Teman, Mibzar, Magdiel and Eram; these are the families of the sons of Esau according to their dukedoms in the land of Seir. **26** And these are the names of the sons of Seir the Horite, inhabitants of the land of Seir, Lotan, Shobal, Zibeon, Anah, Dishan, Ezer and Dishon, being seven sons. **27** And the children of Lotan were Hori, Heman and their sister Timna, that is Timna who came to Jacob and his sons, and they would not give ear to her, and she went and became a concubine to Eliphaz the son of Esau, and she bore to him Amalek. **28** And the sons of Shobal were Alvan, Manahas, Ebal, Shepho, and Onam, and the sons of Zibeon were Ajah, and Anah, this was that Anah who found the Yemim in the wilderness when he fed the asses of Zibeon his father. **29** And while he was feeding his father's asses he led them to the wilderness at different times to feed them. **30** And there was a day that he brought them to one of the deserts on the seashore, opposite the wilderness of the people, and while he was feeding them, behold a very heavy storm came from the other side of the sea and rested upon the asses that were feeding there, and they all stood still. **31** And afterward about one hundred and twenty great and terrible animals came out from the wilderness at the other side of the sea, and they all came to the place where the asses were, and they placed themselves there. **32** And those animals, from their middle downward, were in the shape of the children of men, and from their middle upward, some had the likeness of bears, and some the likeness of the keephas, with tails behind them from between their shoulders reaching down to the earth, like the tails of the ducheephas, and these animals came and mounted and rode upon these asses, and led them away, and they went away unto this day. **33** And one of these animals approached Anah and smote him with his tail, and then fled from that place. **34** And when he saw this work he was exceedingly afraid of his life, and he fled and escaped to the city. **35** And he related to his sons and brothers all that had happened to him, and many men went to seek the asses but could not find them, and Anah and his brothers went no more to that place from that day following, for they were greatly afraid of their lives. **36** And the children of Anah the son of Seir, were Dishon and his sister Ahlibamah, and the children of Dishon were Hemdan, Eshban, Ithran and Cheran, and the children of Ezer were Bilhan, Zaavan and Akan, and the children of Dishon were Uz and Aran. **37** These are the families of the children of Seir the Horite, according to their dukedoms in the land of Seir. **38** And Esau and his children dwelt in the land of Seir the Horite, the inhabitant of the land, and they had possessions in it and were fruitful and multiplied exceedingly, and Jacob and his children and all belonging to them, dwelt with their father Isaac in the land of Canaan, as the Lord had commanded Abraham their father.

CHAPTER 37

1 And in the one hundred and fifth year of the life of Jacob, that is the ninth year of Jacob's dwelling with his children in the land of Canaan, he came from Padan-aram. **2** And in those days Jacob journeyed with his children from Hebron, and they went and returned to the city of Shechem, they and all belonging to them, and they dwelt there, for the children of Jacob obtained good and fat pasture land for their cattle in the city of Shechem, the city of Shechem having then been rebuilt, and there were in it about three hundred men and women. **3** And Jacob and his children and all belonging to him dwelt in the part of the field which Jacob had bought from Hamor the father of Shechem, when he came from Padan-aram before Simeon and Levi had smitten the city. **4** And all those kings of the Canaanites and Amorites that surrounded the city of Shechem, heard that the sons of Jacob had again come to Shechem and dwelt there. **5** And they said, "Will the sons of Jacob the Hebrew again come to the city and dwell therein, after that they have smitten its inhabitants and driven them out? Will they now return and also drive out those who are dwelling in the city or slay them?" **6** And all the kings of Canaan again assembled, and they came together to make war with Jacob and his sons. **7** And Jashub king of Tapnach sent also to all his neighboring kings, to Elan king of Gaash, and to Ihuri king of Shiloh, and to Parathon king of Chazar, and to Susi king of Sarton, and to Laban king of Bethchoran, and to Shabir king of Othnay-mah, saying, **8** Come up to me and assist me, and let us smite Jacob the Hebrew and his sons, and all belonging to him, for they are again come to Shechem to possess it and to slay its inhabitants as before. **9** And all these kings assembled together and came with all their camps, a people exceedingly plentiful like the sand upon the seashore, and they were all opposite to Tapnach. **10** And Jashub king of Tapnach went out to them with all his army, and he encamped with them opposite to Tapnach without the city, and all these kings they divided into seven divisions, being seven camps against the sons of Jacob. **11** And they sent a declaration to Jacob and his son, saying,

"Come you all out to us that we may have an interview together in the plain, and revenge the cause of the men of Shechem whom you slew in their city, and you will now again return to the city of Shechem and dwell therein, and slay its inhabitants as before." **12** And the sons of Jacob heard this and their anger was kindled exceedingly at the words of the kings of Canaan, and ten of the sons of Jacob hastened and rose up, and each of them girt on his weapons of war; and there were one hundred and two of their servants with them equipped in battle array. **13** And all these men, the sons of Jacob with their servants, went toward these kings, and Jacob their father was with them, and they all stood upon the heap of Shechem. **14** And Jacob prayed to the Lord for his sons, and he spread out his hands to the Lord, and he said, "O God, you are an Almighty God, you are our father, you did form us and we are the works of your hands; I pray you deliver my sons through your mercy from the hand of their enemies, who are this day coming to fight with them and save them from their hand, for in your hand is power and might, to save the few from the many. **15** And give unto my sons, your servants, strength of heart and might to fight with their enemies, to subdue them, and make their enemies fall before them, and let not my sons and their servants die through the hands of the children of Canaan. **16** But if it seems good in your eyes to take away the lives of my sons and their servants, take them in your great mercy through the hands of your ministers, that they may not perish this day by the hands of the kings of the Amorites." **17** And when Jacob ceased praying to the Lord the earth shook from its place, and the sun darkened, and all these kings were terrified, and a great consternation seized them. **18** And the Lord hearkened to the prayer of Jacob, and the Lord impressed the hearts of all the kings and their hosts with the terror and awe of the sons of Jacob. **19** For the Lord caused them to hear the voice of chariots, and the voice of mighty horses from the sons of Jacob, and the voice of a great army accompanying them. **20** And these kings were seized with great terror at the sons of Jacob, and while they were standing in their quarters, behold the sons of Jacob advanced upon them, with one hundred and twelve men, with a great and tremendous shouting. **21** And when the kings saw the sons of Jacob advancing toward them, they were still more panic stricken, and they were inclined to retreat from before the sons of

Jacob as at first, and not to fight with them. 22 But they did not retreat, saying, "It would be a disgrace to us thus twice to retreat from before the Hebrews." 23 And the sons of Jacob came near and advanced against all these kings and their armies, and they saw, and behold it was a very mighty people, numerous as the sand of the sea. 24 And the sons of Jacob called unto the Lord and said, "Help us O Lord, help us and answer us, for we trust in you, and let us not die by the hands of these uncircumcised men, who this day have come against us." 25 And the sons of Jacob girt on their weapons of war, and they took in their hands each man his shield and his javelin, and they approached to battle. 26 And Judah, the son of Jacob, ran first before his brethren, and ten of his servants with him, and he went toward these kings. 27 And Jashub, king of Tapnach, also came out first with his army before Judah, and Judah saw Jashub and his army coming toward him, and Judah's wrath was kindled, and his anger burned within him, and he approached to battle in which Judah ventured his life. 28 And Jashub and all his army were advancing toward Judah, and he was riding upon a very strong and powerful horse, and Jashub was a very valiant man, and covered with iron and brass from head to foot. 29 And while he was upon the horse, he shot arrows with both hands from before and behind, as was his manner in all his battles, and he never missed the place to which he aimed his arrows. 30 And when Jashub came to fight with Judah, and was darting many arrows against Judah, the Lord bound the hand of Jashub, and all the arrows that he shot rebounded upon his own men. 31 And notwithstanding this, Jashub kept advancing toward Judah, to challenge him with the arrows, but the distance between them was about thirty cubits, and when Judah saw Jashub darting out his arrows against him, he ran to him with his wrath-excited might. 32 And Judah took up a large stone from the ground, and its weight was sixty shekels, and Judah ran toward Jashub, and with the stone struck him on his shield, that Jashub was stunned with the blow, and fell off from his horse to the ground. 33 And the shield burst asunder out of the hand of Jashub, and through the force of the blow sprang to the distance of about fifteen cubits, and the shield fell before the second camp. 34 And the kings that came with Jashub saw at a distance the strength of Judah, the son of Jacob, and what he had done

to Jashub, and they were terribly afraid of Judah. 35 And they assembled near Jashub's camp, seeing his confusion, and Judah drew his sword and smote forty-two men of the camp of Jashub, and the whole of Jashub's camp fled before Judah, and no man stood against him, and they left Jashub and fled from him, and Jashub was still prostrate upon the ground. 36 And Jashub seeing that all the men of his camp had fled from him, hastened and rose up with terror against Judah, and stood upon his legs opposite Judah. 37 And Jashub had a single combat with Judah, placing shield toward shield, and Jashub's men all fled, for they were greatly afraid of Judah. 38 And Jashub took his spear in his hand to strike Judah upon his head, but Judah had quickly placed his shield to his head against Jashub's spear, so that the shield of Judah received the blow from Jashub's spear, and the shield was split in too. 39 And when Judah saw that his shield was split, he hastily drew his sword and smote Jashub at his ankles and cut off his feet that Jashub fell upon the ground, and the spear fell from his hand. 40 And Judah hastily picked up Jashub's spear, with which he severed his head and cast it next to his feet. 41 And when the sons of Jacob saw what Judah had done to Jashub, they all ran into the ranks of the other kings, and the sons of Jacob fought with the army of Jashub, and the armies of all the kings that were there. 42 And the sons of Jacob caused fifteen thousand of their men to fall, and they smote them as if smiting at gourds, and the rest fled for their lives. 43 And Judah was still standing by the body of Jashub, and stripped Jashub of his coat of mail. 44 And Judah also took off the iron and brass that was about Jashub and behold nine men of the captains of Jashub came along to fight against Judah. 45 And Judah hastened and took up a stone from the ground, and with it smote one of them upon the head, and his skull was fractured, and the body also fell from the horse to the ground. 46 And the eight captains that remained, seeing the strength of Judah, were greatly afraid and they fled, and Judah with his ten men pursued them, and they overtook them and slew them. 47 And the sons of Jacob were still smiting the armies of the kings, and they slew many of them, but those kings daringly kept their stand with their captains, and did not retreat from their places, and they exclaimed against those of their armies that fled from before the sons of Jacob, but none would listen to them, for they were afraid of their lives lest they should die. **48** And all the sons of Jacob, after having smitten the armies of the kings, returned and came before Judah, and Judah was still slaying the eight captains of Jashub, and stripping off their garments. **49** And Levi saw Elon, king of Gaash, advancing toward him, with his fourteen captains to smite him, but Levi did not know it for certain. **50** And Elon with his captains approached nearer, and Levi looked back and saw that battle was given him in the rear, and Levi ran with twelve of his servants, and they went and slew Elon and his captains with the edge of the sword.

CHAPTER 38

1 And Ihuri king of Shiloh came up to assist Elon, and he approached Jacob, when Jacob drew his bow that was in his hand and with an arrow struck Ihuri which caused his death. **2** And when Ihuri king of Shiloh was dead, the four remaining kings fled from their station with the rest of the captains, and they endeavored to retreat, saying, "We have no more strength with the Hebrews after their having killed the three kings and their captains who were more powerful than we are." **3** And when the sons of Jacob saw that the remaining kings had removed from their station, they pursued them, and Jacob also came from the heap of Shechem from the place where he was standing, and they went after the kings and they approached them with their servants. **4** And the kings and the captains with the rest of their armies, seeing that the sons of Jacob approached them, were afraid of their lives and fled until they reached the city of Chazar. **5** And the sons of Jacob pursued them to the gate of the city of Chazar, and they smote a great smiting among the kings and their armies, about four thousand men, and while they were smiting the army of the kings, Jacob was occupied with his bow confining himself to smiting the kings, and he slew them all. **6** And he slew Parathon king of Chazar at the gate of the city of Chazar, and he afterward smote Susi king of Sarton, and Laban king of Bethchorin, and Shabir king of Machnaymah, and he slew them all with arrows, an arrow to each of them, and they died. **7** And the sons of Jacob seeing that all the kings were dead and that they were broken up and retreating, continued to carry on the battle with the armies of the kings opposite the gate of Chazar, and they still smote about four hundred of their men. **8** And three men of the servants of Jacob

fell in that battle, and when Judah saw that three of his servants had died, it grieved him greatly, and his anger burned within him against the Amorites. **9** And all the men that remained of the armies of the kings were greatly afraid of their lives, and they ran and broke the gate of the walls of the city of Chazar, and they all entered the city for safety. **10** And they concealed themselves in the midst of the city of Chazar, for the city of Chazar was very large and extensive, and when all these armies had entered the city, the sons of Jacob ran after them to the city. **11** And four mighty men, experienced in battle, went out from the city and stood against the entrance of the city, with drawn swords and spears in their hands, and they placed themselves opposite the sons of Jacob, and would not suffer them to enter the city. **12** And Naphtali ran and came between them and with his sword smote two of them and cut off their heads at one stroke. **13** And he turned to the other two, and behold they had fled, and he pursued them, overtook them, smote them and slew them. **14** And the sons of Jacob came to the city and saw, and behold there was another wall to the city, and they sought for the gate of the wall and could not find it, and Judah sprang upon the top of the wall, and Simeon and Levi followed him, and they all three descended from the wall into the city. **15** And Simeon and Levi slew all the men who ran for safety into the city, and also the inhabitants of the city with their wives and little ones, they slew with the edge of the sword, and the cries of the city ascended up to heaven. **16** And Dan and Naphtali sprang upon the wall to see what caused the noise of lamentation, for the sons of Jacob felt anxious about their brothers, and they heard the inhabitants of the city speaking with weeping and supplications, saying, "Take all that we possess in the city and go away, only do not put us to death." **17** And when Judah, Simeon, and Levi had ceased smiting the inhabitants of the city, they ascended the wall and called to Dan and Naphtali, who were upon the wall, and to the rest of their brothers, and Simeon and Levi informed them of the entrance into the city, and all the sons of Jacob came to fetch the spoil. **18** And the sons of Jacob took the spoil of the city of Chazar, the flocks and herds, and the property, and they took all that could be captured, and went away that day from the city. **19** And on the next day the sons of Jacob went to Sarton, for they heard that the men of Sarton who had remained in the city were assembling to fight with them for having slain their king, and Sarton was a very high and fortified city, and it had a deep rampart surrounding the city. 20 And the pillar of the rampart was about fifty cubits and its breadth forty cubits, and there was no place for a man to enter the city on account of the rampart, and the sons of Jacob saw the rampart of the city, and they sought an entrance in it but could not find it. 21 For the entrance to the city was at the rear, and every man that wished to come into the city came by that road and went around the whole city, and he afterwards entered the city. 22 And the sons of Jacob seeing they could not find the way into the city, their anger was kindled greatly, and the inhabitants of the city seeing that the sons of Jacob were coming to them were greatly afraid of them, for they had heard of their strength and what they had done to Chazar. 23 And the inhabitants of the city of Sarton could not go out toward the sons of Jacob after having assembled in the city to fight against them, lest they might thereby get into the city, but when they saw that they were coming toward them, they were greatly afraid of them, for they had heard of their strength and what they had done to Chazar. 24 So the inhabitants of Sarton speedily took away the bridge of the road of the city, from its place, before the sons of Jacob came, and they brought it into the city. 25 And the sons of Jacob came and sought the way into the city and could not find it and the inhabitants of the city went up to the top of the wall, and saw, and behold the sons of Jacob were seeking an entrance into the city. 26 And the inhabitants of the city reproached the sons of Jacob from the top of the wall, and they cursed them, and the sons of Jacob heard the reproaches, and they were greatly incensed, and their anger burned within them. 27 And the sons of Jacob were provoked at them, and they all rose and sprang over the rampart with the force of their strength, and through their might passed the forty cubits' breadth of the rampart. 28 And when they had passed the rampart they stood under the wall of the city, and they found all the gates of the city enclosed with iron doors. 29 And the sons of Jacob came near to break open the doors of the gates of the city, and the inhabitants did not let them, for from the top of the wall they were casting stones and arrows upon them. 30 And the number of the people that were upon the wall was about four hundred men, and when the sons of Jacob saw that the men of the city would not let them open the gates of the city, they sprang and ascended the top of the wall, and Judah went up first to the east part of the city. 31 And Gad and Asher went up after him to the west corner of the city, and Simeon and Levi to the north, and Dan and Reuben to the south. 32 And the men who were on the top of the wall, the inhabitants of the city, seeing that the sons of Jacob were coming up to them, they all fled from the wall, descended into the city, and concealed themselves in the midst of the city. 33 And Issachar and Naphtali that remained under the wall approached and broke the gates of the city and kindled a fire at the gates of the city, that the iron melted, and all the sons of Jacob came into the city, they and all their men, and they fought with the inhabitants of the city of Sarton, and smote them with the edge of the sword, and no man stood up before them. 34 And about two hundred men fled from the city, and they all went and hid themselves in a certain tower in the city, and Judah pursued them to the tower and he broke down the tower, which fell upon the men, and they all died. 35 And the sons of Jacob went up the road of the roof of that tower, and they saw, and behold there was another strong and high tower at a distance in the city, and the top of it reached to heaven, and the sons of Jacob hastened and descended, and went with all their men to that tower, and found it filled with about three hundred men, women and little ones. 36 And the sons of Jacob smote a great smiting among those men in the tower and they ran away and fled from them. 37 And Simeon and Levi pursued them, when twelve mighty and valiant men came out to them from the place where they had concealed themselves. 38 And those twelve men maintained a strong battle against Simeon and Levi, and Simeon and Levi could not prevail over them, and those valiant men broke the shields of Simeon and Levi, and one of them struck at Levi's head with his sword, when Levi hastily placed his hand to his head, for he was afraid of the sword, and the sword struck Levi's hand, and it wanted but little to the hand of Levi being cut off. 39 And Levi seized the sword of the valiant man in his hand, and took it forcibly from the man, and with it he struck at the head of the powerful man, and he severed his head. 40 And eleven men approached to fight with Levi, for they saw that one of them was killed, and the sons of Jacob fought, but the sons of Jacob could not prevail over them, for those men were very powerful. **41** And the sons of Jacob seeing that they could not prevail over them, Simeon gave a loud and tremendous shriek, and the eleven powerful men were stunned at the voice of Simeon's shrieking. **42** And Judah at a distance knew the voice of Simeon's shouting, and Naphtali and Judah ran with their shields to Simeon and Levi, and found them fighting with those powerful men, unable to prevail over them as their shields were broken. **43** And Naphtali saw that the shields of Simeon and Levi were broken, and he took two shields from his servants and brought them to Simeon and Levi. **44** And Simeon, Levi and Judah on that day fought all three against the eleven mighty men until the time of sunset, but they could not prevail over them. **45** And this was told unto Jacob, and he was sorely grieved, and he prayed unto the Lord, and he and Naphtali his son went against these mighty men. **46** And Jacob approached and drew his bow, and came nigh unto the mighty men, and slew three of their men with the bow, and the remaining eight turned back, and behold, the war waged against them in the front and rear, and they were greatly afraid of their lives, and could not stand before the sons of Jacob, and they fled from before them. **47** And in their flight they met Dan and Asher coming toward them, and they suddenly fell upon them, and fought with them, and slew two of them, and Judah and his brothers pursued them, and smote the remainder of them, and slew them. **48** And all the sons of Jacob returned and walked about the city, searching if they could find any men, and they found about twenty young men in a cave in the city, and Gad and Asher smote them all, and Dan and Naphtali lighted upon the rest of the men who had fled and escaped from the second tower, and they smote them all. **49** And the sons of Jacob smote all the inhabitants of the city of Sarton, but the women and little ones they left in the city and did not slay them. **50** And all the inhabitants of the city of Sarton were powerful men, one of them would pursue a thousand, and two of them would not flee from ten thousand of the rest of men. **51** And the sons of Jacob slew all the inhabitants of the city of Sarton with the edge of the sword, that no man stood up against them, and they left the women in the city. **52** And the sons of Jacob took all the spoil of the city, and captured what they desired, and they took flocks and herds and property from the city, and the sons of

Jacob did unto Sarton and its inhabitants as they had done to Chazar and its inhabitants, and they turned and went away.

CHAPTER 39

1 And when the sons of Jacob went from the city of Sarton, they had gone about two hundred cubits when they met the inhabitants of Tapnach coming toward them, for they went out to fight with them, because they had smitten the king of Tapnach and all his men. **2** So all that remained in the city of Tapnach came out to fight with the sons of Jacob, and they thought to retake from them the booty and the spoil which they had captured from Chazar and Sarton. **3** And the rest of the men of Tapnach fought with the sons of Jacob in that place, and the sons of Jacob smote them, and they fled before them, and they pursued them to the city of Arbelan, and they all fell before the sons of Jacob. **4** And the sons of Jacob returned and came to Tapnach, to take away the spoil of Tapnach, and when they came to Tapnach they heard that the people of Arbelan had gone out to meet them to save the spoil of their brethren, and the sons of Jacob left ten of their men in Tapnach to plunder the city, and they went out toward the people of Arbelan. **5** And the men of Arbelan went out with their wives to fight with the sons of Jacob, for their wives were experienced in battle, and they went out, about four hundred men and women. **6** And all the sons of Jacob shouted with a loud voice, and they all ran toward the inhabitants of Arbelan, and with a great and tremendous voice. **7** And the inhabitants of Arbelan heard the noise of the shouting of the sons of Jacob, and their roaring like the noise of lions and like the roaring of the sea and its waves. **8** And fear and terror possessed their hearts on account of the sons of Jacob, and they were terribly afraid of them, and they retreated and fled before them into the city, and the sons of Jacob pursued them to the gate of the city, and they came upon them in the city. **9** And the sons of Jacob fought with them in the city, and all their women were engaged in slinging against the sons of Jacob, and the combat was very severe among them the whole of that day until evening. **10** And the sons of Jacob could not prevail over them, and the sons of Jacob had almost perished in that battle, and the sons of Jacob cried unto the Lord and greatly gained strength toward evening, and the sons of Jacob smote all the inhabitants of Arbelan by the edge of the sword, men, women and little ones.

11 And also the remainder of the people who had fled from Sarton, the sons of Jacob smote them in Arbelan, and the sons of Jacob did unto Arbelan and Tapnach as they had done to Chazar and Sarton, and when the women saw that all the men were dead, they went upon the roofs of the city and smote the sons of Jacob by showering down stones like rain. 12 And the sons of Jacob hastened and came into the city and seized all the women and smote them with the edge of the sword, and the sons of Jacob captured all the spoil and booty, flocks and herds and cattle. 13 And the sons of Jacob did unto Machnaymah as they had done to Tapnach, to Chazar and to Shiloh, and they turned from there and went away. 14 And on the fifth day the sons of Jacob heard that the people of Gaash had gathered against them to battle, because they had slain their king and their captains, for there had been fourteen captains in the city of Gaash, and the sons of Jacob had slain them all in the first battle. 15 And the sons of Jacob that day girt on their weapons of war, and they marched to battle against the inhabitants of Gaash, and in Gaash there was a strong and mighty people of the people of the Amorites, and Gaash was the strongest and best fortified city of all the cities of the Amorites, and it had three walls. 16 And the sons of Jacob came to Gaash and they found the gates of the city locked, and about five hundred men standing at the top of the outer-most wall, and a people numerous as the sand upon the seashore were in ambush for the sons of Jacob from without the city at the rear thereof. 17 And the sons of Jacob approached to open the gates of the city, and while they were drawing nigh, behold those who were in ambush at the rear of the city came out from their places and surrounded the sons of Jacob. 18 And the sons of Jacob were enclosed between the people of Gaash, and the battle was both to their front and rear, and all the men that were upon the wall, were casting from the wall upon them, arrows and stones. 19 And Judah, seeing that the men of Gaash were getting too heavy for them, gave a most piercing and tremendous shriek and all the men of Gaash were terrified at the voice of Judah's cry, and men fell from the wall at his powerful shriek, and all those that were from without and within the city were greatly afraid for their lives. 20 And the sons of Jacob still came nigh to break the doors of the city, when the men of Gaash threw stones and arrows upon them from the top of the wall and made them flee from the gate. 21 And the sons of Jacob returned against the men of Gaash who were with them from without the city, and they smote them terribly, as striking against gourds, and they could not stand against the sons of Jacob, for fright and terror had seized them at the shriek of Judah. 22 And the sons of Jacob slew all those men who were without the city, and the sons of Jacob still drew nigh to effect an entrance into the city, and to fight under the city walls, but they could not for all the inhabitants of Gaash who remained in the city had surrounded the walls of Gaash in every direction, so that the sons of Jacob were unable to approach the city to fight with them. 23 And the sons of Jacob came nigh to one corner to fight under the wall, the inhabitants of Gaash threw arrows and stones upon them like showers of rain, and they fled from under the wall. 24 And the people of Gaash who were upon the wall, seeing that the sons of Jacob could not prevail over them from under the wall, reproached the sons of Jacob in these words, saying, 25 "What is the matter with you in the battle that you cannot prevail? Can you then do unto the mighty city of Gaash and its inhabitants as you did to the cities of the Amorites that were not so powerful? Surely to those weak ones among us you did those things, and slew them in the entrance of the city, for they had no strength when they were terrified at the sound of your shouting. 26 And will you now then be able to fight in this place? Surely here you will all die, and we will avenge the cause of those cities that you have laid waste." 27 And the inhabitants of Gaash greatly reproached the sons of Jacob and reviled them with their gods and continued to cast arrows and stones upon them from the wall. 28 And Judah and his brothers heard the words of the inhabitants of Gaash and their anger was greatly roused, and Judah was jealous for his God in this matter, and he called out and said, "O Lord, help, send help to us and our brothers." 29 And he ran at a distance with all his might, with his drawn sword in his hand, and he sprang from the earth and by dint of his strength, mounted the wall, and his sword fell from his hand. 30 And Judah shouted upon the wall, and all the men that were upon the wall were terrified, and some of them fell from the wall into the city and died, and those who were yet upon the wall, when they saw Judah's strength, they were greatly afraid and fled for their lives into the city for safety. 31 And some were emboldened to fight

with Judah upon the wall, and they came nigh to slay him when they saw there was no sword in Judah's hand, and they thought of casting him from the wall to his brothers, and twenty men of the city came up to assist them, and they surrounded Judah and they all shouted over him, and approached him with drawn swords, and they terrified Judah, and Judah cried out to his brothers from the wall. 32 And Jacob and his sons drew the bow from under the wall, and smote three of the men that were upon the top of the wall, and Judah continued to cry and he exclaimed, "O Lord help us, O Lord deliver us," and he cried out with a loud voice upon the wall, and the cry was heard at a great distance. 33 And after this cry he again repeated to shout, and all the men who surrounded Judah on the top of the wall were terrified, and they each threw his sword from his hand at the sound of Judah's shouting and his tremor and fled. 34 And Judah took the swords which had fallen from their hands, and Judah fought with them and slew twenty of their men upon the wall. 35 And about eighty men and women still ascended the wall from the city and they all surrounded Judah, and the Lord impressed the fear of Judah in their hearts, that they were unable to approach him. 36 And Jacob and all who were with him drew the bow from under the wall, and they slew ten men upon the wall, and they fell below the wall, before Jacob and his sons. 37 And the people upon the wall seeing that twenty of their men had fallen, they still ran toward Judah with drawn swords, but they could not approach him for they were greatly terrified at Judah's strength. 38 And one of their mighty men whose name was Arud approached to strike Judah upon the head with his sword, when Judah hastily put his shield to his head, and the sword hit the shield, and it was split in two. 39 And this mighty man after he had struck Judah ran for his life, at the fear of Judah, and his feet slipped upon the wall and he fell among the sons of Jacob who were below the wall, and the sons of Jacob smote him and slew him. 40 And Judah's head pained him from the blow of the powerful man, and Judah had nearly died from it. 41 And Judah cried out upon the wall owing to the pain produced by the blow, when Dan heard him, and his anger burned within him, and he also rose up and went at a distance and ran and sprang from the earth and mounted the wall with his wrath-excited strength. 42 And when Dan came upon the wall near unto Judah

all the men upon the wall fled, who had stood against Judah, and they went up to the second wall, and they threw arrows and stones upon Dan and Judah from the second wall and endeavored to drive them from the wall. 43 And the arrows and stones struck Dan and Judah, and they had nearly been killed upon the wall, and wherever Dan and Judah fled from the wall, they were attacked with arrows and stones from the second wall. 44 And Jacob and his sons were still at the entrance of the city below the first wall, and they were not able to draw their bow against the inhabitants of the city, as they could not be seen by them, being upon the second wall. 45 And Dan and Judah when they could no longer bear the stones and arrows that fell upon them from the second wall, they both sprang upon the second wall near the people of the city, and when the people of the city who were upon the second wall saw that Dan and Judah had come to them upon the second wall, they all cried out and descended below between the walls. 46 And Jacob and his sons heard the noise of the shouting from the people of the city, and they were still at the entrance of the city, and they were anxious about Dan and Judah who were not seen by them, they being upon the second wall. 47 And Naphtali went up with his wrath-excited might and sprang upon the first wall to see what caused the noise of shouting which they had heard in the city, and Issachar and Zebulun drew nigh to break the doors of the city, and they opened the gates of the city and came into the city. 48 And Naphtali leaped from the first wall to the second, and came to assist his brothers, and the inhabitants of Gaash who were upon the wall, seeing that Naphtali was the third who had come up to assist his brothers, they all fled and descended into the city, and Jacob and all his sons and all their young men came into the city to them. 49 And Judah and Dan and Naphtali descended from the wall into the city and pursued the inhabitants of the city, and Simeon and Levi were from without the city and knew not that the gate was opened, and they went up from there to the wall and came down to their brothers into the city. 50 And the inhabitants of the city had all descended into the city, and the sons of Jacob came to them in different directions, and the battle waged against them from the front and the rear, and the sons of Jacob smote them terribly, and slew about twenty thousand of them men and women, not one of them could stand up against the sons of

Jacob. 51 And the blood flowed plentifully in the city, and it was like a brook of water, and the blood flowed like a brook to the outer part of the city and reached the desert of Bethchorin. 52 And the people of Bethchorin saw at a distance the blood flowing from the city of Gaash, and about seventy men from among them ran to see the blood, and they came to the place where the blood was. 53 And they followed the track of the blood and came to the wall of the city of Gaash, and they saw the blood issue from the city, and they heard the voice of crying from the inhabitants of Gaash, for it ascended unto heaven, and the blood was continuing to flow abundantly like a brook of water. 54 And all the sons of Jacob were still smiting the inhabitants of Gaash, and were engaged in slaying them until evening, about twenty thousand men and women, and the people of Chorin said, "Surely this is the work of the Hebrews, for they are still carrying on war in all the cities of the Amorites." 55 And those people hastened and ran to Bethchorin, and each took his weapons of war, and they cried out to all the inhabitants of Bethchorin, who also girt on their weapons of war to go and fight with the sons of Jacob. 56 And when the sons of Jacob had done smiting the inhabitants of Gaash, they walked about the city to strip all the slain and coming in the innermost part of the city and farther on they met three very powerful men, and there was no sword in their hand. 57 And the sons of Jacob came up to the place where they were, and the powerful men ran away, and one of them had taken Zebulun, who he saw was a young lad and of short stature, and with his might dashed him to the ground. 58 And Jacob ran to him with his sword and Jacob smote him below his loins with the sword, and cut him in two, and the body fell upon Zebulun. 59 And the second one approached and seized Jacob to fell him to the ground, and Jacob turned to him and shouted to him, while Simeon and Levi ran and smote him on the hips with the sword and felled him to the ground. 60 And the powerful man rose up from the ground with wrath-excited might, and Judah came to him before he had gained his footing, and struck him upon the head with the sword, and his head was split and he died. 61 And the third powerful man, seeing that his companions were killed, ran from before the sons of Jacob, and the sons of Jacob pursued him in the city; and while the powerful man was fleeing he found one of the swords of the inhabitants of the city, and he picked it up and turned to the sons of Jacob and fought them with that sword. 62 And the powerful man ran to Judah to strike him upon the head with the sword, and there was no shield in the hand of Judah; and while he was aiming to strike him, Naphtali hastily took his shield and put it to Judah's head, and the sword of the powerful man hit the shield of Naphtali and Judah escaped the sword. 63 And Simeon and Levi ran upon the powerful man with their swords and struck at him forcibly with their swords, and the two swords entered the body of the powerful man and divided it in two, length-wise. 64 And the sons of Jacob smote the three mighty men at that time, together with all the inhabitants of Gaash, and the day was about to decline. 65 And the sons of Jacob walked about Gaash and took all the spoil of the city, even the little ones and women they did not suffer to live, and the sons of Jacob did unto Gaash as they had done to Sarton and Shiloh.

CHAPTER 40

1 And the sons of Jacob led away all the spoil of Gaash and went out of the city by night. 2 They were going out marching toward the fortress of Bethchorin, and the inhabitants of Bethchorin were going to the fortress to meet them, and on that night the sons of Jacob fought with the inhabitants of Bethchorin, in the fortress of Bethchorin. 3 And all the inhabitants of Bethchorin were mighty men, one of them would not flee from before a thousand men, and they fought on that night upon the fortress, and their shouts were heard on that night from afar, and the earth quaked at their shouting. 4 And all the sons of Jacob were afraid of those men, as they were not accustomed to fight in the dark, and they were greatly confounded, and the sons of Jacob cried unto the Lord, saying, "Give help to us O Lord, deliver us that we may not die by the hands of these uncircumcised men." 5 And the Lord hearkened to the voice of the sons of Jacob, and the Lord caused great terror and confusion to seize the people of Bethchorin, and they fought among themselves the one with the other in the darkness of night, and smote each other in great numbers. 6 And the sons of Jacob, knowing that the Lord had brought a spirit of perverseness among those men, and that they fought each man with his neighbor, went out from among the bands of the people of Bethchorin and went as far as the descent of the fortress of Bethchorin, and

farther, and they tarried there securely with their young men on that night. **7** And the people of Bethchorin fought the whole night, one man with his brother, and the other with his neighbor, and they cried out in every direction upon the fortress, and their cry was heard at a distance, and the whole earth shook at their voice, for they were powerful above all the people of the earth. **8** And all the inhabitants of the cities of the Canaanites, the Hittites, the Amorites, the Hivites and all the kings of Canaan, and also those who were on the other side of the Jordan, heard the noise of the shouting on that night. **9** And they said, "Surely these are the battles of the Hebrews who are fighting against the seven cities, who came nigh unto them; and who can stand against those Hebrews?" **10** And all the inhabitants of the cities of the Canaanites, and all those who were on the other side of the Jordan, were greatly afraid of the sons of Jacob, for they said, "Behold, the same will be done to us as was done to those cities, for who can stand against their mighty strength?" **11** And the cries of the Chorinites were very great on that night, and continued to increase; and they smote each other until morning, and numbers of them were killed. **12** And the morning appeared, and all the sons of Jacob rose up at daybreak and went up to the fortress, and they smote those who remained of the Chorinites in a terrible manner, and they were all killed in the fortress. **13** And the sixth day appeared, and all the inhabitants of Canaan saw at a distance all the people of Bethchorin lying dead in the fortress of Bethchorin and strewed about as the carcasses of lambs and goats. **14** And the sons of Jacob led all the spoil which they had captured from Gaash and went to Bethchorin, and they found the city full of people like the sand of the sea, and they fought with them, and the sons of Jacob smote them there until evening time. **15** And the sons of Jacob did unto Bethchorin as they had done to Gaash and Tapnach, and as they had done to Chazar, to Sarton and to Shiloh. **16** And the sons of Jacob took with them the spoil of Bethchorin and all the spoil of the cities, and on that day they went home to Shechem. **17** And the sons of Jacob came home to the city of Shechem, and they remained without the city, and they then rested there from the war, and tarried there all night. **18** And all their servants together with all the spoil that they had taken from the cities, they left without the city, and they did not enter the city, for they said, "Perhaps there may be yet more fighting against us, and they may come to besiege us in Shechem." **19** And Jacob and his sons and their servants remained on that night and the next day in the portion of the field which Jacob had purchased from Hamor for five shekels, and all that they had captured was with them. **20** And all the booty which the sons of Jacob had captured, was in the portion of the field, immense as the sand upon the seashore. **21** And the inhabitants of the land observed them from afar, and all the inhabitants of the land were afraid of the sons of Jacob who had done this thing, for no king from the days of old had ever done the like. **22** And the seven kings of the Canaanites resolved to make peace with the sons of Jacob, for they were greatly afraid for their lives, on account of the sons of Jacob. **23** And on that day, being the seventh day, Japhia king of Hebron sent secretly to the king of Ai, and to the king of Gibeon, and to the king of Shalem, and to the king of Adulam, and to the king of Lachish, and to the king of Chazar, and to all the Canaanite kings who were under their subjection, saying, **24** "Go up with me, and come to me that we may go to the sons of Jacob, and I will make peace with them, and form a treaty with them, lest all your lands be destroyed by the swords of the sons of Jacob, as they did to Shechem and the cities around it, as you have heard and seen. **25** And when you come to me, do not come with many men, but let every king bring his three head captains, and every captain bring three of his officers. **26** And come all of you to Hebron, and we will go together to the sons of Jacob and supplicate them that they will form a treaty of peace with us." **27** And all those kings did as the king of Hebron had sent to them, for they were all under his counsel and command, and all the kings of Canaan assembled to go to the sons of Jacob, to make peace with them; and the sons of Jacob returned and went to the portion of the field that was in Shechem, for they did not put confidence in the kings of the land. **28** And the sons of Jacob returned and remained in the portion of the field ten days, and no one came to make war with them. **29** And when the sons of Jacob saw that there was no appearance of war, they all assembled and went to the city of Shechem, and the sons of Jacob remained in Shechem. **30** And at the expiration of forty days, all the kings of the Amorites assembled from all their places and came to Hebron, to Japhia, king of Hebron.

31 And the number of kings that came to Hebron, to make peace with the sons of Jacob, was twenty-one kings, and the number of captains that came with them was sixty-nine, and their men were one hundred and eighty-nine, and all these kings and their men rested by Mount Hebron. 32 And the king of Hebron went out with his three captains and nine men, and these kings resolved to go to the sons of Jacob to make peace. 33 And they said unto the king of Hebron, "Go you before us with your men, and speak for us unto the sons of Jacob, and we will come after you and confirm your words," and the king of Hebron did so. 34 And the sons of Jacob heard that all the kings of Canaan had gathered together and rested in Hebron, and the sons of Jacob sent four of their servants as spies, saying, "Go and spy on these kings, and search and examine their men whether they are few or many, and if they are but few in number, number them all and come back." 35 And the servants of Jacob went secretly to these kings, and did as the sons of Jacob had commanded them, and on that day they came back to the sons of Jacob, and said unto them, "We came unto those kings, and they are but few in number, and we numbered them all, and behold, they were two hundred and eighty-eight, kings and men." 36 And the sons of Jacob said, "They are but few in number, therefore we will not all go out to them"; and in the morning the sons of Jacob rose up and chose sixty two of their men, and ten of the sons of Jacob went with them; and they girt on their weapons of war, for they said, "They are coming to make war with us," for they knew not that they were coming to make peace with them. 37 And the sons of Jacob went with their servants to the gate of Shechem, toward those kings, and their father Jacob was with them. 38 And when they had come out, behold, the king of Hebron and his three captains and nine men with him were coming along the road against the sons of Jacob, and the sons of Jacob lifted up their eyes, and saw at a distance Japhia, king of Hebron, with his captains, coming toward them, and the sons of Jacob took their stand at the place of the gate of Shechem, and did not proceed. 39 And the king of Hebron continued to advance, he and his captains, until he came nigh to the sons of Jacob, and he and his captains bowed down to them to the ground, and the king of Hebron sat with his captains before Jacob and his sons. 40 And the sons of Jacob said unto him, "What has befallen you,

O king of Hebron? Why have you come to us this day? What do you require from us?" And the king of Hebron said unto Jacob, "I implore you my lord, all the kings of the Canaanites have this day come to make peace with you." 41 And the sons of Jacob heard the words of the king of Hebron, and they would not consent to his proposals, for the sons of Jacob had no faith in him, for they imagined that the king of Hebron had spoken deceitfully to them. 42 And the king of Hebron knew from the words of the sons of Jacob, that they did not believe his words, and the king of Hebron approached nearer to Jacob, and said unto him, "I implore you, my lord, to be assured that all these kings have come to you on peaceable terms, for they have not come with all their men, neither did they bring their weapons of war with them, for they have come to seek peace from my lord and his sons." 43 And the sons of Jacob answered the king of Hebron, saying, "Send you to all these kings, and if you speak truth unto us, let them each come singly before us, and if they come unto us unarmed, we will then know that they seek peace from us." 44 And Japhia, king of Hebron, sent one of his men to the kings, and they all came before the sons of Jacob, and bowed down to them to the ground, and these kings sat before Jacob and his sons, and they spoke unto them, saying, 45 "We have heard all that you did unto the kings of the Amorites with your sword and exceedingly mighty arm, so that no man could stand up before you, and we were afraid of you for the sake of our lives, lest it should befall us as it did to them. 46 So we have come unto you to form a treaty of peace between us, and now therefore contract with us a covenant of peace and truth, that you will not meddle with us, inasmuch as we have not meddled with you." 47 And the sons of Jacob knew that they had really come to seek peace from them, and the sons of Jacob listened to them, and formed a covenant with them. 48 And the sons of Jacob swore unto them that they would not meddle with them, and all the kings of the Canaanites swore also to them, and the sons of Jacob made them tributary from that day forward. 49 And after this all the captains of these kings came with their men before Jacob, with presents in their hands for Jacob and his sons, and they bowed down to him to the ground. 50 And these kings then urged the sons of Jacob and begged of them to return all the spoil they had captured from the seven cities of the Amorites, and the sons of

Jacob did so, and they returned all that they had captured, the women, the little ones, the cattle and all the spoil which they had taken, and they sent them off, and they went away each to his city. **51** And all these kings again bowed down to the sons of Jacob, and they sent or brought them many gifts in those days, and the sons of Jacob sent off these kings and their men, and they went peaceably away from them to their cities, and the sons of Jacob also returned to their home, to Shechem. **52** And there was peace from that day forward between the sons of Jacob and the kings of the Canaanites, until the children of Israel came to inherit the land of Canaan.

CHAPTER 41

1 And at the revolution of the year the sons of Jacob journeyed from Shechem, and they came to Hebron, to their father Isaac, and they dwelt there, but their flocks and herds they fed daily in Shechem, for there was there in those days good and fat pasture, and Jacob and his sons and all their household dwelt in the valley of Hebron. **2** And it was in those days, in that year, being the hundred and sixth year of the life of Jacob, in the tenth year of Jacob's coming from Padan-aram, that Leah the wife of Jacob died; she was fifty-one years old when she died in Hebron. **3** And Jacob and his sons buried her in the cave of the field of Machpelah, which is in Hebron, which Abraham had bought from the children of Heth, for the possession of a burial place. **4** And the sons of Jacob dwelt with their father in the valley of Hebron, and all the inhabitants of the land knew their strength and their fame went throughout the land. **5** And Joseph the son of Jacob, and his brother Benjamin, the sons of Rachel, the wife of Jacob, were yet young in those days, and did not go out with their brethren during their battles in all the cities of the Amorites. **6** And when Joseph saw the strength of his brethren, and their greatness, he praised them and extolled them, but he ranked himself greater than them, and extolled himself above them; and Jacob, his father, also loved him more than any of his sons, for he was a son of his old age, and through his love toward him, he made him a coat of many colors. **7** And when Joseph saw that his father loved him more than his brethren, he continued to exalt himself above his brethren, and he brought unto his father evil reports concerning them. **8** And the sons of Jacob seeing the whole of Joseph's conduct

toward them, and that their father loved him more than any of them, they hated him and could not speak peaceably to him all the days. **9** And Joseph was seventeen years old, and he was still magnifying himself above his brethren, and thought of raising himself above them. **10** At that time he dreamed a dream, and he came unto his brothers and told them his dream, and he said unto them, "I dreamed a dream, and behold, we were all binding sheaves in the field, and my sheaf rose and placed itself upon the ground and your sheaves surrounded it and bowed down to it." **11** And his brethren answered him and said unto him, "What means this dream that you did dream? Do you imagine in your heart to reign or rule over us?" **12** And he still came, and told the thing to his father Jacob, and Jacob kissed Joseph when he heard these words from his mouth, and Jacob blessed Joseph. **13** And when the sons of Jacob saw that their father had blessed Joseph and had kissed him, and that he loved him exceedingly, they became jealous of him and hated him the more. **14** And after this Joseph dreamed another dream and related the dream to his father in the presence of his brethren, and Joseph said unto his father and brethren, "Behold I have again dreamed a dream, and behold the sun and the moon and the eleven stars bowed down to me." **15** And his father heard the words of Joseph and his dream, and seeing that his brethren hated Joseph on account of this matter, Jacob therefore rebuked Joseph before his brethren on account of this thing, saying, "What means this dream which you have dreamed, and this magnifying yourself before your brethren who are older than you are? **16** Do you imagine in your heart that I and your mother and your eleven brethren will come and bow down to you, that you speak these things?" **17** And his brethren were jealous of him on account of his words and dreams, and they continued to hate him, and Jacob reserved the dreams in his heart. **18** And the sons of Jacob went one day to feed their father's flock in Shechem, for they were still herdsmen in those days; and while the sons of Jacob were that day feeding in Shechem they delayed, and the time of gathering in the cattle was passed, and they had not arrived. **19** And Jacob saw that his sons were delayed in Shechem, and Jacob said within himself, "Perhaps the people of Shechem have risen up to fight against them, therefore they have delayed coming this day." **20** And Jacob called Joseph his son and commanded him, saying, "Behold, your brethren are feeding in Shechem this day, and behold, they have not yet come back; go now therefore and see where they are, and bring me word back concerning the welfare of your brethren and the welfare of the flock." 21 And Jacob sent his son Joseph to the valley of Hebron, and Joseph came for his brothers to Shechem, and could not find them, and Joseph went about the field which was near Shechem, to see where his brothers had turned, and he missed his road in the wilderness, and knew not which way he should go. 22 And an angel of the Lord found him wandering in the road toward the field, and Joseph said unto the angel of the Lord, "I seek my brethren; have you not heard where they are feeding?" And the angel of the Lord said unto Joseph, "I saw your brethren feeding here, and I heard them say they would go to feed in Doesan." 23 And Joseph hearkened to the voice of the angel of the Lord, and he went to his brethren in Doesan and he found them in Doesan feeding the flock. 24 And Joseph advanced to his brethren, and before he had come nigh unto them, they had resolved to slay him. 25 And Simeon said to his brethren, "Behold the man of dreams is coming unto us this day, and now therefore come and let us kill him and cast him in one of the pits that are in the wilderness, and when his father will seek him from us, we will say an evil beast has devoured him." 26 And Reuben heard the words of his brethren concerning Joseph, and he said unto them, "You should not do this thing, for how can we look up to our father Jacob? Cast him into this pit to die there but stretch not out a hand upon him to spill his blood"; and Reuben said this in order to deliver him from their hand, to bring him back to his father. 27 And when Joseph came to his brethren he sat before them, and they rose upon him and seized him and smote him to the earth and stripped the coat of many colors which he had on. 28 And they took him and cast him into a pit, and in the pit there was no water, but serpents and scorpions. And Joseph was afraid of the serpents and scorpions that were in the pit. And Joseph cried out with a loud voice, and the Lord hid the serpents and scorpions in the sides of the pit, and they did no harm unto Joseph. 29 And Joseph called out from the pit to his brethren, and said unto them, "What have I done unto you, and in what have I sinned? Why do you not fear the Lord concerning me? Am I not of your bones and flesh, and is not Jacob your father, my father? Why do you do this thing unto me this day, and how will you be able to look up to our father Jacob?" 30 And he continued to cry out and call unto his brethren from the pit, and he said, "O Judah, Simeon, and Levi, my brethren, lift me up from the place of darkness in which you have placed me, and come this day to have compassion on me, you children of the Lord, and sons of Jacob my father. And if I have sinned unto you, are you not the sons of Abraham, Isaac, and Jacob? If they saw an orphan they had compassion over him, or one that was hungry, they gave him bread to eat, or one that was thirsty, they gave him water to drink, or one that was naked, they covered him with garments!" 31 And how then will you withhold your pity from your brother, for I am of your flesh and bones, and if I have sinned unto you, surely you will do this on account of my father! 32 And Joseph spoke these words from the pit, and his brethren could not listen to him, nor incline their ears to the words of Joseph, and Joseph was crying and weeping in the pit. 33 And Joseph said, "O that my father knew, this day, the act which my brothers have done unto me, and the words which they have this day spoken unto me." 34 And all his brethren heard his cries and weeping in the pit, and his brethren went and removed themselves from the pit, so that they might not hear the cries of Joseph and his weeping in the pit.

CHAPTER 42

1 And they went and sat on the opposite side, about the distance of a bow-shot, and they sat there to eat bread, and while they were eating, they held counsel together what was to be done with him, whether to slay him or to bring him back to his father. 2 They were holding the counsel, when they lifted up their eyes, and saw, and behold there was a company of Ishmaelites coming at a distance by the road of Gilead, going down to Egypt. 3 And Judah said unto them, "What gain will it be to us if we slay our brother? Perhaps God will require him from us; this then is the counsel proposed concerning him, which you will do unto him: Behold this company of Ishmaelites going down to Egypt. 4 Now therefore, come let us dispose of him to them, and let not our hand be upon him, and they will lead him along with them, and he will be lost among the people of the land, and we will not put him to death with our own hands." And the proposal pleased his brethren and they did according to the word of

Judah. **5** And while they were discoursing about this matter, and before the company of Ishmaelites had come up to them, seven trading men of Midian passed by them, and as they passed they were thirsty, and they lifted up their eyes and saw the pit in which Joseph was immured, and they looked, and behold every species of bird was upon him. **6** And these Midianites ran to the pit to drink water, for they thought that it contained water, and on coming before the pit they heard the voice of Joseph crying and weeping in the pit, and they looked down into the pit, and they saw and behold there was a youth of comely appearance and well favored. **7** And they called unto him and said, "Who are you and who brought you here, and who placed you in this pit, in the wilderness?" And they all assisted to raise up Joseph and they drew him out, and brought him up from the pit, and took him and went away on their journey and passed by his brethren. **8** And these said unto them, "Why do you do this, to take our servant from us and to go away? Surely we placed this youth in the pit because he rebelled against us, and you come and bring him up and lead him away; now then give us back our servant." **9** And the Midianites answered and said unto the sons of Jacob, "Is this your servant, or does this man attend you? Perhaps you are all his servants, for he is more comely and well favored than any of you, and why do you all speak falsely unto us? **10** Now therefore we will not listen to your words, nor attend to you, for we found the youth in the pit in the wilderness, and we took him; we will therefore go on." **11** And all the sons of Jacob approached them and rose up to them and said unto them, "Give us back our servant, and why will you all die by the edge of the sword?" And the Midianites cried out against them, and they drew their swords, and approached to fight with the sons of Jacob. **12** And behold Simeon rose up from his seat against them and sprang upon the ground and drew his sword and approached the Midianites and he gave a terrible shout before them, so that his shouting was heard at a distance, and the earth shook at Simeon's shouting. **13** And the Midianites were terrified on account of Simeon and the noise of his shouting, and they fell upon their faces, and were excessively alarmed. **14** And Simeon said unto them, "Verily I am Simeon, the son of Jacob the Hebrew, who have, only with my brother, destroyed the city of Shechem and the cities of the Amorites; so will

God moreover do unto me, that if all your brethren the people of Midian, and also the kings of Canaan, were to come with you, they could not fight against me. **15** Now therefore give us back the youth whom you have taken, lest I give your flesh to the birds of the skies and the beasts of the earth." **16** And the Midianites were more afraid of Simeon, and they approached the sons of Jacob with terror and fright, and with pathetic words, saying, **17** "Surely you have said that the young man is your servant, and that he rebelled against you, and therefore you placed him in the pit; what then will you do with a servant who rebels against his master? Now therefore sell him unto us, and we will give you all that you require for him"; and the Lord was pleased to do this in order that the sons of Jacob should not slay their brother. **18** And the Midianites saw that Joseph was of a comely appearance and well-favored; they desired him in their hearts and were urgent to purchase him from his brethren. **19** And the sons of Jacob hearkened to the Midianites and they sold their brother Joseph to them for twenty pieces of silver, and Reuben their brother was not with them, and the Midianites took Joseph and continued their journey to Gilead. **20** They were going along the road, and the Midianites repented of what they had done, in having purchased the young man, and one said to the other, "What is this thing that we have done, in taking this youth from the Hebrews, who is of comely appearance and well favored. **21** Perhaps this youth is stolen from the land of the Hebrews, and why then have we done this thing? And if he should be sought for and found in our hands we will die through him. **22** Now surely hardy and powerful men have sold him to us, the strength of one of whom you saw this day; perhaps they stole him from his land with their might and with their powerful arm and have therefore sold him to us for the small value which we gave unto them." **23** And while they were thus discoursing together, they looked, and behold the company of Ishmaelites which was coming at first, and which the sons of Jacob saw, was advancing toward the Midianites, and the Midianites said to each other, "Come let us sell this youth to the company of Ishmaelites who are coming toward us, and we will take for him the little that we gave for him, and we will be delivered from his evil." **24** And they did so, and they reached the Ishmaelites, and the Midianites sold Joseph to the Ishmaelites for twenty pieces of silver which they had given for him to his brethren. 25 And the Midianites went on their road to Gilead, and the Ishmaelites took Joseph and they let him ride upon one of the camels, and they were leading him to Egypt. 26 And Joseph heard that the Ishmaelites were proceeding to Egypt, and Joseph lamented and wept at this thing that he was to be so far removed from the land of Canaan, from his father, and he wept bitterly while he was riding upon the camel, and one of their men observed him, and made him go down from the camel and walk on foot, and notwithstanding this Joseph continued to cry and weep, and he said, "O my father, my father." 27 And one of the Ishmaelites rose up and smote Joseph upon the cheek, and still he continued to weep; and Joseph was fatigued in the road, and was unable to proceed on account of the bitterness of his soul, and they all smote him and afflicted him in the road, and they terrified him in order that he might cease from weeping. 28 And the Lord saw the ambition of Joseph and his trouble, and the Lord brought down upon those men darkness and confusion, and the hand of everyone that smote him became withered. 29 And they said to each other, "What is this thing that God has done to us in the road?" And they knew not that this befell them on account of Joseph. And the men proceeded on the road, and they passed along the road of Ephrath where Rachel was buried. 30 And Joseph reached his mother's grave, and Joseph hastened and ran to his mother's grave, and fell upon the grave and wept. 31 And Joseph cried aloud upon his mother's grave, and he said, "O my mother, my mother, O you who did give me birth, awake now, and rise and see your son, how he has been sold for a slave, and no one to pity him. 32 O rise and see your son, weep with me on account of my troubles, and see the heart of my brethren. 33 Arouse my mother, arouse, awake from your sleep for me, and direct your battles against my brethren. O how have they stripped me of my coat, and sold me already twice for a slave, and separated me from my father, and there is no one to pity me. 34 Arouse and lay your cause against them before God, and see whom God will justify in the judgment, and whom he will condemn. 35 Rise, O my mother, rise, awake from your sleep and see my father how his soul is with me this day, and comfort him and ease his heart." 36 And Joseph continued to speak these words, and Joseph cried aloud and wept

bitterly upon his mother's grave; and he ceased speaking, and from bitterness of heart he became still as a stone upon the grave. 37 And Joseph heard a voice speaking to him from beneath the ground, which answered him with bitterness of heart, and with a voice of weeping and praying in these words: 38 "My son, my son Joseph, I have heard the voice of your weeping and the voice of your lamentation; I have seen your tears; I know your troubles, my son, and it grieves me for your sake, and abundant grief is added to my grief. 39 Now therefore my son, Joseph my son, hope to the Lord, and wait for him and do not fear, for the Lord is with you, he will deliver you from all trouble. 40 Rise my son, go down unto Egypt with your masters, and do not fear, for the Lord is with you, my son." And she continued to speak like unto these words unto Joseph, and she was still. 41 And Joseph heard this, and he wondered greatly at this, and he continued to weep; and after this one of the Ishmaelites observed him crying and weeping upon the grave, and his anger was kindled against him, and he drove him from there, and he smote him and cursed him. 42 And Joseph said unto the men, "May I find grace in your sight to take me back to my father's house, and he will give you abundance of riches." 43 And they answered him, saying, "Are you not a slave, and where is your father? And if you had a father you would not already twice have been sold for a slave for so little value"; and their anger was still roused against him, and they continued to smite him and to chastise him, and Joseph wept bitterly. 44 And the Lord saw Joseph's affliction, and the Lord again smote these men, and chastised them, and the Lord caused darkness to envelope them upon the earth, and the lightning flashed and the thunder roared, and the earth shook at the voice of the thunder and of the mighty wind, and the men were terrified and knew not where they should go. 45 And the beasts and camels stood still, and they led them, but they would not go, they smote them, and they crouched upon the ground; and the men said to each other, "What is this that God has done to us? What are our transgressions, and what are our sins that this thing has thus befallen us?" 46 And one of them answered and said unto them, "Perhaps on account of the sin of afflicting this slave has this thing happened this day to us; now therefore implore him strongly to forgive us, and then we will know on whose account this evil befalls us, and if

God will have compassion over us, then we will know that all this comes to us on account of the sin of afflicting this slave." **47** And the men did so, and they supplicated Joseph and pressed him to forgive them; and they said, "We have sinned to the Lord and to you, now therefore graciously request of your God that he will put away this death from among us, for we have sinned to him." **48** And Joseph did according to their words, and the Lord hearkened to Joseph, and the Lord put away the plague which he had inflicted upon those men on account of Joseph, and the beasts rose up from the ground and they conducted them, and they went on, and the raging storm abated and the earth became tranquilized, and the men proceeded on their journey to go down to Egypt, and the men knew that this evil had befallen them on account of Joseph. **49** And they said to each other, "Behold, we know that it was on account of his affliction that this evil befell us; now therefore why will we bring this death upon our souls? Let us hold counsel what to do to this slave." **50** And one answered and said, "Surely he told us to bring him back to his father; now therefore come, let us take him back and we will go to the place that he will tell us, and take from his family the price that we gave for him and we will then go away." **51** And one answered again and said, "Behold, this counsel is very good, but we cannot do so for the way is very far from us, and we cannot go out of our road." **52** And one more answered and said unto them, "This is the counsel to be adopted, we will not swerve from it; behold we are this day going to Egypt, and when we will have come to Egypt, we will sell him there at a high price, and we will be delivered from his evil." **53** And this thing pleased the men and they did so, and they continued their journey to Egypt with Joseph.

CHAPTER 43

1 And when the sons of Jacob had sold their brother Joseph to the Midianites, their hearts were smitten on account of him, and they repented of their acts, and they sought for him to bring him back, but could not find him. **2** And Reuben returned to the pit in which Joseph had been put, in order to lift him out, and restore him to his father, and Reuben stood by the pit, and he heard not a word, and he called out, "Joseph! Joseph!" And no one answered or uttered a word. **3** And Reuben said, "Joseph has died through fright, or some serpent has caused his death"; and Reuben

descended into the pit, and he searched for Joseph and could not find him in the pit, and he came out again. **4** And Reuben tore his garments and he said, "The child is not there, and how will I reconcile my father about him if he be dead?" And he went to his brethren and found them grieving on account of Joseph, and counseling together how to reconcile their father about him, and Reuben said unto his brethren, "I came to the pit and behold Joseph was not there, what then will we say unto our father, for my father will only seek the lad from me." **5** And his brethren answered him saying, "Thus and thus we did, and our hearts afterward smote us on account of this act, and we now sit to seek a pretext how we will reconcile our father to it." **6** And Reuben said unto them, "What is this you have done to bring down the grey hairs of our father in sorrow to the grave? The thing is not good, that you have done." **7** And Reuben sat with them, and they all rose up and swore to each other not to tell this thing unto Jacob, and they all said, "The man who will tell this to our father or his household, or who will report this to any of the children of the land, we will all rise up against him and slay him with the sword." **8** And the sons of Jacob feared each other in this matter, from the youngest to the oldest, and no one spoke a word, and they concealed the thing in their hearts. **9** And they afterward sat down to determine and invent something to say unto their father Jacob concerning all these things. **10** And Issachar said unto them, "Here is an advice for you if it seem good in your eyes to do this thing, take the coat which belongs to Joseph and tear it, and kill a kid of the goats and dip it in its blood. **11** And send it to our father and when he sees it he will say an evil beast has devoured him, therefore tear you his coat and behold his blood will be upon his coat, and by your doing this we will be free of our father's murmurings." **12** And Issachar's advice pleased them, and they hearkened unto him and they did according to the word of Issachar which he had counselled them. **13** And they hastened and took Joseph's coat and tore it, and they killed a kid of the goats and dipped the coat in the blood of the kid, and then trampled it in the dust, and they sent the coat to their father Jacob by the hand of Naphtali, and they commanded him to say these words: **14** "We had gathered in the cattle and had come as far as the road to Shechem and farther, when we found this coat upon the road in the wilderness dipped in blood and in dust; now therefore know whether it be your son's coat or not." **15** And Naphtali went and he came unto his father and he gave him the coat, and he spoke unto him all the words which his brethren had commanded him. **16** And Jacob saw Joseph's coat and he knew it and he fell upon his face to the ground, and became as still as a stone, and he afterward rose up and cried out with a loud and weeping voice and he said, "It is the coat of my son Joseph!" **17** And Jacob hastened and sent one of his servants to his sons, who went to them and found them coming along the road with the flock. **18** And the sons of Jacob came to their father about evening, and behold their garments were torn and dust was upon their heads, and they found their father crying out and weeping with a loud voice. **19** And Jacob said unto his sons, "Tell me truly what evil you have this day suddenly brought upon me?" And they answered their father Jacob, saying, "We were coming along this day after the flock had been gathered in, and we came as far as the city of Shechem by the road in the wilderness, and we found this coat filled with blood upon the ground, and we knew it and we sent unto you if you could know it." **20** And Jacob heard the words of his sons and he cried out with a loud voice, and he said, "It is the coat of my son, an evil beast has devoured him; Joseph is rent in pieces, for I sent him this day to see whether it was well with you and well with the flocks and to bring me word again from you, and he went as I commanded him, and this has happened to him this day while I thought my son was with you." **21** And the sons of Jacob answered and said, "He did not come to us, neither have we seen him from the time of our going out from you until now." **22** And when Jacob heard their words he again cried out aloud, and he rose up and tore his garments, and he put sackcloth upon his loins, and he wept bitterly and he mourned and lifted up his voice in weeping and exclaimed and said these words, **23** "Joseph my son, O my son Joseph, I sent you this day after the welfare of your brethren, and behold you have been torn in pieces; through my hand has this happened to my son. **24** It grieves me for you Joseph my son, it grieves me for you; how sweet were you to me during life, and now how exceedingly bitter is your death to me. **25** O that I had died in your stead Joseph my son, for it grieves me sadly for you my son, O my son, my son. Joseph my son, where are you, and where have you been drawn? Arouse,

arouse from your place, and come and see my grief for you, O my son Joseph. **26** Come now and number the tears gushing from my eyes down my cheeks, and bring them up before the Lord, that his anger may turn from me. **27** O Joseph my son, how did you fall, by the hand of one by whom no one had fallen from the beginning of the world unto this day; for you have been put to death by the smiting of an enemy, inflicted with cruelty, but surely I know that this has happened to you, on account of the multitude of my sins. **28** Arouse now and see how bitter is my trouble for you my son, although I did not rear you, nor fashion you, nor give you breath and soul, but it was God who formed you and built your bones and covered them with flesh, and breathed in your nostrils the breath of life, and then he gave you unto me. **29** Now truly God who gave you unto me, he has taken you from me, and such then has befallen you." **30** And Jacob continued to speak like unto these words concerning Joseph, and he wept bitterly; he fell to the ground and became still. **31** And all the sons of Jacob seeing their father's trouble, they repented of what they had done, and they also wept bitterly. **32** And Judah rose up and lifted his father's head from the ground, and placed it upon his lap, and he wiped his father's tears from his cheeks, and Judah wept an exceedingly great weeping, while his father's head was reclining upon his lap, still as a stone. **33** And the sons of Jacob saw their father's trouble, and they lifted up their voices and continued to weep, and Jacob was yet lying upon the ground still as a stone. **34** And all his sons and his servants and his servant's children rose up and stood round him to comfort him, and he refused to be comforted. **35** And the whole household of Jacob rose up and mourned a great mourning on account of Joseph and their father's trouble, and the intelligence reached Isaac, the son of Abraham, the father of Jacob, and he wept bitterly on account of Joseph, he and all his household, and he went from the place where he dwelt in Hebron, and his men with him, and he comforted Jacob his son, and he refused to be comforted. **36** And after this, Jacob rose up from the ground, and his tears were running down his cheeks, and he said unto his sons, "Rise up and take your swords and your bows, and go out into the field, and seek whether you can find my son's body and bring it unto me that I may bury it. **37** Seek also, I pray you, among the beasts and hunt them, and that which will come the first before you seize and bring it unto me, perhaps the Lord will this day pity my affliction, and prepare before you that which did tear my son in pieces, and bring it unto me, and I will avenge the cause of my son." 38 And his sons did as their father had commanded them, and they rose up early in the morning, and each took his sword and his bow in his hand, and they went out into the field to hunt the beasts. 39 And Jacob was still crying aloud and weeping and walking to and fro in the house, and smiting his hands together, saying, "Joseph my son, Joseph my son." 40 And the sons of Jacob went into the wilderness to seize the beasts, and behold a wolf came toward them, and they seized him, and brought him unto their father, and they said unto him, "This is the first we have found, and we have brought him unto you as you did command us, and your son's body we could not find." 41 And Jacob took the beast from the hands of his sons, and he cried out with a loud and weeping voice, holding the beast in his hand, and he spoke with a bitter heart unto the beast, "Why did you devour my son Joseph, and how did you have no fear of the God of the earth, or of my trouble for my son Joseph? 42 And you did devour my son for naught, because he committed no violence, and did thereby render me culpable on his account, therefore God will require him that is persecuted." 43 And the Lord opened the mouth of the beast in order to comfort Jacob with its words, and it answered Jacob and spoke these words unto him, 44 "As God lives who created us in the earth, and as your soul lives, my lord, I did not see your son, neither did I tear him to pieces, but from a distant land I also came to seek my son who went from me this day, and I know not whether he be living or dead. 45 And I came this day into the field to seek my son, and your sons found me, and seized me and increased my grief, and have this day brought me before you, and I have now spoken all my words to you. 46 And now therefore, O son of man, I am in your hands, and do unto me this day as it may seem good in your sight, but by the life of God who created me, I did not see your son, nor did I tear him to pieces, neither has the flesh of man entered my mouth all the days of my life." 47 And when Jacob heard the words of the beast he was greatly astonished, and sent out the beast from his hand, and she went her way. 48 And Jacob was still crying aloud and weeping for Joseph day after day, and he mourned for his son many days.

CHAPTER 44

1 And the sons of Ishmael who had bought Joseph from the Midianites, who had bought him from his brethren, went to Egypt with Joseph, and they came upon the borders of Egypt, and when they came near unto Egypt, they met four men of the sons of Medan the son of Abraham, who had gone out from the land of Egypt on their journey. 2 And the Ishmaelites said unto them, "Do you desire to purchase this slave from us?" And they said, "Deliver him over to us," and they delivered Joseph over to them, and they beheld him, that he was a very comely youth and they purchased him for twenty shekels. 3 And the Ishmaelites continued their journey to Egypt and the Medanim also returned that day to Egypt, and the Medanim said to each other, "Behold we have heard that Potiphar, an officer of Pharaoh, captain of the guard, seeks a good servant who will stand before him to attend him, and to make him overseer over his house and all belonging to him. 4 Now therefore come let us sell him to him for what we may desire, if he be able to give unto us that which we will require for him." 5 And these Medanim went and came to the house of Potiphar, and said unto him, "We have heard that you seek a good servant to attend you, behold we have a servant that will please you, if you can give unto us that which we may desire, and we will sell him unto you." 6 And Potiphar said, "Bring him before me, and I will see him, and if he pleases me I will give unto you that which you may require for him." 7 And the Medanim went and brought Joseph and placed him before Potiphar, and he saw him, and he pleased him exceedingly, and Potiphar said unto them, "Tell me what you require for this youth?" 8 And they said, "Four hundred pieces of silver we desire for him," and Potiphar said, "I will give it you if you bring me the record of his sale to you, and will tell me his history, for perhaps he may be stolen, for this youth is neither a slave, nor the son of a slave, but I observe in him the appearance of a goodly and handsome person." 9 And the Medanim went and brought unto him the Ishmaelites who had sold him to them, and they told him, saying, "He is a slave and we sold him to them." 10 And Potiphar heard the words of the Ishmaelites in his giving the silver unto the Medanim, and the

Medanim took the silver and went on their journey, and the Ishmaelites also returned home. 11 And Potiphar took Joseph and brought him to his house that he might serve him, and Joseph found favor in the sight of Potiphar, and he placed confidence in him, and made him overseer over his house, and all that belonged to him he delivered over into his hand. 12 And the Lord was with Joseph and he became a prosperous man, and the Lord blessed the house of Potiphar for the sake of Joseph. 13 And Potiphar left all that he had in the hand of Joseph, and Joseph was one that caused things to come in and go out, and everything was regulated by his wish in the house of Potiphar. 14 And Joseph was eighteen years old, a youth with beautiful eyes and of comely appearance, and like unto him was not in the whole land of Egypt. 15 At that time while he was in his master's house, going in and out of the house and attending his master, Zelicah, his master's wife, lifted up her eyes toward Joseph and she looked at him, and behold he was a youth comely and well favored. 16 And she coveted his beauty in her heart, and her soul was fixed upon Joseph, and she enticed him day after day, and Zelicah persuaded Joseph daily, but Joseph did not lift up his eyes to behold his master's wife. 17 And Zelicah said unto him, "How goodly are your appearance and form, truly I have looked at all the slaves, and have not seen so beautiful a slave as you are"; and Joseph said unto her, "Surely he who created me in my mother's womb created all mankind." 18 And she said unto him, "How beautiful are your eyes, with which you have dazzled all the inhabitants of Egypt, men and women"; and he said unto her, "How beautiful they are while we are alive, but should you behold them in the grave, surely you would move away from them." 19 And she said unto him, "How beautiful and pleasing are all your words; take now, I pray you, the harp which is in the house, and play with your hands and let us hear your words." 20 And he said unto her, "How beautiful and pleasing are my words when I speak the praise of my God and his glory"; and she said unto him, "How very beautiful is the hair of your head, behold the golden comb which is in the house, take it I pray you, and curl the hair of your head." 21 And he said unto her, "How long will you speak these words? Cease to utter these words to me and rise and attend to your domestic affairs." 22 And she said unto him, "There is no one in

my house, and there is nothing to attend to but to your words and to your wish"; yet notwithstanding all this, she could not bring Joseph unto her, neither did he place his eye upon her, but directed his eyes below to the ground. 23 And Zelicah desired Joseph in her heart, that he should lie with her, and at the time that Joseph was sitting in the house doing his work, Zelicah came and sat before him, and she enticed him daily with her discourse to lie with her, or ever to look at her, but Joseph would not hearken to her. 24 And she said unto him, "If you will not do according to my words, I will chastise you with the punishment of death, and put an iron yoke upon you." 25 And Joseph said unto her, "Surely God who created man loosens the fetters of prisoners, and it is he who will deliver me from your prison and from your judgment." 26 And when she could not prevail over him, to persuade him, and her soul being still fixed upon him, her desire threw her into a grievous sickness. 27 And all the women of Egypt came to visit her, and they said unto her, "Why are you in this declining state? You that lack nothing; surely your husband is a great and esteemed prince in the sight of the king, should you lack anything of what your heart desires?" 28 And Zelicah answered them, saying, "This day it will be made known to you, from where this disorder springs in which you see me," and she commanded her maidservants to prepare food for all the women, and she made a banquet for them, and all the women ate in the house of Zelicah. 29 And she gave them knives to peel the citrons to eat them, and she commanded that they should dress Joseph in costly garments, and that he should appear before them, and Joseph came before their eyes and all the women looked on Joseph, and could not take their eyes from off him, and they all cut their hands with the knives that they had in their hands, and all the citrons that were in their hands were filled with blood. 30 And they knew not what they had done but they continued to look at the beauty of Joseph and did not turn their eyelids from him. 31 And Zelicah saw what they had done, and she said unto them, "What is this work that you have done? Behold I gave you citrons to eat and you have all cut your hands." 32 And all the women saw their hands, and behold they were full of blood, and their blood flowed down upon their garments, and they said unto her, "This slave in your house has overcome us, and we could not turn our eyelids from him on account of his beauty." **33** And she said unto them, "Surely this happened to you in the moment that you looked at him, and you could not contain yourselves from him; how then can I refrain when he is constantly in my house, and I see him day after day going in and out of my house? How then can I keep from declining or even from perishing on account of this?" **34** And they said unto her, "The words are true, for who can see this beautiful form in the house and refrain from him, and is he not your slave and attendant in your house, and why do you not tell him that which is in your heart, and suffer your soul to perish through this matter?" **35** And she said unto them, "I am daily endeavoring to persuade him, and he will not consent to my wishes, and I promised him everything that is good, and yet I could meet with no return from him; I am therefore in a declining state as you see." **36** And Zelicah became very ill on account of her desire toward Joseph, and she was desperately lovesick on account of him, and all the people of the house of Zelicah and her husband knew nothing of this matter, that Zelicah was ill on account of her love to Joseph. **37** And all the people of her house asked her, saying, "Why are you ill and declining, and lack nothing?" And she said unto them, "I know not this thing which is daily increasing upon me." **38** And all the women and her friends came daily to see her, and they spoke with her, and she said unto them, "This can only be through the love of Joseph"; and they said unto her, "Entice him and seize him secretly, perhaps he may hearken to you, and put off this death from you." **39** And Zelicah became worse from her love to Joseph, and she continued to decline, until she had scarce strength to stand. **40** And on a certain day Joseph was doing his master's work in the house, and Zelicah came secretly and fell suddenly upon him, and Joseph rose up against her, and he was more powerful than she, and he brought her down to the ground. **41** And Zelicah wept on account of the desire of her heart toward him, and she supplicated him with weeping, and her tears flowed down her cheeks, and she spoke unto him in a voice of supplication and in bitterness of soul, saying, **42** "Have you ever heard, seen or known of so beautiful a woman as I am, or better than myself, who speak daily unto you, fall into a decline through love for you, confer all this honor upon you, and still you will not hearken to my voice? **43** And if it be through fear of your master lest he punish you, as the king lives no harm will come to you from your master through this thing; now, therefore pray listen to me, and consent for the sake of the honor which I have conferred upon you, and put off this death from me, and why should I die for your sake?" And she ceased to speak. **44** And Joseph answered her, saying, "Refrain from me, and leave this matter to my master; behold my master knows not what there is with me in the house, for all that belongs to him he has delivered into my hand, and how will I do these things in my master's house? **45** For he has also greatly honored me in his house, and he has also made me overseer over his house, and he has exalted me, and there is no one greater in this house than I am, and my master has refrained nothing from me, excepting you who are his wife, how then can you speak these words unto me, and how can I do this great evil and sin to God and to your husband? **46** Now therefore refrain from me, and speak no more such words as these, for I will not hearken to your words." But Zelicah would not hearken to Joseph when he spoke these words unto her, but she daily enticed him to listen to her. **47** And it was after this that the brook of Egypt was filled above all its sides, and all the inhabitants of Egypt went out, and also the king and princes went out with timbrels and dances, for it was a great rejoicing in Egypt, and a holiday at the time of the inundation of the sea Sihor, and they went there to rejoice all day long. **48** And when the Egyptians went out to the river to rejoice, as was their custom, all the people of the house of Potiphar went with them, but Zelicah would not go with them, for she said, "I am indisposed," and she remained alone in the house, and no other person was with her in the house. **49** And she rose up and ascended to her temple in the house, and dressed herself in princely garments, and she placed upon her head precious stones of onyx stones, inlaid with silver and gold, and she beautified her face and skin with all sorts of women's purifying liquids, and she perfumed the temple and the house with cassia and frankincense, and she spread myrrh and aloes, and she afterward sat in the entrance of the temple, in the passage of the house, through which Joseph passed to do his work, and behold Joseph came from the field, and entered the house to do his master's work. **50** And he came to the place through which he had to pass, and he saw all the work of Zelicah, and he turned back. **51** And Zelicah saw Joseph turning back from her, and she called out to him, saying, "What ails you Joseph? Come to your work and behold I will make room for you until you will have passed to your seat." **52** And Joseph returned and came to the house and passed from there to the place of his seat, and he sat down to do his master's work as usual and behold Zelicah came to him and stood before him in princely garments, and the scent from her clothes was spread to a distance. **53** And she hastened and caught hold of Joseph and his garments, and she said unto him, "As the king lives if you will not perform my request you will die this day," and she hastened and stretched out her other hand and drew a sword from beneath her garments, and she placed it upon Joseph's neck, and she said, "Rise and perform my request, and if not you die this day." **54** And Joseph was afraid of her at her doing this thing, and he rose up to flee from her, and she seized the front of his garments, and in the terror of his flight the garment which Zelicah seized was torn, and Joseph left the garment in the hand of Zelicah, and he fled and got out, for he was in fear. **55** And when Zelicah saw that Joseph's garment was torn, and that he had left it in her hand, and had fled, she was afraid of her life, lest the report should spread concerning her, and she rose up and acted with cunning, and put off the garments in which she was dressed, and she put on her other garments. **56** And she took Joseph's garment, and she laid it beside her, and she went and seated herself in the place where she had sat in her illness, before the people of her house had gone out to the river, and she called a young lad who was then in the house, and she ordered him to call the people of the house to her. **57** And when she saw them she said unto them with a loud voice and lamentation, "See what a Hebrew your master has brought to me in the house, for he came this day to lie with me. **58** For when you had gone out he came to the house and seeing that there was no person in the house, he came unto me, and caught hold of me, with intent to lie with me. **59** And I seized his garments and tore them and called out against him with a loud voice, and when I had lifted up my voice he was afraid for his life and left his garment before me, and fled." **60** And the people of her house spoke nothing, but their wrath was very much kindled against Joseph, and they went to his master and told him the words of his wife. **61** And Potiphar came home enraged, and his wife cried out to him, saying, "What is this thing that you have done unto me in bringing a Hebrew servant into my house, for he came unto me this day to sport with me; thus did he do unto me this day." **62** And Potiphar heard the words of his wife, and he ordered Joseph to be punished with severe stripes, and they did so to him. **63** And while they were smiting him, Joseph called out with a loud voice, and he lifted up his eyes to heaven, and he said, "O Lord God, you know that I am innocent of all these things, and why will I die this day through falsehood, by the hand of these uncircumcised wicked men, whom you know?" **64** And while Potiphar's men were beating Joseph, he continued to cry out and weep, and there was a child there eleven months old, and the Lord opened the mouth of the child, and he spoke these words before Potiphar's men, who were smiting Joseph, saying, **65** "What do you want of this man, and why do you do this evil unto him? My mother speaks falsely and utters lies; thus was the transaction." **66** And the child told them accurately all that happened, and all the words of Zelicah to Joseph day after day did he declare unto them. **67** And all the men heard the words of the child and they wondered greatly at the child's words, and the child ceased to speak and became still. **68** And Potiphar was very much ashamed at the words of his son, and he commanded his men not to beat Joseph anymore, and the men ceased beating Joseph. **69** And Potiphar took Joseph and ordered him to be brought to justice before the priests, who were judges belonging to the king, in order to judge him concerning this affair. **70** And Potiphar and Joseph came before the priests who were the king's judges, and he said unto them, "Decide I pray you, what judgment is due to a servant, for thus has he done." **71** And the priests said unto Joseph, "Why did you do this thing to your master?" And Joseph answered them, saying, "Not so my lords, thus was the matter"; and Potiphar said unto Joseph, "Surely I entrusted in your hands all that belonged to me, and I withheld nothing from you but my wife, and how could you do this evil?" **72** And Joseph answered saying, "Not so my lord, as the Lord lives, and as your soul lives, my lord, the word which you did hear from your wife is untrue, for thus was the affair this day. **73** A year has elapsed to me since I have been in your house; have you seen any iniquity in me, or anything which might cause you to demand my life?" **74** And the priests said unto Potiphar, "Send, we pray you, and let them bring before us Joseph's torn garment, and let us see the tear in it, and if it will be that the tear is in front of the garment, then his face must have been opposite to her and she must have caught hold of him, to come to her, and with deceit did your wife do all that she has spoken." **75** And they brought Joseph's garment before the priests who were judges, and they saw and behold the tear was in front of Joseph, and all the judging priests knew that she had pressed him, and they said, "The judgment of death is not due to this slave for he has done nothing, but his judgment is, that he be placed in the prison house on account of the report, which through him has gone out against your wife." **76** And Potiphar heard their words, and he placed him in the prison house, the place where the king's prisoners are confined, and Joseph was in the house of confinement twelve years. **77** And notwithstanding this, his master's wife did not turn from him, and she did not cease from speaking to him day after day to hearken to her, and at the end of three months Zelicah continued going to Joseph to the house of confinement day by day, and she enticed him to hearken to her, and Zelicah said unto Joseph, "How long will you remain in this house? But hearken now to my voice, and I will bring you out of this house." **78** And Joseph answered her, saying, "It is better for me to remain in this house than to hearken to your words, to sin against God"; and she said unto him, "If you will not perform my wish, I will pluck out your eyes, add fetters to your feet, and will deliver you into the hands of them whom you did not know before." **79** And Joseph answered her and said, "Behold, the God of the whole earth is able to deliver me from all that you can do unto me, for he opens the eyes of the blind, and loosens those that are bound, and preserves all strangers who are unacquainted with the land." **80** And when Zelicah was unable to persuade Joseph to hearken to her, she left off going to entice him; and Joseph was still confined in the house of confinement. And Jacob the father of Joseph, and all his brethren who were in the land of Canaan still mourned and wept in those days on account of Joseph, for Jacob refused to be comforted for his son Joseph, and Jacob cried aloud, and wept and mourned all those days.

CHAPTER 45

1 And it was at that time in that year, which is the year of Joseph's going down to Egypt after his brothers had sold him, that Reuben the son of Jacob went to Timnah and took unto him for a wife Eliuram, the daughter of Avi the Canaanite, and he came to her. **2** And Eliuram the wife of Reuben conceived and bore him Hanoch, Palu, Chetzron and Carmi, four sons; and Simeon his brother took his sister Dinah for a wife, and she bare unto him Memuel, Yamin, Ohad, Jachin and Zochar, five sons. **3** And he afterward came to Bunah the Canaanite woman, the same is Bunah whom Simeon took captive from the city of Shechem, and Bunah was before Dinah and attended upon her, and Simeon came to her, and she bore unto him Saul. **4** And Judah went at that time to Adulam, and he came to a man of Adulam, and his name was Hirah, and Judah saw there the daughter of a man from Canaan, and her name was Aliyath, the daughter of Shua, and he took her, and came to her, and Aliyath bore unto Judah, Er, Onan and Shiloh; three sons. **5** And Levi and Issachar went to the land of the east, and they took unto themselves for wives the daughters of Jobab the son of Yoktan, the son of Eber; and Jobab the son of Yoktan had two daughters; the name of the elder was Adinah, and the name of the younger was Aridah. **6** And Levi took Adinah, and Issachar took Aridah, and they came to the land of Canaan, to their father's house, and Adinah bore unto Levi, Gershon, Kehas and Merari; three sons. **7** And Aridah bore unto Issachar Tola, Puvah, Job and Shomron, four sons; and Dan went to the land of Moab and took for a wife Aphlaleth, the daughter of Chamudan the Moabite, and he brought her to the land of Canaan. **8** And Aphlaleth was barren, she had no offspring, and God afterward remembered Aphlaleth the wife of Dan, and she conceived and bore a son, and she called his name Chushim. **9** And Gad and Naphtali went to Haran and took from there the daughters of Amuram the son of Uz, the son of Nahor, for wives. **10** And these are the names of the daughters of Amuram; the name of the elder was Merimah, and the name of the younger Uzith; and Naphtali took Merimah, and Gad took Uzith; and brought them to the land of Canaan, to their father's house. **11** And Merimah bare unto Naphtali Yachzeel, Guni, Jazer and Shalem, four sons; and Uzith bore unto Gad Zephion, Chagi, Shuni, Ezbon, Eri, Arodi and Arali, seven sons. **12** And Asher went out and took Adon the daughter of Aphlal, the son of Hadad, the son of Ishmael, for a wife, and he brought her to the land of Canaan. **13** And Adon the wife of Asher died in those days: she had no offspring; and it was after the death of Adon that Asher went to the other side of the river and took for a wife Hadurah the daughter of Abimael, the son of Eber, the son of Shem. **14** And the young woman was of a comely appearance, and a woman of sense, and she had been the wife of Malkiel the son of Elam, the son of Shem. **15** And Hadurah bore a daughter unto Malkiel, and he called her name Serach, and Malkiel died after this, and Hadurah went and remained in her father's house. **16** And after the death of the wife of Asher he went and took Hadurah for a wife, and brought her to the land of Canaan, and Serach her daughter he also brought with them, and she was three years old, and the damsel was brought up in Jacob's house. **17** And the damsel was of a comely appearance, and she went in the sanctified ways of the children of Jacob; she lacked nothing, and the Lord gave her wisdom and understanding. **18** And Hadurah the wife of Asher conceived and bore unto him Yimnah, Yishvah, Yishvi and Beriah; four sons. **19** And Zebulun went to Midian and took for a wife Merishah the daughter of Molad, the son of Abida, the son of Midian, and brought her to the land of Canaan. **20** And Merushah bore unto Zebulun Sered, Elon and Yachleel; three sons. **21** And Jacob sent to Aram, the son of Zoba, the son of Terah, and he took for his son Benjamin Mechalia the daughter of Aram, and she came to the land of Canaan to the house of Jacob; and Benjamin was ten years old when he took Mechalia the daughter of Aram for a wife. **22** And Mechalia conceived and bore unto Benjamin Bela, Becher, Ashbel, Gera and Naaman, five sons; and Benjamin went afterward and took for a wife Aribath, the daughter of Shomron, the son of Abraham, in addition to his first wife, and he was eighteen years old; and Aribath bore unto Benjamin Achi, Vosh, Mupim, Chupim, and Ord; five sons. **23** And in those days Judah went to the house of Shem and took Tamar the daughter of Elam, the son of Shem, for a wife for his firstborn Er. **24** And Er came to his wife Tamar, and she became his wife, and when he came to her he outwardly destroyed his seed, and his work was evil in the sight of the Lord, and the Lord slew him. **25** And it was after the death of Er, Judah's firstborn, that Judah said unto Onan, "Go to your brother's wife and marry her as the next of kin and raise up seed to your brother." **26** And Onan took Tamar for a wife and he came to her, and Onan also did

like unto the work of his brother, and his work was evil in the sight of the Lord, and he slew him also. **27** And when Onan died, Judah said unto Tamar, "Remain in your father's house until my son Shiloh will have grown up, and Judah did no more delight in Tamar, to give her unto Shiloh, for he said, "Perhaps he will also die like his brothers." **28** And Tamar rose up and went and remained in her father's house, and Tamar was in her father's house for some time. **29** And at the revolution of the year, Aliyath the wife of Judah died; and Judah was comforted for his wife, and after the death of Aliyath, Judah went up with his friend Hirah to Timnah to shear their sheep. **30** And Tamar heard that Judah had gone up to Timnah to shear the sheep, and that Shiloh was grown up, and Judah did not delight in her. **31** And Tamar rose up and put off the garments of her widowhood, and she put a vail upon her, and she entirely covered herself, and she went and sat in the public thoroughfare, which is upon the road to Timnah. **32** And Judah passed and saw her and took her and he came to her, and she conceived by him, and at the time of being delivered, behold, there were twins in her womb, and he called the name of the first Perez, and the name of the second Zarah.

CHAPTER 46

1 In those days Joseph was still confined in the prison house in the land of Egypt. **2** At that time the attendants of Pharaoh were standing before him, the chief of the butlers and the chief of the bakers which belonged to the king of Egypt. **3** And the butler took wine and placed it before the king to drink, and the baker placed bread before the king to eat, and the king drank of the wine and ate of the bread, he and his servants and ministers that ate at the king's table. **4** And while they were eating and drinking, the butler and the baker remained there, and Pharaoh's ministers found many flies in the wine, which the butler had brought, and stones of nitre were found in the baker's bread. **5** And the captain of the guard placed Joseph as an attendant on Pharaoh's officers, and Pharaoh's officers were in confinement one year. **6** And at the end of the year, they both dreamed dreams in one night, in the place of confinement where they were, and in the morning Joseph came to them to attend upon them as usual, and he saw them, and behold their countenances were dejected and sad. **7** And Joseph asked them, "Why are your countenances sad and dejected this day?" And they said unto him, "We dreamed a dream, and there is no one to interpret it"; and Joseph said unto them, "Relate, I pray you, your dream unto me, and God will give you an answer of peace as you desire." **8** And the butler related his dream unto Joseph, and he said, "I saw in my dream, and behold a large vine was before me, and upon that vine I saw three branches, and the vine speedily blossomed and reached a great height, and its clusters were ripened and became grapes. **9** And I took the grapes and pressed them in a cup and placed it in Pharaoh's hand and he drank"; and Joseph said unto him, "The three branches that were upon the vine are three days. **10** Yet within three days, the king will order you to be brought out and he will restore you to your office, and you will give the king his wine to drink as at first when you were his butler; but let me find favor in your sight, that you will remember me to Pharaoh when it will be well with you, and do kindness unto me, and get me brought out from this prison, for I was stolen away from the land of Canaan and was sold for a slave in this place. **11** And also that which was told you concerning my master's wife is false, for they placed me in this dungeon for naught"; and the butler answered Joseph, saying, "If the king deal well with me as at first, as you last interpreted to me, I will do all that you desire, and get you brought out of this dungeon." **12** And the baker, seeing that Joseph had accurately interpreted the butler's dream, also approached, and related the whole of his dream to Joseph. **13** And he said unto him, "In my dream I saw and behold three white baskets upon my head, and I looked, and behold there were in the upper-most basket all manner of baked meats for Pharaoh, and behold the birds were eating them from off my head." **14** And Joseph said unto him, "The three baskets which you did see are three days, yet within three days Pharaoh will take off your head, and hang you upon a tree, and the birds will eat your flesh from off you, as you saw in your dream." **15** In those days the queen was about to be delivered, and upon that day she bore a son unto the king of Egypt, and they proclaimed that the king had gotten his firstborn son and all the people of Egypt together with the officers and servants of Pharaoh rejoiced greatly. **16** And upon the third day of his birth Pharaoh made a feast for his officers and servants, for the hosts of the land of Zoar and of the land of Egypt. **17** And all the people of Egypt and the servants of Pharaoh came to eat and drink with the king at the feast of his son, and to rejoice at the king's rejoicing. **18** And all the officers of the king and his servants were rejoicing at that time for eight days at the feast, and they made merry with all sorts of musical instruments, with timbrels and with dances in the king's house for eight days. **19** And the butler, to whom Joseph had interpreted his dream, forgot Joseph, and he did not mention him to the king as he had promised, for this thing was from the Lord in order to punish Joseph because he had trusted in man. **20** And Joseph remained after this in the prison house two years, until he had completed twelve years.

CHAPTER 47

1 And Isaac the son of Abraham was still living in those days in the land of Canaan; he was very aged, one hundred and eighty years old, and Esau his son, the brother of Jacob, was in the land of Edom, and he and his sons had possessions in it among the children of Seir. **2** And Esau heard that his father's time was drawing nigh to die, and he and his sons and household came unto the land of Canaan, unto his father's house, and Jacob and his sons went out from the place where they dwelt in Hebron, and they all came to their father Isaac, and they found Esau and his sons in the tent. **3** And Jacob and his sons sat before his father Isaac, and Jacob was still mourning for his son Joseph. **4** And Isaac said unto Jacob, "Bring me here your sons and I will bless them"; and Jacob brought his eleven children before his father Isaac. **5** And Isaac placed his hands upon all the sons of Jacob, and he took hold of them and embraced them, and kissed them one by one, and Isaac blessed them on that day, and he said unto them, "May the God of your fathers bless you and increase your seed like the stars of heaven for number." **6** And Isaac also blessed the sons of Esau, saying, "May God cause you to be a dread and a terror to all that will behold you, and to all your enemies." **7** And Isaac called Jacob and his sons, and they all came and sat before Isaac, and Isaac said unto Jacob, "The Lord God of the whole earth said unto me, 'Unto your seed will I give this land for an inheritance if your children keep my statutes and my ways, and I will perform unto them the oath which I swore unto your father Abraham.' **8** Now therefore my son, teach your children and your children's children to fear the Lord, and to go in the good way which will please the Lord your God, for if you keep the ways of the Lord and his statutes the Lord will also keep unto you his covenant with Abraham, and will do well with you and your seed all the days." **9** And when Isaac had finished commanding Jacob and his children, he gave up the ghost and died, and was gathered unto his people. **10** And Jacob and Esau fell upon the face of their father Isaac, and they wept, and Isaac was one hundred and eighty years old when he died in the land of Canaan, in Hebron, and his sons carried him to the cave of Machpelah, which Abraham had bought from the children of Heth for a possession of a burial place. **11** And all the kings of the land of Canaan went with Jacob and Esau to bury Isaac, and all the kings of Canaan showed Isaac great honor at his death. **12** And the sons of Jacob and the sons of Esau went barefooted round about, walking and lamenting until they reached Kireath-arba. **13** And Jacob and Esau buried their father Isaac in the cave of Machpelah, which is in Kireath-arba in Hebron, and they buried him with very great honor, as at the funeral of kings. **14** And Jacob and his sons, and Esau and his sons, and all the kings of Canaan made a great and heavy mourning, and they buried him and mourned for him many days. **15** And at the death of Isaac, he left his cattle and his possessions and all belonging to him to his sons; and Esau said unto Jacob, "Behold I pray you, all that our father has left we will divide it in two parts, and I will have the choice," and Jacob said, "We will do so." **16** And Jacob took all that Isaac had left in the land of Canaan, the cattle and the property, and he placed them in two parts before Esau and his sons, and he said unto Esau, "Behold, all this is before you, choose you unto yourself the half which you will take." **17** And Jacob said unto Esau, "Hear you I pray you what I will speak unto you, saying, 'The Lord God of heaven and earth spoke unto our fathers Abraham and Isaac, saying, *Unto your seed will I give this land for an inheritance forever.*' **18** Now therefore all that our father has left is before you, and behold all the land is before you; choose you from them what you desire. **19** If you desire the whole land take it for you and your children forever, and I will take these riches, and it you desire the riches take it unto you, and I will take this land for me and for my children to inherit it forever." **20** And Nebayoth, the son of Ishmael, was then in the land with his children, and Esau went on that day and consulted with him, saying, **21** "Thus has Jacob spoken unto me, and thus has he answered me, now give your advice and we will hear." **22** And Nebayoth said, "What is this that Jacob has spoken unto you? Behold all the children of Canaan are dwelling securely in their land, and Jacob says he will inherit it with his seed all the days. **23** Go now therefore and take all your father's riches and leave Jacob your brother in the land, as he has spoken." **24** And Esau rose up and returned to Jacob, and did all that Nebayoth the son of Ishmael had advised; and Esau took all the riches that Isaac had left, the souls, the beasts, the cattle and the property, and all the riches; he gave nothing to his brother Jacob; and Jacob took all the land of Canaan, from the brook of Egypt unto the river Euphrates, and he took it for an everlasting possession, and for his children and for his seed after him forever. **25** Jacob also took from his brother Esau the cave of Machpelah, which is in Hebron, which Abraham had bought from Ephron for a possession of a burial place for him and his seed forever. **26** And Jacob wrote all these things in the book of purchase, and he signed it, and he testified all this with four faithful witnesses. **27** And these are the words which Jacob wrote in the book, saying: "The land of Canaan and all the cities of the Hittites, the Hivites, the Jebusites, the Amorites, the Perizzites, and the Gergashites, all the seven nations from the river of Egypt unto the river Euphrates. **28** And the city of Hebron Kireath-arba, and the cave which is in it, the whole did Jacob buy from his brother Esau for value, for a possession and for an inheritance for his seed after him forever." **29** And Jacob took the book of purchase and the signature, the command and the statutes and the revealed book, and he placed them in an earthen vessel in order that they should remain for a long time, and he delivered them into the hands of his children. **30** Esau took all that his father had left him after his death from his brother Jacob, and he took all the property, from man and beast, camel and ass, ox and lamb, silver and gold, stones and bdellium, and all the riches which had belonged to Isaac the son of Abraham; there was nothing left which Esau did not take unto himself, from all that Isaac had left after his death. **31** And Esau took all this, and he and his children went home to the land of Seir the Horite, away from his brother Jacob and his children. **32** And Esau had possessions among the children of Seir, and Esau returned not to the land of Canaan from that day forward. **33** And the whole land of Canaan became an inheritance to the children of Israel for an everlasting inheritance, and Esau with all his children inherited the mountain of Seir.

CHAPTER 48

1 In those days, after the death of Isaac, the Lord commanded and caused a famine upon the whole earth. **2** At that time Pharaoh king of Egypt was sitting upon his throne in the land of Egypt, and lay in his bed and dreamed dreams, and Pharaoh saw in his dream that he was standing by the side of the river of Egypt. **3** And while he was standing he saw and behold seven fat fleshed and well favored kine came up out of the river. **4** And seven other kine, lean fleshed and ill favored, came up after them, and the seven ill favored ones swallowed up the well-favored ones, and still their appearance was ill as at first. **5** And he awoke, and he slept again, and he dreamed a second time, and he saw and behold seven ears of corn came up upon one stalk, rank and good, and seven thin ears blasted with the east wind sprang, up after them, and the thin ears swallowed up the full ones, and Pharaoh awoke out of his dream. **6** And in the morning the king remembered his dreams, and his spirit was sadly troubled on account of his dreams, and the king hastened and sent and called for all the magicians of Egypt, and the wise men, and they came and stood before Pharaoh. **7** And the king said unto them, "I have dreamed dreams, and there is none to interpret them"; and they said unto the king, "Relate your dreams to your servants and let us hear them." **8** And the king related his dreams to them, and they all answered and said with one voice to the king, "May the king live forever; and this is the interpretation of your dreams. **9** The seven good kine which you did see denote seven daughters that will be born unto you in the latter days, and the seven kine which you saw come up after them, and swallowed them up, are for a sign that the daughters which will be born unto you will all die in the life-time of the king. **10** And that which you did see in the second dream of seven full good ears of corn coming up upon one stalk, this is their interpretation, that you will build unto yourself in the latter days seven cities throughout the land of Egypt; and that which you saw of the seven blasted ears of corn springing up after them and swallowing them up while you did behold them with your eyes, is for a sign that the cities which you will build will all be destroyed in the latter days, in the life-time of the king." **11** And when they spoke these words the king did not incline his ear to their words, neither did he fix his heart upon them, for the king knew in his wisdom that they did not give a proper interpretation of the dreams; and when they had finished speaking before the king, the king answered them, saying, "What is this thing that you have spoken unto me? Surely you have uttered falsehood and spoken lies; therefore now give the proper interpretation of my dreams, that you may not die." **12** And the king commanded after this, and he sent and called again for other wise men, and they came and stood before the king, and the king related his dreams to them, and they all answered him according to the first interpretation, and the king's anger was kindled and he was very angry, and the king said unto them, "Surely you speak lies and utter falsehood in what you have said." **13** And the king commanded that a proclamation should be issued throughout the land of Egypt, saying, "It is resolved by the king and his great men, that any wise man who knows and understands the interpretation of dreams, and will not come this day before the king, will die. **14** And the man that will declare unto the king the proper interpretation of his dreams, there will be given unto him all that he will require from the king." And all the wise men of the land of Egypt came before the king, together with all the magicians and sorcerers that were in Egypt and in Goshen, in Rameses, in Tachpanches, in Zoar, and in all the places on the borders of Egypt, and they all stood before the king. **15** And all the nobles and the princes, and the attendants belonging to the king, came together from all the cities of Egypt, and they all sat before the king, and the king related his dreams before the wise men, and the princes, and all that sat before the king were astonished at the vision. **16** And all the wise men who were before the king were greatly divided in their interpretation of his dreams; some of them interpreted them to the king, saying, "The seven good kine are seven kings, who from the king's issue will be raised over Egypt. **17** And the seven bad kine are seven princes, who will stand up against them in the latter days and destroy them; and the seven ears of corn are the seven great princes belonging to Egypt, who will fall in the hands of the seven less powerful princes of their enemies, in the wars of our lord the king."

18 And some of them interpreted to the king in this manner, saying, "The seven good kine are the strong cities of Egypt, and the seven bad kine are the seven nations of the land of Canaan, who will come against the seven cities of Egypt in the latter days and destroy them. **19** And that which you saw in the second dream, of seven good and bad ears of corn, is a sign that the government of Egypt will again return to your seed as at first. **20** And in his reign the people of the cities of Egypt will turn against the seven cities of Canaan who are stronger than they are, and will destroy them, and the government of Egypt will return to your seed." **21** And some of them said unto the king, "This is the interpretation of your dreams; the seven good kine are seven queens, whom you will take for wives in the latter days, and the seven bad kine denote that those women will all die in the lifetime of the king. **22** And the seven good and bad ears of corn which you did see in the second dream are fourteen children, and it will be in the latter days that they will stand up and fight among themselves, and seven of them will smite the seven that are more powerful." **23** And some of them said these words unto the king, saying, "The seven good kine denote that seven children will be born to you, and they will slay seven of your children's children in the latter days; and the seven good ears of corn which you did see in the second dream, are those princes against whom seven other less powerful princes will fight and destroy them in the latter days, and avenge your children's cause, and the government will again return to your seed." **24** And the king heard all the words of the wise men of Egypt and their interpretation of his dreams, and none of them pleased the king. **25** And the king knew in his wisdom that they did not altogether speak correctly in all these words, for this was from the Lord to frustrate the words of the wise men of Egypt, in order that Joseph might go out from the house of confinement, and in order that he should become great in Egypt. **26** And the king saw that none among all the wise men and magicians of Egypt spoke correctly to him, and the king's wrath was kindled, and his anger burned within him. **27** And the king commanded that all the wise men and magicians should go out from before him, and they all went out from before the king with shame and disgrace. **28** And the king commanded that a proclamation be sent throughout Egypt to slay all the magicians that were in Egypt, and not one of them should be suffered to live. **29** And the captains of the guards belonging to the king rose up, and each man drew his sword, and they began to smite the magicians of Egypt, and the wise men. **30** And after this Merod, chief butler to the king, came and bowed down before the king and sat before him. **31** And the butler said unto the king, "May the king live forever, and his government be exalted in the land. **32** You were angry with your servant in those days, now two years past, and did place me in the ward, and I was for some time in the ward, I and the chief of the bakers. **33** And there was with us a Hebrew servant belonging to the captain of the guard, his name was Joseph, for his master had been angry with him and placed him in the house of confinement, and he attended us there. **34** And in some time after when we were in the ward, we dreamed dreams in one night, I and the chief of the bakers; we dreamed, each man according to the interpretation of his dream. **35** And we came in the morning and told them to that servant, and he interpreted to us our dreams, to each man according to his dream, did he correctly interpret. **36** And it came to pass as he interpreted to us, so was the event; there fell not to the ground any of his words. **37** And now therefore my lord and king do not slay the people of Egypt for naught; behold that slave is still confined in the house by the captain of the guard his master, in the house of confinement. **38** If it pleases the king let him send for him that he may come before you and he will make known to you, the correct interpretation of the dream which you did dream." **39** And the king heard the words of the chief butler, and the king ordered that the wise men of Egypt should not be slain. **40** And the king ordered his servants to bring Joseph before him, and the king said unto them, "Go to him and do not terrify him lest he be confused and will not know to speak properly." **41** And the servants of the king went to Joseph, and they brought him hastily out of the dungeon, and the king's servants shaved him, and he changed his prison garment and he came before the king. **42** And the king was sitting upon his royal throne in a princely dress girt around with a golden ephod, and the fine gold which was upon it sparkled, and the carbuncle and the ruby and the emerald, together with all the precious stones that were upon the king's head, dazzled the eye, and Joseph wondered greatly at the king.

43 And the throne upon which the king sat was covered with gold and silver, and with onyx stones, and it had seventy steps. **44** And it was their custom throughout the land of Egypt, that every man who came to speak to the king, if he was a prince or one that was estimable in the sight of the king, he ascended to the king's throne as far as the thirty-first step, and the king would descend to the thirty-sixth step, and speak with him. **45** If he was one of the common people, he ascended to the third step, and the king would descend to the fourth and speak to him, and their custom was, moreover, that any man who understood to speak in all the seventy languages, he ascended the seventy steps, and went up and spoke until he reached the king. **46** And any man who could not complete the seventy, he ascended as many steps as the languages which he knew to speak in. **47** And it was customary in those days in Egypt that no one should reign over them, but who understood to speak in the seventy languages. **48** And when Joseph came before the king he bowed down to the ground before the king, and he ascended to the third step, and the king sat upon the fourth step and spoke with Joseph. **49** And the king said unto Joseph, "I dreamed a dream, and there is no interpreter to interpret it properly, and I commanded this day that all the magicians of Egypt and the wise men thereof, should come before me, and I related my dreams to them, and no one has properly interpreted them to me. **50** And after this I this day heard concerning you, that you are a wise man, and can correctly interpret every dream that you hear." **51** And Joseph answered Pharaoh, saying, "Let Pharaoh relate his dreams that he dreamed; surely the interpretations belong to God"; and Pharaoh related his dreams to Joseph, the dream of the kine, and the dream of the ears of corn, and the king left off speaking. **52** And Joseph was then clothed with the Spirit of God before the king, and he knew all the things that would befall the king from that day forward, and he knew the proper interpretation of the king's dream, and he spoke before the king. **53** And Joseph found favor in the sight of the king, and the king inclined his ears and his heart, and he heard all the words of Joseph. And Joseph said unto the king, "Do not imagine that they are two dreams, for it is only one dream, for that which God has chosen to do throughout the land he has shown to the king in his dream, and this is the proper interpretation of your dream: **54** The seven good kine and ears of corn are seven years, and the seven bad kine and ears of corn are also seven years; it is one dream. **55** Behold, the seven years that are coming there will be a great plenty throughout the land, and after that the seven years of famine will follow them, a very grievous famine; and all the plenty will be forgotten from the land, and the famine will consume the inhabitants of the land. **56** The king dreamed one dream, and the dream was therefore repeated unto Pharaoh because the thing is established by God, and God will shortly bring it to pass. **57** Now therefore I will give you counsel and deliver your soul and the souls of the inhabitants of the land from the evil of the famine, that you seek throughout your kingdom for a man very discreet and wise, who knows all the affairs of government, and appoint him to superintend over the land of Egypt. **58** And let the man whom you place over Egypt appoint officers under him, that they gather in all the food of the good years that are coming and let them lay up corn and deposit it in your appointed stores. **59** And let them keep that food for the seven years of famine, that it may be found for you and your people and your whole land, and that you and your land be not cut off by the famine. **60** Let all the inhabitants of the land be also ordered that they gather in, every man the produce of his field, of all sorts of food, during the seven good years, and that they place it in their stores, that it may be found for them in the days of the famine and that they may live upon it. **61** This is the proper interpretation of your dream, and this is the counsel given to save your soul and the souls of all your subjects." **62** And the king answered and said unto Joseph, "Who says and who knows that your words are correct?" And he said unto the king, "This will be a sign for you respecting all my words, that they are true and that my advice is good for you. **63** Behold, your wife sits this day upon the stool of delivery, and she will bear you a son and you will rejoice with him; when your child will have gone out from his mother's womb, your firstborn son that has been born these two years back will die, and you will be comforted in the child that will be born unto you this day." **64** And Joseph finished speaking these words to the king, and he bowed down to the king and he went out, and when Joseph had gone out from the king's presence, those signs which Joseph had spoken unto the king came to pass on that day. **65** And the queen bore a son on that day and the king heard the glad tidings about his son, and he rejoiced, and when the reporter had gone out from the king's presence, the king's servants found the firstborn son of the king fallen dead upon the ground. **66** And there was great lamentation and noise in the king's house, and the king heard it, and he said, "What is the noise and lamentation that I have heard in the house?" And they told the king that his firstborn son had died; then the king knew that all Joseph's words that he had spoken were correct, and the king was consoled for his son by the child that was born to him on that day as Joseph had spoken.

CHAPTER 49

1 After these things the king sent and assembled all his officers and servants, and all the princes and nobles belonging to the king, and they all came before the king. **2** And the king said unto them, "Behold, you have seen and heard all the words of this Hebrew man, and all the signs which he declared would come to pass, and not any of his words have fallen to the ground. **3** You know that he has given a proper interpretation of the dream, and it will surely come to pass, now therefore take counsel, and know what you will do and how the land will be delivered from the famine. **4** Seek now and see whether the like can be found, in whose heart there is wisdom and knowledge, and I will appoint him over the land. **5** For you have heard what the Hebrew man has advised concerning this to save the land from the famine, and I know that the land will not be delivered from the famine but with the advice of the Hebrew man, him that advised me." **6** And they all answered the king and said, "The counsel which the Hebrew has given concerning this is good; now therefore, our lord and king, behold, the whole land is in your hand, do that which seems good in your sight. **7** Him whom you choose, and whom you in your wisdom know to be wise and capable of delivering the land with his wisdom, him will the king appoint to be under him over the land." **8** And the king said to all the officers: "I have thought that since God has made known to the Hebrew man all that he has spoken, there is none so discreet and wise in the whole land as he is; if it seem good in your sight I will place him over the land, for he will save the land with his wisdom." **9** And all the officers answered the king and said, "But surely it is written in the laws of Egypt, and it should not be violated, that no man will reign over Egypt, nor be the second to the king, but

one who has knowledge in all the languages of the sons of men. **10** Now therefore our lord and king, behold, this Hebrew man can only speak the Hebrew language, and how then can he be over us the second under government, a man who not even knows our language? **11** Now we pray you send for him, and let him come before you, and prove him in all things, and do as you see fit." **12** And the king said, "It will be done tomorrow, and the thing that you have spoken is good"; and all the officers came on that day before the king. **13** And on that night the Lord sent one of his ministering angels, and he came into the land of Egypt unto Joseph, and the angel of the Lord stood over Joseph, and behold, Joseph was lying in the bed at night in his master's house in the dungeon, for his master had put him back into the dungeon on account of his wife. **14** And the angel roused him from his sleep, and Joseph rose up and stood upon his legs, and behold, the angel of the Lord was standing opposite to him; and the angel of the Lord spoke with Joseph, and he taught him all the languages of man in that night, and he called his name Jehoseph. **15** And the angel of the Lord went from him, and Joseph returned and lay upon his bed, and Joseph was astonished at the vision which he saw. **16** And it came to pass in the morning that the king sent for all his officers and servants, and they all came and sat before the king, and the king ordered Joseph to be brought, and the king's servants went and brought Joseph before Pharaoh. **17** And the king came out and ascended the steps of the throne, and Joseph spoke unto the king in all languages, and Joseph went up to him and spoke unto the king until he arrived before the king in the seventieth step, and he sat before the king. **18** And the king greatly rejoiced on account of Joseph, and all the king's officers rejoiced greatly with the king when they heard all the words of Joseph. **19** And the thing seemed good in the sight of the king and the officers, to appoint Joseph to be second to the king over the whole land of Egypt, and the king spoke to Joseph, saying, **20** "Now you did give me counsel to appoint a wise man over the land of Egypt, in order with his wisdom to save the land from the famine; now therefore, since God has made all this known to you, and all the words which you have spoken, there is not throughout the land a discreet and wise man like unto you. **21** And your name no more will be called Joseph, but Zaphnath Paaneah will be your name; you will be second to me, and according to your word will be all the affairs of my government, and at your word will my people go out and come in. 22 Also from under your hand will my servants and officers receive their salary which is given to them monthly, and to you will all the people of the land bow down; only in my throne will I be greater than you." 23 And the king took off his ring from his hand and put it upon the hand of Joseph, and the king dressed Joseph in a princely garment, and he put a golden crown upon his head, and he put a golden chain upon his neck. 24 And the king commanded his servants, and they made him ride in the second chariot belonging to the king, that went opposite to the king's chariot, and he caused him to ride upon a great and strong horse from the king's horses, and to be conducted through the streets of the land of Egypt. 25 And the king commanded that all those that played upon timbrels, harps and other musical instruments should go out with Joseph; one thousand timbrels, one thousand mecholoth, and one thousand nebalim went after him. 26 And five thousand men, with drawn swords glittering in their hands, and they went marching and playing before Joseph, and twenty thousand of the great men of the king girt with girdles of skin covered with gold, marched at the right hand of Joseph, and twenty thousand at his left, and all the women and damsels went upon the roofs or stood in the streets playing and rejoicing at Joseph, and gazed at the appearance of Joseph and at his beauty. 27 And the king's people went before him and behind him, perfuming the road with frankincense and with cassia, and with all sorts of fine perfume, and scattered myrrh and aloes along the road, and twenty men proclaimed these words before him throughout the land in a loud voice: 28 "Do you see this man whom the king has chosen to be his second? All the affairs of government will be regulated by him, and he that transgresses his orders, or that does not bow down before him to the ground, will die, for he rebels against the king and his second." 29 And when the heralds had ceased proclaiming, all the people of Egypt bowed down to the ground before Joseph and said, "May the king live, also may his second live"; and all the inhabitants of Egypt bowed down along the road, and when the heralds approached them, they bowed down, and they rejoiced with all sorts of timbrels, mechol and nebal before Joseph. 30 And Joseph upon his horse lifted up his eyes to heaven, and called out and said, "He raises the poor man from the dust, He lifts up the needy from the dunghill. O Lord of Hosts, happy is the man who trusts in you." 31 And Joseph passed throughout the land of Egypt with Pharaoh's servants and officers, and they showed him the whole land of Egypt and all the king's treasures. 32 And Joseph returned and came on that day before Pharaoh, and the king gave unto Joseph a possession in the land of Egypt, a possession of fields and vineyards, and the king gave unto Joseph three thousand talents of silver and one thousand talents of gold, and onyx stones and bdellium and many gifts. 33 And on the next day the king commanded all the people of Egypt to bring unto Joseph offerings and gifts, and that he that violated the command of the king should die; and they made a high place in the street of the city, and they spread out garments there, and whoever brought anything to Joseph put it into the high place. 34 And all the people of Egypt cast something into the high place, one man a golden earring, and the other rings and earrings, and different vessels of gold and silver work, and onyx stones and bdellium did he cast upon the high place; everyone gave something of what he possessed. 35 And Joseph took all these and placed them in his treasuries, and all the officers and nobles belonging to the king exalted Joseph, and they gave him many gifts, seeing that the king had chosen him to be his second. 36 And the king sent to Potiphera, the son of Ahiram priest of On, and he took his young daughter Osnath and gave her unto Joseph for a wife. 37 And the damsel was very comely, a virgin, one whom man had not known, and Joseph took her for a wife; and the king said unto Joseph, "I am Pharaoh, and beside you none will dare to lift up his hand or his foot to regulate my people throughout the land of Egypt." 38 And Joseph was thirty years old when he stood before Pharaoh, and Joseph went out from before the king, and he became the king's second in Egypt. 39 And the king gave Joseph a hundred servants to attend him in his house, and Joseph also sent and purchased many servants and they remained in the house of Joseph. 40 Joseph then built for himself a very magnificent house like unto the houses of kings, before the court of the king's palace, and he made in the house a large temple, very elegant in appearance and convenient for his residence; three years was Joseph in erecting his house. 41 And Joseph made unto himself a very elegant throne of abundance of gold and silver, and he covered it with onyx stones and bdellium, and he made upon it the likeness of the whole land of Egypt, and the likeness of the river of Egypt that waters the whole land of Egypt; and Joseph sat securely upon his throne in his house and the Lord increased Joseph's wisdom. **42** And all the inhabitants of Egypt and Pharaoh's servants and his princes loved Joseph exceedingly, for this thing was from the Lord to Joseph. **43** And Joseph had an army that made war, going out in hosts and troops to the number of forty thousand six hundred men, capable of bearing arms to assist the king and Joseph against the enemy, besides the king's officers and his servants and inhabitants of Egypt without number. **44** And Joseph gave unto his mighty men, and to all his host, shields and javelins, and caps and coats of mail and stones for slinging.

CHAPTER 50

1 At that time the children of Tarshish came against the sons of Ishmael, and made war with them, and the children of Tarshish spoiled the Ishmaelites for a long time. **2** And the children of Ishmael were small in number in those days, and they could not prevail over the children of Tarshish, and they were sorely oppressed. **3** And the old men of the Ishmaelites sent a record to the king of Egypt, saying, "Send I pray you unto your servants officers and hosts to help us to fight against the children of Tarshish, for we have been consuming away for a long time." **4** And Pharaoh sent Joseph with the mighty men and host which were with him, and also his mighty men from the king's house. **5** And they went to the land of Havilah to the children of Ishmael, to assist them against the children of Tarshish, and the children of Ishmael fought with the children of Tarshish, and Joseph smote the Tarshishites and he subdued all their land, and the children of Ishmael dwell therein unto this day. **6** And when the land of Tarshish was subdued, all the Tarshishites ran away, and came on the border of their brethren the children of Javan, and Joseph with all his mighty men and host returned to Egypt, not one man of them missing. **7** And at the revolution of the year, in the second year of Joseph's reigning over Egypt, the Lord gave great plenty throughout the land for seven years as Joseph had spoken, for the Lord blessed all the produce of the earth in those days for seven years, and they ate and were greatly satisfied. **8** And Joseph at that time had officers under him, and they collected all the food of the good years, and heaped corn year by year, and they placed it in the treasuries of Joseph. **9** And at any time when they gathered the food Joseph commanded that they should bring the corn in the ears, and also bring with it some of the soil of the field, that it should not spoil. **10** And Joseph did according to this year by year, and he heaped up corn like the sand of the sea for abundance, for his stores were immense and could not be numbered for abundance. **11** And also all the inhabitants of Egypt gathered all sorts of food in their stores in great abundance during the seven good years, but they did not do unto it as Joseph did. **12** And all the food which Joseph and the Egyptians had gathered during the seven years of plenty, was secured for the land in stores for the seven years of famine, for the support of the whole land. **13** And the inhabitants of Egypt filled each man his store and his concealed place with corn, to be for support during the famine. **14** And Joseph placed all the food that he had gathered in all the cities of Egypt, and he closed all the stores and placed sentinels over them. **15** And Joseph's wife Osnath the daughter of Potiphera bore him two sons, Manasseh and Ephraim, and Joseph was thirty-four years old when he begat them. **16** And the lads grew up and they went in his ways and in his instructions, they did not deviate from the way which their father taught them, either to the right or left. **17** And the Lord was with the lads, and they grew up and had understanding and skill in all wisdom and in all the affairs of government, and all the king's officers and his great men of the inhabitants of Egypt exalted the lads, and they were brought up among the king's children. **18** And the seven years of plenty that were throughout the land were at an end, and the seven years of famine came after them as Joseph had spoken, and the famine was throughout the land. **19** And all the people of Egypt saw that the famine had commenced in the land of Egypt, and all the people of Egypt opened their stores of corn for the famine prevailed over them. **20** And they found all the food that was in their stores, full of vermin and not fit to eat, and the famine prevailed throughout the land, and all the inhabitants of Egypt came and cried before Pharaoh, for the famine was heavy upon them. **21** And they said unto Pharaoh, "Give food unto your servants, and why will we die through hunger before your eyes, even we and our little ones?" 22 And Pharaoh answered them, saying, "And why do you cry unto me? Did not Joseph command that the corn should be laid up during the seven years of plenty for the years of famine? And why did you not hearken to his voice?" 23 And the people of Egypt answered the king, saying, "As your soul lives, our lord, your servants have done all that Joseph ordered, for your servants also gathered in all the produce of their fields during the seven years of plenty and laid it in the stores unto this day. 24 And when the famine prevailed over your servants we opened our stores and behold all our produce was filled with vermin and was not fit for food." 25 And when the king heard all that had befallen the inhabitants of Egypt, the king was greatly afraid on account of the famine, and he was much terrified; and the king answered the people of Egypt, saying, "Since all this has happened unto you, go unto Joseph, do whatever he will say unto you, transgress not his commands. 26 And all the people of Egypt went out and came unto Joseph, and said unto him, "Give unto us food, and why will we die before you through hunger? For we gathered in our produce during the seven years as you did command, and we put it in store, and thus has it befallen us." 27 And when Joseph heard all the words of the people of Egypt and what had befallen them, Joseph opened all his stores of the produce and he sold it unto the people of Egypt. 28 And the famine prevailed throughout the land, and the famine was in all countries, but in the land of Egypt there was produce for sale. 29 And all the inhabitants of Egypt came unto Joseph to buy corn, for the famine prevailed over them, and all their corn was spoiled, and Joseph daily sold it to all the people of Egypt. 30 And all the inhabitants of the land of Canaan and the Philistines, and those beyond the Jordan, and the children of the east and all the cities of the lands far and nigh heard that there was corn in Egypt, and they all came to Egypt to buy corn, for the famine prevailed over them. 31 And Joseph opened the stores of corn and placed officers over them, and they daily stood and sold to all that came. 32 And Joseph knew that his brethren also would come to Egypt to buy corn, for the famine prevailed throughout the earth. And Joseph commanded all his people that they should cause it to be proclaimed throughout the land of Egypt, saying, 33 "It is

the pleasure of the king, of his second and of their great men, that any person who wishes to buy corn in Egypt will not send his servants to Egypt to purchase, but his sons, and also any Egyptian or Canaanite, who will come from any of the stores from buying corn in Egypt, and will go and sell it throughout the land, he will die, for no one will buy but for the support of his household. 34 And any man leading two or three beasts will die, for a man will only lead his own beast." 35 And Joseph placed sentinels at the gates of Egypt, and commanded them, saying, "Any person who may come to buy corn, suffer him not to enter until his name, and the name of his father, and the name of his father's father be written down, and whatever is written by day, send their names unto me in the evening that I may know their names." 36 And Joseph placed officers throughout the land of Egypt, and he commanded them to do all these things. 37 And Joseph did all these things, and made these statutes, in order that he might know when his brethren should come to Egypt to buy corn; and Joseph's people caused it daily to be proclaimed in Egypt according to these words and statutes which Joseph had commanded. 38 And all the inhabitants of the east and west country, and of all the earth, heard of the statutes and regulations which Joseph had enacted in Egypt, and the inhabitants of the extreme parts of the earth came and they bought corn in Egypt day after day, and then went away. 39 And all the officers of Egypt did as Joseph had commanded, and all that came to Egypt to buy corn, the gate keepers would write their names, and their fathers' names, and daily bring them in the evening before Joseph.

CHAPTER 51

1 And Jacob afterward heard that there was corn in Egypt, and he called unto his sons to go to Egypt to buy corn, for upon them also did the famine prevail, and he called unto his sons, saying, 2 "Behold I hear that there is corn in Egypt, and all the people of the earth go there to purchase, now therefore why will you show yourselves satisfied before the whole earth? Go you also down to Egypt and buy us a little corn among those that come there, that we may not die." 3 And the sons of Jacob hearkened to the voice of their father, and they rose up to go down to Egypt in order to buy corn among the rest that came there. 4 And Jacob their father commanded them,

saying, "When you come into the city do not enter together in one gate, on account of the inhabitants of the land." 5 And the sons of Jacob went out and they went to Egypt, and the sons of Jacob did all as their father had commanded them, and Jacob did not send Benjamin, for he said, "Lest an accident might befall him on the road like his brother"; and ten of Jacob's sons went out. 6 And while the sons of Jacob were going on the road, they repented of what they had done to Joseph, and they spoke to each other, saying, "We know that our brother Joseph went down to Egypt, and now we will seek him where we go, and if we find him we will take him from his master for a ransom, and if not, by force, and we will die for him." 7 And the sons of Jacob agreed to this thing and strengthened themselves on account of Joseph, to deliver him from the hand of his master, and the sons of Jacob went to Egypt; and when they came near to Egypt they separated from each other, and they came through ten gates of Egypt, and the gate keepers wrote their names on that day, and brought them to Joseph in the evening. 8 And Joseph read the names from the hand of the gate-keepers of the city, and he found that his brethren had entered at the ten gates of the city, and Joseph at that time commanded that it should be proclaimed throughout the land of Egypt, saying, 9 "Go out all you store guards, close all the corn stores and let only one remain open, that those who come may purchase from it." 10 And all the officers of Joseph did so at that time, and they closed all the stores and left only one open. 11 And Joseph gave the written names of his brethren to him that was set over the open store, and he said unto him, "Whosoever will come to you to buy corn, ask his name, and when men of these names will come before you, seize them and send them, and they did so. 12 And when the sons of Jacob came into the city, they joined together in the city to seek Joseph before they bought themselves corn. 13 And they went to the walls of the harlots, and they sought Joseph in the walls of the harlots for three days, for they thought that Joseph would come in the walls of the harlots, for Joseph was very comely and well favored, and the sons of Jacob sought Joseph for three days, and they could not find him. 14 And the man who was set over the open store sought for those names which Joseph had given him, and he did not find them. 15 And he sent to Joseph, saying, "These three days have passed, and those men

whose names you did give unto me have not come"; and Joseph sent servants to seek the men in all Egypt, and to bring them before Joseph. 16 And Joseph's servants went and came into Egypt and could not find them, and went to Goshen and they were not there, and then went to the city of Rameses and could not find them. 17 And Joseph continued to send sixteen servants to seek his brothers, and they went and spread themselves in the four corners of the city, and four of the servants went into the house of the harlots, and they found the ten men there seeking their brother. 18 And those four men took them and brought them before him, and they bowed down to him to the ground, and Joseph was sitting upon his throne in his temple, clothed with princely garments, and upon his head was a large crown of gold, and all the mighty men were sitting around him. 19 And the sons of Jacob saw Joseph, and his figure and comeliness and dignity of countenance seemed wonderful in their eyes, and they again bowed down to him to the ground. 20 And Joseph saw his brethren, and he knew them, but they knew him not, for Joseph was very great in their eyes, therefore they knew him not. 21 And Joseph spoke to them, saying, "From where do you come?" And they all answered and said, "Your servants have come from the land of Canaan to buy corn, for the famine prevails throughout the earth, and your servants heard that there was corn in Egypt, so they have come among the other comers to buy corn for their support." 22 And Joseph answered them, saying, "If you have come to purchase as you say, why do you come through ten gates of the city? It can only be that you have come to spy through the land." 23 And they all together answered Joseph, and said, "Not so my lord, we are right, your servants are not spies, but we have come to buy corn, for your servants are all brothers, the sons of one man in the land of Canaan, and our father commanded us, saying, 'When you come to the city do not enter together at one gate on account of the inhabitants of the land.'" 24 And Joseph again answered them and said, "That is the thing which I spoke unto you, you have come to spy through the land, therefore you all came through ten gates of the city; you have come to see the nakedness of the land. 25 Surely everyone that comes to buy corn goes his way, and you are already three days in the land, and what do you do in the walls of harlots in which you have been for these three days? Surely spies do like unto these things." **26** And they said unto Joseph, "Far be it from our lord to speak thus, for we are twelve brothers, the sons of our father Jacob, in the land of Canaan, the son of Isaac, the son of Abraham, the Hebrew, and behold the youngest is with our father this day in the land of Canaan, and one is not, for he was lost from us, and we thought perhaps he might be in this land, so we are seeking him throughout the land, and have come even to the houses of harlots to seek him there." **27** And Joseph said unto them, "And have you then sought him throughout the earth, that there only remained Egypt for you to seek him in? And what also should your brother do in the houses of harlots, although he was in Egypt? Have you not said, 'That you are from the sons of Isaac, the son of Abraham, and what will the sons of Jacob do then in the houses of harlots?' " **28** And they said unto him, "Because we heard that Ishmaelites stole him from us, and it was told unto us that they sold him in Egypt, and your servant, our brother, is very comely and well-favored, so we thought he would surely be in the houses of harlots, therefore your servants went there to seek him and give ransom for him." **29** And Joseph still answered them, saying, "Surely you speak falsely and utter lies, to say of yourselves that you are the sons of Abraham; as Pharaoh lives you are spies, therefore have you come to the houses of harlots that you should not be known." **30** And Joseph said unto them, "And now if you find him, and his master requires of you a great price, will you give it for him?" And they said, "It will be given." **31** And he said unto them, "And if his master will not consent to part with him for a great price, what will you do unto him on his account?" And they answered him, saying, "If he will not give him unto us we will slay him, and take our brother and go away." **32** And Joseph said unto them, "That is the thing which I have spoken to you; you are spies, for you are come to slay the inhabitants of the land, for we heard that two of your brethren smote all the inhabitants of Shechem, in the land of Canaan, on account of your sister, and you now come to do the like in Egypt on account of your brother. **33** Only hereby will I know that you are true men; if you will send home one from among you to fetch your youngest brother from your father, and to bring him here unto me, and by doing this thing I will know that you are right." **34** And Joseph called to seventy of his mighty men, and he said unto them, "Take these men

and bring them into the ward." **35** And the mighty men took the ten men, they laid hold of them and put them into the ward, and they were in the ward three days. **36** And on the third day Joseph had them brought out of the ward, and he said unto them, "Do this for yourselves if you be true men, so that you may live, one of your brethren will be confined in the ward while you go and take home the corn for your household to the land of Canaan, and fetch your youngest brother, and bring him here unto me, that I may know that you are true men when you do this thing." **37** And Joseph went out from them and came into the chamber, and wept a great weeping, for his pity was excited for them, and he washed his face, and returned to them again, and he took Simeon from them and ordered him to be bound, but Simeon was not willing to be done so, for he was a very powerful man and they could not bind him. **38** And Joseph called unto his mighty men and seventy valiant men came before him with drawn swords in their hands, and the sons of Jacob were terrified at them. **39** And Joseph said unto them, "Seize this man and confine him in prison until his brethren come to him," and Joseph's valiant men hastened and they all laid hold of Simeon to bind him, and Simeon gave a loud and terrible shriek and the cry was heard at a distance. **40** And all the valiant men of Joseph were terrified at the sound of the shriek, that they fell upon their faces, and they were greatly afraid and fled. **41** And all the men that were with Joseph fled, for they were greatly afraid for their lives, and only Joseph and Manasseh his son remained there, and Manassah the son of Joseph saw the strength of Simeon, and he was exceedingly angry. **42** And Manassah the son of Joseph rose up to Simeon, and Manassah smote Simeon a heavy blow with his fist against the back of his neck, and Simeon was stilled of his rage. **43** And Manassah laid hold of Simeon and he seized him violently and he bound him and brought him into the house of confinement, and all the sons of Jacob were astonished at the act of the youth. **44** And Simeon said unto his brethren, "None of you must say that this is the smiting of an Egyptian, but it is the smiting of the house of my father." **45** And after this Joseph ordered him to be called who was set over the storehouse, to fill their sacks with corn as much as they could carry, and to restore every man's money into his sack, and to give them provision for the road, and thus did he unto them. **46** And Joseph commanded them, saying, "Take heed lest you transgress my orders to bring your brother as I have told you, and it will be when you bring your brother here unto me, then will I know that you are true men, and you will traffic in the land, and I will restore unto you your brother, and you will return in peace to your father." **47** And they all answered and said, "According as our lord speaks so will we do," and they bowed down to him to the ground. **48** And every man lifted his corn upon his ass, and they went out to go to the land of Canaan to their father; and they came to the inn and Levi spread his sack to give provender to his ass, when he saw and behold his money in full weight was still in his sack. **49** And the man was greatly afraid, and he said unto his brethren, "My money is restored, and, behold, it is even in my sack," and the men were greatly afraid, and they said, "What is this that God has done unto us?" **50** And they all said, "And where is the Lord's kindness with our fathers, with Abraham, Isaac, and Jacob, that the Lord has this day delivered us into the hands of the king of Egypt to contrive against us?" **51** And Judah said unto them, "Surely we are guilty sinners before the Lord our God in having sold our brother, our own flesh, and why do you say, 'Where is the Lord's kindness with our fathers?' " **52** And Reuben said unto them, "Had I not said unto you, do not sin against the lad, and you would not listen to me? Now God requires him from us, and how dare you say, 'Where is the Lord's kindness with our fathers, while you have sinned unto the Lord?' " **53** And they tarried overnight in that place, and they rose up early in the morning and laded their asses with their corn, and they led them and went on and came to their father's house in the land of Canaan. **54** And Jacob and his household went out to meet his sons, and Jacob saw and behold their brother Simeon was not with them, and Jacob said unto his sons, "Where is your brother Simeon, whom I do not see?" And his sons told him all that had befallen them in Egypt.

CHAPTER 52

1 And they entered their house, and every man opened his sack and they saw and behold every man's bundle of money was there, at which they and their father were greatly terrified. **2** And Jacob said unto them, "What is this that you have done to me? I sent your brother Joseph to inquire after your welfare and you said unto me, 'A wild beast did devour him.' **3** And Simeon went with you to buy food and you say the king of Egypt has confined him in prison, and you wish to take Benjamin to cause his death also and bring down my grey hairs with sorrow to the grave on account of Benjamin and his brother Joseph. **4** Now therefore my son will not go down with you, for his brother is dead and he is left alone, and mischief may befall him by the way in which you go, as it befell his brother." **5** And Reuben said unto his father, "You will slay my two sons if I do not bring your son and place him before you"; and Jacob said unto his sons, "Abide you here and do not go down to Egypt, for my son will not go down with you to Egypt, nor die like his brother." **6** And Judah said unto them, "Refrain you from him until the corn is finished, and he will then say, 'Take down your brother, when he will find his own life and the life of his household in danger from the famine.' " **7** And in those days the famine was sore throughout the land, and all the people of the earth went and came to Egypt to buy food, for the famine prevailed greatly among them, and the sons of Jacob remained in Canaan a year and two months until their corn was finished. **8** And it came to pass after their corn was finished, the whole household of Jacob was pinched with hunger, and all the infants of the sons of Jacob came together and they approached Jacob, and they all surrounded him, and they said unto him, "Give unto us bread, and why will we all perish through hunger in your presence?" **9** Jacob heard the words of his son's children, and he wept a great weeping, and his pity was roused for them, and Jacob called unto his sons and they all came and sat before him. **10** And Jacob said unto them, "And have you not seen how your children have been weeping over me this day, saying, 'Give unto us bread, and there is none?' Now therefore return and buy for us a little food." **11** And Judah answered and said unto his father, "If you will send our brother with us we will go down and buy corn for you, and if you will not send him then we will not go down, for surely the king of Egypt particularly enjoined us, saying, 'You will not see my face unless your brother be with you,' for the king of Egypt is a strong and mighty king, and behold if we will go to him without our brother we will all be put to death. **12** Do you not know and have you not heard that this king is very powerful and wise, and there is not like unto him in all the earth? Behold we have seen all the kings of the earth and we have not seen one like that king, the king of Egypt; surely among all the kings of the earth there is none greater than Abimelech king of the Philistines, yet the king of Egypt is greater and mightier than he, and Abimelech can only be compared to one of his officers. 13 Father, you have not seen his palace and his throne, and all his servants standing before him; you have not seen that king upon his throne in his pomp and royal appearance, dressed in his kingly robes with a large golden crown upon his head; you have not seen the honor and glory which God has given unto him, for there is not like unto him in all the earth. 14 Father, you have not seen the wisdom, the understanding and the knowledge which God has given in his heart, nor heard his sweet voice when he spoke unto us. 15 We know not, father, who made him acquainted with our names and all that befell us, yet he asked also after you, saying, 'Is your father still living, and is it well with him?' 16 You have not seen the affairs of the government of Egypt regulated by him, without inquiring of Pharaoh his lord; you have not seen the awe and fear which he impressed upon all the Egyptians. 17 And also when we went from him, we threatened to do unto Egypt like unto the rest of the cities of the Amorites, and we were exceedingly angry against all his words which he spoke concerning us as spies, and now when we will again come before him his terror will fall upon us all, and not one of us will be able to speak to him either a little or a great thing. 18 Now therefore father, send we pray you the lad with us, and we will go down and buy you food for our support, and not die through hunger." And Jacob said, "Why have you dealt so ill with me to tell the king you had a brother? What is this thing that you have done unto me?" 19 And Judah said unto Jacob his father, "Give the lad into my care and we will rise up and go down to Egypt and buy corn, and then return, and it will be when we return if the lad be not with us, then let me bear your blame forever. 20 Have you seen all our infants weeping over you through hunger and there is no power in your hand to satisfy them? Now let your pity be roused for them and send our brother with us and we will go. 21 For how will the Lord's kindness to our ancestors be manifested to you when you say that the king of Egypt will take away your son? As the Lord lives I will not leave him until I bring him and place him before you; but pray for us unto the Lord, that

he may deal kindly with us, to cause us to be received favorably and kindly before the king of Egypt and his men, for had we not delayed surely now we had returned a second time with your son." 22 And Jacob said unto his sons, "I trust in the Lord God that he may deliver you and give you favor in the sight of the king of Egypt, and in the sight of all his men. 23 Now therefore rise up and go to the man and take for him in your hands a present from what can be obtained in the land and bring it before him, and may the Almighty God give you mercy before him that he may send Benjamin and Simeon your brethren with you." 24 And all the men rose up, and they took their brother Benjamin, and they took in their hands a large present of the best of the land, and they also took a double portion of silver. 25 And Jacob strictly commanded his sons concerning Benjamin, saying, "Take heed of him in the way in which you are going, and do not separate yourselves from him in the road, neither in Egypt." 26 And Jacob rose up from his sons and spread out his hands and he prayed unto the Lord on account of his sons, saying, "O Lord God of heaven and earth, remember your covenant with our father Abraham, remember it with my father Isaac and deal kindly with my sons and deliver them not into the hands of the king of Egypt; do it I pray you O God for the sake of your mercies and redeem all my children and rescue them from Egyptian power, and send them their two brothers." 27 And all the wives of the sons of Jacob and their children lifted up their eyes to heaven and they all wept before the Lord, and cried unto him to deliver their fathers from the hand of the king of Egypt. 28 And Jacob wrote a record to the king of Egypt and gave it into the hand of Judah and into the hand of his sons for the king of Egypt, saying, 29 "From your servant Jacob, son of Isaac, son of Abraham the Hebrew, the prince of God, to the powerful and wise king, the revealer of secrets, king of Egypt, greeting. 30 Be it known to my lord the king of Egypt, the famine was sore upon us in the land of Canaan, and I sent my sons to you to buy us a little food from you for our support. 31 For my sons surrounded me and I being very old cannot see with my eyes, for my eyes have become very heavy through age, as well as with daily weeping for my son, for Joseph who was lost from before me, and I commanded my sons that they should not enter the gates of the city when they came to Egypt, on account of the inhabitants of the land. **32** And I also commanded them to go about Egypt to seek for my son Joseph, perhaps they might find him there, and they did so, and you did consider them as spies of the land. **33** Have we not heard concerning you that you did interpret Pharaoh's dream and did speak truly unto him? How then do you not know in your wisdom whether my sons are spies or not? **34** Now therefore, my lord and king, behold I have sent my son before you, as you did speak unto my sons; I implore you to put your eyes upon him until he is returned to me in peace with his brethren. **35** For do you not know, or have you not heard that which our God did unto Pharaoh when he took my mother Sarah, and what he did unto Abimelech king of the Philistines on account of her, and also what our father Abraham did unto the nine kings of Elam, how he smote them all with a few men that were with him? **36** And also what my two sons Simeon and Levi did unto the eight cities of the Amorites, how they destroyed them on account of their sister Dinah? **37** And also on account of their brother Benjamin they consoled themselves for the loss of his brother Joseph; what will they then do for him when they see the hand of any people prevailing over them, for his sake? **38** Do you not know, O king of Egypt, that the power of God is with us, and that also God ever hears our prayers and forsakes us not all the days? **39** And when my sons told me of your dealings with them, I called not unto the Lord on account of you, for then you would have perished with your men before my son Benjamin came before you, but I thought that as Simeon my son was in your house, perhaps you might deal kindly with him, therefore I did not do this thing unto you. **40** Now therefore behold Benjamin my son comes unto you with my sons, take heed of him and put your eyes upon him, and then will God place his eyes over you and throughout your kingdom. **41** Now I have told you all that is in my heart, and behold my sons are coming to you with their brother, examine the face of the whole earth for their sake and send them back in peace with their brethren." **42** And Jacob gave the record to his sons into the care of Judah to give it unto the king of Egypt.

CHAPTER 53

1 And the sons of Jacob rose up and took Benjamin and the whole of the presents, and they went and came to Egypt and they stood before Joseph. **2** And Joseph beheld his brother Benjamin with them and he saluted them, and these men came to Joseph's house. **3** And Joseph commanded the superintendent of his house to give to his brethren to eat, and he did so unto them. **4** And at noon time Joseph sent for the men to come before him with Benjamin, and the men told the superintendent of Joseph's house concerning the silver that was returned in their sacks, and he said unto them, "It will be well with you, fear not," and he brought their brother Simeon unto them. **5** And Simeon said unto his brethren, "The lord of the Egyptians has acted very kindly unto me, he did not keep me bound, as you saw with your eyes, for when you went out from the city he let me free and dealt kindly with me in his house." **6** And Judah took Benjamin by the hand, and they came before Joseph, and they bowed down to him to the ground. **7** And the men gave the present unto Joseph and they all sat before him, and Joseph said unto them, "Is it well with you, is it well with your children, is it well with your aged father?" And they said, "It is well," and Judah took the record which Jacob had sent and gave it into the hand of Joseph. **8** And Joseph read the letter and knew his father's writing, and he wished to weep and he went into an inner room and he wept a great weeping; and he went out. **9** And he lifted up his eyes and beheld his brother Benjamin, and he said, "Is this your brother of whom you spoke unto me?" And Benjamin approached Joseph, and Joseph placed his hand upon his head and he said unto him, "May God be gracious unto you my son." **10** And when Joseph saw his brother, the son of his mother, he again wished to weep, and he entered the chamber, and he wept there, and he washed his face, and went out and refrained from weeping, and he said, "Prepare food." **11** And Joseph had a cup from which he drank, and it was of silver beautifully inlaid with onyx stones and bdellium, and Joseph struck the cup in the sight of his brethren while they were sitting to eat with him. **12** And Joseph said unto the men, "I know by this cup that Reuben the firstborn, Simeon and Levi and Judah, Issachar and Zebulun are children from one mother, seat yourselves to eat according to your births." **13** And he also placed the others according to their births, and he said, "I know that this your youngest brother has no brother, and I, like him, have no brother, he will therefore sit down to eat with me." **14** And Benjamin went up before Joseph and sat upon the throne, and the men beheld the acts of Joseph, and they were astonished at them; and the men ate and drank at that time with Joseph, and he then gave presents unto them, and Joseph gave one gift unto Benjamin, and Manasseh and Ephraim saw the acts of their father, and they also gave presents unto him, and Osnath gave him one present, and they were five presents in the hand of Benjamin. **15** And Joseph brought them out wine to drink, and they would not drink, and they said, "From the day on which Joseph was lost we have not drunk wine, nor eaten any delicacies." **16** And Joseph swore unto them, and he pressed them hard, and they drank plentifully with him on that day, and Joseph afterward turned to his brother Benjamin to speak with him, and Benjamin was still sitting upon the throne before Joseph. **17** And Joseph said unto him, "Have you begotten any children?" And he said, "Your servant has ten sons, and these are their names, Bela, Becher, Ashbal, Gera, Naaman, Achi, Rosh, Mupim, Chupim, and Ord, and I called their names after my brother whom I have not seen." **18** And he ordered them to bring before him his map of the stars, whereby Joseph knew all the times, and Joseph said unto Benjamin, "I have heard that the Hebrews are acquainted with all wisdom, do you know anything of this?" **19** And Benjamin said, "Your servant is knowing also in all the wisdom which my father taught me," and Joseph said unto Benjamin, "Look now at this instrument and understand where your brother Joseph is in Egypt, who you said went down to Egypt." **20** And Benjamin beheld that instrument with the map of the stars of heaven, and he was wise and looked therein to know where his brother was, and Benjamin divided the whole land of Egypt into four divisions, and he found that he who was sitting upon the throne before him was his brother Joseph, and Benjamin wondered greatly, and when Joseph saw that his brother Benjamin was so much astonished, he said unto Benjamin, "What have you seen, and why are you astonished?" **21** And Benjamin said unto Joseph, "I can see by this that Joseph my brother sits here with me upon the throne," and Joseph said unto him, "I am Joseph your brother, reveal not this thing unto your brethren; behold I will send you with them when they go away, and I will command them to be brought back again into the city, and I will take you away from them. **22** And if they dare their lives and fight for you, then will

I know that they have repented of what they did unto me, and I will make myself known to them, and if they forsake you when I take you, then will you remain with me, and I will wrangle with them, and they will go away, and I will not become known to them." **23** At that time Joseph commanded his officer to fill their sacks with food, and to put each man's money into his sack, and to put the cup in the sack of Benjamin, and to give them provision for the road, and they did so unto them. **24** And on the next day the men rose up early in the morning, and they loaded their asses with their corn, and they went out with Benjamin, and they went to the land of Canaan with their brother Benjamin. **25** They had not gone far from Egypt when Joseph commanded him that was set over his house, saying, "Rise, pursue these men before they get too far from Egypt, and say unto them, 'Why have you stolen my master's cup?' " **26** And Joseph's officer rose up and he reached them, and he spoke unto them all the words of Joseph; and when they heard this thing they became exceedingly angry, and they said, "He with whom your master's cup will be found will die, and we will also become slaves." **27** And they hastened and each man brought down his sack from his ass, and they looked in their bags and the cup was found in Benjamin's bag, and they all tore their garments and they returned to the city, and they smote Benjamin in the road, continually smiting him until he came into the city, and they stood before Joseph. **28** And Judah's anger was kindled, and he said, "This man has only brought me back to destroy Egypt this day." **29** And the men came to Joseph's house, and they found Joseph sitting upon his throne, and all the mighty men standing at his right and left. **30** And Joseph said unto them, "What is this act that you have done, that you took away my silver cup and went away? But I know that you took my cup in order to know thereby in what part of the land your brother was." **31** And Judah said, "What will we say to our lord, what will we speak and how will we justify ourselves, God has this day found the iniquity of all your servants, therefore has he done this thing to us this day." **32** And Joseph rose up and caught hold of Benjamin and took him from his brethren with violence, and he came to the house and locked the door at them, and Joseph commanded him that was set over his house that he should say unto them, "Thus says the king, 'Go in peace to your father, behold I have taken the man in whose hand my cup was found.' "

CHAPTER 54

1 And when Judah saw the dealings of Joseph with them, Judah approached him and broke open the door, and came with his brethren before Joseph. 2 And Judah said unto Joseph, "Let it not seem grievous in the sight of my lord, may your servant I pray you speak a word before you?" And Joseph said unto him, "Speak." 3 And Judah spoke before Joseph, and his brethren were there standing before them; and Judah said unto Joseph, "Surely when we first came to our lord to buy food, you did consider us as spies of the land, and we brought Benjamin before you, and you still make sport of us this day. 4 Now therefore let the king hear my words, and send I pray you our brother that he may go along with us to our father, lest your soul perish this day with all the souls of the inhabitants of Egypt. 5 Do you not know what two of my brethren, Simeon and Levi, did unto the city of Shechem, and unto seven cities of the Amorites, on account of our sister Dinah, and also what they would do for the sake of their brother Benjamin? 6 And I with my strength, who am greater and mightier than both of them, come this day upon you and your land if you are unwilling to send our brother. 7 Have you not heard what our God who made choice of us did unto Pharaoh on account of Sarah our mother, whom he took away from our father, that he smote him and his household with heavy plagues, that even unto this day the Egyptians relate this wonder to each other? So will our God do unto you on account of Benjamin whom you have this day taken from his father, and on account of the evils which you this day heapest over us in your land; for our God will remember his covenant with our father Abraham and bring evil upon you, because you have grieved the soul of our father this day. 8 Now therefore hear my words that I have this day spoken unto you and send our brother that he may go away lest you and the people of your land die by the sword, for you cannot all prevail over me." 9 And Joseph answered Judah, saying, "Why have you opened wide your mouth and why do you boast over us, saying, 'strength is with you?' As Pharaoh lives, if I command all my valiant men to fight with you, surely you and these your brethren would sink in the mire." 10 And Judah said unto Joseph, "Surely it becomes you and your people to fear me; as the Lord lives if I once draw my sword I will not sheathe it again until I will this day have slain all Egypt, and I will commence with you and finish with Pharaoh your master." 11 And Joseph answered and said unto him, "Surely strength belongs not alone to you; I am stronger and mightier than you, surely if you draw your sword I will put it to your neck and the necks of all your brethren." 12 And Judah said unto him, "Surely if I this day open my mouth against you I would swallow you up that you be destroyed from off the earth and perish this day from your kingdom." And Joseph said, "Surely if you open your mouth I have power and might to close your mouth with a stone until you will not be able to utter a word; see how many stones are before us, truly I can take a stone, and force it into your mouth and break your jaws." 13 And Judah said, "God is witness between us, that we have not so far desired to battle with you, only give us our brother and we will go from you"; and Joseph answered and said, "As Pharaoh lives, if all the kings of Canaan came together with you, you should not take him from my hand. 14 Now therefore go your way to your father, and your brother will be unto me for a slave, for he has robbed the king's house." And Judah said, "What is it to you or to the character of the king, surely the king sends out from his house, throughout the land, silver and gold either in gifts or expenses, and you still talk about your cup which you did place in our brother's bag and say that he has stolen it from you? 15 God forbid that our brother Benjamin or any of the seed of Abraham should do this thing to steal from you, or from anyone else, whether king, prince, or any man. 16 Now therefore cease this accusation lest the whole earth hear your words, saying, 'For a little silver the king of Egypt wrangled with the men, and he accused them and took their brother for a slave.' " 17 And Joseph answered and said, "Take unto you this cup and go from me and leave your brother for a slave, for it is the judgment of a thief to be a slave." 18 And Judah said, "Why are you not ashamed of your words, to leave our brother and to take your cup? Surely if you give us your cup, or a thousand times as much, we will not leave our brother for the silver which is found in the hand of any man, that we will not die over him." 19 And Joseph answered, "And why did you forsake your brother and sell him for twenty pieces of silver unto this day, and why

then will you not do the same to this your brother?" **20** And Judah said, "The Lord is witness between me and you that we desire not your battles; now therefore give us our brother and we will go from you without quarreling." **21** And Joseph answered and said, "If all the kings of the land should assemble they will not be able to take your brother from my hand"; and Judah said, "What will we say unto our father, when he sees that our brother comes not with us, and will grieve over him?" **22** And Joseph answered and said, "This is the thing which you will tell unto your father, saying, 'The rope has gone after the bucket.' " **23** And Judah said, "Surely you are a king, and why speak you these things, giving a false judgment? Woe unto the king who is like unto you." **24** And Joseph answered and said, "There is no false judgment in the word that I spoke on account of your brother Joseph, for all of you sold him to the Midianites for twenty pieces of silver, and you all denied it to your father and said unto him, 'An evil beast has devoured him, Joseph has been torn to pieces.' " **25** And Judah said, "Behold the fire of Shem burns in my heart, now I will burn all your land with fire"; and Joseph answered and said, "Surely your sister-in-law Tamar, who killed your sons, extinguished the fire of Shechem." **26** And Judah said, "If I pluck out a single hair from my flesh, I will fill all Egypt with its blood." **27** And Joseph answered and said, "Such is your custom to do as you did to your brother whom you sold, and you dipped his coat in blood and brought it to your father in order that he might say an evil beast devoured him and here is his blood." **28** And when Judah heard this thing he was exceedingly angry and his anger burned within him, and there was before him in that place a stone, the weight of which was about four hundred shekels, and Judah's anger was kindled and he took the stone in one hand and cast it to the heavens and caught it with his left hand. **29** And he placed it afterward under his legs, and he sat upon it with all his strength and the stone was turned into dust from the force of Judah. **30** And Joseph saw the act of Judah and he was very much afraid, but he commanded Manassah his son and he also did with another stone like unto the act of Judah, and Judah said unto his brethren, "Let not any of you say, this man is an Egyptian, but by his doing this thing he is of our father's family." **31** And Joseph said, "Not to you only is strength given, for we are also powerful men,

and why will you boast over us all?" And Judah said unto Joseph, "Send I pray you our brother and ruin not your country this day." **32** And Joseph answered and said unto them, "Go and tell your father an evil beast has devoured him as you said concerning your brother Joseph." **33** And Judah spoke to his brother Naphtali, and he said unto him, "Make haste, go now and number all the streets of Egypt and come and tell me"; and Simeon said unto him, "Let not this thing be a trouble to you; now I will go to the mount and take up one large stone from the mount and level it at everyone in Egypt, and kill all that are in it." **34** And Joseph heard all these words that his brethren spoke before him, and they did not know that Joseph understood them, for they imagined that he knew not to speak Hebrew. **35** And Joseph was greatly afraid at the words of his brethren lest they should destroy Egypt, and he commanded his son Manasseh, saying, "Go now make haste and gather unto me all the inhabitants of Egypt, and all the valiant men together, and let them come to me now upon horseback and on foot and with all sorts of musical instruments," and Manasseh went and did so. **36** And Naphtali went as Judah had commanded him, for Naphtali was lightfooted as one of the swift stags, and he would go upon the ears of corn and they would not break under him. **37** And he went and numbered all the streets of Egypt, and found them to be twelve, and he came hastily and told Judah, and Judah said unto his brethren, "Hasten you and put on every man his sword upon his loins and we will come over Egypt, and smite them all, and let not a remnant remain." **38** And Judah said, "Behold, I will destroy three of the streets with my strength, and you will each destroy one street"; and when Judah was speaking this thing, behold the inhabitants of Egypt and all the mighty men came toward them with all sorts of musical instruments and with loud shouting. **39** And their number was five hundred cavalry and ten thousand infantry, and four hundred men who could fight without sword or spear, only with their hands and strength. **40** And all the mighty men came with great storming and shouting, and they all surrounded the sons of Jacob and terrified them, and the ground quaked at the sound of their shouting. **41** And when the sons of Jacob saw these troops they were greatly afraid for their lives, and Joseph did so in order to terrify the sons of Jacob to become tranquilized. **42** And Judah, seeing some of his brethren terrified, said unto them, "Why are you afraid while the grace of God is with us?" And when Judah saw all the people of Egypt surrounding them at the command of Joseph to terrify them, only Joseph commanded them, saying, "Do not touch any of them." **43** Then Judah hastened and drew his sword, and uttered a loud and bitter scream, and he smote with his sword, and he sprang upon the ground and he still continued to shout against all the people. **44** And when he did this thing the Lord caused the terror of Judah and his brethren to fall upon the valiant men and all the people that surrounded them. **45** And they all fled at the sound of the shouting, and they were terrified and fell one upon the other, and many of them died as they fell, and they all fled from before Judah and his brethren and from before Joseph. **46** And while they were fleeing, Judah and his brethren pursued them unto the house of Pharaoh, and they all escaped, and Judah again sat before Joseph and roared at him like a lion and gave a great and tremendous shriek at him. **47** And the shriek was heard at a distance, and all the inhabitants of Succoth heard it, and all Egypt quaked at the sound of the shriek, and also the walls of Egypt and of the land of Goshen fell in from the shaking of the earth, and Pharaoh also fell from his throne upon the ground, and also all the pregnant women of Egypt and Goshen miscarried when they heard the noise of the shaking, for they were terribly afraid. **48** And Pharaoh sent word, saying, "What is this thing that has this day happened in the land of Egypt?" And they came and told him all the things from beginning to end, and Pharaoh was alarmed and he wondered and was greatly afraid. **49** And his fright increased when he heard all these things, and he sent unto Joseph, saying, "You have brought unto me the Hebrews to destroy all Egypt; what will you do with that thievish slave? Send him away and let him go with his brethren, and let us not perish through their evil, even we, you and all Egypt. **50** And if you desire not to do this thing, cast off from you all my valuable things, and go with them to their land, if you delight in it, for they will this day destroy my whole country and slay all my people; even all the women of Egypt have miscarried through their screams; see what they have done merely by their shouting and speaking, moreover if they fight with the sword, they will destroy the land; now therefore choose that which you desire, whether me or the Hebrews, whether Egypt or

the land of the Hebrews." **51** And they came and told Joseph all the words of Pharaoh that he had said concerning him, and Joseph was greatly afraid at the words of Pharaoh and Judah and his brethren were still standing before Joseph indignant and enraged, and all the sons of Jacob roared at Joseph, like the roaring of the sea and its waves. **52** And Joseph was greatly afraid of his brethren and on account of Pharaoh, and Joseph sought a pretext to make himself known unto his brethren, lest they should destroy all Egypt. **53** And Joseph commanded his son Manasseh, and Manasseh went and approached Judah, and placed his hand upon his shoulder, and the anger of Judah was stilled. **54** And Judah said unto his brethren, "Let no one of you say that this is the act of an Egyptian youth for this is the work of my father's house." **55** And Joseph seeing and knowing that Judah's anger was stilled, he approached to speak unto Judah in the language of mildness. **56** And Joseph said unto Judah, "Surely you speak truth and have this day verified your assertions concerning your strength, and may your God who delights in you, increase your welfare; but tell me truly why from among all your brethren do you wrangle with me on account of the lad, as none of them have spoken one word to me concerning him." **57** And Judah answered Joseph, saying, "Surely you must know that I was security for the lad to his father, saying, if I brought him not unto him I should bear his blame forever. **58** Therefore have I approached you from among all my brethren, for I saw that you were unwilling to suffer him to go from you; now therefore may I find grace in your sight that you will send him to go with us, and behold I will remain as a substitute for him, to serve you in whatever you desire, for wheresoever you will send me I will go to serve you with great energy. **59** Send me now to a mighty king who has rebelled against you, and you will know what I will do unto him and unto his land; although he may have cavalry and infantry or an exceedingly mighty people, I will slay them all and bring the king's head before you. **60** Do you not know or have you not heard that our father Abraham with his servant Eliezer smote all the kings of Elam with their hosts in one night, they left not one remaining? And ever since that day our father's strength was given unto us for an inheritance, for us and our seed forever." **61** And Joseph answered and said, "You speak truth, and falsehood is not in your mouth, for it was also told unto us that the Hebrews have power and that the Lord their God delights much in them, and who then can stand before them? **62** However, on this condition will I send your brother, if you will bring before me his brother the son of his mother, of whom you said that he had gone from you down to Egypt; and it will come to pass when you bring unto me his brother I will take him in his stead, because not one of you were security for him to your father, and when he will come unto me, I will then send with you his brother for whom you have been security." **63** And Judah's anger was kindled against Joseph when he spoke this thing, and his eyes dropped blood with anger, and he said unto his brethren, "How does this man this day seek his own destruction and that of all Egypt!" **64** And Simeon answered Joseph, saying, "Did we not tell you at first that we knew not the particular spot to which he went, and whether he was dead or alive, and and why does my lord speak about these things?" **65** And Joseph, observing the countenance of Judah, discerned that his anger began to kindle when he spoke unto him, saying, "Bring unto me your other brother instead of this brother." **66** And Joseph said unto his brethren, "Surely you said that your brother was either dead or lost, now if I should call him this day and he should come before you, would you give him unto me instead of his brother?" **67** And Joseph began to speak and call out, "Joseph, Joseph, come this day before me, and appear to your brethren and sit before them." **68** And when Joseph spoke this thing before them, they looked each a different way to see from from where Joseph would come before them. **69** And Joseph observed all their acts, and said unto them, "Why do you look here and there? I am Joseph whom you sold to Egypt, now therefore let it not grieve you that you sold me, for as a support during the famine did God send me before you." **70** And his brethren were terrified at him when they heard the words of Joseph, and Judah was exceedingly terrified at him. **71** And when Benjamin heard the words of Joseph he was before them in the inner part of the house, and Benjamin ran unto Joseph his brother, and embraced him and fell upon his neck, and they wept. **72** And when Joseph's brethren saw that Benjamin had fallen upon his brother's neck and wept with him, they also fell upon Joseph and embraced him, and they wept a great weeping with Joseph. **73** And the voice was heard in the house of Joseph that they were Joseph's brethren, and it pleased Pharaoh exceedingly, for he was afraid of them lest they should destroy Egypt. **74** And Pharaoh sent his servants unto Joseph to congratulate him concerning his brethren who had come to him, and all the captains of the armies and troops that were in Egypt came to rejoice with Joseph, and all Egypt rejoiced greatly about Joseph's brethren. **75** And Pharaoh sent his servants to Joseph, saying, "Tell your brethren to fetch all belonging to them and let them come unto me, and I will place them in the best part of the land of Egypt," and they did so. **76** And Joseph commanded him that was set over his house to bring out to his brethren gifts and garments, and he brought out to them many garments being robes of royalty and many gifts, and Joseph divided them among his brethren. **77** And he gave unto each of his brethren a change of garments of gold and silver, and three hundred pieces of silver, and Joseph commanded them all to be dressed in these garments, and to be brought before Pharaoh. **78** And Pharaoh seeing that all Joseph's brethren were valiant men, and of beautiful appearance, he greatly rejoiced. **79** And they afterward went out from the presence of Pharaoh to go to the land of Canaan, to their father, and their brother Benjamin was with them. **80** And Joseph rose up and gave unto them eleven chariots from Pharaoh, and Joseph gave unto them his chariot, upon which he rode on the day of his being crowned in Egypt, to fetch his father to Egypt; and Joseph sent to all his brothers' children, garments according to their numbers, and a hundred pieces of silver to each of them, and he also sent garments to the wives of his brethren from the garments of the king's wives, and he sent them. **81** And he gave unto each of his brethren ten men to go with them to the land of Canaan to serve them, to serve their children and all belonging to them in coming to Egypt. **82** And Joseph sent by the hand of his brother Benjamin ten suits of garments for his ten sons, a portion above the rest of the children of the sons of Jacob. **83** And he sent to each fifty pieces of silver, and ten chariots on the account of Pharaoh, and he sent to his father ten asses laden with all the luxuries of Egypt, and ten she asses laden with corn and bread and nourishment for his father, and to all that were with him as provisions for the road. **84** And he sent to his sister Dinah garments of silver and gold, and frankincense and myrrh, and aloes and women's ornaments in great plenty, and he sent the same from the wives of Pharaoh to the wives of Benjamin. **85** And he gave unto all his brethren, also to their wives, all sorts of onyx stones and bdellium, and from all the valuable things among the great people of Egypt, nothing of all the costly things was left but what Joseph sent of to his father's household. **86** And he sent his brethren away, and they went, and he sent his brother Benjamin with them. **87** And Joseph went out with them to accompany them on the road unto the borders of Egypt, and he commanded them concerning his father and his household, to come to Egypt. **88** And he said unto them, "Do not quarrel on the road, for this thing was from the Lord to keep a great people from starvation, for there will be yet five years of famine in the land." **89** And he commanded them, saying, "When you come unto the land of Canaan, do not come suddenly before my father in this affair, but act in your wisdom."

90 And Joseph ceased to command them, and he turned and went back to Egypt, and the sons of Jacob went to the land of Canaan with joy and cheerfulness to their father Jacob. **91** And they came unto the borders of the land, and they said to each other, "What will we do in this matter before our father, for if we come suddenly to him and tell him the matter, he will be greatly alarmed at our words and will not believe us." **92** And they went along until they came nigh unto their houses, and they found Serach, the daughter of Asher, going out to meet them, and the damsel was very good and subtle, and knew how to play upon the harp. **93** And they called unto her and she came before them, and she kissed them, and they took her and gave unto her a harp, saying, "Go now before our father, and sit before him, and strike upon the harp, and speak these words." **94** And they commanded her to go to their house, and she took the harp and hastened before them, and she came and sat near Jacob. **95** And she played well and sang, and uttered in the sweetness of her words, "Joseph my uncle is living, and he rules throughout the land of Egypt, and is not dead." **96** And she continued to repeat and utter these words, and Jacob heard her words and they were agreeable to him. **97** He listened while she repeated them twice and thrice, and joy entered the heart of Jacob at the sweetness of her words, and the Spirit of God was upon him, and he knew all her words to be true. **98** And Jacob blessed Serach when she spoke these words before him, and he said unto her, "My daughter, may death never prevail over you, for you have revived my spirit; only speak yet before me as you have spoken, for you have gladdened me with all your words." **99** And she continued to sing these words, and Jacob listened and it pleased him, and he rejoiced, and the Spirit of God was upon him. **100** While he was yet speaking with her, behold his sons came to him with horses and chariots and royal garments and servants running before them. **101** And Jacob rose up to meet them, and saw his sons dressed in royal garments and he saw all the treasures that Joseph had sent to them. **102** And they said unto him, "Be informed that our brother Joseph is living, and it is he who rules throughout the land of Egypt, and it is he who spoke unto us as we told you." **103** And Jacob heard all the words of his sons, and his heart palpitated at their words, for he could not believe them until he saw all that Joseph had given him and what he had sent him, and all the signs which Joseph had spoken unto them. **104** And they opened out before him, and showed him all that Joseph had sent, they gave unto each what Joseph had sent him, and he knew that they had spoken the truth, and he rejoiced exceedingly on account of his son. **105** And Jacob said, "It is enough for me that my son Joseph is still living, I will go and see him before I die." **106** And his sons told him all that had befallen them, and Jacob said, "I will go down to Egypt to see my son and his offspring." **107** And Jacob rose up and put on the garments which Joseph had sent him, and after he had washed, and shaved his hair, he put upon his head the turban which Joseph had sent him. **108** And all the people of Jacob's house and their wives put on the garments which Joseph had sent to them, and they greatly rejoiced at Joseph that he was still living and that he was ruling in Egypt, **109** and all the inhabitants of Canaan heard of this thing, and they came and rejoiced much with Jacob that he was still living. **110** And Jacob made a feast for them for three days, and all the kings of Canaan and nobles of the land ate and drank and rejoiced in the house of Jacob.

CHAPTER 55

1 And it came to pass after this that Jacob said, "I will go and see my son in Egypt and will then come back to the land of Canaan of which God had spoken unto Abraham, for I cannot leave the land of my birth-place." **2** Behold the word of the Lord came unto him, saying, "Go down to Egypt with all your household and remain there, fear not to go down to Egypt for I will there make you a great nation." **3** And Jacob said within himself, "I will go and see my son whether the fear of his God is yet in his heart amidst all the inhabitants of Egypt." **4** And the Lord said unto Jacob, "Fear not about Joseph, for he still retains his integrity to serve me, as will seem good in your sight," and Jacob rejoiced exceedingly concerning his son. **5** At that time Jacob commanded his sons and household to go to Egypt according to the word of the Lord unto him, and Jacob rose up with his sons and all his household, and he went out from the land of Canaan from Beersheba, with joy and gladness of heart, and they went to the land of Egypt. **6** And it came to pass when they came near Egypt, Jacob sent Judah before him to Joseph that he might show him a situation in Egypt, and Judah did according to the word of his father, and he hastened and ran and came to Joseph, and they assigned for them a place in the land of Goshen for all his household, and Judah returned and came along the road to his father. **7** And Joseph harnessed the chariot, and he assembled all his mighty men and his servants and all the officers of Egypt in order to go and meet his father Jacob, and Joseph's mandate was proclaimed in Egypt, saying, "All that do not go to meet Jacob will die." **8** And on the next day Joseph went out with all Egypt a great and mighty host, all dressed in garments of fine linen and purple and with instruments of silver and gold and with their instruments of war with them. **9** And they all went to meet Jacob with all sorts of musical instruments, with drums and timbrels, strewing myrrh and aloes all along the road, and they all went after this fashion, and the earth shook at their shouting. **10** And all the women of Egypt went upon the roofs of Egypt and upon the walls to meet Jacob, and upon the head of Joseph was Pharaoh's regal crown, for Pharaoh had sent it unto him to put on at the time of his going to meet his father. **11** And when Joseph came within fifty cubits of his father, he alighted from the chariot and he walked toward his father, and when all the officers of Egypt and her nobles saw that Joseph had gone on foot toward his father, they also alighted and walked on foot toward Jacob. **12** And when Jacob approached the camp of Joseph, Jacob observed the camp that was coming toward him with Joseph, and it gratified him and

Jacob was astonished at it. **13** And Jacob said unto Judah, "Who is that man whom I see in the camp of Egypt dressed in kingly robes with a very red garment upon him and a royal crown upon his head, who has alighted from his chariot and is coming toward us?" And Judah answered his father, saying, "He is your son Joseph the king"; and Jacob rejoiced in seeing the glory of his son. **14** And Joseph came nigh unto his father and he bowed to his father, and all the men of the camp bowed to the ground with him before Jacob. **15** And behold Jacob ran and hastened to his son Joseph and fell upon his neck and kissed him, and they wept, and Joseph also embraced his father and kissed him, and they wept and all the people of Egypt wept with them. **16** And Jacob said unto Joseph, "Now I will die cheerfully after I have seen your face, that you are still living and with glory." **17** And the sons of Jacob and their wives and their children and their servants, and all the household of Jacob wept exceedingly with Joseph, and they kissed him and wept greatly with him. **18** And Joseph and all his people returned afterward home to Egypt, and Jacob and his sons and all the children of his household came with Joseph to Egypt, and Joseph placed them in the best part of Egypt, in the land of Goshen. **19** And Joseph said unto his father and unto his brethren, "I will go up and tell Pharaoh, saying, 'My brethren and my father's household and all belonging to them have come unto me, and behold they are in the land of Goshen.' " **20** And Joseph did so and took from his brethren Reuben, Issachar Zebulun and his brother Benjamin and he placed them before Pharaoh. **21** And Joseph spoke unto Pharaoh, saying, "My brethren and my father's household and all belonging to them, together with their flocks and cattle have come unto me from the land of Canaan, to sojourn in Egypt; for the famine was sore upon them." **22** And Pharaoh said unto Joseph, "Place your father and brethren in the best part of the land, withhold not from them all that is good, and cause them to eat of the fat of the land." **23** And Joseph answered, saying, "Behold I have stationed them in the land of Goshen, for they are shepherds, therefore let them remain in Goshen to feed their flocks apart from the Egyptians." **24** And Pharaoh said unto Joseph, "Do with your brethren all that they will say unto you"; and the sons of Jacob bowed down to Pharaoh, and they went out from him in peace, and Joseph afterward brought his father before Pharaoh. **25** And

Jacob came and bowed down to Pharaoh, and Jacob blessed Pharaoh, and he then went out; and Jacob and all his sons, and all his household dwelt in the land of Goshen. **26** In the second year, that is in the hundred and thirtieth year of the life of Jacob, Joseph maintained his father and his brethren, and all his father's household, with bread according to their little ones, all the days of the famine; they lacked nothing. **27** And Joseph gave unto them the best part of the whole land; the best of Egypt had they all the days of Joseph; and Joseph also gave unto them and unto the whole of his father's household, clothes and garments year by year; and the sons of Jacob remained securely in Egypt all the days of their brother. **28** And Jacob always ate at Joseph's table, Jacob and his sons did not leave Joseph's table day or night, besides what Jacob's children consumed in their houses. **29** And all Egypt ate bread during the days of the famine from the house of Joseph, for all the Egyptians sold all belonging to them on account of the famine. **30** And Joseph purchased all the lands and fields of Egypt for bread on the account of Pharaoh, and Joseph supplied all Egypt with bread all the days of the famine, and Joseph collected all the silver and gold that came unto him for the corn which they bought throughout the land, and he accumulated much gold and silver, besides an immense quantity of onyx stones, bdellium and valuable garments which they brought unto Joseph from every part of the land when their money was spent. **31** And Joseph took all the silver and gold that came into his hand, about seventy-two talents of gold and silver, and also onyx stones and bdellium in great abundance, and Joseph went and concealed them in four parts, and he concealed one part in the wilderness near the Red Sea, and one part by the river Perath, and the third and fourth part he concealed in the desert opposite to the wilderness of Persia and Media. **32** And he took part of the gold and silver that was left and gave it unto all his brothers and unto all his father's household, and unto all the women of his father's household, and the rest he brought to the house of Pharaoh, about twenty talents of gold and silver. **33** And Joseph gave all the gold and silver that was left unto Pharaoh, and Pharaoh placed it in the treasury, and the days of the famine ceased after that in the land, and they sowed and reaped in the whole land, and they obtained their usual quantity year by year; they lacked nothing.

34 And Joseph dwelt securely in Egypt, and the whole land was under his advice, and his father and all his brethren dwelt in the land of Goshen and took possession of it. **35** And Joseph was very aged, advanced in days, and his two sons, Ephraim and Manasseh, remained constantly in the house of Jacob, together with the children of the sons of Jacob their brethren, to learn the ways of the Lord and his law. **36** And Jacob and his sons dwelt in the land of Egypt in the land of Goshen, and they took possession in it, and they were fruitful and multiplied in it.

CHAPTER 56

1 And Jacob lived in the land of Egypt seventeen years, and the days of Jacob, and the years of his life were a hundred and forty-seven years. **2** At that time Jacob was attacked with that illness of which he died and he sent and called for his son Joseph from Egypt, and Joseph his son came from Egypt and Joseph came unto his father. **3** And Jacob said unto Joseph and unto his sons, "Behold I die, and the God of your ancestors will visit you, and bring you back to the land, which the Lord sware to give unto you and unto your children after you, now therefore when I am dead, bury me in the cave which is in Machpelah in Hebron in the land of Canaan, near my ancestors." **4** And Jacob made his sons swear to bury him in Machpelah, in Hebron, and his sons swore unto him concerning this thing. **5** And he commanded them, saying, "Serve the Lord your God, for he who delivered your fathers will also deliver you from all trouble." **6** And Jacob said, "Call all your children unto me," and all the children of Jacob's sons came and sat before him, and Jacob blessed them, and he said unto them, "The Lord God of your fathers will grant you a thousand times as much and bless you, and may he give you the blessing of your father Abraham"; and all the children of Jacob's sons went out on that day after he had blessed them. **7** And on the next day Jacob again called for his sons, and they all assembled and came to him and sat before him, and Jacob on that day blessed his sons before his death, each man did he bless according to his blessing; behold it is written in the book of the law of the Lord pertaining to Israel. **8** And Jacob said unto Judah, "I know my son that you are a mighty man for your brethren; reign over them, and your sons will reign over their sons forever. **9** Only teach your sons the bow and all the weapons of war, in order that they may fight the battles of their brother who will rule over his enemies." 10 And Jacob again commanded his sons on that day, saying, "Behold I will be this day gathered unto my people; carry me up from Egypt, and bury me in the cave of Machpelah as I have commanded you. 11 Nevertheless, take heed I pray you that none of your sons carry me, only yourselves, and this is the manner you will do unto me, when you carry my body to go with it to the land of Canaan to bury me, 12 Judah, Issachar and Zebulun will carry my bier at the eastern side; Reuben, Simeon and Gad at the south, Ephraim, Manasseh and Benjamin at the west, Dan, Asher and Naphtali at the north. 13 Let not Levi carry with you, for he and his sons will carry the ark of the covenant of the Lord with the Israelites in the camp, neither let Joseph my son carry, for as a king so let his glory be; nevertheless, Ephraim and Manasseh will be in their stead. 14 Thus will you do unto me when you carry me away; do not neglect anything of all that I command you; and it will come to pass when you do this unto me, that the Lord will remember you favorably and your children after you forever. 15 And you my sons, honor each his brother and his relative, and command your children and your children's children after you to serve the Lord God of your ancestors all the days. 16 In order that you may prolong your days in the land, you and your children and your children's children forever, when you do what is good and upright in the sight of the Lord your God, to go in all his ways. 17 And you, Joseph my son, forgive I pray you the prongs of your brethren and all their misdeeds in the injury that they heaped upon you, for God intended it for your and your children's benefit. 18 And O my son leave not your brethren to the inhabitants of Egypt, neither hurt their feelings, for behold I consign them to the hand of God and in your hand to guard them from the Egyptians"; and the sons of Jacob answered their father saying, "O, our father, all that you have commanded us, so will we do; may God only be with us." 19 And Jacob said unto his sons, "So may God be with you when you keep all his ways; turn not from his ways either to the right or the left in performing what is good and upright in his sight. 20 For I know that many and grievous troubles will befall you in the latter days in the land, yea your children and children's children, only serve the Lord and he will save you from all trouble.

21 And it will come to pass when you will go after God to serve him and will teach your children after you, and your children's children, to know the Lord, then will the Lord raise up unto you and your children a servant from among your children, and the Lord will deliver you through his hand from all affliction, and bring you out of Egypt and bring you back to the land of your fathers to inherit it securely." 22 And Jacob ceased commanding his sons, and he drew his feet into the bed, he died and was gathered to his people. 23 And Joseph fell upon his father and he cried out and wept over him and he kissed him, and he called out in a bitter voice, and he said, "O my father, my father." 24 And his son's wives and all his household came and fell upon Jacob, and they wept over him, and cried in a very loud voice concerning Jacob. 25 And all the sons of Jacob rose up together, and they tore their garments, and they all put sackcloth upon their loins, and they fell upon their faces, and they cast dust upon their heads toward the heavens. 26 And the thing was told unto Osnath Joseph's wife, and she rose up and put on a sack and she with all the Egyptian women with her came and mourned and wept for Jacob. 27 And also all the people of Egypt who knew Jacob came all on that day when they heard this thing, and all Egypt wept for many days. 28 And also from the land of Canaan did the women come unto Egypt when they heard that Jacob was dead, and they wept for him in Egypt for seventy days. 29 And it came to pass after this that Joseph commanded his servants the doctors to embalm his father with myrrh and frankincense and all manner of incense and perfume, and the doctors embalmed Jacob as Joseph had commanded them. 30 And all the people of Egypt and the elders and all the inhabitants of the land of Goshen wept and mourned over Jacob, and all his sons and the children of his household lamented and mourned over their father Jacob many days. 31 And after the days of his weeping had passed away, at the end of seventy days, Joseph said unto Pharaoh, "I will go up and bury my father in the land of Canaan as he made me swear, and then I will return." 32 And Pharaoh sent Joseph, saying, "Go up and bury your father as he said, and as he made you swear"; and Joseph rose up with all his brethren to go to the land of Canaan to bury their father Jacob as he had commanded them. 33 And Pharaoh commanded that it should be proclaimed throughout Egypt, saying,

"Whoever goes not up with Joseph and his brethren to the land of Canaan to bury Jacob, will die." **34** And all Egypt heard of Pharaoh's proclamation, and they all rose up together, and all the servants of Pharaoh, and the elders of his house, and all the elders of the land of Egypt went up with Joseph, and all the officers and nobles of Pharaoh went up as the servants of Joseph, and they went to bury Jacob in the land of Canaan. **35** And the sons of Jacob carried the bier upon which he lay; according to all that their father commanded them, so did his sons unto him. **36** And the bier was of pure gold, and it was inlaid around with onyx stones and bdellium; and the covering of the bier was gold woven work, joined with threads, and over them were hooks of onyx stones and bdellium. **37** And Joseph placed upon the head of his father Jacob a large golden crown, and he put a golden scepter in his hand, and they surrounded the bier as was the custom of kings during their lives. **38** And all the troops of Egypt went before him in this array, at first all the mighty men of Pharaoh, and the mighty men of Joseph, and after them the rest of the inhabitants of Egypt, and they were all girded with swords and equipped with coats of mail, and the trappings of war were upon them. **39** And all the weepers and mourners went at a distance opposite to the bier, going and weeping and lamenting, and the rest of the people went after the bier. **40** And Joseph and his household went together near the bier barefooted and weeping, and the rest of Joseph's servants went around him; each man had his ornaments upon him, and they were all armed with their weapons of war. **41** And fifty of Jacob's servants went in front of the bier, and they strewed along the road myrrh and aloes, and all manner of perfume, and all the sons of Jacob that carried the bier walked upon the perfumery, and the servants of Jacob went before them strewing the perfume along the road. **42** And Joseph went up with a heavy camp, and they did after this manner every day until they reached the land of Canaan, and they came to the threshing floor of Atad, which was on the other side of Jordan, and they mourned an exceeding great and heavy mourning in that place. **43** And all the kings of Canaan heard of this thing and they all went out, each man from his house, thirty-one kings of Canaan, and they all came with their men to mourn and weep over Jacob. **44** And all these kings beheld Jacob's bier, and behold Joseph's crown was upon it, and they also put their crowns upon

the bier, and encircled it with crowns. **45** And all these kings made in that place a great and heavy mourning with the sons of Jacob and Egypt over Jacob, for all the kings of Canaan knew the valor of Jacob and his sons. **46** And the report reached Esau, saying, "Jacob died in Egypt, and his sons and all Egypt are conveying him to the land of Canaan to bury him." **47** And Esau heard this thing, and he was dwelling in Mount Seir, and he rose up with his sons and all his people and all his household, a people exceedingly great, and they came to mourn and weep over Jacob. **48** And it came to pass, when Esau came he mourned for his brother Jacob, and all Egypt and all Canaan again rose up and mourned a great mourning with Esau over Jacob in that place. **49** And Joseph and his brethren brought their father Jacob from that place, and they went to Hebron to bury Jacob in the cave by his fathers. **50** And they came unto Kireath-arba, to the cave, and as they came Esau stood with his sons against Joseph and his brethren as a hindrance in the cave, saying, "Jacob will not be buried therein, for it belongs to us and to our father." **51** And Joseph and his brethren heard the words of Esau's sons, and they were exceedingly angry, and Joseph approached unto Esau, saying, "What is this thing which they have spoken? Surely my father Jacob bought it from you for great riches after the death of Isaac, now five and twenty years ago, and also all the land of Canaan he bought from you and from your sons, and your seed after you. **52** And Jacob bought it for his sons and his seed after him for an inheritance forever, and why speak you these things this day?" **53** And Esau answered, saying, "You speak falsely and utter lies, for I sold not anything belonging to me in all this land, as you say, neither did my brother Jacob buy all belonging to me in this land." **54** And Esau spoke these things in order to deceive Joseph with his words, for Esau knew that Joseph was not present in those days when Esau sold all belonging to him in the land of Canaan to Jacob. **55** And Joseph said unto Esau, "Surely my father inserted these things with you in the record of purchase, and testified to the record with witnesses, and behold it is with us in Egypt. **56** And Esau answered, saying unto him, "Bring the record, all that you will find in the record, so will we do." **57** And Joseph called unto Naphtali his brother, and he said, "Hasten quickly, stay not, and run I pray you to Egypt and bring all the records; the record of the purchase, the sealed record and the open record, and also all the first records in which all the transactions of the birth-right are written, fetch you. **58** And you will bring them unto us here, that we may know from them all the words of Esau and his sons which they spoke this day." **59** And Naphtali hearkened to the voice of Joseph and he hastened and ran to go down to Egypt, and Naphtali was lighter on foot than any of the stags that were upon the wilderness, for he would go upon ears of corn without crushing them. **60** And when Esau saw that Naphtali had gone to fetch the records, he and his sons increased their resistance against the cave, and Esau and all his people rose up against Joseph and his brethren to battle. **61** And all the sons of Jacob and the people of Egypt fought with Esau and his men, and the sons of Esau and his people were smitten before the sons of Jacob, and the sons of Jacob slew of Esau's people forty men. **62** And Chushim the son of Dan, the son of Jacob, was at that time with Jacob's sons, but he was about a hundred cubits distant from the place of battle, for he remained with the children of Jacob's sons by Jacob's bier to guard it. **63** And Chushim was dumb and deaf, still he understood the voice of consternation among men. **64** And he asked, saying, "Why do you not bury the dead, and what is this great consternation?" And they answered him the words of Esau and his sons; and he ran to Esau in the midst of the battle, and he slew Esau with a sword, and he cut off his head, and it sprang to a distance, and Esau fell among the people of the battle. **65** And when Chushim did this thing the sons of Jacob prevailed over the sons of Esau, and the sons of Jacob buried their father Jacob by force in the cave, and the sons of Esau beheld it. **66** And Jacob was buried in Hebron, in the cave of Machpelah which Abraham had bought from the sons of Heth for the possession of a burial place, and he was buried in very costly garments. **67** And no king had such honor paid him as Joseph paid unto his father at his death, for he buried him with great honor like unto the burial of kings. **68** And Joseph and his brethren made a mourning of seven days for their father.

CHAPTER 57

1 And it was after this that the sons of Esau waged war with the sons of Jacob, and the sons of Esau fought with the sons of Jacob in Hebron, and Esau was still lying dead, and not buried. **2** And the battle was heavy between them, and the sons of Esau were smitten before the sons of Jacob, and the sons of Jacob slew of the sons of Esau eighty men, and not one died of the people of the sons of Jacob; and the hand of Joseph prevailed over all the people of the sons of Esau, and he took Zepho, the son of Eliphaz, the son of Esau, and fifty of his men captive, and he bound them with chains of iron, and gave them into the hand of his servants to bring them to Egypt. **3** And it came to pass when the sons of Jacob had taken Zepho and his people captive, all those that remained were greatly afraid for their lives from the house of Esau, lest they should also be taken captive, and they all fled with Eliphaz the son of Esau and his people, with Esau's body, and they went on their road to Mount Seir. **4** And they came unto Mount Seir and they buried Esau in Seir, but they had not brought his head with them to Seir, for it was buried in that place where the battle had been in Hebron. **5** And it came to pass when the sons of Esau had fled from before the sons of Jacob, the sons of Jacob pursued them unto the borders of Seir, but they did not slay a single man from among them when they pursued them, for Esau's body which they carried with them excited their confusion, so they fled and the sons of Jacob turned back from them and came up to the place where their brethren were in Hebron, and they remained there on that day, and on the next day until they rested from the battle. **6** And it came to pass on the third day they assembled all the sons of Seir the Horite, and they assembled all the children of the east, a multitude of people like the sand of the sea, and they went and came down to Egypt to fight with Joseph and his brethren, in order to deliver their brethren. **7** And Joseph and all the sons of Jacob heard that the sons of Esau and the children of the east had come upon them to battle in order to deliver their brethren. **8** And Joseph and his brethren and the strong men of Egypt went out and fought in the city of Rameses, and Joseph and his brethren dealt out a tremendous blow among the sons of Esau and the children of the east. **9** And they slew of them six hundred thousand men, and they slew among them all the mighty men of the children of Seir the Horite; there were only a few of them left, and they slew also a great many of the children of the east, and of the children of Esau; and Eliphaz the son of Esau, and the children of the east all fled before Joseph and his brethren. **10** And Joseph and his brethren pursued them until they came unto Succoth, and they yet slew of them in Succoth thirty men, and the rest escaped and they fled each to his city. 11 And Joseph and his brethren and the mighty men of Egypt turned back from them with joy and cheerfulness of heart, for they had smitten all their enemies. 12 And Zepho the son of Eliphaz and his men were still slaves in Egypt to the sons of Jacob, and their pains increased. 13 And when the sons of Esau and the sons of Seir returned to their land, the sons of Seir saw that they had all fallen into the hands of the sons of Jacob, and the people of Egypt, on account of the battle of the sons of Esau. 14 And the sons of Seir said unto the sons of Esau, "You have seen and therefore you know that this camp was on your account, and not one mighty man or an adept in war remains. 15 Now therefore go out from our land, go from us to the land of Canaan to the land of the dwelling of your fathers; why will your children inherit the effects of our children in latter days?" 16 And the children of Esau would not listen to the children of Seir, and the children of Seir considered to make war with them. 17 And the children of Esau sent secretly to Angeas king of Africa, the same is Dinhabah, saying, 18 "Send unto us some of your men and let them come unto us, and we will fight together with the children of Seir the Horite, for they have resolved to fight with us to drive us away from the land." 19 And Angeas king of Dinhabah did so, for he was in those days friendly to the children of Esau, and Angeas sent five hundred valiant infantry to the children of Esau, and eight hundred cavalry. 20 And the children of Seir sent unto the children of the east and unto the children of Midian, saying, "You have seen what the children of Esau have done unto us, upon whose account we are almost all destroyed, in their battle with the sons of Jacob. 21 Now therefore come unto us and assist us, and we will fight them together, and we will drive them from the land and be avenged of the cause of our brethren who died for their sakes in their battle with their brethren the sons of Jacob." 22 And all the children of the east listened to the children of Seir, and they came unto them about eight hundred men with drawn swords, and the children of Esau fought with the children of Seir at that time in the wilderness of Paran. 23 And the children of Seir prevailed then over the sons of Esau, and the children of Seir slew on that day of the children of Esau in that battle about two

hundred men of the people of Angeas king of Dinhabah. 24 And on the second day the children of Esau came again to fight a second time with the children of Seir, and the battle was sore upon the children of Esau this second time, and it troubled them greatly on account of the children of Seir. 25 And when the children of Esau saw that the children of Seir were more powerful than they were, some men of the children of Esau turned and assisted the children of Seir their enemies. 26 And there fell yet of the people of the children of Esau in the second battle fifty-eight men of the people at Angeas king of Dinhabah. 27 And on the third day the children of Esau heard that some of their brethren had turned from them to fight against them in the second battle; and the children of Esau mourned when they heard this thing. 28 And they said, "What will we do unto our brethren who turned from us to assist the children of Seir our enemies?" And the children of Esau again sent to Angeas king of Dinhabah, saying, 29 "Send unto us again other men that with them we may fight with the children of Seir, for they have already twice been heavier than we were." 30 And Angeas again sent to the children of Esau about six hundred valiant men, and they came to assist the children of Esau. 31 And in ten days' time the children of Esau again waged war with the children of Seir in the wilderness of Paran, and the battle was very severe upon the children of Seir, and the children of Esau prevailed at this time over the children of Seir, and the children of Seir were smitten before the children of Esau, and the children of Esau slew from them about two thousand men. 32 And all the mighty men of the children of Seir died in this battle, and there only remained their young children that were left in their cities. 33 And all Midian and the children of the east betook themselves to flight from the battle, and they left the children of Seir and fled when they saw that the battle was severe upon them, and the children of Esau pursued all the children of the east until they reached their land. 34 And the children of Esau slew yet of them about two hundred and fifty men and from the people of the children of Esau there fell in that battle about thirty men, but this evil came upon them through their brethren turning from them to assist the children of Seir the Horite, and the children of Esau again heard of the evil doings of their brethren, and they again mourned on account of this thing. 35 And it came to pass after the battle, the children of Esau turned back and came home unto Seir, and the children of Esau slew those who had remained in the land of the children of Seir; they slew also their wives and little ones, they left not a soul alive except fifty young lads and damsels whom they suffered to live, and the children of Esau did not put them to death, and the lads became their slaves, and the damsels they took for wives. 36 And the children of Esau dwelt in Seir in the place of the children of Seir, and they inherited their land and took possession of it. 37 And the children of Esau took all belonging in the land to the children of Seir, also their flocks, their bullocks and their goods, and all belonging to the children of Seir, did the children of Esau take, and the children of Esau dwelt in Seir in the place of the children of Seir unto this day, and the children of Esau divided the land into divisions to the five sons of Esau, according to their families. 38 And it came to pass in those days, that the children of Esau resolved to crown a king over them in the land of which they became possessed. And they said to each other, "Not so, for he will reign over us in our land, and we will be under his counsel and he will fight our battles, against our enemies," and they did so. 39 And all the children of Esau swore, saying that none of their brethren should ever reign over them, but a strange man who is not of their brethren, for the souls of all the children of Esau were embittered every man against his son, brother and friend, on account of the evil they sustained from their brethren when they fought with the children of Seir. 40 Therefore the sons of Esau swore, saying from that day forward they would not choose a king from their brethren, but one from a strange land unto this day. 41 And there was a man there from the people of Angeas king of Dinhabah; his name was Bela the son of Beor, who was a very valiant man, beautiful and comely and wise in all wisdom, and a man of sense and counsel; and there was none of the people of Angeas like unto him. 42 And all the children of Esau took him and anointed him and they crowned him for a king, and they bowed down to him, and they said unto him, "May the king live, may the king live." 43 And they spread out the sheet, and they brought him each man earrings of gold and silver or rings or bracelets, and they made him very rich in silver and in gold, in onyx stones and bdellium, and they made him a royal throne, and they placed a regal crown upon his head, and they built a palace for him and he dwelt therein, and he became king over all the children of Esau. 44 And the people of Angeas took their hire for their battle from the children of Esau, and they went and returned at that time to their master in Dinhabah. 45 And Bela reigned over the children of Esau thirty years, and the children of Esau dwelt in the land instead of the children of Seir, and they dwelt securely in their stead unto this day.

CHAPTER 58

1 And it came to pass in the thirty-second year of the Israelites going down to Egypt, that is in the seventy-first year of the life of Joseph, in that year died Pharaoh king of Egypt, and Magron his son reigned in his stead. 2 And Pharaoh commanded Joseph before his death to be a father to his son, Magron, and that Magron should be under the care of Joseph and under his counsel. 3 And all Egypt consented to this thing that Joseph should be king over them, for all the Egyptians loved Joseph as before now, only Magron the son of Pharaoh sat upon his father's throne, and he became king in those days in his father's stead. 4 Magron was forty-one years old when he began to reign, and forty years he reigned in Egypt, and all Egypt called his name Pharaoh after the name of his father, as it was their custom to do in Egypt to every king that reigned over them. 5 And it came to pass when Pharaoh reigned in his father's stead, he placed the laws of Egypt and all the affairs of government in the hand of Joseph, as his father had commanded him. 6 And Joseph became king over Egypt, for he superintended over all Egypt, and all Egypt was under his care and under his counsel, for all Egypt inclined to Joseph after the death of Pharaoh, and they loved him exceedingly to reign over them. 7 But there were some people among them, who did not like him, saying, "No stranger will reign over us"; still the whole government of Egypt devolved in those days upon Joseph, after the death of Pharaoh, he being the regulator, doing as he liked throughout the land without anyone interfering. 8 And all Egypt was under the care of Joseph, and Joseph made war with all his surrounding enemies, and he subdued them; also all the land and all the Philistines, unto the borders of Canaan, did Joseph subdue, and they were all under his power and they gave a yearly tax unto Joseph. 9 And Pharaoh king of Egypt sat upon his throne in his father's stead, but he was under the control and counsel of Joseph,

as he was at first under the control of his father. 10 Neither did he reign but in the land of Egypt only, under the counsel of Joseph, but Joseph reigned over the whole country at that time, from Egypt unto the great river Perath. 11 And Joseph was successful in all his ways, and the Lord was with him, and the Lord gave Joseph additional wisdom, and honor, and glory, and love toward him in the hearts of the Egyptians and throughout the land, and Joseph reigned over the whole country forty years. 12 And all the countries of the Philistines and Canaan and Zidon, and on the other side of Jordan, brought presents unto Joseph all his days, and the whole country was in the hand of Joseph, and they brought unto him a yearly tribute as it was regulated, for Joseph had fought against all his surrounding enemies and subdued them, and the whole country was in the hand of Joseph, and Joseph sat securely upon his throne in Egypt. 13 And also all his brethren the sons of Jacob dwelt securely in the land, all the days of Joseph, and they were fruitful and multiplied exceedingly in the land, and they served the Lord all their days, as their father Jacob had commanded them. 14 And it came to pass at the end of many days and years, when the children of Esau were dwelling quietly in their land with Bela their king, that the children of Esau were fruitful and multiplied in the land, and they resolved to go and fight with the sons of Jacob and all Egypt, and to deliver their brother Zepho, the son of Eliphaz, and his men, for they were yet in those days slaves to Joseph. 15 And the children of Esau sent unto all the children of the east, and they made peace with them, and all the children of the east came unto them to go with the children of Esau to Egypt to battle. 16 And there came also unto them of the people of Angeas, king of Dinhabah, and they also sent unto the children of Ishmael and they also came unto them. 17 And all this people assembled and came unto Seir to assist the children of Esau in their battle, and this camp was very large and heavy with people, numerous as the sand of the sea, about eight hundred thousand men, infantry and cavalry, and all these troops went down to Egypt to fight with the sons of Jacob, and they encamped by Rameses. 18 And Joseph went out with his brethren with the mighty men of Egypt, about six hundred men, and they fought with them in the land of Rameses; and the sons of Jacob at that time again fought with the children of Esau, in the fiftieth year of the sons of Jacob going down to Egypt, that is the thirtieth year of the reign of Bela over the children of Esau in Seir. 19 And the Lord gave all the mighty men of Esau and the children of the east into the hand of Joseph and his brethren, and the people of the children of Esau and the children of the east were smitten before Joseph. 20 And of the people of Esau and the children of the east that were slain, there fell before the sons of Jacob about two hundred thousand men, and their king Bela the son of Beor fell with them in the battle, and when the children of Esau saw that their king had fallen in battle and was dead, their hands became weak in the combat. 21 And Joseph and his brethren and all Egypt were still smiting the people of the house of Esau, and all Esau's people were afraid of the sons of Jacob and fled from before them. 22 And Joseph and his brethren and all Egypt pursued them a day's journey, and they slew yet from them about three hundred men, continuing to smite them in the road; and they afterward turned back from them. 23 And Joseph and all his brethren returned to Egypt, not one man was missing from them, but of the Egyptians there fell twelve men. 24 And when Joseph returned to Egypt he ordered Zepho and his men to be additionally bound, and they bound them in irons and they increased their grief. 25 And all the people of the children of Esau, and the children of the east, returned in shame each unto his city, for all the mighty men that were with them had fallen in battle. 26 And when the children of Esau saw that their king had died in battle they hastened and took a man from the people of the children of the east; his name was Jobab the son of Zarach, from the land of Botzrah, and they caused him to reign over them instead of Bela their king. 27 And Jobab sat upon the throne of Bela as king in his stead, and Jobab reigned in Edom over all the children of Esau ten years, and the children of Esau went no more to fight with the sons of Jacob from that day forward, for the sons of Esau knew the valor of the sons of Jacob, and they were greatly afraid of them. 28 But from that day forward the children of Esau hated the sons of Jacob, and the hatred and enmity were very strong between them all the days, unto this day. 29 And it came to pass after this, at the end of ten years, Jobab, the son of Zarach, from Botzrah, died, and the children of Esau took a man whose name was Chusham, from the land of Teman, and they made him king over them instead of Jobab, and Chusham reigned in Edom over all the children of Esau for twenty years. **30** And Joseph, king of Egypt, and his brethren, and all the children of Israel dwelt securely in Egypt in those days, together with all the children of Joseph and his brethren, having no hindrance or evil accident and the land of Egypt was at that time at rest from war in the days of Joseph and his brethren.

CHAPTER 59

1 And these are the names of the sons of Israel who dwelt in Egypt, who had come with Jacob, all the sons of Jacob came unto Egypt, every man with his household. **2** The children of Leah were Reuben, Simeon, Levi, Judah, Issachar and Zebulun, and their sister Dinah. **3** And the sons of Rachel were Joseph and Benjamin. **4** And the sons of Zilpah, the handmaid of Leah, were Gad and Asher. **5** And the sons of Bilhah, the handmaid of Rachel, were Dan and Naphtali. **6** And these were their offspring that were born unto them in the land of Canaan, before they came unto Egypt with their father Jacob. **7** The sons of Reuben were Chanoch, Pallu, Chetzron and Carmi. **8** And the sons of Simeon were Jemuel, Jamin, Ohad, Jachin, Zochar and Saul, the son of the Canaanite woman. **9** And the children of Levi were Gershon, Kehas and Merari, and their sister Jochebed, who was born unto them in their going down to Egypt. **10** And the sons of Judah were Er, Onan, Shelah, Perez and Zarach. **11** And Er and Onan died in the land of Canaan; and the sons of Perez were Chezron and Chamul. **12** And the sons of Issachar were Tola, Puvah, Job and Shomron. **13** And the sons of Zebulun were Sered, Elon and Jachleel, and the son of Dan was Chushim. **14** And the sons of Naphtali were Jachzeel, Guni, Jetzer and Shilam. **15** And the sons of Gad were Ziphion, Chaggi, Shuni, Ezbon, Eri, Arodi and Areli. **16** And the children of Asher were Jimnah, Jishvah, Jishvi, Beriah and their sister Serach; and the sons of Beriah were Cheber and Malchiel. **17** And the sons of Benjamin were Bela, Becher, Ashbel, Gera, Naaman, Achi, Rosh, Mupim, Chupim and Ord. **18** And the sons of Joseph, that were born unto him in Egypt, were Manasseh and Ephraim. **19** And all the souls that went out from the loins of Jacob, were seventy souls; these are they who came with Jacob their father unto Egypt to dwell there: and Joseph and all his brethren dwelt securely in Egypt, and they ate of the best of Egypt all the days

of the life of Joseph. **20** And Joseph lived in the land of Egypt ninety-three years, and Joseph reigned over all Egypt eighty years. **21** And when the days of Joseph drew nigh that he should die, he sent and called for his brethren and all his father's household, and they all came together and sat before him. **22** And Joseph said unto his brethren and unto the whole of his father's household, "Behold I die, and God will surely visit you and bring you up from this land to the land which he swore to your fathers to give unto them. **23** And it will be when God will visit you to bring you up from here to the land of your fathers, then bring up my bones with you from here." **24** And Joseph made the sons of Israel to swear for their seed after them, saying, "God will surely visit you and you will bring up my bones with you from here." **25** And it came to pass after this that Joseph died in that year, the seventy-first year of the Israelites going down to Egypt. **26** And Joseph was one hundred and ten years old when he died in the land of Egypt, and all his brethren and all his servants rose up and they embalmed Joseph, as was their custom, and his brethren and all Egypt mourned over him for seventy days. **27** And they put Joseph in a coffin filled with spices and all sorts of perfume, and they buried him by the side of the river, that is Sihor, and his sons and all his brethren, and the whole of his father's household made a seven day's mourning for him. **28** And it came to pass after the death of Joseph, all the Egyptians began in those days to rule over the children of Israel, and Pharaoh, king of Egypt, who reigned in his father's stead, took all the laws of Egypt and conducted the whole government of Egypt under his counsel, and he reigned securely over his people.

CHAPTER 60

1 And when the year came round, being the seventy-second year from the Israelites going down to Egypt, after the death of Joseph, Zepho, the son of Eliphaz, the son of Esau, fled from Egypt, he and his men, and they went away. **2** And he came to Africa, which is Dinhabah, to Angeas king of Africa, and Angeas received them with great honor, and he made Zepho the captain of his host. **3** And Zepho found favor in the sight of Angeas and in the sight of his people, and Zepho was captain of the host to Angeas king of Africa for many days. **4** And Zepho enticed Angeas king of Africa to collect all his army to go and fight with the Egyptians, and with the sons of Jacob, and to avenge of them the cause of his brethren. **5** But Angeas would not listen to Zepho to do this thing, for Angeas knew the strength of the sons of Jacob, and what they had done to his army in their warfare with the children of Esau. **6** And Zepho was in those days very great in the sight of Angeas and in the sight of all his people, and he continually enticed them to make war against Egypt, but they would not. **7** And it came to pass in those days there was in the land of Chittim a man in the city of Puzimna, whose name was Uzu, and he became degenerately deified by the children of Chittim, and the man died and had no son, only one daughter whose name was Jania. **8** And the damsel was exceedingly beautiful, comely and intelligent, there was none seen like unto her for beauty and wisdom throughout the land. **9** And the people of Angeas king of Africa saw her and they came and praised her unto him, and Angeas sent to the children of Chittim, and he requested to take her unto himself for a wife, and the people of Chittim consented to give her unto him for a wife. **10** And when the messengers of Angeas were going out from the land of Chittim to take their journey, behold the messengers of Turnus king of Bibentu came unto Chittim, for Turnus king of Bibentu also sent his messengers to request Jania for him, to take unto himself for a wife, for all his men had also praised her to him, therefore he sent all his servants unto her. **11** And the servants of Turnus came to Chittim, and they asked for Jania, to be taken unto Turnus their king for a wife. **12** And the people of Chittim said unto them, "We cannot give her, because Angeas king of Africa desired her to take her unto him for a wife before you came, and that we should give her unto him, and now therefore we cannot do this thing to deprive Angeas of the damsel in order to give her unto Turnus. **13** For we are greatly afraid of Angeas lest he come in battle against us and destroy us, and Turnus your master will not be able to deliver us from his hand." **14** And when the messengers of Turnus heard all the words of the children of Chittim, they turned back to their master and told him all the words of the children of Chittim. **15** And the children of Chittim sent a memorial to Angeas, saying, "Behold Turnus has sent for Jania to take her unto him for a wife, and thus have we answered him; and we heard that he has collected his whole army to go to war against

you, and he intends to pass by the road of Sardunia to fight against your brother Lucus, and after that he will come to fight against you." **16** And Angeas heard the words of the children of Chittim which they sent to him in the record, and his anger was kindled and he rose up and assembled his whole army and came through the islands of the sea, the road to Sardunia, unto his brother Lucus king of Sardunia. **17** And Niblos, the son of Lucus, heard that his uncle Angeas was coming, and he went out to meet him with a heavy army, and he kissed him and embraced him, and Niblos said unto Angeas, "When you ask my father after his welfare, when I will go with you to fight with Turnus, ask of him to make me captain of his host," and Angeas did so, and he came unto his brother and his brother came to meet him, and he asked him after his welfare. **18** And Angeas asked his brother Lucus after his welfare, and to make his son Niblos captain of his host, and Lucus did so, and Angeas and his brother Lucus rose up and they went toward Turnus to battle, and there was with them a great army and a heavy people. **19** And he came in ships, and they came into the province of Ashtorash, and behold Turnus came toward them, for he went out to Sardunia, and intended to destroy it and afterward to pass on from there to Angeas to fight with him. **20** And Angeas and Lucus his brother met Turnus in the valley of Canopia, and the battle was strong and mighty between them in that place. **21** And the battle was severe upon Lucus king of Sardunia, and all his army fell, and Niblos his son fell also in that battle. **22** And his uncle Angeas commanded his servants and they made a golden coffin for Niblos and they put him into it, and Angeas again waged battle toward Turnus, and Angeas was stronger than he, and he slew him, and he smote all his people with the edge of the sword, and Angeas avenged the cause of Niblos his brother's son and the cause of the army of his brother Lucus. **23** And when Turnus died, the hands of those that survived the battle became weak, and they fled from before Angeas and Lucus his brother. **24** And Angeas and his brother Lucus pursued them unto the highroad, which is between Alphanu and Romah, and they slew the whole army of Turnus with the edge of the sword. **25** And Lucus king of Sardunia commanded his servants that they should make a coffin of brass, and that they should place therein the body of his son Niblos, and they buried him in that place. **26** And they built upon it a high tower there upon the highroad, and they called its name after the name of Niblos unto this day, and they also buried Turnus king of Bibentu there in that place with Niblos. **27** And behold upon the highroad between Alphanu and Romah the grave of Niblos is on one side and the grave of Turnus on the other, and a pavement between them unto this day. **28** And when Niblos was buried, Lucus his father returned with his army to his land Sardunia, and Angeas his brother king of Africa went with his people unto the city of Bibentu, that is the city of Turnus. **29** And the inhabitants of Bibentu heard of his fame and they were greatly afraid of him, and they went out to meet him with weeping and supplication, and the inhabitants of Bibentu entreated of Angeas not to slay them nor destroy their city; and he did so, for Bibentu was in those days reckoned as one of the cities of the children of Chittim; therefore he did not destroy the city. **30** But from that day forward the troops of the king of Africa would go to Chittim to spoil and plunder it, and whenever they went, Zepho the captain of the host of Angeas would go with them. **31** And it was after this that Angeas turned with his army and they came to the city of Puzimna, and Angeas took from there Jania the daughter of Uzu for a wife and brought her unto his city unto Africa.

CHAPTER 61

1 And it came to pass at that time Pharaoh king of Egypt commanded all his people to make for him a strong palace in Egypt. **2** And he also commanded the sons of Jacob to assist the Egyptians in the building, and the Egyptians made a beautiful and elegant palace for a royal habitation, and he dwelt therein and he renewed his government and he reigned securely. **3** And Zebulun the son of Jacob died in that year, that is the seventy-second year of the going down of the Israelites to Egypt, and Zebulun died a hundred and fourteen years old, and was put into a coffin and given into the hands of his children. **4** And in the seventy-fifth year died his brother Simeon, he was a hundred and twenty years old at his death, and he was also put into a coffin and given into the hands of his children. **5** And Zepho the son of Eliphaz the son of Esau, captain of the host to Angeas king of Dinhabah, was still daily enticing Angeas to prepare for battle to fight with the sons of Jacob in Egypt, and Angeas was unwilling to do this thing, for his servants

had related to him all the might of the sons of Jacob, what they had done unto them in their battle with the children of Esau. **6** And Zepho was in those days daily enticing Angeas to fight with the sons of Jacob in those days. **7** And after some time Angeas hearkened to the words of Zepho and consented to him to fight with the sons of Jacob in Egypt, and Angeas got all his people in order, a people numerous as the sand which is upon the seashore, and he formed his resolution to go to Egypt to battle. **8** And among the servants of Angeas was a youth fifteen years old, Balaam the son of Beor was his name and the youth was very wise and understood the art of witchcraft. **9** And Angeas said unto Balaam, "Conjure for us, I pray you, with the witchcraft, that we may know who will prevail in this battle to which we are now proceeding." **10** And Balaam ordered that they should bring him wax, and he made thereof the likeness of chariots and horsemen representing the army of Angeas and the army of Egypt, and he put them in the cunningly prepared waters that he had for that purpose, and he took in his hand the boughs of myrtle trees, and he exercised his cunning, and he joined them over the water, and there appeared unto him in the water the resembling images of the hosts of Angeas falling before the resembling images of the Egyptians and the sons of Jacob. **11** And Balaam told this thing to Angeas, and Angeas despaired and did not arm himself to go down to Egypt to battle, and he remained in his city. **12** And when Zepho the son of Eliphaz saw that Angeas despaired of going out to battle with the Egyptians, Zepho fled from Angeas from Africa, and he went and came unto Chittim. **13** And all the people of Chittim received him with great honor, and they hired him to fight their battles all the days, and Zepho became exceedingly rich in those days, and the troops of the king of Africa still spread themselves in those days, and the children of Chittim assembled and went to Mount Cuptizia on account of the troops of Angeas king of Africa, who were advancing upon them. **14** And it was one day that Zepho lost a young heifer, and he went to seek it, and he heard it lowing around the mountain. **15** And Zepho went and he saw and behold there was a large cave at the bottom of the mountain, and there was a great stone there at the entrance of the cave, and Zepho split the stone and he came into the cave and he looked and behold, a large animal was devouring the ox; from the middle upward it resembled a man, and from the middle downward it resembled an animal, and Zepho rose up against the animal and slew it with his swords. 16 And the inhabitants of Chittim heard of this thing, and they rejoiced exceedingly, and they said, "What will we do unto this man who has slain this animal that devoured our cattle?" 17 And they all assembled to consecrate one day in the year to him, and they called the name thereof Zepho after his name, and they brought unto him drink offerings year after year on that day, and they brought unto him gifts. 18 At that time Jania the daughter of Uzu wife of king Angeas became ill, and her illness was heavily felt by Angeas and his officers, and Angeas said unto his wise men, "What will I do to Jania and how will I heal her from her illness?" And his wise men said unto him, "Because the air of our country is not like the air of the land of Chittim, and our water is not like their water, therefore from this has the queen become ill. 19 For through the change of air and water she became ill, and also because in her country she drank only the water which came from Purmah, which her ancestors had brought up with bridges." 20 And Angeas commanded his servants, and they brought unto him in vessels of the waters of Purmah belonging to Chittim, and they weighed those waters with all the waters of the land of Africa, and they found those waters lighter than the waters of Africa. 21 And Angeas saw this thing, and he commanded all his officers to assemble the hewers of stone in thousands and tens of thousands, and they hewed stone without number, and the builders came and they built an exceedingly strong bridge, and they conveyed the spring of water from the land of Chittim unto Africa, and those waters were for Jania the queen and for all her concerns, to drink from and to bake, wash and bathe therewith, and also to water therewith all seed from which food can be obtained, and all fruit of the ground. 22 And the king commanded that they should bring of the soil of Chittim in large ships, and they also brought stones to build therewith, and the builders built palaces for Jania the queen, and the queen became healed of her illness. 23 And at the revolution of the year the troops of Africa continued coming to the land of Chittim to plunder as usual, and Zepho son of Eliphaz heard their report, and he gave orders concerning them and he fought with them, and they fled before him, and he delivered the land of Chittim from

them. 24 And the children of Chittim saw the valor of Zepho, and the children of Chittim resolved and they made Zepho king over them, and he became king over them, and while he reigned they went to subdue the children of Tubal, and all the surrounding islands. 25 And their king Zepho went at their head and they made war with Tubal and the islands, and they subdued them, and when they returned from the battle they renewed his government for him, and they built for him a very large palace for his royal habitation and seat, and they made a large throne for him, and Zepho reigned over the whole land of Chittim and over the land of Italia fifty years.

CHAPTER 62

1 In that year, being the seventy-ninth year of the Israelites going down to Egypt, died Reuben the son of Jacob, in the land of Egypt; Reuben was a hundred and twenty-five years old when he died, and they put him into a coffin, and he was given into the hands of his children. 2 And in the eightieth year died his brother Dan; he was a hundred and twenty years at his death, and he was also put into a coffin and given into the hands of his children. 3 And in that year died Chusham king of Edom, and after him reigned Hadad the son of Bedad, for thirty-five years; and in the eighty-first year died Issachar the son of Jacob, in Egypt, and Issachar was a hundred and twenty-two years old at his death, and he was put into a coffin in Egypt, and given into the hands of his children. 4 And in the eighty-second year died Asher his brother, he was a hundred and twenty-three years old at his death, and he was placed in a coffin in Egypt, and given into the hands of his children. 5 And in the eighty-third year died Gad, he was a hundred and twenty-five years old at his death, and he was put into a coffin in Egypt, and given into the hands of his children. 6 And it came to pass in the eighty-fourth year, that is the fiftieth year of the reign of Hadad, son of Bedad, king of Edom, that Hadad assembled all the children of Esau, and he got his whole army in readiness, about four hundred thousand men, and he directed his way to the land of Moab, and he went to fight with Moab and to make them tributary to him. 7 And the children of Moab heard this thing, and they were very much afraid, and they sent to the children of Midian to assist them in fighting with Hadad, son of Bedad, king of Edom. 8 And Hadad came unto the land of Moab, and Moab and the

children of Midian went out to meet him, and they placed themselves in battle array against him in the field of Moab. **9** And Hadad fought with Moab, and there fell of the children of Moab and the children of Midian many slain ones, about two hundred thousand men. **10** And the battle was very severe upon Moab, and when the children of Moab saw that the battle was sore upon them, they weakened their hands and turned their backs, and left the children of Midian to carry on the battle. **11** And the children of Midian knew not the intentions of Moab, but they strengthened themselves in battle and fought with Hadad and all his host, and all Midian fell before him. **12** And Hadad smote all Midian with a heavy smiting, and he slew them with the edge of the sword, he left none remaining of those who came to assist Moab. **13** And when all the children of Midian had perished in battle, and the children at Moab had escaped, Hadad made all Moab at that time tributary to him, and they became under his hand, and they gave a yearly tax as it was ordered, and Hadad turned and went back to his land. **14** And at the revolution of the year, when the rest of the people of Midian that were in the land heard that all their brethren had fallen in battle with Hadad for the sake of Moab, because the children of Moab had turned their backs in battle and left Midian to fight, then five of the princes of Midian resolved with the rest of their brethren who remained in their land, to fight with Moab to avenge the cause of their brethren. **15** And the children of Midian sent to all their brethren the children of the east, and all their brethren, all the children of Keturah came to assist Midian to fight with Moab. **16** And the children of Moab heard this thing, and they were greatly afraid that all the children of the east had assembled together against them for battle, and they the children of Moab sent a memorial to the land of Edom to Hadad the son of Bedad, saying, **17** "Come now unto us and assist us and we will smite Midian, for they all assembled together and have come against us with all their brethren the children of the east to battle, to avenge the cause of Midian that fell in battle." **18** And Hadad, son of Bedad, king of Edom, went out with his whole army and went to the land of Moab to fight with Midian, and Midian and the children of the east fought with Moab in the field of Moab, and the battle was very fierce between them. **19** And Hadad smote all the children of Midian and the children of the east

with the edge of the sword, and Hadad at that time delivered Moab from the hand of Midian, and those that remained of Midian and of the children of the east fled before Hadad and his army, and Hadad pursued them to their land, and smote them with a very heavy slaughter, and the slain fell in the road. **20** And Hadad delivered Moab from the hand of Midian, for all the children of Midian had fallen by the edge of the sword, and Hadad turned and went back to his land. **21** And from that day out, the children of Midian hated the children of Moab, because they had fallen in battle for their sake, and there was a great and mighty enmity between them all the days. **22** And all that were found of Midian in the road of the land of Moab perished by the sword of Moab, and all that were found of Moab in the road of the land of Midian, perished by the sword of Midian; thus did Midian unto Moab and Moab unto Midian for many days. **23** And it came to pass at that time that Judah the son of Jacob died in Egypt, in the eighty-sixth year of Jacob's going down to Egypt, and Judah was a hundred and twenty-nine years old at his death, and they embalmed him and put him into a coffin, and he was given into the hands of his children. **24** And in the eighty-ninth year died Naphtali, he was a hundred and thirty-two years old, and he was put into a coffin and given into the hands of his children. **25** And it came to pass in the ninety-first year of the Israelites going down to Egypt, that is in the thirtieth year of the reign of Zepho the son of Eliphaz, the son of Esau, over the children of Chittim, the children of Africa came upon the children of Chittim to plunder them as usual, but they had not come upon them for these thirteen years. **26** And they came to them in that year, and Zepho the son of Eliphaz went out to them with some of his men and smote them desperately, and the troops of Africa fled from before Zepho and the slain fell before him, and Zepho and his men pursued them, going on and smiting them until they were near unto Africa. **27** And Angeas king of Africa heard the thing which Zepho had done, and it vexed him exceedingly, and Angeas was afraid of Zepho all the days.

CHAPTER 63

1 And in the ninety-third year died Levi, the son of Jacob, in Egypt, and Levi was a hundred and thirty-seven years old when he died, and they put him into a coffin and he was given into the hands of his children. **2** And it came to pass after the death of Levi, when all Egypt saw that the sons of Jacob the brethren of Joseph were dead, all the Egyptians began to afflict the children of Jacob, and to embitter their lives from that day unto the day of their going out from Egypt, and they took from their hands all the vineyards and fields which Joseph had given unto them, and all the elegant houses in which the people of Israel lived, and all the fat of Egypt, the Egyptians took all from the sons of Jacob in those days. 3 And the hand of all Egypt became more grievous in those days against the children of Israel, and the Egyptians injured the Israelites until the children of Israel were wearied of their lives on account of the Egyptians. 4 And it came to pass in those days, in the hundred and second year of Israel's going down to Egypt, that Pharaoh king of Egypt died, and Melol his son reigned in his stead, and all the mighty men of Egypt and all that generation which knew Joseph and his brethren died in those days. 5 And another generation rose up in their stead, which had not known the sons of Jacob and all the good which they had done to them, and all their might in Egypt. 6 Therefore all Egypt began from that day out to embitter the lives of the sons of Jacob, and to afflict them with all manner of hard labor, because they had not known their ancestors who had delivered them in the days of the famine. 7 And this was also from the Lord, for the children of Israel, to benefit them in their latter days, in order that all the children of Israel might know the Lord their God. 8 And in order to know the signs and mighty wonders which the Lord would do in Egypt on account of his people Israel, in order that the children of Israel might fear the Lord God of their ancestors, and walk in all his ways, they and their seed after them all the days. 9 Melol was twenty years old when he began to reign, and he reigned ninety-four years, and all Egypt called his name Pharaoh after the name of his father, as it was their custom to do to every king who reigned over them in Egypt. 10 At that time all the troops of Angeas king of Africa went out to spread along the land of Chittim as usual for plunder. 11 And Zepho the son of Eliphaz the son of Esau heard their report, and he went out to meet them with his army, and he fought them there in the road. 12 And Zepho smote the troops of the king of Africa with the edge of the sword, and left none remaining of them, and not even one returned to his master in Africa. 13 And

Angeas heard of this which Zepho the son of Eliphaz had done to all his troops, that he had destroyed them, and Angeas assembled all his troops, all the men of the land of Africa, a people numerous like the sand by the seashore. 14 And Angeas sent to Lucus his brother, saying, "Come to me with all your men and help me to smite Zepho and all the children of Chittim who have destroyed my men," and Lucus came with his whole army, a very great force, to assist Angeas his brother to fight with Zepho and the children of Chittim. 15 And Zepho and the children of Chittim heard this thing, and they were greatly afraid and a great terror fell upon their hearts. 16 And Zepho also sent a letter to the land of Edom to Hadad the son of Bedad king of Edom and to all the children of Esau, saying, 17 "I have heard that Angeas king of Africa is coming to us with his brother for battle against us, and we are greatly afraid of him, for his army is very great, particularly as he comes against us with his brother and his army likewise. 18 Now therefore come you also up with me and help me, and we will fight together against Angeas and his brother Lucus, and you will save us out of their hands, but if not, know that we will all die." 19 And the children of Esau sent a letter to the children of Chittim and to Zepho their king, saying, "We cannot fight against Angeas and his people for a covenant of peace has been between us these many years, from the days of Bela the first king, and from the days of Joseph the son of Jacob king of Egypt, with whom we fought on the other side of the Jordan when he buried his father." 20 And when Zepho heard the words of his brethren the children of Esau he refrained from them, and Zepho was greatly afraid of Angeas. 21 And Angeas and Lucus his brother arrayed all their forces, about eight hundred thousand men, against the children of Chittim. 22 And all the children of Chittim said unto Zepho, "Pray for us to the God of your ancestors, perhaps he may deliver us from the hand of Angeas and his army, for we have heard that he is a great God and that he delivers all who trust in him." 23 And Zepho heard their words, and Zepho sought the Lord and he said, 24 "O Lord God of Abraham and Isaac my ancestors, this day I know that you are a true God, and all the gods of the nations are vain and useless. 25 Remember now this day unto me your covenant with Abraham our father, which our ancestors related unto us, and do graciously with me this day for the sake of Abraham and

Isaac our fathers and save me and the children of Chittim from the hand of the king of Africa who comes against us for battle." **26** And the Lord hearkened to the voice of Zepho, and he had regard for him on account of Abraham and Isaac, and the Lord delivered Zepho and the children of Chittim from the hand of Angeas and his people. **27** And Zepho fought Angeas king of Africa and all his people on that day, and the Lord gave all the people of Angeas into the hands of the children of Chittim. **28** And the battle was severe upon Angeas, and Zepho smote all the men of Angeas and Lucus his brother, with the edge of the sword, and there fell from them unto the evening of that day about four hundred thousand men. **29** And when Angeas saw that all his men perished, he sent a letter to all the inhabitants of Africa to come to him, to assist him in the battle, and he wrote in the letter, saying, "All who are found in Africa let them come unto me from ten years old and upward; let them all come unto me, and behold if he comes not he will die, and all that he has, with his whole household, the king will take." **30** And all the rest of the inhabitants of Africa were terrified at the words of Angeas, and there went out of the city about three hundred thousand men and boys, from ten years upward, and they came to Angeas. **31** And at the end of ten days Angeas renewed the battle against Zepho and the children of Chittim, and the battle was very great and strong between them. **32** And from the army of Angeas and Lucus, Zepho sent many of the wounded unto his hand, about two thousand men, and Sosiphtar the captain of the host of Angeas fell in that battle. **33** And when Sosiphtar had fallen, the African troops turned their backs to flee, and they fled, and Angeas and Lucus his brother were with them. **34** And Zepho and the children of Chittim pursued them, and they smote them still heavily on the road, about two hundred men, and they pursued Azdrubal the son of Angeas who had fled with his father, and they smote twenty of his men in the road, and Azdrubal escaped from the children of Chittim, and they did not slay him. **35** And Angeas and Lucus his brother fled with the rest of their men, and they escaped and came into Africa with terror and consternation, and Angeas feared all the days lest Zepho the son of Eliphaz should go to war with him.

CHAPTER 64

1 And Balaam the son of Beor was at that time with Angeas in the battle, and when he saw that Zepho prevailed over Angeas, he fled from there and came to Chittim. **2** And Zepho and the children of Chittim received him with great honor, for Zepho knew Balaam's wisdom, and Zepho gave unto Balaam many gifts and he remained with him. **3** And when Zepho had returned from the war, he commanded all the children of Chittim to be numbered who had gone into battle with him and behold not one was missed. **4** And Zepho rejoiced at this thing, and he renewed his kingdom, and he made a feast to all his subjects. **5** But Zepho remembered not the Lord and considered not that the Lord had helped him in battle, and that he had delivered him and his people from the hand of the king of Africa, but still walked in the ways of the children of Chittim and the wicked children of Esau, to serve other gods which his brethren the children of Esau had taught him; it is therefore said, "From the wicked goes out wickedness." **6** And Zepho reigned over all the children of Chittim securely, but knew not the Lord who had delivered him and all his people from the hand of the king of Africa; and the troops of Africa came no more to Chittim to plunder as usual, for they knew of the power of Zepho who had smitten them all at the edge of the sword, so Angeas was afraid of Zepho the son of Eliphaz, and of the children of Chittim all the days. **7** At that time when Zepho had returned from the war, and when Zepho had seen how he prevailed over all the people of Africa and had smitten them in battle at the edge of the sword, then Zepho advised with the children of Chittim, to go to Egypt to fight with the sons of Jacob and with Pharaoh king of Egypt. **8** For Zepho heard that the mighty men of Egypt were dead and that Joseph and his brethren the sons at Jacob were dead, and that all their children the children of Israel remained in Egypt. **9** And Zepho considered to go to fight against them and all Egypt, to avenge the cause of his brethren the children of Esau, whom Joseph with his brethren and all Egypt had smitten in the land of Canaan, when they went up to bury Jacob in Hebron. **10** And Zepho sent messengers to Hadad, son of Bedad, king of Edom, and to all his brethren the children of Esau, saying, **11** "Did you not say that you would not fight against the king of Africa for he is a member of your covenant? Behold I fought with him

415

and smote him and all his people. **12** Now therefore I have resolved to fight against Egypt and the children of Jacob who are there, and I will be revenged of them for what Joseph, his brethren and ancestors did to us in the land of Canaan when they went up to bury their father in Hebron. **13** Now then if you are willing to come to me to assist me in fighting against them and Egypt, then will we avenge the cause of our brethren." **14** And the children of Esau hearkened to the words of Zepho, and the children of Esau gathered themselves together, a very great people, and they went to assist Zepho and the children of Chittim in battle. **15** And Zepho sent to all the children of the east and to all the children of Ishmael with words like unto these, and they gathered themselves and came to the assistance of Zepho and the children of Chittim in the war upon Egypt. **16** And all these kings, the king of Edom and the children of the east, and all the children of Ishmael, and Zepho the king of Chittim went out and arrayed all their hosts in Hebron. **17** And the camp was very heavy, extending in length a distance of three days' journey, a people numerous as the sand upon the seashore which cannot be counted. **18** And all these kings and their hosts went down and came against all Egypt in battle and encamped together in the valley of Pathros. **19** And all Egypt heard their report, and they also gathered themselves together, all the people of the land of Egypt, and of all the cities belonging to Egypt, about three hundred thousand men. **20** And the men of Egypt sent also to the children of Israel who were in those days in the land of Goshen, to come to them in order to go and fight with these kings. **21** And the men of Israel assembled and were about one hundred and fifty men, and they went into battle to assist the Egyptians. **22** And the men of Israel and of Egypt went out, about three hundred thousand men and one hundred and fifty men, and they went toward these kings to battle, and they placed themselves from without the land of Goshen opposite Pathros. **23** And the Egyptians believed not in Israel to go with them in their camps together for battle, for all the Egyptians said, "Perhaps the children of Israel will deliver us into the hand of the children of Esau and Ishmael, for they are their brethren." **24** And all the Egyptians said unto the children of Israel, "Remain you here together in your stand and we will go and fight against the children of Esau and Ishmael, and if these kings should prevail over us, then

come you altogether upon them and assist us," and the children of Israel did so. **25** And Zepho the son of Eliphaz the son of Esau king of Chittim, and Hadad the son of Bedad king of Edom, and all their camps, and all the children of the east, and children of Ishmael, a people numerous as sand, encamped together in the valley of Pathros opposite Tachpanches. **26** And Balaam the son of Beor the Syrian was there in the camp of Zepho, for he came with the children of Chittim to the battle, and Balaam was a man highly honored in the eyes of Zepho and his men. **27** And Zepho said unto Balaam, "Try by divination for us that we may know who will prevail in the battle, we or the Egyptians." **28** And Balaam rose up and tried the art of divination, and he was skillful in the knowledge of it, but he was confused and the work was destroyed in his hand. **29** And he tried it again but it did not succeed, and Balaam despaired of it and left it and did not complete it, for this was from the Lord, in order to cause Zepho and his people to fall into the hand of the children of Israel, who had trusted in the Lord, the God of their ancestors, in their war. **30** And Zepho and Hadad put their forces in battle array, and all the Egyptians went alone against them, about three hundred thousand men, and not one man of Israel was with them. **31** And all the Egyptians fought with these kings opposite Pathros and Tachpanches, and the battle was severe against the Egyptians. **32** And the kings were stronger than the Egyptians in that battle, and about one hundred and eighty men of Egypt fell on that day, and about thirty men of the forces of the kings, and all the men of Egypt fled from before the kings, so the children of Esau and Ishmael pursued the Egyptians, continuing to smite them unto the place where was the camp of the children of Israel. **33** And all the Egyptians cried unto the children of Israel, saying, "Hasten to us and assist us and save us from the hand of Esau, Ishmael and the children of Chittim." **34** And the hundred and fifty men of the children of Israel ran from their station to the camps of these kings, and the children of Israel cried unto the Lord their God to deliver them. **35** And the Lord hearkened to Israel, and the Lord gave all the men of the kings into their hand, and the children of Israel fought against these kings, and the children of Israel smote about four thousand of the kings' men. **36** And the Lord threw a great consternation in the camp of the kings, so that the fear of the children of Israel fell upon them. **37** And all the hosts of the kings fled from before the children of Israel and the children of Israel pursued them continuing to smite them unto the borders of the land of Cush. **38** And the children of Israel slew of them in the road yet two thousand men, and of the children of Israel not one fell. **39** And when the Egyptians saw that the children of Israel had fought with such few men with the kings, and that the battle was so very severe against them, **40** All the Egyptians were greatly afraid of their lives on account of the strong battle, and all Egypt fled, every man hiding himself from the arrayed forces, and they hid themselves in the road, and they left the Israelites to fight. **41** And the children of Israel inflicted a terrible blow upon the kings' men, and they returned from them after they had driven them to the border of the land of Cush. **42** And all Israel knew the thing which the men of Egypt had done to them, that they had fled from them in battle, and had left them to fight alone. **43** So the children of Israel also acted with cunning, and as the children of Israel returned from battle, they found some of the Egyptians in the road and smote them there. **44** And while they slew them, they said unto them these words: **45** "Why did you go from us and leave us, being a few people, to fight against these kings who had a great people to smite us, that you might thereby deliver your own souls?" **46** And of some which the Israelites met on the road, they the children of Israel spoke to each other, saying, "Smite, smite, for he is an Ishmaelite, or an Edomite, or from the children of Chittim," and they stood over him and slew him, and they knew that he was an Egyptian. **47** And the children of Israel did these things cunningly against the Egyptians, because they had deserted them in battle and had fled from them. **48** And the children of Israel slew of the men of Egypt in the road in this manner, about two hundred men. **49** And all the men of Egypt saw the evil which the children of Israel had done to them, so all Egypt feared greatly the children of Israel, for they had seen their great power, and that not one man of them had fallen. **50** So all the children of Israel returned with joy on their road to Goshen, and the rest of Egypt returned each man to his place.

CHAPTER 65

1 And it came to pass after these things, that all the counsellors of Pharaoh, king of Egypt, and all the elders of Egypt assembled and came before the king and bowed down to the ground, and they sat before him. **2** And the counsellors and elders of Egypt spoke unto the king, saying, **3** "Behold the people of the children of Israel are greater and mightier than we are, and you know all the evil which they did to us in the road when we returned from battle. **4** And you have also seen their strong power, for this power is unto them from their fathers, for but a few men stood up against a people numerous as the sand, and smote them at the edge of the sword, and of themselves not one has fallen, so that if they had been numerous they would then have utterly destroyed them. **5** Now therefore give us counsel what to do with them, until we gradually destroy them from among us, lest they become too numerous for us in the land. **6** For if the children of Israel should increase in the land, they will become an obstacle to us, and if any war should happen to take place, they with their great strength will join our enemy against us, and fight against us, destroy us from the land and go away from it." **7** So the king answered the elders of Egypt and said unto them, "This is the plan advised against Israel, from which we will not depart, **8** behold in the land are Pithom and Rameses, cities unfortified against battle, it behooves you and us to build them, and to fortify them. **9** Now therefore go you also and act cunningly toward them, and proclaim a voice in Egypt and in Goshen at the command of the king, saying, **10** 'All you men of Egypt, Goshen, Pathros and all their inhabitants! The king has commanded us to build Pithom and Rameses, and to fortify them for battle; who among you of all Egypt, of the children of Israel and of all the inhabitants of the cities, are willing to build with us, will each have his wages given to him daily at the king's order'; so go you first and do cunningly, and gather yourselves and come to Pithom and Rameses to build. **11** And while you are building, cause a proclamation of this kind to be made throughout Egypt every day at the command of the king. **12** And when some of the children of Israel will come to build with you, you will give them their wages daily for a few days. **13** And after they will have built with you for their daily hire, drag yourselves away from them daily one by one in secret, and then you will rise up and become their task-masters and officers, and you will leave them afterward to build without wages, and should they refuse, then force them with all your might to build. **14** And if you do this it will be well with us to strengthen our land against the children of Israel, for on account of the fatigue of the building and the work, the children of Israel will decrease, because you will deprive them from their wives day by day." **15** And all the elders of Egypt heard the counsel of the king, and the counsel seemed good in their eyes and in the eyes of the servants of Pharaoh, and in the eyes of all Egypt, and they did according to the word of the king. **16** And all the servants went away from the king, and they caused a proclamation to be made in all Egypt, in Tachpanches and in Goshen, and in all the cities which surrounded Egypt, saying, **17** "You have seen what the children of Esau and Ishmael did to us, who came to war against us and wished to destroy us. **18** Now therefore the king commanded us to fortify the land, to build the cities Pithom and Rameses, and to fortify them for battle, if they should again come against us. **19** Whosoever of you from all Egypt and from the children of Israel will come to build with us, he will have his daily wages given by the king, as his command is unto us." **20** And when Egypt and all the children of Israel heard all that the servants of Pharaoh had spoken, there came from the Egyptians, and the children of Israel to build with the servants of Pharaoh, Pithom and Rameses, but none of the children of Levi came with their brethren to build. **21** And all the servants of Pharaoh and his princes came at first with deceit to build with all Israel as daily hired laborers, and they gave to Israel their daily hire at the beginning. **22** And the servants of Pharaoh built with all Israel and were employed in that work with Israel for a month. **23** And at the end of the month, all the servants of Pharaoh began to withdraw secretly from the people of Israel daily. **24** And Israel went on with the work at that time, but they then received their daily hire, because some of the men of Egypt were yet carrying on the work with Israel at that time; therefore the Egyptians gave Israel their hire in those days, in order that they, the Egyptians their fellow-workmen, might also take the pay for their labor. **25** And at the end of a year and four months all the Egyptians had withdrawn from the children of Israel, so that the children of Israel were left alone engaged in the work. **26** And after all the Egyptians had withdrawn from the children of Israel they returned and became oppressors and officers over them, and some of them stood over the children of Israel as task masters, to receive from them all that they gave them for the pay of their labor. **27** And the Egyptians did in this manner to the children of Israel day by day, in order to afflict in their work. **28** And all the children of Israel were alone engaged in the labor, and the Egyptians refrained from giving any pay to the children of Israel from that time forward. **29** And when some of the men of Israel refused to work on account of the wages not being given to them, then the exactors and the servants of Pharaoh oppressed them and smote them with heavy blows, and made them return by force, to labor with their brethren; thus did all the Egyptians unto the children of Israel all the days. **30** And all the children of Israel were greatly afraid of the Egyptians in this matter, and all the children of Israel returned and worked alone without pay. **31** And the children of Israel built Pithom and Rameses, and all the children of Israel did the work, some making bricks, and some building, and the children of Israel built and fortified all the land of Egypt and its walls, and the children of Israel were engaged in work for many years, until the time came when the Lord remembered them and brought them out of Egypt. **32** But the children of Levi were not employed in the work with their brethren of Israel, from the beginning unto the day of their going out from Egypt. **33** For all the children of Levi knew that the Egyptians had spoken all these words with deceit to the Israelites, therefore the children of Levi refrained from approaching to the work with their brethren. **34** And the Egyptians did not direct their attention to make the children of Levi work afterward, since they had not been with their brethren at the beginning, therefore the Egyptians left them alone. **35** And the hands of the men of Egypt were directed with continued severity against the children of Israel in that work, and the Egyptians made the children of Israel work with rigor. **36** And the Egyptians embittered the lives of the children of Israel with hard work, in mortar and bricks, and also in all manner of work in the field. **37** And the children of Israel called Melol the king of Egypt "Meror, king of Egypt," because in his days the Egyptians had embittered their lives with all manner of work. **38** And all the work wherein the Egyptians made the children of Israel labor, they exacted with rigor, in order to afflict the children of Israel, but the more they afflicted them, the more they increased and grew, and the Egyptians were grieved because of the children of Israel.

CHAPTER 66

1 At that time died Hadad the son of Bedad king of Edom, and Samlah from Mesrekah, from the country of the children of the east, reigned in his place. 2 In the thirteenth year of the reign of Pharaoh king of Egypt, which was the hundred and twenty-fifth year of the Israelites going down into Egypt, Samlah had reigned over Edom eighteen years. 3 And when he reigned, he drew out his hosts to go and fight against Zepho the son of Eliphaz and the children of Chittim, because they had made war against Angeas king of Africa, and they destroyed his whole army. 4 But he did not engage with him, for the children of Esau prevented him, saying, "He was their brother," so Samlah listened to the voice of the children of Esau, and turned back with all his forces to the land of Edom, and did not proceed to fight against Zepho the son of Eliphaz. 5 And Pharaoh king of Egypt heard this thing, saying, "Samlah king of Edom has resolved to fight the children of Chittim, and afterward he will come to fight against Egypt." 6 And when the Egyptians heard this matter, they increased the labor upon the children of Israel, lest the Israelites should do unto them as they did unto them in their war with the children of Esau in the days of Hadad. 7 So the Egyptians said unto the children of Israel, "Hasten and do your work, and finish your task, and strengthen the land, lest the children of Esau your brethren should come to fight against us, for on your account will they come against us." 8 And the children of Israel did the work of the men of Egypt day by day, and the Egyptians afflicted the children of Israel in order to lessen them in the land. 9 But as the Egyptians increased the labor upon the children of Israel, so did the children of Israel increase and multiply, and all Egypt was filled with the children of Israel. 10 And in the hundred and twenty-fifth year of Israel's going down into Egypt, all the Egyptians saw that their counsel did not succeed against Israel, but that they increased and grew, and the land of Egypt and the land of Goshen were filled with the children of Israel. 11 So all the elders of Egypt and its wise men came before the king and bowed down to him and sat before him. 12 And all the elders of Egypt and the wise men thereof said unto the king, "May the king live forever; you did counsel us the counsel against the children of Israel, and we did unto them according to the word of the king. 13 But in proportion to the increase of the labor so do they increase and grow in the land, and behold the whole country is filled with them. 14 Now therefore our lord and king, the eyes of all Egypt are upon you to give them advice with your wisdom, by which they may prevail over Israel to destroy them, or to diminish them from the land"; and the king answered them saying, "Give you counsel in this matter that we may know what to do unto them." 15 And an officer, one of the king's counsellors, whose name was Job, from Mesopotamia, in the land of Uz, answered the king, saying, 16 "If it please the king, let him hear the counsel of his servant"; and the king said unto him, "Speak." 17 And Job spoke before the king, the princes, and before all the elders of Egypt, saying, 18 "Behold the counsel of the king which he advised formerly respecting the labor of the children of Israel is very good, and you must not remove from them that labor forever. 19 But this is the advice counselled by which you may lessen them, if it seems good to the king to afflict them. 20 Behold we have feared war for a long time, and we said, 'When Israel becomes fruitful in the land, they will drive us from the land if a war should take place.' 21 If it please the king, let a royal decree go out, and let it be written in the laws of Egypt which will not be revoked, that every male child born to the Israelites, his blood will be spilled upon the ground. 22 And by your doing this, when all the male children of Israel will have died, the evil of their wars will cease; let the king do so and send for all the Hebrew midwives and order them in this matter to execute it"; so the thing pleased the king and the princes, and the king did according to the word of Job. 23 And the king sent for the Hebrew midwives to be called, of which the name of one was Shephrah, and the name of the other Puah. 24 And the midwives came before the king and stood in his presence. 25 And the king said unto them, "When you do the office of a midwife to the Hebrew women, and see them upon the stools, if it be a son, then you will kill him, but if it be a daughter, then she will live. 26 But if you will not do this thing, then will I burn you up and all your houses with fire." 27 But the midwives feared God and did not hearken to the king of Egypt nor to his words, and when the Hebrew women brought out to the midwife son or daughter, then did the midwife do all that was necessary to the child and let it live; thus did the midwives all the days. 28 And this thing was told to the king,

and he sent and called for the midwives and he said to them, "Why have you done this thing and have saved the children alive?" 29 And the midwives answered and spoke together before the king, saying, 30 "Let not the king think that the Hebrew women are as the Egyptian women, for all the children of Israel are vigorous, and before the midwife comes to them they are delivered, and as for us your handmaids, for many days no Hebrew woman has brought out upon us, for all the Hebrew women are their own midwives, because they are vigorous." 31 And Pharaoh heard their words and believed them in this matter, and the midwives went away from the king, and God dealt well with them, and the people multiplied and waxed exceedingly.

CHAPTER 67

1 There was a man in the land of Egypt of the seed of Levi, whose name was Amram, the son of Kehas, the son of Levi, the son of Israel. 2 And this man went and took a wife, namely Jochebed the daughter of Levi his father's sister, and she was one hundred and twenty-six years old, and he came unto her. 3 And the woman conceived and bore a daughter, and she called her name Miriam, because in those days the Egyptians had embittered the lives of the children of Israel. 4 And she conceived again and bore a son and she called his name Aaron, for in the days of her conception, Pharaoh began to spill the blood of the male children of Israel. 5 In those days died Zepho the son of Eliphaz, son of Esau, king of Chittim, and Janeas reigned in his stead. 6 And the time that Zepho reigned over the children of Chittim was fifty years, and he died and was buried in the city of Nabna in the land of Chittim. 7 And Janeas, one of the mighty men of the children of Chittim, reigned after him and he reigned fifty years. 8 And it was after the death of the king of Chittim that Balaam the son of Beor fled from the land of Chittim, and he went and came to Egypt to Pharaoh king of Egypt. 9 And Pharaoh received him with great honor, for he had heard of his wisdom, and he gave him presents and made him for a counsellor and aggrandized him. 10 And Balaam dwelt in Egypt, in honor with all the nobles of the king, and the nobles exalted him, because they all coveted to learn his wisdom. 11 And in the hundred and thirtieth year of Israel's going down to Egypt, Pharaoh dreamed that he was sitting upon his kingly throne and lifted up his eyes and saw an old man standing before him, and there were scales in the hands of the old man, such scales as are used by merchants. 12 And the old man took the scales and hung them before Pharaoh. 13 And the old man took all the elders of Egypt and all its nobles and great men, and he tied them together and put them in one scale. 14 And he took a milk kid and put it into the other scale, and the kid preponderated over all. 15 And Pharaoh was astonished at this dreadful vision, why the kid should preponderate over all, and Pharaoh awoke and behold it was a dream. 16 And Pharaoh rose up early in the morning and called all his servants and related to them the dream, and the men were greatly afraid. 17 And the king said to all his wise men, "Interpret I pray you the dream which I dreamed, that I may know it." 18 And Balaam the son of Beor answered the king and said unto him, "This means nothing else but a great evil that will spring up against Egypt in the latter days. 19 For a son will be born to Israel who will destroy all Egypt and its inhabitants and bring out the Israelites from Egypt with a mighty hand. 20 Now therefore, O king, take counsel upon this matter, that you may destroy the hope of the children of Israel and their expectation, before this evil arises against Egypt." 21 And the king said unto Balaam, "And what will we do unto Israel? Surely after a certain manner did we at first counsel against them and could not prevail over them. 22 Now therefore give you also advice against them by which we may prevail over them." 23 And Balaam answered the king, saying, "Send now and call your two counsellors, and we will see what their advice is upon this matter and afterward your servant will speak." 24 And the king sent and called his two counsellors Reuel the Midianite and Job the Uzite, and they came and sat before the king. 25 And the king said to them, "Behold you have both heard the dream which I have dreamed, and the interpretation thereof; now therefore give counsel and know and see what is to be done to the children of Israel, whereby we may prevail over them, before their evil will spring up against us." 26 And Reuel the Midianite answered the king and said, "May the king live, may the king live forever. 27 If it seems good to the king, let him desist from the Hebrews and leave them, and let him not stretch out his hand against them. 28 For these are they whom the Lord chose in days of old, and took as the lot of his inheritance from among all the nations of the earth and the kings

of the earth; and who is there that stretched his hand against them with impunity, of whom their God was not avenged? **29** Surely you know that when Abraham went down to Egypt, Pharaoh, the former king of Egypt, saw Sarah his wife, and took her for a wife, because Abraham said, 'she is my sister,' for he was afraid, lest the men of Egypt should slay him on account of his wife. **30** And when the king of Egypt had taken Sarah then God smote him and his household with heavy plagues, until he restored unto Abraham his wife Sarah, then was he healed. **31** And Abimelech the Gerarite, king of the Philistines, God punished on account of Sarah wife of Abraham, in stopping up every womb from man to beast. **32** When their God came to Abimelech in the dream of night and terrified him in order that he might restore to Abraham Sarah whom he had taken, and afterward all the people of Gerar were punished on account of Sarah, and Abraham prayed to his God for them, and he was entreated of him, and he healed them. **33** And Abimelech feared all this evil that came upon him and his people, and he returned to Abraham his wife Sarah, and gave him with her many gifts. **34** He did so also to Isaac when he had driven him from Gerar, and God had done wonderful things to him, that all the water courses of Gerar were dried up, and their productive trees did not bring out. **35** Until Abimelech of Gerar, and Ahuzzath one of his friends, and Pichol the captain of his host, went to him and they bent and bowed down before him to the ground. **36** And they requested of him to supplicate for them, and he prayed to the Lord for them, and the Lord was entreated of him and he healed them. **37** Jacob also, the plain man, was delivered through his integrity from the hand of his brother Esau, and the hand of Laban the Syrian his mother's brother, who had sought his life; likewise from the hand of all the kings of Canaan who had come together against him and his children to destroy them, and the Lord delivered them out of their hands, that they turned upon them and smote them, for who had ever stretched out his hand against them with impunity? **38** Surely Pharaoh the former, your father's father, raised Joseph the son of Jacob above all the princes of the land of Egypt, when he saw his wisdom, for through his wisdom he rescued all the inhabitants of the land from the famine. **39** After which he ordered Jacob and his children to come down to Egypt, in order that through their virtue, the land of Egypt and the land of Goshen might be delivered from the famine. **40** Now therefore if it seems good in your eyes, cease from destroying the children of Israel, but if it be not your will that they will dwell in Egypt, send them out from here, that they may go to the land of Canaan, the land where their ancestors sojourned." **41** And when Pharaoh heard the words of Jethro he was very angry with him, so that he rose with shame from the king's presence, and went to Midian, his land, and took Joseph's stick with him. **42** And the king said to Job the Uzite, "What say you Job, and what is your advice respecting the Hebrews?" **43** So Job said to the king, "Behold, all the inhabitants of the land are in your power, let the king do as it seems good in his eyes." **44** And the king said unto Balaam, "What do you say, Balaam, speak your word that we may hear it." **45** And Balaam said to the king, "Of all that the king has counselled against the Hebrews will they be delivered, and the king will not be able to prevail over them with any counsel. **46** For if you think to lessen them by the flaming fire, you cannot prevail over them, for surely their God delivered Abraham their father from Ur of the Chaldeans; and if you think to destroy them with a sword, surely Isaac their father was delivered from it, and a ram was placed in his stead. **47** And if with hard and rigorous labor you think to lessen them, you will not prevail even in this, for their father Jacob served Laban in all manner of hard work and prospered. **48** Now therefore, O King, hear my words, for this is the counsel which is counselled against them, by which you will prevail over them, and from which you should not depart. **49** If it pleases the king let him order all their children which will be born from this day forward, to be thrown into the water, for by this can you wipe away their name, for none of them, nor of their fathers, were tried in this manner." **50** And the king heard the words of Balaam, and the thing pleased the king and the princes, and the king did according to the word of Balaam. **51** And the king ordered a proclamation to be issued and a law to be made throughout the land of Egypt, saying, "Every male child born to the Hebrews from this day forward will be thrown into the water." **52** And Pharaoh called unto all his servants, saying, "Go now and seek throughout the land of Goshen where the children of Israel are, and see that every son born to the Hebrews will be cast into the river, but every daughter you will let live." **53** And when the children of Israel heard this thing which Pharaoh had commanded, to cast their male children into the river, some of the people separated from their wives and others adhered to them. 54 And from that day forward, when the time of delivery arrived for those women of Israel who had remained with their husbands, they went to the field to deliver, and they brought out in the field, and left their children upon the field and returned home. 55 And the Lord who had sworn to their ancestors to multiply them, sent one of his ministering angels which are in heaven to wash each child in water, to anoint and swathe it and to put into its hands two smooth stones from one of which it sucked milk and from the other honey, and he caused its hair to grow to its knees, by which it might cover itself; to comfort it and to cleave to it, through his compassion for it. 56 And when God had compassion over them and had desired to multiply them upon the face of the land, he ordered his earth to receive them to be preserved therein until the time of their growing up, after which the earth opened its mouth and vomited them out and they sprouted out from the city like the herb of the earth, and the grass of the forest, and they returned each to his family and to his father's house, and they remained with them. 57 And the babes of the children of Israel were upon the earth like the herb of the field, through God's grace to them. 58 And when all the Egyptians saw this thing, they went out, each to his field with his yoke of oxen and his ploughshare, and they ploughed it up as one ploughs the earth at seed time. 59 And when they ploughed they were unable to hurt the infants of the children of Israel, so the people increased and waxed exceedingly. 60 And Pharaoh ordered his officers daily to go to Goshen to seek for the babes of the children of Israel. 61 And when they had sought and found one, they took it from its mother's bosom by force, and threw it into the river, but the female child they left with its mother; thus did the Egyptians do to the Israelites all the days.

CHAPTER 68

1 And it was at that time the Spirit of God was upon Miriam the daughter of Amram the sister of Aaron, and she went out and prophesied about the house, saying, "Behold, a son will be born unto us from my father and mother this time, and he will save Israel from the hands of Egypt." 2 And when Amram heard the words of his daughter, he went and took his wife back to the house, after he had driven her away at the time when Pharaoh ordered every male child of the house of Jacob to be thrown into the water. 3 So Amram took Jochebed his wife, three years after he had driven her away, and he came to her and she conceived. 4 And at the end of seven months from her conception she brought out a son, and the whole house was filled with great light as of the light of the sun and moon at the time of their shining. 5 And when the woman saw the child that it was good and pleasing to the sight, she hid it for three months in an inner room. 6 In those days the Egyptians conspired to destroy all the Hebrews there. 7 And the Egyptian women went to Goshen where the children of Israel were, and they carried their young ones upon their shoulders, their babes who could not yet speak. 8 And in those days, when the women of the children of Israel brought out, each woman had hidden her son from before the Egyptians, that the Egyptians might not know of their bringing out and might not destroy them from the land. 9 And the Egyptian women came to Goshen and their children who could not speak were upon their shoulders, and when an Egyptian woman came into the house of a Hebrew woman her babe began to cry. 10 And when it cried the child that was in the inner room answered it, so the Egyptian women went and told it at the house of Pharaoh. 11 And Pharaoh sent his officers to take the children and slay them; thus did the Egyptians to the Hebrew women all the days. 12 And it was at that time, about three months from Jochebed's concealment of her son, that the thing was known in Pharaoh's house. 13 And the woman hastened to take away her son before the officers came, and she took for him an ark of bulrushes, and daubed it with slime and with pitch, and put the child therein, and she laid it in the flags by the river's brink. 14 And his sister Miriam stood afar off to know what would be done to him, and what would become of her words. 15 And God sent out at that time a terrible heat in the land of Egypt, which burned up the flesh of man like the sun in his circuit, and it greatly oppressed the Egyptians. 16 And all the Egyptians went down to bathe in the river, on account of the consuming heat which burned up their flesh. 17 And Bathia, the daughter of Pharaoh, went also to bathe in the river, owing to the consuming heat, and her maidens walked at the riverside, and all the women of Egypt as

well. **18** And Bathia lifted up her eyes to the river, and she saw the ark upon the water, and sent her maid to fetch it. **19** And she opened it and saw the child, and behold the babe wept, and she had compassion on him, and she said, "This is one of the Hebrew children." **20** And all the women of Egypt walking on the riverside desired to give him suck, but he would not suck, for this thing was from the Lord, in order to restore him to his mother's breast. **21** And Miriam his sister was at that time among the Egyptian women at the riverside, and she saw this thing and she said to Pharaoh's daughter, "Will I go and fetch a nurse of the Hebrew women, that she may nurse the child for you?" **22** And Pharaoh's daughter said to her, "Go," and the young woman went and called the child's mother. **23** And Pharaoh's daughter said to Jochebed, "Take this child away and suckle it for me, and I will pay you your wages, two bits of silver daily"; and the woman took the child and nursed it. **24** And at the end of two years, when the child grew up, she brought him to the daughter of Pharaoh, and he was unto her as a son, and she called his name Moses, for she said, "Because I drew him out of the water." **25** And Amram his father called his name Chabar, for he said, "It was for him that he associated with his wife whom he had turned away." **26** And Jochebed his mother called his name Jekuthiel, because, she said, "I have hoped for him to the Almighty, and God restored him unto me." **27** And Miriam his sister called him Jered, for she descended after him to the river to know what his end would be. **28** And Aaron his brother called his name Abi Zanuch, saying, "My father left my mother and returned to her on his account." **29** And Kehas the father of Amram called his name Abigdor, because on his account did God repair the breach of the house of Jacob, that they could no longer throw their male children into the water. **30** And their nurse called him Abi Socho, saying, "In his tabernacle was he hidden for three months, on account of the children of Ham." **31** And all Israel called his name Shemaiah, son of Nethanel, for they said, "In his days has God heard their cries and rescued them from their oppressors." **32** And Moses was in Pharaoh's house, and was unto Bathia, Pharaoh's daughter, as a son, and Moses grew up among the king's children.

CHAPTER 69

1 And the king of Edom died in those days, in the eighteenth year of his reign, and was buried in his temple which he had built for himself as his royal residence in the land of Edom. **2** And the children of Esau sent to Pethor, which is upon the river, and they fetched from there a young man of beautiful eyes and comely aspect, whose name was Saul, and they made him king over them in the place of Samlah. **3** And Saul reigned over all the children of Esau in the land of Edom for forty years. **4** And when Pharaoh king of Egypt saw that the counsel which Balaam had advised respecting the children of Israel did not succeed, but that still they were fruitful, multiplied and increased throughout the land of Egypt, **5** then Pharaoh commanded in those days that a proclamation should be issued throughout Egypt to the children of Israel, saying, "No man will diminish anything of his daily labor. **6** And the man who will be found deficient in his labor which he performs daily, whether in mortar or in bricks, then his youngest son will be put in their place." **7** And the labor of Egypt strengthened upon the children of Israel in those days, and behold, if one brick was deficient in any man's daily labor, the Egyptians took his youngest boy by force from his mother, and put him into the building in the place of the brick which his father had left wanting. **8** And the men of Egypt did so to all the children of Israel day by day, all the days for a long period. **9** But the tribe of Levi did not at that time work with the Israelites their brethren, from the beginning, for the children of Levi knew the cunning of the Egyptians which they exercised at first toward the Israelites.

CHAPTER 70

1 And in the third year from the birth of Moses, Pharaoh was sitting at a banquet, when Alparanith the queen was sitting at his right and Bathia at his left, and the lad Moses was lying upon her bosom, and Balaam the son of Beor with his two sons, and all the princes of the kingdom were sitting at table in the king's presence. **2** And the lad stretched out his hand upon the king's head and took the crown from the king's head and placed it on his own head. **3** And when the king and princes saw the work which the boy had done, the king and princes were terrified, and one man to his neighbor expressed astonishment. **4** And the king said unto the princes who were before him at the table, "What speak you and what say you, O you princes, in this matter, and what is to be the judgment against the boy on account of this act?" **5** And Balaam the son of Beor the magician answered before the king and princes, and he said, "Remember now, O my lord and king, the dream which you did dream many days since, and that which your servant interpreted unto you. **6** Now therefore this is a child from the Hebrew children, in whom is the Spirit of God, and let not my lord the king imagine that this youngster did this thing without knowledge. **7** For he is a Hebrew boy, and wisdom and understanding are with him, although he is yet a child, and with wisdom has he done this and chosen unto himself the kingdom of Egypt. **8** For this is the manner of all the Hebrews to deceive kings and their nobles, to do all these things cunningly, in order to make the kings of the earth and their men tremble. **9** Surely you know that Abraham their father acted thus, who deceived the army of Nimrod king of Babel, and Abimelech king of Gerar, and that he possessed himself of the land of the children of Heth and all the kingdoms of Canaan. **10** And that he descended into Egypt and said of Sarah his wife, 'she is my sister,' in order to mislead Egypt and her king. **11** His son Isaac also did so when he went to Gerar and dwelt there, and his strength prevailed over the army of Abimelech king of the Philistines. **12** He also thought of making the kingdom of the Philistines stumble, in saying that Rebecca his wife was his sister. **13** Jacob also dealt treacherously with his brother and took from his hand his birthright and his blessing. **14** He went then to Padan-aram to the house of Laban his mother's brother, and cunningly obtained from him his daughter, his cattle, and all belonging to him, and fled away and returned to the land of Canaan to his father. **15** His sons sold their brother Joseph, who went down into Egypt and became a slave, and was placed in the prison house for twelve years. **16** Until the former Pharaoh dreamed dreams, and withdrew him from the prison house, and magnified him above all the princes in Egypt on account of his interpreting his dreams to him. **17** And when God caused a famine throughout the land he sent for and brought his father and all his brothers, and the whole of his father's household, and supported them without price or reward, and bought the Egyptians for slaves. **18** Now therefore my lord king, behold, this child has risen up in their stead in Egypt, to do according to their deeds and to trifle with every king, prince and judge. **19** If it pleases the king, let us now spill his blood upon the ground, lest he grow up and take away the government from your hand, and the hope of Egypt perish after he will have reigned." **20** And Balaam said to the king, "Let us moreover call for all the judges of Egypt and the wise men thereof, and let us know if the judgment of death is due to this boy as you did say, and then we will slay him." **21** And Pharaoh sent and called for all the wise men of Egypt and they came before the king, and an angel of the Lord came among them, and he was like one of the wise men of Egypt. **22** And the king said to the wise men, "Surely you have heard what this Hebrew boy who is in the house has done, and thus has Balaam judged in the matter. **23** Now judge you also and see what is due to the boy for the act he has committed." **24** And the angel, who seemed like one of the wise men of Pharaoh, answered and said as follows, before all the wise men of Egypt and before the king and the princes: **25** "If it pleases the king let the king send for men who will bring before him an onyx stone and a coal of fire, and place them before the child, and if the child will stretch out his hand and take the onyx stone, then will we know that with wisdom has the youth done all that he has done, and we must slay him. **26** But if he stretches out his hand upon the coal, then will we know that it was not with knowledge that he did this thing, and he will live." **27** And the thing seemed good in the eyes of the king and the princes, so the king did according to the word of the angel of the Lord. **28** And the king ordered the onyx stone and coal to be brought and placed before Moses. **29** And they placed the boy before them, and the lad endeavored to stretch out his hand to the onyx stone, but the angel of the Lord took his hand and placed it upon the coal, and the coal became extinguished in his hand, and he lifted it up and put it into his mouth and burned part of his lips and part of his tongue, and he became heavy in mouth and tongue. **30** And when the king and princes saw this, they knew that Moses had not acted with wisdom in taking off the crown from the king's head. **31** So the king and princes refrained from slaying the child, so Moses remained in Pharaoh's house, growing up, and the Lord was with him. **32** And while the boy was in the king's house, he was robed in purple and he grew among the children of the king. **33** And when Moses grew up in the king's house, Bathia the daughter of Pharaoh considered him as a son, and all the household of Pharaoh honored him, and all the men of Egypt were afraid of him. 34 And he daily went out and came into the land of Goshen, where his brethren the children of Israel were, and Moses saw them daily in shortness of breath and hard labor. 35 And Moses asked them, saying, "Why is this labor meted out unto you day by day?" 36 And they told him all that had befallen them, and all the injunctions which Pharaoh had put upon them before his birth. 37 And they told him all the counsels which Balaam the son of Beor had counselled against them, and what he had also counselled against him in order to slay him when he had taken the king's crown from off his head. 38 And when Moses heard these things his anger was kindled against Balaam, and he sought to kill him, and he was in ambush for him day by day. 39 And Balaam was afraid of Moses, and he and his two sons rose up and went out from Egypt, and they fled and delivered their souls and went themselves to the land of Cush to Kikianus, king of Cush. 40 And Moses was in the king's house going out and coming in, the Lord gave him favor in the eyes of Pharaoh, and in the eyes of all his servants, and in the eyes of all the people of Egypt, and they loved Moses exceedingly. 41 And the day arrived when Moses went to Goshen to see his brethren, that he saw the children of Israel in their burdens and hard labor, and Moses was grieved on their account. 42 And Moses returned to Egypt and came to the house of Pharaoh, and came before the king, and Moses bowed down before the king. 43 And Moses said unto Pharaoh, "I pray you my lord, I have come to seek a small request from you, turn not away my face empty"; and Pharaoh said unto him, "Speak." 44 And Moses said unto Pharaoh, "Let there be given unto your servants the children of Israel who are in Goshen, one day to rest therein from their labor." 45 And the king answered Moses and said, "Behold, I have lifted up your face in this thing to grant your request." 46 And Pharaoh ordered a proclamation to be issued throughout Egypt and Goshen, saying, 47 "To you, all the children of Israel, thus says the king, for six days you will do your work and labor, but on the seventh day you will rest, and will not perform any work, thus will you do all the days, as the king and Moses the son of Bathia have commanded." 48 And Moses

rejoiced at this thing which the king had granted to him, and all the children of Israel did as Moses ordered them. 49 For this thing was from the Lord to the children of Israel, for the Lord had begun to remember the children of Israel to save them for the sake of their fathers. 50 And the Lord was with Moses and his fame went throughout Egypt. 51 And Moses became great in the eyes of all the Egyptians, and in the eyes of all the children of Israel, seeking good for his people Israel and speaking words of peace regarding them to the king.

CHAPTER 71

1 And when Moses was eighteen years old, he desired to see his father and mother and he went to them to Goshen, and when Moses had come near Goshen, he came to the place where the children of Israel were engaged in work, and he observed their burdens, and he saw an Egyptian smiting one of his Hebrew brethren. 2 And when the man who was beaten saw Moses he ran to him for help, for the man Moses was greatly respected in the house of Pharaoh, and he said to him, "My lord attend to me, this Egyptian came to my house in the night, bound me, and came to my wife in my presence, and now he seeks to take my life away." 3 And when Moses heard this wicked thing, his anger was kindled against the Egyptian, and he turned this way and the other, and when he saw there was no man there he smote the Egyptian and hid him in the sand, and delivered the Hebrew from the hand of him that smote him. 4 And the Hebrew went to his house, and Moses returned to his home, and went out and came back to the king's house. 5 And when the man had returned home, he thought of repudiating his wife, for it was not right in the house of Jacob, for any man to come to his wife after she had been defiled. 6 And the woman went and told her brothers, and the woman's brothers sought to slay him, and he fled to his house and escaped. 7 And on the second day Moses went out to his brethren, and saw, and behold two men were quarreling, and he said to the wicked one, "Why do you smite your neighbor?" 8 And he answered him and said to him, "Who has set you for a prince and judge over us? Do you think to slay me as you did slay the Egyptian?" And Moses was afraid, and he said, "Surely the thing is known?" 9 And Pharaoh heard of this affair, and he ordered Moses to be slain, so God sent his angel, and he appeared unto

Pharaoh in the likeness of a captain of the guard. **10** And the angel of the Lord took the sword from the hand of the captain of the guard, and took his head off with it, for the likeness of the captain of the guard was turned into the likeness of Moses. **11** And the angel of the Lord took hold of the right hand of Moses, and brought him out from Egypt, and placed him from without the borders of Egypt, a distance of forty days' journey. **12** And Aaron his brother alone remained in the land of Egypt, and he prophesied to the children of Israel, saying, **13** "Thus says the Lord God of your ancestors, 'Throw away, each man, the abominations of his eyes, and do not defile yourselves with the idols of Egypt.' " **14** And the children of Israel rebelled and would not hearken to Aaron at that time. **15** And the Lord thought to destroy them, were it not that the Lord remembered the covenant which he had made with Abraham, Isaac and Jacob. **16** In those days the hand of Pharaoh continued to be severe against the children of Israel, and he crushed and oppressed them until the time when God sent out his word and took notice of them.

CHAPTER 72

1 And it was in those days that there was a great war between the children of Cush and the children of the east and Aram, and they rebelled against the king of Cush in whose hands they were. **2** So Kikianus king of Cush went out with all the children of Cush, a people numerous as the sand, and he went to fight against Aram and the children of the east, to bring them under subjection. **3** And when Kikianus went out, he left Balaam the magician, with his two sons, to guard the city, and the lowest sort of the people of the land. **4** So Kikianus went out to Aram and the children of the east, and he fought against them and smote them, and they all fell down wounded before Kikianus and his people. **5** And he took many of them captives and he brought them under subjection as at first, and he encamped upon their land to take tribute from them as usual. **6** And Balaam the son of Beor, when the king of Cush had left him to guard the city and the poor of the city, he rose up and advised with the people of the land to rebel against king Kikianus, not to let him enter the city when he should come home. **7** And the people of the land hearkened to him, and they swore to him and made him king over them, and his two sons for captains of the army. **8** So they rose up and raised the walls of the city at the two corners, and they built an exceeding strong building. **9** And at the third corner they dug ditches without number, between the city and the river which surrounded the whole land of Cush, and they made the waters of the river burst out there. **10** At the fourth corner they collected numerous serpents by their incantations and enchantments, and they fortified the city and dwelt therein, and no one went out or in before them. **11** And Kikianus fought against Aram and the children of the east and he subdued them as before, and they gave him their usual tribute, and he went and returned to his land. **12** And when Kikianus the king of Cush approached his city and all the captains of the forces with him, they lifted up their eyes and saw that the walls of the city were built up and greatly elevated, so the men were astonished at this. **13** And they said one to the other, "It is because they saw that we were delayed, in battle, and were greatly afraid of us, therefore have they done this thing and raised the city walls and fortified them so that the kings of Canaan might not come in battle against them." **14** So the king and the troops approached the city door and they looked up and behold, all the gates of the city were closed, and they called out to the sentinels, saying, "Open unto us, that we may enter the city." **15** But the sentinels refused to open to them by the order of Balaam the magician, their king, they suffered them not to enter their city. **16** So they raised a battle with them opposite the city gate, and one hundred and thirty men of the army at Kikianus fell on that day. **17** And on the next day they continued to fight and they fought at the side of the river; they endeavored to pass but were not able, so some of them sank in the pits and died. **18** So the king ordered them to cut down trees to make rafts, upon which they might pass to them, and they did so. **19** And when they came to the place of the ditches, the waters revolved by mills, and two hundred men upon ten rafts were drowned. **20** And on the third day they came to fight at the side where the serpents were, but they could not approach there, for the serpents slew of them one hundred and seventy men, and they ceased fighting against Cush, and they besieged Cush for nine years, no person came out or in. **21** At that time that the war and the siege were against Cush, Moses fled from Egypt from Pharaoh who sought to kill him for having slain the

Egyptian. **22** And Moses was eighteen years old when he fled from Egypt from the presence of Pharaoh, and he fled and escaped to the camp of Kikianus, which at that time was besieging Cush. **23** And Moses was nine years in the camp of Kikianus king of Cush, all the time that they were besieging Cush, and Moses went out and came in with them. **24** And the king and princes and all the fighting men loved Moses, for he was great and worthy, his stature was like a noble lion, his face was like the sun, and his strength was like that of a lion, and he was counsellor to the king. **25** And at the end of nine years, Kikianus was seized with a mortal disease, and his illness prevailed over him, and he died on the seventh day. **26** So his servants embalmed him and carried him and buried him opposite the city gate to the north of the land of Egypt. **27** And they built over him an elegant strong and high building, and they placed great stones below. **28** And the king's scribes engraved upon those stones all the might of their king Kikianus, and all his battles which he had fought, behold they are written there at this day. **29** Now after the death of Kikianus king of Cush it grieved his men and troops greatly on account of the war. **30** So they said one to the other, "Give us counsel what we are to do at this time, as we have resided in the wilderness nine years away from our homes. **31** If we say we will fight against the city many of us will fall wounded or killed, and if we remain here in the siege we will also die. **32** For now all the kings of Aram and of the children of the east will hear that our king is dead, and they will attack us suddenly in a hostile manner, and they will fight against us and leave no remnant of us. **33** Now therefore let us go and make a king over us and let us remain in the siege until the city is delivered up to us." **34** And they wished to choose on that day a man for king from the army of Kikianus, and they found no object of their choice like Moses to reign over them. **35** And they hastened and stripped off each man his garments and cast them upon the ground, and they made a great heap and placed Moses thereon. **36** And they rose up and blew with trumpets and called out before him, and said, "May the king live, may the king live!" **37** And all the people and nobles swore unto him to give him for a wife Adoniah the queen, the Cushite, wife of Kikianus, and they made Moses king over them on that day. **38** And all the people of Cush issued a proclamation on that day, saying, "Every man must give

something to Moses of what is in his possession." **39** And they spread out a sheet upon the heap, and every man cast into it something of what he had, one a gold earring and the other a coin. **40** Also of onyx stones, bdellium, pearls and marble did the children of Cush cast unto Moses upon the heap, also silver and gold in great abundance. **41** And Moses took all the silver and gold, all the vessels, and the bdellium and onyx stones, which all the children of Cush had given to him, and he placed them among his treasures. **42** And Moses reigned over the children of Cush on that day, in the place of Kikianus king of Cush.

CHAPTER 73

1 In the fifty-fifth year of the reign of Pharaoh king of Egypt, that is in the hundred and fifty-seventh year of the Israelites going down into Egypt, reigned Moses in Cush. **2** Moses was twenty-seven years old when he began to reign over Cush, and forty years did he reign. **3** And the Lord granted Moses favor and grace in the eyes of all the children of Cush, and the children of Cush loved him exceedingly, so Moses was favored by the Lord and by men. **4** And in the seventh day of his reign, all the children of Cush assembled and came before Moses and bowed down to him to the ground. **5** And all the children spoke together in the presence of the king, saying, "Give us counsel that we may see what is to be done to this city. **6** For it is now nine years that we have been besieging round about the city and have not seen our children and our wives." **7** So the king answered them, saying, "If you will hearken to my voice in all that I will command you, then will the Lord give the city into our hands and we will subdue it. **8** For if we fight with them as in the former battle which we had with them before the death of Kikianus, many of us will fall down wounded as before. **9** Now therefore behold here is counsel for you in this matter; if you will hearken to my voice, then will the city be delivered into our hands." **10** So all the forces answered the king, saying, "All that our lord will command that will we do." **11** And Moses said unto them, "Pass through and proclaim a voice in the whole camp unto all the people, saying, **12** 'Thus says the king, *Go into the forest and bring with you of the young ones of the stork, each man a young one in his hand.* **13** *And any person transgressing the word of the king, who will not bring his young one, he will die, and the* *king will take all belonging to him.* **14** *And when you will bring them they will be in your keeping, you will rear them until they grow up, and you will teach them to dart upon, as is the way of the young ones of the hawk.'* " **15** So all the children of Cush heard the words of Moses, and they rose up and caused a proclamation to be issued throughout the camp, saying, **16** "Unto you, all the children of Cush, the king's order is, that you go all together to the forest, and catch there the young storks each man his young one in his hand, and you will bring them home. **17** And any person violating the order of the king will die, and the king will take all that belongs to him." **18** And all the people did so, and they went out to the wood and they climbed the fir trees and caught, each man a young one in his hand, all the young of the storks, and they brought them into the desert and reared them by order of the king, and they taught them to dart upon, similar to the young hawks. **19** And after the young storks were reared, the king ordered them to be hungered for three days, and all the people did so. **20** And on the third day, the king said unto them, "Strengthen yourselves and become valiant men, and put on each man his armor and gird on his sword upon him and ride each man his horse and take each his young stork in his hand. **21** And we will rise up and fight against the city at the place where the serpents are"; and all the people did as the king had ordered. **22** And they took each man his young one in his hand, and they went away, and when they came to the place of the serpents the king said to them, "Send out each man his young stork upon the serpents." **23** And they sent out each man his young stork at the king's order, and the young storks ran upon the serpents and they devoured them all and destroyed them out of that place. **24** And when the king and people had seen that all the serpents were destroyed in that place, all the people set up a great shout. **25** And they approached and fought against the city and took it and subdued it, and they entered the city. **26** And there died on that day one thousand and one hundred men of the people of the city, all that inhabited the city, but of the people besieging not one died. **27** So all the children of Cush went each to his home, to his wife and children and to all belonging to him. **28** And Balaam the magician, when he saw that the city was taken, he opened the gate and he and his two sons and eight brothers fled and returned to Egypt to Pharaoh king of Egypt. **29** They are the sorcerers and magicians who are mentioned in the book of the law, standing against Moses when the Lord brought the plagues upon Egypt. **30** So Moses took the city by his wisdom, and the children of Cush placed him on the throne instead of Kikianus king of Cush. **31** And they placed the royal crown upon his head, and they gave him for a wife Adoniah the Cushite queen, wife of Kikianus. **32** And Moses feared the Lord God of his fathers, so that he came not to her, nor did he turn his eyes to her. **33** For Moses remembered how Abraham had made his servant Eliezer swear, saying unto him, "You will not take a woman from the daughters of Canaan for my son Isaac." **34** Also what Isaac did when Jacob had fled from his brother, when he commanded him, saying, "You will not take a wife from the daughters of Canaan, nor make alliance with any of the children of Ham. **35** For the Lord our God gave Ham the son of Noah, and his children and all his seed, as slaves to the children of Shem and to the children of Japheth, and unto their seed after them for slaves, forever." **36** Therefore Moses turned not his heart nor his eyes to the wife of Kikianus all the days that he reigned over Cush. **37** And Moses feared the Lord his God all his life, and Moses walked before the Lord in truth, with all his heart and soul, he turned not from the right way all the days of his life; he declined not from the way either to the right or to the left, in which Abraham, Isaac and Jacob had walked. **38** And Moses strengthened himself in the kingdom of the children of Cush, and he guided the children of Cush with his usual wisdom, and Moses prospered in his kingdom. **39** And at that time Aram and the children of the east heard that Kikianus king of Cush had died, so Aram and the children of the east rebelled against Cush in those days. **40** And Moses gathered all the children of Cush, a people very mighty, about thirty thousand men, and he went out to fight with Aram and the children of the east. **41** And they went at first to the children of the east, and when the children of the east heard their report, they went to meet them, and engaged in battle with them. **42** And the war was severe against the children of the east, so the Lord gave all the children of the east into the hand of Moses, and about three hundred men fell down slain. **43** And all the children of the east turned back and retreated, so Moses and the children of Cush followed them and subdued them, and put a tax upon them, as was their custom. **44** So Moses and all the people with him passed from there to the land of Aram for battle. **45** And the people of Aram also went to meet them, and they fought against them, and the Lord delivered them into the hand of Moses, and many of the men of Aram fell down wounded. **46** And Aram also were subdued by Moses and the people of Cush, and also gave their usual tax. **47** And Moses brought Aram and the children of the east under subjection to the children of Cush, and Moses and all the people who were with him, turned to the land of Cush. **48** And Moses strengthened himself in the kingdom of the children of Cush, and the Lord was with him, and all the children of Cush were afraid of him.

CHAPTER 74

1 In the end of years died Saul king of Edom, and Baal Chanan the son of Achbor reigned in his place. **2** In the sixteenth year of the reign of Moses over Cush, Baal Chanan the son of Achbor reigned in the land of Edom over all the children of Edom for thirty-eight years. **3** In his days Moab rebelled against the power of Edom, having been under Edom since the days of Hadad the son of Bedad, who smote them and Midian, and brought Moab under subjection to Edom. **4** And when Baal Chanan the son of Achbor reigned over Edom, all the children of Moab withdrew their allegiance from Edom. **5** And Angeas king of Africa died in those days, and Azdrubal his son reigned in his stead. **6** And in those days died Janeas king of the children of Chittim, and they buried him in his temple which he had built for himself in the plain of Canopia for a residence, and Latinus reigned in his stead. **7** In the twenty-second year of the reign of Moses over the children of Cush, Latinus reigned over the children of Chittim forty-five years. **8** And he also built for himself a great and mighty tower, and he built therein an elegant temple for his residence, to conduct his government, as was the custom. **9** In the third year of his reign he caused a proclamation to be made to all his skilful men, who made many ships for him. **10** And Latinus assembled all his forces, and they came in ships, and went therein to fight with Azdrubal son of Angeas king of Africa, and they came to Africa and engaged in battle with Azdrubal and his army. **11** And Latinus prevailed over Azdrubal, and Latinus took from Azdrubal the aqueduct which his father had brought from the children of Chittim, when he took Janiah the daughter of Uzi for a wife, so Latinus overthrew the bridge of the aqueduct, and smote the whole army of Azdrubal a severe blow. **12** And the remaining strong men of Azdrubal strengthened themselves, and their hearts were filled with envy, and they courted death, and again engaged in battle with Latinus king of Chittim. **13** And the battle was severe upon all the men of Africa, and they all fell wounded before Latinus and his people, and Azdrubal the king also fell in that battle. **14** And the king Azdrubal had a very beautiful daughter, whose name was Ushpezena, and all the men of Africa embroidered her likeness on their garments, on account of her great beauty and comely appearance. **15** And the men of Latinus saw Ushpezena, the daughter of Azdrubal, and praised her unto Latinus their king. **16** And Latinus ordered her to be brought to him, and Latinus took Ushpezena for a wife, and he turned back on his way to Chittim. **17** And it was after the death of Azdrubal son of Angeas, when Latinus had turned back to his land from the battle, that all the inhabitants of Africa rose up and took Anibal the son of Angeas, the younger brother of Azdrubal, and made him king instead of his brother over the whole land at Africa. **18** And when he reigned, he resolved to go to Chittim to fight with the children of Chittim, to avenge the cause of Azdrubal his brother, and the cause of the inhabitants of Africa, and he did so. **19** And he made many ships, and he came therein with his whole army, and he went to Chittim. **20** So Anibal fought with the children of Chittim, and the children of Chittim fell wounded before Anibal and his army, and Anibal avenged his brother's cause. **21** And Anibal continued the war for eighteen years with the children of Chittim, and Anibal dwelt in the land of Chittim and encamped there for a long time. **22** And Anibal smote the children of Chittim very severely, and he slew their great men and princes, and of the rest of the people he smote about eighty thousand men. **23** And at the end of days and years, Anibal returned to his land of Africa, and he reigned securely in the place of Azdrubal his brother.

CHAPTER 75

1 At that time, in the hundred and eightieth year of the Israelites going down into Egypt, there went out from Egypt valiant men, thirty thousand on foot, from the children of Israel, who were all of the tribe of Joseph, of the children of Ephraim the son of Joseph. **2** For they said the period was completed which the Lord had appointed to the children of Israel in the times of old, which he had spoken to Abraham. **3** And these men girded themselves, and they put each man his sword at his side, and every man his armor upon him, and they trusted to their strength, and they went out together from Egypt with a mighty hand. **4** But they brought no provision for the road, only silver and gold, not even bread for that day did they bring in their hands, for they thought of getting their provision for pay from the Philistines, and if not they would take it by force. **5** And these men were very mighty and valiant men, one man could pursue a thousand and two could rout ten thousand, so they trusted in their strength and went together as they were. **6** And they directed their course toward the land of Gath, and they went down and found the shepherds of Gath feeding the cattle of the children of Gath. **7** And they said to the shepherds, "Give us some of the sheep for pay, that we may eat, for we are hungry, for we have eaten no bread this day." **8** And the shepherds said, "Are they our sheep or cattle that we should give them to you even for pay?" So the children of Ephraim approached to take them by force. **9** And the shepherds of Gath shouted over them that their cry was heard at a distance, so all the children of Gath went out to them. **10** And when the children of Gath saw the evil doings of the children of Ephraim, they returned and assembled the men of Gath, and they put on each man his armor, and came out to the children of Ephraim for battle. **11** And they engaged with them in the valley of Gath, and the battle was severe, and they smote from each other a great many on that day. **12** And on the second day the children of Gath sent to all the cities of the Philistines that they should come to their help, saying, **13** "Come up unto us and help us, that we may smite the children of Ephraim who have come out from Egypt to take our cattle, and to fight against us without cause." **14** Now the souls of the children of Ephraim were exhausted with hunger and thirst, for they had eaten no bread for three days. And forty thousand men went out from the cities of the Philistines to the assistance of the men of Gath. **15** And these men were engaged in battle with the children of Ephraim, and the Lord delivered the children of Ephraim into the hands of the Philistines. **16** And they smote all the children of Ephraim, all who had gone out from Egypt, none were remaining but ten men who had run

away from the engagement. **17** For this evil was from the Lord against the children of Ephraim, for they transgressed the word of the Lord in going out from Egypt, before the period had arrived which the Lord in the days of old had appointed to Israel. **18** And of the Philistines also there fell a great many, about twenty thousand men, and their brethren carried them and buried them in their cities. **19** And the slain of the children of Ephraim remained forsaken in the valley of Gath for many days and years, and were not brought to burial, and the valley was filled with men's bones. **20** And the men who had escaped from the battle came to Egypt and told all the children of Israel all that had befallen them. **21** And their father Ephraim mourned over them for many days, and his brethren came to console him. **22** And he came unto his wife and she bore a son, and he called his name Beriah, for she was unfortunate in his house.

CHAPTER 76

1 And Moses the son of Amram was still king in the land of Cush in those days, and he prospered in his kingdom, and he conducted the government of the children of Cush in justice, in righteousness, and integrity. **2** And all the children of Cush loved Moses all the days that he reigned over them, and all the inhabitants of the land of Cush were greatly afraid of him. **3** And in the fortieth year of the reign of Moses over Cush, Moses was sitting on the royal throne while Adoniah the queen was before him, and all the nobles were sitting around him. **4** And Adoniah the queen said before the king and the princes, "What is this thing which you, the children of Cush, have done for this long time? **5** Surely you know that for forty years that this man has reigned over Cush he has not approached me, nor has he served the gods of the children of Cush. **6** Now therefore hear, O you children of Cush, and let this man no more reign over you as he is not of our flesh. **7** Behold Menacrus my son is grown up, let him reign over you, for it is better for you to serve the son of your lord, than to serve a stranger, slave of the king of Egypt." **8** And all the people and nobles of the children of Cush heard the words which Adoniah the queen had spoken in their ears. **9** And all the people were preparing until the evening, and in the morning they rose up early and made Menacrus, son of Kikianus, king over them. **10** And all the children of Cush were afraid to stretch out their hand against

Moses, for the Lord was with Moses, and the children of Cush remembered the oath which they swore unto Moses, therefore they did no harm to him. **11** But the children of Cush gave many presents to Moses and sent him from them with great honor. **12** So Moses went out from the land of Cush, and went home and ceased to reign over Cush, and Moses was sixty-six years old when he went out of the land of Cush, for the thing was from the Lord, for the period had arrived which he had appointed in the days of old, to bring out Israel from the affliction of the children of Ham. **13** So Moses went to Midian, for he was afraid to return to Egypt on account of Pharaoh, and he went and sat at a well of water in Midian. **14** And the seven daughters of Reuel the Midianite went out to feed their father's flock. **15** And they came to the well and drew water to water their father's flock. **16** So the shepherds of Midian came and drove them away, and Moses rose up and helped them and watered the flock. **17** And they came home to their father Reuel and told him what Moses did for them. **18** And they said, "An Egyptian man has delivered us from the hands of the shepherds, he drew up water for us and watered the flock." **19** And Reuel said to his daughters, "And where is he? Why have you left the man?" **20** And Reuel sent for him and fetched him and brought him home, and he ate bread with him. **21** And Moses related to Reuel that he had fled from Egypt and that he reigned forty years over Cush, and that they afterward had taken the government from him and had sent him away in peace with honor and with presents. **22** And when Reuel had heard the words of Moses, Reuel said within himself, "I will put this man into the prison house, whereby I will conciliate the children of Cush, for he has fled from them." **23** And they took and put him into the prison house, and Moses was in prison ten years, and while Moses was in the prison house, Zipporah the daughter of Reuel took pity over him, and supported him with bread and water all the time. **24** And all the children of Israel were yet in the land of Egypt serving the Egyptians in all manner of hard work, and the hand of Egypt continued in severity over the children of Israel in those days. **25** At that time the Lord smote Pharaoh king of Egypt, and he afflicted with the plague of leprosy from the sole of his foot to the crown of his head; owing to the cruel treatment of the children of Israel was this plague at that time from the Lord upon Pharaoh king of Egypt. **26** For the Lord had hearkened to the prayer of his people the children of Israel, and their cry reached him on account of their hard work. **27** Still his anger did not turn from them, and the hand of Pharaoh was still stretched out against the children of Israel, and Pharaoh hardened his neck before the Lord, and he increased his yoke over the children of Israel and embittered their lives with all manner of hard work. **28** And when the Lord had inflicted the plague upon Pharaoh king of Egypt, he asked his wise men and sorcerers to cure him. **29** And his wise men and sorcerers said unto him, "That if the blood of little children were put into the wounds he would be healed." **30** And Pharaoh hearkened to them and sent his ministers to Goshen to the children of Israel to take their little children. **31** And Pharaoh's ministers went and took the infants of the children of Israel from the bosoms of their mothers by force, and they brought them to Pharaoh daily, a child each day, and the physicians killed them and applied them to the plague; thus did they all the days. **32** And the number of the children which Pharaoh slew was three hundred and seventy-five. **33** But the Lord hearkened not to the physicians of the king of Egypt, and the plague went on increasing mightily. **34** And Pharaoh was ten years afflicted with that plague, still the heart of Pharaoh was more hardened against the children of Israel. **35** And at the end of ten years the Lord continued to afflict Pharaoh with destructive plagues. **36** And the Lord smote him with a bad tumor and sickness at the stomach, and that plague turned to a severe boil. **37** At that time the two ministers of Pharaoh came from the land of Goshen where all the children of Israel were, and went to the house of Pharaoh and said to him, "We have seen the children of Israel slacken in their work and negligent in their labor." **38** And when Pharaoh heard the words of his ministers, his anger was kindled against the children of Israel exceedingly, for he was greatly grieved at his bodily pain. **39** And he answered and said, "Now that the children of Israel know that I am ill, they turn and scoff at us, now therefore harness my chariot for me, and I will go myself to Goshen and will see the scoff of the children of Israel with which they are deriding me"; so his servants harnessed the chariot for him. **40** And they took and made him ride upon a horse, for he was not able to ride of himself; **41** And he took with him ten horsemen and ten footmen and went to the children of Israel to Goshen. **42** And when they had come to the border of Egypt, the king's horse passed into a narrow place, elevated in the hollow part of the vineyard, fenced on both sides, the low, plain country being on the other side. **43** And the horses ran rapidly in that place and pressed each other, and the other horses pressed the king's horse. **44** And the king's horse fell into the low plain while the king was riding upon it, and when he fell the chariot turned over the king's face and the horse lay upon the king, and the king cried out, for his flesh was very sore. **45** And the flesh of the king was torn from him, and his bones were broken, and he could not ride, for this thing was from the Lord to him, for the Lord had heard the cries of his people the children of Israel and their affliction. **46** And his servants carried him upon their shoulders, a little at a time, and they brought him back to Egypt, and the horsemen who were with him came also back to Egypt. **47** And they placed him in his bed, and the king knew that his end was come to die, so Aparanith the queen his wife came and cried before the king, and the king wept a great weeping with her. **48** And all his nobles and servants came on that day and saw the king in that affliction and wept a great weeping with him. **49** And the princes of the king and all his counselors advised the king to cause one to reign in his stead in the land, whomsoever he should choose from his sons. **50** And the king had three sons and two daughters which Aparanith the queen his wife had borne to him, besides the king's children of concubines. **51** And these were their names, the firstborn Othri, the second Adikam, and the third Morion, and their sisters, the name of the elder Bathia and of the other Acuzi. **52** And Othri the firstborn of the king was an idiot, precipitate and hurried in his words. **53** But Adikam was a cunning and wise man and knowing in all the wisdom of Egypt, but of unseemly aspect, thick in flesh, and very short in stature; his height was one cubit. **54** And when the king saw Adikam his son intelligent and wise in all things, the king resolved that he should be king in his stead after his death. **55** And he took for him a wife Gedudah daughter of Abilot, and he was ten years old, and she bore unto him four sons. **56** And he afterward went and took three wives and begat eight sons and three daughters. **57** And the disorder greatly prevailed over the king, and his flesh stank like the flesh of a carcass cast upon the field in summer time, during the heat of the sun. **58** And when the king saw that his sickness had greatly strengthened itself over him, he ordered his son Adikam to be brought to him, and they made him king over the land in his place. **59** And at the end of three years, the king died, in shame, disgrace, and disgust, and his servants carried him and buried him in the sepulcher of the kings of Egypt in Zoan Mizraim. **60** But they embalmed him not as was usual with kings, for his flesh was putrid, and they could not approach to embalm him on account of the stench, so they buried him in haste. **61** For this evil was from the Lord to him, for the Lord had paid him back evil for the evil which in his days he had done to Israel. **62** And he died with terror and with shame, and his son Adikam reigned in his place.

CHAPTER 77

1 Adikam was twenty years old when he reigned over Egypt, he reigned four years. **2** In the two hundred and sixth year of Israel's going down to Egypt did Adikam reign over Egypt, but he continued not so long in his reign over Egypt as his fathers had continued their reigns. **3** For Melol his father reigned ninety-four years in Egypt, but he was ten years sick and died, for he had been wicked before the Lord. **4** And all the Egyptians called the name of Adikam Pharaoh like the name of his fathers, as was their custom to do in Egypt. **5** And all the wise men of Pharaoh called the name of Adikam Ahuz, for short is called Ahuz in the Egyptian language. **6** And Adikam was exceedingly ugly, and he was a cubit and a span and he had a great beard which reached to the soles of his feet. **7** And Pharaoh sat upon his father's throne to reign over Egypt, and he conducted the government of Egypt in his wisdom. **8** And while he reigned he exceeded his father and all the preceding kings in wickedness, and he increased his yoke over the children of Israel. **9** And he went with his servants to Goshen to the children of Israel, and he strengthened the labor over them and he said unto them, "Complete your work, each day's task, and let not your hands slacken from our work from this day forward as you did in the days of my father." **10** And he placed officers over them from among the children of Israel, and over these officers he placed taskmasters from among his servants. **11** And he placed over them a measure of bricks for them to do according to that number, day by day, and he turned back and went to Egypt.

12 At that time the task-masters of Pharaoh ordered the officers of the children of Israel according to the command of Pharaoh, saying, **13** "Thus says Pharaoh, 'Do your work each day, and finish your task, and observe the daily measure of bricks; diminish not anything. **14** And it will come to pass that if you are deficient in your daily bricks, I will put your young children in their stead.' " **15** And the task-masters of Egypt did so in those days as Pharaoh had ordered them. **16** And whenever any deficiency was found in the children of Israel's measure of their daily bricks, the task-masters of Pharaoh would go to the wives of the children of Israel and take infants of the children of Israel to the number of bricks deficient, they would take them by force from their mother's laps, and put them in the building instead of the bricks; **17** While their fathers and mothers were crying over them and weeping when they heard the weeping voices of their infants in the wall of the building. **18** And the task-masters prevailed over Israel, that the Israelites should place their children in the building, so that a man placed his son in the wall and put mortar over him, while his eyes wept over him, and his tears ran down upon his child. **19** And the task-masters of Egypt did so to the babes of Israel for many days, and no one pitied or had compassion over the babes of the children of Israel. **20** And the number of all the children killed in the building was two hundred and seventy, some whom they had built upon instead of the bricks which had been left deficient by their fathers, and some whom they had drawn out dead from the building. **21** And the labor imposed upon the children of Israel in the days of Adikam exceeded in hardship that which they performed in the days of his father. **22** And the children of Israel sighed every day on account of their heavy work, for they had said to themselves, "Behold when Pharaoh will die, his son will rise up and lighten our work!" **23** But they increased the latter work more than the former, and the children of Israel sighed at this and their cry ascended to God on account of their labor. **24** And God heard the voice of the children of Israel and their cry, in those days, and God remembered his covenant with them which he had made with Abraham, Isaac and Jacob. **25** And God saw the burden of the children of Israel, and their heavy work in those days, and he determined to deliver them. **26** And Moses the son of Amram was still confined in the dungeon in those days, in the house of Reuel the Midianite, and Zipporah the daughter of Reuel did support him with food secretly day by day. **27** And Moses was confined in the dungeon in the house of Reuel for ten years. **28** And at the end of ten years which was the first year of the reign of Pharaoh over Egypt, in the place of his father, **29** Zipporah said to her father Reuel, "No person inquires or seeks after the Hebrew man, whom you did bind in prison now ten years. **30** Now therefore, if it seems good in your sight, let us send and see whether he is living or dead," but her father knew not that she had supported him. **31** And Reuel her father answered and said to her, "Has ever such a thing happened that a man should be shut up in a prison without food for ten years, and that he should live?" **32** And Zipporah answered her father, saying, "Surely you have heard that the God of the Hebrews is great and awful, and does wonders for them at all times. **33** He it was who delivered Abraham from Ur of the Chaldeans, and Isaac from the sword of his father, and Jacob from the angel of the Lord who wrestled with him at the ford of Jabbuk. **34** Also with this man has he done many things, he delivered him from the river in Egypt and from the sword of Pharaoh, and from the children of Cush, so also can he deliver him from famine and make him live." **35** And the thing seemed good in the sight of Reuel, and he did according to the word of his daughter and sent to the dungeon to ascertain what became of Moses. **36** And he saw and, behold, the man Moses was living in the dungeon, standing upon his feet, praising and praying to the God of his ancestors. **37** And Reuel commanded Moses to be brought out of the dungeon, so they shaved him and he changed his prison garments and ate bread. **38** And afterward Moses went into the garden of Reuel which was behind the house, and he there prayed to the Lord his God, who had done mighty wonders for him. **39** And it was that while he prayed he looked opposite to him, and behold a sapphire stick was placed in the ground, which was planted in the midst of the garden. **40** And he approached the stick and he looked and, behold, the name of the Lord God of hosts was engraved thereon, written and developed upon the stick. **41** And he read it and stretched out his hand and he plucked it like a forest tree from the thicket, and the stick was in his hand. **42** And this is the stick with which all the works of our God were performed, after he had created heaven and earth, and all the host of them, seas, rivers and all their fishes. **43** And when God had driven Adam from the garden of Eden, he took the stick in his hand and went and tilled the ground from which he was taken. **44** And the stick came down to Noah and was given to Shem and his descendants, until it came into the hand of Abraham the Hebrew. **45** And when Abraham had given all he had to his son Isaac, he also gave to him this stick. **46** And when Jacob had fled to Padan-aram, he took it into his hand, and when he returned to his father he had not left it behind him. **47** Also when he went down to Egypt he took it into his hand and gave it to Joseph, one portion above his brethren, for Jacob had taken it by force from his brother Esau. **48** And after the death of Joseph, the nobles of Egypt came into the house of Joseph, and the stick came into the hand of Reuel the Midianite, and when he went out of Egypt, he took it in his hand and planted it in his garden. **49** And all the mighty men of the Kinites tried to pluck it when they endeavored to get Zipporah his daughter, but they were unsuccessful. **50** So that stick remained planted in the garden of Reuel, until he came who had a right to it and took it. **51** And when Reuel saw the stick in the hand of Moses, he wondered at it, and he gave him his daughter Zipporah for a wife.

CHAPTER 78

1 At that time died Baal Channan son of Achbor, king of Edom, and was buried in his house in the land of Edom. **2** And after his death the children of Esau sent to the land of Edom and took from there a man who was in Edom, whose name was Hadad, and they made him king over them in the place of Baal Channan, their king. **3** And Hadad reigned over the children of Edom forty-eight years. **4** And when he reigned he resolved to fight against the children of Moab, to bring them under the power of the children of Esau as they were before, but he was not able, because the children of Moab heard this thing, and they rose up and hastened to elect a king over them from among their brethren. **5** And they afterward gathered together a great people and sent to the children of Ammon their brethren for help to fight against Hadad king of Edom. **6** And Hadad heard the thing which the children of Moab had done, and was greatly afraid of them, and refrained from fighting against them. **7** In those days Moses, the son of Amram, in Midian, took Zipporah, the daughter of Reuel the Midianite, for a wife. **8** And Zipporah walked in the ways of the daughters of Jacob, she was nothing short of the righteousness of Sarah, Rebecca, Rachel and Leah. **9** And Zipporah conceived and bore a son and he called his name Gershom, for he said, "I was a stranger in a foreign land"; but he circumcised not his foreskin, at the command of Reuel his father-in-law. **10** And she conceived again and bore a son, but circumcised his foreskin, and called his name Eliezer, for Moses said, "Because the God of my fathers was my help and delivered me from the sword of Pharaoh." **11** And Pharaoh king of Egypt greatly increased the labor of the children of Israel in those days and continued to make his yoke heavier upon the children of Israel. **12** And he ordered a proclamation to be made in Egypt, saying, "Give no more straw to the people to make bricks with, let them go and gather themselves straw as they can find it. **13** Also the tale of bricks which they will make let them give each day, and diminish nothing from them, for they are idle in their work." **14** And the children of Israel heard this, and they mourned and sighed, and they cried unto the Lord on account of the bitterness of their souls. **15** And the Lord heard the cries of the children of Israel and saw the oppression with which the Egyptians oppressed them. **16** And the Lord was jealous of his people and his inheritance, and heard their voice, and he resolved to take them out of the affliction of Egypt, to give them the land of Canaan for a possession.

CHAPTER 79

1 And in those days Moses was feeding the flock of Reuel the Midianite his father-in-law, beyond the wilderness of Sin, and the stick which he took from his father-in-law was in his hand. **2** And it came to pass one day that a kid of goats strayed from the flock, and Moses pursued it and it came to the mountain of God to Horeb. **3** And when he came to Horeb, the Lord appeared there unto him in the bush, and he found the bush burning with fire, but the fire had no power over the bush to consume it. **4** And Moses was greatly astonished at this sight, why the bush was not consumed, and he approached to see this mighty thing, and the Lord called unto Moses out of the fire and commanded him to go down to Egypt, to Pharaoh king of Egypt, to send the children of Israel from his service. **5** And the Lord said unto Moses, "Go, return to Egypt, for all those men who sought your life are dead, and you will speak unto Pharaoh to send out the children of Israel from his land." 6 And the Lord commanded him to do signs and wonders in Egypt before the eyes of Pharaoh and the eyes of his subjects, in order that they might believe that the Lord had sent him. 7 And Moses hearkened to all that the Lord had commanded him, and he returned to his father-in-law and told him the thing, and Reuel said to him, "Go in peace." 8 And Moses rose up to go to Egypt, and he took his wife and sons with him, and he was at an inn in the road, and an angel of God came down, and sought an occasion against him. 9 And he wished to kill him on account of his firstborn son, because he had not circumcised him, and had transgressed the covenant which the Lord had made with Abraham. 10 For Moses had hearkened to the words of his father-in-law which he had spoken to him, not to circumcise his firstborn son, therefore he circumcised him not. 11 And Zipporah saw the angel of the Lord seeking an occasion against Moses, and she knew that this thing was owing to his not having circumcised her son Gershom. 12 And Zipporah hastened and took of the sharp rock stones that were there, and she circumcised her son, and delivered her husband and her son from the hand of the angel of the Lord. 13 And Aaron the son of Amram, the brother of Moses, was in Egypt walking at the riverside on that day. 14 And the Lord appeared to him in that place, and he said to him, "Go now toward Moses in the wilderness," and he went and met him in the mountain of God, and he kissed him. 15 And Aaron lifted up his eyes and saw Zipporah the wife of Moses and her children, and he said unto Moses, "Who are these unto you?" 16 And Moses said unto him, "They are my wife and sons, which God gave to me in Midian; and the thing grieved Aaron on account of the woman and her children. 17 And Aaron said to Moses, "Send away the woman and her children that they may go to her father's house," and Moses hearkened to the words of Aaron, and did so. 18 And Zipporah returned with her children, and they went to the house of Reuel, and remained there until the time arrived when the Lord had visited his people and brought them out from Egypt from the hand of Pharaoh. 19 And Moses and Aaron came to Egypt to the community of the children of Israel, and they spoke to them all the words of the Lord, and the people rejoiced an exceedingly great

rejoicing. 20 And Moses and Aaron rose up early on the next day, and they went to the house of Pharaoh, and they took in their hands the stick of God. 21 And when they came to the king's gate, two young lions were confined there with iron instruments, and no person went out or came in from before them, unless those whom the king ordered to come, when the conjurors came and withdrew the lions by their incantations, and this brought them to the king. 22 And Moses hastened and lifted up the stick upon the lions, and he loosed them, and Moses and Aaron came into the king's house. 23 The lions also came with them in joy, and they followed them and rejoiced as a dog rejoices over his master when he comes from the field. 24 And when Pharaoh saw this thing he was astonished at it, and he was greatly terrified at the report, for their appearance was like the appearance of the children of God. 25 And Pharaoh said to Moses, "What do you require?" And they answered him, saying, "The Lord God of the Hebrews has sent us to you, to say, 'send out my people that they may serve me.' " 26 And when Pharaoh heard their words he was greatly terrified before them, and he said to them, "Go today and come back to me tomorrow," and they did according to the word of the king. 27 And when they had gone Pharaoh sent for Balaam the magician and to Jannes and Jambres his sons, and to all the magicians and conjurors and counsellors which belonged to the king, and they all came and sat before the king. 28 And the king told them all the words which Moses and his brother Aaron had spoken to him, and the magicians said to the king, "But how did the men come to you with the lions which were confined at the gate?" 29 And the king said, "Because they lifted up their rod against the lions and loosed them, and came to me, and the lions also rejoiced at them as a dog rejoices to meet his master." 30 And Balaam the son of Beor the magician answered the king, saying, "These are none else than magicians like ourselves. 31 Now therefore send for them, and let them come and we will try them," and the king did so. 32 And in the morning Pharaoh sent for Moses and Aaron to come before the king, and they took the rod of God, and came to the king and spoke to him, saying, 33 "Thus said the Lord God of the Hebrews, 'send my people that they may serve me.' " 34 And the king said to them, "But who will believe you that you are the messengers of God and that you come to me by his order?

35 Now therefore give a wonder or sign in this matter, and then the words which you speak will be believed." 36 And Aaron hastened and threw the rod out of his hand before Pharaoh and before his servants, and the rod turned into a serpent. 37 And the sorcerers saw this and they cast each man his rod upon the ground and they became serpents. 38 And the serpent of Aaron's rod lifted up its head and opened its mouth to swallow the rods of the magicians. 39 And Balaam the magician answered and said, "This thing has been from the days of old, that a serpent should swallow its fellow, and that living things devour each other. 40 Now therefore restore it to a rod as it was at first, and we will also restore our rods as they were at first, and if your rod will swallow our rods, then will we know that the Spirit of God is in you, and if not, you are only a craftsman like unto ourselves." 41 And Aaron hastened and stretched out his hand and caught hold of the serpent's tail and it became a rod in his hand, and the sorcerers did the like with their rods, and they took hold, each man of the tail of his serpent, and they became rods as at first. 42 And when they were restored to rods, the rod of Aaron swallowed up their rods. 43 And when the king saw this thing, he ordered the book of records that related to the kings of Egypt, to be brought, and they brought the book of records, the chronicles of the kings of Egypt, in which all the idols of Egypt were inscribed, for they thought of finding therein the name of Jehovah, but they found it not. 44 And Pharaoh said to Moses and Aaron, "Behold, I have not found the name of your God written in this book, and his name I know not." 45 And the counsellors and wise men answered the king, "We have heard that the God of the Hebrews is a son of the wise, the son of ancient kings." 46 And Pharaoh turned to Moses and Aaron and said to them, "I know not the Lord whom you have declared, neither will I send his people." 47 And they answered and said to the king, "The Lord God of Gods is his name, and he proclaimed his name over us from the days of our ancestors, and sent us, saying, 'Go to Pharaoh and say unto him, *Send my people that they may serve me.*' 48 Now therefore send us, that we may take a journey for three days in the wilderness, and there may sacrifice to him, for from the days of our going down to Egypt, he has not taken from our hands either burnt offering, oblation or sacrifice, and if you will not send us, his anger will be kindled against you, and he will smite

Egypt either with the plague or with the sword." 49 And Pharaoh said to them, "Tell me now his power and his might"; and they said to him, "He created the heaven and the earth, the seas and all their fishes, he formed the light, created the darkness, caused rain upon the earth and watered it, and made the herbage and grass to sprout, he created man and beast and the animals of the forest, the birds of the air and the fish of the sea, and by his mouth they live and die. 50 Surely, he created you in your mother's womb, and put into you the breath of life, and reared you and placed you upon the royal throne of Egypt, and he will take your breath and soul from you, and return you to the ground from where you were taken." 51 And the anger of the king was kindled at their words, and he said to them, "But who among all the gods of the nations can do this? My river is mine own, and I have made it for myself." 52 And he drove them from him, and he ordered the labor upon Israel to be more severe than it was yesterday and before. 53 And Moses and Aaron went out from the king's presence, and they saw the children of Israel in an evil condition for the task-masters had made their labor exceedingly heavy. 54 And Moses returned to the Lord and said, "Why have you mistreated your people? For since I came to speak to Pharaoh the reason you sent me, he has exceedingly mistreated the children of Israel." 55 And the Lord said to Moses, "Behold, you will see that with an outstretched hand and heavy plagues, Pharaoh will send the children of Israel from his land." 56 And Moses and Aaron dwelt among their brethren the children of Israel in Egypt. 57 And as for the children of Israel the Egyptians embittered their lives, with the heavy work which they imposed upon them.

CHAPTER 80

1 And at the end of two years, the Lord again sent Moses to Pharaoh to bring out the children of Israel, and to send them out of the land of Egypt. 2 And Moses went and came to the house of Pharaoh, and he spoke to him the words of the Lord who had sent him, but Pharaoh would not hearken to the voice of the Lord, and God roused his might in Egypt upon Pharaoh and his subjects, and God smote Pharaoh and his people with very great and sore plagues. 3 And the Lord sent by the hand of Aaron and turned all the waters of Egypt into blood, with all their streams and rivers. 4 And when an Egyptian came to drink and

draw water, he looked into his pitcher, and behold all the water was turned into blood; and when he came to drink from his cup the water in the cup became blood. **5** And when a woman kneaded her dough and cooked her victuals, their appearance was turned to that of blood. **6** And the Lord sent again and caused all their waters to bring out frogs, and all the frogs came into the houses of the Egyptians. **7** And when the Egyptians drank, their bellies were filled with frogs and they danced in their bellies as they dance when in the river. **8** And all their drinking water and cooking water turned to frogs, also when they lay in their beds their perspiration bred frogs. **9** Notwithstanding all this, the anger of the Lord did not turn from them, and his hand was stretched out against all the Egyptians to smite them with every heavy plague. **10** And he sent and smote their dust to lice, and the lice became in Egypt to the height of two cubits upon the earth. **11** The lice were also very numerous, in the flesh of man and beast, in all the inhabitants of Egypt, also upon the king and queen the Lord sent the lice, and it grieved Egypt exceedingly on account of the lice. **12** Notwithstanding this, the anger of the Lord did not turn away, and his hand was still stretched out over Egypt. **13** And the Lord sent all kinds of beasts of the field into Egypt, and they came and destroyed all Egypt, man and beast, and trees, and all things that were in Egypt. **14** And the Lord sent fiery serpents, scorpions, mice, weasels, toads, together with others creeping in dust. **15** Flies, hornets, fleas, bugs and gnats, each swarm according to its kind. **16** And all reptiles and winged animals according to their kind came to Egypt and grieved the Egyptians exceedingly. **17** And the fleas and flies came into the eyes and ears of the Egyptians. **18** And the hornet came upon them and drove them away, and they removed from it into their inner rooms, and it pursued them. **19** And when the Egyptians hid themselves on account of the swarm of animals, they locked their doors after them, and God ordered the Sulanuth which was in the sea, to come up and go into Egypt. **20** And she had long arms, ten cubits in length of the cubit of a man. **21** And she went upon the roofs and uncovered the raftering and flooring and cut them and stretched out her arm into the house and removed the lock and the bolt, and opened the houses of Egypt. **22** Afterward came the swarm of animals into the houses of Egypt, and the swarm of animals destroyed the Egyptians, and it grieved them exceedingly. **23** Notwithstanding this the anger of the Lord did not turn away from the Egyptians, and his hand was yet stretched out against them. **24** And God sent the pestilence, and the pestilence pervaded Egypt, in the horses and asses, and in the camels, in herds of oxen and sheep and in man. **25** And when the Egyptians rose up early in the morning to take their cattle to pasture they found all their cattle dead. **26** And there remained of the cattle of the Egyptians only one in ten, and of the cattle belonging to Israel in Goshen not one died. **27** And God sent a burning inflammation in the flesh of the Egyptians, which burst their skins, and it became a severe itch in all the Egyptians from the soles of their feet to the crowns of their heads. **28** And many boils were in their flesh, that their flesh wasted away until they became rotten and putrid. **29** Notwithstanding this, the anger of the Lord did not turn away, and his hand was still stretched out over all Egypt. **30** And the Lord sent a very heavy hail, which smote their vines and broke their fruit trees and dried them up that they fell upon them. **31** Also every green herb became dry and perished, for a mingling fire descended amidst the hail, therefore the hail and the fire consumed all things. **32** Also men and beasts that were found abroad perished of the flames of fire and of the hail, and all the young lions were exhausted. **33** And the Lord sent and brought numerous locusts into Egypt, the Chasel, Salom, Chargol, and Chagole, locusts each of its kind, which devoured all that the hail had left remaining. **34** Then the Egyptians rejoiced at the locusts, although they consumed the produce of the field, and they caught them in abundance and salted them for food. **35** And the Lord turned a mighty wind of the sea which took away all the locusts, even those that were salted, and thrust them into the Red Sea; not one locust remained within the boundaries of Egypt. **36** And God sent darkness upon Egypt, that the whole land of Egypt and Pathros became dark for three days, so that a man could not see his hand when he lifted it to his mouth. **37** At that time died many of the people of Israel who had rebelled against the Lord and who would not hearken to Moses and Aaron and believed not in them that God had sent them. **38** And who had said, "We will not go out from Egypt lest we perish with hunger in a desolate wilderness," and who would not hearken to the voice of Moses. **39** And the

Lord plagued them in the three days of darkness, and the Israelites buried them in those days, without the Egyptians knowing of them or rejoicing over them. **40** And the darkness was very great in Egypt for three days, and any person who was standing when the darkness came, remained standing in his place, and he that was sitting remained sitting, and he that was lying continued lying in the same state, and he that was walking remained sitting upon the ground in the same spot; and this thing happened to all the Egyptians, until the darkness had passed away. **41** And the days of darkness passed away, and the Lord sent Moses and Aaron to the children of Israel, saying, "Celebrate your feast and make your Passover, for behold I come in the midst of the night among all the Egyptians, and I will smite all their firstborn, from the firstborn of a man to the firstborn of a beast, and when I see your Passover, I will pass over you." **42** And the children of Israel did according to all that the Lord had commanded Moses and Aaron, thus did they in that night. **43** And it came to pass in the middle of the night, that the Lord went out in the midst of Egypt, and smote all the firstborn of the Egyptians, from the firstborn of man to the firstborn of beast. **44** And Pharaoh rose up in the night, he and all his servants and all the Egyptians, and there was a great cry throughout Egypt in that night, for there was not a house in which there was not a corpse. **45** Also the likenesses of the firstborn of Egypt, which were carved in the walls at their houses, were destroyed and fell to the ground. **46** Even the bones of their firstborn who had died before this and whom they had buried in their houses, were raked up by the dogs of Egypt on that night and dragged before the Egyptians and cast before them. **47** And all the Egyptians saw this evil which had suddenly come upon them, and all the Egyptians cried out with a loud voice. **48** And all the families of Egypt wept upon that night, each man for his son and each man for his daughter, being the firstborn, and the tumult of Egypt was heard at a distance on that night. **49** And Bathia the daughter of Pharaoh went out with the king on that night to seek Moses and Aaron in their houses, and they found them in their houses, eating and drinking and rejoicing with all Israel. **50** And Bathia said to Moses, "Is this the reward for the good which I have done to you, who have reared you and stretched you out, and you have brought this evil upon me and my father's house?" **51** And

Moses said to her, "Surely ten plagues did the Lord bring upon Egypt; did any evil accrue to you from any of them? Did one of them affect you?" And she said, "No." **52** And Moses said to her, "Although you are the firstborn to your mother, you will not die, and no evil will reach you in the midst of Egypt." **53** And she said, "What advantage is it to me, when I see the king, my brother, and all his household and subjects in this evil, whose firstborn perish with all the firstborn of Egypt?" **54** And Moses said to her, "Surely your brother and his household, and subjects, the families of Egypt, would not hearken to the words of the Lord, therefore did this evil come upon them." **55** And Pharaoh king of Egypt approached Moses and Aaron, and some of the children of Israel who were with them in that place, and he prayed to them, saying, **56** "Rise up and take your brethren, all the children of Israel who are in the land, with their sheep and oxen, and all belonging to them, they will leave nothing remaining, only pray for me to the Lord your God." **57** And Moses said to Pharaoh, "Behold, though you are your mother's firstborn, yet fear not, for you will not die, for the Lord has commanded that you will live, in order to show you his great might and strong stretched out arm." **58** And Pharaoh ordered the children of Israel to be sent away, and all the Egyptians strengthened themselves to send them, for they said, "We are all perishing." **59** And all the Egyptians sent the Israelites out, with great riches, sheep and oxen and precious things, according to the oath of the Lord between him and our Father Abraham. **60** And the children of Israel delayed going out at night, and when the Egyptians came to them to bring them out, they said to them, "Are we thieves, that we should go out at night?" **61** And the children of Israel asked of the Egyptians, vessels of silver, and vessels of gold, and garments, and the children of Israel stripped the Egyptians. **62** And Moses hastened and rose up and went to the river of Egypt and brought up from there the coffin of Joseph and took it with him. **63** The children of Israel also brought up, each man his father's coffin with him, and each man the coffins of his tribe.

CHAPTER 81

1 And the children of Israel journeyed from Rameses to Succoth, about six hundred thousand men on foot, besides the little ones and their wives. **2** Also a mixed multitude went up with them, and flocks and herds, even much cattle. **3** And the sojourning of the children of Israel, who dwelt in the land of Egypt in hard labor, was two hundred and ten years. **4** And at the end of two hundred and ten years, the Lord brought out the children of Israel from Egypt with a strong hand. **5** And the children of Israel traveled from Egypt and from Goshen and from Rameses and encamped in Succoth on the fifteenth day of the first month. **6** And the Egyptians buried all their firstborn whom the Lord had smitten, and all the Egyptians buried their slain for three days. **7** And the children of Israel traveled from Succoth and encamped in Ethom, at the end of the wilderness. **8** And on the third day after the Egyptians had buried their firstborn, many men rose up from Egypt and went after Israel to make them return to Egypt, for they repented that they had sent the Israelites away from their servitude. **9** And one man said to his neighbor, "Surely Moses and Aaron spoke to Pharaoh, saying, 'We will go a three days' journey in the wilderness and sacrifice to the Lord our God.' **10** Now therefore let us rise up early in the morning and cause them to return, and it will be that if they return with us to Egypt to their masters, then will we know that there is faith in them, but if they will not return, then will we fight with them, and make them come back with great power and a strong hand." **11** And all the nobles of Pharaoh rose up in the morning, and with them about seven hundred thousand men, and they went out from Egypt on that day, and came to the place where the children of Israel were. **12** And all the Egyptians saw and behold Moses and Aaron and all the children of Israel were sitting before Pi-hahiroth, eating and drinking and celebrating the feast of the Lord. **13** And all the Egyptians said to the children of Israel, "Surely you said, 'We will go on a journey for three days in the wilderness and sacrifice to our God and return.' **14** Now therefore this day makes five days since you went, why do you not return to your masters?" **15** And Moses and Aaron answered them, saying, "Because the Lord our God has testified to us, saying, 'You will never return to Egypt,' but we will journey ourselves to a land flowing with milk and honey, as the Lord our God had sworn to our ancestors to give to us." **16** And when the nobles of Egypt saw that the children of Israel did not hearken to them, to return to Egypt, they girded themselves to fight with Israel. **17** And the Lord strengthened the hearts

of the children of Israel over the Egyptians, that they gave them a severe beating, and the battle was sore upon the Egyptians, and all the Egyptians fled from before the children of Israel, for many of them perished by the hand of Israel. **18** And the nobles of Pharaoh went to Egypt and told Pharaoh, saying, "The children of Israel have fled, and will no more return to Egypt, and in this manner did Moses and Aaron speak to us." **19** And Pharaoh heard this thing, and his heart and the hearts of all his subjects were turned against Israel, and they repented that they had sent Israel; and all the Egyptians advised Pharaoh to pursue the children of Israel to make them come back to their burdens. **20** And they said each man to his brother, "What is this which we have done, that we have sent Israel from our servitude?" **21** And the Lord strengthened the hearts of all the Egyptians to pursue the Israelites, for the Lord desired to overthrow the Egyptians in the Red Sea. **22** And Pharaoh rose up and harnessed his chariot, and he ordered all the Egyptians to assemble, not one man was left excepting the little ones and the women. **23** And all the Egyptians went out with Pharaoh to pursue the children of Israel, and the camp of Egypt was an exceedingly large and heavy camp, about ten hundred thousand men. **24** And the whole of this camp went and pursued the children of Israel to bring them back to Egypt, and they reached them encamping by the Red Sea. **25** And the children of Israel lifted up their eyes, and beheld all the Egyptians pursuing them, and the children of Israel were greatly terrified at them, and the children of Israel cried to the Lord. **26** And on account of the Egyptians, the children of Israel divided themselves into four divisions, and they were divided in their opinions, for they were afraid of the Egyptians, and Moses spoke to each of them. **27** The first division was of the children of Reuben, Simeon, and Issachar, and they resolved to cast themselves into the sea, for they were exceedingly afraid of the Egyptians. **28** And Moses said to them, "Fear not, stand still and see the salvation of the Lord which He will effect this day for you." **29** The second division was of the children of Zebulun, Benjamin and Naphtali, and they resolved to go back to Egypt with the Egyptians. **30** And Moses said to them, "Fear not, for as you have seen the Egyptians this day, so will you see them no more forever." **31** The third division was of the children of Judah and Joseph, and they resolved to go to meet the Egyptians to fight with them. 32 And Moses said to them, "Stand in your places, for the Lord will fight for you, and you will remain silent." 33 And the fourth division was of the children of Levi, Gad, and Asher, and they resolved to go into the midst of the Egyptians to confound them, and Moses said to them, "Remain in your stations and fear not, only call unto the Lord that he may save you out of their hands." 34 After this Moses rose up from amidst the people, and he prayed to the Lord and said, 35 "O Lord God of the whole earth, save now your people whom you did bring out from Egypt, and let not the Egyptians boast that power and might are theirs." 36 So the Lord said to Moses, "Why do you cry unto me? Speak to the children of Israel that they will proceed, and you will stretch out your rod upon the sea and divide it, and the children of Israel will pass through it." 37 And Moses did so, and he lifted up his rod upon the sea and divided it. 38 And the waters of the sea were divided into twelve parts, and the children of Israel passed through on foot, with shoes, as a man would pass through a prepared road. 39 And the Lord manifested to the children of Israel his wonders in Egypt and in the sea by the hand of Moses and Aaron. 40 And when the children of Israel had entered the sea, the Egyptians came after them, and the waters of the sea resumed upon them, and they all sank in the water, and not one man was left excepting Pharaoh, who gave thanks to the Lord and believed in him, therefore the Lord did not cause him to perish at that time with the Egyptians. 41 And the Lord ordered an angel to take him from among the Egyptians, who cast him upon the land of Ninevah and he reigned over it for a long time. 42 And on that day the Lord saved Israel from the hand of Egypt, and all the children of Israel saw that the Egyptians had perished, and they beheld the great hand of the Lord, in what he had performed in Egypt and in the sea. 43 Then sang Moses and the children of Israel this song unto the Lord, on the day when the Lord caused the Egyptians to fall before them. 44 And all Israel sang in concert, saying, "I will sing to the Lord for He is greatly exalted, the horse and his rider has he cast into the sea; behold it is written in the book of the law of God." 45 After this the children of Israel proceeded on their journey, and encamped in Marah, and the Lord gave to the children of Israel statutes and judgments in that place in Marah, and the Lord commanded the children of Israel to walk in all his ways and to serve him. 46 And they journeyed from Marah and came to Elim, and in Elim were twelve springs of water and seventy date trees, and the children encamped there by the waters. 47 And they journeyed from Elim and came to the wilderness of Sin, on the fifteenth day of the second month after their departure from Egypt. 48 At that time the Lord gave the manna to the children of Israel to eat, and the Lord caused food to rain from heaven for the children of Israel day by day. 49 And the children of Israel ate the manna for forty years, all the days that they were in the wilderness, until they came to the land of Canaan to possess it. 50 And they proceeded from the wilderness of Sin and encamped in Alush. 51 And they proceeded from Alush and encamped in Rephidim. 52 And when the children of Israel were in Rephidim, Amalek the son of Eliphaz, the son of Esau, the brother of Zepho, came to fight with Israel. 53 And he brought with him eight hundred and one thousand men, magicians and conjurers, and he prepared for battle with Israel in Rephidim. 54 And they carried on a great and severe battle against Israel, and the Lord delivered Amalek and his people into the hands of Moses and the children of Israel, and into the hand of Joshua, the son of Nun, the Ephrathite, the servant of Moses. 55 And the children of Israel smote Amalek and his people at the edge of the sword, but the battle was very sore upon the children of Israel. 56 And the Lord said to Moses, "Write this thing as a memorial for you in a book, and place it in the hand of Joshua, the son of Nun, your servant, and you will command the children of Israel, saying, 'When you will come to the land of Canaan, you will utterly efface the remembrance of Amalek from under heaven.' " 57 And Moses did so, and he took the book and wrote upon it these words, saying, 58 "Remember what Amalek has done to you in the road when you went out from Egypt. 59 Who met you in the road and smote your rear, even those that were feeble behind you when you were faint and weary. 60 Therefore it will be when the Lord your God will have given you rest from all your surrounding enemies in the land which the Lord your God giveth you for an inheritance, to possess it, that you will blot out the remembrance of Amalek from under heaven, you will not forget it. 61 And the king who will have pity on Amalek, or upon his memory or upon his seed, behold I will require it of him, and I will cut him off from among his people." 62 And Moses wrote all these things in a book, and he enjoined the children of Israel respecting all these matters.

CHAPTER 82

1 And the children of Israel proceeded from Rephidim and they encamped in the wilderness of Sinai, in the third month from their going out from Egypt. 2 At that time came Reuel the Midianite, the father-in-law of Moses, with Zipporah his daughter and her two sons, for he had heard of the wonders of the Lord which he had done to Israel, that he had delivered them from the hand of Egypt. 3 And Reuel came to Moses to the wilderness where he was encamped, where was the mountain of God. 4 And Moses went out to meet his father-in-law with great honor, and all Israel was with him. 5 And Reuel and his children remained among the Israelites for many days, and Reuel knew the Lord from that day forward. 6 And in the third month from the children of Israel's departure from Egypt, on the sixth day thereof, the Lord gave to Israel the ten commandments on Mount Sinai. 7 And all Israel heard all these commandments, and all Israel rejoiced exceedingly in the Lord on that day. 8 And the glory of the Lord rested upon Mount Sinai, and he called to Moses, and Moses came in the midst of a cloud and ascended the mountain. 9 And Moses was upon the mount forty days and forty nights; he ate no bread and drank no water, and the Lord instructed him in the statutes and judgments in order to teach the children of Israel. 10 And the Lord wrote the ten commandments which he had commanded the children of Israel upon two tablets of stone, which he gave to Moses to command the children of Israel. 11 And at the end of forty days and forty nights, when the Lord had finished speaking to Moses on Mount Sinai, then the Lord gave to Moses the tablets of stone, written with the finger of God. 12 And when the children of Israel saw that Moses tarried to come down from the mount, they gathered round Aaron, and said, "As for this man Moses we know not what has become of him. 13 Now therefore rise up, make unto us a god who will go before us, so that you will not die." 14 And Aaron was greatly afraid of the people, and he ordered them to bring him gold and he made it into a molten calf for the people. 15 And the Lord said to Moses, before he had come down from the mount, "Get you

down, for your people whom you did bring out from Egypt have corrupted themselves. 16 They have made to themselves a molten calf, and have bowed down to it, now therefore leave me, that I may consume them from off the earth, for they are a stiffnecked people." 17 And Moses beseeched the countenance of the Lord, and he prayed to the Lord for the people on account of the calf which they had made, and he afterward descended from the mount and in his hands were the two tablets of stone, which God had given him to command the Israelites. 18 And when Moses approached the camp and saw the calf which the people had made, the anger of Moses was kindled, and he broke the tablets under the mount. 19 And Moses came to the camp and he took the calf and burned it with fire, and ground it until it became fine dust, and strewed it upon the water and gave it to the Israelites to drink. 20 And there died of the people by the swords of each other about three thousand men who had made the calf. 21 And the next day Moses said to the people, "I will go up to the Lord, perhaps I may make atonement for your sins which you have sinned to the Lord." 22 And Moses again went up to the Lord, and he remained with the Lord forty days and forty nights. 23 And during the forty days did Moses entreat the Lord in behalf of the children of Israel, and the Lord hearkened to the prayer of Moses, and the Lord was entreated of him on behalf of Israel. 24 Then spoke the Lord to Moses to hew two stone tablets and to bring them up to the Lord, who would write upon them the ten commandments. 25 Now Moses did so, and he came down and hewed the two tablets and went up to Mount Sinai to the Lord, and the Lord wrote the ten commandments upon the tablets. 26 And Moses remained yet with the Lord forty days and forty nights, and the Lord instructed him in statutes and judgments to impart to Israel. 27 And the Lord commanded him respecting the children of Israel that they should make a sanctuary for the Lord, that his name might rest therein, and the Lord showed him the likeness of the sanctuary and the likeness of all its vessels. 28 And at the end of the forty days, Moses came down from the mount and the two tablets were in his hand. 29 And Moses came to the children of Israel and spoke to them all the words of the Lord, and he taught them laws, statutes and judgments which the Lord had taught him. 30 And Moses told the children of Israel the word of the Lord, that a sanctuary should be made for him, to dwell among the children of Israel. 31 And the people rejoiced greatly at all the good which the Lord had spoken to them, through Moses, and they said, "We will do all that the Lord has spoken to you." 32 And the people rose up like one man and they made generous offerings to the sanctuary of the Lord, and each man brought the offering of the Lord for the work of the sanctuary, and for all its service. 33 And all the children of Israel brought each man of all that was found in his possession for the work of the sanctuary of the Lord, gold, silver and brass, and everything that was serviceable for the sanctuary. 34 And all the wise men who were practiced in work came and made the sanctuary of the Lord, according to all that the Lord had commanded, every man in the work in which he had been practiced; and all the wise men in heart made the sanctuary, and its furniture and all the vessels for the holy service, as the Lord had commanded Moses. 35 And the work of the sanctuary of the tabernacle was completed at the end of five months, and the children of Israel did all that the Lord had commanded Moses. 36 And they brought the sanctuary and all its furniture to Moses; like unto the representation which the Lord had shown to Moses, so did the children of Israel. 37 And Moses saw the work and, behold, they did it as the Lord had commanded him, so Moses blessed them.

CHAPTER 83

1 And in the twelfth month, in the twenty-third day of the month, Moses took Aaron and his sons, and he dressed them in their garments, and anointed them and did unto them as the Lord had commanded him, and Moses brought up all the offerings which the Lord had on that day commanded him. 2 Moses afterward took Aaron and his sons and said to them, "For seven days will you remain at the door of the tabernacle, for thus am I commanded." 3 And Aaron and his sons did all that the Lord had commanded them through Moses, and they remained for seven days at the door of the tabernacle. 4 And on the eighth day, being the first day of the first month, in the second year from the Israelites' departure from Egypt, Moses erected the sanctuary, and Moses put up all the furniture of the tabernacle and all the furniture of the sanctuary, and he did all that the Lord had commanded him. 5 And Moses called to Aaron and his sons, and they brought the burnt offering and the sin offering for themselves and the children of Israel, as the Lord had commanded Moses. 6 On that day the two sons of Aaron, Nadab and Abihu, took strange fire and brought it before the Lord who had not commanded them, and a fire went out from before the Lord, and consumed them, and they died before the Lord on that day. 7 Then on the day when Moses had completed to erect the sanctuary, the princes of the children of Israel began to bring their offerings before the Lord for the dedication of the altar. 8 And they brought up their offerings each prince for one day, a prince each day for twelve days. 9 And all the offerings which they brought, each man in his day, one silver charger weighing one hundred and thirty shekels, one silver bowl of seventy shekels after the shekel of the sanctuary, both of them full of fine flour, mingled with oil for a meat offering. 10 One spoon, weighing ten shekels of gold, full of incense. 11 One young bullock, one ram, one lamb of the first year for a burnt offering. 12 And one kid of the goats for a sin offering. 13 And for a sacrifice of peace offering, two oxen, five rams, five he-goats, five lambs of a year old. 14 Thus did the twelve princes of Israel day by day, each man in his day. 15 And it was after this, in the thirteenth day of the month, that Moses commanded the children of Israel to observe the Passover. 16 And the children of Israel kept the Passover in its season in the fourteenth day of the month, as the Lord had commanded Moses, so did the children of Israel. 17 And in the second month, on the first day thereof, the Lord spoke unto Moses, saying, 18 "Number the heads of all the males of the children of Israel from twenty years old and upward, you and your brother Aaron and the twelve princes of Israel." 19 And Moses did so, and Aaron came with the twelve princes of Israel, and they numbered the children of Israel in the wilderness of Sinai. 20 And the numbers of the children of Israel by the houses of their fathers, from twenty years old and upward, were six hundred and three thousand, five hundred and fifty. 21 But the children of Levi were not numbered among their brethren the children of Israel. 22 And the number of all the males of the children of Israel from one month old and upward, was twenty-two thousand, two hundred and seventy-three. 23 And the number of the children of Levi from one month old and above, was twenty-two thousand. 24 And Moses placed the priests and

the Levites each man to his service and to his burden to serve the sanctuary of the tabernacle, as the Lord had commanded Moses. **25** And on the twentieth day of the month, the cloud was taken away from the tabernacle of testimony. **26** At that time the children of Israel continued their journey from the wilderness of Sinai, and they took a journey of three days, and the cloud rested upon the wilderness of Paran; there the anger of the Lord was kindled against Israel, for they had provoked the Lord in asking him for meat, that they might eat. **27** And the Lord hearkened to their voice and gave them meat which they ate for one month. **28** But after this the anger of the Lord was kindled against them, and he smote them with a great slaughter, and they were buried there in that place. **29** And the children of Israel called that place Kebroth Hattaavah, because there they buried the people that lusted after flesh. **30** And they departed from Kebroth Hattaavah and pitched in Hazeroth, which is in the wilderness of Paran. **31** And while the children of Israel were in Hazeroth, the anger of the Lord was kindled against Miriam on account of Moses, and she became leprous, white as snow. **32** And she was confined without the camp for seven days, until she had been received again after her leprosy. **33** The children of Israel afterward departed from Hazeroth and pitched in the end of the wilderness of Paran. **34** At that time, the Lord spoke to Moses to send twelve men from the children of Israel, one man to a tribe, to go and explore the land of Canaan. **35** And Moses sent the twelve men, and they came to the land of Canaan to search and examine it, and they explored the whole land from the wilderness of Sin to Rechob as you come to Chamoth. **36** And at the end of forty days they came to Moses and Aaron, and they brought him word as it was in their hearts, and ten of the men brought up an evil report to the children of Israel, of the land which they had explored, saying, "It is better for us to return to Egypt than to go to this land, a land that consumes its inhabitants." **37** But Joshua the son of Nun, and Caleb the son of Jephuneh, who were of those that explored the land, said, "The land is exceedingly good. **38** If the Lord delight in us, then he will bring us to this land and give it to us, for it is a land flowing with milk and honey." **39** But the children of Israel would not hearken to them, and they hearkened to the words of the ten men who had brought up an evil report of the land. **40** And

the Lord heard the murmurings of the children of Israel and he was angry and swore, saying, **41** "Surely not one man of this wicked generation will see the land from twenty years old and upward excepting Caleb the son of Jephuneh and Joshua the son of Nun. **42** But surely this wicked generation will perish in this wilderness, and their children will come to the land and they will possess it"; so the anger of the Lord was kindled against Israel, and he made them wander in the wilderness for forty years until the end of that wicked generation, because they did not follow the Lord. **43** And the people dwelt in the wilderness of Paran a long time, and they afterward proceeded to the wilderness by the way of the Red Sea.

CHAPTER 84

1 At that time Korah the son of Jetzer the son of Kehas the son of Levi, took many men of the children of Israel, and they rose up and quarreled with Moses and Aaron and the whole congregation. **2** And the Lord was angry with them, and the earth opened its mouth, and swallowed them up, with their houses and all belonging to them, and all the men belonging to Korah. **3** And after this God made the people go round by the way of Mount Seir for a long time. **4** At that time the Lord said unto Moses, "Provoke not a war against the children of Esau, for I will not give to you of anything belonging to them, as much as the sole of the foot could tread upon, for I have given Mount Seir for an inheritance to Esau." **5** Therefore did the children of Esau fight against the children of Seir in former times, and the Lord had delivered the children of Seir into the hands of the children of Esau, and destroyed them from before them, and the children of Esau dwelt in their stead unto this day. **6** Therefore the Lord said to the children of Israel, "Fight not against the children of Esau your brethren, for nothing in their land belongs to you, but you may buy food of them for money and eat it, and you may buy water of them for money and drink it." **7** And the children of Israel did according to the word of the Lord. **8** And the children of Israel went about the wilderness, going round by the way of Mount Sinai for a long time, and touched not the children of Esau, and they continued in that district for nineteen years. **9** At that time died Latinus king of the children of Chittim, in the forty-fifth year of his reign, which is the fourteenth year of the children of Israel's departure from Egypt. **10** And they buried him in his place which he had built for himself in the land of Chittim, and Abimnas reigned in his place for thirty-eight years. **11** And the children of Israel passed the boundary of the children of Esau in those days, at the end of nineteen years, and they came and passed the road of the wilderness of Moab. **12** And the Lord said to Moses, "Besiege not Moab, and do not fight against them, for I will give you nothing of their land." **13** And the children of Israel passed the road of the wilderness of Moab for nineteen years, and they did not fight against them. **14** And in the thirty-sixth year of the children of Israel's departing from Egypt the Lord smote the heart of Sihon, king of the Amorites, and he waged war, and went out to fight against the children of Moab. **15** And Sihon sent messengers to Beor the son of Janeas, the son of Balaam, counsellor to the king of Egypt, and to Balaam his son, to curse Moab, in order that it might be delivered into the hand of Sihon. **16** And the messengers went and brought Beor the son of Janeas, and Balaam his son, from Pethor in Mesopotamia, so Beor and Balaam his son came to the city of Sihon and they cursed Moab and their king in the presence of Sihon king of the Amorites. **17** So Sihon went out with his whole army, and he went to Moab and fought against them, and he subdued them, and the Lord delivered them into his hands, and Sihon slew the king of Moab. **18** And Sihon took all the cities of Moab in the battle; he also took Heshbon from them, for Heshbon was one of the cities of Moab, and Sihon placed his princes and his nobles in Heshbon, and Heshbon belonged to Sihon in those days. **19** Therefore the parable speakers Beor and Balaam his son uttered these words, saying, "Come unto Heshbon, the city of Sihon will be built and established. **20** Woe unto you Moab! You are lost, O people of Kemosh! Behold it is written upon the book of the law of God." **21** And when Sihon had conquered Moab, he placed guards in the cities which he had taken from Moab, and a considerable number of the children of Moab fell in battle into the hand of Sihon, and he made a great capture of them, sons and daughters, and he slew their king; so Sihon turned back to his own land. **22** And Sihon gave numerous presents of silver and gold to Beor and Balaam his son, and he dismissed them, and they went to Mesopotamia to their home and country. **23** At that time all the children of Israel passed from the road of the wilderness of Moab and returned and surrounded the wilderness of Edom. **24** So the whole congregation came to the wilderness of Sin in the first month of the fortieth year from their departure from Egypt, and the children of Israel dwelt there in Kadesh, of the wilderness of Sin, and Miriam died there and she was buried there. **25** At that time Moses sent messengers to Hadad king of Edom, saying, "Thus says your brother Israel, 'Let me pass I pray you through your land, we will not pass through field or vineyard, we will not drink the water of the well; we will walk in the king's road.' " **26** And Edom said to him, "You will not pass through my country," and Edom went out to meet the children of Israel with a mighty people. **27** And the children of Esau refused to let the children of Israel pass through their land, so the Israelites removed from them and fought not against them. **28** For before this the Lord had commanded the children of Israel, saying, "You will not fight against the children of Esau," therefore the Israelites removed from them and did not fight against them. **29** So the children of Israel departed from Kadesh, and all the people came to Mount Hor. **30** At that time the Lord said to Moses, "Tell your brother Aaron that he will die there, for he will not come to the land which I have given to the children of Israel." **31** And Aaron went up, at the command of the Lord, to Mount Hor, in the fortieth year, in the fifth month, in the first day of the month. **32** And Aaron was one hundred and twenty-three years old when he died in Mount Hor.

CHAPTER 85

1 And king Arad the Canaanite, who dwelt in the south, heard that the Israelites had come by the way of the spies, and he arranged his forces to fight against the Israelites. **2** And the children of Israel were greatly afraid of him, for he had a great and heavy army, so the children of Israel resolved to return to Egypt. **3** And the children of Israel turned back about the distance of three days' journey unto Maserath Beni Jaakon, for they were greatly afraid on account of the king Arad. **4** And the children of Israel would not get back to their places, so they remained in Beni Jaakon for thirty days. **5** And when the children of Levi saw that the children of Israel would not turn back, they were jealous for the sake of the Lord, and they rose up and fought against the Israelites their brethren, and slew of them a great body, and forced them to turn back to their place, Mount Hor. **6** And when they returned, king Arad was still arranging his host for battle against the Israelites. **7** And Israel vowed a vow, saying, "If you will deliver this people into my hand, then I will utterly destroy their cities." **8** And the Lord hearkened to the voice of Israel, and he delivered the Canaanites into their hand, and he utterly destroyed them and their cities, and he called the name of the place Hormah. **9** And the children of Israel journeyed from Mount Hor and pitched in Oboth, and they journeyed from Oboth and they pitched at Ije-abarim, in the border of Moab. **10** And the children of Israel sent to Moab, saying, "Let us pass now through your land into our place," but the children of Moab would not suffer the children of Israel to pass through their land, for the children of Moab were greatly afraid lest the children of Israel should do unto them as Sihon king of the Amorites had done to them, who had taken their land and had slain many of them. **11** Therefore Moab would not suffer the Israelites to pass through his land, and the Lord commanded the children of Israel, saying that they should not fight against Moab, so the Israelites removed from Moab. **12** And the children of Israel journeyed from the border of Moab, and they came to the other side of Arnon, the border of Moab, between Moab and the Amorites, and they pitched in the border of Sihon, king of the Amorites, in the wilderness of Kedemoth. **13** And the children of Israel sent messengers to Sihon, king of the Amorites, saying, **14** "Let us pass through your land, we will not turn into the fields or into the vineyards, we will go along by the king's highway until we will have passed your border," but Sihon would not suffer the Israelites to pass. **15** So Sihon collected all the people of the Amorites and went out into the wilderness to meet the children of Israel, and he fought against Israel in Jahaz. **16** And the Lord delivered Sihon king of the Amorites into the hand of the children of Israel, and Israel smote all the people of Sihon with the edge of the sword and avenged the cause of Moab. **17** And the children of Israel took possession of the land of Sihon from Aram unto Jabuk, unto the children of Ammon, and they took all the spoil of the cities. **18** And Israel took all these cities, and Israel dwelt in all the cities of the Amorites. **19** And all the children of Israel resolved to fight against the children of Ammon, to take their land also. **20** So the Lord said to the children of Israel, "Do not besiege the children of Ammon, neither stir up battle against them, for I will give nothing to you of their land," and the children of Israel hearkened to the word of the Lord and did not fight against the children of Ammon. **21** And the children of Israel turned and went up by the way of Bashan to the land of Og, king of Bashan, and Og the king of Bashan went out to meet the Israelites in battle, and he had with him many valiant men, and a very strong force from the people of the Amorites. **22** And Og king of Bashan was a very powerful man, but Naaron his son was exceedingly powerful, even stronger than he was. **23** And Og said in his heart, "Behold now the whole camp of Israel takes up a space of seven miles, now will I smite them at once without sword or spear." **24** And Og went up Mount Jahaz, and took from there one large stone, the length of which was seven miles, and he placed it on his head, and resolved to throw it upon the camp of the children of Israel, to smite all the Israelites with that stone. **25** And the angel of the Lord came and pierced the stone upon the head of Og, and the stone fell upon the neck of Og that Og fell to the earth on account of the weight of the stone upon his neck. **26** At that time the Lord said to the children of Israel, "Be not afraid of him, for I have given him and all his people and all his land into your hand, and you will do to him as you did to Sihon." **27** And Moses went down to him with a small number of the children of Israel, and Moses smote Og with a stick at the ankles of his feet and slew him. **28** The children of Israel afterward pursued the children of Og and all his people, and they beat and destroyed them until there was no remnant left of them. **29** Moses afterward sent some of the children of Israel to spy out Jaazer, for Jaazer was a very famous city. **30** And the spies went to Jaazer and explored it, and the spies trusted in the Lord, and they fought against the men of Jaazer. **31** And these men took Jaazer and its villages, and the Lord delivered them into their hand, and they drove out the Amorites who had been there. **32** And the children of Israel took the land of the two kings of the Amorites, sixty cities which were on the other side of Jordan, from the brook of Arnon unto Mount Herman. **33** And the children of Israel journeyed and came into the plain of Moab which is on this side of Jordan, by Jericho. **34** And the children of Moab heard all the evil which the children of Israel had done to the two kings of the Amorites, to Sihon and Og, so all the men of Moab were greatly afraid of the Israelites.

35 And the elders of Moab said, "Behold the two kings of the Amorites, Sihon and Og, who were more powerful than all the kings of the earth, could not stand against the children of Israel, how then can we stand before them? **36** Surely they sent us a message before now to pass through our land on their way, and we would not suffer them, now they will turn upon us with their heavy swords and destroy us"; and Moab was distressed on account of the children of Israel, and they were greatly afraid of them, and they counselled together what was to be done to the children of Israel. **37** And the elders of Moab resolved and took one of their men, Balak the son of Zippor the Moabite, and made him king over them at that time, and Balak was a very wise man. **38** And the elders of Moab rose up and sent to the children of Midian to make peace with them, for a great battle and enmity had been in those days between Moab and Midian, from the days of Hadad the son of Bedad king of Edom, who smote Midian in the field of Moab, unto these days. **39** And the children of Moab sent to the children of Midian, and they made peace with them, and the elders of Midian came to the land of Moab to make peace in behalf of the children of Midian. **40** And the elders of Moab counselled with the elders of Midian what to do in order to save their lives from Israel. **41** And all the children of Moab said to the elders of Midian, "Now therefore the children of Israel lick up all that are around us, as the ox licks up the grass of the field, for thus did they do to the two kings of the Amorites who are stronger than we are." **42** And the elders of Midian said to Moab, "We have heard that at the time when Sihon king of the Amorites fought against you, when he prevailed over you and took your land, he had sent to Beor the son of Janeas and to Balaam his son from Mesopotamia, and they came and cursed you; therefore did the hand of Sihon prevail over you, that he took your land. **43** Now therefore send you also to Balaam his son, for he still remains in his land, and give him his hire, that he may come and curse all the people of whom you are afraid"; so the elders of Moab heard this thing, and it pleased them to send to Balaam the son of Beor. **44** So Balak the son of Zippor king of Moab sent messengers to Balaam, saying, **45** "Behold there is a people come out from Egypt, behold they cover the face of the earth, and they abide over against me. **46** Now therefore come and curse this people for me, for they are too mighty for me,

perhaps I will prevail to fight against them, and drive them out, for I heard that he whom you bless is blessed, and whom you curse is cursed." **47** So the messengers of Balak went to Balaam and brought Balaam to curse the people to fight against Moab. **48** And Balaam came to Balak to curse Israel, and the Lord said to Balaam, "Curse not this people for it is blessed." **49** And Balak urged Balaam day by day to curse Israel, but Balaam hearkened not to Balak on account of the word of the Lord which he had spoken to Balaam. **50** And when Balak saw that Balaam would not accede to his wish, he rose up and went home, and Balaam also returned to his land and he went from there to Midian. **51** And the children of Israel journeyed from the plain of Moab and pitched by the Jordan from Beth-jesimoth even unto Abel-shittim, at the end of the plains of Moab. **52** And when the children of Israel dwelt in the plain of Shittim, they began to commit whoredom with the daughters of Moab. **53** And the children of Israel approached Moab, and the children of Moab pitched their tents opposite to the camp of the children of Israel. **54** And the children of Moab were afraid of the children of Israel, and the children of Moab took all their daughters and their wives of beautiful aspect and comely appearance and dressed them in gold and silver and costly garments. **55** And the children of Moab seated those women at the door of their tents, in order that the children of Israel might see them and turn to them, and not fight against Moab. **56** And all the children of Moab did this thing to the children of Israel, and every man placed his wife and daughter at the door of his tent, and all the children of Israel saw the act of the children of Moab, and the children of Israel turned to the daughters of Moab and coveted them, and they went to them. **57** And it came to pass that when a Hebrew came to the door of the tent of Moab, and saw a daughter of Moab and desired her in his heart, and spoke with her at the door of the tent that he desired, while they were speaking together the men of the tent would come out and speak to the Hebrew like unto these words: **58** "Surely you know that we are brethren, we are all the descendants of Lot and the descendants of Abraham his brother, why then will you not remain with us, and why will you not eat our bread and our sacrifice?" **59** And when the children of Moab had thus overwhelmed him with their speeches, and enticed him by their flattering words, they seated him in the tent and cooked and sacrificed for him, and he ate of their sacrifice and of their bread. **60** They then gave him wine and he drank and became intoxicated, and they placed before him a beautiful damsel, and he did with her as he liked, for he knew not what he was doing, as he had drunk plentifully of wine. **61** Thus did the children of Moab to Israel in that place, in the plain of Shittim, and the anger of the Lord was kindled against Israel on account of this matter, and he sent a pestilence among them, and there died of the Israelites twenty-four thousand men. **62** Now there was a man of the children of Simeon whose name was Zimri, the son of Salu, who connected himself with the Midianite Cosbi, the daughter of Zur, king of Midian, in the sight of all the children of Israel. **63** And Phineas the son of Elazer, the son of Aaron the priest, saw this wicked thing which Zimri had done, and he took a spear and rose up and went after them, and pierced them both and slew them, and the pestilence ceased from the children of Israel.

CHAPTER 86

1 At that time after the pestilence, the Lord said to Moses, and to Elazer the son of Aaron the priest, saying, **2** "Number the heads of the whole community of the children of Israel, from twenty years old and upward, all that went out in the army." **3** And Moses and Elazer numbered the children of Israel after their families, and the number of all Israel was seven hundred thousand, seven hundred and thirty. **4** And the number of the children of Levi, from one month old and upward, was twenty-three thousand, and among these there was not a man of those numbered by Moses and Aaron in the wilderness of Sinai. **5** For the Lord had told them that they would die in the wilderness, so they all died, and not one had been left of them excepting Caleb the son of Jephuneh, and Joshua the son of Nun. **6** And it was after this that the Lord said to Moses, "Say unto the children of Israel to avenge upon Midian the cause of their brethren the children of Israel." **7** And Moses did so, and the children of Israel chose from among them twelve thousand men, being one thousand to a tribe, and they went to Midian. **8** And the children of Israel warred against Midian, and they slew every male, also the five princes of Midian, and Balaam the son of Beor did they slay with the sword. **9** And the children of Israel took the wives of Midian captive, with

their little ones and their cattle, and all belonging to them. **10** And they took all the spoil and all the prey, and they brought it to Moses and to Elazer to the plains of Moab. **11** And Moses and Elazer and all the princes of the congregation went out to meet them with joy. **12** And they divided all the spoil of Midian, and the children of Israel had been revenged upon Midian for the cause of their brethren the children of Israel.

CHAPTER 87

1 At that time the Lord said to Moses, "Behold your days are approaching to an end, take now Joshua the son of Nun your servant and place him in the tabernacle, and I will command him," and Moses did so. **2** And the Lord appeared in the tabernacle in a pillar of cloud, and the pillar of cloud stood at the entrance of the tabernacle. **3** And the Lord commanded Joshua the son of Nun and said unto him, "Be strong and courageous, for you will bring the children of Israel to the land which I swore to give them, and I will be with you." **4** And Moses said to Joshua, "Be strong and courageous, for you will make the children of Israel inherit the land, and the Lord will be with you, he will not leave you nor forsake you, be not afraid nor disheartened." **5** And Moses called to all the children of Israel and said to them, "You have seen all the good which the Lord your God has done for you in the wilderness. **6** Now therefore observe all the words of this law and walk in the way of the Lord your God, turn not from the way which the Lord has commanded you, either to the right or to the left." **7** And Moses taught the children of Israel statutes and judgments and laws to do in the land as the Lord had commanded him. **8** And he taught them the way of the Lord and his laws; behold they are written upon the book of the law of God which he gave to the children of Israel by the hand of Moses. **9** And Moses finished commanding the children of Israel, and the Lord said to him, saying, "Go up to Mount Abarim and die there, and be gathered unto your people as Aaron your brother was gathered." **10** And Moses went up as the Lord had commanded him, and he died there in the land of Moab by the order of the Lord, in the fortieth year from the Israelites going out from the land of Egypt. **11** And the children of Israel wept for Moses in the plains of Moab for thirty days, and the days of weeping and mourning for Moses were completed.

CHAPTER 88

1 And it was after the death of Moses that the Lord said to Joshua the son of Nun, saying, 2 "Rise up and pass the Jordan to the land which I have given to the children of Israel, and you will make the children of Israel inherit the land. 3 Every place upon which the sole of your feet will tread will belong to you, from the wilderness of Lebanon unto the great river the river of Perath will be your boundary. 4 No man will stand up against you all the days of your life; as I was with Moses, so will I be with you, only be strong and of good courage to observe all the law which Moses commanded you, turn not from the way either to the right or to the left, in order that you may prosper in all that you do." 5 And Joshua commanded the officers of Israel, saying, "Pass through the camp and command the people, saying, 'Prepare for yourselves provisions, for in three days more you will pass the Jordan to possess the land.' " 6 And the officers of the children of Israel did so, and they commanded the people and they did all that Joshua had commanded. 7 And Joshua sent two men to spy out the land of Jericho, and the men went and spied out Jericho. 8 And at the end of seven days they came to Joshua in the camp and said to him, "The Lord has delivered the whole land into our hands, and the inhabitants thereof are melted with fear because of us." 9 And it came to pass after that, that Joshua rose up in the morning and all Israel with him, and they journeyed from Shittim, and Joshua and all Israel with him passed the Jordan; and Joshua was eighty-two years old when he passed the Jordan with Israel. 10 And the people went up from Jordan on the tenth day of the first month, and they encamped in Gilgal at the eastern corner of Jericho. 11 And the children of Israel kept the Passover in Gilgal, in the plains of Jericho, on the fourteenth day at the month, as it is written in the law of Moses. 12 And the manna ceased at that time on the morrow of the Passover, and there was no more manna for the children of Israel, and they ate of the produce of the land of Canaan. 13 And Jericho was entirely closed against the children of Israel, no one came out or went in. 14 And it was in the second month, on the first day of the month, that the Lord said to Joshua, "Rise up, behold I have given Jericho into your hand with all the people thereof; and all your fighting men will go round the city, once each day, thus will you do for six days. 15 And the priests will blow upon trumpets, and when you will hear the sound of the trumpet, all the people will give a great shouting, that the walls of the city will fall down; all the people will go up every man against his opponent." 16 And Joshua did so according to all that the Lord had commanded him. 17 And on the seventh day they went around the city seven times, and the priests blew upon trumpets. 18 And at the seventh round, Joshua said to the people, "Shout, for the Lord has delivered the whole city into our hands. 19 Only the city and all that it contains will be accursed to the Lord, and keep yourselves from the accursed thing, lest you make the camp of Israel accursed and trouble it. 20 But all the silver and gold and brass and iron will be consecrated to the Lord, they will come into the treasury of the Lord." 21 And the people blew upon trumpets and made a great shouting, and the walls of Jericho fell down, and all the people went up, every man straight before him, and they took the city and utterly destroyed all that was in it, both man and woman, young and old, ox and sheep and ass, with the edge of the sword. 22 And they burned the whole city with fire; only the vessels of silver and gold, and brass and iron, they put into the treasury of the Lord. 23 And Joshua swore at that time, saying, "Cursed be the man who builds Jericho; he will lay the foundation thereof in his firstborn, and in his youngest son will he set up the gates thereof. 24 And Achan the son of Carmi, the son of Zabdi, the son of Zerah, son of Judah, dealt treacherously in the accursed thing, and he took of the accursed thing and hid it in the tent, and the anger of the Lord was kindled against Israel. 25 And it was after this when the children of Israel had returned from burning Jericho, Joshua sent men to spy out also Ai, and to fight against it. 26 And the men went up and spied out Ai, and they returned and said, "Let not all the people go up with you to Ai, only let about three thousand men go up and smite the city, for the men thereof are but few." 27 And Joshua did so, and there went up with him of the children of Israel about three thousand men, and they fought against the men of Ai. 28 And the battle was severe against Israel, and the men of Ai smote thirty-six men of Israel, and the children of Israel fled from before the men of Ai. 29 And when Joshua saw this thing, he tore his garments and fell upon his face to the ground before the Lord, he, with the elders of Israel, and they put dust upon their heads. 30 And Joshua said, "Why O

Lord did you bring this people over the Jordan? What will I say after the Israelites have turned their backs against their enemies? **31** Now therefore all the Canaanites, inhabitants of the land, will hear this thing, and surround us and cut off our name." **32** And the Lord said to Joshua, "Why do you fall upon your face? Rise, get up, for the Israelites have sinned, and taken of the accursed thing; I will no more be with them unless they destroy the accursed thing from among them." **33** And Joshua rose up and assembled the people, and brought the Urim by the order of the Lord, and the tribe of Judah was taken, and Achan the son of Carmi was taken. **34** And Joshua said to Achan, "Tell me my son, what have you done," and Achan said, "I saw among the spoil a fancy garment of Shinar and two hundred shekels of silver, and a wedge of gold of fifty shekels weight; I coveted them and took them, and behold they are all hid in the earth in the midst of the tent." **35** And Joshua sent men who went and took them from the tent of Achan, and they brought them to Joshua. **36** And Joshua took Achan and these utensils, and his sons and daughters and all belonging to him, and they brought them into the valley of Achor. **37** And Joshua burned them there with fire, and all the Israelites stoned Achan with stones, and they raised over him a heap of stones, therefore did he call that place the valley of Achor, so the Lord's anger was appeased, and Joshua afterward came to the city and fought against it. **38** And the Lord said to Joshua, "Fear not, neither be dismayed, behold I have given into your hand Ai, her king and her people, and you will do unto them as you did to Jericho and her king, only the spoil thereof and the cattle thereof will you take for a prey for yourselves; lay an ambush for the city behind it." **39** So Joshua did according to the word of the Lord, and he chose from among the sons of war thirty thousand valiant men, and he sent them, and they lay in ambush for the city. **40** And he commanded them, saying, "When you will see us we will flee before them with cunning, and they will pursue us, you will then rise out of the ambush and take the city," and they did so. **41** And Joshua fought, and the men of the city went out toward Israel, not knowing that they were lying in ambush for them behind the city. **42** And Joshua and all the Israelites feigned themselves wearied out before them, and they fled by the way of the wilderness with cunning. **43** And the men of Ai gathered all the people who were in the city to pursue the Israelites, and they went out and were drawn away from the city, not one remained, and they left the city open and pursued the Israelites. **44** And those who were lying in ambush rose up out of their places and hastened to come to the city and took it and set it on fire, and the men of Ai turned back, and behold the smoke of the city ascended to the skies, and they had no means of retreating either one way or the other. **45** And all the men of Ai were in the midst of Israel, some on this side and some on that side, and they smote them so that not one of them remained. **46** And the children of Israel took Melosh king of Ai alive, and they brought him to Joshua, and Joshua hanged him on a tree and he died. **47** And the children of Israel returned to the city after having burned it, and they smote all those that were in it with the edge of the sword. **48** And the number of those that had fallen of the men of Ai, both man and woman, was twelve thousand; only the cattle and the spoil of the city they took to themselves, according to the word of the Lord to Joshua. **49** And all the kings on this side Jordan, all the kings of Canaan, heard of the evil which the children of Israel had done to Jericho and to Ai, and they gathered themselves together to fight against Israel. **50** Only the inhabitants of Gibeon were greatly afraid of fighting against the Israelites lest they should perish, so they acted cunningly, and they came to Joshua and to all Israel, and said unto them, "We have come from a distant land, now therefore make a covenant with us." **51** And the inhabitants of Gibeon outwitted the children of Israel, and the children of Israel made a covenant with them, and they made peace with them, and the princes of the congregation swore unto them, but afterward the children of Israel knew that they were neighbors to them and were dwelling among them. **52** But the children of Israel slew them not; for they had sworn to them by the Lord, and they became hewers of wood and drawers of water. **53** And Joshua said to them, "Why did you deceive me, to do this thing to us?" And they answered him, saying, "Because it was told to your servants all that you had done to all the kings of the Amorites, and we were greatly afraid for our lives, and we did this thing." **54** And Joshua appointed them on that day to hew wood and to draw water, and he divided them for slaves to all the tribes of Israel. **55** And when Adonizedek king of Jerusalem heard all that the children of Israel had done to Jericho and to Ai, he sent to Hoham king of Hebron and to Piram king at Jarmuth, and to Japhia king of Lachish and to Deber king of Eglon, saying, **56** "Come up to me and help me, that we may smite the children of Israel and the inhabitants of Gibeon who have made peace with the children of Israel." **57** And they gathered themselves together and the five kings of the Amorites went up with all their camps, a mighty people numerous as the sand of the seashore. **58** And all these kings came and encamped before Gibeon, and they began to fight against the inhabitants of Gibeon, and all the men of Gibeon sent to Joshua, saying, "Come up quickly to us and help us, for all the kings of the Amorites have gathered together to fight against us." **59** And Joshua and all the fighting people went up from Gilgal, and Joshua came suddenly to them, and smote these five kings with a great slaughter. **60** And the Lord confounded them before the children of Israel, who smote them with a terrible slaughter in Gibeon, and pursued them along the way that goes up to Beth Horon unto Makkedah, and they fled from before the children of Israel. **61** And while they were fleeing, the Lord sent upon them hailstones from heaven, and more of them died by the hailstones, than by the slaughter of the children of Israel. **62** And the children of Israel pursued them, and they still smote them in the road, going on and smiting them. **63** And when they were smiting, the day was declining toward evening, and Joshua said in the sight of all the people, "Sun, stand you still upon Gibeon, and you moon in the valley of Ajalon, until the nation will have revenged itself upon its enemies." **64** And the Lord hearkened to the voice of Joshua, and the sun stood still in the midst of the heavens, and it stood still six and thirty moments, and the moon also stood still and hastened not to go down a whole day. **65** And there was no day like that, before it or after it, that the Lord hearkened to the voice of a man, for the Lord fought for Israel.

CHAPTER 89

1 Then spoke Joshua this song, on the day that the Lord had given the Amorites into the hand of Joshua and the children of Israel, and he said in the sight of all Israel, **2** "You have done mighty things, O Lord, you have performed great deeds; who is like unto you? My lips will sing to your name. **3** My goodness and my fortress, my high tower, I will sing a new song unto you, with thanksgiving will I sing to you, you are the strength of my salvation. **4** All the kings of the earth will praise you, the princes of the world will sing to you, the children of Israel will rejoice in your salvation, they will sing and praise your power. **5** To you, O Lord, did we confide; we said you are our God, for you were our shelter and strong tower against our enemies. **6** To you we cried and were not ashamed, in you we trusted and were delivered; when we cried unto you, you did hear our voice, you did deliver our souls from the sword, you did show unto us your grace, you did give unto us your salvation, you did rejoice our hearts with your strength. **7** You did go out for our salvation, with your arm you did redeem your people; you did answer us from the heavens of your holiness, you did save us from tens of thousands of people. **8** The sun and moon stood still in heaven, and you did stand in your wrath against our oppressors and did command your judgments over them. **9** All the princes of the earth stood up, the kings of the nations had gathered themselves together, they were not moved at your presence, they desired your battles. **10** You did rise against them in your anger and did bring down your wrath upon them; you did destroy them in your anger and cut them off in your heart. **11** Nations have been consumed with your fury, kingdoms have declined because of your wrath, you did wound kings in the day of your anger. **12** You did pour out your fury upon them, your wrathful anger took hold of them; you did turn their iniquity upon them and did cut them off in their wickedness. **13** They did spread a trap, they fell therein, in the net they hid, their foot was caught. **14** Your hand was ready for all your enemies who said, 'Through their sword they possessed the land, through their arm they dwelt in the city'; you did fill their faces with shame, you did bring their horns down to the ground, you did terrify them in your wrath, and did destroy them in your anger." **15** The earth trembled and shook at the sound of your storm over them, you did not withhold their souls from death, and did bring down their lives to the grave. **16** You did pursue them in your storm, you did consume them in your whirlwind, you did turn their rain into hail, they fell in deep pits so that they could not rise. **17** Their carcasses were like rubbish cast out in the middle of the streets. **18** They were consumed and destroyed in your anger, you did save your people with your might. **19** Therefore our hearts rejoice in you, our souls exalt in your salvation. **20** Our tongues will relate your might, we will sing and praise your wondrous works. **21** For you did save us from our enemies, you did deliver us from those who rose up against us, you did destroy them from before us and depress them beneath our feet. **22** Thus will all your enemies perish O Lord, and the wicked will be like chaff driven by the wind, and your beloved will be like trees planted by the waters." **23** So Joshua and all Israel with him returned to the camp in Gilgal, after having smitten all the kings, so that not a remnant was left of them. **24** And the five kings fled alone on foot from battle, and hid themselves in a cave, and Joshua sought for them in the field of battle and did not find them. **25** And it was afterward told to Joshua, saying, "The kings are found and behold they are hidden in a cave." **26** And Joshua said, "Appoint men to be at the mouth of the cave, to guard them, lest they escape"; and the children of Israel did so. **27** And Joshua called to all Israel and said to the officers of battle, "Place your feet upon the necks of these kings," and Joshua said, "So will the Lord do to all your enemies." **28** And Joshua commanded afterward that they should slay the kings and cast them into the cave, and to put great stones at the mouth of the cave. **29** And Joshua went afterward with all the people that were with him on that day to Makkedah, and he smote it with the edge of the sword. **30** And he utterly destroyed the souls and all belonging to the city, and he did to the king and people thereof as he had done to Jericho. **31** And he passed from there to Libnah and he fought against it, and the Lord delivered it into his hand, and Joshua smote it with the edge of the sword, and all the souls thereof, and he did to it and to the king thereof as he had done to Jericho. **32** And from there he passed on to Lachish to fight against it, and Horam king of Gaza went up to assist the men of Lachish, and Joshua smote him and his people until there was none left to him. **33** And Joshua took Lachish and all the people thereof, and he did to it as he had done to Libnah. **34** And Joshua passed from there to Eglon, and he took that also, and he smote it and all the people thereof with the edge of the sword. **35** And from there he passed to Hebron and fought against it and took it and utterly destroyed it, and he returned from there with all Israel to Debir and fought against it and smote it with the edge of the sword. **36** And he destroyed every soul in it, he left none

remaining, and he did to it and the king thereof as he had done to Jericho. **37** And Joshua smote all the kings of the Amorites from Kadesh-barnea to Azah, and he took their country at once, for the Lord had fought for Israel. **38** And Joshua with all Israel came to the camp to Gilgal. **39** When at that time Jabin king of Chazor heard all that Joshua had done to the kings of the Amorites, Jabin sent to Jobat king of Midian, and to Laban king of Shimron, to Jephal king of Achshaph, and to all the kings of the Amorites, saying, **40** "Come quickly to us and help us, that we may smite the children of Israel, before they come upon us and do unto us as they have done to the other kings of the Amorites." **41** And all these kings hearkened to the words of Jabin, king of Chazor, and they went out with all their camps, seventeen kings, and their people were as numerous as the sand on the seashore, together with horses and chariots innumerable, and they came and pitched together at the waters of Merom, and they were met together to fight against Israel. **42** And the Lord said to Joshua, "Fear them not, for tomorrow about this time I will deliver them up all slain before you, you will hough their horses and burn their chariots with fire." **43** And Joshua with all the men of war came suddenly upon them and smote them, and they fell into their hands, for the Lord had delivered them into the hands of the children of Israel. **44** So the children of Israel pursued all these kings with their camps and smote them until there was none left of them, and Joshua did to them as the Lord had spoken to him. **45** And Joshua returned at that time to Chazor and smote it with the sword and destroyed every soul in it and burned it with fire, and from Chazor, Joshua passed to Shimron and smote it and utterly destroyed it. **46** From there he passed to Achshaph and he did to it as he had done to Shimron. **47** From there he passed to Adulam and he smote all the people in it, and he did to Adulam as he had done to Achshaph and to Shimron. **48** And he passed from them to all the cities of the kings which he had smitten, and he smote all the people that were left of them and he utterly destroyed them. **49** Only their booty and cattle the Israelites took to themselves as a prey, but every human being they smote, they suffered not a soul to live. **50** As the Lord had commanded Moses so did Joshua and all Israel, they failed not in anything. **51** So Joshua and all the children of Israel smote the whole land of Canaan as the Lord had commanded them, and smote all their kings, being thirty and one kings, and the children of Israel took their whole country. **52** Besides the kingdoms of Sihon and Og which are on the other side Jordan, of which Moses had smitten many cities, and Moses gave them to the Reubenites and the Gadites and to half the tribe of Manasseh. **53** And Joshua smote all the kings that were on this side of the Jordan to the west, and gave them for an inheritance to the nine tribes and to the half tribe of Israel. **54** For five years did Joshua carry on the war with these kings, and he gave their cities to the Israelites, and the land became tranquil from battle throughout the cities of the Amorites and the Canaanites.

CHAPTER 90

1 At that time in the fifth year after the children of Israel had passed over Jordan, after the children of Israel had rested from their war with the Canaanites, at that time great and severe battles arose between Edom and the children of Chittim, and the children of Chittim fought against Edom. **2** And Abianus king of Chittim went out in that year, that is in the thirty-first year of his reign, and a great force with him of the mighty men of the children of Chittim, and he went to Seir to fight against the children of Esau. **3** And Hadad the king of Edom heard of his report, and he went out to meet him with a heavy people and strong force and engaged in battle with him in the field of Edom. **4** And the hand of Chittim prevailed over the children of Esau, and the children of Chittim slew of the children of Esau, two and twenty thousand men, and all the children of Esau fled from before them. **5** And the children of Chittim pursued them and they reached Hadad king of Edom, who was running before them and they caught him alive and brought him to Abianus king of Chittim. **6** And Abianus ordered him to be slain, and Hadad king of Edom died in the forty-eighth year of his reign. **7** And the children of Chittim continued their pursuit of Edom, and they smote them with a great slaughter and Edom became subject to the children of Chittim. **8** And the children of Chittim ruled over Edom, and Edom became under the hand of the children of Chittim and became one kingdom from that day. **9** And from that time they could no more lift up their heads, and their kingdom became one with the children of Chittim. **10** And Abianus placed officers in Edom and all the children of Edom

became subject and tributary to Abianus, and Abianus turned back to his own land, Chittim. **11** And when he returned he renewed his government and built for himself a spacious and fortified palace for a royal residence and reigned securely over the children of Chittim and over Edom. **12** In those days, after the children of Israel had driven away all the Canaanites and the Amorites, Joshua was old and advanced in years. **13** And the Lord said to Joshua, "You are old, advanced in life, and a great part of the land remains to be possessed. **14** Now therefore divide this land for an inheritance to the nine tribes and to the half tribe of Manasseh," and Joshua rose up and did as the Lord had spoken to him. **15** And he divided the whole land to the tribes of Israel as an inheritance according to their divisions. **16** But to the tribe at Levi he gave no inheritance, the offerings of the Lord are their inheritance as the Lord had spoken of them by the hand of Moses. **17** And Joshua gave Mount Hebron to Caleb the son of Jephuneh, one portion above his brethren, as the Lord had spoken through Moses. **18** Therefore Hebron became an inheritance to Caleb and his children unto this day. **19** And Joshua divided the whole land by lots to all Israel for an inheritance, as the Lord had commanded him. **20** And the children of Israel gave cities to the Levites from their own inheritance, and suburbs for their cattle, and property, as the Lord had commanded Moses so did the children of Israel, and they divided the land by lot whether great or small. **21** And they went to inherit the land according to their boundaries, and the children of Israel gave to Joshua the son of Nun an inheritance among them. **22** By the word of the Lord did they give to him the city which he required, Timnath-serach in Mount Ephraim, and he built the city and dwelt therein. **23** These are the inheritances which Elazer the priest and Joshua the son of Nun and the heads of the fathers of the tribes portioned out to the children of Israel by lot in Shiloh, before the Lord, at the door of the tabernacle, and they left off dividing the land. **24** And the Lord gave the land to the Israelites, and they possessed it as the Lord had spoken to them, and as the Lord had sworn to their ancestors. **25** And the Lord gave to the Israelites rest from all their enemies around them, and no man stood up against them, and the Lord delivered all their enemies into their hands, and not one thing failed of all the good which the Lord had spoken to the children of Israel—the Lord performed everything. **26** And Joshua called to all the children of Israel and he blessed them, and commanded them to serve the Lord, and he afterward sent them away, and they went each man to his city, and each man to his inheritance. **27** And the children of Israel served the Lord all the days of Joshua, and the Lord gave them rest from all around them, and they dwelt securely in their cities. **28** And it came to pass in those days, that Abianus king of Chittim died, in the thirty-eighth year of his reign, that is the seventh year of his reign over Edom, and they buried him in his place which he had built for himself, and Latinus reigned in his stead fifty years. **29** And during his reign he brought out an army, and he went and fought against the inhabitants of Britannia and Kernania, the children of Elisha son of Javan, and he prevailed over them and made them tributary. **30** He then heard that Edom had revolted from under the hand of Chittim, and Latinus went to them and smote them and subdued them and placed them under the hand of the children of Chittim, and Edom became one kingdom with the children of Chittim all the days. **31** And for many years there was no king in Edom, and their government was with the children of Chittim and their king. **32** And it was in the twenty-sixth year after the children of Israel had passed the Jordan, that is the sixty-sixth year after the children of Israel had departed from Egypt, that Joshua was old, advanced in years, being one hundred and eight years old in those days. **33** And Joshua called to all Israel, to their elders, their judges and officers, after the Lord had given to all the Israelites rest from all their surrounding enemies, and Joshua said to the elders of Israel, and to their judges, "Behold I am old, advanced in years, and you have seen what the Lord has done to all the nations whom he has driven away from before you, for it is the Lord who has fought for you. **34** Now therefore strengthen yourselves to keep and to do all the words of the law of Moses, not to deviate from it to the right or to the left, and not to come among those nations who are left in the land; neither will you make mention of the name of their gods, but you will cleave to the Lord your God, as you have done to this day." **35** And Joshua greatly exhorted the children of Israel to serve the Lord all their days. **36** And all the Israelites said, "We will serve the Lord our God all our days, we and our children, and our children's children, and

our seed forever." **37** And Joshua made a covenant with the people on that day, and he sent away the children of Israel, and they went each man to his inheritance and to his city. **38** And it was in those days, when the children of Israel were dwelling securely in their cities, that they buried the coffins of the tribes of their ancestors, which they had brought up from Egypt, each man in the inheritance of his children, the twelve sons of Jacob did the children of Israel bury, each man in the possession of his children. **39** And these are the names of the cities wherein they buried the twelve sons of Jacob, whom the children of Israel had brought up from Egypt. **40** And they buried Reuben and Gad on this side of the Jordan, in Romia, which Moses had given to their children. **41** And Simeon and Levi they buried in the city Mauda, which he had given to the children of Simeon, and the suburb of the city was for the children of Levi. **42** And Judah they buried in the city of Benjamin opposite Bethlehem. **43** And the bones of Issachar and Zebulun they buried in Zidon, in the portion which fell to their children. **44** And Dan was buried in the city of his children in Eshtael, and Naphtali and Asher they buried in Kadesh-naphtali, each man in his place which he had given to his children. **45** And the bones of Joseph they buried in Shechem, in the part of the field which Jacob had purchased from Hamor, and which became to Joseph for an inheritance. **46** And they buried Benjamin in Jerusalem opposite the Jebusite, which was given to the children of Benjamin; the children of Israel buried their fathers each man in the city of his children. **47** And at the end of two years, Joshua the son of Nun died, one hundred and ten years old, and the time which Joshua judged Israel was twenty-eight years, and Israel served the Lord all the days of his life. **48** And the other affairs of Joshua and his battles and his reproofs with which he reproved Israel, and all which he had commanded them, and the names of the cities which the children of Israel possessed in his days, behold they are written in the book of the words of Joshua to the children of Israel, and in the book of the wars of the Lord, which Moses and Joshua and the children of Israel had written. **49** And the children of Israel buried Joshua in the border of his inheritance, in Timnath-serach, which was given to him in Mount Ephraim. **50** And Elazer the son of Aaron died in those days, and they buried him in a hill belonging to Phineas his son, which was given him in Mount Ephraim.

CHAPTER 91

1 At that time, after the death of Joshua, the children of the Canaanites were still in the land, and the Israelites resolved to drive them out. 2 And the children of Israel asked of the Lord, saying, "Who will first go up for us to the Canaanites to fight against them?" And the Lord said, "Judah will go up." 3 And the children of Judah said to Simeon, "Go up with us into our lot, and we will fight against the Canaanites and we likewise will go up with you, in your lot," so the children of Simeon went with the children of Judah. 4 And the children of Judah went up and fought against the Canaanites, so the Lord delivered the Canaanites into the hands of the children of Judah, and they smote them in Bezek, ten thousand men. 5 And they fought with Adonibezek in Bezek, and he fled from before them, and they pursued him and caught him, and they took hold of him and cut off his thumbs and great toes. 6 And Adonibezek said, "Three score and ten kings having their thumbs and great toes cut off, gathered their meat under my table, as I have done, so God has paid me back," and they brought him to Jerusalem and he died there. 7 And the children of Simeon went with the children of Judah, and they smote the Canaanites with the edge of the sword. 8 And the Lord was with the children of Judah, and they possessed the mountain, and the children of Joseph went up to Bethel, the same is Luz, and the Lord was with them. 9 And the children of Joseph spied out Bethel, and the watchmen saw a man going out from the city, and they caught him and said unto him, "Show us now the entrance of the city and we will show kindness to you." 10 And that man showed them the entrance of the city, and the children of Joseph came and smote the City with the edge of the sword. 11 And the man with his family they sent away, and he went to the Hittites and he built a city, and he called the name thereof Luz, so all the Israelites dwelt in their cities, and the children at Israel dwelt in their cities, and the children of Israel served the Lord all the days of Joshua, and all the days of the elders, who had lengthened their days after Joshua, and saw the great work of the Lord, which he had performed for Israel. 12 And the elders judged Israel after the death of Joshua for seventeen years. 13 And all the elders also fought the battles of Israel against the Canaanites and the Lord drove the Canaanites from before the children of Israel, in order to place the Israelites in their land. 14 And he accomplished all the words which he had spoken to Abraham, Isaac, and Jacob, and the oath which he had sworn, to give to them and to their children, the land of the Canaanites. 15 And the Lord gave to the children of Israel the whole land of Canaan, as he had sworn to their ancestors, and the Lord gave them rest from those around them, and the children of Israel dwelt securely in their cities. 16 Blessed be the Lord forever, amen, and amen. 17 Strengthen yourselves and let the hearts of all you that trust in the Lord be of good courage.

ADDITIONS TO THE BIBLE

ESTHER

With LXX additions in bold brackets

The Septuagint (LXX) version of Esther contains a number of sections not found in the Hebrew version of the text. The entire book of Esther is included here with these additions denoted by bolded double brackets.

CHAPTER 1

1 **[[In the second year of the reign of Ahasuerus the great king, on the first day of Nisan, Mordecai the son of Jair, the son of Shimei, the son of Kish, of the tribe of Benjamin, a Jew dwelling in the city Susa, a great man, serving in the king's palace, saw a vision. Now he was of the captivity which Nebuchadnezzar king of Babylon had carried captive from Jerusalem, with Jeconiah the king of Judea. This was his dream: Behold, voices and a noise, thunders and earthquake, tumult upon the earth. And, behold, two great serpents came out, both ready for conflict. A great voice came from them. Every nation was prepared for battle by their voice, even to fight against the nation of the just. Behold, a day of darkness and blackness, suffering and anguish, affection and tumult upon the earth. And all the righteous nation was troubled, fearing their own afflictions. They prepared to die and cried to God. Something like a great river from a little spring with much water, came from their cry. Light and the sun arose, and the lowly were exalted, and devoured the honorable. Mordecai, who had seen this vision and what God desired to do, having arisen, kept it in his heart, and desired by all means to interpret it, even until night. Mordecai rested quietly in the palace with Gabatha and Tharrha the king's two chamberlains, eunuchs who guarded the palace. He heard their conversation and searched out their plans. He learned that they were preparing to lay hands on King Ahasuerus; and he informed the king concerning them. The king examined the two chamberlains. They confessed and were led away and executed. The king wrote these things for a record. Mordecai also wrote concerning these matters. The king commanded Mordecai to serve in the palace and gave gifts for this service. But Haman the son of Hammedatha the Bougean was honored in the sight of the king, and he endeavored to harm Mordecai and his people, because of the king's two chamberlains.]]** And it came to pass after these things in the days of Ahasuerus, — (this Ahasuerus ruled over one hundred twenty-seven provinces from India)—2 in those days, when King Ahasuerus was on the throne in the city of Susa. 3 In the third year of his reign, he made a feast for his friends, and the other nations, and for the nobles of the Persians and Medes, and the chief of the local governors. 4 After this, after he had shown them the wealth of his kingdom and the abundant glory of his wealth during one hundred eighty days, 5 when the days of the wedding feast were completed, the king made a banquet for the people of the nations who were present in the city for six days, in the court of the king's house, 6 which was adorned with fine linen and flax on cords of fine linen and purple, fastened to golden and silver studs, on pillars of white marble and stone. There were golden and silver couches on a pavement of emerald stone, and of pearl, and of white marble, with transparent coverings variously flowered, having roses worked around it. 7 There were gold and silver cups, and a small cup of carbuncle set out of the value of thirty thousand talents, with abundant and sweet wine, which the king himself drank. 8 This banquet was not according to the appointed law; but as the king desired to have it. He charged the stewards to perform his will and that of the company. 9 Also Vashti the queen made a banquet for the women in the palace where King Ahasuerus lived. 10 Now on the seventh day, the king, being merry, told Haman, Bazan, Tharrha, Baraze, Zatholtha, Abataza, and Tharaba, the seven chamberlains, servants of King Ahasuerus, 11 to bring in the queen to him, toenthrone her, and crown her with the diadem, and to show her to the princes, and her beauty to the nations: for she was beautiful. 12 But Queen Vashti didn't listen to come with the chamberlains; so the king was grieved and angered. 13 And he said to his friends, "This is what Vashti said. Therefore, pronounce your legal judgement on this case." 14 So Arkesaeus, Sarsathaeus, and Malisear,

the princes of the Persians and Medes, who were near the king, who sat chief in rank by the king, drew near to him, **15** and reported to him according to the laws what it was proper to do to Queen Vashti, because she had not done the things commanded by the king through the chamberlains. **16** And Memucan said to the king and to the princes, "Queen Vashti has not wronged the king only, but also all the king's rulers and princes: **17** for he has told them the words of the queen, and how shedisobeyed the king. As she then refused to obey King Ahasuerus, **18** so this day the other wives of the chiefs of the Persians and Medes, having heard what she said to the king, will dare in the same way to dishonor their husbands. **19** If then it seems good to the king, let him make a royal decree, and let it be written according to the laws of the Medes and Persians, and let him not alter it: 'Don't allow the queen to come in to him any more. Let the king give her royalty to a woman better than she.' **20** Let the law of the king which he will have made be widely proclaimed in his kingdom. Then all the women will give honor to their husbands, from the poor even to the rich." **21** This advice pleased the king and the princes; and the king did as Memucan had said, **22** and sent into all his kingdom through the several provinces, according to their language, so that men might be feared in their own houses.

CHAPTER 2

1 After this, the king's anger was pacified, and he no more mentioned Vashti, bearing in mind what she had said, and how he had condemned her. **2** Then the servants of the king said, "Let chaste, beautiful young virgins be sought for the king. **3** Let the king appoint local governors in all the provinces of his kingdom, and let them select fair, chaste young ladies and bring them to the city Susa, into the women's apartment. Let them be consigned to the king's chamberlain, the keeper of the women. Then let things for purification and other needs be given to them. **4** Let the woman who pleases the king be queen instead of Vashti." This thing pleased the king; and he did so. **5** Now there was a Jew in the city Susa, and his name was Mordecai, the son of Jairus, the son of Shimei, the son of Kish, of the tribe of Benjamin. **6** He had been brought as a prisoner from Jerusalem, which Nebuchadnezzar king of Babylon had carried into captivity. **7** He had a foster child, daughter of Aminadab his father's brother. Her name was Esther. When her parents died, he brought her up to womanhood as his own. This lady was beautiful. **8** And because the king's ordinance was published, many ladies were gathered to the city of Susa under the hand of Hegai; and Esther was brought to Hegai, the keeper of the women. **9** The lady pleased him, and she found favor in his sight. He hurried to give her the things for purification, her portion, and the seven maidens appointed her out of the palace. He treated her and her maidens well in the women's apartment. **10** But Esther didn't reveal her family or her kindred; for Mordecai had charged her not to tell. **11** But Mordecai used to walk every day by the women's court, to see what would become of Esther. **12** Now this was the time for a virgin to go into the king, when she should have fulfilled twelve months; for so are the days of purification fulfilled, six months while they are anointing themselves with oil of myrrh, and six months with spices and women's purifications. **13** And then the lady goes in to the king. The officer that he commands to do so will bring her to come in with him from the women's apartment to the king's chamber. **14** She enters in the evening, and in the morning she departs to the second women's apartment, where Hegai the king's chamberlain is keeper of the women. She doesn't go in to the king again, unless she is called by name. **15** And when the time was fulfilled for Esther the daughter of Aminadab the brother of Mordecai's father to go in to the king, she neglected nothing which the chamberlain, the women's keeper, commanded; for Esther found grace in the sight of all who looked at her. **16** So Esther went in to King Ahasuerus in the twelfth month, which is Adar, in the seventh year of his reign. **17** The king loved Esther, and she found favor beyond all the other virgins. He put the queen's crown on her. **18** The king made a banquet for all his friends and great men for seven days, and he highly celebrated the marriage of Esther; and he granted a remission of taxes to those who were under his dominion. **19** Meanwhile, Mordecai served in the palace. **20** Now Esther had not revealed her kindred; for so Mordecai commanded her, to fear God, and perform his commandments, as when she was with him. Esther didn't change her manner of life. **21** Two chamberlains of the king, the chiefs of the bodyguard, were grieved, because Mordecai was promoted; and they sought to kill King Ahasuerus. **22** And the matter was discovered by Mordecai, and he made it known to Esther, and she declared to the king the matter of the conspiracy. **23** And the king examined the two chamberlains and hanged them. Then the king gave orders to make a note for a memorial in the royal records of the good offices of Mordecai, as a commendation.

CHAPTER 3

1 After this, King Ahasuerus highly honored Haman the son of Hammedatha, the Bugaean. He exalted him and set his seat above all his friends. **2** All in the palace bowed down to him, for so the king had given orders to do; but Mordecai didn't bow down to him. **3** And they in the king's palace said to Mordecai, "Mordecai, why do you transgress the commands of the king?" **4** They questioned him daily, but he didn't listen to them; so they reported to Haman that Mordecai resisted the commands of the king; and Mordecai had shown to them that he was a Jew. **5** When Haman understood that Mordecai didn't bow down to him, he was greatly enraged, **6** and took counsel to utterly destroy all the Jews who were under the rule of Ahasuerus. **7** In the twelfth year of the reign of Ahasuerus in the twelfth year of the reign of Ahasuerus, he made a decision by casting lots by day and month, to kill the race of Mordecai in one day. The lot fell on the fourteenth day of the month of Adar. **8** So he spoke to King Ahasuerus, saying, "There is a nation scattered among the nations in all your kingdom, and their laws differ from all the other nations. They disobey the king's laws. It is not expedient for the king to tolerate them. **9** If it seems good to the king, let him make a decree to destroy them, and I will remit into the king's treasury ten thousand talents of silver." **10** So the king took off his ring, and gave it into the hands of Haman, to seal the decrees against the Jews. **11** The king said to Haman, "Keep the silver, and treat the nation as you will." **12** So the king's recorders were called in the first month, on the thirteenth day, and they wrote as Haman commanded to the captains and governors in every province, from India even to Ethiopia, to one hundred twenty-seven provinces; and to the rulers of the nations according to their languages, in the name of King Ahasuerus. **13** The message was sent by couriers throughout the kingdom of Ahasuerus, to utterly destroy the race of the Jews on the first day of the twelfth month,

which is Adar, and to plunder their goods. [[The following is the copy of the letter. "From the great King Ahasuerus to the rulers and the governors under them of one hundred twenty-seven provinces, from India even to Ethiopia, who hold authority under him: "Ruling over many nations and having obtained dominion over the whole world, I was determined (not elated by the confidence of power, but ever conducting myself with great moderation and gentleness) to make the lives of my subjects continually tranquil, desiring both to maintain the kingdom quiet and orderly to its utmost limits, and to restore the peace desired by all men. When I had asked my counselors how this should be brought to pass, Haman, who excels in soundness of judgment among us, and has been manifestly well inclined without wavering and with unshaken fidelity, and had obtained the second post in the kingdom, informed us that a certain ill-disposed people is mixed up with all the tribes throughout the world, opposed in their law to every other nation, and continually neglecting the commands of the king, so that the united government blamelessly administered by us is not quietly established. Having then conceived that this nation is continually set in opposition to every man, introducing as a change a foreign code of laws, and injuriously plotting to accomplish the worst of evils against our interests, and against the happy establishment of the monarchy; we instruct you in the letter written by Haman, who is set over the public affairs and is our second governor, to destroy them all utterly with their wives and children by the swords of the enemies, without pitying or sparing any, on the fourteenth day of the twelfth month Adar, of the present year; that the people previously and now ill-disposed to us having been violently consigned to death in one day, may hereafter secure to us continually a well constituted and quiet state of affairs."]] **14** Copies of the letters were published in every province; and an order was given to all the nations to be ready for that day. **15** This business was hastened also in Susa. The king and Haman began to drink, but the city was troubled.

CHAPTER 4

1 But Mordecai, having perceived what was done, tore his garments, put on sackcloth, and sprinkled dust upon himself. Having rushed out through the open street of the city, he cried with a loud voice, "A nation that has done no wrong is going to be destroyed!" **2** He came to the king's gate and stood; for it was not lawful for him to enter into the palace wearing sackcloth and ashes. **3** And in every province where the letters were published, there was crying, lamentation, and great mourning on the part of the Jews. They wore sackcloth and ashes. **4** The queen's maids and chamberlains went in and told her; and when she had heard what was done, she was disturbed. She sent to clothe Mordecai and take away his sackcloth; but he refused. **5** So Esther called for her chamberlain Hasach, who waited upon her; and she sent to learn the truth from Mordecai. **7** Mordecai showed him what was done, and the promise which Haman had made the king of ten thousand talents to be paid into the treasury, that he might destroy the Jews. **8** And he gave him the copy of what was published in Susa concerning their destruction to show to Esther; and told him to charge her to go in and entreat the king, and to beg him for the people. "Remember, he said, the days of your humble condition, how you were nursed by my hand; because Haman who holds the next place to the king has spoken against us for death. Call upon the Lord, and speak to the king concerning us, to deliver us from death." **9** So Hasach went in and told her all these words. **10** Esther said to Hasach, "Go to Mordecai, and say, **11** 'All the nations of the empire know than any man or woman who goes in to the king into the inner court without being called, that person can't live; except to whomever the king stretches out his golden scepter, he will live. I haven't been called to go into the king for thirty days.' " **12** So Hasach reported to Mordecai all the words of Esther. **13** Then Mordecai said to Hasach, "Go, and say to her, 'Esther, don't say to yourself that you alone will escape in the kingdom, more than all the other Jews. **14** For if you refuse to listen on this occasion, help and protection will come to the Jews from another place; but you and your father's house will perish. Who knows if you have been made queen for this occasion?' " **15** And Esther sent the man that came to her to Mordecai, saying, **16** "Go and assemble the Jews that are in Susa, and all of you fast for me, and don't eat or drink for three days, night and day. My maidens and I will also fast. Then I will go in to the king contrary to the law, even if I must die." **17** So Mordecai went and did all that Esther commanded him. **18** [[He prayed to the Lord, making mention of all the works of the

Lord. **19** He said, "Lord God, you are king ruling over all, for all things are in your power, and there is no one who can oppose you in your purpose to save Israel; **20** for you have made the heaven and the earth and every wonderful thing under heaven. **21** You are Lord of all, and there is no one who can resist you, Lord. **22** You know all things. You know, Lord, that it is not in insolence, nor arrogance, nor love of glory, that I have done this, to refuse to bow down to the arrogant Haman. **23** For I would gladly have kissed the soles of his feet for the safety of Israel. **24** But I have done this that I might not set the glory of man above the glory of God. I will not worship anyone except you, my Lord, and I will not do these things in arrogance. **25** And now, O Lord God, the King, the God of Abraham, spare your people, for our enemies are planning our destruction, and they have desired to destroy your ancient inheritance. **26** Do not overlook your people, whom you have redeemed for yourself out of the land of Egypt. **27** Listen to my prayer. Have mercy on your inheritance and turn our mourning into gladness, that we may live and sing praise to your name, O Lord. Don't utterly destroy the mouth of those who praise you, O Lord." **28** All Israel cried with all their might, for death was before their eyes. **29** And queen Esther took refuge in the Lord, being taken as it were in the agony of death. **30** Having taken off her glorious apparel, she put on garments of distress and mourning. Instead of grand perfumes she filled her head with ashes and dung. She greatly brought down her body, and she filled every place of her glad adorning with her tangled hair. **31** She implored the Lord God of Israel, and said, "O my Lord, you alone are our king. Help me. I am destitute, and have no helper but you, **32** for my danger is near at hand. **33** I have heard from my birth, in the tribe of my kindred that you, Lord, took Israel out of all the nations, and our fathers out of all their kindred for a perpetual inheritance, and have done for them all that you have said. **34** And now we have sinned before you, and you have delivered us into the hands of our enemies, **35** because we honored their gods. You are righteous, O Lord. **36** But now they have not been content with the bitterness of our slavery, but have laid their hands on the hands of their idols **37** to abolish the decree of your mouth, and utterly to destroy your inheritance, and to stop the mouth of those who praise you, and to extinguish the glory of your house and your alter, **38** and to open the mouth of the Gentiles to speak the praises of vanities, and that a mortal king should be admired forever. **39** O Lord, don't resign your scepter to them that are not, and don't let them laugh at our fall, but turn their counsel against themselves, and make an example of him who has begun to injure us. **40** Remember us, O Lord, manifest yourself in the time of our affliction. Encourage me, O King of gods, and ruler of all dominion! **41** Put harmonious speech into my mouth before the lion and turn his heart to hate him who fights against us, to the utter destruction of him who agrees with him. **42** But deliver us by your hand, and help me who am destitute, and have none but you, O Lord. **43** You know all things, and know that I hate the glory of transgressors, and that I abhor the couch of the uncircumcised, and of every stranger. **44** You know my necessity, for I abhor the symbol of my proud station, which is upon my head in the days of my splendor. I abhor it as a menstruous cloth, and I don't wear it in the days of my tranquility. **45** Your handmaid has not eaten at Haman's table, and I have not honored the banquet of the king, neither have I drunk wine of libations. **46** Neither has your handmaid rejoiced since the day of my promotion until now, except in you, O Lord God of Abraham. **47** O God, who has power over all, listen to the voice of the desperate, and deliver us from the hand of those who devise mischief. Deliver me from my fear.]]

CHAPTER 5

1 It came to pass on the third day, when she had ceased praying, that she took off her servant's dress, and put on her glorious apparel. Being splendidly dressed and having called upon God the Overseer and Preserver of all things, she took her two maids, and she leaned upon one, as a delicate female, and the other followed bearing her train. She was blooming in the perfection of her beauty. Her face was cheerful and looked lovely, but her heart was filled with fear. Having passed through all the doors, she stood before the king. He was sitting on his royal throne. He had put on all his glorious apparel, covered all over with gold and precious stones, and was very terrifying. And having raised his face resplendent with glory, he looked with intense anger. The queen fell and changed her color as she fainted. She bowed herself upon the head of the maid who went before her. But God

changed the spirit of the king to gentleness, and in intense feeling, he sprang from off his throne, and took her into his arms, until she recovered. He comforted her with peaceful words, and said to her, "What is the matter, Esther? I am your relative. Cheer up! You will not die, for our command is openly declared to you: 'Draw near.' " **2** And having raised the golden scepter, he laid it upon her neck, and embraced her. He said, "Speak to me." So, she said to him, "I saw you, my lord, as an angel of God, and my heart was troubled for fear of your glory; for you, my lord, are to be wondered at, and your face is full of grace." While she was speaking, she fainted and fell. Then the king was troubled, and all his servants comforted her. **3** The king said, "What do you desire, Esther? What is your request? Ask even to the half of my kingdom, and it will be yours." **4** Esther said, "Today is a special day. So, if it seems good to the king, let both him and Haman come to the feast which I will prepare this day." **5** The king said, "Hurry and bring Haman here, that we may do as Esther said." So, they both came to the feast about which Esther had spoken. **6** At the banquet, the king said to Esther, "What is your request, queen Esther? You will have all that you require." **7** She said, "My request and my petition are: **8** if I have found favor in the king's sight, let the king and Haman come again tomorrow to the feast which I will prepare for them, and tomorrow I will do the same." **9** So Haman went out from the king very glad and merry; but when Haman saw Mordecai the Jew in the court, he was greatly enraged. **10** Having gone into his own house, he called his friends, and his wife Zeresh. **11** He showed them his wealth and the glory with which the king had invested him, and how he had promoted him to be chief ruler in the kingdom. **12** Haman said, "The queen has called no one to the feast with the king but me, and I am invited tomorrow. **13** But these things don't please me while I see Mordecai the Jew in the court. **14** Then Zeresh his wife and his friends said to him, "Let a fifty-cubit tall gallows be made for you. In the morning you speak to the king, and let Mordecai be hanged on the gallows; but you go in to the feast with the king and be merry." The saying pleased Haman, and the gallows was prepared.

CHAPTER 6

1 The Lord removed sleep from the king that night; so, he told his servant to bring in the books, the registers of daily events, to read to him. **2** And he found the records written concerning Mordecai, how he had told the king about the king's two chamberlains, when they were keeping guard, and sought to lay hands on Ahasuerus. **3** The king said, "What honor or favor have we done for Mordecai?" The king's servants said, "You haven't done anything for him." **4** And while the king was enquiring about the kindness of Mordecai, behold, Haman was in the court. The king said, "Who is in the court? Now Haman had come in to speak to the king about hanging Mordecai on the gallows which he had prepared. **5** The king's servants said, "Behold, Haman stands in the court." And the king said, "Call him!" **6** The king said to Haman, "What should I do for the man whom I wish to honor?" Haman said within himself, "Whom would the king honor but myself?" **7** He said to the king, "As for the man whom the king wishes to honor, **8** let the king's servants bring the robe of fine linen which the king puts on, and the horse on which the king rides, **9** and let him give it to one of the king's noble friends, and let him dress the man whom the king loves. Let him mount him on the horse, and proclaim through the streets of the city, saying, "This is what will be done for every man whom the king honors!" **10** Then the king said to Haman, "You have spoken well. Do so for Mordecai the Jew, who waits in the palace, and let not a word of what you have spoken be neglected!" **11** So Haman took the robe and the horse, dressed Mordecai, mounted him on the horse, and went through the streets of the city, and proclaiming, saying, "This is what will be done for every man whom the king wishes to honor." **12** Then Mordecai returned to the palace; but Haman went home mourning, and having his head covered. **13** Haman related the events that had happened to him to Zeresh his wife, and to his friends. His friends and his wife said to him, "If Mordecai is of the race of the Jews, and you have begun to be humbled before him, you will assuredly fall, and you will not be able to withstand him, for the living God is with him." **14** While they were still speaking, the chamberlains arrived, to rush Haman to the banquet which Esther had prepared.

CHAPTER 7

1 So the king and Haman went in to drink with the queen. **2** The king said to Esther at the banquet on the second day, "What is it, queen Esther? What is your request? What is your petition? It will be done for you, up to half of my kingdom." **3** She answered and said, "If I have found favor in the sight of the king, let my life be granted as my petition, and my people as my request. **4** For both I and my people are sold for destruction, pillage, and genocide. If both we and our children were sold for male and female slaves, I would not have bothered you, for this isn't worthy of the king's palace." **5** The king said, "Who has dared to do this thing?" **6** Esther said, "The enemy is Haman, this wicked man!" Then Haman was troubled before the king and the queen. **7** The king rose up from the banquet to go into the garden. Haman began to beg the queen for mercy; for he saw that he was in trouble. **8** The king returned from the garden; and Haman had fallen upon the bed, begging the queen for mercy. The king said, "Will you even assault my wife in my house?" And when Haman heard it, he changed countenance. **9** And Bugathan, one of the chamberlains, said to the king, "Behold, Haman has also prepared a gallows for Mordecai, who spoke concerning the king, and a fifty-cubit high gallows has been set up on Haman's property." The king said, "Let him be hanged on it!" **10** So Haman was hanged on the gallows that had been prepared for Mordecai. Then the king's wrath was appeased.

CHAPTER 8

1 On that day, King Ahasuerus gave to Esther all that belonged to Haman the slanderer. The king called Mordecai; for Esther had shown that he was related to her. **2** The king took the ring which he had taken away from Haman and gave it to Mordecai. Esther appointed Mordecai over all that had been Haman's. **3** She spoke yet again to the king, and fell at his feet, and implored him to undo Haman's mischief and all that he had done against the Jews. **4** Then the king extended the golden scepter to Esther; and Esther arose to stand near the king. **5** Esther said, "If it seems good to you, and I have found favor in your sight, let an order be sent that the letters sent by Haman may be reversed, that were written for the destruction of the Jews who are in your kingdom. **6** For how could I see the affliction of my people, and how could I survive the destruction of my kindred?" **7** Then the king said to Esther, "If I have given and freely granted you all that was Haman's, and hanged him on a gallows, because he laid his hands upon the Jews, what more do you seek? **8** Write in my name whatever seems good to you, and seal it with my ring; for whatever is written at the command of the king, and sealed with my ring, cannot be countermanded. **9** So the scribes were called in the first month, which is Nisan, on the twenty-third day of the same year; and orders were written to the Jews, whatever the king had commanded to the local governors and chiefs of the local governors, from India even to Ethiopia, one hundred twenty-seven local governors, according to the several provinces, in their own languages. **10** They were written by order of the king, sealed with his ring, and the letters were sent by the couriers. **11** In them, he charged them to use their own laws in every city, to help each other, and to treat their adversaries and those who attacked them as they pleased, **12** on one day in all the kingdom of Ahasuerus, on the thirteenth day of the twelfth month, which is Adar. **13** Let the copies be posted in conspicuous places throughout the kingdom. Let all the Jews be ready against this day, to fight against their enemies. The following is a copy of the letter containing orders. [[The great King Ahasuerus sends greetings to the rulers of provinces in one hundred twenty-seven local governance regions, from India to Ethiopia, even to those who are faithful to our interests. Many who have been frequently honored by the most abundant kindness of their benefactors have conceived ambitious designs, and not only endeavor to hurt our subjects, but moreover, not being able to bear prosperity, they also endeavor to plot against their own benefactors. They not only would utterly abolish gratitude from among men, but also, elated by the boastings of men who are strangers to all that is good, they supposed that they would escape the sin-hating vengeance of the ever-seeing God. And oftentimes evil exhortation has made partakers of the guilt of shedding innocent blood, and has involved in irremediable calamities, many of those who had been appointed to offices of authority, who had been entrusted with the management of their friends' affairs; while men, by the false sophistry of an evil disposition, have deceived the simple candor of the ruling powers. And it is possible to see this, not so much from more ancient traditionary accounts, as it is immediately in your power to see it by examining what things have been wickedly perpetrated by the baseness of men unworthily

holding power. It is right to take heed with regard to the future, that we may maintain the government in undisturbed peace for all men, adopting needful changes, and ever judging those cases which come under our notice with truly equitable decisions. For whereas Haman, a Macedonian, the son of Hammedatha, in reality an alien from the blood of the Persians, and differing widely from our mild course of government, having been hospitably entertained by us, obtained so large a share of our universal kindness as to be called our father, and to continue the person next to the royal throne, reverenced of all; he however, overcome by pride, endeavored to deprive us of our dominion, and our life; having by various and subtle artifices demanded for destruction both Mordecai our deliverer and perpetual benefactor, and Esther the blameless consort of our kingdom, along with their whole nation. For by these methods he thought, having surprised us in a defenseless state, to transfer the dominion of the Persians to the Macedonians. But we find that the Jews, who have been consigned to destruction by the most abominable of men, are not malefactors, but living according to the most just laws, and being the sons of the living God, the most high and mighty, who maintains the kingdom, to us as well as to our forefathers, in the most excellent order. You will therefore do well in refusing to obey the letter sent by Haman the son of Hammedatha, because he who has done these things has been hanged with his whole family at the gates of Susa, Almighty God having swiftly returned to him a worthy punishment. We enjoin you then, having openly published a copy of this letter in every place, to give the Jews permission to use their own lawful customs, and to strengthen them, that on the thirteenth of the twelfth month Adar, on the self-same day, they may defend themselves against those who attack them in a time of affliction. For in the place of the destruction of the chosen race, Almighty God has granted them this time of gladness. Therefore, you also, among your notable feasts, must keep a distinct day with all festivity, that both now and hereafter it may be a day of deliverance to us and who are well disposed toward the Persians, but to those that plotted against us a memorial of destruction. And every city and province collectively, which will not do accordingly, will be consumed with vengeance by spear and fire. It will be made not only inaccessible to men, but most hateful to wild beasts and birds forever.]] Let the copies be posted in conspicuous places throughout the kingdom and let all the Jews be ready against this day, to fight against their enemies. **14** So the horsemen went out with haste to perform the king's commands. The ordinance was also published in Susa. **15** Mordecai went out robed in royal apparel, wearing a golden crown and a diadem of fine purple linen. The people in Susa saw it and rejoiced. **16** The Jews had light and gladness in every city and province where the ordinance was published. **17** Wherever the proclamation took place, the Jews had joy and gladness, feasting and mirth. Many of the Gentiles were circumcised and became Jews, for fear of the Jews.

CHAPTER 9

1 Now in the twelfth month, on the thirteenth day of the month which is Adar, the letters written by the king arrived. **2** In that day, the adversaries of the Jews perished; for no one resisted, through fear of them. **3** For the chiefs of the local governors, and the princes and the royal scribes, honored the Jews; for the fear of Mordecai was upon them. **4** For the order of the king was in force, that he should be celebrated in all the kingdom. **6** In the city Susa the Jews killed five hundred men, **7** including Pharsannes, Delphon, Phasga, **8** Pharadatha, Barea, Sarbaca, **9** Marmasima, Ruphaeus, Arsaeus, and Zabuthaeus, **10** the ten sons of Haman the son of Hammedatha the Bugaean, the enemy of the Jews, and they plundered their property on the same day. **11** The number of those who perished in Susa was reported to the king. **12** Then the king said to Esther, "The Jews have slain five hundred men in the city Susa. What do you think they have done in the rest of the country? What more do you ask, that it may be done for you?" **13** Esther said to the king, "Let it be granted to the Jews to do the same to them tomorrow. Also hang the bodies of the ten sons of Haman." **14** He permitted it to be done; and he gave up to the Jews of the city the bodies of the sons of Haman to hang. **15** The Jews assembled in Susa on the fourteenth day of Adar and killed three hundred men but plundered no property. **16** The rest of the Jews who were in the kingdom assembled, and helped one another, and obtained rest from their enemies; for they destroyed fifteen thousand of them on the thirteenth day of Adar but took no spoil. **17** They rested on the fourteenth of the same month and kept it as a day of rest with joy and gladness. **18** The Jews in the city Susa assembled also on the fourteenth day and rested; and they also observed the fifteenth with joy and gladness. **19** On this account then it is that the Jews dispersed in every foreign land keep the fourteenth of Adar as a holy day with joy, each sending gifts of food to his neighbor. **20** Mordecai wrote these things in a book, and sent them to the Jews, as many as were in the kingdom of Ahasuerus, both those who were near and those who were far away, **21** to establish these as joyful days, and to keep the fourteenth and fifteenth of Adar; **22** for on these days the Jews obtained rest from their enemies; and in that month, which was Adar, in which a change was made for them, from mourning to joy, and from sorrow to a good day, to spend the whole of it in good days of feasting and gladness, sending portions to their friends and to the poor. **23** And the Jews consented to this as Mordecai wrote to them, **24** showing how Haman the son of Hammedatha the Macedonian fought against them, how he made a decree and cast lots to destroy them utterly; **25** also how he went in to the king, telling him to hang Mordecai; but all the calamities he tried to bring upon the Jews came upon himself, and he was hanged, along with his children. **26** Therefore these days were called Purim, because of the lots (for in their language they are called Purim) because of the words of this letter, and because of all they suffered on this account, and all that happened to them. **27** Mordecai established it, and the Jews took upon themselves, and upon their seed, and upon those that were joined to them to observe it, neither would they on any account behave differently; but these days were to be a memorial kept in every generation, city, family, and province. **28** These days of the Purim will be kept forever, and their memorial will not fail in any generation. **29** Queen Esther the daughter of Aminadab, and Mordecai the Jew, wrote all that they had done, and the confirmation of the letter of Purim. **31** Mordecai and Esther the queen established this decision on their own, pledging their own health to their plan. **32** And Esther established it by a command forever, and it was written for a memorial.

CHAPTER 10

1 The king levied a tax upon his kingdom both by land and sea. **2** As for his strength and valor, and the wealth and glory of his kingdom, behold, they are written in the book of the Persians and Medes for a memorial. 3 Mordecai was viceroy to King Ahasuerus, and was a great man in the kingdom, honored by the Jews, and lived his life loved by all his nation. 4 [[Mordecai said, "These things have come from God. 5 For I remember the dream which I had concerning these matters; for not one detail of them has failed. 6 There was the little spring which became a river, and there was light, and the sun and much water. The river is Esther, whom the king married, and made queen. 7 The two serpents are Haman and me. 8 The nations are those *nations* who combined to destroy the name of the Jews. 9 But as for my nation, this is Israel, even those who cried to God and were delivered; for the Lord delivered his people. The Lord rescued us out of all these calamities; and God worked such signs and great wonders as have not been done among the nations. 10 Therefore he ordained two lots. One for the people of God, and one for all the other nations. 11 And these two lots came for an appointed season, and for a day of judgment, before God, and for all the nations. 12 God remembered his people and vindicated his inheritance. 13 They will observe these days in the month Adar, on the fourteenth and on the fifteenth day of the month, with an assembly, joy, and gladness before God, throughout the generations forever among his people Israel. 14 In the fourth year of the reign of Ptolemeus and Cleopatra, Dositheus, who said he was a priest and Levite, and Ptolemeus his son, brought this letter of Purim, which they said was the same, and that Lysimachus the son of Ptolemeus, who was in Jerusalem, had interpreted.]]

PSALM 151

Psalm 151 is a short psalm found in most copies of the Septuagint but not in the Hebrew Bible. The Greek title given to this psalm indicates that it is supernumerary. It is also included in some manuscripts of the Peshitta. The psalm concerns the story of David and Goliath. The Eastern Orthodox Church as well as the Coptic Orthodox Church, Armenian Apostolic Church and the Armenian Catholic Church accept Psalm 151 as deuterocanonical.

This Psalm is ascribed to David and is outside the number. When he slew Goliath in single combat.

1 I was small among my brothers, and youngest in my father's house. I tended my father's sheep. 2 My hands formed a musical instrument, and my fingers tuned a lute. 3 Who will tell my Lord? The Lord himself, he himself hears. 4 He sent out his angel and took me from my father's sheep, and he anointed me with his anointing oil. 5 My brothers were handsome and tall; but the Lord didn't take pleasure in them. 6 I went out to meet the Philistine, and he cursed me by his idols. 7 But I drew his own sword and beheaded him and removed reproach from the children of Israel.

DANIEL

With LXX additions in bold brackets

The Septuagint (LXX) version of Daniel contains three sections not found in the Hebrew version of the text. These are known as "The Prayer of Azariah and Song of the Three Holy Children" (3:24–90); "Susanna and the Elders" (Ch. 13); and "Bel and the Dragon" (Ch. 14). The whole book of Daniel is included here with these additions denoted by bolded double brackets.

CHAPTER 1

1 In the third year of the reign of Jehoiakim king of Judah, Nebuchadnezzar king of Babylon came to Jerusalem and besieged it. 2 The Lord gave Jehoiakim king of Judah into his hand, with part of the vessels of the house of God; and he carried them into the land of Shinar to the house of his god. He brought the vessels into the treasure house of his god. 3 The king spoke to Ashpenaz the master of his eunuchs, that he should bring in some of the children of Israel, even of the royal offspringand of the nobles; 4 youths in whom was no defect, but well-favored, and skillful in all wisdom, and endowed with knowledge, and understanding science, and who had the ability to stand in the king's palace; and that he should teach them the learning and the language of the Chaldeans. 5 The king appointed for them a daily portion of the king's dainties, and of the wine which he drank, and that they should be nourished three years; that at its end they should stand before the king. 6 Now among these were of the children of Judah: Daniel, Hananiah, Mishael, and Azariah. 7 The prince of the eunuchs gave names to them: to Daniel he gave the name Belteshazzar; to Hananiah, Shadrach; to Mishael, Meshach; and to Azariah, Abednego. 8 But Daniel purposed in his heart that he would not defile himself with the king's dainties, nor with the wine which he drank. Therefore, he requested of the prince of the eunuchs that he might not defile himself. 9 Now God made Daniel find kindness and compassion in the sight of the prince of the eunuchs. 10 The prince of the eunuchs said to Daniel, "I fear my lord the king, who has appointed your food and your drink. For why should he see your faces worse looking than the youths who are of your own age? Then you would endanger my head with the king." 11 Then Daniel said to the steward whom the prince of the eunuchs had appointed over Daniel, Hananiah, Mishael, and Azariah: 12 "Test your servants, I beg you, ten days; and let them give us vegetables to eat, and water to drink. 13 Then let our faces be examined before you, and the face of the youths who eat of the king's dainties; and as you see, deal with your servants." 14 So he listened to them in this matter and tested them for ten days. 15 At the end of ten days, their faces appeared fairer, and they were fatter in flesh, than all the youths who ate of the king's dainties. 16 So the steward took away their dainties, and the wine that they would drink, and gave them vegetables. 17 Now as for these four youths, God gave them knowledge and skill in all learning and wisdom; and Daniel had understanding in all visions and dreams. 18 At the end of the days which the king had appointed for bringing them in, the prince of the eunuchs brought them in before Nebuchadnezzar. 19 The king talked with them; and among them all was found no one like Daniel, Hananiah, Mishael, and Azariah. Therefore, stood they before the king. 20 In every matter of wisdom and understanding, concerning which the king inquired of them, he found them ten times better than all the magicians and enchanters who were in all his realm. 21 Daniel continued even to the first year of king Cyrus.

CHAPTER 2

1 In the second year of the reign of Nebuchadnezzar, Nebuchadnezzar dreamed dreams; and his spirit was troubled, and his sleep went from him. 2 Then the king commanded that the magicians, the enchanters, the sorcerers, and the Chaldeans be called to tell the king his dreams. So they came in and stood before the king. 3 The king said to them, "I have dreamed a dream, and my spirit is troubled to know the dream." 4 Then the Chaldeans spoke to the king in the Syrian language, "O king, live forever! Tell your servants the dream, and we will show the interpretation." 5 The king answered the

Chaldeans, "The thing has gone from me. If you don't make known to me the dream and its interpretation, you will be cut in pieces, and your houses will be made a dunghill. **6** But if you show the dream and its interpretation, you will receive from me gifts, rewards, and great honor. Therefore, show me the dream and its interpretation." **7** They answered the second time and said, "Let the king tell his servants the dream, and we will show the interpretation." **8** The king answered, "I know of a certainty that you are trying to gain time, because you see the thing has gone from me. **9** But if you don't make known to me the dream, there is but one law for you; for you have prepared lying and corrupt words to speak before me, until the situation changes. Therefore, tell me the dream, and I will know that you can show me its interpretation." **10** The Chaldeans answered before the king, and said, "There is not a man on the earth who can show the king's matter, because no king, lord, or ruler, has asked such a thing of any magician, enchanter, or Chaldean. **11** It is a rare thing that the king requires, and there is no other who can show it before the king, except the gods, whose dwelling is not with flesh." **12** Because of this, the king was angry and very furious, and commanded that all the wise men of Babylon be destroyed. **13** So the decree went out, and the wise men were to be slain. They sought Daniel and his companions to be slain. **14** Then Daniel returned answer with counsel and prudence to Arioch the captain of the king's guard, who had gone out to kill the wise men of Babylon. **15** He answered Arioch the king's captain, "Why is the decree so urgent from the king?" Then Arioch made the thing known to Daniel. **16** Daniel went in, and desired of the king that he would appoint him a time, and he would show the king the interpretation. **17** Then Daniel went to his house and made the thing known to Hananiah, Mishael, and Azariah, his companions: **18** that they would desire mercies of the God of heaven concerning this secret; that Daniel and his companions would not perish with the rest of the wise men of Babylon. **19** Then the secret was revealed to Daniel in a vision of the night. Then Daniel blessed the God of heaven. **20** Daniel answered, "Blessed be the name of God forever and ever; for wisdom and might are his. **21** He changes the times and the seasons. He removes kings and sets up kings. He gives wisdom to the wise, and knowledge to those who have understanding. **22** He reveals the deep and secret things. He knows what is in the darkness, and the light dwells with him. **23** I thank you and praise you, O God of my fathers, who have given me wisdom and might, and have now made known to me what we desired of you; for you have made known to us the king's matter." **24** Therefore Daniel went in to Arioch, whom the king had appointed to destroy the wise men of Babylon. He went and said this to him: "Don't destroy the wise men of Babylon. Bring me in before the king, and I will show to the king the interpretation." **25** Then Arioch brought in Daniel before the king in haste, and said this to him: "I have found a man of the children of the captivity of Judah who will make known to the king the interpretation." **26** The king answered Daniel, whose name was Belteshazzar, "Are you able to make known to me the dream which I have seen, and its interpretation?" **27** Daniel answered before the king, and said, "The secret which the king has demanded can't be shown to the king by wise men, enchanters, magicians, or soothsayers; **28** but there is a God in heaven who reveals secrets, and he has made known to king Nebuchadnezzar what will be in the latter days. Your dream, and the visions of your head on your bed, are these: **29** "As for you, O king, your thoughts came on your bed, what should happen hereafter; and he who reveals secrets has made known to you what will happen. **30** But as for me, this secret is not revealed to me for any wisdom that I have more than any living, but to the intent that the interpretation may be made known to the king, and that you may know the thoughts of your heart. **31** "You, O king, saw, and behold, a great image. This image, which was mighty, and whose brightness was excellent, stood before you; and its appearance was terrifying. **32** As for this image, its head was of fine gold, its breast and its arms of silver, its belly and its thighs of bronze, **33** its legs of iron, its feet part of iron, and part of clay. **34** You saw until a stone was cut out without hands, which struck the image on its feet that were of iron and clay and broke them in pieces. **35** Then the iron, the clay, the bronze, the silver, and the gold were broken in pieces together, and became like the chaff of the summer threshing floors. The wind carried them away, so that no place was found for them. The stone that struck the image became a great mountain and filled the whole earth. **36** "This is the dream; and we

will tell its interpretation before the king.
37 You, O king, are king of kings, to whom the
God of heaven has given the kingdom, the
power, the strength, and the glory.
38 Wherever the children of men dwell, he has
given the animals of the field and the birds of
the sky into your hand and has made you rule
over them all. You are the head of gold.
39 "After you, another kingdom will arise that
is inferior to you; and another third kingdom
of bronze, which will rule over all the earth.
40 The fourth kingdom will be strong as iron,
because iron breaks in pieces and subdues all
things; and as iron that crushes all these, it will
break in pieces and crush. **41** Whereas you
saw the feet and toes, part of potters' clay, and
part of iron, it will be a divided kingdom; but
there will be in it of the strength of the iron,
because you saw the iron mixed with miry
clay. **42** As the toes of the feet were part of
iron, and part of clay, so the kingdom will be
partly strong, and partly broken. **43** Whereas
you saw the iron mixed with miry clay, they
will mingle themselves with the seed of men;
but they won't cling to one another, even as
iron does not mix with clay. **44** "In the days of
those kings the God of heaven will set up a
kingdom which will never be destroyed, nor
will its sovereignty be left to another people;
but it will break in pieces and consume all
these kingdoms, and it will stand forever.
45 Because you saw that a stone was cut out of
the mountain without hands, and that it broke
in pieces the iron, the bronze, the clay, the
silver, and the gold; the great God has made
known to the king what will happen hereafter.
The dream is certain, and its interpretation
sure." **46** Then king Nebuchadnezzar fell on
his face, worshiped Daniel, and commanded
that they should offer an offering and sweet
odors to him. **47** The king answered to Daniel,
and said, "Of a truth your God is the God of
gods, and the Lord of kings, and a revealer of
secrets, since you have been able to reveal this
secret." **48** Then the king made Daniel great,
and gave him many great gifts, and made him
rule over the whole province of Babylon, and
to be chief governor over all the wise men of
Babylon. **49** Daniel requested of the king, and
he appointed Shadrach, Meshach, and
Abednego over the affairs of the province of
Babylon; but Daniel was in the king's gate.

CHAPTER 3

1 Nebuchadnezzar the king made an image of
gold, whose height was sixty cubits, and its
width six cubits. He set it up in the plain of
Dura, in the province of Babylon. **2** Then
Nebuchadnezzar the king sent to gather
together the local governors, the deputies, and
the governors, the judges, the treasurers, the
counselors, the sheriffs, and all the rulers of
the provinces, to come to the dedication of the
image which Nebuchadnezzar the king had set
up. **3** Then the local governors, the deputies,
and the governors, the judges, the treasurers,
the counselors, the sheriffs, and all the rulers
of the provinces, were gathered together to the
dedication of the image that Nebuchadnezzar
the king had set up; and they stood before the
image that Nebuchadnezzar had set up. **4** Then
the herald cried aloud, "To you it is
commanded, peoples, nations, and languages,
5 that whenever you hear the sound of the
horn, flute, zither, lyre, harp, pipe, and all
kinds of music, you fall down and worship the
golden image that Nebuchadnezzar the king
has set up. **6** Whoever doesn't fall down and
worship will be cast into the middle of a
burning fiery furnace the same hour."
7 Therefore at that time, when all the peoples
heard the sound of the horn, flute, zither, lyre,
harp, pipe, and all kinds of music, all the
peoples, the nations, and the languages, fell
down and worshiped the golden image that
Nebuchadnezzar the king had set up.
8 Therefore at that time certain Chaldeans
came near and brought accusation against the
Jews. **9** They answered Nebuchadnezzar the
king, "O king, live forever! **10** You, O king,
have made a decree that every man who hears
the sound of the horn, flute, zither, lyre, harp,
pipe, and all kinds of music will fall down and
worship the golden image; **11** and whoever
doesn't fall down and worship will be cast into
the middle of a burning fiery furnace. **12** There
are certain Jews whom you have appointed
over the affairs of the province of Babylon:
Shadrach, Meshach, and Abednego. These
men, O king, have not respected you. They
don't serve your gods, and don't worship the
golden image which you have set up." **13** Then
Nebuchadnezzar in rage and fury commanded
that Shadrach, Meshach, and Abednego be
brought. Then these men were brought before
the king. **14** Nebuchadnezzar answered them,
"Is it on purpose, Shadrach, Meshach, and
Abednego, that you don't serve my god, nor
worship the golden image which I have set up?
15 Now if you are ready whenever you hear
the sound of the horn, flute, zither, lyre, harp,
pipe, and all kinds of music to fall down and

worship the image which I have made, good; but if you don't worship, you will be cast the same hour into the middle of a burning fiery furnace. Who is that god who will deliver you out of my hands?" **16** Shadrach, Meshach, and Abednego answered the king, "Nebuchadnezzar, we have no need to answer you in this matter. **17** If it happens, our God whom we serve is able to deliver us from the burning fiery furnace; and he will deliver us out of your hand, O king. **18** But if not, let it be known to you, O king, that we will not serve your gods or worship the golden image which you have set up." **19** Then Nebuchadnezzar was full of fury, and the form of his appearance was changed against Shadrach, Meshach, and Abednego. He spoke and commanded that they should heat the furnace seven times more than it was usually heated. **20** He commanded certain mighty men who were in his army to bind Shadrach, Meshach, and Abednego, and to cast them into the burning fiery furnace. **21** Then these men were bound in their pants, their tunics, and their mantles, and their other clothes, and were cast into the middle of the burning fiery furnace. **22** Therefore because the king's commandment was urgent, and the furnace exceedingly hot, the flame of the fire killed those men who took up Shadrach, Meshach, and Abednego. **23** These three men, Shadrach, Meshach, and Abednego, fell down bound into the middle of the burning fiery furnace. [[**24** They walked in the midst of the fire, praising God, and blessing the Lord. **25** Then Azarias stood and prayed like this. Opening his mouth in the midst of the fire he said: **26** "Blessed are you, O Lord, you God of our fathers! Your name is worthy to be praised and glorified forevermore; **27** for you are righteous in all the things that you have done. Yes, all your works are true. Your ways are right, and all your judgments are truth. **28** In all the things that you have brought upon us, and upon the holy city of our fathers, Jerusalem, you have executed true judgments. For according to truth and justice you have brought all these things upon us because of our sins. **29** For we have sinned and committed iniquity in departing from you. **30** In all things we have trespassed, and not obeyed your commandments or kept them. We haven't done as you have commanded us, that it might go well with us. **31** Therefore all that you have brought upon us, and everything that you have done to us, you have done in true judgement.

32 You delivered us into the hands of lawless enemies, most hateful rebels, and to an unjust king who is the most wicked in all the world. **33** And now we can't open our mouth. Shame and reproach have come on your servants and those who worship you. **34** Don't utterly deliver us up, for your name's sake. Don't annul your covenant. **35** Don't cause your mercy to depart from us, for the sake of Abraham who is loved by you, and for the sake of Isaac your servant, and Israel your holy one, **36** to whom you promised that you would multiply their offspring as the stars of the sky, and as the sand that is on the seashore. **37** For we, O Lord, have become less than any nation, and are kept under this day in all the world because of our sins. **38** There isn't at this time prince, or prophet, or leader, or burnt offering, or sacrifice, or oblation, or incense, or place to offer before you, and to find mercy. **39** Nevertheless in a contrite heart and a humble spirit let us be accepted, **40** like the burnt offerings of rams and bullocks, and like tens of thousands of fat lambs. So let our sacrifice be in your sight this day, that we may wholly go after you, for they will not be ashamed who put their trust in you. **41** And now we follow you with all our heart. We fear you and seek your face. **42** Put us not to shame; but deal with us after your kindness, and according to the multitude of your mercy. **43** Deliver us also according to your marvelous works, and give glory to your name, O Lord. Let all those who harm your servants be confounded. **44** Let them be ashamed of all their power and might, and let their strength be broken. **45** Let them know that you are the Lord, the only God, and glorious over the whole world." **46** The king's servants who put them in didn't stop making the furnace hot with naphtha, pitch, tinder, and small wood, **47** so that the flame streamed out forty-nine cubits above the furnace. **48** It spread and burned those Chaldeans whom it found around the furnace. **49** But the angel of the Lord came down into the furnace together with Azarias and his fellows, and he struck the flame of the fire out of the furnace, **50** and made the midst of the furnace as it had been a moist whistling wind, so that the fire didn't touch them at all. It neither hurt nor troubled them. **51** Then the three, as out of one mouth, praised, glorified, and blessed God in the furnace, saying, **52** "Blessed are you, O Lord, you God of our fathers, to be praised and exalted above all forever! **53** Blessed is your glorious and holy name, to be praised and exalted above all forever! 54 Blessed are you in the temple of your holy glory, to be praised and glorified above all forever! 55 Blessed are you who see the depths and sit upon the cherubim, to be praised and exalted above all forever. 56 Blessed are you on the throne of your kingdom, to be praised and extolled above all forever! 57 Blessed are you in the firmament of heaven, to be praised and glorified forever! 58 O all you works of the Lord, bless the Lord! Praise and exalt him above all forever! 59 O you heavens, bless the Lord! Praise and exalt him above all forever! 60 O you angels of the Lord, bless the Lord! Praise and exalt him above all forever! 61 O all you waters that are above the sky, bless the Lord! Praise and exalt him above all forever! 62 O all you powers of the Lord, bless the Lord! Praise and exalt him above all forever! 63 O you sun and moon, bless the Lord! Praise and exalt him above all forever! 64 O you stars of heaven, bless the Lord! Praise and exalt him above all forever! 65 O every shower and dew, bless the Lord! Praise and exalt him above all forever! 66 O all you winds, bless the Lord! Praise and exalt him above all forever! 67 O you fire and heat, bless the Lord! Praise and exalt him above all forever! 68 O you dews and storms of snow, bless the Lord! Praise and exalt him above all forever! 69 O you nights and days, bless the Lord! Praise and exalt him above all forever! 70 O you light and darkness, bless the Lord! Praise and exalt him above all forever! 71 O you cold and heat, bless the Lord! Praise and exalt him above all forever! 72 O you frost and snow, bless the Lord! Praise and exalt him above all forever! 73 O you lightnings and clouds, bless the Lord! Praise and exalt him above all forever! 74 O let the earth bless the Lord! Let it praise and exalt him above all forever! 75 O you mountains and hills, bless the Lord! Praise and exalt him above all forever! 76 O all you things that grow on the earth, bless the Lord! Praise and exalt him above all forever! 77 O sea and rivers, bless the Lord! Praise and exalt him above all forever! 78 O you springs, bless the Lord! Praise and exalt him above all forever! 79 O you whales and all that move in the waters, bless the Lord! Praise and exalt him above all forever! 80 O all you fowls of the air, bless the Lord! Praise and exalt him above all forever! 81 O all you beasts and cattle, bless the Lord! Praise and exalt him above all forever! 82 O you children of men,

bless the Lord! Praise and exalt him above all forever! 83 O let Israel bless the Lord! Praise and exalt him above all forever. 84 O you priests of the Lord, bless the Lord! Praise and exalt him above all forever! 85 O you servants of the Lord, bless the Lord! Praise and exalt him above all forever! 86 O you spirits and souls of the righteous, bless the Lord! Praise and exalt him above all forever! 87 O you who are holy and humble of heart, bless the Lord! Praise and exalt him above all forever! 88 O Hananiah, Mishael, and Azariah, bless the Lord! Praise and exalt him above all forever; for he has rescued us from Hades and saved us from the hand of death! He has delivered us out of the midst of the furnace and burning flame. He has delivered us out of the midst of the fire. 89 O give thanks to the Lord, for he is good; for his mercy is forever. 90 O all you who worship the Lord, bless the God of gods, praise him, and give him thanks; for his mercy is forever!"]] 91 Then Nebuchadnezzar the king was astonished and rose up in haste. He spoke and said to his counselors, "Didn't we cast three men bound into the middle of the fire?" They answered the king, "True, O king." 92 He answered, "Look, I see four men loose, walking in the middle of the fire, and they are unharmed. The appearance of the fourth is like a son of the gods." 93 Then Nebuchadnezzar came near to the mouth of the burning fiery furnace. He spoke and said, "Shadrach, Meshach, and Abednego, you servants of the Most High God, come out, and come here!" Then Shadrach, Meshach, and Abednego came out of the middle of the fire. 94 The local governors, the deputies, and the governors, and the king's counselors, being gathered together, saw these men, that the fire had no power on their bodies. The hair of their head wasn't singed. Their pants weren't changed, the smell of fire wasn't even on them. 95 Nebuchadnezzar spoke and said, "Blessed be the God of Shadrach, Meshach, and Abednego, who has sent his angel and delivered his servants who trusted in him, and have changed the king's word, and have yielded their bodies, that they might not serve nor worship any god, except their own God. 96 Therefore I make a decree, that every people, nation, and language, which speak anything evil against the God of Shadrach, Meshach, and Abednego, will be cut in pieces, and their houses will be made a dunghill; because there is no other god who is able to deliver like this." 97 Then the king promoted

Shadrach, Meshach, and Abednego in the province of Babylon.

CHAPTER 4

1 Nebuchadnezzar the king, to all the peoples, nations, and languages, who dwell in all the earth: Peace be multiplied to you. 2 It has seemed good to me to show the signs and wonders that the Most High God has worked toward me. 3 How great are his signs! How mighty are his wonders! His kingdom is an everlasting kingdom. His dominion is from generation to generation. 4 I, Nebuchadnezzar, was at rest in my house, and flourishing in my palace. 5 I saw a dream which made me afraid; and the thoughts on my bed and the visions of my head troubled me. 6 Therefore I made a decree to bring in all the wise men of Babylon before me, that they might make known to me the interpretation of the dream. 7 Then the magicians, the enchanters, the Chaldeans, and the soothsayers came in; and I told the dream before them; but they didn't make known to me its interpretation. 8 But at the last Daniel came in before me, whose name was Belteshazzar, according to the name of my god, and in whom is the spirit of the holy gods. I told the dream before him, saying, 9 "Belteshazzar, master of the magicians, because I know that the spirit of the holy gods is in you, and no secret troubles you, tell me the visions of my dream that I have seen, and its interpretation. 10 These were the visions of my head on my bed: I saw, and behold, a tree in the middle of the earth; and its height was great. 11 The tree grew, and was strong, and its height reached to the sky, and its sight to the end of all the earth. 12 Its leaves were beautiful, and it had much fruit, and in it was food for all. The animals of the field had shade under it, and the birds of the sky lived in its branches, and all flesh was fed from it. 13 "I saw in the visions of my head on my bed, and behold, a watcher and a holy one came down from the sky. 14 He cried aloud, and said this, 'Cut down the tree, and cut off its branches! Shake off its leaves and scatter its fruit! Let the animals get away from under it, and the fowls from its branches. 15 Nevertheless leave the stump of its roots in the earth, even with a band of iron and bronze, in the tender grass of the field; and let it be wet with the dew of the sky. Let his portion be with the animals in the grass of the earth. 16 Let his heart be changed from man's and let an animal's heart be given to him. Then let seven times pass over him.

17 "'The sentence is by the decree of the watchers, and the demand by the word of the holy ones; to the intent that the living may know that the Most High rules in the kingdom of men, and gives it to whomever he will, and sets up over it the lowest of men.' 18 "This dream I, king Nebuchadnezzar, have seen; and you, Belteshazzar, declare the interpretation, because all the wise men of my kingdom are not able to make known to me the interpretation; but you are able; for the spirit of the holy gods is in you." 19 Then Daniel, whose name was Belteshazzar, was stricken mute for a while, and his thoughts troubled him. The king answered, "Belteshazzar, don't let the dream, or the interpretation, trouble you." Belteshazzar answered, "My lord, may the dream be for those who hate you, and its interpretation to your adversaries. 20 The tree that you saw, which grew, and was strong, whose height reached to the sky, and its sight to all the earth; 21 whose leaves were beautiful, and its fruit plentiful, and in it was food for all; under which the animals of the field lived, and on whose branches the birds of the sky had their habitation: 22 it is you, O king, that have grown and become strong; for your greatness has grown, and reaches to the sky, and your dominion to the end of the earth. 23 "Whereas the king saw a watcher and a holy one coming down from the sky, and saying, 'Cut down the tree, and destroy it; nevertheless, leave the stump of its roots in the earth, even with a band of iron and bronze, in the tender grass of the field, and let it be wet with the dew of the sky. Let his portion be with the animals of the field, until seven times pass over him.' 24 "This is the interpretation, O king, and it is the decree of the Most High, which has come on my lord the king: 25 that you will be driven from men, and your dwelling will be with the animals of the field. You will be made to eat grass as oxen and will be wet with the dew of the sky, and seven times will pass over you; until you know that the Most High rules in the kingdom of men, and gives it to whomever he will. 26 Whereas they commanded to leave the stump of the roots of the tree; your kingdom will be sure to you, after that you will have known that the heavens do rule. 27 Therefore, O king, let my counsel be acceptable to you, and break off your sins by righteousness, and your iniquities by showing mercy to the poor. Perhaps there may be a lengthening of your tranquility." 28 All this came on the king Nebuchadnezzar.

29 At the end of twelve months he was walking in the royal palace of Babylon. 30 The king spoke and said, "Is not this great Babylon, which I have built for the royal dwelling place, by the might of my power and for the glory of my majesty?" 31 While the word was in the king's mouth, a voice came from the sky, saying, "O king Nebuchadnezzar, to you it is spoken: 'The kingdom has departed from you. 32 You will be driven from men; and your dwelling will be with the animals of the field. You will be made to eat grass as oxen. Seven times will pass over you, until you know that the Most High rules in the kingdom of men and gives it to whomever he will.' " 33 This was fulfilled the same hour on Nebuchadnezzar. He was driven from men, and ate grass as oxen, and his body was wet with the dew of the sky, until his hair had grown like eagles' feathers, and his nails like birds' claws. 34 At the end of the days I, Nebuchadnezzar, lifted up my eyes to heaven, and my understanding returned to me, and I blessed the Most High, and I praised and honored him who lives forever; for his dominion is an everlasting dominion, and his kingdom from generation to generation. 35 All the inhabitants of the earth are reputed as nothing; and he does according to his will in the army of heaven, and among the inhabitants of the earth; and no one can stop his hand, or ask him, "What are you doing?" 36 At the same time my understanding returned to me; and for the glory of my kingdom, my majesty and brightness returned to me. My counselors and my lords sought me; and I was established in my kingdom, and excellent greatness was added to me. 37 Now I, Nebuchadnezzar, praise and extol and honor the King of heaven; for all his works are truth, and his ways justice; and those who walk in pride he is able to abase.

CHAPTER 5

1 Belshazzar the king made a great feast to a thousand of his lords and drank wine before the thousand. 2 Belshazzar, while he tasted the wine, commanded that the golden and silver vessels which Nebuchadnezzar his father had taken out of the temple which was in Jerusalem be brought to him; that the king and his lords, his wives and his concubines, might drink from them. 3 Then they brought the golden vessels that were taken out of the temple of God's house which was at Jerusalem; and the king and his lords, his wives and his concubines, drank from them.

4 They drank wine, and praised the gods of gold, and of silver, of bronze, of iron, of wood, and of stone. 5 In the same hour, the fingers of a man's hand came out and wrote near the lamp stand on the plaster of the wall of the king's palace. The king saw the part of the hand that wrote. 6 Then the king's face was changed in him, and his thoughts troubled him; and the joints of his thighs were loosened, and his knees struck one against another. 7 The king cried aloud to bring in the enchanters, the Chaldeans, and the soothsayers. The king spoke and said to the wise men of Babylon, "Whoever reads this writing, and shows me its interpretation, will be clothed with purple, and have a chain of gold about his neck, and will be the third ruler in the kingdom." 8 Then all the king's wise men came in; but they could not read the writing, and couldn't make known to the king the interpretation. 9 Then king Belshazzar was greatly troubled, and his face was changed in him, and his lords were perplexed. 10 The queen by reason of the words of the king and his lords came into the banquet house. The queen spoke and said, "O king, live forever; don't let your thoughts trouble you, nor let your face be changed. 11 There is a man in your kingdom, in whom is the spirit of the holy gods; and in the days of your father light and understanding and wisdom, like the wisdom of the gods, were found in him. The king, Nebuchadnezzar, your father, yes, the king, your father, made him master of the magicians, enchanters, Chaldeans, and soothsayers; 12 because an excellent spirit, knowledge, understanding, interpreting of dreams, showing of dark sentences, and dissolving of doubts were found in the same Daniel, whom the king named Belteshazzar. Now let Daniel be called, and he will show the interpretation." 13 Then Daniel was brought in before the king. The king spoke and said to Daniel, "Are you that Daniel of the children of the captivity of Judah, whom the king my father brought out of Judah? 14 I have heard of you, that the spirit of the gods is in you, and that light, understanding, and excellent wisdom are found in you. 15 Now the wise men, the enchanters, have been brought in before me, that they should read this writing, and make known to me its interpretation; but they could not show the interpretation of the thing. 16 But I have heard of you, that you can give interpretations, and dissolve doubts. Now if you can read the writing, and make known to

me its interpretation, you will be clothed with purple, and have a chain of gold around your neck, and will be the third ruler in the kingdom." **17** Then Daniel answered before the king, "Let your gifts be to yourself, and give your rewards to another. Nevertheless, I will read the writing to the king, and make known to him the interpretation. **18** "To you, king, the Most High God gave Nebuchadnezzar your father the kingdom, and greatness, and glory, and majesty. **19** Because of the greatness that he gave him, all the peoples, nations, and languages trembled and feared before him. He killed whom he wanted to, and he kept alive whom he wanted to. He raised up whom he wanted to, and he put down whom he wanted to. **20** But when his heart was lifted up, and his spirit was hardened so that he dealt proudly, he was deposed from his kingly throne, and they took his glory from him. **21** He was driven from the sons of men, and his heart was made like the animals', and his dwelling was with the wild donkeys. He was fed with grass like oxen, and his body was wet with the dew of the sky; until he knew that the Most High God rules in the kingdom of men, and that he sets up over it whomever he will. **22** "You, his son, Belshazzar, have not humbled your heart, though you knew all this, **23** but have lifted up yourself against the Lord of heaven; and they have brought the vessels of his house before you, and you and your lords, your wives, and your concubines, have drunk wine from them. You have praised the gods of silver and gold, of bronze, iron, wood, and stone, which don't see, or hear, or know; and you have not glorified the God in whose hand your breath is, and whose are all your ways. **24** Then the part of the hand was sent from before him, and this writing was inscribed. **25** "This is the writing that was inscribed: 'MENE, MENE, TEKEL, UPHARSIN.' **26** "This is the interpretation of the thing: MENE: God has counted your kingdom and brought it to an end. **27** TEKEL: you are weighed in the balances and are found wanting. **28** PERES: your kingdom is divided and given to the Medes and Persians." **29** Then Belshazzar commanded, and they clothed Daniel with purple, and put a chain of gold about his neck, and made proclamation concerning him, that he should be the third ruler in the kingdom. **30** In that night Belshazzar the Chaldean King was slain. **31** Darius the Mede received the kingdom, being about sixty-two years old.

CHAPTER 6

1 It pleased Darius to set over the kingdom one hundred twenty local governors, who should be throughout the whole kingdom; **2** and over them three presidents, of whom Daniel was one; that these local governors might give account to them, and that the king should suffer no loss. **3** Then this Daniel was distinguished above the presidents and the local governors, because an excellent spirit was in him; and the king thought to set him over the whole realm. **4** Then the presidents and the local governors sought to find occasion against Daniel as touching the kingdom; but they could find no occasion or fault, because he was faithful. There wasn't any error or fault found in him. **5** Then these men said, "We won't find any occasion against this Daniel, unless we find it against him concerning the law of his God." **6** Then these presidents and local governors assembled together to the king, and said this to him, "King Darius, live forever! **7** All the presidents of the kingdom, the deputies and the local governors, the counselors and the governors, have consulted together to establish a royal statute, and to make a strong decree, that whoever asks a petition of any god or man for thirty days, except of you, O king, he will be cast into the den of lions. **8** Now, O king, establish the decree, and sign the writing, that it not be changed, according to the law of the Medes and Persians, which doesn't alter." **9** Therefore king Darius signed the writing and the decree. **10** When Daniel knew that the writing was signed, he went into his house (now his windows were open in his room toward Jerusalem) and he kneeled on his knees three times a day, and prayed, and gave thanks before his God, as he did before. **11** Then these men assembled together, and found Daniel making petition and supplication before his God. **12** Then they came near, and spoke before the king concerning the king's decree: "Haven't you signed a decree that every man who makes a petition to any god or man within thirty days, except to you, O king, will be cast into the den of lions?" The king answered, "This thing is true, according to the law of the Medes and Persians, which doesn't alter." **13** Then they answered and said before the king, "That Daniel, who is of the children of the captivity of Judah, doesn't respect you, O king, nor the decree that you have signed, but makes his petition three times a day." **14** Then the king, when he heard these words, was very displeased, and set his heart on Daniel to deliver him; and he labored until the going down of the sun to rescue him. **15** Then these men assembled together to the king, and said to the king, "Know, O king, that it is a law of the Medes and Persians, that no decree nor statute which the king establishes may be changed." **16** Then the king commanded, and they brought Daniel, and cast him into the den of lions. The king spoke and said to Daniel, "Your God whom you serve continually, he will deliver you." **17** A stone was brought and laid on the mouth of the den; and the king sealed it with his own signet, and with the signet of his lords; that nothing might be changed concerning Daniel. **18** Then the king went to his palace and passed the night fasting. No musical instruments were brought before him; and his sleep fled from him. **19** Then the king arose very early in the morning and went in haste to the den of lions. **20** When he came near to the den to Daniel, he cried with a troubled voice. The king spoke and said to Daniel, "Daniel, servant of the living God, is your God, whom you serve continually, able to deliver you from the lions?" **21** Then Daniel said to the king, "O king, live forever! **22** My God has sent his angel, and has shut the lions' mouths, and they have not hurt me; because as before him innocence was found in me; and also before you, O king, I have done no harm." **23** Then the king was exceedingly glad, and commanded that they should take Daniel up out of the den. So Daniel was taken up out of the den, and no kind of harm was found on him, because he had trusted in his God. **24** The king commanded, and they brought those men who had accused Daniel, and they cast them into the den of lions, them, their children, and their wives; and the lions mauled them, and broke all their bones in pieces, before they came to the bottom of the den. **25** Then king Darius wrote to all the peoples, nations, and languages, who dwell in all the earth: "Peace be multiplied to you. **26** "I make a decree that in all the dominion of my kingdom men tremble and fear before the God of Daniel; "for he is the living God, and steadfast forever. His kingdom is that which will not be destroyed. His dominion will be even to the end. **27** He delivers and rescues. He works signs and wonders in heaven and in earth, who has delivered Daniel from the power of the lions." **28** So this Daniel prospered in the reign of Darius, and in the reign of Cyrus the Persian.

CHAPTER 7

1 In the first year of Belshazzar king of Babylon, Daniel had a dream and visions of his head on his bed. Then he wrote the dream and told the sum of the matters. **2** Daniel spoke and said, "I saw in my vision by night, and, behold, the four winds of the sky broke out on the great sea. **3** Four great animals came up from the sea, different from one another. **4** "The first was like a lion and had eagle's wings. I watched until its wings were plucked, and it was lifted up from the earth, and made to stand on two feet as a man. A man's heart was given to it. **5** "Behold, there was another animal, a second, like a bear. It was raised up on one side, and three ribs were in its mouth between its teeth. They said this to it: 'Arise! Devour much flesh!' **6** "After this I saw, and behold, another, like a leopard, which had on its back four wings of a bird. The animal also had four heads; and dominion was given to it. **7** "After this I saw in the night visions, and, behold, there was a fourth animal, awesome and powerful, and exceedingly strong. It had great iron teeth. It devoured and broke in pieces and stamped the residue with its feet. It was different from all the animals that were before it. It had ten horns. **8** "I considered the horns, and behold, there came up among them another horn, a little one, before which three of the first horns were plucked up by the roots: and behold, in this horn were eyes like the eyes of a man, and a mouth speaking great things. **9** "I watched until thrones were placed, and one who was ancient of days sat. His clothing was white as snow, and the hair of his head like pure wool. His throne was fiery flames, and its wheels burning fire. **10** A fiery stream issued and came out from before him. Thousands of thousands ministered to him. Ten thousand times ten thousand stood before him. The judgment was set. The books were opened. **11** "I watched at that time because of the voice of the great words which the horn spoke. I watched even until the animal was slain, and its body destroyed, and it was given to be burned with fire. **12** As for the rest of the animals, their dominion was taken away; yet their lives were prolonged for a season and a time. **13** "I saw in the night visions, and behold, there came with the clouds of the sky one like a son of man, and he came even to the ancient of days, and they brought him near before him. **14** Dominion was given him, and glory, and a kingdom, that all the peoples, nations, and languages should serve him. His dominion is an everlasting dominion, which will not pass away, and his kingdom that which will not be destroyed. **15** "As for me, Daniel, my spirit was grieved within my body, and the visions of my head troubled me. **16** I came near to one of those who stood by and asked him the truth concerning all this. "So he told me, and made me know the interpretation of the things. **17** 'These great animals, which are four, are four kings, who will arise out of the earth. **18** But the saints of the Most High will receive the kingdom, and possess the kingdom forever, even forever and ever.' **19** "Then I desired to know the truth concerning the fourth animal, which was different from all of them, exceedingly terrible, whose teeth were of iron, and its nails of bronze; which devoured, broke in pieces, and stamped the residue with its feet; **20** and concerning the ten horns that were on its head, and the other horn which came up, and before which three fell, even that horn that had eyes, and a mouth that spoke great things, whose look was more stout than its fellows. **21** I saw, and the same horn made war with the saints, and prevailed against them, **22** until the ancient of days came, and judgment was given to the saints of the Most High, and the time came that the saints possessed the kingdom. **23** "So he said, 'The fourth animal will be a fourth kingdom on earth, which will be different from all the kingdoms, and will devour the whole earth, and will tread it down, and break it in pieces. **24** As for the ten horns, ten kings will arise out of this kingdom. Another will arise after them; and he will be different from the former, and he will put down three kings. **25** He will speak words against the Most High and will wear out the saints of the Most High. He will plan to change the times and the law; and they will be given into his hand until a time and times and half a time. **26** "'But the judgment will be set, and they will take away his dominion, to consume and to destroy it to the end. **27** The kingdom and the dominion, and the greatness of the kingdoms under the whole sky, will be given to the people of the saints of the Most High. His kingdom is an everlasting kingdom, and all dominions will serve and obey him.' **28** "Here is the end of the matter. As for me, Daniel, my thoughts troubled me greatly, and my face was changed in me; but I kept the matter in my heart."

CHAPTER 8

1 In the third year of the reign of king Belshazzar, a vision appeared to me, even to me, Daniel, after that which appeared to me at the first. **2** I saw the vision. Now it was so, that when I saw, I was in the citadel of Susa, which is in the province of Elam. I saw in the vision, and I was by the river Ulai. **3** Then I lifted up my eyes, and saw, and behold, there stood before the river a ram which had two horns. The two horns were high; but one was higher than the other, and the higher came up last. **4** I saw the ram pushing westward, northward, and southward. No animals could stand before him. There wasn't any who could deliver out of his hand; but he did according to his will and magnified himself. **5** As I was considering, behold, a male goat came from the west over the surface of the whole earth, and didn't touch the ground. The goat had a notable horn between his eyes. **6** He came to the ram that had the two horns, which I saw standing before the river, and ran on him in the fury of his power. **7** I saw him come close to the ram, and he was moved with anger against him, and struck the ram, and broke his two horns. There was no power in the ram to stand before him; but he cast him down to the ground and trampled on him. There was no one who could deliver the ram out of his hand. **8** The male goat magnified himself exceedingly. When he was strong, the great horn was broken; and instead of it there came up four notable horns toward the four winds of the sky. **9** Out of one of them came out a little horn, which grew exceedingly great, toward the south, and toward the east, and toward the glorious land. **10** It grew great, even to the army of the sky; and it cast down some of the army and of the stars to the ground and trampled on them. **11** Yes, it magnified itself, even to the prince of the army; and it took away from him the continual burnt offering, and the place of his sanctuary was cast down. **12** The army was given over to it together with the continual burnt offering through disobedience. It cast down truth to the ground, and it did its pleasure and prospered. **13** Then I heard a holy one speaking; and another holy one said to that certain one who spoke, "How long will the vision about the continual burnt offering, and the disobedience that makes desolate, to give both the sanctuary and the army to be trodden under foot be?" **14** He said to me, "To two thousand and three hundred evenings and mornings. Then the sanctuary will be cleansed." **15** When I, even I Daniel, had seen the vision, I sought to understand it. Then behold, there stood before me something like the appearance of a man. **16** I heard a man's voice between the banks of the Ulai, which called, and said, "Gabriel, make this man understand the vision." **17** So he came near where I stood; and when he came, I was frightened, and fell on my face; but he said to me, "Understand, son of man; for the vision belongs to the time of the end." **18** Now as he was speaking with me, I fell into a deep sleep with my face toward the ground; but he touched me, and set me upright. **19** He said, "Behold, I will make you know what will be in the latter time of the indignation; for it belongs to the appointed time of the end. **20** The ram which you saw, that had the two horns, they are the kings of Media and Persia. **21** The rough male goat is the king of Greece. The great horn that is between his eyes is the first king. **22** As for that which was broken, in the place where four stood up, four kingdoms will stand up out of the nation, but not with his power. **23** "In the latter time of their kingdom, when the transgressors have come to the full, a king of fierce face, and understanding dark sentences, will stand up. **24** His power will be mighty, but not by his own power. He will destroy awesomely and will prosper in what he does. He will destroy the mighty ones and the holy people. **25** Through his policy he will cause deceit to prosper in his hand. He will magnify himself in his heart, and he will destroy many in their security. He will also stand up against the prince of princes; but he will be broken without hand. **26** "The vision of the evenings and mornings which has been told is true; but seal up the vision, for it belongs to many days to come." **27** I, Daniel, fainted, and was sick for some days. Then I rose up and did the king's business. I wondered at the vision, but no one understood it.

CHAPTER 9

1 In the first year of Darius the son of Ahasuerus, of the offspring of the Medes, who was made king over the realm of the Chaldeans, **2** in the first year of his reign I, Daniel, understood by the books the number of the years about which Yahweh's word came to Jeremiah the prophet, for the accomplishing of the desolations of Jerusalem, even seventy years. **3** I set my face to the Lord God, to seek by prayer and petitions, with fasting and sackcloth and ashes. **4** I prayed to Yahweh my God, and made confession, and said, "Oh, Lord, the great and dreadful God, who keeps covenant and loving kindness with those who love him and keep his commandments, **5** we have sinned, and have dealt perversely, and have done wickedly, and have rebelled, even turning aside from your precepts and from your ordinances. **6** We haven't listened to your servants the prophets, who spoke in your name to our kings, our princes, and our fathers, and to all the people of the land. **7** "Lord, righteousness belongs to you, but to us confusion of face, as it is today; to the men of Judah, and to the inhabitants of Jerusalem, and to all Israel, who are near, and who are far off, through all the countries where you have driven them, because of their trespass that they have trespassed against you. **8** Lord, to us belongs confusion of face, to our kings, to our princes, and to our fathers, because we have sinned against you. **9** To the Lord our God belong mercies and forgiveness; for we have rebelled against him. **10** We haven't obeyed Yahweh our God's voice, to walk in his laws, which he set before us by his servants the prophets. **11** Yes, all Israel have transgressed your law, turning aside, that they should not obey your voice. "Therefore, the curse and the oath written in the law of Moses the servant of God has been poured out on us; for we have sinned against him. **12** He has confirmed his words, which he spoke against us, and against our judges who judged us, by bringing on us a great evil; for under the whole sky, such has not been done as has been done to Jerusalem. **13** As it is written in the law of Moses, all this evil has come on us. Yet we have not entreated the favor of Yahweh our God, that we should turn from our iniquities and have discernment in your truth. **14** Therefore Yahweh has watched over the evil and brought it on us; for Yahweh our God is righteous in all his works which he does, and we have not obeyed his voice. **15** "Now, Lord our God, who has brought your people out of the land of Egypt with a mighty hand, and have gotten yourself renown, as it is today; we have sinned. We have done wickedly. **16** Lord, according to all your righteousness, please let your anger and your wrath be turned away from your city Jerusalem, your holy mountain; because for our sins, and for the iniquities of our fathers, Jerusalem and your people have become a reproach to all who are around us. **17** "Now therefore, our God, listen to the prayer of your servant, and to his petitions, and cause your face to shine on your sanctuary that is desolate, for the Lord's sake. **18** My God, turn your ear, and hear. Open your eyes, and see our desolations, and the city which is called by your name; for we do not present our petitions before you for our righteousness, but for your great mercies' sake. **19** Lord, hear. Lord, forgive. Lord, listen and do. Don't defer, for your own sake, my God, because your city and your people are called by your name." **20** While I was speaking, praying, and confessing my sin and the sin of my people Israel, and presenting my supplication before Yahweh my God for the holy mountain of my God; **21** yes, while I was speaking in prayer, the man Gabriel, whom I had seen in the vision at the beginning, being caused to fly swiftly, touched me about the time of the evening offering. **22** He instructed me and talked with me, and said, "Daniel, I have now come to give you wisdom and understanding. **23** At the beginning of your petitions the commandment went out, and I have come to tell you; for you are greatly beloved. Therefore, consider the matter, and understand the vision. **24** "Seventy weeks are decreed on your people and on your holy city, to finish disobedience, and to make an end of sins, and to make reconciliation for iniquity, and to bring in everlasting righteousness, and to seal up vision and prophecy, and to anoint the most holy. **25** "Know therefore and discern that from the going out of the commandment to restore and to build Jerusalem to the Anointed One, the prince, will be seven weeks and sixty-two weeks. It will be built again, with street and moat, even in troubled times. **26** After the sixty-two weeks the Anointed One will be cut off and will have nothing. The people of the prince who come will destroy the city and the sanctuary. Its end will be with a flood, and war will be even to the end. Desolations are determined. **27** He will make a firm covenant with many for one week. In the middle of the week he will cause the sacrifice and the offering to cease. On the wing of abominations will come one who makes desolate; and even to the full end, and that determined, wrath will be poured out on the desolate."

CHAPTER 10

1 In the third year of Cyrus king of Persia a thing was revealed to Daniel, whose name was called Belteshazzar; and the thing was true, even a great warfare. He understood the thing and had understanding of the vision. **2** In those days I, Daniel, was mourning three whole weeks. **3** I ate no pleasant bread. No meat or wine came into my mouth. I didn't anoint myself at all, until three whole weeks were fulfilled. **4** In the twenty-fourth day of the first month, as I was by the side of the great river, which is Hiddekel, **5** I lifted up my eyes, and looked, and behold, there was a man clothed in linen, whose thighs were adorned with pure gold of Uphaz. **6** His body also was like beryl, and his face as the appearance of lightning, and his eyes as flaming torches. His arms and his feet were like burnished bronze. The voice of his words was like the voice of a multitude. **7** I, Daniel, alone saw the vision; for the men who were with me didn't see the vision; but a great quaking fell on them, and they fled to hide themselves. **8** So I was left alone and saw this great vision. No strength remained in me; for my face grew deathly pale, and I retained no strength. **9** Yet I heard the voice of his words. When I heard the voice of his words, then I fell into a deep sleep on my face, with my face toward the ground. **10** Behold, a hand touched me, which set me on my knees and on the palms of my hands. **11** He said to me, "Daniel, you greatly beloved man, understand the words that I speak to you, and stand upright; for I have been sent to you, now." When he had spoken this word to me, I stood trembling. **12** Then he said to me, "Don't be afraid, Daniel; for from the first day that you set your heart to understand, and to humble yourself before your God, your words were heard. I have come for your words' sake. **13** But the prince of the kingdom of Persia withstood me twenty-one days; but, behold, Michael, one of the chief princes, came to help me because I remained there with the kings of Persia. **14** Now I have come to make you understand what will happen to your people in the latter days; for the vision is yet for many days." **15** When he had spoken these words to me, I set my face toward the ground, and was mute. **16** Behold, one in the likeness of the sons of men touched my lips. Then I opened my mouth and spoke and said to him who stood before me, "My lord, by reason of the vision my sorrows have overtaken me, and I retain no strength. **17** For how can the servant of this my lord talk with this my lord? For as for me, immediately there remained no strength in me. There was no breath left in me." **18** Then one like the appearance of a man touched me again, and he strengthened me. **19** He said,

"Greatly beloved man, don't be afraid. Peace be to you. Be strong. Yes, be strong." When he spoke to me, I was strengthened, and said, "Let my lord speak; for you have strengthened me." 20 Then he said, "Do you know why I have come to you? Now I will return to fight with the prince of Persia. When I go out, behold, the prince of Greece will come. 21 But I will tell you that which is inscribed in the writing of truth. There is no one who holds with me against these, but Michael your prince.

CHAPTER 11

1 "As for me, in the first year of Darius the Mede, I stood up to confirm and strengthen him. 2 "Now I will show you the truth. Behold, three more kings will stand up in Persia; and the fourth will be far richer than all of them. When he has grown strong through his riches, he will stir up all against the realm of Greece. 3 A mighty king will stand up, who will rule with great dominion, and do according to his will. 4 When he stands up, his kingdom will be broken, and will be divided toward the four winds of the sky, but not to his posterity, nor according to his dominion with which he ruled; for his kingdom will be plucked up, even for others besides these. 5 "The king of the south will be strong. One of his princes will become stronger than him and have dominion. His dominion will be a great dominion. 6 At the end of years they will join themselves together; and the daughter of the king of the south will come to the king of the north to make an agreement; but she will not retain the strength of her arm. He will also not stand, nor will his arm; but she will be given up, with those who brought her, and he who became the father of her, and he who strengthened her in those times. 7 "But out of a shoot from her roots one will stand up in his place, who will come to the army, and will enter into the fortress of the king of the north, and will deal against them, and will prevail. 8 He will also carry their gods, with their molten images, and with their goodly vessels of silver and of gold, captive into Egypt. He will refrain some years from the king of the north. 9 He will come into the realm of the king of the south, but he will return into his own land. 10 His sons will wage war, and will assemble a multitude of great forces, which will come on, and overflow, and pass through. They will return and wage war, even to his fortress. 11 "The king of the south will be moved with anger, and will come out and fight with him, even with the king of the north. He will send out a great multitude, and the multitude will be given into his hand. 12 The multitude will be lifted up, and his heart will be exalted. He will cast down tens of thousands, but he won't prevail. 13 The king of the north will return and will send out a multitude greater than the former. He will come on at the end of the times, even of years, with a great army and with much substance. 14 "In those times many will stand up against the king of the south. Also, the children of the violent among your people will lift themselves up to establish the vision; but they will fall. 15 So the king of the north will come and cast up a mound and take a well-fortified city. The forces of the south won't stand, neither will his chosen people, neither will there be any strength to stand. 16 But he who comes against him will do according to his own will, and no one will stand before him. He will stand in the glorious land, and destruction will be in his hand. 17 He will set his face to come with the strength of his whole kingdom, and with him equitable conditions. He will perform them. He will give him the daughter of women, to corrupt her; but she will not stand, and won't be for him. 18 After this he will turn his face to the islands and will take many; but a prince will cause the reproach offered by him to cease. Yes, moreover, he will cause his reproach to turn on him. 19 Then he will turn his face toward the fortresses of his own land; but he will stumble and fall and won't be found. 20 "Then one who will cause a tax collector to pass through the kingdom to maintain its glory will stand up in his place; but within few days he will be destroyed, not in anger, and not in battle. 21 "In his place a contemptible person will stand up, to whom they had not given the honor of the kingdom; but he will come in time of security and will obtain the kingdom by flatteries. 22 The overwhelming forces will be overwhelmed from before him and will be broken. Yes, also the prince of the covenant. 23 After the treaty made with him he will work deceitfully; for he will come up, and will become strong, with a small people. 24 In time of security he will come even on the fattest places of the province. He will do that which his fathers have not done, nor his fathers' fathers. He will scatter among them prey, plunder, and substance. Yes, he will devise his plans against the strongholds, even for a time. 25 "He will stir up his power and his courage against the king of the south with a great army; and the

king of the south will wage war in battle with an exceedingly great and mighty army; but he won't stand; for they will devise plans against him. **26** Yes, those who eat of his dainties will destroy him, and his army will be swept away. Many will fall down slain. **27** As for both these kings, their hearts will be to do mischief, and they will speak lies at one table; but it won't prosper, for the end will still be at the appointed time. **28** Then he will return into his land with great wealth. His heart will be against the holy covenant. He will take action and return to his own land. **29** "He will return at the appointed time and come into the south; but it won't be in the latter time as it was in the former. **30** For ships of Kittim will come against him. Therefore, he will be grieved, and will return, and have indignation against the holy covenant, and will take action. He will even return and have regard to those who forsake the holy covenant. **31** "Forces will stand on his part, and they will profane the sanctuary, even the fortress, and will take away the continual burnt offering. Then they will set up the abomination that makes desolate. **32** He will corrupt those who do wickedly against the covenant by flatteries; but the people who know their God will be strong and take action. **33** "Those who are wise among the people will instruct many; yet they will fall by the sword and by flame, by captivity and by plunder, many days. **34** Now when they fall, they will be helped with a little help; but many will join themselves to them with flatteries. **35** Some of those who are wise will fall, to refine them, and to purify, and to make them white, even to the time of the end; because it is yet for the time appointed. **36** "The king will do according to his will. He will exalt himself, and magnify himself above every god, and will speak marvelous things against the God of gods. He will prosper until the indignation is accomplished; for that which is determined will be done. **37** He won't regard the gods of his fathers, or the desire of women, or regard any god; for he will magnify himself above all. **38** But in his place he will honor the god of fortresses. He will honor a god whom his fathers didn't know with gold, silver, and with precious stones and pleasant things. **39** He will deal with the strongest fortresses by the help of a foreign god. He will increase with glory whoever acknowledges him. He will cause them to rule over many and will divide the land for a price. **40** "At the time of the end the king of the south will contend with him; and the king of the north will come against him like a whirlwind, with chariots, with horsemen, and with many ships. He will enter into the countries and will overflow and pass through. **41** He will enter also into the glorious land, and many countries will be overthrown; but these will be delivered out of his hand: Edom, Moab, and the chief of the children of Ammon. **42** He will also stretch out his hand on the countries. The land of Egypt won't escape. **43** But he will have power over the treasures of gold and of silver, and over all the precious things of Egypt. The Libyans and the Ethiopians will be at his steps. **44** But news out of the east and out of the north will trouble him; and he will go out with great fury to destroy and utterly to sweep away many. **45** He will plant the tents of his palace between the sea and the glorious holy mountain; yet he will come to his end, and no one will help him.

CHAPTER 12

1 "At that time Michael will stand up, the great prince who stands for the children of your people; and there will be a time of trouble, such as never was since there was a nation even to that same time. At that time your people will be delivered, everyone who is found written in the book. **2** Many of those who sleep in the dust of the earth will awake, some to everlasting life, and some to shame and everlasting contempt. **3** Those who are wise will shine as the brightness of the expanse. Those who turn many to righteousness will shine as the stars forever and ever. **4** But you, Daniel, shut up the words, and seal the book, even to the time of the end. Many will run back and out, and knowledge will be increased." **5** Then I, Daniel, looked, and behold, two others stood, one on the river bank on this side, and the other on the river bank on that side. **6** One said to the man clothed in linen, who was above the waters of the river, "How long will it be to the end of these wonders?" **7** I heard the man clothed in linen, who was above the waters of the river, when he held up his right hand and his left hand to heaven, and swore by him who lives forever that it will be for a time, times, and a half; and when they have finished breaking in pieces the power of the holy people, all these things will be finished. **8** I heard, but I didn't understand. Then I said, "My lord, what will be the outcome of these things?" **9** He said, "Go your way, Daniel; for the words are shut up and sealed until the time of the end. **10** Many will purify themselves, and make themselves white, and be refined; but the wicked will do wickedly; and none of the wicked will understand; but those who are wise will understand. **11** "From the time that the continual burnt offering is taken away, and the abomination that makes desolate set up, there will be one thousand two hundred ninety days. **12** Blessed is he who waits and comes to the one thousand three hundred thirty-five days. **13** "But go your way until the end; for you will rest and will stand in your inheritance at the end of the days."

CHAPTER 13

[[**1** A man lived in Babylon, and his name was Joakim. **2** He took a wife, whose name was Susanna, the daughter of Helkias, a very fair woman, and one who feared the Lord. **3** Her parents were also righteous and taught their daughter according to the law of Moses. **4** Now Joakim was a great rich man, and had a fair garden joining to his house. The Jews used to come to him, because he was more honorable than all others. **5** The same year two of the elders of the people were appointed to be judges, such as the Lord spoke of, that wickedness came from Babylon from elders who were judges, who were supposed to govern the people. **6** These were often at Joakim's house. All that had any suits in law came to them. **7** When the people departed away at noon, Susanna went into her husband's garden to walk. **8** The two elders saw her going in every day, and walking; and they were inflamed with lust for her. **9** They perverted their own mind and turned away their eyes, that they might not look to heaven, nor remember just judgments. **10** And although they both were wounded with lust for her yet dared not show the other his grief. **11** For they were ashamed to declare their lust, that they desired to have to do with her. **12** Yet they watched jealously from day to day to see her. **13** The one said to the other, "Let's go home, now; for it is dinner time." **14** So when they had gone out, they parted company, and turning back again, they came to the same place. After they had asked one another the cause, they acknowledged their lust. Then they appointed a time both together, when they might find her alone. **15** It happened, as they watched on an opportune day, she went in as before with only two maids, and she desired to wash herself in the garden; for it was hot.

16 There was nobody there except the two elders who had hid themselves and watched her. **17** Then she said to her maids, "Bring me oil and washing balls, and shut the garden doors, that I may wash myself." **18** They did as she asked them, and shut the garden doors, and went out themselves at the side doors to fetch the things that she had commanded them. They didn't see the elders, because they were hidden. **19** Now when the maids had gone out, the two elders rose up, and ran to her, saying, **20** "Behold, the garden doors are shut, that no man can see us, and we are in love with you. Therefore, consent to us, and lie with us. **21** If you will not, we will testify against you, that a young man was with you; therefore, you sent your maids away from you." **22** Then Susanna sighed, and said, "I am trapped; for if I do this thing, it is death to me. If I don't do it, I can't escape your hands. **23** It is better for me to fall into your hands, and not do it, than to sin in the sight of the Lord." **24** With that Susanna cried with a loud voice; and the two elders cried out against her. **25** Then one of them ran and opened the garden doors. **26** So when the servants of the house heard the cry in the garden, they rushed in at the side door, to see what had happened to her. **27** But when the elders had told their tale, the servants were greatly ashamed; for there was never such a report made of Susanna. **28** It came to pass on the next day, when the people assembled to her husband Joakim, the two elders came full of their wicked intent against Susanna to put her to death, **29** and said before the people, "Send for Susanna, the daughter of Helkias, Joakim's wife." So they sent; **30** and she came with her father and mother, her children, and all her kindred. **31** Now Susanna was a very delicate woman, and beautiful to behold. **32** These wicked men commanded her to be unveiled, for she was veiled, that they might be filled with her beauty. **33** Therefore her friends and all who saw her wept. **34** Then the two elders stood up in the midst of the people and laid their hands upon her head. **35** She, weeping, looked up toward heaven; for her heart trusted in the Lord. **36** The elders said, "As we walked in the garden alone, this woman came in with two maids, shut the garden doors, and sent the maids away. **37** Then a young man, who was hidden there, came to her and lay with her. **38** And we, being in a corner of the garden, saw this wickedness and ran to them. **39** And when we saw them together, we couldn't hold the man; for he was stronger than we, and

DANIEL

opened the doors, and leaped out. **40** But having taken this woman, we asked who the young man was, but she would not tell us. We testify these things. **41** Then the assembly believed them, as those who were elders of the people and judges; so they condemned her to death. **42** Then Susanna cried out with a loud voice, and said, "O everlasting God, you know the secrets, and know all things before they happen, **43** you know that they have testified falsly against me. Behold, I must die, even though I never did such things as these men have maliciously invented against me." **44** The Lord heard her voice. **45** Therefore when she was led away to be put to death, God raised up the holy spirit of a young youth, whose name was Daniel. **46** He cried with a loud voice, "I am clear from the blood of this woman!" **47** Then all the people turned them toward him, and said, "What do these words that you have spoken mean?" **48** So he, standing in the midst of them, said, "Are you all such fools, you sons of Israel, that without examination or knowledge of the truth you have condemned a daughter of Israel? **49** Return again to the place of judgement; for these have testified falsly against her." **50** Therefore all the people turned again in haste, and the elders said to him, "Come, sit down among us, and show it to us, seeing God has given you the honor of an elder." **51** Then Daniel said to them, "Put them far apart from each another, and I will examine them." **52** So when they were put apart one from another, he called one of them, and said to him, "O you who have become old in wickedness, now your sins have returned which you have committed before, **53** in pronouncing unjust judgement, condemning the innocent, and letting the guilty go free; although the Lord says, 'You will not kill the innocent and righteous.' **54** Now then, if you saw her, tell me, under which tree did you see them companying together?" He answered, "Under a mastick tree." **55** And Daniel said, "You have certainly lied against your own head; for even now the angel of God has received the sentence of God and will cut you in two." **56** So he put him aside, and commanded to bring the other, and said to him, "O you seed of Canaan, and not of Judah, beauty has deceived you, and lust has perverted your heart. **57** Thus you have dealt with the daughters of Israel, and they for fear were intimate with you; but the daughter of Judah would not tolerate your wickedness. **58** Now

therefore tell me, under which tree did you take them being intimate together?" He answered, "Under an evergreen oak tree." **59** Then Daniel said to him, "You have also certainly lied against your own head; for the angel of God waits with the sword to cut you in two, that he may destroy you." **60** With that, all the assembly cried out with a loud voice, and blessed God, who saves those who hope in him. **61** Then they arose against the two elders, for Daniel had convicted them of false testimony out of their own mouth. **62** According to the law of Moses they did to them in such sort as they maliciously intended to do to their neighbor. They put them to death, and the innocent blood was saved the same day. **63** Therefore Helkias and his wife praised God for their daughter Susanna, with Joakim her husband, and all the kindred, because there was no dishonesty found in her. **64** And from that day out was Daniel had in great reputation in the sight of the people.]]

CHAPTER 14

[[**1** King Astyages was gathered to his fathers, and Cyrus the Persian received his kingdom. **2** Daniel lived with the king and was honored above all his friends. **3** Now the Babylonians had an idol, called Bel, and every day twelve great measures of fine flour, forty sheep, and six firkinsof wine were spent on him. **4** And the king honored it and went daily to worship it; but Daniel worshiped his own God. The king said to him, "Why don't you worship Bel?" **5** He said, "Because I may not honor idols made with hands, but only the living God, who has created the sky and the earth, and has sovereignty over all flesh." **6** Then the king said to him, "Don't you think that Bel is a living god? Don't you see how much he eats and drinks every day?" **7** Then Daniel laughed, and said, "O king, don't be deceived; for this is just clay inside, and brass outside, and never ate or drank anything." **8** So the king was angry, and called for his priests, and said to them, "If you don't tell me who this is who devours these expenses, you will die. **9** But if you can show me that Bel devours them, then Daniel will die; for he has spoken blasphemy against Bel." Daniel said to the king, "Let it be according to your word." **10** Now there were seventy priests of Bel, besides their wives and children. The king went with Daniel into Bel's temple. **11** So Bel's priests said, "Behold, we will leave; but you, O king, set out the meat, and mix the wine and set it out, shut the door

482

securely, and seal it with your own signet. **12** When you come in the morning, if you don't find that Bel has eaten everything, we will suffer death, or else Daniel, who speaks falsely against us." **13** They weren't concerned, for under the table they had made a secret entrance, whereby they entered in continually, and consumed those things. **14** It happened, when they had gone out, the king set the meat before Bel. Now Daniel had commanded his servants to bring ashes, and they scattered them all over the temple in the presence of the king alone. Then they went out, shut the door, sealed it with the king's signet, and so departed. **15** Now in the night, the priests came with their wives and children, as they usually did, and ate and drank it all. **16** In the morning, the king arose, and Daniel with him. **17** The king said, "Daniel, are the seals whole?" He said, "Yes, O king, they are whole." **18** And as soon as he had opened the door, the king looked at the table, and cried with a loud voice, "You are great, O Bel, and with you is no deceit at all!" **19** Then Daniel laughed, and held the king that he should not go in, and said, "Behold now the pavement, and mark well whose footsteps these are." **20** The king said, "I see the footsteps of men, women, and children." Then the king was angry, **21** and took the priests with their wives and children, who showed him the secret doors, where they came in, and consumed the things that were on the table. **22** Therefore the king killed them, and delivered Bel into Daniel's power, who overthrew him and his temple. **23** In that same place there was a great dragon, which the people of Babylon worshiped. **24** The king said to Daniel, "Will you also say that this is of brass? Behold, he lives, eats and drinks. You can't say that he is no living god. Therefore, worship him." **25** Then Daniel said, "I will worship the Lord my God; for he is a living God. **26** But allow me, O king, and I will kill this dragon without sword or staff." The king said, "I allow you." **27** Then Daniel took pitch, fat, and hair, and melted them together, and made lumps of them. He put these in the dragon's mouth, so the dragon ate and burst apart. Daniel said, "Behold, these are the gods you all worship." **28** When the people of Babylon heard that, they took great indignation, and conspired against the king, saying, "The king has become a Jew. He has pulled down Bel, slain the dragon, and put the priests to the sword." **29** So they came to the king, and said, "Deliver Daniel to us, or else we will destroy you and your house." **30** Now when the king saw that they trapped him, being constrained, the king delivered Daniel to them. **31** They cast him into the lion's den, where he was six days. **32** There were seven lions in the den, and they had been giving them two carcasses and two sheep every day, which then were not given to them, intending that they would devour Daniel. **33** Now there was in Jewry the prophet Habakkuk, who had made stew, and had broken bread into a bowl. He was going into the field to bring it to the reapers. **34** But the angel of the Lord said to Habakkuk, "Go carry the dinner that you have into Babylon to Daniel, in the lions' den." **35** Habakkuk said, "Lord, I never saw Babylon. I don't know where the den is." **36** Then the angel of the Lord took him by the crown and lifted him up by the hair of his head, and with the blast of his breath set him in Babylon over the den. **37** Habakkuk cried, saying, "O Daniel, Daniel, take the dinner which God has sent you." **38** Daniel said, "You have remembered me, O God! You haven't forsaken those who love you!" **39** So Daniel arose and ate; and the angel of God set Habakkuk in his own place again immediately. **40** On the seventh day, the king came to mourn for Daniel. When he came to the den, he looked in, and, behold, Daniel was sitting. **41** Then the king cried with a loud voice, saying, "Great are you, O Lord, you God of Daniel, and there is none other beside you!" **42** So he drew him out, and cast those that were the cause of his destruction into the den; and they were devoured in a moment before his face.]]

THE END OF THE APOCRYPHA

COVENANT OF THE CCC

WE BELIEVE in One God, revealed to the world as YHWH of Israel,
Uncreated, self-existent, eternal, all-powerful, and unchanging.
He knows all things and there is nowhere where He is not.
He is good, His word is inerrant, and His nature is love.

WE BELIEVE God subsists as the mutual indwelling of three persons:
The Father, the Son, and the Holy Spirit, in eternal communion.
God the Son and God the Holy Spirit come from God the Father,
And throughout eternity they have always existed with the Father.

WE BELIEVE God created time, space, matter, and all things,
Accomplishing His initial act of creation in only six days.
On the sixth day God created Man in His own image out of dust,
Adam the first male and Eve the first female.

WE BELIEVE God said the man should be joined to his wife,
And in so doing the two would become one flesh in marriage.
In diversity He created the marital union sacred, monogamous,
And dissoluble only by death or unfaithfulness.

WE BELIEVE God gave Man the choice of obedience or rebellion,
And Adam and Eve willfully rebelled by eating the forbidden fruit,
Which came from the Tree of the Knowledge of Good and Evil.
They suffered spiritual death and passed their sin nature on to us.

WE BELIEVE that God justly judged the world with a flood,
Sparing Noah and his family through whom came the nations.
And from Noah's son Shem came Abraham, Isaac, and Jacob,
And from Jacob the twelve tribes of Israel and the prophets.

WE BELIEVE that in the fullness of time God gave us His Son,
Born under the law to redeem those condemned by the law.
He was born in the town of Bethlehem to a virgin named Mary,
And in accordance with God's command was named Jesus.

WE BELIEVE Jesus was chosen before the creation of the world,
To live a sinless human life in perfect obedience to the Father,
That He might die a substitutionary death in place of sinners,
Giving forgiveness of sins and eternal life to all who trust in Him.

WE BELIEVE Jesus freely gave His life in obedience to the Father,
And at the order of Pontius Pilate was flogged and crucified.
At the ninth hour He declared His purpose in death was finished,
And He died and was buried in the tomb of Joseph of Arimathea.

WE BELIEVE that death had no power over God's perfect Son,
And on the third day He conquered death by rising to life again.
This was literal, physical, and attested to by over 500 witnesses,
And is the event that gives power and validation to our faith.

WE BELIEVE men are only reconciled to God through Jesus Christ,
And receive salvation by grace through faith apart from works.
By the Spirit all believers are baptized into one body, the Church.
Christians baptize, share communion, and love one another.

WE BELIEVE the Church is a universal priesthood of believers.
Membership is not obtained by belonging to a denomination,
But is received by trusting in Jesus for the forgiveness of sins.
The Church awaits Jesus' soon return when He will call us home.

CONVICTIONS OF THE CCC

1. THERE IS ONE GOD WHO IS ETERNAL, SELF-EXISTENT, ALL-POWERFUL, ALL-KNOWING, EVERYWHERE-PRESENT, COMPLETELY GOOD, AND NEVER CHANGING. GOD IS PERFECT IN MORAL CHARACTER AND HIS NATURE IS LOVE. GOD ALONE CAN DECLARE WHETHER CONDUCT IS RIGHT OR WRONG.

Scripture References: Deuteronomy 6:4, Isaiah 44:8, Psalm 90:2, Isaiah 40:28, Exodus 3:14, Revelation 19:6, Psalm 147:5, 1 John 3:20, Psalm 139:7–8, Jeremiah 23:24, Psalm 119:68, James 1:17, Hebrews 13:8, 1 John 4:8, Judges 21:25, Isaiah 45:19

2. GOD SUBSISTS ETERNALLY IN THREE PERSONS: THE FATHER, THE SON, AND THE HOLY SPIRIT. THESE THREE ARE NEITHER PARTS NOR MODES.

Scripture References: Matthew 28:19, Luke 1:35, 3:21–22, John 1:1–2, 10:30, 14:16, 2 Corinthians 13:14, 1 Peter 1:2; see also Genesis 1:26, 3:22, 11:7

3. THE BIBLE IS A COMPILATION OF GOD'S WORDS AND IN ITS ORIGINAL HEBREW, GREEK, AND ARAMAIC FORM IS INERRANT AND SUFFICIENT IN ITSELF FOR TEACHING CHRISTIAN BELIEF AND PRACTICE. IT SHOULD BE INTERPRETED LITERALLY, HISTORICALLY, AND AT FACE VALUE UNLESS THE TEXT ITSELF ALLOWS FOR A DIFFERENT INTERPRETATION IN A SPECIFIC PASSAGE.

Scripture References: Exodus 20:11, Matthew 5:18, 19:4–6, 24:37–39, John 10:35, Acts 1:16, Romans 15:4, 2 Timothy 3:16, 2 Peter 1:20–21, 3:15–16, 2 Thessalonians 2:14–15, Revelation 22:18–19; see also Genesis 41:25–27, Matthew 13:18–23, 13:36–43, Revelation 1:20

4. MANKIND WAS GIVEN THE FREE CHOICE TO OBEY GOD OR REBEL AGAINST HIM IN THE GARDEN OF EDEN AND FREELY CHOSE TO REBEL BY EATING THE FORBIDDEN FRUIT FROM THE TREE OF THE KNOWLEDGE OF GOOD AND EVIL. THIS CHOICE BROUGHT DEATH, SEPARATION FROM GOD, AND A SINFUL NATURE TO THE ENTIRE HUMAN RACE.

Scripture References: Genesis 2:16–17, 3, 6:5, Isaiah 59:1–2, Romans 3:23, 5:12–18, 6:23, 1 Corinthians 15:22

5. GOD PLANNED IN ADVANCE TO SEND HIS SON INTO THE WORLD TO DIE FOR THE SINS OF MANKIND. THIS PLAN INCLUDED THE COVENANT OF BLESSING WITH ABRAHAM AND THE INSTITUTION OF THE NATION OF ISRAEL AND WAS FORESHADOWED BY THE SYSTEM OF ATONING SACRIFICES IN THE LEVITICAL LAW.

Scripture References: Genesis 22:17–18, Isaiah 53, Jeremiah 1:5, Luke 24:27, John 5:39, Acts 8:30–35, Colossians 2:17, Hebrews 10:1–23, Revelation 13:8

6. GOD BECAME MAN IN THE PERSON OF JESUS CHRIST. JESUS LIVED A SINLESS AND MORALLY PERFECT LIFE. HE WAS CRUCIFIED AT THE HANDS OF THE ROMANS AND THROUGH DEATH HE ATONED FOR THE SINS OF MANKIND. HE WAS BURIED AND ON THE THIRD DAY ROSE PHYSICALLY FROM THE DEAD, CONQUERING DEATH AND SIN. SALVATION IS FOUND IN CHRIST ALONE BY GRACE ALONE THROUGH FAITH ALONE AND NOT BY WORKS.

Scripture References: Isaiah 7:14, 9:6, Matthew 1:22–23, Luke 1:35, John 1:14, Philippians 2:6–8, Colossians 1:15, 1 John 4:2, Isaiah 53:9, John 19:4, 2 Corinthians 5:21, 1 Peter 1:18–19, 2:22, Hebrews 4:15, 1 John 3:5, Mark 15:43–47, Matthew 28:1–15, Romans 6:4, 8:11, 1 Corinthians 15:1–32, 1 Peter 1:3, Ephesians 2:8–9

7. JESUS PROMISED THAT IN ACCORDANCE WITH THE SCRIPTURES HE WOULD PHYSICALLY RETURN TO EARTH TO RESCUE HIS CHURCH, PUT AN END TO SIN, AND REIGN AS KING OVER ISRAEL AND THE WHOLE EARTH. BY HIM THE LIVING AND THE DEAD WILL BE JUDGED, SOME INHERITING ETERNAL LIFE AND OTHERS RECEIVING ETERNAL PUNISHMENT. CHRISTIANS MUST BE WATCHFUL AND READY FOR THESE EVENTS.

Scripture References: Psalms 72:8–11, Daniel 2:44, 7:13–14, Ezekiel 33:1–6, Zechariah 14:1–9, Matthew 16:27, 24:37–44, 25:1–13, 25:46, Luke 12:37–40, 17:28–30, 18:8, 21:34–36, John 5:22, 14:3, Romans 2:16, 1 Corinthians 15:52, 1 Thessalonians 4:13–18, Revelation 1:7, 11:15, 20:4–6

POSITIONS OF THE CCC

All believers and associated denominations are strongly exhorted to hold fast to these positions regardless of familial, cultural, or political pressure, recognizing that believing in and practicing biblical morality is strong evidence of one's saving faith.

Abortion is without question the murder of a child made in God's image. It should not be permitted even in the case of rape or incest as the child is innocent of any perpetrator's crime. The commission of the terrible evil of rape or incest can never justify the terrible evil of murder. In exceptional cases a mother's life may be jeopardized by pregnancy and only in this exceptional case does the CCC not take an absolute position. However, the mark of a Christian is love and sacrifice and the exemplary mother will put her child's life before her own, trusting that God will be faithful in the midst of tragic circumstances.

Adultery is intrinsically evil and never permissible under any circumstances, not only the physical act of adultery (Ex. 20:14), but also adulterous thoughts (Mt. 5:27–28).

Alcohol consumption is permissible and is in fact encouraged in some Scriptures (1 Tim. 5:23; Eccl. 9:7), but moderation is necessary. Intoxication and drunkenness are not permissible (Eph. 5:18; 1 Cor. 6:10). The Christian should never drink so much that he or she loses cognitive control and the ability to maintain a Christlike demeanor (Prov. 20:1; Prov. 23:29–35).

Anti-Semitism, a form of racism, should never be found in the thoughts, words, writings, or actions of a believer. Gentile believers have not replaced Jewish believers and in fact salvation has come from the Jews. The Apostle Paul likens the entirety of the people of God to an olive tree, which is Israel. Unbelieving Jews have been cut off from the tree and believing Gentiles have been grafted in (Rom. 11:17–24), but the roots of the tree remain Jewish through Abraham, Isaac, Jacob, and the King of the Jews—Jesus. In fact, the Bible promises that one day the Jews will return to God and all Israel will be saved (Rom. 11:25–28; Isa. 45:17; Jer. 31:1). God gave to the descendants of Abraham through Isaac and Jacob a specific area of land that they still have yet to take full possession of according to the promise. Since God is the ultimate sovereign of the earth and His word is true and the land deed still stands, Christians cannot support efforts such as the two-state solution. The Bible proclaims that judgment will befall those who divide God's covenant land (Jl. 3:1–2).

Contraception is not mentioned in Scripture except in the case of Onan who sinned by preventing his wife from becoming pregnant in order to withhold from her dead husband an heir (Gen. 38:8–10). For this reason only contraception that may result in the death of an embryo or done against the will of one's spouse is forbidden. Christians should be wise about this and research diligently before engaging in intercourse with one's spouse. Drugs such as Plan B are never permissible, but even typical hormonal contraception drugs may result in abortion and their use is thus discouraged. Natural family planning is encouraged and in all cases the husband and wife should be one in heart and mind.

Divorce is inherently evil (Mk. 10:11–12), except in the case of marital unfaithfulness (Mt. 5:32). However, even in the case of adultery it is exemplary and most commendable to extend grace and forgiveness and ultimately reconcile with one's spouse recognizing that Christ died for us while we were yet sinners (Rom. 5:8) and God has reconciled us by the death of His Son (Rom. 5:10).

Embryonic stem cell research is never permissible because the embryos are in fact children in their earliest stage of development and therefore those who destroy embryos are murdering children made in the image of God. The Bible is clear that human life begins in the womb (Job 31:15; Ps. 22:10; 139:13; Jer. 1:5; Ex. 21:22–23) and science is clear that an organism's life begins at conception.

Eugenics in most forms should be understood as evil—especially historic eugenics programs that aimed at eradicating minority populations, killing the mentally handicapped, and murdering the terminally ill. Eugenics continues today in many forms including sex-selective abortions, minority-focused placement of abortion facilities, abortion of babies with trisomy disorders, and many instances of euthanasia. These are all intrinsically evil and Christians should themselves avoid these things while preaching forcefully against them.

Euthanasia, which is the intentional killing of a man or woman by both the perpetrator and the one being killed, is unquestionably murder and must not be committed or advocated by any believer.

Fornication, which is sexual activity outside of marriage, is always sinful (Mt. 15:19; 1 Cor. 6:9). God created sex to be enjoyed within the boundaries of marriage and within those boundaries there is great freedom for husband and wife. God created sex for building unity between husband and wife (Gen. 2:24, Mk. 10:8), for pleasure (1 Cor. 7:3–9; Prov. 5:18–19; Song 4:1–16), and for producing offspring (Gen. 1:28; 9:7; Mal. 2:15) and it is only in the context of marriage that these three purposes find their ultimate fulfillment. Men and women in a romantic relationship should not cohabitate before marriage, so that they avoid fornication and the appearance of evil (1 Thess. 5:22).

Gender roles are biblical and must be upheld in the Christian community. Men and women are equal before God in regard to intrinsic value and salvation (Gen. 1:27; Gal. 3:28), but nevertheless have been given by God specific callings. The man is the head of his family—not as a coercive force, but as a servant leader (1 Cor. 11:3). The man is called by God to protect and manage his family well (1 Tim. 3:4), love his wife, and even lay his life down for her (Eph. 5:25). In regard to church leadership, men are called to exercise authority over the congregation, both in teaching to the collective assembly (1 Cor. 14:34–35) and in shepherding (1 Tim. 2:8–3:13). Women are called to respect their husbands out of willful humility (1 Pet. 3:1) and to help and encourage them (Gen. 2:18). In the Christian community women are uniquely called to teach and disciple other women (Tit. 2:3–5).

Genetic manipulation of plants and animals without combining genes from different species is permissible although the Bible does not appear to speak to this issue. Wisdom should be exercised in regard to this issue. However, the creation of hybrid species is unadvisable since God created plants and animals after their own kind (Gen. 1:11, Gen. 1:24). The creation of human/animal hybrids, three-parent babies, or babies resulting from the genetic material of two men or two women are intrinsically evil acts and Christian geneticists should seriously and prayerfully consider the spiritual implications of these creations.

Homosexuality is repeatedly condemned in the Bible as a sin and an abomination (1 Tim. 1:9–10; 1 Cor. 6:9–10; Lev. 18:22; 20:13), as well as unnatural (Rom. 1:26–28). God created sexuality for the purpose of intimacy and pleasure between a husband and wife and ultimately for bringing children into the world. Christians who struggle with homosexuality should flee temptation by any means necessary and should not define themselves by their struggle (1 Cor. 6:11).

Homosexual marriage is intrinsically evil for two reasons: first, because homosexual acts are sinful and unnatural, and second, because it is diametrically opposed to God's design for marriage, which is repeatedly defined in the Bible as the union of one man and one woman (Gen. 2:24; Mt. 19:5; Mk. 10:7; Eph. 5:31).

In Vitro Fertilization is not permissible for the same reason embryonic stem cell research is not permissible: embryos are necessarily destroyed thus the act of murder is committed.

Marrying unbelievers is not permissible for the committed Christian (2 Cor. 6:14), though having already been married before coming to faith is a common occurrence. In such a case the believer must remain committed to their unbelieving spouse and through love and faithfulness attempt to win them over with the Gospel (1 Cor. 7:12–16; 1 Pet. 3:1).

Media must be monitored and controlled in the Christian life. There is no justification, artistic or otherwise, for Christians to watch or listen to sinful things for the purpose of entertainment. There is much media a believer can enjoy, but that which is full of cursing, wonton violence, or sexuality is never permissible. The martyr Telemachus stands as an eternal symbol of this truth.

Narcotic use for the express purpose of treating an injury or disease is permissible, but narcotic use for the purpose of intoxication is a great and destructive evil to oneself, to one's family, and to one's society. There is evidence that drug intoxication is partly what was intended when the Bible speaks of the sin of sorcery.

Pornography is never permissible in any form as it is a form of adultery, or in the case of the unmarried, fornication. Pornography also promotes the objectification and abuse of women and children, is by some measures more addictive than heroine, causes permanent emotional and physical desensitization, and even induces early puberty in children exposed from a young age.

Racism is not in accord with the character of Christ who has made all believers one (Gal. 3:28; Rom. 3:29) for God does not show partiality (Acts 10:34; Rom. 2:11). Believers must not favor the rich over the poor (Jas. 2:1–9), but must show equal favor to all in regard to wealth, station, fame, or race. However, culture has greatly twisted and abused the word *racism* by extending it to include areas where believers in fact should lovingly discriminate between right and wrong: regarding religion, culture, and sinful behaviors.

Slavery, including and especially sexual slavery and trafficking, is never tolerable. Modern slavery differs greatly from biblical indentured servitude, which in certain times and cultures was lawful, in that modern slavery is illegal, always abusive, and routinely violent and coercive. With more people enslaved today than at any time in history, Christians should advocate zealously for their freedom and protection.

Speech should be Christlike in every way and "seasoned with salt" (Col. 4:6). Lies, curses, crude joking, and malicious gossip should never proceed from the mouth of a believer (Mt. 12:36; Prov. 19:5; Tit. 3:2; Eph. 5:4; 1 Tim. 5:13).

Theft is an obvious and unquestionable sin and is not dependent on circumstance (Ex. 20:15). The poor may not steal from the rich even though the rich have more and the poor have less. Instead, the believer struggling with poverty should work diligently (2 Thess. 3:10), trusting in God to provide (Mt. 6:25–34), and making his or her needs known openly to the Christian community (Acts 2:44–45). Believers should not take anything unlawfully, including intellectual property, music, or media. Believers selling products or services that they know are scams or falsely advertised are committing theft as well as lying and should cease immediately (Prov. 11:1; 20:23), returning the money that was stolen.

Transgenderism is both sinful and a great deceit. Sinful in that it defies God's created order of male and female and deceitful in that it convinces a person that they can be something that they are not nor could ever be. Christians must refer to a man in masculine terms and a female in feminine terms regardless of how that person may define himself—even if this results in physical, emotional, or legal consequences for the believer. Men should strive for masculinity and women for femininity (1 Cor. 6:9; 16:13), fully embracing God's design.

The Covenant Christian Coalition is an international, evangelical, post-denominational coalition of churches still faithful to Christ and the Gospel.

You can learn more at www.ccc.one.

SOLA FIDE · SOLA GRATIA · SOLUS CHRISTUS · SOLA SCRIPTURA · SOLI DEO GLORIA

Made in the USA
Monee, IL
12 December 2021